THE VENETIAN MONEY MARKET

MONEY AND BANKING IN MEDIEVAL AND RENAISSANCE VENICE

♦

VOLUME I

COINS AND MONEYS OF ACCOUNT

Frederic C. Lane
and
Reinhold C. Mueller

♦

VOLUME II

THE VENETIAN MONEY MARKET

BANKS, PANICS, AND THE PUBLIC DEBT,
1200–1500

Reinhold C. Mueller

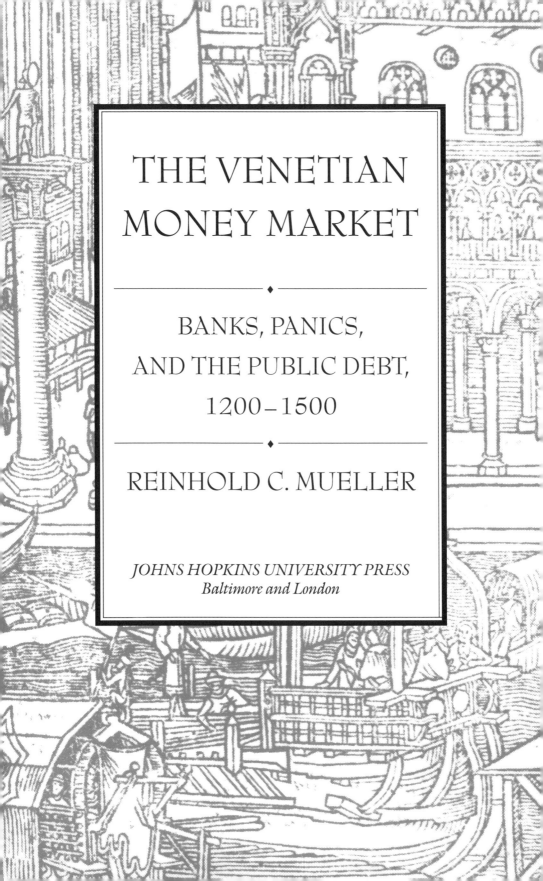

THE VENETIAN MONEY MARKET

◆

BANKS, PANICS, AND THE PUBLIC DEBT, 1200–1500

◆

REINHOLD C. MUELLER

JOHNS HOPKINS UNIVERSITY PRESS
Baltimore and London

*This book has been brought to publication
with the generous assistance of
the Gladys Krieble Delmas Foundation.*

Front case stamping: Lira Tron of 1472.
For a full description, see figure 8b in Chapter 5.

The Johns Hopkins University Press
2715 North Charles Street
Baltimore, Maryland 21218-4319
The Johns Hopkins Press Ltd., London

Library of Congress Cataloging-in-Publication Data
will be found at the end of this book.

A catalog record for this book is available from the British Library.

ISBN 0-8018-5437-7

CONTENTS

CONTENTS

ILLUSTRATIONS

FIGURES

Thanks go to the following individuals and institutions for the figures that appear in the book — Fig. 1: Architects Luigi Fregonese, Francesco Guerra, and Luca Pilot of the Cartographic Center (CIRCE), Institute of Architecture, Venice, authors of the digitalization. Figs. 3–6: Prof. Donatella Calabi and the Diateca, Department of the History of Architecture, Institute of Architecture, Venice. Figs. 7–8: Dr. Roberta Parise, vice-curator of the numismatic collection (Museo Bottacin), and Prof. Andrea Saccocci. By permission of the director of the Musei Civici of Padua. Fig. 9: The Ashmolean Museum,

Cambridge, and Dr. Peter Spufford, who brought the plate to my attention. Fig. 12: Photograph by the Microfilm Section, Archivio di Stato di Venezia, by permission of the Ministero per i Beni Culturali ed Ambientali (authorization number 27/1996). Figs. 13 and 15: Photographs from the Archivio Datini, Prato, by permission of the Archivio di Stato di Firenze (Sezione di Prato) and the Ministero per i Beni Culturali ed Ambientali (authorization number 215/1996). All other credits are specified in the captions.

GRAPHS

TABLES

xiii

PREFACE

HIS BOOK, *The Venetian Money Market: Banks, Panics, and the Public Debt, 1200–1500,* is the second volume of the work originally planned by Frederic C. Lane and myself entitled *Money and Banking in Medieval and Renaissance Venice.*

The first volume, *Coins and Moneys of Account,* coauthored by Lane and Mueller, was published in 1985. Its contents had been revised, about two years before publication, to include all the chapters prepared by Frederic Lane; under the new thematic organization, coins and moneys of account first and then the money market, my institutional chapters on banking in Venice, already drafted and discussed, were no longer appropriate for the first volume and were left for the second. Frederic Lane died on 14 October 1984, shortly before his eighty-fourth birthday, but he had lived to see the first proofs. While he was in the hospital, we worked together on the illustrations and their captions. Lane's principal worry at the time was whether his inexperienced coauthor, left to his own devices, was really up to making an index in the way indexes *ought* to be made. As a guest at the Johns Hopkins University's Charles Singleton Center for Italian Studies at Villa Spelman in Florence at the end of 1984 and the beginning of 1985 (a period punctuated by the killer freeze in Tuscany), I was able to read page proofs and compile, under the patient and expert tutelage of Richard Goldthwaite, an index that, hopefully, turned out to be as indexes ought to be.

This second volume has only one author. Lane left unpublished only a rough draft of a subchapter on the reform of minting in the 1420s, which did not fit into this volume. In fact, the theme of monetary policy has been left out altogether, in part because Alan Stahl is preparing a history of the Venetian mint which will include that reform, and in part to focus attention on the money market, that is, on credit. As a result, the promise to continue through the Quattrocento monetary themes of earlier centuries begun in volume 1 (there are plenty of references — reminders as much to me as to the reader — in footnotes of volume 1 to "see volume 2") has remained unfulfilled. I have published various articles on Venetian monetary policy which are readily available. Fortunately, Venetian moneys of account were simplified in the fifteenth century; explications that are nonetheless essential to an understanding of aspects of the money market have been relegated to Appendix D. That appendix has benefited from the expertise on such knotty problems as the "lira manca" of Giulio Mandich, a faithful friend and constant interlocutor until his death in 1994.

Lane read and commented on drafts of the chapters in Part I and generally on drafts based upon my research at the Datini archive. One evening after supper, at the Pensione Seguso on the Zattere, on his last visit in 1982, he resolved in no time, in his characteristically simple and incisive fashion, my quandary about the strange oscillations of exchange rates between Venice and Milan around 1400. My explanation, in Appendix C, is beneficiary of his extraordinary capacity to solve monetary puzzles, which, if anything, grew with age.

The general plan for this joint effort was to produce a history of money and banking for a commercial and industrial center, Venice, that had not received much attention. Armando Sapori, Raymond de Roover, and Federigo Melis had made Florentine banking famous, and Roberto S. Lopez had recounted the origins of banking in medieval Genoa. As for Venice, historians could only refer to the documents published and commented upon by Elia Lattes and Francesco Ferrara in the context of burning nineteenth-century debates on regulation and deregulation in the banking sector. Gino Luzzatto dealt only en passant with Venetian private banks, in an article centered on the public Banco della Piazza di Rialto and the Banco Giro. He gave a lecture on Venetian banks to the personnel of the Banca Nazionale del Lavoro in 1950, of which three to four pages dealt with the Middle Ages, but he never allowed it to be published. (Federigo Melis kindly lent me the text of that lecture, when I was still a graduate student.) Mario Brunetti and Giovanni Orlandini, finally, once undertook to write a history of the public Banco Giro of Venice; they got as far as drafting a first part, entitled "I banchi privati," based on official deliberations and exemptions ("gratie"); a copy of the unfinished typescript was deposited in the library of the Museo Correr.

The history of Venetian banking, prior to the founding of its famous public banks, then, remained little known, except in general terms. Abbot Payson Usher, Frederic Lane's professor, had planned to study Venice for the second volume of his *Early History of Deposit Banking in Mediterranean Europe*. Lane, too, had meant to undertake a study of Venetian banking. In

1937 he published an article on the rash of bankruptcies beginning in 1499, largely on the basis of Marin Sanudo's diaries; and in 1944 he wrote, "I hope to explain more fully in a separate study both [the banker Francesco] Balbi's operations and Venetian banking methods as they are revealed by [Andrea] Barbarigo's books." Neither man realized his hopes.

The present volume is devoted to the money market, that is, to credit, in Venice from the later thirteenth century to about 1500. It takes as given the general European and comparative treatment with which Volume 1 began, in particular in chapter 6, on the origins of banking in medieval Europe.[1] The sources utilized here are the same as those used in Volume 1, with perhaps somewhat less recourse to official deliberations and more emphasis on account books, commercial correspondence, civil lawsuits, criminal trials, and, for subjects like bank failures, the reports of eyewitnesses, including chroniclers, diarists, and envoys.

This volume consists of five parts. Part I is devoted to the institutional structure of deposit banks. It begins with a discussion of the origin and nature of deposit banking on the Rialto, for which documentation begins only from the end of the thirteenth century. Already at that time it was clear that the banks were essential to the payments system, and this realization caused first the Great Council and then the Senate to attempt to regulate banking, with the aim of increasing the trustworthiness of what was seen as a public service, not only a private enterprise; their deliberations in this sector, many of which up to about 1380 were published by the indefatigable Roberto Cessi, are quite complete. Continual failures of private banks,

---

[1]It is worth noting, nevertheless, some important collections of essays on the history of European and Italian banking in general which have appeared since Volume 1 was completed. Anna Vannini Marx, ed., *Credito, banche e investimenti, secoli XIII–XX*, Acts of the Settimane di Studio, Istituto Datini, Prato, 4 (Florence, 1985), is weak on the Middle Ages and was already rather outdated once it was finally published (the papers were read in 1972). Much more important is a more recent set of acts: *Banchi pubblici, banchi privati e monti di pietà nell'Europa preindustriale*, 2 vols. (Genoa, 1991). An excellent work is that directed by Herman van der Wee, *La banque en occident* (Antwerp, 1991; in English as *A History of European Banking* [Antwerp, 1994]), with three studies by Raymond Bogaert (the ancient world), Herman van der Wee (medieval and early modern Europe), and Ginette Kurgan-Van Hentenryk (modern and contemporary Europe); not only is van der Wee's piece a fine overview, but it also adds new information on the situation in the Low Countries; the volume is superbly illustrated. The most recent collection of studies is that edited by Hans Pohl for the Institut für bankhistorische Forschung: *Europäische Bankengeschichte* (Frankfurt am Main, 1993); the essay dedicated to the Middle Ages, by Martin Körner, is an overview of commercial credit, coinage policy, and banking. Finally, it is worth mentioning Peter Spufford's *Money and Its Use in Medieval Europe* (Cambridge, England, 1988), even though banking and credit do not constitute major themes of the book. As regards Venice in particular, my own studies are listed in the bibliography; overviews of medieval banking and finance by Ugo Tucci and Michael Knapton, respectively, have been announced as forthcoming in the multivolume *Storia di Venezia* (Rome, 1992–).

causing interruptions of the payments cycle and the temporary freezing of deposits, prompted discussion in the later fourteenth century of projects for a public bank, which was not instituted, however, until 1587. During the mid-fourteenth century Tuscan immigrants contributed in an important way to deposit banking in Venice, not only as bankers themselves but also as factors and employees. After the 1370s, however, the number of banks declined, and banking was taken over increasingly by Venetians, both non-noble and noble. Unfortunately, no partnership contract has yet been uncovered; the questions of divisions of profit and loss and of liability in cases of failure can be only partially reconstructed, on the basis of tangential evidence.

While Part I provides an essentially static picture, Part II offers a more dynamic one, for it chronicles panics and bank failures over almost two centuries and presents an analysis of the economic conjuncture in which these took place. The account begins and ends with the two best-known crisis periods in premodern European financial history, namely, the 1340s and 1499–1500. There is an obvious drawback in treating banking history in this fashion, for failures make news — successes do not. Aside from this bias of the sources, however, it is a fact that Rialto banks more often than not met a bad end, and bank failures reflected more profound economic crises. At the same time, this kind of evidence does not lend itself to debates about long-term trends, such as that regarding a general economic crisis of the Trecento or of the late Middle Ages. It contributes, rather, more to complexity than to simplification.

The medieval money market par excellence is the foreign exchange market, which made available, locally, short-term loans at variable rates of interest. Part III is dedicated to a treatment of the exchange market and of the Florentine community of merchant bankers resident in Venice who dominated the market. Florentine merchant manuals single out Venice as a crucial exchange market, in part because it was perhaps the principal bullion market in Europe and in part because of the high demand for money and for credit in a port city that by the late fourteenth century practically monopolized the Levant trade. The discussion is based on examples drawn from the years 1336 to 1506. It is in this context that the question of usury is taken up for the first time, thanks to the discovery of two unpublished tracts devoted specifically to the Venetian marketplace and to investment in loans under the form of rechange contracts with Bruges and London, which were so popular around the mid-fifteenth century.

The last two parts of this volume are dedicated to the public debt and private wealth, first to voluntary loans and the floating debt and then to forced loans and the consolidated or funded debt. The Venetian Camera del Frumento, or Grain Office, administered the floating debt, from the late thirteenth to the late fourteenth century. It developed as a solution both for a state in need of readily available credit and for lords of the mainland, from north-central Italy to the Balkans, who had liquid capital that they wished to have in a secure place, even at low rates of interest, far from the internecine strife of their courts. In short, they needed a sort of "Swiss" bank. Venetians also deposited money with the Camera del Frumento, especially dowry funds, which, under certain conditions, were required by law to be deposited there, where they were guaranteed by the state. The Grain Office also offered long-term loans, of six to ten years' duration, at low interest to entrepreneurs, generally nobles, in sectors of the economy directly involving the commonweal, such as the operation of flour mills and brick kilns, at a time when Venice, before its first expansion on the mainland in 1339, was dependent upon structures situated in what periodically was enemy territory. Finally, some depositors had qualms of conscience about accepting interest from the Grain Office, which permits a brief consideration of how they comported themselves.

Until relatively recently I had no intention whatsoever of treating Venice's funded debt in this book, since that topic had been researched in so exemplary a fashion by Gino Luzzatto; his book is a model, much more successful than books written about the funded debts of cities whose sources are infinitely superior to those extant in Venice. The decision finally to include the topic, presented here in the fifth and last part, derived from the realization, first, that few people actually read Luzzatto's history but simply take it for granted, cite it, and go on to other things; and second, that Luzzatto's treatment includes some misleading passages in crucial points, owing to a misunderstanding of a money of account peculiar to the administration of the public debt. Since I came upon the cause of the problem by studying private account books, I decided to develop especially this private side of the public debt, namely, the effect of forced loans on private patrimonies, a theme that Luzzatto only barely touched upon. In order to do this, I first had to re-create the mechanisms of the Monte Vecchio, in part by rereading Luzzatto, for the benefit of those who do not know Italian or have not read the book. Then, because it is well known that Florentine leaders invoked the "Venetian model" when they debated the reform that instituted the catasto in 1427, I emphasized (in Chapter 12) the criteria used in assessing patrimonies, as a way of leading up to a reconsideration of the role of Venice's experience in the Florentine debates. The matter of usury and the funded debt had to be treated solely on the basis of secondary sources, since I did not turn up new material on this theme. The last chapter deals with foreign investment in the open market in Venetian government obligations. The Venetian term "imprestiti" (the Florentines used "prestanze"), it is worth pointing out from the start, will be rendered here as government obligations or credits; today they could be called bonds. "Paghe" (singular, "paga") will be rendered as claims to interest; today they might be called coupons.

What I did not include in this volume must also be said. I have already mentioned the question of monetary policy and products of the mint. Strictly connected with the themes here discussed are investments by bankers; extant material is minimal and so scattered, however, that it could not be treated separately. Another missing topic intimately a part of the money market is that of consumption credit. Again, documentation on usury and extortion survives only in rare cases. Manifest usury was forbidden in Venice since 1254; that prohibition remained in force until the War of the League of Cambrai, when Jewish pawnbrokers of the Terraferma were driven toward Venice by local revolts and advancing armies. There is only one exception, namely, the period from 1382 to 1397, following the War of Chioggia, when Jews were invited to lend in Venice itself. I have not uncovered new material sufficient to modify or enrich significantly the conclusions reached in my article on that interlude, published twenty years ago; simply to repeat the article, outside the general context of consumption credit, would have been out of place. Similarly, I have not dedicated space to the Procuratia di San Marco, either as a depository of unproductive valuables and coin or as investor of the liquid capital of estates under its administration, having dealt with these topics sufficiently in the past; in the fifteenth century the investments become less interesting, since they were in practice restricted to the purchase of government obligations. As the reader will already have noticed, moreover, I have decided against devoting a separate chapter to usury and the doctrinal debate regarding it, in favor of treating the topic on three different occasions, each time imbedded in the particular context — loans on rechange, deposits in the Grain Office, investments in government obligations — in which moral concern was awakened in some persons. Finally, I have not undertaken an investigation of the origins of the Monte Nuovo, even though it began in 1482, well within the chronological limits of this study. That topic is worthy of a monograph in itself.

What Venetian studies most need is a series of wages and prices which gives an idea of the value or purchasing power of money. In the absence of such a tool, I refer the reader to Appendix I, which presents some scattered data on the value of money, and Appendix J, on wage rates.

The two chapters in Part IV, concerning the floating debt, repropose, with only slight revisions, articles that appeared previously in acts of congresses, one on the Grain Office (Chapter 9, sections i–iv), the other on bank loans to the state (Chapter 10).[2] I had the opportunity to try out

---

[2]"La Camera del frumento: Un 'banco pubblico' veneziano e i gruzzoli dei signori di Terraferma," in *Istituzioni, società e potere nella marca trevigiana e veronese (secoli XIII–XIV): Sulle tracce di G. B. Verci,* ed. Gherardo Ortalli and Michael Knapton (Rome, 1988), 321–60, and "'Quando i banchi no' ha' fede, la terra no' ha credito': Bank loans to the Venetian state in the fifteenth century," *Banchi pubblici, banchi privati,* 275–308.

chapters regarding the public debt and proposals to institute a public bank with audiences at the universities of Marburg and Siegen, the Max-Planck Institut für Geschichte in Göttingen, and the Ecole des Hautes Etudes en Sciences Sociales.

Two databases have made it possible to reduce detail. The first, called CIVES, is a matrix of some thirty-six hundred citizenship privileges, accorded between 1300 and 1500; all archival references regarding new citizens mentioned in the text can be found in CIVES, making it possible to reduce the footnotes. The second contains all the exchange rates (more than seven thousand) regarding Venice collected from the Datini archive (see Appendix C). Both are available to interested persons: the first will be put into a databank with general access as soon as possible; the second is already scheduled to be part of the Medieval and Early Modern Data Bank (MEMDB) at Rutgers University.

The dates of all documents cited have been converted, where necessary, from *more veneto* (with the year beginning 1 March) to the modern style.

I owe thanks to so many people that a page might not suffice to mention them all. That is what happens when work on the same general topic lasts decades. For institutional support, I owe thanks to the Faculty of Letters of the University of Venice for sabbatical leaves, and most especially to the Wissenschaftskolleg zu Berlin, where, in 1989–90, besides living in the highly charged atmosphere of what has come to be called the fall of the Berlin wall, I was nonetheless able to draft about one-third of this book and revise another third. Of the generations of friends and colleagues who have frequented the Archivio di Stato at one time or another and have passed on tesserae that I have been able to fit into my mosaic, I will mention by name only one of the first generation, Susan Connell, who so kindly donated her rich fund of wage rates, here summarized in Appendix I, and the most recent, Annalisa Conterio, Edoardo Demo, Luca Molà, and Stefano Piasentini, former students, and Fabio Carrera, who produced the graphs. Needless to say, the students of my seminars at the Dipartimento di Studi Storici in Venice forced me to express with the greatest clarity I could muster some of the themes dealt with in this book. Directors, archivists, librarians, and personnel especially of the Archivio di Stato and the Biblioteca Marciana, as well as of many other scientific institutions, not only in Venice but from Petrograd to Minneapolis, have done their utmost to assist my research. The editors of the Johns Hopkins University Press have been generous in suggesting creative solutions to problems as they arose and have been full of encouragement. The book would never have seen the light of day, finally, without the constant help and support of Richard Goldthwaite and M. Laura Lepscky Mueller.

I join the Johns Hopkins University Press in thanking the Gladys Krieble Delmas Foundation for choosing generously to support the publication of this volume as a tribute to the memory of Frederic C. Lane, not only as a world-renowned historian but also as a good friend and counsel to the foundation.

One afternoon, Fred Lane and I discussed the possibility of dedicating Volume 1 to Abbot Payson Usher, his mentor at Harvard. As soon as we recalled that he was the author of a volume 1 on deposit banking in the Mediterranean world, the sequel to which, on Venice, never appeared, with wide grins and a toast, we immediately agreed to drop the idea, out of healthy superstition. In fact, a volume 1 is a heavy heritage to bear. This Volume 2 (and the last of two) is dedicated to my father, who constantly cajoled me to produce it but did not live to see it in print.

ABBREVIATIONS

For full titles and facts of publication, see Bibliography.

ADP	Archivio Datini, Prato
ASF	Archivio di Stato, Florence
MAP	Mediceo avanti il Principato
ASI	*Archivio storico italiano*
ASMI	Archivio di Stato, Milan
ASMN	Archivio di Stato, Mantua
AST	Archivio di Stato, Treviso
Osp	Ospedale di S. Maria dei Battuti
PO	Pergamene dell'Ospedale
ASV	Archivio di Stato, Venice
AC	Avogaria di comun
CIN	Cancelleria inferiore, notai
CN	Collegio, Notatorio
GP	Giudici di petizion
Sg	Sentenze a giustizia
MC	Maggior Consiglio, Deliberazioni
NT	Notarile, testamenti
PSM	Procuratori di San Marco
SM	Senato, Misti
SMar	Senato, Mar
SSec	Senato, Secreta
ST	Senato, Terra
AV	*Archivio veneto*
Barbarigo, ledger A, B	ASV, Archivio Grimani Barbarigo, b. 41, ledger A (1431–40); ledger B (1440–49)
BG	Besta, ed., *Bilanci generali*
BMCV	Biblioteca del Museo Civico Correr, Venice
BMV	Biblioteca Marciana, Venice

BNF	Biblioteca Nazionale, Florence
cap.	capitulum, capitula
Cap. Broche	Bonfiglio Dosio, ed., *Il "Capitolar dalle broche"*
commis.	commissaria (estate)
DBI	*Dizionario biografico degli italiani*
de Roover, *Medici Bank*	de Roover, *Rise and Decline of the Medici Bank*
DMC	Cessi, ed., *Deliberazioni del Maggior Consiglio*
Dolfina	Cronaca di Zorzi Dolfin, BMV, It. cl. VII, 794 (8503)
DQ	Lombardo, ed., *Deliberazioni del Consiglio dei Quaranta*
Ferrara, "Antichi banchi"	Ferrara, "Gli antichi banchi di Venezia"
Ferrara, "Documenti"	Ferrara, ed., "Documenti per servire alla storia de' banchi veneziani"
FSV	Fonti per la Storia di Venezia
JEEcH	*Journal of European Economic History*
Lattes, *Libertà*	E. Lattes, *La libertà delle banche*
LCR	Predelli, ed., *I libri commemoriali — regesti*
£/s/d	Lire, soldi, denari (pounds, shillings, pence)
Malipiero, *Annali*	Malipiero, *Annali veneti dall'anno 1457 al 1500*
Morosini, Cronaca, 1, 2	BMV, Mss. it., cl. VII, 2048 (8331) = 1; 2049 (8332) = 2. Antonio Morosini, Cronaca. Nineteenth-century transcription of the original (in Österreichische Nationalbibliothek, Vienna, Hs. 6586–87); longer passages were checked against the original or the microfilm of it at the Fondazione Cini, Venice, and are so noted.
NAV	*Nuovo archivio veneto*
Papadopoli	Papadopoli-Aldobrandini, *Le monete di Venezia*
PMV	Cessi, ed., *Problemi monetari veneziani*
Priuli, *Diarii*	Priuli, *I diarii*
PRV	Luzzatto, ed., *I prestiti pubblici della Repubblica di Venezia*
qd.	quondam (son of the deceased, Ital. "del fu")
RES	Cessi, ed., *La regolazione delle entrate e delle spese*
Sanudo, *De origine*	Marin Sanudo, *De origine, situ et magistratibus*
Sanudo, *Diarii*	Marin Sanudo, *I diarii*
Soranzo ledger	ASV, Miscellanea Gregolin, b. 14, libro real nuovo (1406–36)
SV	*Studi veneziani*
Traictie	Braunstein and Mueller, eds., *Description ou traictie du gouvernement de Venise*
Vol. 1	Lane and Mueller, *Coins and Moneys of Account*, vol. 1 of *Money and Banking*

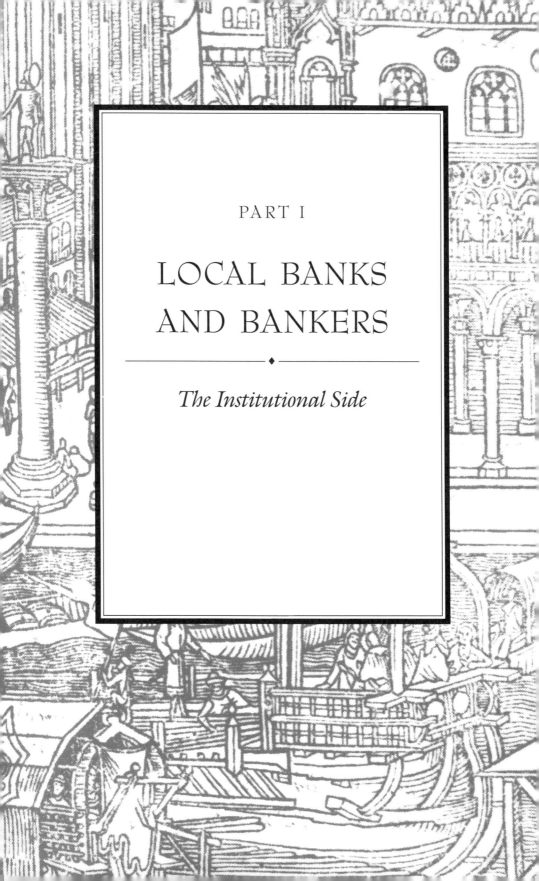

PART I

LOCAL BANKS
AND BANKERS

◆

The Institutional Side

1

FROM MONEYCHANGING TO DEPOSIT BANKING

i. LITERARY EVIDENCE: THE RIALTO MAKES NEWS

THE MANY KINDS AND qualities of coins that circulated within a given marketplace and the practically infinite varieties and qualities that circulated between marketplaces made the activity of the moneychanger indispensable for both local and interregional trade, especially in a large port city such as Venice. The local moneychanger then developed into the deposit banker, that figure who facilitated even more than his predecessor the conclusion of commercial transactions, whether wholesale or retail, by reducing the confusion of coins and sundry moneys of account to the simple device of bank money, a fiduciary money transferable upon oral order without recourse to specie (see Vol. 1, chap. 6).

The principal instrument of commercial mediation was the distinctive transfer bank, or banco di scritta, of the Rialto. Venetians took this institution for granted and do not provide particularly useful descriptions of its operation. Foreigners, on the other hand, generally more used to handling coins, found the Rialto banks to be particularly newsworthy.

Two poems in praise of Venice dating from the first half of the fifteenth century do not fail to mention the Rialto banks. The earlier, anonymous, probably written by a Venetian sometime between 1420 and 1430, merely expresses wonder at the banks ("i cambi") situated around the square and at the amount of money circulating at the Rialto—so much so that it seemed "to flow from a vein of ore."[1] The second, written in 1443 by

---

[1] "Chi vuol danari qui convien che passa / perché l'è fonte de molto trexoro / e tanto arzento e oro / se trova qui, che par che essa de vena. / . . . In el Rialto ognum con suo tabaro / chi

the Florentine Jacopo d'Albizzotto Guidi, a merchant resident in Venice at least by 1409, is more precise. Jacopo asserts that the three banks then operating accepted deposits from whoever desired to use his account for making payments and that everyone had to be satisfied with the payment made, whether by transfer or in cash.[2]

At the end of the century four prose tracts contain increasingly clearer explications of the functioning of Rialto banks and their creation of bank money. The first, dated 1493, is by Marin Sanudo, the only Venetian among the four authors to mention the banks, however fleetingly, in the course of his sketch of things worthy of note in Venice. He names the four bankers operating in that year and says that large sums of money were deposited with them which could be passed by transfer from account to account.[3] In the course of writing his *Diarii* over the following decades, furthermore, Sanudo showed himself to be a careful observer of the workings of the Rialto banks, but then his reports refer to specific problems and conditions.[4]

The best known of the contemporary descriptions is that of Fra Luca Pacioli, the Tuscan mathematician who studied at the school located at the Rialto sometime during the third quarter of the fifteenth century, when he was also a tutor in arithmetic and accounting to two young Venetians; he returned to the Rialto to lecture there in 1508.[5] In his famous tract on

---

compra con dinari e poi revende / e tal chredenza prende / per trapassar suo vita con honore / I cambi sono atorno a tute l'ore / pur con la moneda d'oro e d'arzento / chi ben sa zir con tempo / chi più nella sua chassa ne ritrova." *Quartine in lode di Venezia tratta fidelmente da un'antica stampa di Treviso, 1473,* Nozze Albrizzi-Galvagna (Venice, 1839), 37, 51. The introduction dates the poem from internal evidence at 1420, while Vittorio Rossi makes a case for 1431; see his "Jacopo d'Albizzotto Guidi e il suo inedito poema su Venezia," *NAV* 5 (1893): 412–13.

[2]"Sonvi tre banchi di tant'afezione / Di scritte, che son tanti suficienti / Cho lor duchati ciaschedun vi pone / Per fare e pagamenti a tutte gienti / D'ongni merchato e anche de soldati, / Sicchè chonviene che ciaschedun contenti / Di scritta od di danari anoverati." Roberto Cessi and Annibale Alberti, *Rialto: L'isola, il ponte, il mercato* (Bologna, 1934), 439. According to Rossi, "Jacopo d'Albizzotto Guidi," the author is registered in the Florentine catasto of 1427 as age fifty-two and "recently" emigrated to Venice; he was supposedly close to Cosimo de' Medici during the latter's exile in Venice (1433–34), and his brother Guido was buried in Venice in 1406. In Venetian documents, however, we find that Jacopo was a factor in the firm of Luigi Davanzati, which specialized in foreign exchange on the Rialto, in 1409. ASV, GP, Frammenti antichi, b. 11, testificationes, for 18 February 1410. Actually, the familiarity of the Guidi with Venice was of an early date. Bonagiunta qd. Guido Guidi was naturalized "de intus" in 1333; perhaps from him Guido and Jacopo d'Albizzotto inherited Venetian citizenship; on the basis of extant sources, they did not themselves receive a privilege.

[3]"Sono . . . quattro banchi de scritta: Pisani et Lippomani, patrizi, et Garzoni et Augustini, cittadini, nelli qual sono assaissimi danari, et con partide vien dati et scritti in varij nomi; sono ditti banchieri creti e le loro partide sono sententie fatte." Sanudo, *De origine,* 27–28.

[4]See Frederic C. Lane, "Venetian Bankers, 1496–1533," reprinted in his *Venice and History: The Collected Papers of Frederic C. Lane* (Baltimore, 1966), 80 and passim.

[5]Luca Pacioli, *Summa de arithmetica, geometria, proportioni e proportionalità* (Venice, 1494),

double-entry bookkeeping published in Venice in 1494 (*De divina propor-tione, Tractatus XI, De scripturis*), he has the banks of Venice in particular in mind when he writes:

> It is common practice to deal directly with a transfer bank, where you can deposit your money for greater security or for the purpose of making your daily payments to Piero, Giovanni, and Martino through the bank, because the registration of the transferred claim [la ditta del banco] is as authoritative as a notarial instrument since it is backed by the government. . . . Now suppose you are a banker . . . performing a transfer: if your creditor, without withdrawing cash, orders payment to another party, in your journal you debit that depositor and credit the assignee. Thus you make a transfer from one creditor to another, while you yourself remain debtor. Here you function as an intermediary [persona meççana], as witness and agent of the parties and you justly receive a commission.[6]

There is no evidence that commissions were actually charged, but otherwise the operation described was commonplace at the Rialto.

The feudatory Arnold von Harff, in Venice on his way from Cologne to the Holy Land in the 1490s, was struck by the bankers active at the Rialto: "The moneychangers are seated around the square, and they hold the money that merchants consigned to them in order to avoid the count-ing out of cash. When one merchant pays off another, he gives that person an assignment in bank [dat oeverwijst eyn dem anderen in den bencken], so that very little cash passes among the merchants."[7]

An acute French observer, who was well acquainted with Venetian institutions and wrote an extensive tract on the government and constitu-tion of Venice around 1500, went to great lengths to describe the city's

---

fol. 206, and in the critical edition *Trattato di partita doppia,* ed. Annalisa Conterio (Venice, 1994), 90–91. In his examples of the accounting of "li banchi de scripta" of Venice, he uses the firm of "Gerolamo Lippomano dal banco e compagni," which was active at the time but which failed in 1499.

[6]Pacioli studied under Domenego Bragadin, who taught at the Rialto school from 1455 to 1484; he was in Venice as the tutor of a merchant's sons in 1470. See Bruno Nardi, "La scuola di Rialto e l'umanesimo veneziani," in *Umanesimo europeo e umanesimo veneziano,* ed. Vittore Branca (Florence, 1963), 101, 112–15, and idem, "Letteratura e cultura veneziana del Quat-trocento," in *La civiltà veneziana del Quattrocento* (Florence, 1957), 118. See also the introduc-tory essays of Annalisa Conterio and Gino Belloni in Pacioli, *Trattato di partita doppia.*

[7]"Dae hart umb den platz sittzen die wesseler und die der koufflude geld under henden haven, die it dar inne gelaicht haven, off dat man de myn darff tzellen. As eyn kouffman dem anderen aeff hait gegolden, dat oeverwijst eyn dem anderen in den bencken, so dat wenich geltz dae under den kouffluden over getzalt wyrt." Arnold von Harff, *Die Pilgerfahrt des Ritters Arnold von Harff . . . in den Jahren 1496 bis 1499,* ed. E. von Groote (Cologne, 1860), 41.

"banquiers d'escriptes": "Individuals leave large sums of money with a banker merely for the convenience, and not in order to earn interest. Most purchases, sales, and other contracts are paid for in bank, without any counting out of coin but solely in bank money [en escript], for the banker merely debits the buyer's account, and credits that of the seller." The anonymous writer, like Pacioli, points out, furthermore, that the entry in the banker's account book signifies total extinction of the debt involved in the transaction "as though it had been written by some authentic and great notary."[8]

What caught the interest of these authors was that assignments in bank were made by oral order, for the entry that the banker made in his journal was no more and no less than a written record of an order-to-pay made orally.[9] According to a senatorial deliberation of the sixteenth century, both parties were to be physically present at the banker's table when the banker recorded the debtor's order-to-pay. In practice, however, the creditor's acceptance of the assignment was probably taken for granted in most cases, and his physical presence could then be dispensed with.[10] This was the case, for example, when the banker served as collection agent for house rents or for interest on government obligations, which he often did. As Pacioli wrote, the banker merely mediated the transaction between two parties by giving his word to effect a convertible transfer, which thus came to be called a "ditta (or detta) di banco." Complete faith was placed in the oral order so recorded, as the above-mentioned commentators underscored.

---

[8]"Les banquiers . . . ont en leur banque trés grant somme d'argent de particulieres personnes, lequel argent est laissé a demourer a ladicte banque, seullement pour la commodité d'iceulx a qui apartient ledit argent et sans point de gaing d'iceulx; lesquelz gens a qui est ledit argent sont marchans la plus grant part, et, selon ce qu'ilz achantent ou vendent quelque marchandise ou qu'ilz font aultre contract ou il advient quelque payement ou desboursement d'argent, ilz font ledit payement ou desboursement d'argent ausdicts banques, et pour la plus grant part sans aucune numeracion d'argent, mais seulleument en escript; c'est assavoir que lesdiz banquiers ou ilz ont aucuns crediteurs en leurs livres et comptes, si lesdiz crediteurs veulleunt distribuer et bailler leurdit argent a quelque ung, lesdiz banquiers escripvent en leurs livres par façon que celuy qui doit avoir l'argent demeure crediteur de ladicte banque et l'aultre est acquicté par la somme qu'il a distribuée." *Traictie,* chap. 32; previously in Paul M. Perret, ed., *Histoire des relations de la France avec Venise du XIIIᵉ siècle a l'avènment de Charles VIII,* 2 vols. (Paris, 1896), 2:281.

[9]Abbot P. Usher, *The Early History of Deposit Banking in Mediterranean Europe* (Cambridge, Mass., 1943; reprint, New York, 1967), 91.

[10]Ibid., 22, 91. A question arose only when an agio developed between bank money and specie, thus temporarily creating two different standards of value. Such was the case in 1526 when the presence of both parties was mandated; the assumption is, of course, that one party was often not present. Lattes, *Libertà,* doc. 32, para. 8. That acceptance of an assignment was normally taken for granted is clear from practice but also from paragraph 7 of the same law, which states that a beneficiary was free to accept or refuse payment in bank for past contracts but that for future contracts he could not refuse payment in bank unless it was specifically stated that payment was due in specie or "fuora di banco."

The use of the oral order in Venice has been considered backward in contrast to the advance in Florentine banking which brought the written order, or check.[11] It must be remembered, however, that the few principal transfer banks at Venice were situated only a few steps apart on Campo San Giacomo di Rialto, where most commercial transactions, large and small, were negotiated. In short, to pass by one's bank was no hardship, and written orders would have provided little advantage. Furthermore, should a client have been absent from the city or otherwise unable to appear in person, he could always send an employee or servant, bearer of an informal memorandum addressed to the banker, or a person with a formal notarized power of attorney.[12] It was easy for a client to compare his record of accounts with that of his banker. This situation of ready contact with few bankers on a small square contrasts with that of Florence, where there were a great many more local bankers and moneychangers (about eighty at any given time in the first half of the fourteenth century, about thirty during most of the fifteenth century) and as many as four different concentrations of bankers, situated at a distance one from the other.[13] At the same time, most of these members of the Cambio guild operated on a small scale, while all the major local bankers had their counting houses at the Mercato Nuovo, the principal site, where many merchant bankers were also situated. Some of the genuine checks uncovered were written outside the city and on Florentine banks. While there is no way of knowing how generalized the use of written orders in Tuscany was, in such cases they constituted a real facilitation in making payments.[14] Relations between the city of Venice and the surrounding subject provinces, on the other hand, lack comparable documentation, and the use of written orders in the Veneto can be excluded; their use in the banking sector of the capital city is doubtful, and no example has been uncovered.[15]

[11]See, in particular, Federigo Melis, *Documenti per la storia economica dei secoli XIII–XVI* (Florence, 1972), 103. In an earlier, more comparative treatment, Melis was less dogmatic. See his *Note di storia della banca pisana nel Trecento* (Pisa, 1955), chap. 8. Reprinted in Melis, *La banca pisana e le origini della banca moderna*, ed. by Marco Spallanzani (Florence, 1987).

[12]Usher, *Early History*, 91. See also Gino Luzzatto, *Storia economica di Venezia dall'XI al XVI secolo* (Venice, 1961), 100–102.

[13]Raymond de Roover, "New Interpretations of the History of Banking," as reprinted in his *Business, Banking, and Economic Thought in Late Medieval and Early Modern Europe*, ed. Julius Kirshner (Chicago, 1974), 217, and "La structure des banques au Moyen Age," *Third International Conference of Economic History, Munich 1965*, (Paris, 1974), 5:165 n. 1. For a critical reevaluation, see Richard A. Goldthwaite, "Local Banking in Renaissance Florence," *JEEcH* 14 (1985): 5–55, reprinted as chap. 4 in his *Banks, Palaces, and Entrepreneurs in Renaissance Florence* (London, 1995).

[14]See Marco Spallanzani, "A Note on Florentine Banking in the Renaissance: Orders of Payment and Cheques," *JEEcH* 7 (1978): 145–68, and "L'apside dell'Alberti a San Martino a Gangalandi: Nota di storia economica," *Mitteilungen des kunsthistorischen Institutes in Florenz* 19 (1975): 241–50.

[15]Giulio Mandich, "Monete di conto veneziane in un libro di commercio del 1336–1339,"

ii. EARLIEST DOCUMENTARY EVIDENCE

The banking system installed at the Rialto and described by these observers of the Quattrocento had been developed long before them. Documentation for the early period, however, is extremely scanty, and it is not until almost 1300 that we can be sure that the process of transformation from moneychanging to transfer banking had taken place.

One must assume the presence and activity of moneychangers in Venice in the early centuries, for the Rialto was already a hub of interregional commercial activity by the eleventh century. At the end of that century, precisely in 1097, a large part of the Rialto passed by donation into the public domain. The government thereby became the landlord also of the tables of moneychangers, which were rented out at public auction to the benefit of the communal treasury.[16] The earliest reference to rent income derived from the public marketplace is also the first reference to tables of moneychangers ("tabule"). A notarized contract of 1164, by which the rents from the Rialto were turned over for a period of eleven years to a group of citizens who had made a large loan to the Commune, distinguished the tabule from the generic category of shops ("stationes") and other rent-producing stands and storage rooms under which they were generally included.[17]

The earliest occasion on which the names of moneychangers who rented tabule are preserved dates from 1225. In that year the doge and his council confirmed a three-year rental agreement at 15 lire per year for a tabula assigned to Marinus Decaçatus. It was described as being situated "next to the table of Vidotus Sinolo and across from that of Çordanus."[18] The names are those of commoners, persons who, despite the importance of their profession for the functioning of the marketplace, probably had no voice in political decision making.

The earliest extant regulations of the Great Council regarding moneychangers date from the 1260s. They show that "campsores" were active not only at the Rialto but also on Piazza San Marco and that in both locations they were involved in the bullion trade. In 1266 officials of the Gold Office were called upon to test all the weights and scales of the campsores at the Rialto and at San Marco at least once each month.[19] In 1268 German

---

SV, n.s., 8 (1984): 30–36, assumes a clear distinction between "contadi di banco," as good as specie, and "buona scrittura," which could be used only in book transfers. He does not take a position on eventual written orders. The only written order I have uncovered is an IOU with a bearer clause, purchased (and probably discounted) by Melchiore de Coltis e nipoti, bankers (or at least former bankers) at the Rialto. See below, App. G.

[16]Cessi and Alberti, *Rialto,* 20–23.

[17]*PRV,* doc. 1.

[18]*PMV,* doc. 5, and *DMC,* 1:93.

[19]*DMC,* 2:312.

importers of silver and silver coins were required to sell at the Rialto or on the San Marco exchange ("ad cambium Sancti Marci") whatever they did not sell to the mint.[20] Ten years later further laws regulating the bullion market required the moneychangers to swear a solemn oath before the doge himself to abide by them.[21] But continual policing of the market was necessary. In 1283 the moneychangers were accused of trying to forestall, leaving their exchange tables to corner an importer ("causa capiendi aliquem theotonicum vel mercatorem") and negotiate a purchase. The Signori di Notte therefore were given the responsibility of seeing to it that the merchants were left free to approach whomever they wished in order to sell their silver.[22] At the same time, the regulatory officials themselves might be held to account before the moneychangers for their activity. In 1274 the doge and his council selected three unnamed campsores to examine the records of a public assayer who, as a result of their investigation, was deprived of his office.[23]

Contemporaneous with the regulation of the role of campsores in the bullion market, authorities expressed concern over the trustworthiness of the moneychangers and the solidity of their operations as bankers. On three occasions between 1270 and 1318 the Great Council formulated and amended the requirement that any person wishing to operate as campsor in Venice first post bond. What was involved was a personal guarantee put up by persons other than the moneychanger and his partners. As discussed more fully below, the bond, demanded of moneychangers in many cities (see Vol. 1, chap. 6), was in Venice probably also a guarantee of obedience both to the law of the state and to the law of the marketplace, for guarantors were liable in case of the insolvency of the moneychanger. This policy was inaugurated because moneychangers were no longer merely exchanging one coin for another on the spot but accepting deposits, making transfers, extending loans exceeding their reserves — in short, they had become bankers.

iii. DEPOSITS AND CURRENT ACCOUNTS: THE ORIGINS OF THE BANCO DI SCRITTA

It is Raymond de Roover's generally accepted thesis that banking developed out of moneychanging; to this he added that the manual exchange of coins — foreign for local, gold for silver, and vice versa — was "one of [the local bankers'] principal sources of profit." No Florentine accounting source has yet been found that corroborates de Roover's assumption by

---

[20]*PMV*, doc. 14, and *DMC*, 2:299.

[21]*PMV*, doc. 26 (1278) and *DMC*, 2:248–49. Also from 1278 is the rule that any moneychanger seeking to purchase silver in the mint while the mintmasters were negotiating with foreign purveyors be sent away. *PMV*, doc. 25, p. 24, para. 38.

[22]Melchiore Roberti, ed., *Le magistrature giudiziarie veneziane e i loro capitolari fino al 1300*, 3 vols. (Padua and Venice, 1906–11), 3:40, cap. 38.

[23]*DMC*, 2:427.

showing how profits made on manual exchange were recorded. I have only a few references, scattered and inconclusive, to fees taken on the exchange of coins in Venice. Magistrates and commentators held that moneychangers actually made their profits from passing off inferior coins to the unaware or by accepting coins by weight and paying them out by tale. That way, bankers contributed directly to the deterioration of the currency, the integrity of which they were supposed to uphold. A banker in 1345 charged one-half bagattino per ducat (0.065%) in consigning gold ducats in exchange for soldini. A century later a banker charged a government office a fee of 1.6 percent for changing Hungarian florins into ducats. About that time bankers took their commission on gold-silver exchanges by withholding one or more soldini from the going exchange rate of 124 soldi per ducat; during the monetary crisis of 1472, the state limited the commission to one soldino, that is, 0.8 percent.[24] It is easy enough to imagine how, in the course of manipulating coins, the banker could convince a client to leave money with him in a savings deposit or a current account.

Venetian law and practice recognized the distinction between the *depositum regulare* and the *depositum irregulare* developed by jurists in the later Middle Ages.[25] The former involved the consignment of valuables (including money, if in sealed bags), merchandise, or other goods for safekeeping. The custodian, whether merchant or moneychanger, had no right to use what was so left on deposit; it was nonfungible and sterile, and he had to restore to the owner on demand exactly what had been left with him. For the service rendered, he could charge a fee.

The irregular deposit, on the other hand, involved coin. As a fungible,

---

[24]For Florence, see de Roover, *Medici Bank,* 17 (the source he cites refers to a brokerage fee, however, not an exchange fee), and Goldthwaite, "Local Banking," 17–19. The Officiales Grossorum Tonsorum fined the banker Andreolo Sanador in 1345 for not making an exchange at his bank, a way of evading controls on bad soldini; they testified at his appeal "quod nichil lucrantur de bonis soldinis . . . , sed de male bene lucrantur, quos ipsi [campsores] emunt occulte et parvo precio, et ipsos dant personis ignorabilibus." The fee was not at issue. ASV, Grazie, reg. 11, fol. 40v. This judgment was shared completely by Tommaso Contarini, writing in 1584; Lattes, *Libertà,* 126–27. In 1463, the Ziera bank took 6½ ducats for changing 184 Hungarian florins into ducats; since those coins, very current in Venice and the Terraferma, were valued at 122 soldi, half the 3.5 percent charge was for the difference in exchange, half for the commission. ASV, PSM, Ultra, b. 424, fasc. 2, fol. 18 (17 March 1463). In June 1472, Giovanni de Strigis wrote to the marquis of Mantua that Venetian bankers had been taking 2 and 3 soldi per ducat (1.6–2.4%) as commission ("per la sua merzede del cambio"), reduced by decree to 1 soldo (0.8%). ASMN, Carteggio estero, Carteggio da inviati, b. 1431 (6 June).

[25]See Umberto Santarelli, *La categoria dei contratti irregolari: Lezioni di storia del diritto* (Turin, 1990), who treats in exemplary fashion the historical development of the juridical category of the irregular deposit and its differentiation also from the *mutuum* in the works of medieval and early modern jurists. It must be noted that in commercial parlance throughout the Quattrocento to invest "nel cambio e in depositi" meant simply to make loans — generally investment loans — at interest; in that context the term *deposito* does not refer to current accounts and deposit banking. This is corroborated both by correspondence and by lawsuits.

money deposited with a shopkeeper or banker was not repaid upon demand in the exact same coins originally deposited but merely in coins of equal value; the depositary had the obligation to "restore the equivalent" ("restituere tantundem"), as the jurists put it. The person making an irregular deposit at least tacitly permitted the depositary to employ the funds, which implied both the passage of ownership from depositor to depositary and some kind of participation by the depositor in the risk of the enterprise, whether the deposit was interest bearing or not.

The distinction between these two kinds of deposits is reflected in a law concerning bankruptcy passed by the Great Council in 1330 and then incorporated into the statutes of the city.[26] The law states that anyone who deposits for safekeeping ("occasione depositi seu salvamenti") any valuables or merchandise, or the keys providing access thereto, into the hands of a shopkeeper or moneychanger ("in statione sive volta seu ad tabulam cambii") had the right to reclaim the deposit in full in the case of insolvency of the depositary. In other words, it was not to be considered part of the assets divided among the creditors in the process of liquidation. In order to distinguish the legal nature of such a regular deposit from that of an irregular deposit, the statute specifically denied the same right to anyone who had deposited money for ends other than safekeeping in a bank that then defaulted: "excepto pecunia tamen quam aliquis posuerit ad aliquam tabulam plenius exceptata."[27] Funds so placed with a banker formed part of his liabilities, with all the risks involved, and the depositors had to wait their turn for repayment, as determined by the committee of creditors.

It is hardly surprising that a person might wish to deposit money with a moneychanger primarily for safekeeping.[28] But when was that deposit to be considered regular? when irregular? when an investment? In 1342 Isabetta Querini, a depositor at the bank of Marino Vendelino, filed suit in the

---

[26]ASV, MC, Spiritus, fol. 44r–v, published by Giovanni Cassandro, *Le rappresaglie e il fallimento a Venezia nei secoli XIII–XVI* (Turin, 1938), 139–41, doc. 6.

[27]Ibid., 141. The legal rationale, explained later by Baldus (1327–1400), was this: in the case of the regular deposit, ownership of the nonfungible remained with the depositor; in the irregular deposit, by contrast, coin, a fungible, was counted out in paying and only the "tantundem," the equivalent value in coin, was counted out in repaying, and here the ownership passed from the depositor to the depositary ("quia consuetudo est ad numerum dare et ad numerum reddere, praesumitur dominium translatum"). In the former case, the depositor, as owner, could claim the whole good; in the latter, he owned only a credit and had to await liquidation of the banker's liabilities and payment "pro rata creditorum." Santarelli, *La categoria dei contratti irregolari*, 108–9. The law of 1330 and the lawsuit of 1342 presently to be discussed show that Venetian lawmakers and judges, all nonprofessionals, understood and applied these concepts.

[28]See, for example, the deposition of a German merchant in 1343: "Et videns periculosum erat tenere penes se dictos florenos, recomendavit eos ad tabulam ser Filippi Marmora, ut melius essent ibi salvi." Heinrich Simonsfeld, *Der Fondaco dei Tedeschi in Venedig und die deutsch-venetianischen Handelsbeziehungen*, 2 vols. (Stuttgart, 1887; reprint, Aalen, 1968), 1:484–85, doc. 804. For a similar case, see ASV, Grazie, reg. 12, fol. 91v (1 December 1350).

court of the Consoli dei Mercanti against the guarantors of the bank when it failed, claiming repayment in full, outside the context of the liquidation process, of money she had left ("dedisse et deponisse") at the bank. As proof of her deposit, which she claimed to be regular, she exhibited two receipts she had received from the banker. Voting two to one, the Consoli agreed with Isabetta and ruled that the guarantors were to pay part of the credit "as a deposit at the Vendelino bank" [tamquam pecuniam depositam in tabulam dicti Marini Vendelini campsoris], sidestepping as clear a distinction as would have been required in Roman law. The dissenting consul, however, promoted the appeal of the guarantors before the Avogadori di Comun and the Quarantia. In that forum the guarantors repeated their position, "saying that the money had not been deposited in the bank but had merely been invested with the banker in the hope of earning a profit" [dicti pleçii se defendentes respondebant dicentes dictam quantitatem pecunie non fuisse depositam in tabulam dicti Marini sed solum datam per ipsam dominam dicto Marino in lucrum et sub specie lucri]. The Quarantia was so sharply divided over the case that it took seven ballots before a decision in favor of the guarantors was reached and the ruling of the Consoli overturned.[29] Areas of doubt were bound to exist in this early period in the development of banking.

Deposits of money in a bank which were clearly irregular according to Roman law were in Venetian practice either conditioned or credited to current account. A conditioned deposit was a kind of time deposit (or certificate of deposit) in which the terms for repayment were fixed by agreement between depositor and depositary and tied to the fulfillment of specific conditions, such as the coming of age of a son, the dowering of a daughter, a particular investment, or a court order. Since it was not payable on demand, a conditioned deposit was a particularly important kind of bank credit which the banker could use for financing enterprises, and he thus paid an interest or dividend, the rate of which depended on the success of the banking firm or of business in general. This practice was judged legitimate by civil authorities as early as 1301, on condition that the bank or other similar business firm was known customarily to accept such deposits.[30] The fluctuating rates of interest they paid on capital left with them were common knowledge in the business community. In fact, throughout most of the fourteenth century their rates constituted a standard for the

---

[29] The whole case is related in ASV, AC, reg. 3642, fol. 44r–v (6 September 1342). It is interesting to note that guarantors of bankers in Bruges during the same period, 1340–80, also refused to be liable for deposits on which interest was paid. Raymond de Roover, *Money, Banking, and Credit in Mediaeval Bruges: Italian Merchant-Bankers, Lombards, and Money-Changers: A Study in the Origins of Banking* (Cambridge, Mass., 1948), 249 and app. 1.

[30] The text of this memorandum of 1301 on usury was transcribed in Reinhold C. Mueller, *The Procuratori di San Marco and the Venetian Credit Market: A Study of the Development of Credit and Banking in the Trecento* (Ph.D. diss., 1969; New York, 1977), app. 1.

rates due on loan contracts called "local colleganze," notarial acts that provide further proof that bankers paid interest on conditioned deposits.[31] Not only might the capital deposited be conditioned, but the depositor's profit might also be conditioned in order to provide an income, for example, for orphans or for some pious purpose. The earliest extant reference to a bank deposit involves a conditioned deposit with some of these characteristics. In 1274 the Great Council ordered a man said to be "in mala via" to provide alimony for his separated wife and child, and it directed that interest paid on his government obligations and eventual amortization payments, in excess of the annual allowance of 60 lire, be deposited with a banker in the name of the wife and son ("ponatur ad unam tabulam ad nomen predicte mulieris et filii").[32] Although the authorities did not specify in this instance that the money was to constitute an interest-bearing deposit, later cases show that contemporaries took it for granted they could earn interest by leaving money in a bank. For example, the 230 ducats left to a minor son in 1332 were ordered placed "ad unam tabulam pro lucrando."[33] Even foreigners were aware of such opportunities in Venice. In 1374 a nobleman of the island of Cherso (or Cres, in Dalmatia), Dragogna de Balbas, requested that his executors transfer 1,500 ducats of his assets to Venice and deposit the money at some bank ("super aliquo bancho") so that from the interest ("de usufructu") two priests could be paid for saying masses for the salvation of his soul.[34]

That bankers paid interest on such conditioned deposits is also reflected in the tradition that lasted throughout much of the fourteenth century whereby the interest or return on private loan contracts called local colleganze was tied to the rate of interest which a specific moneychanger or other capitalist paid on money left with him.[35]

References to conditioned deposits in the fifteenth century do not mention interest, but they do offer further examples of the kinds of conditions which could be applied to deposits. In 1445 the Giudici di Petizion conditioned an account pending conclusion of legal action, when they ordered the freezing of all bank accounts held in the name of a Ser Bartolomeo Soranzo.[36] When in 1449 the Patroni of the arsenal were ordered to set aside 80 ducats per month to pay for construction of a roof over an area of the

---

[31]The earliest case yet found in which the rate of interest paid by a campsor is given as the standard also dates from 1301; see ibid., 78–79.

[32]*DMC,* 2:161.

[33]ASV, AC, reg. 3641, fol. 17 (6 May 1332).

[34]Surely because of the banking crisis in Venice, as elsewhere, in 1374, the executors of the estate, who in their petition quoted from the testament of the deceased, asked and received permission to invest the sum instead in Venetian government obligations. ASV, Grazie, reg. 17, fol. 47v. For the dissenting official's testimony, see below, Chap. 14, n. 5.

[35]On local colleganze and banks, see Mueller, *Procuratori di San Marco,* 72–97.

[36]ASV, GP, Frammenti antichi, b. 13, terminationes, 1445 (under the date 20 August 1445).

arsenal, they were told to deposit the money in the Soranzo bank; the sum could not be touched for any other purpose.[37] A final example is that of Lena Nani, widow of Bertuccio Morosini, who in 1478 bequeathed to the Franciscans of the Frari, among other things, a deposit of 140 ducats in the Garzoni bank, which could not be withdrawn for any purpose other than to buy revenue-producing land ("terreni fructiferi") in the Terraferma.[38] Very likely, contemporaries simply assumed such deposits would earn interest, for a case from the mid-sixteenth century speaks with the same clarity as the fourteenth-century cases. In her testament of 1556, Lucietta da Pozzo ordered her executors to deposit 100 lire di grossi in the Dolfin bank as a "partita condizionata," on which the interest ("prode") was to be spent "amore Dei."[39]

There is, practically speaking, little difference between a conditioned bank deposit and a loan to a banker. Documents reflecting the investor's preference of a notarized contract of loan over a time deposit seem to be restricted to the period of the mid-fourteenth century and to cases involving inheritances, or perhaps also to doubts about the solidity of the depositary. In 1330 and 1331, just before his death, Stefano Manolesso made three sizeable loans (for a total of 970 ducats) in the form of local colleganze to Zonino Alberegno, campsor. Following the usual form for such loans, the contracts foresaw payment of a return ("prode") and named one or more guarantors. It is not possible to know whether or not the lender had had premonitions, but in 1332 Alberegno failed. Thanks to Manolesso's caution, the loans had to be repaid to his estate by the guarantors of the loans; that way they seem to have avoided the problems tied to the liquidation of the bank.[40] Another example is practically coeval. In her testament of 1329 Margherita da Mosto instructed her executors, the Procurators of San Marco, to deposit 100 lire at a bank as legacies for each of her two daughters, who were to receive the interest. In 1333 the Procurators chose the form of the local colleganza over the conditioned deposit when they lent 100 lire to Francesco Corner, campsor. Each year for four years the banker paid a 7 percent return to the estate.[41] In a third case the Procurators used the same formula when they lent 500 ducats from the estate of Andriolo Betino to Marco Stornado, campsor. Stornado, coopted into the Great

---

[37]ASV, CN, reg. 8, fol. 101 (9 September 1449).

[38]ASV, CIN, Miscellanea testamenti notai diversi, b. 27, n. 2594.

[39]ASV, PSM, Supra, commissarie, b. 35.

[40]Ibid., Misti, b. 83, reg., fols. 11–12. The third loan, however, ran into problems and may not have been fully repaid.

[41]Ibid., Ultra, b. 207. The legacy for the first daughter reads: "Item, dimitto Gratolde filie mee libras denariorum venetialium centum, tali quidem condicione quod poni debeant per comissarios meos dicte libre centum ad unam tabulam campsorum ad utilitatem et lucrum dicte filie mee, et prode . . . debeat habere dicta Gratolda filia mea." For the accounts, see the reg., under "Dare in collegantiis."

Council after the War of Chioggia, enjoyed the use of the money from 1372 to 1383, paying 5 percent interest annually.[42]

Distinguishable from conditioned accounts, time deposits, and notarized loans to bankers are deposits on current account. Such "giro" accounts early became the hallmark of Venetian banking and were what so impressed the observers quoted earlier. A deposit on current account in medieval Venice served a function comparable to that of checking accounts today, that is, it was not intended primarily for safekeeping or for earning interest but rather as a means of payment which facilitated the clearance of debts incurred in the process of doing business. In short, the current account constituted "bank money," money based on the banker's promise to pay, which the client could transfer to his creditor by oral order to settle a debt without the use of coin. With the agreement of the banker, he could make a payment also by overdrawing his account.

Once moneychangers began accepting regular and irregular deposits, as they did in Venice during the thirteenth century, the step toward the ready transferability of deposits on current account was short. Still, it is impossible to be precise about when that step was taken. The earliest evidence dates from the end of the thirteenth century, from a suit aired before the commercial court of the Giudici di Petizion. The claimant in the case, the nobleman Andrea Grussoni, related in 1298 that during the lifetime of the moneychanger Bernardo de Bernardo he had regularly deposited money and had money deposited by others in his name at Bernardo's exchange table, confident of the latter's trustworthiness and legality. The statement reflects the fact that it was an accepted practice to have debtors pay by transferring sums to the account of their creditor.[43]

---

[42]Ibid., Misti, b. 145, commis. A. Betino, reg. 1 (Dare in collegantiis), and parchment notarial act of 3 September 1378. Beginning in 1376 the value of the loan was lent in turn by Stornado to Donato Moro, father-in-law of the guarantor, "under the same conditions"; renegotiated for the last time in 1378, the loan was repaid only in 1383. Stornado, who had an exceptionally high assessment (19,500 lire d'estimo), made his testament on 16 August 1383 and died the following year, sometime before July. See the profile in Maria Teresa Todesco, "Aggregati ed esclusi: Le cooptazioni al Maggior Consiglio al tempo della guerra di Chioggia" (laurea thesis, University of Venice, 1986–87).

[43]ASV, PSM, Ultra, b. 43, commis. Bernardo de Bernardo. A partial transcription of the case was published by Bartolomeo Cecchetti, "Appunti sulle finanze antiche della Repubblica Veneta," *AV* 35 (1888): 41 n. 3. The text just paraphrased reads: "dictus nobilis Andreas Grussoni allegabat sic dicens, quod dum viveret Bernardus de Bernardo campsor, confidens de bonitate et legalitate ipsius, deponebat et faciebat deponi penes illum et ad suum tabulam de pecunia sua." The entry that Grussoni presented to the court from his own account books as evidence in his claim for repayment of a loan against Bernardo's son and heir Marco de Bernardo seems also to involve a simple in-bank transfer of 78 lire a grossi from Grussoni's account to that of Marco, as a loan mediated by the banker to his own son. The extract, in vernacular, reads as follows: "1294, dì XII in decembre, et libre LXXVIIJ a grossi ke ò dé a lo dito ser Marco de Bernardo lo dito dì ke vu l'inpreste." The judges awarded the amount plus court costs to the claimant Grussoni.

A second early occasion on which a similar kind of in-bank transfer is reported involves the administration of the estate of the famous Marco Polo. A relative bearing the same name as the author of *Il milione* reported the manner in which he had repaid, in four installments in the course of the year 1325, a sum that he owed the estate for a loan. He quoted from his own account book to show that he had paid the executor partly in cash, partly with a credit rendered at the Salt Office, and partly with transfers at two different banks. In the case of each transfer it is a third party, probably one who in turn owed him money, who actually ordered the transfer "per mi," the first at the bank of Nicoletto Zuchol, the second at the bank of Nicoletto Lanzuol.[44]

The earliest evidence from government sources of the existence of a full-fledged system of transfer banking in Venice dates from the same decade as the Polo case. In the early 1320s the Great Council had to deal with a tight money situation. Three laws were passed in those years which, taken together, prove the existence in current banking practice of three factors crucial to the definition of a banking system: that payment in bank money was a legitimate means of extinguishing a debt, as long as the creditor party agreed; that bankers kept a cash reserve for only a fraction of their liabilities; and that one banker kept current accounts with the other bankers.

The law of October 1322 reflects all three of these factors.[45] It begins by admitting the existence of interbank accounts that made it possible for a banker who did not wish to (or who could not) meet a demand for a cash withdrawal to send the client-depositor to another bank for collection. The law forbade that approach to discouraging cash withdrawals by outlawing the circulation of liabilities among banks. Such a provision, which inhibited the potential creation of bank money via multiple expansion, could only have worsened the tight money situation—and in fact, it was repealed four years later.[46] The law then reiterated a provision of the previous

---

[44]The loan, for 550 ducats, seems to have been in the usual form of a local colleganza; repaid "per cavedal e per pro'," it earned 12.5 percent interest, for an undefined period of time. The two relevant entries read: "Item diè a li diti comessarii, die XVI de luio, li qual avè ser Marco Bragadin in tolla de ser Nicolleto Zuchol, dèlili ser Donado Diedo per mi, libre XXI de grossi ... Item, li qual avè del dito ser Marco, dì V de decenbrio, in bancho de ser Nicolleto Lanzuol, pagalli per mi ser Donado Diedho, libre III, soldi III, denari III de grossi." Quoted in a quittance of 1364, published by Rudolfo Gallo, "Marco Polo, la sua famiglia e il suo libro," in *Nel VII Centenario della nascita di Marco Polo,* ed. Istituto veneto di scienze, lettere ed arti (Venice, 1955), app. 6, p. 117.

[45]*PMV,* liv and doc. 80.

[46]Ibid., doc. 87 (the year should be corrected to 1326). Venice was not unique in this regard. Depositors in Barcelona also complained about being sent from bank to bank to collect; see Abbott P. Usher, "Deposit Banking in Barcelona, 1300–1700," *Journal of Economic and Business History* 4 (1931): 140. An attempt was made in Genoa in 1399 to restrict the practice of sending clients to other banks by permitting it only for sums exceeding 100 lire. See John Day, *Les douanes des Gênes, 1376–1377,* 2 vols. (Paris, 1963), 1:xiv n. 4. In Venice in 1526 the practice was again confronted; see Lattes, *Libertà,* doc. 32, para. 11.

year,[47] when it insisted that a banker convert a demand liability into specie at his own bank within three days of the request for withdrawal. This provision reflects the fact that bankers discouraged cash withdrawals precisely because they operated on a system of fractional reserve, that is, they kept as little cash as possible in the till, while lending and investing the rest. The obligation to pay up in three days' time remained on the books, and the Officiales Grossorum Tonsorum, who had jurisdiction, seem at least occasionally to have applied it to the letter.[48] But the law of 1322 was not only restrictive, for it also recognized the legitimacy of payment via transfer of the banker's promise to pay. The beneficiary of a transfer (take, for example, the borrower, Marco de Bernardo, in the case of 1294 documented above, n. 43) did not have to accept coins from the banker in order to conclude the payment process definitively but could choose to accept payment on the books of the banker, who merely credited his account. And on two occasions in the same law, the procedure of transferring a credit in bank with the mere stroke of a pen is clearly referred to with the verb *scribere,* to mean that service particularly characteristic of Venetian banks, for which they would later be called "banchi di scritta."[49]

In the course of the following decades, the verb *scribere* came to be used to refer to the transfer of money on current account, while the verb *deponere* and the noun *depositum* came to be reserved for conditioned deposits, left for safekeeping and for earning interest. This distinction was clearly intended in a proposal for the establishment of a state bank pre-

---

[47]*PMV,* doc. 79, p. 73. Cf. Alessandro Lattes, *Il diritto commerciale nella legislazione statutaria delle città italiane* (Milan, 1884), 208.

[48]Jacobello Dandolo accused Nicolò Lanzolo, campsor at the Rialto and the same banker mentioned above in the Polo case, of not paying within three days the 100 ducats he had asked to withdraw, even though the third day fell on a Sunday. The officials proceeded to fine him the 10 percent required by the law. In his successful petition for a pardon, Lanzolo declared that he had prepared the money but the client had not returned to claim it and that the office had not followed due process (giving a warning, "ut moris est"). He expressed surprise, furthermore, at the comportment of the client: "mirando tamen de tali peticione, cum sua non sit consuetudo de faciendo sibi petere denarios." ASV, Grazie, reg. 8, fol. 65 (27 June 1340). See also reg. 5, fol. 22v (17 March 1333) for a stay of sentence in favor of Maffeo Gritti, campsor, who was delaying payment of more than 150 ducats to Nicolò Zuccol, himself a banker (or at least he had been one in 1325–26). Prompt payment of demand deposits concerned lawmakers in the 1520s as well; see Lattes, *Libertà,* doc. 30, p. 82. Bankers even had to leave a cash deposit of 500 ducats with the Bank Supervisors; ibid., doc. 31, para. 3, and doc. 32, para. 10.

[49]The text is of particular interest: "Quia campsores faciunt dure solutiones, quas facere debeat, et aliquando conducunt homines de tabula in tabulam . . . , capta fuit pars quod campsores non possint ullo modo sibi ad invicem seu unus alteri scribere aliquod debitum. Insuper teneantur omnes campsores facere solutiones suas super suis propris tabulis, et non alibi, infra diem tercium, postquam fuerint requisiti. . . . Salvo quod si aliqua specialis persona, que recipere debebit aliquid ab aliquo campsore, contentabitur quod ille campsor scribat sibi ipsum debitum super quaterno ipsius campsoris, possit ipsum debitum libere scribere sibi super suo quaterno proprio." *PMV,* doc. 80.

sented by Giovanni Dolfin in 1356. The administrators of the bank, it was proposed, would not be permitted to accept any conditioned deposit but only money left on current account for the sake of facilitating payments by transfer.[50]

Brief extracts from bankers' books brought as evidence before commercial and probate courts become more frequent beginning in the second half of the fourteenth century, when court records survive in greater number. Extracts were produced from the banker's book of first entry, his journal, which was the authoritative document in these cases. A clear early example of this kind of evidence is a claim filed in 1367 by Zanino Soranzo against the estate of his father Piero for his wife's dowry. In support of his claim he brought an extract from the journal of the bank of Jacomello Zancani and Brothers, which showed two payments by transfer; in each the ultimate beneficiary had been his father. In fact, Piero Soranzo had the right, "tamquam pater familias," to hold his son's dowry, and he had done so for more than a year in a kind of familial conditioned deposit. The stylized journal entries (the first of which is a double transfer) read as follows:

> 1366, a dì 7 março, per ser Zacharia Contarini
> [the father-in-law], a ser Zanni Sovrançó de meser
> Piero, e per lui a meser Piero Sovranzo da
> S. Ançollo . . . £50 di grossi.
> 1366, a dì 19 zugno, per ser Zanni Sovranzo a ser
> Piero Sovranzo . . . £26, 12s di grossi.

The probate court ordered immediate payment from the estate.[51]

Much more significant sources than such traces from the accounts of bankers themselves are the few private account books that are still extant. The three earliest, which fall in the period 1350–80, have been preserved among the estate papers of the Procurators of San Marco. Although they are small and surely atypical, they reflect the regular use of current bank accounts. The first two were kept by noblemen of mediocre wealth and little interest in commerce; nonetheless, they contain active current accounts with Rialto bankers, accounts that occasionally contain examples of trans-

---

[50] "Non recipiant nec teneant aliquam quantitatem pecunie vel aliquem denarium seu deposi-
tu.... ....ucto bancho . . . , sed solum teneantur facere scribi omnes solutiones, que fient de persona ad personam." *PMV*, doc. 124, and Gino Luzzatto, "Les banques publiques de Venise: Siècles XVIᶜ–XVIIIᶜ," as reprinted in his *Studi di storia economica veneziana* (Padua, 1954), 228.

[51] The rationale for the transfers was "quia quidem doctem suam ipse pater suus habuit tamquam pater familias in deposito et salvamento." Sentence of the Giudici del Procurator, parchment dated 14 June 1367, in ASV, PSM, Misti, b. 73, commis. of Pietro Soranzo qd. Lorenzo. Claims were also filed against the estate by the bankers Jacobello Zancani and Brothers (30 March 1367) and Bartolomeo Micheli (22 June 1367) "pro resto racionis banchi," that is, probably for overdrafts uncovered at the death of their client.

fers into and out of the account. The third belonged to wealthy merchants of Florentine origin but naturalized citizens of Venice. In all three, the terse entries reflect the banker's intermediary role as he transferred his promise to pay from debtor to creditor.

The account book of the nobleman Andrea Malipiero, which covers the years 1350–62, is derived or carried over from another account book (it was entitled "Debitori e creditori trato de altro quaderno").[52] Although there are current accounts with three bankers, and mentions of two others, Malipiero dealt most often with Alvise Viaro, "cambiator." The account with Viaro opens with a credit balance carried over from the old ledger ("lo quaderno veio"). The great majority of operations, in both the debit and credit accounts, involve cash. One entry, on the other hand, clearly expresses the banker's intermediary role in partial payment of a dowry: "Alvise Viaro owes 1 lira to Cataruça . . . which I told him to transfer to her account."

In the second account book the nobleman Daniele Emo opens his current account with the banker Piero Zancani in February 1362 with a transfer of 20 ducats from Emo's debtor, Piero Dalmer.[53] The corresponding personal account expresses the banker's intermediary role: "The banker Zancani owes me 20 ducats in Dalmer's name." Of the twenty-four deposits recorded during the eighteen months the account was open, eight were credited in this manner; sixteen were made in cash, and a cash account was credited. On the credit side one finds that Emo withdrew cash to make most of his sixty-two payments, but nine entries show Emo paying his debts in bank, and they use terse phrases that mean, in effect, that Emo was transferring to his creditor his banker's promise to pay.

The first extant account book of an active merchant is that of Tommaso Talenti, immigrant from Florence and naturalized citizen of Venice.[54] Although the Talenti family had invested heavily in the production and distribution of silk cloth, as we know from company contracts of the 1360s,[55] Tommaso and his brother Zaccaria decided in 1380 to exploit the crisis in Venice caused by the War of Chioggia by importing wheat from the mainland to feed a population whose usual provisioning by sea had been

---

[52]ASV, PSM, Misti, b. 94. Malipiero dealt also with the banks of Armelino da Mosto (fol. 10) and Marino Baffo and Marco Trevisan (fol. 11). Descriptions of this account book and those next to be discussed, along with transcriptions of sample entries, are in Reinhold C. Mueller, "The Role of Bank Money in Venice, 1300 – 1500," *SV,* n.s., 3 (1979): 53–56.

[53]ASV, PSM, Misti, b. 106. Of the two account books in Daniele Emo's commissaria, only the second carries the current account with the banker Piero Zancani (fols. 3v–4r, 7v–8r, 15v–16r).

[54]Ibid., Citra, b. 141, commis. Talenti, and Mueller, *Procuratori di San Marco,* 201–6. On Talenti's role in Venetian cultural life, see Nardi, "Letteratura e cultura veneziana," which also provides the full text of Talenti's testament (130–35).

[55]Luca Molà, *La comunità dei lucchesi a Venezia: Immigrazione e industria della seta nel tardo Medioevo,* Istituto veneto di scienze, lettere ed arti, Memorie, 53 (Venice, 1994), 198–99.

cut off by the Genoese fleet. Purchasers of the wheat paid their debts in silver coin, which Talenti promptly deposited at the Rialto bank of Gabriele Soranzo. The credits were recorded in money of account and were then immediately available for making payments; as Talenti put it, he deposited the cash with Soranzo so that the latter could then debit the account upon order by Talenti to pay creditors: "per tener il conto seco e scontarmi con il suo libro." In fact, almost all the payments recorded were made via transfer of bank money.

Each of these three early Venetian account books reveals that active accounts were kept with a favorite banker, while short, transitory accounts were kept with other bankers in order to facilitate the collection of accounts receivable. This was true also in the following century.

An idea of the frequency with which clients had recourse to their bankers can be had from the early accounts. Daniele Emo, the petty lender who used his bank account mostly for cash dealings, made eighty-six transactions on seventy-seven business days, over an eighteen-month period. Tommaso Talenti frequented his bank at nearly the same rate: over a period of four and one-half months he made twenty-nine transactions on eighteen business days.

As would be expected, it was at the banks where an operator was a regular client that he could expect preferential treatment and the liberty of overdrawing his account in case of need. All three books record overdrafts, although for relatively small sums and for relatively short periods. Emo's account was in the red on nine occasions totaling a quarter of the time covered by the account. Talenti overdrew his account on three occasions and remained in the red only 13 percent of the time.[56]

Many more private account books — large ledgers, some with matching journals — are extant for the following century, the most important of which are well known to economic historians.[57] By the early Quattrocento the manner of registering accounts in the ledger, especially accounts with bankers, had become highly stylized. An examination of the current accounts maintained by the Soranzo brothers and by Andrea Barbarigo shows that banks were absolutely central to the payments system and that bankers regularly allowed their principal clients to overdraw. When banks were in difficulty, as at the end of the century, one can note increased activity on the cash account as the merchant seems to have relied more and more on specie and less and less on bank money.

[56] On the use of overdrafts in the fourteenth century, see Mueller, *Procuratori di San Marco,* 197–99, 205–6.

[57] The list in Mueller, "Role of Bank Money," 56 n. 21, can fortunately be added to today, with reference to several account books in the Archivio Privato Donà, within ASV, Archivio Marcello-Grimani-Giustinian, bb. 165–68, beginning in the 1460s, as well as one or two of the Quattrocento (and several later) in the Biblioteca Querini Stampalia, Venice, of the Querini family itself.

The frequency of recourse to a bank, as reflected in the Quattrocento sources, was quite varied. The Soranzo fraterna, a very large firm of cotton importers, had dealings with the Priuli banks surprisingly rarely and generally for large sums: a count for six random years between 1407 and 1428 shows the brothers making only twenty-five to thirty operations on about twenty business days per year. On the debit side of the current accounts, we find the receipts from sales of cotton to German merchants; on the credit side are often registered large withdrawals of specie "per navegar," that is, for loading on cogs and galleys as an exchange commodity for Syrian cotton. Andrea Barbarigo, on the other hand, was a smaller merchant who operated alone with a small capital base. He had recourse to the banker Francesco Balbi much more often: some 140 to 150 operations per year, on 75 to 100 business days. The entries are often for smaller sums and for a wider variety of operations.[58]

These same large ledgers also reflect the readiness of bankers to extend credit to their clients by permitting them to overdraw their current accounts. For example, the Soranzo fraterna in 1407 had rather inactive accounts with the Priuli and the Corner-Miorati banks; with the former, its account was overdrawn for nine months, with the latter for five months, but for sums ranging only from 30 to 60 ducats. Thereafter, if one limits the analysis to the times balances were carried forward, the fraterna was regularly in the black with the Priuli bank, and in the red twice with the bank of Giovanni Orsini and Brothers in 1427 and 1428, but for sums of only 10 to 20 ducats. Andrea Barbarigo, on the other hand, overdrew his account more often, especially in the early years of his business career. In 1431, for example, his account was in the red for ten weeks, for sums ranging between 400 and 1,700 ducats; but what had pulled the balance down was a very large payment of 2,000 ducats, by transfer, to another Balbi company —distinct from the bank—on 6 February. Thereafter, we find balances

[58]An examination of the current account kept with Balbi revealed the following:

Year	Operations	Business Days
1431	135	88
1432	147	91
1433	143	99
1441	118	75
1442	91	58
1443	98	70

In the first three years, the number of operations concluded at the bank of Cristoforo Soranzo was insignificant; in 1441 Barbarigo also dealt 22 times with the bank of Nicolò Bernardo and, in 1443, 44 times with the bank of Bernardo Ziera — operations concentrated in the months of June and July. The prevalence of debit or credit operations varied widely, except in 1443, when there were 49 on either side. See Barbarigo, ledgers A and B, and the Soranzo ledger; that the latter was in many ways anomalous, being a later copy compiled from other accounts, will be seen in more detail below.

carried forward in the red in June 1431, for 250 ducats; in May 1432, for 220 ducats; and four times in 1433 (March, July, October, and December), for sums ranging from as little as 20 ducats to as much as 550 ducats. The accounts were very mobile, however; the amounts changed rapidly, and the bank balance shifted between debit and credit. In the years 1441–43, by contrast, Barbarigo was always in the black when he carried balances forward, even though often for very small sums. These random samples are sufficient to show that overdrafts were common. Writing more than a century later about the pros and cons of Venetian banking, Tommaso Contarini asserted that in his time the majority of transactions on the Rialto were facilitated by overdrafts, not uncommonly of as high as 1,000 ducats.[59] Of course, not even a systematic analysis of the current accounts of private clients of Rialto banks would help to understand the extent of "float," that is, the money created by the banking system as a whole; for that, the banks' credits with the state were more significant, although similarly unmeasurable, as will be seen in Chapter 10.

A banker and his client had to meet occasionally to verify their separately kept records of the current account. The moment a balance had to be carried forward, for lack of space on a page, was one occasion; a date could be another occasion. For example, in a ledger kept by Donato and Jacomo Soranzo, the balance in the Orsini bank, in the red by 11 ducats in July 1427, was carried forward to the credit side "by agreement" ("per resto fato d'achordo"). Andrea Barbarigo recorded on his current account, in this case in the middle of a page, that his accounts agreed with those of Francesco Balbi; on the Venetian new year, 1 March 1431, he wrote, "per resto d'acordo." These were ways of verifying the credit status of the accounts, as well as the accuracy of the accounting of each party.[60]

Given the facility with which payments could be made in bank money, persons who frequented the Rialto market came to accept bank money early in a wide variety of transactions. The current accounts that active merchants kept at the banks were thoroughly integrated into the cycle of payments growing out of wholesale and retail transactions alike. Payment in bank for commodities is the most common use of bank money. Even those Florentine international bankers who established themselves in Venice, primarily as lenders and speculators in foreign exchange, maintained current accounts with the Rialto bankers. It was on the books of Venetian local bankers that exchange experts shifted the assets they drew and remitted all across Europe. Such operations are reflected in the account books kept in Venice by Florentine companies as early as the 1330s. Rialto

---

[59]Lattes, *Libertà,* 152.
[60]Soranzo ledger, fols. 129, 137; Barbarigo, ledger A, fol. 14. "Per resto tratto, d'accordo" is also the phrase recorded in the 1460s by Alvise Michiel when he had compared notes with the banker Piero Guerrucci; ASV, Miscellanea Gregolin, b. 15, ledger, fol. 55.

banks became so essential a part of the cycle that when they were closed, foreign exchange operations could not be concluded![61] Furthermore, holders of large and small accounts often lent money by ordering their banker to write the amount to the credit of the borrower. Real estate rents were similarly often paid in bank, whereby the banker became a kind of collection agent for his clients; the same is true when he was entrusted with collecting interest on their government obligations. Obviously, their presence at the bank was not called for on such occasions. The most risky operations involving bank accounts were those that combined high-value commodities and credit. Purchases and sales of gold and especially of silver were often concluded in bank. But because of the speculative nature of the deals involved, the government sometimes tried to control the expansion of bank money by requiring payment in specie for bullion purchased on the Rialto. The extent to which it was successful in maintaining some kind of control over these and similar credit operations is open to doubt; recourse to bank money offered such simple solutions in the cycle of payments that it is not surprising if it was widespread.

But were current accounts used by people below the level of middling wholesale and retail merchants? Tommaso Contarini, in the late sixteenth century, seems to reply affirmatively, even though he insisted especially on the utility of the banks for merchants.[62] For our period, in the absence of accounts kept by bankers themselves, a few scattered examples drawn from private accounts and referring to various categories can provide a glimpse of the wider role of banks in society. Women, especially widows, could be holders of conditioned or savings accounts, and an example was mentioned above, but they do not appear in extant ledgers as payers or beneficiaries of payments on current account. In cases in which government obligations were purchased from a woman, the value, while paid in bank, was credited to the account of a male, who acted in her name. Retail merchants are not much better represented in the sources. When Andrea Barbarigo purchased some pelts from the furrier Mafio "varoter," he paid the small sums he owed in cash; on the other hand, when he sold large quantities of cheese from his lands in Crete, presumably to retailers, one buyer brought cash to the banker Balbi and had it credited to Andrea's account, whereas another paid directly by transfer from his own account at the same bank.

The extent to which artisans may have held bank accounts will remain even more in doubt, especially since building records are rare. In 1400, the Florentine Bindo Piaciti, writing from Venice to Francesco di Marco

---

[61]For example, Zanobi Gaddi once acknowledged receipt of 135 lire remitted to Venice from Florence and continued: "ieri e ogi si può dire essere qua festa, che banchi non tenghono, sichè no' gli abiamo rimesi." ADP, 710, Gaddi to Florence, 6 February 1391.

[62]He wrote that banks involve "il beneficio di tutte le sorte et di tutte le condition di persone; non è alcun habbia o poco o molto che in quei non sia interessado. Sostenendosi il banco, si mantien il ben de tutti; cascando, tira con se universal ruina." Lattes, *Libertà*, 123.

Datini, blamed the run that brought down the bank of Pietro Benedetto on artisans and smaller depositors ("molti artigiani e altri Viniziani assai"), while merchant bankers, like himself, had left their money on deposit (see below, Chap. 5, sec. i.). Marino qd. Antonio Contarini, builder of the Ca' d'Oro in the 1420s, paid all his stonemasons and carpenters exclusively in cash; only a supplier of Istrian stone and roof tiles, a nobleman, was paid in bank.[63] Andrea Barbarigo paid his tailor in cash for a mantle (in three installments), but sums he owed to artisans in the building trades were sometimes handled in bank. In 1435, for example, he had extensive work done on the palace at S. Barnaba which he rented from "Zan Davanzo e compagni"; traces of the accounts remain because he subtracted the expenditures from the rent. The banker Balbi, who handled Barbarigo's rent payments, paid certain residual sums, ranging from ½ ducat to 5 ducats, from Andrea's current account to a carpenter, a mason, a maker of glass windows, a producer of nails, and a smith. Whereas in some cases the banker may have effected payment in cash, in others, such as the 5 ducats owed to Ser Bartolomeo da Crema, "muraro," he seems to have credited the artisan's current account. Ten years later, when Barbarigo was building a summer house at Montebelluna, again a small residual payment for the work done there by the master carpenter Marco was paid on current account at the bank of Bernardo Ziera and Company. Marco "marangon" presumably lived in Venice and was sent on occasion to the Trevigiano as the family's trusted artisan; in any case, he received in partial payment the small sum of 3s 6d di grossi, or about 1½ ducats, as a credit on a Venetian bank, collectable only there. Evidence such as this is inconclusive on several scores; the doubts raised cannot be answered on the basis merely of the client's accounts — to know exactly how the banker acted vis-à-vis the beneficiaries, one would need to see his accounts. The evidence is sufficient to show, however, that bankers mediated payments right down to the artisan class, providing a service for their clients, not inconceivably on the basis of simple orders-to-pay.[64]

[63]ASV, PSM, Citra, b. 269bis, vacchette III and IV, 1425–26. The supplier, Marco Bembo, was paid in the Bernardo bank on 8 June 1429. The building of the Ca' d'Oro was recently studied by Richard Goy, but without particular concern for modalities of payment; see *The House of Gold: The Contarini and the Ca' d'Oro: Building a Palace in Medieval Venice (1420–1440)* (Cambridge, England, 1993).

[64]For payment in the Bernardo bank of government obligations purchased from Giacomella, widow of Giacomello Longo, credited for her to the account of Michele d'Uberto, see ASV, Archivio Grimani-Barbarigo, b. 43, ledger of Nicolò and Alvise Barbarigo, fol. 10. For Andrea's account for the sale of cheese, with payment in bank for a total of 64 ducats, see Barbarigo, ledger A, fol. 190 (1435). For the account with his landlord and the payments for work done by "Mateo marangon," "Bortolameo da Crema, muraro," the "maistro da le finestre de vero," the "maistro di agudi" — both unnamed — and to "Zan Bagoto, favro," "per conzar la casa stemo," see ibid., fol. 154, and the current account, fol. 177. In both places, the phrases

Are we any better able to provide overall quantitative parameters? How many Venetians and foreigners, nobles and non-nobles, the very wealthy and those hardly so, active merchants or not, maintained current accounts at Rialto banks? Just how widespread was the use of this fiduciary money that circulated more rapidly and economically than specie and increased the quantity of money in circulation? It is, of course, impossible to answer these questions, but some approximations are possible for the period around 1500, at the time of the great bank failures. Frederic Lane estimated, on the basis of information culled from the diaries of Marin Sanudo, that about one Venetian in thirty held a current account at the Rialto. Although a relatively coarse estimate (there is no way of distinguishing, for example, how many accounts were held by foreigners or how many persons held accounts in more than one bank), the figure translates more understandably into about one in seven to ten heads of households. At this point, of course, one can legitimately argue whether that represents many or few![65] Another element regards the amount of assets so held at any given time. Again, Lane estimated that Rialto bankers together held about 1 million ducats in their accounts. That estimate corroborates the statement of a contemporary, the above-mentioned anonymous French observer, who asserted that each of three or four banks active on the Rialto held 300,000 ducats "or more" in deposits — for a total of some 900,000 to 1,200,000 ducats — which, he says, "est grant chose."[66] That was about the same amount as the gross annual revenues of the state. One can argue, once again, whether that is much or little, in a city of about 100,000 inhabitants. Whatever the point of view (for answers can only be subjective), the more holders of current accounts in Venice used those accounts as means of payment, the more credit was created and the more specie was freed for export to the Levant, which suffered from a chronic bullion famine and which attracted Venetian coin as an exchange commodity.[67]

"promise per me a . . ." or "i promese e de' per me a . . . ," which signify transfers, appear. For cash payments to "Mafio varoter" (1432), see ibid., fol. 83, and to "Zan de Renaldo, sartor," ledger B, fol. 212 (1448). For work done in Montebelluna by Marco, "marangon," see ibid., fol. 183. The building contractor, "maistro Zanin comascho muraro e compagni, che fexe la mia caxa da Montebeluna," in 1445, is not registered as having been paid in bank; ibid., fol. 160. For the payment of an artisan by check on a Florentine bank, see Spallanzani, "L'apside dell' Alberti"; for payment of "working men" on current account in Florence, see Goldthwaite, "Local Banking," 20–21.

[65]Lane, "Venetian Bankers," 72, and Peter Spufford, *Handbook of Medieval Exchange* (London, 1986), xxx.

[66]Lane, "Venetian Bankers," 72, and *Traictie,* chap. 32. Lane's estimates, from the time of the banking crisis, probably undershoot total liabilities in "normal" times, for persons who were concerned about the stability of the banks tended to reduce the amounts of their bank deposits.

[67]See the statement in this vein by Adam Smith, *Wealth of Nations* (New York, 1937), 277–78.

iv. A TENDENCY TOWARD SPECIALIZATION WITHIN THE FINANCIAL COMMUNITY

Only bankers created "bank money" as such, but there were many persons in the Venetian financial community who also handled money and precious metals. True specialization was never achieved — nor probably was it considered something to strive for — in any particular category, but there was a tendency in the course of time to differentiate among the primary roles assumed by institutions and to an extent also by individual members of the financial community, who were merchants at heart. Some categories came to have distinct labels from an early date. Even the second level below the merchants, that of the brokers, was quite specialized. By the fifteenth century, the documents often distinguish bond brokers and bill brokers from the normal commodity brokers, and specie brokers were probably specialized commodity brokers. A certain ambiguity of roles was normal, however; operators in each distinguishable category of manipulators of money, for example, might also lend money under some guise, often illegally, or deal at least occasionally in bullion as well as in worked silver and jewelry, tasks that we might expect to find only among goldsmiths.

Manifest usurers or pawnbrokers came closest to being true professionals. They lent money, usually legally and under supervision, on the security of pawns and were called "feneratores." Venice outlawed them from the city proper in 1254, when they were Christians particularly from Tuscany, but suspended the prohibition in 1382 when it invited Jewish lenders to establish themselves there long enough to help the city over the crisis caused by the War of Chioggia and the resultant monetary famine. They were expelled in 1397 to nearby Mestre, where they had already supplanted the Christian usurers; after the conquest of the Terraferma, they were permitted to lend in provincial cities and towns, where they often remained even after the establishment of "monti di pietà." They were allowed back to Venice officially during the War of the League of Cambrai, when, in 1516, they were restricted to the area of the ghetto, the former copper foundry, or "getto."[68]

The terms *campsor* and *cambiator* at first embraced three major categories of money managers: small exchangers of coins, local transfer bankers who ran what we might call full-service banks, and international bankers,

---

[68]Reinhold C. Mueller, "Les prêteurs juifs de Venise au Moyen Age," *Annales, économies, sociétés, civilisations* 30 (1975): 1277–1302. Of the many relevant studies by Benjamin Ravid, see especially "The Legal Status of the Jew In Venice to 1509," *Proceedings of the American Academy for Jewish Research* 54 (1987): 169–202. See also David Jacoby, "Les Juifs à Venise du XIVᶜ au Milieu du XVIᶜ Siècle," *Venezia centro di mediazione tra oriente e occidente (secoli XV–XVI),* acts of the congress of 1973 (Florence, 1977), 1:163–216. Now see also Reinhold C. Mueller, "The Jewish Moneylenders of Late Trecento Venice: A Revisitation," in *Intercultural Contacts in the Medieval Mediterranean: Studies in Honour of David Jacoby* (London, 1996), and as a special issue of the *Mediterranean Historical Review* 10 (1995): 202–17.

specialists in foreign exchange. In the preceding sections the term *campsor* was rendered in English both as moneychanger and as banker, reflecting an ambiguity that was very real in the thirteenth century and much of the fourteenth, when many moneychangers performed banking functions. A distinction in functions was first indicated by reference to the topographical location of an enterprise, and only later by applying different labels.

The earliest references to the functions of moneychangers, as we have seen, are to their counter or booth, the tabula or banco.[69] The term *campsor* is found in a decree of 1266 which gave the task of checking the scales of moneychangers to the Gold Office and legal jurisdiction to the Justiciares.[70] Of course, the first act of the moneychanger in evaluating a coin was to weigh it, and it underscores the responsibility of the government, in Venice as in all medieval cities, to guarantee as much as possible the trustworthiness of the vital operation of exchanging coins.

Two years later another decree regulated the role of campsores as bullion merchants, that is, as the principal purchasers of gold and silver imported especially by German merchants and sometimes by Ragusans.[71] It indicates that campsores were active at two strategic locations in the city: at the Rialto, where they were close to the regulating offices for gold and silver and the auction area at the communal scales, and at San Marco, where they were close to the mint. The distinction in location within a short time corresponded to a distinction in rank. The campsor "in Rivoalto," situated in the midst of the international wholesale merchants, was more important than his counterpart "in platea Sancti Marci," who, although close to the

---

[69]*PRV,* doc. 1 (1164); *DMC,* 1:93 (1225), 2:161 (1274). Also "tabula cambii" (1318) in *PMV,* doc. 75; "tabula de cambio" (1324) in ASV, NT, b. 1189, n. 12, testament of M. Bondumier; "tabula campsoria" (1356) in PSM, Ultra, b. 113, commis. Marco Dandolo, sentenza della Curia del Procurator (24 February 1356). The Venetian "tolla" and "bancho" are employed indistinguishably in reference to the same banker in 1325; see Rodolfo Gallo, "Marco Polo," doc. 6, p. 117 of the offprint. Around 1350 the accountants of the Procurators of San Marco tended to substitute "bancum" for "tabula." Also "bancum cambii," in Grazie, reg. 7, fol. 29v (1336); "bancum campsoris" in *PMV,* doc. 148 (1367). A "cambium sive bancum" is mentioned in 1354, *PMV,* doc. 121. A clipper of coins was accused of selling the coins "per banchos et per cambios"; ASV, AC, reg. 3643, fol. 81v (1366). Florentines in Venice simply called any Rialto banker "banchiere"; see ASF, Del Bene, 64, Libro nero of Duccio di Banchello, 1336–39.

[70]*DMC,* 2:312; see Vol. 1, 148–49. Luzzatto, *Storia,* 100, speaks of finding references to campsores in both private and official documents of the first half of the thirteenth century, but he cites no texts. The crucial commercial documents of the twelfth and early thirteenth centuries edited by Raimondo Morozzo della Rocca and Antonino Lombardo (*Documenti del commercio veneziano nei secoli XI–XIII,* 2 vols. [Turin, 1940; reprint, Turin, 1971], and *Nuovi documenti del commercio veneto dei sec. XI–XIII* [Venice, 1953]) do not identify any Venetian as campsor. Not even in the thousands of regestes, prepared by Luigi Lanfranchi, of documents preceding the year 1300 is reference made to indigenous campsores. The Venetian terms *cambiador* and *incambiador* are found in a text of 1311; see Alfredo Stussi, ed., *Zibaldone da Canal: Manoscritto mercantile del sec. XIV,* FSV (Venice, 1967), 5, 7.

[71]*PMV,* doc. 14, and *DMC,* 2:299.

mint, was far from the wholesale market. The latter catered more to retail trade and to the pilgrim and tourist business and was primarily a money-changer. The former — on the Rialto — became principally a deposit and transfer banker. Such a ranking in order of importance, in opportunities for profit, and thus also in risk is reflected in a law of 1283 which confirmed the existing prerequisite of a bond totaling 3,000 lire for Rialto bankers but reduced the requirement for campsores situated at San Marco to only 1,000 lire.[72] Still, specialization was not complete, since one occasionally finds, especially early on, a campsor at San Marco who accepted conditioned deposits and paid interest on them.[73] At the same time, no documentary evidence has been found that campsores at San Marco maintained current accounts; although there is no particular reason why they could not, such was not their principal function.

Moneychangers located at San Marco were not completely cut out of the bullion trade. They dealt with silver merchants sometimes at San Marco itself[74] and sometimes at the auctions held at the Silver Office at the Rialto,[75] where they competed directly with Rialto bankers. But both Rialto bankers and moneychangers at San Marco competed with gold- and silversmiths, for they regularly bought and sold items of worked silver. Some quantities were imported already in the form of silver belts and the like, primarily from Ragusa.[76] Worked silver of foreign origin, offered for sale by campsores, was often judged to be below the legal fineness required at Venice,[77] but Venetian moneychangers were as liable as any dealer in bullion to have articles fabricated below legal fineness within Venice itself.[78] Sale of worked silver by Venetian campsores was so common that even when, as in 1374, attempts were made to exclude them from the wholesale bullion market, an exception was envisioned for their dealing in worked silver, "which every day they display[ed] for sale at their banks."[79]

Since banks thus seem almost to have served as outlets for gold- and

[72]*DMC*, 3:17.

[73]ASV, PSM, Ultra, b. 180, commis. Marcello, parchment "J" dated 1311, which quotes contracts of 1300 and 1301.

[74]Vol. 1, app. G, doc. 5.

[75]ASV, AC, reg. 3643, fols. 85–86 (10 June 1366).

[76]Susan Mosher Stuard, "The Adriatic Trade in Silver, c. 1300," *SV* 17–18 (1975–76): 95–143.

[77]ASV, Zecca, reg. 6bis, Capitolare dei massari all'argento, fols. 27v–28v (21 November 1351); Grazie, reg. 15, fol. 51v (May 1362).

[78]ASV, AC, reg. 3642, in 1349, fols. 4 (21 January), 6 (11 February), 7 (22 April); fol. 78 (17 April 1353).

[79]*PMV*, doc. 160, p. 149 ("quod omni die tenetur super banchis pro vendendo"). Another hint that they dealt much in trinkets and ornaments is the account of a scuffle that occurred at a bank when a public official tried to get the moneychanger to pay a small fine; upon the latter's refusal, he tried to take a handful of ornaments ("unum mazum frisadurarum") as pledge of payment. ASV, AC, reg. 3643, fol. 18v (5 November 1361).

silversmiths, the latter had to struggle to maintain certain direct retail channels. In 1394 goldsmiths and other sellers of jewelry and trinkets obtained the right, against the opposition of the officials concerned with guilds (the Justiciares of the Giustizia vecchia), to set up their stalls at San Marco and San Polo on market days as by longstanding tradition ("sic antiquiter existerat consuetum"). Not long after, the silver officials at the Rialto tried to prohibit their benefiting from the lucrative market-day trade. These officials readily admitted that they were representing the interests of the moneychangers of San Marco ("quod hoc faciunt pro campsoribus Sancti Marci"), who were trying to restrict the competition of the goldsmiths. Although goldsmiths did not have the same ties to the authorities, however, the legitimacy of their claims was upheld by the Collegio, which ruled that market days were open to all and that goldsmiths could not be discriminated against.[80] This conflict between retail artisans and moneychangers at San Marco further underscores the difference between bankers at the Rialto, less interested in retailing worked objects, and their counterparts at San Marco. Thus it is not surprising to discover that Rialto bankers kept what we call "bankers' hours," while moneychangers at San Marco sought to remain open even on feast days.

If Rialto bankers were less interested in retailing worked silver, they were more involved in making loans on collateral — as long as the pawns were valuable and easily stored jewels. This is the reason why the Rialto banks that failed in 1499–1500 listed among their assets holdings in jewels worth astounding sums. Furthermore, even though they were not retailers of jewels, nor were they in direct competition with the goldsmiths located only a few steps away in the Ruga dei Oresi, they probably also kept or bought a certain number of unredeemed pawns as a store of value.[81]

Although a consideration of the interests of Venice's campsores in dealing in worked silver and jewelry permits a first measure of the distinction between those located at the Rialto and those at San Marco, it is obvious that such interests constituted a sideline activity. When one turns to their specifically monetary functions, manual exchange and deposit banking, one finds also here that an attempt was made, in the course of the fourteenth century, to differentiate between the two functions and to distinguish, even terminologically, between persons who tended to specialize in one or the other.

As was mentioned above, the term *banco* came to replace *tavola* to indicate the workplace of the campsor in the first half of the fourteenth century. From that point it was only a short step to calling the person who operated a "banco" "bancherius" or "banchiere." In the mid-fourteenth

---

[80]ASV, CN, reg. 5, fol. 78 (14 August 1417), which also furnishes the content of the decree of 14 April 1394.

[81]See Lane, "Venetian Bankers," 77.

century the term, current in Genoa and Florence but new to Venice, was used interchangeably with the term *campsor*,[82] but it was not long before a distinction developed. An important law of 1374 equated the banker and the moneychanger who operated a deposit and transfer bank when it applied restrictions on the activity of any "bancherius vel campsor qui teneat bancum de scripta."[83] At the same time, the concept of book transfer (the verbs *scribere* and *scribi facere* are used in laws of 1322 and 1356)[84] was added to the concept of bank and banker. From about 1380 onward the new form ("bancherius" or "bancherius a scripta") came to predominate over the term *campsor* when referring to a deposit banker installed at the Rialto,[85] whereas the earlier term came to be reserved for persons specializing in manual exchange. Venetians and foreigners alike then took to calling Rialto banks "banchi di scritta," the distinctive place of business of the Venetian local bankers.[86] About the same time bankers and even the genealogical lines of families of bankers or formerly of bankers came to be distinguished by use of the appellative "dal banco," attached to their name.[87] This does not mean, of course, that the biggest of the bankers spent all their time at the bank. They gave their name to the bank and had ultimate responsibility, but they usually left the daily administration of the enterprise to managers or to head cashiers.

[82]In the account book kept in the 1350s by Andrea Malipiero, two bankers are called "banchier" and one "cambiator" without thereby intending to differentiate their functions. In fact, it is with Alvise Viaro, "cambiator," that he keeps his principal current bank account. ASV, PSM, Misti, b. 94.

[83]*PMV,* doc. 160, p. 147, and the same in Lattes, *Libertà,* doc. 8. The proposal of Michele Morosini, of the same date, speaks of "banca cambiorum a scripta"; *PMV,* doc. 160, p. 149.

[84]*PMV,* docs. 80 and 124.

[85]Ibid., docs. 160, p. 152, and 166, p. 169. In 1382 Ludovico Emo is called "campsor et bancherius in Rivoalto"; ASV, AC, reg. 3644, fol. 45v. In 1387 one still finds the term *campsor a scripta* (Lattes, *Libertà,* doc. 10). The Soranzo brothers, bankers, are called "campsores" as late as 1430, but merely because reference is made then to an enabling act of 1387 which used that term; ibid., docs. 16, 9, and Lattes's note, p. 28.

[86]See, for example, ADP, 927, Commis. Zanobi Gaddi in Venice to Barcelona, 2 October 1400, and 715, Paoluccio di maestro Paolo in Venice to Florence, 8 November 1404. See also *Traictie,* chap. 32.

[87]As early as 1363 Bernardo Emo, member of a fraterna of bankers, is referred to in the account book of a relative as "de la tola"; ASV, PSM, Misti, b. 106, commis. Daniele Emo, account book n. 2, fol. 27v. The appellative "dal banco," used throughout the fifteenth and sixteenth centuries for Rialto bankers and from the sixteenth century onward also for Jewish pawnbrokers in the ghetto, is first encountered in an account book of 1406–11, which contains a current account with the banker and silver merchant Guglielmo Condulmer "dal bancho." Miscellanea atti non appartenenti a nessun archivio, b. 28, rent book of Donato Soranzo, fols. 30–31; the banker is here also referred to as "cambiador"; in fact, he was not one of the principal bankers operating on the Rialto at that time. An important branch of the Pisani family continued to be called "dal banco" for centuries after the last Pisani bank had liquidated. See Giuseppe Gullino, *I Pisani "dal banco" e "moretta": Storia di due famiglie veneziane in età moderna e delle loro vicende patrimoniali tra 1705 e 1836* (Rome, 1984).

By the early fifteenth century, then, the term *campsor* became restricted to moneychangers who were located at the base of the campanile at San Marco and (in the case of one or two) at the Rialto. Whichever their location, these were businessmen of lesser importance, but they rendered an essential service to citizens and foreigners alike. Their names are preserved, not in merchants' account books (exchange of coins technically needs no accounting record), but in criminal and civil cases generally divorced from their economic activity.[88]

The presence at the Rialto of specialists in manual exchange, operating in the shadow of—and in competition with—the famous banchi di scritta, probably never more than one or two, is only rarely documented. In 1478, for example, Antonio Fantini, "campsor" (also "cambiator") at the Rialto, was robbed while he was involved in his trade. In the extant criminal records his bank is distinguished from the banchi di scritta by being called a "mensa numularia," that is, a table for the exchange of coins.[89] The temptation must have been strong for moneychangers at the Rialto, given their location, occasionally to assume functions appropriate to full-service deposit banks. That was illegal, since, at least around 1500, moneychangers did not have to post bond. At the time of the clamorous failures of the banchi di scritta in 1499–1500, Marin Sanudo reported the failure also of two small exchange banks—banks "per cambiar moneta et non de scripta" —which had nonetheless accepted deposits and invested them.[90] Again in 1528 the small banks were found to be attracting deposits away from the banchi di scritta by offering an agio, or premium, on specie brought for deposit and to be keeping journals and alphabetized ledgers in which they performed transfers, just like the banchi di scritta. Such operations were forbidden as contrary to the law that made surety a prerequisite for banking operations.[91] Problems in the regulation of their activities persisted, for in 1554 private moneychanging was actually prohibited and two "banchetti" were instituted and operated by the state, one at the Rialto and one at San Marco. Eight years later private enterprise was reintroduced, but the

---

[88]The court recorder in a commercial suit in the year 1400 must have had some kind of distinction in mind when he began writing "bancherius" after the name of Antonio Contarini, only to cross it out and substitute the term *campsor*. Contarini, bankrupt in 1390, seems surely to have accepted deposits, but it is true enough that he had not been one of the principal Rialto bankers in his time. ASV, GP, Sg, reg. 6, fol. 84 (27 September 1400). For criminal cases regarding campsores at San Marco, see, for example, AC, reg. 3647, fols. 91 (1420) and 106 (1421); reg. 3651, fol. 97v (Melchior "claudus," campsor, 1460); reg. 3657, fol. 25 (Alvise de Tomasiis, campsor, 1490).

[89]ASV, AC, reg. 3654, fol. 55v.

[90]Luzzatto, *Storia*, 247. In the same context Sanudo speaks of them as a "bancho picolo" and a "banco de incambiar"; *Diarii*, 3:726–27, 1040. Sanudo does not mention these moneychangers when he lists the banchi di scritta in operation in 1493, 1512, and 1530; *De origine*, 27–28, 56–57, 175.

[91]Lattes, *Libertà*, doc. 34.

moneychangers were required to post bond of 1,000 ducats as assurance that they would obey the law and destroy all underweight coins.[92]

The third specialization identifiable within the financial community in Venice is that of dealers in foreign exchange. In Italy generally during the sixteenth century, the period of the great exchange fairs, they were called "cambisti"; today they are usually called merchant bankers or international bankers. On the Venetian money market these highly specialized operators, in large part Florentines, were called, in Italian, "cambiatori." For example, in the late fourteenth century, the Florentine merchant Zanobi Gaddi, resident in Venice, referred to the specialized dealers in bills of exchange on the Rialto as "questi cambiatori."[93] Around 1420 Giovanni di Bernardo da Uzzano, in a section dealing with Venice in his merchant manual, distinguishes between Venetian "banchieri," that is, deposit bankers, and "cambiatori," or dealers in foreign exchange, both active on the Rialto. He adds that "others," by whom he seems to mean Venetians, did not regard the work of the cambiatori to constitute that of a banco, in contrast to the Florentine usage with which he was familiar.[94] At bottom, the distinction in terminology implied a functional distinction, for the dealers in foreign exchange, like all merchants, maintained current accounts with the Venetian deposit bankers or banchieri di scritta, through whose mediation they made and received payment for bills of exchange, as well as for merchandise. (On the foreign exchange market, see Part III.)

[92]ASV, Consiglio dei Dieci, Comuni, filza 84, 26 May 1562.

[93]See, for example, ADP, 710, Gaddi in Venice to Florence, 4 January 1390.

[94]*Pratica della mercatura,* in *Della decima,* ed. G. F. Pagnini (Lisbon, 1766), 4:151. Da Uzzano's context concerns bank money; he warns dealers in bills of exchange not to deal with beneficiaries who would withdraw cash from the local bank on which payment would be made; in referring to the beneficiary, he says, "cioè a Cambiatori, che altre giente non riguarda banco," in order to distinguish (to a Florentine audience) between exchange dealers and the Venetian deposit bankers with whom they kept their accounts. For the term *cambiadori* used for foreign exchange dealers in Venice later in the century, see ASV, ST, reg. 7, fol. 89r–v, 92v (1475), and reg. 10, fol. 131 (1489).

2

THE SUPERVISION
AND REGULATION
OF BANKING

i. RENTING BANKS FROM STATE AUTHORITIES

The Rialto

THE CENTER OF BUSINESS activity in Venice — the Rialto, or *insula Rivoalti* — was an area bounded on two sides by the Grand Canal, at the point where it bends at a tight angle, and internally by a canal (thus forming an "island"), embracing the parishes of S. Giovanni di Rialto and S. Matteo. Within this larger area was a third small church, S. Giacomo Apostolo or S. Giacometto, probably built in the second half of the twelfth century. A church without a parish (it was run by a rector, directly subordinate to the bishop of Castello), S. Giacomo was probably intended for the use of the merchants who frequented the campo and the area up to the Grand Canal and the Rialto bridge. Campo S. Giacomo was the core of the Rialto market. The office of the Treasurers (the Camerlenghi di Comun) was located two steps away, where the canal bends, at the foot of the Rialto bridge (see fig. 1).[1]

Most of the area and structures of the marketplace, including the campo, the shops and tables of moneychangers, the loggia (or loggias), and many warehouses above and behind the campo, were donated by their

---

[1]Cessi and Alberti, *Rialto,* 1–35. See also Donatella Calabi and Paolo Morachiello, *Rialto: Le fabbriche e il Ponte* (Turin, 1987), esp. pt. 1.

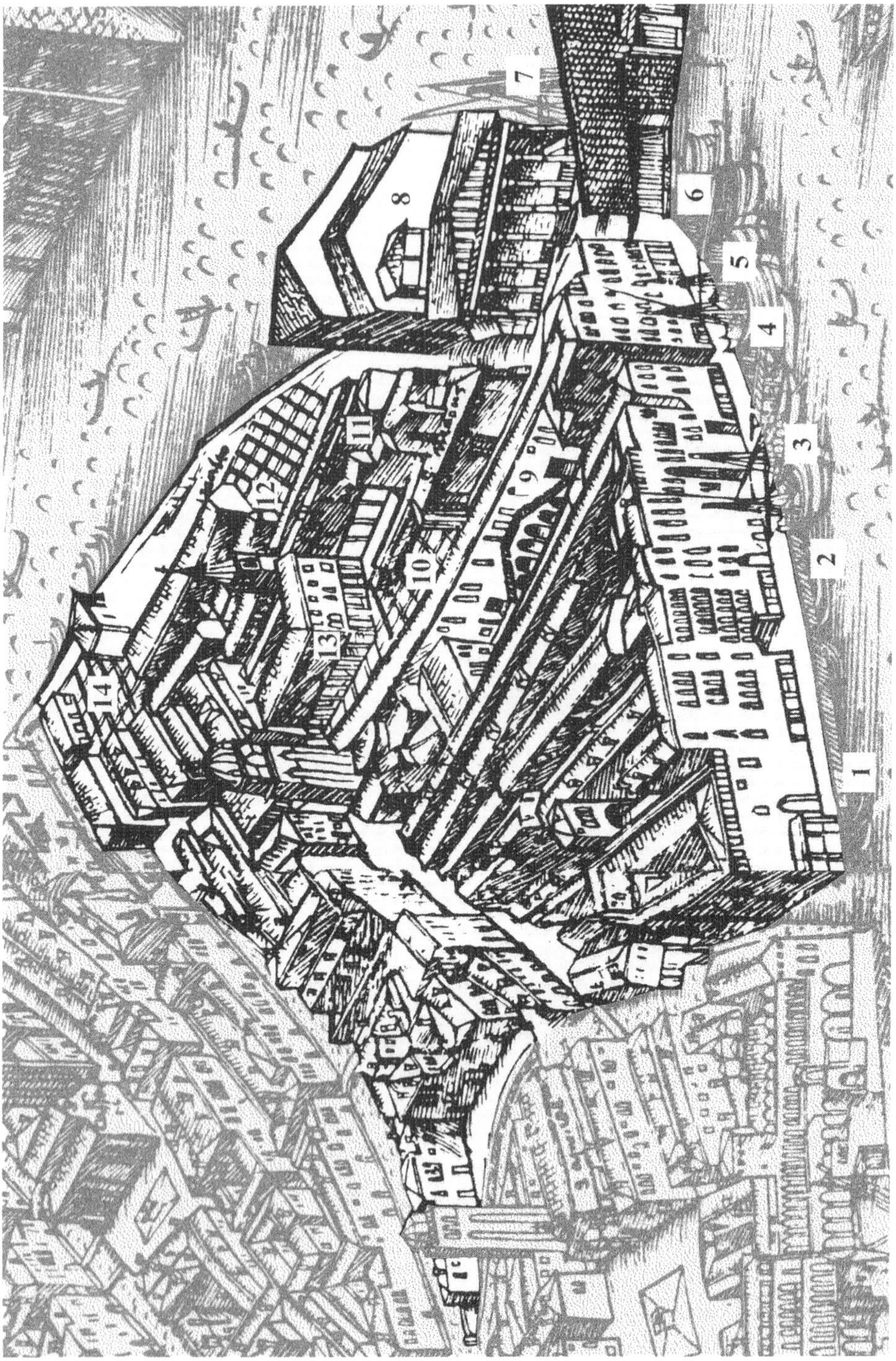

Fig. 1. The "Island of Rialto": The Financial Quarter of Venice (from Jacopo de' Barbari's View of 1500)

KEY

1.	Camera del Frumento Fondaco della Farina	Grain Office Flour warehouse
2.	Giudici del Piovego Dazio del Vin	Piovego magistracy Wine tax office
3.	Messetteria	Brokerage tax office
4.	Camera del Sal	Salt Office
5.	Savi alle Decime Sopraconsoli dei Mercanti Ufficio dei Cazudi Ufficio dell'Argento	Decima tax officials Sopraconsoli dei Mercanti Office of tax delinquents Silver Office
6.	Stadera	Public steelyard and weighers
7.	Loggia dei Mercanti	Loggia of merchants
8.	Camerlenghi di Comun Consoli dei Mercanti	Communal Treasury Consoli dei Mercanti
9.	Governatori alle Entrate	State Revenue Office
10.	Campo S. Giacomo Banchi di scritta	Campo S. Giacomo Private banks of deposit
11.	Provveditori di Comun	Provveditori di Comun
12.	Varoteria	Sellers of furs and pelts
13.	Sicurtà	Maritime insurance underwriters
14.	Pescheria	Fish market

Locations identified from contemporary sources by Calabi and Moracchiello (see Rialto, fig. 9). Digitalization by the CIRCE, Institute of Architecture, Venice.

original owners, the Orio family, "to the signoria and the whole people of Venice" in the year 1097.[2] With this act the market became part of the public domain. Official services for weighing and measuring were early provided at the Rialto, as indicated by the inscription, dating from not later than the twelfth century, affixed to the outside apse of the church of S.Giacomo, at the location of the steelyard or communal weighing station (fig. 2). It reminded merchants that salvation was to be found in the cross and recommended honesty in their dealings: " 'Round about this church may the law-merchant be equitable, the weights just, and may no fraudulent contract be negotiated."[3]

The tables of the moneychangers, who of course used delicate scales more than members of any other profession except assayers and goldsmiths, thus came doubly under communal jurisdiction. The tables, along with all the shops and warehouses of the Rialto, were rented out at auction to the highest bidder, and rents soon became an important category in the Commune's revenues. The procedure of renting, carried out by customs officials called Visdomini, who received jurisdiction over the marketplace,[4] made possible an initial kind of supervision over persons who wished to exercise the delicate profession of moneychanger.

The jurisdiction of the Visdomini over the rental of communal tables to moneychangers at the Rialto continued until about 1230, when their office, reformed and subdivided, was restricted to the collection of customs. The supervision of communal rentals and of the whole marketplace was then given to a new magistracy called the Rialto Office (Officiales Rivoalti). Its mid-thirteenth-century capitolare opens directly with the affirmation that its jurisdiction embraced "the whole Rialto market, all the shops at the Rialto, both on the ground floor and in upper stories, and the moneychangers' tables located at the Rialto." The activity of this magistracy in regard to bankers' tables, however, is documented only for the following century, and thinly at that. In 1371 the Rialto Office was absorbed by the Salt Office, which thereafter administered the public domain at the Rialto.[5]

[2]Cessi and Alberti, *Rialto*, 20–23. The document was published by Samuele Romanin, *Storia documentata di Venezia*, 2d ed., 10 vols. (Venice, 1925), 1:396, doc. 20.

[3]On the cross is legible "Sit crux tua vera salus huic, Christe, loco," and below the cross "Hoc circa templum sit ius mercantibus aequum, pondera nec vergant, nec sit conventio prava." John Ruskin, *Venezia,* translation and notes by M. Pezzè Pascolato (Florence, 1901), 42–44 and notes; photograph on p. 43. See also Cessi and Alberti, *Rialto,* 20 and n. 5, 23 and n. 2.

[4]Cessi and Alberti, *Rialto,* 233. On various Visdomini, see Giorgio Zordan, *I visdomini di Venezia nel secolo XIII* (Padua, 1971).

[5]Cessi and Alberti, *Rialto,* 241–44, and Alessandra Princivalli, ed., *Capitolare degli Ufficiali sopra Rialto: Nei luoghi al centro del sistema economico veneziano (secoli XIII–XIV),* (Milan, 1994), introductory essays by Gherardo Ortalli and A. Princivalli, and cap. 1, 116, 129, 147, 174. Specific operating regulations for "cambiatores, stationarii et sartores qui habent stationes ad fictum a comuni in Rivoalto" in ASV, MC, Capricornus, fol. 43 (18 May 1307).

Fig. 2. Inscription on the apse of S. Giacomo di Rialto.
Dating perhaps from the mid-twelfth century, it reminds merchants to be
honest. It reads: "Sit crux tua vera salus huic, Christe, loco," and,
below the cross, "Hoc circa templum sit ius mercantibus aequum, pondera
nec vergant, nec sit conventio prava."

Photograph by Dida Biggi

A deliberation of the Quarantia of about 1330 reaffirms the right of the Rialto Office to rent out the banks and to supervise their operation. At the Rialto, it states, no transaction that involved moneychanging could take place anywhere except at the Commune's tables and banks, under pain of a 500 lire fine for each violation.[6] Furthermore, renters of communal banks were required to post bond at the conclusion of the annual auction period, so that operation thus legitimated could begin immediately.[7]

There were probably three or four banks at the Rialto in the thirteenth century, eight to ten in the first half of the fourteenth century, and again no more than three or four principal bankers beginning in the 1370s and throughout the fifteenth and sixteenth centuries. In the latter period they were probably all located around the two sides of Campo S. Giacomo. Earlier, when there were more banks, the state also rented out three exchange tables situated between the apse of the church and the foot of the

[6]Princivalli, *Capitolare degli Ufficiali sopra Rialto,* cap. 129, undated but inserted between laws dated 1332 and 1333.
[7]ASV, Grazie, reg. 5, fol. 33 (18 November 1333).

37

Rialto bridge, next to or even under a loggia first constructed in 1322 close to the public weighing station and readily identifiable in de' Barbari's map of 1500 (fig. 3) and Carpaccio's *Miracle of the True Cross*.[8] According to the regulations, these three tables could be put up for rent only after those situated around the square itself had been leased. Occasionally exceptions were made, however, for some bankers seem to have preferred that location, perhaps because of its proximity both to the public scales and to the office of the Camerlenghi.[9] The desire to remain at his previous location caused Marco Stornado, campsor, to offer to pay in advance four years' rent, and he thus convinced the authorities, in 1356, to assign him one of these three tables.[10] With the reduction in the number of moneychangers in the fifteenth century, these banks disappeared, and the loggia was instead reserved as a meeting place for Venetian noblemen.[11] The plan for restoration at the Rialto under Doge Francesco Foscari in 1424–25, which included reconstruction of the loggia, implies furthermore that some banks were located under the portico that begins at the northwest corner of the square and goes westward, bordering the original pescheria (fish market). The banks located farther down the portico were demolished during the restoration, in order to expand the sheltered area available to nobles and merchants for conversing and bargaining, and no banks, it seems, were thenceforth to be located beyond the corner.[12]

In 1459 a more thorough restoration was undertaken. The portico on the west side of the square, that facing the church of S. Giacomo, was enlarged and closed at the back to form a loggia more central and suitable as a meeting place for nobles and merchants than the loggia located at the foot of the bridge. In order to accomplish this, the two banks at either end of the portico, one of which had been leased to Giovanni Soranzo, were demolished and relocated under the north portico, where the fur dealers ("varoteri") were, to leave room for the stone bench reserved for nobles.[13] By 1494, however, two lesser moneychangers had managed to establish themselves under the new loggia just the same.[14] The bankers operating on the Rialto in 1514, at the time of the great fire, found their banks on the square

---

[8]Cessi and Alberti, *Rialto,* 39, 314. A deliberation of 1322 speaks of the need to shorten the "tabula de ca' Pisani" situated near the new loggia, because it jutted out; ibid., 38 n. 4. The possibility that the three tables were actually situated under the loggia arises from a deliberation of 1344 which speaks of them as being "apud pontem Rivoalti sub archis"; ASV, MC, Spiritus, fol. 140.

[9]ASV, MC, Spiritus, fol. 133v (28 October 1343) and fol. 140 (3 November 1344). See also *DQ* 1:7 (1342), 88 (1343); *DQ* 2, doc. 287 (1349).

[10]ASV, Grazie, reg. 14, fol. 2.

[11]Cessi and Alberti, *Rialto,* 61–62.

[12]This seems to be the implication of documents discussed in ibid., 61–64, esp. 64 n. 1.

[13]Ibid., docs. VI and VII, and pp. 67–70.

[14]Ibid., 77 n. 1.

Fig. 3. Loggia at the foot of the Rialto bridge, with, behind it, the
Camerlenghi di Comun and the offices of the Raxon Vecchie and Raxon
Nuove. Meant as a meeting place for nobles and merchants, the loggia often
attracted common gamblers and was used on occasion as a temporary shelter
for bankers' tables (from Jacopo de' Barbari's View of 1500).

Diateca, Department of the History of Architecture, Institute of Architecture, Venice

destroyed, but they were able to reopen almost immediately under the old
loggia at the foot of the bridge while the Rialto was being rebuilt.[15]

Communal tables at the Rialto were to be put up for auction annually,
and the bidding was to be concluded by the feast of St. Michael (29 September), the traditional deadline for rent agreements which coincided, as

[15]Ibid., 93, from Sanudo. The loggia is briefly mentioned by Deborah Howard, *Jacopo
Sansovino: Architecture and Patronage in Renaissance Venice* (New Haven, 1975), 49.

we shall see, with a lull in the activity of the banks. As usual, we know about these regulations from attempts made to skirt them. One way of avoiding an annual headache was offering to pay immediately a fixed rent for future years. In 1352 Armelino da Mosto offered to pay 600 ducats for ten years' rent for the two tables he habitually kept at the Rialto. While the campsor demonstrated considerable faith in his own longevity and that of his bank with such an offer, the state obviously was moved by fiscal considerations, for it was at war with Genoa, and it accepted the proposal.[16] Despite the fact that there was active bidding in 1428, similar considerations (the war in Lombardy) prompted the state to accept offers made by the bankers Giovanni Orsini and Leonardo and Jacomo Priuli; the rent, established by assessment, was set at 110 ducats per year for five years. If they paid all in advance, it was a bad bet, since they suffered a run and were forced to liquidate only seven months after the agreement.[17] Only three years earlier the Salt Office had been reminded of its duty to auction state-owned banks and shops at the Rialto to the highest bidder alone and not to conclude such agreements with the bankers, for — it was noted in the Senate — it had become habitual for banks to be passed on to brothers, sons, and other relatives without being reauctioned by the Salt Office.[18] This tendency is not surprising if one considers the reduced number of potential renters bidding in the fifteenth century and the development of some banking dynasties, like that of the Soranzo, which lasted several generations. Anticipations and other mechanisms, however, also served a fiscally hard-pressed state, as is clear again during the War of Ferrara in 1482.[19]

In the previous century attempts had been made by the bankers themselves to reduce competition in bidding. In 1352 and 1355 the Quarantia intervened against manipulation of the auctions by "conspiration" and other fraudulent methods.[20] The terminal date was one weapon the state had against such combinations. The regulations provided that anyone who so procrastinated in trying to get a favorable rent that he let the feast of St. Michael pass without making an official bid would have to pay a fine of one-fourth more if he wanted to lease a table. Exceptions were made when there was danger that no one at all would rent the bankers' tables — as in the months following the onslaught of the Black Death in 1348,[21] or when war against the Genoese in 1352 made every source of revenue important.[22]

---

[16]ASV, Grazie, reg. 12, fol. 123 (20 March), and Princivalli, *Capitolare degli Ufficiali sopra Rialto,* cap. 172 (23 April). See also the example of 1356, above, n. 12.

[17]ASV, Grazie, reg. 22, fol. 112v (February 1429).

[18]ASV, SM, reg. 55, fol. 127v (18 June 1425).

[19]Cessi and Alberti, *Rialto,* 290–91.

[20]Princivalli, *Capitolare degli Ufficiali sopra Rialto,* cap. 174, 177.

[21]ASV, MC, Spiritus, fol. 158 (19 October).

[22]The hard line taken by the Quarantia on 5 October 1352, cited above, n. 22, was contradicted by the Great Council: ASV, MC, Novella, fol. 19 (18 October); this suspension of the law was repeated in the following year: ibid., fol. 27 (20 October 1353).

Piazza San Marco

Moneychanging, with some related banking services, was also conducted in Piazza San Marco at tables situated at the base of the campanile.[23] Jurisdiction over the Piazza was in the hands of the Procurators of San Marco "de supra," who collected rents from shops and exchange tables. In 1351 the Quarantia denounced cases of the same kind of combination in restraint of competitive bidding at San Marco as that mentioned above regarding the Rialto. Bids judged to have been fixed were declared null and void, for any loss of revenue to the church of San Marco was to be taken as seriously as though it had been a loss to communal revenues. The Quarantia hastened to add, however, that the provision was not intended to infringe upon the rights of partners in a company to bid on one or more exchange tables.[24]

Open competition, on the other hand, had its negative aspects. Moneychangers active at Piazza San Marco served a clientele consisting more of pilgrims and tourists than wholesale merchants and dealt in sidelines such as worked silver articles, and they were, economically and socially speaking, usually a cut or two below their colleagues at the Rialto. Since opportunities for profits were not lacking, however, competition for well-placed tables could be keen. In at least two cases, the contenders who lost out resorted to their knives. In 1331 Zanino Acotanto had to defend himself with a knife against the ire of loser Bertucio Lando.[25] In 1340 Marco Rosso, with an offer of 60 ducats' annual rent, outbid the de Buora family, campsores, for a table that had been run at San Marco by Marco Stornado before his transfer to Rialto but more recently had been held by the de Buora. Nicoletto de Buora, along with his six brothers, approached Rosso, threatening the winner and saying, "Ever shall we be ill-met" [mai ben se trovaremo]; upon hearing this the Procurators (including Andrea Dandolo, future doge) rebuked the de Buora clan for their pride ("nimia superbia"), saying that it seemed they wanted to appropriate the entire Piazza as their own. Later the same day Nicoletto attacked Rosso with a knife and injured him so seriously that his hand had to be amputated. The attacker was sentenced to prison and deprived of the right to operate a banking table on Piazza San Marco — even though his brothers continued to do so in later years.[26]

Auctions probably went as they often do, with considerable confusion of roles between bidder, renter of record, actual operator, and partner. A lawsuit of 1391 describes some of the background to an auction of booths

---

[23]Usually the location is given as simply the Piazza; for the specific location, see, for example, ASV, AC, reg. 3653, fol. 74r–v (1471), regarding a "campsor . . . qui tenebat banchum ad campanilem Sancti Marci."

[24]Princivalli, *Capitolare degli Ufficiali sopra Rialto,* cap. 170 (9 December 1351).

[25]ASV, Grazie, reg. 3, fol. 21v (25 February 1331).

[26]ASV, AC, reg. 3641, fol. 42v (13 March 1340). The victim, unable any longer to change coins with just one hand, asked for a post as a broker at the Silver Office; Grazie, reg. 9, fol. 60 (1 September 1342).

at San Marco in 1389, when one moneychanger asked another to bid for him "as soon as I signal you by touching your foot." Subletting was also possible, and the same case recounts that 100 ducats were offered by one moneychanger for the four months remaining on a lease of yet another who had become ill. Very likely the confusion that reigned among the bankers of San Marco was not matched at the Rialto, where the operators had much higher stakes.[27]

The offices that rented out the tables — the Visdomini, the Rialto Office, the Salt Office, the Procurators of San Marco — thus provided an initial system of control over the banks and the suitability of those who intended to operate them. With the rent contract in proper form, these offices, together with the Consoli dei Mercanti, who had to approve the bank's sureties, could permit the bank to display a carpet on the countertop and begin operations (see fig. 4).[28]

ii. JURISDICTIONS AND REGULATIONS

A comprehensive regulation or supervision, internal or external, of banking was entirely lacking in Venice until 1524, when the Provveditori sopra Banchi were established. No guild organization existed to provide self-government, and the Commune passed and repealed more or less restrictive legislation, the jurisdiction over which was parceled out among several different and often competing magistracies.

The magistracy that as a court of law was most regularly involved with banking in Venice was that of the Consoli dei Mercanti, already in existence in 1233.[29] Beginning in 1270, it became the task of the Consoli to license the bankers, upon verification of the surety that they posted, a task in which they were flanked by the Governatori delle Entrate beginning in 1455. Furthermore, they had jurisdiction over the bankruptcy and liquidation of banks, in which role they regularly had to be confirmed by the Signoria against the contestation of the Sopraconsoli, who dealt with all other bankruptcies. In the fifteenth century, however, when bank failures became veri-

[27]ASV, GP, Frammenti antichi, b. 10, quaternus testificationum, under 7 September 1391; GP, Estraordinari nodari, reg. 1, under 9 and 18 September.

[28]I have found only one direct reference to the use of a carpet in Venice. Evidence presented at a trial that resulted from a scuffle at the bank of Antonio di Paolo at San Marco reports that a sack of coins had broken open, its contents falling "super tapeto banchi." ASV, AC, reg. 3647, fol. 106 (30 July 1421). A carpet covers the countertop in Carpaccio's representation of the bureau of the tax collector St. Matthew, presumably a typical bank at the Rialto (see fig. 4). For the use elsewhere of a cloth or carpet, generally as a sign of a licensed bank, see Vol. 1, pp. 85; for Genoa, where the jurist Bartolomeo Bosco in the early fifteenth century underscored the importance of the symbol as designating a particularly qualified operation, recognized by the Commune, see Vito Piergiovanni, "I banchieri nel diritto genovese e nella tecnica giuridica tra Medioevo e Età Moderna," in *Banchi pubblici, banchi privati,* 1:218.

[29]Cassandro, *Le rappresaglie e il fallimento,* 174.

Fig. 4. Vittore Carpaccio's *The Calling of St. Matthew.* This painting provides a glimpse of what a licensed deposit bank at the Rialto probably looked like about 1500, complete with its carpet and the characteristic funnel tray for counting and sacking coins (at the saint's right hand).

Scuola di S. Giorgio degli Schiavoni, Venice. Diateca, Department of the History of Architecture, Institute of Architecture, Venice

table affairs of state, in part because of the lines of credit continually extended by the banks to the state and in part because of the negative effects produced on the economy as a whole, the Consoli were often reduced to executors of decisions made in the highest organs of government.

The four Consoli had investigative and judicial duties regarding many aspects of commerce,[30] for which they had a large staff (twelve officials raised to twenty in 1476, to forty by 1493), with the right to bear arms during the day and up to two hours after sunset.[31] They were located at the Rialto, in the midst of the merchants and bankers,[32] and provided summary justice on the spot as a commercial court of first instance. Suits between bankers and their clients, initiated by either party, were presented orally before the Consoli, without written plea, and the sentence, consisting of only a few words written on a bit of paper ("in forma di cartolina"), was handed down at the latest on the third day of court following the plea.[33] Cases brought against a banker by a creditor had precedence over any current lawsuit; the latter had to be suspended until "expeditious and summary justice" was rendered to the bank's creditor.[34] While the Consoli adjudicated cases in the first instance, merchants could appeal to the Giudici di Petizion.[35]

As regards the evidence presented before the Consoli and other courts, all commentators note that the entries in the banker's account books, in particular his journal, carried the force of law, "as though they were notarial contracts" or even "court sentences."[36] This was so not only in cases involving banks directly but also those involving two or more merchants, for essential court evidence virtually always included presentation of

[30]A fourth official was added in 1423; ASV, MC, Ursus, fols. 51v–52.

[31]ASV, Consoli dei Mercanti, b. 1 (capitolare), fols. 154v–55 (1476); Sanudo, *De origine,* 135 (1493) and 264–65 (1515); *Traictie,* cap. 31. A consul who served a notice of debt to the former moneychanger Nicoletto de Buora in 1347 was assaulted for his efforts; AC, reg. 3642, fol. 26v.

[32]Cessi and Alberti, *Rialto,* 72 n. 4.

[33]Sanudo, *De origine,* 264–65, and *Traictie,* chap. 31.

[34]Lattes, *Libertà,* doc. 30 (1523), referring to past practice. In 1426 the banker Donato di Filippo Nati, an immigrant from Florence, asked special permission to have a "persona docta" to plead his case against the liquidating bank of the late Andrea Priuli and Brothers before the Consoli; ASV, Grazie, reg. 22, fol. 68.

[35]See, for example, the arbitration between the two moneychangers Donato Alemanni and ~~Gi~~ amii Rizzo, perhaps partners, in ASV, GP, Frammenti antichi, b. 6, fasc. 1352, fol. 69v ff. (3 April 1352). The loser of a suit against the Bernardo-Garzoni bank, presented orally before the Consoli, "che è superiori del bancho," in the first instance, appealed to the Giudici di Petizion; see GP, Sg, reg. 60, fols. 21–22 (20 November 1431).

[36]The expressions used by Luca Pacioli and by the author of the *Traictie* were discussed above, Chap. 1, sec. i. See also Sanudo, as cited above, n. 35. Cf. Abbott P. Usher, "The Origins of Banking: The Primitive Bank of Deposit, 1200–1600," reprinted in *Enterprise and Secular Change: Readings in Economic History,* ed. by Frederic C. Lane and Jelle C. Riemiersma (Homewood, Ill., 1953), 274–75.

a certified extract from the journal of the bank that had mediated the transaction. The extract was always transcribed in the court record, and occasionally the original can be found attached to the transcript.[37] Even when a bank was no longer in operation, the books were preserved either by the successor bank or by the Consoli and could still be consulted and used as evidence.

It is pertinent at this point, after having mentioned the problem of court evidence, to underscore the faith placed by Venetian law in particular in the veracity of a banker's journal. Since an entry in the journal was merely the transcription of an oral order, at least the debtor party, if not both parties to a payment via bank transfer, must have initially approved the entry. Furthermore, each holder of a current account occasionally compared his own record of his bank balance with that registered at the bank, so that any discrepancy would readily come to light.[38] Only two cases in more than two centuries of banking history are known in which bankers were caught falsifying their accounts.

In the first case, an immigrant from Padua and naturalized Venetian by the name of Petrus de Mortisse (also de Mortisio), who was a campsor at San Marco at the time, was charged before the Avogadori di Comun by a debtor for having ripped one or two pages out of the "quaderno" of his bank, pages which proved that the debtor had already paid his debt. The charge was brought while the Black Death was raging, and Petrus did not appear in court to defend himself. Fined in absentia, he was forbidden ever again to run a bank ("tenere cambium") in Venice.[39] After the passing of the plague, however, Petrus proved before the Judices Forinsecorum that his debtor, along with the latter's brother, surety for a loan of 200 lire di piccoli, had defrauded him of his due. In fact, the debtor had agreed to assign him real estate in Padua in lieu of payment; since Petrus was no longer a Paduan and could not have a house there in his own name, the property was transferred to the name of the guarantor. But once Petrus had entered receipt of payment in his accounts, the guarantor claimed to owe him nothing. Seeing that he would have to try to get back at the original

[37]A great many of the cases tried before courts like the Giudici di Petizion adduced "cedule" or "scripture" of the banks as evidence. For example, see ASV, GP, Sg, reg. 4, fols. 22v–23 and insert (1375); also GP, Sentenze e interdetti, reg. 9, fol. 22 (1421), where the extract reads: "1417 a dì 21 luio. Per ser Francesco Nicoloxi, a ser Antonio de le Arme, per ser Petruzo de Ismanini, £iii. [Signed] Andrea de Priolli et fradelli."

[38]In order to maintain "public faith," the Senate in 1467 reminded bankers of their obligation to show their account books to depositors upon request, for the sake of comparing records. In case of discrepancy, the Consoli were to decide. Penalty for noncompliance was set at 1,000 ducats. Lattes, *Libertà,* doc. 24.

[39]Ibid., doc. 2 (from a copy, with misreadings; see the original in ASV, AC, reg. 3642, fol. 40), and *DQ,* 2:14. Lattes rendered the name "de Cortesiis," which misled Ferrara, "Antichi banchi" and "Documenti."

debtor, he tore the page with the record of receipt out of his account book. Fearing incarceration during the plague and thus increased danger of contagion, he had not defended himself at the first hearing. Having now proven that no one's rights had been infringed upon by his action, since he was still creditor, Petrus was permitted to take up banking again — in fact, he transferred his operation to the Rialto once he had become a full-fledged citizen of Venice — even though the fine for the infraction stood.[40]

In the following century Agostino di Bernardo Ziera, a banker on the Rialto, was found to have transferred 300 ducats from one current account, unbeknownst to its holder ("in absentia et nesciente aliquid"), to the account of Ziera's own son-in-law, a nobleman. Ziera was also discovered to have appropriated illegally a credit instrument for 590 ducats. Brought before the Senate itself in 1468, the criminal case was resolved with rectification of the frauds committed, the levy of a heavy fine, and the requirement to liquidate the bank immediately; Ziera was thereupon to begin a prison term and was prohibited from ever again running a bank in Venice. He succeeded in avoiding imprisonment, however, by fleeing to Rome, where he became an apostolic protonotary; using his connections with the papacy, the former banker was able to pay up his debts in Venice four years later (see the treatment below, Chap. 5, sec. v).

It might legitimately be said that these two exceptions merely prove the rule, namely, that bankers' account books reflected the true state of clients' accounts and thus could be taken as comparable to proven court evidence of payment, as they were so regularly.

While bankers' records regarding clients who held current accounts were assumed to be true, this was not the case as regards the records of the bank's own undertakings — the purchase and sale of gold and silver, the coin kept in the till, the consignment of bullion to the mint. In these matters, bankers were subject to several jurisdictions, such as the Gold and Silver Offices (Extimatores Auri, Officiales Argenti), and the offices concerned with the condition of circulating coins (the Officiales Grossorum Tonsorum et de Rascia, and the mintmasters).

One of the earliest regulations concerning moneychangers dates from 1266, when the Gold Office was called upon to test at least once a month the weights and scales that campsores used at San Marco and the Rialto.[41] A century later the Silver Office was reminded to check the scales, now once every three months.[42] A century later still, when the Council of Ten had taken jurisdiction over the Venetian mint, the mintmasters themselves were given the task of checking the scales "of all public offices, of transfer banks and of moneychangers."[43]

[40]ASV, Grazie, reg. 12, fol. 47v (2 July 1349).
[41]*DMC*, 2:312.
[42]*PMV*, doc. 164, p. 166 (the proposal had been made by the banker Pietro Benedetto).
[43]*Cap. Broche*, 206–9 (13 October 1484).

Since the primary duty of the Silver Office was to register bullion imports and sales, with the aim of keeping track of supply, exacting dues, and seeing to it that buyers consigned the quinto or other percentage of the gross purchase to the mint, the first requirement was that all the silver imported be sold only at the approved location at the Rialto ("inter duas scalas"). It was there that those campsores who were particularly interested in the bullion trade competed in buying from the German importers.[44] The Silver Office fined the moneychanger Nicoletto di Lorenzo for buying silver surreptitiously in 1334,[45] but similar infractions could also be prosecuted by officials whose primary responsibility was preventing moneychangers from circulating clipped grossi (Officiales Grossorum Tonsorum).[46] Supervision of bullion sales made it possible for the Silver Office to keep track of the quinto, the silver that had to be consigned to the mint within fifteen days of the purchase. Occasionally campsores were among those fined for failure to consign the quinto to the mint, an infraction sometimes uncovered by auditing the bankers' account books.[47] A monthly audit of the books of silver buyers was required beginning in 1354, and an attempt was made to exclude contravening bankers from practicing their trade for one year.[48] Mintmasters were empowered to compare their records with those of the Silver Office, and if there was a discrepancy, the mintmasters had the right also to audit the silver merchant's books. This was the case in 1412, for example, when the banker and silver merchant Guglielmo Condulmer extracted from his accounts his purchases and consignments of the quinto for more than two decades of activity — a valuable record of quantities and prices — at the request of the mintmasters.[49]

[44]In Vol. 1, app. G, docs. 3 and 4. For prohibitions against campsores combining to reduce competition, see *DMC*, III, 458 (28 July 1299), *PMV*, doc. 125 (1356), and ASV, AC, reg. 3643, fol. 85 ff. (10 June 1366).

[45]ASV, Grazie, regs. 5, fol. 55, and 6, fol. 36; see also 11, fol. 69v (3 April 1346), regarding Marco Stornado, who received a two-year prison term for this offense.

[46]For example, ibid., reg. 10, fol. 1v (26 July 1343), regarding Petrus de Mortisio, campsor at San Marco, and fol. 69 (31 November 1344), regarding Guarnerius Volpe, campsor at the Rialto. At times the Officium Argenti and the Officium Grossorum Tonsorum were one and the same; the label used depended on the case at hand.

[47]Ibid., regs. 6, fol. 56 (5 May 1336), regarding Piero Serafini, and 12, fol. 78 (9 April 1350), fol. 88v (10 August 1350), regarding Andreolo Sanador.

[48]*PMV*, doc. 121. That the Silver Office carried out its duty to audit the accounts of habitual buyers "pro affinando" to determine their adherence to the regulations is clear from the case against Nicoletto Michiel, campsor, in ASV, Grazie, reg. 14, fol. 50v (September 1358), which mentions both the monthly audit and the fifteen days allowed between purchase and consignment of the quinto to the mint.

[49]On the last page of his last account book, he wrote, under the date 2 January 1412, "Mi Vielmo Condolmer son stado cho' i signori de la moneda, miser Fantin Morexini e miser Daniel da Chanal e Miser Tomado da cha' de la Fontana [pesador], i qual voiando veder le raxion de' quinti de chomun, e in fin a el dì dito de sera son romaxo d'achordo cho' i diti signori me avanza chon la zecha marche vinti e onze quatro." ASV, PSM, Misti, b. 182, commis. G.

At one point, following Emperor Sigismund's trade war against Venice and the abolition of the quinto, the Silver Office was considered capable of taking over some banking functions, even the book transfer of funds negotiated via bills of exchange, enough to prompt Roberto Cessi to call the relevant law, passed in 1421, a step toward establishment of a state bank.[50] The project was as ambiguously worded as it was unacceptable to private banks, and twenty-five years later it was admitted that the Silver Office had never actually sought to carry out the function that had been ascribed to it.[51]

Another major area requiring policing was that of the circulation of counterfeit and clipped coins. An oath required of Venetian merchants in general, dating from sometime before 1280 until 1324, contained several clauses to this effect: if I am or ever will be a campsor, I swear I will cut up all grossi I find to have been counterfeited or clipped; and I will not employ any factor ("puer") who takes in or pays out cash, unless he similarly has sworn to destroy all counterfeit and clipped coins.[52] The supervision that the Silver Office was required to exercise over bankers as bullion merchants, in one form or other, also gave the officials the opportunity to check on the coin they handled.[53] But the magistracy more directly responsible in the thirteenth century and first half of the fourteenth was the Officium Grossorum Tonsorum. Occasionally it was even given general jurisdiction over banks, as in 1322, at a time when the use of interbank accounts and fractional reserves was first recognized as creating problems for holders of current accounts.[54] Its authority, however, was usually restricted to the integrity of coins. A regulation that aimed at making their supervision easier was one that required moneychangers to keep their coin on top of their tables and to exchange coins only "above board."[55] In 1354 these officials, seconded by various other policing agencies, were directed by the

Condulmer. On Condulmer and the quinto, see also Vol. 1, p. 195 n. 39. Between 1388 and 1413 Condulmer produced 37,246 marks, nearly 9 metric tons, of refined silver.

[50]Lattes, *Libertà*, doc. 14, at p. 49, and Cessi and Alberti, *Rialto,* 271.

[51]Lattes, *Libertà,* doc. 21. See also below, Chap. 3, sec. vi.

[52]ASV, Miscellanea atti diplomatici e privati, b. 9, no. 326; the oath, a strange kind of capitolare, includes many categories of commercial activity; it also binds merchants to pay their forced loans when ordered to do so. It merits closer scrutiny.

[53]For example, ASV, Grazie, reg. 16, fol. 104v (1369), regarding Andrea Acotanto, campsor at San Marco, who had purchased false bolognini.

[54]*PMV,* docs. 80, 87.

[55]ASV, Grazie, reg. 9, fol. 63 (24 September 1342). Concern for the extensive circulation of clipped coins caused the Quarantia to order that exchange of coins take place on top of the counter, in full view, and only with displayed coins: "quod quicumque cambiator, tam de Rivoalto quam de Sancto Marco, teneatur tenere omnes monetas, quas volet cambiare, sparsas super bancum palam, nec possit cambiare de aliis monetis, quam de illis que erunt sparse super banco palam." In Lattes, *Libertà,* doc. 4, and *PMV,* doc. 134. See also below in this chapter, sec. vi, in the context of bank security.

Quarantia to investigate the tills of bankers in search of counterfeit coins. Campsores caught with such coin were to be severely punished: they were to be fined in the amount of the false coin discovered, plus its nominal equivalent in good coin, and they were deprived of the license to practice their profession for five years.[56] Among the staff of the Officium Grossorum Tonsorum were coin checkers who seem to have gone from bank to bank, and there was a weigher at the office who weighed coins brought by private parties desirous to know the intrinsic value of the coins they held.[57] The same office is mentioned as late as 1421 as having jurisdiction over illegal coin dealt in by bankers and moneychangers.[58] Solemn oaths and more or less draconian laws notwithstanding, the problem was a recurrent one. Criminal prosecutions of bankers and others for illegally manipulating coins show that these regulations were taken seriously, at least in specific and identifiable periods, in the early Trecento and the mid-Quattrocento.

Between 1324 and 1332 several moneychangers were prosecuted, along with many other persons, first for buying or passing off "aquilini," foreign coins meant to be worth 20 and 22 denari, then for clipping the same kinds of coins. These were years in which Venetian grossi were undervalued and disappeared from circulation as good money, according to "Gresham's law"; the severe dearth of good coin was resolved only with the minting of the new mezzanino and soldino in 1332. Specifically identified in the court record as campsores were Francesco Baffo, Donato Bobizo, Nicolò Sanino, and Francesco "Rizzo" da ca' Contarini; Giovanni Acotanto and Lorenzo Grimani seem also to have been in the same profession. Sanino was sentenced on both counts, to a fine in 1326 and to three years in prison in 1332. Acotanto and Grimani, both noblemen, were sentenced for clipping coin, the former to a two-year prison term, the latter to a heavy fine; both were banned from all councils and public offices, and Grimani was banned also from operating a "banchum cambii."[59]

---

[56]*PMV,* doc. 121, a regulation that held also for Venice's small dominion on the Terraferma ("a Quarnario citra").

[57]These two jobs are known from cases against "famuli" of the office who collected kickbacks from the "banchi cambiorum subiecti dicto officio," obviously for not reporting infractions, and against the noble "ponderator" at the office, who substituted bad coins for the good ones he was given to weigh. ASV, AC, reg. 3642, fol. 88v–89 (21 February 1360). While these cases still concern the Officium Grossorum Tonsorum, in 1358 the Quarantia gave jurisdiction to the officials of the mint and the Silver Office to search the banks and even the homes of moneychangers for clipped coins; no matter who connected with the bank was found with such coin, the "caput banchi" was to be held responsible; see Vincenzo Padovan, *Le monete dei Veneziani: Sommario* (Venice, 1881), doc. 13, p. 213 (from the capitolare of the Cattaver). In Florence the task of evaluating and weighing coin was performed by the Arte del Cambio.

[58]Lattes, *Libertà,* doc. 13.

[59]ASV, AC, reg. 3641/I, fols. 2, 5v–6 (1324), 31v–32 (1326), and reg. 3641/II, fols. 13–16 (February–March, 1332). Cf. Reinhold C. Mueller, "Il circolante manipolato: L'impatto di imitazione, contraffazione e tosatura di monete a Venezia nel tardo Medioevo," in *Italia, 1350–*

During the monetary confusion created by the coining of massive quantities of black money and the resultant scarcity of good coin in the mid-fifteenth century, a moneychanger and two partners in a bank were discovered to have been the principal suppliers of mint-fresh coin to a veritable workshop of coin clippers. Antonio Zane, a small operator about whom little else is known, was sentenced in absentia to banishment from Venice for ten years and forbidden ever to run a bank again. The other two were members of the Garzoni family and partners in the prominent Bernardo-Garzoni bank. Giovanni Garzoni, who, like Zane, had fled Venice to avoid arrest, was banished for five years and similarly prohibited from operating a bank; his brother Antonio was sentenced to a one-year prison term for having known about the operation without reporting it. The condemnation of the two Garzoni brothers, declared to have been "carried away by avarice," was handled in such a manner as to absolve this important bank from responsibility, thus permitting it to continue to function on the Rialto as before. Finally, in 1472, during another period of serious monetary confusion, the accountant of the Guerrucci bank was arrested in broad daylight at the crowded Rialto for clipping coins. Fearing that the banker himself might be involved, depositors began a run on the bank, which was saved only by the swift action of the Signoria and other depositors who came to its support. Again, the owner himself was not arrested, nor was he judged responsible for the crime of his employee, and the bank was permitted to carry on. Keeping circulating metallic money free of counterfeit and underweight coins was indeed considered the responsibility of moneychangers and bankers, but it was often not in their interests to do so; policing their countertops was not a simple matter, and they probably were only rarely caught violating the law.[60]

The old Officium Grossorum Tonsorum is rarely mentioned after the mid-fourteenth century, when it was perhaps more thoroughly absorbed into the Silver Office, but its jurisdictions were not abandoned. In 1389 official investigators charged with seeking out the clipped and sweated coins at the banks of moneychangers were given a raise (from one-third to one-half) in the cut due them from fines, as an incentive to carry out their duty.[61] Once the Council of Ten assumed jurisdiction over matters relating to the production and circulation of coins in Venice and its subject territories in 1472, it moved quickly to assert its authority. In 1473 coin checkers operating under the insignia of the lion of St. Mark ("bancherii publici cum

---

1450: Tra crisi, trasformazione, sviluppo (Pistoia, 1993), 225–26. Idem, "Domanda e offerta di moneta metallica nell'Italia settentrionale durante il medioevo," in *Die Friesacher Münze im Alpen-Adria-Raum/La moneta frisacense nell'Alpe Adria,* ed. Reinhard Härtel, acts of the conference of Friesach, 1992 (Graz, 1996), pt. 3.2.

[60]See, below, Chap. 5, at the end of sec. iv, and at the end of sec. v.

[61]*PMV,* doc. 180.

signo S. Marci") were hired, one for the Rialto and one for Piazza San Marco, with the task of evaluating all coin brought to them, so as to take out of circulation counterfeit and underweight coins. Rectors were instructed to do the same in the subject cities they governed. These coin checkers were distinct from bankers and moneychangers, who were enjoined to perform the same service in dealing with their clients; they were salaried and could neither buy coin nor charge a fee.[62] While this office continued to operate as a public service at least into the 1490s,[63] the Council of Ten seems to have placed little faith in the willingness of the Rialto bankers to destroy bad coins. Beginning in 1485 a coin checker ("revisor et ponderator") was assigned to each of the four banchi di scritta then operating at the Rialto and was provided with a set of special standard weights.[64]

Before the arrival of computerized and automated banking facilities, and perhaps even then, the problem of "bankers' hours" often plagued clients. Venetian authorities determined the days on which banks should open, and the Provveditori di Comun — in the fifteenth century — were to see to it that they remained open at least four hours per day. Moneychangers at San Marco generally petitioned to remain open longer hours and more days. In 1379 bankers at both the Rialto and San Marco were prohibited from opening on solemn feast days, with the exception that moneychangers at San Marco could remain open regularly from the first day of Lent to the octave of Ascension. A decade later the operators at San Marco petitioned to remain open also on feast days that fell on Saturday, since that was market day on the Piazza. In 1390, while a special indulgence was being preached, the moneychangers were permitted to stay open on feast days, in view of the fact that they were paying particularly high rents for their banks and because their services were needed by pilgrims and travelers.[65]

Rialto bankers, on the other hand, ran a different kind of operation and stayed open as little as necessary. In the mid-fifteenth century, the Provveditori di Comun noted that a bad habit had arisen among the banchi di scritta of opening only when and for as long as they liked, to the detriment of merchants and others. It was therefore decided by the Senate that the bankers would remain open (literally that they would "sit and write") four hours per day, two hours in the morning, beginning with terce, and two hours after dinner, beginning with vespers. The Provveditori were to

[62]ASV, Consiglio dei Dieci, Miste, reg. 18, fol. 28r–v (21 October 1473) and fol. 30 (3 November). Capi del Consiglio dei Dieci, lettere, b. 1, fol. 240 (20 June 1474).

[63]ASV, AC, reg. 3658, fol. 20 (13 September 1494), in a case against coin checkers who had tried to defraud the lord of Rimini.

[64]ASV, Consiglio dei Dieci, Miste, reg. 22, fols. 162v–64 (27 April 1485), for the deliberation; for the assignments, see Capi dei Dieci, Notatorio, reg. 1, fols. 45 (28 April), and 57 (31 May 1486). *Cap. broche*, 210 (9 May 1485).

[65]The deliberation of 4 May 1379, referred to in ASV, SM, reg. 41, fol. 54v (18 January 1390), is in *PMV*, doc. 164, pp. 165–66. ASV, MC, Leona, fol. 17v (1 October 1387).

activate a "two-hour clock" (presumably a sand-filled hourglass) when the church bells rang terce and vespers, and at the end of the two hours they were to ring a bell, "like that used by the Silver Office," before which no banker could close, under pain of a 50 lire fine.[66] It is likely that bankers tried especially to reduce hours when their cash reserves were low, and in fact the above provision dates from a period of extensive cash withdrawals for a planned crusade, a situation that paved the way for the liquidation of the bank of Francesco Balbi. In June 1478 bankers were not opening at all, leading to "murmuring in the city," and the Senate required that they open at least in the morning until the usual hour.[67] Not even fines, however, would convince bankers to open if they were afraid of a run or were simply unwilling to convert deposits into cash, and the problem of bankers' hours remained recurrent.[68]

iii. POSTING BOND

An essential condition that had to be met before a banker could open for business was the posting of bond. The obligation to provide personal surety was a longstanding tradition in Venetian public offices of particular importance. Mintmasters, for instance, were to provide 1,000 lire in personal surety, as a pledge to honesty and to upholding their oath to obey the capitolare (see Vol. 1, pp. 216–17). Private moneychangers and bankers were also required to post bond. Initially the sums were so small as to be purely symbolic, as was the case with public offices; that is, bankers provided guarantees that they would comply with the law, for example, by withdrawing nonlegal tender coins from circulation. Beginning in the midfifteenth century, however, the pledge required of bankers became so large as to be real rather than symbolic and greatly exceeded that required of government officials. The bond then came to be a guarantee meant to reassure depositors that their money was safe.

No one expected a moneychanger to keep 100 percent reserves behind his deposit liabilities. He would naturally invest his own and his depositors' money in loans and commerce, up to a reasonable sum necessary to keep on reserve. That placed him in a risk category similar to that of any merchant, for he, too, made short-term contracts of colleganza, entered joint ventures, and made long-term partnerships. Perhaps more than most, he was interested in dealing in such speculative commodities as gold and silver. Like all other merchants, then, he was plagued by slow turnover, risk of loss by

---

[66]ASV, ST, reg. 1, fol. 157v (27 June 1445); also in Provveditori di Comun, reg. 1 (capitolare), fols. 79v–80v, but misdated 1455; printed in Lattes, *Libertà*, doc. 17.

[67]ASV, ST, reg. 8, fol. 12 (23 June 1478).

[68]ASV, Provveditori di Comun, reg. 1, fol. 102v (17 December 1488), from the Council of Ten.

shipwreck, and reversal of predicted market trends. In contrast to other merchants, however, the moneychanger-banker made loans with other people's money, without having to ask for consent.

Many governments sought to provide protection for depositors against some part of the risk by requiring bankers to post bond before being considered fully licensed to practice their trade (see Vol. 1, p. 87). Bond was normally personal, that is, in the form of a personal guarantee made by the bondsman and backed generically by the latter's patrimony. But it could also be real, that is, consist in enumerated assets of the banker or of his guarantors or both. In either case, the bond was surely never intended to cover all the banker's liabilities, for it must have been assumed that he would never lose all his depositors' assets. As a result, the bond was probably more often a psychological support for public trust than a proper guarantee that deposits would be repaid in full in case of failure or liquidation. Moreover, neither did the capital of the bank itself and the patrimony of the banker or bank partners constitute a similar guarantee, for the total liabilities of the bank were bound to be many times greater. Taken together, however, individual, family, or partnership capital, patrimony, and sureties were sufficient to prompt depositors in need of banking services to leave their money with a bank or bankers.

Venetian authorities became concerned for the safety of depositors' assets when it became particularly evident, perhaps as a result of a bankruptcy that has left no other trace, that campsores were investing depositors' assets. The bond they decided to call for initially consisted of the personal guarantee offered by persons other than the banker and his partners. The bondsmen, at least by the early fourteenth century, had to be renewed annually and approved by the Consoli dei Mercanti by Michaelmas (29 September), the same date by which the banker had to have rented his table and quarters from the state. Only upon having met both requirements could he practice his profession as a licensed banker.[69]

The earliest provision in this regard, passed in 1270, required each campsor to furnish the Consoli with surety for a minimum of 3,000 lire.[70] Thirteen years later, in 1283, the requirement was amended, with the aim of distinguishing between the two categories of bankers operating in Venice. While the earlier provision was confirmed with respect to campsores at the Rialto, those operating on the Piazza San Marco had to provide surety of only 1,000 lire — the same amount required of mintmasters. This law makes it obvious that Rialto bankers carried greater liabilities than bankers operating at San Marco. At the same time it recognizes that the latter were not

---

[69]ASV, Grazie, reg. 7, fol. 36 (15 October 1336). In 1374 Zaccaria Contarini, who proposed very restrictive banking legislation, sought, in vain, to require bankers to swear on that same date each year that they would uphold the regulations. *PMV*, doc. 160, p. 154.

[70]Lattes, *Libertà*, doc. 1α, and *DMC*, 2:255.

merely moneychangers: they also accepted deposits, with which they might do business.[71] As we have seen above, the campsores at San Marco, given their proximity to the mint, were involved in buying bullion from foreigners and, after refining, reselling it. Furthermore, the fact that they accepted deposits on which they paid interest is documented by a notarial act of the year 1300 in which the interest on a loan (a local colleganza) was tied to the rate of return that Marco Trevisan, moneychanger at San Marco, was paying on funds left with him.[72] A century later, when the bank of Marino Dandolo (a non-noble) failed, it was said that he was indebted to many persons, presumably depositors, as well as to the mint.[73] At the same time, such banking activity was exceptional at San Marco, whereas it was normal at Rialto.

Once bond requirements were established, it remained to be seen just what the liability of the bondsmen would be. During a period of uncertainty, around the time of the coining of the gold ducat, bondsmen seem to have tried to avoid their obligations by claiming that the persons who were actually handling the money ("qui tenerent cambium in predictis tabulis") were not those for whom they had agreed to act as surety. A law of February 1285 therefore ruled bondsmen as well as persons having legal title to the bank liable for the debts of the bank, no matter who had actually run the operation. From this it is clear that there were individuals who founded banks at the Rialto and at San Marco but who, having concluded the rent agreement with the state and having posted bond, turned the operation over to relatives, partners, or employees.[74]

The added risk to depositors involved in such arrangements prompted the Great Council in 1318 to try to provide depositors with a more solid guarantee. The prologue to the new regulation delineated a complicated arrangement, similar to that evoked by bondsmen in 1285, which could — and obviously did — mislead depositors. A merchant might rent a bank, sign it over to a minor son or to others, and then arrange the guarantee, reads the preamble. The person with legal title to the bank and backed by surety, then, was not the one who ran the operation, and depositors were misled to think they were leaving their money with the bonded and licensed banker. Two provisions were intended to rectify the situation. First, only the person holding full title to the bank and who had thus been bonded would henceforth be permitted to receive deposits, under pain of a fine of 25 percent of all sums illegally deposited. Second, the amount of the bond, which the

[71]*DMC*, 3:17. Cf. Alessandro Lattes, *Il diritto commerciale nella legislazione statutaria delle città italiane* (Milan, 1884), 200–201, 216 n. 16.

[72]ASV, PSM, Ultra, b. 180, commis. Marcello, parchment J, dated 1311 but containing copies of contracts from 1300 and 1301.

[73]ASV, Grazie, reg. 20, fol. 95v (15 September 1415).

[74]Lattes, *Libertà*, doc. 1β; same in *DMC*, 3:95, and *PMV*, doc. 38.

law says had to be renewed annually before the Consoli dei Mercanti, was raised from 3,000 to 5,000 lire for Rialto bankers (those at San Marco were not mentioned). No campsor could pledge himself as surety for another campsor, nor could any single bondsman pledge himself for more than 1,000 lire.[75]

Only one case has come to light in which this provision was enforced. In 1353 the Florentine Pietro Fastelli was fined nearly 5,000 ducats by the Consoli dei Mercanti for having accepted some 20,000 ducats on deposit while he was working in the bank of the partners Alessandro degli Agolanti and Donato Alemanni, also immigrants from Florence. When Pietro appealed for a grazia on the grounds that he had run the bank without malice ("pure sine aliqua malicia"), the Consoli testified that their predecessors had also fined Pietro for the same offense when he had accepted deposits at the bank registered in the name of Donato Alemanni alone. Pietro himself had not posted bond on the assumption that he could carry on the activity of the banks under the bond posted by his employers. The motion for a grazia, which reduced the fine to a mere 100 lire, was passed by both the Quarantia and the Great Council. Perhaps the cashier's only mistake was that he had acted in his own name rather than in that of his employer.[76] In any case, the law of 1318 and the attempt to enforce it reflect the extent to which economic relationships traditionally were considered personal relationships, that is, between client and banker, not between client and bank qua institution. In that sense, by the mid-fourteenth century tradition was already superceded by practice.

The effectiveness of the legislation regarding the kind of deposit insurance required of bankers could be tested only in case of liquidation or failure, but the records of the Consoli are lost. For the fourteenth century, only two cases have come to light which indicate that guarantors could indeed be called upon to pay a bankers' liabilities. During the banking crisis of 1342 a depositor brought suit before the Consoli against the guarantors of the bank of Marino Vendelino and insisted that they repay a deposit she had made in the bank. Even though a majority of the Consoli ruled in favor of the depositor, the guarantors won the case on appeal, asserting that they were not liable for debts on which interest ("lucrum") was paid but only for deposits on current account.[77]

---

[75]Lattes, *Libertà,* doc. 1, and *PMV,* doc. 175. The earliest extant capitolare of the Consoli dei Mercanti dates from the mid-fourteenth century. Its capitula 59–62, undated, are the four above-mentioned provisions concerning the posting of bond. Padua, Archivio Giusti Lanfranchi, cod. 175.

[76]ASV, Grazie, reg. 13, fol. 32 (8 November 1353).

[77]"Dicti pleçii se defendentes respondebant dicentes dictam quantitatem pecunie non fuisse depositam in tabulam dicti Marini [Vendelino] sed solum datam per ipsam dominam [Isabetam Quirino] dicto Marino in lucrum et sub specie lucri." ASV, AC, reg. 3642, fol. 44 (6 September 1342). Guarantors of a bank in Bruges which failed in the very same period also

The second case concerns the debts of the small-scale banker Franceschino Spirito, who failed in 1369. Francesco Spirito, presumably his grandfather, once campsor at San Marco and then weigher at the mint, was one of the guarantors and asked for a raise in salary in order to help him meet his obligations.[78] Another guarantor was Nicoletto Servodio, who in 1385 declared that he was owed 1,200 ducats as a result of his connection with the bank. At that time Pietro, brother of Franceschino and cappellanus of San Marco, made an out-of-court settlement with Servodio in lieu of pro rata payments owed him by Franceschino, as recorded at the office of the Consoli. Although the accord was for a small sum (60 ducats at the time, and 2 ducats per annum as long as Franceschino lived), it indicates two significant facts. First, the guarantor was liable for the debts of the bank as soon as its assets were exhausted. It was the guarantor, then, rather than the original creditors, who was owed the pro rata payments established by the agreements with the liquidators. Second, it takes for granted the liability, probably unlimited, of the family. Not only did the guarantor claim that the debt was owed him "by Franceschino Spirito, his heirs and successors," but the bankrupt's brother, despite being a cleric, was constrained to pay his debts.[79]

The validity of requiring surety of bankers was asserted by some but rejected by others during the third quarter of the fourteenth century. Those forces who proposed in 1356 that Venice legalize pawnbroking at fixed and controlled rates of interest included in their bill the requirement that the moneylenders, very likely Jews, be invited on a five-year charter, or condotta, to rent banks from the Rialto Office and supply surety of 5,000 lire with the Consoli — just like the transfer banks.[80] Only two weeks after that bill failed in the Great Council, after having been passed by the Quarantia, Giovanni Dolfin, one of the heads of the Quarantia, proposed the establishment of a public bank that would protect holders of current accounts by maintaining 100 percent reserves. When that proposal also failed, this time in the Senate, Dolfin suggested that the requirement that bankers post 5,000 lire bond be abolished, presumably as ineffectual, a proposal that was similarly defeated.[81] When the establishment of a public bank was again proposed in 1374, which this time would have replaced private banks al-

---

refused to consider themselves liable for interest-bearing deposits; see de Roover, *Money, Banking, and Credit in Mediaeval Bruges,* 249. See also the discussion of deposits, above, Chap. I, sec. iii.

[78]ASV, Grazie, reg. 16, fol. 111.

[79]ASV, CIN, b. 189, notaio P. Sagredo, fragment of an imbreviatura, fol. 3 (14 April 1385).

[80]*PMV,* doc. 122, and, for the context, Mueller, "Les prêteurs juifs," 1279–80.

[81]*PMV,* doc. 124. The investigation of moneychangers ordered in 1359 as a result of the confusion in circulating media ("magnum incommodum denariorum contatorum") included their sureties and partners: "tam in plegiariis quam aliis pertinentibus." Ibid., doc. 133; same in Lattes, *Libertà,* doc. 3.

together, the bill's proponent stated that no surety would be necessary, on the assumption that 100 percent reserves would be maintained (on this theme, see below, Chap. 3, sec. vi).[82]

It is not impossible that surety requirements lapsed some time later. In any case, for more than half a century there is no echo of any role played by guarantors, even in those bankruptcy cases that are well documented. Furthermore, as we shall see, the next law regarding surety for bankers, passed in 1455, makes no reference at all to previous legislation, and, as Elia Lattes commented, it sounds more like an innovation than a reform.[83]

In the meantime, however, another approach to guaranteeing the safety of depositors' assets had been attempted. In 1404, in the midst of a serious banking crisis that in Venice was attributed to overinvestment in the Levant trade by partners in the principal transfer bank on the Rialto, that of the heirs of Pietro Benedetto, the senator Bulgaro Vettori sought to re-establish faith in the banks by curtailing sharply the amount of their commercial investments, thus raising their reserve. The expedient he settled on was that restrictive mechanism employed at various times during the previous century and enforced by the Officium de Navigantibus. The preamble of his bill asserts that it was clear to all that bankers were investing in commerce the money that depositors left with them, in excessive amounts and with the greatest risk to depositors. He thus proposed that a banker's total investments by land or sea be restricted to 150 percent of the same banker's assessed patrimony as recorded in the estimo at the state Loan Office. Although an exception was made for the importation of wheat, which would have no ceiling, the proposal had teeth: severe penalties were envisioned, and a mere proposition to relax the penalties was itself to be punished by a sizeable fine. The bill, which made no provision for the eventuality that a bank was run by two or more partners, passed only narrowly, with 48 ayes against 42 votes to adjourn discussion and 3 abstentions. While Florentine observers in Venice remarked at the severity of the law, the lack of wholehearted support, or the impossibility of policing the measure, seems to have doomed the law to failure from the start. Its attempt to raise cash reserves has no legislative or judicial sequel. And it did not succeed — it could hardly have been expected to — in avoiding the run that engulfed the Benedetto Estate bank only six weeks later.[84]

Another half century, marred by the failure of at least six major banks, passed before the organs of government decided to intervene in the area of

---

[82]*PMV,* doc. 160, p. 151.

[83]Lattes, *Libertà,* 69.

[84]Ibid., doc. 12, but for a fuller discussion and complete references, see below, Pt. II, regarding the bankruptcies. Unfamiliarity with the terms used in the law caused de Roover to interpret the meaning as "total holdings in bonds" (*Money, Banking, and Credit,* 310 and nn. 84–85), whereas what is unequivocally meant is the assessment for which one was inscribed on the estimo, as is clarified below, Pt. V.

bank guarantees. A law of 1455 reinstated the requirement that bankers post surety, but it makes no reference to the earlier law of 1318, still technically in force, or to the law of 1404. The minimum bond required was set at 20,000 ducats, ten or twelve times the amount fixed in 1318.[85] It is important to note that the law was drafted in the midst of a very serious conjuncture for Venetian money and banking. The inflation of black money and the scarcity of gold had just forced the domestic exchange rate up to 124 soldi di piccoli per ducat. The finances of the state were depleted by the war that had engaged Venice in Italy until the Peace of Lodi and by preparations for eventual war against the Turks after the fall of Constantinople; the system of public debt had reached the breaking point. All these factors were involved in some way in the failure of two banks run by Benetto Soranzo and Brothers, the first in September 1453, the second in September 1455. It was only a month after the failure of the second bank that the new bonding law was drafted and passed by the Senate.

The preamble to the law states that it was common knowledge that during the preceding twenty-five years many ("quamplures") Rialto banks had failed or had encountered misfortune ("fefellerint et in viam sinistram inciderint"), to the detriment of the state and the great loss of citizens and others, large portions of whose liquid patrimony had been blocked by the courts as a result of the failure. It was therefore to preserve the reputation of Venice — says the law — that it was necessary to avoid such trouble in the future. The law provided that no banker could make an entry in his books before providing surety for 20,000 ducats to the Governatori delle Entrate and the Consoli dei Mercanti, a majority of whom were to approve the surety. No banker could pledge himself for another banker, nor could any single bondsman pledge more than 2,000 ducats. Although the law of 1318 required a simple personal guarantee, this regulation made it possible for the banker and his guarantors to provide a real guarantee in the form of government obligations, as long as they were conditioned as such, that is, rendered inalienable. Real estate, furthermore, was specifically excluded from the wealth that guarantors could put up as security, and a proposed amendment to the contrary was roundly defeated. Moreover, continues the law, "since the wealth of men usually varies over time," the bankers' sureties would have to be renewed every three years and approved by a majority of the above-mentioned officials, "for the greater security of all." Between renewals one or more bondsmen might be replaced, as long as official approval was obtained. Finally, in order to avoid confusion in the case of bankruptcy, guarantors who were also creditors of the bank were not to be included in the installment payments made to creditors in general.[86]

---

[85]If the 5,000 lire are considered lire a grossi, the equivalent is 1,915 ducats; if lire di piccoli were meant, as is more likely, the bond was equal to 1,562.5 ducats.

[86]Lattes, *Libertà*, doc. 23. The defeated amendment reads: "Quod securitates suprascipte

From this point on it seems that bond requirements were effectively adhered to by bankers at the Rialto. When in 1473 the bank of Piero Guerrucci (Veruzzi in Venetian), survivor of a run during the drastic monetary reforms of the previous year, actually failed, the Senate concerned itself first and foremost with the condition of the bank's guarantors. Guerrucci claimed that, in order to pay all creditors in full, he needed only a moratorium of eight months free of legal action against himself and his assets and the repayment by the state of loans totaling 10,000 ducats. The Senate agreed in principle, but before the agreement became effective, Guerrucci had to reconfirm within three days the support of at least three-fourths of his bondsmen, for a total of 15,000 ducats, and he had five days to come up with new sureties for the balance of 5,000 ducats. The 8,000 ducats that the Salt Office owed the bank since 1464 could be considered obligated to the guarantors, thus facilitating the search for new ones; the state promised to pay that sum after eight months to the bank's creditors or to the guarantors who had made payments for the bank ("qui pro eo solvissent"). All guarantors, new and old, were to be equally liable to all creditors of the bank.[87] A contemporary chronicle supports the bank's claim that it could pay off its creditors, and it sets at only about 30,000 ducats the liabilities on which the bank was forced to delay payment. The chronicler reports that the bank was able to come up with the surety ("bona piezaria") required and that the Senate therefore granted the requested moratorium and safe-conduct. The only damage inflicted, he says, was the "loss of time," with reference to the fact that the depositors' credits were frozen.[88] Even though the delay extended beyond the promised eight months,[89] the case of Guerrucci's failure is one piece of concrete evidence that bank sureties were provided and that on occasion they actually played an active role in the process of liquidation.

The conviction that posting bond provided a kind of insurance for depositors surely existed among Venetian legislators in the later fifteenth century. In 1493 the law of 1455 was extended to the drapers of the Rialto, who thus were to provide surety, at 2,000 ducats per guarantor, "just as was provided — most wisely — in the case of our bankers." The extension was probably due to some kind of custom whereby drapers accepted discretion-

---

etiam fieri possint super possessionibus et bonis stabilibus, detractis et defalcatis dottibus et aliis obligationibus si que essent super dictis possessionibus et bonis stabilibus." The law was passed 107 to 1, with 3 "non sinceri." ASV, ST, reg. 3, fol. 180.

[87]Lattes, *Libertà*, doc. 27, which incorrectly renders the name Veruzzi as "Venier," however, an error that Ferrara, "Documenti," doc. 156, repeats; see the original in ASV, ST, reg. 7, fol. 22r–v. If new liabilities were contracted, or more probably if new debts turned up upon closer audit, further surety was to be posted.

[88]BMV, It. cl. VII, 791 (7589), the "cronaca Veniera," fol. 158; the chronicler gives the period as one year rather than as eight months.

[89]The banker applied for a further four-month safe-conduct in the period around February 1475. See ASV, AC, reg. 3654, fol. 7 (20 February 1475).

ary deposits, as was common in Florence; but nothing further is known about such a practice in the Venetian Quattrocento.[90]

Enforcement of the law with regard to bankers was, of course, no real defense against those panics that precipitated bankruptcy. First of all, a crisis of faith in the solidity of private banks very likely coincided with a decline in faith in government obligations — those very assets that bankers and guarantors alike were permitted to set aside as security.[91] Furthermore, the sum of 20,000 ducats was only a small portion of total liabilities. The anonymous French treatise of about 1500, already referred to in the previous chapter, reports the requirement of bankers to provide sureties who were "bons et riches" for a total of 20,000 ducats, but it remarks that this was a small amount in comparison to a bank's total liabilities in the form of deposits, which sometimes exceeded 300,000 ducats at a single bank, as we have seen. That proportion constituted a mere 6.67 percent, and the treatise relates that mishandling of depositors' funds led to failures despite the guarantees — failures that caused great loss in money and time.[92]

The writer had in mind the failures that threw the Rialto into confusion beginning in 1499, when surety became particularly important. The Bernardo-Garzoni bank failed in 1499; when it tried to reopen in early 1500, the bankers put up surety of more than 50,000 ducats from approved private guarantors, to which the state added a pledge of 20,000 "for the merits of the house of Garzoni." Beyond this the Garzoni had "stable assets" at the Loan Office and liquid assets totaling more than 100,000 ducats. The bank failed again only a few months later, however, and the state named three nobles (provisores super rationibus banchi de Bernardis et Garzonibus) to oversee the liquidation both of the previous bank and of its successor. Among the documents they produced is one that lists all the bank's guarantors, from 1470 to 1499; every three years ten persons pledging 2,000 ducats each had been approved by the Consoli and the Governatori, as prescribed by the law of 1455. The scope of the investigation was probably to see whether the law had been obeyed in the past and to check on the liability of individual guarantors.[93] Between 1506 and 1508 the Garzoni made pacts for repayment of their debt, not with the creditors or their "capi," the liquidators, but with the guarantors. This is a clear indication that the guarantors had stepped in and advanced to the original creditors the sums owed them by the bank. The installments that the bank agreed to pay on its debts therefore passed directly to the guarantors.[94]

[90]ASV, ST, reg. 12, fol. 49 v (21 March 1493). That such shops accepted deposits beginning in the thirteenth century is reflected in the antiusury memorandum of about 1300, in various contracts of local colleganza, and in the partnership contracts of Tommaso Talenti's silk firm; see Mueller, *Procuratori di San Marco,* 71–95, 178–85, and app. I.

[91]Lane, "Venetian Bankers," 79.

[92]*Traictie,* cap. 32; previously published in Perret, *Histoire des relations,* 282.

[93]ASV, PSM, Misti, b. 189, and Ferrara, "Documenti," docs. 136–37.

[94]Ferrara, "Documenti," docs. 147–50.

When the Lippomano also failed and fled the city and the pressure was heavy on the banks of Alvise Pisani and Maffeo Agostini, Pisani is reported to have cried out at the Rialto that the Lippomano were thieves and that the security required of bankers should have been set at 50,000 ducats, not at 20,000. In fact, it was shortly thereafter that the Garzoni put up 50,000 ducats from private sources for their new bank. And Pisani himself was able to convince sixty nobles, citizens, and foreigners to pledge the incredible total of 324,00 ducats, which stopped the run and permitted his bank, "nearly bankrupt" [mezzo rotto], to liquidate and reopen in 1504.[95]

The tremendous difficulties of the Rialto banks around the turn of the century caused the Senate in 1523 to reform and strengthen the bonding procedure. The reform, a prelude to the broad reorganization that saw the establishment of the Provveditori sopra Banchi in 1524, provided that all individuals and firms who wished to open a bank first had to be approved by a majority of a quorum of 150 voting members of the Senate. Once approved, they had to post surety, now for 25,000 ducats, and each bondsman had to be approved by the Senate in the same fashion. As regards the nature of the security, the new law stated that government obligations might no longer be put up, either by the banker or by his bondsmen, and that the only acceptable security was the patrimony ("facoltà") and the person of the bondsmen themselves.[96] The new law was first applied in the case of the Arimondo bank. On 7 March 1524 the Senate voted first on the person of the banker, Andrea Arimondo, and then on each bondsman on the list, as Sanudo duly reported.[97] Even this new regulation, which made the banks more nearly public institutions than ever before, of course did not suffice to stave off bank failures; Arimondo himself failed only two and one-half years later.[98]

From a provision of 1528 it is clear that bonding requirements were limited to the major Rialto banks, the banchi di scritta. The small banks supposedly specializing in manual exchange of coins did not have to post bond. They were found to be attracting deposits away from the banchi di scritta, however, by offering a premium, or agio, on specie brought for deposit and to be keeping alphabetized ledgers and vacchette, or journals, in which they performed transfers, just like the banchi di scritta. This was

---

[95]Malipiero, *Annali*, 715–18; the passage is quoted by Vincenzo Manzini, "La bancarotta e la procedura fallimentare nel diritto veneziano, con cenni sui grandi fallimenti del secolo XV," *Atti dell'Istituto veneto di scienze, lettere ed arti* 85 (1925–26): 1133–34, and Lattes, *Libertà*, 17–18. The Pisani bond is confirmed in ASV, CN, reg. 15, fols. 7–8 (17 July 1499). See also Lane, "Venetian Bankers," 71, and, regarding "insurance" of debts in 1508, 1524, 1526, p. 74 n. 30; idem, *Venice: A Maritime Republic* (Baltimore, 1972), 328–29.

[96]Lattes, *Libertà*, doc. 30.

[97]*Diarii*, 36:33–35; Arimondo did not receive a large majority: 86 ayes to 65 nays. Because of a procedural problem, the voting had to be repeated in May, when all the banks were balloted; ibid., 36:355.

[98]Ibid., 43:57 (12 October 1526); Lane, "Venetian Bankers," 71.

forbidden as contrary to the bonding law.[99] In 1554 private moneychanging was actually prohibited, and two "banchetti" were instituted by the state, one at the Rialto and one at San Marco, operated by salaried employees, expert in identifying coins ("due huomini legali et periti di ori et monede"), but that regulation was overturned in 1562. At that time private parties were again permitted to operate small exchange banks ("levar banchetti da scambiar ori et monede"), but they annually had to provide surety of 1,000 ducats that they would obey the law and destroy all lightweight coins ("monede scarse").[100]

Given the loss of the records of the Consoli dei Mercanti, it is impossible to judge the utility of the Venetian policy of insisting that bankers post surety before beginning operations, since there is no way of knowing just how the guarantors became liable at the critical moment of a banker's actual insolvency. The total silence regarding their role between 1374 and 1455 makes one wonder whether the regulation of 1318 had not in the meantime fallen into disuse. Furthermore, the nature of the reform of 1523 makes one wonder whether the option to condition holdings in government obligations as security, as had been sanctioned by the law of 1455, had not proven in practice to be a rather feeble kind of insurance. Very likely the requirement that bankers show that they were backed by men who were "bons et riches," even if only to a relatively small percentage of total liabilities, at least contributed to the faith that the market placed in the solvency of their operation, which was so central to the functioning of both private and public sectors of the Venetian economy. Thus one can readily agree with the banker Alvise Pisani, who cried out at the Rialto in 1499 that the bond ought to be more than doubled and continued, "For when there is no faith in the banks, Venice has no credit."[101]

iv. CONFLICTS OF INTEREST

It is obvious that moneychangers and bankers would be very interested in the operation of the mint and in the decisions made by the mintmasters. A constant tension existed in fourteenth-century Venice, but probably not only there, between concern for eliminating conflicts of interest damaging to the commonweal and the realization that bankers could bring to the mint an expertise that few nonbankers could match. Florence opted for a pragmatic solution beginning in 1299, when it was decided that of the three mintmasters ("domini monetae") one would always be a banker, chosen by the consuls of the Arte del Cambio from among the members of

---

[99]Lattes, *Libertà,* doc. 34.

[100]ASV, Consiglio dei Dieci, Comuni, filza 84 (26 May 1562).

[101]Malipiero, *Annali,* 716. It is difficult to be sure whether these words are Malipiero's or whether he attributes them to Pisani, as the phrase immediately preceding.

the guild. Similarly, Florentine law made no attempt to prohibit Florentine citizens from accepting contracts for the farming of foreign mints, and Florentines can be found as mintmasters elsewhere in Italy and throughout Europe.[102]

Venetian authorities, on the other hand, early considered it in conflict with the city's interests that Venetians operate foreign mints and consequently prohibited such operations.[103] They were therefore all the more concerned to keep moneychangers and bankers out of positions in which they might influence mint policy or profit personally from advance knowledge of decisions. There seems to have been a regulation or at least a consensus that rendered active bankers ineligible for the higher offices of the mint, and active bankers are absent from the lists of noblemen who held the major rotating offices of mintmaster.[104] In 1328 the Quarantia forbade any campsor or partner in a bank even to pledge himself as surety for the election of a mintmaster.[105]

Lesser offices were similarly protected against conflicts of interest. Active bankers or moneychangers had to suspend operations in order to accept a position at the mint or related offices. Former bankers, on the other hand, were periodically elected to such positions, while, conversely, one case finds a former mintmaster who became a moneychanger.

No incompatibility was seen to exist between the profession of moneychanger and that of refiner of bullion. Refining involved a half-private, half-public status and was done sometimes inside, sometimes outside the mint

[102]A. Lattes, *Il diritto commerciale,* 203, 222 n. 44. Winfried Reichert, "Mercanti e monetieri italiani nel regno di Boemia nella prima metà del XIV secolo," in *Sistema di rapporti ed élites economiche in Europa (secoli XII–XVII),* ed. Mario Del Treppo (Napoli, 1994), 337–48.

[103]Three Venetians operated the mint of the patriarch of Aquileia in 1255; see Giulio Bernardi, *Monetazione del Patriarcato di Aquileia* (Trieste, 1975), 197. The first prohibition was passed in 1284; see Roberti, *Le magistrature giudiziarie,* 2:192. The prohibition was repeated in 1328 and 1437 in a more general context: no mint, tax, or customs could be farmed by a Venetian in any territory not subject to Venice; ASV, SM, reg. 60, fol. 21 (8 June 1437).

[104]The lists prepared by Padovan and reprinted in his *Le monete dei Veneziani* are superceded by those in Papadopoli, 1, app. 2, and 2, app. 2; even these are incomplete, however, and they similarly lack the patronymic crucial for identification. An example of the problems one may encounter: the Benedetto Soranzo listed as mintmaster in 1452 is qd. Antonio, while the Rialto banker Benedetto Soranzo a banco, active at the same time, was qd. Cristoforo; the latter was elected to the Senate in 1451 and to the Zonta in 1452; see ASV, Segretario alle voci, Misti, reg. 4. fols. 26, 130v. A possible exception to the rule is the election of Giovanni Papaziza as mintmaster for gold in 1348, when he is called campsor. Giovanni, mintmaster in 1338, during one of at least eight terms, belonged to a family of persons often elected to that post, and he may have briefly tried his hand at moneychanging. *DQ* 2:14, doc. 50, and Papadopoli, 1, app. 2, and especially Alan Stahl, "Office-holding and the Mint in Early Renaissance Venice," *Renaissance Studies* 8 (1994): 404–15.

[105]"Quod nulla campsor nec qui habeat partem in tabula cambii possit essere plezius communi pro aliquo massario monete, nec etiam complezius aliquo modo," under pain of 1,000 lire fine. ASV, AC, reg. 2, fol. 175, cap. 238, to which A. Lattes seems to refer in *Il diritto commerciale,* 222 n. 44.

premises (as explained in Vol. 1, pp. 219–22). Thus in 1338–39 Marco Stor-lato, a moneychanger at San Marco, was called "campsor et afinator pro comuni" in a court case.[106] A decade later, the banker Donato Alemanni, an immigrant from Florence and partner of Alessandro Agolanti, ran a shop for refining gold.[107] Around 1400, the banker Guglielmo Condulmer, as we have seen, refined silver in his own furnaces, but his accounts were subject to close scrutiny by the mintmasters for fiscal and provisioning reasons, namely, the proper consignment of the quinto, as required of all bullion dealers. Donato di Filippo Nati, another immigrant from Florence, was at the same time a large-scale refiner, the owner of two goldbeaters' shops, and a partner in three successive banks. It was he, as "argentarius," who main-tained the bank's relationships between the mint and clients.[108] Vettor Sor-anzo — brother of Gabriele, who founded the Soranzo bank — and his heirs were wholesale bullion dealers. Giovanni di Vettor reopened the Soranzo bank after the bank operated by Benetto di Gabriele Soranzo had failed twice, while other members of his branch continued to deal in bullion. One of them, Matteo, was called "argentarius" of the Garzoni bank when both of them failed in 1499.[109] Other campsores, as we shall see, also invested in furnaces used for refining.

Full-time government offices required greater vigilance. Francesco Vielmo, campsor, who customarily operated a moneychanger's table at San Marco, was required in 1346 to give up his concession in order to accept a position as an official at the mint. To keep a hand in his preferred profession, however, Vielmo feigned a partnership with a moneychanger so that he could occasionally sit at the bank. Such anomalous behavior caused him to be fined for buying silver without being in that year a licensed campsor and for contravening the capitolare of his office.[110] In 1349 Filippo Dandolo was declared ineligible for the position of weigher at the silver mint ("pondera-tor super argento") because he was a partner in a bank ("quia habet partem in cambio").[111] An exception was made in the case of Pietro Emo, a banker on the Rialto, who, in the 1370s, was also an assayer of gold. But when he died in October 1375, shortly after admitting bankruptcy, the Great Council decreed that conflict of interest be avoided in the future; his replacement could have no ties with a banco di scritta nor any interest in the gold trade.[112]

---

[106]ASV, AC, reg. 3641, fol. 31v (9 July 1338), and reg. 3642, fol. 14 (10 September 1341).

[107]ASV, Signori di Notte al Criminal, reg. 6, fol. 30 (17 December 1350).

[108]Reinhold C. Mueller, "Mercanti e imprenditori fiorentini a Venezia nel tardo Medioevo," *Societa e storia* 55 (1992): 50.

[109]See below, Chap. 6, on the bankruptcies of that year.

[110]Vol. 1, app. G, doc. 5.

[111]*DQ*, 2, doc. 164 (30 March 1349).

[112]"Et iste qui fiet nunc et decetero fiendi non possint habere partem in bancho de scripta, nec partem in auro." ASV, MC, Novella, fol. 155 (28 October 1375). His replacement was probably Alvise Viaro, a banker who had failed in 1361; see Grazie, reg. 17, fol. 92v (1377).

In 1417, however, Pietro di Bernardo de Arsengo, campsor, could still compete for such lesser positions as scribe and weigher at the mint.[113]

Steps were also taken to regulate the relations between officials and bankers. In 1382 special ducat weighers ("officiales deputati ad ponderandum ducatos") were enjoined not to accept loans from bankers,[114] and again in 1410 the Great Council insisted that officials at the gold mint, given the importance of the position, be not only monetary experts but also free of any tie with a banco di scritta, be it through favors or loans of any amount.[115] Family ties were more difficult to control, but even here efforts were made to avoid conflicts of interest. For example, when in 1459 the bullion supplier Giovanni Corner consigned a quantity of gold to the mint, it was considered improper that his brother Michele, official assayer, should test the gold, and a substitute was named for the occasion.[116]

Former moneychangers could offer a certain level of expertise to the state. Marco Rosso, the campsor at San Marco who, as we have already seen, was injured in the hand by a member of the de Buora clan and was therefore unable to continue his profession, received a position as broker at the Silver Office in 1342.[117] Donato Quintavalle, campsor in 1340, when he seems to have failed, received a post as "pensator ad argentum" in 1354 and then went on to serve several terms as mintmaster in a long public career at the mint.[118] A rather similar case is that of Francesco Spirito, campsor at San Marco in 1346, who was soon made a full-time weigher at the gold mint, where he stayed on for more than twenty-two years.[119]

One could, of course, also move from service to the state to a private profession. Cristoforo Zancani, who was elected mintmaster of silver in 1381 and of gold in 1385 and 1386, established himself as campsor at the base of the campanile in Piazza San Marco, but probably only after his last term of office. He failed in 1389 or 1390, blaming bankruptcy on losses suffered in purchasing a Viennese merchant's silver coins ("vianenses") — a strange miscalculation for a former mintmaster and moneychanger.[120]

[113]ASV, CN, reg. 5, fols. 86v, 87v.

[114]ASV, SM, reg. 37, fol. 89v.

[115]"Verum declaretur quod nullo modo vel ingenio possint accipere seu accipi facere servicium aliquod, aut mutuum alicuius pecunie quantitatis a banchis de scripta pro se vel aliis, sub pena perpetue privationis ipsius officii." ASV, MC, Leona, fol. 195v (11 September 1410).

[116]ASV, CN, reg. 9, fol. 170 (15 December 1459).

[117]ASV, Grazie, reg. 9, fol. 60. The same man began as a wine dealer in 1344; see reg. 10, fol. 38.

[118]Ibid., reg. 13, fol. 44v, and Papadopoli, 1, app. 2. A Donato Quintavalle is "massarius monete nostre auri" as late as 1387 and 1395, which means the former banker either lived to age seventy-five or was replaced at some point by a homonym. For the latest reference, see MC, Leona, fol. 76v (17 January 1395).

[119]Vol. 1, app. G, doc. 5; also ASV, Grazie, regs. 13, fol. 48v (20 June 1354), and 16, fol. 111 (1369, approved April 1370).

[120]Cap. broche, 42–44; Papadopoli, 1, app. 2; Simonsfeld, Der Fondaco, 1, docs. 263, 264, 265. The existence of homonyms cannot be excluded.

It was only logical that bankers who were noblemen and therefore members of the ruling councils were occasionally elected to committees of experts who had to formulate monetary or financial policy. In 1274, for example, three campsores were named to a committee to examine the record of an employee of the Gold Office, subsequently dismissed for malfeasance.[121] In 1353, the moneychanger Andrea Gabriel was elected, with two others, to serve on a committee on mint policy in the Council of Forty; his proposals for reform of the coinage did not pass but were heavily debated.[122] Pietro Benedetto, a prominent Rialto banker, was one of three "sapientes super monetis" in the crucial years 1379–80, even though their decisions involved bankers at nearly every step.[123] And in 1417 Cristoforo Soranzo, director of the bank of the estate of his father, Gabriele, was a member of the committee for reform of the currency and of mint procedures.[124]

When ties between bankers and the state became ever closer after the War of Chioggia, and when the banks came to constitute the state's primary floating debt, it is obvious that bankers were in a position to acquire a more direct influence in decisions regarding financial policy. An especially blatant concession to the realities of war finance was made in 1440. In that year the Signoria, which had been borrowing heavily from the bank of Luca Soranzo and Brothers for the campaigns in Lombardy and had no alternative to further borrowing, invited one of the brothers, Benetto, who was "solicitous in lending to the Signoria," to be present daily at meetings of the highest organs of the state so that he might receive orders to pay, as well as solicit repayment. He was permitted to sit in the Collegio at will ("ad beneplacitum suum"), "as though he were a sapiens terre nove."[125] The military situation at that time was undoubtedly exceptional, but the invitation extended by the government headed by Francesco Foscari to a Soranzo qua banker was completely outside Venetian constitutional procedure. As such, it is an exceptional case. In fact, the figure of the banker-politician probably did not develop before the end of the fifteenth century, and the role of the banker Alvise Pisani in politics and on the Rialto between 1499 and 1526 was probably unique in Venetian history, at least up to that time. Whatever their political connections or their wealth, banker-politicians might have been mistrusted; only three were named Procurator of San Marco, and no banker was ever elected doge.[126]

[121]*DMC*, 2, appendix, p. 427.

[122]In 1360 he was prosecuted for falsifying receipts on a purchase of gold and was prohibited from operating a bank in the future. Stahl, "Office-holding and the Mint," 407–10.

[123]*PMV*, docs. 163–64. The same banker was elected to a committee of auditors of the accounts of the Loan Office; ASV, MC, Novella, fol. 170v (23 February 1382).

[124]Papadopoli, 1:245.

[125]ASV, CN, reg. 7, fol. 23 (23 December 1440): Benetto "habuit et habet hanc praticam et sollecitudinem serviendi nostro dominio, nomine suo et fratrum."

[126]On Alvise Pisani, see Lane, *Venice*, 328–30.

v. BANK SECRECY AND THE FISC

Bankers prepared their tax declarations for the assessors as private citizens and heads of households, not as bankers, even though their role as mediators in the payments system was practically public. Because of their peculiar position, bankers were regularly given preferential treatment, as was admitted by a law of 1446 that, as we will see shortly, insisted that they be treated instead like any taxpayer. That was common knowledge, according to the accuser in a lawsuit against two members of the Garzoni family a decade later. "They pay according to the assessment that suits them," he testified, and he presented as proof the surprisingly low assessments for which the two were inscribed on the estimo; "That tells you," he concluded ironically, "just how rich they are."[127]

Bankers also had a public relation to the system of forced loans and hence to the fisc, deriving from their position as mediators. Since bankers held in the form of deposits portions of the liquid capital of a great many persons who were obliged to contribute to the loan funds, government policymakers were concerned about whether or not to support bank secrecy. In the course of the first half of the fifteenth century, the policy changed from complete approval of bank secrecy to its total elimination.

The assessors elected in 1403 to revise the estimo were instructed to examine taxpayers' declarations, or "condizioni," for accuracy. They were permitted to place the principals and "other persons" under oath and to collect pertinent information from any and all government offices by consulting their account books for the current and past years, so as to learn the truth ("pro possendo habere bene veritatem"). At this point, two exceptions were made. The first concerned the office of the Procurators of San Marco, which traditionally had been trusted to declare what was owed by the estates and the bequests they administered without their declarations being subject to outside audit. The second exception involved the bankers, who were declared immune from being placed under oath regarding others; nor could they be questioned concerning the sums of money they held on deposit in their banks, in the name of any contributor to the public debt.[128] This provision, of course, was a consciously created loophole that favored the practice of evading one's legal obligations, safe from the scrutiny of the auditors, by depositing liquid capital in a bank and failing to declare it. Such a policy of bank secrecy, then as today, must at the same time have favored the bankers by providing more and bigger clients, raising

---

[127]"Segondo, questi da cha' di Garzoni non habuto angaria de tal raxione, perchè sono banchi de scripta, e fano le angarie per quelo che i piaxe, avixando le Reverentie Vostre che uno di loro fratelli fano di £2000, l'altro di 2400, che dixe chotanto àno." ASV, GP, Sg, reg. 123, fols. 65–69v (24 May 1456).

[128]"Verum, bancherii qui sunt ad presens et erunt infra hoc tempus non possint poni ad sacramentum nec peti de quantitate pecunie quam haberent de aliqua alia persona in eorum banchis." ASV, SM, reg. 46, fols. 112v–13.

their reserves and promoting further investments, especially during the period devoted to revision of the estimo.

The loophole was partially closed by a law of 1427 which defined the criteria for a revision of the estimo in that year. The senatorial decree again instructs the assessors to study the returns and clarifies certain specific deductions, including those for dependents and for debts. A separate clause was dedicated to bank loans, which contributors claimed as deductions: "If any citizen claims he is debtor to any of our transfer banks, the bankers concerned are bound under oath to declare the truth concerning that debt upon request of the auditors."[129] The loans declared could have been long-term contracts, medium-term loans via bills of exchange, or short-term loans via overdraft. It is not impossible that permitting deductions for loans promoted indebtedness. This law opened a first breach in the wall of bank secrecy. At this time the principle seems to have remained intact as far as deposits are concerned, however, for no permission was given the assessors to audit active bankers' ledgers in order to determine the credits recorded on depositors' accounts.

The authorities could intervene, on the other hand, and audit accounts in the case of bankrupt and insolvent banks. In 1431 the Senate repeated an order previously given to the assessors who revised the estimo to proceed against persons who had fraudulently claimed to be debtors of the Orsini bank, then in the hands of liquidators. It then expanded the order to include all persons who had failed to declare that they were creditors of the Orsini or of other former banks, all persons who claimed to be creditors for sums inferior to their actual credits, and all those who had received cash payments from the liquidators of the banks just before turning in their "condizioni" but did not declare them.[130] Until the former banks had paid in full, their books were deposited at the office of the Consoli dei Mercanti, where they could easily be consulted by the assessors. That implied much work, for two banks had liquidated (Cocco-Miorati, 1424, and Orsini, 1428), and three had declared insolvency (Andrea Priuli estate, 1425; Priuli estate and Bartolomeo Priuli, 1429; Jacopo Priuli and Orsini, 1429).

All this changed in 1446 during the last serious revision of the estimo for the Monte Vecchio. At that time the authorities threatened with a heavy fine anyone who concealed any part of the patrimony of any Venetian who

---

[129]"Se alguno nostro çitadin se darà per debitor a algun dei nostri banchi de scrita, sia tegnudi i diti banchieri la veritade dir ai nostri savi da chi i sarano rechiesti, e con sacramento afermar quelo che serà la veritade del dito debito. E si i darà altri suo crededori, sia tegnudi i diti far clari i diti nostri savii dei diti tal debiti." ASV, SM, reg. 56, fol. 90r–v.

[130]Ibid., reg. 58, fol. 73 (9 August 1431). The vote on the same day to include banks other than the Orsini who had been active in the 1420s but were no more ("etiam intelligatur pro aliis banchis a scripta qui erant tempore sapientum predictorum") drew considerable opposition.

was required to contribute by standing in for or substituting his name for ("tanxare") such a person. The fine was set at 25 percent of the amount occulted and was payable to the assessors and their staff who discovered the deception.[131] On the same day, the Senate pointed a finger at the bankers as the principal concealers of wealth and goods of Venetian citizens, a situation that is not surprising given the bank secrecy law of 1403. In order to remedy the situation, the assessors who audited the condizioni were permitted to examine the entries in the bankers' books relevant to the return being audited. Furthermore, they were empowered to investigate bankers suspected of concealing the wealth of other citizens, and if any money or assets of others were uncovered which should have appeared on the accounts maintained by the banker but did not, the guilty banker was to be fined 25 percent of the total concealed. Finally, the Senate ruled that this regulation be read in the Great Council, "ad informationem omnium."[132]

Several months later, for some unexplained reason, some of the assessors were in doubt whether the deliberation regarding revision of the estimo, which required all persons ("omnes indifferenter") to compile returns, included bankers. The Senate responded that all bankers and all partners in banks had to prepare their declarations of patrimony distinctly and precisely ("distincte et particulariter") as all others had to, so that bankers not be given preferential treatment ("ita quod in hoc non sint melioris conditionis aliorum"). The subcommittee of five assessors which had jurisdiction over the Rialto bankers and their partners was to examine their returns with particular care and then consult the other two subcommittees before arriving at a vote (requiring a majority of nine of fifteen or eight of fourteen) on the acceptability of the returns that the bankers had prepared.[133]

While this law required the assessors to keep "secretissima" all their investigations and discussions, the policy of bank secrecy, which had facilitated tax evasion, was legally ended. It is somewhat surprising that it lasted

[131]Lattes, *Libertà,* 66, in the notes.

[132]"Verum, quia etiam necessario providendum est quod bancherii pretendentes occultare et tanxare facultates et bona civium nostrorum caveant ab istis inconvenientiis committendis, ex nunc captum sit et commissum sapientibus nostris ad aptandum terram quod, pro intelligendo veritatem in conditionibus quas aptare habebunt, mittere possint quando eis videbitur pro illis bancheriis quos voluerint et ab eis cum sacramento intelligere veritatem super illa vel illis conditionibus quas aptare volent; et possendo examinare et videre partita vel partitas contentas in libris banchorum suorum pro declaratione eorum que agere habebunt. Et ultra hoc habeant libertatem prefati sapientes intelligere et diligenter investigare de predictis bancheriis, qui tanxarent seu occultarent bona et facultates civium nostrorum facientium seu qui facere possint de imprestitis." ASV, ST, reg. 1, fol. 187v, in Lattes, *Libertà,* doc. 19. The law was passed 97 to 24 with 10 "non sinceri." One of the assessors whose term began 29 November 1446 was Bernardo Balbi, a member of the banking fraterna Francesco Balbi and Brothers, which had been forced into liquidation the year before; see ST, reg. 1, fol. 183v.

[133]Lattes, *Libertà,* doc. 20.

as long as it did (almost half a century, although what policy was followed before 1403 is not known), given the readiness with which Venetian authorities usually legislated interference and government controls on the daily activities of the Rialto bankers.

vi. BANK SECURITY AND BANK ROBBERS

While, on the one hand, bankers avoided the use of coin by mediating much of the business transacted on the Rialto by the simple book transfer of sums from account to account, on the other hand, banker and money-changer alike derived considerable profit from the manual exchange of coins. They handled large amounts of all denominations of coins, local and foreign, as well as valuables, as part and parcel of their daily activity. The temptation for bankers themselves to commit crimes connected with their particular activity was ever present, as much then as in any age. Quite often, in fact, we find bankers accused of buying counterfeit coins as well as stolen valuables such as gems and silver belts. As we have seen above (in sec. ii of this chapter), sometimes they themselves were discovered to be partners in the production and distribution of counterfeit coins, or they were found to have ordered the wholesale clipping and filing of mint coins, even though culling was a criminal activity.

At this point, however, I mean to investigate the role of bankers, not as malefactors, but as victims. Given the importance of the banks for the functioning of the marketplace and for the lines of credit they provided for the state, the authorities in Venice took pains to provide security for bankers, for their money and valuables, and, failing that, they sought to punish bank robbers in such an exemplary manner as to deter others from similar undertakings.

The problem of security regarded both the location of the bank and the person of the banker. The locations were not separate buildings, it must be remembered, but tables under a loggia with a room or rooms behind, or — as at San Marco, at the foot of the campanile — separate and precarious booths. Specie for immediate exchange of coins was often kept in a bowl or bowls on the table, and all exchanges, by law, were to take place "above board." Specie needed to meet normal daily demand for withdrawals and exchange of coins was more likely kept for the day in a strongbox in the back room. Policing the area of the Rialto day and night were two non-noble captains of the guard ("custodes Rivoalti"), each with a squadron of as many as twelve men.[134] Despite the show of force, police protection was not considered sufficient. For the night, bankers tended to bring the cash-

---

[134]See Guido Ruggiero, *Violence in Early Renaissance Venice* (New Brunswick, N.J., 1980), 12–17. The captains were under the authority of the Signori di Notte; Sanudo, *De origine,* 261; cf. *Traictie,* cap. 24.

Fig. 5. Palace of the Camerlenghi, or Treasurers, as rebuilt about 1525–30.
This office building also housed other magistracies, and jail rooms were
situated on the ground floor. The Camerlenghi provided space for the
strongboxes of the private deposit banks, situated a few steps away.

Diateca, Department of the History of Architecture, Institute of Architecture, Venice

box — or have it brought — to their private homes, a potentially risky operation. In an effort to resolve this problem, the state in time provided space in
a government office and licenses to bear arms.

Sometime in the first half of the fifteenth century, clearly as a result of
the robberies (especially one of the year 1410, which will be discussed
shortly), each banker was permitted to keep a strongbox in the Treasury,
seat of the Camerlenghi di Comun. This office was located very close to the
transfer banks, at the bend in the Grand Canal, at the foot of the Rialto
bridge. Sanudo describes the building in 1493 as recently constructed and
most beautiful (*"noviter* fabricato sopra Canal Grando, che è bellissimo"*);
it survived the fire of 1514 but was then rebuilt about 1525–30 (see fig.
5).[135] Many tax-collecting offices were required each evening to bring their
day's proceeds to the Treasury, and since much of the state's liquid resources
lay there, it was well guarded. To that extent it is understandable that
bankers found the offer useful; on the other hand, leaving much cash in
safes under the physical control of the state could have raised some doubts,

[135]*De origine,* 110–11, 247–48; in both places he mentions that there "si tien le casse delli
denari di banchi di scritta." See also Calabi and Morachiello, *Rialto,* chap. 6.

and bankers seem to have kept some cash there, some at home, and perhaps some at the bank.

The deliberation of the Collegio in September 1453 which first informs us of the failure of the Soranzo bank reports that the principals themselves learned of the problem only when the cashier failed to appear either at their home or at the Treasury: "It happened that Alvise qd. Pietro Venier, manager and accountant at the bank of the noble Soranzo family, who always brought the accounts either to the home of Benetto Soranzo and his brothers or to the safe assigned to them at the Treasury, yesterday, after closing the bank, took the accounts and the money of the bank but did not take them either to the Soranzo home or to the Treasurers; where he went is not known."[136] In short, the alternative was open and subject, it seems, to a daily, perhaps arbitrary, decision.

That bankers were perhaps right to keep open an alternative is indicated by a single isolated case. Although protection of a private bank's assets in a government office building probably did not lead the contemporary to imagine the state's getting its hands on specie in a moment of need, it did give the authorities the possibility of prohibiting the banker's access to his bank's strongbox. When the Garzoni failed in 1499, access was blocked throughout the whole one-year moratorium; when the bankers got their surety together and were permitted to reopen, access was once again granted (see below, Chap. 6, sec. ii).

The same bank's application for the right to keep a safe ("unum capsonum ferratum") at the Camerlenghi for the security of its liquid assets dates from a generation earlier. When they applied in 1461, the Garzoni stated that other banks already kept such safes at the Treasury.[137] Only four years later it became necessary to enlarge the quarters occupied by the office, because the working space necessary for the accountants had been cramped by the safes of all revenue-collecting offices of the city, as well as those containing "all the money of the transfer banks of the city" [tutti li danari de li banchi de scripta de questa nostra città].[138] Since a special nightwatch was mounted at the Rialto precisely to protect the quarters of the Camerlenghi, bankers continued throughout the sixteenth century as well to make use of the secure space offered them by the state.[139]

Even though his bank's assets were watched over by the state, the banker still had to concern himself with his own safety against the ill intentioned. The state authorities, therefore, at least from the early fifteenth

---

[136]Lattes, *Libertà,* doc. 26.

[137]ASV, CN, reg. 10, fol. 19v (13 January 1461).

[138]Cessi and Alberti, *Rialto,* doc. VIII, pp. 320–21.

[139]Sanudo, *De origine,* 110–11 (1493), 248 (1515); Arturo Magnocavallo, "Proposta di riforma bancaria del banchiere veneziano Angelo Sanudo (secolo XVI)," *Atti del Congresso internazionale di scienze storiche, Roma, 1–9 Aprile 1903,* vol. 9 (Rome, 1904), 415, an inventory of about 1570.

century, granted bankers the license to carry arms, which assumes some ability to use them. Licenses were first granted upon application through the "grazia" procedure, as we know from cases beginning 1409, with the consent of the Signori di Notte, and were usually renewable year by year.[140] Later the Senate had jurisdiction. Application to the Senate was one of the first concerns of Francesco and Giovanni Pisani, for example, when they founded their bank in 1475; it was readily granted, "as customary for other bankers."[141] In later years private armed guards were hired to protect the operations of banks at the Rialto.[142]

As mentioned above, these security precautions were perhaps taken as a result of some robberies that occurred in the late fourteenth and early fifteenth centuries, but they did not altogether prevent robbers from trying their hand. The following cases exemplify three situations in which bankers of the Rialto and San Marco were targets of robbers. They could be victims in broad daylight, while they exchanged coins on their counters; in the evening, after closing, when they transported the cash reserve; or during the night, when the safes at their banks presented a different kind of challenge. Each case adds some detail to the general picture of banking operations. The guilty were in all cases foreigners to Venice.

In 1352 Zanino da Bergamo, "vagabundus," watched a monk of S. Giustina count out silver mezzanini at the bank of Francesco Teldi, opposite the loggia of the nobles at the Rialto; he went up and stole 4 ducats' worth of the coins, only to be caught after a short chase and condemned to blinding.[143] Four years later a Bartolomeo da Verona, desperate after losing money at gambling, went to San Marco and watched a few exchanges being made at the bank of Matteo Spiati; when he saw his chance, he snatched a small sack containing 36 ducats and small change; he, too, was captured immediately and sentenced to hanging.[144] Again at San Marco later the

---

[140]See, for example, ASV, Grazie, reg. 20, fols. 16v (1409: "consideratis periculis quibus subjacet"), 50v (1411), 63 (1413), for Bernardo Giustinian; ibid., fol. 19v (1409: "attentis dubiis et periculis"), bank of Giovanni Corner, Antonio Miorati, and Donato di Filippo Nati; ibid., fol. 30 (1410) for Gabriele Soranzo and his son Nicolò, "cum tribus apud eos, attentis dubiis"; fol. 60 (1413) for Andrea Priuli and Brothers and for Nicolò Cocco and Partners. Ibid., reg. 21, fols. 4v (1417), Cristoforo Soranzo and Brothers, and 74r (1423), Andrea Priuli and Brothers. Ibid., reg. 22, fol. 6v (1424), a one-year renewal for the bank of Nicolò Cocco and Antonio Miorati; ibid., fol. 63v (1426), bank of Leonardo and Jacopo Priuli and Brothers, "sicut aliis bancheriis Rivoalti concessum est"; renewed in 1427, fol. 88, and 1428, fol. 106; ibid., fol. 69 (1426), bank of Giovanni Orsini and Brother; fol. 147v (October 1430), bank of Francesco Balbi and Brothers. Ibid., reg. 24, fol. 30 (1438), Luca Soranzo and Partners, "secundum consuetudinem hactenus observatam."

[141]ASV, ST, reg. 7, fol. 76v (9 June 1475), and Ferrara, "Antichi banchi," 198.

[142]ASV, Consiglio dei Dieci, Comuni, reg. 18, fol. 184, authorization granted to the Dolfin bank (28 November 1548).

[143]ASV, Signori di Notte al Criminal, reg. 6, fol. 52.

[144]Ibid., reg. 7, fol. 1 (11 July 1356).

same year Otto from Salzburg, "vagabundus," feigned the desire to exchange small coins for a ducat at the bank of Francesco Contarini and made off with 3 ducats; under interrogation (with the help of an interpreter), he was unable to say whether he had taken them from a wooden bowl or from a wooden counting board (presumably a board with a kind of funnel at one end to facilitate slipping coins into a sack; see fig. 6). The culprit was sentenced to blinding of his left eye.[145] On a similar pretense, a courier from Bologna asked to change a ducat into bolognini or aquilini at an exchange table at the Rialto. Because the moneychanger had none on hand, the courier said he would accept old soldini, but while the moneychanger was selecting the coins, he snatched 4 ducats. Again he did not get far before being caught; this time, the sentence called for amputation of the right hand as well as blinding of the left eye.[146]

The exposed condition of bankers and the fragile nature of banks were no different in the Quattrocento, as two further examples demonstrate. In 1419 a unemployed German baker, Cristoforo qd. Enrico, vagabond, seeing a bowlful ("scudelotum") of ducats on the table run by Pietro Venier, managing partner in the bank of Andrea Priuli and Brothers, picked up a handful of dirt and threw it in Venier's eyes and made off with the bowl. Venier gave chase, forcing Cristoforo to drop the bowl containing 340 ducats, and he was captured in the pescheria. The punishment was exemplary: after being conducted along the Grand Canal on a barge tied to a pole, in the usual manner, his right hand was amputated in front of the bank and tied about his neck, before he was hung on gallows strategically set up in the canal in front of the pescheria, where his body was to remain two days.[147] Later in the century a similar robbery occurred which caught the attention of chroniclers. In 1478 a Greek from Candia succeeded in getting his hands on 21 ducats at the table ("mensa numularia") of the moneychanger Antonio Fantini when the latter's attention was distracted. After a short chase, the guards of the Rialto captured the thief and took him to the office of the Signori di Notte, where he was tortured and confessed. The very next day he was sentenced and executed: in the usual manner, his right hand was amputated at the scene of the crime, after which he was hung on high gallows erected "between the bridge and the loggia at the Rialto," where his body was to remain suspended for two days.[148]

---

[145]Ibid., fol. 13, and Simonsfeld, *Der Fondaco,* 2:298, doc. 21 (1356–57). He "posuit manum in quodam ordegno ligni, quem nescit an sit platena vel nombratoria, et inde furtive accepit tres ducatos."

[146]ASV, Signori di Notte al Criminal, reg. 8, fol. 2v (10 September 1361).

[147]ASV, AC, reg. 3647, fol. 62v. It is worth noting that these first three cases were among the criminal cases that attracted Marin Sanudo's special attention, as he studied the registers of the Quarantia: Quarantia Criminal, reg. 14bis, fol. 99v (5 July 1419).

[148]ASV, AC, reg. 3654, fol. 55v (18 February 1478); BMV, It. cl. VII, 791 (7589), fol. 162, and 519 (8438), fol. 288.

Fig. 6. Depiction of a Treasurer (Camerlengo di Comun). The official is
emptying out a sack of coins onto a funnel tray used by financial
offices and private operators alike for counting and sacking coins.
Miniature in the margin of a page of Livy's history of Rome, in the
Biblioteca Ambrosiana, Milan.

Diateca, Department of the History of Architecture, Institute of Architecture, Venice

In these examples of hardly premeditated crimes, the banker himself did not run any mortal risk, and it was usually he who began giving chase. But the opposite could also happen, for the habit of taking the daily cash reserve home at night invited robbers to plan an ambush.

On 12 January 1382 four men from Padua and the Padovano executed a plan to rob Ludovico Emo, whose bank was located under the loggia near the Rialto bridge. When the nobleman Emo and his assistant ("famulus") headed for home after closing time with a sack of money and other items, the robbers followed them. Upon reaching a bridge near S. Aponal they attacked, threw the banker into the canal, beat his servant, grabbed the assets of the bank, and disappeared. On the following day, the Quarantia announced a reward of 3,000 lire di piccoli for information leading to the arrest of the guilty parties.[149] Some time thereafter, three of the same men, obviously feeling confident, went into action again. They appeared at the house of Gabriele Soranzo, one of the principal bankers of the city, pretending to be bearers of a letter from Remigio Soranzo, then in Padua. When Gabriele descended the steps to receive the letter, they grabbed and bound him, threatening to kill him if he shouted, and proceeded to rob him. The summary court record stops at this point, and the events leading to the arrests are not explained. In any case, it was not until August that the Quarantia voted to proceed against the suspects. Antonio di Nerio of Padua, the ring leader, was sentenced to be dragged through the city to the scenes of the crime; at S. Aponal his right hand was amputated and hung about his neck; his left hand was severed in front of the bank of Gabriele Soranzo and similarly hung about his neck. Once his crime had been proclaimed by the crier at the Rialto, he was dragged to San Marco, where, between the columns, he was beheaded and quartered. The quarters then were strategically placed to warn other provincials of the consequences of crimes perpetrated against the bankers of Venice and the money of Venetians: one of each on the roads to Castro Carro, to Piove di Sacco, to Padua; the fourth was hung for one day outside the house of Gabriele Soranzo and then placed on the route to Mestre. Two of Antonio's companions were saved from capital punishment, but they both lost their right hand, were blinded in both eyes, and were banished from Venice. The sentences were executed the same day they were handed down. The fourth accomplice, Antonio's brother, seems not to have been captured.[150]

Small moneychangers at the Rialto in the following century probably did not have the privilege of keeping a safe at the Camerlenghi. In 1460 the factor of a silk shop, Francesco di Giovanni, developed a friendship with the

---

[149]ASV, AC, reg. 3644, fols. 45v–46v (20 August 1382); Quarantia Criminal, reg. 17, fol. 103 (13 January 1382), and reg. 14bis (Marin Sanudo's notes), fols. 61v–62.

[150]ASV, AC, as cited in the previous note; it is recorded in the margin that the sentence was executed the same day.

campsor Stefano Marino, who granted him loans. On one occasion, the moneychanger, who does not appear in account books of the period, agreed to a loan of 200 ducats, with some bolts of silk cloth as collateral. Giovanni consigned the bolts by boat, in which he accompanied the campsor home. The boatman was taken by the fact that Marino, after locking up at night, took his accounts and a sack of money ("computum et saculum pecunie banchi") home with him. After dropping off the moneychanger, the boat-man exclaimed to the factor that the man was rich and ought to be killed ("à tanti danari! el se voria amazarlo!"), to which Francesco agreed. They accompanied him home again, on another occasion, to get into his confi-dence, and the third time brutally murdered him in the boat by fracturing his skull; they weighted the body with heavy stones, threw it overboard, and divided the booty: 800 florins, some jewels and other objects, and a few silver coins. The body must have surfaced, however, for the authorities arrested Francesco, while the boatman, who supposedly killed the man, succeeded in fleeing the city. The accomplice was decapitated and quar-tered; hanging and quartering awaited the boatman, should he ever return to Venetian lands.[151] Here the murderers, though immigrants, seem to have been resident in Venice and were easily identified by the authorities.

Conditions were just as risky for moneychangers at San Marco, who seem to have had neither the right to bear arms nor a safe place, private or public, to keep their reserves. As in the preceding case, Marco Sagredo did not have an assistant. In 1440 this non-noble campsor was easy prey for two robbers and cutthroats, Enrico of Lubiana and "Ancius [Hans] sive Johan-nes teotonicus." Seeing that Sagredo had, as usual, a large amount of coin on his counter ("ut moris est, super banco suo satis bonam pecunie sum-mam"), they decided to rob him on his way home after closing. They confessed to having tried three times without success. On the fourth occa-sion (it was Saturday — thus market day at San Marco — 12 November at nightfall), as Sagredo was leaving his bank with a sack containing about 300 ducats and with his account books, they assaulted him, wounding him several times, and robbed him. Persons who had heard the banker's cries succeeded in capturing the robbers as they fled toward S. Angelo, where they came up against an impassable bridge. Judged to be murderers as well as robbers, these foreigners were, as usual, hung, drawn, and quartered and the quarters displayed "in loca solita," about thirty-six hours after their capture.[152]

Attempts were also made, with varying degrees of success, to break into banks after hours. At the Rialto, in contrast to the mean booths under the campanile at San Marco, situated next to and between sellers of sau-sages, there was a solid back room behind the counter, and above it a

[151]Ibid., reg. 3651, fols. 101r–2v (7–20 November 1460).

[152]Ibid., reg. 3648, fols. 73v–74 (14 November 1440).

storage room with a safe. The evidence is largely from the fifteenth century. In July 1410 Antonello of Catania noted a hunchback named Domenico (surely Domenico di Masino di Manetto), factor at the Cocco-Miorati bank, while, with an assistant, he carried two large sacks of coin to the bank's storage room on the mezzanine. Antonello confessed that he had followed them to see where they went, before going home to S. Samuele to get his tools; he broke the lock of the vault, then that of the safe, and stole two sacks containing Venetian coin and one of "viannari," silver pennies often imported in large quantities by Austrian merchants. The record of the trial does not say how he was caught or what happened to the money or how much it was worth, but the Council of Forty was present in force and voted unanimously that he be hanged on gallows planted in the Grand Canal opposite the fish market — for the crime had been committed "to the detriment of the whole city, considering the place where the money was stored," that is, in the locale of a bank on the Rialto.[153]

Six years later the bank of Bernardo Giustinian, situated next to the church of S. Giacomo, became the target of another thief whose nighttime operation was so elaborate and so unlucky that the authorities did not ask capital punishment. On 27 March 1416 "Jacobus qd. Jacobi Coquus de Alemania, vagabundus," used an iron bar to break a hole in the wall inside the church of S. Giacomo; this hole gave him access to the mezzanine of the magistracy called the Raxon Nuova, where he broke another hole in the floor through which he lowered himself into the quarters occupied by the Giustinian bank. Here he forced the safe, thinking he would find money ("putans reperire pecunias"), but he found only 54 soldi in silver coins, worth half a ducat, and one small ring. The culprit was captured while still in the bank by the guards patrolling the Rialto. Obviously struck both by the ingenuity required by the enterprise and by the meager results (the bank's liquid assets were probably in care of the Camerlenghi), the Quarantia voted twenty times in vain before finally reaching agreement on a sentence that amounted to leniency: Jacobus was taken between the two columns where he was branded and blinded in his right eye; then at the Rialto, opposite the Giustinian bank, his right hand was amputated and hung from the column of the town crier. After his guilt was proclaimed at the Rialto and at San Marco, the unfortunate robber was banished from Venice and threatened with hanging should he ever return.[154]

---

[153]Antonello saw that a "gibus, nomine Dominicus, qui moratur in banco viri nobilis Nicolai Caucho et ser Anthonii Miorato campsorum scripte in Rivoalto, cum uno alio puero portaverat duos sachos pecunie satis magnos hora prandii ad voltam dicti banchi super solaria." He broke in and stole the sacks, "predicta committendo in magnum onus tocius terre, considerato loco in quo ipsa pecunia adderat." Ibid., reg. 3646, fol. 85 (4 July 1410). In an early case of 1333 lacking in detail, the night watch discovered Menico of Orvieto in the act of breaking into the bank of Marino Vendelino on the Rialto; Signori di Notte al Criminal, reg. 16, fol. 91v.

[154]ASV, AC, reg. 3646, fol. 108v; Quarantia Criminal, reg. 14bis, fol. 98v (3 June 1416).

The mirage of finding a treasure never dies, as two final cases reported by Marin Sanudo indicate. In 1497, during the night of 26 November, the Agostini bank at the Rialto was broken into. The strongboxes were forced open, but the thief got very little because the cash reserve had been placed in the bank's safe in care of the Camerlenghi.[155] Rather more successful was a break-in at the bank of the great Alvise Pisani in 1519, where the take amounted to 4,000 lire di piccoli, worth about 600 ducats but in heavy small coin. That daring act ("enorme caso," "temerario ardimento," wrote Sanudo) struck at the financial and political heart of the state, and the reaction was strong: the Senate offered a reward of the same amount for information, put up half by the state and half by Alvise Pisani; for turning over the culprit or culprits to the Signoria the reward was 6,000 lire, similarly divided; anyone who concealed information was threatened with a year's imprisonment. The coup of the offer was this: if one of the malefactors turned himself in, he would be acquitted and receive the reward just the same.[156] This last extraordinary clause must mean that the authorities had little hope of finding the robbers. In neither case is a sequel recounted.

These criminal cases reflect, more than do many laws, that side of moneychanging and deposit banking which concerns daily operations and the handling of cash reserves. The fragile nature of the structure — a table or counter set out in front of a small shop room — and the habit of keeping coins for immediate use on the countertop itself, as a sign of solvency as well as of capacity to meet demand, are indicated by the prevalence of unpremeditated thefts of small amounts of coins. Even before they were armed, bankers or their acting managers did not hesitate to give chase. Their vaults were not considered secure, however, and in the fourteenth century bankers left their reserves at home and took to work and back only the amount of cash foreseen as useful to meet demand on a given day. Security became an urgent problem early in the following century: licenses to bear arms were issued beginning in 1409, and, probably shortly after the break-in of 1410, the state began making space available at the Camerlenghi where bankers could keep a safe. At the same time, not all took advantage of the offer, if the Garzoni, who opened in 1430, did not apply for space till 1461. Now there were three options for storing reserves — the rented vault at the Rialto, the strongbox at the Camerlenghi, the private home — played off one against the other according to assumed convenience. Trials for

---

[155]Malipiero, *Annali,* cited by both Ferrara, "Antichi banchi," 198, and Giorgio Ferrari, s.v. "Agostini, Agostino," and "Agostini, Maffio," in *DBI,* 1 (1960), 459, 468–69. See also Sanudo, *Diarii,* 1:823, who adds that a reward was announced for information leading to the capture of the thief. Sanudo recorded a break-in at night at the "bank" of Zuanne Trevisan by Bernardino di Valcamonica in 1491 (ASV, Quarantia Criminal, reg. 14bis, fol. 127v); although the locale is called a "bancum," however, Trevisan is labeled "a securitatibus," that is, he was an insurance underwriter; see AC, reg. 3657, fol. 67v (15 April 1493).

[156]Sanudo, *Diarii,* 27:218, 230, 232.

breaking into bank vaults and safes show that they usually held little or nothing; the sacks kept there by the Cocco-Miorati bank in 1410 were robbed in July, in a season of high demand for specie; even the sum of 4,000 lire di piccoli taken from the Pisani bank in 1519 was nothing next to his liabilities.

From the point of view of the condemned, the sentences — perhaps only somewhat more exemplary than those normally meted out — show that one does not need to look to the famed procedures of the Council of Ten to find examples of summary justice. Bank robbers, especially those caught in the act, were swiftly sentenced to exemplary punishment, generally capital, for crimes against the banks of Venice constituted crimes against the patrimony of the wealthy classes and their commercial organization and were perpetrated, furthermore, generally by foreigners and marginals. For their part, such needy criminals could not find hiding places and were, in any case, little deterred by the threat of capital punishment.[157]

---

[157]On robbery and theft, see Stefano Piasentini, *Alla luce della luna: Il furto a Venezia, 1275–1403* (Venice, 1992); at p. 211, no. 1124, he records also the theft of 4 florins from the bank of the Lucchese Bartolomeo Micheli in 1362, confessed to by a thief accused of multiple crimes. For the role of criminal bands and the use of the term *vagabond* in general, see also Bronesław Geremek, ed., *Truands et misérables dans l'Europe moderne (1350–1600)* (Paris, 1980).

3

THE ORGANIZATION AND OPERATION OF BANKING ENTERPRISES

i. AN OVERVIEW

HE ORGANIZATION AND OPERATION of local banking enterprises in Venice can be discussed only on the basis of indirect documentation, largely lawsuits. Not only have no banker's account books survived (most of them were preserved by the Consoli dei Mercanti, whose archive has been lost), but not even a single partnership contract for a bank, either notarial or informal, has been turned up. This means that one can piece together only a very incomplete and unsatisfactory picture, and at that regarding only certain themes essential to an understanding of banking. The discussion here, therefore, is limited to forms of business organization and the question of liability; it is based largely on elements that emerge from the sources discussed in Part II, which is dedicated to an examination of bankruptcies and liquidations. A separate treatment of such an important topic as the investments of bankers, on the other hand, could not be undertaken at all, since the references found were simply too few and far between.

It is once again useful to look outside Venice for help in understanding what was happening inside Venice, first regarding the primary function of local banks, namely, the creation of bank money, then regarding moments of overcreation of credit, when lawmakers debated whether to eliminate private banks altogether and substitute for them a public bank.

What kind of men undertook local banking in Venice, in part to earn on commissions, in part to garner investment capital in the form of clients' deposits? A glance at Appendix A, below, a chronological listing of bankers known to have operated in Venice, is sufficient to get an idea of the numbers of bankers, their social and "national" backgrounds, and the general types of operation.

In the period from about 1330 to 1370, eight to ten bankers operated on the Rialto at any given time. They seem to have been relatively small operators on the average, so that a banker like Giovanni Stornado, who dominated banking activity from about 1328 to 1342, as the accounts of Florentine firms indicate, stands out as an exception. There was much flexibility and movement within the group: short- and long-term operations, Venetians and foreigners or "new citizens," mergers and separations; relatively few bankers were nobles. Even Giovanni Stornado, who bore a noble surname, was actually non-noble; his attempt to gain entry to the Great Council failed, as we will see below. The da Mosto, who operated banks between the 1330s and 1350s, were immigrants from Lodi and became naturalized citizens. Also non-noble despite the surname was the branch of the Zancani family which dominated the Rialto in the 1360s and 1370s. Probably half the bankers in that period operated as individuals, but many tended sooner or later to merge with other operators in relatively flexible partnership arrangements that might last only from one annual rent auction to another. The bankruptcies of the early 1340s, the mortality caused by the Black Death and the recurrences of plague, the response by way of facilitations to immigration and naturalization, and, finally, the monetary crises of the 1350s and 1360s kept the Rialto in a state of considerable flux. Many names of moneychangers and bankers appear in the documents only briefly and sporadically.

Around 1370, however, the situation changed. Individual operators became rare, recent immigrants disappeared, and Venetian noble families began to dominate the marketplace. After the banking crisis of the 1370s and the War of Chioggia, the number of banchi di scritta operating at any given time on the Rialto dropped to about four, sometimes as few as three. These banks tended, therefore, to be larger and more important than before. Their organizational form was generally either that of the fraterna or that of the partnership, the latter often concluded between a citizen and a noble.

The progressive change in the social rank of bankers is noteworthy. A further glance at Appendix A shows the following examples of partnerships between non-nobles and nobles in the first half of the Quattrocento: Antonio Miorati, member of a family of immigrants naturalized two generations earlier, operated first with Giovanni Corner, then with Nicolò Cocco; the Orsini brothers, sons of an immigrant, at one point associated with the Priuli brothers; the Garzoni, who stemmed from the branch that was not coopted into the Great Council after the Chioggia war, were partners of the

Bernardo family in a bank that lasted nearly seventy years and is referred to in the documents alternatively by one name or the other; finally, Agostino Ziera, member of an old citizen family, at one point associated with Jacomo Corner. It was obviously advantageous for non-nobles to have a partner who had direct access to the political organs of the state. After midcentury, an individual operator, of the type the nobleman Bernardo Giustinian had been, is no longer to be found. In the second half of the fifteenth century there were very often two noble and two non-noble banks, as was the case observed by Marin Sanudo in 1493 (he counted the Garzoni bank non-noble, for even though the Bernardo were legally still partners, their name had disappeared from the style).[1] After the failure of the Agostini in 1508 and until the founding of the public bank in 1587, Rialto banks were run solely by Venetian nobles. Documented investment by nobles in the banking sector, however, involved only some families; many surnames of noble families are conspicuously absent from the list.

The political activity of noble Rialto bankers has not been specifically investigated here. They took their turns as members of the organs of government — Francesco Balbi, for example, was a member of the Council of Ten that tried and sentenced Count Carmagnola, the mercenary captain suspected of treason, in 1432 — but not many achieved or seem particularly to have sought careers in politics. There are notable exceptions. Giovanni di Vettor Soranzo showed in his testament of 1468, as we shall see, that he could deal on equal terms with the very top echelon of the political establishment. Only Nicolò Bernardo, in 1458, and Alvise Pisani, in 1516, were elected Procurators of San Marco in our period; Antonio Priuli and Andrea qd. Silvano Capello followed suit in 1528 and 1537, respectively.[2]

The banks of moneychangers situated at the base of the campanile in the Piazza of course reflect a very different situation, especially in the fifteenth century. They were much smaller operations, probably less long-lasting, more rarely headed by nobles (although four nobles, albeit of minor standing, were still operating there in 1390), more open to new entrants. Although partnerships existed, bankers at San Marco could more easily operate as individuals, and the principals were generally also the managers. In 1391, for example, a moneychanger at San Marco testified that the bank next to his was run by two men and that he could not tell

---

[1]*De origine,* 27.

[2]For the fifteenth century, see, for example, ASV, Segretario alle voci, Miste, reg. 4, fols. 92–93, 96v–97, where Balbi and his brother Bernardo appear as ducal councillors in the 1440s, while Giorgio qd. Gabriele Soranzo and Luca di Cristoforo qd. Gabriele were both in the Senate in 1438 and Maffeo qd. Gabriele Soranzo was in a "zonta" of the Quarantia in the same year. Nicolò qd. Francesco Bernardo was in the Senate in 1438, whereas he was an Avogador in 1458 when elected Procurator. A handy listing of Procurators is Fulgentio Manfredi, *Degnità procuratoria di San Marco di Venetia* (Venice, 1602).

which was the principal ("maior"), because both partners could always be found together in the booth.[3]

Before returning with more detail to some of the questions raised above, we can get another view of the functions of Rialto banks by looking at Venice from abroad.

ii. VENETIAN BANKS OUTSIDE VENICE

Although it is true enough that Venetian banks were local and that they did not maintain branches outside the capital city, it is nonetheless clear from scattered evidence that local deposit banks that were often run by Venetians existed in cities or quarters of cities especially but not only subject to Venetian domination. Some of the evidence is more explicit and clear than anything relating directly to banks in Venice. That is the case with a unique defense of bank money, the nature of which was simply taken for granted in Venice and never explicated in that setting.

In territories both of the Stato da Mar and of the Terraferma, banking tables were owned by the state and rented out by local Venetian authorities to the highest bidder, just as in Venice. The bankers were deposit and transfer bankers, exchangers of coin, and intermediaries in transactions involving bills of exchange, just as were those at the Rialto. They were similarly called "a banco" and "banchiere." Banks in Tana were explicitly called "banchi a scripta," and the extensive accounts kept in Constantinople in the 1430s by Giacomo Badoer reflect the operation there of eight to ten bankers, of which one, the Venetian Carlo Capello "a banco," was Badoer's principal banker. From the accounts it is clear that he acted no differently in Constantinople than if he had been located at the Rialto—except in his daily relationships with members of the local Jewish community, which Venice at the time did not have.

Of the scanty information available on banks outside the Venetian capital, most concerns Constantinople in the last century of Venetian administration of its quarter. At least three banks were operating there by the early 1340s. It was a clever investment decision, particularly in those years, to locate a bank in Constantinople, for there a banker could accumulate the silver sent eastward from Venice, a veritable flood in the 1340s (see Vol. 1, chap. 17), assign the value in bank money to depositors, and sell to the local mints. Some silver was reexported overland to Tartary, where it was traded for gold and gems. A "bancum campsoris" was operated in this context by the firm of the Venetian Marco Soranzo; another bank was run by Giuliano da Mar, "campsor"; and a third by Zanone Visdomino, called both "ban-

---

[3]ASV, GP, Frammenti antichi, b. 10, testificationes, under 7 September 1391. A number of moneychangers at San Marco bore noble surnames but were non-nobles; that was rarely the case at the Rialto.

cherius" and "campsor" in the documents. The banks were clearly tied together through interlocking accounts, for in one case we find a payment made in the Soranzo bank, credited to Zanone Visdomino, with an order to the latter to credit the first party's account at the Soranzo bank for a bill of exchange.[4] It is documented furthermore that silver bars were deposited in the bank run by Marco Soranzo's company, an association that specialized in trade in Romania, where it retained a factor.[5]

The locations of the banks were under the jurisdiction of the bailo, the principal authority of the Venetian quarter, and they seem to have been rented out, as usual, as a source of revenue. A century later, in any case, at least one of the banks in operation was called a "banchum comunis," and it was to be rented out at public auction to the Venetian who offered the most. The deliberation of 1447 echoes the concern of authorities at the Rialto: the bank was a "banchum cambii nostri dominii," and it should not be treated as private but as communal property and be rented out to the highest bidder, rather than "per amicitiam vel amorem."[6] The eight to ten banks mentioned in the ledger kept in Constantinople by Giacomo Badoer, from 1436 to 1440, were operated by persons with local interests. Some were Greeks, like Costantin Critopulo or Caloiani Sofiano; some were Italians of indeterminate origin, like Tomà Spinola, surely a Genoese; only one, Carlo Capello, is clearly a Venetian nobleman, and it was he who operated the "banchum comunis."[7]

While Badoer kept current accounts with several bankers, as was habitual also on the Rialto, his principal banker was Carlo Capello. The latter

---

[4]Ibid., b. 5, reg. bound in leather and dated 1341, containing transcripts of testimony under the dates 30 January and 26 February 1342. A party "fecerat scribi [in bancho ser Marci Superancio campsoris in Constantinopoli] eidem Zanono de voluntate ipsius Zanoni faciens ibi scribi quod erant pro cambio dicti ser Garzoni, et ordinavit eidem Zanono quod debeat scribere . . . ad rationem dicti ser Garzoni." The bank at that time was managed by the scribe Giorgio Pisano. A "Zane da Mar dal banco," that is, of the same surname as one of the three, was active in Constantinople a century later; see Umberto Dorini and Tommaso Bertelè, eds., *Il libro dei conti di Giacomo Badoer* (Rome, 1956), index.

[5]ASV, GP, Sentenze e interdetti, reg. 6, fol. 64 (9 April 1348). The silver bars were deposited in order to facilitate payments in a deal calling for the delivery of wheat in Caffa. The transfer of payment is already referred to here as a "promissio." It is likely that Soranzo's operation in Constantinople was used by the commercial expedition to Delhi led by Giovanni Loredan in 1338–43, which included another Marco Soranzo, of SS. Apostoli (whereas the banker's residence in Venice was at S. Moisè). For the stopover of the expedition, see Roberto S. Lopez, "Venezia e le grandi linee dell'espansione commerciale," in *La civiltà veneziana nel secolo di Marco Polo* (Florence, 1955), 53–55. It was Pegolotti who suggested the exchange of Western silver for Eastern gold and gems; see Ugo Tucci, "I primi viaggiatori e l'opera di Marco Polo," in *Storia della cultura veneta* (Vicenza, 1976), 1:662–63.

[6]ASV, SMar, reg. 3, fol. 8 or 9, cited in Freddy Thiriet, *Regestes des délibérations du Sénat de Venise concernant la Romanie,* 3 vols. (Paris, 1958–61), 3, no. 2739, and in Chryssa A. Maltesou, *L'istituzione del bailo di Venezia a Costantinopoli, 1268–1453* [in Greek] (Athens, 1970), 81.

[7]Dorini and Bertelè, *Il libro dei conti di Giacomo Badoer.*

carefully distinguished between affairs of his bank and investments he made as a private merchant ("in spizialità"), just as the Rialto banker Francesco Balbi did in the very same years, even though the distinction was difficult to maintain in case of failure. Badoer's current accounts indicate a preponderance of in-bank transfers for payments made (avere), while sums credited to his account (dare) were often cash deposits. Perhaps for this reason Capello was ready to permit his client to overdraw occasionally (accounts are carried forward in the red on fols. 183 and 356). The banker mediated between the various parties in bills of exchange, incoming and outgoing, in which Badoer was often involved. He operated, in sum, just like the principal banchieri di scritta at the Rialto, and the Badoer accounts reflect how the Venetian quarter at Constantinople hummed with activity around its banks, until 1453.

Farther north, in the area of the Black Sea, the Genoese colonies at Chilia and Caffa[8] and the Venetian colony at Tana also had need of the services of local bankers. The Venetian quarter in Tana, capital of the slave trade, had banks very much on the Venetian model. An early mention of a bank operated there by Marino and Polo Contarini dates from the early 1340s, shortly after the founding of the colony in 1333. At that time the location of banks was already part of the public domain, as were the houses of the Venetian consul and the merchants, and were rented out by Venetian authorities.[9] In 1397, among the orders that accompanied an ambassador to Tana, in the wake of the sack of the city by Timur (Tamerlane) in 1395, the Senate included the resolution that three "banchi a scripta" located there could be rented at auction to Venetian nobles, as long as they agreed to lend 90 lire to the state.[10] A short time later, in the aftermath of the serious losses — estimated at 120,000 ducats — suffered by Venetians during another sack of Tana, this time by the khan of Kiptchak on 12 August 1410, we learn that those banks were the exact image of those in Venice and Constantinople. Two cases came before the Giudici di Petizion after the sack of 1410 on the basis of suits brought by Venetian merchants with interests in Tana. They had sent their agents specie, and the agents, before proceeding to carry out their principals' orders, deposited the money in the banco di scritta of Ser Lion Lion; one of those deposits, made possible by the con-

---

[8]Geo Pistarino, "Banchi e banchieri del '300 nei centri genovesi del Mar Nero," in *Cronache Finmare*, no. 5/6 (May–June 1974): 8–13, on the basis of notarial documents.

[9]Restricted to the slave trade is Charles Verlinden, "La colonie vénetienne de Tana, centre de la traite des esclaves au XIV^c et au debut du XV^c s.," in *Studi in onore di Gino Luzzatto*, 4 vols. (Milan, 1949), 2:1–25. See esp. E. C. Skrzinskaja, "Storia della Tana," *SV* 10 (1968): 3–45, and Marie Nystazopoulou Pélékidis, "Venise et la Mer Noire du XIe au XVe siècle," in *Venezia e il Levante fino al sec. XV*, ed. Agostino Pertusi (Florence, 1973), 541–82, and exactly the same in *Thesaurismata* (Venice) 7 (1970): 15–51. The Contarini bank is mentioned in ASV, Grazie, reg. 10, fol. 23 (4 February 1344).

[10]ASV, SM, reg. 43, fol. 111v (22 February 1397).

signment of the specie by the Venetian consul, had been made on 11 August, the very day before the sack during which the bank was cleaned out. The agents defended themselves against their accusers, who insisted that they should not have deposited the money, by describing the advantages of the banking system in Tana's Venetian quarter. One said that all agents and factors were authorized to make deposits in a banco di scritta.[11] The other agent repeated the same conviction and reported that practically all payments in Tana were made in bank in order to achieve greater clarity in the process of clearing, as was the case in Venice itself. But in Tana, he testified, there were two special reasons for dealing through the banks: first, because the coin current in Tana was small silver and troublesome to count; second, during the busy season many counterfeit coins circulated, which the bankers identified, culled out, and returned to the payer, who was required to take them back. Finally, bank money was to be considered the equivalent of specie, that is, fully convertible — at the very time, the defendant might have added, that there was an agio on full-weight coin as against bank money in Venice.[12] This statement is perhaps the best surviving defense of bank money, and it was made before a Venetian court but concerning a faraway commercial colony. The banking system in operation in Tana presumably revived once again and continued until the collapse of the colony in the years following the conquest of Constantinople.

One final document regarding banking in the Levant mentions the situation in Alexandria. Even though the papacy had lifted its ban on trade with the infidel and had permitted Venice to send ships to Egypt in 1344, two years later the Senate passed a series of regulations against dealings with the Saracens. Among these was the prohibition against any Venetian operating an exchange bank inside or outside the Venetian fondaco in Alex-

---

[11]Regarding the sack, see Wilhelm Heyd, *Histoire du commerce du Levant au Moyen-Age* (Leipzig, 1886; reprint, Amsterdam, 1959), 2:377–78. The agent testified that a "recordatio" gave him "plenam libertatem . . . , et etiam quia erat bancum de scripta in quo concessum est omnes ponere denarios." ASV, GP, Sg, reg. 21, fol. 39r–v (11 May 1411). A Ser Lion de Lion, perhaps the same person, turns up in 1437 as Treasurer (Camerlengo di Comun) in Constantinople; Dorini and Bertelè, *Il libro dei conti di Giacomo Badoer*, 274.

[12]The testimony reads: "quod omnes solutiones aut maior pars solutionum que fiunt in Tana fiunt per banchum, sicut etiam hic fit pro maiori claritudine et adhuc magis ibi in Tana duabus occasionibus principalibus: primo, quia moneta est de argento et fastidiossa ad contandum, et spetialiter tempore facendarum; secundo, quia reperitur multa pecunia falsa, et quia campsores ipsas monetas cognoscitur et quasi non habent aliud agere quam cernere bonam monetam. Et si reperiunt de falsis, restituuntur; et qui ipsas dederint tenentur ad reacipiendi. Et ad quid opportet movere istam exceptionem quia cognitum fuit ad istud judicium et ubique, quod denarii de banchis sunt denarii contati; et quod semper factores possint ponere denarios in bancho et similiter extrahere." Finally, it states, all money chests ("capsa"), whether in the bank or not, were plundered during the sack. ASV, GP, Sg, reg. 20, fols. 91–96 (30 August 1412). On the agio in Venice in 1410, see Mueller, "Role of Bank Money," 86–88. The Tana case was discussed in Reinhold C. Mueller, "I banchi locali a Venezia nel tardo Medioevo," *Studi storici* 28 (1987): 150–51.

andria or accepting on deposit any assets of Saracens or other persons.[13] This law is proof enough that Venetians had operated banks in Alexandria in the past, but there seems to be no further reference to banking there, even though Venice maintained a consulate ("cottimo") in that Egyptian port.

Given the Venetian propensity to the Levant trade, finding sedentary Venetian deposit bankers in key market cities in Romania and Oltremare perhaps does not come as a surprise. It is more surprising, on the other hand, to find traces of Venetian banks in Sicily, in port cities serving the western Mediterranean trade. In the mid-fifteenth century, Francesco Morosini opened a bank in Palermo.[14] About the same time, as we are informed by a civil lawsuit of 1467, a Venetian-style deposit bank was operated in Syracuse by another nobleman, Ser Piero Barbo (a man with the same name as a rather better-known contemporary who became Pope Paul II). The defendant, Marco Querini, recounted that Sebastiano Querini had paid him in Syracuse a certain sum of money in "oncie," part of which he ordered deposited in Barbo's bank, so that it would be available there for a payment he owed on a purchase of wheat.[15] After the fall of Constantinople, Sicily had become more important, along with Apulia, for provisioning Venice with wheat, and operating a deposit bank in Syracuse was probably a strategic investment decision.

These are fleeting references to probably small operations, small but useful to Venetians doing business in those parts and especially for merchants coming and going on Venetian ships and galleys.

Also as regards moneychangers in cities of the Venetian Terraferma, only scanty information has been found on the Venetian side. In Treviso, just before Venice's occupation of the city, one of the six campsores — mostly Florentines, then as later — operating there was a moneychanger called "Donato of Venice." Later the Venetian podestà was ordered, in 1366, to follow Venetian regulations regarding the rental of publicly owned shops. Among these shops, situated under the loggia of the Palazzo and at the herald's proclamation stone, were the "tabule cambiorum." At the time of the deliberation, they were being rented out for periods of several years without Senate approval, to the detriment of communal revenues. A book of rents of properties in the public domain, extant for the years 1389–91, includes thirteen exchange banks, rented out to Florentines and local people labeled both "campsores" and "bancherii."[16]

[13]No Venetian might "tenere bancum in Alexandria in fontico vel extra in aliquo loco pro cambio, nec possit tenere in depositum aliquid de havere saracenorum vel aliarum personarum." ASV, SM, reg. 23, fol. 64v (26 October 1346).

[14]Rosa M. Dentici Buccellato, "Forestieri e stranieri nelle città siciliane del basso Medioevo," *Forestieri e stranieri nelle città basso-medievali* (Florence, 1988), 243, where the author mentions also the fixed presence of a commercial company of the Contarini family in Syracuse.

[15]"Mi dixe dovessi meterli in bancho di ser Piero Barbo, perchè l'aveva di bisogno di far lo pagamento di certi frumenti." ASV, GP, Sg, reg. 154, fols. 118v–21 (24 July 1471).

[16]Rambaldo Azzoni Avogaro, "Delle monete di Trivigi," in *Nuova raccolta delle monete e delle*

The same policy, informed by a concern for revenues but also for supervision, was followed when Venice expanded its dominion over the Terraferma in the fifteenth century. Venetian authorities *in loco* rented out the booths, as usual, sometimes under central directives. In 1406, for example, the Senate itself confirmed the privilege of two brothers, citizens of Vicenza, to operate a bank ("statio cambii") on the main square of the city.[17] Such banks located in the subject cities, however, probably did little more than exchange coins. Pawnbroking was then handled by Jews, under license. On the other hand, wholesale operations concluded in the Terraferma cities were probably cleared in Venice at the deposit banks of the Rialto.[18]

iii. FOREIGNERS AND CITIZENS

Venetian citizenship was not a prerequisite for opening a bank on the Rialto, as one might have assumed, and in fact, a number of foreigners established banks in Venice. Within a short time, however, the incentives were felt strongly enough that practically all applied for some form of naturalization. First, foreigners paid higher brokerage taxes and customs dues than did Venetians. Second, it was prohibited for a foreigner to enter a commercial or industrial partnership with a Venetian.[19] Among some 3,600 extant citizenship privileges granted over two centuries, almost no immigrant indicated his occupation as that of campsor.[20] If we start, vice versa, from our list of campsores, we can identify quite a few new citizens who engaged in moneychanging, especially in the period preceding the War of

---

zecche d'Italia, ed. Guid'Antonio Zanetti, 4 vols. (Bologna, 1775–89), 4:166–67 (1332). A "Cinus campsor qd. ser Tegna de Florentia" operated in Treviso in 1365; ASV, CIN, b. 37, fasc. 4 (notaio Francesco di Marsilio da Corona). The order to the podestà is in MC, Novella, fol. 104 (10 September 1366). The rent book, in Biblioteca Civica di Treviso, ms. 675, is discussed in Luigi Pesce, *Vita socio-culturale della diocesi di Treviso nel primo Quattrocento* (Venice, 1983), 40, 269, 319–20.

[17]"Quod confirmentur privilegia que habuerunt et habent providi viri Antonius et Raynaldus fratres de Gilino, cives et fideles nostri Vicentini, a dominationibus preteritis de una statione cambii posita super platea civitatis Vincentie," at 8 lire di piccoli per year. The case went to the Collegio and the Senate because the capitano Gabriele Emo favored the confirmation whereas the podestà Giovanni Moro opposed it. ASV, SSec, reg. 3, fol. 35v (29 July 1406).

[18]For example, in the 1330s the Covoni operations in Padua went through Venice, as did those of the Del Bene in the 1390s.

[19]This fact was expressed by the Florentine Bindo Piaciti when he wrote from Venice, "Non si può avere compagnia un forestiere chon un citadino." ADP, 714, 9 December 1402.

[20]For a brief outline of the legislation, see Mueller, "Mercanti e imprenditori fiorentini," 38–41, and Luca Molà and Reinhold C. Mueller, "Essere straniero a Venezia nel tardo Medioevo: Accoglienza e rifiuto nei privilegi di cittadinanza e nelle sentenze criminali," in *Le migrazioni in Europa, secoli XIII–XVII,* ed. Simonetta Cavaciocchi, Acts of the Settimane di Studio, Istituto Datini, Prato, 25 (Florence, 1994), 841–43. In what follows, archival references to citizenship privileges have been dispensed with; they are contained in the database "CIVES," which is open to consultation.

Chioggia, when the profession was more open and there were places to fill, as a result of the bankruptcies of the early 1340s and the plague of 1348 and its recurrences. Beginning in August 1348, a policy of incentives to immigration eliminated for a time the residence requirement for the "de intus" privilege for retail trade, previously fifteen years, and reduced the requisite for the "de extra" privilege for overseas trade from twenty-five years to ten years. For two years, the lesser privilege was granted directly upon application, without the need for senatorial confirmation; these simplified registrations have not survived.

Despite the fact that his surname corresponds to that of a Venetian noble family, Jacobino qd. Donato da Mosto was an immigrant from Lodi. Called "Pestamosto" by Florentine merchant bankers, Jacobino was a campsor at the Rialto from the late 1330s; he received the de extra privilege in 1347. Armelino da Mosto, who operated two banks at the Rialto in the 1340s and 1350s, was presumably Jacobino's brother and partner; he was murdered while on his way between the Rialto and home (S. Geremia) one day in 1355 at the hands of an assassin, who had been hired by another campsor, a native Venetian.[21] Filippo Mafei of Verona, a financial agent in Venice of Cangrande II della Scala, had a regular tabula at the Rialto as early as 1342; making use of the facilitations passed in 1348, he received the de intus privilege in that same year and the de extra privilege in 1358. Pietro de Mortisse, formerly from Padua, whom we encountered above in connection with the charge that he had torn a page from his account book, was a campsor at San Marco by 1343. After he was pardoned, he was granted the de extra privilege in 1352, which permitted him to expand into foreign trade; thereafter, he moved his operation to the more important market at the Rialto.[22] Alessandro degli Agolanti of Florence was active at the Rialto from 1348 to 1356; he was naturalized by special privilege in 1349. His compatriot Donato Alemanni was active as a campsor from 1350 to 1353 and as a refiner of silver, and the two merged their operations about 1352. While two members of Donato's family, Alemanno and Giannino qd. Donato, had been naturalized twenty years earlier, Donato probably profited from the facilitations of 1348 to get the first privilege upon application.[23] Ughettus de Cavariis of Bologna, probably attracted to Venice by the same law, called himself "novus campsor" in an act of 1351.[24] Bartolomeo

---

[21]ASV, AC, reg. 3642, fols. 25v–26. The case was underscored by Guido Ruggiero as a rare example of murder of one nobleman by another, but even the other campsor, Zannino Soranzo, who hired the assassin, was non-noble despite his name (he is called "ser" in a source that regularly labels nobles with the title "nobilis vir"). *Violence,* 72–73.

[22]He is identified as "campsor in Rivoalto" in ASV, AC, reg. 3642, fol. 64v (14 March 1358).

[23]Donato Alemanni is documented as an active Rialto banker from 1350 to 1353. For the bank partnership of Donato with Giannino Rizzo, terminated in 1351–52, see ASV, GP, Frammenti antichi, b. 6, fasc. 1352, fols. 69vff. (3 April 1352); for mention of that which Donato had with Alessandro, see Grazie, reg. 13, fol. 32 (8 November 1353).

[24]ASV, Grazie, reg. 12, fol. 97v.

Micheli of Lucca, made a citizen in 1356, is documented as an active banker on the Rialto between 1358 and 1371; during at least the last four years of his banking activity, he was in partnership in a Rialto bank with Giovanni dei Bugni, a wealthy Cremonese who had been naturalized in 1345.[25]

Bartolomeo d'Acarisio, an immigrant from Ferrara, where his father, Checchino, had been a campsor, opened a bank at the Rialto shortly after his arrival. In 1375, perhaps at the time he inaugurated his operation, he received a grant of citizenship de intus on condition that he reside in Venice and buy a house worth at least 1,000 ducats within two years. In 1378 Bartolomeo, now resident at S. Silvestro and listed as a campsor, was made a citizen de extra. During the War of Chioggia he voluntarily raised his assessment for forced loans and made numerous noncompulsory loans as well. As a very recent immigrant, he had no chance of being included in the number of persons eligible to be coopted in the Great Council, but after the war, in 1382, he petitioned that he and his heirs receive the privilege of "original citizenship," in view of his contributions to the war effort. The petition was granted eighteen months before his violent death — d'Acarisio and his wife were murdered in their bed on 7 September 1383. The fact was a clamorous one, and the Collegio itself intervened immediately. Suspicion was directed from the very beginning toward a band of five young thugs, all with fine noble names. Warrants for their arrest were sent out to the Venetian governors of Chioggia and Mestre, and a request for information was sent to the Venetian Visdomino of Ferrara. Two were arrested and interrogated as to their alibis, but no criminal case was brought against them, and the murderers, whoever they were, went unpunished. Like the killing of the citizen-banker Armelino da Mosto, commissioned by Zannino Soranzo in 1355, the murder of citizen-banker d'Acarisio and his wife, seemingly at the hands of nobles, was premeditated and probably also on commission. Perhaps this recent immigrant had been seen as too eager to be patriotic, had risen to the highest citizen status too quickly — albeit with the condescension of the noble organs of state — and had been too successful as a banker on the Rialto. To be sure, he was perfectly solvent, for no problem with the liquidation arose. The case seems to have dissolved into thin air within a matter of days, and one can only wonder what was behind the ambiguous comportment of the noble order faced with this crime.[26]

Three other non-nobles who turned to banking came from immigrant families that were, by contrast, established in Venice and naturalized as citizens for some time. The first is Antonio Miorati (Venetian for Mi-

---

[25]The privilege of Micheli is published in Molà, *La comunità dei lucchesi,* 43 n. 62.

[26]ASV, Secreta, Collegio, Secreti, reg. 1382–85, fols. 24 and (upside down) 154–56. The suspects were Nicoletto di Michele Gradenigo, Zannino di Pietro Erizo, Fantino di Pietro Gritti, Zannino di Orso Gradenigo, and "a certain youth of ca' Soranzo." Three of these same men were arrested in 1390, tried on three counts of theft, and acquitted without explanation; Signori di Notte al Criminal, reg. 12, fol. 8 and (for Pietro Gritti, father of Fantino) fol. 126.

gliorati), most likely a son or grandson of Ranieri or Benedetto Miorati, registered as an immigrant from Florence although more correctly from Prato, who received the de extra privilege in 1358 and 1359, respectively. Miorati opened a bank in partnership with the nobleman Giovanni Corner in 1399 and formed a new partnership, this time with the nobleman Nicolò Cocco, in 1410. The second is Donato di Filippo Nati, a Florentine bullion dealer, refiner, and goldbeater, who became a sleeping partner in the bank of Miorati and Corner and perhaps also of its successor. He asserted to the Florentine catasto officials that he had gone to Venice in the late 1380s; he gained citizenship privileges in 1404 and 1414. After Miorati died and Cocco liquidated in 1424, Nati is still labeled "bancherius in Rivoalto," when he was sleeping partner and "argentarius" in the bank of Giacomo Priuli and Partners; and the banker Francesco Priuli was a partner in one of Nati's goldbeating shops.[27] The third is the Orsini family, immigrants from Como; Ziliolo, head of the household, received three citizenship privileges, like d'Acarisio, the first in 1373, the "originarius" privilege in 1392. His four sons—no longer in a "fraterna"—opened a bank at the Rialto in 1425; in 1428 they formed a partnership with Giacomo Priuli under the style "Jacomo Priuli e Zan Orsini e compagni," which failed the very next year. Theirs was a very short and unfortunate experience in running a bank.[28] These three were the last immigrants to set up banks; they all ended up making partnerships with nobles, in the hope that that would increase their security, perhaps in more ways than one.

As mentioned above, the man or men whose names appeared in the style of a bank were not necessarily the same persons that actually managed the business. Working partners and factors were sometimes also chosen from among immigrants.

iv. PARTNERS AND FACTORS

Venice's bankers, especially those located at the Rialto, generally employed a factor who served as accountant and cashier when they did not have an actual business partner who performed the same functions.[29]

---

[27]Mueller, "Mercanti e imprenditori fiorentini," 49–50. Nati is named along with the partners in ASV, Grazie, reg. 22, fol. 123 (1429).

[28]For the division of their "bona conpagnia et fraterna societas," see ASV, CIN, Miscellanea atti notai diversi, b. 32, reg. for S. Polo, fol. 1v (20 December 1413).

[29]In the 1350s Jacopo de Lisca formed a partnership with the Florentine Martino Sasso precisely "ut facta sua regeret." ASV, Grazie, reg. 14, fol. 18 (March 1357). On the other hand, in the sixteenth century, the banker Angelo Sanudo "el gobbo" purposely avoided the expense of an employee, for when he turns in his accounts as a bankrupt in 1569, he notes, "Con questa appresento il mio libro imperfetto con quattro vachette, che serve più tosto per memorial che per libro ordinario, fatto di mia mano per il levar del banco, non havendo voluto accresser la spesa de homini per tal conto, e riputando, facendo io pochi negotii, che il medesimo libro del

Moneychangers at the campanile on Piazza San Marco, on the other hand, tended to operate their own exchange tables personally, aided perhaps by a boy.[30] Specific regulations covered bank employees who had some responsibility. One regulation forbade mergers between formerly independent bankers; a second required that employees of banks be citizens of Venice.

In the years immediately following the Black Death, during Venice's third war against archrival Genoa, Venice was concerned about revenues, among which, as we have seen, was the rent collected from banking booths. The Council of Forty complained in October 1352 that most of the banks on the Rialto had remained unrented that year because a few renters had invited the collaboration, as partners or as administrators, of persons who had previously rented banks in their own right. It was thus forbidden for any moneychanger to hire as administrator of his bank anyone who had previously rented a bank as an independent operator ("cavo de taule"). Such a person was not allowed to exchange coins or to transfer deposits, under pain of a 500 lire fine against both the principal and the administrator.[31]

This law was prompted by cases such as that involving Donato di Alemanno Alemanni. In 1352 Donato was in the process of dissolving a partnership in a bank which he had with the Venetian Giannino di Marco Rizzo. The liquidation of affairs between the two required the intervention of two arbiters, a Venetian (Francesco Morosini) and an immigrant from Florence (Giovanni di Filippo Talenti, a naturalized citizen like Donato). The arbitration included the entire gamut of their operations: from the bank, to commerce in bullion, to operation of a shop for refining precious metals. The arbiters' decision that Rizzo owed Donato 650 ducats was sanctioned by the Giudici di Petizion, and Rizzo's brother Nicoletto agreed to abide by it.[32] That freed Donato to go into a new bank partnership with his compatriot Alessandro degli Agolanti, also a new citizen; as bank man-

---

Banco potesse supplire come libro mio particulare." Magnocavallo, "Proposta di riforma bancaria," 417.

[30]During interrogation concerning a partnership at a bank at San Marco, a neighboring moneychanger was asked, "Quis erat maior in dicto bancho? . . . Respondit nescire, qui semper ipsi ambo stabant in dicto bancho." ASV, GP, Frammenti antichi, b. 10, testificationes, 7 September 1391. In another case reported in the same register, a witness was asked whether others were present during a transaction; "respondit quod nulus aliud erat ibi nisi dictus ser Christoforus [Zancani, the banker] cum quodam juvene existente in dicto suo bancho." Published by Simonsfeld, *Der Fondaco,* 1, doc. 265.

[31]Princivalli, *Capitolare degli Ufficiali sopra Rialto,* cap. 174 (5 October 1352, that is, just after 29 September, day of the rent auction).

[32]ASV, GP, Frammenti antichi, b. 6, fasc. 1352, fol. 69v ff.; the arbitration dealt "tam de ratione tabule campsorie, quam de argentis, quam de stacione, de traffico auri et argenti, et quamcumque mercationum datarum ad invicem, private vel occulte vel palam, per scripturam quaternorum campsorie vel sine." That the shop was for refining appears from the trial for theft of a fragment of gold by his servant, hired to tend the fires; Signori di Notte al Criminal, reg. 6, fol. 30 (17 December 1350).

ager they seem to have hired the Florentine Pietro Fastelli.[33] It was Fastelli who, in the following year, 1353, was accused by the Consoli of illegally having accepted deposits at the Alemanni-Agolanti bank, without having himself posted bond as a banker (see above, Chap. 2, sec. iii). After what might be considered an apprenticeship as bank manager in Venice, under the direction of his compatriots, Fastelli returned to Florence, where he appears later as a member of the Arte del Cambio.[34]

The aim of the antimerger law of 1352 was strictly fiscal — namely, to increase revenues in a moment of financial crisis — and had nothing at all to do with partnerships as such. Notice of only one indictment based on it has survived. The Rialto Office, responsible for renting out banks to the highest bidder, prosecuted a little-known banker, Jacopo de Lisca, for violation of the law some five years later. The Consoli dei Mercanti, responsible for licensing bankers, took his side, however, and supported his successful appeal. They testified that the bank's administrator, the Florentine Martino Sasso, "civis de extra" in 1362, had indeed been a "caput tabularum" in the past but that he had entered into a regular partnership with the principal some time before the latter had rented the bank, so that the case was not to be considered a merger between existing banks at all.[35]

A second law that helps us gain an insight into the operation of banks was one that prohibited bankers from hiring foreigners as employees at their banks. Particularly in demand, as we have already seen, were Tuscans and especially Florentines. In 1329 a derogation from the law was made in favor of the Rialto banker Giovanni Stornado so that he could retain the services of a certain Jacopo, formerly a scribe at the Officium Grossorum Tonsorum and thus a man with useful experience, a resident of Venice for some thirteen years, not enough to make him eligible for citizenship.[36] Ten years later, when Jacopo left Stornado to go into business for himself, the banker asked for and received another derogation, this time to hire a Pistoian, Pietro Pugni, to work at his bank. On this occasion it was stated that the grant was made in recognition of the reputation of Stornado and of the importance of his bank to the state and as well as to his private clients.[37]

When residency requirements for naturalization were drastically re-

---

[33]ASV, Grazie, reg. 13, fol. 32.

[34]ASF, Arte del Cambio, reg. 14. At fol. 62v, in 1370–71, is listed an Ubaldino Fastelli, in partnership with Jacobo Ubaldini; for Piero Fastelli, listed as operating alone in 1381, see fol. 77. Matteo di Piero Fastelli continued the bank, for he is listed as "tavoliere" in the estimo of 1403; Lauro Martines, *The Social World of Florentine Humanists* (London, 1963), 360.

[35]ASV, Grazie, reg. 14, fol. 18 (March 1357).

[36]Ibid., reg. 3, fol. 5 (31 July — 20 August 1329); Jacopo's provenance is not indicated.

[37]Ibid., reg. 8, fol. 10 (13 March 1339). The privilege to hire Pietro "ad servicium dicte sue tabule" was granted "nonobstante consilio in contrarium ordinato, cum, sicut dicunt Provisores, magna erit curialitas, considerata conditione ipsius Johannis Stornado, fructuosa comuni et specialibus personis, ut est notum." (It is conceivable that the employee is the same "Petrus qd. Perucii de Vani de Pistorio" who received a citizenship privilege in 1350.)

duced beginning in August 1348, this law no longer presented an obstacle, and it became easier to hire an immigrant Florentine as director, cashier, or accountant. There are only a few cases from the fourteenth century in which otherwise anonymous employees are named. We have already encountered Pietro Fastelli and Martino Sasso. The former probably was naturalized under the facilitations passed beginning in 1348; the latter received the de intus privilege in 1348 and full citizenship rights in 1362.[38] Apparently Florentine was Taddeo de Muçole, who worked as a factor for Marco Stornado at the latter's bank at the Rialto until 1361, when he resigned and left Venice.[39] In the 1360s the important bank of Jacobello Zancani and Brothers employed as "scribanus" Giovanni di Guccio Gucci, a Florentine who became a naturalized citizen of Venice with full rights in 1366.[40] A contemporary Rialto banker of Lucchese origin, Bartolomeo Micheli, normally turned over the management of his bank when he was absent from Venice to a Giovanni Zudi, of unknown origin.[41] The bank of Roberto Priuli and Brothers (1399–1402) employed as scribe a Giovanni Fioravanti.[42] A final case provides somewhat more detail. Early in the Quattrocento, the immigrant from Florence Domenico di Masino di Manetto was a factor in the Corner-Miorati and Cocco-Miorati banks. After the latter began the liquidation procedure in 1424, Domenico became a factor in the goldbeater shops of Donato di Filippo Nati, who had been a sleeping partner in both banks.[43]

The preference that some Venetian bankers seemed to display toward employees of Tuscan and especially Florentine origin is surely significant. It dated from even before the Black Death, that is, before one would expect to find immigrants replacing the deceased. There are two possible explanations for the phenomenon. First of all, it might have been a way of tapping Tuscan expertise in the field of accounting; second and more important, it could have served as a ploy for attracting wealthy Tuscan merchants and exchange dealers as clients—a goal that Giovanni Stornado, for example, clearly achieved, according to the account books of the Florentine firms of the Covoni and of Duccio di Banchello, both active in Venice in the 1330s and both dependent on the Stornado bank for handling the payments side of their foreign exchange dealings. To that extent, it was related to the

---

[38]Sasso was among the first to receive the de intus privilege, only ten days after the facilitations passed on 11 August 1348. From 1351 to 1354 he was a partner of the Albizzi in Venice "for wool cloth and exchange"; see Hidetoshi Hoshino, *L'arte della lana in Firenze nel basso Medioevo: Il commercio della lana e il mercato dei panni fiorentini nei secoli XIII–XV* (Florence, 1980), 319–20.

[39]ASV, GP, Frammenti antichi, b. 7, fasc. 1363–64 (5 December 1363).

[40]Ibid., Sg, reg. 6, fol. 53r–v, evidence presented in a case of the year 1400. The privilege was registered in the names of "Gucius qd. Gucii et Johannes, Girardus et Bartolomeus eius filii, qui fuerunt de Florentia."

[41]Luzzatto, *Storia*, 107–8.

[42]ASV, GP, Sg, reg. 38, fols. 53–54 (May 1426).

[43]Mueller, "Mercanti e imprenditori fiorentini," 50–51.

presence in Venice of dozens of companies of Florentine experts in foreign exchange, a topic treated below (see Part III). From the point of view of the Florentines, it constituted a chance for employment and experience; while some stayed on, others returned to their native city. The phenomenon did not last much beyond the Trecento. In the fifteenth century, bank managers were apt to be Venetians — like Lorenzo Loredan, a factor for Francesco Balbi, or like Alvise Venier, the cashier of the bank of Benedetto Soranzo and Brothers, who brought on a crash in 1453 by fleeing Venice with the bank's ledgers and its cash reserves. By that time banking in Venice had long since taken on a native character, for bankers themselves were either Venetian nobles or members of citizen families of long standing.

v. FORMS OF BUSINESS ORGANIZATION AND LIABILITY

Venice had no law that recognized limited liability, such as the statute of Siena of 1339 or the famous law of Florence which legalized the "accomandita" in 1408.[44] Nor have any articles of association for local banking enterprises survived, on the basis of which one could test how partners protected themselves against unlimited liability and how they kept open the possibility of investing outside that company or even of forming another company in a different sector. The question is important because unlimited liability was inherent in the Venetian family company, or fraterna; the only defense against it was the formal division among brothers and the emancipation of son by father.[45] In the present section, I have merely extracted what information is available, especially from lawsuits arising from the liquidation of failed banks, which sheds some light on the question. The results are ambiguous and contradictory, but perhaps Venetian commercial law in this sector was itself not exactly limpid.

[44]The partners of the Tolomei company of Siena which liquidated in 1319 were "limited in their liability to their share of the capital invested in the company." The statute, which seems to have formalized current practice, stated that partners were to "satisdare de dictis creditis pro rata eorum et cuiusque eorum capitalium que miserint seu haberent in societate predicta." Edward English, *Enterprise and Liability in Sienese Banking, 1230–1350* (Toronto, 1988), 96. For the Florentine accomandita, see Federigo Melis, "Le società commerciali a Firenze dalla seconda metà del XIV al XVI secolo," reprinted in *L'azienda nel Medioevo,* ed. Marco Spallanzani (Florence, 1991), 170–73. Richard A. Goldthwaite, "The Medici Bank and the World of Florentine Capitalism," *Past and Present* 114 (1987): 13–16, and "Urban Values and the Entrepreneur," in *L'impresa: Industria commercio banca, secc. XIII–XVIII,* Acts of the Settimane di Studio, Istituto Datini, Prato, 22 (Florence, 1991), 647–49, both now also in his *Banks, Palaces, and Entrepreneurs.*

[45]A. Lattes, *Il diritto commerciale,* 124–25, 130 n. 6. This is explicit in Roberto Cessi, ed., *Gli statuti veneziani di Jacopo Tiepolo del 1242 e le loro glosse,* Istituto veneto di scienze, lettere ed arti, *Memorie,* 30 (Venice, 1938), fasc. 2; book III, art. 4, pp. 124–25. Official copies of acts of division and emancipation were kept by the Cancelleria Inferiore; those parchment fascicles with wood covers which are extant today can be found in ASV, CIN, Miscellanea notai diversi, buste 32 and 33, circa 1360–1478, divided by sestiere.

Little capital was needed—then as today—to institute a bank, perhaps only enough to convince guarantors to pledge their limited backing and clients to deposit their money, for it was deposits rather than funds invested by partners which provided bankers with investable capital. In the final analysis, it was the visible patrimony of the banker—alone or as part of a fraterna compagnia—and his reputation as an operator on the marketplace in general which were placed on the balance to offset risk and win trust. That a deposit could also be intended as an investment can be seen in the contribution of 15,000 ducats which Lorenzo Priuli made toward the banking enterprise of his son Gerolamo, the diarist, four days before the grand opening on 15 March 1507. Of that sum, 10,000 remained to his credit until 1514, almost a year after the bank was forced into liquidation. That was, of course, a peculiar arrangement, strictly within the family.[46]

Partnerships in the moneychangers' booths at San Marco could be even more informal, as is indicated—much earlier—by the testimony presented in his own defense in 1346 by Francesco Vielmo, usually a campsor but in that year an official at the mint. He reported that he had an agreement with Francesco Spirito for a share in the latter's bank. In order to symbolize the share, he made an advance of 5 ducats in partial payment, Vielmo testified, "as is customarily done, so that two or three can have a share in banks located on the Piazza, . . . which [practice] has never been contradicted." Even though Spirito testified under oath that he had no partnership with Vielmo, the latter's assertion that partnerships could be so readily contracted is significant in itself.[47]

Investments in a bank by outsiders were handled in various ways. The nature of the investment had to be carefully defined because participation in the profits pointed to a form of partnership, which could involve the investor in unlimited liability.[48] In the fourteenth century the local colleganza was sometimes employed. This notarized credit instrument, commonly used in commercial enterprises, became very similar to a certificate of deposit when the borrower was a banker, and it provided more security against risk than a simple deposit—for a guarantor was generally required

[46]BMCV, PD 912/II, under the dates 11 March 1507 and 13 September 1514. Found and underscored by Nicola Di Lernia, "Il giornale di Lorenzo Priuli e figli (1505–1533). Aspetti economico-sociali di una fraterna veneziana" (laurea thesis, 2 vols., University of Venice, 1988–89), 1:110–11, and 2:14, 52, 115 of the reconstructed ledger. Perhaps his father's investment in the bank, as well as his own patriotism, prompted him to make a loan to the state when his father was the ranking official in control of military funds during the War of the League of Cambrai; see Felix Gilbert, *The Pope, His Banker, and Venice* (Cambridge, Mass., 1980), 34.

[47]Vol. 1, app. G, doc. 5. It is important to note that the advance, like the handshake, "costituisce una vera solennità necessaria alla perfezione del contratto [di società]"; A. Lattes, *Il diritto commerciale*, 125–26. A witness testified in 1410 that he saw parties to a freight contract "dir . . . e thocare la mano"; ASV, GP, Frammenti antichi, b. 11, testificationes 1409–10, under 8 May 1410.

[48]Frederic C. Lane, *Andrea Barbarigo, Merchant of Venice, 1418–1449* (Baltimore, 1944), 95.

— and more assurance of earning a return. As in all local colleganze (in contrast to the earlier colleganze of maritime trade), the return was not so much a share in profits as a form of interest, the rate of which varied according to the market. This rate, often pegged to the rate paid by another leading banking firm or firms, was determined only at the maturity of the loan (generally after one year), a practice that protected the contract and the lender from the accusation of usury.[49]

Estate funds were sometimes invested in this manner. For example, in 1329 Margherita da Mosto provided in her testament that the money she left for dowries for each of her daughters be left in a bank at profit ("poni debeant . . . ad unam tabulam campsorum ad utilitatem et lucrum dicte filie mee"). Beginning in 1333 the Procurators of San Marco, executors of the estate, put the money out in the form of local colleganze to Francesco Corner, campsor. Over the next twelve years the investment brought in generally 5 percent but occasionally 7 percent interest.[50] Again in 1352 the Procurators as executors of the estate of Marchesina Bocco lent 30 lire (di grossi a monete) in the form of a local colleganza to the banker Andreolo Sanador, which returned less than 5 percent.[51] In his testament of 1371 Andreolo Betino ordered his executors to invest his liquid capital "ad lucrum, secundum consuetudinem" in favor of his daughters, who were to receive the money as dowries of 1,000 ducats each. The Procurators lent 500 ducats of the total to the banker Marco Stornado in the form of a local colleganza, beginning in 1372. The contract, renewed six times with different guarantors, brought 5 percent per annum, the customary rate of interest for estate funds lent in that form to entrepreneurs of any kind after the middle of the fourteenth century.[52] Clearly, such investments did not render the investor liable for the losses of the banker.

A different approach was taken at the end of the fourteenth century by Bono Arian, who invested in the Rialto bank of his brother Marco. Even though the two already owned some properties "in fraterna," Bono sought protection against the unlimited liability inherent in the family company. He turned over 1,000 ducats to his brother for commercial investment, at one-half the profit or loss ("causa utendi et trafficandi ad medietatem lucri et damni pro me et pro ipso"). Upon making his testament, Bono left the

---

[49]Frederic C. Lane, "Investment and Usury," reprinted in his *Venice and History*, 56–68. On the role of the time deposit as a way of increasing working capital, see also the comments of Goldthwaite, "Urban Values and the Entrepreneur," 647–48.

[50]ASV, PSM, Ultra, b. 207, and Reinhold C. Mueller, "The Procurators of San Marco in the Thirteenth and Fourteenth Centuries: A Study of the Office as a Financial and Trust Institution," *SV* 13 (1971): 169, 171.

[51]ASV, PSM, Misti, b. 148, commis. Marchesina Bocco.

[52]Oddly enough, between 1376 and 1378 the colleganza was passed on by the banker to Donato Moro, on the same terms as bound the former to the Procurators. See, besides the testament and register of accounts, a notarial document dated 3 September 1378 in ASV, PSM, Misti, b. 145, commis. A. Betino; also Mueller, "Procurators of San Marco," 170–73.

investment at the bank but instructed his executors to reclaim it as soon as it no longer yielded a profit and as soon as his brother no longer rendered account of the money. The problems foreseen by the testator soon became reality, leading to the lawsuit that provided the above particulars.[53]

Banks invested in trade directly, or indirectly by lending money to long-distance merchants, while bankers also personally entered into partnerships for commercial activity which were meant to be distinct from the operation of the bank. There was clearly no obstacle to the formation of long- or short-term commercial partnerships or to individual investments by a Rialto banker, even though he might be a member of a local banking firm.[54] In these cases it is impossible to know whether the banker invested by overdrawing his account with the bank or to what extent he tried to keep the accounts of the two operations separate. Legally, however, the two operations seem to have been treated as distinct. Some examples. In the early 1350s the Rialto banker Armelino da Mosto was "socius et caput" in a partnership with two other persons which was involved in exporting great quantities of salt to Lombardy.[55] One of the most powerful and rich commercial companies operating in Venice at the end of the fourteenth century was formed by the Rialto banker Gabriele Soranzo and Francesco Corner, son of the late doge Marco. Florentine merchant bankers competed for their business; at least for a time they were represented in Majorca and Barcelona, where they made enormous purchases of Barbary and Spanish wool, by the affiliates of the firm of Francesco di Marco Datini.[56] About two decades later both partners in the bank of Antonio Miorati and Nicolò

---

[53]For the property, see ASV, GP, Sg, reg. 10, fol. 98r–v (13 September 1403); for the investment, see GP, Sentenze e interdetti, reg. 7, fol. 19 (3 December 1404).

[54]For some examples of direct investment by banks (two Garzoni, Luca Soranzo and Brothers, Nicolò Bernardo and Brothers) in the spice trade, see Eliahu Ashtor, "The Volume of Levantine Trade in the Later Middle Ages (1370–1498)," reprinted in his *Studies on the Levantine Trade in the Middle Ages* (London, 1978), art. X, 602–4. For an example of a bank loan (Giovanni Orsini and Brothers) to a patrono of the Flanders galleys in 1428, see ASV, GP, Sg, reg. 48, fols. 51–85 (3 April 1430). Cf. A. Lattes, *Il diritto commerciale,* 161, where the author points out that in partnership contracts the working partner was generally forbidden to enter into other associations or invest outside. This is clear also from the articles of association published by Melis, *Documenti.*

[55]ASV, Grazie, reg. 14, fol. 19v (June 1357). The partners in a purchase of 6,000 ducats' worth of salt from the Salt Office were Guglielmo de Guffredis and Barnaba Zancani. For the importance of the salt trade in that period, see fol. 23, where two Milanese merchants are identified as purchasers of 30,000 florins' worth of salt in a single transaction.

[56]ADP, 710, Zanobi Gaddi to Florence, beginning with the letter of 31 December 1395, where they are called "2 grandi e richi cittadini e merchatanti di qui." See also b. 1082, fourteen letters from Francesco Corner "che fo de meser lo doxe" and Gabriele Soranzo to Majorca, 1396–97. They often sent as many as four cogs at a time to load wool; they paid both with remittances sent via bills of exchange and with such exchange commodities as pearls and large quantities of metals. Their partnership is often mentioned in the records of the court of the Petizion, for example, ASV, GP, Sg, reg. 18, fol. 28ff, 68–69.

Cocco invested in separate arrangements outside the bank. Cocco, for example, joined his brother in 1417 in the purchase of three carats of the tavern tax.[57] Miorati, too, formed a partnership with others, among them his son, for trade between Venice and Tana, as we shall see shortly. In the very same years Andrea Priuli, director of a banking fraterna on the Rialto, was partner in a commercial company with Pietro Venier, who, in turn, was also manager of the bank. The bank owed money to Venier when it failed in 1425, and lawsuits that went on for decades were filed by the heirs of Venier against the heirs of the bank in order to collect the last installments owed by the liquidators to creditors of the bank. Finally, one should mention the network of firms affiliated with the Pisani family in the late fifteenth and early sixteenth centuries. A privileged place in the family was held by the bank of Alvise Pisani, one of the most influential men in Venice, but his brothers Lorenzo and Almorò operated "in fraterna" without him. Here the bank appears as part of a larger whole.[58] Two organizational structures, a banking company and a commercial company, in short, could be rather separate operations, although there were points of contact.

Further indications about forms of business organization can be gathered from a consideration of liability when banks were forced to liquidate. Here again rare and ambiguous sources have to be used in lieu of more direct evidence.

The creditors of Marco Storlado, "campsor et afinator pro comuni," who fled Venice with a quantity of silver in late 1339 or early 1340, had the banker's son imprisoned. Nicoletto remained in prison for twenty-two months before his father's creditors finally agreed to his release (in September 1341). He was obviously not emancipated and was therefore considered fully liable for his father's debts.[59]

The failure of another Rialto banker, Piero Serafini, during the same financial crisis led to a legal dispute between two magistracies regarding the existence—or not—of a fraterna compagnia. The Sopraconsoli, ruling in favor of the creditors, declared Giovanni, the banker's brother, similarly bankrupt and "liable for all debts contracted by his brother Pietro in whole and in part, together with said Pietro, as full partner [socius generalis] of his brother Pietro." The Avogadori di Comun, acting as state's attorneys, explained before the Great Council during the appeal of the sentence that one of the Sopraconsoli, since deceased, had recognized the illegality of the first sentence and had supported their proposal to overturn the decision. The Great Council finally agreed on the second ballot to the nullification of

---

[57]See ASV, GP, Sg, reg. 29, fol. 81v (21 July 1417). At 120 ducats per carat, this was a small investment.

[58]Frederic C. Lane, "Family Partnerships and Joint Ventures," reprinted in his *Venice and History,* esp. 40–44.

[59]ASV, AC, reg. 3642, fol. 15, two acts dated 10 September 1341. See also A. Lattes, *Il diritto commerciale,* 85, 124.

the sentence; a bare majority felt that the brother was not to be considered fully liable for the bankrupt campsor's debts. Clearly, the arguments used by both sides — not explicated in the sources — were not particularly convincing. In fact, the revocation produced lasting rancor among the creditors, for Giovanni was later attacked at the Rialto by one of the liquidators ("capi dei creditori"), who was fined for assault.[60]

A better-documented case involving a bank partnership dates from the early fifteenth century. The Rialto banker Pietro Benedetto, member of a small noble family, had tried in 1389 to initiate his son Giovanni (Zanino) into the world of business by constituting a partnership consisting of three young men — Giovanni, his cousin Marco Condulmer, and his future brother-in-law Jacobello Zane — obviously with the hope that the experience would prepare the partners to take over the bank in due time. Two days before the partnership contract was notarized, the banker emancipated his son and made him a free gift of 2,000 ducats.[61] The contract of commercial apprenticeship, as one might call it, was backed by the banker, who was declared arbiter of any differences that might arise among the partners. The contract itself, while not particularly revealing, can be viewed as a forerunner of the bank partnership that would be formed in the year 1400. The founding capital of the company of youths was considerable: 2,000 ducats in specie or approved merchandise each. All three were to operate exclusively in favor of the company; profits and losses were to be divided equally among the three. The duration of the agreement was fixed at a minimum of one year. As Roberto Cessi underscored, the contract makes no mention of a limitation on liability, as a result of which liability seems to have been unlimited. The company lasted only a short time, however.[62] After fifteen months, the banker's son decided formally to abandon the world of commerce and devote himself to God. Giovanni returned to his father the gift of 2,000 ducats, plus the profits — unspecified — which the gift had earned in the company. He then entered the Dominican order, in a ferment of reform at that time, and began, at the convent of SS. Giovanni e Paolo, an ecclesiastical career that would take him, with his father's simoniacal help, as far as the bishopric of Treviso.[63]

[60]The Sopraconsoli "sententiarunt et determinarunt dictum Johannem Saraphyno fugitivum esse et teneri ad omnia debita contracta per dictum Petrum eius fratrem in parte et in toto simul cum dicto Petro tanquam socium generalem ipsi Petri fratris sui." ASV, AC, reg. 3642, fols. 21r–v (20 November 1341) and 23r–v (21 January 1342).

[61]ASV, CIN, b. 34, Atti P. de Compostellis, fol. 53v (two acts dated 6 February 1389).

[62]The contract (ibid., fol. 54), was published by Roberto Cessi in his "Note per la storia delle società di commercio nel medioevo in Italia," *Rivista italiana per le scienze giuridiche* 59 (1917): 53–54 (also published separately as a book, Rome, 1917). The manuscript has the added notation "revoked on 25 May 1389" (an error for 1390), when it was crossed out.

[63]The renunciation of the gift and of the secular world was formalized by the same notary: ASV, CIN, b. 34, Atti P. de Compostellis, fol. 58 (12 May 1390). For more detail, see Reinhold C. Mueller, "Sull'establishment bancario veneziano: Il banchiere davanti a Dio (secoli XIV–

On 29 September 1400 the banker Pietro Benedetto fell ill from plague and made his testament. Because the news produced a run on his bank, as will be seen below, he provided for its liquidation and the institution of a successor bank, constituted of four partners: his estate, Jacobello Zane and Marco Condulmer (from the above-mentioned partnership with the banker's son), and Simone Condulmer (brother of Gabriele, the future pope Eugenius IV). The banker died on 2 October, and the successor bank immediately replaced the first. The new bank itself lasted only little more than four years before it failed in early 1405.

No articles of association for the new bank are extant, but its failure produced documentation that reflects its structure. A suit arose in 1407 concerning an investment or deposit of 2,000 ducats made by a foreigner, Gasparotto Leccacorvo of Piacenza. The money was left with Simone Condulmer, and Leccacorvo received a receipt ("scriptum") written by Simone but signed "Marco Condulmer and Partners," meaning the bank. The creditor sought to prove that the balance of 750 ducats due him stood outside the debts of the bank, which had merely guaranteed the credit, and that it should be paid by Simone as his personal obligation ("in specialitate") rather than as partner in the bank. Such an arrangement would have made it possible for him to receive early payment, that is, before the conclusion of the one-year moratorium that the bank seems to have arranged with its creditors, but the Consoli dei Mercanti ruled that Leccacorvo's credit was a liability of the bank as principal debtor. As such, it was to be paid in installments by all four partners or their heirs. At this point a concept of limited liability is expressed, for according to the testimony of the claimant himself, Simone Condulmer as partner was liable for only one-fourth of the debts of the bank: "Dictus ser Simon participat in debito dicti banc[h]i pro uno quarto." Although there is no indication how the other three shares were divided among the heirs of Pietro Benedetto and of the now deceased partners Marco Condulmer and Jacobello Zane, the phrase seems to show that liability was divided proportionally according to the investment made at the time of the bank's constitution. While the Giudici di Petizion ruled in favor of the claimant, the Avogadori di Comun overturned their decision, reinstating the ruling of the Consoli, which favored the defendant, Simone Condulmer, by defining the debt as one to be paid, in installments, by the partnership as a whole.[64]

A contemporary bank partnership, with a somewhat longer life, also sheds some light on the relationship between personal and general liability among partners. In 1410 Antonio Miorati, who had operated a bank on the

---

XV)," in *Mercanti e vita economica nella Repubblica Veneta (Secoli XIII–XVIII)*, ed. Giorgio Borelli, 2 vols. (Verona, 1985), 1:78–86.

[64]For particulars on the bankruptcies, see below, Chap. 5, sec. i. The lawsuit is in ASV, GP, Sg, reg. 16, fols. 25–27 (24 February 1408).

Rialto with Giovanni Corner since 1399, went into partnership with another nobleman, Nicolò Cocco. Two months after Miorati died during a ravaging plague epidemic, in 1424, his estate was forced to declare bankruptcy. Cocco recounted in court later that on the day after his partner's death he had decided not to continue the bank, neither in his own name nor in that of his partner's estate. Thereupon, but perhaps prompted by the possibility of a run owing to heavy demand for specie (as he noted, the galleys departed for Alexandria that day), he closed the bank and took the account books to the Consoli so that they could oversee the liquidation. At that point he accepted unlimited liability, but only for the debts of the bank styled "Cocco-Miorati" ("me oblegai de pagar tuti quelli doveva aver per el bancho 'da Nicolò Chocho e ser Antonio Meiorato'"), that is, to all those who appeared on the books as creditors and who were verified by the Consoli as the responsibility of Nicolò. In short order, he testified, he paid off all creditors: "E così de presente pagai cadauna persona che deveva aver dal bancho."

Cocco was then forced to defend himself against the claim that before his partner's death he had assumed — in writing — liability also for debts deriving from his partner's private investments, those contracted "in soa spizilitade." Miorati's good name was such, said Cocco, that there was never any lack of trust among his creditors, until after his death, and no occasion ever arose in which he might have been asked to pledge "tal obligation universal." Miorati's executors never let him examine the books of the estate, explained Cocco, neither as partner nor as individual, until he himself was named chief liquidator by the Giudici di Petizion on 12March 1425. Now he refused to pay as individual, since he had never done business with the claimants; as liquidator, he could do no more than pay creditors the first installment due on the estate, that is, just under 50 percent, on what was a separate company for trade in the Tana organized by Miorati along with the claimants.[65]

Within a day or two of the death of Antonio Miorati, in August 1424, Andrea Priuli, head of probably the most prominent Rialto bank, also died of the plague. This bank was a fraterna, for Andrea managed it in the name of several brothers. On 14 May 1425 the Priuli estate bank was declared insolvent. After two generations the liquidation process was still not resolved, and extant documents reflect three major questions: the role of a commercial company in which Andrea had been a partner and which had a claim against the bank; the liability of Andrea's sons in the debts of the bank; and the division of the fraterna into two separate banks.

---

[65]The claimants, Nicolò and Taddeo Bevilacqua, took pains to distinguish between the compagnia formed by another brother of theirs with the deceased banker and other private affairs. Cocco sued them in turn for what they owed the Miorati estate from the Tana trade. ASV, GP, Sg, reg. 13, fols. 162–64v, 171 (July 1427).

Regarding the collateral company, little can be said beyond the fact that suits brought against the bank and the heirs of its principal by Pietro Venier and his heirs lasted at least until 1454, when creditors were still trying to collect the last 7 percent of the total debt of the bank. Even though there is no way of knowing how the debt had been contracted originally, the lawsuits indicate that the bank and the commercial company had been separate entities.[66]

More information is forthcoming when one considers the liability of Andrea's sons, for creditors were still suing the heirs of the banker as late as 1481. In that year the Procurators of San Marco, as executors of the estate of Michele, Andrea's last son, traced a history of the family in order to show that neither Michele nor his elder brothers had been liable for the debts contracted by their father as banker. The whole situation is complicated by two factors. First, the fraterna split up around the time of the failure of the Priuli estate bank. Second, the estate of Andrea was used as the basis of a successor bank, in partnership with Andrea's brother Bartolomeo, while the other surviving brothers, Leonardo and Giacomo, formed another bank with partners outside the family, including the Orsini brothers, previously bankers in their own right. Both these new Priuli banks failed in 1429. In the decades that followed, the debts of the original bank ("qd. Andrea Priuli e fratelli") and its successor ("la commissaria di Andrea Priuli e Bartolomeo Priuli") were often confused (or fused) into one and the same fund of liabilities.[67]

The Procurators, in the role of executors for Michele Priuli, summarized the case as follows. At Andrea's death in 1424 only one son, Alvise, was of age (eighteen years); the others were age ten or less. Their uncles administered Andrea's estate as well as the bank. When they declared the bank insolvent in 1425, two Procurators of San Marco, Leonardo Mocenigo and Antonio Contarini, were formally named by the state as receivers of the bank, and they sequestered the whole patrimony of Andrea and of the bank, "down to the very beds," so that the sons were left nothing for their subsistence but the dowry of their mother. The four surviving sons were therefore self-made men who had picked themselves up and rebuilt their fortune by the sweat of their brow, both by serving as officials of the state and through

---

[66]Andrea Priuli and Pietro, qd. Mafeo Venier, often appear in civil suits as "socii." See, for example, ASV, GP, Sg, reg. 11, fol. 45 (20 March 1404), reg. 19, fol. 42 (1 April 1413), and reg. 36, fols. 48, 52 (1424). Also SM, reg. 49, fol. 127v (22 July 1412).

[67]The confusion was noted in 1430 when the Great Council was called upon to resolve the procedural problem arising from the fact that no council could maintain a quorum after interested parties, debtors and creditors of the banks, had left the hall. "Et sint tot creditores et debitores dicti banchi [qd. Andree de Priolis et fratrum] et banchi comissarie qd. ser Andree et Bartolomei de Priolis, qui sunt illimet persone nominate superius quibus tangit causa predicta, quavis sint duo banchi." ASV, MC, Ursa, fol. 85 (22 October 1430).

investments in the Levant, after the first bank had failed.[68] Even when the second bank failed in 1429, the sons had successfully defended themselves against the creditors using the same argument, as was recorded in a case heard by the Quarantia. Furthermore, since the first sons, Alvise and Alessandro, had received nothing from their father's estate, they passed nothing from it on to their brother Michele. Even if Alvise had earned 10,000 ducats from the bank, the Procurators hypothesized, that money would not have been inherited by his brother Michele, who was therefore not liable as individual ("in suo spizialità"). Moreover, Alessandro drowned while on a voyage of the Flanders galleys, when he went down with all the merchandise sent by Alvise. The accounts adduced by the claimants as evidence of receipts by the two elder brothers from the successor bank, the Procurators asserted, merely showed the two acting as messengers between the bank of their father's estate and that of their uncles Leonardo and Jacomo Priuli. But the crowning defense employed by the Procurators was this: when the bank of the Priuli estate and Bartolomeo Priuli failed in 1429, the Quarantia had clearly ruled that the sons were not liable for any debts of the bank.[69] The Giudici del Procurator agreed with the defense, namely, that Daniele Priuli, the claimant and liquidator of the first bank, could not sue Michele or his estate, but at most the estate of Andrea, still being managed by the Sopragastaldi, and Daniele was charged with the court costs.

Finally, a word about the first bank of Andrea Priuli as fraterna. According to the entry made by the contemporary chronicler Antonio Morosini in May 1425, the failure of the bank was rumored to be the consequence of squabbles among the surviving brothers ("fo dito fo per alguna controversia de parole queli fradeli aver abudo in non esser stadi d'accordo").[70] Whether cause or effect of the failure, a division of the patrimony of the fraterna resulted, for within a short time two separate Priuli banks went into operation, as was mentioned above, styled "la commissaria di ser Andrea e ser Bartolomeo Priuli" and "ser Leonardo e ser Jacomo

---

[68]ASV, Giudici del Procurator, Sentenze a legge, reg. 10, fols. 85v–90v (15 May 1481). "Dapoi s'à del 1425 el banco fallì, e 'l fu fato capo di credadori del banco le magnificentie de misser Lunardo Mocenigo e misser Antonio Contarini; per loro fo tolto e 'struiato tutta la facoltà de misser Andrea e quella del banco et ogni sustancia fin ai leti, come per libri del banco apar esser sta' messo a conto, per modo che a quelli fioli non rimaxe substancia alguna salvo la dote e dimissoria de la madre per sustentarse, et se loro se àno voluto sostentarse, lor l'àno vadagnato cum suo sudor, sì in offitii come in Levante et altre facende."

[69]After listing property and liabilities, in order to show that nothing had passed from his brothers to Michele, the Procurators concluded "che, falido el bancho de ser Andrea e ser Bartolomeo di Prioli e per la Quarantia in contraditorio zudizio fo dichiarido i diti [fioli] non dover nè non poder eser astricti ad algun debito del soraschrito bancho, e provasi per i libri de quel tempo de la Quarantia." Ibid., fol. 88v. The deliberations of the Quarantia, unfortunately, are not extant for that period, so the allegation cannot be confirmed.

[70]Cronaca, 2:542.

Priuli e compagni." The latter two brothers probably sought out the device of legal division of the family patrimony, not as a way of escaping liability in the bank of their deceased brother, but out of disagreement about either the distribution of liability or the form that the successor bank was to take. No act of division, however, has as yet been found. The two new banks were at least as closely tied as Rialto banks normally were, if the above-mentioned account of 1481 shows Andrea's sons acting as messengers and bearers of specie between the two. (For the genealogy, see table H.2.)

While the Priuli banks lasted one generation, the banks of the Soranzo family lasted several generations. The misfortunes of one of them provide ample documentation in the area of bankruptcy, as we shall see below, but some indications are useful here in the context of business organization and liability.

When in September 1455 the bank of the Soranzo fraterna, directed by Benetto Soranzo, failed for the second time, Benetto and his brother Giovanni (sons of Cristoforo, son of Gabriele) fled Venice with the bank's reserves and with all its account books. Vain attempts were made to gain extradition of the two or, failing that, at least the sequestration of the account books. Some time between January and May 1456 Benetto — from a distance — made an agreement with the bank's creditors, and it was very likely about that time that his brother Giovanni first decided to return to Venice to face up to his responsibility. Whatever the exact date of his return, we know that he was granted an open-ended safe-conduct against imprisonment for the debts of the bank in May 1458. The grant was made by the Senate at the very same session in which that organ, upon the plea presented by the Avogadori, took the drastic and unusual step of divesting Benetto and his numerous sons of their title of nobility as punishment for his fraudulent bankruptcy. Giovanni, on the other hand, had returned and had admitted his unlimited liability in the debts of the bank of the fraterna. Even though it was recognized that he was innocent of the crime of his brother, he turned over all his belongings to the creditors and was left as a result "quasi nudus." Although Giovanni's act was considered honorable, no doubt was expressed that it was also his obligation as a result of unlimited liability, and, in fact, the safe-conduct was limited to his person, while his goods remained bound to the liquidators ("remanentibus tamen omnibus eius bonis obligatis sicut sunt ad presens").[71]

A new bank, registered under the style "Giovanni Soranzo," was in operation at the latest by 28 January 1456, when it made an advance to the state.[72] As we shall see below, the banker was not the above-mentioned Giovanni di Cristoforo di Gabriele, who had been left "quasi nudus" by the failure of Benetto di Cristoforo, but Giovanni, son of Vettor; Vettor was the

[71]ASV, ST, reg. 4, fol. 71v, and Ferrara, "Documenti," doc.22.
[72]Ferrara, "Documenti," doc. 16.

deceased brother of Gabriele, who had founded the bank before the War of Chioggia (see the genealogy in App. H, below). The sons of Giovanni di Vettor continued the operation and upheld the good name of the house until the bank's triumphant closing and liquidation "a trombe e pifferi" in 1491.[73]

Just how those sons succeeded their father offers a final, albeit fleeting, insight into the Soranzo bank as a family firm, although now run by a collateral branch, on a matter not of liability but of legitimization as an enterprise. The bank had traditionally been a regular lender to the Venetian government. Upon the failure of Benetto, the state was probably worried, not only about the citizens and foreigners who took considerable losses as its creditors but also about its own sources of short-term credit. Very likely the state therefore supported the proposal of Giovanni di Vettor to "levare banco," but the event of the opening is not mentioned by the chroniclers. Over the next decade the bank of Giovanni Soranzo is the principal lender to the state, in advancing well over half the total credit extended by the Rialto banks as a whole (see below, Chap. 10). When Giovanni di Vettor redacted his testament in 1468, he ordered his many executors, which included the Procurators of San Marco de citra and three of his sons who had passed their eighteenth birthday, to meet with Doge Cristoforo Moro himself to deliberate "whether or not his sons should carry on the operation of the bank" ("utrum filii mei tenere debeant banchum de scripta vel non").[74] Obviously the testator sought to involve the doge himself in the decision in order to assure the support of the state for the continuation of the enterprise. He knew how badly the state needed the services of this bank and probably wanted to constrain the state to guarantee repayment of outstanding loans. This would increase public trust in the firm when the management of the bank passed to his sons. The informal blessing of the state was obviously imparted, and to good effect, for the bank survived the critical moment of transition, and in March 1469 Piero and Francesco, qd. Giovanni, qd. Vettor, "persuaded by the exhortations of the doge and because of the singular devotion and charity they [had] toward [the] state," made a loan of 15,000 ducats to the Signoria.[75]

Only two further specific references to liability have been turned up. The first appears in the context of the registration in 1499 of guarantors for the second Garzoni bank. At the head of the final list is the style of the bank, plus the names of all the sons and nephews of Andrea d'Andrea Garzoni, who were all involved in the fraterna. There follows then the notation, probably taken for granted, that each was liable for all: "E chadaun de loro

---

[73]The same Vettor is called "dal banco" in marriage records (see ASV, AC, regs. 106 and 107, under Soranzo) and was probably involved in the administration of the bank of Gabriele's estate before the latter's sons succeeded in their own right.

[74]ASV, NT, b. 1240, n. 203 (28 May 1468).

[75]ASV, ST, reg. 6, fol. 53; on the same occasion the Veruzzi bank lent 11,000 ducats.

in parte e in tutto."[76] This was certainly the law regarding the fraterna compagnia. At this point, however, other Garzoni documents reflect a more complex reality. One of them seems to reconfirm unlimited liability even for persons who were minors at the time of the failure — in contrast to the ruling in the Priuli case, discussed above; the other identifies one of the partners in the fraterna as liable for only one-third of the debt.

Six years after the failure in 1500 of the revived Garzoni bank, two sons of Andrea qd. Andrea, namely, Francesco and Garzone, applied for a safe-conduct in order to be able to live in Venice. In their petition they asserted that they were innocent of all matters regarding the bank, that they had never had anything to do with it, and that they had never received anything from it, having been made liable while still minors ("per esser sta' in puerile età obligati"). In the end, they concluded, they had inherited only misery and perpetual servitude and were deprived of their fatherland. It is true that they were liable, for their names were listed as such in the above-mentioned document of 1500, even though they were too young to have been involved personally in the operation of the bank. In response to their petition, they received an open-ended personal safe-conduct, left to the discretion of the Signoria. By contrast, their father, brothers, and cousins shortly thereafter received a personal safe-conduct limited to one year only, leaving the impression that in practice, even within a structure presumably of unlimited liability, some were more liable than others.[77]

The cousin of the two petitioners, Agostino di Garzone, had other difficulties, since the patrimony of his wife, Alba d'Alban, was tied up in Ferrara at the beginning of the War of the League of Cambrai and was not available to repay the guarantors of the second bank. When Agostino applied for a renewal of his safe-conduct and drew up an accord with the guarantors in 1508, he declared that he had been partner in the bank for one-third ("participante per terzo in dicto banco") and that he promised to pay them only the third that he owed ("solo per el terzo a mi aspectante de tutto el loro credito hanno cum el bancho"). As regards the remaining two-thirds, he insisted that the guarantors free him completely and definitively from any liability. Here we are fortunate enough to have the text of the "concordium" that was subscribed to by a large majority of the forty-two persons who had put up the guarantee (corresponding to 91% of the total of 50,000 ducats) and which was approved by the Senate and solemnized by transcription in the register of the Senate, which also renewed the safe-conduct for a further year.[78] Thus we have, first, the confirmation of the fact

---

[76]The papers for the reconstitution of the bank, together with the lists of guarantors, are in ASV, PSM, Misti, b. 189.

[77]Ferrara, "Documenti," docs. 146, 147.

[78]Ibid., doc. 150. Among the subscribers we find "Alvise Pisani e fratelli." The concordat called for installment payments either in assets of the Salt Office, at par, or in cash.

that guarantors had to step in as soon as the relatively liquid assets of the principals were exhausted, so that they had to recoup losses directly from the principals; and second, the admission that even in a company constituted as a partnership, even though the partners were all members of a very extended family, including cousins, a single member could successfully claim to represent only one-third of the total liability and no more.

A final reference to organization and liability comes from the pen of Angelo Sanudo "el gobbo," whose bank failed in 1569. While in debtors' prison in 1570, he wrote up a declaration of his assets, in which he distinguished between his bank, as an operation restricted to himself personally, and the fraterna. At the same time, he considered the fraterna as an overlapping entity ("l'istessa persona") with his personal account.[79]

In summary, some general observations can be made on the basis of such fragments of indirect evidence. First of all, the business organization of banks was initially flexible and relatively informal. Although it probably remained so on Piazza San Marco, it tended to become more structured on the Rialto beginning with the last third of the fourteenth century. Forms of investment in banks were sought which circumscribed the liability of the investor. Presumably the liability of the guarantor was limited (otherwise, who would ever pledge himself as surety to a bank?), but whether it was limited to the amount pledged when the bank was licensed or to a part of the outstanding debt, proportional to the total guarantee (precisely one-tenth, 2,000/20,000 ducats), is not known; alas, for the manner of limiting the liability of guarantors might have served as a model for the limitation of liability for partners. Commercial investments made and partnerships formed by bankers outside their deposit banks were considered separate entities, for which partners in the bank were not considered liable. A distinction was generally made and maintained. In 1429 the Consoli dei Mercanti, qua adjudicators of matters regarding banks, even sought to withdraw from a lawsuit regarding the Priuli-Orsini bank when it appeared that the "spetialitates" of the bank partners were involved.[80] On the other hand, when in 1453 the Benetto Soranzo bank failed for the first time, the authorities made an effort to get hold of all account books, listed as those of the bank, of the "spezialità," of partnerships, and of the cashier. Thus, while clearly distinguishing the kinds of account books, the state still wanted them all.[81] Even though in the case of Cocco and Miorati the former was

---

[79]"Ducati 820 in circa che sono il restante di tutti quelli che ho io maneggiato così del banco come della nostra fraterna . . . Essendo passate alcune partite tra la fraterna e me, che ho però sempre reputata una e l'istessa persona, che io fuori de Banco accomodai la ditta fraterna de ducati 5000, gr. 6 per pagar la Magnifica Madama Iustina Zana nostra zermana, che era creditrice di altri tanti scrittine in Cecca per avanti." Magnacavallo, "Proposta di riforma bancaria," 416–17.

[80]Lattes, *Libertà,* doc. 15.

[81]Ibid., doc. 26α.

not liable for the latter's "spezialità," the juridical status of a banker's personal account remains uncertain and problematic.[82]

Second, in the realm of the fraterna compagnia, unlimited liability was generally not contested but could be — and occasionally was. The very existence of a fraterna could be denied, by showing proof of a preexisting division of patrimony or act of emancipation, but no example has emerged. Alternatively, liability could be contested in specific cases, by showing that since no assets had been inherited, liability could not be inherited, or by arguing that a member had been a minor at the time of the failure and thus was blameless in regard to it.[83]

Third, there are two indications, a century apart, that bank partnerships could be of limited liability. Simone Condulmer paid a debt of the Benedetto successor bank only up to the limit of his one-fourth investment. Agostino Garzoni agreed, similarly, to pay only one-third of the debts of the Garzoni successor bank to the guarantors, since his contribution to the partnership's capital had been one-third. Nicolò Cocco, on the other hand, did not contest his obligation to pay the debts of his bank partnership with the deceased Antonio Miorati — but that might have been because the debts were easily within his capacity to pay.

A fourth phenomenon is that of the successor bank itself, instituted in the wake of the failure or forced liquidation of the original bank, often at the death of the principal. A distinction was presumed to exist between the bank and the fraterna or the estate of the deceased. The bank could be forced to liquidate, perhaps following a run, but as long as the fraterna or the estate was considered solvent, it could serve as the basis for instituting a successor bank.

When the same business organization was unable to reorganize after a failure, a new enterprise quickly took its place on the Rialto, so that there were always three or four major banks in operation. The frequency with which deposit banks on the Rialto failed, however, caused the authorities in the second half of the Trecento to debate the possibility of instituting a public bank that would guarantee what had become a public service, that of transfer, or giro.

vi. PROPOSALS FOR THE INSTITUTION OF A PUBLIC BANK

Neither better definition of the structures of private banking enterprises nor regulation of their activities by the government succeeded in

---

[82]Alessandro Lattes, *Il fallimento nel diritto comune e nella legislazione bancaria della Repubblica di Venezia* (Venice, 1880), 55.

[83]Cf. Richard A. Goldthwaite, *The Building of Renaissance Florence: An Economic and Social History* (Baltimore, 1981), 62–63, where the author contrasts the obligation placed by the Peruzzi on their heirs for one hundred years in 1345 with the fragmented and circumscribed investments made by Florentines in the following century.

stemming the cadenced demise of banks through failure. Insolvency and bankruptcy of banks periodically created havoc in the Venetian money market. Failure, as we shall see shortly, tied up bankers' assets and clients' deposits in lengthy and litigious liquidation procedures. It did not matter whether the bank was the victim of a chain reaction initiated by the failure of commercial companies or whether it was a bank that had set off the chain. The tight money situation that inevitably resulted caused serious problems for citizens and foreigners alike. The role of the local deposit bank situated at the Rialto was too central to the credit system and the clearing system to be taken lightly. In moments of frustration, civic leaders and legislators judged private banks to be incapable of providing the public service for which they had been licensed to operate; to be too free with funds left by depositors to be worthy of the public trust; to be too uncontrollable, too unregulatable. Discussions of the feasibility of instituting a public transfer bank took place in the second half of the fourteenth century. On three occasions, each time in the midst of monetary and banking crises, the authorities discussed publicly more or less concrete proposals for such an institution; twice specific recommendations were voted down. In the early fifteenth century, a provision for instituting a kind of public bank was inserted into a proposal aimed at regulating banking activity; although the bill was passed into law, the plan, as we shall see, was never put into effect. These proposals seem to have aroused considerable debate and received serious consideration. None of them, however, even mentions the possibility of expanding the activities of the Grain Office, which was the existing depositary for private hoards and other funds as well as the principal administrator of the state's floating debt but which did not offer the service of transfer. Nor did they consider expanding the role of the Salt Office, which did transfer credits, at least those of nominal owners of salt stored in the warehouses, and which administered some of the state's floating debt, to the extent that it was regularly in arrears in paying importers and was constantly obliged, in the fifteenth century, to repay the banks that had lent money to the state.[84]

---

[84]These aspects of the activity of the Salt Office are explained by Jean-Claude Hocquet, *Le sel et la fortune de Venise*, 2 vols., vol. 2, *Voiliers et commerce en Méditerranée* (Lille, 1978–79), chap. 9. Using a specific example, the author also discusses the discounting of salt credits, sold in the 1360s at prices ranging from 70 to 86 percent of par; the discount derived both from the changing value of salt which stood behind the credit and from the delays of the office in paying off its credits–at par (pp. 456–64). Tax farmers were particularly interested in purchasing the credits of importers (408–11). Hocquet poses the question, finally, of the extent to which the Salt Office performed functions similar to those of a public bank (422–28). It is worth pointing out a case in private accounts of transfers and sales of salt credits (at 80 and 90 percent of par) at the Salt Office; see the small ledger of the Giustinian fraterna in ASV, PSM, Misti, b. 91A, fol. 7 (1417). See also Hocquet's "Guerre et finance dans l'etat de la Renaissance (la Chambre du Sel et la dette publique à Venise)," in *Actes du 102ᵉ Congrès National des Sociétés Savantes, Limoges 1977* (Paris, 1979), vol. 1.

The first proposal for a state bank was aired before the Senate in 1356 by Giovanni Dolfin, one of the heads of the Council of Forty, a body that most likely had already discussed the matter. As will be seen below, in the immediate aftermath of the third war with Genoa, at least one bank had failed; speculation in copper and silver and usurious interest rates created anxiety and aroused debate. One of the several solutions proposed and rejected involved the legalization of pawnbanks through state licensing of the lenders. All these questions were topics of the day in 1355–57 and were intimately tied to concern for the condition of the banks.

The public bank to be created by the Commune ("unum bancum [constituatur] per Comune"), as envisioned by Giovanni Dolfin, would have coexisted with private banks. It was to be headed by three noble officials, as were most Venetian offices and magistracies. Its primary function would have been that of accepting deposits on current account and of transferring bank money from person to person upon oral order. A fee of 1 soldo was to have been exacted, in order to pay the salaries of the officials and the staff of three accountants. The bank — or perhaps more correctly the public clearing institution — would have been prohibited from accepting conditioned deposits, from lending or investing money, and from paying interest. Obliged as it would have been to maintain 100 percent reserves, Dolfin's proposed institution was meant simply to be a solid and trustworthy intermediary in the traditional clearing process operative on the Rialto, a public service.

The fact that on the same day the Senate attempted to put an end to "the deceit and fraud committed in commerce in silver" by regulating the refinement and sale of bullion is a sign that the banks, once again, had given cause for concern by speculating too freely in this commodity. The proposal to place a carefully controlled public bank at their side was intended to guarantee continuity in the clearing of payments even when private banks were insecure. Dolfin's proposal was voted down by a wide margin. Probably in a pique he immediately offered another proposal: given that private banks were to operate alone on the Rialto, it was best to admit the ineffectiveness of the surety of 5,000 lire which had been demanded of them since 1318; communal revenues would be best served simply by seeking the best possible rent for the banks that, in that moment, remained to be leased. This proposal was similarly defeated.[85]

---

[85]*PMV*, docs. 124, 125 (15 December 1356). The preamble to the two documents refers to copper and silver brought by Germans ("et in milliaribus fontici Teutonicorum et in argento eciam modus incongruus teneatur"). Copper was sold by thousandweight. The officials of the public bank were to be instructed that they "non recipiant nec teneant aliquam quantitatem pecunie vel aliquem denarium seu depositum super dicto bancho per se nec per alium, sed solum teneantur facere scribi omnes solutiones, que fient de persona ad personam." Each official was to have his own accountant (scriba), and all three would administer a strong box into which they would place their money. See also Luzzatto, "Les banques publiques," 227–28.

Only a few years later, in September 1361, the Council of Forty actively discussed the problem of tight money. There was a dearth of gold and full-weight silver coin, clipped coins were circulating freely, and recent bank failures — one just a month earlier, in August 1361, four in 1359 — had exacerbated the situation. Once again the Forty debated whether to promote the establishment of new private banks or to insist on the institution of one or more banks by the state. A committee was created to discuss the question, and concern was expressed: "Unless one or more banks be provided by the Commune, business is apt to be seriously compromised." Again in October the committee was reminded to weigh the alternative of public and private banks and to present concrete proposals. No proposals, however, if any were actually drafted by the committee, have survived. Very likely, the emergency had passed, rendering further consideration less pressing.[86]

Nearly fifteen years went by before another banking crisis in Venice prompted another formal attempt to institute a public bank. The institution proposed by Michele Morosini in 1374 repeated almost verbatim the proposal made nearly two decades earlier by Dolfin. Morosini, probably the same extremely wealthy man who would be elected doge in 1382, formulated his proposal as a member of an ad hoc Senate banking committee (the "sapientes cambiorum") named to deal with the banks and the bullion market. The fact that he reformulated Dolfin's proposal — in part awkwardly — means that he had the earlier text in hand and supports the assumption that the idea of establishing a public bank had continued in the interim to interest certain circles in the ruling group.[87]

Morosini went a step further than Giovanni Dolfin, however, and proposed first the drastic solution of prohibiting private deposit banking altogether; he envisioned heavy penalties against nobles or citizens who would open banks. The place of the private banks would be taken by a state bank ("unum banchum [fiat et deputetur] per Comune") that would have a monopoly on transfer operations. It would be headed by two nobles elected in the Senate, each with one accountant; if the officials proved to be good, they could be reconfirmed year by year. As in Dolfin's proposal, they were forbidden to accept deposits at interest or make loans but were only to "transfer payments from person to person." Obviously, the bank was to

---

[86]The committee had time through October to conclude its investigation. The deliberation expresses a general preoccupation, "quia dicitur quod nisi provideatur de aliquo banco vel banchis pro communi, status mercationum est pro recipiendo maximum sinistrum." Lattes, *Libertà*, doc. 5 (15 September 1361). The sages "possint et debeant consulere de banchis cambii tenendis, vel pro communi, vel pro spetialibus personis, sicut videbitur bonum et cum illis conditionibus et modis quibus videbitur." Ibid., doc. 6 (20 October 1361).

[87]The text of the proposal that he turned in for registration by the scribe says that "aliquis bancherius" need no longer provide surety, "quia non erit necessarium," even though the foregoing paragraph had already forbidden anyone from running a bank. *PMV*, doc. 160, pp. 149–52; see also Luzzatto, "Les banques publiques," 228.

maintain 100 percent reserves. Since there would no longer be private banks ever ready to purchase the bullion and coin imported by German merchants, Morosini suggested that the Treasury accommodate the silver and specie they imported; in practice, the Treasury would have had to accept bullion as "regular" deposits of nonfungibles and render them upon request. The fee to be charged for the service of making transfers at the public bank was here more carefully spelled out than before: 6 denari piccoli for sums from 1 to 200 ducats, 8 denari for sums from 200 to 1,000 ducats, 1 soldo (12 denari) for sums exceeding 1,000 ducats. Provisions for the maintenance and safety of the account books and the cashbox as well as for the hours to be kept by the officials are again almost verbatim those of Dolfin. The proposal garnered only seventeen "aye" votes in the Senate.

The desire to find an alternative to private banking clearly did not die down. Men in authoritative positions — men like Michele Morosini himself and Zaccaria Contarini, another influential member of the banking committee — also seem to have discussed plans for the institution of a public bank with foreign dignitaries. One of these was Philippe de Mézières (1327–1405), French nobleman and chancellor of the kingdom of Cyprus, who knew Venice well and admired its institutions, which he described at some length. He was in Venice on many occasions, en route between Avignon and Cyprus on diplomatic missions: in 1365, when he was made an honorary citizen; in 1369, when he donated a relic of the true cross to the Scuola Grande of S. Giovanni Evangelista, a relic that immediately became famous for the miracles it worked; in 1371–72, when he spent almost two consecutive years in Venice; in the 1380s, as we know from evidence in his *Dream of the Old Pilgrim,* a call for reform of French institutions, written in 1388.[88] This work includes a description of what was supposedly Venice's public bank — part of his dream, to be sure, but detailed enough to make it quite obvious that the author himself had heard the project extensively debated.

De Mézières's vision of the Bank of Venice is at once fantasy and reality. The author praises the Venetians and their "well-known" bank as a way of attacking the inefficiency of the French financial bureaucracy and its

[88]For the donation and its place in art, see Patricia Fortini Brown, *Venetian Narrative Painting in the Age of Carpaccio* (New Haven, 1988), 45, 60, 139–42. Philippe de Mézières, *Le songe du vieil pelerin,* ed. G. W. Coopland, 2 vols. (Cambridge, England, 1969), 1:134–35 and 254–55, 413–15, 460–61. The author gives two fixed equivalences in a (complicated) Venetian money of account (1 ducato a monete = 64 soldi or 16 grossi) and one market equivalence (1 ducato d'oro = 80 soldi); the latter was the rate of exchange current in Venice only between 1380 and 1387, while the former was a money of account then in its last two decades of use (ibid., 2:371–72); for the explanations, see Vol. 1:354–55 and its app. D.3. Other visits to Venice, in December 1362, "probably" in 1364, in June 1366, August 1367, January 1369 (when he visited the Certosa in the Trevigiano, which he made beneficiary of a donation of land in 1378), are recalled by Luigi Pesce, "Filippo de Mézières e la Certosa del Montello," *AV* 134 (1990): 12–26, 33.

inability to control royal expenditures. The bank is treated as an example of a just institution, founded for the common good. The description, which de Mézières, in his allegory, put into the mouth of Hardiesse, the attendant of Justice, can be rendered in translation as follows:

> In the noble city of Venice there is an exchange called the public bank ["un change qui s'appelle le banc du commun"]. The elected governor of the bank receives and pays out three or four million ducats annually, [in payment for imports and exports, such as] gold and silver, precious stones, plate, jewels, and spices. No noble or merchant or even the Signoria in their affairs, in buying, selling or exchanging, ever pays with circulating currency but they all have the money delivered, accredited and transferred at the public bank. The governor of the bank or exchange satisfies every seller and buyer, for all transactions pass through his hands. He alone is master of the accounts, treasurer, depositary and paymaster, as it were, of the whole wealth of Venice. Sometimes he handles large transactions, of 1000 ducats, 40–60 times per year, or he exchanges ducats into petty coins, grossi and bagattini, and all is duly recorded. The service and solicitude of the bank's directorship and the large sums of silver and gold received and exchanged may seem incredible to the French, with their disorganized bureaucracy, but they are true and meet the approval of all the merchants of Venice.
>
> The staff is efficient; the governor has only two or three scribes who are hardly ever idle. They maintain accounts of all transactions, large and small, for a whole year in journals and in a single great ledger. And they do so in such a manner that even 10–20,000 clients can receive, in less than four days from the date of the request, an overview of all the accounts that concern them, large or small.
>
> This fine institution clearly benefits the public ["au prouffit du commun"]. The office is authentic, unbureaucratic and so generally sanctioned that all merchants judge their money safer there than in their own homes. However, for the greater security of the institution, should the governor ever fail to render true account to any merchant, through error, malice or negligence, he is required to make good by paying out of his own pocket. That rarely happens, however, for the governor is elected as a prudent and wise man and he has to provide good sureties that he will perform his office loyally and satisfy each and every client. The administration of the bank is hard work and requires subtlety, fidelity, diligence, memory and experience. Therefore the governor receives a just retribution for his

labors, in the form of a commission of one-half or one percent or whatever the Signoria and the Consoli dei Mercanti ordain.

Thus each year, on the basis of a simple ledger, one can have an overview of the whole condition of the city of Venice, as concerns the large sums of money that turn over in commerce, and to a considerable extent as concerns the finances and treasury of the Signoria. And this suffices to demonstrate the artfulness and experience necessary for the common good of the Italians, who manage public affairs as regards finance better than any other people.[89]

The detail and the precision with which the author describes this would-be state bank of Venice are not the fruit of mere wishful thinking. It is clear from his formulations that de Mézières was well acquainted with the Venetian payments system, based upon transfers of bank money and the avoidance, in large transactions, of the use of specie. He even got almost right the name of the office that had jurisdiction over the Rialto banks, the Consoli dei Mercanti (rendered by him "le conseil des marchans"). Just as clearly, he was echoing a proposal that he had heard described firsthand, perhaps by someone who convinced him it was sure to be passed before long by the responsible organs of government. His descriptions of other Venetian institutions, furthermore, are close enough to reality that we can assume he took notes on what he saw and heard during his sojourns in Venice. For de Mézières, at the time he wrote his work, the Bank of Venice was not a dream but a reality, "a well-known example" worthy of being followed.[90]

After the defeat of Morosini's proposal, we hear again of a proposed public initiative in the banking sector only half a century later. In the meantime, the first public banks had been established in Barcelona and perhaps in Majorca in 1401, in Genoa in 1407, and in Valencia in 1408. These were cities in which Venetian merchants were quite used to doing business, and they were surely acquainted with the functions of the new municipal banks. These were not monopoly banks, for private banking continued to be permitted in those cities, but certain kinds of patrimonies and incomes had by law to be deposited there; bills of exchange, especially in Barcelona, were to

---

[89]*Le songe du vieil pelerin,* 1:460–61 (text) and 1:413–15 (Coopland's paraphrase). The description is introduced thus: "Cy recite la chambriere Hardiesse un exemple notoire pour abreger l'outrageux nombre des officiers royaulx et de tranchier raisonnablement la despence royalle." The phrase "du commun," in fourteenth-century French usage, means more correctly "of the commonweal" or "of the public," rather than "of the Commune," as one might have assumed proceeding from the Venetian Latin texts; I am grateful to my colleague Henri Dubois for this clarification.

[90]For Coopland, de Mézières's "knowledge of Venice was probably closer than that of any other city in the West except Paris." Ibid., 1:134.

be bought and sold exclusively on the books of the bank. All of them served as fiscal agents and depositaries of their respective cities — functions that are not mentioned in what is known of the Venetian proposals but seem to have been taken for granted by Philippe de Mézières.[91] In central and southern Germany, moreover, an area admittedly less well known to Venetian merchants through personal experience, a number of cities, beginning with Frankfurt in 1402, also instituted public banks "for the sake of the common good." Actually, these involved solely the manual exchange of coins and merely sought to divert to the common chest the profits that could be made from exchanging coins; giro seems not to have been so common a service there as to constitute a motive for public initiative in banking.[92]

In 1421, immediately following King Sigismund's "Continental blockade," which had created difficulties in the silver market, several restrictions on banking practices were passed by the Venetian Senate. The law, voted in September, was to take effect the following Christmas. Its primary aim was to bring an end to the existence of an agio between bank money and specie. Restrictions were placed on the use of bank money; bills of exchange, for example, were to be paid in specie. In order to meet the needs of the marketplace, which could not do without bank money as a means of payment, moreover, the Senate ordered the Silver Office to provide the service of accepting deposits and making transfers — in effect, to act as a public clearing bank. All transfers were to be made in the presence of both parties to a transaction. Fees were specified for certain operations, especially for those involving payments for bills of exchange.[93]

Although the law passed, the provision for a public clearing service was never put into effect. Not only is there no reflection in merchants' account books of transfer operations having taken place at the Silver Office,

[91]Usher, *Early History*; recent treatments with bibliography are Manuel Riu, "Banking and Society in Late Medieval and Early Modern Aragon," in *The Dawn of Modern Banking,* ed. Center for Medieval and Renaissance Studies, University of California, Los Angeles (New Haven, 1979), 131–67, expanded and updated fifteen years later as "La banca i la societat a la corona d'Aragó, a finals de l'edat mitjana i començaments de la moderna," *Acta mediaevalia* 11–12 (1990–91): 187–224; Esteban Hernandez Esteve, "Aspectos organizativos, operativos, administrativos y contables del proyecto de erarios publicos," in *Banchi pubblici, banchi privati,* 2:971–74; Giuseppe Felloni, "I primi banchi pubblici della Casa di San Giorgio (1408–45)," in *Banchi pubblici, banchi privati,* 1:225–46.

[92]Karl Günther, *Die städtischen Wechselbanken Deutschlands im Mittelalter und im 16. Jahrhundert* (Munich, 1932), 16–30. For the existence of giro banking in Nuremberg, see Wolfgang von Stromer, "Funktionen und Rechtsnatur der Wechselstuben als Banken im internationalen Vergleich," in Marx, *Credito, banche e investimenti,* 248.

[93]Lattes, *Libertà,* doc. 14, p. 49. Cessi mistook the Officium Argenti for the mint. Roberto Cessi, "Alcuni aspetti della crisi economica veneziana al principio del secolo XV," *Economia: Rassegna mensile di politica economica* (Trieste) 1 (july 1923): 155–56, and Cessi and Alberti, *Rialto,* 271.

but the law of 1447 which specifically revoked this provision of the law states that the operation of deposit and transfer had in fact never been inaugurated.[94] Thus, once again, the option of instituting a public bank in Venice was rejected. Only in 1587 would the public Banco della Piazza di Rialto be substituted for private banks, of which the last major one, the Pisani-Tiepolo bank, had declared insolvency in 1584 under the pressure of a run by depositors. Finally Venice had the bank envisioned more than two centuries earlier, which held, at least at the outset, 100 percent reserves and provided the service of clearing debts via giro among its depositors.[95]

[94]Lattes, *Libertà,* doc. 21, pp. 69–70.

[95]Ugo Tucci, "Il Banco della Piazza di Rialto, prima banca pubblica veneziana," reprinted in his *Mercanti, navi, monete nel Cinquecento veneziano* (Bologna, 1981), 231–50, in particular 240. Idem, "Il banco pubblico a Venezia," in *Banchi pubblici, banchi privati,* 1:309–25. It is interesting to note that the governors of the public bank had much the responsibility that de Mézières had envisioned — so much so that notarial acts referring to the bank give it the name of the governor currently in office.

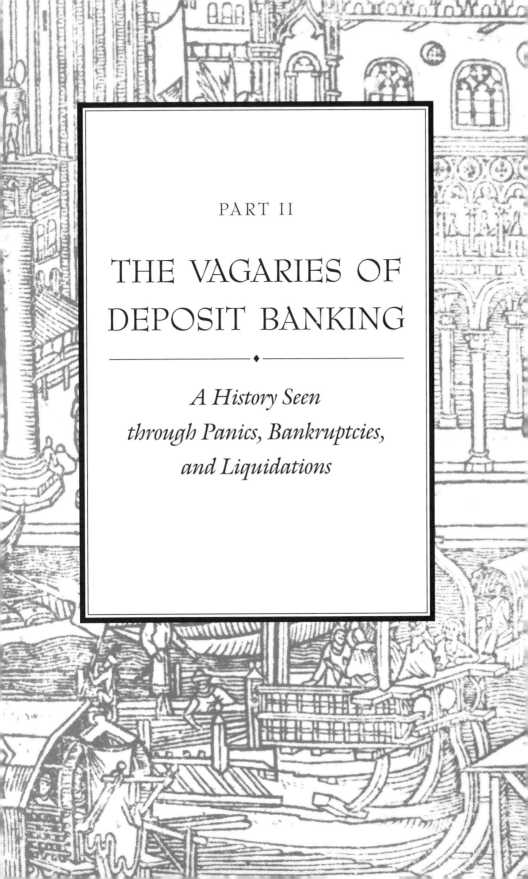

PART II

THE VAGARIES OF DEPOSIT BANKING

*A History Seen
through Panics, Bankruptcies,
and Liquidations*

4

BANK FAILURES
IN THE TRECENTO

i. CASH, CREDIT, AND CALAMITY: TOWARD A TYPOLOGY

The Dimensions of the Problem

THAT "BANK MONEY IS AS GOOD AS CASH" was the argument used in their defense by the commission agents who had deposited their principals' cash investment in the local bank of Tana the day before the colony was sacked and the bank cleaned out, as we saw above. That bank money was often not "as good as cash" can also be learned from the cries of despair which arose on the Rialto when banks closed their doors and were forced into liquidation or bankruptcy. Such closings occurred in response to panics and runs by depositors which exhausted the bank's liquid reserves and meant, for the unlucky depositor who failed to withdraw his money in time, at best a loss of time and thus a temporary loss of liquidity, at worst a partial loss of assets as well. In an age in which the largest investments were in maritime trade, in which the mere turnaround time of ships and galleys meant months or even a year or more, it could take a long time to collect the banker's assets.

We have seen how bank transfers played a pivotal role in the payments system of the Rialto. Banks collectively — that is, the banking system — were the "cashier of all the money of the market place," as the senator Tommaso Contarini wrote in 1584 in a discussion of the feasibility of instituting a public bank, after the failure of the last large private bank on the Rialto.[1]

---

[1]Lattes, *Libertà*, docs. 42–43, pp. 118–60, are the two supposed "orations" of Tommaso Contarini in the Senate, one pro, the other contra the institution of a public bank. Each uses some of the same arguments.

Two hundred years earlier Philippe de Mézières had said the same about the would-be public bank he was describing. The mere entry in a banker's journal constituted legal proof of payment. Its utility rendered the bank indispensable, but it was a fragile, unstable institution.

As Contarini wrote, it did not take much to upset public trust and unleash a run. A rumor was sufficient: that there were insufficient reserves; that the banker had sustained a loss in a commercial venture; that a depositor had been seen withdrawing his money in cash; that a debtor of the bank had failed; that war was declared. Some such event was bound to occur sooner or later, he wrote, and convince panicking creditors to forgo the facility of making payments in bank and get their hands on the cash, in order to avoid a lengthy liquidation process and the risk of loss. Sometimes those who initiated the runs were merchant bankers, sometimes artisans and holders of small current accounts.

It is difficult to say whether Contarini had access to documentation preserved by the office of the Consoli dei Mercanti in order to prepare his position papers, but he gives a summary of the history of failures which seems informed, even though he employed it for effect. Looking back over the history of the city's banks, he noted their unique rate of failure: "In the 1,200 years during which this Republic exists by the grace of God, one finds that 103 private banks were erected, of which 96 failed . . . and 7 alone succeeded."[2] Of course, he was not counting from A.D. 420, the mythical founding of Venice, but from about 1250 or 1300. Perhaps he had consulted records of the public contracts for rental of the banks. Let us assume that he included the banks of small moneychangers, about whom little is known, and maybe even those situated at San Marco. Whatever the case may be, the survival rate that he indicated is not far from the truth, to the extent that a reconstruction is possible. As can be seen from Appendix B, below, information survives for about 50 failures between 1340 and 1500; few major banks avoided a bitter end. On the other hand, the attraction of being able to invest and make loans with other people's money was such that there was always someone who was ready to take the place of the last loser and hope for better prospects. Or, if the pressed banker was merely temporarily insolvent and not bankrupt, he might found a successor bank, as long as a sufficient number of creditors were ready to accept their credits as deposits on the new bank, payable at certain specified intervals, in order to limit the freezing of their assets.

Part II begins and ends with the two best-known panics in European history prior to John Law. In the first period, the 1340s, the famous bankruptcies are those of Florentine firms, all of which had a branch or an agency in Venice; the failure of Venetian banks, quite unknown and certainly sec-

---

[2]Ibid., 124, 157.

ondary by comparison, anticipated that of the Florentines by a year or two and is indicative of the "international" character of the crisis. In the last period, 1499–1500, it is the Venetian situation that is best known, thanks to the reports of Venetian eyewitnesses and the analysis of those reports in a classic article by Frederic Lane. To conclude the discussion of bankruptcies with an examination of the conjuncture that spawned the panic of 1499–1500 is not meant, however, to signify the end of the phenomenon, for bank failures on the Rialto continued for most of the following century.

Legal Considerations

Fortunately historians of commercial law have dealt fairly extensively with the Venetian situation, as regards both bankruptcy in general and the failure of banks in particular.[3] Each time there was a rash of failures, reforms of laws were undertaken or derogations to existing laws were granted, with a typically Venetian concern for flexibility in practice. Just the same, some points of general validity can be made.

Jurisdictions, first of all, were relatively clear, although often contested in given situations. Bank failures were handled by the Consoli dei Mercanti. According to a deliberation of 1301, failures of merchants labeled "burdened by debt" ("gravati di debito") were under the Giudici di Petizion, whereas "fugitives" were under the Sopraconsoli dei Mercanti; that remained in effect until 1425, when jurisdiction over both categories passed to the Sopraconsoli dei Mercanti. The actions of each magistracy were subject to the approval of the Council of Forty; particularly clamorous cases were simply arrogated by the Senate or Council of Ten.[4]

The terminology employed in discussing the legal status of insolvents was also quite clear, in theory. "Fugitivus" was an officially proclaimed bankrupt, whether he actually fled the city or not; most did flee, in order to avoid arrest and incarceration, to abscond with the account books and with

---

[3]A. Lattes, *Il fallimento*; Manzini, "La bancarotta e la procedura fallimentare"; and Cassandro, *Le rappresaglie e il fallimento*; Cassandro examined only nonbank failures, "since bank failures always have an occasional and sporadic character" (vii). The importance of distinguishing jurisdictions and regulations regarding banks from those regarding merchants in general was underscored in early-fifteenth-century Genoa by the jurist Bartolomeo Bosco; licensing created a special trust in the citizenry vis-à-vis the bankers and obligated the state to judge defaulting bankers with particular severity. It should be noted that revisions of laws concerning banking in Genoa were undertaken in practically the same years as those of Venice, reflecting the international character of banking crises. Vito Piergiovanni, "Banchieri e falliti nelle 'Decisiones de mercatura' della Rota civile di Genova," in *Diritto comune, diritto commerciale, diritto veneziano*, ed. Karin Nehlsen–von Stryk and Dieter Nörr, Centro tedesco di studi veneziani, Quaderni, 31 (Venice, 1985), 17–38. See also idem, "I banchieri nel diritto genovese."

[4]By the time Sanudo wrote, the authority of the Consoli was much reduced (a jurisdiction over bankrupts is not even mentioned), and the Sopraconsoli, he writes, were more important. See *De origine*, 135–36 (1493) and 265–66 (1515).

what liquidity remained, and to be able to extract a safe-conduct from the authorities. The official proclamation of failure was the "stridatio" or "strida," which initiated procedures for the sequester of the bankrupt's goods and the attempt of liquidators elected by the creditors ("capita creditorum") to collect assets from his debtors and to ascertain the correctness of the claims presented by creditors; liquidators were paid a salary from the assets collected; the relevant magistracy supervised and intervened when necessary. Flight was obviously against the law and created the suspicion of fraud, but, once outside the jurisdiction of Venetian authorities, the bankrupt was in a position of strength: not only his assets (at that point "havere aliorum") but also the account books were essential to the liquidation process, and the issue of a safe-conduct ("fida" or "salvacondotto") was guaranteed. The personal safe-conduct, meaning immunity from arrest for the period indicated, often involved a kind of moratorium, during which the insolvent could not be sued, in order to give him time to liquidate his assets as favorably as possible. The "gravato di debito," on the other hand, was the person who admitted insolvency by consigning his account books voluntarily to the proper magistracy, which initiated the procedure for ascertaining the level of liabilities and the nature of assets. The distinction between the two categories of insolvent, however, lost significance in the Quattrocento, and actual flight from the city became infrequent, since safe-conducts were readily obtained. In 1500, 1501, and 1508 failed bankers, the Garzoni, the Lippomano (after breaking out of prison on a ruse), and the Agostini, respectively, fled to the sanctuary of monasteries within Venice; in 1513 Gerolamo Priuli fled to the patriarch of Venice, in the cathedral church of S. Pietro di Castello.

Once back in Venice and safe from incarceration, the "fugitivus" could better arrive at an agreement or concordat ("pactum") with his creditors regarding the amount he could pay, if less than 100 percent, and the modality of payment (amount and timing of installments), always formulated as a number of soldi per lira of debt (that is, in twentieths). Concordats had to be approved by the Council of Forty, in whose archives, however, very few have survived. In important cases of the failure of banks, the Senate stepped in, first to authorize safe-conducts, then to approve the concordats; by the late fifteenth century, the Council of Ten arrogated to itself the issuance of safe-conducts. Finally, the state assumed more direct responsibility in the most serious cases of bank failure. In 1375 two noble receivers were elected by the Forty to liquidate as rapidly as possible the credits of the defaulting bank; beginning in 1425, when it was judged that the reputation of the republic was at stake, the Senate named two of the prestigious Procurators of San Marco as official receivers, with the duty of overseeing the task of liquidation. That gives the measure of the extent to which Rialto banks were considered institutions in the public interest.

The insolvents who failed to pay in full were excluded from the public and economic life of the city. If they were nobles, they could not take part in the councils or hold any office; if they were non-nobles, they were prohibited from entering the areas of the Rialto or San Marco, which practically excluded them from doing business or from dealing on their own initiative with the courts situated at the Rialto and in the ducal palace. That and the public proclamation were infamy enough; Venice did not resort to the public rituals of infamy reserved for bankrupts on the Terraferma and in much of Italy, namely, the bankrupt's striking his naked buttocks three times on the "stone of infamy," usually situated in the main square, while pronouncing the words of total surrender, "Cedo bonis."[5] The term *bancarotta* ("bancum est ruptum") was occasionally used in the late fourteenth century but simply to signify a bank failure, without reference to any ritual act of breaking the banker's table or bancum.

Toward a Typology of Bank Failures in Venice

The historical record provides a number of recurring aspects of failure, both exogenous and endogenous.[6]

Public trust, or fiducia, in private banks was labile. It resided actually more in the person (and to a certain extent the family) of the banker than in the bank as institution. It could be built up by display and a bit of theater, just as it could be deflated quickly by the rumor, for example, that the banker had taken ill.

It was a custom to celebrate the opening of a bank with much fanfare. The principals first attended solemn mass at S. Giovanni Elemosinario and then proceeded in procession to the bank, accompanied by fifes and trumpets and escorted by their relatives and guarantors and sometimes by high government officials. The culmination of the show was the display of sacks of gold and silver coins, sometimes poured out on the countertop in order to assure potential depositors of the existence of a healthy reserve. Clients then began to line up to open an account by depositing further specie; those at the head of the line were surely put up to the act. Such staged spectacles were also used by rescue committees to alleviate the pressure on a bank when a run was threatened, when the names of underwriters of guarantee funds were solemnly announced. The first recorded celebration was actually a "grand closing," when Pietro di Giovanni di Vettor Soranzo liquidated his

---

[5]See, for example, Nilo Faldon, ed., *Gli antichi statuti e le provvisioni ducali della magnifica comunità di Conegliano (1488)* (Conegliano, 1974), 49, 177, 239 n. 11. For Verona, see Manzini, "La bancarotta e la procedura fallimentare," 1097 n. 2; for Padua, where the inscription on the stone reads "Lapis vituperii et cessationis bonorum," see Andrea Gloria, *La pietra del vituperio nel salone di Padova: Lettera* (Padua, 1851), 8, 15–17.

[6]Stimulating on this theme is Charles Kindleberger, *Manias, Panics, and Crashes: A History of Financial Crises* (New York, 1978; rev. ed., New York, 1989), even though it begins only with John Law.

bank "with trumpets and fifes" on 21 April 1491. But when Sanudo recounted the reopening of the Garzoni bank on 3 February 1500 and noted that Andrea Garzoni dressed in black and had dismissed with music, he made it clear that the principal had gone against tradition. The next day, after the rumor had spread that the sacks that had been displayed at the opening were not all full of coins, the bankers had them emptied out for all to see.[7]

The importance of the person of the banker was expressed in the midfourteenth century when it was legislated that only the principal, in whose name bond had been posted, could accept deposits and not his manager or cashier. That the person of the banker remained crucial can be seen in the bonding law of 1523, according to which the prospective banker himself, as well as his guarantors, had to be approved by a majority vote in the Senate.

The connection between the health of the principal and the stability of the bank was underscored in the case of Pietro Benedetto, who was struck with the plague in the fall of the year 1400. The rumor that he had died, spread by the envious or by competing bankers, according to observers, caused a furious run on the bank, and the cashier had to close at sunset and admit insolvency at the office of the Consoli. Actually, the banker lived another two days and had time to prepare the way for the opening of a successor bank on the following Monday. In other instances, there was a concomitance between failure and death of the principal. Pietro Emo died shortly after his bank was declared bankrupt in June 1375. Shortly after Antonio Miorati's death in 1424, his executors were forced to file for bankruptcy. Less than one year after the death of Andrea Priuli, also in 1424, the bank of his estate defaulted, and dissention among his surviving brothers came to a head. By contrast, Giovanni di Vettor Soranzo in 1468 resolved not to abandon his bank and his sons to their fate and the risk of a run at his death; by involving the highest organs of the state in bolstering public trust, he successfully prepared the passage of the management to his sons. Finally, two cases from the following century are noteworthy. During the night of 12 October 1526, only two and one-half years after opening, the banker Andrea Arimondo died, as Sanudo reports, "of melancholy of the bank, since he did not have the money to pay his creditors and was paying high interest on loans contracted via dry exchange." Shortly after this report was written, the bank failed.[8] Finally, when Vettor Pisani, of the Pisani-Tiepolo bank, the last survivor among the major Rialto banks, died in early July 1576, the immediate reaction was a turbulent run on the bank ("una gran furia"). The bank was saved only by the intervention of a lender of last resort: the Council of Ten ordered the mint (where the bank held government securities) to lend the bank 65,000 ducats for three months, at 4

---

[7]*Diarii*, 3:96–97.
[8]Ibid., 43:57, and Lane, "Venetian Bankers," 74–75.

percent interest. The bank survived only until 1584, when it succumbed to another run (provoking the tracts by the senator Tommaso Contarini, mentioned above).[9] The banker, not the bank, was thus the object of careful scrutiny; unless it was known that a succession was planned and organized, the impending death of the principal could awaken fears of a difficult execution of the testament. Not providing specifically for the continuity of management and responsibility was a serious weakness of Venetian practice and commercial law in this sector.

Endogenous factors are even more recurrent. They fall into three categories: the seasonal demand for money; the creation of chains of indebtedness; famine and high prices. Chance failures, independent of such conjunctural factors, are rare.

As we will see in Part III, the demand for money, in terms both of credit and of bank balances convertible into specie, was highest in July and August, when the galley fleets were preparing for departure to the Levant. Merchants made large cash withdrawals from banks in order to load specie and silver bars onto the galleys as an exchange commodity. The supply came from matured term payments and from Germans who brought silver and some gold to exchange for spices and cotton. Bankers were often the immediate suppliers of coin, for they often extended credit to the German importers, arranged for refining, consigned the bullion to the mint, collected the finished product, and distributed it among their clients. When the last galleys were out of the port, demand dropped sharply, but bank reserves stood at their lowest point in the year; the slightest demand could reveal their weakness. It is not surprising, therefore, to learn that almost all failures occurred between July and October (see below, App. B). Closely connected with demand was the bankers' role in the bullion trade and in direct or indirect speculation in silver; and that varied, as both cause and effect, according to the state's mint policy and the reaction to changes in the bimetallic ratio. The occasional prohibition of direct speculation by bankers could not have the hoped-for effect of stabilization of the bullion market. The condition of tight money which reigned in periods of banking crises during the fourteenth century, finally, meant high interest rates, as emerges from a heightened concern in those periods for the question of usury.

The concatenation of commercial failures with bank failures was a constant feature. Speculative manias involving commodities with unstable prices, such as precious and nonprecious metals or pepper and other spices, were essential ingredients of many of the financial crises that will be examined. War or the threat of war was sufficient to close off a flourishing foreign

---

[9]ASV, Council of Ten, Zecca, filza 2 (5 and 9 July 1576). On the failures of the Sanudo and Dolfin banks in 1569–70 and the Pisani-Tiepolo bank in 1584, see the important account by Brian Pullan in "The Occupations and Investments of the Venetian Nobility in the Middle and Late Sixteenth Century," in *Renaissance Venice*, ed. J. R. Hale (London, 1973), 383–85.

market suddenly with the result that stocks accumulated locally; gluts brought a fall in prices which, in turn, caused failures. Banks might have invested directly in such commodities, offered lines of credit to speculators, or furnished guarantees. While chain reactions are part of any local financial crisis, furthermore, the foreign exchange market brought distant markets close together. Thus in some periods it can be observed, if not satisfactorily explained, that a crisis in Florence, for example, paralleled a crisis in Venice.

Finally, famine, meaning exceptionally high wheat prices, was in several cases concomitant with a crisis in the banking system. Venice provisioned itself largely by sea—from the Black Sea (until 1453), from Apulia and Sicily—even after its expansion on the Terraferma. It was a credit-hungry trade; merchants required investment credit, and the state guaranteed them payment on schedule with bank guarantees (called "dette"). That meant the creation of float, since the state was ever behind in repaying the bankers. Moreover, Rialto bankers themselves invested in the importation of wheat, as we know from the exemption of that staple from the law of 1404 which tried to place a ceiling on the level of investment permitted to bankers.

These are the major recurrent elements in the banking crises of late medieval and Renaissance Venice. They are observable as parallel factors in the conjunctures; unfortunately, direct cause and effect relationships cannot be explained with the scattered nature of the extant documentation.

In what follows, I recount chronologically what can be known about specific runs, failures, and liquidations and about the conjuncture in which each banking crisis was produced. Treating causal and contributing factors, chains of indebtedness, and the reactions provoked by the failures constitutes the occasion to present broader sketches of Venetian financial history for those periods. The material is almost completely new for the fifteenth century; only one crash was well known heretofore, namely that of 1499–1500, described and analyzed by Frederic Lane. Regarding that episode, therefore, I have attempted to provide, not simply a reiteration of known material, but some new corroborative testimony, in particular that of the Milanese ambassador. For the fourteenth century, until about 1375, many of the legislative documents that will be used have been published, but even so they have been largely ignored; they are here contextualized.

ii. THE CRISIS OF 1340–1342

There were already several signs of trouble in the banking system, perhaps involving failures, in the thirteenth century. The bonding laws themselves would not have been proposed if serious problems had not arisen in 1270, 1285, and 1318, even though no further corroborative documentation has been uncovered for those years. The decade of the 1320s, moreover, was marked by the scarcity of full-weight grossi and the circulation of foreign, clipped, and sweated coins, and bankers had to be ordered to convert a deposit claim into specie within three days of the request and to refrain from sending the client from bank to bank for collection. In 1328, finally, the state placed a floor under the ducat when it was made legal tender for 24 grossi, in the face of the unforeseen and rapid fall of gold (see Vol. 1, chap. 15). The effect of all this on specific banks, however, is not known, even though trouble occurred which was serious enough to have prompted the discussion and passage by the Great Council of an important law on bankruptcy in 1330. The law established that "regular" deposits at banks be returned to their owners before the liquidation procedure, while deposits on current account and savings deposits be considered together with all the bank's liabilities.[10] It can only have been prompted by problems then encountered in the forced liquidation of one or more banks.

New possibilities for profits in a bullion market characterized by the onset of a fall in gold seem to have interested new people in taking up banking in the 1330s. Quite a few operators and many new names are recorded. An idea of the number of bankers operating simultaneously on the Rialto can best be had from the following list of persons identified as "banchiere" (one as "cambiatore") by Piero del Buono and Partners, who kept the accounts in Venice for the Florentine company of Duccio di Banchello and Banco Bencivenni and Partners in the years 1336–40.[11] There were eleven; the dates following the names are the limits of their activity on the Rialto, as far as has been determined on the basis of extant documentation:

> Piero Alberegno, active 1331–47
> Marco Arian, active 1333–38
> Bianco (Biancolino) Capello, 1338 (perhaps continuator of the
>   bank run 1319–21 by Pantaleone and Bertuccio Capello)
> Jacobello (Jacomello) Gabriel, active 1335–49
> Giannino Gritti, 1338 (only reference to him)
> Filippo Marmora, active 1340–43
> Nicoletto Onorato, 1340 (only reference to him)
> Jacomino da Mosto ("Pestamosto"), 1339–48 (continuator:
>   Armellino da Mosto, 1349–55)
> Piero Serafini, 1335–41
> Gianni (Giovanni) Stornado, active 1328–1342
> Marino Vendelino, 1336–42

The bankers most often used by this Florentine company were Jacomello Gabriel, Piero Serafini, Giovanni Stornado, and Marino Vendelino.

---

[10]Printed by Cassandro, *Le rappresaglie e il fallimento,* 139–41 (comment on 103). In 1327 a Nicoletto Michiel, factor of the campsor Lorenzo di Nicolò Diedo, fled Venice; the principal was imprisoned, but only until he paid the rent on the bank. ASV, AC, reg. 22, fol. 51v.

[11]ASF, Del Bene, 64, rubric. The names were also published by Mandich in "Monete di conto veneziane," 28 n. 29.

Giovanni Stornado was the principal banker on the marketplace; here he mediated payments in bank money for most of the over four hundred bills of exchange registered in the surviving ledger. Several of the payments to other bankers were also handled by him in bank money, in clear examples of interbank clearances. Of the eleven, three or four seem not to have survived the temporal limits of the account book (and the expulsion of Florentine merchants from Venice in early 1340). But other records name other bankers also active in the same four years — Giuliano Adoldo, Giovanni Baffo, Nicolò Lanzuolo, Nicoletto Michiel, Donato Quintavalle — so that at any given moment there were at least ten men or partnerships active on the Rialto. That number probably represents a high point; those who now rented a table from the state and set up business must have considered the chances for profits, especially in the burgeoning silver market, to be particularly good.

In the history of banking, the decade of the 1340s is best known for the failures of the great merchant-banking companies of Florence which Villani had called the "pillars of Christendom." In Venice, several of the very much smaller deposit banks of the Rialto also failed, in a wave that anticipated the Florentine bankruptcies, in part perhaps because Venice, as a bullion market, was more sensitive to the changes taking place worldwide in the bullion trade in reaction to the fall of gold. As always on the basis of scanty documentation, we know of seven or eight failures of Rialto banks between 1340 and 1342.

The first bank to fall was that of Donato Quintavalle, probably in early 1340. Donato's bank was closely tied to members of the Quintavalle family who were bullion merchants. Some were active in Ragusa (Dubrovnik) as buyers of Serbian silver, and Donato's uncle, the noble Catarino Quintavalle, and the latter's son Francesco were bullion merchants in Venice.[12] Donato was, as usual, forced to turn over his account books. While the accounts were being scrutinized, it was discovered that some illegal deposits had been made in his bank. That information must have been turned over directly to the Piovego, for the office charged at least three depositors with usury for having received interest at fixed rates, not tied, that is, to "danger and risk."

One of these loans, a deposit by a goldsmith, sheds some light on the kind of speculation in silver which was current. The defendant, Marco Giusto, declared that he had lent 200 ducats to Donato at the insistence of the latter's uncle, Catarino. The profit that had been promised him was tied

---

[12]Mosher Stuard, "The Adriatic Trade in Silver," 118–19. Francesco was charged in 1337 with failure to consign the quinto of his silver imports; ASV, Grazie, reg. 7, fol. 52. Catarino, found to have purchased 9,000 marks of silver in 1344, was also charged with incorrect consignments, in 1345; ibid., reg. 11, fols. 11v, 48v, 50.

to the yield that a quantity of silver, in which the banker wished to invest, would bring. The usury officials countered that they had it from credible witnesses that Marco was to earn 20 percent profit after two months. Whatever the truth, it is important here to emphasize that profits in silver were such that a banker would solicit interest-bearing loans (deposits) to use in speculation, that is, in the purchase, refinement, and resale of a highly risky commodity.[13] Quintavalle was not alone, but in competition with the whole Rialto; about the same time, another banker, Marco Storlado, who was also a refiner for the Commune, fled Venice taking with him silver he was to have refined. His son spent twenty-two months in prison in his stead.[14]

The principal failure of the year 1341 was that of Piero Serafini. When he fled Venice, the Sopraconsoli required his brother Giovanni to pay his debts. When that decision regarding liability was overturned by the Great Council in November, the liquidators were clearly frustrated, for one of them, the nobleman Nicoletto Polani, along with his son, resorted to physical aggression and struck Giovanni in the face.[15] When and to what extent the debts of the bank were paid is unknown. In time Piero returned to Venice, but after two decades the ignominy of bankruptcy continued to hang over him: as a "fugitivus" he was still denied access to the areas of the Rialto and San Marco.[16]

In Venice the climax in the series of bank failures was reached in 1342, whereas in Florence the series of bankruptcies of the smaller firms had just begun in late 1341.[17] Smaller Venetian banks like that of Marco "Gallina" Bobiço[18] and Marco and Guido Michiel[19] defaulted in 1342 — even though

[13]Mueller, *Procuratori di San Marco,* 310–13, from ASV, Grazie, reg. 8, fols. 60, 63v, 67; the first regards the silver speculation, the last provides the indication that Donato had failed.

[14]ASV, AC, reg. 3642, fol. 15; at the date of the sentence, 10 September 1341, the son had already spent twenty-two months in jail in place of his father. The creditors of Marco agreed that he should be released. Assuming the accuracy of the information, Marco must have failed in December 1339. In July 1338 he is called campsor in Piazza San Marco; ibid., reg. 3641, fol. 31v.

[15]Ibid., reg. 3642, fols. 21, 23.

[16]He had been fined 25 lire di piccoli by the Sopraconsoli "quia existens sub iugo ipsorum officialium ivit in Rivoalto"; he asked for a grazia as "pauperimus." ASV, Grazie, reg. 14, fol. 142v (1360). On the penalties, see Cassandro, *Le rappresaglie e il fallimento,* 98–99.

[17]Armando Sapori, *La crisi delle compagnie mercantili dei Bardi e dei Peruzzi* (Florence, 1926), 140. Brucker mentions the existence of an alphabetical list of bankrupts, chronologically undifferentiated but ranging from 1333 to 1346, which names 350 under the letters A to S. Gene A. Brucker, *Florentine Politics and Society, 1343–1378* (Princeton, 1962), 16–17 and n. 64.

[18]Marco Bobiço was a debtor of the noble Marino Magno, weigher at the mint, who seems himself to have failed (in his testament of 25 January 1342 he mentions that the Sopraconsoli had sold his house at S. Margherita — obviously for debts); the estate accounts record the installments "pro parte debiti Marci Bobici canpsoris" paid in the decade following Magno's death (July 1344). ASV, PSM, Ultra, b. 177. Inexplicably, a man with the same name and nickname, also "campsor," is found dealing in silver in 1357 and 1366. AC, reg. 3642, fol. 48v, and PSM, Misti, b. 141, commis. Andrea Bollani, reg., under those years.

[19]*DQ,* 1:11, 13, docs. 32, 38 (6 and 13 November, for Guido), and 1:14, doc. 42 (22 November, for Marco "dictus Blanchus"). Guido Michiel continued to have trouble with his

we find banks bearing similar names again after a few years. A third smaller bank, that of the nobleman Filippo Marmora and Brothers, also failed in 1342.[20] But the failures that must have been most felt in that year were those of Marino Vendelino and especially of Giovanni di Marco Stornado.

Vendelino was probably established at the Rialto by 1336, for in early 1337 he appears in several accounts of the company of Duccio di Banchello. There he was involved, however, primarily in cash transactions.[21] He, too, speculated in silver, for there is a charge against him of buying Hungarian silver at the home of a Ragusan, that is, not at the authorized bullion market.[22] When he failed, the Consoli dei Mercanti constrained the guarantors of the bank to pay specific claims.[23]

Giovanni Stornado, a non-noble despite his surname, was both a refiner and a banker, the foremost one, having been in operation at least since 1328.[24] As seen reflected in the accounts of two Florentine firms from 1336 to 1340, Stornado was very active in mediating payments among Florentine merchant bankers especially as dealers in bills of exchange; in that specific role the banker profited from the oscillating agio between bank money and specie.[25] Furthermore, he was in the best position to mediate the huge payments sent from Florence to pay for mercenaries during the Scaliger War (1336–39). In 1341 (or early 1342) he was riding high enough in his role that he applied for admission into the Great Council, but the petition for recognition as a noble failed to pass, and he was fined, as by law, 300 lire for having tried and failed.[26]

---

creditors; an application for safe-conduct to reach an accord was denied him on 9 June 1343 (ibid., 1:52, doc. 172). It remains unclear what connection, if any, there was between these two and Nicoletto Michiel, active on the Rialto from 1337 to 1358 (e.g., ASV, Grazie, reg. 11, fol. 93v; a homonym had failed in 1327, as mentioned above), or to the Guido Michiel who in 1345–46 as silver merchant was in continual trouble with the Silver Office and the mint and at one point was imprisoned at the request of his creditors (ibid., fols. 11v, 15v, 34, 70, 77v).

[20]*DQ*, 1:10, doc. 29 (23 October). It is possible that there were many more failures, also of nonbankers, but extant records begin only in the fall of 1342. See, for example, the safe-conduct granted to Giovanni and Gabriele Natale on 23 November; ibid., 1:14, doc. 43.

[21]ASF, Del Bene, 64, fols. 8v, 66v, 67, 71v, 139v, 145v, 157v.

[22]ASV, Grazie, reg. 8, fol. 43. He also had to defend himself against a false charge of adultery; AC, reg. 3648, fols. 18v, 28v.

[23]On appeal, the guarantors were able to free themselves from the obligation to pay for a deposit "ad lucrum" made by Elisabetta Querini. ASV, AC, reg. 3642, fol. 44.

[24]In 1340 he was fined by the Giustizieri Vecchi in a case regarding the provisioning of his "fornelli" with firewood; ASV, Grazie, reg. 8, fol. 53v.

[25]ASF, Del Bene, 64, where he is mentioned on practically every page as mediating payments; in this "libro nero" there is no current account opened to Stornado — it seems to have been in the lost "libro nero F" or in the "libro bianco." Also Armando Sapori, ed., *Libro giallo della compagnia dei Covoni* (Milan, 1970) and the introduction by Guilio Mandich.

[26]The family belonged to Venice's most ancient nobility (see Gerhard Rösch, *Der Venezianische Adel bis zur Schließung des Großen Rats. Zur Genese einer Führungsschicht* [Sigmaringen, 1989], index), but this Giovanni di Marco was obviously part of a cadet line left out in the

Very likely Venice's controversy with Florence over the latter's debit balance remaining after the Scaliger War and the resulting expulsion hurt Giovanni Stornado particularly. A hint of that is extant. In 1339 Lappo Amidei of Florence, in preparation for his forced departure for Padua, along with many other Florentine merchants, withdrew the considerable sum of 3,300 ducats from the Stornado bank and invested it with Alemanno Alemanni, a naturalized Venetian who had arrived from Florence early in the century. That action was not a sign of distrust in Stornado but was a response to Venice's decision to expel Florentine merchants. In fact, Amidei wrote from Padua authorizing Alemanni to invest the money in a trip of his own to Cyprus, probably a speculation in bullion, which he did, although it was illegal for a citizen to do business with foreign capital — especially Florentine capital at that moment.[27] A sudden void and considerable confusion created by the expulsion of the Florentines and the export of their capital must have aggravated an already difficult situation on the local money market.

In October 1342 Giovanni Stornado was forced to close his bank and flee Venice ("se absentavit pro debitis"). On 23 October he was granted a first safe-conduct (of only eight days' duration) in order to come to terms with his creditors — the same day as the concession to Filippo Marmora. The safe-conduct was renewed four times,[28] but the outcome of the affair, how soon and to what extent Stornado was able to satisfy his creditors, is not known. Nor is there any sure connection between Giovanni and the silver merchant Marco Stornado, who, also in 1342, was fined and then imprisoned for occult sales of silver and for failure to consign the quinto to the mint.[29]

It was surely no exaggeration to assert, as did the Senate in a delibera-

---

process that closed the Great Council. Probably owing to the existence of homonyms (there were at least two others, both noble), this man is always identified as a campsor. ASV, AC, reg. 3642, fol. 27v (28 February 1342). For the law of 1316 permitting applications under the grazia procedure, see Stanley Chojnacki, "In Search of the Venetian Nobility," in Hale, *Renaissance Venice*, 53.

[27]ASV, Grazie, reg. 9, fol. 19 (petition: 2 September 1341; first vote by Quarantia: 14 August 1342). Two months after leaving, Amidei wrote from Padua with instructions to "tenere et traficare cum suis denariis." Alemanno qd. Donato Alemanni, citizen de intus in 1320, de extra in 1328, must have arrived about 1303. His son Donato, a refiner of bullion, opened a bank at the Rialto at the latest in 1350.

[28]*DQ*, 1:10, 11, 13 (the last extension was dated 20 November).

[29]Since he was able to pay only part of the fine, Marco Stornado was imprisoned for two years before he escaped and fled Venice. Application for a grazia in ASV, Grazie, reg. 11, fol. 69v (3 April 1346). Other persons named Marco Stornado or Storlado (surnames that were sometimes but not always interchangeable) were active bankers in 1349–56 and 1362–69; one of them was the Marco (qd. Andrea) Stornado, campsor, who was coopted into the Great Council in 1381. His son, Alvise qd. Marco, had the name Stornado formally changed to Storlado in 1417, in order to avoid further confusion. Ibid., reg. 21, fol. 2. See also Maria Teresa Todesco, "Aggregati ed esclusi: Le cooptazioni al Maggior Consiglio al tempo della guerra di Chioggia" (laurea thesis, University of Venice, 1986–87).

tion of 3 November, that the banks of moneychangers were "in a weak condition."[30] Most of them, including the principal ones, were no longer operating.

It is impossible to attribute this rash of at least seven or eight bank failures over the short space of two to three years to specific causal factors, given the terse and often indirect documentation extant. As mentioned, the crisis on the Rialto anticipated the bankruptcies in Florence, where the large merchant-banking firms held out until the Peruzzi failed in 1343, followed by the Acciaiuoli, while the Bardi survived until 1346. The causes of these failures (the suspension of payments by Edward III, the indebtedness of a belligerent Florentine state to the banks, the fall of gold) need not be repeated here.[31] But there are points of contact with the economic situation in Venice.

In sketching the background of the crisis in Venice, attention will be given to three major factors, namely, (1) the grain trade and famine, (2) war, and (3) the fall of gold, speculation in bullion, and monetary policy; all these factors, furthermore, were intimately tied to the foreign exchange market.

First, Venice had to import wheat from Apulia, Sicily, and the Black Sea, since it had no political control over the hinterland (the first acquisitions of Terraferma provinces date from 1339, at the conclusion of the Scaliger War). Just the same, when famine struck north-central Italy generally and Florence in particular between 1338 and 1341,[32] Venice was also severely affected. The city's annona registered surpluses in 1338 and 1340, famine and high prices in 1339, 1341 (until April), and 1342. Famine years alternated with the occasional glut, provoked in part by the premiums offered by the annona to grain merchants. Gluts meant spoiling stocks and the forced sale of excess surpluses, a form of taxation.[33] The importers played off the free market and the annona: the state, in order to create an incentive, guaranteed a high price floor to importers; when market prices

---

[30]"Cum banchi campssorum presencialiter in debili condicione consistant." ASV, SM, reg. 20, fol. 95 (3 November), printed in A. Scialoija, "Un precedente medioevale dei 'pools' marittimi," in *Studi in memoria di B. Scorza* (Rome, 1940), 758 n.

[31]See Vol. 1, pp. 439–42, 452–55. The most recent treatments of these failures are Carlo M. Cipolla, "Uomini duri," in his *Tre storie extra vaganti* (Bologna, 1994), 9–55, which regards members of the Bardi firm in the 1340s who concerned themselves, among other things, with counterfeiting coins, and Edwin S. Hunt, *The Medieval Super-companies: A Study of the Peruzzi Company of Florence* (New York, 1994). The latter (pp. 179–81) takes exception to the affirmation (Vol. 1, pp. 440–41) that Florentine merchant bankers insisted on particularly favorable exchange rates, as long as they could, in their dealings with the English Crown; or, more correctly, he dismisses the fall of gold as irrelevant in the rise and decline of the Peruzzi company.

[32]Giuliano Pinto, ed., *Il libro del Biadaiolo: Carestia e annona a Firenze dalla metà del '200 al 1348* (Florence, 1978), 100. Idem, *La Toscana nel tardo Medio Evo: Ambiente, economia rurale, società* (Florence, 1982), 335.

[33]For forced sales in these years, see, for example, ASV, MC, Spiritus, fols. 110v (22 June 1340) and 127 (30 December 1342).

fell, merchants sold to the state, which absorbed the losses, some of which it tried to recoup via the highly unpopular forced sales. That this was the system was openly admitted but also criticized.[34] It is not surprising, therefore, that the reigning doge, Bartolomeo Gradenigo (1339–42), was reported to be much loved by the nobility but very unpopular with the people.[35]

Surpluses created serious problems from May to December 1341, when export licenses were granted.[36] In that year construction was begun on a huge new granary next to San Marco. In April 1342 an inventory revealed that of 370,000 measures (staia) of wheat on hand, less than 100,000 were judged good, the rest mediocre, bad, or very bad.[37] By September there was again dearth.[38] The deficits run by the communal Grain Office (then a combination of annona and a kind of public bank, as we shall see below) nearly brought it to bankruptcy in 1343–45.

Rialto bankers were probably involved in the grain trade directly (that would be the case in the following century) or at least indirectly, to the extent that they granted and guaranteed loans to the importers in this notoriously credit-hungry and risky trade. Wholesale merchants stood to make handsome profits, but prices could reverse direction suddenly, and the state's premium incentive was probably not a total guarantee of their safety.

The second general factor was Venice's alliance with Florence in the war against Scaliger Verona (1336–39). The war proved advantageous to Venice, which gained its first extensive territories on the Terraferma, less so to Florence. Florence, whose sights were set on the subjugation of Lucca, was obliged by the alliance to pay for the armies of German mercenaries fighting in the Veneto; this meant flows of specie from Florence to Venice.[39] The Commune of Florence established special committees, the "Dieci da Vinegia," the "Seidici da Vinegia," which had the task of raising money, usually via costly loans, and transmitting it to Venice—in amounts of as

---

[34]An example: when the importer Marco Falier failed in 1340, the state agreed to buy up the 7,000 staia of wheat he had just received from the Black Sea, at specified prices deemed equitable by the grain officials upon inspection of the shipment. ASV, Grazie, reg. 8, fol. 77 (29 September). For clear statements of how the system functioned and of its consequences, see MC, Spiritus, fols. 115 (15 April 1341) and 123 (15 September 1342); cf. Cessi in *RES,* civ n. 1, cviii n. 1.

[35]BMV, Lat. X, 136 (3026), fol. 47. Cf. Roberto Cessi and Fanny Bennato, eds., *Venetiarum historia vulgo Petro Iustiniano Iustiniani filio adiudicata* (Venice, 1964), 224, 229.

[36]There are many licenses in ASV, Grazie, end of reg. 8 and the beginning of reg. 9; cf., for example, reg. 9, fol. 16 (12 August 1341).

[37]ASV, MC, Spiritus, fol. 120v.

[38]The deliberations of the Great Council in these years reflect serious preoccupation with the problem of provisioning. Importers tended to wait for higher prices; when prices fell and their stocks were threatened with spoilage, they sold to the state at the guaranteed price (thus in a deliberation of 15 April 1341). See also Cessi in *RES,* civ and passim.

[39]On the war and its costs, see also Luigi Simeoni's introduction to Jacopo Piacentino's *Cronaca della guerra Veneto-Scaligera* (Venice, 1931), 12–13.

high as 100,000 florins at a time, for a total of some 600,000 florins. The ledger of the Covoni company reflects how the exchange market and the firms operating in Venice were used by these committees to move coin and credit (see below, Chap. 8, sec. v). Venice had to advance some of the money, and at war's end (Venice had made a separate peace, and Florence could only follow suit) Florence still owed some 37,000 ducats.[40] Florence was unable to pay that relatively small debt, and it became for both cities a pretext for breaking off diplomatic and commercial relations. As mentioned, Venice expelled Florentine merchants in February 1340 — though they had begun leaving earlier — and Florence retaliated with reprisals. All in all, it seems that a very active market in specie and bills of exchange, on which Venetian bankers earned agios and commissions if they did nothing other than mediate payments, suddenly reversed itself: capital was pulled out, trade between the two cities came to a standstill. Neither could afford to hold out. Florence sent representatives to negotiate a settlement with Venice in late November 1341; the Senate announced on 20 December that an accord had been reached, bringing an end to reprisals; Florence ratified the agreement the next day. But the hiatus in commercial and banking relations had lasted very nearly two years.[41]

Although Venice did not organize a special office similar to the Dieci or Sedici da Vinegia in Florence, it also raised voluntary loans from local bankers. The organizer, perhaps unofficial, was the nobleman Giovanni Papaçiça, of a minor family, a sometime mintmaster and sometime campsor, who raised the loans from other bankers and moneychangers and passed them on to the Commune. He personally borrowed 6,000 ducats and lent the sum, in turn, to the Treasury. Just how much the voluntary system garnered in all and how it was repaid is not recorded.[42]

At the same time, some potential profits and possibly unsettling cash flows continued between Tuscany and the Veneto. In July 1341 Florence was reduced to buying Lucca from Mastino della Scala of Verona for 250,000 florins, and the sum was paid in full by the end of 1345. That money must also have come through Venice or somehow affected it, for Verona was not a money market and could hardly have handled such sums.

Taken together, between 1337 and 1345 probably something nearing 1 million florins passed from Florence to or through Venice, only for a war and a purchase, both useless to Florence. Not surprisingly, Giovanni Villani reported in 1341 that there was "almost no specie to be found in Florence."[43]

---

[40]A contemporary chronicle relates that at one point Venice had advanced 60,000 ducats "ex propria animi largitate." Marghereta Merores, "Un codice veneziano del secolo XIV nell'Haus-Hof- und Staatsarchiv di Vienna," *NAV,* n.s., 29 (1915): 164.

[41]*LCR,* 2, lib. 3, docs. 442, 559; summarized in *RES,* lxxxviii n. 4.

[42]ASV, Grazie, reg. 8, fols. 2v (15 December 1338) and 37 (which refers to the loan of 6,000 ducats from Lotto da Montagnana).

[43]The best account is Sapori, *La crisi delle compagnie mercantili,* 107–40, 158–59. The price for Lucca had to be paid in full also because Mastino della Scala held Florentine hostages to

Much of this money was handled by the exchange market in Venice, where the Rialto banks held the current accounts of the Florentine cambisti.

The libro giallo of the Covoni shows how active Florentines were on the Venetian exchange market in the years 1336–39. Some sixty individuals and companies are named. The Covoni alone offered loans in Florence on the exchange with Venice ranging between 1,700 and 4,000 ducats per month. Interest rates, based on fluctuating exchange rates, averaged 12–14 percent per year. Venetian deposit bankers handled the accounts of both Venetian and Florentine operators; such turnover meant the chance for earning commissions and for profiting from the agio between specie and bank money. The sudden departure of the Florentines must have tightened the credit market drastically and reduced the opportunities of the Rialto bankers for making profits.[44]

The third general problem, speculation in bullion, was caused by the fall of gold and led to record imports of gold and silver to and through Venice, Italy's largest bullion market. Gold had peaked by 1328 and thereafter began to decline rapidly — by 26 percent over the next two decades. Silver rose and became a commodity of particular interest to bankers; it was they who made possible the preparation of the galleys that carried previously unheard-of quantities of silver to the Levant, by granting credits, supervising the refinement of bullion, and organizing the collection of specie at the mint.

As we have seen, the first banker to fail, in 1340, belonged to a family that had invested heavily in Ragusan silver (and continued to do so); the second was also a refiner, who fled Venice with the bullion he was to have refined. The demand for silver in the Levant grew rapidly and consistently; in 1342 six merchant galleys were sent to the Black Sea area to trade silver for slaves and furs at the recently established Venetian colony in Tana (Azov), while seven were sent to Cyprus, the intermediary for trade with Moslem Egypt (for direct trade had been forbidden by the papacy). That year four major bankers still active on the Rialto, led by Giovanni Stornado, failed; at least Stornado, if not also others, failed after the galleys had departed.

Opportunities for profit in silver were so great, despite the failures, that in 1343 the Senate authorized silver to be sent not only on the planned sixteen galleys but also on round ships, albeit escorted by the patrol fleet

---

that end; Roberto Barducci, "Politica e speculazione finanziaria a Firenze dopo la crisi del primo Trecento (1343–1358)," *ASI* 137 (1979): 187, 191–92. See also below, Chap. 8, sec. v.

[44]A reflection of tight money may be found in the maximum rates quoted on local colleganze, tied to yields earned by bankers, in the crucial years. A contract of December 1339 which gives Pietro Albergno's yield as the standard sets the maximum at 10 percent; a contract of exactly one year later which quotes the yield of the campsor Giovanni Baffo sets the maximum at 20 percent. But so many factors come into play in such loan agreements that it is best not to lay too much weight on such evidence. Luciano Gargan, *Cultura e arte nel Veneto al tempo del Petrarca* (Padua, 1978), 28–29, taken from ASV, CIN, b. 180, acts of Santo Viviano.

(see Vol. 1, pp. 367–70). Speculation increased still more in 1343 and in 1344, until news arrived that the Tatar ruler had destroyed the Venetian and Genoese colonies in Tana. Optimistic forecasts were shattered. Bullion merchants who had invested on the basis of those forecasts were very likely hurt, but now there is no evidence of involvement by surviving banks. As regards earlier bankers, on the other hand, silver was surely a major factor in their failure, as in the weakness of the survivors, if only because of overextension of credit on the books to speculators.

How might the fall of gold have affected local bankers? Shrewd entrepreneurs should have foreseen the fall and might have turned it to a profit. But there are many intangibles. Venetians were extremely active in exporting silver to the Levant, in all possible forms: various kinds of coin, large certified bars, and small silver bars called "summi" destined for the market in Tana. Rialto bankers were pivotal in the speculative cycle of buying, refining, and exporting bullion. They not only had a near monopoly on buying bullion imported to the city, but they often refined it, consigned it to the mint, and collected the resulting specie or certified bars for their clients. The trade was highly speculative and risky, all the more now with the reversal in trend of bimetallic ratios. Some might have made long-term investments or held credits in gold which lost value, or had debts in silver which would cost them more to repay. Some may have sought to remedy their situation by defying the regulations more than usual, or perhaps the authorities merely applied sanctions with greater persistence than usual. In any case, the "Grazie" series is full of petitions for pardons from convictions against persons — largely bankers and bullion merchants tied to bankers — who had sought to circumvent the numerous ordinances by selling or buying silver outside the official market ("furtively"), by tampering with the purity of the refined silver, or by failing to consign the proper amount (a quinto or a decimo) to the mint. Confusion might have been increased by conflicts of interest, since many of the silver brokers nominated by the government beginning in 1341 were active silver merchants.[45]

On the monetary front, the divergence between the official and the market prices or rates for the conversion of the gold ducat also created problems. Evidence comes from a deliberation of 11 April 1342 regarding the revenues and expenditures of government offices and magistracies. Many officials, says the deliberation, take in gold ducats but must make certain payments in silver; to do so, they buy silver with their ducats on the open market, profiting personally from the agio ("lazium," "l'azio") while the state received no benefit from the operation, thus the complaint. Officials were ordered, therefore, to buy needed silver coin at the Grain Office, which always had plenty ("que semper de ipsis habet in maxima quantitate"); the grain officials, then in serious economic straits, were to provide

[45]*DQ*, 1:5, doc. 11; 1:39, doc. 138.

the silver to government offices without agio ("sine lazio") and — presumably — go on the open market and profit from the agio. What this seems to have meant in practice was that the Grain Office paid out 64 soldini for one ducat (the official price) and then turned around and bought 68 soldini from the bankers with the same ducat, thereby earning, for the Commune, a profit of about 6 percent on the operation.[46] Permitting such a high differential to persist was bound to promote speculation among private individuals as well as among bankers and moneychangers and aggravate problems of circulation.

Similarly, civil servants would be very concerned about just how they themselves were paid. Only three weeks before this law was passed, Marino Falier, for example, then podestà in Treviso, claimed that his salary, owed him in ducats, had been paid him in silver ("in monetis"). He petitioned the Senate that, if he was to be paid in silver, he was also owed the "laçium." His petition was rejected, but it reflects an understandably general concern for a chance to increase earnings by 6 percent — or not to lose that much.[47]

Despite the great abundance of gold and silver in circulation, the existence of an agio might have offered the occasion to some to raise interest rates. In any case, there was in these very years a particular preoccupation with the question of usury. In 1340 a committee was named to study the problem. Among those elected was Marino Falier, who was then borrowing large sums of money in the form of local colleganze at 6 and 7 percent. The Piovego, the usury magistracy, became especially active in prosecuting offenders. Those sentenced promptly appealed for pardons. More than half of the ninety-seven appeals found are concentrated in these years: twenty-four in 1340 and 1341, twenty-six between 1342 and 1346.[48] These cases reflect nervousness about legitimacy in lending and probably about rates of interest.

The reader may legitimately wonder how this bleak picture of the early 1340s can be reconciled with the rosy picture that Gino Luzzatto painted of the very same years. There was, to be sure, a building boom. Just to mention public commissions, one side of the ducal palace was being extensively changed in order to expand the hall of the Great Council to accommodate the enlarged membership that resulted from the constitu-

---

[46]*RES,* doc. 149 and p. cvii; also *PMV,* lxix. A good analysis of the provision is Roberto Cessi, "Studi sulla moneta veneta: II. La coniazione del ducato aureo," *Economia: Rassegna mensile di politica economica* 2 (1924): 49–50. See also Vol. 1, p. 332, app. D, and tables 19 and 20, pp. 394–95.

[47]ASV, SM, reg. 20, fol. 43 (23 March) and Vittorio Lazzarini, *Marino Faliero* (Florence, 1963), 74–75. At that time Venice had ruled Treviso for barely three years; it quickly became a tradition to pay rectors in the Terraferma in silver coin, even when their salaries were stated in gold-based money of account, as was the case in Florence.

[48]Seventy percent of all appeals are concentrated in the years 1334–46; see Mueller, *Procuratori di San Marco,* 269–70, 285–86; for an important usury law of 1333, see ibid., 267–68.

tional reform known as the Serrata. Nearby, the huge new grain warehouse was being built. These projects surely increased employment, offered occasions for profitable investment, and probably heightened the feeling of a booming economy, already present in the bullion market. Luzzatto then points to market prices of government obligations as another sign of prosperity. It is true that the price of obligations rose from 96 to 100 percent of par in 1340–41 and reached 102 in 1344. But it rose for two reasons: first, because the state was amortizing numerous issues at 100 percent, and second, because of the atmosphere of financial uneasiness. Investors could no longer trust the banks, which were failing one by one, and the Florentine cambisti, who had readily invested funds in loans, were absent from the city in 1340–41; the only handy refuge was the market for government credits, where the price naturally rose.[49]

As is so often the case, what is a boom for one is a bust for another, or, better, every boom at some point turns into a bust for some. Such was the case in the agitated early 1340s.

iii. PLAGUE, WAR, AND CREDIT CRISES, 1348–1363

The survival rate of bankers — or at least of banks — during the Black Death, to the extent that it can be observed, is surprising. At least five banks survived: the nobleman Giacomello Gabriel, active on the Rialto with his brothers Maffeo and Andrea from about 1335 until about 1349, while his brothers carried on until 1360; the brothers Giovanni and Marino Baffo, of whom at least Marino survived and continued in partnership with Marco Trevisan until 1355; of the da Mosto family, immigrants from Lodi, Jacopo seems to have died in 1348, but Armellino, presumably his brother, carried on from 1349 until he was murdered in 1355; Pietro de Mortisse, an immigrant from Padua who was a moneychanger at San Marco from 1343 to 1348, saved himself from the contagion by fleeing the city during the plague (thereby also avoiding imprisonment for a criminal conviction regarding his banking operation) and established himself on the Rialto from 1349 to 1364; and finally Andreolo and Alvise Sanador, members of a citizen family and active at least from 1345 until their failure in 1359. Others seem to begin in 1348, as though they had found new opportunities by taking the places of those deceased. The Florentines Alessandro Agolante and Donato Alemanni, who merged their operations in 1353, were new entries.

Very soon after the onslaught of the plague, which must have carried away one-third to one-half of the population, Venice undertook its third war against Genoa. It was costly: in four years contributors to the public debt had to pay 15 percent of their assessed patrimony; the market price

---

[49]Luzzatto, *Storia,* 135–39, and *PRV,* cxxviii–ix.

of government obligations dropped from 98 to 77 over the period, even though the state continued to pay interest with perfect regularity.[50] Peace was signed on 1 June 1355. Only then could galley voyages with Romania be resumed, but only two galleys were sent there that summer.[51]

Not long after the last galleys had departed, probably carrying with them much of the remaining liquidity in the city, the bank of Marino Baffo and Marco Trevisan failed when the principals fled, allegedly absconding with 20,000 ducats. The situation was serious enough that a reward of 500 lire was offered to whoever brought them to justice; a fine of the same amount and a six-month prison term were imposed against anyone who failed to turn them in or report what they knew. The system seems to have worked, for Marco Trevisan was in prison some months later — when Baffo and Marco's brother, Stefano, were charged with providing the "iron instruments" necessary for his escape.[52]

The bank, which had been active on the Rialto since about 1340, when it was run by Marino Baffo's brother Giovanni, was unable to pay in full. The accounts of a client, Andrea Malipiero, who had an interest-bearing deposit (or a loan "at profit" [in vadagno]) in the bank, allow one to follow the liquidation procedure. The Sopraconsoli had jurisdiction and paid installments for each former banker separately. The client received 65 percent of his 250 ducat credit. He notes that the Signoria then made an accord with Baffo and Trevisan that they repay the balance due (35 percent) on the total debt in installments of 250 ducats per year. Malipiero then seems to have made a separate deal by which he received a payoff of 28 ducats and agreed to write off the balance (59.5 ducats) as a loss.[53]

When this bank closed in the fall of 1355, liquidity in the city must

---

[50]Luzzatto, in *PRV,* p. c, where the author states that levies totaled "40 percent," whereby he should have said 40 lire d'estimo per 100 lire a grossi; 40 divided by 2.611 = 15.3 percent (for an explanation of this problem, see below, App. D, sec. i).

[51]ASV, SM, reg. 27, fols. 14v–15v, 18v, 19v–20r. By contrast, even during the war with Genoa, Venice was able to continue shipping silver to Cyprus; see Grazie, reg. 13, fols. 28 (25 October 1353), 40v (3 May 1354); AC, reg. 3642/II, fol. 8 (11 August 1354).

[52]ASV, Quarantia Criminal, b. 14bis (Sanudo's notes on lost registers of the Quarantia), fol. 21 (25 October, a Sunday; the printed version gives 15 October). Sanudo noted the proceedings carefully, indicating that the first provisions made against the bankers passed unanimously, whereas the proposal to give the Collegio special authority to interrogate them once arrested took five ballots before it passed, 17 to 12, with 3 neutral. On the other hand, it might be more credible to understand the alleged absconding with 20,000 ducats as a "flight with assets" than an estimation of liabilities of the bank at 20,000 ducats. The case against Stefano Trevisan: ibid., fol. 21v (18 December). In the printed version of Sanudo's *Vite de' duchi di Venezia,* Rerum Italicarum Scriptores, vol. 22 (Milan, 1733), 782, there is only a short summary of the case. A Stefano Trevisan was executed for having taken part in the Falier conspiracy; see Lazzarini, *Marino Faliero,* index.

[53]ASV, PSM, Misti, b. 94, commis. Andrea Malipiero, vacchetta, fol. 11. The final payment is undated.

have been seriously reduced. Interest rates clearly had risen, to such a point as to inflame a new discussion about usury and pawnbroking in 1356 and 1357. In 1356 a state bank was first proposed before the Senate.

The controversy over usury involved both theory and practice. A proposal of December 1356 stated that interest rates in Venice were as high as 25, 30, or even 40 percent per year, whereas in the neighboring territories money was being lent "at usury" of only 10 or 12 percent. What was being proposed was to invite pawnbrokers into Venice as a way of controlling interest rates via the negotiation of a charter or condotta, probably with Jews (or with Christians and Jews alike, for there were still Christian usurers active in nearby Mestre). When that proposal failed to pass, another was presented which criticized usury, illegal exchange, and other contracts and asked that a committee be nominated to study the matter. The committee's proposal, passed in March 1357, overturned traditional Venetian practice by bluntly forbidding the local coll_eganza, on which the interest was tied to the market rate current at maturity (as defined by named banking operations), as well as all dubious forms of foreign exchange. The law was so restrictive that it could only have tightened the credit market and liquidity still further — and in fact it was revoked six months later.[54]

The traditional formula for avoiding the charge of usury by tying a loan to a future, uncertain rate came under indirect attack also in the proposal for a state bank. The "bancum per Comune" would flank, not replace, private banks; it would limit itself to clearing functions through giro; it would be specifically forbidden from accepting deposits that participated in the profits of the bank — as private bankers were wont to accept, thereby determining that strange phenomenon, the "future, uncertain market rate." The proposal failed, but the preoccupation regarding that kind of credit was voiced again a few months later in the above-mentioned radical usury law.

The same day on which the public bank was proposed (15 December 1356), the Senate passed legislation showing its concern for a seemingly uncontrolled silver market. "In order to avoid the frauds that are continuously being committed in silver transactions," the law forbade forestalling and any kind of combination in restraint of trade which would allow a merchant to see, analyze, or purchase silver brought to Venice before it was refined. Nor could refiners make partnerships with importers or buyers. Refiners were to turn in weekly reports to the Silver Office, giving the name of the client and the amounts of silver and gold separated and refined. Clearly, the state wanted to have complete information on imports and exports, to be sure it was collecting the quinto and able to provision the mint. But the preoccupation was a continuing one in these years.[55]

---

[54]Mueller, "Les prêteurs juifs," 1280.

[55]*PMV,* doc. 125, also in Princivalli, *Capitolare degli Ufficiali sopra Rialto,* cap. 178. Four

Hardly had peace been established with Genoa when Venice was at war with Hungary, the result of which was the loss of Dalmatia in 1357. Increased expenditures and reduced revenues created serious budgetary problems: a chronicler reported that the state Treasury was practically empty ("erraria publica diminuita").[56] The inevitable financial crisis came to a head beginning in 1359. Actual failures spawned a cycle of frauds — fraudulent bankruptcy of the debtors of the bankrupt, fraudulent claims to be creditors of those who had failed. In order to meet their debts, the insolvent had to stand by and watch the Sopraconsoli sell their real property and other assets at auction. Provisions concerning bankruptcy made by the Great Council were numerous but seemingly ineffectual.[57] Not surprisingly, the bankers' tables on the Rialto could not long remain immune from the general contagion; four bankers failed in 1359, a major failure occurred in 1361, a lesser one (the former's debtor) in 1363. The documentation provides only sparse details about the failures.

The first operation to fail was a moneychanger's table at San Marco run by Francesco Spirito. He was arrested by the Consoli dei Mercanti, but on the way to prison he convinced the accompanying officer to let him stop off at home — whence he escaped and fled, "to the detriment of his creditors."[58]

Shortly thereafter, in July 1359, followed the moneychangers Andreolo Saimben and Andreolo Sanador. Both were speculators in silver; one used the other as straw man in silver purchases. Sanador admitted that he was a debtor to the mint for the quinto for a total of 140 marks of silver since November 1354; he asked for leniency, because of his "many misfortunes" and "considering his poverty."[59]

Late in the same year the bank of Francesco Iuda (or Giuda) failed. Francesco, a member of a family that had immigrated from Florence, had operated a bank only since about 1355, in partnership with his noble father-in-law Pietro da Mosto.[60]

The bank of Alvise Viaro and Partners failed in August 1361. It had been in operation at least since 1353 and must have been an important bank, for "the whole city" was somehow involved in its assets and lia-

---

people falsely accused Marco Bobizo, campsor, of exporting silver "ad furthonum." ASV, AC, reg. 3642, fol. 48v (3 February 1357). Unsupervised purchases were decried a few months later in the Quarantia; see Zecca, reg. 6bis, fol. 29v (5 May).

[56]Cessi and Bennato, *Venetiarum historia*, 252–53.

[57]ASV, MC, Novella, fols. 67 (17 February), 69r–v (15 and 29 September), 70 (6 October). One of the deliberations of 15 September was raised to the status of a statute; it is printed in Cassandro, *Le rappresaglie e il fallimento*, 145, doc. 14.

[58]ASV, AC, reg. 3642, fol. 79v (3 July 1359).

[59]ASV, Grazie, reg. 14, fol. 83v (29 July 1359).

[60]Ibid., fol. 111v (January 1360); this document, which involves two clients of the bank, reveals that Iuda's account books were in the office of the Consoli, who had to approve a clearing operation, whereby it can be assumed that the bank had failed.

bilities.[61] Provision had therefore to be made to restrict the conflict-of-interest legislation so that the Consoli could hear the case. At the same time, the jurisdictional powers ("arbitrium") of the Consoli were increased; later they were given a large raise in pay because of the burden of work they were called upon to resolve.[62]

Finally, one of Viaro's debtors, the silver merchant Marco Gritti, who is identified as a campsor in 1358, declared himself insolvent in January 1363. When Viaro failed, Gritti owed 226 marks of silver to the mint for the quinto. At that time Gritti had been absent from the city, and the Consoli had sequestered his money and the silver he had placed in care of the banker Marco Stornado, for his debts to the state and to Viaro. Just the same, he was able to survive for more than a year before admitting insolvency. Very likely he had overextended himself in purchases of silver.[63]

The context of this series of failures was typical: a famine, with wheat prices at nearly 1 ducat per staio in September 1360, and speculation in silver.

Speculation in bullion was rife, in part owing to the existence of an agio between coined gold and coined silver. The agio promoted the work of coin clippers, which was more of a concern than usual. In 1359 it was stated that circulating coin was in such bad condition that it was damaging the economy within the city and without.[64] Strong laws were passed against clippers and sweaters of coins in February 1360,[65] but even the threat of amputation of a hand, blinding, a fine, and banishment did not deter certain experts. One of them, Ermolao Dolce, had a system of exchanging ducats for mint soldini, clipping them, melting the clippings, selling the bullion, and exchanging the clipped coins for ducats, with which he began the cycle again.[66] Even officials and staff of the Officium Grossorum Tonsorum, who were supposed to weigh and sort coins brought to them for verification, succumbed to the temptation to cull out good coins and substitute clipped ones.[67]

A direct reflection of problems with agio, similar to that of 1342

[61]Andrea Malipiero held a current account with Viaro from 1353 to 1357; see ASV, PSM, Misti, b. 94, vacchetta, fols. 7, 12, 19, 21.

[62]ASV, MC, Novella, fol. 80v (12 August 1361). The raise in salary from 80 to 120 ducats per year is in ibid., fol. 82 (16 January 1362). The failure is mentioned in Grazie, reg. 15, fol. 41.

[63]ASV, Grazie, reg. 15, fol. 41 (March 1362) and Sopraconsoli, b. 1, capitolare, fol. 81r–v (24 January 1363).

[64]*PMV*, doc. 133; same in Lattes, *Libertà*, doc. 3; it begins "Quia in terra habetur ad presens magnum incommodum denariorum contatorum . . ." Most widely clipped were mezzanini and soldini; *PMV*, doc. 134 (the same in Lattes, *Libertà*, doc. 4).

[65]*PMV*, doc. 134, and ASV, Zecca, b. 6bis, fol. 33 (6 February).

[66]ASV, AC, reg. 3643, fol. 14 (15 September 1361); similar sentences against a surgeon and his servant for clipping in ibid., fols. 19–20 (10 November 1361).

[67]Ibid., reg. 3642, fols. 88–89 (21 February to 11 March 1360).

encountered above, was the desire of officials, authorized to pay their own salaries out of their office's revenues, to profit from the differential. Officers of the arsenal were especially singled out for this usage in calculating their "utilità," or cut. If they took in silver coin, they would pay themselves in ducats; in so doing, they would gain an added 12.5 percent, for they would exchange the silver coins in the office at the official rate of only 64 soldini per ducat, whereas outside it took 72 soldini to make a ducat. The Great Council tried to move against this practice, which it branded as inequitable ("non sit equum"), by requiring officials to take their percentage cuts in gold for revenues collected as gold, and in silver for revenues collected in silver.[68]

Clearly implicated in this situation were the bankers, and from 1358 to 1360 attempts were made to call them to order, to remind them of their obligation to keep circulating media pristine. In 1358 it was stated that badly clipped coins were to be found at the banks. Mint officials and the Silver Office were given the jurisdiction to investigate the banks and to hold the principal ("caput banchi") as the sole person responsible for transgression of the law.[69] The bad state of circulating silver coins meant that ducats were being exported — which could only force up the value of gold. Bankers were ordered to exchange coins only aboveboard, on top of their counters, and not to hold or exchange clipped coins but retire them for melting down, as they were obligated to do by law.[70] It was surely true that moneychangers could profit from passing off bad coins for good; but the general atmosphere of speculation probably made them and bankers think of wider horizons and larger profit margins. Insolvency and failure were the end results.

iv. THE CRISIS OF 1374–1375

The decade of the 1370s witnessed two major crises, both of which contributed to fundamental changes in the nature of the credit market in Venice. The first is the economic crisis that brought down the two principal banks operating on the Rialto, namely, Jacobello Zancani and Brothers and Pietro Emo and Brother, as well as other merchants, in 1374 and 1375. The second is the War of Chioggia (1378–81), which taxed Venice's strength to the limit. Both involved tight money situations and thus prompted the search for new sources of credit under new legal forms. No banks defaulted during the war, however, and that period will be treated in the context of the public debt (below, Chap. 11).

[68]Ibid., reg. 2, fol. 96 (28 December 1361).
[69]Padovan, *Le monete dei Veneziani,* doc. 13, p. 213.
[70]As above, n. 64.

Reflections of a General Economic Crisis

The crisis of the 1370s was not restricted to Venice. The Florentine Provvisioni, which register only twenty bankruptcies in the period 1349–65, record no fewer than seventy-three between 1366 and 1378.[71]

Another sign of potential trouble is the value of silver against gold, which began rising again after two decades of stability, 1353–74, at a bimetallic ratio of slightly below 10:1. Although it cannot be proven that this brusque movement caught bankers and merchants unawares, it did have a rather direct effect on domestic exchange in several cities. What data there are indicate a rise of silver currency, that is, a drop in the exchange rate against gold, in Italy generally and especially in Tuscany.[72] The tendency might be a first signal of a silver famine.[73]

The result of such a de facto revaluation of silver would normally be the fall of the prices of commodities usually paid for in silver coins. However, the general price level for foodstuffs rose sharply in exactly the same period, as a result of the exceptionally bad harvests that brought famine to much of Europe.[74] Florentine documentation shows increases in the prices of meat, oil, and wine ranging from 65 to 85 percent in the years around 1370 in comparison with the years around the middle of the century. The price level for wheat in Florence also rose sharply in 1368 but reached a peak hardly matched before or since precisely in 1375.[75]

[71]That is, an average of six per year in 1366–70, of seven per year in 1371–76. Brucker, *Florentine Politics and Society,* 15, and G. De Leonardis, "Tra depressione e sviluppo: Tendenze dell'economia fiorentina nel secolo XIV, attraverso la storiografia più recente," *Bollettino dell'Istituto storico italiano per il medioevo e Archivio muratoriano* 84 (1972–73): 297.

[72]In Florence the rise was particularly sharp between 1371 and 1374—until October 1375, then a drop. In Pisa there was a sharp fluctuation between June 1374 and May 1376, when the drop occurred. In Siena there was a rise from July 1374 to August 1375 and a slight drop in 1377. In Piedmont a first drop occurred in 1368, a sharp one in 1374–75. In Zara the drop occurred sometime before October 1372. Spufford, *Handbook,* 7, 46, 56, 112; Carlo M. Cipolla, *Studi di storia della moneta,* vol. 1, *I movimenti dei cambi in Italia dal secolo XIII al XV,* Pubblicazioni dell'Università di Pavia, Studi nelle scienze giuridiche e sociali, 101 (Pavia, 1948), 107; cf. Vol. 1, p. 582. Although the above indications take no account of changes in the silver content of white money, it is highly doubtful that mints would have undertaken a revaluation of silver currency during a time of silver famine.

[73]John Day, "The Great Bullion Famine of the Fifteenth Century," reprinted in his *The Medieval Market Economy* (Oxford, 1987); for sharp contractions in mint production in the 1370s in England and Genoa, see ibid., 17, 26, and his "Monetary Contraction in Late Medieval Europe," in *Medieval Market Economy,* table 2.2, also for France. The author did not utilize domestic exchange as an indicator of trouble.

[74]Elizabeth Carpentier, "Autour de la Peste Noire: Famine et épidémies dans l'histoire du XIVe siècle," *Annales, économies, sociétés, civilisations* 17 (1962): 1075–78. For England, Douai, and Florence, see the graph in Day, "Late Medieval Price Movements," in his *Medieval Market Economy,* app. 4.1

[75]De Leonardis, "Tra depressione e sviluppo," 296. Richard A. Goldthwaite, "I prezzi del grano a Firenze nei secoli XIV–XVI," *Quaderni storici,* 28 (1975): 19, 33 (now also in his *Banks, Palaces, and Entrepreneurs*).

Reflections of the Crisis in Venice

Venice, too, experienced a rash of bankruptcies in the mid-1370s; the failures of the Zancani and Emo banks merely head the list, for they were involved in a chain reaction of failures.[76] The liquidity of the banks would perhaps have sufficed in normal times, but the failure of many of their debtors made collection so difficult that the state stepped in by naming two official receivers. To the factors reflected generally — problems in the bullion market and famine — one must add changes in the nature of credit and a period of belligerency to the north which compromised both importation and exportation of commodities essential to Venice's commercial turnover.

In the credit sector, one cannot help but note while reading notarial documents that the local colleganza, which had been so popular for almost a century, an instrument that applied a market rate of interest to a loan only at the time of its maturity, fell out of use among private parties beginning around 1375. The reason for such a rapid demise should be sought in the heavy involvement in local colleganze by major bankers and wealthy entrepreneurs, in the roles of both lenders and borrowers. Since the rates that they paid and received were taken to be the market rates for this kind of credit generally in the city, the rash of failures probably dissolved public trust in the predictability of rates and the security of this credit instrument. In 1375, moreover, the public debt was definitively declared to be permanent and unredeemable. While that merely legalized a situation of fact, from that point on issues were amortized only by the state's intervening on the open market by purchasing government obligations at market prices, rather than at par, as had been the practice before. The open market grew livelier as investors became interested in the rates of yield which Venetian government credits offered (see below, Chap. 11).

Venice experienced the same rise in the value of silver as other commercial cities since about 1328 but was perhaps better able to turn the rise and consequent divergences in gold-silver ratios between East and West to good account. In the late 1360s the trend accelerated. Senatorial deliberations indicate that the market price of a mark of certified silver in October 1368 stood at 5.9 ducats; fourteen months later, in December 1369, the mint offered 6.3 ducats for a mark, a rise of 6.4 percent.[77] Higher prices must have been offered elsewhere, since full-weight silver coins were being culled and exported as bullion.[78] In an attempt to remedy the situation, the Senate cut the tax on silver imports by raising the mint's price for requisi-

[76]An accord was reached with the patriarch of Aquileia for the extradition, upon presentation of a formal request, of the many bankrupts who fled to the area of Portogruaro with their assets ("Nostri fugitivi qui continue affugiunt de Veneciis ad terram Portusgruari darentur nobis cum personis et havere"); ASV, SM, reg. 34, fol. 88 (9 March 1374).

[77]PMV, docs. 151, 158.

[78]Ibid., doc. 153.

tioned silver (the "quinto") by almost 9 percent. At the same time the soldino was debased by 8.4 percent. Such was the rise in the value of silver in this period, however, that the quotation of the ducat, which had been very stable at 74 soldini from 1361 to 1369, did not increase, as one would have expected with the new lighter soldini, but rather decreased to 70–72, that is, by about 4 percent.[79]

A trade embargo imposed in the course of wars between Venice and the metal-producing countries of Austria and Hungary caused the price of silver to jump unexpectedly sometime in the autumn of 1374. The disturbance is reflected in a senatorial resolution and in the value of the ducat, which dropped by 2 soldi in September. On 21 November the preamble to a provision instituting a committee of inquiry on the silver market states that there had been in recent days a "magna mutatio" in the price of silver, that the prices of other commodities were following suit, but that the cause of all this lay elsewhere. That "mutatio" meant a rise was common usage in the exchange market, confirmed here by two factors. First, that word had been substituted in the official record for the word "requisitio," meaning there had been heavy demand for silver. Second, it is stated that other prices "vadunt retro," that is, they followed suit, and in fact the prices of consumables certainly did rise, contrary to expectations. Unfortunately, there is no echo of any action taken by this committee, although it had been ordered to report in December.[80]

In the absence of market prices for silver in Venice, figures from nearby Zara may be taken as indicative. These show an increase in the price of silver in bars from 16 lire di piccoli per mark in June 1372 to 22 lire in March 1377. In ducats, at 72 soldi per ducat, that meant a jump from a low of 4.4 to a high of 6.1 ducats.[81] Available information on the money and bond markets in this period is insufficient to corroborate the tendency.

Although wheat prices are lacking for 1374–75, all indications point to a serious famine. The scanty figures available in a charitable endowment suggest considerable stability around the price of 18 grossi per staio in the 1360s (a stability that matches that of the domestic exchange); a sharp rise to 24 and 30 grossi occurred in 1370, when bad harvests were being widely experienced; the endowment suspended purchases between 1374 and 1377.

---

[79]See Vol. 1, app. A and table D.3. The mint price (*PMV*, doc. 157), valid for two years, was reconfirmed for two more years on 16 December 1371; ASV, SM, reg. 33, fol. 144v. The denaro piccolo was ordered "lightened" in February 1370 (*PMV*, doc. 158).

[80]*PMV*, doc. 161, and the original, with the word "requisitio" crossed out, in ASV, SM, reg. 34, fol. 145v. Known rates of the ducat (Vol. 1, table D.3) are 73 soldi on 8 August, 71 on 13 September, 73 again on 22 November. Cessi's paraphrase of the provision is noncommittal: "Restrictions placed on bankers' bullion dealings determined an immediate alteration in the silver market, with strong repercussions on business in general." *RES*, cclv.

[81]Antonio Teja, *Aspetti della vita economica di Zara dal 1289 al 1409*, 3 vols. (Zara, 1936–42), vol. 1, *La pratica bancaria*, 27.

The situation was so serious that even the Franciscans of the great convent of the Frari had to appeal to the Gonzaga of Mantua for a delivery, writing that the penury of wheat and legumes was such that they could not be had even for money.[82] In February 1375 a Lucchese merchant reported that wheat flour was selling at 14 lire per staio (about 4 ducats or 96 grossi) and that meat was unavailable.[83] In March galley commanders were permitted to increase the rates charged merchants and their servants for meals on board, since victuals were very dear ("quia omnia sunt in carissimo precio").[84] Wine prices began rising by May, so that the price ceilings usually in effect had to be suspended as an incentive to importation.[85] (In December, for example, it was stated that malmsey wine was not available because the price ceiling ["pretium limitatum"] was 25 ducats per amphora, while the market price was 32 to 35 ducats.)[86] Wine imports were also favored by reducing tariffs and raising export duties, in support of the wool industry, which paid part of its salaries to artisans and the "popolo minuto" in wine ("quod requirit ubertatem pro laboratoribus et alijs gentibus minutis").[87] Despite the famine, in May the Senate was forced to step in and nullify wheat futures that had been contracted with peasants of the Trevigiano and Cenedese because the transactions were judged extortionate and usurious and would have increased the already pressing poverty of the peasants in the current conjuncture.[88]

While bad harvests rather than speculation in silver determined the high prices of consumables (the rise of silver, in fact, should have prompted a deflation), there was a connection — albeit a political-military one — between the prices of silver and of Levantine products. The latter suffered from a glut on the Rialto market, and the prices they could command fell.[89] The reason is that spices (along with fustians) were the commodities desired by German merchants (a category that included Austrians and Hun-

---

[82]Prices in ASV, PSM, Misti, b. 67, commis. Jacobello Gabriel. In a letter bearing only the year 1374, the Franciscans wrote, "Sic universaliter potest constare in civitate Veneciarum est magna penuria frumenti et leguminum, in tantum quod eciam pro pecuniam non potest reperiri." ASMN, Archivio Gonzaga, Estere, b. 1430; reported by Cesare Cenci, "I Gonzaga e i Frati minori," *Archivium Franciscanum Historicum* 58 (1965): 26–29.

[83]Teleseforo Bini, *I lucchesi a Venezia,* 2 vols. (Lucca, 1853–56), 2:390.

[84]ASV, SM, reg. 35, fols. 6v, 24v.

[85]Ibid., fols. 18, 55, 73.

[86]Ibid., fol. 73.

[87]Ibid., fols. 56, 58, 68, 144v.

[88]Ibid., fol. 25v; price ranges are given for wheat (3 lire di piccoli to 1 ducat per staio "ad recoltum") and four other grains; in forbidding these futures, the Senate stated, "quidem mercata sunt causa inducendi caritudinem et consumptionem rusticorum, qui propter maximam paupertatem faciunt dicta mercata que observare non poterunt nisi cum maximis usuris."

[89]Pepper, which had sold well above 200 lire a grossi per carico in the 1360s, stood at 189–86 lire in the fall of 1374 and was destined to decline further. A purchase by a Johannes de Norimbergo on 15 June 1368 went at 220 lire (ASV, PSM, Misti, b. 67, commis. Pietro Soranzo, reg. 2, fol. 1); for 1374 see ibid., Ultra, b. 168, commis. Marino Lion.

garians) in exchange for the metals, precious and nonprecious, which they brought with them. In fact, the recurrent situation of belligerency between Venice and central European powers in this period disrupted trade, causing a dearth of metals in Venice and a lack of demand for the merchandise offered by Venetian merchants in exchange. Venice had sought during the 1360s to secure trade routes to the northeast by making commercial treaties with the dukes of Austria, who had recently acquired the Tirol with its mines and passes, and the count of Gorizia. When Trieste revolted in January 1369, the dukes of Austria agreed to aid the city in return for its submission to Austrian rule. Venice retook the city in November of the same year but did not make peace with the dukes until November 1370. In December 1371 Francesco da Carrara began his expansion in the Terraferma and was joined by the troops of the king of Hungary. Since the dukes of Austria seem also to have joined the fray, this war periodically blocked the passes in Friuli and cut off the importation of metals from the mines of Austria and Hungary. Despite the treaty Venice made in September 1373 with the lord of Padua (who had tried hard to subvert Venice from within), the state of belligerency with the king of Hungary was not ended immediately.[90] Hostile relations between Venice and the dukes of Austria evolved into a trade war in 1374 which continued until late in 1375. An embargo was imposed by protectionist forces in the Senate, which specifically prohibited the importation of gold, silver, copper, tin, and lead, called "mercationes Austrie," and the exportation of spices, fustians, wine, and other merchandise via subjects of the dukes.[91] It is not surprising, then, that by late 1375 Venice's

[90]Political and military highlights of these wars are reported by contemporary chroniclers. BMV, It. cl. VII, 559 (7888), a continuation of the chronicle of Enrico Dandolo, fols. 99v–110v. Raffaino de Caresinis, *Chronica*, ed. E. Pastorello, Rerum Italicarum Scriptores, vol. 12, pt. 2 (Bologna, 1923), 18–30. See also Romanin, *Storia documentata*, 3:234–51, and Paolo Sambin, "La guerra del 1372–73 tra Venezia e Padova", *AV*, s. 5, 38–41 (1946–47): 1–76, esp. 46–47, 50–51, 53, on closing the passes.

[91]Imposition of an embargo, probably in 1373, is documented by successful attempts to lift it, if only temporarily, on 20 December 1375. Two very similar bills were presented; since they describe the situation with great clarity, I shall give the text of the bill that failed and describe that which passed. "Quia sicut notum est fortitudo et status huius civitatis est mercadantia, ad quam augendam vigilandum est summopere, et vita mercationis sit habere largitatem et non stricturam, et quod habeat introitum et exitum, quibus defficientibus vel altero eorum deficit ipsa mercatio, Vadit pars, consideratis predictis et pro bono mercatorum ac expeditione multarum spetiarum et mercationum que ad presens sunt in terra et expectantur de die in diem, quod, in Christi nomine et bone gratie, mercationes Austrie et illarum partium, videlicet aurum, argentum, ramum, stagnum, plumbum, et alia milliaria et mercationes qui sunt nunc stricte et non possunt huc conduci, elargatur quod possint huc conduci et vendi iuxta solitum in fontico theotonicorum, remanentibus stricturis fontici in omnibus et per omnia sicut erant ante guerram Padue, pro quo quidem auro, argento, milliariis et mercationibus possint extrahi species Monovasie et Romanie et alie mercationes. Alia vero victualia et grassa que stricta sunt non posse portari ad dictas partes remaneant in statu et strictura quo sunt ad presens." ASV, SM, reg. 35, fol. 74. Although this motion failed to garner more than 25 aye votes, the bill that passed with 37 (see fol. 76) was merely somewhat more vehement regarding the need to lift

supply of metals was at a dangerously low level and that her own market of Levantine products was glutted.[92]

This state of the Venetian marketplace rekindled the debate between exponents of free trade and exponents of protectionism. The free-traders, who had lost in 1374, succeeded in reopening trade with Austrian merchants in late 1375, and in the following months they were able to defeat attempts to exhume the restrictive mechanism of the Officium de Navigantibus, which was reproposed in various forms.[93] The process of liberalization, which was clearly geared at reducing the price of silver and other metals by making them more available and, at the same time, raising the demand (and the prices) for Levantine products, soon met new obstacles. In March 1376 the dukes of Austria again invaded Venetian territory.[94]

Restrictions against credit transactions contracted with subjects of the sultan were confirmed in June, and in the autumn Venetian goods in Damascus were sequestered.[95] But by this time the economic crisis had in a sense stabilized itself, and open war with archrival Genoa was already more than an eventuality.

The Bankruptcies

In early August 1374, in a season normally of tight money, the prominent bank of Jacobello Zancani and Brothers failed. On Monday, 7 August, the Consoli dei Mercanti were already concerned with casting a trial balance and identifying the debtors and creditors of the bank.[96] It is likely that the bank had been the victim of a run and had turned in its books to the magistracy, as the procedure required. On 31 August the Senate, averring that the Rialto banks could not be in a worse condition, to the detriment of the whole state, named a committee of five to study the problem and

---

trade restrictions in order to sell off accumulating inventories and "ut ista utilitas sit generalis et non in specie aliquorum paucorum," probably a reference to persons profiting from contraband.

[92]Because of a prohibition passed in July against foreigners having copper refined in the "geto" (later "ghetto"), an element of the restrictions desired by the protectionists, in November 1375 only a one and one-half months' supply remained in Venice. ASV, SM, reg. 35, fol. 72v.

[93]Roberto Cessi, "L'ufficium de Navigantibus e i sistemi della politica commerciale veneziana nel sec. XIV," reprinted in his *Politica ed economia di Venezia nel Trecento* (Rome, 1952), 46–47. A proposal of 5 February 1376 would have imposed investment quotas in a staggered fashion favoring persons with lower assessments in the estimo. On 12 February a new attempt to reinstitute the Officium was defeated in favor of a more carefully articulated bill that promised complete freedom to "original" citizens, imposed a ceiling equal to the estimo assessment for naturalized citizens, and forbade Venetians to stand in ("tanxare") for foreign capital destined for the Levant trade but permitted the same for trade with the West. ASV, SM, reg. 35, fols. 87v–88.

[94]Romanin, *Storia documentata,* 3:249.

[95]ASV, SM, reg. 35, fols. 120, 176v.

[96]Ibid., reg. 34, fol. 131.

propose solutions.[97] Because the situation was pressing, with one bank already in liquidation and the others weak, the committee was ready with its proposals more than one month early.

All five members seemed to agree that the reason for the profound lack of trust in the banks was their tendency to make long-term investments in speculative commodities, or to lend to those who did, risking depositors' money rather than their own funds. Transactions in silver were singled out for particular criticism. But the search for a solution caused the formulation of four different proposals.[98]

The most interesting one was that which would have outlawed private banks entirely, establishing in their place a public bank (see above, Chap. 3, sec. vi). This institution would have limited itself to the operation of transfer, that is, it would have merely offset debits and credits among the merchants. It was a drastic proposal that assumed the futility of bank regulation. It was not only pessimistic but dangerous, for such a reform would have greatly reduced the quantity of money in circulation by eliminating bank credit backed only by a fractional reserve of specie. The bill received only seventeen votes.

More optimistic about the chances of regulating private banks was the proposal presented by the prominent senator Zaccaria Contarini. Although his bill attracted only two votes, it is quite instructive concerning banking practices and problems. Very likely with an eye on the history of Florence as well as on the reputation of the Zancani bank, Contarini affirmed that Venice had no use for banks that were "too powerful" [nimium potens] and proposed that the approach to controlling them was to set limits on their credit activities. Ceilings were set on transfers, at 100 ducats per person per day; on bank loans, whether in the form of specie, overdrafts, or guarantees, at 200 ducats total to any one person; and on foreign exchange, in which the banker would be a debtor party (taker or payer) in a bill of exchange, at 500 ducats total exchange obligation. Finally, the bill would have prohibited bankers from buying silver, whether refined or unrefined, as well as copper, tin, lead, and saffron, and from selling gold or silver coin or gold bars on credit. To enforce this legislation, Contarini envisioned a new magistracy of bank examiners who would have provided daily oversight at the Rialto; and bankers would have had to take solemn oaths each year to uphold the provisions of the law. Perhaps it is not surprising that the bill received only two votes.

---

[97]*PMV,* doc. 159.

[98]Ibid., doc. 160, which publishes all four texts, pp. 147–54. The text of the successful bill is also in Lattes, *Libertà,* doc. 8, who published in a note (p. 34, n. 11) a crucial phrase erroneously dropped in Cessi's edition; after "nec taxare aliquem ementem argentum," add "nec mutuare nec facere scriptam argenti alicui qui emeret argentum ad campanellum." Precisely that clause was revoked at some point after 1374, then reinstated in 1388 (ASV, SSec, reg. E, fol. 22), and revoked again in 1429 (SM, reg. 57, fol. 126v).

The two proposals that competed for votes in the Senate were actually in substantial agreement. They left most of the internal mechanisms of banking alone and concentrated on the problem of speculation, especially in silver. The one that failed to pass was the more concise. Its proposer sought to eliminate abuses simply by prohibiting bankers from purchasing or participating in the purchase of unworked silver, copper, or tin. The successful bill merely expanded the list of forbidden commodities — quite similar to Contarini's list — by adding lead, fustians, saffron, and honey. But it was explicit concerning the operations involved in silver deals. Not only was the banker forbidden to buy silver — which he had obviously been paying for by crediting an account in the seller's name — but neither could he extend credit to another buyer, nor stand in as a straw man ("tanxare") for a buyer, nor even mediate a payment by transferring a credit from buyer to seller. All silver purchases had to be paid for (in specie or by barter only, it must be presumed) in the presence of the supervisors of the public sale.

This heterogeneous list of forbidden commodities matches closely the products interdicted by Venice in the trade war against the dukes of Austria. While the importance of silver and copper in the trade between the two powers is obvious (copper was now in great demand in Venice, as elsewhere, for casting cannon),[99] the addition of fustians to the list also matches the current demand among Austrian merchants for that kind of cloth, which at this time they were still buying in Venice.[100] In fact, cases in which Venice sequestered goods traded in violation of the embargo show Austrians importing to Venice silver, copper, and tin and buying for export fustians as well as spices.[101] Prices of these commodities had probably dropped sharply because of the state of war and the resultant glut, creating losses for bankers and clients alike; investment by bankers in the same was thought to constitute a danger to deposit holders, but at the time it meant also aiding and abetting the enemy.

The situation meanwhile at the bank of Jacobello Zancani was ambiguous. Since August 1374 the bank was under the supervision of the Consoli dei Mercanti, perhaps with bank auditors regularly on the scene. Bankruptcy had not yet been officially declared, or else the bank was permitted to

---

[99]Cannons were used by Venetian troops in the war in Friuli in 1376; see Eliahu Ashtor, "Aspetti della espansione italiana nel Basso Medioevo," reprinted in his *Technology, Industry, and Trade: The Levant versus Europe, 1250–1500* (London, 1992), art. V, 22.

[100]Simonsfeld, *Der Fondaco,* 1, doc. 236. Also ASV, SM, reg. 35, fol. 21v. Wolfgang von Stromer, *Die Gründung der Baumwollindustrie in Mitteleuropa* (Stuttgart, 1978), esp. 79–82; the author does not treat the military situation in these years as concerns Venice.

[101]Simonsfeld, *Der Fondaco,* 1, docs. 216, 225, 233, 234. For general information, see Carl Schalk, "Rapporti commerciali fra Venezia e Vienna," *NAV,* n.s., 23 (1912): 52–95, 285–317, and Theodor Mayer, *Der auswärtige Handel des Herzogtums Österreich im Mittelalter* (Innsbruck, 1909; reprint, Aalen, 1973), esp. 44, where it is affirmed that honey and wax, as well as metals, were important export items in the fourteenth century.

perform some operations in the process of collecting on debts. Accounts maintained by the Procurators of San Marco as executors of the estate of the wealthy merchant Marino Lion, deceased in late August or early September 1374, show that among the revenues of the estate were 4,000 ducats in eight payments made "in the bank of Jacobello Zancani" between 23 February and 13 March 1375. (Much of this sum came from remittances from Bruges for which the estate was beneficiary.) The Procurators were forced to accept these credits in bank money, despite the difficulties the bank was experiencing. Of the many merchants who borrowed large sums of money from the estate in the form of local colleganze of the type used by the Procurators, namely, at 5 percent interest, three received the principal of 600 ducats each in bank money on the Zancani bank in March.[102]

Ambiguities about the status of the bank began to dissolve in the following months. Marin Sanudo's notes on deliberations of the Council of Forty (the original deliberations have since been lost) indicate that on 21 April 1375 the Consoli had been empowered to issue a safe-conduct to Jacobello Zancani. This was probably the first "fida" issued and suggests that the banker had finally admitted bankruptcy, most likely by fleeing from the city to avoid imprisonment.[103] The safe-conduct was approved by the Forty on 13 May, valid through June.[104] On 20 June the Quarantia recognized that many debtors of the banker were unable to pay what they owed; many of them were themselves bankrupt and had fled the city or had been imprisoned for debt. The liquidators were given permission, at the request of a majority of creditors, to arrange with these persons as advantageously as possible for the payment of their debts. By this time it was clear that a kind of chain reaction was occurring and that one could hardly expect full payment of bank claims if the bank's debtors themselves had failed and were making agreements for partial payment, by installment, of their own debts.[105]

Realization of this state of affairs was too much for another banking operation, that of Pietro and Bernardo Emo: the two bankers fled Venice on 21 June 1375. On the next day the Quarantia, averring that this fact affected many people, authorized the Consoli to grant a safe-conduct to the brothers, even though these officials were personally involved as debtors and creditors. On 30 July a ten-day extension was granted, indicating that difficulties had arisen in negotiations with the creditors.[106] One complication was surely Pietro Emo's official position in the Gold Office as "extimator auri." When he died in the autumn of 1375, the Great Council ruled that his successor could have no conflict of interest, that is, could not have a

[102]ASV, PSM, Ultra, b. 168, reg. 1, fols. 1v, 42r–v.

[103]ASV, Quarantia Criminal, reg. 14bis, fol. 52v.

[104]Ibid. reg. 16, fol. 98.

[105]Ibid., fol. 99v. Some Milanese merchants had fled Venice in May "cum magno havere nostrorum civium." ASV, SM, reg. 35, fol. 18v.

[106]ASV, Quarantia Criminal, reg. 16, fols. 99v, 103.

banchum de scripta or be a partner in a concern dealing in gold.[107] Upon Pietro's death, moreover, liability was passed officially to Bernardo, who seems to have settled with the bank's creditors, for, although neither Bernardo nor a third brother, Alvise, appears in the estimo of 1379, some years later Alvise Emo can be found running a bank at the Rialto.[108] There is in any case no further echo of the liquidation of the earlier bank.

The Zancani failure, on the other hand, continued to disturb the economic life of the city and thus is reflected in the documents. In July 1375 the Consoli and the receivers of the bank were concluding the preliminary investigations regarding assets and liabilities and began to take steps. On 16 July some creditors appealed certain of their decisions to the court of the Auditori.[109] But in the course of a month a compromise agreement was reached between the majority of the creditors (represented by the liquidators) and the banker. Liabilities were calculated to be the very considerable sum of 208,000 ducats. A sizeable portion of this amount must have been owed to Florentine merchants, since one of the elected representatives of the creditors was a certain Filippo di Giovanni di Firenze.[110]

By the end of July the liquidators realized that the problems of collecting the assets of the bank were so vast that they could not handle all the necessary business, especially the collection of sums owed by the debtors of the bank, "qui multi sunt." Since delay damaged the creditors as well as the banker, they petitioned successfully before the Forty for the nomination of two or three nobles who would serve as receivers of all the bank's credits.[111] Three nobles were elected by the ducal council and by the Forty to a one-year term. They were to establish an office and attend to the affairs daily, morning and afternoon, with a small staff of a scribe and two aides ("famuli") appointed by the Consoli. The officials could not accept another position; in addition, they would be fined if they resigned and fined if they did not keep the established hours. The attraction of the job was a cut of 6 denari per lira (2.5%) of all the money collected, of which 1½ denari would go to the scribe and 4½ to the officials. The banker himself was in full agreement with this plan, and he offered to pay if possible half of their cut

---

[107]ASV, MC, Novella, fol. 155 (28 October).

[108]When Pietro died, an act of the Consoli was required to transfer to Bernardo the "honus et ius banchi condam ser Petri fratris sui." Cited in ASV, GP, Frammenti antichi, b. 8, fasc. 1376, fol. 38 (18 December 1376). It will be recalled that Alvise Emo was robbed in 1382, while returning home with the day's cash reserve (above, Chap. 2, sec. vi). The Signoria had previously supported the Emo fraterna by intervening, first with Francesco da Carrara for a debt of more than 3,000 ducats owed them by Francesco di Corte of Padua, then with the podestà of Treviso for a small debt. Collegio, Secreti, fasc. dated 1366–72 (in a busta dated 1375–77), fols. 21v, 23 (1372).

[109]ASV, Quarantia Criminal, reg. 16, fol. 100v.

[110]This agreement, not extant, is reflected in the amendments passed on 11 August, discussed below.

[111]ASV, Quarantia Criminal, reg. 16, fol. 103 (in pencil: 236).

from his own funds; otherwise, the whole amount would be taken from the "monte" of assets accrued in the course of the liquidation. While two men paid a fine to reject election to the post, three accepted and were reconfirmed for another one-year term as their work dragged on.

After the signing of the concordat and the naming of the receivers, some further debts of the bank were uncovered. These gave rise to differences between the liquidators and the banker which had to be resolved by amending the concordat itself. The amendments were recorded by the Forty, and they are of some help in understanding the nature of the "pactum," which unfortunately is not extant.[112] First, the banker would receive no part of the collections made until the sum of 208,000 ducats due to creditors had been reached. While the first installment had been fixed at 20,000 ducats, the creditors insisted on the right to charge a further 4,000 ducats due at the same maturity date to cover damages, any credits that might be offset against debits and thus not add to the liquid assets, and any declared credit that proved not to be owed to the bank. At the same maturity date, Jacobello Zancani was to pay an account of Donato di Guido, very likely a bankrupt Florentine, for the balance due on a sale of ginger, which the banker had probably guaranteed. These amendments were approved by the liquidators, the former banker, the Consoli, an adjunct committee of five noble creditors, two supervisors of the grain magistracy, and finally by the Quarantia. There is no indication why the grain officials appeared among the creditors, but they may have advanced money to the bank for wheat that had not been delivered. That the bank owed money to the Commune is attested by a document of 1390, fifteen years later, which says the former bank still owed 6,000 ducats, probably to the grain magistracy.[113]

The year 1376 brought little respite to the local economy. Of the two remaining banks active on the Rialto, that of Gabriele Soranzo experienced serious payment difficulties in July. Probably the victim of a run by depositors, he duly turned his ledgers over to the office of the Consoli.[114] Most likely the office ascertained his solvency and permitted him to reopen, since he remained in business and went on to become one of the city's two principal bankers. For the marketplace, however, the difficulties encountered by Soranzo, which left only one bank (out of four) fully active, must have seriously reduced the quantity of money available for making payments.

Jacobello Zancani was still not out of trouble. He was unable to meet the first installment of 20,000 or more ducats and fled Venice in August 1376. On the 20th he was given a three-month safe-conduct to return to the city.[115] The process of liquidation became long and drawn out. A testator in

[112]Ibid., fol. 96 (in pencil: 228).
[113]ASV, CN, reg. 2, fol. 172.
[114]ASV, Quarantia Criminal, reg. 17, fol. 12.
[115]Ibid., fol. 12v.

1377 ordered, "If anything should be collected on what Jacobello Zancani owes me for the installment of 5 soldi per lira [25%] that he agreed upon with his creditors, that should be turned over to my wife."[116] The estimo of 1379 places his personal patrimony at 2,000 lire, which would be high for a bankrupt, but it probably includes his wife's dowry, which could not be sequestered by the liquidators.[117] In 1390, the year in which Cristoforo Zancani, moneychanger on Piazza San Marco, failed, Jacobello Zancani, as we have seen, still owed some 6,000 ducats to the Venetian Commune.

[116]ASV, NT, b. 1039, n. 216, testament of Marcus Belonor (5 April 1377).

[117]*PRV*, 181, parish of S. Tomà. His brother Andriolo in S. Leonardo (ibid., 164) had the high assessment of 8,000 lire, but the figure, which would otherwise raise questions about the matter of liability, is attributable to the dowry of 8,000 ducats brought by his wife Cristina (2,000 ducats of which had been secured in 1372 by Jacobello, the banker); see ASV, AC, reg. 3644, fol. 25r–v (15 December 1380). It is interesting to note that Cristina later sold real estate to Isabetta, wife of the banker Pietro Benedetto; Giorgio Tamba, ed., *Bernardo de Rodolfis, notaio di Venezia (1392–1399)*, FSV (Venice, 1974), docs. 191, 193, 197.

5

BANK FAILURES
IN THE QUATTROCENTO

i. INSOLVENCY AND FAILURE OF THE BENEDETTO BANKS, 1400 AND 1405

The Postwar Decades

ALTHOUGH THE FIRST SIGNIFICANT and well-documented bank failures after 1376 took place in 1400, there were, of course, periods of economic crisis in the interim which brought down commercial companies, as well as two small banks. The enterprise of banking had changed considerably in the 1370s. The business of the Rialto was concentrated in the hands of fewer, larger banks. The liabilities of the Zancani bank, of well over 200,000 ducats, are one reflection of the trend. Only two principal banks (those of the noblemen Gabriele Soranzo and Pietro Benedetto) and a few lesser ones survived the two devastating financial crises of 1374–76 and of the War of Chioggia (1378–81). Although it did not bring down banks, the war—one of the most serious military crises in Venetian history—absorbed the liquid assets of Venetians through impositions of forced loans amounting to more than 40 percent of their assessed valuations, causing a partial redistribution of wealth which merits separate study.[1]

A reflection of the redistribution can be found in the fate of the patrimonies of the top four non-nobles registered in the estimo of 1379: Bandino Garzoni and Giovanni de' Bugni, both in second position at

---

[1]Reinhold C. Mueller, "Effetti della guerra di Chioggia (1378–1381) sulla vita economica e sociale di Venezia," *Ateneo veneto* 19 (1981): 27–41.

50,000 lire; Maffeo Giuda, fifth at 35,000 lire; and Marino Carlo, sixth along with four nobles at 30,000 lire. Bandino Garzoni, an immigrant from Lucca via Bologna early in the century, was coopted into the Great Council posthumously (in favor of two of his four sons) in September 1381; the family encountered financial difficulties in the following decades and never matched the wealth of the non-noble branch (the extension, it seems, of the other two sons) that entered banking in 1430. Maffeo Giuda, son of Lippo, an immigrant from Florence and a new citizen at the beginning of the Trecento, and relative of Francesco Giuda, Rialto banker in the 1350s and 1360s, was declared bankrupt on 18 February 1387. Pietro Carlo, a draper like his father, Marino, was declared bankrupt by the Consoli in 1392; in his testament of 1388 he admitted having serious financial problems, which he attributed to the War of Chioggia, that is, to the forced loans. Omobono, son of Giovanni de' Bugni, an immigrant from Cremona, who had operated for a time as partner of the Rialto banker Bartolomeo Micheli of Lucca, was declared bankrupt in March 1400, at the same time as the death of his brother Pino.[2] The difficulties of these families is perhaps not surprising. During the three and one-half years of the war, Garzoni and Bugni had to pay, in cash, for forced loans, 20,500 ducats each; Giuda, 14,350; Carlo, 12,300; the total for four families was nearly 78,000 ducats. Liquidating assets sufficient for making such massive contributions to the funded debt must have changed the nature of their fortune as well as diminishing it.

The failure of Maffeo Giuda in March 1387 was part of a rash of bankruptcies which seems to have shaken various commercial cities. Zanobi Gaddi, the principal correspondent in Venice of Francesco di Marco Datini, acknowledged on 5 February receipt of the news of failures in Florence. By 12 March Gaddi had heard of the failure of Damiano Piccon in Genoa (on which he commented with the ritual "Idio ristori e perdenti").[3] In the following year the drapers Franceschino Valier and Piero Giudice and Partners failed in Venice. Although they had liabilities of some 8,000 ducats, more than half of which was owed to Florentine cloth merchants, they were

[2]For the estimo, *PRV,* 145, 174, 186, 189. For Garzoni, see Todesco, "Aggregati ed esclusi," 193–215. For Giuda (Iuda), ASV, Sopraconsoli, b. 1, capitolare, fols. 86v–87, from the Collegio. Zanobi Gaddi, who had reported Giuda to be in trouble and borrowing money on the exchange in 1386 (ADP, 709, 25 and 31 October), wrote on 26 February 1387: "Chon ser Mafio Giuda non abiamo a fare niente; avi a fare asai; de' nostro non perderanno niente, se non un pocho di tenpo." This Venetian citizen was mistaken for a Jew by A. Ciscato, *Gli ebrei in Padova (1300–1800)* (Padova, 1901), 20, an error often repeated since. His testament of 1389 and estate papers are in PSM, Ultra, b. 157. For Carlo: MC, Leona, fol. 61; his testament is in PSM, Ultra, b. 81. He died, surely of the plague then raging, on 22 October 1400. The failure of Omobono de' Bugni and the death of his brother were reported by Gaddi, ADP, 712, letter of 16 March 1400, where it is said they owned real estate valued at 7,000 ducats. Their father's testament is in ASV, NT, b. 920, n. 191 (notary N. Saiabianca).

[3]ADP, 709.

judged wealthy enough to pay off their creditors, who would "lose only time" in the liquidation process.[4] Another draper, Pietro Carlo, as we have seen, followed suit in 1392.

Of the failures of two banks in these years only the scarcest of evidence is extant. The failure of Antonio Contarini in January 1390 is reported in a deliberation of the Great Council; the liquidation seems to have dragged on for some years. He is known to have had close ties with German importers of gold and silver ingots and silverware, such as the Kress company of Nuremberg.[5] Cristoforo Zancani — perhaps a relative of Jacobello, who failed in 1374–75 — was a moneychanger who operated a bank at San Marco. He had probably gained expertise in handling money as mintmaster of silver (1381) and of gold (1385–86).[6] Zancani dealt in large sums of money and transferred deposits like Rialto bankers, but he specialized in the exchange of coins, in large quantities, with German customers. After he failed ("fefelerat") in 1390, he met his creditors in the church of S. Salvador and explained to them that he had incurred serious losses on the Viennese pennies ("vianensi," "vianari") that he had bought from a German merchant, Ser Rigo Rocco.[7] He may have misjudged their quality or the demand for that kind of silver, but the general business climate was also unfavorable. Pepper prices fluctuated wildly, and trade on the Rialto was so depressed during the summer months that Florentine correspondents in Venice did not bother to write to their principals in Florence.[8]

---

[4]Ibid., Manetto Davanzati to Florence, 1 August 1388; similar in Antonio di Benincasa e Jacopo di Tedaldo, ibid., same date.

[5]ASV, MC, Leona, fol. 37 (27 January 1390). Since "hoc factum tangat multas et diversas personas," continues the deliberation, conflict of interest clauses were suspended in order to facilitate the work of the Consoli. Mentioned in A. Lattes, *Il fallimento,* 42 n. A Pietro Contarini, qd. Francesco, was declared bankrupt shortly thereafter; CN, reg. 1, fol. 97 (also numbered 77), (19 February 1390); GP, Sg, reg. 6, fol. 28v (27 September 1400). Hilpolt Kress, active in Venice in 1389–97, had accounts with Antonio Contarini, as well as with the larger banks of Pietro Benedetto and Gabriele Soranzo. Philippe Braunstein, "Relations d'affaires entre Nurembergeois et Venitiens à la fin du XIV^c siècle," *Mélanges d'archéologie e d'histoire,* Ecole Française de Rome, 76 (1964): 235–52.

[6]*Cap. broche,* 42–43, 147 n., and Padovan, *Le monete dei Veneziani,* 142–43.

[7]Simonsfeld, *Der Fondaco,* 1, docs. 263, 264. Mayer (*Der auswärtige Handel,* 16–19) insists that such "denarii viennenses" actually came from Hungary. A letter written by a Del Bene factor in Trieste in December 1390 suggests opportunities for profits on these coins. He reported that Slavs had been buying them in Trieste at 8 denari each (that is, at 123 per ducat, with the ducat at 82 soldi), while he had heard that they were current in Venice at 135 or 134 per ducat; he requested the shipment of some from Venice at those rates — for a possible gross profit of 8.8 percent. It might be added here that he ordered also "ducati scarsi," since the Slavs, he wrote, "exchange readily and don't weigh ducats"; he also wanted "aquilini" and "carrarini" going for 2 soldi in Trieste, but no Venetian silver. ASF, Archivio Del Bene, 49, no. 162, to Francesco di Jacopo Del Bene in Venice. Spufford, *Handbook,* 271, shows rapid devaluation of "Viennese pennies" against the Hungarian ducat: 126 d. (1390), 132 d. (1391), 138 d. (1392).

[8]In May news of record prices in the Levant caused pepper to soar from 72 to 127 ducats, only to fall and climb again. In June Gaddi wrote: "Di merchantatia non si fa qui nulla; al tutto

The situation improved in the rest of the decade, enough to convince merchants to open two new banks. On 15 and 20 October 1399 banks were opened by Giovanni Corner and Antonio Miorati and by Roberto di Lorenzo Priuli, with his many brothers. The Florentines on the Rialto, who announced the fact to their correspondents, judged them to be solid.[9]

The Rialto in the Year 1400

Venice and its merchant community had at least three major preoccupations in the summer and fall of the year 1400. First of all, the city was stricken with the plague, the worst since 1348, just as was Florence. According to a late chronicle, people died at a rate that peaked at five hundred per day, for a total of sixteen thousand in a few months.[10] Many of those who could, fled the city.[11] The successor of Zanobi Gaddi, who had died of the plague in July, complained that the epidemic was worsening in October, a fact that disturbed him, as he said, "not only because of the certain death involved but because it is bad for business; you cannot sell, or collect, or do anything."[12] Earlier he had written that Venice seemed like a country defeated in war ("pare una terra schonfitta"), because of the raging plague.[13] Pietro Benedetto, the principal banker of the city, died of this plague, as we shall see. Second, Tamerlane was active in the northern Levant. The Venetians sustained considerable losses when they fled, leaving behind all heavy goods.[14] In September the Beirut galleys were diverted to Alexandria.[15] A third cause for concern was the war between Florence and Giangaleazzo Visconti — republic against despot. Although Venice's role was that of a nonbelligerent ally, Florentine pressure for a full alliance and for financial aid was strong. In September Venice threatened reprisals if Florence failed to repay a loan of 15,000 ducats (which recalls the situation in 1339–40!).[16]

---

pare spenta e noi siamo serati, che in niuna parte posiamo mandare." Only nine letters are extant for the whole year — "there's no need to write," explained Gaddi in August. ADP, 710.

[9]"A dì 15 s'aprise un bancho di scritta, che è ser Gianino Chornero e Antonio Migliorati; e lunedì a dì 20 se ne de'e aprire un altro, che sia ser Ruberto di Prioli e fratelli. Tutti ci paiono sichuri e buoni; siate avisati; che Idio dia loro buona 'ventura." ADP, 712, Manetto Davanzati to Francesco Datini, 17 October 1399.

[10]G. B. Galicciolli, *Delle memorie venete antiche profane ed ecclesiastiche*, 8 vols. (Venice, 1795), 2:208. Manetto Davanzati wrote from Venice on 19 June, "Siamo avisati la mortalità s'à pur da noi cossta, che Idio piacie porvi fine; qui, e 'per tutto il mondo, ci pare anche se ne sente; è tempo da fare pocho e da fare bene con messer Domenedio." ADP, 713.

[11]ADP, 713, Antonio di Ser Bartholomeo to Florence, 7 September.

[12]Ibid., Commissaria Gaddi to Florence, 20 October.

[13]Ibid., 927, Commissaria Gaddi to Barcelona, 8 October.

[14]Morosini, Cronaca, 1:280.

[15]ADP, 927, Commissaria Gaddi to Barcelona, 25 September.

[16]ASV, SM, reg. 45, fol. 32v (3 September). Tension between the allies had already, in the previous February, led to the exclusion of Florentines from any action before a Venetian court of law, a reprisal that had depressed commerce and exchange in both cities. ADP, 712, 10 and 14 February and 16 March 1400.

But Venice was more concerned about the movements of the Paduans, who were in a position to block trade routes, as in fact they later did.

On the more immediately economic level, the situation appears complex. The market in bullion and coin in central and northern Italy was extremely active in 1399 and early 1400. Foreign exchange experts in Venice, such as Manetto Davanzati, speculated vigorously. Special couriers were sent out with bills of exchange, news of exchange rates and bullion prices, and bullion itself. The hub of activity for the collection and distribution of culled coins, clippings, coins no longer legal tender, and small pellets of partially refined bullion — all of which were generically called "bolzono" or "rottame" — was Bologna, from which bullion was transported periodically in order to exploit the tight market. The banker Guglielmo Condulmer's list of prices of silver shows that market prices of certified silver bars in Venice held steady until August 1399, when the price hit a low of £14 16s and then rose to a peak of £16 8s in January 1400. Thereafter, however, the price returned to a stable average. The Venetian Senate was surely reacting to this situation when in October 1399 it ordered the mint to devaluate the grosso and the soldino by 3 percent.[17]

It will be recalled that dealing in silver by bankers had been forbidden in 1374. Exceptions were made in 1387 and 1390 which allowed bankers to purchase annually up to 4,000 ducats' worth of certified silver to ship to the Levant, so that they could legally compete in the Levant trade.[18] Accounts maintained by the moneychanger Guglielmo Condulmer, on the other hand, indicate clearly that his own trading in silver, between 1389 and 1413, was virtually unhindered, even though total annual values exceeded 4,000 ducats. He did not export, however, but sold locally after refining. It could be said that his dealings were officially countenanced, even though they were against the law, since the mint officials audited the banker's books to make sure that he had consigned the "quinto."[19] Speculation in silver, in other words, this time seems not to have compromised the Rialto banks in 1400 or in 1405, although the Levant trade, as we shall see, constituted a serious problem in the latter year.

Wheat prices show that there was also no famine in this conjuncture, for they seem to have been quite stable from 1397 to 1405. Wage rates similarly remained stable, despite the devastating effects of the plague and the devaluation of the grosso and soldino in 1399. The only echo of these events is in the price commanded by a baker for having wheat milled and for producing a measure of loaves of bread, which went from 16 soldi, which had been the price for a decade, to 20 soldi in December 1402.[20]

[17]*PMV,* doc. 192, and Vol. 1, app. A and table A.2.
[18]Lattes, *Libertà,* docs. 8 and 9.
[19]ASV, PSM, Misti, b. 182. Also SM, reg. 45, fols. 39v–41v (16 November 1400).
[20]For wheat prices and the prices bakers commanded, see the estate papers of Manfredo V di Saluzzo in ASV, PSM, Supra, commissarie, b. 35. For wage rates, see App. J, below.

In the fall of 1400, with the plague still raging, business was slow, and with so many merchants out of the city to flee contagion, debts due from old and recent bankrupts could not be collected. The Datini correspondents reported regularly about the fate of the merchants Jacopo Squarcia, who had failed in 1395, and Nicolò Orsato and Omobono Gritti, who had failed more recently. As a result of the plague, liquidation procedures could not proceed, for the liquidators themselves had either died or fled the city.[21]

The Bank of Pietro Benedetto

On Thursday, 30 September 1400, late in the day, the rumor that one of the two principal bankers of the city, the nobleman Pietro Benedetto, had died of the plague was sufficient to provoke a run on his bank. The dynamics of the case are described in detail by the Florentine Bindo Piaciti, a correspondent of Francesco Datini, who (fortunately for us) was one of the principal creditors and thus directly interested. In fact, earlier in the day his account had been credited with 200 ducats as beneficiary of a bill of exchange remitted from Florence.[22]

On Monday, 27 September, late in the evening, Pietro Benedetto had indeed been stricken with the plague. Two days later he made his testament.[23] This fact had fed the rumor that was maliciously spread on the 30th. As Piaciti reported, some blamed the false report on the envious in general, others on the very bankers who competed with the unfortunate Pietro on the Rialto. Who was it who ran to convert his claim into specie? Not the wealthy merchants, nor the Florentine exchange dealers, who had every reason to hope that the bank would hold out, but the middling and smaller depositors. Piaciti wrote, "At that point, many artisans and other Venetians ran to the bank in a fury to demand payment of their credits." Seeing that he could not sustain "tanta furia," the cashier of the bank closed down the operation at sunset. Following the usual practice, he took his ledgers to the Consoli dei Mercanti, declared that he could pay all creditors, and petitioned the Consoli to compel the bank's debtors to pay up. On the following day (Friday, 1 October) he convoked the creditors and demonstrated that there were sufficient assets to pay all and still leave 15,000–20,000 ducats to the children of Ser Pietro. Piaciti himself was elected by the creditors to be part of the committee that was to study the bank's "libro segreto." The trial balance cast by this group showed the closed bank to be in excellent condition. Benedetto's assets in merchandise and real estate were calculated at 55,000–56,000 ducats, while total liabilities stood at only

[21]See, for example, ADP, 713, Commissaria Gaddi to Florence, 4 and 18 September.

[22]The letters from which most of what follows was reconstructed are ADP, 713, Piaciti to Florence, 2, 9, 16, 23 October (carried by four successive Saturday evening couriers); and 927, Commissaria Gaddi to Barcelona, 2 October.

[23]The original is in ASV, CIN, Miscellanea testamenti notai diversi, b. 23, n. 1025 (atti Guglielmo Vicensi). A copy of 1449 is in NT, b. 364, atti B. Darvasio, fol. 54r ff.

18,000–19,000 ducats, most of which was owed to the Florentines.[24] The condition of the latter was reported as follows:

Filippo di Michele	200 lire di grossi
Manetto Davanzati	95 lire di grossi
Martino Martini	200 lire di grossi
Matteo di Sangallo	110 lire di grossi
Bindo di Gherardo Piaciti	174 lire di grossi
Maffio d'Ansingho	200 lire di grossi
Salvi di Giovanni Lippi e altri	(blank)
Total	979 lire di grossi

Most of this sum, clearly well over 1,000 lire or 10,000 ducats, was probably owed for foreign exchange recently credited to their accounts as beneficiaries of drafts on Venice. The same day, Friday, in fact, the foreign exchange market immediately reflected the tight money situation resulting from the run on the Benedetto bank the previous evening. Word about the solidity of the bank, however, brought the rates back down on Saturday: it had been a false alarm ("è stato un fuocho di paglia"), wrote Gaddi's successor.[25]

At dawn on Saturday, 2 October, the banker did indeed die, victim of the plague. Despite preparations for the funeral, which took place on the same day, Piaciti found the opportunity to approach some of the relatives and ascertained that both heirs and relatives intended to carry out the banker's last will and establish a successor bank. The plan was to collect as much specie as possible in order to be able to open up for business as usual on Monday morning and to offer payment to any creditor of the old bank who so wished. Piaciti reckoned that no one would lose a penny ("uno baghatino"), but at most a month or two of time.

As Piaciti's later letters attest, the new bank opened as planned on Monday morning, 4 October, and promised to pay by January all creditors of the old bank who desired payment. This means (although it is not expressly stated here) that creditors of the old bank who agreed were given at once (or were promised) credit on the books of the new bank. The Florentines breathed a sigh of relief, since, as they noted, a full liquidation would have taken from as little as one to two months to as long as eighteen months, if real estate had to be sold. But the condition of the new bank was so strong that the estimated time for liquidating the old bank was reckoned at two months or less by Piaciti. The promises had the intended effect: on the first day some 25,000–30,000 ducats in coin were brought for deposit—a staged spectacle, in part, to be sure, but much was probably brought by the artisans and others who had staged the run on the old bank the week before.

[24]The above-mentioned letter sent by Gaddi's successor (ADP, 927, 2 October) claimed that the bank owed Florentines alone 25,000 ducats, but Piaciti had seen the accounts.
[25]Ibid.

The testament and other documents describe the successor bank. As stipulated in the concluding paragraph of the testament, the new bank, styled "La commissaria di Piero Benedetto e Marco Condulmer e Compagni," was a partnership of four: (1) the Benedetto estate; (2) Marco Condulmer; (3) Simone Condulmer; and (4) Jacobello Zane. Each, it seems, contributed one-quarter of the founding capital, the amount of which is not revealed. Piaciti wrote to Florence that all four were "gran ricchi" and "soficientisimi." As we have already seen (Chap. 3, sec. iv), Marco (qd. Andrea) Condulmer and Jacobello (qd. Lorenzo) Zane had formed a partnership in 1389 with Pietro Benedetto's son, Giovanni (Zanino), each contributing 2,000 ducats, in order to learn business under the tutelage of the experienced banker.[26] After sixteen months, Giovanni returned the money, renounced his inheritance, and entered the Dominican order,[27] but Jacobello Zane married the banker's daughter Cristina.[28] Marco Condulmer, called nephew ("nievo") in the testament, redacted the banker's last will. His debt to the old bank was not to be called in, but otherwise little is known of him. Simone, also called "nievo" in the testament, on the other hand, was the son of Angelo di Fiornovello Condulmer and brother of Gabriele, former merchant, cofounder of the reform congregation of the canons at S. Giorgio in Alga, the future Pope Eugenius IV—in short, a member of a family very much in the public eye, although not of the branch that had been ennobled in 1381.[29] Simone and Gabriele had operated as a fraterna before the latter's entry into the clerical world.[30] Thus it is not surprising that the successor bank inspired the confidence of Venetians and foreigners alike. On 16 October Piaciti reported that the partners were more active than ever ("fanno più che mai") and predicted that the new bank would be the strongest in the city if it made good its promise to liquidate the debts of the old bank in full in four months or less.

Along with a flourishing banking business the new company inherited an industrial obligation. The testator ordered it to continue financial support of two silk shops ("botege") in which he obviously had a substantial interest, namely, those of Jacomello Menegi and Bartolomeo Gardellino, both immigrants from Lucca. The interest probably involved an outright investment—or a line of credit which had become such, since the

[26]Cessi, "Note per la storia delle società di commercio," 53–55.

[27]ASV, CIN, b. 34, Atti P. de Compostellis, fol. 58 (12 May 1390).

[28]There are two copies of Christina's testament: ASV, CIN, b. 22, fasc. 8 (atti Barzacchi), and NT, b. 1232, n. 336, fol. 141. Jacobello Zane's testament is in CIN, Misc. testamenti notai diversi, b. 23 nn. 1094–95.

[29]In general, on the connections between banking and religious reform, see Mueller, "Sull'establishment bancario veneziano."

[30]ADP, 550, seven letters from Simone and Gabriele Condulmer in Venice to the Datini branch in Pisa, 22 June to 30 August 1396. Gaddi recommended the brothers to Datini's Florence office on 17 August, saying "sono genti da servire." Ibid., 711.

banker's concern was to avoid immediate liquidation. Marco Condulmer was to oversee the operations, permit completion of production that was under way, and direct the orderly sale of the finished silk cloths. Liquidation was probably avoided altogether, since at least the second shop continued to operate for several years with the successor bank and Marco Condulmer as partners.[31]

The Benedetto Successor Bank, 1405

The new bank was uniquely successful over the next four years. Although it was flanked at the Rialto by the banks of the Soranzo, the Priuli, Cocco-Miorati, and Guglielmo Condulmer, it was asserted in late 1404 that the successor bank nearly monopolized the market ("fa quasi il tutto"), especially for the foreigners who dealt in bills of exchange.

Signs of serious trouble in the Venetian money market, however, had begun to appear in the autumn of 1404. Exogenous factors directly affected the health of the successor bank, although in this it was not alone. Venice was at war — a bloody war, wrote the Florentines — with the Carraresi of Padua. Venice was on the verge of becoming a mainland power. In September and October specie was flowing out of the city to pay the troops. The result, mirrored on the exchange, was a rise in interest rates. And, since bank reserves probably declined, an agio, or differential, developed between bank money and specie. On 4 October the agio was fixed at 1.5 percent, which meant that 100 ducats in a bank account were worth only 98½ ducats in cash.[32] Liquidity was further compromised by the death in October of Salvi di Giovanni Lippi, a wealthy Florentine exchange dealer. He had started out in Venice as partner and factor of the Del Bene firm and then stayed on as an independent merchant banker. Upon his death, his wife and children fled Venice, seriously complicating the collection of his credits.[33]

At some distance from Venice trouble loomed as well. Sometime in October 1404 news reached Venice that the important exchange bank of the Florentine Filippozzo Soldani in Barcelona had gone bankrupt. Little hope

---

[31]Besides Benedetto's testament, cited above, see also ASV, GP, Sg, reg. 39, fol. 5 (21 November 1415 but concerning 1405). In a power of attorney granted in 1398 to Marco Condulmer, Gardellino, and Ramaldo d'Andrea di San Canciano, Jacobello Menegi mentioned having instituted a company that same day in which he had invested 3,000 ducats, which investment plus potential profits he "obligated" to the banker Pietro Benedetto. The two acts he mentions, however, are not to be found among acts of the same notary. CIN, b. 92, fasc. cartacei, 1398, 25 September. A new power of attorney was granted to Nicolino di Lappo, with a similar duty "ad respondendum" to the banker; see the same notary (G. di Gibellino), protocollo 2, 7 October 1399. Also Molà, *La comunità dei lucchesi*, 258–59.

[32]Mueller, "Role of Bank Money," 87.

[33]ASV, AC, reg. 3645, fols. 75v–76 (1 December 1404). I did not note a reference to this fact in the Datini letters.

existed among the exchange dealers in Venice that Soldani, a partner of Nicolò Alberti, would pay his debts in full.[34] On the other end of the Mediterranean, the Genoese were preying on Venetian shipping. They captured and sacked several Venetian ships in the Black Sea, news of which reached Venice in November: two cogs laden with merchandise worth 40,000–45,000 ducats had been taken, and three Venetian merchants ("2 gentiluomini e 1° di popolo") had been taken captive; and a "grepperia" laden with malmsey wine had been captured off Modon. Would this be "la vigilia di mala festa?" the correspondents asked themselves.[35]

It is perhaps not surprising, then, that Venetians turned their attention to the investments made by bankers. The evidence is very clear that the Benedetto estate bank was deeply involved in the Levant trade. The new partners of the Condulmer and Zane families had been merchants before they joined the banking enterprise, and they did not change the nature of their interests. On the contrary, the bank gave them a new source of investment capital. They seem, however, not to have operated in the name of the bank but as individuals and through different partnerships and ventures. The distinction was made for purposes of liability, but for the solidity of the bank, it must have made little difference. The surviving minutes of the Venetian Council of Twelve in Alexandria show that Leonardo Zane, Jacobello's brother, was active there in 1401 and 1402 in at least three roles: "in sua spetialitate" and with partners; as agent for Simone, Zorzi Zane, and Federico Michiel; and in partnership with Marco Condulmer. Simone Condulmer was the most active among them. The commodities they dealt in, mentioned because of litigation, were oil, honey, lead, pepper, ginger, and jewels.[36] At some point, however, the aggregate activity of the bank partners would be assessed in the marketplace as overinvestment.

In early November 1404 the Benedetto estate bank was reported to be in trouble ("non istanno i lloro 'fari bene").[37] A kind of run developed, in which depositors tried to pass off their holdings. This time the big exchange speculators who had been accepting and making all their payments in this bank were caught up in the atmosphere of apprehension. Their reaction was to try to sell their bank deposits by offering them on the exchange to

[34]ADP, 929, Luigi di Manetto Davanzati to Barcelona, 2 October; 715, Paoluccio di maestro Paolo to Florence, 15 October. Losses were heavy; see Giovanni di Ser Nigi to Florence, ibid., 27 January 1405. On the connection of Soldani with Alberti, see Raymond de Roover, *The Bruges Money Market around 1400* (Brussels, 1968), 19–20.

[35]Pirates attacked and robbed a pilgrim ship near Candia; ADP, 715, Paoluccio, 14 October. On the Genoese attacks, see the letters written to Florence on 25 November by Giovanni di Ser Nigi e Gherardo Davizi and by Bindo Piaciti, ibid.

[36]Simone, for example, chartered cogs in 1402 and 1403 (for 355 and 400 ducats) and sent them to Alexandria. ASV, CIN, b. 229, fasc. 5; AC, reg. 3645, fol. 46v (22 November 1402), GP, Sg, reg. 12, fols. 16v–17 (16 January 1404).

[37]ADP, 715, Paoluccio to Florence, 8 November.

any taker who would promise repayment in another city. The rates mirror the sudden supply of money offered by dipping abruptly by more than 25 percent, which means that buyers of bills of exchange were willing to take a possible loss now and have a credit payable elsewhere rather than get caught holding balances in a bankrupt bank.[38]

The pendulum of fortune then swung in the opposite direction: on 23 November 1404 the Alexandria galleys arrived safe and sound. Their return temporarily lifted the suspicion that had hung over the bank, for they carried 480 carghi of pepper belonging to the bankers. At the market rate, that meant a value of almost 27,000 ducats; but the bank had other spices and merchandise aboard the galleys, as well as on a cog that had also arrived. "The suspicion with which people viewed the bank has lifted, but only because much merchandise has arrived in the bankers' name," wrote Giovanni di Ser Nigi to Florence.[39]

The Venetian Signoria did not permit the momentary safety of the Benedetto estate bank, however, to divert its attention from the causes of potential danger. The ducal councillor Bulgaro Vettori introduced a bill in the Senate to limit overseas investments by banks. Vettori was a very active merchant as well as a member of the inner circles of government; that he had an interest in the problem of bank regulation is obvious from the fact that he would also introduce, in 1421, the famous regulatory act prompted by King Sigismund's trade war.[40] Now, clearly reacting to the vulnerability of the Benedetto estate bank, he stated that Venetian bankers were making excessively large investments in maritime commerce with the money that depositors left at the bank — at the serious risk of the depositors themselves. The mechanism of control which he suggested was that of the old Officium de Navigantibus, that is, that investments in commerce by land or sea be restricted to 150 percent of the banker's personal worth as assessed and registered in the estimo. The only commodity exempt from this limitation on the banker's investments was wheat, whose importation was too vital to permit of any restriction. The discussion in the Senate must have been lively, for Vettori's bill just passed with forty-eight votes, while forty-two Senators voted to postpone the matter for further discussion (and three abstained).[41] But as a correspondent wrote to Datini in Florence, the law

---

[38]Ibid.; also Giovanni di Ser Nigi, same day.

[39]ADP, 715, Paoluccio to Florence, 23 November; Giovanni di Ser Nigi, 10 December: "Il sospetto di quello bancho è levato, ma perchè è loro venuta molta roba."

[40]Lattes, *Libertà,* doc. 14. See also Mueller, "Role of Bank Money," 74.

[41]Lattes, *Libertà,* doc. 12, misdated. See the original, with voting records, in ASV, SM, reg. 46, fol. 162v (28 November 1404). Elia Lattes (p. 43) mistakenly interpreted this law to mean 150 percent of bankers' bond holdings. His brother Alessandro Lattes corrected him; what is meant is the patrimony on which levies were based ("la quota con cui participava . . . ai prestiti publici forzosi"); *Il fallimento,* 44. While Cessi avoided interpretation by quoting crucial phrases in Latin, the usage is clarified by the 1361 addition to cap. 8 of the capitolare of the

had teeth: no pardon (grazia) could be granted, under pain of a 2,000 ducat fine levied against any official who would propose the same; no one was allowed to ship goods for a bank, that is, by acting as straw man for the bank, and anyone who so carried goods for a bank in excess of the limit imposed would never have to render account for the shipment or pay for it. The writer concluded, "It is a very strict law" [è molto forte ordine sopra-ciò].[42] The aim of the law was laudable, from the point of view of the middling and smaller depositors especially, but it must have been difficult to enforce; and even if it worked, it could close only one leak — and not immediately, at that — in the structure of the Venetian bank as a credit institution. Plenty of legal loopholes must surely have remained.[43]

It was not long before another and unforeseen crisis engulfed this bank, eliminating it altogether from competition at the Rialto — as well as in the Levant. The proximate cause in this case was the failure on Tuesday, 6 January 1405, of the great Bolognese merchant-banking firm of Romeo and Rafaello Foscherari. The Foscherari were members of the Arte del Cambio in Bologna, where they, along with the del Caro family, were the most important dealers in foreign exchange.[44] They had a branch in Venice, run by a partner and resident factor, the Florentine Antonio di Giovanni. As typical merchant bankers, they had very diversified interests in Venice, including insurance underwriting.[45] They maintained close ties with the Benedetto estate bank, where they held a current account.[46] News of the failure in Bologna reached Venice on Saturday, the 10th, carried by a special messenger of the cardinal-legate of Bologna, Baldassare Cossa (the future antipope John XXIII), a prelate with important interests in Venice as well as in the Foscherari firm.[47] Since the Signoria received the news before anyone

---

Officium de Navigantibus. Cessi, "L'ufficium de Navigantibus," 106–46, reprinted in his *Politica ed economia*. See also Lane, *Venice,* 140, and Benjamin Kedar, *Merchants in Crisis: Genoese and Venetian Men of Affairs and the Fourteenth-Century Depression* (New Haven, 1976), 27.

[42]ADP, 715, Giovanni di Ser Nigi, 10 December.

[43]This law, for example, did not hinder Cristoforo Soranzo, son of the banker Gabriele, from winning bids as patrone of an Alexandria galley in 1405 and a Flanders galley in 1407. ASV, SM, reg. 47, fol. 10 (9 July 1405), fol. 87v (January 1407). The Provveditori di Comun were to prosecute violations, but their acts are unfortunately not extant.

[44]Both these families were active for decades; see, for example, ASV, PSM, Citra, b. 141, Talenti account book, fol. 5v, for a bill of 1380. Published mentions of the Foscherari appear in Enrico Bensa, *Francesco di Marco da Prato* (Milan, 1928), 342, 346. In the Venice correspondence, see, for example, ADP, 714, Piaciti to Datini in Florence, 9 December 1402 and 1 October 1403. The Foscherari, with their partner Zono di Pietro de la Volta, were called "soci in arte et misterio artis cambii" in Bologna, in ASV, GP, Sg, reg. 12, fol. 11 (12 November 1403). Virtually unstudied are the several buste of letters written to Datini from Bologna, a major center of the trade in specie; see ADP, 645–46, for the years 1399–1400.

[45]ADP, 715, Piaciti to Florence, 24 May 1404.

[46]Act of the Petizion, cited above, n. 44.

[47]On Cardinal Cossa's connections, see his suit against the Venetian branch of the firm Gabion e Giacomo Gozzadini e Compagni, in the person of the partner and factor Jacopo de'

else, it had time to arrest the factor as debtor to the state. Some time shortly before, in fact, the Signoria had remitted 12,000 ducats to Mantua via bills drawn by the firm's Venetian representative. There were also other remittances to Mantua via Bologna, as well as a shipment of 3,070 "pezi" of gold worth 9,000 ducats. When Antonio di Giovanni was arrested, the state sequestered jewels worth 10,000 ducats as surety for the bills, as well as merchandise and credits ("debitori") for an additional 8,000 ducats.[48] Preliminary estimates showed that the Foscherari had debits in Venice of 35,000–36,000 ducats, of which most were owed to Florentines and at least 6,000 were owed directly to the Signoria.[49] On Sunday, 11 January 1405, it was realized that the Benedetto estate bank had been guarantor of the Foscherari to the state for the remittance of 12,000 ducats. Not surprisingly, on Monday the 12th there was a run on the bank, and by the end of the day the partners, "finding themselves in debt for 80,000 ducats or more," had to close and take their account books to the Consoli dei Mercanti. According to custom, they declared that they intended to pay all and asked help in the collection of debts as well as an immediate safe-conduct to protect themselves from arrest.

The foreign community in Venice was very much disturbed. Paoluccio, who had a credit of only 75 ducats in the bank, could not help commenting pessimistically, "It's very risky to do business in these times" [Gran pericholo è a fare al dì d'oggi la merchatantia].[50] Piaciti warned that the Foscherari firm was "deeply indebted" to the Venetian bank. Even though he estimated Florentine credits in the second Benedetto bank at only 4,000 ducats and predicted payment in full, he averred that bankrupt Bolognese never pay in full.[51] Other correspondents also reported that the Bolognese debt was "grande e non buono."[52] By 19 January word of the agreement between the Foscherari and their creditors was out: they would pay up only two-thirds of their debts, half in two months and the balance (one-sixth) in one year. Later it was said that Cardinal Cossa had agreed to put up one-twelfth in order to bring the total to 75 percent. For Venetian debts of the Foscherari the correspondents also predicted a settlement at 75 percent.[53]

Foschi, a naturalized Venetian of Bolognese origin. The suit speaks of 10,000–16,000 ducats deposited in the bank "qui non reperiuntur" in Venice or Rome, from which the cardinal had ordered payments to other prelates. ASV, GP, Sg, reg. 12, fols. 110v–14v (17 September 1404). His involvement in the Foscherari failure is mentioned by Domenico d'Andrea to Barcelona, ADP, 929, 28 February 1405.

[48]The most detailed account of the whole affair is provided by the long letters of Giovanni di Ser Nigi e Gherardo Davizi to Florence, of 13–16 January and 27 January 1405, in ADP, 715.

[49]ADP, 715, Piaciti to Florence, 3–15 January; also Domenico d'Andrea to Barcelona, ADP, 929, 13–16 January 1405.

[50]ADP, 929, Paoluccio to Barcelona, 13 January 1405.

[51]"Non è usanza de' Bologniesi uscire tropo buon debiti quando venghono a simili casi." ADP, 715, Piaciti to Florence, 3–15 January.

[52]ADP, 647, Jacopo e Giovanni de' Cari in Bologna to Florence, 12 January 1405.

[53]Ibid., 19 January, and ibid., 929, Domenico d'Andrea to Barcelona, 28 February 1405.

As regards the Benedetto estate bank, the forecast was for full payment over time. The trial balance cast by 16 January 1405 showed the financial situation to be the following:

Liabilities:		110,000 ducats
Assets:	real estate (but inalienable):	40,000
	good loans ("buoni debitori"), plus gold and silver at the mint:	45,000
	in a bottega di seta:	13,000
	"mercantie in più parti," viz. Alexandria, Syria, Turkey, and Seville:	"denari assai"

At the same time the partners made their opening offer to the creditors: they would pay 50 percent after one year, and 25 percent at the end of each of the subsequent six-month periods. The final agreement on a debt now set at 114,000 ducats was ready by the 27th; the debt would be paid in full ("20 soldi per lira") over 28 months, in four installments:[54]

8s	(40%)	in 4 months
5s	(25%)	in 8 months
3s 6d	(17.5%)	in 8 months
3s 6d	(17.5%)	in 8 months
20s	(100%)	in 28 months

The first payment was to be financed by collections from debtors; subsequent payments were to be backed by guarantors.

The reaction of the Venetian money market to the failure and to the negotiations is interesting and instructive. First, exchange rates shot up and remained high for one month. Giovanni di Ser Nigi explained that the reason for this was the failure of the Benedetto estate bank; because of its near monopoly of business with dealers in foreign exchange, funds normally available for buying bills were now largely tied up.[55] Then some creditors, seeing that the collection process would be protracted, began offering their claims ("dette") at a one-third discount! Again it was Giovanni di Ser Nigi who reported this tendency, and he gave the example of a

[54]ADP, 715, Giovanni di Ser Nigi and Gherardo Davizi to Florence, 13–16 January. Terms of the agreement are described also by Domenico d'Andrea (ADP, 929, 28 January and 28 February) and by the Gaddi estate (ADP, 715, 27 January).

[55]"Qui sarà gran charestia di danari per chagione di questo bancho rotto, e la chagione è che tutti questi forestieri davano danari in chanbio gli avieno o in sul bancho o in questi Foscherari e prima in Salvi, perchè quasi il tutto faceva quello bancho; sichè fuori di là non n'erano molti." Salvi di Giovanni Lippi, the merchant banker, had died in October. This passage seems to indicate that some foreign exchange was carried on the books of merchant bankers but that most was handled by the transfer banks of the Rialto. ADP, 715, Giovanni di Ser Nigi, 13–16 January; repeated on 27 January.

Ragusan merchant who had sold his credit of 3,000 ducats to the exchange dealer Alessandro Borromei for 2,000 ducats cash. Noting that the latter now owned 8,000 ducats in claims on the bank, the correspondent wrote that this was an astute move ("à fatto buona compera"). As always, some would profit and some would lose. There was room for optimism in the fact that a chain of bankruptcies, similar to that of 1374–75, did not develop in Venice. But upon hearing a rumor that the administrator of the bank was considering the possibility of reopening, the successor of Gaddi wrote, "I don't know who should trust him."[56] The trial balloon, if that it was, did not lift off. The remaining banks took over the business of the foreign community. In late February 1405 merchants in Florence were assured that none of the remaining banks in Venice was suspect and that one could place full trust in them.[57]

Up to this point we have been able to reconstruct the affair and its effect on the money market largely on the basis of reports written by the bank's foreign clients. With the addition of the meager Venetian documentation, we can look more closely at organizational and legal problems, some of which shed light on general procedures and practices.

The safe-conduct, or "fida," requested by the partners was immediately conceded.[58] Jurisdictional questions were resolved on 15 January when full powers over the "banchum . . . ruptum" were conferred upon the Consoli dei Mercanti, despite their personal interests in the bank.[59] The firm remained open for the initial period of liquidation, but a "massarius" of the Consoli supervised operations. No payments could be made by the bank without prior verification of the debt by the Consoli.[60] Clients were called upon to cooperate. The Sienese Domenico d'Andrea, himself a creditor of the bank for 1,400 ducats, explained that all depositors would turn in records of their current accounts with the bank for activity subsequent to the last balance each had cast in agreement with the banker. This, he said, was the traditional way of proceeding in Venice.[61]

---

[56]ADP, 715, Commis. Gaddi, 27 January: "E dicesi ritornare a bancho; non so chi ssi dovrà fidare di lui." The person meant here was the active partner, either Stefano Benedetto (Pietro's second son) or more likely Marco or Simone Condulmer.

[57]"E non ciè di bisongnio avere sospetto di nullo bancho ci sia." ADP, 715, Giovanni di Ser Nigi, 23 February.

[58]ADP, 929, Paoluccio to Barcelona, 13 January.

[59]Lost deliberation of 15 January, cited in ASV, MC, Ursa, fol. 34v (18 March 1421).

[60]ASV, GP, Sg, reg. 16, fols. 25–27 (24 February 1408). This case, along with another of 1 September 1407 (ibid., reg. 27, fol. 75), represent attempts to get around the Consoli and the agreement on installments by appealing to the Petizion against Simone Condulmer. Both were in fact voided; see AC, reg. 3646, fols. 41v–42 (1 June 1408).

[61]"Tutti se mandaranno le partitte dal bancho da l'ultimo saldo in qua, sichè posono vedere chome vi sono, e così è usanza di fare." ADP, 929, Domenico d'Andrea to Barcelona, 28 February. This is the first documented indication that interim balances (saldi) were periodically agreed upon between Venetian banchieri di scritta and their clients, even though the need for such a practice is self-evident.

The state took steps to help the families of the partners but also protected its own interests. Upon petition of the heirs of Pietro Benedetto and Jacobello Zane (who had died in 1403), and with the agreement of the Consoli and a majority of creditors, a moratorium was placed on the sale of real estate to prevent the "destruction" of the more than thirty-five dependents ("creature") of those families.[62] A further moratorium was granted when forced loan levies ("impositiones") on Marco and Simone Condulmer were suspended.[63] On the other hand, customs dues and freights owed by Simone were ordered paid "primo et ante omnia," which probably meant that the officials (the Estraordinari) did not consider themselves bound by the agreement made with private creditors.[64] The state, however, was ready to use its authority, if necessary, to help collect debts.[65] And it cooperated with the private creditors of the Foscherari firm by giving power of attorney to one of their representatives to negotiate in Bologna for payment of the bills remitted to Mantua, while keeping open its claims against the Venetian bank that had guaranteed them.[66]

As had been established in the agreement made with the creditors, the bank partners were to put up bond to ensure payment of the later installments. This was accomplished by having guarantors pay money to the Consoli, while the partners turned over merchandise or its sale value to the guarantors. Civil suits have preserved the names of some of those who pledged themselves in 1405 and the amounts guaranteed:

Andreolo di Cristofano:	1,000 ducats
Francesco Pavoni, archbishop of Crete:	1,000 ducats
Leonardo Zane, Giannino Zane, and Federigo Michiel, commercial partners of the bankers:	500 ducats each

Some goods in the Levant were ordered signed over to Andreolo.[67] A

---

[62]On 13 January Giovanni di Ser Nigi had written, "Non bisogna vendere nulla loro possessione, che vale anchora si tiene di largho duchati 40,000." ADP, 715. The petition was entered in the copy of deliberations of the Great Council maintained by the Avogaria and dated 8 February (ASV, AC, reg. 28, fols. 30v–31). It is not clear whether the children of Marco and Simone Condulmer were included in the count of the offspring. The executors of the Benedetto and Zane estates were also permitted to act in the name of the bank as principals along with the two Condulmer.

[63]Lost deliberation, mentioned in ASV, SM, reg. 47, fol. 14 (5 August 1405).

[64]ASV, CN, reg. 3, fol. 129 (18 February).

[65]Debts owed by Bolognese to the heirs and executors of Pietro Benedetto much later, but probably still as a result of the failures of 1405, were ordered collected by reprisal. ASV, SM, reg. 52, fol. 27v (17 June 1417), and CN, reg. 6, fol. 1 (18 November 1424).

[66]ASV, MC, Leona, fol. 153r–v (13 May 1406). The liquidators were Pietro Trevisan and Bernardo Buora, Venetians, and Pietro Dini, a Florentine. The Raxon Vecchia maintained these contacts for the state; Marco Condulmer and Pietro Dini made an agreement that required their ratification; ibid., and 23 May.

[67]ASV, GP, Sg, reg. 15, fols. 38v–39v (18 May 1408), with a "copia scripti" of 25 September 1405.

shipment of five cases of velvets and cloths of gold from the bank's silk shop was sent to the agent Jacopo Erizzo in Alexandria, which was worth 10,000 ducats (4,000 due to the Benedetto estate, 6,000 to Marco Condulmer and the silk entrepreneur Bartolomeo Gardellino); from the proceeds of the sale, Erizzo was to invest 2,500 ducats in the name of the other four guarantors, using their own merchant symbols.[68]

The bank met its initial obligations, probably even on time,[69] but full liquidation took much longer than the promised twenty-eight months. As late as 1418 a piece of real estate belonging to Simone Condulmer was to be sold to meet debts of the bank.[70] The liquidation, however, did not prevent this wealthy merchant from continuing to do business, and in grand style.

ii. REORGANIZATIONS AND FAILURES IN THE 1420s

The two decades following the failure of the Benedetto estate bank in 1405 were free of banking crises, despite the existence — more elsewhere than in Venice — of the so-called bullion famine. Venice had its own bullion famine from 1417 to 1423, as a result of a trade blockade imposed by King Sigismund which made it difficult for German merchants to reach Venice with their usual cargos of silver. The famous law of 1421 which tried to limit the use of bank money and the agio that had developed between full-weight coin and bank money is best seen in the context of that blockade, rather than as a reflection of a crisis in the banking system.[71]

The demise of the Benedetto bank and its successor left four banks operating on the Rialto, to which number a fifth was added. The five banks were (1) that of Gabriele Soranzo, who had opened his bank in the 1370s, not long after Pietro Benedetto's start; (2) that of Guglielmo Condulmer, the bullion dealer, who, having begun about 1389, continued to function until about 1413 and seems to have simply wound down and closed without incident (the banker himself died in 1421); (3) that of Ser Giovanni Corner and Antonio Miorati, which opened in 1399; (4) that founded by Roberto Priuli and Brothers in the same year; and, finally, (5) that of Bernardo di Pietro Giustinian, a single operator who opened in 1409 and closed in 1424 or 1425, without any recorded incident.[72] Banks, probably of

---

[68]Ibid., reg. 39, fol. 4 (21 November 1415).

[69]Soranzo ledger, fols. 1 and 2 (1406).

[70]ASV, MC, Ursa, fol. 20v (17 July 1418); there were still complications on the Zane side in 1421, ibid., fol. 34v (18 March). Petty sums regarding Simone Condulmer's one-fourth liabilities in the bank were still outstanding in 1454; see GP, Sg, reg. 144, fols. 33v–42, 63v–67v (22 February and 3 April 1465).

[71]Lattes, *Libertà,* doc. 14; Mueller, "Role of Bank Money," 84–94; and Mandich, "Monete di conto veneziane," 30–36

[72]Little is known about this bank; it was not connected with the fraterna of Bernardo, Paolo e Gerolamo Giustinian, sons of Giustiniano Giustinian, who used the bank solely for transitory accounts in 1418–20. ASV, PSM, Misti, b. 91a, fasc. 7, small ledger, fol. 3.

moneychangers, with little echo in the documents were those of Marco Arian, who closed in August 1403, and Giovanni della Torre, active between 1412 and 1416.

The principal competitor of the Benedetto banks was that of the nobleman Gabriele di Giovanni Soranzo, in operation by 1374. That bank weathered the crises that brought the demise of others in 1374–76, 1400, 1405. It had to weather a crisis of its own around 1393. In that year Gabriele's close friend Verde della Scala, a Veronese noblewoman, daughter of Mastino della Scala and widow of Nicolò d'Este, then a citizen of and resident in Venice, having named the banker one of her executors, willed him the palazzo she had just purchased plus a pension of 200 ducats per year "should at any time he fall into poverty"; and on the following day she made over to him, should her testamentary provisions not be carried out for some reason, the large sum of 30,000 ducats.[73] Clearly, Gabriele found himself in difficult straits (imagine an established banker being offered a pension by an admiring old gentlewoman!), but he managed to ride out the storm. Besides the bank, however, Gabriele in the same years had a commercial company, which specialized in the importation of raw wool from Catalonia and which figures prominently in the Datini correspondence, with Francesco Corner, son of the deceased doge, Marco Corner. When Gabriele died in 1410, the bank continued as an estate under the style "Commissaria di Gabriele Soranzo"; it was run by his several sons until 1430, when Cristoforo, the eldest surviving son and survivor of two major banking crises, changed the style in his own right to "Cristoforo Soranzo e fratelli."

Another major bank of those years was that formed by the nobleman Giovanni Corner and the non-noble Antonio Miorati, which opened on 15 October 1399. The bank was interested in the bullion trade; in fact, "Giannino Chornero," as he was called in a Florentine account book, was a bullion dealer before opening the bank, and at some point the bank took in two immigrants from Florence with the aim of increasing its strength in that sector. Domenico di Masino di Manetto was made factor, at a salary of 100 ducats per year, and at least by 1409 the refiner and bullion merchant Donato di Filippo Nati was made full partner of the bank.[74] In 1410, the same year as Gabriele Soranzo's death, Giovanni Corner presumably died, and his place in the partnership, which otherwise remained the same, was taken by Nicolò Cocco, another nobleman.

---

[73]For the testament, see Reinhold C. Mueller, "Veronesi e capitali veronesi a Venezia in epoca scaligera," *Gli Scaligeri, 1277–1387*, ed. Gian Maria Varanini (Verona, 1988), 370. For the assurance of 30,000 ducats, never referred to as covering a debt, see ASV, CIN, b. 169 (notaio M. Raffanelli), reg. 1, under 5 December 1393; in the act Verde calls the banker "compater fidentissimus meus"; highly placed witnesses to the act included Gabriele's business partner, Francesco Corner.

[74]See above, Chap. 3, sec. iv. In 1391 Corner furnished the Del Bene bank in Padua with silver bars. ASF, Del Bene, n. 20 (journal), fol. 6, and n. 19 (ledger), fols. 13, 88–89.

As was common in Venice, both Miorati and Cocco also had private commercial ventures in the Levant trade in which the bank technically did not figure (they were recorded as being "in mia spizialità" or "spizialitade"). In practice, the distinctions were labile, and bankers invested their own liabilities in commercial ventures. Furthermore, Miorati named his current bank partners as his executors in the extant testaments of 1405 and 1422. The latter text was drafted more under the pressure of economic difficulties than of the plague season. In recommending his family to the tutelage of Nicolò Cocco, Antonio states that he was in trouble because of losses sustained on voyages to England and Romania (he had interests in Tana, where his son Ranieri was active).[75] A week before his death, Miorati added a codicil to the testament in which he stated that the bank he had with Nicolò Cocco could be continued by Cocco alone or, should he so choose, with another partner or partners, a statement made surely in order to forestall the trouble that usually arose in Venice at the death of a banker.[76] When Cocco was sued by Antonio's commercial partners to pay the deceased's debts, he contended that he was not liable personally for his former partner's personal debts and recounted the story of Antonio's death and the sequel—his own decision not to carry on the banking enterprise.[77]

Miorati died on 31 August 1424. On 1 September, "the day the [Alexandria] galleys departed," Cocco met with the executors of Miorati's estate to discuss "the matter of the bank and to see how much the bank owed the estate." On that occasion, Cocco decided he did not want to continue the bank, neither in his own name nor in that of the estate, or sign any obliga-

[75]He wrote, "Perchè i mie fati enno andadi stranamente di uno bon pezo in qua, e questo è per lo viazio da Sio [Scio] e di Inghilterra e senpre son stado suxo grandissima spexa, e per questa chaxion rechomando questa mia fameglia a ser Nicolò Chocho. . . . Perchè al prexente mal poso veder di quelo me truovo sea la mia condizion, e per questa chaxion laso in libertade de la plu parte di mie chomesari." ASV, NT, b. 1230, no. 17.

[76]The two testaments are in ibid., b. 858 (notary Marco de Raffanelli) and 1230, n. 17.

[77]ASV, GP, Sg, reg. 13, fols. 162–64v, 170v (countersuit) (21 July 1427). Neither case was resolved in court with a sentence, an unusual event, which might mean the matter was referred to arbitration and resolved out of court. The commercial company for the Tana voyage was formed in 1421 by Miorati, Nicolò Morosini, and Stefano Bevilaqua; the latter was a traveling partner and sent to Venice "sementina, robarbaro, teste [slaves]," and other things. When Stefano died in Tana, Miorati sent his son Ranieri to close out affairs. Antonio Morosini reports on the voyages likely involved. The three galleys to the Black Sea, on which Stefano must have sailed in July 1421, departed with goods and bullion valued at 260,000 ducats. A cog was wrecked in 1422, while another was captured by pirates in 1423 when only two of three galleys returned, carrying little merchandise (silk, few spices, wax, and skins), reporting war and sacking in the areas controlled by the Tatars. See Morosini, Cronaca, 2:303, 361, 427, 440. Cocco himself had, with partners, invested in cotton; see ASV, GP, Sg, reg. 31, fol. 18v (5 February 1414). In 1427 Cocco recalled that the solvency of the estate had been believed by all up until "about 1 November 1424," after which the estate was declared bankrupt. The date of that declaration was 12 March 1425, according to a deliberation of 25 September 1425, in Cassandro, Le rappresaglie e il fallimento, 158, doc. 29.

tion with the executors, so he opted for liquidation in the usual fashion: he went with the account books to the Consoli dei Mercanti so that they would oversee the task of collecting the credits and paying the debts of the bank. The private commercial investments of Miorati, "who was as wonderfully trustworthy as any merchant of Venice," were considered solid until the executors declared the estate bankrupt on 12 March 1425. Cocco paid the bank's debts and received the credits verified by the Consoli. Then, on 12 March 1425 (two days before the failure of the Priuli bank), Cocco was formally named chief liquidator ("cavo") of the Miorati estate, which, after paying out a settlement of nearly 2,000 ducats to the son Ranieri, was able to pay only slightly less than 50 percent of the estate's debts. The former commercial partners and the former banking partner accused one another of hiding crucial account books. The liquidation of the bank, on the other hand, proceeded in an orderly fashion, and the bank probably paid in full. Cocco himself seems to have died in 1430.[78]

The history of the Priuli bank was much more complicated. It opened, as we have seen, with the style "Ser Ruberto di Prioli e fratelli" on 20 October 1399, five days after the opening of the Corner-Miorati bank, as we know from the report of Manetto Davanzati (who judged both safe and wished them Godspeed). Roberto di Lorenzo,[79] who had some five brothers, died in 1402, after which the bank, now styled "La commissaria di Roberto Priuli e fratelli," was run by Andrea, executor and the next brother in line. In February 1405, just after the fall of the Benedetto estate bank, Andrea began in his own right, styling the bank "Ser Andrea di Priuli e fratelli."[80]

If the Benedetto estate bank nearly monopolized business (especially the exchange business, as the Florentine operator had observed), it seems there was more competition later. It is true that evidence is one sided, for we have only one major ledger for the first three decades of the century. That commercial company, the Soranzo fraterna, did most of its banking business with Andrea Priuli and its successor and with Corner and Miorati and its successor, Cocco and Miorati, as long and solid current accounts attest. Bernardo Giustinian was used only infrequently, and the fraterna kept only two brief transitory accounts with the bank of Gabriele Soranzo and its successor.

Andrea Priuli also had a commercial company on the side, but this time the bank and the company became inextricably intertwined. Accord-

---

[78]ASV, GP, Sg, reg. 58, fols. 33v–35r (2 December 1430), and reg. 74, fol. 93bis r–v (4 July 1437). The Soranzo fraterna (ledger, fol. 105) balanced and closed its account with the bank on 1 September 1424.

[79]The branch was that of S. Giovanni Decollato; Lorenzo was inscribed in the estimo of 1379 for 5,500 lire; PRV, 191; cf. Ferrara, "Antichi banchi," 194.

[80]The reader who wishes to distinguish among the eight different styles used by members of this family in just thirty years is referred to the entry in App. A for the Priuli banks, under the year 1399.

ing to an heir of his major commercial partner, Pietro (di Maffeo) Venier,[81] the bank was a partner of the commercial company ("ne la qual [compagnia] el bancho ne intervegnia e participava"), so that it was proper that the liquidation of both entities be handled by the Consoli dei Mercanti, who had jurisdiction over banks.[82] We are fairly well informed about the failure of the bank in 1425 from litigation that generated many court briefs and deliberations over nearly fifty years, in suits both between Priuli and Venier heirs and between the two together and creditors of the bank, as we have seen above (Chap. 3, sec. v).

At the end of an illustrious career as a banker on the Rialto, Andrea Priuli died in late August 1424.[83] That was, of course, a dangerous season, not only for the plague but also for the tight money situation created by the departure of the last galleys, those sailing to Alexandria. There must have been tension on the market, but the brothers refounded the bank immediately under the style "La commissaria di Andrea Priuli e fratelli." In that form the bank continued to operate for another year, until it was forced to close because of insolvency, probably under the pressure of a run by depositors, on the morning of Monday, 14 May 1425. Venetians at the time judged the cause to have been serious quarreling among the surviving brothers.[84] Later chroniclers all report the failure, which was among the more clamorous in Venetian history; liabilities, according to these later reports, were placed at 240,000–250,000 ducats, and the failure was attributed to the death of Andrea Priuli, who had directed operations for twenty-two years.[85]

---

[81]So called in ASV, GP, Sg, reg. 11, fol. 45 (20 March 1404). A Pietro qd. Andrea Venier of S. Croce is called "campsor" in the vote for a position (won by another) as scribe and weigher at the gold mint; CN, reg. 5, fol. 86v (31 November 1417). It is probably the latter whose bank was robbed in 1419 (Quarantia Criminal, reg. 14bis, fol. 99v, and AC, reg. 3647, fol. 62v), presumably a small-time operator. The other Pietro, occasionally found working at the bank of Andrea Priuli and thus called "dal banco" (e.g., in 1415: GP, Sg, reg. 60, fol. 18v), was a partner of the bank and of a formally separate commercial company.

[82]ASV, GP, Sg, reg. 128, fols. 1–5 (16 October 1459).

[83]The testament, not as yet found, was registered in the chancery on 29 August; this and many similar details are drawn from the lawsuit in ASV, Giudici del Procurator, Sentenze a legge, reg. 10, fols. 85v–90v (15 May 1481), fols. 86r, 88–89.

[84]The contemporary chronicler Antonio Morosini (Cronaca, 2:542; original, fol. 422) recorded the event: "1425. Nota fazio a memuoria de tuti, chomo in l'ano de 1425 de luni, dì 14 mazio in Veniexia falì el bancho de la comesaria de ser Andrea d'i Prioli e fradeli, da matina, e fo dito fo per alguna controversia de parole queli fradeli aver abudo insembre in non eser stadi d'acordo, e non se sa como queli fati ancora se troverà in li suo prededori ben in ordene."

[85]Of these the best-informed report comes from the cronaca Veniera, BMV, It. cl. VII, 793 (8477), fol. 146v, and (very similar) ibid., 791 (7589), fol. 114v. It reads: "Faccio memoria come 1425 a dì 14 mazo falì el bancho de scritta de ser Andrea di Priuli et fradeli, qual era uno notablissimo bancho et questo intervene per la morte del ditto ser Andrea di Priuli, el qual governava el ditto bancho et tròvase debitor de ducati 250,000 et era anchora el bancho creditor de più persone de bona suma de danari." Cf. also ibid., 1568 (8016), under the date. Sixteenth-century chronicles continued to carry the event, but in a very summary fashion; see,

Even the later chronicles were not far from wrong: the death of the experienced banker, even though it had occurred more than eight months before the liquidation procedure began, must have set the surviving brothers to quarreling. But if that was the proximate cause, the economic causes were more profound. A rash of failures in Venice and Florence was causing chain reactions that made collection of credits difficult. Perhaps the series of failures had already started in 1424,[86] but the signs are clearer in the following year. On 12 March 1425, only two months before the Priuli failure, the estate of the deceased banker Miorati was declared bankrupt, as mentioned above. Then the freezing of private assets in bank deposits worth a quarter of a million ducats — assuming the veracity of that report — in the Priuli liquidation only two months prior to the "termini" at the beginning of the sailing season surely provided further pretext for declarations of bankruptcy. After the departure of the galleys in late summer, the Sandelli fraterna, the important Lucchese family of silk entrepreneurs in Venice, failed,[87] and in September the Great Council, in reminding other courts that only the Sopraconsoli had jurisdiction to deal with (nonbank) bankrupts, complained that in that period many persons were feigning bankruptcy and fleeing Venice in order to get the best possible terms ("bonissimi pati") with their creditors, which brought infamy on the city and was "an outright robbery, odious to God and mankind."[88]

In May, furthermore, Venice and Florence were negotiating their military alliance against Visconti Milan. The prospect of heavy impositions of forced loans for a war effort caused the price of government obligations to fall from 67 to 64½. That drop, in turn, reduced the value of assets that had to be liquidated by debtors to the failed bank, thus tightening the credit market still further.[89]

The Sandelli case, which involved many protested bills of exchange,

for example, BMCV, cod. Cicogna 2569 (cronaca Alberegno), fol. 140v (liabilities: 240,000 ducats). One late chronicle, which belonged to an unknown "Francesco Soranzo dal banco," set *net* liabilities at 240,000 ducats: "batudo i debitori e chredidori, restavano debitori a particular persone ducati 240,000"; Seminario patriarcale, Venice, ms. 191, fol. 137.

[86]A bankrupt debtor of the banker Bernardo Giustinian was Marco Bocchetta, and the banker was his "caput creditorum"; in that capacity Bernardo had words with Daniele Venier, Sopraconsolo, which cost him a fine of 100 lire. ASV, AC, reg. 3647, fol. 53 (17 March 1424). It was also the year of the death of both Andrea Priuli and Antonio Miorati.

[87]ASV, GP, Sg, reg. 48, between fols. 74 and 75, copy of a letter dated 20 August 1425 of Giorgio Orselli to Ettore Belloni, who had lent the Sandei 3,000 ducats via bills of exchange, now being protested. On the failure, see Molà, *La comunità dei lucchesi,* 203–4. An earlier example is the flight of the Ragusan Biagio di Buona, probably a silver merchant, who absconded in 1423 with money and goods "of nobles and other Venetians" worth 8,000 ducats; see SM, reg. 54, fols. 94r, 95r, 96r–v, 132v, 163r.

[88]ASV, MC, Ursa, fol. 64v, printed in Cassandro, *Le rappresaglie e il fallimento,* 158–59.

[89]The story is recounted in testimony presented in a suit by Maffeo qd. Maffeo Malipiero against Tomà qd. Marino Malipiero, in ASV, GP, Sg, reg. 96, fols. 87v–96v (27 April 1444).

and the movement of funds necessary for the war effort underscore the importance of interregional financial connections. In Florence, the closest money market and Venice's ally, the economic situation was characterized by a general lack of liquidity later in the same year. The state was unable to repay bankers for short-term loans (usually contracted on the bill market), and several large merchant-banking firms, including those of Palla di Palla Strozzi, Nicolò d'Agnolo Serragli, and Salomone di Carlo Strozzi, declared bankruptcy; the Medici, according to de Roover, decided to discontinue their Naples branch.[90]

In Venice the situation must have been tense; both private parties and the state intervened quickly. Private creditors acted to make sure their interests would be represented.[91] The state, in an unusual move, named as receivers two of the most prominent nobles of Venice, Leonardo Mocenigo and Antonio Contarini, both Procurators of San Marco, aided by two nobles selected by them, Francesco Zane and Pietro Pisani.[92] So many noblemen and their relatives were involved in some way with the insolvent bank that, under conflict-of-interest regulations, the Forty could not reach a quorum for discussion of the case.[93] The liquidators worked rapidly, however, for on 20 August they were able to pay what Antonio Morosini announced as a large first installment of two-thirds of the debt, with the promise of another installment of 20 percent the following Christmas.[94] The concordat, reached "pleasantly" (according to the chronicler) and approved by the Forty on 22 October, promised payment of the final balance due in two years' time. In a climate of renewed trust, a successor bank, styled "La commissaria di Andrea Priuli e Ser Bartolomeo Priuli, banchieri," was able to open on the same location a week later.[95]

---

[90]Anthony Molho, *Florentine Public Finances in the Early Renaissance* (Cambridge, Mass., 1971), 153–54; de Roover, *Medici Bank*, 48.

[91]Two powers of attorney were drafted precisely for "asking, demanding and collecting what I am owed by the bank of the estate of Andrea Priuli." ASV, CIN, b. 194, notary Enrico de Sileris, fol. 4v: Francesco Bevilacqua of Mantua on 15 May, and (fol. 5v) Johannes Oder of Salzburg on 4 June.

[92]This procedure would also be used in 1453, when this precedent was mentioned; see Ferrara, "Documenti," doc. 12, p. 115.

[93]ASV, MC, Ursa, fol. 63 (24 June 1425).

[94]"Fazo nota ad memuoria de tute persone, per i signor chavi credadori del bancho de scrita fo de ser Andrea di Prioli e suo fradeli paga e chomenza a dar a dì 20 d'avosto de 1425 per la prima paga a tute persone de' aver da quela, per i do terzi di quelo i die' aver — soldi 13, denari 4 di grossi per livra de grosi — e dise de' dar una altra parte per 'sto nadal prosimo de 1425 circha soldi 4 per livra de grosi." Morosini, Cronaca, 2:565; original, fol. 426. In fact, on 25 August the Soranzo fraterna, which had only a minute claim against this bank, received something less than 5 ducats cash from the liquidators as its first installment (Soranzo ledger, fol. 107).

[95]See the terse note by Marin Sanudo in ASV, Quarantia Criminal, reg. 14bis, fol. 101v. Morosini wrote, "Femo mencion in nome de Cristo che el bancho d'i Prioli tegniva miser Andrea e fradeli, el qual falì de Veniexia, se aconza con i suo credadori piaxevelmente e queli s'acorda de conplirli de pagar con intrigitade; e retornadi può suxo el so bancho uno luni a dì

Even though the Soranzo fraterna accepted what it called a final settlement in June 1428 as a credit on their current account on the successor bank,[96] actual liquidation of the last perhaps 15 percent of the debt dragged on for half a century. The liquidators gave chase to the big debtors.[97] Big creditors must have been seriously hurt, first by the loss of liquidity but also by absolute loss of capital. The delays were aggravated by constant suits and countersuits between the heirs of Andrea Priuli and those of Pietro Venier as to how much of whose money was to go toward paying the bank's debt. Venier seems to have been a silent partner of the bank and probably also took his turn in handling daily business, since he is sometimes called "dal banco"; at the same time, he was a partner of Andrea Priuli in commercial ventures. Special provisions had to be made in the organs of government in order to ensure a quorum when the case was discussed, and courts of appeal such as the Auditori Vecchi and Nuovi, which had to present cases before the Forty, also constantly overturned earlier decisions. As we have seen in more detail in discussing liability (above, Chap. 3, sec. v), in 1453, twenty-eight years after the failure, the litigation and "subtle questions" that kept the innumerable creditors of the bank ("assai e de grandissimo numero") from receiving their due, then calculated to be 1⅓ soldi on a lira, or 7 percent, threatened to become "immortal." Together the Senate and Great Council acted to reduce procedure to a minimum so as to get the executors of the Venier estate (the Procurators of San Marco) to reach an accord with the current liquidators.[98] An agreement was in fact reached: the litigants together were to pay out the balance due in nine equal annual installments. But in 1459 the heirs of Antonio Contarini, the Procurator and first liquidator, claimed that they had yet to receive anything at all; representatives of the Priuli and Venier families, now in unison, rejected the claim and recounted how Contarini and the other capi had refused to show them the account books until the pact had been signed.[99] So matters dragged on further, and in 1481, nearly fifty years since the failure, Daniele Priuli, then in the role of liquidator, was still trying to get money out of the estate of Michele, Andrea Priuli's youngest son. The Procurators, as executors of

29 otubrio de l'ano de 1425, pagando tuti con intrigitade, infin a ani do chonplidi." Morosini, Cronaca, 2:595; original, fol. 431. The Soranzo fraterna registered its first operations at the bank in December (ledger, fol. 125).

[96]Soranzo ledger, fol. 107.

[97]For example, Tomà qd. Marino Malipiero was forced to borrow money because "li era per rizever grande inchargo, per la chaza i dava i chavi di chrededori del bancho." GP, Sg, reg. 96, fols. 87v–96v (27 April 1444). Donato di Filippo Nati, the bullion dealer who seems to have been a silent partner of the bank, was forced to flee Venice for debts in 1427.

[98]ASV, MC, Ursa, fols. 119 (1438), 171 (1450), 185 (1453), 187v and 192r (1454); ST, reg. 2, fol. 157v (1450), reg. 4, fol. 185r (1453).

[99]The agreement of 19 May 1453 is copied into the record: ASV, GP, Sg, reg. 128, fol. 4v; the case is fols. 1–5; defendants were Daniele di Nicolò (di Lorenzo) Priuli and Francesco di Pietro Venier.

that estate, successfully defended the position that Michele had been considerably less than ten years old at the time of the failure and that he was not liable for the debts of the bank.[100] Whether the relatively small balance due on the bank's debts was ever paid in full cannot be known.

The quarrel among Andrea's brothers and the liquidation of the Priuli estate bank did not exclude the brothers from operating on the Rialto. On the contrary, they may well have already planned the sequel when they declared bankruptcy that Monday morning, for the brothers split, and from the ashes of the one bank sprang two: a successor bank styled, as we have seen, "La commissaria di Ser Andrea Priuli e Ser Bartolomeo Priuli, banchieri" and a bank of the other two brothers, styled "Ser Leonardo e Ser Jacomo Priuli fratelli, banchieri." In the first bank, directed by Bartolomeo, partner for one-half, worked two of Andrea's sons, Alvise (age eighteen at his father's death) and Alessandro; in the second worked some other members of the next generation, including Francesco di Leonardo and Marco (probably his brother). The estate bank reopened in October 1425 on the same site held by the previous bank, while Leonardo Priuli, in September 1425, rented the bank formerly held by Bernardo Giustinian.[101] (For a genealogy of this branch of the Priuli, see table H.2, below.)

The deaths of Antonio Miorati and Andrea Priuli, the retirement of Nicolò Cocco and Bernardo Giustinian from banking — all in 1424 — and, finally, the failure of the Priuli estate bank on 14 May 1425 made room for restructuring and for the entry of a new family on the Rialto. This time the new bankers, four Orsini brothers — Giovanni, Francesco, Bernardo, and Agostino — were of immigrant stock. Their father, Ziliolo, originally from Como and an arms importer, had received all three citizenship privileges (de intus in 1373, de extra in 1382, originarius in 1392) and had married off all his children to noble families.[102] As we saw above, the four sons had dissolved their "fraterna societas" in 1413, but they joined forces for this new endeavor, styled "Zan Orsini e fradelli, banchieri."

So the Rialto in late 1425 once again had four banks, a survivor and three new ones: the Soranzo estate bank, run by Cristoforo di Gabriele, the two Priuli banks, and the Orsini bank.[103]

---

[100]ASV, Giudici del Procurator, Sentenze a legge, reg. 10, fols. 85v–90v.

[101]ASV, Grazie, reg. 22, fol. 56: "Quod concedatur viri nobilis ser Leonardo de Priulis quod, cum velit facere teneri unum banchum a scripta, habere debeat illum banchum quem tenebat alias vir nobilis ser Bernardo Justiniano."

[102]In petitioning for the highest citizenship privilege, Ziliolo, who here for the first time uses a surname, informs that he had seven children born in Venice and that he was an arms merchant; ASV, Grazie, reg. 18, fol. 24v.

[103]A moneychanger's bank located at the head of the loggia of the nobles was operated by a Tarquinio Orso (Cessi and Alberti, *Rialto,* 64 n. 1). Donato di Filippo Nati, a partner of the Cocco-Miorati bank until 1424, is called "bancherius in Rivoalto" in April 1426 when he asked the right to counsel in dealing with the failed Andrea Priuli estate bank (ASV, Grazie, reg. 22, fol. 68r). Donato's position is ambiguous, for a partner of one of his goldbeater shops was

"And the Rialto was left like an orphan": The Failures of 1429

The new banks seem to have done well. The two Priuli banks were on good terms; in fact, regular contacts were reflected in the account books, as Leonardo used his two nephews Alvise and Alessandro as errand boys ("mesi") to carry cash from his bank to theirs to cover payments he had made on the latter bank.[104] As late as 1428, prospects in banking were good, for banks brought high rents, on five-year contracts, at the state auctions. Giovanni Orsini got his for 110 ducats per year, while Leonardo and Giacomo Priuli initially had to bid 138 ducats per year to get theirs before asking for — and receiving — equal treatment.[105] Giovanni Orsini made large bank loans and investments, including the construction of a soap-manufacturing plant, for which the contract with the master mason alone was for 1,000 ducats.[106] In the same year, however, Leonardo Priuli died,[107] and perhaps also Agostino Orsini (his testament is dated 1428). In any case, events prompted a unique solution: the formation of a new company, by merger, styled "Ser Jacomo Priuli e Zuane Orsini e compagni, banchieri." The partners clearly pooled their respective assets and liabilities, for there is no evidence of liquidation of the previous banks.

In 1429 the sky fell in. The causes of the failures of that year are myriad, and they will be examined in due course, but first, what can be known about the dynamics of the failures themselves?

Both the bank of the Andrea Priuli estate and Bartolomeo Priuli and that of Priuli-Orsini failed in September 1429, causing untold problems on the Rialto. Early in the month, after the departure of seven galleys (one more than usual) for the Levant, Giacomo Priuli, according to the report of his nephew Giovanni Diedo, found himself in a serious crisis of liquidity; trying to conceal his straits, he begged and cajoled Diedo and surely other trusted friends and relatives for cash loans "in order to maintain the bank with honor." Diedo testified that he arranged for a total of about 2,500 ducats in all possible ways, via bills of exchange, the sale of government

---

Francesco di Leonardo Priuli, which indicates an investment by the Jacomo and Leonardo Priuli bank, and he had large debts with that bank, as provider of silver and coin, when he failed in 1427; GP, Sg, reg. 66, fols. 20v–21v, 44v–45, and 5 unnumbered fols.

[104]ASV, Giudici del Procurator, Sentenze a legge, reg. 10, fols. 86v–88r (1481).

[105]ASV, Grazie, reg. 22, fol. 112v. The Priuli brothers had bid 691 ducats, 9 grossi a oro for the five years (138 ducats per year).

[106]Lawsuit between Ziliolo di Giovanni Orsini and magister Giovanni da Cremona, "murer," who had traveled to Cremona to attract other "maistri" to Venice to work on the project, an expense not accepted by Ziliolo, "perchè qua se trova maistri assai." ASV, GP, Sg, reg. 76, fols. 85–87v (10 May 1438).

[107]The Soranzo fraterna (ledger, fols. 140, 144) opened an account with "Commissaria Lunardo Priuli e Jacomo Priuli" on 30 January 1428, which means that Leonardo was dead by then. There is no trace of a rapport with the bank of Jacomo Priuli and Francesco Orsini in the ledger.

obligations, outright loans, all in cash that entered Giacomo's bank.[108] One of the creditors, Maffeo di Benetto Contarini, related how he had been approached. Diedo asked him, on or before 6 September, for a loan of 4,000 ducats that he would deposit in the bank of Giacomo Priuli and partners; if he did not have it in cash, he was told, he should withdraw it from the bank of the Priuli estate and Bartolomeo Priuli — and here is a first indication of disloyal competition. But Contarini had only 100 ducats cash and little interest in lending it. On Friday the 9th, when the banks reopened after dinner, Diedo returned, saying with insistence that he should deposit at least the 100 ducats, which Contarini finally agreed to do, using 40 ducats of that, however, to pay by transfer a debt he owed. After a weekend spent in the Trevigiano, Contarini returned to Venice on Monday the 12th to hear that the bank had failed. Since Diedo had known of the difficulties of the bank, asserted Contarini, Diedo had done him, a relative, a bad turn, "one you wouldn't do even to a Jew." Diedo, who replied that he had been working under pressure from Giacomo Priuli to find 1,000 ducats cash, admitted that others also were critical of his comportment and that he had tried in the days following to mollify Contarini with a pair of capons and a promise to make good on the balance due.[109]

Contarini and Diedo were not alone. Antonio Morosini, who seems to have had money in these banks, reported the failure and the mood of the marketplace, which was estimating losses. Liabilities were placed at 114,000 ducats, against assets of only 85,500–86,000 ducats, of which 5,500–6,000 were in cash, 60,000 in "good debtors," and 20,000 in doubtful debtors. Worst hit were judged to be Germans, Florentines, and then non-noble and noble Venetians. A safe-conduct was made valid for six months; ten liquidators (instead of the usual three), their names recorded by Morosini, were elected from among the creditors.[110]

---

[108]ASV, GP, Sg, reg. 56, fols. 42v–43 (25 September 1431). In response to Jacomo's suit to recover a chest of valuables he had turned over for security, Diedo said: "Tegnando mio barba el bancho, et siando in grandissimo bixogno et sinestro di danari, forzandosse celare el suo incargo quanto plui potea, et cognosando la carità et el mio bon servire, me rechiesse plui et diverse volte e tempi li dovesse dinari per mantegnirse in honor sul bancho, astrenzendome cum pregierie et pietade chomo è consueto a queli sono in adversitade, per modo io me inzengnai et retrarsi cercha ducati 2500, tuti al suo beneficio et destro, hora per cambii, hora a la Camera di impresdedi, hora a imprestedo et per altre vie, chomo se costuma, i quali tuti intrò in suo bancho, a suo beneficio, et io reçevi di danno ducati 200 et plui."

[109]For the judges that was not sufficient, and they ordered Diedo to pay some 55 ducats, via transfer on the books of the same failed bank; thus they favored Diedo by letting him use his otherwise frozen credit balance in the bank and forced Contarini in any case to await the liquidation of the bank itself. Ibid., reg. 52, fol. 6r–v (15 October 1429).

[110]Despite the report of credits held by foreigners, all ten seem to have been Venetians and eight of them nobles: Silvestro Morosini, Francesco Loredan, Domenico Bembo, Francesco Zorzi, Maffeo Viaro (a GP document of 1437 says Stefano Viaro), Nicolò Lippomano, Marino Giustinian. Morosini, Cronaca, 2:1018; original, fol. 508. The account repeated in later chronicles set losses at 5,000 ducats each to Germans and Florentines, 9,000 ducats to Vene-

Not surprisingly, on that same Monday the 12th a run was begun against the bank of the Priuli estate and Bartolomeo Priuli. The report comes from Leonardo qd. Pietro Venier (son of Andrea Priuli's former partner), one of those who asked to have their money in cash. After lunch on the 12th he came to withdraw all of the approximately 300 ducats he had to his credit. Milling around the bank, to give their support, were numerous nobles, among them Federigo Contarini, who tried to reassure Venier with soothing words and convince him to leave his money there, "for the bank was very safe and strong." Venier remained unconvinced, "having already lost money in this bank in the past," until Contarini offered to guarantee half the amount, on his word. Contarini, who substantially confirmed the story, said that he had been present "for the honor of the city, to avoid that the bank of Bartolomeo Priuli be put on the run."[111]

The strategy of the noble merchants worked on that afternoon of the 12th, but the bank, under continual pressure, lasted only two more weeks. On Monday, 26 September, the bank of the Priuli estate and Bartolomeo Priuli, located below the office of the Sopraconsoli, failed. Bartolomeo brought the account books to the Consoli dei Mercanti, and the Signoria and the Quarantia granted the usual safe-conduct for six months. Along with the books, the banker brought 5,000 ducats' worth of jewels and specie. While the observer Antonio Morosini was writing in his diary, it was too early to know the nature of the debt, but he recorded the fact that people were estimating assets, in the form of "good debtors," some at 63,000, others at 85,000 ducats, without counting the amount that his guarantors would cover. He did not yet know the terms of any agreement with the creditors but he was distraught: "Considering the fact that within a short time two transfer banks have failed, the city of Venice has been seriously harmed and it is evident to all that the Rialto has been orphaned, like a child without father or mother. Only time will tell what will happen; may God be praised."[112] He had just written that he did not yet know the names of the liquidators when the names were announced by the Consoli;

---

tians, and asserted that only 40 percent (8 soldi on a lira) would be paid, the balance lost. For example, BMV, It. cl. VII, 50 (9275), the pseudo-Zancaruola, fol. 534, and ibid., 794 (8503), the Dolfina, fol. 347.

[111]ASV, GP, Sg, reg. 52, fols. 1–2 (12 October 1429): "trovandome per evitar e per honor di questa terra che 'l bancho di ser Bortholamio di Prioli non fosse messo in fuga." Contarini disclaimed responsibility, however, citing first the jurisdiction of the liquidators rather than of the Petizion, then claiming that the obligation had lost all validity because all or part of the deposit had been "mosso"; in any case, he said, the claimant had asked much less after the failure ("dapuo' roto el bancho"). The sentence went against him, but, as in the case previously considered, Contarini was told to transfer the sum due on the books of the failed bank.

[112]Cronaca, 2:1019–20; original, fol. 509: "che con vero eser seguido notabel dano e incargo de tuta la citade de Veniexia, considerando in puocho de tenpo do banchi de scrita eser presto falidi, ch'è aparso a tuto el Rialto sia stado orfano de fioli senza padre e mare eser manchadi; ma per avanti aparerà quelo seguirà; Dio sia regraciado."

this time there were five "capi," three Venetian nobles, one non-noble, and a Bolognese who, in 1405, had been factor of the Gozzadini company. As to the debt, Morosini feared the bank might not be able to pay but 11–12 soldi on the lira (55–60%) and added, "I pray to God they pay more than one thinks — or knows — they will. Amen."[113]

The effects of the two failures made themselves felt immediately in both the private and the public spheres. As regards the first failure, the Consoli dei Mercanti, in the name of the creditors, sequestered, as Francesco Orsini testified, "everything we had in the world," from merchandise to real estate. For example, in 1428 Giovanni and Francesco Orsini had invested 3,580 ducats (in cash and merchandise) in Syrian cotton, which they entrusted to their nephew Donato di Domenico Malipiero, who acted as their agent; the Consoli had already noted this account on the day of the failure. When the cotton started coming in, as early as October 1429, the liquidators found 129 sacks sent by Donato; they paid a draft of 500 ducats for 30 sacks, sequestered all, took them through customs, and placed them in a warehouse. When Donato appeared on the scene personally, he summoned the liquidators to appear before the Consoli, with the intention of getting the cotton out of hock. Instead, the Consoli, having checked the entries in the books of the bank, identified the cotton as being an investment of the bank "and sent him on his way."[114] The sale of house property belonging to the Orsini continued as late as 1431.[115] One house seems to have been pledged to Donato Malipiero, not for the cotton but for a sizeable loan of 1,600 ducats he had made to the liquidators, in the form of transfers on banks then in operation. The house was sold for 1,050 ducats, but he had to compete for years with another creditor in an effort to recover his money.[116]

[113]Ibid. The liquidators were Piero Pisani, Jacomo Soranzo, Leonardo Contarini, Jacomo de' Foschi, Piero Inglostro. The second was a member of the Soranzo fraterna, which, as we know from its ledger, had constant dealings with the bank. The fourth had been a factor in Venice of the Bolognese Gozzadini bank earlier on in the century. Morosini's prayer: "Prego Dio el sia mior de quelo se crede over se sapia, Amen." Later chronicles repeat a stylized dark forecast: on liabilities of 80,000 ducats, the bank would pay only 10 or 12 soldi a lira. The Dolfina, fol. 347, which, like all the others, says four capi were chosen, leaves the number of soldi per lira blank. Ibid., 50 (9275), fol. 534, says 10 soldi, "el resto se perde." Ibid., 1 (8356), fol. 105v, says 12 soldi. A last example, ibid., 2034 (8834), fol. 395v, adds the comment, "Questo romper de questi banchi fa uno grande incargo . . . ad questa Signoria."

[114]ASV GP, 3g, reg. 73, fols. 52–54 (22 January 1436). Orsini testified (despite having denied that the Petizion had any jurisdiction) that the investment had been registered in the name of Donato and of Michele di Giovanni Orsini, even though the latter was only ten years old at the time, "per farli condizion et fama." When Donato asked for a ruling, "per quelli signori Consoli, visti i nostri libri del bancho, fo chognossudo quelli [gotoni] esser de raxon del bancho, e fo mandado chon Dio." The matter dragged on: ibid., reg. 82, fols. 13–16v (24 November 1438) and 53–57v (21 May 1439).

[115]Ibid., reg. 56, fols. 83v–84v (18 April 1431).

[116]Ibid., reg. 57, fol. 87v (18 August 1439), reg. 86, fols. 104v–7v (2 May 1442), reg. 87, fols. 110v–12 (7 July 1442); each time the defendant was Agostino Coppo.

Just how much the Priuli-Orsini bank was able to pay in the end is not clear; it did at least pay one installment of 50 percent, but the liquidation was still incomplete a decade later.[117] Clearer is the social demise of the Orsini family. The brothers' immigrant father had woven a clever web of marriage alliances with noble families, but the failure and the subsequent liquidation seem to have knocked the family out of contention for a high place in the ranks of the cittadini. Michele, "fio di fameia" of Giovanni, went into orders and made a very modest ecclesiastical career culminating in his consecration as bishop of Pola in Istria, a position he held until his retirement in 1497. Another Orsini tried to go into banking again in mid-century, but the enterprise was minor and lasted only a short time.[118] The rise and fall of this citizen family proved very rapid; the banking enterprise and the merger with Jacopo Priuli lasted only four years and contributed little to the family's upward social mobility but much to its undoing.

The failure of the second bank, hardly as "solid and strong" as one of its noble supporters had claimed during the run on 12 September, also froze the liquidity of its creditors. Although we do not have the concordat, the creditors aimed for payment of installments coinciding with the summer "termini." Evidence comes from the ledger of the Soranzo fraterna, a member of which, Jacopo, was represented on the commission of liquidators, given the fraterna's total credit of nearly 900 ducats with the bank. The accounts show that the first installment of 5 soldi (25%) was paid in cash on 4 July 1430, by the liquidator ("chavo") Jacopo de' Foschi; the second, also of 5 soldi, was paid at the termini of the Beirut galleys (as the entry reads), on the following 7 August, this time as a credit on the books of the bank of Cristoforo Soranzo and Brothers. Another year passed before any more was paid: on 4 August 1431 the liquidators paid in cash an installment of 3 soldi. With this total of 13 soldi, or 65 percent, paid in two years, the account dies out. The worst fears of the chronicler Antonio Morosini had been realized.[119]

Now this promising branch of the Priuli family, like the Orsini family, seems doomed. Andrea's sons received no inheritance, at least no positive inheritance. True, they were judged not liable for the debts, on the grounds they had been minors at the time of the failure, but they constantly had to

---

[117]Ibid., reg. 125, fols. 125v–28 (27 January 1458), where an accounting entry, alas undated, is copied into the court record, to the effect that an estate had received a sum "per rata de s. 10 per £ del bancho de ser Jacomo di Prioli e compagni come debitori de la dita compagnia." A trace of continuing problems is reflected in the usual question of conflict of interest and the quorum in the Forty; see ASV, MC, Ursa, fol. 119 (22 September 1438).

[118]ASV, GP, Sg, fols. 92–93 (15 November 1457); involved was a Nicolò Orsini, partner with Antonio de' Tommasi, "in uno bancho de cambio in Rialto," dissolved in 1454. The family should not be confused with the Orsini of Rome, of whom some members were made honorary nobles of Venice. For Michele Orsini, see Cesare Cenci, "Senato veneto: 'Probae' ai benefizi ecclesiatici," in C. Piana and C. Cenci, *Promozioni agli ordini sacri a Bologna e alle dignità ecclesiastiche nel Veneto nei secoli XIV–XV* (Quaracchi, 1968), 413, 430 n. 1.

[119]Soranzo ledger, fols. 138, 156.

defend that favorable verdict. What they had in the world they had earned in office holding and in commerce, so their executors testified late in the century. Alvise, the eldest, invested all he had in a voyage of the Flanders galleys, on which he sent his brother Alessandro. But the galley ship-wrecked, and Alessandro, intestate, drowned. The families of the other brothers had little better luck. So this family, which at the outset in 1399 hàd all the genealogical strength necessary to carry on a lasting enterprise, was undone — first by the death of Andrea, then by the dissention among his brothers, and in the end by three failures![120]

In the public sphere, the failure of the two banks in 1429 indeed created a serious problem for the government, asserted Antonio Morosini ("Questo romper de questi banchi fa uno grande incargo . . . ad questa Signoria"). Leaving the role of the two in public credit aside, since nothing can be known about the topic, the "incargo" can be seen reflected institutionally and in connection with taxes.

As early as 14 September the Great Council deliberated a delimitation of the conflict-of-interest clause which required all debtor and creditor parties as well as relatives of the Priuli-Orsini bankers to leave the hall, so that it would refer only to the principals and their immediate family members (father, brother, son); this was in order to provide more rapid justice, especially in the Quarantia, which had to deliberate on the safe-conduct and the concordat.[121] In the following year in a case involving both Andrea Priuli estate banks (failed in 1425 and 1429), legal exclusions for conflicts of interest made it impossible to reach a quorum in either the Quarantia or the Senate, and they had to be sharply reduced.[122] The Consoli dei Mercanti were also overburdened with work; in order to encourage the staff to track down debtors of the banks (which meant much accounting work as well as accepting and keeping track of collateral), the cut ("utilitas") on all collateral received or sold was to be thus divided: one-third to the Consoli themselves, and one-third each to the two head accountants ("massari").[123]

Finally, the failure of the banks was the occasion for much falsification of tax declarations ("conditiones"). As discussed below (Chap. 12, sec. iii), this was discovered when the estimo was revised in February 1431. A favorite ruse in tax evasion was to declare oneself a debtor to one of the failed banks, in particular the Priuli-Orsini bank; debts were deductible, and such

[120]ASV, Giudici del Procurator, Sentenze a legge, reg. 10, fols. 85v–90v, esp. 88v.

[121]ASV, MC, Ursa, fol. 79r.

[122]Ibid., fol. 85.

[123]The office had been accorded a fourth consul in 1423 for the same basic reasons; ibid., fols. 51v–52. For the 1429 decision, see SM, reg. 57, fol. 167 (13 November). The Consoli tried to pass off jurisdiction regarding some creditors of the Priuli-Orsini bank, only to have the Collegio confirm their jurisdiction. Originals in CN, reg. 6, fols. 77 (4 December) and 78v (12 December); printed from the capitolare of the Consoli in Lattes, *Libertà*, doc. 15, and Ferrara, "Documenti," doc. 152.

claims were difficult to contradict. Thus in March the assessors were given the right to investigate the books of the bank itself. As they worked, they also discovered the opposite ruse: creditors were not declaring either the full value of their credits or the receipt of cash from the banks' liquidators. In August the investigation was extended to include just such cases.[124]

The Conjuncture in 1429

When we turn to the causes of the failure of the two banks in 1429, we are again met by contributing factors of differing natures, familial and economic. First, "some months" before 12 September Giovanni Orsini had died, as his brother Francesco affirmed during testimony given later.[125] That event seems to have had no direct or immediate effect on trust in the bank, in part perhaps because Jacomo Priuli remained as titular head and in part because behind Jacomo there was a "company"; Francesco Orsini merely stepped in as the major representative of his family's interests in the bank.

The marketplace, on the contrary, showed signs of serious problems, first of all in the bullion market, which was of such immediate interest to Venice's bankers. Silver had been on the rise for the past few years; prices paid by the Soranzo fraterna for certified silver bars to ship east went from 5.625 ducats per mark in July 1426 to 6 ducats (up 6.67%) in July 1427, to 5.92 in February 1428 (up 4.9% in relation to 1426).[126] The rise probably continued in the following year, for in order to attract supplies of good silver, Filippo Maria Visconti of Milan flooded north-central Italy with coins that commanded the same value in money of account as Venetian coins, although of an alloy worth less by at least 20 percent. "Gresham's law" did the rest, as good Venetian coin disappeared. In response, on 9 July 1429, only shortly before the departure of the galleys, the Senate intervened decisively on three fronts. It ordered, first, the devaluation of Venetian soldini and grossi (in demand in Syria) by 4.2 percent, calibrated to sustain the value of the ducat, which probably had threatened to decline, at the current rate of 104 soldi.[127] Second, it ordered the coining of a new, larger silver coin, the grossone, worth 8 soldi of the Venetian lira di piccoli, specifically for the new provinces of Bergamo and Brescia, recently won over from Milan, where it was worth 4 soldi imperiali (see fig. 7). The third step, coordinated in a secret colloquy with the Florentine ambassador on 1 August, as Antonio Morosini recounts, was to outlaw the circulation of the "evil and dolorous" Milanese coins.[128] The response to the Milanese move,

---

[124]Luzzatto in *PRV,* ccxxxiv n. 1, and ASV, SM, reg. 58, fols. 36v, 73.

[125]ASV, GP, Sg, reg. 73, fol. 52.

[126]Soranzo ledger, fols. 129v, 131, 135v, 140.

[127]*Cap. Broche,* 110–11.

[128]Reinhold C. Mueller, "L'imperialismo monetario veneziano nel Quattrocento," *Società e storia* 8 (1980): 284.

Fig. 7. Venetian coins in circulation after the mint reform of 1429. Of the nine different coins — gold, fine silver, and billon — shown here in their actual size, seven were minted under Doge Francesco Foscari (1423–57), under whom the reform was carried out; two (both billon coins) were struck under his predecessor Tommaso Mocenigo (1414–23).

a. Gold ducat.

Obv.: **FRANC FOSCARI DVX. S.M.VENETI** St. Mark, facing three-quarters right, presents the banner to the kneeling doge.

Rev.: **.SIT.T.XPE.DAT.Q.TV REGIS.ISTE.DVCAT.** (Sit tibi Christe datus qui tu regis iste Ducatus). Christ in the act of blessing, in a mandorla with nine stars in the field.

AV, 21.2 mm, 3.528 gr. Museo Bottacin, inv. no. 280A (Papadopoli, 1:269, no. 1).

b. Grossone of 8 soldi.

Obv.: **FRANCISCVS.FOSCARI DVX** The doge, facing left, holds the banner in both hands.

Rev.: **+. SANCTVS.MARCVS.VENETI.** Bust of St. Mark, facing front, holding the gospel in his left hand, his right hand raised in blessing.

AR, 26.0 mm, 3.018 gr. Museo Bottacin, inv. no. 282 (Papadopoli, 1:269, no. 3).

c. Grosso or grossetto of 4 soldi.

Obv.: **FRA.FOSCARI DVX.S.M.VENETI** St. Mark, on the right facing front, hands the banner to the doge, in profile. **K** in the left field, **P** in the right field.

Rev.: **+.TIBI.LAVS.7.GLORI.A** Christ enthroned.

AR, 19.6 mm, 1.364 gr. Museo Bottacin, inv. no. 289 (Papadopoli, 1:270, no. 5).

d. Mezzogrosso of 2 soldi.

Obv.: **FRA FOSCARI.DVX.** The doge, facing left, holds the banner in both hands.

Rev.: **.SMARC/. .VENETI**. Bust of St. Mark, facing front, holding the gospel in his left hand, his right hand raised in blessing.

AR, 19.4 mm, 0.708 gr. Museo Bottacin, inv. no. 300 (Papadopoli, 1:270, no. 7).

e. Soldino.

Obv.: **FRA.FOSCARI.DVX** The doge, facing left, holds the banner in both hands. **BS** in the right field.

Rev.: **+.S.MARCVS.VENETI** Winged lion crouching and facing front, holding the gospel in his front paws.

AR, 13.1 mm, 0329 gr. Museo Bottacin, inv. no. 301 (Papadopoli, 1:270–71, no. 8).

f. Cupped piccolo.

Obv.: **+.TO.MOC.DVX** Cross patée in a circle.

Rev.: Type of *Obv.* incuse.

B, 10.0 mm, 0.206 gr. Museo Bottacin, inv. no. 266 (Papadopoli, 1:253, no. 6).

Fig. 7 *(cont.)*

g. Piccolo or bagattino for Verona and Vicenza.
Obv.: **FR AF OD VX** Letters intersected by a cross, with annulets in the quadrants.
Rev.: **+.S.M.VENETI** Head of St. Mark, facing front.

B, 10.4 mm, 0.241 gr. Museo Bottacin, inv. no. 325 (Papadopoli, 1:273, no. 17).

h. Piccolo or bagattino for Friuli (?).
Obv.: **+ TOM MOCENICO DVX** Cross patée with wedge points in the quadrants.
Rev.: Bust of St. Mark with pearled halo, in a circle.

B, 13.3 mm, 0.400 gr. Museo Bottacin, inv. no. 265 (Papadopoli, 1:253, no. 8).

i. Piccolo or bagattino for Brescia.
Obv.: **F F D V** Letters in the quadrants of a cross patée.
Rev.: Winged lion crouching and facing front, holding the gospel in his front paws.

B, 13.3 mm, 0.415 gr. Museo Bottacin, inv. no. 326 (Papadopoli, 1:273, no. 16).

an effective weapon in monetary warfare, obviously could not be delayed despite the delicate moment, marked by the preparation of seven galleys and many cogs for departure to the Levant and by the peak demand for money. Behind this rise in silver was new demand for silver in the Levant, which had previously (since 1407) "clamored" for gold. As the Soranzo bank expressed it in 1430, when requesting an export license for silver, "gold is no longer exported as it was earlier."[129]

The need to ask for such licenses derived from another senatorial decision of 9 July 1429. That was to reinstate, in modified form, the old and obviously no longer observed restriction of 1374 on bankers' bullion transactions. That meant that bankers could not purchase silver, but it did allow them to mediate payments of bullion merchants on current account, "for the greater convenience of the merchants." Furthermore, firm controls over the purchase and sale of silver were reinstituted after having been suspended in 1419, as a countermeasure to the trade blockade imposed by King Sigismund. Once again, silver could be dealt in only at the public auction at the Rialto, under careful supervision of government officials.[130] Surely the law was meant to limit speculative buying that might cause the price of silver to rise even higher; and bankers were always in the midst of the bullion market. The demand for silver and the price it commanded, moreover, were such as to provoke a veritable "silver rush" in the mountains above Vicenza, in the same summer months of 1429, when the Senate accorded mining privileges to companies of German entrepreneurs.[131]

At the same time, Venice was once again experiencing a glut in the spice market. Unsold stocks were so large that a warehouse, usually used for meat and wine, had to be cleaned out to make room for them; pepper prices, which had been falling for some time, collapsed by nearly 40 percent.[132] Needless to say, spices, along with raw cotton, constituted the major exchange commodities for Germans who came to Venice with silver.

What were the bankers doing? They were probably continuing to grant overdrafts to buyers and guaranteeing purchases, even if they them-

---

[129]Lattes, *Libertà*, doc. 16.

[130]ASV, SM, reg. 57, fols. 130v–31r; in Venetian in *Cap. Broche,* 111–12. The law was reported, not in the clearest terms, by Antonio Morosini: Cronaca, 2:978. The law of 1374 is printed in *PMV,* doc. 160, pp. 147–48, taken, not from the original, as stated, but from the capitolare that dropped the phrase about paying on current account, revoked in 1429; cf. the version in Lattes, *Libertà*, doc. 8 and n. 11.

[131]ASV, SM, reg. 57, fols. 127 (14 July), 148 (23 August 1429). By 1430 (fol. 242) others had also begun to mine veins, without license, and without reserving for Venice the one-tenth of all silver and other metals extracted, as had been accorded with the first arrived. Discussed by Philippe Braunstein, "Les entreprises minières en Vénétie au XVe siècle," *Mélanges d'archéologie et d'histoire,* Ecole Française de Rome, 77 (1965): 533, 553–55, 589.

[132]Dolfina, fol. 346, under the date 6 May 1429. For pepper prices, see Lane, *Venice,* 288–89, and "Pepper Prices before Da Gama," reprinted in his *Studies in Venetian Social and Economic History,* ed. Benjamin G. Kohl and Reinhold C. Mueller (London, 1987), art. V, 593–96.

selves were forbidden by the newly reinstated law to deal directly in silver.[133] Clearly, opportunities for speculation existed, for news from the Levant must have promised good profits on exported silver. In fact, four cogs left for Syria on 26 July bearing merchandise, silver bars, and coin worth 250,000 ducats — values usually carried only by galleys — and seven galleys also went out laden! Our two banks failed only weeks after the departure of the galleys. Very likely they were completely overextended and illiquid and prey to the first small request for a cash withdrawal.

iii. NEW FOUNDATIONS, A CRUSADE, AND A FAILURE, 1430–1445

New Foundations

Three months after the two Priuli failures, the only major bank that had survived the crisis on the Rialto, that of the estate of Gabriele Soranzo, reconstituted itself and reopened under a new style. On Monday, 14 November 1429, records Antonio Morosini, the bank of "Ser Cristoforo Soranzo e fradeli," sons of Gabriele and like him resident in the parish of S. Maria Formosa, opened on the Rialto "with the good wishes and God-speed of the whole corporation of Venice."[134] Such hopes were sincere and widespread, given the liquidity crisis that persisted. One bank could hardly handle the business of the marketplace, however, and now there was plenty of room for new investment in the sector.

In the following March two new banks opened, as Morosini was happy to relate (and as all later chroniclers noted). On 1 March 1430 — an interesting choice, for that was both the first day of the Venetian New Year and the first day of Lent — Francesco Balbi and Brothers opened operations. The location chosen was next to the rostrum from which edicts were publicly announced, a bank most recently held by Andrea Priuli and the two Priuli successor banks. On that first festive business day, the bank took in deposits totaling 9,000–10,000 ducats. Morosini, still in shock from the previous failures, prayed "that Christ allow him to finish in good form, Amen," a prayer that was only partially heard, as we shall see. Another

---

[133]The phrase of the 1374 law revoked in 1429 reads "nec mutuare nec facere scriptam argenti aliqui qui emeret argentum"; ASV, SM, reg. 57, fols. 130v–31; in Venetian in *Cap. Broche*, 111–12; duely reported by Antonio Morosini, Cronaca, 2:978. An example of such operations can be seen in the Soranzo ledger, fol. 129v, in 1426 when Zan Orsini and Brothers allowed the Soranzo fraterna on 27 July to overdraw by 310 ducats in paying for silver that the bank itself was selling, an overdraft not completely covered until 2 September. The following year (fol. 135v) a similar purchase called for an overdraft of 600 ducats, though only for one day, after which it was largely covered by an interbank transfer from the Priuli Estate and Bartolomeo Priuli bank.

[134]"Fo levado bancho de scrita in Rialto dito in nome de 'Ser Cristofalo Soranzo e fradeli' de la contrada de S. Maria Formosa in bona ventura e con bona gracia de tuta la universitade de Veniexia, Amen." Morosini, Cronaca, 2:1033.

chronicler stated more simply, "May God grant them good fortune."[135] The second bank was opened on 23 March by a partnership headed by the nobleman Nicolò Bernardo and including Matteo and Giovanni Garzoni (qd. Francesco) of the non-noble branch of that family, residing at S. Cassian, under the style "Ser Nicolò de Bernardo e compagni." The quarters they occupied were those where Nicolò Cocco had been six years earlier. Again a prayer from the lips of Morosini: "May Christ allow them to persevere for a long time in good form and in good grace, Amen." Another chronicler put it more bluntly: "May God grant them profit." In any case, an atmosphere of nervous optimism seems to have reigned on the Rialto.[136]

Both banks were strong. One has the impression that the Balbi bank was small in structure but efficient and well financed. Only Francesco and his brothers received a license to bear arms, although the wealthy Francesco surely did not run the bank personally at all times.[137] Francesco quickly developed a reputation as a shrewd banker. One creditor testified that he was "deaf like a merchant" when it came to paying; a debtor, defendant in a lawsuit begun by Balbi, testified, with a certain irony, that the banker was surely one who "never left money idle."[138] In the early years of his activity as a banker, he came to know Lorenzo and Cosimo de' Medici, in Venice as exiles, and he continued a correspondence with them after their return to Florence in 1434. He was the banker, financier, and advisor of Andrea Barbarigo (and as such was given a claim to fame by Frederic Lane). When he died in 1470, at age eighty-four, Balbi was reputed to be one of the

[135]Morosini: "Che Cristo i lasa fenir in bon stado, Amen." Ibid., 2:1066–67 (original, fol. 517). The other phrase, "Che Dio li dia bona ventura," in BMV, It. cl. VII, 50 (9275), fol. 535v. See also ibid., 791 (7589), fol. 122; ibid., 793 (8477), fol. 150v; ibid., 48 (7143), fol. 177v. Actually Morosini, who defines the site so precisely, says the bank had previously been held by Jacomello Zancani (failed in 1374–75); it is the later chronicles that say the bank was that of Andrea Priuli. Surely the same is meant, for it is difficult to imagine that a site would have been left unrented for fifty-five years, but it is interesting that the memory of the earlier bank survived so long.

[136]Cronaca, 2:1069–70 (original, fol. 518): "Cristo 'i lasa perseverar per longo tenpo in bon stado e con bona gratia, Amen." BMV, It. cl. VII, 793 (8477), fol. 122: "Che Dio li dia vadagno." Terse reports in the chronicles cited in the previous note.

[137]ASV, Grazie, reg. 22, fol. 147v (October 1430). Regarding Balbi's staff, there are notices from 1442 that a Marino Darmano was cashier (GP, Sg, reg. 111, fol. 143r (1 August 1450) and from 1445 that a Zuan Charlier was "longamente fatore e governadore de le scriture de miser Francesco Balbi" (ibid., reg. 107, fols. 118–24 (26 May 1449). The Barbarigo accounts show that the nobleman Lorenzo Loredan, once called "dal banco," was a factor of the bank.

[138]The creditor of nearly 1,000 ducats said, "Et el ditto ser Francesco habi fatto et faza rechie de marcadante et diga 'bem . . . , faremo . . . ,' et questo perchè la moneda i torna destra." ASV, GP, Sg, reg. 77, fols. 78–79 (21 May 1438). When Balbi sued a client for unrecovered overdrafts, the defendant's lawyer stated that the banker had allowed the overdrafts: "Cognosando miser Francesco, che non lassi star i suo dinari morti, et che non habia facto risistentia nel trar dei diti denari, nè impedimento alcuno non 'i ha dato." Ibid., reg. 84, fols. 68v–69v (16 June 1441).

wealthiest men in Venice, able, on one occasion, to dispatch three Flanders galleys on his own.

The Bernardo-Garzoni bank was a strong noble–non-noble partnership. Nicolò Bernardo was very well placed politically; for his merits he was elected Procurator of San Marco in 1458. For a long time, the bank's style bore only his name: "Ser Nicolò Bernardo e compagni," later "Nicolò Bernardo el Procurator e compagni, banchieri." The Garzoni must have been the men actually visible behind the bank, the day-to-day managers. They derived from the branch of the family not ennobled in 1381 and were demographically particularly strong. Their administrative structure seems larger than usual, for the license to bear arms, granted to Nicolò Bernardo and his brothers and to Matteo and Giovanni Garzoni, was extended also to a staff of five persons: Alessandro de Cagnolis, Simone di Giovanni, Marco Fove, Angelo de Nani, and even the scribe Vettor Negro.[139]

Thus in the 1430s there were three major banks active on the Rialto: Soranzo, Balbi, and Bernardo-Garzoni. About 1441 Melchiore De Coltis, an immigrant from Pisa (his brothers, the "circumspecti juvenes" Gasparo and Baldassarre, had received the citizenship privilege de intus in 1422), opened a bank that left little trace but was still in operation in 1455. More significant was the bank partnership opened in 1442 by Bernardo Ziera, member of an old citizen family. The bank was taken over in 1454 by Bernardo's son Agostino, in partnership with his noble brother-in-law Giacomo qd. Donato Corner.

The bank that was to meet the quickest end was financially the strongest, that of Francesco Balbi, victim in 1445 indeed of a general credit crisis, especially in the exchange market, but in the end victim of a mere mischance. A rare extant register of the deliberations of the Council of Forty, which had to approve the concordats negotiated by the Sopraconsoli between bankrupts and their creditors, reflects growing problems in the 1440s. There were two serious bankruptcies in 1443, six in 1444; then, after a hiatus of seven months, serious failures came fast and furious beginning in June 1445. In June and July alone there were six, five of which involved companies headed by nobles. One of these was the firm of Andrea and Federico Corner, who had clearly borrowed money via drafts on Bruges and London; most of their creditors, in fact, were unable to prove their credits with exactitude "because they could not have news from persons to whom they had remitted money from place to place, given the distances involved."[140] This was clearly a year in which large speculative profits could

---

[139]ASV, Banco Giro, unnumbered volume, bound in white, entitled "Terminationi e decreti," fol. 2 (from the capitolare of the Signori di Notte al Civil, fol. 55), privilege granted "occasione banchi et pecuniarum" (11 November 1430).

[140]ASV, Quarantia Criminal, reg. 18, fols. 65v–66 (14–16 July 1445): "pro non habendo notitiam et claritudines a personis quibus remiserint suos denarios de loco ad locum, propter distantiam locorum."

be made by lending on the bill market, with all the risk that entailed.[141] More unsettling yet to the money market were the failures of Bernardo Zane, a local noble, and the merchant banker Lazzaro di Giovanni, partner and factor in Venice of the Borromei. The former, who defined himself as "miserable and naked" [misero e nudo], made his "pacta" on 11 August — the same day on which Lazzaro's flight from Venice for debt was recorded, in the season when money was at its tightest. Zane's creditors, for some 16,000 ducats, included the local branches of the biggest Florentine merchant-banking companies: Cosimo de' Medici and Company, Giovanni Rucellai and Company, Giovanni Portinari and Company, and many others, often in the role of guarantors for Venetian firms, as was the case of the Medici, who had stood surety for 1,400 ducats for Andrea Zen and Brother. The chain reaction effect, furthermore, is quite visible if one only compares the lists of creditors with the names of those who later applied for protection under the bankruptcy laws.[142]

In the midst of all this, the Venetian pope Eugenius IV (Gabriele Condulmer) was trying to actualize his plan for a crusade against the Turks. In the port of Venice, not only the usual Levant galleys were preparing for departure but also the Cyprus, or war, galleys, which were to meet and pay the crews of a force of galleys already armed.[143] The pope, in support of his project, remitted 12,000 ducats to Venice via the Medici. The Medici branch in Venice promised payment in mid-August on the current accounts it held with Venetian bankers. Since the money was supposed to be loaded onto the galleys, it had to be withdrawn in cash by the beneficiaries of the bills, Michele Zon and the bishop of Coron. The banks balked and refused to pay, on the pretext that the bishop of Coron was not present. On 13 August the Senate, at the same time as it set up a special commission to study the problem of bankrupts "fleeing the city daily with the assets of citizens," overrode the objections of the bankers and ordered them to pay out the cash to Zon so that it could be sent as quickly as possible to the naval expedition, led by the cardinal-legate Francesco Condulmer, nephew of the pope, and the captain general, Alvise Loredan. The Senate recognized the danger that its decree constituted for the banks — but it did nothing to avert

---

[141]The noble Prosdocimo Arimondo had ordered his factor Andrea Bembo "che de tuti mie danar li chapitasse ne le mano, quelli dovesse chambiare per Londra e Bruza e d'altri luogi dove che plui mia utilità se dovesse conseguire." ASV, GP, Sg, reg. 98, fol. 105r–v (1 February 1445).

[142]ASV, Quarantia Criminal, reg. 18, fols. 68–69v.

[143]For the crusade in general, see Kenneth M. Setton, *The Papacy and the Levant (1204–1571)*, 4 vols. (Philadelphia, 1976–84), vol. 2, chap. 3, "The Crusade of Varna and Its Aftermath." For Venice's contributions and the financial dealings involving more than 61,000 ducats, very important accounts, not heretofore noted, were copied into ASV, CN, reg. 8, fols. 178v–81v, dated 1443 but beginning in 1438 and ending in 1446. In spring 1444 the duke of Burgundy remitted 35,000 ducats to Venice in order to arm four galleys at his expense. BMV, It. cl. VII, 50 (9275), fols. 592v, 598v (for the celebration of victory in October 1445); Dolfina, fols. 396v, 400v.

trouble; on the contrary, by unanimous decision it threatened a fine of 500 ducats to be collected "from disobedient bankers" by the powerful Avogadori themselves.[144]

The "unwilling bankers" mentioned in the documents in practice boiled down to Francesco Balbi, who was the principal transfer banker of the Medici in Venice. On the morning of the next business day, Zon appeared at the bank to withdraw the money due him. The amount requested — 10,000–12,000 ducats[145] — exhausted Balbi's reserves, leaving him unable to meet the demands for cash withdrawals of other depositors and with no alternative but to close, declaring his insolvency.[146]

What the politics of the case were are difficult to imagine. The Senate knew the consequences; had there been any doubts, Francesco's brother and partner, Bernardo Balbi, was at that time a member of the Ducal Council. Eugenius himself, whose brother Simone had been a partner in the successor bank of Pietro Benedetto, also knew well the possible effects of his remittances. Perhaps there was an element of good sportsmanship on the part of Francesco, but it cannot be excluded that the ruling group in the Senate stood against him, for the government could easily have invented alternatives: it could have anticipated the cash, or have guaranteed the other depositors, or have granted a moratorium, perhaps pressuring the Medici in the meanwhile to help in collecting sufficient specie. The facts of the matter were that at this time of year, money was at its tightest in Venice and the state itself had promised to contribute to the crusade project. When a German creditor of the bank at the time of the failure blurted out such angry words against the Venetian nobility that he had to flee the city to avoid the ire of the Council of Ten, the object of his wrath was probably more the Senate than the unfortunate banker Balbi.[147]

[144]ASV, ST, reg. 1, fol. 161v: "cum hoc quod nostra dominatio teneatur conservare dictos bancherios sine damno omni tempore." The bills of exchange of Eugenius IV are mentioned by Setton, *Papacy and the Levant*, 2:91–92.

[145]Zon asked the Collegio to record officially that of the 12,000 ducats remitted by the pope, he had loaded 6,000 ducats in four sacks ("groppi") on the Cyprus galleys, 4,478 ducats in three sacks on the Alexandria galleys (for a total of 10,478 ducats). ASV, CN, reg. 8, fol. 28 (14 September).

[146]Malipiero (*Annali*, 659) wrote in 1470, on the occasion of Balbi's death, "E' morto Francesco Balbi, homo di 84 anni, el qual ha essercita' la marcadantia fin in ultima, con bona fama, senza querela de nissun. Altre volte el tene banco, e un anno el spazzete tre galie in Fiandra; e del '43 [*sic* for 1445] el falite, quando Papa Eugenio armò alcune galie in questa Terra per mandarle in Danubio, legato Francesco Condolmer Cardenal, Capitanio Zeneral Alvise Loredan. Li danari fo remissi da Roma nel so Banco, e fo tratti tutti in una mattina; de modo che le non havè da suplir a i altri credadori." (Also quoted, in translation, by Lane, *Andrea Barbarigo*, 24.) The first formal notice of the failure is in ASV, CN, reg. 8, fol. 27 (16 August), when the Ducal Counsellors, less Bernardo Balbi, confirmed the jurisdiction of the Consoli dei Mercanti in the case; printed in Lattes, *Libertà*, doc. 18.

[147]ASV, Consiglio dei Dieci, Miste, reg. 13, fol. 23 (19 January 1446); a reprieve was granted

The liquidity crisis made it difficult for Balbi to collect on debts owed him. The Senate intervened — rather late and in an unusual manner — by insisting that debts owed to his bank be paid by 15 October, under penalty of 10 percent on sums paid after that time. Offsetting between debtors and creditors was declared possible, which reduced the demand for specie. At the same time, with so many bankrupts about (and the Senate made special provision for collection of the bank debts of a Genoese draper who had failed in Venice), there was no saying when Balbi would actually be paid.[148] Lawsuits brought by the former banker reflect his difficulty in collecting on investments made both as bank and separately ("in sua spizialità"); during heated and lengthy debates in court, some of the modalities of investment (not to speak of the character of the banker) emerge. In 1439, for example, he had formed a commercial company with three young brothers, Francesco, Andrea, and Nicolò Venier, who invested 8,000 ducats; Balbi, who took the initiative, contributed 5,000 ducats "cash" as a silent partner and styled the company "Ser Francesco Venier e fratelli." The extraordinarily high capital was matched by a unique duration: the agreement called for liquidation after ten years. The company had credits from Romania to Catalonia, which the brothers were trying hard to collect, they testified, "especially in view of the failure of the bank in August 1445." If the company had not been successful, they claimed, it was due in part to Balbi's distractions with other investments.[149] A second suit recounts an initial loan made in 1442 to Giovanni di Francesco Giustinian, patrono of one of the Romania galleys, so he could pay his crew, followed by a series of measures taken by Balbi to cover himself. The mix involved rechange (or reexchange) on Bruges, Geneva, and Constantinople (the latter declared by the debtor to have been "fictitious and illicit") and the banker's purchase — in cash — of 2,300 ducats' worth of claims to freights on the galley, at a discount of 30 percent. Obviously, Balbi had been rightly concerned, for after six years he still had not been paid — not even the freights.[150] These

---

to this Petrus at the request of the city council of Nuremberg, "consideretur quod dolor denariorum suorum fecit illum loqui non ita sapienter sicut equum erat."

[148]ASV, ST, reg. 1, fol. 165v (24 September). The Senate continued in September and October to debate how to reform the office of the Sopraconsoli, in an attempt to reduce the damage from the many bankruptcies; ibid., fols. 66v, 68v–69v. Loans via bills of exchange created problems: bills were redrawn, accumulated interest, were protested, were only partially paid; see, for example, GP, Sg, reg. 102, fol. 55 (28 February 1446).

[149]The court record is fascinating; the brothers described Balbi as having acted as their father, as having "induced" them to form the company when they were "in tenera e dire' chosì pupilar etade, innespertissimi, masime de la marchadantia, per non esser sta' fata in nostro tempo in chaxa nostra." ASV, GP, Sg, reg. 107, fols. 118–24 (26 May 1449).

[150]Ibid., reg. 111, fols. 125–48 (1 August 1450). This defendant did not mention the failure but accused Balbi of many tricks used by bankers. He pointed out that the initial loan had been kept on rechange for six years, that the purchase of freight claims at a discount was "per

cases confirm the statement cited earlier, that Balbi was not the type to leave money idle and was ready to risk it, but they also indicate that he had been encountering problems before the arrival of the fatal drafts from Rome.

In the meantime, Balbi founded a short-lived successor bank (Andrea Barbarigo, his faithful client, entitled the new account "Ser Francesco Balbi per lo banco nuovo") with the sole aim of facilitating liquidation, which seems to have been just a matter of time.[151] Balbi, who was wealthy and moved in high places,[152] no longer needed the bank as a source of capital, to make loans with other people's money. Very likely he lost all interest in deposit banking as a result of the unfortunate insolvency. He could easily have salvaged his name as a banker and his banking enterprise, but he did not need to and obviously decided to direct his attention solely to commerce, where he remained extremely successful, one of the wealthiest men of the city.

iv. THE TWO BANKS OF BENETTO SORANZO AND THE FALL OF CONSTANTINOPLE

The First Bankruptcy

On the evening of Monday, 10 September, Alvise (qd. Pietro) Venier, cashier and manager of the bank of Benetto Soranzo e fratelli, who had always consigned the account books and the ready cash reserve at the end of the day's work either to the home of the banker or to the safe at the office of the Camerlenghi, failed to do so and disappeared. The next morning the principal and his brothers asked the College (the Council of Forty did not meet that day) for a safe-conduct, which they received, valid for a single day. The request was an admission of insolvency, and the city was in turmoil. On Wednesday the Senate authorized the last of the Beirut galleys to delay departure for a day so that everyone could "learn his situation and set his affairs in order."[153]

The bankers naturally placed the blame on the absent cashier, who had taken refuge in Trieste. In fact, Alvise Venier had granted loans totaling

---

ingrassar el so bancho de contadi" with a profit of 800 ducats in cash, and that the money was turned over in silver at 113 soldi per ducat, when the rate was 115 soldi. The last allegation inflated the actual differential, but it is true that gold was rising rapidly just then, and the payment in silver in order to receive gold would have been another occasion for profit—had the banker been paid!

[151]See Barbarigo, ledger B, fol. 158, for the successor bank; the account is not balanced.

[152]Francesco's brother Bernardo is often found in high organs of government; Francesco himself sat on the Council of Ten that decided the fate of Count Carmagnola. A few months before the failure, he attended a party at the palace of the Marquis d'Este of Ferrara (where his servant wounded another servant in a fight). ASV, AC, reg. 3649, fol. 81 (7 April 1445).

[153]ASV, CN, reg. 9, fol. 9v (in Lattes, *Libertà,* doc. 26); SMar, reg. 5, fol. 5v.

49,000 ducats, supposedly without the authorization of the bankers, to Donato Barisano, an Apulian importer of wheat and other grains. Furthermore, Venier, a non-noble, had occasionally acted on his own account while running the bank, so that (as the chronicler Zorzi Dolfin recounts) he convinced clients to make deposits into his own hands rather than into the bank. Such was his credit standing on the Rialto, writes Dolfin, that he was able to attract some 20,000 ducats in this manner, including 4,000 from Gerolamo qd. Ruggiero Contarini alone. On the 14th the Senate, which dedicated the whole day to the failure, sent a secretary to Trieste to explain the case and ask for the extradition of Venier as administrator of the failed bank and "well informed of all its dealings." At the end of the instructions, the Senate added that he should similarly ask for the extradition of Barisano, "should he be there."[154]

The situation of the Soranzo brothers, as might be expected, was not exactly limpid. Zorzi Dolfin placed their liabilities at 140,000 ducats.[155] After having received a safe-conduct from the Council of Forty on the 12th, they delayed in turning over their account books and papers. The Senate ordered them to consign forthwith all the accounts relating to the bank and to the brothers individually or in partnerships, as well as to those of the cashier Venier. If it was discovered that they had occulted documents, the Senate threatened to exclude them from all councils and magistracies. Threats of punishments reserved for fraudulent bankrupts were made to debtors of the bank, of the family, or of the cashier; they were given eight days to inform the authorities of all they knew about such debts or about other assets of the insolvents.[156]

As regards jurisdiction over the liquidation, the Senate, acting on the same day, deviated from previous practice when it withdrew the case from the Consoli dei Mercanti, on the claim that they were too busy with pending cases, and turned it over to the Provveditori sopra Camere, judged to be "worthy persons and not particularly occupied." Then, on the basis of the precedent of 1425, it selected two Procurators of San Marco to act as special commissioners, to be flanked by the three liquidators elected by the creditors. On both points, however, there was serious disagreement, for the ayes won by only eight and eleven votes respectively.[157]

Only four days later the Senate was again preoccupied with the failure, this time with the effects on the credit market and with related prob-

---

[154]Dolfina, fol. 436v; ASV, ST, reg. 3, fol. 78. In April Barisano had contracted to deliver 10,000 staia of wheat to Venice, under a guarantee provided by the Bernardo-Garzoni bank; ASV, ST, reg. 3, fol. 63.

[155]Dolfina, fol. 436v.

[156]ASV, ST, reg. 3, fol. 78v (in Lattes, *Libertà*, doc. 26α).

[157]ASV, ST, reg. 3, fol. 78v (in Ferrara, "Documenti," doc. 12). The Procurators elected were Andrea Donà and Stefano Moro; the "capita creditorum," to whom were assigned 100 ducats each from the assets of the bank, were Carlo Pisani, Domenico Zorzi, and Gerolamo Loredan.

lems of mint policy. Creditors of the bank, first of all, were using the failure and the resultant freezing of deposits as an excuse for not paying forced loans — in the midst of the costly war in Lombardy. Then the captain of the Alexandria galleys could not get the cash needed to pay advances on wages and salaries in order to depart, and he had to be authorized to borrow the money on the exchange, charging interest ("damnum cambii") to freight owed by the merchants. Third, a secretary was sent to the orator of Venice's ally, King Alfonso of Aragon, in Apulia, in order to assure him that Venice was capable of paying cash for the 20,000 staia of barley then being loaded onto ships (urgently needed for the cavalry fighting against Milan and Florence), despite the flight of Venier and the failure of the bank.[158]

The senators were aware of the concourse of many factors in this crisis, for on the same day they dealt with the mint. One factor was the rapid rise of gold, exactly the opposite of what was experienced at the time of the failures of 1429, coupled with a general bullion famine. They complained that too little gold was being coined and too much silver, a situation reflected in the rapid increase in the value of the ducat from 114 to 120 soldi. Worse yet, the mint was producing huge quantities of a billon penny, for the revenue (seigniorage) it produced. The only solution they came up with was to suspend production of the "denaro piccolo" for two years; but that wishful thinking lasted only a short time, for, with the same large majority, they had to revoke the suspension for reasons of fiscal necessity and even to order production of another billon coin, the "quattrino."[159]

In the following month little progress was made toward resolving the question of culpability and the definition of assets of the failed bank. Alvise Venier had returned to Venice, willingly or not, but his presence availed little; no one seemed prepared to reveal how much money was missing and who had absconded with it. Clearly Benetto Soranzo was not cooperating, or his testimony was not credible, for on 15 October the Avogadori di Comun asked that he be arrested for interrogation, along with Venier and Angelo Orsini, guarantor of the large loans Venier had made to the grain wholesaler Barisano. Should the truth not come out, a special committee ("collegium") was to be formed "according to usual procedure," with the right to interrogate the three even under torture. The committee was formed, but opinion within it was so divided that it could reach no decision, and the Avogadori, clearly frustrated, had the Senate expand membership to include a ducal counselor, an Avogador, and a police official (Signore di Notte). Even this further investigation was inconclusive, and the Senate on 20 December ordered the release of the three from prison and recognized the validity of their safe-conducts and of the concordats that Venier, the "casserius," and Orsini had made with their creditors and which

[158]ASV, ST, reg. 3, fol. 79r–v, and SMar, reg. 5, fol. 5v, both 18 September.
[159]ASV, ST, reg. 3, fol. 79r–v, and Mueller, "L'imperialismo monetario," 288–89.

the bank had made both with its creditors and its guarantors — this in order to permit them to appear before the civil courts.[160]

Of these courts, the Consoli dei Mercanti recovered at least partial jurisdiction in the case. They were to force debtors of the bank to pay up and apply a 10 percent fine — which they could keep as incentive money — on sums not turned over by the end of December. Even this pressure, however, brought no results, and the deadline was extended for another month.[161]

After the release of Benetto Soranzo from prison, the family resumed its place on the Rialto, perhaps at the head of a successor bank. The basis of their claim to the trust of the population was their success in pinning the blame for the failure of the first bank on the cashier. The longer-term validity of that claim depended upon the outcome of a suit brought by the bankers against Venier, and that was a path strewn with hurdles. First, forgers became involved, and then a sentence favorable to the Soranzo passed by the Consoli was appealed to the Senate itself.

The primary evidence in the case pending before the Consoli was a piece of paper (a "scriptum") that had been found on which Venier admitted to having made the loan of 49,000 ducats to Barisano "with money of the bank" [de pecuniis dicti banchi]. A forger, Alvise Santo of Padua, offered his services as false witness to Venier, saying that he had documents in Benetto's handwriting which would support Venier's case. The conspiracy involved playing each side against the other. First, Santo secretly convened such powerful men as Andrea Vendramin, currently chief ducal councillor, and Venier's lawyer, Giovanni Giustinian, at the house of a certain Gasparino at S. Felice and told them the following story: Benetto Soranzo had met with him at the house of Andrea di Giorgio Corner and had tried to "seduce him and others with many promises" if he would testify that Venier had told him that Venier and not the bank was debtor for the 49,000 ducat loan, suggesting that he hire others to give similar false witness, against a recompense of 3,000 ducats and a safe-conduct. When interrogated by the Soranzo side, Santo said that he had in fact so testified, as had an accomplice, Bertoldino of Castelfranco.

The Soranzo brothers, perhaps not in on the scheme at all, began to distrust the witness and asked for a receipt for the 3,000 ducats (thus Santo's testimony in the criminal trial). Santo supposedly went to Benetto's house, where he saw many assets of the bank, including 18,000 ducats in cash. Here Santo said he was given a note for 2,000 ducats. Whether the

---

[160]ASV, ST, reg. 3, fols. 84v (15 October, with 44 abstentions), 87v (20 November), 94v (20 December). Zorzi Dolfin states that the bank had promised to pay its debt "over two years, without guarantors"; Dolfina, fol. 436v.

[161]Ferrara, "Documenti," doc. 13 (17 November), and ASV, ST, reg. 3, fol. 96v (14 January 1454).

"scriptum" was genuine or forged, Santo planned to use it to get money out of the defendant's side.

The next step, then, was to meet with Venier and his creditors. To these Santo recounted another story, that he had received an advance of 60 ducats from Benetto Soranzo on the "many ducats" he was owed. He asked them for the money with which to repay Benetto and get a signed receipt that could be used against him. So the creditors gave him 50 ducats, which Santo used to hire two more false witnesses; these he introduced to Venier's lawyer, and he showed him a note ("scriptum") for 3,000 ducats, supposedly made out by Benetto. Giustinian examined the document and said he would call the two as witnesses. But the two were not called when they had expected to be, and, suspecting betrayal on the part of Santo, they called the Soranzo side to SS. Giovanni e Paolo and related the whole plan. The Soranzo brothers passed on the information to the Avogadori, who had Santo and Bartolino arrested. Tried and sentenced before the Council of Forty, the two, in the usual fashion, were paraded down the Grand Canal on a barge and then overland to San Marco, where Santo's right hand and nose and Bartolino's nose were amputated and both were banished.[162]

There is no record of an attempt to get corroborating evidence, but the Avogadori must have interrogated the nobles of rank named in the confessions. Whatever the truth, the lawsuit must have been one in which no holds were barred. Even though Benetto Soranzo may not have been above such deals, his case was strengthened. The Consoli, in fact, ruled in his favor and against Alvise Venier, on the grounds that the latter had acted on his own.[163] But Soranzo was still not in the clear.

One of the Auditori Vecchi, Nicolò Cocco, overturned the decision on appeal. Thus the suit reached the hall of the Senate itself, which had to decide between the two opposing verdicts. Setting the agenda for the Senate to sit as a court of law was itself a problem, and no quorum could be reached until the Great Council limited the conflict-of-interest clause to those directly involved; other creditors and debtors of the two sides could sit in judgment.[164] The case brought by the appeal judge, according to the Dolfin chronicle, required the Senate to convene four times. First the sentences were read, until midnight ("the fourth hour of night"); in the second, third, and fourth sessions there were debates, in which the position of

---

[162]ASV, AC, reg. 3650, fol. 11r–v (21 June 1454).

[163]The Consoli who reached the decision were Francesco qd. Gerolamo Malipiero, Biagio Michiel, and Piero Bembo (the last probably a substitute); so named in the Dolfina, fol. 436v, and corroborated in ASV, Segretario alle voci, reg. 4, fol. 25.

[164]A hearing was set for 8 December and then moved to the 10th; ASV, ST, reg. 3, fol. 137 (30 November). Cocco tried, without success, to bring the case before the Great Council; CN, reg. 9, fol. 35v (3 December). The decision regarding which senators could remain in the hall and which had to absent themselves, "quia res est maxime importantie bonum est quod solenniter iudicetur," is in MC, Ursa, fol. 192 (8 December).

the Consoli was defended by Domenico Zorzi, one of the liquidators of the bank. The first two debates lasted ten and eight hours respectively, each ending in balloting unfavorable to the appeal judge; the third debate lasted only four hours because Cocco, realizing he would lose on the final ballot as well, had abandoned the hall. The Senate expressed itself unambiguously, once it came to a vote, in favor of the noble Soranzo brothers and against the non-noble cashier Venier.[165] With this victory, the Soranzo family (often called in this period the "Soranzi") could take up their activity as bankers with renewed confidence.[166]

The Second Bankruptcy

After the Peace of Lodi (9 April 1454) Venice was also able to make peace with the Turkish conqueror of Constantinople. Despite a generally improved economic situation, however, the new or revived bank of Benetto and Giovanni (qd. Cristoforo) Soranzo lasted only a very short time: it failed again on Monday, 1 September 1455. This time it was the principals themselves, Benetto with his ten sons and Giovanni, who fled Venice and took refuge in the Rodigiano (not yet under Venetian domination). The Dolfin chronicle this time placed liabilities at 40,000 ducats.[167]

---

[165]The minutes were not kept by the Senate but by the Auditori and are not extant; the voting on each ballot is recorded in the Dolfina (fol. 437):

ayes	nays	non sinceri
18	38	68
28	45	56
37	61	23

Alvise was considered both an independent debtor and the cashier of the failed bank; he received several safe-conducts: for the third time in 1457, "pro possendo declarare dubia que intervenire possent" regarding missing funds of the bank; a one-year extension was granted in 1459. ASV, Consiglio dei Dieci, Miste, reg. 15, fol. 142 (also in Ferrara, "Documenti," doc. 21) and fol. 176v.

[166]In August the Senate had ordered the Salt Office to pay a debt of 714 ducats it owed to the bank; perhaps the "new bank" was meant, or payment would have more correctly been ordered made to the liquidators. ASV, ST, reg. 3, fol. 125 (8 Aug 1454). Assuming Domenico Zorzi's defense of the bank before the Senate was in the role of liquidator, the liquidators were active as late as December 1454. Whether liquidation was suspended after the legal victory of the Soranzo before the Senate or whether a new entity was created cannot be determined on the basis of extant documentation, where no distinction has been found between an "old" and a "new" bank styled "Benetto Soranzo and brother." The last movement in the current account of Francesco Contarini is dated 12 July 1454, when the account is closed out with a transfer; BMCV, P.D.C. 912, fol. 129. On 15 February 1455 the Collegio delle Biave ordered payment to the Soranzo bank of a debt of 3,000 ducats, almost two years overdue; ASV, Provveditori alle Biave, b. 1, libro II, fol. 95.

[167]The Dolfina mentions the failure twice, first right after having spoken of the concordat for the first bank and of the fact that some creditors had indeed received installments: "Et alcuni havè la sua rata, e avanti fusse passato l'anno iterum fallitino, debiti ducati 40,000. Et Beneto Soranzo andò a Mantoa dove do anni dapoi morite in miseria, benchè li figlioli dapoi mon-

The Consoli intervened immediately on the afternoon of the 1st, but there was little they could do to alleviate the situation. The concomitance of the failure with the departure of the galleys created a serious liquidity crisis ("carentia pecuniarum"), such that the Senate had to extend the deadline for payment of customs and taxes. Similarly, debtors both of the bank and of individual members of the Soranzo family were having difficulty paying and were ordered to turn over what they owed by the end of October or face the usual fine of 10 percent.[168]

If in the case of the first failure two years earlier the Venetian nobility finally sided with the bankers against their cashier, this time the culpability of the Soranzo brothers was beyond doubt: they had fled with the account books and with money and other goods legally belonging to their creditors. On 26 and 27 October the Senate made two important decisions, the first regarding the case at hand, the second attempting to reduce the risk of similar bank failures in the future.

First, it was resolved to send a very prestigious special ambassador, Vitale qd. Marino Lando, "artium et utriusque juris doctor," to the duke of Modena, in whose lands the family had taken asylum. The commission did not contain a request for extradition (was that a sign of noble solidarity?), but the ambassador was to ask that the duke force the former bankers to turn over their account books, without which no progress could be made in the liquidation, and to deny them asylum in his lands. The last request drew a large negative vote in the Senate, reflecting disagreement on how to proceed. In fact, the departure of Lando was delayed several times, at first by a lack of funding (when the liquidators were ordered to lend 80 ducats) and then by other, indefinite factors.[169]

The second provision involved a radical change in banking law. Who-

---

strono haver facultade" (fol. 436v). Here various facts are telescoped, for Benetto did not die until much later. The second mention is found under the autumn months of 1455: "Benetto Soranzo dal bancho, non possendo satisfar a' sui creditori, fuzite a Ruigo, designato legato a Ferrara Vitale Lando, doctor" (fol. 442v), where the chronicler inserted immediately the election of the ambassador who was to plead Venice's case against Soranzo, as we shall see below.

[168]ASV, CN, reg. 9, fol. 56v (2 September 1455), which declared of dubious legality the "molte subventiones," of unknown nature, granted by the Consoli. But the suspension of the "subventiones" was in turn suspended because a creditor, Polo Bernardo (probably of the Bernardo-Garzoni bank), had illegally sat in on the decision; AC, reg. 3650/II, fol. 60 (27 February 1456). The rationale for extending the deadline was so phrased: "Cum propter rupturam sive fugam banchi nobilium de cha' Superantio et propter recessum galearum et navium, cives et mercatores nostri habent carentiam pecuniarum, et sit facienda omnes honestas comoditas nostris mercatoribus." ST, reg. 3, fol. 175v (23 September 1455). For the order to pay debts owed to the bank, see ibid., fol. 177v, partially in Ferrara, "Documenti," doc. 15.

[169]The decision to send an ambassador was taken on 26 October, when Lando was also elected (ASV, ST, reg. 3, fol. 179v); his commission was formulated and passed on 7 November (SSec, reg. 20, fol. 72v); the manner of funding was ordered and reiterated on 20 November and 15 December (ST, reg. 3, fols. 182, 186r–v); on 30 December Lando was ordered to depart by 3 January or face a fine of 500 ducats (ibid., fol. 188).

ever in the future wished to open a bank at Venice would have to provide surety for 20,000 ducats — a tenfold increase over the guaranty ordered in 1318 and probably by then a dead letter. A single person could guarantee a maximum of 2,000 ducats, in movable goods. More important, the Soranzo experience of dual failure convinced the Senate to give jurisdiction to a committee formed by the Consoli and by the Governatori delle Entrate to consider the suitability of the guarantors and to reconsider it every three years, voting on each person, one by one. But a law for the future, however valid, left the current situation unresolved (see above, Chap. 2, sec. iii).

The liquidators were having difficulty collecting sums owed the bank. They may have still been operating on the basis of the agreement reached between the first bank and its creditors in 1453.[170] Private account books show that the first two installments were made between January and April 1457, for a total of 6 soldi, or 30 percent of the debt.[171] In March it was ordered that all goods entering Venice which belonged to debtors of the bank be blocked at customs for sale at auction, under the direction of the liquidators.[172] Alvise Venier, who had fled Venice again, was given a personal safe-conduct of six months, because his presence was needed in order to clarify doubts as they arose in the process of liquidation.[173]

At this point, two developments ensued. First, a cousin of the bankrupts, Giovanni di Vettor Soranzo, opened a bank on the Rialto. There was no fanfare, and there is no mention of the event in the chronicles. It was probably an attempt to pick up where the cousins had failed and to rescue the family name by providing some continuity; the new banker's grandfather, in fact, was the brother of Gabriele, founder of the bank around 1370. (For the genealogy, see table H.3, below.) The first indication that he was operating is a loan of 1,000 ducats to the state in January 1456, only a few months after the flight of Benetto and Giovanni di Cristoforo.[174] The failed bank then comes to be called "the bank of the old line" ("bancho di Soranzi vechi").[175] The fact that the new principal bore the same name as Benetto's brother has been a source of confusion,[176] but the brother resurfaces to clarify matters in the second unusual development.

---

[170]A "conventio" made by Benetto but not respected by him is mentioned in a deliberation of 1459 (Ferrara, "Documenti," doc. 25).

[171]ASV, GP, b. 955, cashbook of Leonardo Sanudo, fols. 60, 67; Archivio Grimani-Barbarigo, b. 43, reg. 6, fol. 6, shows a payment in March 1457, a second in April 1459. Early payment of the first installment was accorded to the Brothers of Mt. Sion in Jerusalem, who were in dire need. CN, reg. 9, fol. 78 (21 May 1456).

[172]ASV, ST, reg. 4, fol. 32 (16 March 1457); see also fol. 69 (20 March 1458) and Malipiero, *Annali*, 561.

[173]Ferrara, "Documenti," doc. 21 (Council of Ten, 14 December 1457).

[174]Ibid., doc. 16.

[175]For example, ASV, GP, Sg, regs. 124, fol. 85 (15 October 1457), and 132, fol. 6r–v (3 February 1961).

[176]Ferrara, "Antichi banchi," 190.

In 1458 Giovanni di Cristoforo returned to Venice from the Modenese and recounted the misdeeds and frauds of his brother Benetto; perhaps he brought some account books, and he divested himself of all he owned, in favor of both his own creditors and those of Benetto. When he received a safe-conduct whereby he could avoid imprisonment, the Senate deliberation that pronounced him innocent of his brother's crimes said that he was reduced to rags ("remansit quasi nudus").[177] On the same day, 5 May 1458, the Senate, which had been so protective of Benetto in 1453, took drastic action against the fugitive and his sons. The Avogadori, acting on the authority of the Signoria, had investigated criminal aspects, using information provided by Giovanni, and presented the results before the Senate: Benetto had falsified a cash account, thus depriving his creditors of 18,752 ducats, with which he had absconded, and had claimed to have made payments to four government offices for a total of 26,600 ducats which he had in fact never made. The Avogadori (one of whom was the Procurator and banker Nicolò Bernardo) proposed the following sentence, which the Senate then passed. Benetto Soranzo had brought intolerable loss to citizens and foreigners and ignominy on the state by having fled with assets robbed from the bank. He had been summoned several times and had not heeded. Proceeding "humanely," the Senate decided to give him two months to appear, after which he and his sons would be perpetually banned from Venice and all subject territories, with dire consequences (decapitation for Benetto, imprisonment for the sons) should they be caught. Furthermore, a reward of 10,000 lire (1,613 ducats) was offered to anyone who would capture Benetto alive and bring him to justice. His sons, should they come on their own to make satisfaction, could be absolved from the penalties.[178]

Benetto did not appear, then or ever. The ban took effect, which meant, in practice, that the bankrupt and his ten sons were disennobled. That was a drastic and rarely imposed punishment (in a case of bank failure it would be imposed only one other time, a century later)[179] and raised some eyebrows in the Great Council. First, further attempts were made to have the duke of Modena convince Benetto to pay up or to extradite him; when the duke finally agreed to intervene, Benetto merely moved to lands under the jurisdiction of the duke of Mantua.[180] Then in 1464 another group of Avogadori sought to overturn the sentence in a plea before the Great Council. Ever since the sentence of banishment, they reported, the ten sons, deprived of their nobility, had lived in "the greatest misery and calamity"; "by the most holy laws of this republic" they should never have

---

[177]Ferrara, "Documenti," doc. 22.

[178]ASV, ST, reg. 4, fol. 72v; the same sentence, but with the evidence presented before the Senate, is in AC, reg. 3651, fol. 27r–v. The sentence is summarized in Malipiero, *Annali*, 652.

[179]In the case of the Dolfin family, in the 1570s; Ferrara, "Antichi banchi," 439.

[180]Ferrara, "Documenti," doc. 25 (16 April 1459), and ASV, ST, reg. 4, fol. 156 (30 October 1460).

been condemned, for they themselves had not been summoned to appear and could not defend themselves. These and other procedural irregularities meant that the "illegal and inhuman sentence" against these youths, innocent of the crime of their father, had to be annulled. The Avogadori marshaled the support of all those still living who had proposed the resolution six years earlier, and the annulment was passed almost unanimously.[181]

A further act of noble mercy for nobles was the reinstatement of Benetto's brother Giovanni to office holding. Since the bank was a debtor to the state, Giovanni had been disqualified, even though the Senate had declared him innocent of the crimes of his brother. Very likely, Giovanni remained impoverished and needed the opportunity to earn the salary provided by an office.[182]

The liquidation procedure continued but brought little satisfaction to the creditors. By 1477 some creditors had received three or more installments (probably at 3 soldi per lira each) but were liable to have to return some of it to the liquidators, for the failure had taken on a diplomatic aspect, and Venetian merchants were threatened with reprisals. Philip the Good of Burgundy (d. 1467) had deposited money in the Soranzo bank, earmarked for the congregation of the Brothers of Mt. Sion and for the Knights Hospitalers of St. John of Jerusalem. These deposits, made perhaps as early as 1444 when the duke had armed galleys for Eugenius IV's crusade, were, of course, frozen by the liquidation procedure. In 1456 the Brothers of Mt. Sion had successfully petitioned for an early payment of the first installment, given their position in the forefront of the struggle against the Turks. Charles the Bold (1467–77), through his ambassador, insisted on release of the alms to the beneficiaries and threatened reprisals, whereupon Venice tried various ways of raising the money (that owed to the Hospitalers totaled 3,227 ducats, as had been certified in the bank's ledgers, which had in the meantime surfaced in Venice). Even in the months following Charles's death, the Signoria was still trying to avoid having to pay out of the state Treasury a debt of the "primo bancho di Soranzi." But very likely no more than 45 percent of the debt was ever paid to the bank's creditors, lay or religious.[183]

Benetto Soranzo died in the 1470s, still a fugitive and disennobled,

[181]ASV, AC, reg. 3651, fol. 68 (20 March 1464); the vote was 506 to 13, with 9 abstentions.

[182]ASV, CN, reg. 11, fol. 142v (29 January 1473).

[183]For the petition of 1456, mentioned above, see ASV, CN, reg. 9, fol. 78; renewed pressure, for the same order, is found in CN, reg. 12, fol. 39 (1 March 1476). In favor of the Hospitalers are the following deliberations: SSec, reg. 27, fol. 75 (30 May 1476); ST, reg. 7, fols. 172 (7 July 1477), 178 (12 August), 186 (18 October), 191v–92 (16 December). The two, three, and more installments mentioned on 7 July would have meant at 3 soldi per lira: 2 = 30 percent, 3 = 45 percent, 4 = 60 percent; Nicolò Barbarigo, in any case, closed his ledger in 1483 with less than 30 percent paid (as above, n. 171). Other relevant litigation is reflected in Consiglio dei Dieci, Miste, reg. 17, fol. 33 (23 September 1467); MC, Regina, under the date 25 October 1467; CN, reg. 11, fol. 141v (25 January 1473).

unreconciled with his creditors and with his city. If he died in "miseria," as the Dolfin chronicle says, his misery was very likely not economic, for he had absconded with enough money to live very comfortably, as well as to pay for protection — against the diplomatic pressures applied by Venice on his new sovereigns, as well as against reward hunters.

Benetto Soranzo's Reputation

When looking for causes of the Soranzo failures of midcentury, one should first look at the people, then at the local credit market, and finally at the international situation.

"Human interest" elements of the story of the dual failure of the firm of Benetto Soranzo and Brother, bankers, force one to look at personages. Alvise Venier, the cashier, seems to have used his position of prestige to accumulate deposits on his own. The complicated criminal case against false witnesses and the successful defense of the interests of the bank over against Venier's before the Senate meant that Soranzo's peers assumed that he himself was relatively clean, that Venier had indeed made the huge loan of 49,000 ducats on his own and alone should bear the responsibility. On the other hand, the second failure showed up Benetto as the culprit; he took no interest in defending himself or his house and earned the enmity of the Senate that had previously defended him.

Actually, Benetto was a problematic leader of a banking concern. In his father's testament, Benetto had already earned special, negative mention. When Cristoforo made disposition for the three slave women of the household, he ordered that two serve his sons but that Benetto was not to have anything to do with one of them, Lucia, with whom it may be assumed he, as a youth, had had some kind of illicit relationship. At the same time, he seems to have been a litigious type. In 1445 he appealed from a sentence and a fine of 300 lire for a bad row ("pro certa pura et inopinata rixa"), an accusation that had been brought by the podestà of Padua.[184] Nonetheless, he was elected to positions of some rank: as a young man, to the Council of Forty (1438), in 1451 to the Senate, and in the following year to the Zonta of the Senate, for one-year terms.[185] Although his power or influence was probably more economic than political, the Senate in which he had sat so recently defended him. The detailed story told by the false witnesses who had tried to blackmail both Soranzo and Venier, which could have been rather easily confirmed, seems to have damaged only them-

---

[184]His father wrote: "Intendando e chusì laso che Benedetto mai non debi aver algun servizio nè afar con la dita Luzia"; ASV, NT, b. 1230, n. 147 e b. 1232, not. Stefani, fol. 154, n. 385 (23 June 1431). The appeal is in Grazie, reg. 24, fol. 138v (1 May 1445).

[185]ASV, Segretario alle voci, Misti, reg. 4, fols. 96 (18 May 1438), 130v (29 August 1451), 134v (30 September 1452) — all as "Benedetto qd. Cristoforo Soranzo a bancho." The Benedetto Soranzo elected mintmaster on 14 May 1452 was qd. Antonio (ibid., fol. 26).

selves, leaving both litigants unscathed. Is it possible that neither had bought or suborned witnesses? or tried to? Benetto Soranzo's comportment after the second failure leaves at least some doubt, as it must have done among many senators.

The Fall of Constantinople

The economic problems that very likely had contributed to the failures were both immediate and longer term. Immediately preceding the first failure was the fall of Constantinople. Since two chroniclers seem to make some connection between the fall of the Byzantine capital on 29 May 1453 and the failure of the Soranzo bank on the following 10–11 September, saying the bank claimed losses at Pera, some attempt must be made to estimate the losses, economic as well as psychological. Venice had been paying attention primarily to the war against Milan and Florence, and the news of the conquest by the Turks, which arrived in Venice as rumor on 29 June and was verified on 4 July by the Romania galleys that had succeeded in escaping, took the city by surprise and provoked criticism of the organs of state for lack of foresight and action on the eastern front.[186]

Contemporary estimates of Venetian financial losses vary widely. Jacopo Tedaldi, who reports that total damages were 4 million ducats, places the Venetians after the Byzantines in his list of losers with a figure of 50,000 ducats, probably a copyist's error for 500,000.[187] Giacomo Languschi's ac-

---

[186]Zorzi Dolfin (1396–1468) juxtaposes the two events but with a sibylline phrase that was not necessarily meant to convey a causal relationship: "1453, 11 septembre, marti, sotto el partir de le gallie de Levante scampono falidi de Venexia Benetto Soranzo e fradelli dal bancho, fo di ser Christofalo, debito duc. 140,000, el falir del quale è de grandissimo danno a Venexia per la prexa de Constantinopoli, che fu dì 29 de Maxo 1453, per la qual se havè de danno duc. CC millia, oltra la morte de molti nostri citadini occisi. Fu caxon del suo fallir . . ." Dolfina, fol. 436v. One version of the Venier chronicle says the banker failed and fled the city "perchè fu giudicato che l'havesse in Pera i danari, ma perchè non se vedeva che i havesseno havuto danno alcuno, el ditto ser Benetto fu bandito de tutte terre et luochi della Segnoria de Venetia et tutti suoi fiogli de Gran Consiglio, i quali dapoi molti anni cognosciuti innocento forno ritronati nel suo stato di esser del Gran Conseglio, cioè suoi fiogli, et ser Benetto morì misseramente fora di Venetia" (BMV, It. cl. VII, 791 [7589], fol. 148; also ibid., 1568 [8016], fol. 331v), while another version suggests that a copyist's error was involved, for it reads "et perchè el fu zudegado che havese portado i dinari via." It is doubtful, first, that a Venetian would have made extensive investments in the Genoese colony, even though bankers, like all merchants, regularly invested in the Romania; furthermore, the second version, which connects the failure with the flight with depositors' money, is more credible; ibid., 793 (8477), fol. 179. All the chroniclers seem to fuse the two failures, confusing the flight of the cashier Venier in 1453 (when the Soranzo stayed in Venice, "fugitivi" only in the legal sense of bankrupt) with that of the Soranzo themselves in 1455. Same in ibid., 519 (8438), the "Trevisana," fol. 265v. See also Agostino Pertusi, ed., *La caduta di Costantinopoli*, 2 vols. (Milan, 1976), 1:369, 2:18, and Lane, *Venice*, 235.

[187]Pertusi, *La caduta*, 1:186, 413–14 n. 33. General survey in Setton, *Papacy and the Levant*, 2:132–33 nn.

count, copied by Zorzi Dolfin, places losses to Venetians at 200,000 ducats and to their subjects in Crete at 100,000.[188] The so-called Venier chronicle assesses Venetian losses at more than 1 million ducats, but only a few lines later it states that Christians in general lost 1 million ducats in Constantinople and in the Genoese colony of Pera together.[189] Nicolò Soderini, writing from Genoa, where he was Florentine ambassador, reported that the Genoese were reckoning total losses to Christians at 4 million ducats, 3 million in Constantinople, 1 million in Pera (Genoese losses), and that the news had caused a sharp fall in the price of government obligations at San Giorgio.[190]

Leaving aside the internal contradictions, the above-mentioned Venier chronicle is more specific than others. It states that Venetian losses were "in merchandise of debtors and ransoms" and goes on to recount the number of round ships and light galleys lost and tells of the three Romania galleys that escaped. By "merchandise of debtors" is probably meant goods purchased on funds advanced in Venice; intended was probably a chain of indebtedness which would at some point involve a bank like that of Benetto Soranzo — whose failure the chronicler then discussed in his succeeding paragraph.

Ransoms asked of the living and doubts about the fate of the missing must also have constituted both psychological and economic strains. Nicolò Barbaro related that twenty nobles were ransomed for sums ranging from 800 to 2,000 ducats each, which might have cost Venice some 25,000–30,000 ducats. Relatives and creditors of the missing, furthermore, took the probate court by assault in the month after the first news had arrived. Finally, despite the fact that Venice was at war, the Senate is said to have voted pensions to bereaved families and damages — probably a vain promise — to those who had suffered loss of property.[191]

A calculation of damages would have to take into account the value

---

[188]This passage in the Dolfina was published by Georg M. Thomas, "Belagerung und Eroberung von Constantinopel im Jahre 1453," *Sitzungsberichte der königlichen bayerischen Akademie der Wissenschaften* 2 (1868): 41, and Pertusi, *La caduta*, 1:341.

[189]As cited above, n. 186.

[190]Pertusi, *La caduta*, 1:414; idem, ed., *Testi inediti e poco noti sulla caduta di Costantinopoli*, ed. Antonio Carile (Bologna, 1983), 61–62.

[191]E. Cornet, ed., *Giornale dell'assedio di Constantinopoli, 1453* (Vienna, 1856), 59; see also Fernand Braudel, "L'Italia fuori d'Italia: Due secoli e tre Italie," *Storia d'Italia* 2 (Turin, 1974): 2104, who says that Bartolomeo Marcello was sent to the sultan and succeeded in liberating 117 prisoners, of whom 47 were nobles (Sanudo's figure), and that he recovered merchandise worth 7,000 ducats. That human problems were also economic is shown by a deliberation of the Minor Consiglio on 19 August 1453. There was still no news of the light galleys and other vessels that had been at Constantinople, and there was no way of knowing whether merchants and crews were dead or alive. It was decided, therefore, that the Giudici del Proprio were authorized to presume death, paying first dowries and then other creditors but keeping careful accounts; ASV, CN, reg. 9, fol. 6v. Finally, on the Senate's promises, see David M. Nicol, *Byzantium and Venice* (Cambridge, England, 1989), 404–7.

both of the three Romania galleys that escaped and of the round ships that did not. But the evidence is ambiguous. The question hinges on the problem of whether the galleys sailed full (usually they carried some 200,000–300,000 ducats' worth of goods) or only half full, as the Venier chronicle relates. If we say as a hypothesis that half was lost, and if we say the three roundships that were captured carried at least 50,000 ducats' worth of goods each, we have a total of 300,000 ducats, without counting ransoms, the value of the many other vessels lost, real estate in the colony, and the like. So an estimate of one-half million in losses is not at all far-fetched.[192] Clearly, large profits on the voyages of galleys and roundships to Constantinople and to the Black Sea that year had been forecast, if the Senate felt it could impose a special tax totaling 16,000 ducats on merchants having interests in the Romania.[193] So much the greater must have been the consternation in Venice upon arrival of the news of the fall of the Byzantine capital and the confirmation of the worst reports in late summer.

What all this had to do directly with the failure of the Soranzo bank is hard to say, except in terms of timing. Had Benetto really lost personally, he would have used that as an excuse. That many Venetians did lose heavily is clear, and more than likely some — survivors and not — were debtors to the Soranzo bank.[194] The inevitable chains of indebtedness were perhaps more important — but none of this is mentioned as a justification by the Soranzo brothers, who accused solely the fraud and embezzlement of their cashier (whose principal debtor had invested in safe Apulia). The galleys to Romania could not sail, neither then nor until a peace was signed in 1479, after an extenuating naval war.[195] Shocked by the cruelty exhibited by the sultan, owners of roundships that sailed in the years following the fall supposedly carried little of value "because they did not trust him" [per non si fidar di

---

[192]Both the Dolfina and the Veniera (see n. 186, above) say many merchants had goods unloaded, considering the land safer than the galleys. But whereas the Dolfina says that the galleys made sail "cargando tutto quello poteno cargar et alevar per la occasion," the Veniera says they fled "con li marchadanti et robbe che si atrovorno haver," arriving therefore in Venice half empty. On the other hand, Barbaro, an eyewitness, says the galleotti had refused to permit unloading of the merchandise (Lane, *Venice*, 349). Tedaldi says a Genoese ship that was sunk by the Turks was worth 80,000 ducats (Pertusi, *La caduta*, 1:414). On the positive side, it seems that some Greek refugees loaded specie onto the Venetian galleys, which was then confiscated by Venice to help pay debts that Greeks owed to Venetians (including 17,163 perperi owed by the emperor). See Steven Runciman, *The Fall of Constantinople, 1453* (Cambridge, England, 1965), 162, and Nicol, *Byzantium and Venice*, 406.

[193]Freddy Thiriet, *La Romanie vénitienne au Moyen Age* (Paris, 1959), 381 (24 February 1453).

[194]One might look for more references to individual losses, but they do not abound. One example is the wool shop of a draper, Jacopo Toxon, which reported no profits from 1454 to 1457, "ch'el falì, per dano hauto a Costantinopoli." ASV, GP, Sg, reg. 142, fols. 76v–84v (24 May 1464).

[195]Lane, *Venice*, 349.

lui].[196] Failure to sail in late summer meant upsetting plans made in June, including those regarding the export of specie, central to the interests of a Rialto banker.

Public finance had more than ever become central to banking since the collapse of the system of forced loans by the beginning of the 1450s (the last levy would be made in February 1454). Government obligations dropped to 25, interest payments were reduced and already years behind, new levies could not be honored. Faith in the system had dwindled. New schemes were invented to deal with the pressing problem of financing the war against Milan and Florence. A plan for increasing revenues ("per recuperar denari") of 8 December 1453 estimated, optimistically, annual expenditures in the land war at 550,000 ducats and costs of the military armada at 120,000, for a total of 670,000.[197] A seriously aggravating factor was Venice's expulsion of Florentine merchant-banking firms, which must have had the immediate result of a sharp reduction in the availability of specie and credit on the Rialto and probably a concomitant increase in interest rates.

Among the long-range policies for increasing revenues were two that could have dire consequences for the economy, namely, the formulation of mint policy so as to provide revenue, and the use of banks as carriers of the floating debt. Let us take the second first, since Luzzatto expressed the opinion that excessive government borrowing and not any fraud perpetrated by Venier was the true cause of the downfall of the Soranzo bank.[198]

While admittedly not all bank loans to the state were registered by the Senate, a listing of loans in 1448–55 shows that from 1448 to 1452 the Soranzo bank was almost the sole lender. It surely led the others, lending 41,000 ducats in the second semester of 1448 alone; in late 1449 it was still out for 25,000 ducats, though willing in February 1450 to lend an additional 10,000 ducats so that, as the Senate deliberated, "we can avoid imposing a forced loan." On the other hand, a report of May of the same year shows that the Ziera bank was then out for 19,000 ducats, and it continued to make loans. Still, the Soranzo bank was the most faithful: in 1451 the Senate — when Benetto Soranzo was a member of the Zonta — asked the bank for a "detta" or guarantee that it would pay importers of 10,000 staia of wheat, an open grant the bank made "with its customary readiness freely to serve the state" if it was itself guaranteed repayment from specific revenues.[199] The last Soranzo loan for which there is evidence from Senate

[196]As in n. 186, above. On the other hand, in the very next year galley voyages shifted to Aleppo, a rapidly established alternative reflected in the account books of Francesco Contarini.

[197]*BG*, 1, docs. 98–106, and the long extract from the Dolfina, *BG*, 1:125–26.

[198]*PRV*, ccliv.

[199]"Pro consueto more suo serviendi libenter nostro dominio"; ASV, ST, reg. 3, fol. 2v (20 December). For these loans, see below, Chap. 10.

records is one of 16 December 1452 of 5,000–5,500 ducats in specie to be sent in sacks to the army on the front, repayable from the forced loan just levied.[200] In January 1453 the bank had made a small loan of some 3,000 ducats to the Provveditori alle Biave, but no further large loans by the Soranzo bank are recorded. Perhaps it simply did not offer its services any longer, realizing it was overextended. Its place as the foremost lender was taken by the Corner bank, which merged in late 1454 or early 1455 with the Ziera bank. The difference was that Corner lent smaller sums, and, in a period of a rapid rise of gold, he insisted on being repaid in gold (see below, Chap. 10).

Such was the recourse of the state to bank loans to pay mercenaries, and such was the practice of the bankers to lend if at all possible in bank money, that the state lost control of the flows. On the eve of new hostilities against Florence and Milan an accounting review was ordered, on the records both of the several mercenary captains and of the banks, with the aim of verifying and liquidating any balances due.[201]

The debts, of course, were not cumulative, but very often the revenues earmarked for repayment were simply not forthcoming: taxpayers were late in meeting levies; treasuries of the subject cities (especially Treviso and Padua) were not taking in the sums foreseen; the revenues might have already been obligated to another creditor; or a new emergency may have diverted revenues meant to repay a bank to a more pressing need. This meant a nearly certain dilation of payments, beyond that initially prospected, and a general swelling of credit.

But just what the effect of this situation was on the failure of the Soranzo bank is impossible to determine. Indebtedness to the state was not mentioned by the bankers as a cause or as an excuse, nor did the state admit to owing large sums to the bank which it rushed to repay.[202]

The chain of indebtedness of private parties and companies probably had little to do directly with government indebtedness. In the chain there was only one major failure, that of the Tuscan firm of Jacopo Benci and Ludovico di S. Cassiano, in February 1454. That bankruptcy involved so many nobles that the Quarantia Civil could not get a quorum, and members of the Quarantia Criminal had to fill in.[203]

More serious in general terms was the bullion famine. Connected with the decision to make the mint produce a revenue, the scarcity of raw material for the mint meant a flooding of the market, both in Venice and in the subject territories, with petty or black coins, on which high rates of

[200]ASV, ST, reg. 3, fol. 48v.

[201]Ibid., reg. 2, fol. 186 (15 May 1451).

[202]The only hint is the belated order of 1454 to the Salt Office to pay the Soranzo bank a small sum of 770 ducats, as we saw above.

[203]ASV, MC, Ursa, fols. 187v (17 February 1454) and 189 (26 May).

seigniorage could be charged. Literally tons of such largely copper coins circulated; they were so highly overvalued that they attracted innumerable counterfeiters, whose products merely aggravated the situation. Payments made in such coins required an agio, above the official or silver price of gold ducats.[204]

Silver brought to the mint and registered by the "pesador" declined drastically, from 18,389 marks in 1450 to 4,198 marks in 1451; amounts brought in the next two years hardly exceeded that low figure, while the accounts, perhaps incomplete, fade away with a figure of a mere 59 marks in 1454. Even if incomplete, these figures probably reflect the actual situation, a wartime situation that Venice seriously aggravated. In an attempt at promoting Venetian products, especially woolens, the Senate required Ragusan importers of Serbian silver to invest one-quarter of their earnings in Venetian goods. The reaction of the Ragusans, who probably preferred Florentine cloth anyway, was to take their silver to Florence. The counselors, who proposed the tardy revocation of the protectionist legislation, admitted that little silver had been brought to the silver mint, whose activity had been sharply curtailed.[205]

Gold became more rare than silver, causing the value of the gold ducat in stable silver soldini and grossi to rise from 114 to 120 soldi in 1453, and again to 124 in 1455, for a total increase of 9 percent. But the mint did not react to raise its bimetallic ratio to that of the market. Mercenaries in the field complained of receiving only counterfeit or light ducats,[206] but the situation was little different in Venice itself. In 1452 "florins of various kinds" were ousting Venetian ducats; while being exchanged at only 2 soldi below the rate for ducats, they were 6–8 percent lighter; all were ordered brought to the mint except for Hungarian florins, judged to be "perfectly good."[207] The order fell on deaf ears, if in 1454 it was said in the Senate that only Hungarian and other foreign gold coins were circulating in Venice.[208] At the close of the same year it was admitted that foreigners were taking their gold to Ferrara and elsewhere, rather than to Venice, to have it minted, and attempts were made to facilitate the entry into Venice of merchants who might also bring gold.[209] Venice was in a vortex: bimetallic ratios in Italy and in the rest of Europe were vacillating, moving by no means always in the same direction (in France silver rose!); demand in the Levant had been for silver when in 1453–54 it suddenly changed to gold.

---

[204]Mueller, "L'imperialismo monetario."

[205]Reinhold C. Mueller, "La crisi economica-monetaria veneziana di metà Quattrocento nel contesto generale," in *Aspetti della vita economica medievale: Atti del convegno di studi nel X anniversario della morte di F. Melis* (Florence, 1985), 552 n. 50, 553–54.

[206]ASV, ST, reg. 2, fol. 151 (8 August 1450).

[207]Ibid., reg. 3, fol. 35v (30 August 1452).

[208]Ibid., fol. 128v (13 September 1454).

[209]Ibid., fol. 139 (6 December 1454) and fol. 79r–v (September 1453).

Citizens and dealers in money reacted to such stimuli in various ways: by hoarding, by lightening and counterfeiting coins, by avoiding the use of specie where possible, by speculating. Examples of each abound in the few years that here interest us.

Hoarding, whether covert or conspicuous, kept money "dead." In December 1453 a first attempt at passing a sumptuary law — "so that superfluous expense be avoided and money not be kept dead, while inordinate expenditures are made in ornaments for our women" — was roundly defeated. Little more than a year later a sumptuary law was passed with a different rationale: conspicuous expenditure displeased the Creator and brought about illicit gains and the squandering of patrimonies.[210] Renewed preoccupation with unproductive investments was clearly a product of the general bullion famine and scarcity of coins.

In 1450 a workshop for clipping mint-fresh coins, run by the priest Giovanni of Todi, was discovered. Most prominent among those who had furnished the mint coins were bankers, in the best position to acquire coins from the mint and pass off the clipped coins. The banker-moneychanger Antonio Zane (seemingly not of the noble family of that name) was identified as the worst offender and was banished for ten years and forbidden ever to run a bank again. More surprising is the condemnation of two partners of the Bernardo-Garzoni bank, who, "avaritia ducti," also wanted to be in on a business that guaranteed a quick profit of 7 percent. Giovanni Garzoni, the more active, who like Zane had fled the city, was banished for five years and forbidden ever again to run a bank; his brother Antonio was sentenced to one year in prison for having known of the operation. It is interesting that the bank itself was not closed; there were many other members of the Garzoni family who could continue to run the bank, and the noble principal, Nicolò Bernardo, was in high government circles in those years. Of course, neither the government nor the marketplace could do without this prominent bank, even though everyone involved must have known what was going on. A new draconian law against clippers and counterfeiters was passed in reaction to the case, but it had little effect: a workshop for grossetti which collected itinerant experts in making dies and "whitening copper" was discovered in Conegliano in 1455, not to mention the large-scale fabrication of black money.[211]

The scarcity of good coin caused citizens to resort to offsetting probably more than before. It was an old practice to offset debits with credits at

---

[210]Ibid., fols. 93 (21 December 1453) and 146 (28 February 1455), and Margaret M. Newett, "The Sumptuary Laws of Venice in the Fourteenth and Fifteenth Centuries," in *Historical Essays by Members of Owens College, Manchester,* ed. T. F. Tout and J. Tait (London, 1902), 245–78.

[211]ASV, Quarantia Criminal, reg. 18, fols. 86v, 89v–90r; reg. 14bis (Sanudo's notes), fol. 107. AC, regs. 3649, fols. 106v–7v, and 3650, fol. 30r–v (14 March 1455).

the office of the Estraordinari, which took in freight charges and other customs duties. But in the years 1449 to 1455 the office, whose revenues were earmarked for the arsenal, was not taking in specie at all, as a result of the widespread use of offsetting, and was unable to pass much or anything to the arsenal. In 1449 it was forbidden to make offsets unless an initial deposit in cash had been made, but the practice continued, and in 1451 and 1455 the office, which was not taking in a penny ("non exigit unum denarium"), was told to permit offsetting only if one-fifth of the amount transferred had been rendered as cash.[212]

What was the position of the banker who, like Soranzo, did not put clippers to work (or did not get caught for doing it)? Surely he continued, perhaps with greater zeal than ever, to cull coins, and he obviously sent the worst to the front for the mercenaries. When his loans to the state could not be in bank money but, as in the case of mercenaries, had to be in cash, then he hoped for repayment in good mint coin, thereby to profit from the difference. A bind in which the banker was clearly caught in the critical first half of the 1450s was making loans in ducats (or in gold-based bank money) and getting repaid in silver, which was falling. That could have meant losses, even though the market pushed up the conversion rate for ducats. To avoid loss, or perhaps to guarantee a profit, bankers sometimes agreed they would make a loan to the state only if they were repaid in gold. That Benetto Soranzo did as early as 1449 on a large but unspecified loan, having foreseen the coming trend.[213] Giacomo Corner insisted on repayment in gold in 1453 and 1454 when risk was much greater.[214] By then Soranzo had stopped lending to the state, or so it seems, but he probably continued to lend to private parties and could have gotten into a squeeze between the supply and demand of one metal over against the other.

Between failures the banking scene at the Rialto changed, and another disaster beset Venetian commerce. First to the configuration of the banks.

About February 1454 the banker Bernardo Ziera, active since 1442, died. Rather than continue the bank on his own, Bernardo's son Agostino merged the bank he had inherited with that of his brother-in-law, the bullion merchant Giacomo Corner. Sometime in the same year the small bank of Nicolò Orsini and partners (namely, Antonio e Cosimo de' Tomasi) closed down.[215] Both actions reduced competition but also reinforced two conceivably threatened operations while eliminating a third altogether.

Second, a disaster in commercial shipping which impressed public opinion in Venice as a whole occurred on 17 January 1455. Two galleys arriving from Acquamorte shipwrecked at the entry to the port of Venice, at

[212]Mueller, "La crisi economica-monetaria," 555.

[213]ASV, ST, reg. 2, fol. 107 (26 April 1449), for "as much as possible of 33,000 ducats."

[214]Ibid., reg. 3, fols. 85 (2 November 1453) and 102 (25 January 1454).

[215]ASV, GP, Sg, reg. 125, fols. 92–93 (15 November 1457): "del 1454 desfexe el bancho" (92v).

S. Nicolò del Lido, in a terrible storm of wind, rain, and snow. Zorzi Dolfin wrote that he had never before seen galleys wrecked at the Lido. The decision to chance the crossing from Istria, while a hundred sails, including the roundships from Syria, had decided not to lift anchor at Parenzo because of the forecast of bad weather ("luna da greco"), was a bad one. It was impossible for witnesses to lend aid, and seventy men drowned. Merchandise lost was valued at 100,000 ducats, including 500 caratelli of sugar from Palermo and the dyestuff kermes (grana), as well as wool, hides, and other goods that were water damaged or stolen during salvage operations. Furthermore, wrote Dolfin, the government lost 15,000 ducats in customs revenues, freight taxes, and the value of the vessels themselves.[216] This was just another link in the chains of indebtedness which would bring down the Benetto Soranzo bank, for the second time.

v. A LIQUIDATION BY COURT ORDER AND A QUIET FAILURE

An Overview of the Later Quattrocento

Most of the half century following the failures of Benetto Soranzo's banks was — unusually — calm on the Rialto. It is difficult to characterize the state of the Venetian economy in general in that period; signs of stagnation are mixed with signs of renewed entrepreneurial endeavor. If fewer heavy merchantmen were built in the arsenal, emphasis shifted to light war galleys and a permanent war fleet. In military terms, the Peace of Lodi brought only a short respite. There followed a long war with the Turks (1463–79), the short but very costly war of Ferrara (1482–84), involvement in the Italian wars beginning with the French invasions in 1494, and a new naval war with the Turks (1499–1501). They meant heavy taxation and a reorganization of public finance. On the other hand, the market for silver and for copper became very lively beginning in the 1460s with the reopening of the Tyrolian mines. Mining rights in the Veneto were expanded and reorganized. The importation of silver became so extensive in the 1480s that new legislation was called for to redefine the role of the bankers in that sector. Along with the metals came such rapidly growing German companies as the Fugger, and along with copper and tin came the movable type of a printing industry that quickly rose to first place in Europe. If anything, the need for secure banks grew, and there were enough positive signs to convince new people to establish themselves as bankers on the Rialto.

Two major banks continued to operate throughout the period. The Soranzo bank, under the new family line of Giovanni di Vettor, was run by Giovanni's sons Pietro and Vettor (the style was changed to Pietro Soranzo

---

[216]Dolfina, fol. 440. Mention of one of the victims in ASV, GP, reg. 123, fol. 40 (6 March 1456).

e fratelli in 1473); it liquidated in 1491, as we shall see. The other bank was that of Bernardo-Garzoni, founded in 1430, which after about 1470 went mostly under the name of Garzoni, with the Bernardo as something like silent partners. It succumbed in 1499 and again in 1500.

The bank of the Ziera, opened by Bernardo in 1442, taken over by his son Agostino and merged with the recently opened bank of Giacomo Corner and partners in 1454, was forced by court order to liquidate in 1468, when Agostino was caught falsifying his accounts. Giacomo Corner, Agostino Ziera's brother-in-law, may have begun in 1453, exploiting the situation created by the first failure of Benetto Soranzo.

There were five major new entries. Piero Guerrucci (Veruzzi in Venetian) was in operation by 1459 and was forced to liquidate in 1473. Ziera's location was taken over by Andrea di Pietro Barbarigo, of the branch of the Barbarigo family nicknamed "Brocca," in 1468, in partnership with Vettor and Zuanbattista Contarini; the bank reportedly liquidated after fourteen years of activity.[217] Francesco, Giovanni, and Alvise Pisani, sons of Almorò, opened a bank on the Venetian new year, 1 March 1475, in effect taking over the position of Guerrucci; this bank liquidated in 1500, was reopened in 1504 by Alvise Pisani, one of the most powerful men in Venice, and operated until 1528. Tomà Lippomano opened in 1480, in partnership at first with Andrea di Vettor Capello and brothers; his was the second bank to succumb to the runs that began in 1499. The last newcomer was Matteo Agostini, in operation by 1493; his family had for many decades been one of the city's major bullion importers, and banking was a natural development of this interest; the bank survived the crash of 1499, only to fail in 1508.[218]

Smaller banks, like those of Francesco Fedele and Alvise Nicchetta, who primarily changed coins on the Rialto but also took deposits, were also in danger, and at least Nicchetta defaulted in 1499, for the second time.

The Ziera Affair

The Ziera family was of old citizen stock, with strong interests — and perhaps their origins — in the Venetian fortress colony of Coron in the Morea (Peloponnesus). Bernardo, who founded the bank in 1442, was reported to be a man of noble bearing. A chronicler who saw a portrait of the man said he went about dressed in red with a black cape and beret.[219] We will meet him below as executor of the estate of his cousin Giacomo Ziera, bishop of Coron, who died in 1437; in that role, he purchased some

---

[217]Malipiero, *Annali*, 655, says the grand opening took place on 7 June 1467, "Su 'l canton sotto 'l Razo, dove era 'l Banco de Bernardo Ciera; e fu saldà in cao de 14 anni." Sanudo writes, "Sotto 'l razzo di le ore appresso la chiesa di S. Giacomo dove era il banco di Bernardo Ciera che fallì," as reported in Ferrara, "Antichi banchi," 196. But since Ziera operated until 1468, the location cannot have been taken over earlier.

[218]Lane, "Venetian Bankers," for all these names.

[219]Ferrara, "Antichi banchi," 196 (from Cicogna's *Iscrizioni*).

5,000 ducats' worth of government obligations to provide an endowment for the deceased's pious legacies, an activity that might have set him to thinking about running a bank. Bernardo, son of a noblewoman, married all his children and grandchildren into noble families. When he died, in late 1453 or early 1454, his son and successor Agostino merged the Ziera bank with that of his noble brother-in-law Giacomo Corner, as was mentioned above. The bank operated under both names until Giacomo died (between 1462 and 1464), after which it was known under the name only of Agostino Ziera, even though Giacomo's son Piero succeeded his father as partner. Agostino also had a son Piero, who is referred to as "a banco" in 1464.

Agostino controlled sufficient capital to make himself and his children interesting marriage partners to noble families, but he seems not to have controlled the sympathies of many nobles. He gained leverage outside Venice, in rapport first with Nicholas V, who granted a special indulgence for him and his family in 1450, and then with the emperor Frederick III, who, while in Venice in 1452, where he hardly cut a good figure, asked the personal favor of receiving Ziera into the nobility—a request rejected by the Senate as constitutionally unfeasible.[220]

In Venice, Ziera moved in a circle of disreputable, cantankerous types. His daughter Filippa was married (in 1462) to Giovanni di Marino Capello of S. Polo—the same Marino who had hosted the Florentine *malelingua* Benedetto Dei in the latter's youth. Capello's own testament reflects the atmosphere of the circle and bars no holds when discussing the misdeeds of his own son, whom he disowns. In what was virtually a deposition, Marino accused his son of collusion with Ziera against him, especially as regards the dowry Zuanne controlled and a false entry in the books of Ziera's bank which had cost Marino dearly. Not surprisingly, Marino Capello recalls Ziera in his testament of 1475 as "ribaldo et amicho del diavolo."[221] Agostino Ziera's son Piero was of the same stamp; he even spent a year in prison for insulting the captain of Suave in the Veronese and the Signoria itself "in front of the whole population."[222] Agostino caused embarrassment for his daughter Brigida when he sued her husband—a lawsuit filled with ran-

---

[220]Ferrara, "Antichi banchi," 196–98, and Laura Giannasi, "Ciera, Bernardo" and "Ciera, Agostino," in *DBI,* 25 (1981), 443–47. (Note that Ziera or Çiera was only occasionally rendered Ciera in contemporary documents.) An interest in dealing with the feudal aristocracy is also reflected in Ziera's banking activity, for he had large credits on pawns with a certain noble Giovanni da Castro. In 1454 da Castro owed some 4,200 ducats to Ziera, on which some 650 ducats were still due in 1461; some pawns ("arzenti" and cloths, the object of a joint investment) had already been sold. The nobleman's procurators, Andrea and Marco Corner (the latter a "miles"), gave the excuse that da Castro was currently under siege in his castle. ASV, GP, Sg, reg. 133, fols. 15–19v.

[221]ASV, NT, b. 69, fols. 3–4v (31 May 1475); original in b. 68, num. 217 (8–12 May).

[222]He was sentenced in joint session of the Quarantia Criminal and Civil to a one-year prison term and 500 ducats fine and was banned from the district of Verona for five years. A marginal note states that he was released on 16 August 1465 after doing his time. ASV, AC, reg. 3651, fols. 78v–79.

corous language, as we shall see, which probably reflected longstanding conflicts. Considerable interest was aroused among the nobility when Agostino was discovered to have falsified some entries in his bank's account books, an unpardonable offense, given the nearly sacred nature of bankers' books in Venice.

The case against Agostino Ziera was brought before the Senate itself by the Avogadori di Comun on 19 December 1468. The charges read against him were basically two:

1. He had made a fraudulent entry in the name of Antonio da Vico, without the latter's knowledge, in which he debited da Vico and credited Agostino's own son-in-law Bartolomeo Lion for 300 ducats, including in the registration other falsehoods that damaged other persons;
2. In 1465 he had stolen from the office of the Sopraconsoli an order to pay 590 ducats obtained from the Consoli by Antonio da Vico against Giovanni Tron; following a series of offsets, the order had been presented to the Sopraconsoli by Bartolomeo Miliotto, creditor of da Vico, asking for payment from Ziera, debtor of Tron.

The proposal to proceed against Ziera passed by a wide margin: 119 to 6, with 24 neutral votes. Then began the discussion on how to discipline Ziera.

There was one major proposal plus three amendments, each of which asked for increasingly longer prison terms. The proposal that passed deprived Ziera and his company ("dicta") of the right to operate a deposit bank in Venice; ordered him to balance the books and liquidate in three months; ordered him in the interim to answer all requests for information from clients about their accounts; nullified the fraudulent entry; confirmed the validity of the order-to-pay and restored it to Miliotto; and assigned 500 ducats to the Avogadori. The amendment that passed reduced the latter assignment to 300 ducats and added another, for 100 ducats, to Miliotto for damages and condemned Ziera to enter prison for a two-month term in March 1469, once the liquidation was concluded. Then several other crimes came to light, such as the illegal appropriation of a shop in Padua; a fraud committed while he held the tax farm for salt in the Terraferma, when he had illegal salt measures made; and, finally, the nonobservance of the bequests of the deceased bishop of Coron, whose executor he had become, in which case his bad faith was explicitly condemned.[223]

Not surprisingly, liquidation took longer than had been foreseen. In 1471 the Senate, recognizing that interested parties were not being permitted to see their accounts, ordered them put in a public place and gave Agostino eight days to turn over to the Provveditori di Comun all account books of all kinds, from the beginning of the operation of the bank to the

---

[223]Ferrara, "Documenti," doc. 160, and "Antichi banchi," 197, with misunderstandings of the balloting on the amendments and of the series of offsets. Giannasi, "Ciera, Agostino," 444–45.

present.[224] At some point Agostino, to avoid imprisonment, fled Venice for Rome, where he sought protection from Sixtus IV (1471–84), who, as Francesco della Rovere, had supposedly been his mentor at the University of Padua, who promptly made him protonotary apostolic;[225] Agostino's son Piero and the rest of the family remained in charge of the liquidation. In September 1472 a lawsuit between Agostino, represented by Piero, and the former's son-in-law Francesco Girardo still involved affairs of the bank. In 1475 Piero Ziera, in a tirade against Girardo, affirmed that he, Piero, with his mother and sister, had liquidated all accounts. As late as that year, however, the authorities were still finding irregularities in Agostino's accounts.[226] The story has it that Agostino returned to Venice from Rome in 1473 to announce successful liquidation of all the bank's debts, "with solemn pomp and to universal applause." He died in Rome in 1476, where his epitaph recounts that he had given up business, in which he had been laudably involved ("in quibus fuerat cum laude versatus"!), for higher things. In short, the ignominy of the banker Agostino Ziera, a fraud and a villain with the right connections, was at least superficially overcome, through ecclesiastical intervention and benefices.[227] The forced closure of the bank of this "friend of the devil" had nothing to do with the general economic conjuncture but was strictly personal in nature.

The Case of Piero Guerrucci

The case of Piero Guerrucci is rather more honorable. Guerrucci was of Lucchese stock (his ancestors came to Venice in the early fourteenth century), and his family had been involved in the silk industry. He was married to the daughter of Andrea Zusto, a non-noble from whom he received the modest dowry of 800 ducats.[228] The first we know of his operating a bank is in December 1459, when Nicolò Barbarigo opened a

---

[224]Ferrara, "Documenti," doc. 161.

[225]Ferrara, "Antichi banchi," 198.

[226]"E tanto fixi tra la benedeta anima di mia madre, mia sorela et io, che condussimo a saldo tutte le nostre raxon." ASV, GP, Sg, reg. 160, fols. 127–41v, 143v, at fol. 133; copy of the document of 1472 on fol. 141v. A last intervention by the authorities to balance an account on the books of the bank was made in 1475: a debit of the lumber merchant Andrea Zusto of 1455 was nullified as false; the account appeared "viva," although it had been "quasi ex toto satisfacta." ASV, Quarantia Criminal, reg. 19, fol. 16 (pencil), and AC, reg. 3654, fol. 34 (20 September 1475). At some point, Agostino had pledged surety for Giacomo Surian, abbot of S. Zeno of Verona, to Giovanfrancesco Strozzi, merchant banker in Venice; Pietro, representing his cleric father, was ordered to pay 240 ducats. GP, Sg, reg. 159, fols. 29v–30 (7 September 1473).

[227]Pietro Ziera, Agostino's son and self-styled cardinal (d. 1507), wrote a rather strange humanistic tract, "De origine venetorum et de civitate Venetiarum," in British Library, London, Add. ms 8573 (Fondazione G. Cini, Venice, microfilm BML 61).

[228]ASV, GP, Sg, reg. 134, fols. 16v–17 (11 March 1462). For the family, see Molà, *La comunità dei lucchesi,* 266–67.

current account with him.[229] Most likely he had opened a year or two earlier, for in 1458 his brother Michele returned to Lucca to enter politics, with the support of his banker brother. Michele soon plotted to overthrow the government and, with the favor of both Cosimo de' Medici and Francesco Sforza, sought to make himself *signore* of Lucca. Discovered, he was condemned to death for treason, but the sentence was conditionally commuted to a fine of 10,000 ducats, payable in two installments. His banker brother in Venice did not come across with the ransom money, however, and Michele was executed in January 1460. Even had Piero wished to pay, political pressures in Venice would probably have tied his hands, for his family connections had become, for a moment, a matter of international politics and intrigue.[230]

The bank quickly became one of the pillars of Venetian state finance, not far behind the banks of Soranzo and Garzoni in maintaining the floating debt. The primary need for liquidity which the state had at this time was the protracted and costly war against the Turks (1463–79); peace was signed in January 1479, after a clear defeat of Venice. In the "Terra" series of Senate deliberations alone, the bank turns up some thirteen times as lender. Its maximum credit line was in the year from May 1465 to May 1466, when it extended a total of some 60,000 ducats. On 8 May 1465, when it was still a creditor for 17,700 ducats, it lent an additional 20,000, so that it was "out" for nearly 38,000 ducats at a single date. The last large loan (50,000 ducats divided among three banks) was made in April 1471; it was to be repaid first through July, then through September, then through April 1472 — and even that promise could probably not be held. So the state had reason to be interested in the bank's health.

The state had the opportunity to demonstrate its concern for the bank in May 1472. That was the month in which the vastest demonetization and reorganization of Venice's currency were undertaken (see fig. 8). The city feared an inundation of counterfeits, and circulating grossi and grossoni were badly clipped. When the value of these coins was cried down for that reason, Giacomo Feletro, accountant ("scrivan") of the Guerrucci bank, was arrested in the midst of the Rialto for clipping coins. The diarist Malipiero writes that the public arrest created the fear that Guerrucci himself might be found guilty of the same crime, and depositors began a run to withdraw their money. The bank was about to fail, says Malipiero, when the Signoria, along with many citizens and foreigners, came to its aid with money, so that the bank could survive the pressure.[231]

---

[229]ASV, Archivio Grimani-Barbarigo, b. 43, reg. 6, fols. 22, 40, 85, 111.

[230]M. E. Bratchel, *Lucca, 1430–1494: The Reconstruction of an Italian City-Republic* (Oxford, 1995), 68–73.

[231]Malipiero, *Annali*, 659: "e perchè se dubitava che 'l Veruzzi fosse in dolo, molti andava a trazer i so danari, tal che el Banco era per falir; ma la Signoria e molti cittadini e altri forestieri l'ha aiutà de denari, tal che 'l se ha prevalso."

Fig. 8. Venetian coins in circulation after the mint reform of 1472.
Of the six coins — gold, fine silver, billon, and copper — shown here in
their actual size, five were struck under Doge Nicolò Tron (1471–74),
under whom the reform was carried out; one, a billon coin, was struck under
Doge Pasquale Malipiero (1457–62).

a. Gold ducat.

Obv.: **NICOL.TRONVS DVX.S.M.VENETI** St. Mark, facing three-
quarters right, presents the banner to the kneeling doge.
Rev.: **.SIT.T.XPE.DAT.Q.TV REGIS.ISTE.DVCAT.** (Sit tibi Christe
datus qui tu regis iste Ducatus). Christ in the act of blessing, in a mandorla
with nine stars in the field.

AV, 20.4 mm, 3.534 gr. Museo Bottacin, inv. no. 340A (Papadopoli, 2:10, no. 1).

b. Lira Tron.

Obv.: Leaf **NICOLAVS TRONVS DVX** Bust of bearded doge, facing left,
wearing the ducal cap.
Rev.: **SANCTVS MARCVS** Winged lion crouching and facing front,
holding the gospel in his front paws, encircled by a garland tied with a bow.

AR, 28.9 mm, 6.372 gr. Museo Bottacin, inv. no. 342 (Papadopoli, 2:10–11, no. 5).

c. Marchetto or soldino.

Obv.: **NI.TRONVS.DVX.** Bearded doge facing left, holding the banner
with both hands. **LM** in the right field.
Rev.: Winged lion crouching and facing front, holding the gospel in his front
paws, in a lobed circle with annulets in each quadrant.

AR, 13.1 mm, 0.329 gr. Museo Bottacin, inv. no. 348 (Papadopoli, 2:12, no. 17).

Fig. 8 (*cont.*)

d. Piccolo or bagattino.
Obv.: **.NICOLAVS.TRONVS.DVX.** Bust of bearded doge, facing left.
Rev.: **.SANCTVS.MARCVS.V.** Lion rampant left, holding the banner.

AE, 18.5 mm, 2.092 gr. Museo Bottacin, inv. no. 352 (Papadopoli, 2:13, no. 21).

e. Piccolo or bagattino for Friuli (?).
Obv.: **+.PA.MARIPETRO** Cross patée in a circle.
Rev.: **+.S MARCUS.** Bust of St. Mark with pearled halo, in a circle.

B, 13.5 mm, 0.570 gr. Museo Bottacin, inv. no. 332 (Papadopoli, 1:279, no. 5).

f. Bagattino for Verona and Vicenza.
Obv.: **NICOLAVS TRONVS** Bust of bearded doge, facing left.
Rev.: Winged lion crouching and holding the gospel in his front paws.

AE, 14.2 mm, 2.415 gr. Museo Bottacin, inv. no. 353a (Papadopoli, 2:14, no. 27).

Guerrucci had, of course, also extended credit to private citizens. One example is a loan of 535 ducats to the Procurator Andrea d'Antonio Contarini; his estate was unable to repay, and Guerrucci had to get a court order to be able to divert to himself the interest payments on government obligations due to the estate.[232] Only three weeks before his bank failed, Guerrucci had made a large contract for the importation of wheat with Luca di Triadano Gritti.[233] Only a week before the fact, Giovanni Lanfredini, Medici partner and factor in Venice, who had had dealings with the Guerrucci bank, knew that it was on the verge of defaulting and had himself designated procurator by a Florentine (Giovanni di Vanni) and a Venetian (Valeriano Amadi) to deal in the name of all three for a surety of 1,000 ducats that they had posted for the banker and which they had already been called upon by the Consoli to pay.[234]

Whether it was a second run that caused the Guerrucci bank to close on 21 October 1473 is not known. Neither the banker nor the populace, however, seems to have been worried about losing money. The chroniclers report that liabilities were only about 30,000 ducats and that all that would be lost was time ("non si hebbe alcuno danno, salvo di tempo").[235] It would seem that the admission of insolvency was more an accident than the logical consequence of a panic, even less dramatic than the earlier case of Francesco Balbi.

On 4 November the banker appeared before the Signoria to plead his case. His difficulty derived, he said, not from lack of assets, of which he had plenty to cover all debts, but from his generosity in lending to the state. Those loans to the state were indeed considerable, as we will see below (Chap. 10). If the state would repay some of his own capital but especially grant him time (that is, a moratorium), it would be to his benefit, to that of his creditors, and to the honor of the state, he petitioned. The Senate responded positively, as follows: Guerrucci had three days to gain the approval of three-quarters of his guarantors (for 15,000 ducats) and an additional five days to produce new surety for the remaining 5,000 ducats—all to be approved, as usual, by the Governatori delle Entrate and the Consoli dei Mercanti; full surety, in short, was the precondition for the granting of a moratorium. Guerrucci in return promised to pay in full within eight

---

[232]ASV, GP, Sg, reg. 156, fols. 71v–73v (27 January 1473).

[233]Ibid., reg. 170, fols. 23–27 (a case of 2 October 1479, referring to "patti" of 2 October 1473).

[234]BNF, mss. II.V.13 (Carte Lanfredini), fol. 146 (13 October 1473). Lanfredini had told the others "ch'el ditto ser Piero Guerrucci sarà gravato in qualche acor[d]o over compoxizione." Two years earlier Guerrucci had consigned to Lanfredini, as representative of the firm Pierfrancesco e Giuliano de' Medici, a remarkable cache of jewels (pearls, rubies, and the like), each described by weight and quality but not by price; there is no indication whether Guerrucci was the seller, depositary, or pawner of the cache. Ibid., fol. 136.

[235]BMV, Cronaca Veniera, It. cl. VII, cod. 791 (7589), fol. 158.

months. The state also agreed to repay him 2,000 ducats it owed; an additional 8,000 ducats under lien at the Salt Office would be released at the end of the eight months, an old credit dating from 1464 which had served as surety for a loan from the Medici bank. The 8,000 ducats could be obligated to the guarantors, as an incentive to stand surety. As usual, the arm of the state would be used to force debtors to pay up or provide surety themselves at the office of the Consoli. Once the moratorium ran out, creditors were free to sue both the bank and its guarantors.[236]

The optimistic prediction of the former banker turned out to be wrong, especially as regards the time needed to liquidate. In 1474 Guerrucci pawned a dozen silken cloths ("spaliere di razo") bearing his coat of arms to Luca Gritti, who seems to have been his former partner in the importation of wheat, as well as a guarantor; for the silks, which were worth 300 ducats to Guerrucci but estimated at only 148 by a "straxaruol," or used clothes dealer, Gritti lent only 140 ducats, and he then had the coat of arms changed to his own.[237] In 1475 Guerrucci was still in need of a four-month safe-conduct; perhaps the failure of some debtors had complicated his plans.[238] Extant account books are unenlightening,[239] but the liquidation had been completed by 1479, when Guerrucci was in a position to sue the estate of Luca Gritti for return of the pawns and the defendants spoke of the loan as having been granted in the banker's time of need ("nel tenpo de le suo necessità"). Moreover, in 1478 he had been able to dower his daughter Giovanna, who was married to the noble Nicolò Corner, great-great grandson of the doge Marco Corner.[240] Again, somewhat as in the case of Ziera, it

---

[236]ASV, ST, reg. 7, fol. 22r–v. Published from an incomplete copy by Lattes, *Libertà*, doc. xxvii (where Veruzzi was misread "Venerius," repeated by Ferrara, "Documenti," doc. 156). While the deliberation was supported by 81 votes, a counterproposal to give Guerrucci nothing, since he owed 190 ducats to the Cazudi, received 46 votes (there were 21 nays and 9 neutral). The actual safe-conduct was granted by the Quarantia, as usual; the text was on a lost fol. 14, as the rubric indicates: Quarantia Criminal, reg. 19, last folio.

[237]ASV, GP, Sg, reg. 69, fols. 169–70 (8 June 1479, the date on which Guerrucci successfully sued to get the spaliere back from the Gritti estate).

[238]ASV, AC, reg. 3654, fol. 7 (20 February); the grant, made by the Signoria, was nullified on a procedural question. Bartolomeo Zorzi was in debt for more than 100,000 ducats; creditors twice had him excommunicated, but, reduced to "summa inopia et miseria," he appealed to the Senate for intervention at the Roman Curia; ST, reg. 7, fol. 108v (28 March 1476). It seems he had, or also had, a debt of 100,000 ducats with the sultan for an "apalto," which open question was made part of the peace treaty of 1479; see Marin Sanudo, *Le vite dei dogi (1474–1494)*, ed. Angela Caracciolo Aricò (Padua, 1989), 1:137.

[239]Nicolò Barbarigo's last operation at the bank is dated 18 August 1472; a balance was closed out to "debitori-creditori" when the account book was balanced in 1483. ASV, Archivio Grimani-Barbarigo, b. 43, reg. 6. Alvise Michiel had a very small credit balance of £1 19s when Guerrucci failed; of that he was able to transfer the bulk, or 15 ducats, in October 1474. The remaining less than 5 ducats were unpaid in October 1476 when the account was carried to a new ledger, not extant. Miscellanea Gregolin, b. 15, fol. 55.

[240]ASV, AC, reg. 107, fol. 71.

seems that the insolvency of this bank was an isolated incident and not part of a particularly negative conjuncture. For the first time, however, a banker specifically indicted the state for contributing to his insolvency by delaying the repayment of the loans he had made.

The war against the Turks strained the economy, to be sure, but those chains of indebtedness which undid banks in other settings did not develop in either of these two cases.

6

THE MAKING OF THE PANIC
OF 1499–1500

i. THE CONJUNCTURE IN THE DECADE 1488–1498

HE CONJUNCTURE IN THE decade beginning in 1488, leading up to the crash of 1499, perhaps presented more opportunity for profitable investment than usual but also greater risk. More than ever, market indicators provide negative signals. Those signals were noted and the effects of the negative conjuncture felt by the Rialto bankers Pietro and Vettor Soranzo (sons of Giovanni di Vettor), who decided to abandon banking while the enterprise was still solvent. Actually, in a letter to their brother, the archbishop of Cyprus, they wrote as early as 1485 that the affairs of the bank had taken a bad turn over the preceding eight years; and in 1490 they urged their brother to return to Venice for the impending division of the family patrimony which threatened them with ruin and would force them to liquidate. The famous bank was in fact successfully liquidated on 21 April 1491, to the sound of trumpets and fifes, as Malipiero reports.[1] That must have been a painful decision for a bank with a more than secular history, but it was taken with foresight, for conditions were destined to worsen.

---

[1]*Annali*, 688; in Ferrara, "Antichi banchi," 191. Nothing more is known of this liquidation. It was foreseen in 1485, when the brothers warned the prelate that the time would come in which "non è che andate a tavola per zenar la sera." In 1490 they wrote of the division that threatened the "ruina di tuti nui" and forced them to "saldar 'sto bancho." The two bankers had actively aided the career of their prelate brother; their correspondence is extant in ASV, Archivio del vescovo di Cipro, especially buste 3b and 4; it was reported on by Giuseppe dalla Santa, "Benedetto Soranzo patrizio veneziano, arcivescovo di Cipro e Gerolamo Riario: Una pagina nuova della guerra di Ferrara degli anni 1482–1484," *NAV*, n.s., 28 (1914), esp. 310 n. 1 and 312 n. 3.

The sectors that involved Rialto banks most closely were the usual ones: importation and exportation of silver and copper, famine and the importation of wheat, and the credit market in general. They will be treated in that order, along with a consideration of a few of the outstanding personalities involved.

Markets for Silver

The revival of the extraction of silver and copper from mines situated from Tyrol to Hungary which began in the 1460s merely enhanced the role of Venice as Europe's major market for precious and nonprecious metals, the major entrepôt between West and East. Demand in the Levant increased contemporaneously, but just when the seaways became ever less secure, owing to the growing might of the Turks.

As ever, the Rialto banks were in an ambiguous position as regards the bullion market; their intervention and mediation were essential to the smooth operation of the market, but the risks involved caused the government again and again to limit or to prohibit altogether their direct investment. Although strong restrictive laws had been passed again in 1450 and 1465,[2] the financial needs of the War of Ferrara in 1482 had introduced a system whereby banks were officially permitted, on an ad hoc basis, to purchase silver and bring it to the mint for transformation into coin and certified bars, as long as the coin was lent to the state. The circuit worked as follows: the importer sold to the banker, who paid with a credit on current account; the bank brought the bullion to the mint, where normally one-fourth was turned into coin, three-fourths into bars; when the coin was produced, in about forty days on the average, a portion of it (for example, half according to a provision of 1485) went directly from the mint to the Treasury as a loan, while remaining credited to the banker on the books of the mint; when the Treasury was able, after a variable delay, it repaid the banker in coin. Licenses were issued by the Council of Ten alone, which, since the demonetization of 1472, had jurisdiction over the mint. The system could obviously produce float, that is, expand the money supply. Potential profits — and risk — were considerable.[3]

The silver market was dominated by five to ten persons and companies, generally connected more or less directly to the banks. Two major figures in those years were Antonio Cavalli and Zorzi Orese, an outsider and an insider, both of whom failed in 1491. Large deliveries of silver in 1490 by Cavalli in partnership with the Paumgartner firm and in 1489–91 by their competitor the Fugger company caused the price of silver to drop.[4]

---

[2]ASV, ST, reg. 2, fol. 152, and *Cap. Broche,* 134–37; ST, reg. 5, fol. 108v (8 February 1465).

[3]*Cap. Broche,* 194–245 and passim (the example from 1485 on 212–13), and below, Chap. 10. For practical implementation of the enabling legislation in two cases, see ASV, Capi del Consiglio dei Dieci, Notatorio, reg. 2, fols. 45 (20 June 1492) and 88 (24–26 October 1495).

[4]The paragraph that follows is derived from Braunstein, "Les entreprises minières," 559–80

This inversion of the price curve probably caught speculators in Venice unawares. Despite the abundance of silver available, however, the temptation persisted for bullion merchants and refiners, closely connected to the banks, to falsify the alloy of the plate they produced; two of them were caught at the act in 1490 and were sentenced to banishment for ten years.[5]

Antonio Cavalli (de Caballis), known in German lands as Anton vom Roß, probably had a patent of Venetian nobility, inherited from an ancestor who lived a century earlier. Be that as it may, his primary interests lay in Tyrol, where, through a system of loans to Archduke Sigismund, he had gained monopoly control over the extraction of copper and silver. For a time he was finance minister to the archduke, and he fell out of favor and back into favor several times. In 1488, when he had been dismissed, he appeared in Venice offering a plan to reform the whole system of mining in Venetian lands, for which he wanted to be named general director. The Council of Ten did not trust him enough to take up the offer, although it did undertake a reform. About the same time, at the conclusion of a short but bloody war between Venice and Sigismund, Cavalli was able to make one more loan to the archduke, probably in partnership with the Venetian Paolo Contarini. Then in 1490 Cavalli accompanied a large delivery of Tyrolian silver, in which he had invested along with his partners, the Paumgartner firm. The market price was low (it had probably dropped on occasion of an even larger delivery by the Fugger company in 1489 or 1490, when they had been repaid in Tyrolian silver for a loan to Sigismund of 150,000 Rhenish florins), and he could find no buyers. He complained of the matter directly to the Council of Ten, which responded with irony, saying that the price of silver, as of all other commodities, varied in Venice according to supply and demand and that, if he were to try lowering the asking price, he would discover a myriad of takers. In 1491, Cavalli, who had made his testament in Venice in 1490, finally defaulted in Tyrol and had to divest himself of all his properties and rights. The precise effects in Venice

---

(who published the telling response of the Ten to Cavalli's complaint of 1490, pp. 579–80), and from Hermann Kellenbenz, "Le miniere di Primiero e le relazioni dei Fugger con Venezia nel Quattrocento," *Il Trentino in età veneziana*, in *Atti dell'Accademia roveretana degli agiati* 238 (1988; Rovereto, 1990): 371–77. See also A. A. Strnad, "Cavalli, Antonio di," *DBI*, 22 (1979), 714–16. Giacomo Cavalli, mercenary captain for Venice during the War of Chioggia, had been coopted into the Great Council in 1381 (L. Miglio, "Cavalli, Giacomo," *DBI*, 22 (1979), 727–31, but direct genealogical proof of Antonio's status as heir and thus as Venetian noble has yet to be found; the fact that a member of the family, born in the 1450s of Nicolò and the Venetian noblewoman Adriana Foscolo and clearly a Venetian nobleman, was given the name Sigismondo could well reflect an early connection of the Cavalli with Archduke Sigismund (1446–90/96), Antonio's employer. Sigismondo was also concerned with mines, in the Veronese. See Achille Olivieri, "Cavalli, Sigismondo," *DBI*, 22 (1979), 758–60.

[5]Malipiero, *Annali*, 686, recounts that the Council of Ten banished Vettor di Vettor Soranzo and Giacomo Agostini for ten years and forbade their having dealings with the mint thereafter, "per haver falsificà le piastre che i fondeva."

of the failure have not been studied, but there was at least one local victim of the general state of the market.

When he died in late 1491, Giorgio de Allegretis of Ragusa, master goldsmith, better known simply as Zorzi Orese, the principal bullion dealer in Venice, left debts of 40,000 ducats, so that his estate was declared insolvent. Zorzi had received full citizenship in Venice in 1460, and for a generation he was one of a handful of leading bullion dealers and refiners in the city. Needless to say, he worked with and through the Rialto bankers. When Zorzi's son and heir Polo asked for a safe-conduct in January 1492, he stated in his petition to the Senate that the debt his father had left was large enough to have unsettled even a deposit bank ("la qual summa veramente haveria smarito uno bancho de scritta"). The son had himself lost more than 8,000 ducats in Cairo, and many of his debtors and his father's had themselves failed, and their debts had to be written off as losses; nonetheless, he had already succeeded in paying off more than 37,000 ducats of his father's debts. He had to ask for a safe-conduct because he did not wish to flee, he said, and because two difficult creditors remained to be paid off. The biggest debts Zorzi had accumulated were with Anselm the Jew (9,100 ducats), the archbishop of Spalato (7,700 ducats), and the bank of Francesco and Giovanni Pisani (6,620 ducats). Anselm was the powerful Jewish lender Asher Meshullam, based in Mestre, who later became head of the Jewish community in Venice;[6] the prelate was the Brescian Bartolomeo Averoldi. The Pisani bank had clearly been financing Zorzi's speculations in silver, probably by advancing him money for deliveries they needed. The bankers Lippomano and Agostini were also creditors of the bullion expert, but for sums of only 200–300 ducats at the time of the failure of his estate. The major outstanding creditor was the prelate, who was owed some 2,200 ducats, secured on a jeweled ornament.[7] As had been the case with Donato di Filippo Nati at the beginning of the century (see above, Chap. 3, sec. iii), Zorzi Orese was so involved with the banks, as an expert refiner and bullion wholesaler, as to be considered nearly a banker.

In the following years the silver market remained volatile. At least two further failures are tied to it, both of German firms that were major importers of silver and copper to Venice. In 1493 Heinrich Stammler and Brothers defaulted and fled Venice "with vast assets of Venetians and foreigners." This company, later judged by Sanudo — when it failed a second time — one of the foremost firms at the Fontego, had sixty-three creditors and total liabilities of 20,000 ducats. Somehow it was able to pay off its creditors in full, for it was back in operation by 1499, when we shall meet it again.[8] A much better known firm, that of Lucas Fugger, of the "roebuck" branch of

---

[6]Brian S. Pullan, *Rich and Poor in Renaissance Venice* (Oxford, 1971), 479–83.

[7]ASV, ST, 11, fols. 92–93v (9 January 1492).

[8]Simonsfeld, *Der Fondaco,* 1:321–22, docs. 591–92; 2:38.

the family, defaulted, and the principal fled Venice on 2 June 1494. With the agreement of twenty-five of the thirty creditors, the Senate granted a three-month safe-conduct. Liquidation dragged on over several years. In 1497 further safe-conducts were granted to Lucas Fugger and to his son Marcus, but only on 5 February 1499 (four days after the failure of the Garzoni) is there mention of an accord between them and their creditors, ratified at that time by the Senate.[9]

A practical example of the demand for silver in Venice as an exchange commodity for Levantine products will be useful. During the summer of 1497, the Rialto experienced a particular euphoria in the opportunities offered by the Levant trade, and there was competition to export large quantities of silver. The mint must have worked at full capacity to produce the "mocenighi," or 1 lira pieces, that were most in demand. The profit margin possible on bars of certified silver this time was judged to be too low to make them desirable, given their high gold price (which had recently risen by 7 percent).[10] What was loaded, then, were coins, mostly "mocenighi" but also foreign coins, such as Milanese "testoni," soldi of Bologna, Ferrara, and Mantua, papal "carlini," and even German "bezi." The total value of the specie, all silver, which went east is given by Malipiero as 300,000 ducats' worth on four galleys to Alexandria, 60,000 ducats' worth on the galleys to Beirut, not counting merchandise.[11] Thus the Alexandria galleys alone carried well over 12 metric tons of silver coin.[12]

Fortunately, the market in 1497 can also be seen from the point of view of a single investor. The record book and accounts of the nobleman Michele da Lezze register the investment made on those very galleys, although not the profits that were generated. Michele listed on his bill of lading ten numbered sacks, or "groppi," of mocenighi, worth 700 ducats each, by weight, for a total of 7,000 ducats. Six sacks were loaded on one galley, four on another, all headed for Alexandria. In other words, this merchant alone loaded 283 kilograms of silver coin, to be traded for spices.

[9]Unfortunately, no details of the accord are mentioned. See ibid., 1:323–29, docs. 594, 603, 604, 606; 2:61. Very terse references to the matter in Sanudo, *Diarii,* 2:10, 14, 17. It may be useful to note how a traveling German merchant, later a factor of the Fuggers in Venice, was dependent on the banks. On 5 August 1489, in time for the "termini," Hans Keller of Ulm arrived in Venice and received payment of some 2,000 ducats on current account at the Lippomano bank, more than half from the Fuggers; he then paid his IOUs ("brieflin"), that is, the notes obligatory deriving from purchases he had made earlier at deferred payment (he does not specify having paid in bank). After seventeen days, he departed once again. Adolf Bruder, ed., "Reiserechenbuch des Hans Keller aus den Jahren 1489–90," *Zeitschrift für die gesammte Staatswissenschaft* 37 (1881): 831–51.

[10]*Cap. broche,* 245, law of 23 August 1497, gives old price as 11 soldi or 5 ducats, 12 grossi a oro per mark; Malipiero (*Annali,* 640) gives the new price as 5 ducats, 21 grossi, a 6.8 percent increase.

[11]*Annali,* 640; Sanudo, *Diarii,* 1:736.

[12]Figured on the basis of the "mocenigo," the best of the coin, which weighed 6.52 grams; 1 ducat was worth £6 4s, that is, 6.2 of them.

Fig. 9. Doge Agostino Barbarigo overseeing the loading of sacks of coin on board a galley. The occasion for this maiolica plate was the arming of a fleet to aid Naples, invaded by Charles VIII, immediately upon the signing of the Holy Alliance in 1495 — thus the inscription "fate, fate, fate et non parole" [deeds, deeds, deeds and not words]. The sacks are labeled with the kind of coin each contained: "marcelli" and "troni" (Venetian silver pieces of one-half and one lira, respectively), on the back of the stevedore; "docatti anconetani," "-ungari," "-venetiani" (two sacks), and "-papali," all gold ducats, already on board. Similar sacks or "groppi" were used by merchants for loading coin on the Levant galleys.

Ashmolean Museum, Cambridge

The bill of lading for the return voyage lists just as carefully all the pepper and ginger delivered, but without giving a monetary value. The accompanying letter shows that two sacks of coin came back, meaning that, of the 7,000 ducats' worth that went out, 1,400 ducats' worth could not profitably be exchanged, and the commission agent had judged it worthwhile to pay the freight for the return voyage rather than sell too low. Supply continued to be excellent; the real question concerned the demand and the ability of Venice to meet it.[13]

Markets for Copper

Closely linked to silver as an exchange commodity is copper: in the ore, in the refining process, and in the marketing.[14] Importation of copper to Venice, in part for local consumption and in part for export, especially to the Levant, was an important enterprise in the 1490s.

That Venice's Rialto banks were involved in the importation, on public initiative, of copper, as well as of silver, from German lands is made clear by this example of 1495: the Venetian government bought more than 38 tons (80 migliaria) of copper from Germans (probably the Fugger enterprise) for casting bombards in the arsenal. The importers asked for payment in bank, and Andrea Garzoni gave his word ("detta") to credit their account for the (unspecified) contracted sale price, as long as he was — doubly — guaranteed to be repaid.[15] Private parties were also interested in the importation, sometimes in the re-refining, and reexport of copper. Malipiero relates that in 1498 the Alexandria galleys carried, besides 200,000 ducats' worth of specie and other merchandise, 1,100 coffers ("coffe") of worked copper; the Beirut galleys carried 164 such coffers, as well as large quantities of tin and mercury.[16] Heavy demand by such exporters as Michele Foscari, the major client of the Fugger company, probably created a speculative climate. Even though much copper was exported eastward, unsold stocks still built up in Venice. Tension with the Turks, leading up to the major war of 1499–1502, meant that for three years no copper could go out; no galleys at all sailed in 1499. A copper glut developed in Venice;

---

[13]Fernand Braudel and Alberto Tenenti, "Michiel da Lezze, Marchand Venitien (1497–1514)," in *Wirtschaft, Geschichte und Wirtschaftsgeschichte: Festschrift zum 65. Geburtstag von Friedrich Lütge* (Stuttgart, 1966), 40, 42–43. The coins were sacked by weight, not by tale, and were referred to as "monede veneciane pexade." What da Lezze sent out in 1498 is not recorded, only what returned; during the years of the war with the Turks (1499–1502) the records are silent. No galleys went out at all in 1499. The evidence, here and for 1499, as we shall see, points, if anything, to an oversupply of bullion, not to a drop in imports of silver and gold, which one author pointed to as a factor that exacerbated the crisis of 1499; see Vitorino Magalhaes Godinho, "Le repli vénitien et égyptien et la route du Cap, 1496–1533," in *Eventail de l'histoire vivante: Hommage à Lucien Febvre* (Paris, 1953), 2:283–300 (based, as the dates indicate, on the diaries of Sanudo). Rather than supply, which was abundant and caused, if anything, a drop in prices, the question was one of demand in the Levant and the capability of Venice in meeting demand; the Cape route becomes crucial but is not a factor in supply in 1490–1500.

[14]The best overview of these aspects is Hermann Kellenbenz, "Europäisches Kupfer, Ende 15. bis Mitte 17. Jahrhundert: Ergebnisse eines Kolloquiums," in *Schwerpunkte der Kupferproduktion und des Kupferhandels in Europa 1500–1650,* ed. Hermann Kellenbenz (Cologne, 1977), 290–351, esp. pt. 6.

[15]Simonsfeld, *Der Fondaco,* 1:324, doc. 597.

[16]*Annali,* 646.

stocks totaled 1,120 tons in May 1499, 2,000 tons at Christmas. Only in 1502 could Foscari and other merchants return to exporting copper, and then in record quantities.[17] A copper craze, checkmated by an unlucky military situation, seriously worsened the economic situation in 1499 and must have affected the banks, directly and indirectly.

Famine and the Wheat Market

The famine began in 1496, a "universally bad year for wheat" [mala annata universal de formenti], and it worsened in the following year, when wheat reached 8 lire per staio; Malipiero called it the worst since 1478 (when the price had peaked at 7 lire). Even wheat of bad quality imported by certain Marranos in late 1497, which the state refused to accept, sold for 6.2 lire or 1 ducat the staio. Only in late February 1499, after the Garzoni failure, did the price fall to 5 lire upon arrival of a shipment from the Maghreb. In August 1499 prices dropped from £4 16s to £3 12s per measure.

This is important in the present context, first of all because high prices and the promise of a bonus spurred speculative buying, with costly credit; the fall of prices may have come earlier than foreseen by some and may have contributed to the chains of defaulting debtors. It is also important because probably all the contracts made by the state with Venetian and foreign importers alike called for payment in bank money, that is, each contract called for a "detta di banco," that guarantee whereby a bank agreed to step in and pay the importer at the times scheduled in the contract and await repayment by the state. Huge sums of money were involved. Sanudo reports in early 1497 that the authorities had contracted for a total of 200,000 staia of wheat. A single contract with the Spanish Jews Alfonso and Giovanni Sanchez for 50,000 staia meant more than 60,000 ducats plus 10,000 ducats bonus ("dono"). This surely put banks under pressure. In early 1499 wheat importers were still calling for payment in bank promises, but in February, after the Garzoni failure, the remaining banks pulled out of the contracts they had previously agreed to, and the Council of Ten had quickly to seek other solutions.[18]

---

[17]See Philippe Braunstein, "Le marché du cuivre à Venise à la fin du Moyen-Age," in Kellenbenz, *Schwerpunkte,* 78–94; the statistics are based largely on Priuli's diaries.

[18]For prices and descriptions of the situation, see Sanudo, *Diarii,* 1:507, 535; Malipiero, *Annali,* 700, 703–4, 707–9, 719. For the handling of wheat imports on government account with use of the "detta," see Mueller, "Role of Bank Money," 81–83, and below, Chap. 10. For the importers, see Pullan, *Rich and Poor,* 513–14, and for prices in Venice, Pierre Sardella, *Nouvelles et spéculations a Venise au début du XVIᵉ siècle* (Paris, 1948), 19–21. For prices in nearby Mestre, not as protected as Venice, see Alessandra Checchin, *La scuola e l'ospedale di S. Maria dei Battuti di Mestre, dalle origini al 1520,* Quaderno di studi e notizie, n.s., no. 6, of the Centro Studi Storici, Mestre (Venice, 1996), appendices. Florence was in a similar situation in the same three years; see Goldthwaite, "I prezzi del grano a Firenze," 34–35. The use of bank guarantees was commonplace even outside of specific commercial contracts; as late as 15–17 February 1499, two of the dozen candidates for operating a state-owned ship produced guar-

War with Florence, 1496–1499

The problem of famine and high wheat prices in Venice itself was exacerbated by the deliveries that Venice made to beleaguered Pisa. Venice, in fact, was in open warfare with Florence, having decided to support the Pisan revolt beginning in 1496. For the first two years — during the famine — it was willing to spend what was necessary, but by the end of 1498 Venice had made it clear to Pisa that it wished to withdraw from the conflict, which had already cost the Venetian taxpayer at least ten impositions of the decima. The compromise that the duke of Ferrara, as mediator, worked out between Venice and Florence bears the date 6 April 1499, well after the Garzoni failure; the accord called for reparations payments of 180,000 ducats on the part of Florence. Venice finally abandoned Pisa to its destiny in early May, before the Lippomano failure. In short, military and diplomatic disengagement from the Pisan war was not a result of the failures, as some rumors had it, but rather of the threat of war with the Turks. In April Antonio Grimani was elected captain general of a fleet that had been in preparation for some time, in part through the recall of galleys and ships that had been engaged at Pisa.[19]

A related aspect of the state of belligerency between the two republics was the tension it caused locally between Venice and its community of Florentine merchant-bankers, which was not about to sustain the Venetian cause; tension probably led to a tightening of the money market.

The Money Market and the Financial Market

When the diarist Domenico Malipiero returned from Pisa, where he had overseen Venetian operations, he tried to analyze the causes of the bank failures, in which he seems to have lost money. For him, just as for Marin Sanudo, with whom he must have compared notes, tight money, resulting from a policy of war finance over the previous sixteen years, was the major cause as well as, in exacerbated form, the major effect. A series of wars had been financed by the Monte Nuovo and by constant recourse to the tax called the decima. Both diarists write — before the beginning of the costly

---

antees, the first of the Lippomano bank, the other of the Pisani bank; the candidate supported by the Lippomano was approved by the Signoria. Both banks pledged themselves "de tute le obligation haverà . . . per dicta caxon" — a risky, all-inclusive obligation, especially at that date! See ASV, CN, reg. 14, fol. 190.

[19]Malipiero, *Annali*, 716 (also in Lattes, *Libertà*, 18). See Michele Luzzati, *Una guerra di popolo: Lettere private del tempo dell'assedio di Pisa (1494–1509)* (Pisa, 1973), 30, 34, 37, 42–44, 120–21, and Frederic C. Lane, "Naval Actions and Fleet Organization, 1499–1502," reprinted in his *Studies*, art. VIII, 147–48. Precise dates of accords with Duke Ercole d'Este and with Florence in *LCR*, 6:36–40, docs. 139, 143–48, 151. Also Malipiero, *Annali*, 427–28, 538–41, and Romanin, *Storia documentata*, 5:105–8. According to the treaty, Florence owed Venice 15,000 ducats per year for twelve years.

naval war against the Turks (1499-1502) — that there had been a total of seventy impositions since 1482, distributed as follows:

Ferrara war (1482-84):	37 decime
war against Archduke Sigismund of Austria (1487):	5 decime
war against France (1494-99):	18 decime
war against Florence in support of Pisa (1496-99):	10 decime

Some of the decime were lifted as a direct tax; others were credited to the Monte Nuovo, where they earned 5 percent interest. Moreover, Monte Nuovo credits were also occasionally available voluntarily, sometimes at 75, thus offering an interesting yield of 6⅔ percent. The new issue thus gained widespread popularity, after the abandonment of the Monte Vecchio and the arrears in interest payments on that debt.[20]

The state's return to the financial market had damaging effects on the banks, however. Whether the issues were purchased as forced loans or voluntarily, the result was that cash flowed out of the banks, where deposits did not fructify. In order to counter the tendency and attract deposits, both the Garzoni and the Lippomano banks had taken to offering 3 percent interest on current accounts — a complete novelty in Venetian banking practice. With that offer, says Malipiero, the Garzoni had "lost" 20,000 ducats, that is, they had paid that much in interest over an unspecified number of years.

In the same way that the banks competed in attracting deposits, they competed in importing silver in order to increase their liquidity. Malipiero reports that the Garzoni had been offering 2-3 grossi per mark above market prices, that is, a premium of something over 2 percent.[21] The speculation and the added costs brought the Garzoni further losses totaling 30,000 ducats, reported Malipiero.[22] Finally, bankers were also extensively overdrawing their own accounts at the banks to finance their purchases of silver. Some had their own suppliers: the Lippomano financed Matteo di Vettor Soranzo, who failed; the Pisani, who earlier had financed Zorzi Orese, came to be the major customers of another branch of the Fugger.[23]

[20]Malipiero writes, "La Terra è restà vacua de danari in sedese anni per el far de Monte Nuovo, per i falimenti che son stai, e per le guerre che se ha habuo." *Annali*, 532. To explain the condition of tight money, Sanudo added, besides the decime and the rush to invest in Monte Nuovo credits, expenditure in palaces and sumptuous clothing, concluding, "sichè la terra è stretta." *Diarii*, 2:391-92. For an example of a voluntary issue of Monte Nuovo credits, see *BG*, 1, doc. 132 (1495).

[21]When one mark cost 6 ducats, then 3 grossi a oro represented a premium of 2.1 percent.

[22]The lines are worth citing: "e da quattro anni in qua, s'ha habù danno de 30,000 ducati d'arzenti che i comprava in concorrentia, a do e tre grossi de più la marcha, per far vegnir i danari in Banco; per el qual effetto i pagava anche tre per cento, e de questa rason i ha perso 20,000 ducati." *Annali*, 531. Sanudo wrote (*Diarii*, 2:332): "et si dice tolevano contadi a tre per cento"; for the premium on silver, see ibid., 2:391.

[23]A company of German merchants, probably involved in silver, failed and received a safe-

The difficulties of the banks in maintaining their dominant role in the local money market left room for alternatives tied to more or less manifest usury. In 1490 a Jewish pawnbroker, Jacob qd. Moisè, operator of a bank located at the base of the castle of Mestre, overextended himself and failed.[24] Three years later the Sopraconsoli denounced the Jews of the Mestran banks before the Senate for fraud and extortion in lending to persons in Venice itself.[25] After the moneychanger Alvise Nichetta defaulted in July 1497, it was revealed that he had indebted himself to Angelo Levi, Jew of Monopoli (Apulia), and was paying usury. Levi was tried and sentenced for having defied the prohibition to lend at usury in Venice.[26]

The case against Angelo Levi was the first of a series of trials for usury, which focused both on Jews and on Florentines in Venice who were charged with having lent money over the past years at usury, through the mediation of Jews. An anonymous denunciation led to the sequester of the account books of all involved and the discovery of the fraudulent movement of capital. The Florentines were Giovan Filippo Frescobaldi, his partner and brother-in-law Bartolo Nerli, and Pietro Corsini, all charged and fined between December 1498 and March 1499.[27] The Frescobaldi firm alone was charged with having lent a total of 55,800 ducats, at 12 percent interest, on the security of pawns. The intermediary, Aaron qd. Jacob de Castellatio, judeus, was fined 1,900 ducats, while the Florentines were fined 3,000 ducats.[28] These actions probably must be seen in connection with the state of

---

conduct in January 1499, but nothing is known of their connections. Simonsfeld, *Der Fondaco,* 1:329, doc. 605.

[24]The Sopraconsoli granted him a safe-conduct and had jurisdiction over Venetian creditors and agreements with the liquidators, while the podestà-capitano of Mestre dealt with Mestran creditors. ASV, CN, reg. 14, fol. 21 (19 August).

[25]ASV, ST, reg. 12, fol. 36 (22 December 1493).

[26]In granting the safe-conduct, the Senate recognized it was making an exception to the law, "la qual [leze] dice che non puol tuor fida infra sei mesi et maxime essendo danari de bancho, visto etiam che altre volte l'è sta' facto ad altri." ASV, ST, reg. 13, fol. 6v (2 August). The sum Nichetta had borrowed is not specified but was "in non parva quantitate." The Jew was fined 80 ducats for lending at usury in Venice against the law. Unable to appear in court himself, he was represented by Asher Meshullam. Nichetta failed a second time on the heels of the Lippomano bank and a year later was arrested for clipping ducats. AC, reg. 3658, fol. 195v (16 November 1498).

[27]ASV, AC, reg. 3658, fols. 198r–v, 203r–205. There was no concensus in the Forty to condemn any of the parties involved; in almost every ballot, the decision to condemn passed by a single vote. Most seriously damaged by "fraud and deception" was Marco qd. Antonio Loredan, on a "diabolical" contract of sale for 5,600 ducats in 1495. Sanudo reports that a valuable jewel of Loredan's wife was involved and that he (Sanudo), as Signore di Notte, was present at the interrogation of Aaron when the latter was fined 1,800 ducats. The Jew was later arrested again and fined an additional 100 ducats, which Sanudo judged "et fu troppo." *Diarii,* 2:505, 510. Shortly before, however, a claim of the Florentine Lorenzo Tornabuoni against Andrea Bragadin for a credit had been confirmed by the Forty on appeal, providing Sanudo with the opportunity to praise the objectivity of Venetian justice; ibid., 1:496.

[28]The Piovego, who had legal jurisdiction over usury, charged the Avogadori with arrogat-

tension between Venice and its Florentine community which resulted from Venetian support of the Pisan revolt.

Finally, the liquidity of the state itself seems to have been in doubt. Rather than awaiting payment, some creditors, who had obviously not asked for a bank guarantee, were ready to sell their credits against the Treasury at a discount, for as low as 52 percent. One buyer turned out to be one of the state Treasurers, who then proceeded to repay himself from the till at 100 percent. He was tried and sentenced for malfeasance in office.[29] The situation at the Salt Office was similar: in 1492–99 the state was in arrears for a total of 225,000 ducats in paying importers of salt; and in 1493 the Senate sought to circumscribe the practice of offsetting credits and debits on the books of the office — normally at a discount — with the aim of increasing liquidity.[30]

ii. THE PANIC AND THE CRASH

Rumors about the solidity of the Garzoni bank circulated since Christmas 1498. During the month of January 1499 some 130,000 ducats were withdrawn by worried depositors, of which 40,000 were withdrawn, mostly by Florentines, in the last week. A major client who pulled out was, in fact, Bartolo Nerli, of the Frescobaldi firm, who over a period of time had made daily withdrawals for a total of 45,000 ducats, to send to Florence; besides concern for his assets, he probably was retaliating for his condemnation for usury as well as for Venice's support of Pisa. On Thursday, 31 January, the Garzoni knew they could no longer withstand the pressure, and on the next day they admitted insolvency and succeeded in obtaining from the Council of Ten a one-year moratorium to protect their patrimony, especially their real estate, from angry creditors.[31]

Reports of the Venetian eyewitnesses Sanudo and Priuli, joined by Malipiero upon his return from Pisa, are well known. Completely unknown, on the other hand, are the reports of another observer on the scene, the Milanese ambassador to Venice, Bishop Cristoforo Latuada. He had

---

ing to themselves jurisdiction in the case and then engaging in plea bargaining so as better to divide among themselves the fines of 3,000 ducats. Sanudo, *Diarii,* 2:322 (10 January 1499). Aaron, like Angelo Levi, must have been a licensed lender in Mestre, where Jews could lend at 15 percent.

[29]ASV, AC, reg. 3658, fol. 155 (28 November 1497). The treasurer, Marino Morosini, was ordered to make full restitution and to pay a fine of 100 ducats to the Avogadori.

[30]Hocquet, *Le sel et la fortune de Venise,* 2:396, 410–11, 413.

[31]In what follows I shall take as given Lane, "Venetian Bankers" and "News on the Rialto" (art. XV of his *Studies*). Both are based heavily on Sanudo's diaries (the title of the former bears the dates of the diaries themselves, rather than those of the failures). Not always clear in the chronology is Mario Brunetti, "Banche e Banchieri veneziani nei 'Diari' di Marin Sanudo (Garzoni e Lippomano)," in *Studi in onore di Gino Luzzatto,* 2:26–47. Generally forgotten although quite useful on these failures is Manzini, "La bancarotta e la procedura fallimentare."

already written a letter on 1 February to Lodovico il Moro, but he was able to add the news of the Garzoni failure to the end of his letter before the courier departed: the bank, he wrote, was "probably the principal bank of the city, . . . the one that handled more and larger business transactions than the others"; the fact that it defaulted "has left people speechless and confused, and there is concern that as a result of this crash others will fail." Initial estimates, he wrote, set liabilities at about 100,000 ducats, of which about 15,000 were owed to Milanese merchants; at the same time, he concluded, the bank had considerable credits and real estate, so that there was hope that in time everyone would receive his due.[32]

Ten days later the ambassador wrote again and provided further detail and analysis. He stressed even more strongly the size of the bank and the impact of its failure upon the populace: liabilities were now estimated at 150,000 ducats, and "anyone who did business in Venice [was] involved, for in truth three-fourths of all business transactions were registered at the Garzoni bank." Still, he expressed hope of full payment in time and estimated the value of Garzoni properties alone at 70,000 ducats. The credits of Milanese merchants in the bank were also revised downward, no longer to exceed 10,000 ducats.[33]

The proximate causes identified by the ambassador were two: envy of the other banks and unabated pressure of depositors. He goes so far as to assert that the other banks, those run by nobles (the Garzoni were popolani), applied the pressure themselves, both withdrawing funds and asking others to make withdrawals. All in all, the bank was bound to fail, he wrote, given the fact that since Christmas it had already paid out 130,000 ducats.[34]

In the long run, the cause of the failure was to be found in war finance, which the ambassador considers beginning only from the invasion of Italy by the king of France (1494). Otherwise, on the financial roots of the crisis, Latuada agrees with Sanudo and Malipiero. Much money was taken out of deposits at the bank and put into the Monte Nuovo; the latter, after all, gave a return of 5 percent, whereas leaving money in the bank normally

---

[32]"Questa matina el bancho di Garzoni, quasi primo bancho di questa terra, è fallito. Et per lo Consiglio di X li è facto uno salvoconduto per uno anno per le persone. Per quello se dice, ha uno debito più de cento milia ducati, et la natione Milanesa è sotto de circa XV milia. Hanno anche crediti et beni stabili honorevoli, per modo che cum tempo si spera che ogni uno sarano pagati. Ma la rottura di questo bancho, quale era pur quello che faceva le più et mazore facende de li altri, ha lassato le brigate molto attonite et suspese, sichè se dubita che per causa di questa rottura non ne habiano fallire multi altri." ASMI, Archivio Ducale, carteggio, b. 1271 (1 February 1499). (I owe the identification of the writer to the kindness of Dr. Cristina Belloni.)

[33]Ibid., under the date 11 February 1499 (a full page, fol. 94, old numbering): "ogni uno che facesse facende qua ne partecipa, perchè in verità de le quattro scripture, le 3 passavano per mane del bancho de' Garzoni." Sanudo reported estimates of liabilities first of 96,000, then 250,000 ducats.

[34]"Doppo invidiato esso bancho da li altri banchi, che sono de zentilhomeni; è stato talmente incalzato, cum farli levare li denari dal bancho." Ibid.

brought no return. Furthermore, he continued, in the beginning it was generally assumed that the bank defaulted because it was creditor of the state for a large sum of money; in fact, this turned out not to be the case at all: the bank was currently creditor of the state for only some 5,000 ducats. On the other hand, it had been true fifteen days before the failure that the bank was owed 30,000 ducats, but the Signoria had repaid that amount.[35] Although the ambassador provides the facts, it is probably nonetheless true that this bank's readiness to lend to the state contributed in January to general nervousness about its solidity; on the other hand, the state's willingness to repay the bulk of the debt during the crisis shows its desire to alleviate the pressure on the bank. When the Garzoni asked for special treatment by the authorities, the bankers were careful to mention their history of readiness to maintain a line of credit for the government and provided data that proved they had, since 1470, lent a total of 1,200,000 ducats to the state.[36]

Worries about the beginning of a chain reaction did not materialize — not right away. The only failure attributed directly to that of the Garzoni was that of the small moneychanger's table ("banchetto") of Andrea and Gerolamo Rizzo. Further trouble was not long in coming, however, for, as the Milanese ambassador observed, people were no longer making deposits but rather continuing to make withdrawals. Money became tighter. As government credits on the Monte Nuovo dropped from 75 to 59, remaining bankers had ever more difficulty in rendering their reserves liquid.

The Lippomano bank was under great pressure in May. Malipiero and Sanudo relate that depositors had withdrawn a total of 300,000 ducats since the Garzoni failure and 30,000 on 15 or 16 May alone. On the evening of the 15th they procured a safe-conduct and moratorium from the Council of Ten; on the 16th they admitted failure. What is particularly interesting is one episode of that peak of the panic. The Signoria, as a kind of lender of last resort, lent 10,000 ducats to sustain the bank money that the state itself had received on loan from private parties, says Malipiero. Once that money was available at the bank, who came to withdraw it all in cash but the very members of the Collegio who had just approved the loan to sustain the bank! The report, again from Malipiero, cannot be corroborated, but if true it surely represents the very limit of panic and bad faith on the part of the authorities themselves. Admission of failure on the 16th was inevitable.[37]

---

[35]"Perchè, havendo esso bancho dinari assai de depositi, sono tutti stati levati per metterli a Monte novo, . . . dove se ne cava emolumento de 5 per cento, che lassarli in bancho, talmente che 'l si è frustato. . . . E' stato opinione nel principio che 'l dovesse essere stato causa de questa Signoria, presuppondossi che dovessero essere grossamente creditori d'essa. Ma si trova che da essa Signoria non se li h' a dare più che circa 5 milia ducati." Ibid.

[36]Ferrara, "Documenti," doc. 136.

[37]*Annali*, 715: "Dopo che el banco di Garzoni ha fallito, è stà cavà dal Banco Lipamano tresentomile e più ducati; e oggi, 16 de Marzo, ne è stà cavà 30,000; e la Signoria, per

News of this second failure, wrote Malipiero, was the worst news possible — worse than if Venice had lost dominion over Brescia. It set the international financial community abuzz, for the Lippomano had a reputation "in the whole world," according to Priuli. A reflection of this might be the fact that the Milanese ambassador wrote two letters on the 16th, one to Lodovico il Moro, another to his own brother; of these, unfortunately, only the covering letter of the second is extant, in which the writer asks the chancellor, Bartolomeo Calco, to deliver the letter to his brother, who obviously had financial interests in the bank. On the cover of the letter are the address and the words "Cito Cito Cito" — Fast! Fast! Fast![38]

The storm then shifted to the remaining two banks. On the next day, 16,000 ducats were withdrawn from the Agostini bank, but the crowd pressed the Pisani bank hardest. Alvise Pisani, however, knew what to expect after the Lippomano had defaulted and had prepared for the worst overnight by collecting support from relatives. When the press of the depositors reached a limit, Alvise sent his uncle, a member of the Ten, to report to the doge, and the Signoria replied by sending three top officials to announce the creation of a guarantee fund of 100,000 ducats. That turned the tide: there was then competition among those present, Venetians as well as members of all the foreign communities in Venice, to join the guarantee fund that swelled to some 320,000 ducats. People began returning to redeposit money they had just withdrawn, and the Milanese ambassador wrote, "What the morning withdraws the afternoon deposits, for a total of over 50,000 ducats, from what I understand."[39]

Latuada's analysis of the panic is interesting, once again, because of the social consideration he brings to bear. In February he had noted the "envy" of the other banks and nobles intent on toppling the non-noble Garzoni, while Venetian observers (all nobles) had pointed their finger at the role of the Florentines. Now the ambassador put the blame on Venetian

---

sovvenirlo, l'ha accomodato de 10,000 ducati, de quei che particulari ghe ha imprestà a essa; e tutti questi 10,000 ducati è stà tratti da quei de Colegio: e finalmente, el banco ha fallito." The month as printed in Malipiero ("marzo") is a misreading of "mazo" by the text's seventeenth-century manipulator or its nineteenth-century editor; the date of 16–17 May is corroborated by all other sources.

[38]Malipiero, *Annali*, 715–16 (also in Lattes, *Libertà*, 17–18). Priuli, *Diarii*, 1:122. Latuada noted to Calco that news of the failure was "of great importance" for his brother Aloisio; ASMI, Autografi, cart. 42 (vescovi), fasc. 6. Malipiero also reports (*Annali*, 715) that all ten banks then active in Florence withstood the financial turmoil in Venice and remained strong ("saldi").

[39]The scribe of the Signoria reported the run thus, "tumultuariter concurrerat magnus numerus personarum ad extrahendum pecunias suas cum periculo banchi predicti." Under the date of the 17th follows a long list of those who had pledged 309,000 ducats, beyond the 20,000 required by law. ASV, CN, reg. 15, fols. 7–8 (16–17 May 1499). Malipiero (715) gives the figure of 324,000 ducats, while the Milanese ambassador, who underscored the offer also of Milanese merchants to join the guarantee fund, reported the figure of 320,000 ducats. ASMI, Archivio Ducale, carteggio, cart. 1271 (17 May 1499). Also Priuli, *Diarii*, 1:123–24.

nobles themselves and their internal rivalry. He wrote, "Such was the press at the Pisani bank, of people seeking to withdraw their money, that the Rialto was topsy-turvy. . . . The cause of the run this time was no foreigner at all, but some Venetian patricians, who, because of the rivalry existing among them, tried to force the bank to its knees — perhaps to alleviate the burden of the Lippomano failure. In short — he concluded — these Venetians have only themselves to blame."[40]

If the Pisani saved themselves, the mood worsened as regards the Lippomano. Alvise Pisani himself called them "thieves" in public and blamed them for having unleashed the runs. "The guarantee fund should be set at 50,000, not at 20,000, and should be renewed every three years," he shouted.[41] A merchant from Corfu, a creditor of the Lippomano, sought them out at their palace and tried to kill Gerolamo, who was defended by a servant. After that they closed themselves into their palazzo and did not venture out. The shadow of a fraudulent bankruptcy on their part was taking shape. The Milanese ambassador, who at first reported their liabilities to be about 100,000 ducats, later corrected the figure to 120,000 ducats and wrote that the failure was "discovered to have been maliciously premeditated, since third parties acted in their stead in shifting money from the bank to the Monte Nuovo. It was rumored that the safe-conduct might be suspended."[42]

The communities of German and Milanese merchants, in turn, asked the government for a safe-conduct to protect their members. The Germans, represented by Johannes Keller, factor of the Fuggers, and their lawyer, reported that they had assets of 10,000 ducats tied up at the Lippomano bank, 30,000 at the Garzoni bank. Furthermore, they did not know what to do with the gold and silver they had imported, for no one had the liquidity with which to buy bullion. Since they reckoned that direct consignment to the mint for coinage would have brought revenues of 4,000 ducats to the state, that means that, after a large number of sales, they were still saddled

---

[40]"Questa matina a hora de li banchi, per il caso seguito de' Lyppomani, fo tanta furia al bancho de' Pisani, per volere levare dinari, per non fidarsi più dei banchi, che 'l Realto era sotto sopra. . . . Di questa furia non ne fo causa alcuno forestero, ma pur de' loro zentilhomeni, per le gare che sono tra epsi per volere fare fallire el dicto bancho, forsi per aleviare la gravezza de' Lippomani; sichè de questi casi non se possono dolere, se non de se stessi." ASMI, Archivio Ducale, carteggio, cart. 1271 (17 May 1499). By "la gravezza de' Lippomani" he meant the burden of being at the center of attention as well as the infamy of their condition.

[41]Malipiero, *Annali*, 716 (in Lattes, *Libertà*, 17).

[42]ASMI, Archivio Ducale, carteggio, cart. 1271, letter of 17 May. The letter of 25 May corrected the figure of the Lippomano liabilities to 120,000 ducats, similar to the figure (119,000) that Malipiero (*Annali*, 716) says was derived from an investigation of the account books. Sanudo (*Diarii*, 2:730–31) gives 120,000 ducats, quoting the words of the doge. He also names (ibid., 723) two straw men and beneficiaries of the supposed transfers to the Monte Nuovo, one of whom was the family Barbarigo "Brocca," represented not long before among the bankers on the Rialto.

with about 165,000 ducats' worth of silver; in short, a considerable glut was developing and prospects were grim, since no galleys were going to sail in any direction in 1499. The Milanese ambassador, on his part, proposed, in vain, that Milanese merchants be able to offset their debts to third parties with the assets they held on the two failed banks.[43]

In the immediate wake of the Lippomano failure came other, lesser failures. Heading the group was the bank's principal bullion dealer and refiner ("arzentier"), Maffeo di Vettor Soranzo; his debts stood at some 40,000 ducats, half of them with the Lippomano bank, which had been financing his deals. Then came two moneychanger's tables, one of them belonging to Alvise Nichetta, located by the office of the Consoli, who thus defaulted for the second time, along with his father-in-law, who was his guarantor. Two other non-noble Venetians also failed. But this was all nothing, wrote the ambassador, next to what was expected to follow, in Venice and elsewhere, from the failure of these two banks; the situation was such, he reported, that "no one dares doing business, not knowing whom to trust, and thus the Rialto appears widowed and like a place under interdict."[44]

The worst effects were quickly palpable, for even the government felt the effects of tight money. Tax-delinquent property valued at 300,000 ducats found no buyers at its real value. A tax of 25,000 ducats was imposed on the Jews of the Terraferma dominions, but even that had to be advanced by the Pisani bank.[45] Venice's enemies rubbed their hands. Machiavelli mentioned the failures and the run on the Pisani bank in two dispatches to the Dieci di Balia in Florence, although only after Venice had already withdrawn from the Pisan conflict.[46] Malipiero reports a speech in the consistory attributed to the Borgia pope Alexander VI, who judged Venice to be finished as a military power, most recently as a result of the bankruptcies; it had been forced to call upon the duke of Ferrara to act as an arbiter of peace in the conflict with Florence, in the same way that it was arbitrating with safe-

---

[43]The mint fee was 3½ grossi a oro per mark, with each mark worth about 6 ducats (of 24 grossi a oro each). Sanudo, *Diarii,* 2:736–37 (20 May). The ambassador Latuada made his requests on 24 May (ibid., 752).

[44]"Quello dì che fallite questo bancho [de' Lippomani] fallite anche uno messer Mapheo Soranzo . . . e un altro bancho de poco conto, Alvise Nichetto et suo suocero, quale era sua segurtà, et doi altri merchadanti veneti popolari. Ma questo è niente a quello se stima habij seguire e qui et altrove per causa de questo fallire de' banchi, per modo che niuno hora ardisse fare facende, non sapendo a chi credere et così el Realto pare sviduato et como loco bandito." ASMI, Archivio Ducale, carteggio, cart. 1271, letter of 17 May. Also Sanudo, *Diarii,* 2:726–27 (17 May 1499).

[45]ASMI, Archivio Ducale, carteggio, cart. 1271, the letter dated 25 May 1499, under the rubric "Avisi de Venezia," mentions first the imposition of 25,000 ducats on the "Judei del dominio suo, et si crede ne sarà servita dal bancho de' Pisani sopra questo assignamento."

[46]*Le opere,* ed. Luigi Passerini et al., 5 vols. (Rome and Florence, 1873–79), 2:154: "Fallirono a Venezia e Lippomani ed i Garzoni, ed i Pisani [the bankers] balenarono." And p. 265: "Fallirono banchi a Vinegia con gran danno della terra." Dated April by the editors, the two undated dispatches must be redated to after 17 May.

conducts between defaulting bankers and their creditors. "We conclude," he said, "that the affairs of that Signoria are finished." Cardinal Ascanio Maria Sforza of Milan, Venice's ally at the time, is said to have risen to Venice's defense, answering as follows: "The Venetians have more money than ever; they have given up the Pisan enterprise because they are attending to other matters [the impending war with the Turks]. And if their banks have failed, that is the result of bad management of the banks and not of the impotence of the state. In a matter of days you will hear other news from that Republic."[47]

In the following months the situation remained critical. The Milanese ambassador reported on state finances as follows: "As I have written you often, here there is a great dearth of money and for this reason there is talk that the state might lay its hands on the money collected from the Garzoni bank to pay its creditors at the end of the year's safe-conduct, which amounts to 36,000 ducats. The same may be done with the Lippomano, who had 15,000 ducats in cash when they failed and since have paid out 5,000. So far there is no certainty, but if money continues to tighten, I think they will." Earlier he had related that the government had named three nobles as receivers to exact the Lippomano bank's credits, with the consent of the liquidators. Such funds obviously were withdrawn from circulation, thus contributing to the tight money situation, and, at the same time, provided a reservoir that might entice the impecunious government.[48] The ambassador informed his lord, Lodovico il Moro, furthermore, that there was a good chance that the Senate would ask him for repayment of a loan of 50,000 ducats, for which the Venetians had pawns. Finally, he reported the next fiscal actions of the government: two decime applied to the clergy, from which 30,000–40,000 ducats in revenue were foreseen, and a tax ("sussidio") for nearly 60,000 ducats to be exacted from the subject territories of the Terraferma.[49]

Unmentioned by the ambassador in his letters of July, perhaps because too insignificant in relative terms or simply too commonplace given the general situation, is the second failure of the firm of Heinrich Stammler and Brothers. The case reflects how the panic of 1499 constantly spawned

[47]*Annali*, 716.

[48]"Como più volte ho scripto, qui c'è molta penuria de dinari, et per questo se ragiona molto che 'l sij misso mane ne li dinari che se sono scossi dal bancho di Garzoni per pagare li creditori a cappo de anno, che sono ducati 36,000. . . . El medesimo se farà de li dinari de li Lyppomani . . . ; pur fino qui non ne ho certeza, ma strenzendossi le cose, credo se farà." ASMI, Archivio Ducale, carteggio, cart. 1273 (5 July 1499). Gerolamo Priuli also recorded that money was particularly tight; *Diarii*, 1:123.

[49]ASMI, Archivio Ducale, carteggio, cart. 1273, letters of 8 and 12–13 July 1499. The government had collected the money necessary for making the loan by selling an issue of Monte Nuovo bonds; see *BG,* 1, doc. 132 (1495). This did not constitute a serious threat, since there was little demand or liquidity should an attempt have been made to auction them at the time. On the other hand, little time remained before Lodovico il Moro would be deposed by the French (2 September).

further failures. The German firm, which seven years before had been forced to liquidate with liabilities of 20,000 ducats, now registered liabilities of 12,000 ducats. It reached agreement with three-fourths of its creditors quite quickly. In his first proposal for repayment in cash in five and one-half years, the principal laid blame: "on the very bad condition of the moment and of commerce, for the failure of many of our business plans, and of many of our debtors who have fled from Venice."[50] But even that pact of August 1499 turned out to be wishful thinking, given the linking of failed firms. Unable to meet the first payment, the principals fled Venice again in 1501, and negotiations with the firm's creditors began anew. Again there is a preamble to the pact: "As you creditors know, the cause of our great misfortune and the inability to live up to the first pact was the fact that many of our debtors have failed and have absconded with great quantities of money. Thus, in these strange times, we have been unable to do anything." Proof of what the Germans claimed can be found among the signatures. Vincenzo d'Antonio Grimani signed to indicate his acceptance of the pact but added that his act was in no way to prejudice his claims against Maffeo Soranzo and the Perducci, who had been guarantors of the Stammler company; both, in fact, had defaulted and fled Venice on 16 May 1499 on the heals of the Lippomano failure.[51]

The collection of credits also proceeded slowly for the defaulting banks. Notaries in the office of receivers for the Garzoni bank (the "Provisores super rationibus banchi de Bernardis et Garzonibus" were Giorgio Loredan and Gerolamo Marino) registered the agreements and the eventual payments. Only a single one of the many hundreds of cases that had to be clarified has as yet been found, but it can serve as an example. On 12 June 1499 Giovanbattista Garzoni, son of the aged and respected banker Andrea (here called "magnificus dominus"!), negotiated an arrangement with the monastery of S. Maria delle Carceri of Padua, indebted to the bank for 314 ducats. Of that sum, 155 ducats were offset on a credit of the monastery of S. Michele di Murano (but in the form of credits on the Monte Nuovo), while the balance was advanced by the Procurator, who was in turn repaid

---

[50]"Nui Rigo Stameler et fradelli per la pessima condition dei tempi et del corso de le marchadantie et per esserne andati falliti molti nostri pensieri et desegni et per esserne falliti molti nostri debitori de fuora de questa terra et etiam per molti altri respecti . . . , se atrovamo cargi de debiti." It is useful to mention, as do the documents, that ratification by the Senate itself was required because the Sopraconsoli did not have jurisdiction over defaulting foreigners who had operated in Venice. Simonsfeld, *Der Fondaco*, 1, docs. 608–9.

[51]"La adversa fortuna et li grandi infortunii occorsi a nui Rigo Stameler et fratelli sono stati causa (che) non habiamo posuto far el debito nostro in satisfarvi . . . , per esserne stà, come a vostre magnificentie è noto, dapoi portato via assai quantità de danari da nostri debitori falliti, et andati tempi stranii che non se ha potuto far cosa alcuna." Ibid., doc. 615. See also Sanudo, *Diarii*, 2:727, and Priuli, *Diarii*, 1:122–23.

after six months.[52] The complexity of the operation, for such a relatively small amount of money, was surely not unique. Transactions costs soared under liquidation procedures, but offsetting reduced pressure on limited liquidity.

Slowly but surely, however, the Garzoni strengthened their position. By the time their moratorium ran out on 1 February 1500, they had collected 50,000 ducats from debtors and had convinced many of their principal creditors to take their due as credits on the books of a successor bank — one-half at once, one-half after one year. Small accounts of up to 20 ducats would be paid at once. The Garzoni had signed up sureties for 50,000 ducats, and the Senate decided, "in the name of the Holy Spirit," to contribute a guarantee of 20,000 ducats to the new bank. Furthermore, the government ordered the release of money the Treasury owed the old bank.[53] On 3 February the new Garzoni bank was able to open, after solemn mass and after the traditional show of sacks full of money. But Andrea, the patriarch of the family, with his sons and grandsons, came dressed in black and did not wish to have fifes and trumpets announce the opening. Following the religious ceremony, the Garzoni were accompanied by high officers of the state to the bank, where the names of the guarantors were proclaimed. The cash in the sacks was judged to be 60,000–70,000 ducats, and deposits were attracted from Venetians and foreigners alike. The Fugger firm deposited 10,000 Hungarian ducats. But suspicion remained: on the next day, to counter the rumor that the sacks were not full only of money, they were emptied out for all to see. Sanudo concluded his report by saying that it would be a good bank and by predicting that the Lippomano would follow suit at the conclusion of their moratorium in May.

However, the nuovo banco Garzoni lasted only six weeks; it failed on 16 March. Andrea Garzoni fled to the Frari for sanctuary, supposedly with the cash reserves, but on the next day the bankers heeded the order of the Avogadori, confirmed by the Senate, to turn over all their account books,[54] and a first meeting of the creditors was held in the church of S. Giovanni di Rialto. The proximate cause of the failure, the doge seemed to suggest in council, was the fact that Spanish Marranos had withdrawn 30,000 ducats, credits surely resulting from their deliveries of wheat. Again the Venetians pointed fingers at foreigners, implying that they had sabotaged the solidity of the bank and Venice's reputation. If true, the withdrawals might have been in retaliation for the government's expulsion order, issued in 1497 but

---

[52]ASV, PSM, Misti, b. 189, booklet of copies of acts regarding the Garzoni liquidation.

[53]See Ferrara, "Documenti," doc. 136 (30 January), and ASV, CN, reg. 15, fol. 15v (2 February).

[54]The order is in ASV, AC, reg. 3659, fols. 2v–3 (16 March 1500); the failure, the order said, brought great damage to nobles, citizens, and foreigners alike and happened not without contempt of and neglect for justice.

seemingly not carried out; in that case, the action by the Marranos might have a political tinge, just like that of the Florentines one year before.[55]

Pressure once again shifted to the Pisani and the Agostini, the two remaining banks. On 20 March depositors withdrew 20,000 ducats. A great show of twelve porters carrying bags of money to the Rialto did not convince the crowd, and on Monday, 23 March, the Pisani, dressed in scarlet and after having attended mass at S. Giacomo, announced that they wished to liquidate and invited all creditors to come and take their money. If liquidation by the Pisani at 100 percent was a marvel that did honor to Venice, it also left the city with only one bank, the smallest of the four.

The crash of the new Garzoni bank so soon after it had opened created a series of contrasts between two committees of liquidators and two committees of guarantors, since many creditors of the old bank had agreed to take payment on the new bank. Three commissioners were elected by the Great Council to try to settle the controversies between the two groups.[56] The liquidators began to contest the guarantors, and a list was ordered drawn up of all the guarantors and sureties ("plegii et securitates") approved for this bank according to the law of 1455, from the year 1470 to 1499.[57] Just what the relevance was of knowing who the guarantors had been previous to the last renewal of their nomination is unclear. What is clear is that the guarantors undertook to pay the creditors, for it was they who then received the installment payments distributed by the bank liquidators. The process dragged on for at least a decade. The Garzoni fled Venice and then were given safe-conduct after safe-conduct. When a landed estate received through the marriage of one of the Garzoni seemed to set everything straight, the area was occupied by troops of the league that beset Venice beginning in 1508. A new concordat was reached and signed in that year, but the War of the League of Cambrai rendered impossible its realization.[58]

The second Garzoni crash and the Pisani liquidation (Alvise Pisani reopened only in 1504) occurred not long before the Lippomano had planned to reopen, at the conclusion of their moratorium. The rapid failure of the new Garzoni bank rendered the plan of the Lippomano to open a successor bank impossible. Now a decision had to be made on how to deal with the Lippomano creditors. Over the year the bankers had collected 42,000 ducats in cash—including 13,000 from their former partners the

---

[55]Malipiero, *Annali,* 708, where the author infers that the Marranos had assets of half a million ducats in Venice; Pullan, *Rich and Poor,* 513–14. See also Sanudo, *Diarii,* 3:148.

[56]Ferrara, "Documenti," doc. 137 (8 April 1500). The interaction of these "Provisores" with the receivers can be seen in such individual actions as the sequestration, "mandato dictorum Provisorum ad instantiam capitum creditorum dicti banchi," of all sums held by the Avogaria belonging to the moneychanger Alvise Nichetta, debtor of the Garzoni. ASV, AC, reg. 2051 (Notatorio, reg. 1), under 3 March 1501.

[57]ASV, PSM, Misti, b. 189.

[58]Ferrara, "Documenti," docs. 138–51.

Capello, who had sold a jeweled collar of the emperor Maximilian to agents of Ivan the Great—on a debt that had grown to 135,000 ducats. The creditors of the Lippomano refused to accept a plan, approved by the Senate,[59] to pay over two years; in June the family was formally judged bankrupt, and the creditors began a frantic and retaliatory liquidation of the family's assets, which meant largely selling to themselves at derisory prices. The state unfroze 7,000 ducats it owed the bank, and the Council of Ten arranged short-term loans.[60] The creditors, insatiable, succeeded in luring Gerolamo and two brothers out of the safety of their palace on a ruse and had them arrested and thrown into prison, where they remained for a year, from 3 September 1500 until 9 September 1501. They were finally able to make an audacious escape to sanctuary at the monastery of S. Elena.

The government continued periodically to be concerned with the case, as creditors charged fraud.[61] But once the Lippomano were free under safe-conduct to explain their case, it was easy to see how the creditors had enriched themselves at the expense of the family, for example, by buying government obligations at 50 which then quickly returned to 75. The government began to take the side of the defaulting bankers: the creditors' committee was replaced by government receivers. In 1504 a solution was reached in which creditors accepted 65 ducats on the hundred. The Lippomano were able to take their place again in civil society and in the ecclesiastical hierarchy. But their sacrifices would not end for a long time to come: years later they still had to rent out their family palace at S. Fosca to the family of Lorenzo Priuli, whose son Gerolamo, who had followed the liquidation as diarist, had set himself up in business—as a banker on the Rialto.[62]

[59]ASV, ST, reg. 13, fol. 128v (4 May).

[60]Ibid., fol. 129v (16 May); one of the Lippomano, a senator, had to exit when the decision was made. The account book of an estate administered by the Procurators of San Marco shows that the Council of Ten borrowed 800 ducats in the name of the bank on 25 August; it was repaid on 22 September. PSM, Citra, b. 189, fasc. 7, reg., fols. 15 (dare) and 2v (recipere).

[61]See, for example, the order to all persons who had money or pawns or any kind of order-to-pay regarding the bank to report it to the receivers within eight days, "so that it can be known whether fraud was committed." AST, ST, reg. 13, fol. 155r–v (13 November 1500).

[62]BMCV, PD C 912/2, fol. 45: Lorenzo Priuli and sons rent for 80 ducats per year the ca' grande at S. Fosca from Boaretto Lippomano and brothers, sons of qd. Tommaso dal banco, for ten years, paying in advance 1,000 ducats. The sum, paid by transfer on Gerolamo's bank, was registered as a loan ("per imprestedo") on 4 April 1510. Underscored by Di Lernia, "Il giornale di Lorenzo Priuli e figli," 1:49–50, 126–27; vol. 2, fol. 89, of the reconstructed ledger. When Gerolamo failed in 1513, he too fled to sanctuary, under the protection of the patriarch at S. Pietro di Castello; Sanudo, *Diarii*, 17:354.

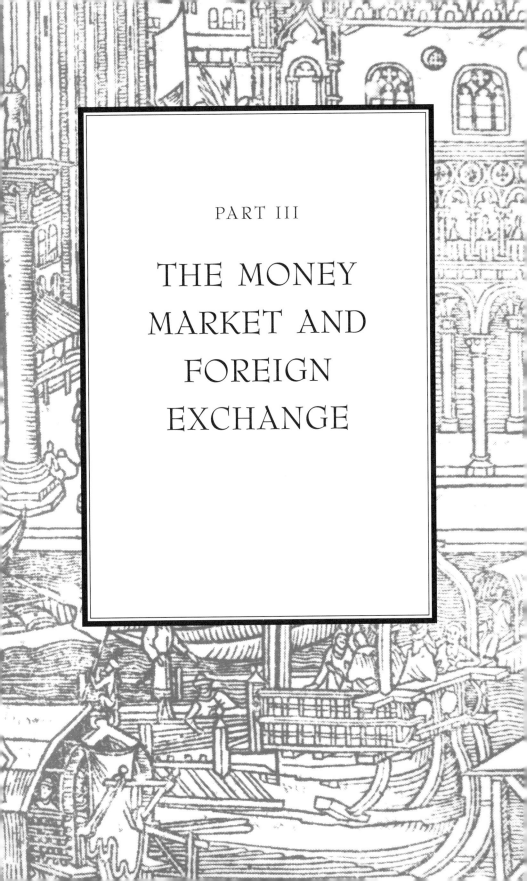

PART III

THE MONEY
MARKET AND
FOREIGN
EXCHANGE

7

FLORENTINE MERCHANT BANKERS AND THEIR COMMUNITY

i. THE FLORENTINE PRESENCE IN VENICE

VENETIANS ARE BEST KNOWN as long-distance merchants, interested in Levantine, Mediterranean, and Western markets, from Tana and Alexandria to Bruges and London; when they acted as bankers, their field of action, as we have seen, was restricted to the Rialto, a local market that served as an international clearinghouse. They were not interested in merchant banking or international banking, that is, in dealing in bills of exchange with the aims of transferring, especially for others, the large sums of money necessary for commerce and of making available to the merchant community more or less short-term loans via exchange and re-change between more or less distant markets. Florentine merchant bankers, from the Bardi to the Medici, are perhaps best known for their loans to kings and princes, even though that kind of lending was by no means their principal activity. Venetians clearly are not known for such activity, even though there were exceptions. For example, sizeable loans were made by the noblemen Nero Cocco, one of the most powerful merchants in the Venice of his time, and Bertuccio Pisani to Edward III of England.[1] Other-

---

[1] Edmund B. Fryde, "Financial Resources of Edward III in the Netherlands, 1337–40," in his *Studies in Medieval Trade and Finance* (London, 1983), art. VII, p. 1184. Cocco, represented by Pietro Miane, lent £3,737 and received as interest 300 sarplars of wool, while Pisani lent £1,050 and received £316 17s 6d as interest in April 1339. Nero Cocco's stature can be measured in part from entries in ASV, Grazie, regs. 4–6, and from the accounts in the ledgers of the company of Duccio di Banchello e Banco Bencivenni (ASF, Del Bene, reg. 64) and of the Alberti (Richard A. Goldthwaite, Enzo Settesoldi, and Marco Spallanzani, eds., *Due libri mastri degli Alberti: Una grande compagnia di Calimala, 1348–1358*, 2 vols. [Florence, 1995]).

wise, Venetians acceded to the virtual monopoly of exchange which Florentine merchant bankers held in Venice, as in all the major banking places of Europe. Venetians kept control of the bill trade with the Levant, but, as we shall see, the sums involved and the rhythm of activity were nothing compared with the level of operation maintained for more than two centuries by Florentines in the West.

The Florentine presence in Venice depended upon various factors. In positive terms, Venice was a major international entrepôt. Woolens produced or refinished in Florence found in Venice a natural market and seaport for transport eastward. Second, the rhythm of the Venetian marketplace was so regular and foreseeable, given the system of state-owned and -operated galley fleets and their regular departures, that Florentine experts in bills of exchange were able to create there a crucial hub in their Europewide network of exchange dealings. Third, foreigners in general were attracted by the equitable execution of contract law by Venetian commercial courts, a point underscored by Doge Tommaso Mocenigo in his so-called deathbed oration. Finally, Venice accepted immigrants, even political exiles, with open arms, men ready to come with their families, capital, and skills. In negative terms, Venice, especially in the fourteenth century, periodically enacted protectionist legislation aimed at limiting and even excluding investment by foreigners in the Levant trade. Defining foreigners and identifying who was really Venetian became a preoccupation of public policy. Periods of particularly adverse legislation had the effect of making Venice less attractive to Florentine merchant bankers. War and diplomacy were other factors that impinged on good relations. On various occasions when the two republics were at odds over their alliances or were in open conflict, Venice expelled the Florentines, meaning, in the end, particularly the merchant bankers.

Some idea of the importance, real or imagined, of the presence of Florentine merchants on the Rialto is provided by the oration of 1423 attributed to Tommaso Mocenigo. The policy of free trade and incentives, on which the doge prided himself, had been most successful with the Florentines, who, according to the doge, made the largest contribution by a foreign community:

> You have seen that Florentines import each year 16,000 bolts of woolen cloth, of finest, fine and medium quality, which we then transport throughout the Mediterranean. Each month these Florentines import 70,000 ducats' worth of merchandise of all kinds, which makes 840,000 ducats per year, and more. And they purchase English and Catalan wool, dyes, silk, wax, spun gold and silver thread, sugar, spices of all kinds, hides and jewels, to the great benefit of our land.[2]

[2] I have mixed two texts and have translated very freely. *BG,* 1, docs. 8obis (pp. 577–80) and 81

The text is corrupt and its source is dubious at best, but it may reflect at least what was considered a high order of magnitude.

Naturalization was one manner of defining newcomers and of granting commercial privileges (especially tariff reductions) otherwise reserved for Venetians. At the time of the "serrata," when nobility was defined as membership in the Great Council, the definition of Venetianness in general was made restrictive and acquisition of citizenship more difficult.[3] From the Black Death onward, by contrast, granting citizenship was simplified in an effort to attract foreigners—especially those who would contribute to the growth of local industries—to settle in Venice. Of the approximately 4,000 novi cives whose record of naturalization has survived for the period between 1300 and 1500, some 83 percent supplied their place of origin. First place by city was held by Florentines; first place by region was held by Tuscans, for Lucca was the second major city of origin.[4]

Only relatively rarely did Florentine merchant bankers seek to acquire Venetian citizenship. That privilege was advantageous for artisan-entrepreneurs and merchants, but foreign status did not constitute a handicap for merchant bankers, who tended to stay in one place only a limited number of years before being transferred to another branch in another banking place. At the same time, it was precisely the merchant bankers who dominated the three institutions that represented the interests of the Florentine "nation" in Venice: the "universitas mercatorum Florentinorum," referred to in those terms in 1387 but in existence long before—in fact, a "sindicho de' merchadanti fiorentini in Vinegia" is mentioned in 1348; the consulate; and the confraternity, or "scuola" ("schola et fraternitas Florentinorum"). As was often the case, the three institutions are not always easily distinguished one from the other.[5]

The confraternity, dedicated to St. John the Baptist, patron saint of the Arno city, existed at least by 1409 but was officially refounded in 1435,

---

(pp. 94–97); in the note on p. 577 Besta suggests alternative readings of the figures for doc. 81, which do not help to clarify a highly corrupt text. Other versions can be found in Romanin, *Storia documentata*, 4:93–95, and Heinrich Kretschmayr, *Geschichte von Venedig*, 3 vols. (Gotha, 1905–34), 2:617–19. The list of the traditional ports of call in the Mediterranean concludes with Lisbon (Besta and Kretschmayr versions) or Istria (Romanin version). Romanin's interpretation, which makes "ducats of all kinds, 7,000 per week," to read "70,000 ducats' worth of merchandise," is more sensible, if admittedly arbitrary. Luzzatto did not attempt an interpretation of this passage in "Sull'attendibilità di alcune statistiche economiche medievali," reprinted in his *Studi*.

[3]Frederic C. Lane, "The Enlargement of the Great Council of Venice," reprinted in his *Studies*, art. III, pp. 258–60, and Reinhold C. Mueller, "Espressioni di *status* sociale a Venezia dopo la 'Serrata' del Maggior Consiglio," in *Studi veneti offerti a Gaetano Cozzi* (Venice, 1992), 53–54.

[4]Molà and Mueller, "Essere straniero a Venezia," 839–51.

[5]Mueller, "Mercanti e imprenditori fiorentini," 29–32, also for the following paragraph. For the quotation of 1348, see the order-to-pay of 4 October recorded in Goldthwaite, Settesoldi, and Spallanzani, *Due libri mastri*, 1: 189.

with the necessary approval of the Council of Ten, when construction of a chapel at the church of the Frari was decided upon. Ninety-seven members of the confraternity were present for that historic decision, and although there were artisans among the leaders, the meeting was dominated by representatives of merchant-banking families then present in Venice: Barbo Altoviti, who was "guardiano," or top official, of the confraternity, Raniero di Pietro Davanzati, Antonio Canigiani, and Tommaso di Gianozzo Alberti, as well as Antonio di Nicolò Martelli, the Florentine consul, who was then assistant manager of the Medici bank in Venice, and Lotto di Tanino Bozzi, who was manager. Perhaps it is not surprising that Bozzi and Martelli were elected to the committee that was to negotiate with the Franciscans, only shortly after Cosimo and Lorenzo de' Medici had returned to Florence from a year's exile spent in Venice. Cosimo was later asked to make a contribution to the building expenses. The original location of the chapel is still marked today with the Florentine lily — "l'arma di Fiorenza" which the scuola ordered made for the chapel; the altar, crowned by Donatello's wooden statue of St. John the Baptist, dated 1438, flanked by Saints Zanobi and Reparata, was moved to the apse in the nineteenth century.

The following consideration of some of the numerous Florentine companies of merchant bankers opens and closes with expulsions: at the beginning, that related to the War of Ferrara, when, even in the absence of a formal "national" structure, the Florentine merchant bankers probably already exercised a dominant role in their community; at the end, that with which Venice responded to Cosimo de' Medici's volte-face, from the traditional "republican" alliance with Venice to support for the cause of the "tyrant" Francesco Sforza of Milan.

ii. COMPANIES ACTIVE ON THE RIALTO, 1310–1451

The period up to the famous bankruptcies of Florentine merchant-banking companies in the 1340s is marked by Venice's first two mainland wars, the War of Ferrara (1308–13) and the Scaliger War (1336–39). Both directly involved relations between Venice and the Florentine merchant bankers present on the Rialto.

The first important encounter with particular Florentine firms in the early fourteenth century comes at the conclusion of the War of Ferrara and involves precisely their expertise in foreign exchange. Venice lost the war over Ferrara with the papacy, which had excommunicated the doge and placed the city under interdict in 1308; even at war's end, the interdict was not to be lifted until a substantial portion of the indemnity — 100,000 florins — was paid.[6] Full powers were granted to the doge, his councillors, and

---

[6]Giovanni Soranzo, *La guerra fra Venezia e la Santa Sede per il dominio di Ferrara (1308–1313)* (Città di Castello, 1905). On the amount of the indemnity and the manner of levying forced

a Council of Fifteen to contract loans with any willing Venetian or foreigner. The Florentine companies were crucial, both for loans and for providing the service of exchange on Avignon, which they monopolized. In July 1312 Jacopo and Cipriano Alberti of the Alberti del Giudice company made an interest-free loan of 100 lire di grossi. Thereafter it was more a question of transferring to Avignon at a favorable rate of exchange sums collected via forced loans from Venetians, rather than the need of further loans. After an initial promise, the Florentines seem to have balked at applying the rate they had previously agreed upon. Venice, still under interdict, was desperate and threatened the Florentines with expulsion and gave them eight days to comply.[7] The merchant bankers obtained delays of a month in order to permit correspondence with their partners in Florence. By 26 October only the factor of the Scali firm had come forward with an offer to transfer to the Venetian ambassador in Avignon one-third of the installment then due; all the other representatives of firms were ordered to leave. Two days later Donato Peruzzi, a principal of the Peruzzi bank, made an offer from the safety of Mestre to exchange 20,000 florins, thus gaining permission for himself and his company to return to Venice and conclude the accord. Perhaps other bankers received a similar reprieve at the time, but failure to meet further Venetian demands for exchange brought orders of expulsion in July 1313 for specific bankers, among whom were Giovanni and Vieri de' Macci, and Meo Palmieri and Salvino di Benincasa of the Buonaccorsi firm.[8]

One Venetian historian called the expulsion "an act of violence" against the Florentines, while the historian of the Ferrara war accused the Florentines, guests of Venice, of intransigence for demanding higher-than-customary rates of exchange when their hosts were in trouble.[9] Clearly, Venice had to free itself of the interdict as soon as possible for commercial reasons, and the Florentines, who had already demonstrated their control of the exchange market at that early date, had every interest in gaining

---

loans to pay it, see Frederic C. Lane, "The Funded Debt of the Venetian Republic, 1262–1482," in his *Venice and History,* 93. For earlier contacts — in 1293 — between the two communes regarding debts owed by Venetians to Florentine merchants, see ASV, Miscellanea atti diplomatici e privati, b. 8, parchments 296–99.

[7]*RES,* doc. 51; *PRV,* docs. 85, 87. Luzzatto (*PRV,* xlii n. 2) takes the position that Venice pressured the Florentine firms active in Venice to lend the value of the bills of exchange. It seems, however, that the falling-out concerned the rate of exchange. A deliberation of 21 September 1312 affirmed that exchange could be had only from the Florentines who handled papal business ("et haberi non possit cambium nisi per Florentinos"), that they should accept the funds in Venice for transfer ("recipiendo hic pecuniam a nobis"), at the agreed rate of exchange ("pro illo pretio quo promiserunt alias").

[8]ASV, MC, Presbiter, fols. 80v, 81v–82 (9–28 October); Commemoriali, reg. 1, fol. 199, and *LCR,* 1:129, nos. 573–74.

[9]Romanin, *Storia documentata,* 3:24, and Soranzo, *La guerra fra Venezia e la Santa Sede,* 225.

readmittance. Just how the reconciliation was made, and when, are not clear, but there was business as usual on the Rialto by 1314.

In the period between the two wars, considerable problems arose from the failures of the Pillestri and the Scali, two important companies with branches in Venice. Florentine authorities, upon informing Venice in early 1326, estimated that the Pillestri had assets of only 10,000 florins and liabilities with Florentines alone of 30,000 florins. Many Venetians also had credits with that company, but the Sopraconsoli, who had jurisdiction, had a difficult time collecting debts that had accrued locally. Venetians, in both cases, seem to have been accorded less than half of their outstanding credits.[10]

The second war pitched Venice and Florence against Mastino della Scala of Verona, lord of ten important towns, including Lucca, Padua, and Treviso. Venice sought to gain the Trevigiano; Florence, which sought to gain Lucca, agreed to contribute half the costs of the military operations and formed a commission, the "Dieci da Vinegia," made up of representatives of the great merchant-banking houses, which had the task of sending monthly installments to Venice to pay the troops. Some funds were transferred in specie, others by exchange agreements; the Covoni, for example, ordered their factor in Venice to pay the Florentine ambassadors by drawing on Florence; the Dieci paid the draft and interest accruing to a rechange operation. It was probably in the context of these payments that the factors of the Bardi and Peruzzi contracted for more than 5,000 ducats in loans in Venice from the recently naturalized nobleman Vitaliano Dente.[11] When the allies dislodged the Scaligeri from Padua, they restored the Carrara signory but only "ad dispositionem et beneplacitum" of both republics; to mark their role, the insignia of Venice and Florence were affixed to the doors of the major church and the city hall of Padua in 1337. When Venice was assured of gaining Treviso, it concluded a separate peace (on 18 December 1338); Florence, whose financiers had just heard of the defeat of their English debtor at the hands of France, was forced to sue for peace the following January without gaining Lucca.[12] The Arno city, which had spent 400,000–600,000 florins in a useless effort, refused to send the last months' installments to pay the mercenaries in the Veneto. Over a disputed sum of only 25,000–36,000 florins came the break: Venice announced the expul-

[10]*LCR,* 1:271, no. 461, and 2:113, no. 2. See also ASV, AC, reg. 3641/I, fols. 45, 48 (12 September and 5 October 1327), and 3641/II, fol. 18 (30 May 1329).

[11]Giulio Mandich, "Per una ricostruzione delle operazioni mercantili e bancarie della compagnia dei Covoni," in Sapori, *Libro giallo,* clxi, cxcii–iii, and Sapori, *La crisi,* 107–10; the Dente loans are discussed in Lane, "Investment and Usury," 65, and in Mueller, *Procuratori di San Marco,* 305–9.

[12]The war was chronicled in both republics by Giovanni Villani and Jacopo Piacentino. The best modern account is Romanin, *Storia documentata,* 3:116–32. See also Giorgio Cracco, *Società e stato nel medioevo veneziano* (Florence, 1967), 392–93, Gioachino Volpe, "L'Italia e Venezia," in *La civiltà veneziana del Trecento* (Florence, 1956), 58–59, and Marvin Becker, *Florence in Transition,* 2 vols. (Baltimore, 1967–68), vol. 1, chap. 4.

TABLE 7.1

The Alberti del Giudice Company:
Assets of the Venice Branch Relative to Total Assets, 1304–1329

1304–7	15%	1315–19	42%	1323–25	42%
1307–10	—	1319–21	39%	1325–27	—
1310–15	19%	1321–23	35%	1327–29	9%

Source: de Roover, "The Story of the Alberti Company of Florence."

sion of all Florentine citizens on 12 February 1340, and Florence responded by announcing reprisals and prohibiting trade with Venice and its subject territories in the Levant. Despite various exceptions decided upon by Florence, the reprisals, combined with the Venetian order of expulsion, meant that trade in goods and foreign exchange between the two cities came to a standstill. Relations were reestablished in the following year, when an accord on the payment via installments of the outstanding debt (less than 32,000 florins) was reached—just when Florence was devoid of specie and the bankruptcies of the smaller companies had already begun.[13]

Extant Florentine account books from this period shed some light on the activity of the branches operating in Venice, on the level of investments there in relation to total assets, and on the importance of their foreign exchange transactions. Both the War of Ferrara and the Scaliger War left their mark on the Florentine presence.

Some of the earliest records are fragments of account books of the Alberti del Giudice company. Extant financial statements seem to reflect a generally increasing level of investment in Venice. The level of goods and money in the hands of the Venetian factor in relation to the assets of the company as a whole can be seen in table 7.1; liabilities specific to the branch seem not to have been itemized. No factor is reported operating in Venice from 1307 to 1310, early in the Ferrara war. The statement of 1315 included real estate in Tuscany valued at 18,000 lire, but despite that, the share of assets held by the Venice branch was 19 percent of the total. In the last

[13]Sapori, *La crisi,* 114–16; Angelo Marchesan (*Treviso medievale,* 2 vols. [Treviso, 1923], 1:239) recounts that at the same date "Tuscan" pawnbrokers in Treviso were also expelled and replaced by Jews. Villani (cited by Mandich, "Per una ricostruzione," clxxv n.), one of the advisors of the Dieci da Vinegia, wrote, "Feciono [i Veneziani] rappresaglia sopra i Fiorentini con forti ed aspre leggi, onde tutti i Fiorentini se ne partirono alla uscita di gennaio 1339 [s.f.]. E simili leggi e più forti furono fatte per li fiorentini sopra i Veneziani e sopra quel Fiorentino vi stesse o v'avesse affare." A convenient summary of the negotiations surrounding the settlement of the debt can be found in Cessi's introduction to *RES,* lxxxviii–ix, esp. n. 4. The sindaci sent from Florence agreed to pay the principal plus interest and damages in ten annual installments; the patrimony of the Marchese d'Este was pledged as surety. The debt was settled in full in 1352.

statement extant, a sum due by the company to Marco Bonsignori, factor in Venice, amounted to nearly half the assets of the Venice branch.

In 1325–26 Agnolo degli Alberti himself was in Venice; from 1329 through 1337, when he headed the company, he was represented in Venice by Rigaletto Tucci. The Alberti weathered the bankruptcies of the 1340s and became bankers to the papacy. They continued to maintain a branch in Venice, directed by Giovanni Ducci, but their investments there did not match the levels maintained earlier. Just the same, their account books of 1348–56 mention dozens of Florentines active on the Rialto.[14]

Practically contemporary with the accounts of the Alberti are those of the Bardi. The Bardi company maintained a salaried factor in Venice fairly continuously. Alessandro di Guccio is the first factor recorded as operating in Venice, from before 1310 until 1313, when he was conceivably expelled. The records note that he had been in Venice "quite a few years" but that he had "comported himself badly" and had "caused serious loss to the company." His successor, Baldinaccio de Verre, was a factor from 1314, when the Bardi were obviously readmitted, until 1328, when his employment also was terminated because "he had comported himself badly in Venice." Other figures were present for shorter periods. Lippo di Tecco Buonaccorsi, who received a high salary, is recorded as having been in Venice before his death in 1318. Giovanni Mafei traveled to Venice for specific tasks: in January 1320 to buy wheat, in March of the same year to load woolens on the galleys; he then remained in Venice until 1323, resigned in the following year, "and did not again return" to Florence. Lotto di Cino Lamberti was first a commission agent for the Bardi in Venice in 1329–30 and then became a factor there from 1333 to 1336. A Venetian account book names Giovanni di Boninsegna Gherardi, "socius de Bardis," as principal of the Venice branch from 1325 to 1337; he was represented before Venetian authorities by various persons: "Calenius de Bardis" (1325–26, 1328), Sandro di Vanni Lamberti (1326, 1331–32), Filippo di Gherardino (1333), Boccaccino "dictus Gallini" de Bardis, who was Giovanni Boccaccio's father (1334), and Andrea di Biagio Boccadibue (1337). The last known Bardi factor was Lotto Franceschi, sent to Venice in 1337–39, perhaps in connection with the Scaliger War.[15]

[14]See Raymond de Roover's analysis of Sapori's edition of the accounts: "The Story of the Alberti Company of Florence," in his *Business, Banking, and Economic Thought*, 39–84. See also Armando Sapori, "La famiglia e le compagnie degli Alberti del Giudice," in his *Studi di storia economica*, 3 vols. (Florence, 1955–67), 2:975–1012. The Sopraconsoli accounts (see next note) record the company as that of "Pagnus del Giudice"; these and the Covoni accounts both record the role of Tucci. For Ducci, see Goldthwaite, Settesoldi, and Spallanzani, *Due libri mastri*.

[15]Sapori, *La crisi*, 254, 256, 267, 271, 272; also idem, "Il personale delle compagnie mercantili del Medioevo," in his *Studi*, 2:700, 711, 717, 730–32, 737, 741, 745–46, 751. The Venetian record is an official account book of creditors of the bankrupt company of two Falier brothers; in it we can watch just who went to collect claims for each of some fifty creditors as they were

Lotto was very active on the exchange market, basically following orders from Ridolfo dei Bardi in Florence to pay his drafts and redraw, while the Bardi were borrowing large sums of money from the Covoni company under the guise of bills of exchange. He also contracted a loan of 2,500 ducats from Vitaliano Dente, the above-mentioned Venetian nobleman of Paduan origin, perhaps in connection with sums owed by the Florentine "Dieci da Vinegia" for the Scaliger War. In 1338–39, finally, Lotto also acted as agent of the patriarch of Aquileia for collecting rents on Istrian lands owed to the prelate by the Commune of Venice.[16]

Lotto Franceschi's brother-in-law, Filippo di Guido del Maestro Fagno, was in Venice in the same years (1337–38) as representative of the Peruzzi bank. In that role he had been preceded by Piero di Giotto Peruzzi (1335–37), who in turn had taken the place of Lippo Sardi, in Venice from 1331 to 1335. But the factor who was most involved in the exchange market was Giovanni Bonducci Cambi, in Venice from 1335 to 1339. From September 1336 until August 1338, Giovanni played a part similar to that of Lotto with the Bardi, namely, he accepted dozens of drafts from Bonifazio Peruzzi and Company in Florence and redrew. As in the case of the Bardi, the Peruzzi branch in Venice drew on Florence to pay its debts and accepted drafts by redrawing in order to cover the loans via bills of exchange which the Peruzzi contracted with the Covoni company.[17] One of these Peruzzi factors, unnamed, accepted a conditioned deposit for 2,500 ducats from the same Vitaliano Dente who had lent a similar sum to the Bardi; this contract, too, was condemned by the Venetian usury officials, whose sentence, similarly, was then lifted. Probably the resident factor was expelled in 1339–40, as part of the aftereffects of the Scaliger War. Not long after being readmitted, the Peruzzi firm failed. The biggest Venetian creditors of the Peruzzi were Vitaliano Dente — perhaps for the same deposit — and the great merchants Nero Cocco and Bertucci Pisani, whom we encountered previously as lend-

---

paid over the years by the Sopraconsoli dei Mercanti; the Bardi were the first non-Venetians on the list. See ASV, PSM, Ultra, b. 125, commis. Nicoletto e Bertucci Falier. For many of the factors, the information goes considerably beyond the names of Bardi personnel, their dates, and branches as collected by Sapori. Giovanni Boccaccio's father, Boccaccio Chellini, is registered as "Bocaçius dictus Gallini de Bardis" when he collected the payment "pro eius societate" in May 1334; he signed the "pacta" with other creditors in August of the same year as "Bochatinus de Certaldo, socius Bardorum" (see under the dates). He was known to have been a Bardi factor in Naples from 1327 to 1338 (see Sapori, "Il personale," 735), whereas here he is called partner ("socius").

[16]For the exchange business, see the tables compiled by Mandich, "Per una ricostruzione." For Lotto and the patriarch, see Donata Degrassi, "I rapporti tra compagnie bancarie toscane e patriarchi d'Aquileia (metà XIII secolo–metà XIV secolo)," in *I toscani in Friuli*, ed. Alessandro Malcagni (Florence, 1992), 192. See also above, n. 11.

[17]Sapori, "Il personale," 721, 723, 726–28; Mandich, "Per una ricostruzione," appendix, tables; for contacts between Filippo di Guido and Lotto Franceschi, see the entry in Armando Sapori, ed., *I libri di commercio dei Peruzzi* (Milan, 1934), 64 (1338).

ers to the English Crown. In their favor, the doge was forced to intervene directly with the priors of Florence on various occasions in 1344.[18]

A unique Venetian source names at least seven Florentine companies that were creditors of the Falier company, which was declared bankrupt in 1325; from that year until 1337 all the representatives of those companies can be watched as they lined up periodically to receive the installments on the liquidation as they were paid out by the court of the Sopraconsoli. Besides the Bardi, who headed the list of foreigner creditors, the following companies were present: Giacomo di Francesco and Pietro Corsini (called Gherardo Corsini and Company in the Covoni accounts; factors were Gherardo, Duccio, and Filippo Corsini), a company doomed to fail in Florence in 1342; Andrea Pillestri, who failed in 1326, so that the money paid by the court after the first year went directly to Pillestri's creditors; Pietro Geri; Guglielmo Niccoli Guglielmi (represented by his partner Nicolò di Pietro), who was hired by the Bardi beginning in 1334; Forte Pieri; and Bertuccio (or Duccio) di Banchello del Buono (represented by his brother Pietro and by Ambrogio Guidi).[19]

An account book (the "libro nero") of the company of Duccio di Banchello del Buono and Banco Bencivenni, kept in Venice by their associates Pietro del Buono e compagni, has survived for the years 1336–40; it includes payments from the Sopraconsoli for the Falier failure. The enterprise was directed toward commerce and exchange ("merchatantia e chanbiora"). The goods dealt in were very heterogeneous; both parties supplied themselves with capital by drawing bills of exchange on the other, but those operations were recorded in a special "libro delle mandate" which has been lost. The Venetian affiliate handled the payments side of its exchange operations through the several Rialto banks then in operation, most notably that of Giovanni Stornado. Both exchange and commercial operations slow down in the latter months of 1339 and stop altogether in the following January, when Venice expelled the Florentine merchant bankers.[20]

A similar picture, for the exact same years, is supplied by the libro giallo, a ledger of the Covoni company, kept in Florence but regarding primarily exchange relations with Venice. The ledger records the activity in Venice of some sixty different Florentine companies (branches, affiliates, and agencies) between 1336 and January 1340; they appear almost exclusively as parties to foreign exchange transactions. The Covoni, as we shall

---

[18]Mueller, *Procuratori di San Marco,* 307–9. ASF, Repubblica, Signori, Missive, Prima cancelleria, reg. 8, fols. 92, 103v. On the difficulty foreigners had in collecting, see Sapori, *La crisi,* 174, 186–92.

[19]ASV, PSM, Ultra, b. 125, commis. Nicoletto e Bertucci Falier. See also Sapori, "Il personale," 743.

[20]ASF, Del Bene, reg. 64, has been described by Giulio Mandich, "Una compagnia fiorentina a Venezia nel quarto decennio del secolo quattordicesimo (un libro di conti)," *Rivista storica italiana* 96 (1984): 129–49.

see below, were primarily lenders on exchange and thus appear as deliverers or beneficiaries, the others as drawers or drawees. The principal commission agent of the Covoni was Giovanni Vai and Company, but other representatives also appear, including for a time Tommaso di Covone Covoni.

Of the numerous drawers and drawees, besides Giovanni Bonducci and Lotto Franceschi discussed above as factors of the Peruzzi and the Bardi, two are worth mentioning: Tosco Ghinazzi and Noddo d'Andrea. In the Covoni ledger, the former represented the company of Dino Guidi and Jacopo Guardi; the latter was a partner of Branca Guidalotti and Company. Both are mentioned in a novella by Franco Sacchetti (about 1390) as members of the Florentine community in Venice who had played a joke on some other members, a story recounted by Sacchetti's father, Benci, who had taken part in the prank. Both became citizens of Venice, which was rather exceptional for persons involved in merchant banking. Tosco Ghinazzi was made citizen de intus in 1344 (he had therefore arrived in Venice by 1329), and Noddo d'Andrea received the privilege de extra in 1358. At the same time, both maintained ties with Florence: Tosco was a prior in 1355, and Noddo, "ammonito" by the Guelf Party in 1359, returned to Florence and matriculated in the Wool Guild in July 1361. Both are mentioned in the Alberti ledgers as being in Venice, Noddo by 1348.[21]

The Covoni company's foreign exchange accounts close, as do those of Duccio di Banchello, in January 1340, as a result of the expulsion of the Florentine merchant bankers from Venice, in the aftermath of the Scaliger War.

Following the bankruptcies of the Florentine merchant banks and the Venetian transfer banks in the 1340s and the Black Death, the business climate in Venice seems to have been less favorable to foreign investment. From 1350 to 1354 Venice was at war with Genoa; thereupon followed the conspiracy of Doge Marino Falier (1355). The ruling councils showed themselves to be completely indecisive on such crucial options as a crackdown on usury or the invitation of pawnbrokers, the regulation of private banks or the establishment of a state bank, a policy of free trade or protectionism. The Guidalotti closed their office in Venice in 1360; the Del Bene seem to have abandoned the Venetian market in 1364. Even though the Officium de Navigantibus was suppressed definitively in 1363, the rule that new citizens could not invest in maritime commerce sums exceeding their assessed valuation as registered in the estimo was maintained, and the shift

---

[21]Mandich, "Per una ricostruzione," tables. Tosco was identified in Florence as a speziale; Noddo also dealt in wool cloth produced by the Del Bene in Florence; neither gave his profession upon registering as a new citizen. Franco Sacchetti, *Il trecentonovelle*, ed. Antonio Lanza (Florence, 1984), 195–200 (novella 98) and notes. The prank involved the theft of a prized tripe while it was cooking in the house of Giovanni Ducci, mentioned above as factor of the Alberti company. See also Mueller, "Mercanti e imprenditori fiorentini," 29–30, 40, and Hoshino, *L'arte della lana in Firenze,* 165. See also Goldthwaite, Settesoldi, and Spallanzani, *Due libri mastri,* index.

away from protectionism was hesitant and halfhearted.[22] By contrast, a local company, renewed in 1362 and 1365 by the naturalized citizens Tommaso di Giovanni Talenti, Florentine, and the Lucchese silk merchants Francesco Volpelli (in the first contract) and Marco Pisanelli and Giovanni di Biagio Bartolomei (in the second), clearly flourished despite the seemingly negative business climate. It had a very considerable capital (15,800 ducats in 1362, raised to 18,245 in 1365) and was directed primarily toward the production and sale of silk cloth but also toward "other goods and to exchange."[23] Just how much the company actually dealt in foreign exchange or how exceptional its level of capital might have been in that period is impossible to determine.

Not until 1375, under pressure of a plethora of inventories, did Venice liberalize its export policy.[24] Florentines were foremost among the foreign merchants who stood to benefit from a reduction of trade barriers. The importance of good relations between the city and its Florentine community is underscored in the formal refusal by Venice, expressed in a senatorial deliberation, to publish the papal interdict against Florence (at war with the papacy) in 1377: "It is clear that our city is sustained, grows, and is conserved solely through the exercise of trade. And these Florentines especially are among those with whom our merchants trade heavily, if not most heavily." Acceptance of the interdict, the deliberation continued, would bring incalculable harm to Venetians, "who through trade and other contacts are owed large sums of money by the Florentines and would force many—even an infinite number—of our merchants into bankruptcy."[25] Nonetheless, a broad policy of free trade, in which the Florentines would play a central role, was formulated only after the political and military crises that confronted each republic: the war of the "Eight Saints" and the Ciompi revolt on the one hand, the War of Chioggia against Genoa on the other.

Between August 1380 and 1382, privileges rained upon foreigners, as a cure for the profound liquidity crisis brought on by the War of Chioggia. They were permitted to purchase real estate and government obligations and to invest in maritime trade sums equal to their investments in houses

[22]Goldthwaite, Settesoldi, and Spallanzani, *Due libri mastri,* 165–66, and chap. 5 of Cessi's introduction to *RES.*

[23]Mueller, *Procuratori di San Marco,* 178–84; Molà, *La comunità dei lucchesi,* 198–99. The second contract mentions the Florentine Girardino Del Bene as a factor of the Talenti, which means that the Del Bene did not disappear altogether from the Venetian scene in the 1360s, as Hoshino thought.

[24]The need found unequivocal expression in the orations of two senators in December 1375 who insisted that "fortitudo et status civitatis est mercadantia" and that "mercationes requirunt exitum," otherwise "mercatores remaneant deserti et consumpti cum notabili damno Comunis Veneciarum." *RES,* cclvii and n. 1.

[25]See the orders sent to the Venetian ambassadors in Avignon, published by Arturo Segre, "Di alcune relazioni tra la Repubblica di Venezia e la S. Sede ai tempi di Urbano V e di Gregorio XI (1367–1378), *NAV* 9 (1905): 213–14.

and government credits "just like original citizens"; prerequisites for naturalization were reduced; Jewish pawnbrokers were invited to lend in the city. Florentine merchants, whose government (represented by the immigrant merchant banker Zanobi di Taddeo Gaddi) was made guarantor of the Peace of Turin, were exempted from the "tratta," a tax on imports. That exemption was renewed after five years, at the request of the "universitas mercatorum Florentinorum," when the Provveditori di Comun advised the Senate that "Florentines export[ed] much larger quantities of goods than they import[ed]."[26] Regulations regarding the brokerage tax ("messetteria"), which foreigners paid at higher rates than Venetians, were made more transparent, although it was reconfirmed that foreigners were not permitted to transact business among themselves or to form companies with Venetians.[27]

In 1382 begins a period of flourishing contacts. Exiles such as the wool entrepreneurs Alessandro and Francesco Gucci and Bernardo Velluti arrived from Florence in response to incentives for foreign investments in the wool industry.[28] Information on the merchant-banking companies active on the Rialto is considerable, thanks to the preservation of the archive of Francesco di Marco Datini (ca. 1335–1410). Datini returned to Prato from Avignon in January 1383 and almost immediately turned his attention to the formation of branch offices in several major cities, beginning with Pisa. He never opened a branch in Venice, preferring to do business with the Florentine firms already established there and to play on the competition among them to promote his interests in trade and foreign exchange.[29] In November 1383 Piero di Guccio Torrigiani, the representative in Venice

---

[26]Luzzatto in *PRV,* clxxii–iii and doc. 169; Mueller, "Mercanti e imprenditori fiorentini," 39, 44–45; Roberto Cessi, "La finanza veneziana al tempo della guerra di Chioggia," in his *Politica ed economia,* 222–23. For the tratta, see ASV, SM, reg. 40, fol. 63 (12 March 1387, the date of the renewal).

[27]ASV, SM, reg. 40, fol. 63, a deliberation passed the same day and recorded on the same page as that concerning the tratta. On differentiated customs duties, see Francesco Balducci Pegolotti, *La pratica della mercatura,* ed. Allan Evans (Cambridge, Mass., 1936), 140–41. On 19 April 1404, the Gaddi firm, which had just received an export license for wool, reported: "Avisoti che vendendo a citadino v'è bene ¾ per cento di mesetteria; ma vendendo a forestiere, v'è 2¼ per cento per parte, che viene 4½ in tutto. ADP, 715. On another occasion, Piaciti reported, "Non si può avere compagnia un forestiere chon un citadino;" ADP, 714, 9 December 1402.

[28]Mueller, "Mercanti e imprenditori fiorentini," 34, 54–55.

[29]For Datini, his firm, and his archive, see Federigo Melis, *Aspetti della vita economica medievale: Studi nell'Archivio Datini di Prato* (Siena, 1962), and Iris Origo, *The Merchant of Prato* (London, 1957). Melis (218–20) mentions about twenty correspondents who wrote from Venice from 1383 to 1410; these were only some of the companies present. Later in life Datini thought of establishing himself in Venice, as he wrote, "to finish my days"; this in conversation with Leonardo Dandolo, Procurator of San Marco and ambassador to Florence in 1397 (on which occasion he visited the Sacra Cintola in Prato, in the company of Datini); Melis, *Aspetti,* 57 n. 9, 73–74.

of his partnership with Inghilese d'Inghilese, wrote his first letter to Francesco di Marco and Company in Pisa, in order to establish a correspondent relationship. Introducing himself, he tells the Pisan factor to take note of his handwriting and suggests that they begin making agreements and keep each other informed on all matters concerning their respective markets, "like brothers": "I shall keep you posted on news from [Venice and] Alexandria and you do the same for all news from Pisa and Genoa; write regarding any change [in the situation] and write often; it can only be advantageous."[30]

In March of the following year began the most important and lasting agency relationship between Venice and the Datini network, that with Zanobi di Taddeo Gaddi, son and brother, respectively, of the famous Florentine painters Taddeo and Agnolo and founder of the Gaddi merchant-banking house. Zanobi, resident in Venice since 1369 and thus eligible for full citizenship in 1384, also introduced himself to the Datini factor in Pisa; he wrote that he would be needing things from Pisa "daily" and continues, "I am in pretty good order and becoming well established; opportunities do exist here — may God preserve them and make them grow. If God grants me life and grace, as he has done so far, my hope is to do well. But enough of that; I am at your service."[31] From the date of this letter until his death on 21 July 1400 during the terrible plague of that year, Gaddi and his employees in Venice wrote regularly to all the Datini branches; more than fifteen hundred of those letters are still extant.[32] Just before he died, Zanobi broke with Francesco Datini, upon hearing that Datini had planned to shift his business in Venice to Bindo Piaciti and Company. Datini later did not deny the allegation.

After Zanobi's death a company was formed in the name of his minor sons, who had returned to Florence with their mother. Run by Antonio di Ser Bartolomeo (and styled "Commissaria di Zanobi di Taddeo e Antonio di Ser Bartolomeo"), it continued to serve the Datini network until Francesco himself died; of this company, an additional seven hundred letters are preserved. It had the typical structure of Florentine companies; in 1400 it was known to have attracted a deposit of 1,200 florins on sopracorpo, at 8 percent, while in 1402 it was reported to have a capital (corpo) of 6,000

---

[30]ADP, 548, Inghilese to Pisa, 26 November 1383. Melchiore and Pietro Torrigiani fled Venice as bankrupts in 1390; see Cassandro, *Le rappresaglie e il fallimento*, 82, doc. 38.

[31]ADP, 548, Gaddi to Pisa, 26 March 1384: "Io sono inn asai buono ordine o buono e bello inviamento, e anche ciè qualche cosa — Dio m'el conservi e piaciagli accresciello; e se Dio mi presta vita e della sua grazia com' à fato in sino qui, ò speranza di star bene e più sopraciò non dicho; vostro sono."

[32]See Melis, *Aspetti*, 219–20, for approximate numbers of letters and for names of all the correspondents who wrote from Venice. A new, complete inventory of the letters is being undertaken under the direction of Bruno Dini and Elena Cecchi.

The labels within the painting read (left to right):

✠ TADDEVS GHADDI ✠ :GADDVS ZENOBII: ✠ :ANGELVS TADDEI: ✠

Fig. 10. From painting to commerce: three generations of painters in the Gaddi family. From left to right: the father (Taddeo di Gaddo), grandfather (Gaddo di Zanobi) and brother (Agnolo di Taddeo), respectively, of the Florentine merchant banker Zanobi di Taddeo Gaddi. The latter was the principal correspondent of Francesco di Marco Datini in Venice, where he founded a merchant-banking operation that lasted three more generations.

Galleria degli Uffizi, Florence

269

ducats.[33] Both Zanobi and the successor company (with a single branch operation, in Montpellier) were unspecialized; they dealt in buying and selling all kinds of commodities for import and export, as well as acting as agents on the exchange market. When they came of age, Zanobi's sons Taddeo and Agnolo followed in their father's footsteps, and Venice continued to hold a privileged position in their enterprise. In fact, Taddeo di Zanobi complained to the officials of the catasto in 1427 that double citizenship meant double jeopardy, since he had to pay forced loans both in Venice, where he was a citizen by birth, son of a naturalized father, and in Florence. He and Agnolo reported, furthermore, that they had invested 6,000 ducats in a firm based in Venice, administered at the time by Domenico di Tommaso di Francesco della Vacca. After Taddeo's death, his son Alessandro represented in Venice the firm of his uncle, Agnolo di Zanobi, which appears in Venetian account books in the late 1430s. Taddeo's other sons, Francesco and Zanobi, were active in Venice in the 1440s, most likely also as factors of their uncle. Agnolo, who was generally at his headquarters on the Mercato Nuovo of Florence in that decade, maintained a learned correspondence with Mariano di Volterra, vicar of the Carthusian monastery of S. Andrea on the Lido of Venice.[34] His second wife, Maddelena Ridolfi, registered as age twenty-one in the catasto of 1427, made her testament in May 1450 in Venice, a document that shows her to be at home in the Venetian context. Under the direction of their two sons, Francesco and Taddeo, the Gaddi merchant-banking company gave up the Venetian connection, preferring the Florence-Rome axis. Francesco d'Agnolo became a noted humanist, eminent ambassador of Florence, and papal collector. But the merchant-banking house he managed had been founded in Venice by his grandfather, Zanobi di Taddeo, who, from a family of artists, had started it on its way to fame and fortune (for the genealogy, see table H.1, below).[35]

Other firms also made Venice an important base for their operations. In the Datini years, the specialized dealer in foreign exchange and in ar-

[33]Notification of Zanobi's death was sent to Pisa on 22 July 1400 by Antonio di Ser Bartolomeo, and he reported "e lasciò per testamento che qui si ritenesse questo suo traficho per filiuoli suoi e per me in chonpagnia." ADP, 550. References to the company's capital in ADP, 713, Commis. Gaddi to Florence (23 December 1400) and 714, Bindo Piaciti to Florence (2 September 1402). It should be noted that the term *commissaria* (here used in the style of the Gaddi successor firm) in Venice is the same as *redi di* . . . in Florence, meaning, that is, an estate; it does not mean "commission agency," as has mistakenly been affirmed.

[34]Tammaro de Marinis and Alessandro Perosa, eds., *Nuovi documenti per la storia del Rinascimento* (Florence, 1970), 13–22 (eleven letters, 1442–48).

[35]See Mueller, "Mercanti e imprenditori fiorentini," 45–47, where the catasto returns and other sources are cited. See also the cashbook of the Medici branch in Venice in 1437, in ASF, MAP, 134/1, fols. 147v, 280v. Maddelena's testament is in ASV, NT, Miscellanea testamenti notai diversi, b. 25, n. 1994; she left her husband only three books, an icon, and silverware; her executors were Venetian women: Lucia Diedo, noblewoman and residuary heir, and Bertucia, a seamstress ("sartoressa") at the orphanage of the Pietà.

bitrage was Manetto Davanzati and Company. On 4 October 1384 the factor of the Davanzati firm wrote to the Datini company in Pisa announcing its new Venetian branch ("la compagnia nuova che qui abiamo cominciato"): "We are taking note of your handwriting, and you take note of ours. Tell us what is available in Pisa, and here you will be well served." In fact, this company became involved in commodities only rarely (and with negative consequences); its letters (some 300) and those of its successor (some 175 after 1402) constitute the best-informed sources of information on exchange and give the largest number of quotations; the market analyses they contain are the most insightful of the whole Datini archive. In the early fifteenth century, Manetto's son Luigi managed the operation.[36]

Many others offered their services as commission agents to Datini. In 1387 Antonio di Benincasa Alemanni and Jacopo di Tedaldo Benozzi and Company wrote to the main office in Florence: "I know that Zanobi di Taddeo keeps you fully informed on the condition of merchandise here; still, I too will write you and keep you apprised of the situation."[37]

A close friend of Datini's, Bindo di Gherardo Piaciti, came to Venice in 1394. In November of that year he wrote saying that he had heard that the Florence branch would use him as a commission agent and expressed thanks for that decision. He assured Datini's partner, Stoldo di Lorenzo, that he was working alone and that he would not handle commissions from others; "your business will be handled like my own," he concluded. Piaciti became a methodical correspondent who often wrote separately to Datini and to Stoldo.[38] Maintaining several agency relationships in the same city created difficulties revealed in a letter from Datini to Piaciti in 1401, when he recounts that Gaddi had broken with him just before he died and had tried to undermine his friendship and business connections with his best clients in the Catalan trade, Francesco Corner and Antonio Contarini. The break had been brought on by the well-founded rumor, which Zanobi had heard from Datini's bookkeeper, that Datini had planned to shift the bulk of

[36]ADP, b. 548. The branch was probably run mostly by factors, even though members of the Davanzati family, namely, Piero di Chiarino in 1395–96, Piero di Bernardo in 1400, were sometimes in Venice; see Gene Brucker, *The Civic World of Early Renaissance Florence* (Princeton, 1977), 21, 170. Named factor in a three-year (notarized) contract beginning in 1387 was Bartolomeo di Francesco di Piero Stefani; as his cousin and surety, Jacopo di Rosso di Piero, recorded: "andò a stare a Vinegia per Manetto Davanzati e chompagnia tavolieri . . . e io Jacopo gli fa mallevadore che renderebbe buono conto."; see ASF, Conventi soppressi, 102 (S. M. Novella), n. 469.

[37]ADP, 709, letter of 19 September 1387. There are some one hundred letters, covering eighteen months.

[38]ADP, 710, 24 November 1394. Nearly seven hundred of his concise and neat letters are extant; the Venetian series was transcribed by P. Gonnelli in a laurea thesis under the direction of F. Melis: "Momenti e aspetti dell'economia veneziana, rivissuti attraverso la corrispondenza Venezia-Firenze dell'azienda fiorentina di Bindo Piaciti, 1394–1407 (con trascrizione di 445 lettere)," Istituto di Storia Economica, University of Florence, 1971. See Melis, *Aspetti,* 219 n. 11.

his business in Venice from Gaddi to Piaciti. Datini felt it was necessary to travel to Venice personally to rectify matters with his clients.[39] Piaciti's interests, like Gaddi's, lay more in commodities than in foreign exchange. He stayed on in Venice long after Datini's death.[40]

Other operators, large and small, also wrote from Venice to Datini branches but are represented by distinctly fewer letters than the above. Some are Donato Dini, Giorgio Niccoli and Giovanni di Buonaccorso, Giovanni di Ser Nigi and Gherardo Davizi, Domenico d'Andrea (a Sienese and naturalized Venetian who, at least for a time, was a partner of Alessandro Borromei), Andrea Lamberteschi and Company, and even Giovanni di Bicci de' Medici, who visited Venice briefly in the years 1398–1401; several companies of the Alberti family are also represented: that of Ricciardo, of Bernardo, of Giannozzo and Antonio, and of Diamante and Altobianco.[41]

Some large companies had little or no connection with the Datini network and are known from other sources. Francesco di Jacopo del Bene, exiled in 1383 on account of his ties with leaders of the Ciompi revolt, established himself on the Rialto until his rehabilitation in 1391. In that year his sons, Borgognone and Jacopo, founded a bank in Padua in partnership with Salvi di Giovanni Lippi, who managed the branch in Venice as long as it lasted and continued to operate there until his death — in a state of bankruptcy — in 1404.[42]

In the same years a Florentine and a Bolognese firm were used as commission agents by Averardo de' Medici. Antonio Dietifeci (of Antonio and Bonaccorso Dietifeci and Company), who resided in Venice (as the ledger reports), handled the bulk of the numerous exchange operations in Venice in 1395. His partner, beginning in 1384, was Giovanni d'Adoardo Portinari, the future manager of the Venice branch of the Medici bank. In

---

[39]ADP, 721, letter of 12 January 1401 from Francesco Datini in Bologna to Bindo Piaciti in Venice.

[40]He is involved in importing Florentine cloth and exporting English wool in 1416 as partner of Gianozzo and Antonio Alberti and Company. He was still active in the same line of business in 1423. ASV, AC, reg. 3647, fols. 5v–6 (16 June 1417), and GP, Sg, reg. 34, fol. 19v (19 February 1424).

[41]Melis, *Aspetti*, 218–20. On bills of exchange, one Alberti company identified its branches as "Bernardo degli Alberti e compagni di Venezia" and "Bernardo degli Alberti e Francesco Davizi in Bologna." ADP, 1142 and 1145bis. Domenico d'Andrea became a Venetian citizen de extra in the year 1400.

[42]Hidetoshi Hoshino, "Francesco di Iacopo Del Bene cittadino Fiorentino del Trecento," *Annuario* of the Istituto giapponese di cultura, 4 (1966–67): 64–65. ASF, Carte Del Bene, n. 49, which contains some fifty letters written in Venice and Padua (1389–92), which are matched by a journal (n. 20) and a ledger (n. 19) of the bank in Padua for the same period. This bank was involved in speculation in specie and bullion, rather than in exchange. Salvi di Giovanni died intestate and bankrupt in October 1404; his wife fled Venice with their six children; Domenico d'Andrea was elected representative of the creditors. ASV, AC, reg. 3645, fols. 75v–76 (1 December 1404).

1398–99 Antonio went bankrupt and fled Venice with assets "ad magnum valorem" belonging to Venetians. The inequity of the subsequent payments to creditors — with Florentines favored over Venetians — brought the Senate to threaten and then carry out legal reprisals against the Florentine community.[43] The Bolognese correspondent was Nanni and Bonifazio Gozzadini and Company; the branch was directed by Bonifazio, in Venice at least during the years 1395–99.[44]

Other companies had longer histories, such as the firm created by the Borromei in Venice. Alessandro, the third son of that Filippo Borromei who had been banished from Florence in 1370 and had moved his family to Milan, set himself up in Venice in partnership with the Sienese Domenico d'Andrea, beginning about 1395. At some point, Alessandro's brother Borromeo and the latter's son Galeazzo joined the partnership in Venice, and when this head office began to specialize in foreign exchange, Galeazzo founded branches in Bruges and London, in 1420. Borromeo died first and was succeeded by Alessandro, who died in 1431; in 1436 Galeazzo died, and his place was taken by his brother Antonio in directing the partnership with their associate of many years, Lazzaro di Giovanni. The same Lazzaro fled Venice for debts in 1445. Whether the roots of the firm were deep enough to overcome this crisis and continue to operate is unclear. Alessandro built the family chapel at S. Elena in Venice, and Galeazzo paid for rebuilding at the church of S. Elena itself; both were buried there, as were other members of the family who died over the decades of the company's activity in Venice.[45]

Similarly active in Venice beginning in the 1430s was the "compagnia

[43]ASF, MAP, 133, and de Roover, *Medici Bank,* 40. ASV, SM, reg. 44, fol. 126 (26 September 1399). The threat, not to hear the claims of Florentines before Venetian courts of law, was carried out. Zanobi Gaddi wrote: "Ànno comandato costoro a ongni corte non sia tenuto ragione a niuno fiorentino per fati d'Antonio di Nicholò; sichè se prima si schotea male, ora si farà male in peggio." And again: "Qui non n'è tenuto ragione a' fiorentini . . . ; giterà grandisimo danno l'ordine fato qui." And later still: "Qui non si può usare niuna nostra ragione a corte niuna, senza costà non si provede per altro modo. . . . A noi gita chativisima ragione e a voi anche tocha protesta come a noi." ADP, 712, Gaddi to Florence, 31 December 1399, 10 January and 10 February 1400. Another Giovanni Portinari, di Sandro, became a naturalized citizen in 1372.

[44]De Roover, *Medici Bank,* 40. There is a fascicle of letters to Bonifazio in Venice (1395–99) in Biblioteca dell'Arciginnasio, Bologna, Archivio Gozzadini, no. 58. The family was on the losing side in a struggle with Baldassare Cossa, the future antipope John XXIII, beginning in 1400; that was the year of Datini's sojourn in Bologna, when he was close friends with the Gozzadini.

[45]Florence Edler de Roover, "Borromeo, Galeazzo," in *DBI,* 13 (1971), 47–49. Gerolamo Biscaro, "Il banco Filippo Borromei e compagni di Londra," *Archivio storico lombardo,* a. 40, fasc. 37 (1913): 39–40. The Borromei sued Domenico d'Andrea in 1410; see ASV, GP, Sg, reg. 18, fol. 94vff. Galeazzo's testament was revised in 1436; Antonio Borromei and Lazzaro di Giovanni were still involved in settling his estate in 1441, in a case reflecting far-flung business interests; AC, reg. 3648, pt. 1, fol. 113v (15 June 1436), and pt. 2, fols. 76v–77 (20 January 1441). When Lazzaro di Giovanni fled, the Venice firm had creditors in Bruges, London, Valenza, and Barcelona; Quarantia Criminal, reg. 18, fol. 69v (11 August 1445).

di Vinegia" of Giovanni Rucellai, Florentine merchant banker and humanist. When the partnership was renewed in 1441 (with Giannozzo di Bernardo Manetti, statesman and humanist, Mariotto Banchi, and Giovanni di Francesco della Luna), it had a capital of 12,000 florins. Its declared goals were "to deal in commerce and foreign exchange as well as in the production of silks and other things, and to maintain a house, a shop and a warehouse in Venice." For decades, beginning in 1445, the operation was directed by Giovanfrancesco di Palla Strozzi (of the exiled branch of the family), who was already active in Venice. Giovanni Rucellai records that he himself was on hand in 1451, when Venice expelled the Florentine merchant bankers as a result of Cosimo de' Medici's decision to support Francesco Sforza of Milan against Venice. Business picked up quickly after the war, if the compagnia di Vinegia could report a balanced account of 33,000 ducats to the catasto officials in 1458. In a senatorial deliberation of 1470, where one learns that the Florentine Matteo Baroncelli had asked the pope to excommunicate the factors Filippo Rucellai and Giovanfrancesco Strozzi for defaulting on a debt, the two are called "cives et habitatores" of Venice. Just how much longer the company was active is not known.[46]

A very dynamic company was that of Giovanni and Angelo Baldesi; while the former operated in Florence, his brother administered affairs in Venice from at least 1454 to 1476. Their correspondence and other documents show that they dealt in exchange and especially in the importation of wheat. In 1464 they mediated a payment by five Benedictine abbots of Venice and the area to Pius II; two years later they were involved in a lawsuit with the commercial courts of Florence, Bologna, and Venice regarding an exchange for 12,000 florins. In 1465 Angelo promised to deliver up to 30,000 staia of Calabrian wheat to the Rialto banker Agostino Ziera, who planned to resell it—a deal worth more than 31,000 ducats. A decade later, as we shall see, Angelo formed a partnership in the same sector with Giovanni Lanfredini, factor of the Medici in Venice.[47]

Numerous other Florentine companies can be traced by chance survival of bills of exchange. Thus we know from four drafts in the estate papers of Guglielmo Querini that in the 1430s Bardo Altoviti was the factor in Venice of the firm of Giovanni Panciatichi and Giovanni Portinari and Company and that Nicolò Tommasi represented Cecco Tommasi and

---

[46]Mueller, "Mercanti e imprenditori fiorentini," 53, 58–60. Giovanfrancesco was in Venice in 1440, when he appealed a sentence involving a debt of 1,500 ducats that his father Palla (exiled to Padua after the return of Cosimo) owed the firm of Antonio Borromei e Lazzaro di Giovanni; ASV, Grazie, reg. 24, fol. 5. See also ST, reg. 6, fol. 102v (24 September 1470). The contract of 1441 is in ASF, MAP, filza 89, no. 289; see also Catasto, 817, fols. 207–12.

[47]ASV, S. Giorgio Maggiore, b. 172. Seven letters to Angelo Baldesi in Venice (1458–60) have ended up at the Library of the University of Minnesota in Minneapolis, James Ford Bell Collection, Bell, 1426 fIt, no. 3–4, and 1436 fIt, no. 2–6.

Brothers.[48] Bills preserved today in St. Petersburg reflect the activity in Venice of an aging Luigi Ardinghelli in 1466 and show that Giovanfrancesco Strozzi was represented in 1468 by Piero Bosso. The list could surely grow a great deal longer, especially for the period up to 1451, the year of the expulsion, discussed below.[49]

Concluding this incomplete overview is the rather uncommon case of a "cambista" who was not Florentine or of Florentine origin: Arrighino Panigaruola of Milan, who ran a foreign exchange bank in Venice in the 1430s and 1440s. We know of his activity because he was a correspondent of the Borromei of Bruges and London, in which role he appears in the Borromeo ledger of London and in the ledgers of Andrea Barbarigo. Even though it seems that his operation in Venice was completely independent, he also represented the Milanese company of the Panigaruola. Venice, in fact, was a much more important banking place than Milan, and a big merchant like Marco Serraineri had to run all of his exchange business from Bruges, Antwerp, Florence, and Rome through Venice, where he had numerous correspondents, rather than through Milan, where he was based.[50]

iii. THE "COMPAGNIA DI VINEGIA" OF THE MEDICI BANK

A separate discussion is called for when we come to the Medici bank, primarily because of the kind and amount of information available. As was the case in Florence, the political stature of the family conferred status on the branch in Venice, even though it was not the biggest Florentine opera-

---

[48]ASV, PSM, Citra, b. 271, and below, Chap. 8, sec. vi.

[49]It is worth noting the presence of a family of silk producers, for, even though they were not merchant bankers, they understood high finance. Andrea di Jacopo Arnoldi, who probably founded the firm in Venice, was made a citizen de extra in 1396. Francesco d'Andrea, who reported economic difficulties in the Venice operation to the catasto officials in 1427, proposed in 1430 that Florentines monetize their funded debt—a proposal clearly based on his experience with Venetian banchi di scritta. See Raymond de Roover, "A Florence: Un projet de monetisation de la dette publique au XVe siècle," in *Histoire économique du monde mediterranéen, 1450–1650 (Mélanges Braudel)* (Toulouse, 1973), 511–19. Given their difficulties, the Arnoldi received a reduction of their estimo assessment in Venice from 2,100 lire d'estimo in 1427 to 1,800 lire in 1431 and 1433. Andrea di Francesco was consul of the Florentine community in 1444, when he was imprisoned for insulting an official of the Consoli dei Mercanti "and other nobles of this republic." ASV, AC, reg. 3649, fols. 69v, 70v. In the Florentine tax roll of 1447, Jacopo di Francesco e fratelli are recorded as still residing in Venice, "e là sono citadini e paghano la graveza personale e albitraria in su' loro asercizio." Elio Conti, *L'imposta diretta a Firenze nel Quattrocento (1427–1494),* Istituto storico italiano per il Medio Evo, Studi storici (Rome, 1984), 119 n. 1; Mueller, "Mercanti e imprenditori fiorentini," 52.

[50]Patrizia Mainoni, "Un mercante milanese del primo Quattrocento: Marco Serraineri," *Nuova rivista storica* 59 (1975): 363, and idem, "Milano di fronte a Venezia, un'interpretazione in chiave economica di un rapporto difficile," in *Venezia Milano* (Milan, 1984), 9–24.

tion and certainly did not have a monopoly in the merchant-banking sector of the Rialto.[51]

First to be considered are the predecessors of the better-known Medici bank. By 1385 Vieri di Cambio de' Medici had established a partnership in Venice with Jacopo di Francesco Venturi. When the bank was dissolved, of the three successors, two continued their ties with Venice: Averardo di Francesco worked through the above-mentioned agents Dietifeci and Gozzadini, according to the remaining ledger of 1395; when Giovanni di Bicci de' Medici moved the center of his operations from Rome to Florence in 1397, he immediately began to consider the situation in Venice. In the following year he sent Neri di Cipriano Tornaquinci, a factor in the Rome office, to Venice, where he stayed on as a salaried agent through 1401.[52]

A regular branch was established in March 1402, and Neri was made the first manager. The corpo of the branch firm consisted of 8,000 florins invested by Giovanni di Bicci and Benedetto de' Bardi plus 1,000 florins by Neri Tornaquinci. The branch, like the other Florentine merchant-banking firms, existed primarily for the sake of the business of foreign exchange. This scope is clearly stated in the contract of 1406: the new manager, Giovanni da Gagliano, was instructed as follows: "to remain in Venice and diligently, as is called for, apply himself to the business of exchange, as is our custom, and also to commerce, should we so decide."[53] Successive contracts reasserted this point, often adding some phrase about the necessity that the exchange dealings be licit before God and the Venetian state.[54] Exchange or international banking, in short, was primary, and that was the case down to the directorship of Giovanni Lanfredini, who diversified Medici investments considerably but caused the failure of the branch company in 1477 and was forced to liquidate the operation.

[51]See in general Goldthwaite, "Medici Bank."

[52]Raymond de Roover, "The Antecedents of the Medici Bank: The Banking House of Messer Vieri di Cambio de' Medici," reprinted in his *Business, Banking, and Economic Thought*, 261, 264. Idem, *Medici Bank*, 37–40 (partial analysis of ASF, MAP, 133/1). Jacopo Venturi waged a claim against the estate of a deceased Venetian debtor in his name and that of Vieri di Cambio on 20 January 1384; see ASV, PSM, Ultra, b. 201, commis. Pietro da Molin.

[53]De Roover, *Medici Bank*, 40, 240–41, and in general on the Venice branch, chap. 10. Melis, *Documenti*, 336, doc. 102. On the Bueri brothers, who went to work in Venice during the validity of the 1406 contract, see Raymond de Roover, "Bueri, Gherardo," in *DBI*, 14 (1972), 792–93. Gherardo is known for having tried to found a branch in Lübeck.

[54]In 1420 Giovanni Portinari was to "trafichare in detto trafico in chanbiare, secondo messer Domenedio ne conciederà la grazia e chome si richiede in simele mestiero e traficho, e sopratutto deba fare buoni e liciti contratti e degl'utili che Idio ne concedesse." ASF, MAP, 153, libro segreto 2, fols. 7–8. In 1435 the contract reads again "in chambiare e merchatantie"; ibid., libro segreto 3, fol. 3r–v. Following the Peace of Lodi, Alessandro Martelli was ordered to reestablish the company, the fondaco, and the house in Venice and to dedicate himself to "chanbi reali e contratti leciti e leali merchatantie e cche non sieno proibite agli ordini di Vinegia." MAP, 146, fol. 176r–v (20 January 1455). The formula in 1460, written by Alessandro Martelli, is practically the same (ibid., fols. 183–84).

TABLE 7.2

Managers and Personnel of the Venetian Branch of the Medici Bank, 1398–1481

1398–1406	Neri di Cipriano Tornaquinci	
	Employees:	Andrea di Giovanni del Belaccio (cashier)
		Cristofano di Francesco da Gagliano
		Zanobi di ser Paolo Ricoldi
1406–16	Giovanni di Francesco da Gagliano	
	Employees:	Andrea di Lancelotto
		Francesco (Checco) d'Antonio de' Medici
		Gherardo di Nicola Bueri
		Francesco di Nicola Bueri (from 1410)
		Antonio di Lazzaro Bertini
		Giovanni Bruscolini
		Lotto di Tanino Bozzi (1414–15)
1416–35	Giovanni d'Adoardo Portinari	
	Employees:	Lotto di Tanino Bozzi (junior partner from 1428)
		Antonio di Niccolò Martelli (from 1427)
		Francesco d'Antonio de' Medici
		Paolo di Domenico Guasconi
		Maria Rossa (slave)
1435–48	Lotto di Tanino Bozzi (Tanini)	
	Asst. manager:	Antonio di Niccolò Martelli
	Employees:	Gerardo di Giovanni Portinari (1435–36)
		Francesco Davizi
		Alessandro di Niccolò Martelli
		Pigello Portinari
		Angelo Tani
		Cristofano (servant)
1448–65	Alessandro di Niccolò Martelli	
1466–69	Giovanni d'Oddo Altoviti	
	Employees:	seven
1469–71	(Discontinued)	
1471–80	Giovanni d'Orsino Lanfredini (liquidator, 1477–80)	
	Asst. manager:	Giovambattista Ridolfi
	Factors:	Alessandro Tornabuoni
		Agnolo Stralzi (liquidator)
1481		Piero d'Antonio di Taddeo (liquidator)

Source: de Roover, *Medici Bank*, 44, 95, 240–53, 377–78; for A. Tornabuoni: ASV, GP, Sg, regs. 169, fol. 106 ff., 171, fols. 149v f.

Table 7.2 shows the managers and personnel of the Venice branch, partnership by partnership. It is worth noting that in only six years, 1435–40, we find in Venice five future partners destined to manage branches in the whole Medici network; and there were more later. In other words, Venice served the Medici as a school for future managers and partners, just as would be the case with the Fuggers later in the century. The staff of the Venice branch produced profits that contributed substantially to the total

TABLE 7.3

Capital and Annual Distributed Profits of the "Compagnia di Vinegia" of the Medici Bank, 1398–1481

Dates	Style of the "Compagnia di Vinegia"	Capital		Agio (%)	Profits	Rate (% p.a.)
		du.	fl.[a]			
1398	(Giovanni de' Medici e Co. of Rome)	5,000 9,000	5,225 [9,405]	4.5		
1401					1,720 fl.	18
15.3.1402[b]	Giovanni de' Medici e Co.	[8,681]	9,000	3.7		
1402–6					−1,339 fl.[c]	−15
25.4.1406[b]		8,000				
1.5.1410[b]		8,000	[8,296]			
1406–1415					1,710 fl.	20.5
1416[b]		11,000 +3,000				
23.10.1420[b]	Cosimo e Lorenzo de' Medici e Co.	8,000	8,570	7.1		
1420–34[d]					1,630 fl.	19
15.7.1435[b]		8,000	[8,640]			
1435–40					6,525.5 du.	75
1439					8,000 du.	100
1.11.1441[ef]		8,000	[8,640]	8.0		
1441[b]–48[b]		8,000			4,827.7 du.	60[g]
1449–50		7,000			2,638 du.	38
24.3.1451[e]		7,000	7,700[h]	10.0		
20.1.1455[b]	Pierfrancesco di Lorenzo de' Medici e Co.	14,000				
25.3.1460[b]		15,000				
1461–63					5,959 du.	40
25.3.1465[b]		15,000				
1469	Voluntary liquidation begun					
1471[b]	Pierfrancesco e Giuliano de' Medici e Co.					
1477–?	Insolvency and forced liquidation					

Source: de Roover, Medici Bank, 41, 44, 50, 53, 56, 61, 66–67, 82, 106, 240–53, 393.
[a]De Roover's figures are recorded sometimes as fiorini affiorino (e.g., p. 55), sometimes as both fiorini a fiorino and di suggello. The rising agio between the figures in ducats and those in florins (registered in the next column) parallels closely the rates found in contemporary Florentine sources for the agio of the fiorino di suggello, indicating that these florins are to be considered fiorini a fiorino di suggello. That is also the money of account used in the catasto of 1427, where Agnolo di Zanobi Gaddi gives the agio between ducats and florins as 8 percent ("Ragiono i detti danari di Vinegia 8 per C° meglio che fiorini"), ASF, Catasto, 52, fol. 10, as well as in the quotation of exchange rates. Figures in brackets on the table were calculated by

earnings of the Medici bank as a holding company. That contribution has been quantified as follows:

period	percentage of total
1398–1420	14.9
1420–35	13.1
1435–50	21.8

Except in the first period, Venice was second only to the Rome branch.[55] Table 7.3 shows at a glance the formation of capital and the rate of net profits derived from the Venice branch. It can be seen how the Medici doubled their investment in Venice over the years and how the reorganization of the bank decided upon by Cosimo and Lorenzo during their exile in Venice in 1433–34 brought immediate results—including profits that in one year (1439) went as high as 100 percent.

The story of the exile of Cosimo and Lorenzo in September 1433 has some bearing on the role of the bank in Venice. Lorenzo was assigned to Venice; Cosimo, who had been assigned to Padua, was permitted to join him, thanks to the intercession of Venice. Near the end of the exile the aged Averardo di Francesco, who had been assigned to Naples and had been banished because of his refusal to go there, turned up in Venice to be with his relatives. Averardo's grandson Francesco, through whose correspondence much of this period is known, was put to work in the counting house, copying letters and learning the abacus under the direction of Antonio Martelli, who was about to be named assistant manager. It was clearly a year of slow business. Cosimo dedicated himself to politics and, with the support of Doge Francesco Foscari and Venetian diplomacy, prepared the way

---

[55]De Roover, *Medici Bank*, 47, 55, 69.

---

proportion, the first two using given data of the nearest date, the third and fourth data of the same date. For the fiorino a fiorino di suggello, see Richard A. Goldthwaite and Giulio Mandich, *Studi sulla moneta fiorentina (secoli XIII–XVI)* (Florence, 1994).

[b]Dates of company contracts.

[c]Total net loss of 5,356 fl. over four years under Neri Tornaquinci. Capital in 1402 is given (p. 41) as 8,000 fl. (7,716 du.) for the Medici plus 1,000 fl. for Tornaquinci, for a total of 9,000 fl. or (by proportion) 8,680.5 du.

[d]In 1427 there were an additional 8,000 du. on deposit from the Rome branch. In 1431 profits increased by 50 percent over the previous year (p. 53).

[e]Dates of balance sheets.

[f]The Medici of Florence invested 7,000 du. or 7,560 fl. (an agio of 8.0%) in the branch, plus a sovracorpo of 6,587 fl., for a total of 14,147 fl. (pp. 61, 249). Presumably the managers in Venice added 1,000 du. as they had in 1435.

[g]Even counting the years 1446–47, in which no profits were distributed because of losses of 8,100 du. in drafts on Barcelona (p. 249).

[h]Alessandro Martelli, managing partner since 1448, made no investment in the capital account until 1455, when he contributed 2,000 ducats. Equity of the partnership was falsified in initial balances prepared for the catasto of 1457; see de Roover, *Medici Bank*, 73, 423 n. 92.

for the return from exile, while Lorenzo dedicated himself to the affairs of the bank. For almost exactly one year the Venice branch constituted the "casa madre" of the whole Medici bank. It was during that year that the two brothers excogitated the reorganization of the bank that was put into effect soon after they returned to Florence (in October 1434). The positive results were almost immediate, and the Venice branch, as can be seen from table 7.3, flourished under the new direction. Upon their departure, Cosimo offered Venice a loan of 30,000 ducats for the current war against the Visconti, as a sign of gratitude for the help and hospitality received.[56]

It is unnecessary to repeat the rest of the history of the Medici branch in Venice, so well recounted by Raymond de Roover from the point of view of the enterprise. The last years, however, those covering the liquidation of 1469, the reopening under the direction of Giovanni d'Orsino Lanfredini in 1471, and the final liquidation, treated in a few lines by de Roover, merit more careful attention, for the story ends on a rather different note than that on which de Roover concludes.[57] First of all, Lanfredini was no newcomer to Venice; his father had been active there earlier in the century.[58] Giovanni himself, according to Sanudo, was a citizen and had many connections ("compari") in Venice; his son Orsino was an "original citizen," having been born in Venice of a citizen (a condition confirmed by the Senate in 1474). In 1463 Lanfredini represented Giovanni Canigiani in a lawsuit before a Venetian court,[59] and in the same decade, on orders from the Medici, he must have inaugurated, as Medici factor, the construction of a "small but beautiful library" for the Benedictines at S. Giorgio Maggiore, conceivably in fulfillment of a promise made by Cosimo during his exile long before.

As we shall see below (Chap. 10), Lanfredini invested heavily in the importation of wheat in that decade. He imported wheat for the Venetian state as Medici factor, sometimes in partnership with the Florentine Angelo Baldesi, in 1475–78. But he also used the port of Venice to import wheat for foreign powers. There is one example, from 1476, when Leonardo Botta, ambassador of Milan, contracted with him in Venice for 40,000 staia of wheat from Apulia at £4 10s per staio. The ambassador must have previously cleared the deal with the Signoria, for to import wheat to Venice for reexportation required a special license. That was a large contract, worth

[56]Mueller, "Mercanti e imprenditori fiorentini," 35–38.

[57]*Medici Bank,* 253, 367; he incorrectly dated the "liquidation" 1479–81; as we shall see, it took at least a decade longer.

[58]Orsino Lanfredini was client of the Priuli bank in 1423 and sued a Venetian nobleman in the following year; ASV, GP, Sg, reg. 34, fol. 19v.

[59]*Le vite dei dogi,* 1:173 (where the library is described as "picola, ma polita"); Mueller, "Mercanti e imprenditori fiorentini," 37 n. 19. For the mention of Lanfredini as representing Canigiani, see ASV, GP, Sg, reg. 158, fols. 126–27v (15 February 1474).

more than 29,000 ducats.[60] The wholesale wheat market was a notoriously risky one, for prices tended to change rapidly according to supply, and it is not impossible that Lanfredini began encountering problems precisely with his investments in this sector.

In fact, Venetian sources show that the last years of the administration of Lanfredini involved, not a voluntary liquidation of the branch, as de Roover wrote, but outright bankruptcy. On 28 August 1477 the Venetian Signoria accorded the company an unlimited safe-conduct, clearly negotiated in the absence of the persons responsible, who must have fled to the mainland to avoid arrest and court suits. The safe-conduct involved a moratorium, for the Medici could sue but not be sued, that is, as one debtor exclaimed, the branch "could collect from its debtors without honoring its own debts."[61] Finally, in 1481, Venetian creditors of the branch convinced the Senate to apply a limit to the validity of the safe-conduct, so that they could sue the Medici with the same freedom with which the Medici branch was able to sue its debtors. The Senate gave the branch six months to liquidate affairs with its creditors, after which time it would no longer be protected from lawsuits.[62]

Clearly, Lanfredini was the principal liquidator after 1477, as partner and manager of the branch, even though Alessandro Tornabuoni was sent to the scene for a time. In March 1480 Lanfredini sent his factor Giovambattista Ridolfi, along with Lorenzo Rucellai, to Florence, Rome, and Na-

[60]BNF, mss. II.V.13, fol. 159r–v (7 September 1476). Bartolomeo da Como also signed the contract, together with Ambassador Botta and Lanfredini (who signed for Lorenzo and Giuliano de' Medici, as well as for himself, "come comesso e compagno"). Payment was to be made in Venetian gold ducats; but Lanfredini agreed to accept up to half the sum in "fiorini largi de peso" as ducats, as long as the Milanese paid an agio of 2 soldi di piccoli per fiorino largo; in other words, the full-weight fiorino largo of Florence was rated — by the Medici branch itself — 122 soldi in Venice, against 124 soldi for the ducat. Risk capital was to be had in discretionary deposits accepted by the branch, like the one for 7,000 ducats made by the Cypriot Guiotin de Nores in 1474; ibid., fols. 150v–51r.

[61]Several cases were heard by the Giudici di Petizion. See, for example, ASV, GP, Sg, reg. 169, fols. 106v–7v, a case against Domenico di Piero for a pawn, a brooch worth 600 ducats (16 March 1479), where the representative of the branch explained the changed name or "style" of the partnership after the death of Piero and Giuliano de' Medici — a change seen as a trick aimed at facilitating collection while avoiding payment ("soto diversi nomi poder schoder e non pagar"); the sentence was canceled at the end of the month at the request of Alessandro Tornabuoni after an out-of-court settlement had been reached. See also ibid., reg. 170, fols. 146v–47v (13 March 1480), a claim for 1,000 ducats owed by the patriarch Antonio Zane; and reg. 171, fols. 149v–50 (10 November 1480), registration of an accord reached in arbitration between Alessandro Tornabuoni, representing the Medici, and the nobleman Giacomo Polani.

[62]The act of the Signoria is summarized in the Senate deliberation: ASV, ST, reg. 8, fol. 127 (9 August 1481). The decision reads: "El sia admoniti i factori over negotiatori de' dicti Medici, che qui al presente si atrovano, che fin a mexi 6 proximi debino haver composte le cosse sue con i suo creditori."

ples to plead his case and to collect his credits. First they were to show the balance sheets to "il Magnifico" and the managers in Florence and Rome, Francesco Sassetti and Giovanni Tornabuoni, and ask advice. Lanfredini's position was defensive, to show that his insolvency was not his fault but that of other branches that did not pay their debts. Here it will suffice to mention just some of the points made in the "ricordo." The branch was owed money by the government of Florence (for the condotta of the duke of Urbino and the Ufficio de' Ribelli); by the lord of Rimini; by Luigi Guicciardini; by an unnamed Veronese, who had been sentenced in Florence; for drafts from the Bruges branch, then falling due; and, finally, for malmsey wine delivered to Pisa. Furthermore, the branch had in the warehouse, under its control, 160 *miara* of olive oil ordered by Francesco Morosini and 120 *miara* ordered by Doge Andrea Vendramin, who was still involved in the management of his huge soap industry. Credits with the branch in Naples were large, including a loan of nearly 4,000 ducats which Lanfredini had supplied by borrowing on the exchange ("gli tenemo . . . in su' chanbi"); despite his having done a favor for another Medici branch, he was worried he would be saddled with the costs of the loan. The biggest open accounts were with Apulia, probably for wheat as well as for oil. The thrust of the orders given to Ridolfi, in sum, was to solicit payment and demonstrate the good faith of the Venice branch.[63] But it was in Venice that the situation precipitated, unexpectedly.

On 20 July 1480 Giovanni Lanfredini was arrested by the Council of Ten for revealing state secrets to Lorenzo de' Medici. Given the delicate nature of the accusation, a special addition, or Zonta, was elected to deliberate with the Council of Ten, and a special "collegio" was named to interrogate and, if necessary, torture him. He was kept in a special secret cell. Finally, on 11 August he was banished from Venice and all its territories, but he was given two months, while remaining in prison, to settle his affairs (a motion to grant him house arrest failed). He, his son, and any heirs were stripped of Venetian citizenship. Clearly he did not have a very free hand in seeing to affairs of the Medici bank before actual banishment; he was replaced in September, even though as late as December in Florence he was still called "partner and manager" of the Venetian branch.[64]

[63]BNF, mss. II.V.13, fols. 167r–68v (29 March 1480).

[64]Sanudo, *Le vite dei dogi*, 1:173–74 and n. 286. Sanudo called Lanfredini Medici factor and cambista ("fator d'i Medici . . . et stava fermo in questa Terra su cambij"). Sanudo's information was taken from ASV, Consiglio dei Dieci, Miste, reg. 20, fols. 13v, 14–15, 17v–18r. The secret seems to have involved the arrest and exile of Gerolamo Lando, titular patriarch of Constantinople (Sanudo, 1:172). The Ten were not so concerned about the secret ("notitia") itself as for problems of diplomacy ("per celar la pratica tra nui e Lorenzo"); see reg. 20, fol. 14v, letter to Zaccaria Barbaro, ambassador to the Curia. The sentence (ibid., fol. 17v) left in doubt whether Giovanni Lanfredini had actually received a citizenship privilege or not but so formulated the condemnation as to cover that eventuality. See also de Roover, *Medici Bank*, 252–53 and notes.

The liquidation dragged on for years. One company that refused to reconcile itself to its losses was the fraterna of Andrea Capello and Brothers. The Capello had a credit dating from 1477 of nearly 2,500 ducats for a shipment of 200 *miara* of Apulian olive oil, plus a bank loan of 300 ducats and other credits contracted in the years 1480–85, when the brothers were partners in the Rialto bank styled "Ser Tomà Lippomano e Ser Andrea Capello e fradelli." None of the credits had ever been paid because of the insolvency of the Medici branch in the same year. In 1486–87 Andrea Capello wrote at least five letters to Lorenzo the Magnificent asking for repayment, to which he seems never to have received a reply. He even obtained a court order at the Curia del Forestier, communicated to the Sei della Mercanzia in Florence, citing Lorenzo to appear in Venice on 8 August 1486, all to no avail. The letters reflect just how frustrated Capello was with Lorenzo and the latter's former factors at the Venice branch. Finally, in January 1488, the parties came to terms. Paolo Antonio Soderini, Florentine ambassador to Venice, signed an accord in the name of two factors sent by Lorenzo whereby the Medici would pay a total debt of nearly 4,000 ducats within one year — but in Calabrian wheat, at the risk of the Capello fraterna. On the Venetian side, the accord was signed by Andrea Capello (the document is in his hand) and by the wealthy and prestigious statesman Zorzi Corner. Whether the tenacity of the Capello brothers, for a time bankers on the Rialto, was matched by other Venetian creditors of the Medici branch is not known, but others also reached agreements. The failure of the branch in Venice was just part of the progressive decline of the economic position of the Medici bank as a whole.[65]

Venice maintained good relations with the Medici, however, even after Piero di Lorenzo de' Medici and his family were exiled from Florence in 1494. For a few days after being expelled, they were hosted in the palace of the Lippomano bankers, and in the following year the Signoria, in the

---

[65]Five letters are extant because copies had to be supplied to the capi of the Council of Ten. The letter of 26 May 1486 recalls that the initial deal had been made by Vettor and Gerolamo, Andrea Capello's sons, and warns Lorenzo that if he treated them that way, their friendship would suffer ("muterà nostra amicizia . . . [se] siamo tratadi a questo modo"); on the Medici side of the deal were Agnolo Stralzi and Giovanni Lanfredini (see, for example, the letter of 24 March 1487). ASV, Capi del Consiglio dei Dieci, Notatorio, reg. 1, a loose sheet at fol. 57v and fols. 116, 118–20 at the end of the volume. The final accord is in BNF, mss. II.V.13, fol. 177r–v (2 January 1488). The next day Soderini came to terms on Medici debts owed to Priamo and Andrea da Lezze (ibid., fol. 179); and a "ricordo" of June addressed to the factor Domenico Mati, who had been sent to Venice along with Agnolo degli Agli, lists the remaining credits of four other Rialto banks as well as other creditors (ibid., fols. 185–86). On 4 October 1488 the Medici admitted that they still owed Capello 1,300 ducats, after having delivered large amounts of wheat (ibid., fol. 189r–v). For the bank partnership, from which the Capello withdrew in 1485, at least from the style of the company, see Ugo Tucci, "Cappello, Andrea," *DBI*, 18 (1975), 738–40. In 1486 Capello referred to a six-year-old credit of "lo bancho nostro," and in 1488 to another "che è creditor el bancho di Lipomano e Chapelli."

"secret back room" of the Lippomano bank, gave Piero's secretary a loan of 5,000 ducats — as "surety" for which, he wrote, he left his son, guest of the Lippomano. The hospitality of the Lippomano family toward the Medici in times of trouble subsequently (Giuliano and Piero were guests at the family palace on Murano in April and September 1499 respectively) was remembered as late as 1515 by the Medici pope Leo X and rewarded with a grant of 4,000 ducats — much needed by the former Rialto bankers, pressed by creditors ever since their own bankruptcy in 1499.[66]

iv. THE FLORENTINE COMMUNITY IN THE LATER QUATTROCENTO

The presence in Venice of Cosimo and Lorenzo in 1433–34 had clearly enhanced the stature of the Florentine community as a whole. The next seventeen years mark the high point of power and prestige of the Florentine community in Venice.

When in 1451 Cosimo decided definitively to side with Francesco Sforza against former ally Venice, the Signoria moved immediately to expel all Florentines as enemy aliens. The process of definition of just who was to be considered Florentine under this proclamation was tense and agitated. In the end, only those whose profits went to support the Florentine cause — insurance underwriters, long-distance merchants, and exchange dealers — were actually expelled. That meant the staff of the Medici branch, headed by Alessandro Martelli, the managers of the Rucellai bank, Giovanfrancesco Strozzi and Filippo Rucellai, and others whose names we do not know, in short, the kingpins of the Venetian foreign exchange market. The suspension of business involved losses for both sides. Large losses on the part of Florentine merchants were lamented by Giovanni Rucellai and Domenico Boninsegni; news of the expulsion caused market values of Monte commune stock in Florence to fall from 30 to 20. Gianozzo Manetti, who wrote to Alfonso of Naples, Venice's ally, that the assets of Florentines in Venice and Naples involved — in cash — 150,000 and 200,000 ducats respectively, made it clear that the withdrawal from the local economies of such imposing sums by the expelled bankers would hurt Venice and Naples as much as Florence. Pasquale Malipiero, the future doge, when he was ambassador to the Curia, confessed to Manetti that the expulsion was the biggest mistake the Venetians had ever committed; Vespasiano da Bistici, who reported the conversation, says that Malipiero's conciliatory message to Cosimo, carried by Manetti, brought an indignant reply that closed the door to negotiations for the

---

[66]See Sanudo, *Diarii*, 2:639, 1288, and 19:424. ASV, Commemoriali, reg. 18, fols. 51v, 52v, and *LCR*, 6:12–13, no. 28. The loan to Piero's secretary was made "in camera secreta banchi Lippamanorum in Rivoalto."

time being.[67] As soon as the Peace of Lodi was signed (9 April 1454), however, the Florentine merchant bankers were back on the Rialto and business returned to normal — or almost to normal.[68]

During the war, the exchange fairs in Geneva had probably benefited from the exclusion of Venice from the traditional exchange circuits. The very institution of the exchange fairs, which in the 1460s moved from Geneva to Lyons, probably constituted strong competition for the role of Venice in the interests of the Florentine cambisti. The calendar of the fairs, four per year, was fixed and perfectly predictable, thus making the regularity of annual demand on the Rialto a much less useful factor in loans made on exchange and rechange. This may be a partial explanation for the reduction of the Florentine community in Venice in the later Quattrocento.[69] Another factor was the rise of the Fugger company of Augsburg, which quickly dominated the bullion market in bullion-hungary Venice and became involved in the exchange market, as well. Finally, the failure and liquidation of the Medici branch, which had always been a pole of attraction, probably had a strongly negative impact on the Florentine presence in the city.[70]

What happened to the Florentine community of merchant bankers after the departure of the Medici and the Rucellai banks around 1480 cannot yet be discerned. Two members failed in the 1480s.[71] The confraternity, or "scuola," continued to function, but its position weakened. In 1489, when Matteo Cini was guardiano, it was said that the scuola at the Frari was "threatened with ruin" but that there was no money for repairs owing to a

---

[67]"Il maggiore errore che avessino mai fatto i Viniziani si era d'avergli cacciati da Vinegia"; Malipiero "aveva commessione da quella Signoria d'offerire a' Fiorentini piena commessione d'acconciare le cose come eglino volessino." Cosimo replied to Manetti "che rispondesse che i Fiorentini non volevano che di questo accordo si parlasse." See Francesca Trivellato, "La missione diplomatica a Venezia del fiorentino Giannozzo Manetti a metà Quattrocento," *SV,* n.s., 28 (1994): 203–35.

[68]Mueller, "Mercanti e imprenditori fiorentini," 56–60. For Boninsegni and the quotation of Monte shares, see Conti, *L'imposta diretta,* 35; for the return of the Medici, de Roover, *Medici Bank,* 251; for the return of the Rucellai-Strozzi bank, which in the meantime had retired to Ferrara, see Michele Cassandro, ed., *Il libro giallo di Ginevra della compagnia fiorentina di Antonio Della Casa* (Florence, 1976), 462–63, 480, 492–93, 589, and tables 52–53.

[69]Cassandro expressed surprise that there were so few exchange operations transacted with Venice in a ledger covering 1453–54, having failed to consider the impact of the war and the mutual expulsions; *Il libro giallo,* 118–19, and, on the fairs, 17, 53–57. See also de Roover, *Medici Bank,* chap. 12.

[70]For the replacement of the Florentine merchant bank as a type by that of the German mining entrepreneurs, see Jean-François Bergier, "From the Fifteenth Century in Italy to the Sixteenth Century in Germany: A New Banking Concept?" in *Dawn of Modern Banking,* 105–29.

[71]Angelo Serragli was granted a safe-conduct in 1488 to return to Venice and reach an accord with his creditors; see ASV, ST, reg. 10, fol. 124v. Bartolomeo Benincasa defaulted with liabilities of 3,700 ducats in 1490 and had trouble reaching a concordat with his creditors; see ibid., reg. 11, fol. 29v.

decline in membership ("pro diminutione ipsorum mercatorum florentinorum et schole in his partibus"). In 1504, when it was directed by Alessandro de' Nerli (guardiano), Matteo Cini, and Pietro Corboli, the scuola was threatened with excommunication in a suit brought by the Franciscans before the papal legate on account of the state of the "building and chapel," which by then was "demolished and devastated." The Florentines countered that they were unable to meet the costs of repairs alone.[72]

The community had shrunk, but Florentines had not abandoned the Rialto. The principal exchange dealer in the last decade of the fifteenth century was Giovanni Frescobaldi, related by marriage to the de' Nerli. After Giovanni's death his brother, Filippo (or Giovanni Filippo), was accused of and sentenced in 1498 for lending at usury in grand style, for a total of 55,800 ducats at 12 percent interest, with the intermediation of the Jew Aaron; the same charge was made against Bartolo de' Nerli, while Pietro Corsini was fined for lending at usury to the Malatesta of Rimini. Very likely the credit market was open to such illicit dealings, since the precarious situation of the Rialto banks was already visible and the Garzoni and Lippomano failures lay just around the corner. Actually, it was the Florentine community and especially de' Nerli, factor of the Frescobaldi firm, which helped force the Garzoni bank to its knees by withdrawing tens of thousands of ducats in the weeks before the crash — perhaps in retaliation both for the condemnation for usury and for Venice's support of the Pisan revolt against Florence (see above, Chap. 6). The third person who represented the "nation" before the legate, Pietro Corboli, was also an exchange banker, active in Venice for many years. His firm failed, with liabilities estimated at 80,000 ducats, in 1518.[73]

[72]Mueller, "Mercanti e imprenditori fiorentini," 30–32. It should be recalled that the century ended with Venice in a close military alliance with Pisa in its revolt against Florence, 1497–99; and in 1500 reprisals were announced against Florentines in Venice for nonpayment of an installment of 15,000 ducats on the reparation payments fixed in the peace treaty. See Romanin, *Storia documentata,* 5:105–7. Pietro Corboli, "che habita in questa Terra," represented Florence's position to the Signoria, before the Senate decided to take the side of Pisa; the doge, in responding to him, addressed him by his Christian name, meaning he must have been a well-known personage in Venice. Romanin, *Storia documentata,* 5:86–87, and Malipiero, *Annali,* 427–28.

[73]For the scuola, see ASV, S. Maria dei Frari, reg. 7, fols. 9–11v (20 May 1489) and 13v (30 June 1504). Luca Pacioli, in his tract on double-entry bookkeeping of 1494, gives an example of exchange handled at the bank of Giovanni Frescobaldi in Venice; see *Trattato di partita doppia,* 92–93. For the trials of Frescobaldi, de' Nerli, and a Corsini for extortion on loans, see ASV, AC, reg. 3658, fols. 198r–v (10 December 1498) and 203v (7 March 1499); see also Sanudo, *Diarii,* 2:322, 505, 510. Sanudo, when recounting the exploits of eight Florentines who dressed for Carneval as seahorses, mentions that they were led by Bartolo de' Nerli, son-in-law of Giovanni Frescobaldi (1:874). For the case against Giovanni Filippo Frescobaldi, see Sanudo, *Diarii,* 2:322 (10 January 1500); for the Corboli failure, 26:17, 20, 27. Luca Pacioli mentioned the presence of the following Florentines at his lecture on Euclid at Venice on 11 August 1508: Matteo Cini, Nicolò Corboli, Bernardo Rucellai and his son Giovanni, and Francesco Rosselli the cosmographer. See Nardi, "La scuola di Rialto," 117.

Other families arrived, if at a much slower pace than a century earlier. The famous Salviati bank, for example, established a branch in Venice perhaps as early as the 1530s. By the middle of the sixteenth century there was enough of a revival of the Florentine community to call for a renewal and reform of the statute of the confraternity of San Giovanni Battista (the official Florentine version is dated 1548, the Venetian copy 1556).[74] Judging from the survival of Florentine account books, however, it would not be until the last third of the century that merchant-banking companies, such as the Arrighi, Strozzi, Riccardi, Tornaquinci, and Galli, would return to Venice in large numbers, once again principally as exchange experts, this time in connection with the Genoese fairs. A parallel study of Venetian notarial records, on the other hand, would reveal the broader base of the revived community and permit a more accurate chronological reconstruction.[75]

[74]Mueller, "Mercanti e imprenditori fiorentini," 32 n. 5.

[75]Dozens of account books of the later sixteenth century have been identified and recorded in a database by Richard A. Goldthwaite, who noted their foreign branches. A hint of even earlier activity in Venice of the Salviati comes from a lawsuit. Benedetto Salviati and Company made an eight-day loan to a Venetian in February 1474, in the bank of Andrea Barbarigo "Broca"; ASV, GP, Sg, reg. 159, fol. 105r–v. Gigi Corazzol reports that the archival series Notarile, Atti, for the later sixteenth century is brimming with Florentine operators in Venice; for the example of Florentine exchange brokers, see his "Varietà notarile: Scorci di vita economica e sociale," in *Storia di Venezia,* 6 (Rome, 1994), 775. See also Renzo Pecchioli, "Uomini d'affari fiorentini a Venezia nella seconda metà del Cinquecento," in his *Dal "mito" di Venezia alla "ideologia" americana* (Venice, 1983).

8

EXCHANGE AND THE
MONEY MARKET

i. INTRODUCTION

ONCERNING EXCHANGE THE Ragusan merchant Benedetto Cotrugli had this to say in the mid-fifteenth century: "It is a delicate
invention, a condiment of all things mercantile, as necessary to
commerce as air is to the human body." If exchange was the "condiment" of
commerce in the commodities market, it was the very staple of the money
market. The bill of exchange was a credit instrument, at the same time that
it served as a means of transferring assets and balancing foreign accounts
without having to ship specie. But it was a complicated instrument; as
Cotrugli went on to say, "Exchange is a most subtle activity to investigate."[1]
One can only agree.

In the discussion that follows, no attempt at completeness in dealing
with the "subtlety" of exchange will be made. The bill of exchange was—
and is—many things to many people. The most authoritative historical
research done on the bill remains that by Raymond de Roover, in a dozen
or more articles and in several books.[2] His work was admittedly rather

[1]"Cambio è gientile trovato ed è quasi uno elemento et condimento di tucte le cose mercantili, senza lo quale, come l'humana conpositione senza li elementi essere non può, così la
mercantia sanza il cambio. . . . Il cambio è una induxtria subtilissima a investigare et difficile a
imitarla et però ci vuole saldo capo a trafficarlo, et tucto dipende dal bene intendere et che così
sia." *Il libro dell'arte di mercatura*, ed. Ugo Tucci (Venice, 1992), 165–66.

[2]See the bibliography in his *Business, Banking, and Economic Thought*. See also Giovanni
Cassandro, "Vicende storiche della lettera di cambio," critical of de Roover, and "Breve storia
della cambiale," both reprinted in his *Saggi di storia del diritto commerciale* (Naples, 1976), 29–
123, 395–423. For a useful summary, see John H. Munro, "Wechsel," in *Von Aktie bis Zoll: Ein
historisches Lexikon des Geldes,* ed. Michael North (Munich, 1995), 413–16.

insistent and repetitive, but efforts to disprove him, on the technical side, have simply failed (see below, n. 63). No one denied — or denies — the importance of the bill in transferring funds necessary for the payment of goods in long-distance commerce. It is essential to understand, however, that experts in exchange, especially Florentines, used the bill of exchange from the very beginning as the major instrument for extending short-term credit. Thus the bill became the very basis of the money market, or, better, of each and every major money market or "banking place" (as de Roover called them) in the European network, for the cambisti extended credit locally, moved assets about by bill of exchange, and calculated the rate of interest on their loans on the basis of pairs of rates of foreign exchange.

This chapter focuses on the crucial role that Venice played in the international money market monopolized by the Florentines. The technical part of the discussion presents nothing new in itself; it leans heavily on traditional explanations provided long ago by de Roover and by Giulio Mandich. While de Roover's analyses have become, willy-nilly, a generally accepted part of historiography, Mandich's contributions have been quite ignored, perhaps because of their often exasperating technicality, but wrongly so. Here the emphasis will be placed on the seasonality of exchange in Venice and thus on the predictability of peaks and troughs in the rates of exchange quoted there — an important factor, since the profitability or the cost of a loan depended upon pairs of ever oscillating exchange rates. The predictability of demand for money on the Rialto is the major reason why Venice was chosen for the classic contracts of rechange: in the fourteenth century, that between Venice and Florence (later called "cambium ad Venetias"), in practice a one-month loan, and that between Venice and Bruges or London, in practice four- and six-month loans respectively, which replaced the shorter-term loan in the early fifteenth century. It will not come as a surprise, then, when we see that the cases studied by de Roover to explain the mechanism of rechange hinge on Venice; the same is true of those elaborated by Mandich, who pushed our knowledge of the contract back by nearly a century. Concrete cases bridging two centuries will be discussed, in order to clarify the nature of the contract and the role of the Rialto.

The debate among theologians and lawyers whether rechange (or reexchange) was licit in light of the church's usury doctrine has been studied by various scholars, foremost among them — once again — Raymond de Roover, whose position, namely, that the bill was used as a widely accepted means of circumventing the ecclesiastical prohibition of usury and that interest was "hidden" in the exchange, has often been contested. This topic and the controversy surrounding it is avoided here, except as regards Venice specifically. The two unpublished tracts that are analyzed (in sec. viii, below) do not reveal new lines of argumentation; what is of interest is that they are born in the Venetian environment, are commissioned by Venetians and by persons close to the money market of the Rialto, and concern the most popular forms of rechange employed in the mid-fifteenth century, those between Venice and Bruges or London.

The chapter ends with an analysis of the operations of the Priuli fraterna in Venice and London in the first years of the sixteenth century. The fortunate survival of two account books, kept in the same years in each of the two cities, makes it possible to bring to light a very complex mix of drafts, remittances, and shipments of specie between the two capitals and adds a new dimension to our understanding of commercial and financial contacts in that period.

Licit or illicit in the eyes of lender or borrower, of jurist or moralist, judged as disguised or undisguised usury, the bill of exchange was used daily for centuries by merchant bankers as a way of lending money and by merchants and nonmerchants alike as a way of borrowing money. Some businessmen were concerned about the ethical side; others were not. Writers of the traditional merchant manuals, for example, took it all in stride as simply a technical mechanism; Benedetto Cotrugli is an exception because he mixes concern with information—in fact, his manual is more ethical than informative on the matter of exchange. Even such hardened Florentine merchant bankers as Giovanni di Bicci and Cosimo de' Medici asked help (respectively) of Popes Martin V, a Roman, and Eugenius IV, a Venetian, to clear their consciences ("per iscarire de la nostra cocienza") regarding the matter of lending money. In both instances, their qualms of conscience were quieted with the modest contribution of 350 ducats toward the repair of churches in Rome. Giovanni Rucellai built into the partnership contract of his "compagnia di Vinegia," which was heavily involved in lending on rechange, a cut of 2 percent of gross revenues "per l'amor di Dio," and the accounts presented to the Catasto Office in 1458 contain an entry for the poor ("Poveri di Dio").[3]

Regardless of the church's teaching on usury, however, rechange presented certain advantages that guaranteed its popularity. It was, in practice, a functional, short-term, interest-bearing note. Its duration, defined by the usance on the particular kind chosen, went from a minimum of one month to a maximum of six months. Furthermore, when the obligation fell due, it was self-liquidating; but the parties to the loan-via-exchange could agree to renew it for one or more "returns." Borrowing on renewed rechange operations was called "stare in su cambi" or "stare su interessi" in lawsuits and commercial letters.[4]

[3]See Cotrugli, *Il libro,* 199–200, a source completely overlooked by scholars interested in such matters. Similarly overlooked is the Medici solution, for which see George Holmes, "How the Medici Became the Pope's Bankers," in *Florentine Studies,* ed. Nicolai Rubinstein (London, 1968), 380. For Rucellai, see above, Chap. 7, n. 46.

[4]Examples are myriad. Omobono de' Bugni, son of one of the wealthiest men in Venice but fallen upon bad times, borrowed nearly 3,000 ducats from Domenico di Monaldi, partner of

The principal of a loan would remain the same on each return if the borrower was capable of paying the interest; otherwise, interest due could be added to the principal on the next renewal. A borrower who was unable to repay the principal at maturity and was forced continually to renew the drafts when they fell due might well complain of being "gnawed to the bone by usury and interest."[5] The fact that "interesse"—the precise term most used by contemporaries in the context of loans on exchange—was not fixed at the time of the contract but fluctuated according to uncertain future market rates provided some protection against condemnation by the church, which did not countenance fixed-interest loans. The direction of fluctuation, however, was largely foreseeable, especially in Venice, and this reduced the risk of loss. Exchange, finally, was extremely sensitive to variations in market factors, and interest on loans tied to it quickly reflected those changes. Profits accruing to merchant bankers consisted not only of interest on their own loans but also of commissions—at the rate of ½ or 1 percent—charged for drawing or remitting for others.

In Venice, the way to acceptance of rechange was probably prepared by a certain similarity the contract had with a typically Venetian credit instrument, the local colleganza. That contract, as we have seen, tied interest to a market rate that would be in force when it matured, a rate that could not be known precisely at the time the contract was made, and this uncertainty assured its legitimacy. The local colleganza required the intervention of a notary, however, whereas in exchange a broker sufficed, and his fee was much lower than that charged by a notary.

In a loan on rechange, the rate of interest was not expressed directly by the rate of exchange between two moneys quoted in the city in which the loan was made. One had to know also the rate quoted at maturity (usance) in the city abroad for which the draft was made out, since interest was calculated by subtracting the rate of exchange on the outgoing draft ("an-

---

the firm of Alessandro Borromei, and assented to paying him "quel costo che seguirà dei diti denari sui cambii e la so provision"; he had to "stay on the exchange" for nearly two years, for which he owed about 12 percent interest. ASV, GP, Sg, reg. 27, fol. 37v. The same company lent Nicolò Adoldo 250 ducats in 1401 "que tanto tempore steterunt super cambiis" with Florence, that the sum due was 287 ducats; the loan was secured on jewelry. Ibid., regs. 20, fol. 109, and 32, fols. 32v–36. A Venetian nobleman lent a shipowner 800 ducats, with the right to draw the sum and keep it "super cambiis et recambiis per omnem partem," especially with Bruges, "et secutus sit multas expensas et interesse"; the lender was made beneficiary of an insurance policy, as surety. Ibid., reg. 46, fol. 77. In 1454 another wealthy merchant fallen upon bad times was forced to borrow on the exchange to feed his family: "diu stetit et continue stat super cambiis cum incredibili interesse et detrimento suo." ST, reg. 3, fol. 133.

[5]In a long brief regarding his debts of twenty years earlier, Giovanni Lio di ca' Ursiolo, in litigation with the estate of Lorenzo Bembo, assured the court that his factor knew "chomo i chanbii e le ussure chontinuamente me magnava e rossegava fin a susso le osse, mi e i mie fioli, e de tuti questi datii et interessi el dito fator fo avixado"; ASV, GP, Sg, reg. 70, bound between fols. 11 and 12.

data") from that of the redraft ("ritorno"). Since all that the parties to a loan really needed to know in order to make the calculation was the rate quoted abroad upon maturity of the draft, it made little practical difference to them whether bills were actually sent, with instructions to redraw; it was sufficient for the foreign correspondent merely to report the rate current abroad on the day of maturity of the would-be draft. This led to the invention of various forms of "dry" and fictitious exchange, which maintained the advantages of exchange while simplifying procedures and reducing transactions costs. In one variety, the bill would actually be sent but with instructions, or an understanding, not to accept it; that way it returned automatically for collection, now at a higher rate, but with added charges of the notary for the formal protest. As long as a bill was actually sent, one of the parties to the bill might have the intention of transferring assets; otherwise, if a bill did not feed the currents of trade, it was considered "dry" (cambio secco, cambium siccum). The "pactum de ricorsa" of the seventeenth century was simply a further refinement by which a bill drawn on a fair was automatically redrawn at rates established by fair officials. In the most fictitious form of exchange, the rate of the redraft — and thus the rate of interest — was fixed at the time the loan contract was made and the bill was never sent; this was exchange in name only.[6] Some lenders insisted on surety, real (usually merchandise) or personal, as becomes clear from extant bills and from lawsuits brought in commercial court against defaulting debtors or cantankerous creditors; in this manner, with the avoidance of all risk of loss, no matter what formal type of exchange contract had been chosen for the loan, the last fig leaf of commercial exchange and thus legitimacy dropped.[7]

Most of the technical apparatus concerning the bill market and rates of exchange in Venice during the years covered by the letters extant in the archive of Francesco di Marco Datini, from late 1383 to early 1411, has been relegated to Appendix C, below. There one will find the methods used for quoting exchange rates between Venice and eleven other European cities and statistical elaborations of the data extracted from the letters.

[6]See Reinhold C. Mueller, "Ricorsa" and "Trockenwechsel," in North, *Von Aktie bis Zoll,* 343–44, 398–99. See also M. M. Postan, "Credit in Medieval Trade," reprinted in *Essays in Economic History,* 2 vols., ed. E. M. Carus-Wilson (London, 1954–62), 1:72–73, where the author emphasizes "genuine exchange transaction[s] employed for the purpose of credit."

[7]For example, in 1411 Domenico d'Andrea di Siena was the guarantor (plezius, contraplezius) for a bill on London, seemingly with an agreement for rechange; ASV, GP, Sg, reg. 35, fol. 26. Peter Engel, a mercer of Cologne, had to leave silk cloth worth 525 ducats in the hands of Bernardo Stella in order to get a loan of 200 ducats which would permit him to meet certain debts upon his departure from Venice; Stella agreed to borrow the money on rechange ("di tuorli a cambio . . . , per un torno"), the interest on which he obviously charged the German; ibid., reg. 152, fols. 92–94 (16 August 1469). Lane assumed that the banker Balbi had rights to some of Barbarigo's merchandise when he lent money under various forms, including exchange; *Andrea Barbarigo,* 26.

ii. TECHNICAL ASPECTS OF THE BILL OF EXCHANGE

An exchange transaction, simply put, consisted of supplying local currency against the future delivery of foreign currency abroad. The essential elements of a classic bill of exchange, then, can be summarized as follows: (1) an exchange of currencies; (2) a transfer of assets over distances without the risk and cost of transferring coin; (3) a loan, to the extent that one party advanced money locally, on the spot, which he could dispose of abroad only after the maturity of the contract, while the taker disposed of the funds immediately. Rechange involved the repayment, not abroad but locally, after the arrival of a return draft.

The classic commercial bill involved four parties. In the first city, the remitter, who wanted to make a payment abroad, provided the value of the bill, in local currency, and the taker, who received the money, made out the draft on his correspondent. In the second city, the beneficiary received the bill and presented it to the payer, the drawer's correspondent, who accepted it and, at maturity, paid its value in the currency of the second city. Figure 11 shows the parties and their technical names and indicates the direction of movement of the bill, the money, and commercial correspondence.[8] The financial bill, or rechange, involved merely repeating the operation, in the reverse. In the redraft, the beneficiary became the remitter and the payer the drawer, whereas in the first city the original drawer or borrower became the payer, and the remitter became the beneficiary — who was thus repaid for his loan, in the same currency in which he had made it. Simplifications were often used for rechange and dry exchange, whereby the two parties in either city were fused into one and the same person, who merely remitted and drew at the same time, or — abroad — accepted and redrew, in a fictional operation. Prospective buyers and sellers of bills, both commercial and financial, in a given city were generally brought together by specialized brokers, who earned a fee.

Crucial for credit is the element of time; and the Florentine merchant bankers, in fixing the rules of their game, set the maturity dates, or "usances," among all the banking places of western Europe in such a way as to allow for credit. In all cases, usance was longer than average postal times, as is made clear in table 8.1.[9] On the Florence-Venice axis, for example, usance

[8]Note that the technical terms in German for the first two parties are the exact reverse of the terms used in other languages; they were inherited–Michael North informed me–from an anomalous usage inaugurated by Levin Goldschmidt in the nineteenth century.

[9]R. de Roover once suggested the comparison of usance with postal times as a manner of underscoring the credit factor in exchange; see "Le marché monétaire au Moyen Age et au début des temps modernes," *Revue historique* 244 (1970): 20. The comparison, in tabular form, was made possible by the useful study of postal times undertaken by Federigo Melis and his assistants (on the basis of some 150,000 letters in the Datini archive); see "Intensità e regolarità nella diffusione dell'informazione economica generale nel Mediterraneo e in Occidente alla fine del Medioevo," in *Mélanges en l'honneur de Fernand Braudel* (Toulouse, 1973),

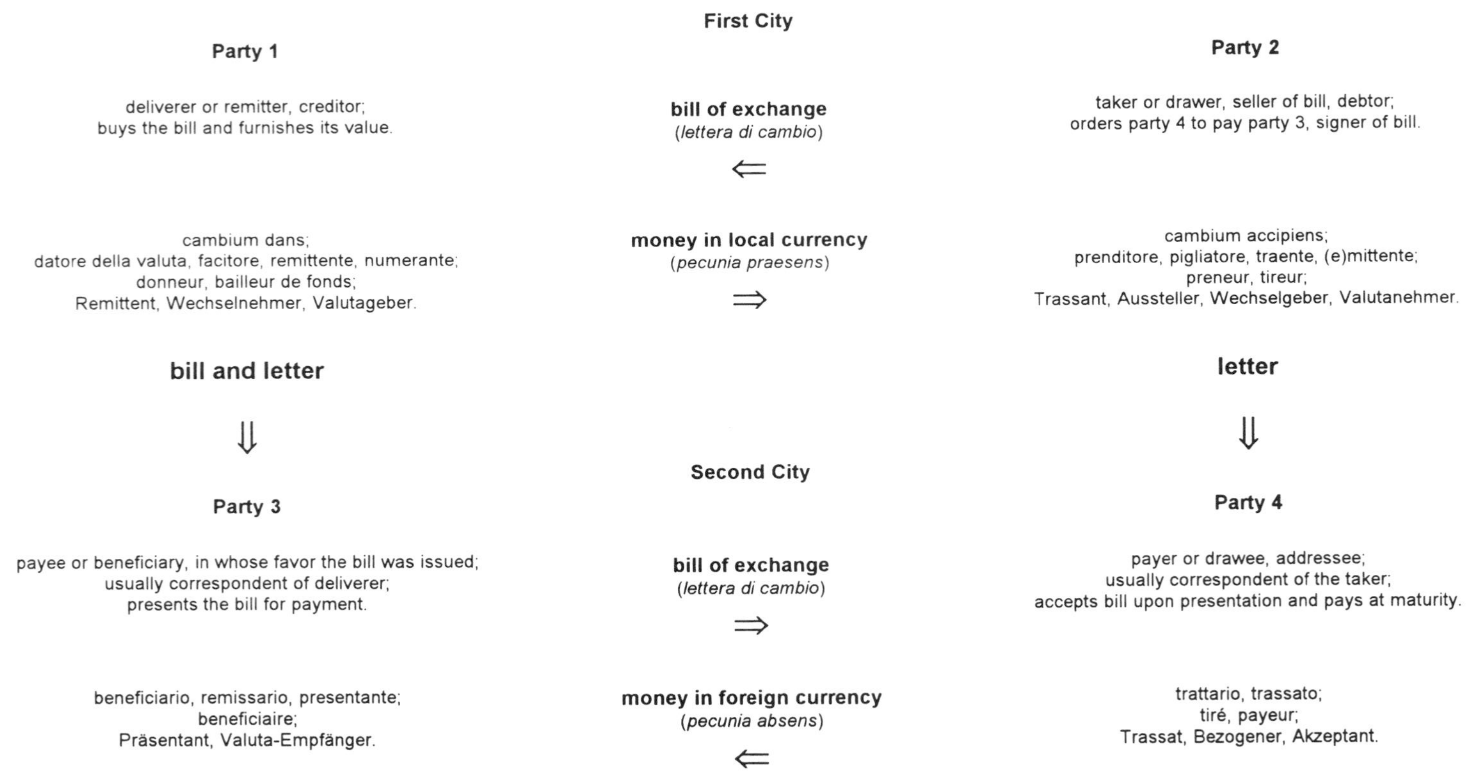

First City

Party 1

$\Rightarrow$

deliverer or remitter, creditor;
buys the bill and furnishes its value.

cambium dans;
datore della valuta, factore, remittente, numerante;
donneur, bailleur de fonds;
Remittent, Wechselnehmer, Valutageber.

Party 2

taker or drawer, seller of bill, debtor;
orders party 4 to pay party 3, signer of bill.

cambium accipiens;
prenditore, pigliatore, traente, (e)mittente;
preneur, tireur;
Trassant, Aussteller, Wechselgeber, Valutanehmer.

bill of exchange
(*lettera di cambio*)

$\Downarrow$

money in local currency
(*pecunia praesens*)

$\Uparrow$

letter

$\Rightarrow$

Second City

bill and letter

$\Rightarrow$

Party 3

payee or beneficiary, in whose favor the bill was issued;
usually correspondent of deliverer;
presents the bill for payment.

beneficiario, remissario, presentante, beneficiario;
bénéficiaire;
Präsentant, Valuta-Empfänger.

Party 4

payer or drawee, addressee;
usually correspondent of the taker;
accepts bill upon presentation and pays at maturity.

trattario, trassato;
tiré, payeur;
Trassat, Bezogener, Akzeptant.

bill of exchange
(*lettera di cambio*)

$\Uparrow$

money in foreign currency
(*pecunia absens*)

$\Leftarrow$

Fig. 11. Parties to a traditional bill of exchange. After de Roover, *Bruges Money Market*, 23–26, and "Marché monétaire," 8; Mandich, "Per una ricostruzione," cxlv; Spufford, Handbook, xxxii.

Fabio Carrera

TABLE 8.1

Usance, Postal Times, and the Mechanics of Exchange
between Venice and Eleven Cities, about 1400

City	Postal Times	Usance	Manner of Quoting Exchange in Venice
Florence	6	and.: 20 days date rit.: 5 days sight	N £ a fiorino di suggello for £1 di grossi; or in percentage of par. Par: £1 = 10 du. = £14.5 affiorino
Pisa	8	20 days date	Percentage of par
Bologna	4	and.: 15 days date rit.: 5 days sight	Percentage of par
Genoa	15	10 days sight	Percentage of par (gold-based lira in Venice against silver-based lira in Genoa)
Milan	4	15 days date	Percentage of par (gold-based lira in Venice against silver-based lira imperiale in Milan)
Rome	10	10 days sight	Percentage of par
Lucca	?	?	Percentage of par
Bruges	26	2 months date	N grossi a oro Venetian for 1 gold franc Flemish; N groats for 1 gold ducat; uncertain — until ca. 1420, when Venice quotes certain
Paris	20	2 months date	N grossi a oro Venetian for 1 gold franc French
Barcelona	21	2 months date	N soldi and denari Barcelonese for 1 gold ducat; certain
London	33	3 months date	N pence sterling for 1 gold ducat; certain

Sources: See below, Appendix C, and the merchant manuals cited in Mueller, "'Chome l'ucciello di passagio.'" Postal times are modal, from Melis, "Intensità e regolarità nella diffusione dell'informazione," based on data culled from tens of thousands of letters in ADP.
Note: "And." = andata, the draft; "rit." = ritorno, the redraft.

was so defined in mixing terms of "sight" (five days "vista" plus six days postal time, Florence to Venice) and "date" (twenty days "fatta," from Venice to Florence) as to create a perfect one-month loan on rechange, a popular short-term loan called "cambium ad Venetias" or "cambium ad grossos venetos," which we shall see at work below. Or again, usance to Bruges was two months, to London three months, against average postal

1:389–424. The results are much more valuable than the list given in da Uzzano's merchant manual and reprinted in Spufford's *Handbook*. Postal times from Venice to Bruges and London in 1439–40 in Lane, *Andrea Barbarigo*, 199–200 (similarly overlooked by Spufford). On usances, now see also Markus A. Denzel, *"La pratica della cambiatura": Europäischer Zahlungsverkehr vom 14. bis zum 17. Jahrhundert* (Stuttgart, 1994), esp. 190–201.

times of twenty-six and thirty-three days respectively. Pegolotti wrote in the early fourteenth century that Florentines knew all the usance periods by heart — among themselves there was no need to specify the maturity; however, he continued, "If you exchange with someone other than a Florentine, you had better specify exactly which usance or which alternative maturity, in order to avoid trouble."[10]

The importance of usance — and forecasting — in the game of exchange can be readily perceived in the area of arbitrage, a fairly common speculation involving buying and selling exchange contemporaneously on different markets. A form of arbitrage is explained in the merchant manuals as a way of keeping funds moving, while maintaining the use of them as long as possible, and it is Venice that serves as the cornerstone in the examples. Antonio Salutati, who wrote on the basis of his experience as a Medici factor in Venice, tells the apprentice cambista in Florence who wants to transfer assets to Bruges or Paris not to do so directly from Florence, at two months' usance; instead, he could gain twenty days' use of his money by ordering his correspondent in Venice to remit from there (where usance was the same) and to pay the cost of the remittance by drawing on him in Florence, where the draft would fall due only after twenty days. Similarly, Benedetto Cotrugli advises the cambista in Barcelona to order his correspondent in Valencia to remit to Venice at 18 soldi and draw on him; when the draft falls due, he pays it by drawing on Venice at, say, 17½ soldi, for a net gain of fifteen days and the difference between the two rates.[11] In practice, of course, expertise in forecasting future rates had to be combined with luck — as in any game — and many orders of this kind in the Datini

---

[10]*La pratica*, 196; the passage follows his list of "termini di cambiora" or usance periods, in the section on Florence. Giulio Mandich expressed the conviction that Florentines fixed the rules of the game. Rechange, he says, was not so much a question of selling in Venice an absent currency for a local currency, as one of "rispettando una certa regola del giuoco, escogitata per negozi che saranno presto chiamati cambi 'ad grossos.'" Florentine experts in foreign exchange were the "principali autrici, o fautrici, del suo stesso progresso tecnico"; see "Per una ricostruzione," clxxxi, clxxxix. Cf. de Roover, *Medici Bank,* 122. Mandich is even more explicit later, when he writes that Florentines fixed the Florence-to-Venice usance as short, in order to facilitate the forecasting in Florence of the return rate from Venice; see his "La prassi delle assegnazioni e delle lettere di pagamento a Venezia nel 1336–1339 (da un libro di conti)," in *SV,* n.s., 11 (1986): 39. It is significant that Venetian merchant manuals of the Middle Ages make no mention of the foreign exchange market, whereas Florentine handbooks are full of advice on how to wheel and deal in bills of exchange. The first Venetian manual to deal with exchange was A. Casanova's *Specchio lucidissimo . . .* (Venice, 1558), on which see Raymond de Roover, "Early Accounting Problems of Foreign Exchange," *Accounting Review* 19 (1944): 398–99.

[11]Of course the remittance would arrive later at its destination, later by the postal time necessary for sending the order. Antonia Borlandi, ed., *Il manuale di mercatura di Saminiato de' Ricci* (Genoa, 1963), 138–40; Salutati warns against doing the opposite (namely, ordering Venice to draw on Bruges and to remit to Florence) as an unjustifiable loss of time. A similar passage in the manual of da Uzzano is referred to in the editor's notes. See also Cotrugli, *Il libro,* 166–67, and the anonymous merchant manual in BNF, Cod. Palatino 601, fol. 72v.

correspondence had to be ignored upon arrival of the letter when the rates foreseen were no longer those in force.[12]

The bill itself is a mere slip of paper. Figures 12a and 12b are perhaps the earliest examples of bills of exchange extant in the original anywhere in Europe, the first drawn in Bruges on Venice, the second in Venice on Bruges, both in the year 1360; they contain all the elements of an order-to-pay in another currency at maturity, but the language—Venetian rather than Florentine—is quite unstylized. (For the texts, see below, App. G, sec. i; for their explanation, see App. C.) They survived because their payment was involved in a case of inheritance, following on the death of one of the parties.[13]

For present purposes, it is better to analyze a completely stylized bill:

Al nome di Dio, dì 25 d'aghosto 1402
Paghate per questa prima a usanza a Paliano di Falcho e
compagni fiorini 215, 21s 8d a fiorino per £20 di grossi qui da
la comesseria di Zanobi di Tadeo e Antonio di Ser Bartolomeo,
a [£15], 12s 10d a fiorino per £. Al termine gli paghate e metete
a conto per voi.

Bindo Piaciti
in Vinegia   Cristo vi ghuardi

Acietta' a dì 2
settembre 1402

verso: Franciescho di Marcho e Stoldo di Lorenzo in Firenze

per dì 14 settembre
pagato

Applying the scheme of figure 11 to this bill, we see that:

Party 1 is the estate of Zanobi Gaddi, which remitted 215 fl. (di suggello), 21s 8d a fiorino, by paying 20 lire di grossi in Venice.

---

[12]The expert in arbitrage was Manetto Davanzati and Company; see, for example, ADP, 712, letters of 5 February and 11 March 1400; or that of Gaddi to Pisa, 5 July 1399, b. 550.

[13]ASV, PSM, Misti, b. 67, commis. Giacomello Gabriel. Payment for the draft on Venice is registered in the accounts of the estate (reg. 1, fol. 9v). Several remittances from Bruges follow in the accounts (reg. 2, fol. 1, and two loose letters, one sent on 28 February 1361, arrived in Venice 27 March, the other sent on 17 March and arrived on 13 April), as Ferigo Bon in Bruges closed out the affairs of Gabriel—himself a former Rialto banker, who had been forced to leave Venice; the Procurators, as executors, were generally credited on the books of a bank. For the exchange rates applied in these bills, see below, App. C, under Bruges. These are merely the first bills extant in the original; evidence from accounts comes much earlier. See, for example, the remittances sent from Venice by Lippo di Fede, 1315–23, the proceeds of his sales of grossi coins; Charles M. de La Roncière, *Un changeur florentin du Trecento: Lippo di Fede del Sega (1285 env.–1363 env.)* (Paris, 1973), 54.

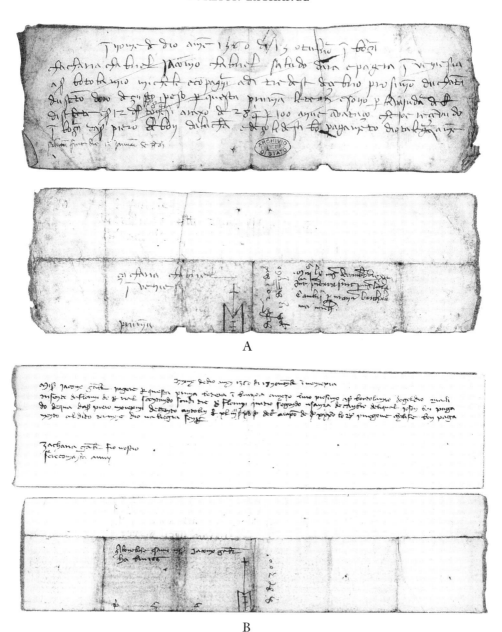

Fig. 12. The earliest original Venetian bills of exchange. The first was drawn in Bruges on Venice, the second in Venice on Bruges, in 1360 (recto and verso; complete transcription in app. G).

ASV, PSM, Misti, b. 67. Photograph by the Microfilm Section, ASV

Party 2 is Bindo Piaciti, who drew the bill at the exchange rate of £15 (understood), 12s 10d a fiorino per lira di grossi and received 20 lire di grossi, or 200 ducats; he signed the bill.

Party 3 is the Datini company in Florence, which is ordered to pay 215 fl. (di suggello), 21s 8d a fiorino, and which accepted the bill on 2 September and paid it on the 14th, that is, at usance: twenty days from the date of the bill; the company is the addressee, on the reverse of the bill.

Party 4 is Paliano di Falco in Florence, who received the bill from the Gaddi firm and presented it to the Datini company for acceptance on 2 September, eight days after the bill was made out.

Parties 1 and 2, as expected, both wrote letters to Florence on 26 August (a Saturday, the day the regular mail pouch left Venice), advising their respective correspondents of the transaction. Piaciti's letter states that in redrawing he had merely followed orders he had received from the Datini firm; the redraft had permitted him to honor the bill (not extant) that previously had been drawn on him, payable to the Venetian branch of the Davanzati company. In short, we learn from the correspondence that the bill, in the traditional form of an autonomous commercial exchange, was just one-half of a rechange operation. On the face of it, the Datini company in Florence was the debtor party on a one-month loan, but it seems, from the journal entry, rather to have acted as a stand-in for a client-borrower who did not have a correspondent abroad, as was often the case; it then charged the client for the costs of the rechange.[14]

We shall see this kind of contract in operation more clearly below, in the treatment of "cambium ad Venetias" (sec. v). For present purposes, let it suffice to demonstrate how the Datini company calculated the rate of interest. So many bills went back and forth in a given week or month that the respective accounting entries are not easily discerned, but the draft on Piaciti can be plausibly reconstructed. It had been drawn in Florence eleven days earlier, on 14 August; if we apply the surviving exchange rate closest to that date (from 7 August), namely, £15 5s 2d a fiorini for 1 lira di grossi Venetian, we can see that Datini (or his client) would have received 210.56 florins as taker. The rate of exchange in Florence was meant to be lower than

---

[14]ADP, 1142, bill of exchange of 25 August; 714, letter of Piaciti of 26 August (that of the Gaddi Estate has been lost); 578, memoriale "FF," fol. 94v (16 September); 559, campione bianco "F," fol. 263v. Piaciti's letter informs Datini as follows: "Paghamo £20 di grossi ci traeste ne' Davanzati, e a vostro conto sono. E per le dette vi traiano in Paliano di Falcho a usanza la valuta di £20 di grossi a [£15], s. 12, d. 10 a fiorini per £ auti qui da la comesseria di Zanobi di Tadeo e Antonio di ser Bartolomeo; paghategli al termine e metete a nostro conto." It is important to note that Florentines in Venice often dropped the figure in lire a fiorino, for years always 15, when quoting Florence, a shorthand procedure — exemplified by the text of this bill — which could cause confusion today (as in Melis, *Documenti*, 101–2).

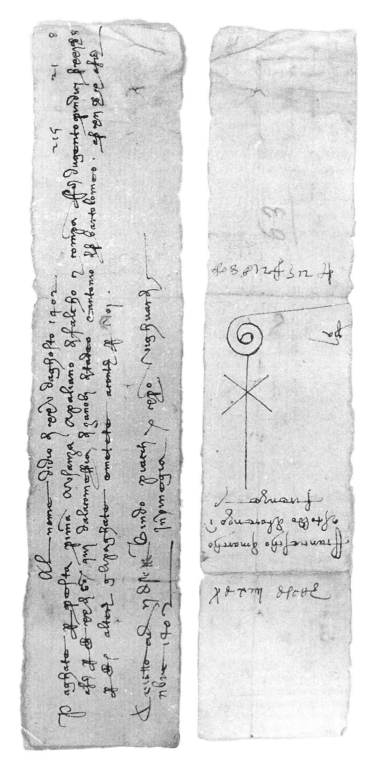

Fig. 13. A bill of exchange drawn in Venice on Florence, 1402 (recto and verso).

ADP, 1142, "lettere di cambio"

that in Venice according to a device invented by the cambisti, whereby Florence "gave certain" to Venice, that is, a variable number of Florentine lire a fiorino were worth 1 Venetian lira di grossi; and such was the case, as we know from the rate applied to the redraft. Perhaps the simplest methods for calculating the interest rate are to subtract the draft rate (£15 5s 2d, Florence on Venice) from the redraft rate (£15 12s 10d, Venice on Florence), which leaves 7s 8d a fiorino for 1 lira for one month; or to subtract the amount borrowed from the amount to be repaid: 215 fl., 21s 8d (215.85) − 210.56 = 5.29 fl. After carrying out the necessary calculations (relegated to the footnote), one arrives either way at a monthly rate of 2.5 percent, which corresponds to an annual rate of 30 percent interest.[15] This was an exceptionally high rate, even for August, but on 2 September Piaciti confirmed that rates were "hot" and "devastating" for anyone who was forced to borrow on the exchange at the time.[16]

This technical step, a banal and quotidian arithmetical calculation for Florentine cambisti, is essential for understanding how profit or interest on a short-term loan was linked to exchange. The rate of interest was tied to two rates of exchange of currencies defined by supply and demand, the first at the time of the contract, the second in another financial market or "banking place" at a future date, defined by usance. In this manner, the parties to a loan contract avoided fixing a rate of interest at the outset, which would have been patently usurious; to the extent that elements of risk of loss and uncertainty of the level of gain remained, it can be said that this credit instrument circumvented important aspects of the ecclesiastical prohibition of usury. In economic terms, however, its popularity lay in its being an agile, self-extinguishing, but renewable note, the terms of which reacted quickly to changes in market factors.

Rechanges that invoked only three parties were as common as the type just analyzed. Bills dated in the weeks following, on 6 and 13 September 1402, were drawn by the same Bindo Piaciti in Venice on the same Datini company in Florence and payable to Barnaba degli Agli. In these redrafts, Piaciti, who had been payer and beneficiary (parties 3 and 4)

---

[15]In this case, there are three ways of arriving at the same result. Method 1: after subtracting the amount borrowed from that owed, divide the difference by the amount of the loan and multiply by 12 months (215.85−210.56 = 5.29/210.56 × 12 = 30 percent). The other methods require reducing the figures to the lowest common denominator, denari. Method 2: the difference between the two rates, 7s 8d = 92 d; the draft rate, £15/5/2, = 3,662d; dividing the former by the latter leaves 0.025, the rate for one month; multiplying by 12 gives the annual rate: 30 percent. Method 3: the draft rate, £15/5/2, meant a loan in Florence of £305.167 a fi. (3,662 × 20 £ di gr./240d, or, multiplying by 0.69 fl. per lira a fi., 210.56 florins); the redraft rate, £15/12/10 or 3,754d × 20/240 gives the sum to be paid upon the return, namely, £312.83 a fi. or 215.85 florins (di suggello). Dividing the difference, 5.29 fl., by 210.56 = 0.025 for one month; multiplying by 12 gives the annual rate of 30 percent.

[16]"I chanbi sono tropo chocenti a tochare ora ed è chosa di disfare altrui." ADP, 714, Bindo Piaciti to Florence, 2 September 1402.

contemporaneously on the "andata," turned around and was both taker and remitter on the "ritorno," a role that he expresses by saying, "Pay to Barnaba a sum received here from myself" ("qui da noi"). Otherwise, the bills are traditional.[17] A dryer alternative common in the fifteenth century, which Datini might have already used, finds the drawer lending money to a client who was extraneous to the money market, thus acting contemporaneously as both remitter and taker (parties 1 and 2); upon the bill's return, the lender paid to himself the increased value of the bill as his profit, which he proceeded to collect from the client-borrower.

A useful diagram explaining a rechange operation on a fair in the sixteenth century, for all practical purposes the same as rechanges of the preceding two centuries, was published by Bernardo Davanzati in his tract *Notizia de' cambi* (1581; see fig. 14). The parties are presented in a slightly different manner than the scheme applied in figure 11, but readers will quickly be able to orient themselves. The bill, drawn in Florence for 102⅔ scudi and redrawn in Lyons for 104⅔ scudi, brought a return, at an annual rate, of 3.8 percent.[18]

The success of a cambista, a lender on exchange, lay in his ability to foresee the movement of various curves of exchange rates, in his own city and in other commercial and financial centers. He had to plan his credit supply in such a way as to exploit the moment of widest divergence between two different rates of exchange, which corresponded to the moment of highest demand for credit. In the case of 1402, discussed just above, a rise in the local rate or a fall in the foreign rate would have reduced the lender's profit. The cambista, therefore, had to know the seasonal tendencies of Europe's money markets and, at the same time, keep up to date with any and all news that might influence the rates of exchange on the short term. The writer of an anonymous manual for merchant bankers, dated 1443, compared exchange to a bird in flight and warned the dealer that he had to be ready to capture it when it approached, for, once past, the bird, which is the golden opportunity for a handsome profit, would not return.[19] The concern of the borrower, of course, was the opposite, namely, to seek credit when the two curves were closest; but he generally had little choice in the matter. These factors are presented graphically below, on the basis of series of actual exchange quotations.

Today the Italian term for a bill of exchange, *cambiale*, has taken on

[17]Ibid., 1142.

[18]Reprinted in *Schisma d'Inghilterra, con altre operette del signor B. Davanzati* (Padua, 1759), 113. See also the diagrams for "real" and "dry" types of rechange prepared by de Roover, *Medici Bank,* 114, 133 (both from Medici examples, both based on Venice).

[19]"Il chanbio è chome l'ucciello di passagio, e vuolsi prendere quando viene altrui davanti, che lasciandolo passare non tornna. Et però chonviene che il chanbiatore n'abi senpre avanti pensato il vantaggio e faccisi inchontro a prendello." BNF, Cod. palatini, 601, pt. 3, "Zibaldone di notizie utili a' mercatanti," fol. 72. Also quoted by de Roover, *Medici Bank,* 122.

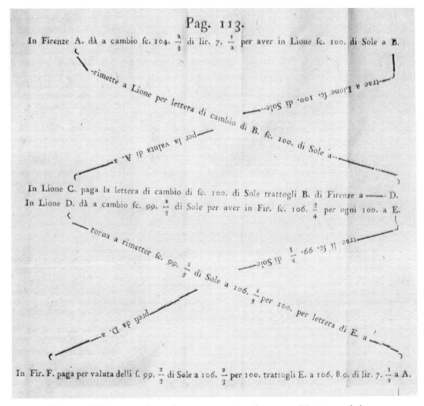

Fig. 14. Diagram of a rechange operation between Venice and the
exchange fairs of Lyons.

From Bernardo Davanzati's Notizia de' cambi, *first published in 1581.*

the meaning of an interest-bearing promissory note, which is precisely what
rechange was in the later Middle Ages and early modern period; moreover,
firmare cambiali (technically "to sign bills") now means to borrow money
on such notes, just as *stare su interessi* meant to borrow on exchange in the
period under study here.

iii. FACTORS AFFECTING THE VENETIAN MONEY MARKET

The exchange market in Venice was organized and run by Florentines,
under the form of a tacitly accepted monopoly. Florentines were particularly numerous on the Rialto because they had given Venice a pivotal role in
their dealings, after the decline of the fairs of Champagne, where bills had
already been used extensively. They had chosen it for three closely interre-
lated reasons: in part as a bullion market, in part because of the high demand for credit, and in part because the pulse of the commercial year beat

there so regularly, which simplified forecasting. Venice assumed a central role in the network of exchange markets, especially as a hinge between the banking places of northwestern Europe and those of Italy, by the early years of the fourteenth century and maintained it for nearly two centuries. One can legitimately say that Venice was made into a more important exchange market than Florence by the Florentines themselves.[20]

It may appear an anomaly, but exchange, designed by Florentine merchant bankers to render unnecessary the movement of specie, was governed by market prices for credit and coin which reflected and actually stimulated the movement of specie and of bullion and defined the direction of bullion flows, interregionally and internationally.[21] This is an important point, for Venice was perhaps Europe's largest bullion market before the arrival of American silver. Following the ups and downs of exchange rates and the market analyses provided by the merchant bankers who scrutinized the "big board," that is, the daily "listini," one can see how much the availability of coin or of bullion (often in the form of "bolzone," that is, scrap and voided coins) on the market conditioned the rates. A rise in the price of exchange reflected a scarcity of coin or mintable bullion and meant high interest rates; a drop in rates occurred as soon as bullion arrived to meet the demand. All markets sought to remit to Venice in time for the peak season; Bologna and Pisa were the markets most concerned with cornering specie to send to Venice in July and August, or whenever demand in Venice warranted the expense.[22] But the relationship between exchange and specie can be even more complex and unexpected, as in two cases with which this chapter closes: in the first, loans in the form of drafts on London made possible the loading of gold ducats on board Venetian galleys bound for the Levant; in the other, Venetian gold and silver coin flowed northward to London, some of it in the same mail pouches that carried bills of exchange.

---

[20]Gerolamo Biscaro reached this conclusion on the basis of his study of the ledger (1436–40) of the Borromei company of London and Bruges; see "Il banco Borromei," esp. 39 and 74–75. See also Gino Luzzatto, "Politica ed economia nella storia di Venezia," *Atti dell'Istituto veneto di scienze, lettere ed arti* 121 (1962–63): 505. Patrizia Mainoni, "Un mercante milanese," 356, 363–64. The situation was the same as late as 1558, according to the accounts of Lorenz Meder of Nuremberg; see Hermann Kellenbenz, "Die Münzen und die internationale Bank, Ende 15. bis Anfang 17. Jahrhundert (Das oberdeutsche Beispiel)," in *La moneta nell'economia europea, secoli XIII–XVIII,* ed. Vera Barbagli Bagnoli, Acts of the Settimane di Studio, Istituto Datini, Prato, 7 (Florence, 1981), 669. The same conclusion was reached most recently in George Holmes' study of an account book kept in London by the Salviati company, where he writes of "the central position of Venice in the European exchange system through which went all the transfers from Florence to north-west Europe." "Anglo-Florentine Trade in 1451," *English Historical Review* 108 (1993): 376.

[21]See my "'Chome l'ucciello di passagio': La demande saisonnière des espèces et le marché des changes à Venise au Moyen Age," in *Etudes d'histoire monétaire,* ed. John Day (Lille, 1981a), 195–219.

[22]Besides the anonymous merchant manual, see also Giovanni da Uzzano, *Pratica della mercatura,* in Pagnini, *Della decima,* 4:155–58.

The connection between coin and credit is essential, for the exchange market was based, in the final analysis, on someone's having a credit balance in bank money, convertible into metallic money at the opportune time. In medieval parlance, to say that money was tight ("carestia di danari," "strettezza di danari") did not mean only that credit was costly but also that demand for specie was high. To say that money was easy ("larghezza di danari," "dovizia di danari") meant that coin was available in abundance with respect to demand. That "danari" meant both credit and metallic money or convertible bank balances was overlooked by Raymond de Roover, who was too prone to exalt a medieval business technique that avoided the use of specie. The merchant manuals, as well as commercial correspondence, explain unequivocally, however, that exchange rates reflected the demand both for credit and for cash.

Tight and easy money and the nexus between exchange and specie were explained in this broader sense by Bernardo Davanzati in 1581, when the situation on the bill fairs was still quite the same. The exportation of a large quantity of specie to pay a prince or to meet demand elsewhere, he writes, would reduce supply locally; owners of coin would hold on to it tightly and not let go of it except at a high rate of exchange. The image he used was that of a hand that tightened or loosened its grasp on the money, forcing up or down the rates of exchange and the interest they reflected. Further on, the author provides another useful image in which specie is likened to water that seeks its own level, rushing to a banking place that is dry, flowing out of one that had an oversupply; similarly, he says, exchange rates cannot stand still but rise and fall according to demand and according to the profit margin that exchange was to provide.[23] Cambisti writing from Venice in the preceding centuries were well aware of these same phenomena and took them into account each time they analyzed an exchange market for a correspondent.

Although it is not incorrect to say that Venice constituted a permanent fair,[24] the Venetian economic calendar had specific high and low points, and the curve that best marks the pulse of the year is the curve of

---

[23]"Quando si dice la Piazza ristrignere, o allargare, s'intende esser pochi, o molti danari ne' mercanti da cambiarsi; il che nasce da varie cagioni. Accaderà che della Piazza esca grossa somma di contanti per far un pagamento a un Principe, o per mandare alle incette, o per altro; onde a pochi ne restano, e chi n'ha, gli ten cari, e stretti, e non gli vuol dare a pregio ordinario, ma a migliore, e chi ha bisogno di pigliare, fa come e' può; e piglierà, poniamo, ducati cento, per rendere in Vinezia fra tre settimane ducati cento dua, o più. Il contrario nelle larghezze avviene . . . ; chiamasi larghezza, e strettezza con parlare figurato, e bello, per vocaboli trasportati gentilmente da quello strignere, o allargar la mano. . . . [F]ate conto, che il contanto, come acqua, corre ne' luoghi più bassi; e viene, e va, secondo che una piazza ne diviene asciutta, o traboccante. . . . Non possono anco i pregi del cambio star fermi in su la pari, ma vanno in su e 'n giù, secondo le strettezze, o larghezze, e secondo che richiede l'utile che dee porgere il cambio." *Notizie de' chambi,* 108–9, 117.

[24]Gino Luzzatto, "Vi furono fiere a Venezia?" in his *Studi,* 201–9.

exchange rates. The Senate fixed the times for sailing at practically the same dates each year, according to the prevailing winds. Around 1400 the schedule, outlined in merchants' manuals and in their correspondence, was this: mid-July for the galleys to Romania, mid-August for those to Beirut, late August to early September for those to Alexandria; all of them carried specie and bars of silver as well as merchandise and thus drove up demand and rates of exchange. The Flanders galleys departed less regularly, usually in March or April, but they carried relatively little bullion. The summer "termini," or designated periods of preparation for departure, coincided with the most common maturity dates—similarly called "termini"—for contracts of sale on deferred payment; the hottest were those of the Romania galleys, and the set period, 4 to 15 July, constituted a kind of financial fair on the Rialto. Merchants scrambled for credit with which to pay their obligations as well as the merchandise and bullion they wished to load onto the departing galleys as exchange commodities. Florentine cambisti were there to satisfy demand. Actual sailing dates were often postponed by the Senate itself, sometimes more than once, but this did not affect payment schedules. Around 1430 the sailing schedule became more crowded, and the departure of the Flanders galleys was shifted, but it was still the departures to the bullion-hungry Levant, which remained the same, which most affected exchange rates.[25] Another maturity date that was commonly fixed was the Christmas fair, which it was hoped would coincide with the return of the galleys. This calendar meant that supply and demand for credit and for specie were largely foreseeable, and Florentine merchant bankers could plan ahead so as to have all possible assets on hand in Venice when demand was highest—that is, when exchange rates and thus interest rates peaked.

The anonymous merchant manual cited earlier states that the "termini" of August coincided with fewer deadlines for payment of debts than those of July but that demand for specie for export was so high in the last ten days of the month that the banks were "cooked" by the heat of cash withdrawals; money was dearer in that moment than in the whole rest of the year. As soon as the Alexandria galleys left the port, rates collapse. If we plot the monthly average exchange rates quoted in Venice on Florence (graph 8.1) and on Pisa, Bologna, Lucca, and Rome (graph 8.2) over the years covered by the Datini correspondence, we find nearly complete corroboration of the anonymous cambista's description of the economic calendar. There is a single minor exception, namely, that in those years rates tended to be just a little (6%) higher in July than in August. The steepest

---

[25]Bernard Doumerc, "La crise structurelle de la marine vénitiénne au XVe siècle: le probleme du retard des 'mude,'" *Annales, économies, sociétés, civilisations* 40 (1985): 605–23, and Frederic C. Lane, "Rhythm and Rapidity of Turnover in Venetian Trade of the Fifteenth Century," in *Venice and History,* 110–11.

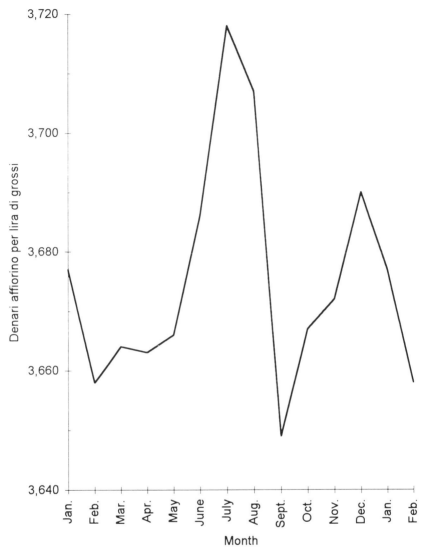

GRAPH 8.1. Seasonal Pattern of Exchange Rates in Venice quoting Florence, 1383–1410

rise was between June and July (18%), the sharpest fall between August and September (25%), as the graphs show.[26]

Any given year, of course, had its own peculiarities, not foreseen by the calendar: war and the need for specie for paying troops and arming war

[26]Mueller, " 'Come l'ucciello di passagio,' " appendix.

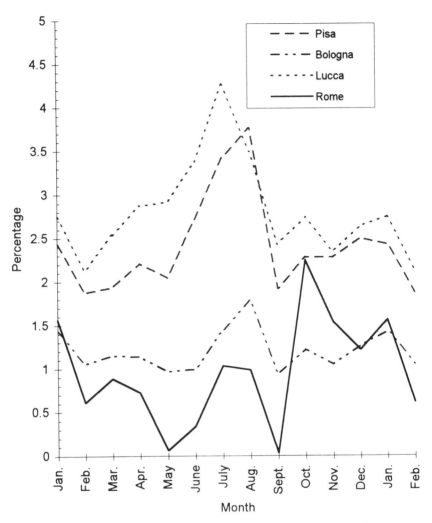

GRAPH 8.2. Seasonal Pattern of Exchange Rates in Venice quoting Pisa, Bologna, Lucca, and Rome, 1383–1410

galleys; news about the depredations of Tamerlane (Timur) or the conquests of the Turks; rumors about shipwrecks and losses sustained; the arrival of representatives of the papal Curia who, instead of accepting credits on Rialto banks, insisted on receiving cash for bills in which the Curia was beneficiary — all such variables caused the market to tighten suddenly. The immediate reaction of the cambisti on the Rialto was to import specie from the closest banking place, which was Bologna, in order to lend cash on the exchange at the high rates then current. Evidence from the Datini

correspondence is myriad, the best of it from the letters of Manetto Davanzati and Company, genuine specialists in exchange.

The year 1389, for example, was one of war between Florence and
Milan. Although exchange rates were expected to decline after the Christmas fair, they failed to do so, when news arrived that a factor of Giangaleazzo Visconti was en route to Venice to withdraw 30,000 ducats' worth of
specie for paying troops. They were given a further boost when he actually
appeared on the scene and made significant withdrawals. In response, specie began to flow toward Venice from Bologna, Verona, and Milan, as the
company reported on 9 and 14 January. But the level remained high, owing
to speculation by a certain cambista, and it was not until the 19th that rates
finally dropped. Again in March a modest payment due by the Signoria of
Venice to the lord of Milan—4,000 ducats drawn by bill on Verona plus
another 4,000 in cash—was enough to cause rates to rise. They remained
high because the companies of Vieri di Cambio de' Medici and the Portinari
were cornering specie for export elsewhere. The Davanzati factor ordered
his correspondent in Bologna to send specie, for which he paid by bill of
exchange; on that operation he hoped to make considerable profit ("bas-
tevole profitto"). The drop foreseen for March did not occur until after
another war-related withdrawal, this time of 5,000 ducats, by the factor of
Giangaleazzo Visconti. Thus far, the source of our information has been the
letters of the Davanzati firm.[27]

When the seasonal rise began in late May—we are still in the year
1389—it is Zanobi Gaddi who informs us of the situation. He knows that
Francesco Datini owes money at the "termini" of July and urges him to send
the funds early in the month, before the specie famine ("gran charestia di
danari") that was foreseen. On 26 June Gaddi reported that Venetian
wholesalers of pepper were beginning to drop their prices in order to attract
buyers, especially Germans, and thus build up convertible assets on their
current accounts at the Rialto banks. Rates peaked on 3 July, as Gaddi had
predicted, and then dropped in response to the arrival of specie from Bologna and elsewhere. Despite Gaddi's prodding, Datini was unable to remit
funds on time, and Gaddi was forced to draw on Florence at a high rate, on
the eve of the departure of the Romania galleys on 25 July. The arrival of
plague in Venice seems to have cut off the correspondence for the rest of the
high season.

To see the difference between the strong reactions of the market to
small off-season demands on liquidity, which reflected limited availability
of funds, and high-season demand, it will be useful to peruse the letters
from the summer of 1399. In July the Davanzati firm was particularly active

---

[27]The letters are found in ADP, 709; since they are arranged by sender in chronological
order, repeated references are unnecessary.

as the agent for Datini's banking operation, sending off market reports every two to three days by special courier. It reported on the 15th the receipt of a shipment of specie sent from Florence; on the 21st and 23d it ascribed a drop in rates on Florence and Bologna to news of a rise in those two cities and to the arrival of more specie; on the 28th and 29th it wrote that rates had climbed in Venice, in part because a speculator with excess cash on hand had actually drawn in order to force up the rates; on the 31st it reported that Vieri di Cambio de' Medici and Company, acting for third parties, had drawn large sums of money and that the two Romania galleys and seven roundships bound for the cotton muda or fair in Syria had departed, the latter alone taking 250,000 gold ducats as well as silver bars and merchandise. In August the rates held high until the 19th, when both specie and remittances arrived; the market was nervous, the same firm reported, and any small change in supply and demand made the rates oscillate. Again on the 23d rates declined for the same reasons and also because demand was down. The Alexandria galleys departed on 3–4 September, and, as forecast, the rates plummeted.[28] One could go on endlessly, given the wealth of the Datini correspondence in this sector, but further examples of normal and abnormal conditions of supply and demand would not differ essentially from those just given.

A final example ties exchange rates to a governmental provision. On 20 July 1403, at the peak of the season, the Senate prohibited the export of specie on the ships loading for departure to the Levant, because of the danger of Genoese warships operating near Alexandria, under the command of Maréchal Boucicault, French governor of Genoa. Commercial letters sent to Florence the next day reported that the exchange had dropped 6 soldi affiorino, a sharp — and unforeseen — fall.[29]

In short, demand for money ("danaro") meant at one and the same time demand for specie or for bank balances convertible into specie when the need arose, demand for exchange, and demand for credit. Exchange rates reflected all these factors: they rose when money was tight; they fell when money was easy.

Two final aspects of the Venetian market on which there is little solid information need at least to be mentioned before we can move on to a series of actual cases. The first is the order of magnitude of the credit made available on the Rialto, especially by Florentine merchant bankers via exchange. The second is the contribution of foreign exchange to total profits in the large merchant-banking enterprises.

There are only scattered and heterogeneous indications of the level of credit which could be raised in medieval and Renaissance Venice, and

---

[28]"'Chome l'ucciello di passagio,'" 209–13, and ADP, 712, letters of Davanzati and Gaddi to Florence.

[29]ASV, SM, reg. 46, fol. 92v; ADP, 714.

points of comparison are lacking. Those uncovered are listed here for the impressions they may provide.

A. In a suit before the commercial court in 1374, a certain Giacomo Bellom demanded payment from a client of commissions due on exchange-rechange transactions ("pro cambiis cambitis et recambitis pro sua provisione"); at 1 percent, the 1,600 ducats charged meant that the principal of the bills totaled, over an unspecified period of time, 160,000 ducats. The dealer also sued for 100 ducats to cover brokerage and other fees. The client responded that the dealer had arranged innumerable exchanges previously, without charging a commission, which means that the sums dealt in reached even higher totals.[30]

B. At the battle of Nicopolis in 1396, the Turks captured John the Fearless, future duke of Burgundy, and the sultan demanded a ransom of 200,000 florins. In order to organize the operation, the Lucchese merchant banker and de facto treasurer of Burgundy Dino Rapondi had to travel from Paris to Venice (he was a naturalized citizen in both places). Once on the Rialto, he remitted the money by advancing it to Italian merchants based in the Levant; it seems that he paid for the bills by drawing contemporaneously on Paris and Bruges.[31]

C. A few years later, in the heat of the battle of republican Florence against the expansionism of Giangaleazzo Visconti, the Arno city sought to enlist the help of Robert of the Palatinate, king of the Romans and treated by the Italians as Holy Roman Emperor, by convincing him to attack Lombardy from the north. He was promised a subsidy of 200,000 florins by ambassadors of Florence, including the memorialist Buonaccorso Pitti, who did not fail to discuss his role. The first problem was collecting that much in specie in August, when demand was at a peak. On the 30th the Senate responded to the embassy of Pitti, Andrea Vettori, and the banker Giovanni di Bicci de' Medici himself that it would not contribute; but on the same day the Alexandria galleys (carrying 130,000 ducats in coin) departed, causing a drop in exchange rates. In September the first installment of 55,000 florins was finally raised by the Florentine community when its members drew on their principals in Florence. Giovanni di Bicci was able to guarantee a ceiling on the exchange rates, so as to contain the costs. A second installment of 90,000 ducats due in October, which kept rates high,

---

[30]Luzzatto, *Storia,* 108. The court reduced the commission to ½ percent. Behind the names of the otherwise unknown Giacomo Bellom and Giorgio Grassi were surely some Florentine companies, such as that of Giovanni Portinari, active in Venice at that time. Of course the figure derives from a total number of self-liquidating drafts and cannot serve as an indication of the amount of credit extended at any give time.

[31]Raymond de Roover, *Money, Banking, and Credit in Mediaeval Bruges,* 86, and *Bruges Money Market,* 43; Edmund B. Fryde and M. M. Fryde, "Public Credit, with Special Reference to North-Western Europe," in *The Cambridge Economic History of Europe* (Cambridge, England, 1963), 3:502–3 (based on the work of L. Mirot).

was reportedly available on the Rialto in specie. An additional 65,000 ducats were agreed upon during King Robert's stay in Padua and in Venice in December and January 1402. The Florentine community in Venice was kept in a state of constant tension but was prepared to make the large payments ordered by their fatherland. Money for the subsidies — made in vain, since the German king's forces were roundly defeated in Lombardy — were more easily raised and distributed on the Rialto than on Florence's Mercato Nuovo itself.[32]

D. When in 1414 John XXIII asked the Alberti for a loan — seemingly a cash loan, to be provided in Bologna — the company had its London branch remit to the Alberti in Venice. Most of the "incredible" sum of 80,000 ducats was amassed on the Rialto in short order and transferred to Bologna, "an amount never before seen in the hands of a private citizen," recounted Leon Battista Alberti years later, in wonderment.[33]

E. A more significant source is a large fragment of the cash book covering the activity of the Medici operation in Venice in 1436–37, kept by the employee Agnolo di Jacopo Tani; it records an impressive cash flow, of assets kept in constant circulation. For example, when the branch closed out the cash account of the third quarter, there was little more than 1,400 ducats' worth of coin in the till; there were also modest sums on current account with the Rialto bankers Francesco Balbi (friend and correspondent of Cosimo de' Medici), Nicolò Bernardo, and Cristoforo Soranzo. But the outflow ("uscita") over three quarters is recorded as follows (in lire di grossi):

first (short) quarter:	10,500
second quarter:	14,275
fourth quarter:	14,493

If we assume about 14,000 lire di grossi, that is, 140,000 ducats, also for the third quarter, the accounts of which are not complete, the total for the year would be 532,680 ducats on the debit side. Since the debit side, plus the cash in the till, was obviously balanced by the same amount on the credit side, we can say that in 1436–37 the cash flow of the Medici branch in Venice easily exceeded 1 million ducats. In other words, there was an aver-

---

[32] The best study of the subsidy from the German side is that of Wolfgang von Stromer, "Das Zusammenspiel Oberdeutscher und Florentiner Geldleute bei der Finanzierung von König Ruprechts Italienzug, 1401–02," in *Forschungen zur Sozial- und Wirtschaftsgeschichte,* ed. Hermann Kellenbenz (Stuttgart, 1971), 16:50–86; German merchants of the Fondaco dei Tedeschi were also involved. See also Brucker, *Civic World,* 176–77, 298. For the Florentine side, a full account, briefly summarized here, is found in the letters sent from Venice by the Gaddi estate and by Bindo Piaciti to Florence; see ADP, b. 713, from August 1401 through January 1402. The letters, not consulted by von Stromer or Brucker, put into relief the leadership of Giovanni di Bicci, as merchant banker and as representative of the Commune of Florence simultaneously.

[33] *I libri della famiglia,* ed. by Ruggiero Romano and Alberto Tenenti (Turin, 1980), 342.

age cash flow per working day (figuring about 270 working days in a year) of at least 3,700 ducats, played out primarily in the game of exchange, "il mestiero del canbio." That must have represented the minimum liquidity necessary for total transactions of a much larger amount, since all that has survived for the local operation is the cash book and, in Florence, the "libro segreto," which shows the Venetian branch to have contributed profits in that year of a nearly record 75 percent.[34] Loans via instruments other than exchange were also regularly made.[35]

F. Fifteen years later, Gianozzo Manetti, a merchant banker, humanist, and diplomat who was conversant with Venice, affirmed (as has been mentioned above) that Florentine operators on the Rialto held more than 150,000 florins in cash, which, he infers, they made available on the exchange to the local credit market.[36] That was about the same as the amount of cash dealt out by the Medici branch alone in three months. Whether Manetti meant cash in hand or merely the capacity of Florentine cambisti to mobilize that much on short notice is not clear.

G. In 1516, finally, the Venetian branch of the Fugger firm is reported to have had a turnover of about 100,000 ducats in its exchange dealings with Antwerp alone. Of that, nine-tenths were remittances in the direction of Venice, only one-tenth in the other direction. In the same year, the branch sent about 175,000 ducats in coin to the Roman Curia. Exchange with Lyons totaled only some 16,000 ducats, that with Nuremberg about 20,000 ducats.[37]

Since no ledgers of even a single cambista who operated on the Rialto

[34]ASF, MAP, 134/1, large fragment of a "libro di entrata e uscita di cassa" of the branch, 1436–37. When closing the third quarter, Tani states that it was he who kept the cash account (fol. 160v). To exemplify the relations with the banks: on 30 January 1337 the Medici withdrew 2,730 ducats from the Balbi bank on three occasions (fol. 147v); on 19 April they paid 200 ducats to Balbi, 300 to Bernardo (fol. 176). For Medici assets (about 60 ducats) and liabilities (about 125 ducats, including 60 on the security of a ring) with four Rialto banks as declared in 1427, see Catasto, 49, fols. 1187–90. In the balance drawn up for the catasto of 1457, the Medici declared having 6,000 ducats in cash on hand at the Venice branch, the highest amount declared in the whole system; see MAP, 82, fol. 593v, account entitled "Danari contanti atroviamo ne' nostri traffichi." For the profits, see above, table 7.3.

[35]For loans called "deposits" of 300, 400, and 1,000 ducats made by the Medici to Venetian noblemen, see ASV, GP, Sg, reg. 85, fols. 54–57 (February 1441), and reg. 114, fols. 31v–34v (1451 but regarding 1427); for a loan of 500 ducats made by Giovanfrancesco Strozzi on current account at the Soranzo bank, see ibid., reg. 142, fol. 2r–v (1463); for an eight-day loan of 65 ducats by Benedetto Salviati and Company, on current account at the Barbarigo bank, see ibid., reg. 159, fol. 105r–v (1474). For the use of the term *deposit* to mean a loan, see Santarelli, *La categoria dei depositi irregolari,* esp. chap. 4, pt. 3.

[36]Cited in my "Mercanti e imprenditori fiorentini," 58. Manetti placed Venice second only to Naples, where Florentines supposedly had 200,000 gold florins. It is difficult to verify or disprove such statements, although it is hard to imagine that Manetti meant cash available in any one moment.

[37]Alfred Weitnauer, *Venezianischer Handel der Fugger, nach der Musterbuchhaltung des Matthäus Schwarz,* Studien zur Fugger-Geschichte, 9 (Munich, 1931), 74, 77, 80.

have survived, these seven cases are provided as mere examples of what the Venetian exchange market was capable of accumulating and turning over in given situations. A judgment about whether the sums were high or low, whether they were exceptional or quotidian, would require better documentation and, above all, the opportunity of comparing them with other marketplaces. The impression one gets, however, is that Venice was particularly well placed to handle large sums, as a result of its dual role of bullion market and pivotal exchange market.

As regards the second question posed above, namely, the role of exchange in the accumulation of profits, our best information comes from the balance sheets of the London branch of a company of the Borromei, a family that had been exiled from Florence in the later fourteenth century. In the years 1436–39 exchange transactions at this branch, which had extensive connections with the Venetian market, contributed between 50 and 60 percent of net profits, even though losses on the exchange were often very high (see table 8.2). We have no similar breakdowns in the Medici balance sheets. For that firm one can only repeat that the Venice branch, which was deeply involved in lending via exchange, was second only to Rome during the first half century of its operation in contributing from 13 to 22 percent of total net profits (see above, Chap. 7, sec. iii).[38]

Before turning to exemplary cases of rechange, first with Florence, then with Bruges and London, it will be useful to turn our attention briefly to the one sector in which Venetians retained a monopoly: exchange with markets in the eastern Mediterranean.

iv. EXCHANGE WITH THE LEVANT

Venetians were most interested in commerce with the Levant, which, if need be, could be financed in Venice by rechange on the West through the mediation of Florentine cambisti. Venice had an unfavorable balance of trade with the East to the extent that its merchants regularly had to load coin and bullion, along with Western goods, on the ships and galleys heading eastward. But since Venetians maintained trading colonies in all the major cities of the Levant, they dealt often with bills of exchange, to and from these areas; the parties are all Venetians.

Obviously there was some interest in providing letters of credit to pilgrims embarking in Venice bound for the Holy Land. An example is provided by the knight of Cologne, Arnold von Harff, who recounts that he purchased letters of credit (which he calls bills of exchange, "wessel brieve") from an unnamed Venetian nobleman, on Alexandria, Damascus,

---

[38]Venice was third after Rome and Florence with 15 percent in 1397–1420, and second only to Rome with 13 percent in 1420–35 and with 22 percent in 1435–50; see de Roover, *Medici Bank*, 47, 55, 69.

TABLE 8.2

The Contribution of Foreign Exchange to Net Profits of
Filippo Borromei and Company in London, 1436–1439
(in pounds sterling, shillings, and pence)

	1436	1437	1438	1439
Merchandise				
Profits	46/ 0/0	149/17/ 6	136/ 8/7	207/ 2/11
Losses	—	1/ 3/ 5	53/ 3/0	44/19/ 6
Net	46/ 0/0	148/14/ 1	83/ 5/7	162/ 3/ 5
Exchange				
Profits	75/17/9	255/ 4/10	199/15/1	207/ 3/11
Losses	—	136/ 2/11	103/14/1	14/ 2/ 7
Net	75/17/9	119/ 1/11	96/ 1/0	193/ 1/ 4
Commissions (ave.) (£117 in 4 years)	30/	30/	30/	30/
Net + commissions	105/17/9	149/ 1/11	126/ 1/0	223/ 1/ 4
Global net profits of the company	24/17/8	303/ 4/ 5	215/ 1/8	387/12/ 1
Approximate contribution of exchange to net profits	—	49%	58%	57%

Source: Derived from de Roover, "Early Accounting Problems of Foreign Exchange," table 5
(in turn an adaptation of Biscaro, "Il banco Filippo Borromei," 381–85); also ibid., 308.

Beirut, Antioch, and Constantinople. He was surprised that he could collect easily abroad, even when he could not communicate with the merchant who honored the letters.[39]

Suits before the commercial court of the Petizion and account books mention bills of exchange on Damascus, Tripoli, and Alexandria,[40] Beirut,[41] Cyprus,[42] Crete, and Constantinople. The sums exchanged in a single bill were on the average less than half those involved in exchanges to the west (100–150 ducats, against 300–400 ducats). It is not surprising that rechange is only rarely encountered. Two examples concerning Alexandria are found in suits of 1444–45, but the sums involved are quite small. The first includes evidence from an accounting entry which doubles the exchange

[39]*Die Pilgerfahrt,* 58–59.

[40]Eliahu Ashtor lists 21 cases involving these three cities, in "Le taux d'intérêt dans l'orient médiéval," reprinted in his *The Medieval Near East: Social and Economic History* (London, 1978), art. XII, 204–7.

[41]See the Bembo letterbook in ASV, Miscellanea Gregolin, b. 13, fols. 13 (20 February 1420), 27 (28 June).

[42]ASV, GP, Sg, reg. 19, fols. 53–54 (1413); PSM, Misti, b. 70, commis. Antonio Contarini, reg. 1 (about 1400) and, among the papers, the bill itself.

rate for "recambio"; the second speaks clearly of interest due ("per danno . . . al rechambio").[43]

As is to be expected, more nearly regular dealings can be found with Candia (Crete) and Constantinople. As early as the 1330s and 1340s there is clear evidence in merchants' letters of exchanges by bill between Venice and Candia and of borrowing on the exchange.[44] Balances continued to be drawn upon or remitted, as the need arose; and some orders-to-pay foresaw the possibility of redrawing ("de recanbiar").[45] In the fifteenth century the government rather often paid debts or borrowed money in Venice by drawing on revenues in Candia—a way, perhaps, of avoiding the transfer of specie.[46]

The most solid source for exchange on Constantinople is the well-known account book of Giacomo Badoer. During the years covered by the accounts (1436–39), we find some twenty-eight drafts from Venice on Constantinople and some eighteen in the reverse direction. The entries are generally incomplete; the dates of the transactions in Venice are missing, and the maturity date is at best vague. The latter, in fact, was tied to the arrival of the galley that carried the mail and thus also the bills themselves. It is clear that Badoer applied to himself a commission of 1 percent, even on the bills in which he was beneficiary. As was the case in Venice, bills in Constantinople were handled on current account in the local deposit banks.

It comes as a mild surprise that the Badoer fraterna and the companies of which it was partner balanced their accounts almost completely with merchandise; what remained was handled, not by shipments of specie, of which there is no trace, but by bill of exchange, in both directions. Moreover, some of the bills on Constantinople were clearly destined to be redrawn. For example, there are four drafts by Pietro Soranzo on Badoer which arrived in September 1437 on the galleys captained by Giorgio Soranzo. All four fell due on the 16th of the same month, and Badoer drew

---

[43]ASV, GP, Sg, reg. 100, fol. 7v: "Ser Zanmathio over Ser Piero Soranzo de dare per una lettera di cambio de ducati 108 ritornada in Alexandria per canbio et recambio, zoè de ritorno, a 14 per centenario, et per lo ritorno de qui altri 14 per centenario, summa 28 per centenario, monta lire 13, soldi 14, denari 2, piccoli 16." Ibid., reg. 99, fols. 153–57v.

[44]Four letters to Pignol Zucchello (*Lettere di mercanti a Pignol Zucchello [1336–1350]*, ed. Raimondo Morozzo della Rocca [Venice, 1957], nos. 2, 22, 25, 32) were analyzed by G. Cassandro, "Note minime per la storia del 'cambio,' " reprinted in his *Saggi*, 209–32. A letter of 1346 orders the correspondent to sell merchandise to pay a draft; in case the goods could not be sold on time, the agent was to redraw at interest ("tolere a presa e mandatemegli a pagare").

[45]Examples in ASV, PSM, Misti, b. 141, commis. Bartolomeo Dallesmannini, reg. 1, fol. 6 (1375), and in Giulio Mandich, *Le pacte de "ricorsa" et le marché italien des changes au XVIIIe siécle* (Paris, 1953), 128–29.

[46]See Cassandro, "Note minime," 226 (who cites documents in Thiriet, *Regestes*). Money was so borrowed in 1441 for the war effort; the government in Candia was ordered to honor the bill immediately—and if it could not, to borrow the money from Jews. ASV, SMar, reg. 1, fol. 88. For funds raised in the same fashion to send troops to Negroponte, see SM, reg. 60, fol. 230 (1440).

back with four bills dated 18 September, 23 October, and 13 November, for the identical value of 900 ducats, bills that he sent off on the return voyage of the same galleys. Calculating the difference between the rates in Venice (undated but very likely in early August, as those of three other bills due the same time), at 3 perperi plus between 7 and 10 carats, and those in Constantinople, which were very close to the par of 3 perperi per ducat, and allowing one month for the return voyage and a maturity of eight days' sight (as is expressly stated in one of the redrafts), we arrive at interest rates, on an annual basis, of from 20 to 30 percent on the four redrafts.[47] Three other bills sent from Venice, one in 1437, two in 1439, find Badoer in the role of both payer and beneficiary; one of them clearly involved a simple balancing of accounts, while the others may have constituted a form of dry exchange; the "payments" in any case were mere book entries.[48] As regards the rates of exchange, suffice it to say that the ducat was constantly rated higher in Venice than in Constantinople, with differentials varying between about 4 and 10 percent. Giacomo Badoer settled accounts with his brother Gerolamo at par, namely, 3 perperi per ducat.[49]

The exchange activity of Venetians with the Levant was not particularly significant, however, in comparison with the known examples of exchange and rechange with the West.

v. CAMBIUM AD VENETIAS, 1336–1426

The Covoni Family Company, 1336–1340

A published ledger of the company of the Covoni, kept in Florence during the years 1336–40, constitutes the earliest solid record of the exchange markets of the two Italian city-republics.[50] It registers, in little more than three years, 443 exchange operations: 70 purely commercial remit-

---

[47]Dorini and Bertelé, *Il libro dei conti di Giacomo Badoer,* fol. 105, accounts entitled "Chambi mandadime a pagar da Venixia per Ser Piero Soranzo . . . diè dar" and "Chanbii mandadi a pagar a Veniexia a Ser Piero Soranzo . . . diè aver." Luzzatto's brief analysis of the same data (*Storia,* 179) is mistaken, to the extent that he did not recognize the element of rechange and sought to calculate profits on single exchanges.

[48]Dorini and Bertelé, *Il libro dei conti,* fols. 362/390, 390/389, 106; Badoer "paid" "in me medemo." Cf. de Roover, *Medici Bank,* 132–34.

[49]Further exchanges can be found in the account books of Francesco Contarini (BMCV, PD, C. 911–12); in suits, for example, ASV, GP, Frammenti antichi, b. 13 (1445, involving Francesco Contarini); ibid., Sg, regs. 130, fols. 57–62v, and 137, fol. 137 (with a copy of a bill dated 1452). In 1478 it was Giovanni Lanfredini, Medici factor in Venice, who advanced 3,200 ducats via remittances to Florentine merchants in Constantinople to pay the ransom of three Venetian captains captured by the Turks; ST, reg. 8, fol. 31v.

[50]Sapori, *Libro giallo,* with the indispensable technical introduction by Giulio Mandich; the accounts make continual reference to a more important book for present purposes, a "quaderno delle mandate di grossi," which has been lost.

tances from Venice to Florence, covering liabilities incurred; 335 speculative remittances (159 from Florence to Venice, 176 from Venice to Florence); and 38 dry exchange contracts, of the kind later called "cambium ad Venetias" or "ad grossos Venetos" by theoreticians, or "cambio per Vinegia senza lettera" by merchants. In both cases, interest rates averaged about 12 to 14 percent per year.

The speculative exchanges were not connected with the movement of goods but were simply loans extended in Florence via remittances that awaited, for repayment, a return remittance from Venice. Since the rate of exchange in Venice quoted certain over against Florence—that is, one Venetian lira di grossi "manca" was quoted as a variable number of Florentine lire a fiorino—the ducat, *pecunia praesens*, was rated higher than in Florence and remittances returned increased in value. Involved was a short-term, one-month investment in rechange, as we have seen above. The speculative element consisted both of the possibility of losing, as rates of exchange fluctuated, and of the uncertain, variable rate of profit. The primary use of exchange made by the Covoni company in the years 1336–38 was the speculative investment of between 2,000 and 3,500 florins per month in Florence at one rate and the expectation of returns from Venice at another, higher rate.[51] Rechanges are plotted on graph 8.3, along with the corresponding annual rates of interest or profit earned. As can be seen at a glance, the closer the two exchange curves, the lower the rate of interest; the greater the spread between the two curves, the higher the rate of profit.

The system of speculative remittances and rechanges (the accounts do not reveal whether with or without the actual sending of bills) was dropped very suddenly in 1338 and replaced by a contract clearly of dry exchange which worked in the following manner. The Covoni, as lenders of money in Florence, gave a round number of Venetian lire at the then current rate of exchange in lire a fiorino; the amount due after one month was calculated on the basis of the exchange rate current in Venice ten days after the contract had been made in Florence—an exchange rate communicated most likely by simple commercial letters containing market information. The return rate is invariably higher than the rate current in Florence, as was the case with the rechanges just discussed.[52]

Table 8.3 shows one example of the six cases in which takers or borrowers in Florence were so in need of credit as to have to "stay on the exchange" ("stare in su cambi") with Venice for more than one month. The company of Antonio Albizzi resorted to this form of borrowing twelve

---

[51]Mandich, "Per una ricostruzione," clxxx–xxxii.

[52]Mandich suggests that in some cases the return rate might have been fixed from the start, making the operation completely fictitious. If this were the case, the fact was well disguised, for the data provided in the accounts clearly show that the rates mirrored completely the traditional seasonality of supply and demand in Venice.

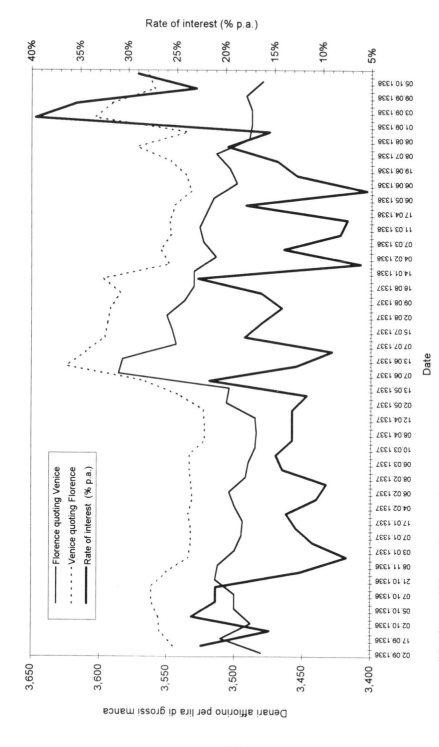

GRAPH 8.3. "Cambium ad Venetias": Rates of Exchange and Rates of Interest, 1336–1338. *Source:* Mandich, "Per una ricostruzione," ccxv–xxii.

TABLE 8.3

An Early Example of "Cambium ad Venetias" in the Covoni Accounts:
Loans by Antonio di Lando Albizzi and Company, 1338–1340
(in lire a fiorino)

Amount (£ gr)	In Florence		In Venice		Difference		Interest per Loan
	date	rate	date	rate	s	d	
45	17. 7.38	14/14/0	27. 7	14/17/ 4	3	4	
	17. 8.38						13.6
50	3. 2.39	14/ 9/7	13. 2	14/12/ 0	2	5	
50	3. 3.39	14/11/6	13. 3	14/13/ 8	2	2	
50	3. 4.39	14/10/6	13. 4	14/12/ 9	2	3	
	3. 5.39				t 6	10	9.4
50	14. 6.39	14/10/5	24. 6	14/14/10	4	5	
40	14. 7.39	14/11/9	24. 7	14/15/ 8	3	11	
80	13. 8.39	14/11/4	23. 8	14/17/10	6	6	
	13. 9.39				t 14	10	20.4
50	29.10.39	14/ 6/9	8.11	14/14/ 2	7	5	
50	29.11.39	14/ 9/8	9.12	14/12/ 4	2	8	
50	29.12.39	14/ 5/9	8. 1.40	14/10/ 4	4	7	
	29. 1.40				t 14	7	20.3
20	4. 1.40	14/ 5/6	14. 1	14/11/ 6	6	0	
	4. 2.40						25.2
50	29. 2.40	14/ 7/0	10. 3	14/11/ 6	4	6	
	30. 3.40						18.8

Source: Mandich, "Per una ricostruzione," ccxxiii.
Note: The first and last two loans lasted a single month, or one return; the second, third, and fourth loans each lasted three returns, so that the differences had to be added (t = total).

times in eighteen months as a means of garnering investment credit, for itself or for unnamed third parties. Plotted on graph 8.4, the results are quite similar to those obtained with the more traditional rechange contract analyzed just above, and, as can be seen, a profit was very nearly guaranteed. The graph shows the annual rate of interest on single returns as well as on single loans with several returns. The element of uncertainty in the rate of profit is demonstrated by the divergence between the two curves; just when a loan kept "on the exchange" was terminated could make an appreciable difference.

This form of dry exchange, with no bill sent, takes over so suddenly in the Covoni accounts as to suggest that "cambium ad Venetias" was invented or at least perfected in the course of the year 1338; the Covoni company, in any case, discovered its utility at that time, perhaps as a result of problems relating to the Scaliger War, then being fought. The Covoni themselves resorted to this form of borrowing on a single one-month loan, on which they — or the party they represented — had to pay interest at the high annual

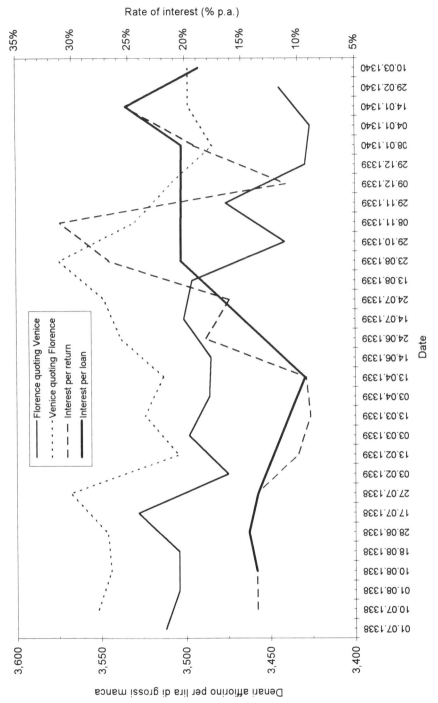

GRAPH 8.4. Dry Exchange in the Covoni Accounts: Rates of Exchange and Rates of Interest, 1338–1340. *Source:* Mandich, "Per una ricostruzione," ccxxiii.

rate of 27 percent.[53] Since the accounts of the factors in Venice, Giovanni Vai and Company, are not extant, it cannot be known whether and at what levels credit was similarly made available on the Rialto.

On the Venetian side, fortunately, those exact same years are covered by another account book, kept by Duccio di Banchello e Banco Bencivenni and Company. In the role of drawer, the Venetian branch of this company took many loans, paying as interest the difference between the rate in Venice and the lower rate current in Florence after twenty days' usance — that is, in just the same manner but in the opposite direction as the system employed by the Florence-based Covoni company. It also accepted many bills drawn on it by the head office in Florence. (The company appears in both roles in the accounts of the Covoni firm, in 1336–37.) Nearly forty cases of rechange handled by this company were found and analyzed by Giulio Mandich. Again, 12–14 percent was the normal rate of annual interest (the extremes were 3.5 and 40%), deriving from the differential between two curves of rates.[54]

The modes of operation on the exchange in Florence and in Venice differed throughout the late Middle Ages. Accounts and merchant manuals show that exchange activity in Venice was mediated by the Rialto banks: bills were bought and sold, received and paid by debiting and crediting current accounts handled by Rialto bankers, as third parties. Bills could be honored only when the Rialto banks were open for business. In the ledger of Duccio di Banchello, payments were made generally in the bank of Giovanni Stornado, the most prominent bank on the Rialto in those years. A century later the Medici branch similarly maintained current accounts at the banks of the Rialto. In Florence, on the other hand, no local bank mediated a transaction between the two principal parties to a bill, for payment was to be made in cash. Thus the ledger entries always mention the name of the man who brought ("annoverò," "portò") or received ("rechò") the money. In fact, the Florentine statutes of 1393 state that bills were to be presented for payment when the local assay office, run by the Arte del Cambio, was open, so that the coins used could be evaluated.[55] It is difficult to imagine porters coming and going around the Mercato Nuovo carrying sacks of coin; perhaps the phrases became mere accounting formulas meant to uphold the letter of the law, while debits and credits resulting from exchange transactions were actually balanced on the current accounts of the parties to the bills. In both cities, finally, there were specialized bill brokers ("sensales cambiorum," "sansarii cambiorum").

Later instances of "cambium ad Venetias" can be adduced to show

<hr/>

[53]Mandich, "Per una ricostruzione," clxxxvii.

[54]See "La prassi delle assegnazioni," 15–46; the rates on 36 rechanges and the calculations are in his appendix. See also idem, "Una compagnia fiorentina a Venezia," 145–46, and "Per una ricostruzione," ccxiv–xix.

[55]A. Lattes, *Il diritto commerciale*, 133 n. 20.

Fig. 15. A loan on rechange. Francesco di Marco Datini's record
of a loan extended to his friend Guelfo de' Pugliesi on a contract of
"cambium ad Venetias," 1398 (a note sent from headquarters in Florence
to Prato in early 1399).

ADP, 1171, fasc. 6, "valute di Firenze"

how common this form of lending became. The Datini archive offers end-
less examples.

Examples from the Datini Firm, 1398–1402

Figure 15 shows a small, damaged slip of paper on which are recorded
the rates of exchange current in Florence and Venice during five months in
1398. It was sent by Datini's office in Florence to Francesco Datini himself
in Prato in early 1399. The note (called "Chonto di valute di ghrossi") was
the record of a loan made by Datini to a good friend and neighbor, the
nobleman Messer Guelfo de' Pugliesi of Prato.[56] The loan was set at 6
Venetian lire di grossi on 20 September 1398, when 1 lira was quoted in
Florence at £15 5s 6d a fiorino, as though Messer Guelfo had sold a bill of
exchange to his banker. At that rate, what Guelfo received in hand ("el
chapitale ch' ebbe") was 63 gold florins.[57] Messer Guelfo kept the money
"on the exchange" for five returns, that is, for five months. The "Chonto," in
fact, goes on to register the rates of the drafts ("andate") in Florence and
the redrafts ("ritorni") from Venice on the basis of generally known market

[56]ADP, 1171, fasc. 6, "valute di Firenze." Messer Guelfo was a man of great prestige; he was
made an honorary citizen of Florence in 1375 and senator of Rome; he served as podestà in
Bologna, Perugia, and Genoa. Upon his death in Prato in 1402, the government of Florence
sent three knights to honor him. See Ser Lapo Mazzei, *Lettere di un notaro a un mercante del
secolo XIV,* ed. Cesare Guasti, 2. vols. (Florence, 1880), 1:23 n, 414 n; idem, ed., *Le commissioni
di Rinaldo degli Albizzi,* 2 vols. (Florence, 1867–73), 1:396 n.

[57]£15/5/6 a fior. = 3,666d a fior., × £6 di gr, ÷ 240d per lira, = £91.65 a fior.; × 0.69 florins
per £ a fior., = 63.2 gold florins.

information on the dates determined by usance: after ten days, the rate in Venice; after an additional twenty days, once again the recorded rate in Florence ("[grossi] valsono"). The rates in Venice, consumed by a mouse or by mold, can be reconstructed from commercial letters—the same source used by the Datini bank. The accountant merely added up the five differentials between the two rates to calculate Guelfo's loss ("che perde"), namely, 3 fl., 8s 3d a fiorino for five months, or 12.5 percent interest at an annual rate (see table 8.4). In this example, it is particularly easy to see how the creditor could lose: it was sufficient that one of the rates of the second column drop below that of the first. In fact, this loan was terminated just before a considerable drop in rates in Venice, of which Datini had surely been forewarned by his correspondents. In contrast to the cases of the 1330s discussed above, here it is sure that no bill was ever sent, no broker was paid, no commission ("provvigione") was paid to a correspondent; rather than rechange, the case involves pure dry exchange—a manner for Datini to calculate the rate of interest to charge his friend Guelfo, without fixing the rate in advance, which would have been usury.

Another example, this time from a Datini "memoriale," or record book, is reported in a slightly different fashion, although the end result is quite the same.[58] After the death from plague in 1400 of Zanobi Gaddi, Datini's principal correspondent in Venice, the merchant banker from Prato felt some obligation toward the deceased's three sons, probably all still minors, and their mother. (They lived then in Florence, while the firm continued to function in Venice under the style "La commissaria di Zanobi di Taddeo e Antonio di Ser Bartolomeo".) When they were in need of liquidity in 1402 in order to meet prestanze obligations, Datini arranged a loan on exchange with Tommaso di Jacopo de' Bardi, for 10 lire di grossi. The differentials were calculated, not beginning in Florence but from the successive Venetian rate. The family must have been in considerable need, for it was forced to borrow in the summer, when rates in Venice were known to peak. On 7 June it received 104.2 florins; on 16 September, after three returns (three months plus ten days), it had to pay interest of 6.54 florins, that is, an annual rate of 22.9 percent. The principal, however, remained "on the exchange" as a continuing loan—a dear one. Bindo Piaciti wrote from Venice to the office in Florence on 2 September 1402 saying that it would have been better to borrow for the heirs by attracting deposits in sopracorpo and pay the relevant "discrezione," since exchange rates were too hot to touch on that day. In the next letter, in fact, Piaciti complained

---

[58]ADP, 578, Memoriale FF, fol. 94v; the operation was posted to Libro d'entrata e uscita FF, fol. 173, and to Libro bianco F, fol. 173. Further transactions of exchange, rechange, and dry exchange ("sanza lettera") in the same period can be studied in ASF, MAP, 133/1, the ledger of 1395 of Averardo de' Medici; when dealing with Venice, his chief agent was Antonio Dietifeci.

TABLE 8.4

Francesco Datini's Loan on Dry Exchange to
Guelfo de' Pugliesi of Prato, 1398

In Florence				In Venice				Difference	
	exchange				exchange				
date	£	s	d	date	£	s	d	s	d
20 Sept. 1398	15	5	6	30 Sept. 1398	15	7	10	2	4
21 Oct.	15	5	8	31 Oct.	15	12	2	6	6
21 Nov.	15	8	8	2 Dec.ª	15	12	8	5	0
23 Dec.	15	10	8	2 Jan. 1399ᵇ	15	11	6	0	10
23 Jan. 1399	15	11	2	2 Feb.ᵇ	15	12	4	1	2
							Total:	15s	10d
							per £1 di grossi		

Source: ADP, 1171, fasc. 6, "Valute di Firenze."
Note: Amount lent: £6 di grossi Venetian, which, on 20 September, brought 63 florins. Amount due on 23 February: 63 florins, plus 3 florins, 8s, 3d a fiorino as interest, or 12.5 percent.
ªMistakenly entered as "10 di novenbre."
ᵇDocument damaged; rate taken from other sources.

that Venetian payers on a remittance from Majorca were stalling and accusing Florentine cambisti of forcing them to pay "usury" of 30–40 percent. In short, the route chosen to help Zanobi's minor heirs by borrowing on exchange in that conjuncture was proving to be particularly costly, as it was also for Venetian borrowers.[59]

The Case of the Aretine Lazzaro Bracci, 1415–1418

The last example, again Florentine, was elucidated by de Roover in his article "Cambium ad Venetias." It is worthwhile recalling it briefly here only because it shows how a lender (or "remitter") could actually, if rarely,

[59]On 2 September Piaciti reported that the partnership instituted in Venice for the heirs was to have a corpo of 6,000 ducats; Piaciti was to invest 500 ducats in the sopracorpo, but there was some doubt whether that amount would not be diverted to paying their prestanze; but, the writer continued, "sarebe meglio per via di diposito farne nostra possa," because "i chanbi sono tropo chocenti a tochare ora, ed è chosa di disfare altrui." The observation that interest could destroy someone was applied to friends who had to pay; when it was a matter of collecting, however, Piaciti was virulent against Venetian debtors on a small bill from Majorca ("non posiamo avere da loro se non parole e frasche"), and he rejected out of hand their accusations of having to pay usury: "e dichono stanno loro a usura a più di 30 per cento, e abominano altrui e questo ne diviene a servire simile gente ingrata"; and again: "e anche dichono altrui vilania e che sono usure di 36 in 40 per cento." ADP, 714, letters of 2, 9, 16 September 1402.

lose on this kind of loan. In fact, in the cases discussed thus far, the lenders never lost. The investor here was Lazzaro Bracci, an Aretine active in Florence. In 1415 he decided to lend idle funds in dry exchange ("io diedi a chanbio per Vinegia") to twelve different borrowers (nine of whom were local bankers at the Mercato Nuovo) — all in the peak summer months. The loans were renewed for a total of fifty-two one-month "returns." That these business loans were at risk is shown by the fact that on nine returns the rate in Florence exceeded that in Venice and the lender absorbed a loss. All told, however, he lost on only one loan of the twelve made, a loan kept on the exchange for three returns; in that instance, the borrower, a local banker, actually earned, at a rate of 1.2 percent. On all the other loans, the lender profited, albeit at a low average rate of 6.6 percent. Once again, no assets passed from one city to the other, no bills were sent; only the difference in current rates in the two cities, foreseeable and nearly guaranteed, was utilized to calculate the rate of interest due in the future, on the "return." As de Roover wrote, "The cards were stacked in his favor," and Bracci continued to lend in the same fashion in the following years. The mere risk of loss (which here became reality) and the uncertainty of the rate of profit made this kind of dry exchange very popular and widely thought to be licit.[60]

The same system, of course, worked also in the opposite direction, permitting Venetians and other merchants active on the Rialto to borrow money on the exchange. The Florentine silk entrepreneur Jacopo d'Andrea Arnoldi, a man with double citizenship who ran silk shops in both cities, declared in 1427 that, in order to meet his forced loan commitments in Venice, he was forced to borrow on the exchange. In fact, in his catasto statement he listed debts for drafts from Venice on Florence: three rechanges and two dry exchanges ("sanza lettera").[61]

vi. RECHANGE ON BRUGES AND LONDON IN THE MID-FIFTEENTH CENTURY

Turning to the documentation for the succeeding decades of the fifteenth century, one notes that longer-term credit than that provided by the one-month, renewable "cambium ad Venetias" was desired by long-distance merchants in Venice and in the network of the Florentine cambisti. Loans via rechange and dry exchange during the central decades of the fifteenth century are between Venice and Bruges and, even more, between Venice and London, thus for double-usance periods of four and six months respectively.

---

[60]Raymond de Roover, "Cambium ad Venetias: Contribution to the History of Foreign Exchange," in his *Business, Banking, and Economic Thought*, 239–59.

[61]See Mueller, "Mercanti e imprenditori fiorentini," 52.

The Borromei of London, 1436–1440

An account book of the London branch of the bank of Filippo Borromei and Company of Bruges shows that London was at the head of two exchange triangles, Venice-London-Bruges and Genoa-London-Bruges, circuits that served primarily for keeping funds moving and earning, often via forms of arbitrage. For example, in 1436 London, acting as principal, ordered the head office in Bruges to draw 1,720 ducats (in five bills) on the bank in Venice of the Milanese merchant banker Arrighino Panigaruola. At about the same time, London remitted 7,100 ducats to Panigaruola, with bills many of which were to mature between May and August, that is, just when rates in Venice were foreseen to peak. Slightly later in the same year, the London company, acting as agent of the Bruges bank, paid drafts arriving especially from Genoa. Those drafts were paid in part with new drafts (six on Genoa, four on Venice), in part with remittances from Bruges. Rechange, like commercial exchange, on the other hand, retained its traditional, linear character.[62]

If we limit ourselves to the rates involving Venice and London, we can see immediately in graph 8.5 that the curves fit perfectly the pattern so often explained by de Roover: the Florentine-made rules of the game had it that rates in Venice, which quoted certain, were going to be generally higher than those current in London, and so it was; in other words, the ducat in Venice, where it was *pecunia praesens*, was worth more than in London, where it was *pecunia absens*. In Venice the price of the ducat averaged about 45 pence sterling, while the price in London averaged about 41 pence. As a result, the remitter generally profited from the differential on rechanges, that is, on loans of six months' duration.[63]

From the Account Books of Andrea Barbarigo

Further examples of the functioning of the money market in Venice in the same decade are found in the accounts of Andrea Barbarigo, the mer-

[62]Biscaro, "Il banco Filippo Borromei," 327, 329 (Panigaruolo, avere), 334, 336 (Borromei-Bruges, dare); 326, 328 (Panigaruola, dare); 336–41.

[63]It should be noted in this context that Spufford's data (*Handbook*, 201–5) regarding exchange between Venice and London in these years and the relative explanation (ibid., intro.) are wrong. Unfortunately, his assistants mistakenly inverted the two curves, reading into the computer program the rates current in Venice as though current in London and vice versa. The result prompted the author to formulate a novel thesis about exchange, in contradiction to "the de Roover orthodoxy," a thesis that is totally fallacious, based as it is on false premises. The author sought to disprove de Roover's explanation of the rule of thumb that the curve of rates in the city whose market quoted "certain" (*N* units foreign money for 1 unit local money) was regularly higher than that of the correspondent city that quoted "uncertain" (*N* units local money for 1 unit foreign money). See my "The Spufford Thesis on Foreign Exchange: The Evidence of Exchange Rates," in *JEEcH* 24 (1995): 121–29.

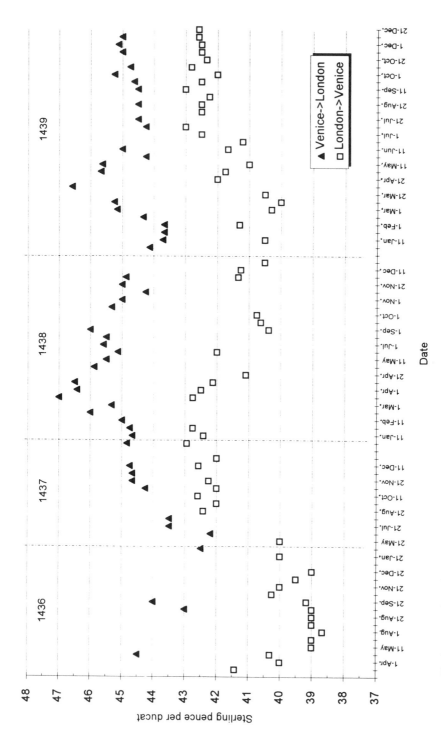

GRAPH 8.5. Exchange and Rechange between Venice and London: The Venetian Ducat in Pence Sterling, 1436–1440. *Source:* Biscaro, "Il banco Filippo Borromei," 376–79.

chant made famous by Frederic Lane. Andrea was a middling merchant, interested primarily in trade in commodities. For his interests in London, Bruges, and Valencia he used bills regularly, remitting money to his correspondents and paying their drafts on him, when the merchandise he shipped to those markets was insufficient to cover the purchases he desired.[64] Occasionally he dabbled in the money market, sometimes on account of third parties;[65] twice he intervened resolutely on his own account, once to borrow, once to lend. Later he sought shorter-term loans via rechanges on Milan and on the Geneva exchange fairs.[66]

On the first occasion, Andrea made a small loan of 80 ducats to a cousin, Giovanni di Almorò Barbarigo, and he himself borrowed that amount from the Medici by selling a bill on London, at 44 pence sterling per ducat. Giovanni knew that, after double the usance of three months, he would have to pay the difference on the redraft; the latter, in fact, was negotiated at 42 pence per ducat. The amount due in six months, 84.4 ducats, constituted an increment (including 26 pence sterling for brokerage and commission) which corresponded, at an annual rate, to 11 percent.[67]

Again acting in the name of others, Andrea also tried his hand at two shorter-term operations on Bruges (usance two months in each direction). In 1435, he invested 300 ducats in the name of his faithful agent Troilo Pacaron, by buying a bill on Bruges, at 49 groats per ducat. The rechange, at a lower rate, as usual, garnered for Pacaron a gain of 10 ducats, or 10 percent per annum.[68] The second operation, in 1436, involved a loan of 120 ducats to his agent Alberto Dolcetto, which Andrea covered with a draft on Bruges at 50 groats per ducat; in Bruges the draft was protested and returned (at 46¾ groats per ducat), so that Dolcetto was debited with interest and charges amounting to almost 9 ducats, or 22.5 percent per annum.[69]

Andrea Barbarigo himself turned to the exchange, both on London and on Bruges, to find funds for investment in 1434. Between late February

---

[64]See Lane, *Andrea Barbarigo*. An excellent example of a letter from London, sent to Venice in 1441, explaining the current prices of Levantine products and of those products Venetians were buying in London to ship back, is published in Melis, *Documenti*, doc. 29. The commercial bills are found in the ledgers' indices under the names of Andrea's correspondents (in particular Vettor Capello e fratelli and Giovanni e Lorenzo di Marcanovo); loans are indexed under "Denari tolti a cambio per . . ." and "Cambi per . . . di mia raxon."

[65]For example, in 1436 he acted in Francesco Balbi's name in drawing 900 ducats on Milan; the two bills returned protested, and Balbi paid Andrea a gift ("dono") of 12.1 percent for the costs of a forty-two-day loan (Barbarigo, ledger A, fol. 248).

[66]Barbarigo, ledger B, fols. 77, 110, 133, 179.

[67]Andrea entitled the account "Danari tolti a canbio per Londra a prò e dano di ser Zan Barbarigo fo de ser Almorò." The parties in London were Vettor Capello e fratelli, Andrea's correspondents; those of the Medici were Galeazzo Borromei e Antonio di Francesco. Barbarigo, ledger A, fol. 111.

[68]Ibid., fols. 146, 173 ("Danari dadi a canbio per Bruza per conto de ser Troilo Pacaron").

[69]Ibid., fol. 136.

and October, but always in periods during which demand was foreseeably low in Venice, he sold five bills on London for a total of 1,300 ducats. Twice it was the Medici branch in Venice which acted as deliverer or lender, and twice it was the Milanese Arrighino Panigaruola; once three of the four parties were the same company, namely, Andrea's agents Vettor Capello e fratelli, whom he ordered to draw back on him ("con ordene me trazese adrieto").

Then he summarized his losses this way: "For Vettor Capello & Bros., London, for 1,300 ducats which I drew on them at 45 and 44 pence sterling per ducat and more, and they redrew at about 40 pence sterling, in four bills, so that I lose more than 140 ducats." And then: "for brokerage and commission charges in London, on drafts which they paid and redrew, 5½ ducats." The wide spread between the rates of exchange in Venice and in London made for a considerable loss: in Venice Andrea had to pay out 1,445.5 ducats, including charges, for an annual rate of "loss" — mostly interest — of 22.4 percent (see table 8.5).[70]

In September 1434 Andrea also turned to the exchange on Bruges. He obtained 410 ducats by selling bills at 49 and 49⅓ Flemish groats per ducat; redrafts from Bruges, where the ducat was quoted lower (just above 46 groats), caused him to pay out 435 ducats. The cost of 25 ducats, equivalent to 18.3 percent per year, was debited to profit and loss.[71]

In short, Andrea was able, in a moment of need, to obtain investment credits totaling 1,710 ducats; his sales of bills on London and Bruges constituted loans of six and four months respectively, on which the exchange market established the cost or interest.

What were the investment needs that caused Andrea to resort to the exchange market? First of all, drafts from London were falling due which he had to honor without redrawing; second, he was interested in investing in Acre, where, in September 1434, he sent 600 gold ducats, in two sacks bearing his coat of arms as identification. In short, rechange with the north provided credits convertible into specie, then in demand in the Levant.[72]

The second major excursion by Andrea Barbarigo into the rechange market was in 1439, when Andrea convinced his banker (Francesco Balbi) to advance sums owed him by purchasers of wool, so that he could invest

[70]Despite the fact that more than one year elapsed between the first draft in Venice (22 February 1434) and the payment of the last redraft, which should have been about 7 April 1435, none of the sums "remained on the exchange," that is, they were not again drawn at once in order to pay the redraft. The only two temporally close operations were these: on 7 October Andrea drew his last bill on London, thus borrowing 300 ducats in Venice; on 10 October he had to pay 100 ducats on a redraft that must have fallen due then (figuring double the usance, from 10 April).

[71]Barbarigo, ledger A, fols. 136, 188.

[72]See ibid., fol. 135, for Andrea's payments of drafts from London; fol. 137 for the shipment of ducats to Acre. All these operations can be followed even better in chronological fashion, in Journal A.

TABLE 8.5

Andrea Barbarigo's Drafts and Rechange on London, 1434

Date	Value (ducats)	Rate (d. ster. per du.)	Remitter (in Venice)	Beneficiary (in London)
22 Feb.	200	45¾	Arrighino Panigaruola	Galeazzo Borromei and Antonio di Francesco
10 Apr.	100	45¼	Medici bank, local branch	Galeazzo Borromei and Antonio di Francesco
18 Sept.	500	44¼	Vettor Capello, Venice branch	Vettor Capello, London branch
24 Sept.	200	441⅛	Medici bank, local branch	Bartolomeo Lomellino
7 Oct.	300	44	Arrighino Panigaruola	Galeazzo Borromei and Antonio di Francesco
Total	1,300	44½ (ave.)		
Rechange:	1,440	40 (ave.)		
Expenses:	5.5			
	1,445.5			

Total cost: 145.5 ducats, or 22.4 percent

Source: Barbarigo, ledger A, fols. 119, 161.
Note: In London, payer on the drafts and taker on the redrafts were Vettor Capello and brothers.

that money in buying bills on London (see table 8.6). Between 6 June and 13 August, just when the rates in Venice were highest, Andrea, represented by Balbi, bought nine bills on London, at rates averaging 45 pence sterling per ducat, for a total of 2,900 ducats, all of it paid in bank money, that is, by transfers on the books of Balbi's bank. On Andrea's orders, the Capello brothers in London bought ten bills on Venice, at rates averaging 42.7 pence sterling per ducat, so that Andrea found himself, after the double usance of six months, between mid-December 1439 and late February 1440, with the value of 3,060 ducats. In short, he had made a profit of 160 ducats; at an annual rate, he earned 11 percent, surely less than he had hoped for. As can be seen from table 8.6, the rates in London, albeit always lower than the rates in Venice, in fact remained relatively high, thus reducing the spread and the chances for higher profits.[73]

[73]Barbarigo, ledger A, fols. 260 (Balbi per conto di lana), 259 (Cambi per Londra per mia raxon), and 277 (Vettor Capello e fradelli). The Capello brothers charged him for the brokerage in London ("coratazo," of 0.083 percent) and for their own commission ("provixion," of one-half of 1 percent).

TABLE 8.6

Andrea Barbarigo's Investment in Rechange, 1439–1440

(a) 9 bills remitted by Andrea Barbarigo from Venice to Vettor Capello and Brothers in London ("cambio di andata"), 1439

Date	Value (ducats)	Rate (d. ster. per du.)	Drawer	Payer
3 June	500	45	Polo and Jacopo Zane	Pasquale Zane
10 June	500	45	Francesco Balbi	Bertucio Contarini
12 July	500	44⅞	Francesco Balbi	Bertucio Contarini
15 July	200	44⅞	Leonardo Contarini	Bertucio Contarini
20 July	300	44⅞	?	Bertucio Contarini
4 Aug.	300	45½	Battista Contarini	Andrea Corner
8 Aug.	300	45¼	Mafeo Michiel	Vettor Capello and brothers
13 Aug.?	100	45⅓	Carlo e Polo Marin	Alvise Marin
13 Aug.	200	45¼	Gabriele Trevisan	Bertucio Contarini
Total:	2,900	45.1 (ave.)		

(b) 10 bills remitted by Vettor Capello and Brothers in London to Andrea Barbarigo in Venice ("cambio di ritorno"), 1439–40

Date	Value (ducats)	Rate (d. ster. per du.)	Payer
3 Sept.	220	42¾	Francesco Balbi
10 Sept.	536	42¼	Polo e Jacopo Zane
12 Oct.	310	42¼	Giovanni Priuli, treasurer
15 Oct.	200	42½	Vettor Capello and brothers
20 Oct.	213.16	42½	Matteo Vetturi e compagni
4 Nov.	250	42½	Leonardo Contarini
8 Nov.	350	42½	Zan Teiazzi
8 Nov.	50	42½	Bernardo Contarini (partial)
8 Nov.	289.25	42½	Andrea Zen (protested bill)
13 Nov.	300	42⁷⁄₁₂	Arrighino Panigaruolo
13 Nov.	250	42⁷⁄₁₂	Zan di Marcanovo
—	60	—	Zan di Marcanovo (balance)
—	31.75	—	Vettor Capello and brothers (balance)
Total:	3,060.16	42.7 ave.	

Source: Barbarigo, ledger A, fols. 259, 269, 272.

Note: The difference between andata (a) and ritorno (b) was 160.16 ducats, or a profit of 11 percent p.a.

Examples from the Medici Branch in Venice

In borrowing and then lending on Bruges and London, Barbarigo operated on longer terms than had been possible with the traditional rechange between Venice and Florence. While the shorter-term variety of dry exchange may have continued to be used by some, we lose sight of it when merchants opted in favor of exchanges on London and on Bruges.

Well known are the examples of dry exchange given by Raymond de Roover for the Medici bank, but it might easily be overlooked that all of them, without exception, concern the branch in Venice. The reason is that, as we have seen above, the cambista operating in Florence saved twenty days' time—and money—exchanging with Bruges and London through Venice. Since de Roover's tables are so readily accessible, I have merely reduced his data, from the central decades of the fifteenth century, to graphic form (see graphs 8.6 and 8.7). All of the data concern bills that were protested, that is, the payer abroad had been instructed not to honor the bill presented for payment and to return it with a protest. This becomes a very popular form of dry exchange. The result was the same as that of any rechange operation, except that the original borrower had to pay the protest fees, as well as the interest defined by the difference between the two rates of exchange.

Of the rechanges between Venice and Bruges nine originated in Bruges, thirty-six in Venice (see graph 8.6). One loan brought an exceptional return of 29 percent, while the others reflect more normal commercial rates ranging between 8 and 20 percent. Only one rechange resulted in a loss: in 1465 it happened that the rechange rate in Venice dropped below the rate applied to the original exchange in Bruges; the result was that the borrower, as well as having had the use of the money, earned 2.8 percent— part of which was certainly absorbed by the protest and other fees.[74] But the loss to the remitter in that one case was real, and the possibility of loss was what rendered rechange licit—or at least sufficiently dubious—for many contemporaries.

In the second case, de Roover collected eleven rechanges between Venice and London, scattered between 1444 and 1463. The annual rate of profit varied from 8 to 21 percent, in relation to the distance between the two curves of exchange rates (see graph 8.7).

Two small collections of actual bills made out in Venice can be used to exemplify just how loans via exchange were handled in practice.

The first group contains six bills involving four drafts on Bruges by the borrower Giacomo Lamberti, a Florentine involved in the wool trade. It survives in the estate papers of Guglielmo Querini, since Querini was the guarantor on each loan. The bills that survive are the first and third copies

[74]De Roover, *Medici Bank,* 113–23, esp. tables 22–24.

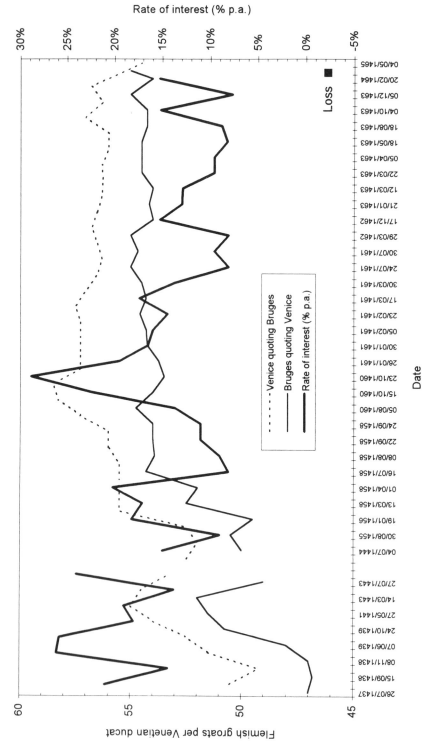

GRAPH 8.6. Exchange and Rechange between Venice and Bruges, with Annual Rate of Interest, 1437–1465. *Source:* de Roover, *Medici Bank,* tables 23–24.

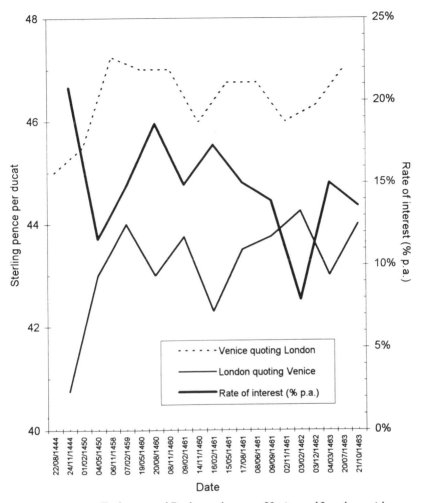

GRAPH 8.7. Exchange and Rechange between Venice and London, with Annual Rate of Interest, 1444–1463. *Source*: de Roover, *Medici Bank*, table 22.

("Pagate per questa prima . . . ," "Pagate per questa terza . . ."). The practice was to give the first copy to the guarantor, who, at the time of payment, had the lender sign the receipt on the bill itself. The third copy, signed by the guarantor with his promise to pay, went to the lender. At the conclusion of the rechange, Querini tried to gain possession of both copies, for his own security. The second copy seems actually to have been sent to the drawee, in each case Bernardo Zorzi in Bruges, ordering him to pay three different firms in Flanders. The three lenders in Venice were the firms of Giovanni Panciatichi and Giovanni Portinari and Company, Cosimo and Lorenzo de' Medici and Company, and Cecco Tommasi and Brothers. Only on the first bill, dated 17 July 1437 and made out for 300 ducats at 51 Flemish groats per ducat, do we find a complete receipt (for 326 ducats), signed by Bardo Alto-viti, factor of the Panciatichi-Portinari firm, which permits calculation of the rate of interest at 24 percent. Lamberti clearly had to redraw in order to pay drafts returning from Bruges, for the value of each successive bill is increased by 25 ducats, that is, the principal included all or most of the unpaid interest, which was in effect compounded. It is obvious why the guarantor jealously guarded the proof that payment had actually been made.[75]

The second group contains twelve bills of exchange involving eight drafts, mostly for rechange, all drawn on London over the period 1451–69. Three are in duplicate, in each case the first and third copies, and, as in the Querini case, it is the third copy that contains the guarantee. All name only three parties: seven name only one party abroad (thus the order reads "pagate a voi medesimi"); in one, the payer and drawer are the same. Two are commercial bills, involving balancing accounts abroad, and the rest are destined to be redrawn, as per instructions ("fategli il dover"). These constitute loans, mostly for very considerable sums, much larger than one finds in commercial bills. Surprising is the role assumed, in this later period, by Venetian Rialto bankers: in only one case is the lender (remitter) a Florentine company (the Rucellai-Strozzi firm appears once as lender, once as borrower), while in six cases the lender is a local transfer banker active on the Rialto. Three different bankers, discussed above in Part I, were involved. Agostino Ziera made three loans, two in 1451 for the huge sums of 10,000 and 3,000 ducats to the same borrower (drawer), Broccardo de' Conti "de Persicho"; in the third bill, in 1466, he advanced 1,700 ducats to the Florentine Luigi Ardinghelli. Pietro di Giovanni Soranzo advanced 500 ducats to the Strozzi factor in Venice in 1468. Andrea qd. Piero Barbarigo lent 1,250 ducats in 1467 to Bartolomeo Pagan and 700 ducats to Giovanni di Michele "dal sal" in 1469. In these last three cases, the duplicate copies of the bills (each time the "terza") were countersigned by Agostino Ziera as guarantor — the last also by his son Piero — specifically "for the above exchange and rechange." The Ziera were known as speculators, and here we have the proof of their readiness to take risks on the rechange market.[76]

Rechange, with or without protests, had become a completely quotidian mode of investing funds, not only by merchant bankers but also by

---

[75]ASV, PSM, Citra, b. 271, fasc. 3, bills bearing the consecutive numbering (albeit not in chonological order) 151–55bis. The beneficiaries in Bruges were Ubertino de' Bardi, Bernardo di Giovanni Portinari, and Filippo Borromei. Antonio Martelli signed the receipts on the two remittances by the Medici, Nicolò Tommasi that of Cecco Tommasi and Brothers. The bills and Querini's guarantees were mentioned by Gino Luzzatto, "L'attività commerciale di un patrizio veneziano del Quattrocento," reprinted in his *Studi*, 186.

[76]Russian Academy of Sciences, St. Petersburg Branch, Archive of the Institute of Russian History, West European Section, box 602, nos. 43–52. My thanks to Dr. Lev G. Klimanov for drawing these bills to my attention in St. Petersburg and for lending me a microfilm of them.

Venetians who found themselves with liquid capital. Orders to agents and powers of attorney included exchange as an investment opportunity to be exploited.[77] The most popular kind of loan on exchange, after about 1420, was from Venice on Bruges and London, but there were also varieties of triangular exchange as well as of rechange simply between London and Bruges by Venetians resident in those two cities. After the 1450s, this kind of loan was often worked out among Venetians; the mediation of Florentines was not necessary to protest a bill.[78]

vii. EXCHANGE AND THE GOVERNMENT

The government became involved with exchange early on various accounts. It tried, first of all, to control illicit kinds of exchange; then it resorted to borrowing on rechange; finally, it tried to tax this form of lending.

A vague order of 1328 to the courts to identify illicit contracts was clarified in 1357, in a climate of heated debate regarding high rates of interest and usury, so as to include illicit exchanges, which were placed under the jurisdiction of the Consoli dei Mercanti. That law, according to which the Consoli were to reduce patently illegal transactions to the mere payment of the principal, seems very rarely to have been invoked, and then in vain.[79] In 1411 the Senate passed, by a wide margin, a vehement law against lending money under all the forms of rechange and dry exchange which we have already encountered: "asking surety for exchange, not sending bills at all, or even sending bills but not really exchanging at all, or

---

[77]See Mandich, *Le pacte de "ricorsa,"* 128–29; ASV, GP, Sg, reg. 98, fol. 105r–v.

[78]For cases of rechange with protest on London, see Rawdon Brown, ed., *Calendar of State Papers — Venetian,* vol. 1 (London, 1864), and the journal of Marco di Colti, 1473–76, in ASV, Miscellanea carte non appartenente a nessun archivio, b. 29, for example, under the dates 30 October, 16 November, and 1 December, 1473, and 17 June 1474. See also CN, reg. 5, fol. 79v (1417). For examples of suits centered on rechange transactions, often with guarantors and IOUs for renewed exchanges, see especially GP, Sg, regs. 109, fols. 161–87 and 114, fols. 74–76v; also regs. 60, fols. 36v–37; 102, fols. 55–56; 105, fol. 58v; 111, fols. 125–48; 115, fols. 199–210; 126, fols. 90–100v and 105r–v; 136, fols. 81v–85; 150, fols. 20v–22v; 152, fol. 18; 162, fols. 79v–82 (on Lyons), 97v–99v, 179–184v, 197; 162, fols. 101r–v and 129v. Especially important is a lawsuit of 1479 regarding a guaranteed loan contract of 1468 (the text was copied verbatim into the court record), in which the creditor stated clearly that interest would be calculated on a bill that would be protested in London; ibid., reg. 168, fols. 100–101v, 129v. Perhaps an agent in London was being facetious in a case of 1465 when he averred that exchange got its name from constantly changing market rates: "e però se chiameno canbii, perchè da uno zorno a l'altra cambiano prexio." In any case, actual exchange of currencies was not foremost in his mind; ibid., reg. 144, fols. 134v–38v.

[79]*PMV,* doc. 127, and Mueller, *Procuratori di San Marco,* 265–66, 274. The only instance I have found in which the law was invoked was a suit of Pietro Lando against the Medici, in which Giovanni di Bicci himself seems to have testified; Lando lost both before the Consoli and, in appeal, before the Petizion; ASV, GP, Sg, reg. 27, fols. 45v–46v.

covering an exchange transaction with a false sale of jewels — all of which reflects the sin of usury, at rates that are worse than usury and are the cause of the consumption of our citizenry and of their insolvency." Object of the law was "any citizen, subject, 'fidelis' or foreigner." But the penalty clauses were tame; it merely threatened consentient brokers with the loss of their job or other mediators with a fine of 50 percent of the value of the bill. If a borrower became insolvent or went bankrupt and there was a pawn involved, that was to be sequestered and returned to its owner. Jurisdiction was given to the Provveditori di Comun and the Piovego if usury was involved, to the Consoli and Sopraconsoli dei Mercanti if bankruptcy was involved. No investigative powers were conferred.[80]

The law came after the death of Francesco Datini, so there is no commercial correspondence extant in which to seek an echo. It may be that the law convinced the Medici, as a precautionary measure, thereafter to add a clause to their partnership contracts for the Venetian branch which specifies investment in "good and licit exchange transactions" (1420) or "real exchanges and licit contracts" (1435). The extent to which the law may have been invoked cannot be known, given the loss of the archives of all four of the magistracies to which the lawmakers assigned jurisdiction. In any case, no one felt it had to be rescinded, as was the Florentine law of 1429 against dry exchange, upon the return of the Medici from their exile in Venice.[81]

Among the many lawsuits regarding loans on exchange heard by the Giudici di Petizion, a commercial court not mentioned in the law of 1411, there are some in which claimants seem to have appealed to this law; one of them bears recounting. Accusers were Bartolomeo Zorzi and Gerolamo Michiel, two very prominent merchants active in London; defendants were Francesco and Marino Dandolo, the latter Venetian vice-consul in London. The object of the suit was a commercial contract for the delivery of alum to England, made in 1463, on which there was a balance due of 20,000 ducats. The crux of the matter was a penalty clause that called for charging interest on the balance, by putting it on the exchange ("star sui interessi"). This, the accusers stated, was "uxuratissimo," since the Dandolo brothers would make the sum earn interest by exchanging with themselves (that is, by acting contemporaneously as remitters and drawers), and without sending a bill, while controlling the collateral. Both these elements were against Venetian law, said the accusers. The judges nullified some of the clauses of the contract, but not all of those contested. The accusations indeed echo

---

[80]ASV, SM, reg. 49, fol. 56 (26 September 1411); it passed 47 to 7, with 5 absentions. The copy in Consoli dei Mercanti, b. 1, capitolare, fol. 71v, bears the erroneous date of 1406, which was then repeated by later scholars (see Mandich, *Le pacte de "ricorsa,"* 121–22).

[81]De Roover, *Medici Bank,* 135.

specific provisions of the law of 1411 regarding pawns and certain kinds of dry exchange.[82]

Again in 1479 a college formed by the Provveditori di Comun and the Consoli dei Mercanti thundered against "dishonest profits and usury earned through bills of exchange and other illicit contracts" but then concerned itself solely with sales of merchandise on credit.[83]

Prohibited or not, even the state itself was forced, at least in one period of heavy disbursements for war, to borrow in that manner, at high rates of interest. Overt borrowing from Rialto bankers "ad cambium" may have been limited to the spring and summer of 1440. In the two surviving instances of approval of such loans, the Signoria went so far as to fix the rate of the "andata" on London at 47 and 48 pence sterling per ducat, clearly two to three points above the market rate, so as to guarantee a handsome return ("interesse et consto") to the Soranzo bank. Assuming the return rate was five or six points lower, these loans totaling 16,000 ducats would have brought as much as 25 percent interest.[84]

"If you cannot beat them, tax them" was the philosophy of the government beginning sometime before 1469, when the fisc started applying a "tansa" on all loans made via exchange. In that year, when a "tansa" was renewed for two years, the Senate listed the usual forms of dry exchange but without any concern for branding them illicit. Clearly, this was one highly liquid form of investment which left little trace and was thus difficult to tax.[85] In 1475 a retroactive tansa was applied: all citizens who had lent or borrowed on exchange over the previous two years were given eight days to declare the transactions and name the parties before a committee called the Cinque Savi in Rialto. A similar declaration was expected of those who had

---

[82]The accusers charged that some of the clauses were "desonesti, inliziti ed uxurarii," while for the Dandolo brothers the contract was a model to be emulated on the Rialto, "honesta, licita e raxonevole." To "star sui interessi" and pay "de tempo in tempo la utilità de' chambi, come se lo i havesse chambiati . . . non solo è dixonesto ma uxurario, perchè el non puol nè die tuor utilità de denari contadi . . . et maxime con el pegno in man; ac etiam non pol chambiar contra sì medeximi, per esser contra lege nostre," the accusers stated. ASV, GP, Sg, reg. 145, fols. 13–15, 37v–44 (1465). It is not clear why such powerful merchants as Zorzi and Michiel had accepted the contract in the first place and then contested it.

[83]The original is lost; copies in ASV, Piovego, b. 1, capitolare, fol. 18r–v, and Compilazione delle leggi, b. 303, fol. 343.

[84]ASV, CN, reg. 7, fols. 11 and 18v, and below, Chap. 10.

[85]ASV, ST, reg. 6, fol. 72, discussed by Mandich, Le pacte de "ricorsa," 121–22. The only previous tax found was a brokerage tax on bills of exchange, applied in 1371 for three years, at differing rates according to the banking places involved, of which half went to the broker, half to the office of the Messetteria as a tax. RES, doc. 270 (16 May). But only six weeks later the Great Council recognized the fact that the tax was "multipliciter dannosa mercatoribus et mercationibus, absque utilitate nostri communis" and paved the way for its repeal. ASV, MC, Novella, fol. 132 (29 June).

lent money under the guise of exchange outside Venice, and a special paragraph was dedicated to Venetians resident in Bruges and London who, as cambiatores, lent money on rechange between those two cities; to get behind their transactions, the Five were to order the Venetian consuls there to investigate and to supply the amounts lent and the names of the parties to the transactions. In Venice, the Five were authorized to investigate the books of the Consoli and the Esaminador, to place under oath nobles, citizens, brokers, and even foreigners, that is, the cambisti, who had in their care the money of Venetians destined for investment via exchange.[86]

The imposition of 1475 brought revenues of 4,000 ducats; thereafter, as we are told in 1483, brokers were absolved of their obligation, and only a third of the loans previously declared were registered, bringing a revenue of only 700 ducats. At that point, in the midst of the War of Ferrara, the Five were once again called upon to collect information on loans made since 1478. As an incentive, borrowers on loans whose lenders did not report the transaction could keep the loan as theirs. But this law, which "ordered cambiadori to register their loans so that they be taxed," brought in only a paltry revenue and had the adverse effect of creating an atmosphere of uneasiness amongst the cambisti, who had supplied the city's credit market. As a result, the cambisti began abandoning Venice, to the great detriment of merchants, of commerce, and of the city's customs revenues. The Senate therefore in 1489 revoked the law of 1483 as well as the deliberation of the special college of 1479, which obviously had unsettled the foreign lending community, on account of its damning preamble. The remaining cambisti, members of the dwindling Florentine community, suppliers of credit to the Venetian marketplace, had to be favored rather than hindered.[87]

viii. *PRO ET CONTRA*: A JURIST AND A THEOLOGIAN ON RECHANGE IN VENICE

The question of the permissibility of exchange and rechange according to lawyers and theologians of the Middle Ages has been treated many times and at length.[88] It is taken up briefly here because two unpublished

---

[86]ASV, ST, reg. 7, fols. 89–90, 92v, and Mandich, *Le pacte de "ricorsa,"* 121–22.

[87]ASV, ST, reg. 10, fol. 131 (28 January 1489).

[88]See Raymond de Roover, *La pensée économique des scolastiques: Doctrines et méthodes* (Montreal, 1971), and Julius Kirshner, "Raymond de Roover on Scholastic Economic Thought," in de Roover's *Business, Banking, and Economic Thought*, 15–36. See also, in the same volume, de Roover's "Cambium ad Venetias," 251–57, and John T. Noonan, *The Scholastic Analysis of Usury* (Cambridge, Mass., 1957), 317–18. An important recent treatment of the positions of Genoese merchant bankers, as well as of lawyers and moralists, regarding the question of usury and exchange is Rodolfo Savelli, "Between Law and Morals: Interest in the Dispute on Exchanges during the Sixteenth Century," in *The Courts and the Development of Commercial Law*, ed. Vito Piergiovanni (Berlin, 1987), 39–102. While the author emphasizes the sixteenth-century debate, his contribution sheds light also on the late Middle Ages; he points out that the Genoese

tracts have come to light which are interesting in the present context because their authors knew the Venetian marketplace firsthand and addressed themselves directly to the problem of whether rechange, specifically that between Venice and Bruges or London, was licit or not. The audience — at least that of the jurist — was the Venetian investor. The two men were contemporaries, lived relatively close to each other — in the Venetian subject cities of Treviso and Udine — and traveled often to Venice, but there is no way of knowing whether they knew each other or whether one intended to respond to the other. While the approach of each is traditionally scholastic and their "auctores" those usually referred to in debates on usury, they reached opposing conclusions.

Francesco di Sergio Pola (also da Pola or da Castropola) came from a noble family of Treviso of recent origin. He earned a degree in civil and canon law at the University of Padua in 1431 and was in the good graces of the Venetian pope Eugenius IV, who provided him with titles; in 1448 he was made procurator of the bishop of Treviso.[89] In the 1440s he was called upon to deliver opinions on suits involving the very highest Venetian ecclesiastical institutions and authorities, from the Benedictine convent of S. Zaccaria to the Venetian patriarch of Constantinople and his son, and the bishop of Castello, at the time the saintly Lorenzo Giustinian. He was obviously a minor lawyer, but his high ecclesiastical connections may have given his opinion added authority.

It was probably in the late 1440s that Pola turned his attention to the matter of exchange on Bruges and put into writing his opinion "whether the contract was to be considered licit," having been solicited "often, by many Venetian nobles and merchants of good conscience, very wary of illicit transactions, considering that it would be of no use to them if they 'gained the whole world but suffered the loss of their souls.'" He submitted his treatise, he wrote, "as though forced by the entreaties of friends,"[90] that is, by his contacts who invested money on the Rialto.

---

were not at all as calloused toward — and oblivious to — the usury prohibition as had previously been thought. At the same time, the decision of the Genoese Rota with which the study concludes states very pragmatically that exchange and lending are one and the same; since free loans are not to be had, yet to charge interest would be usurious, it states, exchange was invented ("inventum est cambium"). Ibid., 101.

[89]For a profile, see Luigi Pesce, *Vita socio-culturale,* 98–99, and idem, *La chiesa di Treviso nel primo quattrocento,* 2 vols. Rome, 1987), 1:137, 349. Pola was named "avvocato concistoriale" and judge and captain of the Roman people by the pope. It was Pesce (*Vita,* 98–99) who pointed out the existence of his consulta, including that on rechange. The author suggests that — possibly — there existed ties of friendship between the Pola family of Treviso and the Condulmer family of Venice, of which the pope was a member.

[90]Biblioteca Comunale, Treviso, ms. 439, entitled "Consiliorum civilium diversorum iuris consultorum liber, per me Nicolaum Maurum iuris consultum tarvisii collectus," late sixteenth century, fols. 53–57v (Pola's other consulta begin on fol. 40). The tract begins: "Cum saepe ac saepius a quampluribus illustrissime civitatis Venetiarum viris nobilibus et mercatoribus, op-

The case he posed was one we have seen in action: the merchant in Venice gives 1,000 ducats today, at 52 Flemish groats per ducat, the market rate of exchange, to have that value in Bruges in two months' time. But in Bruges ducats are worth less, namely, 50 or 49 groats, and if the beneficiary in Bruges decides not to invest in goods but in a draft on Venice, the merchant earns 80 ducats in four months. (To be precise, that rate of profit, 8 percent or 24 percent per annum, means the return rate was about 48.) But sometimes it happens, continues the Trevisan jurist, that the merchant loses, if heavy demand for exchange on Venice ("propter multitudinem mercatorem volentium pecunias Venetiis remittere") should raise the rate in Bruges to 53 groats. But this happens only rarely, he says, so that generally one earns rather than loses on those exchanges, which is the reason many persons in Venice, who have no need for money in Bruges, make such exchanges, namely, to earn on the difference,[91] — whence the doubt, concludes the author, whether the contract is illicit and usurious or not.

The matter is resolved in the usual scholastic manner. Prima facie, says Pola, the answer is yes, and he gives four reasons for considering the contract basically a loan (*mutuum*) and thus usurious, citing among his authorities Hostiensis (Henry of Susa, d. 1271), Goffredo of Trani (d. 1245), and the decretal *Naviganti* (1234) — that is, all from long before the development of the bill of exchange and of rechange. But then he says that he believes it to be truer ("verius") to say that the contract is not usurious at all, for which he supplies fourteen reasons.

Briefly, his argument is that transactions of exchange by bill do not constitute loans but contracts of sale or exchange of currencies (*emptio-venditio* or *permutatio*). His rationales concern specifically the bill of exchange: the anticipation of sums by Florentine merchant bankers for payment elsewhere and later ("propter distantiam locorum," "ratione periculi et interesse" [§ 10], and "ex intervallo temporis" [§ 11]); the difference between *pecunia praesens* and *pecunia absens* (although he does not use these terms) in determining the level of exchange rates (§ 6); the legitimacy of earning a speculative profit after sustaining risk of losing even on the principal, which, he now states, happens often ("cum multotiens occurat") (§ 13). Among his authorities are men closer to his own time: Bartolus (d.

---

time conscientie et ab illicitis contractibus summopere praecavere cupientibus, parum sibi fore arbitrantibus si totum mundum lucrarentur, animae vero suae detrimentum paterentur, admonitus existerem ut super ista contractu canbii de Brugis, an licitus censeri debeat, opinionem meam in scriptis sub compendio redigerem. Ea de re (et si ad presens familiaribus negotiis impeditur existam, et vix otium studio suppeditare valeam) tamen, ne me noluisse, aut laborem nunc effugisse, sibi persuadeant. Hoc opus, veluti amicorum precibus coactus, aggrediendum decrevi, eo semper premissa, ut si quid a me dictam prolatumur foret, aliquorum aceribus indignum, ex nunc cuiuscumque correctioni, melius me in hac materia sentientis, submitto."

[91]"Et sic comuniter potius lucrum consequitur quam damnum ex ipsis canbiis, ea propter

1357) and especially Lorenzo Ridolfi (d. 1442), brought forward as defender of the legitimacy of the one-month "cambium ad Venetias" (§ 5, 8).[92] Pola refers specifically to rechange only in § 14, in which he draws his conclusion from the preceding articles: rechange between Venice and Bruges is not illicit or usurious. After countering his first four points, however, Francesco Pola adds the telling caveat: the contract is indeed legitimate, *unless* done with a will to lend and in fraud of usury ("nisi animo mutuandi et in fraudem usurarum hoc fieret"); intention was essential, even to the jurist.

In concluding his tract, Francesco Pola asserts that this was his position on the matter about which he had been questioned, that he perhaps had gone into the subject at greater length than necessary, but that he had done so in order that not only experts but also the "illiterate" could understand clearly what was involved.[93] It is unfortunate that we cannot know who his referents were in Venice, but one gets the impression that the active market in lending on rechange at the Rialto included a number of investors with scruples concerning the contract. And one wonders how many of them allowed their doubts be laid to rest by the arguments proposed by this jurist, minor and hardly very original but with important connections in the ecclesiastical hierarchy, a situation, again, that may have added force to his arguments.

The second scholastic commentator was Leonardo Mattei, a Dominican based at the friary of Udine. Sometime preacher in Venice, Leonardo compiled a tract on exchange in 1453, only a few years after that of Francesco Pola, at the request of his confreres and in the context of his lectures in theology at the Dominican *studium* in Udine.[94] The tract begins, in the vernacular, with practically the same case as that posed by the jurist: an investor in Venice has 1,000 ducats to invest on the exchange, while another person is in search of credit. The passage merits paraphrasing.

> First, Piero needs 1,000 ducats and agrees to sell a bill on
> Bruges at 52 groats Flemish per ducat; the deliverer has his
> correspondent remit back to Venice, and that will be at 48 to 52
> groats, and thus will the bill be repaid in Venice. At the end of

apud nonnullos non indigentes pecuniis in Brugis faciunt talia cambia, ut ex ista permutatione tantum lucrentur." Ibid.

[92]De Roover, "Cambium ad Venetias," 252–53.

[93]"Haec sunt quae sentio ego Franciscus de domo Castripolae de Tarvisio, minimus utriusque juris doctor et consistorialis advocatus, in hac materia de qua rogatus fui, quam nixus sum longiori forsan verborum sermone quam parerat explicare, sed hoc feci, ut non solum periti sed et illiterati claram intelligentiam de superdictis percipere valeant. Laus Deo."

[94]The *Tractatus de canbis,* dated Udine, 14 August 1453, is preserved in the Biblioteca Apostolica Vaticana, Chigi B.V. 86; it was edited and analyzed, along with other texts, by Maria Grazia Candotto Mis, "Leonardo da Udine, un domenicano del Quattrocento" (laurea thesis, University of Padua, 1983–84, under the direction of Giorgio Cracco and Fernanda Sorelli).

four months, the deliverer earns 50 ducats. Or again: Giovanni needs 1,000 ducats, which I give him in return for a bill on London at 44 pence sterling per ducat; my factor remits back to Venice at 40 pence, or more or less, and after six months I earn 40 ducats.

In short, Leonardo provides two classic examples of the kind reviewed above in practice, with rates of exchange perfectly in line with market rates on the Rialto at the time and with perfectly credible rates of profit (in the former case 15 percent, in the latter 8 percent).

Then Leonardo makes two points that were often identified as crucial by Raymond de Roover. First, he writes, you cannot know your profit in Venice until you have your returns from Bruges after four months or from London after six ("Et tal guadagno non si può intendere se non tornati e danari . . . in Vinegia"). Second, and here he formulates the question of speculative risk and changing rates as did Francesco Pola, "it happens sometimes that you will lose on such an exchange, and it will cost you in capital — but in most cases you earn a profit, I say nine times out of ten." The rationale is very matter of fact: "The Venetian ducat does not have a set price either in Bruges or in London; in fact, you will not find ducats current in Bruges, should you need, say, 100, and even if you found some, you would have to pay 50, 51, 52 groats or more, according to demand; and the same is true in London." In other words, Fra Leonardo — like Pola — merely corroborated the fact that ducats on the exchange constitute *pecunia absens* abroad and are thus usually cheaper than in Venice; gold ducats, on the other hand, if at all available, are worth a premium.

After such a lively and market-minded introduction, in Italian, Leonardo proceeds, now in Latin, in typically scholastic form, again with fourteen points, backed by many of the same authorities used by Francesco Pola (with the addition of much Thomas Aquinas and including Lorenzo Ridolfi), to show that rechange is illicit. He returns to the firm ground of the sterility of money, and his attack on the rechange contract as usurious turns in the end on the intention of the remitter or lender to profit from a loan — the same caveat with which the jurist closed his argumentation, which, however, saw the contract as licit. From a theological point of view, Leonardo writes, such exchanges constituted mortal sin; but even seen juridically, it was best to refrain from their use, because of the danger they presented to the soul. They are known as dry exchanges, he writes, "quia spiritum contristant et conscientiam desiccant ab omni humore divine gratie, ideo tales campsores sunt velut ligna sicca apta eterno igni, de quibus dicitur 'sicut palmes exarescet et in ignem mictetur et ardet' " [They are dry because they depress the spirit and dessicate the conscience of the moisture of divine grace; thus such exchangers are like dry wood fit for eternal fire, of whom it is said 'like branches he withers and is thrown into the fire and burns'] (John 15:6). With the single exception of a loan connected with domestic exchange, "cambio" for Leonardo is rechange; he considers no other variety, and he condemns it, without appeal.[95]

Both tracts, one judging rechange to be a licit contract of *permutatio,* the other judging it to be a usurious loan, reflect the fact that a certain number of habitual investors in this kind of short-term loan in Venice had scruples about the legality of the contract. Very likely the tract of the jurist, solicited by interested Venetian investors, if we believe the author, had the greater circulation. That of the Dominican preacher was perhaps limited to the convent school of theology. In any case, rechange remained a very popular way of investing money.

ix. THE PRIULI FRATERNA AND EXCHANGE WITH LONDON IN THE EARLY SIXTEENTH CENTURY

Let us take it as proven — or, better, proven once again, on the basis of both new and old data — that the system of foreign exchange widely served the local money market.

If the examples presented above are convincing enough on this score, others can be adduced from the first years of the next century which are more complex. The case now to be discussed is that of the fraterna of the Priuli family, consisting of the father Lorenzo and his three sons, Gerolamo, diarist and for a time Rialto banker; Vincenzo, agent in London; and Francesco, who kept the household accounts. Two journals are extant for their operation: one maintained by Vincenzo and kept in London during the years 1503–6, the other kept by Lorenzo in Venice beginning in 1505.[96] In the present context, what is of interest is the operation of the London representative and his exchange relationship with the rest of his family in Venice. Simple rechange transactions are absent.

Vincenzo's primary task in London was the purchase of raw wool of the Cotswolds, woolen cloth especially of the kersey type, fine "bastardi" cloths, tin, and lead, to ship back to Venice. The family sent him as exchange commodities spices such as nutmeg and ginger, and malmsey wine.

---

[95]That the author was attuned to Venetian contemporary realities is reflected in a point he makes involving domestic exchange. He knew that the ducat had long been exchanged locally for 114 Venetian soldi and that it had just gone to 116 and 118: was the loan of a ducat usurious if returned when it was worth more, he asks? Rates had in fact remained stable between 1440 and 1452 and rose to 116 and 118 soldi in the summer of 1453, just when he was writing his tract. (They then rose further, before stabilizing again at 124 soldi in 1455.) See Vol. 1, app. D, table D.3.

[96]BMCV, PD C. 911/II, journal of Vincenzo Priuli in London, 1503–8 (hereafter cited as "Vincenzo Priuli, journal"; PD C. 912/II, Journal of Lorenzo Priuli and sons, 1505–35. The latter was rendered as a ledger and analyzed by Di Lernia, "Il giornale di Lorenzo Priuli e figli."

But the capital available to Vincenzo from the sale of such goods was insufficient for his level of operation. Further capital was provided via exchange: Vincenzo drew on Venice, while Venice sent both remittances and specie.

First, we turn to Vincenzo's drafts, here summarized in table 8.7. As drawer on Venice, Vincenzo assumed the role of a veritable merchant banker: he accepted pounds sterling from members of the London priory of the Knights Hospitalers of St. John of Rhodes and drew bills on his father and brother, thus transferring funds from London to the Venetian priory of the Knights. He also issued a kind of "bearer bill" to English members of the order traveling to Venice. For his services, he charged a fixed and completely artificial rate of exchange: 56 pence sterling per ducat, a rate that stands in sharp contrast to the rate of 48–50 pence quoted on the marketplace in the very same period, even on the very same days as those on which operations for the Knights Hospitalers were concluded. How could Vincenzo charge such a rate and continue to attract the business of the Knights? Only upon watching the Venetian end can one begin to see the rationality of the fixed rate for one-way bills, higher than the market by fully 12 percent for what under usual procedure would have been a three-month contract. In contrast to the merchants with whom the Priuli did business, who made and accepted payment on current account at Rialto banks, the Knights (a) needed cash, (b) they asked for payment in Venice earlier than at usance — usually at sight or shortly after, and (c) their remittances were subject to a royal tax of 1 penny per Venetian ducat, which Vincenzo paid and debited to the family. Despite the added costs (about which anon), the business was still very profitable; clearly Vincenzo Priuli was not the only merchant who could offer such transfer services, and he had to go after it actively. When he made a general accounting for his father of more than 2,000 ducats drawn on the fraterna, he added that the costs of the operation included not only the royal tax but also certain gifts he had to make to get the business ("e per prexenti fati a li ditti per aver ditti danari").[97] At the same time, however, a close rapport with the order was established, for we find on one occasion that a member acted as vector, probably gratis, for specie sent by the Priuli from Venice to London (see table 8.9).

Each of these aspects involved a cost, albeit inferior to the 12 percent taken at the source in London. First of all, as Giovanni da Uzzano wrote in his merchant manual of the earlier fifteenth century, the drawer had to hedge his losses vis-à-vis remitters whose beneficiaries in Venice were liable to ask for payment in cash, for cash had a cost over and above bank money, a premium or agio ("l'azo"). In the cases considered here, the Priuli in Venice had to resort to a cash broker who purchased specie in the form of mint ducats at an agio of 2 to 2½ percent over bank money and who of course

[97]Vincenzo Priuli, journal, fol. 27v (22 July 1505).

TABLE 8.7

Drafts on Venice by Vincenzo Priuli in London, 1505–1506

Vincenzo in London	Lorenzo in Venice		Value				
date of draft	accepted	maturity	£ ster.	du.	gr.	Rate	Beneficiary
28 Mar. 1505	14 May	26 May	233/ 6/ 8	1,000		56	Fra Andrea Martini
2 July	3 Sept.	11 Sept.	170/10/ 8	730	20	56	Fra Andrea Martini
2 July	—	10 Oct.	58/ 6/ 8	250		56	Mons. Bartolomeo Zigli
3 July	16 Sept.	24 Sept.	58/ 6/ 8	250		56	Tomaxo Newport
22 July	15 Sept.	vista	20/	85	17	56	Carlo Lister
24 July	3 Sept.	vista	20/	85	17	56	Guglielmo Hasseldon
24 July	10 Sept.	vista	12/	51	11	56	Gualfredo Mideldon[a]
16 Sept.	—	16 Dec.	43/ 5	213	11	49¾	Zuan Gritti di Luca
11 Nov.	22 Dec.	11 Feb.	104/ 3/ 4	500		50	Nicolò Doria and bros.
19 Nov.	19 Jan.	vista	11/ 5	50		54	Ricardo Anbre a Ferrara[b]
15 Dec.	19 Jan.	vista	16/13/ 4	500		56	Tomaxo Newport
2 Jan. 1506	21 Feb.	vista	60/	257	8	56	Fra Andrea Martini
2 Jan.	21 Feb.	vista	65/	278	13	56	Fra Andrea Martini
10 Feb.	17 March	vista	233/ 6/ 8	1,000		56	Fra Lancelot Docuray
10 Feb.	17 March	vista	20/	85	17	56	Ser James Grim[a]
5 Aug.	—	—	156/ 4/11	669	15	56	Redraft: (⅔ of 1,000)
29 Aug.	3 Nov.	6 Dec.	100/	428	14	56	Fra Andrea Martini
Post 29 Aug.	4 Dec.	—	100/	428	14	56	Fra Andrea Martini
Circa 18 months			Total:	6,865	13		

Source: BMCV, PD C 911–12, Priuli journals (under the dates).

[a]Bearer bills (remitter = beneficiary).

[b]Received from the master of St. John's; payable through the Matavelli bank in Ferrara, in fiorini larghi d'oro in oro (Vincenzo journal, fol. 35).

applied a commission as well. Furthermore, the royal tax ("dover de la maistà del re"), paid by Vincenzo in London but debited to Venice, added a further cost of 2 percent (1 penny per ducat on a market rate of 50 pence).[98] Finally, the fact that the payers in Venice, Lorenzo and Gerolamo Priuli,

[98]One entry in Lorenzo's journal for the royal tax on the remittances of the Knights of Rhodes reads as follows: "28 Febraio [1506]. Per cambi tratimi da Londra per Vincenzo mio fiol / a Vincenzo dito, asegna per danaro 1 per ducato per il re de ducati 2202 tratimi per mano de queli de San Zuane in diverse partite, £9/3/6 de sterline, a 48 per ducato, £4 11s 9d."

had little or no time to collect the cash needed to meet their obligations upon presentation of the bills for acceptance, since the drafts always matured at or shortly after presentation, forced them to pay the agio then current, without being able to negotiate for a better price. One final element of cost, which may or may not have played a role in setting the exchange rate, is the credit that the Knights in London could get from Vincenzo. In at least one case in 1505, Vincenzo signed a draft for 500 ducats on his father without having received anything in London; the prior of the order in London and the representatives of the beneficiary, Thomas Newport, gave him a letter obligatory ("mi sono obligati e fato una obligation") promising payment of the value of the bill in two installments — but long after the bill had to be honored in Venice.[99]

Table 8.7 gives an overview of the drafts signed by Vincenzo himself until late August 1506, when he took ship to return to Venice. From then on his agent Nicolò Duodo continued his practices, but the eighteen drafts are sufficient to show at a glance the difference between market rates and the fixed rate agreed upon by the Order of St. John of Rhodes.

Of the nearly 7,000 ducats drawn on Venice in one and one-half years, about 6,000 were payable to members of the Knights Hospitalers of St. John, mostly to Monsignor Andrea di Martini, prior of the order in Venice. The source of the funds in London was the general treasury (the "comun tesoro di Rodi").

The other way of getting funds in London was via remittances from Venice. The remittances signed by Lorenzo Priuli in Venice are summarized in table 8.8. They do not match up with remittances from London to Venice, and thus rechanges are not involved.

Shipments of Specie

The matter of exchange becomes further complicated by the fact that it was often considered profitable to send specie from Venice to London, in the form of gold ducats and silver "marchetti" or soldini, which brings up a

---

[99]Vincenzo Priuli, journal, fol. 35 (15 December 1505); Newport is called the "bailo" of the priory. The sight bill was honored on 19 January 1506 (Lorenzo journal), while the installments called for were due at the following feasts of St. John (24 June) and St. Bartholomew (24 August). Vincenzo made another loan, to the prior, Thomas Docrai, on 2 July 1505, with a letter obligatory ("per sua obligation," ibid., fol. 24v). The accounting procedure followed by Lorenzo is peculiar but consistent for all accounts dealing with London. Whatever the rate of exchange, whether market or fixed, Lorenzo applied a conventional rate of 48 pence sterling per ducat when debiting his son Vincenzo for the amount paid out. This fact initially created some confusion in the registration of bills of exchange, for it seemed as though redrafts, at a lower rate, were involved. Actually, all Lorenzo was doing was getting his accounts in order, making the last double entries for business already concluded long before, tasks to which he applied himself in September and February, that is, in the slowest seasons of the Venetian business year. This accounting convention meant debiting Vincenzo for sums that exceeded by as much as 14 percent those paid out for the drafts themselves — with what aim is not clear.

TABLE 8.8

Remittances to London by the Priuli in Venice, 1505–1507

Date in Venice	Maturity in London	Value £ ster.	du.	Rate (d. st.)	Beneficiary
Pre 1 Mar. 1505	?	110/14/3	501	53	Nicolò Quaratesi
Pre 1 Mar.	?	88/ 6/4	400	53	Zuan Paolo Zigli
Pre 1 Mar.	?	110/ 8/2	500	53	Francesco e Antonio Grimani
?	10 Feb.	65/12/6	300	52½	Nicolò Doria e frat.
17 Apr.	17 July	54/ 2/7	250	52	Piero Ca' da Pesaro
7 May 1506	7 Aug.	140/16/8	650	52	Agostino e Battista Spinola
14 May	14 Aug.	75/16/8	350	52	Piero Ca' da Pesaro
16 July	11 Sept.	61/16/8	280	53	Nicolò Bonvixi
14 May	12 Aug.	75/16/8	350	52	Piero Ca' da Pesaro
4 Dec.	?	66/17/6	300	53½	Piero Ca' da Pesaro
28 Feb. 1507	28 May	54/ 3/4	250	52	Piero Ca' da Pesaro
1 June	1 Sept.	54/ 8/6	250	52¼	A. Priuli and Piero Ca' da Pesaro[a]
Circa 2½ years		Total: 4,381			

Source: BMCV, PD C 911–12, Priuli journals (under the dates).
Note: Almost all the bills of exchange were paid in bank.
[a]"In loro medeximi."

point made by the Dominican preacher Leonardo of Udine. Ducats were worth between 53 and 54 pence sterling in London, depending on their weight; marchetti went at ½ pence sterling and in fact were often called "galyhalpens" (galley halfpence) in England and were sought after at that value at least a century before.[100] In the early sixteenth century, Vincenzo Priuli records in his journal the arrival in London, both by porter ("fachino") and by postman ("scarsella di corrier"), of large and small quantities of coin. As can be seen in table 8.9, in seven months in 1505, Vincenzo credited his cash account for the arrival of 4,888.5 ducats' worth of coin, of which 113.5 ducats' worth were silver marchetti. The number of ducats shipped at a given time with a given vector probably did not exceed 600 (or 2.1 kilograms); in one case it is recorded that 50 ducats (175 grams) were included in a letter. During the period here examined, silver marchetti were imported in five lots ranging from 6 to 55 ducats' worth, that is, in lots of from 744 coins (or 223 grams) to 6,820 coins (or just over 2 kilograms). The costs of transport from Bruges to London, generally specified by the

[100]See Vol. 1, p. 547, and Frederic C. Lane, "Exportations vénitiennes d'or et d'argent de 1200 à 1450," in Day, *Etudes,* 39.

company Nicolò Balbani of Bruges, amount to less than one-half of 1 percent; those from Venice are not recorded.

The profitability of importing coin can be seen by comparing rates for foreign exchange with rates for manual exchange. As can be seen from table 8.10, the market rate of exchange in London on Venice fluctuated between 49 and 50 pence sterling per ducat, while mint ducats commanded a price of 53–54, a difference of 3–4 pence sterling or 6–8 percent — a differential that Fra Leonardo of Udine wrote was to be expected. Even the foreign exchange rates on the ducat in Venice itself were one to two points lower than the rates for manual exchange current in London (see table 8.9), and this, too, prompted Venetians to send specie.

Not surprisingly, we find in combination the two kinds of exchange operation, that is, the remittance of specie to London and of bills to Venice. In this sense, the sending of specie was not meant primarily to increase working capital in London but to exploit a difference in exchange values. Some examples: On 4 September 1505 Vincenzo received the large sum of 600 gold ducats as well as 55 ducats' worth of marchetti (that is, 6,820 silver coins, weighing about 2 kilograms). He figured the ducats at 53 pence. Between 13 and 16 September he remitted five bills to Venice, at between 49¼ and 50 pence (see table 8.10). In two cases he records having paid the value of the bills to Venetian drawers in London in gold ducats, at 54 pence, while remitting at 50 pence; that way he garnered for the Priuli fraterna a profit of 8 percent.[101]

What else did Vincenzo do with the coins he received? There were various approaches to passing them off. Most commonly, he simply sold them by tale (although they were usually weighed one by one), crediting his cash account for the amount. Another way was to sell a lot by weight. For example, on 3 October 1505 Vincenzo sold 249 ducats at 39s 9½d per ounce; on that occasion, credit was also a factor, for the buyer paid on the spot in sterling only half the amount due. The credit element is often present, for Vincenzo often sold ducats on deferred payment of one or one and one-half months — conceivably the time necessary for the buyer to receive from the Tower mint the corresponding value in nobles or sterling. On 13 February 1506, for example, Luchino Grimaldi sent his clerk ("suo chierego") to pick up 250 ducats, valued at 54d, and promised payment in a month's time ("e mi promese pagarli fino uno mexe"). In most of these cases involving credit, the ducats were probably turned over by tale and without much discussion — they were simply valued at 54d. Of course, much depended upon Vincenzo's leverage or "forza contrattuale"![102]

---

[101]Vincenzo Priuli, journal, fol. 31v (4–16 September 1505); the difference is not calculated separately or posted to profit and loss.

[102]Another example comes from 29 July when Vincenzo lends 63 ducats to Nicolò Quaratesi, who promised payment on 10 September. Ibid., fol. 28v.

TABLE 8.9

Batches of Specie Sent from Venice to Vincenzo Priuli in London, 1505–1506

Date Received	Sender	Vector	Amount in ducats	Exchange rate (d. ster.)	Value in £/s/d ster.
9 May 1505	Lorenzo Priuli	Grava	250	54	56/ 0/ 6
"	"	"fachin"	300	54	67/10/ 0
"	"	Anselin	200	54	45/
13 May	"	Balbani	500[a]	54	112/ 2
"	Francesco Priuli	Anselin	50	54	11/ 5
"	Gerolamo Priuli	"	30	54	6/15
"	Matteo Alberto	Grava	50	53 ¾	11/ 4
20 May	Gerolamo Priuli	Rado	150	54	33/15
"	"	Balbani	330	54	73/18[b]
"	"	"	6[c]	½	1/11
17 June	"	"	250	54	together
"	"	"	27.5[c]	½	63/ 1/ 1[d]
"	"	Treasurer of St. John's	500	54	112/10
"	Matteo Alberto	"	50	54	11/ 5
26 June	Gerolamo Priuli	Damiano	300	54	67/10
"	"	"	15[c]	½	3/17/ 6
"	Francesco Priuli	"	60	54	13/10
"	Matteo Alberto	"	50	54	11/ 5
"	Morosini bros.	"	50	54	11/ 5[e]
7 July	Lorenzo Priuli	Modrusa	100	53 ½	22/ 5/10
"	Gerolamo Priuli	"	100	54	22/10
18 Aug.	"	Balbani	140	54	31/10
27 Aug.	"	"	90	54	20/
4 Sept.	"	"	600	53	132/10
"	"	"	55[c]	½	14/ 4
16 Sept.	"	"	50	54	11/ 5
"	"	"fante"	175	54	39/ 7/ 6
"	"	"	10[c]	½	2/ 5
19 Nov.	"	Modrusa	120	54	27/
12 Dec.	"	"	30	54	6/15
29 Dec.	"	?	100	54	22/10
15 Jan. 1506 1506	"	Rado	150	53.53 ave.[f]	33/ 9/ 2

Total: 4,888.5 (4,775 gold ducats, 113.5 du. worth of soldini)

Source: BMCV, PD C 911–12, Priuli journals (under the dates).

[a]Of these 500, 200 actually were taken at only 53d, which called for rectification in profit and loss by both Vincenzo and Lorenzo.

[b]Less 5s, 1d in vectoring charges and 2s paid to the ambassador in Bruges.

[c]Ducats' worth of soldini, valued at ½d per coin.

[d]Less vectoring charges of 6s.

[e]"Mi mandò in una sua lettera."

[f]These ducats, "posti in zecha," were valued at various rates, averaging 53.53d.

TABLE 8.10

Remittances to Venice by Vincenzo Priuli in London, 1505–1506

Date in London	Maturity in Venice	Value			Rate	Payer
		£ ster.	du.	gr.		
28 May 1505	?	45/ 4/9	228		49¾	Jacopo Doria and bros.
1 July	15 Oct.	61/ 5	300		49	Polo e Gerolamo Tiepolo
27 Aug.	?	20/ 5/3	100		48¾	Polo e Gerolamo Tiepolo
13 Sept.	?	61/18/6	300		49½	Sebastiano e Polo Poggi
"	?	25/13	125		49¼	Gerolamo Dada
"	?	61/18/6	300		49½	Nicolò Ca' da Pesaro
16 Sept.	24 Dec.	45/	216		50	Piero Ca' da Pesaro[a]
"	9 Jan. 1506	39/ 7/6	189		50	Piero Ca' da Pesaro[a]
13 Nov.	13 Feb.[b]	61/ 9/3	296	12	49¾	Piero Corboli heirs
10 Jan. 1506	10 Apr.	51/ 6	250		49¼	Pietro Bembo
15 Jan.	28 Apr.	142/ 7/8	686	21	49¾	Pandolfo Cenami
		Total: 2,991		9		

Source: BMCV, PD C 911–12, Priuli journals (under the dates).
[a]In London these bills were paid for in gold ducats at 54d; the beneficiaries in Venice were the heirs of Piero Corboli.
[b]Accepted on 22 December.

On at least three occasions it was Vincenzo himself who brought the ducats to the mint, which credited him by weight. When in July 1505 he brought to the mint 500 ducats sent him by his father, he had the unpleasant surprise that only 300 were judged worth 54d each, while 200 were valued at 53d; more disappointing yet was a batch of 800 ducats from Gerolamo which brought only 53d. In January 1506 the mint gave him from 53 to 54½d (an average of 53.53d per ducat) on 150 ducats.[103] It is not clear how the mint paid him; in one case Nicolò Quaratesi, with whom Vincenzo did much business, is credited with having delivered some gold nobles ("mi porta . . . i nobeli").[104] But the losses — or rather the incomplete attainment of foreseen profits — were not so serious, and in the process of all this, Vincenzo accumulated assets in pounds sterling which he remitted back to Venice by bill of exchange at the low rates current in London, in order to earn on the differential.[105]

Exactly what happened to the "marchetti" or soldini that brought ½d

[103]Ibid., fol. 27 (20 and 222 July).
[104]Ibid., fol. 29v (26 August).
[105]Ibid., fols. 28 (26 July 1505), 28v (29 July), 31 (3 October), 37v (13 February 1506), and passim.

each is not recorded. These "galley halfpence" probably could not circulate legally and presumably had to be taken to the Tower mint for recoinage.

If we limit our attention to the whole six- to eight-month period of the year 1505 for which we have consistent documentation, we can summarize the approaches of the Priuli to the provisioning of monetary assets and speculation. First, the remittances from Venice to London in 1505 (table 8.8) stop at about the time when the home company begins sending shipments of specie (table 8.9). Second, Vincenzo remitted back to Venice (table 8.10) about two-thirds of the value of specie received in the same period; in other words, specie was sent primarily in order to profit from the difference between the rates of foreign and manual exchange on the London market; only about a third remained in London for investment there.[106] Third, Vincenzo's drafts on Venice (table 8.7) were relatively continual and coincided with the period during which he also received specie shipments; in other words, these one-way drafts were a primary means of finding investment capital in London while, at the same time, profiting from the difference between market rates of exchange and the high, fixed rate contracted with the Knights of Rhodes for collection in Venice. It seems, in this case, that mint parities and "specie points," those magic calculations that explain at what point a merchant decides it is worth his while to ship specie,[107] as well as considerations of "balance of payments" are irrelevant; specie and bills of exchange sometimes traveled northward from Venice in the same mail pouch.

x. CONCLUSION

The material presented in this chapter is largely practical and financial rather than theoretical; it merely confirms what has long been known, namely, that the bill of exchange was the backbone of the money market. Undoubtedly, the bill served and continued to serve as a means of long-distance transfer and exchange of balances for commercial purposes, but it was, from its very beginning and precisely through a careful "fixing" of the rules of the game by the Florentine cambisti, the principal form utilized for lending money locally on the short term. Furthermore, the bill, a surrogate of coin, never really supplanted the need for specie, and rates of exchange were an expression of the supply and demand both of coin and of credit, in short, of interest rates. Whether or not merchant bankers and other lenders really considered profits on the instrument sufficiently speculative and uncertain as to make the instrument licit before God, the bill of exchange

---

[106]At some point prior to the data here collected, Vincenzo clearly had remitted more funds. On 20 July 1505 he accounts for brokerage fees ("corattazo") of 11s 5d on 1872 ducats remitted to Gerolamo (a rate of 0.15 percent). Ibid., fol. 27v.

[107]See Spufford, *Handbook*, xlix.

embodied such considerable advantages that, regardless of usury theory, it would have been used for extending credit: it was self-liquidating, after usance or slightly variable maturity periods; it was easily renewable, by rechange and continued rechanges, as agreed upon by the parties; exchange rates and thus rates of interest oscillated according to the vagaries of the market but, while requiring from the investor a knack for risk, were largely predictable within certain parameters and reacted quickly to changes in market conditions.

Given these advantages, in the context of the late medieval economy, a whole gamut of forms of exchange was spawned: rechange, with or without bills, with or without the actual sending of bills, with or without surety, with or without previously agreed-upon protest. In all these forms, the advantages remained, and in many of them transactions costs were reduced.

Venice was the most bullion-hungry and credit-hungry commercial market in Europe, and the rhythm of demand, tied largely to the departure of galleys and ships to the Levant, made the Rialto the most predictable of Europe's banking places. Florentine dealers in exchange and lenders thus chose Venice for a central role in their exchange network. Exchange between some Italian markets, including Florence, and those of northwestern Europe, was for a long time channeled primarily through Venice. After about 1460 the importance of Venice for the Florentine exchange network is sharply diminished. As was mentioned in the preceding chapter regarding the fate of the Florentine community, the cause is most likely to be sought in the exchange fairs, first of Geneva and then of Lyons. The predictability of demand and the manipulation of usances which had made Venice central were no longer useful; Florentine cambisti dealt directly with those fairs and did not go through Venice. Both Geneva and Lyons organized four fairs per year, perfectly defined on the calendar, and the longest maturity for a loan on rechange was six months, the same as rechange between Venice and London. Even the Medici branch, under Giovanni Lanfredini, before its failure in 1477 seems, on the basis of surviving evidence, to have dedicated itself more to speculation in deliveries of wheat and oil than to foreign exchange; as Lanfredini reported, he resorted to exchange in order to lend money to other Medici branches, such as Naples or Rome, then much more important than Venice.[108] When Venetians lent or borrowed on dry exchange in those same decades, they arranged the contracts among themselves; the intervention of Florentine merchant bankers was no longer necessary simply to instruct a correspondent in London to protest a bill from Venice.

In the Priuli journals, which begin after the crash of 1499–1500, there is no trace of rechange operations. The movement in 1505–6 of drafts,

---

[108]See above, the conclusion to Chap. 7. Andrea Barbarigo in two short periods in the 1440s borrowed money on the exchange for Geneva; see Barbarigo, ledger B, fols. 75 and 179.

remittances, and coin between Venice and London, on the basis of various different rates of exchange, is dizzying. And it might well be that the mix was not very different, at least in certain periods, one or two centuries earlier. The case underscores the importance, in particular situations, of what Giulio Mandich called leverage ("forza contrattuale") in establishing rates of exchange.

In the end, we can accept Benedetto Cotrugli's characterization of exchange as the "condiment" of commerce by adding to the role of the instrument designed to render unnecessary the movement of specie in making payments abroad that of credit, for most of the credit supplied via exchange involved commercial or business loans.

We can stay with the notion of exchange as "condiment" and conclude after the manner of Antonio Salutati, a former employee of the Medici bank in Venice, when in 1416 he brought to a close his merchant's manual and its extensive treatment of foreign exchange with an outburst of exasperation. The only respite he could imagine for a stressed cambista faced with another order for a complex operation of arbitrage on Bruges and Paris — like a stockbroker on a Friday night — was a supper among friends, with lasagna or macaroni:[109]

> He who deals in exchanges and he who deals in merchandise is always anxious and beset by worries. I will instead give you a recipe for lasagna and macaroni.
>
> For lasagna, you need three fat capons and a piece of beef; set them to cooking. In another pan, put the lasagna in boiling water, one at a time, and never stir. Grate some Parmesan cheese. When the lasagna are ready, drain them. Pour over them the fat from the capons and the beef and let it all stand, covered, so that the flavor penetrates — you'll never have tasted anything so good.
>
> For macaroni you do much the same.
>
> Let him who wants to draw on Bruges and remit to Paris do it. I for my part prefer to enjoy supper with my companions. Amen.

[109]Borlandi, *Il manuale*, 163.

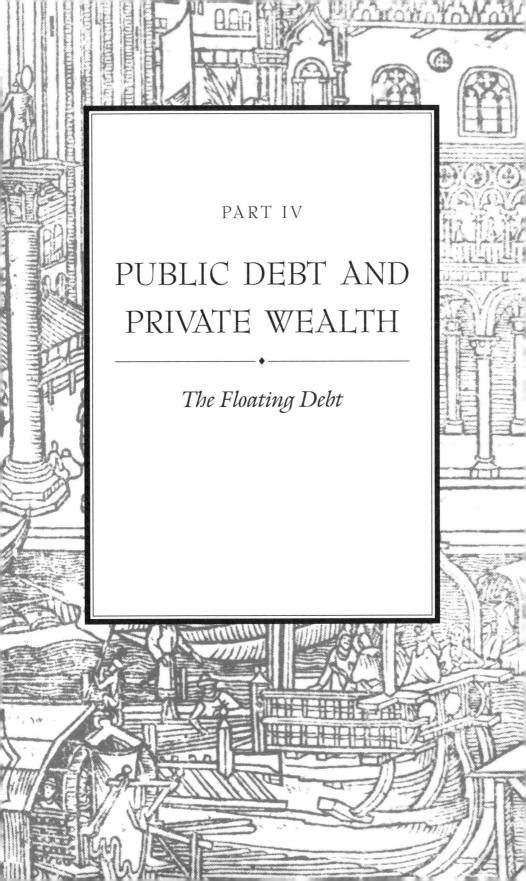

PART IV

PUBLIC DEBT AND PRIVATE WEALTH

◆

The Floating Debt

9

THE GRAIN OFFICE

A "Swiss Bank" for the Nest Eggs of Terraferma Lords, A Quasi-Public Bank for Venetians

i. A PREMISE

THE IMPORTANCE OF THE Grain Office (Camera Frumenti or Camera del Frumento) for Venetian finance in the Trecento was underscored by Gino Luzzatto, who was able to touch on the topic only tangentially, however, in his study of the funded debt.[1] The scope of this chapter is to analyze the various financial roles of the office as administrator of a public floating debt which responded to the needs both of the state and of private wealth.

We begin with a brief look at the institutional structure before passing to the subject of deposits and foreign depositors. While Venetians could deposit money at will and without formalities, foreigners first had to receive permission. Since the archive of the Grain Office has been completely lost, traces of the day-to-day activity of Venetians are practically nonexistent. The primary evidence for the operation of this institution, therefore, is limited to the petitions of foreigners for permission to deposit money at the Grain Office and to those of their heirs to collect interest and withdraw principal. Behind the documentation for each case — generally skeletal and extremely uneven — there is often a story of plot and counterplot, reflecting the concern of urban signori and feudatories alike to stow away their hoards

---

[1]*PRV,* lxxv–lxxviii.

359

in a public institution that for about a century served a function similar to that of a Swiss bank.

Despite the paucity of documentation regarding Venetian clients, a separate discussion is reserved for a special category of interest-bearing deposits, that of dowries, or the liquid part of dowries, which were ordered by statute to be left with the Grain Office. Some cases involve sentences for rape and carnal knowledge whereby the fine exacted from the guilty party was deposited at the Grain Office to constitute a dowry for the victim.

The state, for its part, had the use of the money, for its own extraordinary expenses, examples of which are given. The more interesting aspect of the role of the office as lender, however, is its occasional loans to Venetian entrepreneurs, mostly but not solely nobles, in sectors involving the common good — mills for grinding wheat and kilns for baking bricks and roof tile, above all — but the office also financed a medical doctor particularly dedicated to the care of poor seamen but rather inept at keeping his accounts. A huge loan, finally, made to the emperor in Constantinople on the collateral of the crown jewels, ended up on the books of the Grain Office, which could neither sell the pawns nor collect on the debt (it is recorded as a bad debt, for 96,000 lire, on the balance sheet summarized in table 9.1, below).

These are all aspects of a rather peculiar floating debt administered by the state for its own benefit, to be sure, but also in the private interest. When the Grain Office declined, the role of managers of the floating debt was taken over in the Quattrocento by the private banks of the Rialto, which assumed more than ever the nature of an institution in the public interest.

Before turning to the role of the banks (below, Chap. 10), however, I will treat the question of rates of interest applied at the Grain Office and of the qualms of conscience aroused in some clients by having accepted interest on their deposits.

The problem of provisioning any city in the Middle Ages was serious and required constant vigilance. This was especially so for Venice, which for centuries had no hinterland at all; even when it did, it continued for a long time to rely on importing wheat by sea from distant parts. A separate administration of the annona was supposedly created under Sebastiano Ziani (1172–78); "Offitiales supra granum" are mentioned in 1224; the Officium or Camera Frumenti existed by 1256 and was governed by a first collection of laws or capitolare dated 1276. Some kind of reorganization of the office was undertaken in 1283 by the doge Giovanni Dandolo, according to an early chronicle, but no details are provided. The doge, in fact, had the principal responsibility for provisioning the city, according to his "promissio" or election capitulation, the document to which he had to swear upon taking office. He delegated responsibility to the Grain Office, but he was to be kept informed, even daily, about the state of the city's reserves of wheat and other grains. The first extensive capitolare of the Grain Office which is extant dates from the years immediately following the Black Death.[2]

At about the time of the reported reorganization of 1283, as we shall see shortly, government finance was added to the duties of the Grain Office, and it grew very rapidly into one of the most important institutions of the communal administration in terms of monetary turnover: in 1320 it was called "magnum officium"; in 1342 the office and the Arsenal were described as "officia ponderosa," and in 1348 a law of the Great Council began with the affirmation that it was the foremost office of the city ("Officium frumenti est maximum officium comuni et totius terre").[3] In 1365, however, its annonary responsibilities were handed over to a new magistracy, the Provveditori alle Biave, and after the War of Chioggia (1378–81) it declined quickly to secondary rank. The Camera del Frumento survived as supervisor of the warehouse for flour (Fondaco della Farina) at the Rialto; the Provveditori alle Biave had their headquarters in the Ducal Palace (see fig. 16).[4]

The role of the Camera del Frumento in government finance is never clearly delineated in official documents that regulated the functioning of the office. In typically Venetian fashion, the role was in part assumed, in part authorized on a completely ad hoc basis; the office simply evolved into a kind of state bank. Since the first traces date from the 1280s, the brief and generic capitolary of 1276 says nothing about it; but even the more exten-

---

[2]Sanudo, *De origine,* 140. Hans Conrad Peyer, *Zur Getreidepolitik oberitalienischer Städte im 13. Jahrhundert* (Vienna, 1950), 157. *DMC,* 1:60 and 2:286–89 (capitulary of the Domini super frumento, 1276). For the doge's responsibility, see, for example, the promissione of Andrea Dandolo, in *Andree Dandoli Chronica per extensum descripta,* ed. E. Pastorello, Rerum Italicarum Scriptores, vol. 12, pt. 1 (Bologna, 1941). Under the year 1283, the *Venetiarum historia* (Cessi and Bennato, 191) records: "Hic dux, iam aucto populo Veneciarum, fertilitatem ei facere volens, de novo statuit officium frumenti." The Capitolar de li offitiali dal formento, of about 1350, is in BMCV, mss., cl. III (Commissioni), n. 351 (an edition is planned by M. A. and F. X. Leduc). Many documents concerning this office were collected by Bartolomeo Cecchetti, *La vita dei Veneziani nel 1300* (Venice, 1870–86; reprint, Bologna, 1980), pt. 2: "Il vitto."

[3]ASV, MC, Fronesis, fol. 52 (7 October 1320); *RES,* doc. 159; MC, Spiritus, fol. 157v (18 August 1348).

[4]Numerous deliberations were made in the century following 1276 varying the number of officials, their salaries, and terms of office. In ASV, MC, Leona, alone one finds at least six administrative provisions from 1385 to 1401: fols. 7v, 10v, 25v, 32v–33, 47v, 120v. For Sanudo's summaries of the obligations of both offices, in 1493 and 1515, see *De origine,* 140–41, 271–72, and 108–9, 245. For the institution of the Provisores Bladi, see MC, Spiritus, fols. 150v, 151 (1347), 157 (1348); *RES,* docs. 196 (1348), 209 (1349); MC, Novella, fols. 97 (1365), 131v–32 (1371), 164v (1380), 191 (1383) — at which time they received an increase in salary from 80 to 120 ducats because of their responsibility for "facta . . . que sunt magna et ardua."

Fig. 16. Madonna of the Magistrato alle Biave, attributed to Pietro Lombardo or Giovanni Lascari, about 1475–80. The Provveditori, whose office was at the Ducal Palace, had to inform the doge daily, in writing, of the stocks of flour stored at the Fondaco della Farina, Rialto, and of wheat stored in various warehouses. The coats of arms of one group of officials are seen on the bottom of the relief, while those of another group, perhaps somewhat later, adorn the inscription.

Palazzo Ducale, Venice. Photograph by Cameraphoto

sive capitolary of about 1350, when the financial role of the office was at its height, provides only two opaque hints: one article instructs the accountants to open personal accounts in the ledgers for the "depositi e promesse" of individuals; another tells the staff to remind debtors to redeem their pawns — without further explanation.[5] Only two further traces are furnished by the sources: a robbery during the conspiracy of 1310 and the only balance sheet of the office.

On the day of the attempted coup of Baiamonte Tiepolo in July 1310, one column of conspirators was directed via the Rialto; they stopped there long enough to loot the Grain Office and the Treasury, where they took a large amount of money, most of which was not recovered. Terse, indeed, but the contemporary report of the incident shows that the plotters knew well where to go to get their hands on cash.[6]

Only one balance sheet exists for the Grain Office, the result of an audit made in the spring of 1345. The document is very generic, often incorporating categories that would have been more revealing if kept separate. See Table 9.1. Besides showing the office to be seriously in the red (but its position was improved over 1342!), the balance sheet indicates liabilities — sums owed to individuals — of a quarter of a million ducats. Even though the accounting makes no distinction between deposits and sums owed to importers of wheat, it may be assumed that the latter involved the lesser part of the total (more precision is not possible). Despite the ambiguity, this very considerable sum of money reflects the importance of the Grain Office at that date and its capacity to attract deposits from third parties. Within a short time, moreover, liabilities would soar much further — as we shall see below, the Scaligeri and the Gonzaga alone would have credits of 160,000 ducats shortly thereafter.[7]

Clearly, the office's experience in credit operations for the very large sums of money necessary for the grain trade caused it to be chosen as a kind of broker and administrator for the state's floating debt. As is self-evident, a conspicuous floating debt permitted the state to draw on funds for extraordinary expenditures faster and with less formality than that necessary for levying and collecting forced loans.

---

[5]BMCV, ms., III, n. 351, cap. 38 and 59.

[6]A letter of 10 July from the Collegio to the Venetian ambassador at the Curia reported "cameram frumenti similiter fregerunt et pecuniam ibi inventam in quantitate non modica abstulerunt." From ASV, Collegio, lettere (1308–10), fol. 95v, in G. A. Avogadro, "La congiura Tiepolo-Querini," *AV* 2 (1871): 218. See also Cristoforo Tentori, *Saggio sulla storia civile, politica, ecclesiastica e sulla corografia topografica degli stati della repubblica di Venezia*, 12 vols. (Venice, 1785–90), 5:210–12, 217.

[7]*RES*, docs. 178, 198–204. When, in the spring of 1349, creditors of 22,000 ducats were clamoring to liquidate their assets, the office had no alternative but to attract further loans at interest for a similar amount (doc. 203).

TABLE 9.1

Balance Sheet of the Grain Office, 1345

Assets	Liabilities

854,000 lire di piccoli
of which:
long-term loans (bad):
  96,000
  100,000
bad debts and spoiled wheat:
  130,000
  ─────
  326,000
	755,000 lire di piccoli
	[235,938 du.]
	(debts to "speciales persone")

Net ("boni denari et debiti"): 528,000 [165,000 ducats]	Net negative balance: 227,000 [70,740 du.]

Source: RES, doc. 178.

ii. THE ORIGINS OF THE DEPOSITORY

In its role as a financial arm of the state, the Grain Office garnered funds by contracting loans with private parties, a practice that by about 1300 meant accepting deposits, secured and interest bearing. While seemingly used at the very beginning for the purchase of wheat, in the late thirteenth century the funds were used by the government as a floating debt.

According to a chronicle, the Grain Office was reorganized in 1283, under the aegis of Doge Giovanni Dandolo, and that reorganization might have involved greater authority to borrow money.[8] In that same year the office was authorized to contract a loan at interest ("ad unum certum proficuum"), to pay for 50,000 staia of wheat; security was to be the wheat itself.[9] In August 1290 a similar loan was required, for a sum set at 15,000 lire; certain government revenues, at the discretion of the doge, were to serve as security.[10] To be sure, in those years other offices were also permitted to go into debt for their own affairs, but the Grain Office led the way. For example, when in 1294 the Tana, or state rope factory, was initiated, the three officers were given freedom to contract a loan of 10,000 lire as the

[8]Cessi and Bennato, *Venetiarum historia,* 191. As early as 1256 cash balances at the Grain Office seem to have attracted the interest probably of other government institutions; on that occasion it was ordered that balances be retained by the officials for the sole purpose of buying grain. The capitolare of 1276, included in the Liber Officiorum of the Great Council, says nothing about financial operations with third parties and orders that any cash balance exceeding 5,000 lire be deposited with the Procurators of San Marco for safekeeping; see *DMC,* 2:286–89.

[9]*DMC,* 3:24, doc. 26.

[10]Ibid., 281, doc. 114; same in *PRV,* doc. 55.

grain officials did ("sicut faciunt illi qui sunt super frumento"), in order to buy up hemp stores.[11]

The state guaranteed the loans and deposits and funneled revenues into the office to pay off principal and interest on its liabilities. In terms of assets, the sale ("tratta") of imported wheat represented revenue, as long as the office was also the principal annonary administration. For a number of years (about 1297–1342), the office administered a tax on grants of wine and wood, sometimes as export licenses, and enjoyed the revenue; for much longer it administered funds relating to the operation in Venice of the papal inquisitor for the Veneto.[12] The revenue was never sufficient, however, and the state continually had to earmark other funds for the office, above all forced loan levies, but it often had to apply the most varied stopgap measures.

While especially military expenditures by the Commune in the last quarter of the thirteenth century required continual recourse to forced loans, at 5 percent interest, voluntary loans were contracted at considerably higher rates. In 1285, for example, a loan of 16 lire di grossi was arranged to pay the costs of an embassy to Sicily; the lender was to receive a return ("lucrum") tied to the profits of the Bollani firm, a local banking and business enterprise ("statio," "tabula"), but not exceeding 8 percent, in short, a kind of local colleganza.[13] Beginning in 1288, the task of negotiating similar loans was given to the Grain Office. In that year, the office was to find a loan of up to 20,000 lire, secured on the revenues of the Salt Office. According to the usage that was becoming more and more common in this period, interest was to be calculated at maturity on the basis of the rate of return ("presa") of a local business enterprise, not exceeding 10 percent.[14] A mere six weeks later authorization for a further loan of 20,000 lire was passed, with terms similar to those established earlier ("secundum conditionem alias eis ordinatam").[15] The credit market was tightening, however, and in July the Grain Office announced that it was unable to attract a loan with an offer of only 10 percent interest. The Great Council then authorized a limit of 12 percent, so that it could honor its commitments to those nobles who had previously lent money "pro negociis Crete." In the following

---

[11]*DMC*, 3:352, doc. 127. For a loan made by the mint to promote production of the new gold ducat in 1285 (at 8 percent for nine months or 11 percent per annum), see Vol. 1, p. 283.

[12]For the "gratia vini et lignamini," see *DMC*, 3:427, doc. 38; *RES*, docs. 12. 57, 65, 89, 92, 159. The Grain Office was called upon to administer funds, both income and expenditure, according to a promise made to the pope; *DMC*, 3:250, no. 135; also Romanin, *Storia documentata*, 2:253–54 n. 5.

[13]*PRV*, docs. 39, 47, and Luzzatto's discussion of the context, ibid., xxxiv–xxxv.

[14]*DMC*, III, p. 201, doc. 17; same in *PRV*, doc. 49. The text is quoted in the main also by Gino Luzzatto, "Tasso d'interesse e usura a Venezia nei sec. XIII–XV," in *Miscellanea in onore di Roberto Cessi* (Rome, 1958), 192.

[15]*DMC*, 3:204, doc. 39.

years, similar loans were negotiated, one to pay off several earlier loans that had matured.[16]

More efficient, of course, was a regular floating debt that would avoid ad hoc searches for voluntary lenders. In fact, around 1300 the Grain Office began accepting time deposits that required six months' advance notice before withdrawal. The deposits earned interest at rates that initially varied according to the period and the parties involved. The state requested loans from the Grain Office and promised repayment of principal and interest at the rates that had been promised to the depositors. Being administrator of a floating debt of this kind endowed the Grain Office with some of the functions of a state bank.[17]

Accounts were also opened for suppliers to the state, first of wheat but also of other goods, whose contracts could not be honored at maturity because funds were not immediately available. Early in the fourteenth century a specific authorization was required if those credits were to be interest bearing,[18] while later in the century crediting an account to a supplier and offering interest on the balance due was an option followed often in times of tight money, such as during the War of Chioggia.

The transition made by the Grain Office from its role as occasional credit agent for specific needs of the state to that of a government agency accepting unallocated deposits seems to have taken place in the 1290s. In 1291 a loan contract between two private parties stipulated that the rate of interest (8 percent) and the nature of the risk be those currently in force at the Grain Office.[19] In 1300 specific revenues of the office were earmarked for payment of interest and principal to depositors ("illis personis que mutuaverunt Camere desuper frumento").[20] And sometime before 1304 a woman made restitution to the Commune of interest ("utilitas ordinata") received from the office.[21] On the other hand, as late as 1297 a loan to two nobles for repair of their flour mills involved an authorization by the Great

---

[16]*PRV,* doc. 50; same in *DMC,* 3:207, doc. 60, and cf. p. 153 (13 August 1286). Luzzatto, "Tasso d'interesse," 192. Peyer, *Zur Getreidepolitik,* 123, assumes that increasing the rate offered was due to skepticism concerning the ability of the Grain Office to pay. The loan of 1289 which consolidated previous loans set a maximum of 10 percent interest; in *PRV,* doc. 52, and *DMC,* 3:238, doc. 51. (For some of the original loans, see ibid., 3:159, doc. 99, and pp. 178, 180, 210.) See also ibid., 3:334, doc. 2 (1293).

[17]See the important pages and especially the notes of Luzzatto in *PRV,* lxxv–lxxviii.

[18]*RES,* doc. 49 (1310).

[19]Manuela Baroni, ed., *Notaio di Venezia del sec. XIII (1290–1292),* FSV (Venice, 1977), doc. 302.

[20]*RES,* doc. 12; same in Elena Favaro, ed., *Cassiere della bolla ducale: Grazie — novus liber, 1299–1305,* FSV (Venice, 1962), 226 (hereafter cited as Favaro, *Grazie — novus liber*). The provision was canceled in 1340 because those particular revenues were no longer administered by the office (ASV, MC, Magnus, fol. 12).

[21]Favaro, *Grazie — novus liber,* doc. 494.

Council to the Grain Office to contract a specific loan to that end, while a similar loan authorized in 1314 was made available from general funds held by the Grain Office "from private parties in interest-bearing deposits."[22] Finally, administrative changes and regulations also reflect the fact that a change had taken place. In 1307 the number of officials was increased from three to four and their salary raised. More significant is the order, passed in the following year, requiring the Grain Office to inform potential depositors specifically if their money was to be used for purposes other than for purchasing wheat.[23] In short, by about 1300 the structure and procedures of this credit institution were well established.

Since no accounts of the depository have survived, the normal, daily activity of accepting and paying out money can only be imagined. What documentation has survived regards exceptional cases of deposits by foreign lords and feudatories who required special authorization or who sought special conditions. Such financial ties between Venice and neighboring lords on the Terraferma and in the Balkans strengthened diplomatic and military ties before the period of direct Venetian domination over the Terraferma and reflect the changing fortunes of families and of alliances. So many of them were honorary citizens of Venice that this fact will be mentioned only rarely in what follows — that also was part of building alliances.

iii. THE EARLIEST DEPOSITS

The earliest documentation of an actual deposit of money in the Grain Office is exceptional in that it was interest-free, but it marks the beginning of a century of contacts between Venice and foreign lords in which the former sought cheap credit, the latter a safe place for their nest eggs. In 1316 Guglielmo da Castelbarco, nobleman of the Trentino and moneylender himself, applied to the Signoria for permission to deposit funds in Venice, on condition that they would be safe from reprisals by Venetians against citizens of Trent or others. The Great Council assured him of immunity from sequester and granted him the option of placing the money in the care of churchmen, of the Procurators of San Marco, or of the Commune, as he desired.[24] The next year the nobleman specified that he

---

[22]*DMC,* 3:425, and ASV, MC, Presbiter, fols. 111, 131; see also the discussion, below, on loans to mill operators.

[23]*RES,* docs. 42, 43, 45. In 1310 the office, in financial straits, was ordered to guarantee 10 percent interest on unspecified liabilities, which it was then unable to amortize (ibid., doc. 49).

[24]ASV, MC, Clericus civicus, fol. 43v, partially transcribed by Luzzatto in *PRV,* lxxv n. 3. See also *Relazioni di Guglielmo da Castelbarco con Venezia (Documenti del R. Archivio di Stato in Venezia),* Nozze Jacob-Schizzi (Trent, 1887), docs. 1–2 (1310). In general, see Giuseppe Gerola, "Guglielmo Castelbarco," *Annuario degli studenti trentini* 7 (1901) (offprint), and Elisa Occhipinti, "Castelbarco, Guglielmo," in *DBI,* 21 (1978), 570–74. That Castelbarco had

would deposit 10,000–20,000 florins in Venice, which he would agree to lend to the Commune on suitable surety. On 6 March 1317 the Great Council accepted the offer and decided to place the money "at the Grain Office or at the Salt Office,"[25] and on 29 March it decreed that any funds deposited at either of the two agencies by private parties could not be sequestered for reprisal or for any other legal action.[26] The decision to guarantee the immunity of deposits from legal action — similar to guarantees maintained by Swiss banks until recently — took on the nature of a statute and was later included in a special collection of legislation by Andrea Dandolo.[27] In May an agent of Guglielmo, in the presence of several Dominican friars and others gathered together in the house of a Venetian in Verona, consigned 20,000 florins in two installments to a representative of the doge, with various conditions and for a two-year term. The Commune agreed to repay the sum in two years' time, with two months' notice, and turned the sum over to the Grain Office.[28] In November 1319, shortly before repayment was due, the Great Council voted a gift worth 250 ducats to thank Castelbarco for his interest-free loan.[29] But the foreigner did not yet want his money back, and he protested his disinterest in the promised gifts of wool cloth or silk cloth-of-gold. Through the intercession of the jurist Riccardo Malombra, he succeeded in prolonging the agreement while maintaining his right to repayment on demand.[30] In January 1320 this

---

habitually lent money to local feudal lords, in amounts of 100 to 600 marks at a time, is reported by Josef Riedmann, *Die Beziehungen der Grafen und Landesfürsten von Tirol zu Italien bis zum Jahre 1335,* Österreichische Akademie der Wissenschaften, Sitzungsberichte, 307 (Vienna, 1977), 346–47.

[25]Luzzatto, as in previous note.

[26]ASV, MC, Clericus civicus, fol. 89: "Quod aliqui denarii specialium personarum qui nunc et decetero essent ad cameras frumenti vel salis vel causa mutui vel alia causa non possint intromitti vel impediri pro aliquibus represaliis vel processibus comunis Veneciarum factis vel fiendis aliquo modo vel ingenio." This important safeguard was reinforced, as will be seen shortly, in the case of Marsilio da Carrara.

[27]Luigi Genuardi, "La 'Summula statuorum floridorum Veneciarum' di Andrea Dandolo," *NAV,* n.s., a. 11, 21 (1911): 459. Strangely enough, however, the deliberation did not pass into Dandolo's liber sextus of the Venetian statutes.

[28]*LCR,* 1:178, no. 43, 1:228, no. 263 (misdated 1318), and 1:178, no. 44. The first and third of these documents were printed in full in *Relazioni di Guglielmo da Castelbarco con Venezia,* docs. 3–4. In the first installment, 9,000 florins were "ad pondus pisanum" and 1,000 "ad pondus florentiae," and in the second 8,300 florins were at the former weight, 1,700 at the latter. Each party had a copy of the two standard weights, under seal, so that at maturity perfectly correct repayment could be made. The loan, in short, was fungible, but although the same coins did not have to be returned, similar coins of the same weights were expected. Whether such a costly and time-consuming procedure was actually followed later may legitimately be doubted, even though the executors in 1321 insisted on repayment in the same kind of coins and in the same proportion; in fact, one of the two loans was repaid in part in silver coin (see ibid., docs. 3, p. 17, and 7, pp. 28–29).

[29]*PRV,* doc. 99; see also doc. 9 cited in the following note.

[30]See docs. 7–9 (from ASV, Commemoriali), in Enrico Besta, *Riccardo Malombra, professore*

deposit was among the funds lent by the Grain Office for arming the galleys, whose income from freights was earmarked for repayment.[31]

The depositor died on 6 January 1320. His testament, dated 13 August of the previous year, orders that this nest egg, as well as others carefully spread about among his feudal holdings in Trent, Verona, and elsewhere, was to be used for restitution of ill-gotten gain ("pro male ablatis").[32] A very small part of Castelbarco's loan was repaid to his nephew and executor Aldrighetto in March 1321, but just when the bulk of the deposit was restored is not clearly recorded.[33] This is a case of a foreigner concerned about the safety of his fortune and, in the final analysis, of his soul, for he was uninterested in his last years in earning a return on his capital.

Castelbarco's decision to deposit his nest egg in Venice was probably influenced by his correspondent, Riccardo Malombra, a naturalized citizen of Venice and native of Cremona. In 1312 Malombra, official legal councillor to the Commune of Venice, had lent 200 lire di grossi to the communal Treasury "pura liberalitate," and at some unspecified date he had also deposited 100 lire at the Grain Office. When in 1320 the Great Council ordered the Treasury to repay the amount of 200 lire, Malombra agreed that the money be deposited at the Grain Office, surely with the intention finally of earning a return on it. The state already knew what the loan could be used for, and, in the same deliberation that authorized the transfer, the Great Council ordered the grain officials to lend 100 lire to the Venetian colony at Trebisond for the construction of public buildings and 100 lire to private parties for the construction of brick furnaces. According to the famous jurist Baldus, Malombra's student, Malombra suffered pangs of conscience on his deathbed for having accepted usury on such deposits.[34]

Another noteworthy depositor at the Grain Office in the same years and in the same ambience was Marsilio da Carrara of Padua, honorary citizen of Venice (1320) and later lord of Padua (1328–38). In 1319 the Paduan nobleman lent 9,000 lire di piccoli to the Venetian subject city of Pirano in Istria. The loan, plus "prode, lucrum sive dampnum," at a rate to

---

nello studio di Padova, consultore di stato in Venezia (Venice, 1894), 38–40; two of the letters are also in *Relazioni di Guglielmo da Castelbarco con Venezia* (as cited above), docs. 5–6 (misdated 1318).

[31]*RES,* doc. 87.

[32]Gerola, "Guglielmo Castelbarco," 190–91 (pp. 24–25 of offprint); see especially the edition of the testament in I. C. Lünig, ed., *Codex Italiae diplomaticus,* 4 vols. (Frankfurt, 1725–35), vol. 3 (1732), cols. 1937–50, at col. 1939.

[33]At the time, payment of 1,500 lire di piccoli and 1,000 florins was made on one of the installments; the balance was not then requested. The other installment of 10,000 florins was paid in full, according to a note added to the registration, in 1321, of the instrument of 18 May 1317. *Relazioni di Guglielmo da Castelbarco con Venezia,* doc. 9 and doc. 3, p. 15. As Luzzatto noted (*PRV,* lxxvi), the deliberation of 6 June 1316, accepting the offer of the loan, was judged to be still in force as late as 1339.

[34]Luzzatto in *PRV,* lxxvii n, and doc. 102; also Besta, *Riccardo Malombra,* 31–32.

be defined by that applied by a certain Venetian commercial and banking establishment (the "statio sive tabula" of the brothers Pantalon and Bertucci Capello), was to be repaid in four equal annual installments; Venice guaranteed the loan and directed its podestà in Pirano to enforce compliance with the terms of the accord.[35] Four years later, in September 1323, Marsilio empowered his agent Pietro de Gizi to deposit in the Grain Office 12,800 lire di piccoli, "in good silver coin spendable in Venice," a fund that clearly had accumulated from sums repaid by the Commune of Pirano on the principal, plus interest, at an average annual rate of 10.6 percent. The officials were directed to accept the sum "secundum modum et consuetudinem nostram et dicte camere." For this modest nest egg, worth an equivalent of about 4,000 gold ducats, the depositor received special considerations and assurances concerning the safety of his money in the face of local reprisal laws, assurances that were even more carefully formulated than the general law of 1317, passed in the context of the deposit made by Guglielmo da Castelbarco. Two days later the identical sum, "in toto et parte," was lent by the Grain Office to the state "pro oportunitatibus comunis." Repayment to the grain administration was promised "as soon as possible."[36] At the death of the lord of Padua and according to his testament, this deposit in the Grain Office joined another much larger sum (some 89,000–100,000 ducats) that Marsilio had committed to the care of the Procurators of San Marco, the executors of his estate, and went toward restitution of ill-gotten gain ("male ablata") and the construction of a monastery and several chapels.[37]

Word of the agreement made by Marsilio da Carrara and the Venetian Commune concerning the deposit spread to certain other unnamed persons ("aliqui"), probably also foreigners, who came forward offering to lend some 20,000 lire, on condition that they receive the same assurances that Marsilio had received. On 20 December 1323 the Great Council advised the Grain Office that it should accede to their requests. Here it is explicitly stated, in contrast to the earlier agreement, that the money be accepted as one-year time deposits.[38]

[35] Darja Mihelič, *Neagrarno gospodarstvo Pirana od 1280 do 1320 [La produzione non rurale di Pirano dal 1280 al 1320]*, Academia scientiarum et artium slovenca, cl. I, 27 (Ljubljana, Slovenia, 1985), 151–52; the act, notarized by Andrea Dotto of Venice on 19 February 1319, is summarized in a power of attorney of 1321, in Camillo de Franceschi, ed., "Chartularium piranense — Raccolta dei documenti medievali di Pirano," *Atti e memorie della Società istriana di archeologia e storia patria*, 44 (1932), 275–77, doc. 42; cf. also *PRV*, doc. 101 (29 April 1320). For general information on the lender, see Maria Chiara Billanovich, "Carrara, Marsilio da," *DBI*, 20 (1977), 688–91.

[36] *PRV*, doc. 112, and *RES*, doc. 97.

[37] For the testament, see Museo Civico di Padova, Documenti carraresi, BP 990–91; for the administration of the estate, see ASV, PSM, Ultra, b. 82–87. For information on the deposits in the Procuratia, see Mueller, *Procuratori di San Marco*, 27, 143.

[38] The earlier agreement called for reimbursement on demand, although surely there was a

During these same years the Grain Office also served a special function as depository: it acted as the financial agent of the Council of Ten in the latter's involvement in the Tiepolo-Querini conspiracy of 1310. Funds of one kind or another, sequestered from the families concerned, were deposited in the Grain Office. (The role involves a certain irony, since the conspiracy itself may have failed in part because of the delay caused by the sacking of the Grain Office by the column of armed men due to approach San Marco from the Rialto, as was mentioned above.)[39] In 1320 a sum of 200 lire, which was considered to belong to one of the conspirators, was ordered deposited in the Grain Office, at the disposal of the Council of Ten.[40] Another sum of 24 lire di grossi belonging to the estate of Jacopo Querini had been ordered deposited at the Grain Office; in 1322 it was given to Francesco Querini, executor of the estate.[41] Earlier in the same year the dowry of Maria, late wife of the late conspirator Pietro Querini, on deposit at the Grain Office, was made available to their daughter, under strict conditions. Those conditions were probably met in 1323 when the heir collected some 545 lire.[42]

Those sums of the Querini clan which involved dowries seem to have accrued interest regularly. In 1324 the Grain Office was ordered to administer certain provisions of the will of Galvani Querini. In particular, it was to turn over some rent moneys of the estate to the Hospital of S. Bartolomeo, in the sestiere of Castello, and with other rents to constitute a dowry for the daughter, Agnes. The dowry was to gain interest in the same manner as the officials paid others, that is, at 5 percent.[43]

Although these funds controlled by the Council of Ten were somewhat peculiar in nature, in practice they formed a part of the deposits in the floating debt of the Commune which the Grain Office and the Commune could utilize, with authorization, until the conditions governing the deposits had been met and reimbursement had to be made.

The individual cases discussed so far were exceptional, both for the nature of the persons, foreigners and conspirators, and for the amounts of money involved. Contemporaneously the Grain Office was accepting deposits from individuals, Venetians and foreigners, without specific action

---

mutual understanding that the deposit could be employed for a considerable period of time. The deliberation of December (in *RES,* doc. 99) reads: "Quod usque ad unum annum ad minus, mutuantes non possint petere dictos denarios."

[39]See above, n. 6.

[40]Ferruccio Zago, ed., *Consiglio dei Dieci, deliberazioni miste, registri I–II* (Venice, 1962), doc. 56; the money was claimed three years later (doc. 407).

[41]Ibid., doc. 310.

[42]Ibid., docs. 269, 441, 442; the other half of the 1,000 lire dowry was made up from the sale of government credits.

[43]The obligation of the Grain Office to retain on deposit and administer the rents of the estate was reiterated later, as was the obligation to pay interest. Ibid., docs. 491 and 546.

each time by the Great Council and therefore leaving little or no trace in the documents. By the late 1320s the government was convinced of the utility of this form of floating debt and sought to augment available funds and reduce red tape. First, in February 1328 the Great Council gave the Procurators of San Marco discretionary powers to invest in the Grain Office bequests under their administration which had been earmarked by the testators for investment in Venice under the form of "local colleganze."[44] This option seems in fact not to have been used by the Procurators, most probably since credit extended in the form of local colleganze at the time was still bringing a return of 6 to 12 percent per annum, more than the interest the Grain Office was offering, namely, 3 percent to foreigners, 4 percent to citizens, 5 percent on dowries.[45] A few weeks later the Great Council, noting the interest of private parties in depositing money in the Grain Office "at the usual conditions," delegated its responsibility in the matter of reaching specific agreements with potential depositors to the Signoria plus the grain officials. In practice, this decision gave discretionary authority to the officials of the Grain Office in accepting deposits, within limits, from Venetians and foreigners alike and guaranteeing complete security.[46] A limit of something over 2,000 ducats was probably set about this time; below that amount the officials operated at their own discretion.[47] As a result, evidence of smaller deposits by Venetians is at best sporadic and comes almost exclusively from testaments and account books. The last important decision of the Great Council in regard to the financial operations of the Grain Office comes in 1329; at that time, dowries in liquid form and surety for the same were no longer to be left—without interest—in care of the Procurators of San Marco but were to be deposited in the Grain Office, at 5 percent interest.[48] For the next fifteen years the officials of the Grain Office

---

[44]ASV, MC, Spiritus, fol. 26v.

[45]See Mueller, *Procuratori di San Marco*, 93–95.

[46]"Cum sint aliqui volentes deponere et mutuare peccuniam ad cameram nostram frumenti per modum solitum dicte camere, et cum pactis et condicionibus quibus de sua peccunia possint esse securi, vadit pars quod dicta peccunia possit recipi per dictos officiales et nomine comunis et dicte camere promiti et fieri mutuantibus et deponentibus omnia pacta, promissiones, obligaciones et securitates, que videbuntur domino duci, consiliariis, capitibus, et officialibus frumenti, vel maiori parti eorum et quecumque acta, promissa, et ordinata fuerint in predictis et quolibet predictorum, sint valida et firma, sicut facta essent per maius consilium, et sic debeant observari, non obstantibus aliquibus consiliis vel capitularibus que quantum in hac parte sint revocata. ASV, MC, Spiritus, fol. 27 (9 April 1328).

[47]In the case to be discussed below regarding the deposit made by Ludovico Gonzaga in 1374, the officials claimed the "ancient right" to accept sums up to 2,134 ducats, but they needed authorization to accept more than that from any given person at a given time: "Et officiales predicti ex quadam libertate antiqua possint recipere in deposito ducatos 2134." That amount corresponds, although not exactly, to 7,000 lire di piccoli (2,187.5 ducats at 64 soldi per ducat) or 5,500 lire a grossi (2,115 ducats), the moneys of account in which the ceiling had probably been expressed sometime in the early fourteenth century. ASV, SM, reg. 34, fol. 73v.

[48]ASV, MC, Spiritus, fol. 35v (10 August 1329), and Mueller, *Procuratori di San Marco*, 108 nn.

operated with considerable independence, and little evidence of their activity remains. In late 1344, during a serious crisis in the finances of the Grain Office, the discretionary powers of the officials were strictly limited;[49] from that point on what we know about sizeable deposits made by foreigners comes largely from the deliberations of the Senate, a fact reflected in the source column of table E.1 below, which lists the authorizations to deposit funds.

Having thus traced the origins and the first years of activity of the depository, we can now turn to some of the major figures who appear in the documents over the remaining century of financial activity of the Grain Office. Table E.2 provides a list of names in chronological order, by date of deposit. Rather than treating the cases in that order, however, in the subsections that follow they have been grouped together by geographical area of provenance.

iv. OTHER DEPOSITORS, BY PROVENANCE

The Veneto

Padua is also represented, after the groundbreaking example of Marsilio da Carrara, by the latter's father-in-law, Enrico Scrovegni, son of the usurer Rinaldo of Dantesque fame and patron of Giotto and the Arena chapel. Admittedly, Scrovegni's deposit in the Grain Office was very small: 1,000 lire di piccoli (little more than 300 ducats). Clearly Scrovegni, a naturalized citizen and wealthy moneylender in Venice before his death in 1336, knew how to get at least 8 percent interest on his loans, more than the Grain Office offered at that time.[50] His widow, Jacobina d'Este, also resident in Venice, had a considerably larger deposit at her death, most of which passed to their heirs, first Ugolino and then Caterina. Much larger sums — over 6,000 ducats — were deposited around 1344 by Pietro and Sachetto Campagnola, notables of Padua; after the death of both by plague, the claims to inheritance by relatives multiplied, especially in the 1360s.[51] Deposits made later by numerous other Paduans, not recorded by name in

---

[49]*RES*, doc. 174.

[50]At his death Scrovegni had outstanding credits of more than 16,000 ducats, mostly in the form of local colleganze. See Gino Luzzatto, "La commenda nella vita economica dei secoli XIII e XIV, con particolare riguardo a Venezia," reprinted in his *Studi,* 77–78.

[51]Regarding the nest egg of the da Campagnola brothers, see *LCR,* 3:57–58, nos. 330–36, and Silvana Collodo, "Credito, movimento della proprietà fondiaria e selezione sociale a Padova nel Trecento," reprinted in her *Una società in trasformazione: Padova tra XI e XV secolo* (Padua, 1990), 228 n. 108. One might hypothesize a role of the Venetian podestà of Padua, Andreasio Morosini, in the investment decisions of Paduans; while he himself preferred government obligations, in his testament of 1348 (he died of the plague) he inserted a contingency clause whereby funds could be deposited alternatively at the grain or salt magistracies. ASV, CIN, b. 32, notaio Raffaino Caresini, imbreviatura grande, fols. 4–5.

Venetian sources, can be assumed to have followed the ups and downs of relations between Venice and the Carrara lords. That further and significant deposits had been made and maintained at the Grain Office is underscored in the chronicle of the Gatari brothers in the context of the War of Chioggia. The stake of Paduans, enemies of Venice in that war and after, was such that Francesco il Vecchio insisted upon the insertion in the Treaty of Turin, which ended that war, of guarantees of the security and integrity of investments in government obligations as well as in deposits in the Grain Office by citizens of Padua. In particular, he wanted assurance that interest would be paid on all funds and that investments and deposits made by his deceased wife (and citizen of Venice), Fina Buzzacarini—later estimated at 20,000 ducats—would be restored.[52]

For the Vicentino the only known case is a very important one, that of Pietro "Nan" da Marano, a dwarf. Knighted by Mastino I della Scala in 1291, Pietro served as advisor to the Scaligeri and as moneylender to many persons, both weak and powerful. In 1329 he was made a citizen of Venice. It seems that prior to the Scaliger War (1336–39), which pitted Verona against Florence and Venice, Pietro cautioned his master against undertaking the venture. At just about that time he deposited 10,000 ducats at the Venetian Grain Office for safekeeping. After the war, and under the influence of his confessors the Franciscans Pace da Lugo and Tommaso "de Çenerino," then inquisitor in Verona, Pietro reformulated his testament and left the deposit plus interest (which he called a gift, "dono") for restitution of ill-gotten gain ("male ablata") to specific persons who could prove their claim in court. In 1342, according to the dispositions that Pietro had inscribed in the account books of the Grain Office, the officials turned over 12,153 ducats to the

[52]*Cronaca carrarese,* in Rerum Italicarum Scriptores, ser. 2, vol. 17, pt. I (Città di Castello, 1909–31), 201–2, hereafter cited as Gatari, *Cronaca carrarese,* mentioned by Collodo, "Credito," 272 n. 260. In the list of demands sent by Francesco, that regarding the bond holdings and other sums of money ("altro dinaro") of his wife is number 6. Demand number 11 regards all citizens and all possible funds (bonds, deposits at the Salt Office and at the Grain Office), which, it was hoped, they would be able to enjoy in the future as they had before the war: "volle . . . che tuti i danari ch'è agli inprestii, al salle, al formento, che fosse de' citadini overo abitanti da Padoa, ch'a quilli sia datto il suo utille e pro' del tenpo ch'è a venire e che a loro possa goderlli sì come faxiea prima che fosse la guerra." Of these demands only the former was included, and that in more specific form: at the request that Francesco as heir receive the 20,000 ducats that Fina had kept in Venice, it was agreed that an investigation would be conducted and that, should the sums have meanwhile gotten into private hands, justice would be done. See the text of the treaty in Gianbattista Verci, *Storia della marca trevigiana e veronese,* 17 vols. (Venice, 1786–90), 15:93, and in Šime Ljubić, ed., *Listine o odnošajih izmedju Južnoga Slavenstva i Mletačke republike,* 10 vols., Monumenta spectantia historiam Slavorum meridionalium (vols. 1–5, 9, 12, 17, 21–22), (Zagreb, 1868–91), 4:138. For Francesco's large deposits at Paduan banks, see Francesca Zen Benetti, "Prestatori ebraici e cristiani nel Padovano fra Trecento e Quattrocento," in *Gli Ebrei e Venezia, secoli XIV–XVIII* (Milan, 1987), 632–33.

Procurators of San Marco de Citra, who, together with the above-mentioned Franciscan friars, initiated the task of aiding the soul of the deceased Pietro by making restitution to some thirty claimants and by paying out pious bequests. None of the parties, including the inquisitor, who had jurisdiction over both heresy and usury, were in the least disturbed by using, for restitution of usury and related forms of extortion, not only the principal but also the interest, gained probably at a rate of 4 percent per year.[53]

It is at the Scaliger court at Verona, frequented by Pietro da Marano, that perhaps the most interesting case develops, for the inheritance of a very large deposit, claimed by various parties at various times, caused serious problems for the Venetian state. The deposits made by Cangrande II della Scala, lord of Verona, date from 1355, the year following the unsuccessful revolt of his half-brother Fregnano against his signory. During the revolt, Fregnano died, and dozens of his supporters were executed. Finding himself in a very unstable political and familial situation, the lord of Verona began making deposits in the Grain Office, as well as in the Procuratia di San Marco, clearly as a way of squirreling away an immense liquid patrimony.[54] Between 1355 and his assassination in 1359 at the hands of his brother Cansignorio, Cangrande deposited large sums of money and then changed three times the conditions governing the inheritability of the deposits, to take account of changing family fortunes and specifically of the birth of new bastard sons. According to the later chronicler Torello Saraina, Cangrande was concerned about the future of these minors, since he wished to make them his successors.[55] Very likely with this end in mind, Cangrande contacted both the Grain Office and the Procurators of San Marco, the latter in their capacity (the chronicler reminds us) as guardians of the patrimonies of widows and minors. In fact, he would divide his nest egg between the two Venetian institutions, making in the former an interest-bearing "irregular" deposit, in the latter an unproductive "regular" deposit. In so doing, he

[53]Natascia Carlotto, "Pietro Nan da Marano, miles e civis veneto: Accumulazione e restituzione di un patrimonio nel primo Trecento" (laurea thesis, University of Venice, 1983), 30–33, 63–66, 89–98, and idem, "I da Marano: Una famiglia vicentina dall'età ezzeliniana al dominio veneto," in Ortalli and Knapton, *Istituzioni, società e potere*, 213–15.

[54]The rapid accumulation of great wealth by the Scaligeri can be understood only in the context of that combination of what one might call *Hausgut* and *Krongut*. For the revenues from rents and taxes, see Gian Maria Varanini, "Patrimonio e fattoria scaligera: Tra gestione patrimoniale e funzione pubblica," in *Gli scaligeri, 1277–1387*, ed. Gian Maria Varanini (Verona, 1988), 383–87.

[55]*Le historie e fatti de Veronesi nei tempi del popolo e signori scaligeri* (Verona, 1542), lib. 2, p. 37. See also Parisio da Cerea, *Chronacon veronense*, in Rerum Italicarum Scriptores, 8 (Milan, 1728), 654–55. Secondary sources give at best incomplete information; see Luigi Simeoni, "La ribellione di Fregnano della Scala e la politica generale italiana," *Studi storici veronesi* 11 (1961): 36, and Egidio Rossini, "La signoria scaligera dopo Cangrande," in *Verona e il suo territorio*, vol. 3, pt. 1 (Verona, 1975), 689–700.

exemplified that high degree of trust which the Venetian system of government was able to instill in foreign lords with excess liquid assets.[56]

The authorizations passed by the Senate in May and December of that year, for a total of 90,000 ducats, clearly regard this case, although the depositor's name is not mentioned (see below, table E.1). By December 1355 some funds had already been deposited in the Grain Office in Cangrande's name by Azzone da Correggio and other emissaries.[57] The next year Cangrande was ready to deposit further sums of money and named Antonio di Rolandino Maffei his attorney in the matter. Part of the funds for which he sought a safe haven were probably those 10,000 ducats paid to him by the marquis of Mantua (out of a total debt of 30,000 ducats). In March one of these payments was mediated by the Rialto bank of Antonio's brother Filippo Maffei.[58] But before placing further amounts in the Grain Office, Cangrande desired reassurance about the safety of the money. In a letter of reply, Doge Giovanni Dolfin repeated the text of the regulation passed in 1317 concerning the safety from sequester and reprisals of deposits in the Grain and Salt Offices and continued: "If anyone's money is so guaranteed, how much more yours, dearest friend?"; he concluded: "We firmly promise to hold said funds safely and securely" [Firmiter promittimus quod pecunias supradictas . . . salvas et securas habebimus]. In 1357 Cangrande replied that he was in accord with the agreements made between his representatives and the Commune of Venice.[59]

In the fall of 1358 Cangrande granted power of attorney once again to Antonio Maffei, himself at the time a citizen of Venice (resident at S. Polo) and now a Rialto banker, like his brother Filippo. His task this time was to withdraw — symbolically — and renew the deposit at the Grain Office of 77,500 ducats plus interest ("cum utilitate sive proficuo").[60] Then again in the spring of 1359 he named Filippo Maffei his attorney to renew all the agreements with both the Grain Office and the Procurators of San Marco.[61] On the basis of a later claim, we know that on 2 and 27 May Filippo Maffei reached agreements with the Procurators on a deposit, without interest, of 110,000 ducats, while on 4 May he renewed a deposit of 81,643 ducats (plus some small change in silver coin) at the Grain Office.[62] The lord's testament

[56]On the depository of the Procurators, see Mueller, *Procuratori di San Marco*, 22–35. Further information on this institution will probably be found in archives outside Venice; an example is the deposit of 80,000 ducats made by Mercenarius qd. Generalis de Monteverde for his son Cola, who organized its recovery in 1374 from Treviso; see AST, Notarile I, b. 43, fols. 1v–6v, 23v–25v, kindly brought to my attention by Paolo Cagnin.

[57]ASV, SM, reg. 27, fol. 47 (3 December 1355).

[58]*LCR,* 2:243, no. 145.

[59]ASV, Commemoriali, reg. 5, fols. 61v, 106.

[60]*LCR,* 2:285, no. 48.

[61]Ibid., 2:300, no. 120.

[62]Ibid., 3:175, no. 206 for the dates; for the amounts, see the testament, dated 24 November 1359, in ASV, Secreta, Collegio, Secreti, reg. for 1354–63, fols. 63–66v, and published by

of 24 November changed the definition of the heirs once again and replaced all previously made agreements, including those so recently drawn up by Filippo Maffei. The heirs of nearly 200,000 ducats, divided between the Grain Office and the Procuratia, were to be his bastards Fregnano, probably just born, and Tebaldo, both under the guardianship of Riguccio Pegolotti, Cangrande's faithful factor. The third natural son, Guglielmo, was left 60,000 ducats stored in the castle at Peschieria on Lake Garda.[63]

After Cangrande's death, several attempts were made to recoup the money. First, in 1372 Venice seems to have tried, in the war against Carrara Padua, to win over to its side Cansignorio, Cangrande's assassin (and universal heir, or "residuarius," along with his brother Paolo Alboino), with the promise of at least part of the money left on deposit in Venice for Cangrande's natural sons, a figure then set at 275,000 ducats, in return for permission for the powerful Venetian nobleman, Pantaleone Barbo, to recruit mercenaries in the districts of Verona and Vicenza. This, in any case, is the story as told in some detail by Paduan chroniclers. If it was true, it would complicate the resolution of the case. The chronicle reports that Barbo accompanied the hoard on 9 March 1372 on its way from Venice to Verona, as though the authors had seen the baggage train (the coin would have weighed nearly a ton) and armed guards passing near Padua. No corroboration has been found in official deliberations. In any case, such an agreement would have constituted an arbitrary redefinition of the inheritance, in disregard of the clauses laid down in the depositors's testament. Perhaps Venice merely made a promise to pay, enough to secure the alliance against the Carraresi. Or the report could simply be spurious, made as it was by Carrara partisans.[64] If it had been meant for a wider audience, the report did not reduce interest in the hoard, and in subsequent claims made on the money no mention is made by any party of any previous payment to Cansignorio or to anyone else.

In 1384 Bernabò Visconti, lord of Milan, made a futile attempt to get his hands on the money, specifically that deposited at the Procuratia. He advanced his claim probably as husband of Beatrice, alias Regina, sister of Cangrande II, but he was surely prompted to make the move by knowledge of a nearly contemporaneous rival claim. Bernabò's pique at having his

Gaetano Cogo in "Fregnano della Scala bastardo di Cangrande II," *Atti dell'Accademia di Udine*, ser. 2, 3 (1896):33–51, doc. 1; as Cogo rightly states, the version published by G. Biancolini, *Serie cronologica dei vescovi e governatori di Verona* (Verona, 1760), doc. xxix, pp. 110–16, is an uncritical collage of documents.

[63]Cogo, "Fregnano della Scala," doc. 1. Filippo Maffei, the banker, was interrogated by the Procurators of San Marco as to the intentions of Cangrande; the conditions now governing the deposits were repeated, albeit in a sketchy and incomplete manner, in ASV, Secreta, Collegio, Secreti (1354–63), fols. 72–73v, following the registration of the testament.

[64]See Gatari, *Cronaca carrarese*, 47, 48. The story was picked up by Verci, *Storia*, 14:159. Both Verci and, following him, Cogo ("Fregnano della Scala," 35) speak simply of a "promise" on the part of Venice.

claim dismissed by Venice provoked a significant rhetorical disquisition in the Senate on the world-renowned tradition of Venetian justice whereby everyone is given his due.[65]

The concern of Venice's rulers was not rhetorical but real, for the rival claims to a large sum of money placed them in a difficult position. In the spring of the same year, some months before the harangue on justice, a man who claimed to be Fregnano della Scala (also known as Fregnanino), illegitimate son of Cangrande II and presumably the sole surviving heir to this fortune with a right based on Cangrande's testament, filed suit before a probate court (the Curia del Procurator) claiming his right to the money left with the Procurators of San Marco; contemporaneously he petitioned the grain officials, out of court, for the sums left on deposit at the Grain Office, plus accrued interest. On 20 June the doge, with four councillors and a head of the Forty, arguing that the claims of this Fregnano were serious and affected greatly the Commune and the honor of the whole state, proposed the creation of a committee of ten nobles to advise the three Giudici del Procurator, while guaranteeing the judges complete freedom to arrive independently at a final decision. After four ballots the bill was defeated. It was re-presented on 28 June and 1 July when it was again defeated, but only after further eight ballots, despite the support of the Giudici del Procurator themselves. Finally, on the thirteenth try, it was voted that the three probate judges plus the Procurator Giovanni Gradenigo could meet with the Senate and air their views.[66] The matter was not resolved in this fashion, and the Senate later empowered the full Collegio to negotiate an agreement with that man "qui facit se vocari Fregnanum de la Scala" and report back. That report was redacted more than a year later and presented in late August 1385. It outlined what was to be the final compromise between the parties; only a few loose ends remained. Before the Senate gave its approval, it insisted that more secure formulas be sought for the claimant's renunciation of all that he had coming, "if anything"; the formulation was to be worked out with the Commune's legal advisors.[67]

The report to the Senate plus the much more extensive formal agreement make it possible to learn something about both the procedure followed in the negotiations and the conclusion.[68] As regards the procedure,

---

[65]ASV, SM, reg. 39, fol. 9v (20 September 1384).

[66]Ibid., reg. 28, fol. 139.

[67]Ib. l., reg. 39, fol. 134 (29 August 1385). As the deliberation states, authority had been granted to the full Collegio sometime previously. The quittance demanded was to be "de omni et toto eo quod sibi spectat vel spectare posset, si aliquod ei spectat" and the agreement drafted "cum omnibus cautelis et clausulis opportunis, cum consilio sapientum juris." A rider, asking greater security, was added to the proposal presented by the College (same fol.).

[68]Most of the story is recorded in a very important document four sides long (some 240 lines) in ASV, Commemoriali, reg. 8, fols. 126r–27v, dated 25 September 1385 but containing information and copies of documents both earlier and later. Insufficiently summarized in *LCR*,

very likely the full Collegio had, in turn, delegated authority to the Procurators of San Marco (de Supra) and the grain officials, for it seems to be they who actually carried on the negotiations, although both denied the legitimacy of the claimant's contention. Initially the Procurators Giovanni Gradenigo and Pietro Corner stated that they had it on good authority that Fregnano and Tebaldo had died in prison and that they would therefore not pay out the money. The grain officials likewise refused to pay out the principal and interest ("lucra sive prode") accrued and later asked that it be entered in the court record that they had never believed the man's claim to be Cangrande's heir. But either the case was not as clear as they made it, or there were pressures from other quarters to reach an accommodation. The claimant was first given time to prove his case with witnesses, and later he said that he could produce more, only not "ad presens." Specific documentation of the probatory phase of the case has not survived.

The final document, drawn up in the offices of the Procurators of San Marco, transcribed in the registers of the Commemoriali, and notarized by Pietro de Compostellis, was in fact redacted under the advice of the noted jurist Pietro d'Ancarano (at the time a salaried jurisconsult of the Commune) and is a classic in cautious legal language and hedging. It presents the presumed Fregnano's side, complete with reference to each deposit, with dates, names, and powers of attorney as granted at different times by Cangrande II and corroborated by the record ("catasticus vel liber autenticus") of the Procuratia and the ledger ("quaternus") of the Grain Office. It records the opposition of the Procurators and the grain officials. The text of the agreement follows, which was basically the same as that approved by the Senate (except that the "gift" of 250 ducats had been eliminated). The compromise ("donatio, compositio, transactio, concordia et pacta") included the following terms. The presumed Fregnano promised to give definitive quittance to the Procurators and the grain officials for all sums deposited by Cangrande and accrued interest, in his own name and that of his heirs; in short, he would drop all claims to the hoard. On their part, the Venetian authorities promised to pay him an annuity of 1,500 ducats as long as he lived and after his death pay an annuity of 1,000 ducats to his eventual legitimate male heirs. The accord was to become effective one month from the date of the document (23 September). Two final clauses were added: first, the presumed Fregnano swore that he would not resort in the future to cavils, such as having been underage (twenty-five years) at the time of the stipulation; and second, Venice promised that the annuity would be safe from sequester, even if claimed by eventual creditors.

All that was lacking was pomp and circumstance, and that was

3:175, no. 206. (No reference to the case is extant in ASV, Curia del Procurator, Sentenze a legge, of which the only surviving register close to the case is dated 1383–84.)

promptly provided. The agreement was solemnized in the church of San Marco itself on 17 October, in the presence of the primicerius of San Marco and of the notary Giovanni Vido, "sindic and representative" of the doge for this occasion, as well as the parties to the pact (the Procurators, the grain officials, and the so-called Fregnano). Witnesses were three noble and three non-noble Venetians. The "solemn stipulation" repeated the clauses regarding the annuity, the renunciation, and the affirmation of the supposed heir that he was over twenty-five years of age.[69]

The concern of the highest authorities of the land and the ritual surrounding the final act reflect the importance of the matter: a claim against the state to by now more than 250,000 ducats, part at the Procuratia di San Marco, most at the Grain Office. Clearly, the authorities did not want to have to pay out that amount of money. No reference is made anywhere in the extensive documentation to payment having been made previously to Cansignorio, something that would have come out in court sooner or later, if only via "leaks" on the part of members of the staffs in question.[70] It is difficult to explain Venice's refusal to recognize this nobleman as the real Fregnano, natural son of Cangrande II, except as a way of avoiding payment, for he was well known in the city, where he was "habitator." There had been two assassination attempts against him in Venice which in time involved important organs of the state. In the first case the Avogadori and the Quarantia condemned the principal conspirator, called simply "Regutius de Verona," to life imprisonment. In the second attempt, made on 13 April 1384, probably around the very time of Fregnano's claim to the money, twelve hired assassins tried to break into his house in Venice through a hole they had made in the wall, an attempt that Fregnano himself reported to the Quarantia Criminal the morning after. Again the Quarantia took action, this time offering a reward of 500 lire, "in the name of justice and for the honor of the state."[71] In short, he was a personality in the city, known to the authorities;

---

[69]The concern for Fregnano's age derives from the fact that he had to have been born in the month or two preceding the formulation of Cangrande's will, dated 24 November 1359; it may also be one of the reasons for the delay between the suit (spring 1384) and its resolution.

[70]A law of 1410 which ordered that old records, namely of deposits on which interest had not been collected for five years, be kept separately under lock and key in care of the Procurators of San Marco implied clearly that accountants at the Grain Office were advising unknowing heirs of their rights to deposits made long before, obviously for a fee. ASV, SM, reg. 48, fol. 174.

[71]Cogo, "Fregnano della Scala," 36–39 and docs. 2 and 3. In the earlier case (ASV, Quarantia Criminal, reg. 3, fol. 112r–v [13–17 May 1382]), the sentence passed (out of four proposed solutions) against the prime suspect was not capital punishment (as Cogo has it) but blinding in both eyes and life imprisonment, as is also corroborated by ASV, AC, reg. 3644, fol. 42. The author denies, surely correctly, the possibility that this Riguccio could be identified as Riguccio di Lotto Pegolotti, Cangrande II's "collaterale" in 1357 and guardian of Tebaldo and Fregnanino according to the testament of 1359, in both roles deeply involved in matters of the deposits at the Procuratia and at the Grain Office. (He had already been in the Scaliger court under Mastino II in 1342; see *LCR*, 2:100, no. 567, where he witnessed a document involving the bequests of Pietro Nan da Marano.) The second case, following Fregnano's report, was

he is never referred to as the "presumed" Fregnano della Scala in these criminal cases (in the first he is called "dominus," in the second "egregius vir"), and the Venetian police and judicial system wished at least to look as though they were protecting him. But as soon as he formally sued to establish his claim to the Scaliger nest egg, his paternity came to be doubted. Whether the doubts were raised honestly or not is impossible to say; to be sure, the claimant had been constrained to accept a deal extremely advantageous to Venice: the annuity he was offered was far below even the figure owed by the Grain Office alone in simple interest on the original deposit of over twenty-five years previous. Any nobleman could live quite lavishly, however, on an annuity of 1,500 ducats. Again Venice was fortunate, in that the amount had to be paid out only for a short time, for the beneficiary was dead by early 1391.[72]

The last Scaliger lord, Antonio, son of Cansignorio, also had dealings with the Grain Office, but not as heir or claimant to Cangrande's nest egg.[73] Antonio was a close ally of Venice at least by 1385, when he received honorary membership in the Great Council. He fought for Venice in Friuli as a mercenary captain, for which he received a monthly income. But this did not resolve his financial straits. In 1387 he pawned his jewels to the Jews then lending in Venice for 47,500 ducats, an amount that the Commune agreed to guarantee. The allied armies of Francesco da Carrara and Giangaleazzo Visconti forced him to flee Verona in October 1387. In 1388 the Signoria granted him a pension of 100 ducats per month, money that was conceivably credited to his name at the Grain Office. When in 1388, the year of his death, Antonio sought permission to withdraw from the Grain Office 3,000 ducats credited to his account, the Senate agreed, not to a withdrawal, but to a "loan" of that amount by the Grain Office. Since his jewels were then being sold to cover his huge loans with the Jews, the Senate insisted that Antonio reaffirm his commitments, should the auction not cover the whole loan, requiring the Commune to pay the balance due.[74]

---

turned over to the Avogadori di Comun, and the reward was set "in favorem iustitie et pro nostro honore." Cogo explains Venice's solicitude as repayment for Scaliger military support for the Venetian cause in Friuli, for which he can only cite Antonio della Scala's activity. The relations between Fregnanino and Antonio, if any, are not discernible; no one thought to call Antonio (son of Cansignorio) to testify to the former's identity, nor did Antonio formulate a claim in the inheritance case.

[72]Cf. Cogo, "Fregnano della Scala," 38–39. At 3 percent, the 81,643 ducats registered on 4 May 1359 would have brought about 2,450 ducats annual interest.

[73]An early but unclear reference is that of a decision of the Consoli dei Mercanti in favor of the grain officials and against Crescimbene Maffei, in a case favoring Antonio and his brother Bartolomeo della Scala for a settlement of 2,000 ducats. See ASV, Sindicati, 1, fol. 139v (17 June 1381). In general, see John Law, "La caduta degli Scaligeri," in Ortalli and Knapton, Istituzioni, società e potere, 83–98.

[74]See Mueller, "Les prêteurs juifs," pt. 4. For the loan/withdrawal from the Grain Office, see ASV, SSec, liber E, fol. 18 (29 April 1389 [sic for 1388]). For mention of the sale, see SM, reg. 41 (4 November 1390). See also LCR, 3:178–79, nos. 217, 222.

There is information on deposits by only one other Veronese, a certain Giovanni della Torre. In 1389 he petitioned that 1,000 ducats of the interest due him be added to the principal and the balance paid him in cash by the Camerlenghi di Comun. In 1407 his son Domenico used the balance of more than 3,000 ducats due him by the Grain Office as partial payment to Venetian authorities in Verona for some 9,000 ducats' worth of real estate that he had purchased from them after Venice's takeover of Verona.[75]

Treviso, which passed under direct Venetian domination in 1339, is represented in table E.2 by only the local notable Oliverio Forzetta. The case is unique because the deposits became a perpetual pious legacy. Son and grandson of manifest usurers in serious trouble with the ecclesiastical authorities, Forzetta was a man of culture and a frequent visitor to Venice, where he collected books, works of art, medals, and coins.[76] His several deposits in the Grain Office reached the second-highest figure after that of Cangrande II della Scala. By 1345 Forzetta already had a credit of 15,800 ducats, on which he earned a return of 3 percent.[77] In 1364, the Senate authorized the Grain Office to accept a deposit of 1,800 ducats at 3 percent—but the sum very likely represented accumulated interest added to principal.[78] By the time he died in 1374 (his testament is dated 16 July 1368), Forzetta's credits totaled 37,150 ducats, 17 grossi, 6 piccoli a oro.

Having failed with five wives to produce offspring, Forzetta made the Scuola dei Battuti of Treviso and its hospital his universal heir. The interest payments on the deposit, to the sum of 1,114.5 ducats per year, then became, in effect, a regular and perpetual income for the hospital; the principal was intangible. The hospital's account books indicate that interest was paid at varying dates of maturity: around 1400, once annually, on the feast of St. Lucy (13 December, the date in 1388 when Venice took jurisdiction over Treviso definitively);[79] about 1440 in three equal installments;[80] about 1500 in twelve installments, due on the fifth day of each month.[81] Initially, the money was paid directly by the Grain Office or by the Treasury (upon written order by the Grain Office) to agents sent first by the executors of

---

[75]See the sources cited in table E.2, below.

[76]See Gerolamo Biscaro, *L'ospedale [di Treviso] ed i suoi benefattori* (Treviso, 1903), 49–69; Giovanni Netto, *Nel '300 a Treviso: Vita cittadina vista nell'attività della "Scuola" Santa Maria dei Battuti e del suo Ospedale* (Treviso, 1976), 96–97 and app. 7; Gargan, *Cultura e arte.*

[77]Guid'Antonio Zanetti, ed., *Nuova raccolta delle monete e delle zecche d'Italia,* 4 vols. (Bologna, 1775–89), 4:171, and *PMV,* lxix–lxx. (Forzetta registered the sum as 50,560 lire di piccoli, having converted from ducats at the legal rate of 64 soldi per ducat.) It is interesting to note that only shortly before, in 1339–40, Forzetta occasionally sought loans on the Rialto, in a form similar to that of the local colleganza, on which he paid 10–20 percent interest; see Gargan, *Cultura e arte,* 28–29.

[78]ASV, SM, reg. 31, fol. 53v.

[79]AST, Osp, b. 334, reg. of the commissaria, 1401, fol. 5.

[80]Ibid., b. 1, loose sheet at fol. 45 (1441–42).

[81]Ibid., b. 11–12 (1499–1501).

the estate and then by the administrators of the hospital. Often the hospital had to solicit payment, and the gastaldi had to spend money to send representatives to Venice—sometimes with gifts of hens and sweet cheeses for persons who would intervene on behalf of the hospital (as was the case in 1401).[82] In order to eliminate unnecessary expenses for trips to Venice, Doge Francesco Foscari and the Senate in 1423 ordered payment made to the hospital directly by the Camera Fiscale of Treviso.[83] With that act, the state transformed the original deposit at the Grain Office into a perpetual income, owed by Venice to the hospital; it no longer mattered what office paid it out.

Despite the guarantees provided in the above-mentioned law of 1317, the extraordinary situation of the War of Chioggia and the loss of Treviso caused the Signoria to freeze the Forzetta bequest. From at least 1383 to 1388, when Treviso was dominated first by Austria and then by Padua, Venice refused to pay out the interest due. When in 1389 Venice finally freed the funds, it agreed to resume payments beginning only from 13 December 1388, the day Venetian domination was reestablished.[84]

From that time on, payments were relatively continuous, within the limits of state finances, as one can ascertain by consulting the hospital's remarkable series of huge ledgers.[85] The income was rendered sometimes in gold ducats, often in silver coin, occasionally in both; but since the sum on deposit at Forzetta's death was registered in gold, the interest never lost value over the first century and a half: even when paid in silver, the amount was calculated at the current rate of exchange on the basis of a stable gold value of 1,114.5 ducats, 1 grosso, 30 piccoli a oro per year. After the War of the League of Cambrai, however, when the rate of the gold ducat began rising again after two generations of stability, the amount due was conveniently interpreted in silver ducats of account, at £6 4s (or 124 soldi) di piccoli per ducat, so that the amount turned over by the Camera Fiscale of Treviso in the centuries following 1520 was a stable £575 17s 4d di piccoli per month.[86] As the gold ducat, then called zecchino, gradually moved from

---

[82]Ibid., b. 334, reg. for 1401, fol. 41v.

[83]ASV, SM, reg. 54, fol. 157 (5 November 1423), and the ducale of 11 February 1424 in AST, Osp, b. 364, parchment reg., fol. 2.

[84]See the attempts of the estate in 1381 to collect for the previous two years (AST, PO, n. 2402, 8 October) and early 1389 (ibid., n. 6352, 4 March). The Senate discussed the request and reached its decision on 18 May 1389; ASV, SM, reg. 41, fol. 4v (the text of which was copied into fol. IV of AST, Osp, b. 355, fasc. 1). The deliberation states that interest had not been paid for six years, beginning with a balance due for 1383, "tamquam bona tunc existentia subditorum domini Padue."

[85]I consulted 15 volumes of "entrata-uscita" up to 1526 (AST, Osp, b. 1–15; there are 247 reaching until 1811); the following registers of the Forzetta estate: b. 334–35, 356, 364–65, 383, 393; the libro rosso, b. 355; as well as b. 248, 284, 292.

[86]That is the figure then continually cited in the account books and in the ducal orders to the rectors as the amount due monthly.

6.5 lire di piccoli in 1520 to 22 lire in 1797, it is clear that in gold value the hospital's fixed income diminished progressively.[87]

During the years when Venice was involved in wars on the Terra-ferma, delays in making the payments were common. In 1419 the Senate admitted that the current balance due of 5,000 ducats could not be paid "ex defectu et carentia pecuniarum," a situation of dearth caused in part by King Sigismund's commercial blockade. Since the hospital cared for soldiers wounded in the war in Friuli, however, the Salt Office was ordered to come up with 1,000 ducats for the time being.[88] In 1423, with payments still in arrears, the Camera Fiscale of Treviso took over the obligation.[89] In the following decade, while the hospital was undertaking an important construction project, Doge Francesco Foscari caused the Venetian rector to intervene and order the treasurers to pay sums in arrears "owed to God and the Virgin . . . , lest divine matters be overlooked in favor of this-worldly affairs."[90] A century later Doge Andrea Gritti, upon petition of the gastaldi of the hospital, ordered the transfer of revenues from the butchery tax, "for the sake of the poor, beneficiaries of the interest payments."[91] But it seems that the Camera made the monthly payments of 575.85 lire di piccoli on schedule most of the time, until the fall of the republic.[92]

We can now distance ourselves from Venice and confirm the role of the Grain Office in Venice's relations with seignorial families elsewhere in central-northern Italy and even in the Balkans.

Milan

The active interest shown by Bernabò Visconti in the deposits created by Cangrande II della Scala has already been mentioned. But Bernabò's concern in that case was very likely rooted in an earlier and more direct connection of his forebears with Venice and the Venetian Grain Office. In

---

[87]For the prices of the ducat, see Vol. 1, pp. 567–68. The comment by Netto that the value of the income depreciated as a result of the continual drop in value of the Venetian lira is correct only for the period following the War of the League of Cambrai; *Nel '300 a Treviso*, 96.

[88]ASV, SM, reg. 52, fol. 179v (21 June 1419).

[89]Ibid., reg. 54, fol. 157, and AST, Osp, b. 364, fols. 1v–2. In January 1421 only 100 ducats were turned over; see AST, Osp, b. 334, fol. 43.

[90]AST, Osp, b. 364, fol. 2, and PO, no. 13,922: "ne divina pro secularibus omittant." A similar "ducale" was sent on 15 December 1488 ordering payment by Christmas so that the hospital could minister to its orphans; PO, no. 16,363.

[91]AST, PO, no. 16,078 (27 January 1534): "essendo da proveder per reverentia del nostro Signor Dio alli poveri del qual sono dedicati essi pro." On that date payments were about two years in arrears. The doge, reporting a deliberation of the Council of Ten, states that Forzetta's deposit was originally made at 5 percent interest but had been reduced to the highly advantageous rate of 3 percent. Extant documents do not corroborate this affirmation.

[92]In 1565 the gastaldi complained that the Camera Fiscale was three monthly payments behind (ibid., no. 16,362); in 1626 they complained about a delay of two months (no. 16,086).

1335 Luchino Visconti and his sons were granted honorary membership in the Great Council.[93] In 1342 or 1343 Luchino and his brother Giovanni, who ruled jointly, sent an unspecified hoard of coined silver to Venice in order to deposit it at the Grain Office ("pro peccunia deponendi apud officiales nostros frumenti"). The lords sent an embassy to Venice to complain that, despite the existence of official agreements permitting Milanese merchants to import and export coined bullion freely, a tax had been levied on the hoard; the tax took the form of the "quinto," that one-fifth of all silver imports that was to be consigned to the mint at a fixed price. On that occasion, the Senate refused to concede the point, "so as not to grant foreigners conditions that were more advantageous than those enjoyed by Venetian citizens."[94] Despite this setback, the deposit was made, but its value remains an unknown.

Claims to ownership over the deposit by supposed heirs created a headache for Venice, which must mean that the amount of money credited at the Grain Office was not insignificant. When Luchino died in 1349, his son Luchino Novello (or Luchinetto) remained under the protection of his uncle, Giovanni; but shortly after the latter's death in 1354, Luchino Novello was forced by an uprising to flee to Genova with his mother, Isabella Fieschi. When he reached majority (age fourteen) in 1360, he petitioned, at the prodding of Doge Simone Boccanegra, whose daughter he was to marry, to recover his father's deposit. Immediately his cousin, Galeazzo II, who in the meantime had become lord of Milan, wrote to the doge of Venice that Luchinetto was not the son and heir of Luchino at all but the bastard of his own relationship with Isabella; as a result, the money deposited at the Grain Office was really the legitimate property of Galeazzo and his brother Bernabò, not of Luchinetto. It seems clear that Venice at that point asked for proof from both claimants, for in 1362 Galeazzo wrote again to say that Isabella Fieschi herself was on her way to Venice to justify Luchinetto's petition and to ask that she not be given credence, for he had a written document in which she herself admitted Galeazzo's paternity. Venice then set a deadline on the production of proof by the claimants. In January 1363 Simone Boccanegra wrote to Doge Lorenzo Celsi, asking him to facilitate acceptance of the claims of Isabella and Luchinetto. And in May of the same year Bernabò and Galeazzo wrote to admit that they could not muster in time the proof and witnesses requested by Venice. They reaffirmed the validity of the supposed written admission by Isabella regarding Luchinetto's paternity and added they would not lie for such a small sum.[95] Just how

[93]*LCR,* 2:61, no. 364.

[94]ASV, SM, reg. 21, fol. 13 (10 February 1343); cf. Vol. 1, pp. 194, 372, where the case is mentioned, and 194–96, on the quinto.

[95]Much of this story is recounted by Francesco Cognasso, "L'unificazione della Lombardia sotto Milano," in *Storia di Milano,* 17 vols. (Milan, 1953–66), 5:326–28. The only sources

the Venetian authorities unraveled this knotty dynastic problem is not known, but in the end they very likely made payment to Luchino Novello and his mother Isabella. Although no documentary trace of the deposit at the Grain Office has turned up, it is known that Luchino Novello, who never was able to return to Milan, remained on good terms with Venice, where he was a citizen, made his testament, and, at the time of his death in 1400, held a portfolio of 20,000 ducats in government obligations.[96]

Two other Milanese, both connected with the Visconti court, figure on the list of depositors. Donnina de Porris, mistress of Bernabò, sold grain to Venice during the War of Chioggia, when the Genoese had blockaded the port. Venice was very likely unable to pay in cash, and Donnina accepted payment on 1 October 1380 in the form of a credit for 20,000 ducats on the books of the Grain Office, at 4 percent interest. In April of the following year she sent agents to the Provveditori alle Biave (who then administered the accounts of the Grain Office) to petition to withdraw the whole sum after the agreed-upon six-month term. They were paid 400 ducats as the semiannual interest due. Presumably in recognition of the crucial imports of wheat and of her acceptance of deferred payment during a time of crisis, Donnina was granted Venetian citizenship "de intus et extra" on 8 August 1381, the day the Peace of Turin was signed.[97]

Another person connected with the Visconti, Pietro Stampa, was credited with a deposit of 12,000 ducats at the Grain Office in 1382; the motive of the credit is not clear but could have involved grain imports. As in the case of Donnina de Porris, the deposit earned 4 percent and required six months' notice for withdrawal.[98]

Pesaro and Mantua

Other Italian signori, friends of Venice, can also be found among the foreign depositors at the Grain Office. Pandolfo II Malatesta, a mercenary captain with a sorry record, first for Galeazzo Visconti, then for Florence,

---

cited, however, are the Venetian Commemoriali, which it will be useful to indicate here for the claims and counterclaims, 1360–63: *LCR*, 2:313, no. 200; 3:10–12, nos. 35, 42, 47.

[96]See especially Mario Brunetti, "Nuovi documenti viscontei tratti dall'Archivio di Stato di Venezia: Figli e nipoti di Bernabò Visconti," *Archivio storico lombardo,* 4th ser., 12 (1909): 5–90.

[97]ASV, Commemoriali, reg. 8, fol. 37v (3 April 1381). For the negotiation of wheat deals with Donnina and with Bernabò's wife, Regina della Scala, see Vittorio Lazzarini, ed., *Dispacci di Pietro Cornaro, ambasciatore a Milano durante la guerra di Chioggia* (Venice, 1939), nos. 34, 54, 102. Cf. Gino Barbieri, "Donne ed affari a sostegno della signoria viscontea," in *Scritti in onore di Catarina Vasalini* (Verona, 1974), 105. See also Cognasso, "L'unificazione della Lombardia," 5:494, 503.

[98]ASV, SM, reg. 37, fol. 52 (15 February). Pietro represented Piosello Serego (a Vicentine in the Scaliger court in Verona) in the latter's sales of wheat to Venice; see Lazzarini, *Dispacci di Pietro Cornaro,* nos. 86, 97. He is identified as "familiaris" of Galeazzo Visconti in 1369 in Caterina Santoro, ed., *La politica finanziaria dei Visconti: Documenti* (Milan, 1976), doc. 255. His son was domiciled in Venice in 1386: *LCR,* 3:178, no. 216.

and founder of the Pesaro branch of his family, deposited 10,000 ducats at 3 percent sometime before his death in late 1372. A man of letters and friend of Petrarch, Pandolfo got into trouble with Bernabò Visconti for paying too much attention to one of the latter's mistresses and was imprisoned in Milan for a time. Perhaps he learned of the financial services offered by the Venetian Grain Office while at the Milanese court, where the deposits made by Luchino Visconti and by Cangrande II della Scala were surely discussed, given the claims the Visconti advanced against both. In 1377, after Pandolfo's death, the guardians of his minor son Malatesta agreed that the interest accrued over the previous five years be added to principal — which is how we know of the deposit in the first place.[99] When in 1404 Malatesta was Venice's captain general and seemingly heir to the nest egg in Venice, he did not wish to accept interest (prode) on the deposit from the Grain Office, in fear for his soul. So he formally restored to the Commune the amount he had been given but contemporaneously accepted the same (unspecified) sum in the form of a gift from the Signoria.[100] If we assume that Malatesta's credit still derived from his father's deposit and that his guardians had regularly assigned interest to principal during his wardship, he was receiving something like compound interest, which might have provoked his qualms of conscience.

Another signore, of rather similar stature to that of Pandolfo, Ludovico Gonzaga of Mantua (1334–82), had an important, more diversified, credit relationship with Venice. Ludovico, in the course of establishing himself as lord, was both plotter and object of plots. In 1368 he assassinated his brother Francesco, who in turn had killed their brother Ugolino; and in 1373 he succeeded in uncovering a plot by Antonio Gonzaga against himself and immediately executed the would-be assassins.[101] Thereupon, early in 1374, Ludovico deposited the considerable sum of 33,334 ducats in the Grain Office, at 3 percent interest and on the usual condition of six months' notice for withdrawal, with the intention of securing a patrimony abroad.[102]

[99]ASV, SM, reg. 36, fol. 18v. The deposit was noted by the early-sixteenth-century chronicler Caroldo; see BMV, It. cl. VII, cod. 803 (7295), bk. 10, fol. 82v. For some biographical information, see Philip J. Jones, *The Malatesta of Rimini and the Papal State: A Political History* (Cambridge, England, 1974), 84–85, 89–90, and Gino Franceschini, *I Malatesta* (Milan, 1973), 133 and chap. 15.

[100]ASV, SSec, reg. 2, fol. 22v (26 June 1404). The deliberation reads: "Quod de istis denariis prodis denariorum quos magnificus Dominus Malatesta, capitaneus noster, habuit a Camera nostra frumenti, de quibus idem dominus habet conscientiam accepisse, ordinetur in hunc modum pro salvanda conscientia sua, quod dicti denarii habeantur pro restitutis nostro Comuni per dictum dominum Malatestam, et quod, auctoritate nostrorum consiliorum, dicti denarii sint ei largiti per nostrum Dominium." For Malatesta's position as captain general, offered and accepted the previous month, see Michael Mallett and John Hale, *The Military Organization of a Renaissance State: Venice c. 1400 to 1617* (Cambridge, England, 1984), 21–23.

[101]For biographical details, see Giuseppe Coniglio, *I Gonzaga* (Milan, 1967), 28–30.

[102]ASV, SM, reg. 34, fol. 73r–v (3 and 8 January). Also mentioned by Caroldo (as in n. 99, above), fol. 76v.

The origin of that sum (obviously one-third of an inheritance of 100,000 ducats) is not clear. What is clear is that Ludovico had stocks of wheat and began speculating on the Venetian market in times of dearth. In fact, 1374 was a year of serious famine in Venice and the Veneto, and his agents kept him apprised of the situation and prompted him to export large amounts of wheat to Venice.[103] In December he asked for and received permission to credit the (unspecified) value of the imports, plus other moneys he was sending, to his account at the Grain Office, on the same conditions as his previous deposit.[104] The famine, plus the bullion and banking crisis of that year, must have raised prices considerably and made the deposit a particularly advisable solution.

A few years later, during the Chioggia war, the lord of Mantua again kept careful track, via his agent Bartolino Codelupi and others, of the city's alimentary needs and the current prices. Venice was storing all the grain it could get, in preparation for an eventual total blockade. Ludovico exploited the occasion and again exported wheat to Venice. In 1381, as a result of the "magna denariorum penuria" that Codelupi reported, he was unable to extract payment in cash and had to accept payment in unneeded salt at a fixed price.[105] Even though Venice's stocks of grain seem to have been considerable, more was imported from Mantua immediately after the war; this time the value, totaling 20,000 ducats, was credited to Ludovico's account at the Grain Office, on the previous conditions.[106]

In the same decade of active speculation in wheat on Ludovico Gonzaga's part, the lord of Mantua also invested heavily in Venetian government obligations, accumulating a portfolio of some 90,000 ducats, par value. In the process, he and his family secured for themselves interest revenues from a second Venetian source. The market value of the large sums invested in bonds dropped sharply during the war, and after the war interest rates were lowered; Codelupi and his signore were much disturbed by their losses, but they failed to receive favored treatment.[107]

By contrast, the real value of deposits in the Grain Office remained the same as their nominal value, even though it was not possible to make speculative profits on them, as it was with government obligations. The

[103]The other two-thirds of the 100,000 ducats were in the hands of Francesco Gonzaga (see immediately below). In an otherwise undated letter of 1374 a Franciscan friend wrote from Venice, asking Ludovico for a subsidy of wheat for the Frari, and added: "sicut universaliter potest constare in civitate Veneciarum est magna penuria frumenti et leguminum, in tantum quod eciam pro pecuniam non potest reperiri." ASMN, Estere, b. 1430, published by Cesare Cenci, "I Gonzaga e i frati minori," 32. (See also above, Chap. 4, sec. iv.)

[104]ASV, SM, reg. 34, fol. 146v (11 December); Ludovico's name is attached to the earlier deposit for the first time in this deliberation.

[105]Cessi in RES, cclxx–lxxi nn., and Hocquet, "Guerre et finance," at nn. 21–23.

[106]ASV, SM, reg. 37, fol. 56. Cf. Hocquet, "Guerre et finance," and Luzzatto in PRV, cliii–iv.

[107]PRV, cliii–viii and notes. See also Cessi, "La finanza veneziana," 193–95, 212–14.

greater part of the assets of Ludovico, who died in late 1382, was transferred to his son Francesco, who in 1385 could claim deposits totaling 87,667 ducats. Ownership of the deposits, which were six-month time deposits, was to be proven, not only with proper powers of attorney but by two beads, one of jasper, the other of chalcedony, each broken in half, of which one-half was to be preserved by the depositors, the other half by the Grain Office; naturally, the two halves were to match, to avoid disputes at the time of restitution and possible fraud. The last deposit made by Ludovico, for a value of 20,000 ducats, was inscribed to the name of his daughter Isabetta as part of her dowry. The registration of that deposit contained the same conditions: Isabetta had to give the usual six months' notice before withdrawal and present a letter with seals along with "one-half of a black bead," the other half of which was to remain at the Grain Office. In time, the deposit passed to the woman's husband, Carlo di Galeotto Malatesta, of the Rimini branch of the family and first cousin of Pandolfo II. Carlo, in need of specie on various occasions, tried in vain to withdraw the 20,000 ducats. His requests were rejected as contrary to Venetian law on dowries.[108]

The Balkans

The Balkan peninsula is represented by four depositors. The first instance is an anomalous one concerning Venetian interests in Greece, where the Grain Office is involved only tangentially. The other three regard Croatian feudatories, much more important for the establishment and maintenance of Venetian hegemony; here the public depository was clearly an instrument of foreign policy in Dalmatia.

There was a small marquisate in Frankish Greece, that of Boudonitza, which first came into Venetian hands in the early Trecento when a marchioness, Maria dalle Carceri, a wealthy heiress from Negroponte (Euboea), married Andrea Corner of Crete and Baron of Skarpanto, in 1312. Her daughter by the first marriage, Guglielma Pallavicini, in time married another Venetian feudatory, Nicolò I Zorzi, who began a new line upon entering the marquisate, escorted by a Venetian galley, in 1335. (This branch of the Zorzi was based in Negroponte, where they had a castle.) Relations between the two soured within a decade, and Guglielma forced Nicolò to flee, first to Negroponte and thence to Venice, leaving behind his property and his son (by an earlier marriage), Francesco. Venice took up Nicolò's cause and tried various means of diplomatic persuasion to have him reinstated in his marquisate, but Guglielma refused reconciliation. Venice then ordered the bailo of Negroponte to sequester assets worth

[108]See Marzio A. Romani, "Il credito nella formazione dello stato gonzaghesco (fine XIV sec.)," in *Studi storici Luigi Simeoni,* 33 (1983): 191–99. I am grateful to Dr. Adele Bellù for information regarding the dowry and for registers of documents she uncovered in ASMN, Archivio Gonzaga, D.III.9, b. 215, fols. 87–84, 98, and E.XXVII.2, b. 1081, fols. 38–40.

some 8,400 perperi which Guglielma had deposited in care of Tomà Lippomano and Nicolò di Gandolfo in Negroponte in the name of her daughter Marulla. The valuables were to be sold and the money used on site for the "armata unionis"; the amount in Venetian coin (a small sum of 1,233 ducats) was to be credited in Venice for Nicolò. In fact, Venice advanced the sum in ducats and deposited it in the Grain Office at interest, in Nicolò's name, according to a Senate deliberation of 1346. In time, other sums made their way to Venice, where some were deposited in the Grain Office, some invested in government credits. After serving the republic, but far from his fief, Nicolò died in Venice in 1354; Guglielma Pallavicini died in early 1358 and Marulla shortly thereafter, leaving Francesco Zorzi sole marquis of Boudonitza. At that point he successfully petitioned to receive back the money originally confiscated from his half-sister, both principal and interest — but in unspecified amounts. Venice was happy to comply, since a Venetian was once more ruling Boudonitza.[109]

On the other side of the peninsula the situation of Venetian interests was rather different. To begin with, there are two closely connected instances that concern major Croatian feudatories and warlords of the Dalmatian hinterland involved in rapidly changing relations of friendship and enmity toward Venice: they were alternatively protectors and allies of Venetian subject cities of the coast or ravagers of the countryside. Venice's policy in the first half of the fourteenth century was to bind them to Venetian fortunes in the area, both by securing their assets in Venice and by conferring Venetian citizenship on them, an act that required an oath of fealty.[110]

In 1335 one of these barons, Gregorio qd. Curiaco, count of Corbavia (to the north and east of Zara) and citizen of Venice since 1331, made initial deposits in the Grain Office of 10,000 ducats, at 5 percent interest.[111] In 1341 Gregorio and his brother Budislavo allied themselves with the citizens of Sibenico against a former ally of Venice, Count Nelipich of Tenin or Knin (southeast of Zara), whose castle was a key to control over Dalmatia. After two years of war, Venice forced Nelipich to sign a peace treaty, of which the Curiacovich were a part, and as a guarantee of the peace Venice

<hr>

[109] The fortress fell to the Turks in 1414. For the political part of the story, see William Miller, "The Marquisate of Boudonitza (1204–1414)," in his *Essays in the Latin Orient* (Cambridge, England, 1921; reprint, Amsterdam, 1964), 245–61, including an appendix of five documents from ASV, SM. For the deposits at the Grain Office and the claims, see ASV, SM, reg. 23, fols. 60v–61 (16 September 1346), and reg. 28, fols. 61v (7 July 1358, claim of Marulla and Francesco together) and 81v (13 December). (Incomplete summaries of most of the relevent documents are in Thiriet, *Régestes,* 1, nos. 88, 181, 188, 193, 266, 333.) Useful on Venetian policy in the area in general is George T. Dennis, "Venezia e le signorie feudali nelle isole greche," in *Venezia e il Levante fino al secolo XV,* ed. Agostino Pertusi (Florence, 1973), 219–35.

[110]For the situation in general, see Giuseppe Praga, *Storia della Dalmazia* (Zara, 1941; here I used the Varese, 1981, edition), chap. 5; and V. Klaić, *Geschichte Bosniens,* trans. from the Croat (Leipzig, 1885), chap. 7, pp. 139–83.

[111]ASV, SM, reg. 59, fol. 168v (9 August 1436).

required that Nelipich deposit 20,000 lire (di piccoli) at the Grain Office. The deposit (worth 6,250 ducats in gold) was to bear interest "at the usual rate," which at the time meant 5 percent (the same rate granted to the Curiacovich). Contemporaneously, Venice granted citizenship to Nelipich and his heirs.[112]

Nelipich was dead by June 1344,[113] but an heir turned up fifty years later to claim his rights. From a senatorial deliberation of 1394 we learn that the deposit had indeed been made following the treaty and that interest at 5 percent had been paid for many years; but because of wars and "other novelties" (that is, the conquest of Dalmatia by the kingdom of Hungary in 1357), no claimant had appeared to receive his due till then. The Grain Office was ordered to investigate the legitimacy of the heredity and the claim, "as they always do," and if all was in order to pay him the principal and accrued interest.[114]

At the time of the loss of Dalmatia to Hungary, Gregorio Curiacovich remained faithful to Venice, and as an enemy of the crown he was despoiled and taken off to a Hungarian prison. In 1357 or 1358 he wrote to Doge Giovanni Dolfin saying that all he owned was what he had in Venice; and he asked that his income (that is, the interest on the deposit) be held for him and that nothing be paid out to his sons. But in 1360 he sent an agent to Venice with orders to petition for money; the agent returned empty-handed, and he asked again for a pension of 100 ducats per year plus expenses. This time he named his son Gregorio (alias Giorgio) as his representative.[115] As later documents indicate, Gregorio senior had tried in vain to have accumulated interest added to principal, so that at his death he had a principal of 10,000 ducats earning interest and a sterile deposit of 4,000 ducats in accrued interest. That was the nest egg to which his surviving sons Gregorio and Budislavo were heirs. These brought suit before the Giudici di Petizion in 1376 against the grain officials, and the judges ruled that as of November

[112]Matters can be followed closely in Venetian documents published by Ljubić, *Listine,* for the Curiacovich, 1:392–94 (1332), 2:77–78, 92, 194–95, 204, and for Nelipich, 2:169, 181, 185, 193 (where Venice in 1343 insists on the deposit "ut remaneamus bene securi de pace predicta"); the peace treaty is to be found in 2:196–200, and the clause regarding the deposit reads as follows: "quod comes Neliptius depositum quoddam in Veneciis de libris viginti millibus facere teneatur, quos denarios dictum ducale dominium recipi faciet et deponi ad cameram suam frumenti cum lucro et condicionibus omnibus dicte camere consuetis" (198). See also 2:209–10. Many of the same documents were published almost contemporaneously in *Monumenta Hungariae Historica,* ser. IV/A, Acta extera andegavorum, 3 vols. (Budapest, 1874–76), covering the years 1268–1395.

[113]Klaić, *Geschichte Bosniens,* 165, (where Nelipich is called "der hervorragendste kroatische Magnat"), and *Monumenta Hungariae Historica,* ser. IV/A, 3:48–49, no. 52, where Venice's interest in the castle of Knin is indicated: "Quum istud castrum Tinini sit clavis Sclavonie."

[114]Ljubić, *Listine,* 2:239–40 (1345), and ASV, SM, reg. 43, fol. 27 (27 August 1394).

[115]Ljubić, *Listine,* 3:384 and 4:16–17, and V. Klaić, "Rodoslovje knezova Krbavskih od plemena Gusić," *Rad Jugoslavenske akademije znanosti i umjetnesti,* 134 (1898), 197–98. (Gregorio had broken his oath of fidelity to Venice by hostile action briefly in 1346; ivi, 195–96.)

1375 they were due 2,000 ducats in interest.[116] By 1384 Budislavo was dead, and his widow, as guardian of their minor son Nicolò, sent a representative to file suit against the grain officials for the half due to Nicolò. The judges, correctly, assigned to the guardian one-half of the sterile deposit, plus 1,750 ducats for one-half of the interest due on the principal for the seven years intervening since the last lawsuit and payment, for a total of 3,750 ducats. One month later the Grain Office turned over 1,050 ducats as partial payment; it is not known whether the balance was paid.[117]

When in 1388 Gregorio (qd. Gregorio, even though he is called "nepos" here) claimed his due, it was reported in the Senate that he had a principal of 5,000 ducats and accrued interest of an equal amount. On that occasion it was decided that he be paid 1,500 ducats cash and that the balance in accrued interest be added to the principal, as was the interest due from the following semester onward; in short, in the future he would be owed compound interest on 8,500 ducats. Finally, he was given an advance of 250 ducats.[118] When he made his testament in 1393, Gregorio stated that he had a deposit of 10,000 ducats in Venice on which he earned 5 percent interest.[119]

But the story is still not over. In 1436, 101 years after the initial deposit, with Dalmatia back under Venetian domination, one of the counts of Corbavia came to Venice personally to ask his due. Having checked their books, the Provveditori alle Biave reported that the deposit had originally been made in 1335; that interest had been withdrawn by heirs up until 1409, when the wars with King Sigismund, now Holy Roman Emperor, interrupted relations; and that the present claimant, having already received 500 ducats, was owed 9,500 ducats. The Senate instructed the Signoria to respond with fitting words to this effect: we are not bound to restitution of either principal or interest, but, given the affection demonstrated toward Venice by the claimant's forebears, especially by the first Count Gregorio,

---

[116]This decision is referred to in the sentence of 1384; it is not recorded in the surviving register for 1376 (ASV, GP, Sg, reg. 4). A transcript of the sentence of 11 January 1384 was preserved in the Commemoriali and was published in Ljubić, *Listine,* 4:203–5, and in *Monumenta Hungariae Historica,* ser. IV/A, 3:528–31, no. 287; no original register is extant for that date.

[117]Sentence cited in the previous note. The transcription reduces the response to the suit to a sibylline phrase: the grain officials "respondebant aliqua, que domini iudices bene intellexerint."

[118]ASV, SM, reg. 40, fol. 115 (21 May 1388). Since the real "nepos" of Gregorio qd. Curiaco, namely Gregorio qd. Budislavo qd. Curiaco, was dead by 1387, the claimant must be Gregorio senior's son. See Klaić, "Rodoslovje knezova krbavskih," 202, and the genealogical chart published there.

[119]G. Szekely, "Hongrie et Venise à l'epoque de Sigismond," in *Venezia e l'Ungheria nel Rinascimento,* ed. Vittore Branca (Florence, 1973), 42. The heir is here called Gregoire Kuryak de Atinaszentmàrton, count of Gresencha. The source is not clearly cited.

we shall be happy to repay the principal that he can prove to be owed him, namely 9,500 ducats, in annual installments of 1,000 ducats — but only if he can prove his claim before an ad hoc committee. At this late date the Grain Office, of course, was nearly defunct as a financial institution (which might have been behind the disclaimer of legal obligation to pay), and the Senate had to instruct one of the customs offices, the Tabula Introitus, to set aside 100 ducats per month as first priority to meet the payment. Three years later the heir, Wenceslaus, son of Count Zachary, was permitted to invest his receipts in government obligations and in a house in Venice.[120]

The last foreigner known to have deposited money in the Grain Office was also a Croat, the great nobleman Sandalj Hranic, voivode of Bosnia. We are now in the period of the reacquisition of Dalmatia. After Venice purchased Zara from King Ladislaus in July 1409, it immediately became necessary to consolidate the dominion via dedication, purchase, and conquest. On 13 April 1411 Sandalj, who had been made an honorary member of the Great Council three months earlier, sold Ostroviza and ceded Scardona to Venice.[121] Sandalj asked to invest in Venice the 5,000 ducats that he had received in cash plus other sums for a total of 12,000 ducats, specifying that the investment could be either in government obligations or in a deposit at the Grain Office at interest. The latter was the manner chosen. Of the total, 8,000 ducats were to be sent to Venice, and the balance was to stay with the Venetian rectors in Zara for use on construction of the new fortifications. But the ambassadors of the magnate needed cash in order to make the deposit! So the Signoria asked for loans from unnamed bankers so that the ambassadors could complete their task and return to Zara. With a strange series of fictions, the money, once deposited, was taken on loan by the state from the Grain Office and used to repay the bankers! The rate of interest was set "by privilege" at 4 percent. Just how the money was transferred or further credits offset is not clear.[122] In 1412 Sandalj petitioned

---

[120]The response was to be of this tenor, "quod licet habeamus nichil teneri vel obligari dare pro capitale neque prode, attamen inspecta affectionem quam ipse predecessoresque sui, et spetialiter quondam comes Gregorius, habuerunt ad nostrum dominium"; ASV, Senato, Misti, reg. 59, fol. 168v, passed on the third ballot (9 August and 7 September 1436). The heir is so named in the license to invest in bonds worth 10,000 ducats par value and in a house worth 7,000 ducats; see Grazie, reg. 25, fol. 51 (2 April 1439); no such name is mentioned by Klaić, ("Rodoslovje knezova krbavskih," 208–9 and genealogical chart).

[121]Praga, *Storia della Dalmazia,* 153–54, and Ljubić, *Listine,* 6:147–49 (the purchase of Ostrovize for 5,000 ducats). The chronicler Antonio Morosini described the passage of the castle at Ostrovize to Venice as a "donacion" by Sandalj, for which he in turn received a gift of 5,000 ducats from Venice; the payment was made "con speranza presta de aver Sibinicho chon tuty luoghi suo soto la posanza de la dogal Signoria." See Morosini, Cronaca, 1:623–24. Morosini confused the sale of Ostrovize and the contemporary cession of Scardona; cf. the summary in *LCR,* 3:349–50, no. 123.

[122]Ljubić, *Listine,* 6:156–57 (28 April, when government obligations were spoken of), 159

to divide the deposit and withdraw the money. A special procedure was deemed necessary, since the petition contradicted the conditions under which the deposit had originally been made. Even after reformulating the conditions, Venetian authorities still balked (a withdrawal would be "contra leges et ordines urbis nostre"), but they finally agreed to make an exception and authorized export of the specie.[123]

Six months after the deposit by Sandalj what seems to have been the last request to deposit money was made by Paolo Guinigi, lord of Lucca and honorary noble citizen of Venice. The petition was to invest "part of his hoard," 25,000–50,000 ducats, in his own name and that of his heirs "either in government obligations or at the Grain Office." The alternative presented was the same formulated in the case of Sandalj, but we know from the accounts maintained in Lucca that the money in this case did not go to the Grain Office but was invested in government credits on the open market, where the yield rate was about double the interest offered by the Grain Office. The case therefore will be dealt with in detail under the open market for government obligations (see below, Chap. 14).

Here it is useful merely to recall the rationales, stated and unstated, behind Guinigi's petition: turbulent times in the court and danger to the person of the lord; the desire to stow away a nest egg in genuine safety, in a republic where there was continuity in the law and in respect for promises made; concern for the destiny of one's heirs — such were the preoccupations of most of the depositors. Ever since the 1360s and 1370s, however, most foreigners preferred investing in Venetian government bonds to depositing their money at the Grain Office. Government credits assured them a higher rate of yield than deposits at the Grain Office, albeit with added risk. Since it did not revise its schedule of interest rates as soon as the competition made itself felt, this quasi-public bank outlived its usefulness as a depository for the savings of foreigners. To complete safety of their funds at low rates of interest, they preferred some risk but higher returns. Thus we will meet the same categories of persons and even some of the same personages below, in the discussion of the funded debt.

(13 May); also 8:73 (1421), where it is said that Sandalo had been receiving revenues from Cattaro, perhaps to cover interest due him. ASV, SM, reg. 49, fol. 20v (10 and 15 May 1411), the major deliberations regarding the deposit and the rate of interest; also fol. 22v (19 May), where the officials were instructed to give the ambassadors a letter with the seal of the Grain Office declaring formally the fact of the deposit and its nature, as entered on the books of the office.

[123]The petition, reply, and final authorization show that half the total belonged to Sandalj, half to Baniza, widow of Volcobano, and her daughter, perhaps in the form of a dowry. ASV, SSec, reg. 5, fol. 16v (22 April 1412); LCR, 3:362, nos. 168–69, and ASV, Commemoriali, reg. 10, fol. 134 (29 November 1412).

v. A VENETIAN DOWRY FUND

The Legal Setting

Dowries constituted a significant category of deposits at the Grain Office. In order to see how they became a separate fund, it will be necessary to take a step backward.

The dowry, as is well known, was the property of the woman in whose name it was made. The husband could invest it only if its value was secured and he enjoyed the income during his lifetime. The most common security was a lien on real estate; if the property was sold, the value of the dowry had to be deposited—or secured with a deposit—at the Procuratia di San Marco.[124] According to a revision of the statutes in 1233, the deposit could consist of gold and silver plate, thus releasing the cash value for investment. If the Procurators held both the liquid capital and the security, they themselves could invest the dowry — in local colleganze — and pass on the returns to the beneficiary. In 1316 the depository at the Grain Office was declared an alternative investment opportunity for the Procurators: the Grain Office could borrow dowry funds lying idle at the Procuratia for lack of surety; it was the Commune that provided the surety in gold and silver, as required by statute.[125]

In 1329 this provision was revised with the aim of making the liquid assets of a dowry more liquid and of placing them at the disposal of the state. The preamble of the new law stated that in the past the requirement to deposit in the Procuratia the value of a dowry not guaranteed on real property meant that the husband earned no return unless he first put up surety in valuables; this, it continues, was rarely done and then to the disadvantage of the wife. It was thus passed that all dowries then on deposit at the Procuratia, plus any surety, as well as all unsecured dowries in the future could be turned over instead to the Grain Office. The Commune assumed the risk and stood surety for the liabilities, but now without immobilizing any assets. The Grain Office promised to pay an annual return of 5 percent on this particular type of deposit. That matched the rate paid on forced loans and was higher than the rates promised by the Grain Office on normal deposits by Venetians and by foreigners (4 and 3 percent respectively).[126]

---

[124]References for this paragraph and the next can be found in Mueller, "Procurators of San Marco," 175–80.

[125]In 1328 the authorization accorded to the Procurators to invest in the Grain Office was extended to estate funds in general. On 10 March 1329 the Grain Office, which owed 60,000 lire on wheat en route to Venice, was told to borrow the money from deposits on hand at the Procuratia and repay them from proceeds of the sale; ASV, AC, reg. 22, fol. 99.

[126]This dowry fund differed essentially from the Florentine Monte delle Doti of a century later in that it lacks any speculative or actuarial element. For dowry funds ("monti de novisse")

The law of 1329, which later was made a statute and was included in the "liber sextus" of Venetian statutory law in 1346 by Andrea Dandolo, was first the object of disagreement between the two Procurators of San Marco "de Supra," precisely Andrea Dandolo, the future doge, and Pietro Grimani. The latter held that the new statute, where it read "potest accipi et deposui apud Cameram Frumenti," was an enabling act, not an order; Dandolo, on the other hand, held that the sense of "potere" was "debere," that is, the Procurators were required to turn over all or part of the dowry funds in their care upon receipt of a request to that effect by the officials of the grain magistracy. Grimani brought the case first to the Giudici dell'Esaminator and then appealed to the Avogadori di Comun and finally to the Quarantia—all of which supported Dandolo's reading.[127] That the grain officials, on the basis of the statute, did not ask to have all the money at once, or that dowry funds continued to accumulate at the Procuratia, is reflected in a senatorial decision of 1347 which authorized the Grain Office to accept deposits totaling 5,000 ducats "from dowries held by the Procurators and from others."[128]

Documentary Traces

Traces of dowries deposited in the Grain Office can be found in testaments, in the administration of estates, and in sentences passed down against men charged with rape. The documentation is scanty but sufficient to reveal applications of the law.

Early evidence comes from the year 1323, in the form of a quittance redacted by Benedetta Corner and her daughter for two dowries, principal and interest, collected from the Grain Office and a widow's grant of her dowry, left on deposit, to the convent of S. Paolo in Treviso, where she had entered.[129] Another comes from a decade later when, in 1331, Stefano Manolesso bequeathed the large sum of 100 lire di grossi (1,000 ducats) to be deposited "at the Salt Office or at the Grain Office" as a dowry for his daughter Cristina. In May 1332 the accounts show that the Procurators deposited the sum at the Grain Office and that the money was repaid with interest ("cum prode") some seven months later.[130]

In the same years dealings with the Grain Office are reflected in the records of bankruptcy proceedings against members of the Falier family and

---

administered by the scuole grandi in Venice for the daughters of poor members and invested in government obligations, see William B. Wurthmann, "The Council of Ten and the Scuole Grandi in Early Renaissance Venice," *SV*, n.s., 18 (1989): 50–53.

[127]ASV, AC, reg. 3641, fol. 10v (14 November 1331).

[128]ASV, SM, reg. 24, fol. 33v (4 September).

[129]ASV, PSM, Citra, b. 50, commis. Donadello Donà (10 March 1323). AST, Corporazioni soppresse, S. Paolo, Pergamene, scattola 6, parchment dated 16 February 1323 (kindly passed on to me by Paolo Cagnin).

[130]ASV, PSM, Misti, b. 83, commis. Stefano Manolesso, reg., fols. 14 and 24 (entries for 6 May and 23 November 1332).

in their estate accounts. In 1333 interest on the dowry of Lucia Falier, daughter-in-law of Pietro Falier, was paid by the Grain Office and divided up among the creditors by the Sopraconsoli. But when Pietro left his daughters Orsa and Cristina 8 lire di grossi each for their dowry, to be deposited at the Grain Office, with the interest earmarked for their maintenance until marriage, the grain officials refused to accept the money (perhaps on account of foreseen complications arising from the bankruptcy), and the Procurators invested it instead in local colleganze, where it earned considerably higher interest, at rates ranging from 6 to 10 percent. But investment in colleganze required that real estate of equal value be registered in the name of the beneficiary or that security in gold or silver be deposited with the Procurators — conditions that were obviously not met in full each year; as a result, Falier dowry funds passed back and forth between the Grain Office (whose deposits were secured by the Commune) and the Procurators of San Marco. Thus a sentence by the Curia del Procurator in 1339 ordered part of Lucia's dowry, for a total of 18 lire di grossi, to be deposited at the Grain Office, an order that was observed only two years later, when the gastaldo of the doge sequestered the sum from the Procurators and deposited it directly in the Grain Office. Similarly, the bulk of Cristina's small dowry was taken out of colleganze in 1341 and placed in the Grain Office, where it earned the usual 5 percent interest, only to be withdrawn again in 1343 and reinvested in colleganze, where it earned exactly twice that rate until 1345.[131]

Dowries were probably not often voluntarily deposited at the Grain Office, as long as higher returns could be gotten in other investments. Probate courts based themselves on the statute of the "usus novus" regarding the sale of real property as well as that of 1329: if security was lacking, the value of the dowry had to be deposited in the Grain Office. The Giudici del Procurator ordered the Procurators in 1342 to deposit 6 lire di grossi, the dowry of the wife of Nicolino della Rosa, with the grain magistracy, and the accounts show the payment of interest (sometimes annually, sometimes biannually) by the Grain Office for at least a decade.[132] When the nobleman Domenico Gussoni sold real estate at the Rialto, which had been security for his wife's dowry, the value was ordered turned over to the Procurators and by these to the Grain Office.[133] Whether one deposited the liquid value of a dowry or surety for a dowry otherwise employed made little difference. Sums totaling 1,300 ducats were deposited in the name of Maddalena Pagan, as surety ("pleçaria") for the dowry of her daughter Caterina, wife

---

[131]The whole story is found in ibid., Ultra, b. 125, commis. Pietro Falier, account book of the estate; single documents are in the fascicle entitled "Pergamene Falier." Mention of the interest paid on the dowry of Lucia (wife of Pietro's son Giovanni) was made by Lazzarini, *Marino Faliero*, 165.

[132]ASV, PSM, Ultra, b. 249, fasc. 7, commis. Nigrino della Rosa.

[133]ASV, Quarantia Criminal, reg. 16, fol. 69v (11 January 1369).

of Pietro Loredan. Interest at the usual rate of 5 percent accrued to the estate of Maddalena at least from 1374 into the 1390s.[134]

Venetian usage struck the foreigner as peculiar and negative. In 1375 Zuccaro Parisi, Lucchese factor in Venice of Giusfredo Cenami, wrote to his principal in Lucca for information regarding the law on dowries in his native city. He had become a Venetian citizen de extra in 1354 and had purchased a house, the value of which he had registered in the name of his wife. If he sold the property, as he was about to do for 160 "fiorini di grosso" (presumably 1,600 ducats), he reported, he would be required by Venetian law to deposit the value of the dowry in the Grain Office at 5 percent interest, whereas he preferred to invest the money in his own shop (he was a dyer), where it could earn more. His hope was that, he wrote, "being a foreigner, and the woman is a foreigner," he could claim to be under Lucchese law.[135]

The period of the War of Chioggia created many insolvent debtors for forced loans, persons who for tax delinquency were constrained to sell real estate to meet their debts. A law of 1380 tried to stimulate prospective buyers by making it possible to pay in government obligations valued at 33 1/3, the current market price. The authorities realized, however, that much property thus put up for sale constituted surety for dowries, and they were concerned to preserve the dowries intact. The state therefore offered the women creditors an option: they could take payment in government obligations or be credited for the full monetary value of their dowry at the Grain Office, at the usual conditions — that is, at 5 percent interest — the bonds remaining in the hands of the Commune.[136] Surely the second option was preferable, since government credits were falling in value, interest had been suspended, and the rate was about to be reduced. While the authorities did not have to pay debt service on credits held by the state, they were burdening the Grain Office with new liabilities that were not covered by deposits of specie — and to that extent it might be said that there was a creation of money, an expansion of deposits. An example is furnished by the sale of the palace on the Grand Canal of Andrea da ca' Pesaro and his brothers, then purchased by the state for Nicolò d'Este and which much later would become the Fondaco dei Turchi. Of the sale price of 10,000 ducats, half was to be in government

[134]ASV, PSM, Misti, b. 126, commis. Maddelena Pagan, who made her testament in 1366; reg. 1 is completely ruined and illegible, but payments of interest from 1374 to the 1390s are contained in reg. 2. The sum of 250 ducats "pro capitale" was paid by the Grain Office to the Procurators, as executors, in 1391.

[135]Bini, *I lucchesi a Venezia*, vol. 2, appendix, docs. 1 and 4 (22 and 28 February 1375). The first letter reads "E' occorso caso che i' ho venduta la casa e, secondo l'usanza da Vinegia, mi conviene mettere i denari della dota al fondago del formento a cinque percento. A me gitta migliore ragione a tenerli nella stazione."

[136]*PRV*, doc. 172: "Si vero mulieres sepedicte noluerint imprestita, remaneant ipsa imprestita comuni, et scribatur eisdem mulieribus tanta quantitas pecunie quanta fuerit earum dotes ad cameram frumenti, cum prode et condicionibus ipsius camere consuetis."

credits valued at 26, half in cash, payable in fifteen months, or in offsets on his debt; of the cash, Andrea had the option of taking the value of his wife's dowry (which had been guaranteed by the real estate) as a credit written on the books of the Grain Office.[137]

Another particular kind of document sheds further light on the function of the office as depository for dowries. A handful of sentences passed by the Avogadori di Comun against rapists specify that part of the fine levied on them be deposited in the Grain Office as a dowry for the victim, should she marry or enter a convent. In 1330 Chesino, a silk dyer from Lucca, sentenced for having "seduced" a girl of seven, was fined 100 lire di piccoli and banished. By order of the court, half of the fine was deposited at interest at the Grain Office and the officials of the grain magistracy were made tutors of the victim, to the extent that they were to give their consent to the planned marriage or entry in a convent, when the time came.[138] A similar case in 1335 called for a fine of 700 lire, of which 200 were deposited at interest at the Grain Office to serve toward a dowry for the victim ("pro suo maritare vel monachare").[139] Two cases of carnal knowledge judged on the same day in 1347 called for the deposit of half of the fines (amounting to 20 and 30 ducats respectively) in the names of the victims.[140] More than a century later, dowry fines were much higher. In 1468 a rape victim ten years of age was assigned 200 ducats of the fine levied on the condemned criminal as a dowry to be deposited at the Grain Office. A decade later, however, two dowries of 100 ducats each were ordered consigned, no longer to the Grain Office, but to the Procurators of San Marco (de Supra) until the victims married.[141] By then the courts seem to have preferred deposits without interest in the Procuratia to deposits at interest in an institution that had to a large extent lost its former financial function.

Further traces of dowry deposits indicate that the Grain Office continued, though probably on an ever decreasing scale, to guarantee the value of dowries during the decades between the War of Chioggia and the mid-fifteenth century. But there is no way of following the daily transactions of the office as it paid out interest to husbands, for we are left only with

[137]Ibid., doc. 178: "Et etiamdio, s'el dicto ser Andrea vorà de la dicta quantitade fare scrivere alla Camera del Formento la impromessa de soa muier, che, se ducati mille, queli debia essere scripti, non debiando havere el pro' se no passadi li dicti mesi XV." For the transaction, see Mueller, "Effetti della guerra di Chioggia," 36–37.

[138]ASV, AC, reg. 3641, fol. 29v (10 January 1330). On 8 February the dyer Tomasino paid a balance due on the fine in "libre parvorum in monetis" plus £4 3s 4d as "agio" — probably because he paid in billon pennies.

[139]Ibid., fol. 11 (14 August 1335).

[140]Ibid., reg. 3642, fol. 25 (27 April 1347).

[141]Ibid., regs. 3652, fol. 84v (22 June 1468, mentioned by Guido Ruggiero, *The Boundries of Eros: Sex Crime and Sexuality in Renaissance Venice* [Oxford, 1985], 107), and 3654, fol. 68r–v (9 September 1478); also Quarantia Criminal, reg. 19, fol. 133 (22 August 1477), a case in which the rapist had promised to marry the victim but then married another.

scattered cases concerning estates, litigation in favor of widows,[142] and, in general, problems concerning modes of payment of the principal to beneficiaries when the office was in irreversible decline.

Only three documents mention banks active on the Rialto, even though they must have been involved on a regular basis in payments due on dowries. Depositing a dowry at a bank was permitted only if the value of the dowry was secured by real estate or valuable plate. Thus a deposit was ordered withdrawn from the bank of Gabriele Soranzo in 1409 and deposited at the Grain Office as surety for a dowry ("pro cautione repromisse"), and in 1454 the proceeds of a sale of property, on deposit at the bank of Benedetto Soranzo, was ordered deposited either at the Procuratia or at the Grain Office.[143] The third instance regards an inexplicably complicated mediation of a bank: at the death of Cristoforo qd. Ferigo Corner, his widow received her dowry of 1,000 ducats from the Procurators "de Ultra," executors of the estate of Ferigo, who had received it from the bank of Pietro Benedetto, where it had been deposited by the officials of the Grain Office (where previously it had been earning interest).[144]

By the fifteenth century the Grain Office seems no longer to have had either financial autonomy or funds with which to meet claims. Creditors of dowry funds on deposit at the office, largely widows, met increasing difficulty in receiving their due when it came time to collect the principal. In the 1430s the Senate had to intervene twice against the inefficiency of the institutions of public finance to make good those credits. In 1433 it was stated that it was the custom of the Grain Office, when a dowry was to be paid out, to write an order-to-pay ("cedula") to the Treasury. Once the order had been issued, the Grain Office stopped paying interest, but the Treasury often let as much as five or ten years pass before paying the debt, during which time the widows had neither their dowry nor the interest on it.

---

[142]See ASV, PSM, Misti, b. 166, commis. Catarino Donà, reg., entry for 26 May 1383 (a deposit ordered by probate court); Tamba, *Bernardo de Rodolfis*, doc. 85; ASV, CIN, b. 207, atti della Torre, loose parchment dated 17 August 1403, a quittance and notice of two withdrawals of dowries from the Grain Office by widows; GP, Sg, reg. 73, fols. 16v–17v (7 November 1436), and reg. 86, fols. 2v–5r (24 October 1441). In the last of these cases it is stated that the creditrix had the right to interest only during the six months between her first and second marriages in 1427 and after the death of her second husband; otherwise it went to the husbands. The grazia procedure was also used to permit the sale of real estate under lien for dowries. In 1424 Marco da Ponte received permission to sell, as long as the value of the dowries, "iuxta tenorem statuti," was deposited at the Grain Office. Grazie, reg. 22, fol. 9.

[143]ASV, GP, Sg, reg. 17, fol. 78v (4 September 1409), and Giudici del Procurator, Sentenze a legge, reg. 4, fols. 27–28 (26 September 1454). An anomalous case provides evidence that a bank account was unacceptable whereas government credits were: the liquid capital of a dowry was withdrawn from the bank of Andrea Priuli and Partners in 1414 and used to purchase bonds, which, in turn, were conditioned as security for the dowry; GP, Sg, reg. 68, fol. 3 (14 October 1434).

[144]ASV, PSM, Ultra, b. 106, commis. Ferigo Corner di S. Aponal, reg. 2, under 6 June 1393 and 26 June 1394.

Acknowledging that it was "pious to come to the aid of these women," the Senate ordered the Salt Office to bring the necessary money to the Treasurers for payment to the creditors — under pain of heavy fines for both administrations, in case the money was used first for other purposes. This procedure was to be followed also in the future, as credits "pro depositis dotium" matured.[145] It was probably the realities of war finance which rendered the deliberation ineffectual, even though it was passed almost unanimously and imposed heavy fines for nonobservance. Almost three years later the Senate noted that "an infinite number of very poor widows" with dowries deposited at the Grain Office but payable at the Treasury "were never paid and were dying of hunger." Now the duty of furnishing the necessary funds was passed to the Fondaco dei Tedeschi, which was to turn over to the Treasury what of its tax revenues it had left after meeting its monthly obligations (which involved, in particular, payment of the salaries of the Councils of Forty).[146]

Just who was to pay claims and how remained an open question, however. In early 1454, a period of severe economic strain, Gerolamo Dolfin needed a senatorial order to withdraw money from the Grain Office to dower his daughter.[147] In 1461 the Provveditori alle Biave refused to refund the principal of a dowry, saying the Treasury should pay; it took a decision of the Collegio to force the Provveditori to do so, on the principle that "where money is paid in, there [also] should it be paid out."[148] Not long after, a poor widow ("paupercula fidelis nostra"), in the hope of receiving her 60 ducats more rapidly from the Treasury, asked that the sum be transferred there by the Grain Office; but when the Treasury did not honor the claim, the Senate had to order the transfer of the credit back to the Grain Office, from which it was to be paid "when possible."[149] Yet again in the same decade the intervention of the Senate was requested, this time by the noblewoman Maria Bembo, owed 225 ducats for the dowry of her daughter; this time the Grain Office was ordered to pay "from its own funds, as is customary."[150]

By the early sixteenth century at the latest, the financial obligations of the Grain Office were completely out of its hands. In 1502 a claim to correct an error made in the distant past by the Grain Office in calculating the interest on a dowry passed through the Provveditori sopra Uffici, the Provveditori alle Biave, and the Collegio alle Biave. These organs inspected the

---

[145]ASV, SM, reg. 58, fol. 177v (26 February 1433).

[146]Ibid., reg. 59, fol. 131v (25 October 1435).

[147]ASV, ST, reg. 3, fol. 101 (18 February 1454); the office was ordered to pay "de denariis extrahendis de fontico tam de farinis nostris quam aliter."

[148]ASV, CN, reg. 10, fol. 26 (22 May 1461).

[149]ASV, ST, reg. 5, fol. 153 (28 March 1466).

[150]Ibid., reg. 6, fol. 63v (14 July 1469): "de denariis officii sui, sicut in similibus fieri est consuetum."

account books ("catastici" and "libri") of the Grain Office to verify the deposit of 800 ducats in 1425 and 1427 of the dowry of Nicolosa da Ponte, wife of Piero da Ponte, "cum pro' de 5 per cento." But only 4 percent had been paid on balances remaining on deposit from 1457 to 1487, complained the creditor, Misser Zuan Capello fo de Misser Francesco; that is, the creditor had been paid the rate due on normal deposits made by Venetian citizens rather than that due on dowries. The correctness of the petition was ascertained: Capello had been "defrauded" of 1 percent interest through an "inadvertent error"; calculations were done on the spot and the sum of 107½ ducats was ordered paid — as 655 lire di piccoli.[151]

As with regular deposits made by foreign lords, authorities recognized the state's liabilities for dowries as much as a century after the debt had been contracted, and even though the Grain Office itself had ceased functioning as a financial institution. In a balance sheet dated 1490 recorded by Marin Sanudo, the "Camera del Formento" was still listed as having expenditures of 400 ducats per year "per depositi"; assuming the sum represented interest payments of 5 percent on dowry deposits, as must have been the case, the total principal held at that late date was a mere 8,000 ducats.[152]

vi. A LENDING BANK

The floating debt administered by the Grain Office in the fourteenth century began, as was explained above, with the annonary institution acting as agent for the Commune in contracting specific loans for specific purposes. Quickly the procedure changed to the acceptance of deposits for the creation of a fund into which the state could dip more readily and quickly for relatively short term loans. This was a way of handling emergencies for which there was insufficient time to levy and collect forced loans. A few examples will be sufficient to show how that part of the system worked; after a certain point, authorizations at the legislative level were probably no longer necessary, so that no echo remains of the practice followed on a daily basis.

Alongside loans to the state, this financial institution also made long-term investment loans to private entrepreneurs, more often than not nobles, upon authorization and in areas of strategic importance for the Venetian economy. At the same time, the office was saddled with unrecoverable credits of a political nature — like the very large loan to the Byzantine emperor — which condemned it to operating continually in the red.[153]

---

[151]Remaining balances were 360½ ducats from 1457 to 1485, 265 ducats in 1486, and 34 ducats in 1487. The conversion in lire di piccoli was done at 122 soldi per ducat instead of the current rate of 124 soldi. Were the error to be found in the period preceding 1457, it was similarly to be made good. ASV, Provveditori alle Biave, b. 2, reg. 4, fol. 71v (14 October 1502).

[152]BG, 1, doc. 129, p. 164.

[153]See Luzzatto in PRV, lxxvi–viii n.

Loans to the State

Loans made to the state involved the usual problems of extraordinary expenditures: getting off the galleys, sending an ambassador on his way, meeting a pressing but limited military obligation.

Where trade or commercial relations with other states were involved, principal and interest were ordered paid by freights or by a special customs duty levied against merchants who were expected to benefit from the ambassadorial intervention. In 1320, for example, large loans were required for sending off the galley fleets, and restitution was promised from freight charges. Further loans, one (for 200 lire di grossi) for the same reason, another generically "pro oportunitatibus comunis," were authorized three years later.[154]

Diplomatic engagements and the maintenance of Venice's trading colonies also commonly required loans. Most of them probably did not leave a record; again the bulk of the recorded examples comes from the 1320s. The Grain Office had to lend money needed for an indemnity owed to the crown of Hungary, with whom Venice's envoy had signed a peace treaty; the money was to be sent by bill of exchange, and repayment was guaranteed by forced loans. The cost of a treaty with England and the repayment of a debt to a citizen of Majorca were similarly to be anticipated from the depository and repaid by the interested parties.[155] An embassy sent to the Curia in Avignon on occasion of the consecration of Clement VI in 1342 was financed in the same manner, as was an embassy to England in 1374.[156] Again in the 1320s the Grain Office was ordered to finance the Venetian consulate in Tunis and the construction of houses for Venetian merchants in Trebisond and, in 1333, in Tana; these undertakings were also supported by the intervention of Venetian envoys.[157] Even in 1345, when the Grain Office was under pressure from creditors who wished to withdraw their deposits, and received monthly injections of public funds to help it meet its obligations, it was ordered to come up with the considerable sum of 12,000 ducats for the war in Istria; if funds currently available in the depository were insufficient, the deliberation stated, the officials were to seek out new loans and deposits.[158] In this last case it is particularly clear

---

[154]*RES*, docs. 87, 97; *PRV*, docs. 103, 107.

[155]*PRV*, doc. 104 and p. lxxvii.

[156]*RES*, doc. 152; ASV, SM, reg. 34, fol. 126, also in Brown, *Calendar of State Papers*, vol. 1, docs. 46, 48 (decree suspending the embassy). Repayment was to come from a duty of 0.5 percent on all trade at Bruges. An embassy to Armenia in 1333 was to be financed by the Salt Office; see Roberto Cessi et al., eds., *Le deliberazioni del Consiglio dei Rogati (Senato)*, 2 vols. (Venice, 1960–62), 2:185, doc. 108.

[157]Cessi et al., *Le deliberazioni del Consiglio dei Rogati*, 1:460, doc. 245, and 1:465, doc. 310; 2:11, doc. 33. *PRV*, docs. 100, 102, 106. In the end the loan for the houses in Tana was canceled; ibid., 2:120–21, docs. 428–29, and 2:186, doc. 112.

[158]*RES*, docs. 174, 178–79, and pp. cxix–xx.

that the communal Treasury, itself indebted for 30,000 ducats, was incapable of financing the state's local needs and its foreign and military policy; it was probably considered inopportune to levy new forced loans after fourteen years of extensive amortizations; the lender of last resort to an insolvent state, therefore, was the Grain Office and its floating debt.

Loans to Private Individuals

Legislative bodies also called upon the Grain Office to make investment loans to private individuals. In its original function, the magistracy, as responsible for provisioning the city, sometimes advanced money to specific merchants and shipowners willing to depart for distant ports in Apulia, Sicily, and the Black Sea in search of wheat as long as they had initial capital and a guaranteed price floor for sale to the state upon arrival in Venice, or to communities that showed promise in producing a surplus exportable to Venice. The office also made long-term loans, however, of five to ten years' duration, to small industrial entrepreneurs in areas of strategic importance for the economy: flour mills and brick kilns. The former were part of the same annonary sector that was the office's original concern; the latter were vital for maintaining productivity in the construction sector, in a period — the first half of the fourteenth century — of considerable building activity in Venice. Finally, exceptional loans were made to the emperor in Constantinople and to a medical doctor in state pay, with interests both in the wheat trade and in providing health care, who often needed loans and advances.

It is impossible to know how common it was for the office to advance money to importers. Perhaps it was a matter of contingency, for it seems to have been more common for the state to make contracts for delivery on deferred payment: the state paid for grain it imported with the "tratta" — the returns from its resale. But the exceptions are interesting. An early loan of 200 lire di grossi was made in 1270 to the Commune of Recanati in the Marches for delivery of wheat — an advance that Venice could decide to call in, either in kind or in money.[159] In 1301 the government authorized loans to individual importers who would provide surety and contract with the Grain Office for delivery of wheat in fixed periods.[160]

Loan contracts, aimed at promoting agricultural production in Venetian-controlled Istria and garnering monopsonist privileges on surplus wheat, were made in 1330 with six Istrian towns. The loans, contracted at the Grain Office for a total of 12,350 lire di piccoli, were earmarked for the purchase of oxen and other beasts of burden to work the soil; prices per staio of wheat were prefixed. Repayment was to be made in three years' time at 5 percent interest.[161]

---

[159]*DMC*, 2:126, a contract for June to September of 1271.

[160]Favaro, *Grazie — novus liber*, appendix, p. 226, doc. 87.

[161]ASV, Commemoriali, reg. 3, fols. 59r–60r, and *LCR*, 3:31–33, nos. 179–81, 184, 186–87. Funds were turned over "pro emendis bobus et bestias oportunas ad laborandum terras et

More like futures contracts were the loans made to members of the Kalergi family in Crete, of which two examples survive. In 1304, Alexis Kalergi received 6,000 perperi, on good security, in return for delivery over the successive four years of 1,500 perperi worth of wheat at 15 perperi per 100 measures. Kalergi was actually only one of several exporters from Crete, whose grain administration sent thousands of measures of wheat to Venice, much of it on loans repayable in Venice.[162] In 1333 the Grain Office stipulated an agreement with Alexis's son Giovanni, but in the context of a general agreement with the "universitas" of the feudatories of Crete. In January Venice agreed to purchase 80,000 measures of wheat per year for five years at 18 perperi per hundred.[163] Then in February the deal with Giovanni Kalergi: the Grain Office would send off 300 lire di grossi on the next galleys departing for Cyprus in return for 47,000 measures of good and marketable wheat to be shipped at his expense to Venice in installments of 6,000 measures per year. The Grain Office gave its assent to the request for a loan, stating that by setting the price at 15 perperi per 100 measures, the Commune would be receiving its interest on the loan simultaneously with the wheat deliveries.[164] Similar cash loans repayable in wheat seem to have been requested so regularly via the chancery at Candia that the Great Council acted in 1339 to make approval more difficult.[165] One of the contracts had been made with Pieraccio Gradenigo, feudatory of Candia, for 10,000 perperi; he was required to supply about 18,000 measures of wheat per year, for sale to Venice at 18 perperi per 100 measures and at the same time pay 5 percent interest on the loan. But a famine in the years around 1341 caused a sharp rise in prices ("caritudo bladi"), and he was forced to borrow large sums of money at usury in order honor the contract, for he had to buy

---

territorium" against the pledge to "ipsas terras . . . diligenter laborare et laborari facere et in laborerio tenere" and to consign wheat that exceeded internal demand directly to the ships for export to Venice. The interest due was at the same rate that the Grain Office paid its depositors ("sicut solvit aliis dicta camera").

[162]The document in ASV, Commemoriali, reg. 1, fol. 48v, and *LCR* 1:34, no. 145, provides an accounting (of December 1303 or 1304) of the administration of the annona in Candia, of wheat sent to Venice (nearly 16,000 perperi' worth), and of the balance due in wheat by the annona and by the Kalergi. The Cretan officials wrote: "Per lo pagamento de lo sovradecto furmento, nui avemo tolto impresteddho per pagare a Venesia." In 1329 the doge authorized the Venetian governor or "duca" to borrow at the most favorable rates possible in order to buy wheat to send to Venice; Sindacati, reg. 1, fol. 1 (28 June 1329) and passim. The series ASV, Duca di Candia, would surely reveal much more on this theme.

[163]ASV, SM, reg. 15, copia, fols. 112v–13 (21 January 1333).

[164]Ibid., fol. 115r, and Cessi et al., *Le deliberazioni del Consiglio dei Rogati,* 2:116, doc. 409 (6 February). Figuring the perpero of Crete at 26 soldi a grossi (see Vol. 1, p. 298, table 8), 300 lire di grossi manchi would buy 40,000 measures, whereas the contract was for 47,000, a modest interest of 2.2 percent, figuring eight years for the life of the contract. The next year Giovanni died, deeply indebted, but his son promised to carry out the terms of the contract; Cessi et al., *Le deliberazioni del Consiglio dei Rogati,* 2:289, doc. 411.

[165]ASV, MC, Spiritus, fol. 97v, registered in Freddy Thiriet, *Deliberations des assemblées vénitiennes concernant la Romanie,* 2 vols. (Paris, 1966–71), vol. 1, doc. 473.

wheat at 25–33 perperi per 100 measures. At his request, Venice agreed to relieve the situation somewhat by granting him a ten-year export license and a price ceiling of 25 perperi.[166]

The famines of the 1340s grew worse, as is well known, and the Grain Office had a difficult time securing supplies. We know little about particulars, aside from the office's growing indebtedness; in the worst year, 1347, even galleys were put into service for the importation of wheat.[167]

The Provveditori alle Biave, the annonary administration that took over from the Grain Office, continued to make loans and advances, but little trace of them remains. In 1385 auditors of the accounts of both offices found traces of loans made to shipowners for repair of ships to be sent abroad for loading wheat, and they charged the Provveditori with serious deficiencies in their accounting and in failing to call in the loans.[168] At the same time, when a debtor-importer went bankrupt, the government refused to grant the Provveditori any preemptive rights over his goods: the office was to be treated like any private creditor and take the installment payments as they came.[169]

With the decline of the Grain Office as a financial institution in the late fourteenth century, the Rialto banks took over the credit arrangements for grain imports, by guaranteeing payment on terms that the state could not possibly meet as long as it had to await the returns on sales of the grain imported before paying importers (see below, Chap. 10).

For Flour Mills

Intimately tied to the annonary responsibilities of the Grain Office was the milling of wheat. It must be remembered that Venice did not have political control even over its own immediate hinterland until the conclusion of the Scaliger War in 1339. It is well known that Venetians owned land in the Terraferma long before that time, and mills on rivers and canals were among those properties. Such wheels were at the mercy of marauding armies, however, which caused Venetian authorities to experiment with tide mills and windmills situated in the lagoons, by financing private entrepreneurs and inventors. After 1339 milling was handled more efficiently in a vast territory, the Trevigiano, now under direct control of Venice. The

---

[166]ASV, Grazie, reg. 9, fol. 4v (26 May 1341). Such long-term plans as described in this paragraph, theoretically efficient because they made forecasting need possible, must often have run against the realities of individual harvests. In 1336 we find the Peruzzi and Bardi firms delivering Sicilian wheat to Canea in Crete, chargeable to the Commune of Venice; see Sapori, *I libri di commercio dei Peruzzi,* 104.

[167]ASV, SM, reg. 24, fol. 33 (1 September): the Grain Office advanced 200 ducats for freight charges on a galley awaited from Sicily.

[168]Ibid., reg. 39, fol. 120v (4 August 1385).

[169]ASV, CN, reg. 5, fol. 29v (7 July 1399), mentioned by Cassandro, *Le rappresaglie e il fallimento,* 107 n. 4.

concern that remained thereafter was the "just price" of flour; inability to control prices adequately caused the state at one point in the second half of the fifteenth century to build some mill wheels itself. By that time, population pressure was once again similar to that of the early fourteenth century.

The earliest evidence of loans made by the Grain Office to investors, nearly all of whom were nobles, in the construction and repair of mills for grinding wheat comes from the late thirteenth century. Three times between 1297 and 1299 the Great Council authorized loans totaling 2,300 lire di piccoli for repair of mills — tide mills in the lagoons — belonging to members of the Capello and Zane families. Income from operation of the mills was to go toward paying the principal and an unspecified rate of interest ("capitale et proficuum") on the loans.[170]

More solid evidence, beyond the mere authorizations, has survived regarding loans made to the Marcello family in 1314, when the depository was in full operation. Angelo Marcello, a nobleman from the parish of S. Angelo Raffaele, proposed to build mills at the edge of the lagoon for milling wheat, for which the office came up with a total of 74 lire di grossi "manchi" on two occasions. These were guaranteed loans due for repayment within three years, at the same rate of interest which the office paid its depositors. The fact that debit and credit rates of interest were equal shows the office was intentionally a nonprofit institution.[171]

Details about the case survive in a lawsuit brought by Angelo Marcello in 1323 against the estate of his brother Filippo (d. 21 November 1318).[172] Angelo's aim in suing was to constrain the executors of his broth-

[170]Since the Grain Office was not yet an organized depository, it was to borrow the money, at interest, from the funds administered by the Procurators of San Marco for mentally deficient persons. *DMC,* 3:425 (doc. 27), 430 (doc. 56), 448 (doc. 51). That the mills of the ca' Capello and the ca' Zane were tide mills is indicated by specific toponyms in the northern lagoon as well as from archeological remains; see the map of Antonio G. Vestri of 1692 (ASV, Savi ed esecutori alle acque, no. 68): north of Torcello is the "Valle di ca' Zane" (F2) and a "ramo di ca' Zane" (no. 156); in the western lagoon, near Fusina, a canal "detto Capello" (no. 114); several canals and branches called "molino," "del molino," or "di molini" (nos. 135, 360, 371, 376). For many further locations of mills in the lagoon (mulino a Cannaregio, mulino a Diano, and so on), see Bianca Lanfranchi Strina, ed., *Codex publicorum (Codice del Piovego),* FSV (Venice, l985), 1:48 and sent. 10. Regarding mills on the edge of the lagoon which exploited the current of inflowing rivers as well as tide mills in the lagoon itself, see Eugenia Bevilacqua, "Un particolare aspetto del passato nella laguna di Venezia: I molini," *Memorie dell'Accademia patavina di scienze, lettere ed arti,* classe morale, 72 (1959–60): 155–60. A French traveler in 1533 reported seeing a tide mill at Murano; Fernand Braudel, *Civilization matérielle, économie et capitalisme,* 3 vols. (Paris, 1979), 1:271. For the technology of tide mills, see W. E. Minchinton, "Early Tide Mills: Some Problems," *Technology and Culture* 20 (1979): 777–86.

[171]ASV, MC, Presbiter, fols. 111 (6 January) and 131 (17 December); the latter, also in AC, reg. 21, fol. 18v, is mentioned by Luzzatto in *PRV,* lxxvi.

[172]ASV, PSM, Ultra, b. 180, commis. Marcello, a large parchment bearing the no. 4, a sentence of the Curia del Procurator of 28 September 1323. The sentence transcribes in full many documents that clarify the terse deliberations of the Great Council (specifying, for example, that the lire indicated were lire di grossi "manchi" and that the total actually advanced

er's estate to lend him about 20 lire di grossi (on which he offered 10 percent interest payable from profits ("de l'usofruto") but at the risk and fortune of the estate. The executors had denied the request on the grounds that the testament had expressly excluded Angelo from any part in the estate. First of all, Angelo showed that he had asked for the loans (worth about 734 gold ducats) in his own name but at the request of Filippo, for the two were to collaborate in the enterprise. Second, the Grain Office provided, among other documents, a list of seven guarantors (six of whom were nobles) for the first loan of 40 lire di grossi "manchi." Listed also are the six installments in which the principal was paid off; the last payment, a year late, was made by Filippo upon order by the Giudici di Petizion. Payments on the principal for the second loan of 34 lire di grossi "manchi" are also extant. The accounts produced by the Grain Office indicate that interest, calculated to the very day, was paid together for both loans, at annual rates of 7 percent in 1315 and 6 percent from 1316 to 1318 — presumably the rates paid by the Grain Office itself on deposits in those years.

Angelo explained before the court that on the second loan, despite an authorization of 80 lire di grossi, he had received only 34 lire from the Grain Office, which he had invested in equipment and in getting a certain Lorenzo (obviously the artisan-engineer) to work on the project of building six mills at the Lago di Vigo, near the western edge of the lagoons, and on that sum more than 6 lire had been paid out in interest. The work had not been completed, however, and he needed further investment capital, which he sought from the estate.

The rebuttal was presented by Jacopo Romano, lawyer for the Procurators and the estate, who cited the clause of the testament which excluded Angelo from any part in it, reminded the judges that there were other partners in the project who had not advanced similar requests, and warned that Angelo was a tremendous quibbler ("tante caviliacionis vir").

The judges, on the contrary, ruled in Angelo's favor, considering him to be credible ("fide dignus") and the work on the mills necessary and useful. Since he had received only 34 lire from the second loan, and since both loans had been duly repaid, principal and interest, by both brothers equally, the court gave the executors fifteen days to advance 18 lire di grossi for five and one-half years to match the sum that Angelo had spent "for his part of the construction"; Angelo was obliged to complete the mills and put them into operation as soon as construction of the necessary canals or

---

by the Grain Office on the second loan was only 34 lire, on an authorization of 80 lire). The estate papers include Filippo's testament and two registers of estate accounts. Angelo continued to have a rapport with the Grain Office; probably as guarantor for a similar loan to Penzino Babilonio, Angelo paid 10 lire di grossi to the office; he was repaid in small installments until at least 1360. ASV, CIN, b. 32, fasc. 8 (13 June 1335). In 1331 an investigation was ordered to clarify a charge that Angelo Marcello "et consortes" were occupying lands in the public domain (which might refer to land connected with the mills); see AC, reg. 22, fol. 131.

spillways ("taiate") was complete. In short, the judges wanted the project, which the Commune had supported financially from the start via loans from the Grain Office, given the great need for mills, to be brought to completion for the sake of the common good; a clause in a testament was not to stand in the way.[173]

Extant documentation of further loans of the same kind probably does not match the extent of the practice, for some petitions specifically request a loan "like those conceded to others and on similar terms." In 1315 the Grain Office was authorized to lend up to 24 lire di grossi for three years to Francesco Valier for construction of two new wheels next to others that he owned.[174] And Caterino Zane requested 110 lire di grossi to repair and rebuild twelve mill wheels, since a petition supported by the officials reads, "the whole city suffers from the lack of milling facilities." The term was set at seven years, with interest to be paid annually at the same rate the Grain Office paid its depositors. The work was still proceeding a year later, delayed in part because of a suit filed against him by the Capello family, but Zane asked and received a further loan of 20 lire. Presumably a relatively large enterprise was involved. In 1321, with only eighteen months left before repayment was due, work was still not completed, and the total investment had risen to an estimated 200 lire di grossi. The Great Council, noting that interest had been paid regularly until then, gave an extension on repayment of the principal and remaining interest, while insisting upon renewal of the guarantee.[175]

In 1322 at least three loans were made for the construction or repair of mills, two of which were approved in August. In the first case, the noble partners Giovanni da Molin and Zannino Polani requested and received 80

---

[173]The locations mentioned in the documents are, besides the Lago di Vigo, Visignone and Linçina. The sentence ordered the beneficiary of the loans to cut canals where necessary ("debeat fieri facere taiatam in loco qui dicitur Scharlata et alias taiatas alibi ubi necesse fuerit"). The mills were driven by current and were located in territory subject to the abbot of SS. Ilario e Benedetto e S. Gregorio, seemingly near the mainland, west of Lizza Fusina (a Canal de Vigo runs from the Lago de Vigo to the island of S. Giorgio in Alga); other canals or "taiade" come off the Brenta River, including the "Fossa de' Molini," the Volpadego (with four "molini de Volpadego"), and the Laroncello (with four mills). See the map of Nicolò dal Cortivo in ASV, Savi ed esecutori alle acque, dis. 5. (Mill locations were found with the generous help of Giovanni Caniato.) Accounts in the estate papers register the names of renters and the incomes and expenses of the whole operation of a changing number of wheels (and parts of wheels), 1319–30.

[174]ASV, MC, Clericus Civicus, fol. 9v. It is difficult to say whether by new wheels was meant the construction of new mills or the addition of new wheels to an existing structure. For a large structure with six wheels on the Sile River, see Mauro Pitteri, *Segar le acque: Quinto e Santa Cristina al Tiveron: Storia e cultura di due villaggi ai bordi del Sile* (Treviso, 1984), plates 11–12 (1653).

[175]ASV, MC, Clericus Civicus, fols. 19 (30 September), containing the clause "sicut concessum est aliis simili modo," and 47v (24 July). For the extension: AC, reg. 21, fol. 132 (8 March 1321).

lire di grossi from the Grain Office for the construction of six wheels, as the authorization reads, "in certain waters which they claim to own near the mills of Visignone," for three years, at the usual conditions. The Great Council approved the loan but ordered the Piovego to check the property rights of the Commune and of private parties before construction could begin; furthermore, the Grain Office was to keep apprised of the work and of the expenditures made for the six wheels.[176] Only a few days later three brothers, sons of the deceased Turco Morosini, asked for 150 lire di grossi in order to repair mills destroyed during the recent war with Padua. The operation, they declared, had in the past produced 18 lire or 180 ducats profit annually for the family. The loan was authorized; interest, at the rate the Grain Office paid, was due in the first year, while repayment on principal in annual installments of 20 lire was to begin in the second year. As in the previous case, the grain officials were ordered to keep track of progress on the construction site and to see to it that the work was completed and the money well spent.[177] Finally, on the advice of the grain officials, a loan of 50 lire di grossi was made to Ungarello Natale and partners, owners of mills at the Turris Babie (behind Chioggia), for the construction of a fulling mill; it was due in four years with interest, and on the same conditions as the loan made to the Morosini brothers.[178]

In the following year, the Commune financed — most probably through the Grain Office — the construction of a mill invented by "magister Johannes teothonicus, ençegnerius mollendinorum," with 16 lire di grossi; the Giustizia Nuova was the magistracy delegated to inspect progress twice monthly.[179] That mill — probably a windmill — was assigned in 1324 to the scribe Marcellino and to Dardi Albizzo of Castello, who had offered to build a mill if they could receive a credit of 50 lire di grossi; their petition was approved, but the assessed value of the German's mill was subtracted from the amount requested.[180]

Not surprisingly, flour mills located on rivers in the mainland, even after Venice's expansion, were a primary target of marauding armies. Sometime during the war with Hungary, which Venice lost in 1358, certain mills belonging to Lorenzo Querini had been destroyed, and the owner had received a loan of 1,000 ducats toward the cost of their reconstruction. When he died, his minor sons were reduced to "extreme poverty" and

[176]ASV, MC, Clericus Civicus, fol. 174 (17 August).

[177]Ibid., fols. 189v–90, mentioned by Luzzatto in PRV, lxxvii n. The benefit of the Commune and concern for the welfare of the brothers and their "domus," deprived of the guardianship of their "avus" Albertino Morosini, who had in the past seen to the upkeep of the mills, were expressed by the Great Council.

[178]ASV, AC, reg. 21, fol. 201 (20 December).

[179]Ibid., fols. 190 (27–28 January 1323), 195 (3 March), and 215 (12 November).

[180]Ibid., reg. 22 (Brutus), fol. 5v; completion within one year was ordered.

received two "grazie," which reduced the installments on principal first to 50 then to 30 ducats per year.[181] Following the War of Chioggia, Roberto Morosini had received a loan from the Grain Office for the reconstruction of mills; when he failed to repay the loan, an equivalent value in his holdings in government credits was sequestered.[182] During that war the mills of Fantin Malipiero had been protected from burning by the enemy, as the owner reported in 1424 by way of indicating their vital importance, when he asked for a loan of 300 ducats for necessary repairs; he received the money, no longer from the Grain Office but from the Provveditori alle Biave. He promised to repay the sum in part by milling 150 staia of wheat per month and by paying the balance due over four years. In the same months two other owners — members of families whose names recur in this connection — requested loans: Polo Valier, who asked for 150 ducats, and Piero and Giacomo Morosini, who asked for 400 ducats, on the promise to grind wheat at 4 to 5 soldi per staio "segondo i tempi."[183] By that time the depository was no longer active.

In the mid-fifteenth century mills again become a major concern, probably as population pressure began to grow. The Collegio delle Biave had granted loans for milling and for repairing mills, but the borrowers were lax in meeting their repayment schedules.[184] Despite the fact that the Collegio had expressed assurance in 1459 that there were enough private mills, the state itself undertook to build mills, to avoid the frauds being committed against the poor by the mixing of base grains with wheat; with that rationale, the Senate ordered eight wheels to be built on the Sile River at the Castello of Treviso in 1466.[185] Now the state, under population pressure similar to that of the early fourteenth century, decided to intervene

---

[181]ASV, Grazie, reg. 15, fol. 92v (1363). The condition of milling facilities was declining in the 1360s, and in 1364 a committee was selected to study the situation; MC, Novella, fol. 92 (15 September).

[182]ASV, CN, reg. 2, fol. 60 (20 January 1386). Another debtor of the annona, the "camera provisorum bladi," was the estate of Nicoletto Floreni, whose heirs agreed to the sale at auction of a mill on the Lido (probably damaged during the war and object of a loan) and other properties; MC, Novella, fol. 192v (19 July 1383).

[183]ASV, Compilazione delle leggi, b. 88, fols. 43–46; the first request was approved by the Minor Consiglio, the others by the Collegio delle Biave.

[184]An estimo of Treviso for 1499 shows the Venetian nobleman Bernardo Donà as proprietor of a mill with four wheels (as well as two villas and lands) at Quinto trevigiano; see Pitteri, *Segar le acque,* 34, 43 n. 4. Patent rights, as well as loans, were the object of petitions; see ASV, CN, reg. 8, fol. 125 (for water-driven mills), and reg. 10, fols. 164–66; ST, reg. 7, fol. 91 (1475) for "dry" mills (probably windmills) in Venice; for dozens of such patents for mills, 1443–1550, see Giulio Mandich, "Le privative industriali veneziane (1450–1550)," *Rivista del diritto commerciale,* a. 34 (1936). Regarding the unrepaid loans "de maxenadure et anche per conzar molini," see CN, reg. 9, fol. 161r–v (1459).

[185]ASV, ST, reg. 5, fol. 161v. Three mill wheels owned by the state in Treviso were "destructe" in 1470, and 300 ducats were allocated for their repair.

directly as miller of wheat for the poor, rather than by subsidizing private entrepreneurs with cheap, long-term loans like those once provided by the Grain Office.[186]

For Kilns

The manufacture of bricks and roof tiles constituted another area in which the state intervened with long-term loans in periods of particular dearth; most known cases come from the years 1317 to 1330, obviously boom years in the construction industry, a period during which the Grain Office itself—beginning in 1322—was rebuilding the granary at S. Biagio near the arsenal.[187] In 1317 Nicola, a mason turned entrepreneur, received a loan of 1,000 lire di piccoli, repayable in five years at the same rate of interest which the Grain Office paid on deposits—that is, the same terms as on the loans granted for flour mills in the same years.[188] Three years later the Great Council authorized a large loan of 100 lire di grossi, expandable according to need, to be divided among any parties willing to construct kilns.[189] In 1321 the nobleman Giovanni Michiel was beneficiary of a loan of 1,000 lire di piccoli for the construction of a second much needed kiln at Tombello, near Mestre. He had, as usual, to post good bond, but he did not have to begin repaying the principal for two years, after which he had five years to pay—at the usual rate of interest; but the generous terms had a condition: the kiln had to be completed within three months.[190]

Five years later the dearth of building materials was still acute. In 1327 the Great Council invited bids for the construction of kilns; each of the top

---

[186]A last instance of a loan by the Grain Office for a mill, this time not for milling wheat but for fulling cloth, dates from 1374. This was a period in which Venice had decided to promote the local wool industry, and the Provveditori di Comun, who had jurisdiction over the wool guild, organized a loan from the Grain Office from funds deposited by Ludovico Gonzaga. Of the amount lent, 1,000 ducats were to go toward the construction of fulling mills, of which the Arte della Lana had great need. Once built, they were to be auctioned by the state in order to recover costs. BMCV, mss., cl. IV, no. 129 (mariegola dell'Arte della Lana), fol. 221, records, without date, a loan of nearly the whole deposit of Ludovico Gonzaga, that is, of 30,300 ducats, which is highly doubtful. The only reference to a larger loan to the guild is that earmarking 1,000 ducats for the construction of fulling mills, "de denariis deputatis ad prestantiam pannorum venetorum"; ASV, SM, reg. 34, fol. 150v (12 January 1375). Both documents are discussed by Nellie Fano, "Ricerche sull'arte della lana a Venezia nel XIII e XIV secolo", *AV*, ser. 5, 18 (1936): 97, 141.

[187]ASV, MC, Fronesis, fols. 96v (18 September 1322), 107v (14 and 20 April 1323), 137 (31 July 1324). For a treatment of kilns in the district of Florence, but with full bibliography on the situation in Europe as a whole, see Goldthwaite, *Building of Renaissance Florence,* chap. 4.

[188]Giovanni Monticolo, ed., *I capitolari delle arti veneziane (dalle origini al 1330),* 3 vols. (Rome, 1896–1914), 1:215, doc. 5.

[189]Ibid., 1:216, doc. 7; complete in *PRV,* doc. 102. The money was to come from the deposit made by Rizzardo Malombra.

[190]Monticolo, *I capitolari delle arti,* 1:217, doc. 8, and 224, doc. 14; mentioned in *PRV,* lxxvii n.

four bidders, to be selected by the Council of Forty, was promised a loan of 60 lire di grossi for eight years; interest, at 6 percent, was to be paid only after the first year. A condition called for completion of a kiln within six months after the loan was accepted.[191] In the same year two other loans are recorded, one to the noble Pancino Babilonio for 1,000 lire di piccoli, for repair of an existing kiln located in Quarto trevigiano, the second for the large sum of 160 lire di grossi (1,600 ducats) to the noble Nicolò Grimani for construction of two kilns in Venice, payable, at interest, over ten years. The yield of Grimani's first kiln, in bricks, lime, and roof tiles was reserved for work on the arsenal and on the second kiln. But the entrepreneur quickly encountered problems: a large batch of bricks was ruined, for which he was fined, and in 1330, with 90 lire still to be repaid, Grimani was unable to continue payments, nor could he renew his surety; on the petition of the guarantors, the Great Council authorized the Grain Office to sequester the kilns, the building, and the bricks and sell them at auction.[192] Very likely there were many other such loans that left no trace when no particular problems arose.[193]

Even though the 1340s were years of intense construction by the state, both for the expansion of the hall of the Great Council in the Ducal Palace and for the huge granary that occupied the area west of the mint (until it was torn down under Napoleon to create the Giardini Reali), there is no evidence of a dearth of bricks such that the state had to intervene to subsidize the industry.[194] When new public works called for subvention via loans, they involved the defenses of Mestre, seriously damaged during the War of Chioggia; again the entrepreneurs are nobles, but there is by this time — the 1390s — no mention of the Grain Office.[195]

[191]Monticolo, *I capitolari delle arti*, 1:218–20, doc. 11. The Grain Office is not specifically mentioned, but it may be assumed to have been the lending agency.

[192]Ibid., 1:225–30, docs. 15–17, 21, 23. By late 1328 Babilonio (for whom, as we have seen, Angelo Marcello was a guarantor to the Grain Office) was bankrupt; see ASV, AC, reg. 22, fol. 92 (10 November).

[193]Two further documents of 1328 speak of a kiln operator who died without heirs before repaying his loan; see Monticolo, *I capitolari delle arti*, 1:227, docs. 18–19.

[194]A fine was imposed by the Giustizia Vecchia on four brickmakers who furnished the Grain Office with roof tiles larger than regulation size; see ASV, Grazie, reg. 9, fol. 78 (4 March 1343). Evidence that work on the granary was proceeding upward so as to cut off the sun from the back of the Procuratia is in MC, Spiritus, fol. 130v (26 August 1343).

[195]An offer of loans to persons interested in building kilns "pro faciendo et coquendo lapites" in Mestre was raised from 2,000 to 4,000 lire di piccoli when the first offer found no takers; ASV, MC, Leona, fol. 72 (28 June 1394), which mentions a deliberation by the Senate of May 1393. In 1396 a loan of 8,000 lire di piccoli was made to Fantino di Marco Marcello and Francesco di Dardo Dolfin for construction of two kilns in Mestre; they repaid 6,000 lire before the war for conquest of the Terraferma broke out but claimed to be unable to pay the balance, since the operators of the kiln, their debtors, had died under the walls of Padua while serving in the army, into which they had been conscripted; see CN, reg. 4, fol. 52v (June 1409).

For Religious Houses

Traces exist for loans made to the monasteries of S. Nicolò del Lido and S. Giorgio Maggiore in the early years of the Trecento. In 1315 the Great Council called on the Grain Office to resolve an untenable condition of indebtedness at S. Nicolò: the previous abbot had borrowed "at usury" to pay for needed repairs and had mortgaged the monastery's holdings in the district of Padua for a total debt of about 5,000 lire. The property in the Padovano stood in danger of being lost to the creditor, a situation that obviously ran counter to Venice's interests, also because the land produced wheat that the monastery imported to Venice. The Grain Office was to find the funds with which to pay off the monastery's loan; the monastery was obliged to pay 1,000 lire per year on the new loan, first on the interest, the balance toward the principal.[196] A second case concerns the monastery of S. Giorgio. Here the Grain Office, in 1319, lent 6,000 lire a grossi (2,300 ducats), repayable in six years, to the abbot to finance his trip to Rome for confirmation and consecration. All the property of the monastery was obligated for the loan, and as specific security a "ruga" or street of urban real estate in the parish of S. Zulian (with rental income of 45½ lire di grossi per year) was consigned to the state. Furthermore, the Great Council asked for surety in the persons of three brothers (Tomà, Bartolomeo, and Menego) of the prestigious merchant-banking firm of the ca' Bollani. Three years later a further loan of 100 lire di grossi was made to the monastery, repayable in four years with the usual interest ("proficuum"), making the total the significant sum of 3,300 ducats.[197]

Miscellaneous Loans

Requests for economical loans and the readiness of the Great Council to provide them were such in the years around 1320 as to compromise the

[196]ASV, MC, Clericus Civicus, fol. 2 (20 May 1315). The Procurators were to contribute to the loan fund about 25 lire di grossi that they administered, money earmarked by testators for a crusade.

[197]*PRV*, doc. 96 (1319), and ASV, AC, reg. 21, fols. 145v (a first "dilatio" during construction of the altar for the relics of S. Stefano) and 181 (mentioned by Luzzatto in *PRV*, lxxvii–viii n). In 1323 the Commune pledged itself guarantor for a loan at interest of 100 lire di grossi which the abbot was to contract "pro aleviatione debitorum," and one of the bondsmen to the Grain Office for the previous loans was Giovanni Papaziza; five years were given for payment in full of principal and interest later in the same year. An interest-free loan in the Salt Office was ordered transferred to the Grain Office in October to substitute for the loans made to S. Giorgio, so that it could profit the beneficiary. AC, reg. 21, fols. 203v (31 May), 211 (6 September), and 214v (29 October). The Commune's concern for local prelates' expenses for confirmation and consecration is evidenced also by the two-year loan of 10 lire di grossi made to Tommaso Contarini, bishop of Capodistria, without which he purportedly would have been unable to go to his see. Ibid., fol. 20v (4 February 1315).

liquidity of the Grain Office and to require strict curtailment in 1326. Only a few of what seem to have been many successful applications have left a trace; the following petitions involve the state's concern for public health, for noble indigence, and for foreign policy.

The colorful career of the famous Venetian surgeon magister Gualterius (d. 1346) involved numerous credit dealings with the communal government, several of which specifically concerned the Grain Office. Gualtiero was one of the twenty-four physicians and surgeons in Venice who were public servants; in 1305 his annual salary was a substantial 12 lire di grossi.[198] His service, his readiness to stand bond for others, and his investments, however, continuously got him into economic straits. The state intervened first of all with several advances on his salary, one such while he was part of an official embassy to Avignon. He had also been taken prisoner during the War of Ferrara (1308–12), and in order to pay his ransom, he had used the dowry set aside for a niece or granddaughter ("nepta"); when the dowry was needed in 1320, the Grain Office lent him 18 lire di grossi, due in six annual installments of 4 lire (which would come to 5.5 percent interest per year).[199] Gualtiero's major project from that time on was the construction of a hospital for disabled and retired seamen at S. Elena, an island just beyond the arsenal. In 1321 he received a license to purchase quantities of wheat for export to allies of Venice, with the profits to go toward the hospital. In the next year another loan of 30 lire di grossi from the Grain Office was authorized, due in six years at the usual conditions, to be used only for the projected hospital.[200] His indebtedness to the grain magistracy grew: he received advances on his government salary so as to meet the payments due in 1324 and 1327, and in the latter year the Grain Office was ordered to advance a year's rent on a granary owned by Gualtiero in which communal grain was stored — money usually placed in the hands of trustees; in 1329 he was authorized to sell or mortgage his house to pay his debts — with any balance to be deposited in the Grain Office "for safekeeping, for his own good."[201] Finally, in 1332, when Gualtiero's house in S. Vio was already

---

[198]Many of the documents were published by Monticolo, *I capitolari delle arti*, vol. 1, on medical doctors. See also Bartolomeo Cecchetti, "La medicina in Venezia nel 1300," *AV* 26 (1883): 107–11, and Ugo Stefanutti, *Documentazioni cronologiche per la storia della medicina, chirurgia e farmacia in Venezia dal 1258 al 1332* (Venice, 1961).

[199]Monticolo, *I capitolari delle arti*, 1:338–39, doc. 136; the authorization by the Great Council states that the ransom had cost 20 lire di grossi, that the interest due on the loan be at the same rate as that paid by the Grain Office, and that the loan of 18 lire be repaid in six installments, "videlicet libras IIII grossorum et prode annuatim," which comes to 5.5 percent.

[200]For the license mentioned and two earlier ones, ibid., 1:345, doc. 146 (cf. docs. 95 and 121); for the loan, ibid., 1:349–50, doc. 159.

[201]Ibid., 1:352, doc. 165, 1:361–62, docs. 177–78, 1:364–65, doc. 187, 1:366, doc. 194. The total owed to the Grain Office in 1329 was 65 lire di grossi; the license was needed because all contracts concluded by Gualtiero on his own had been declared null and void (doc. 187). Total

mortgaged "in manu aliena," the Grain Office agreed to purchase his granaries for the large sum of 1,100 ducats.[202]

In this unique case the communal government, generally with the mediation of the grain magistracy, was protecting its interests by supporting an individual whose skills and services were considered vital to the city. When he died in 1346, Gualtiero was still indebted, and the Procurators of San Marco, as his executors, auctioned his furniture and other belongings.

In a second case, a large sum of money was lent to Count Federico, son of the deceased Doimo, feudal lord of the strategically placed island of Veglia (Krk) in the Quarnero, at the head of the Adriatic. In 1319, on the eve of the maturity date, and after having made some payments, the count still owed 120 lire di grossi to the Grain Office. At that time the Great Council, besides granting an extension of eighteen months, lent him an additional 20 lire at interest so that he could repay a noble creditor. But in 1321 and 1322 he still could not pay and received further extensions, on condition that he could renew his bondsmen.[203]

Only two petitions have turned up which concern Venetian noblemen, although there must have been many. In 1321 three members of the Contarini family received a five-year loan of 50 lire di grossi, at interest, to enable them to rebuild their palace, which had burned. And in 1325 Giovanni Minotto received a two-year loan (then extended for two more years) "at the usual conditions" regarding surety and interest, "because of his misfortune and indigence."[204]

In the 1320s the requests for such cheap long-term loans from the Grain Office were myriad, so much so that in 1326 the Great Council made authorization both for loans and for extensions of terms via the "grazia" procedure, which was much more difficult to obtain; from then on a petition needed approval of all six councillors, thirty-five of the Forty, and two-thirds of the Great Council. Too easy credit, it was recognized, could quickly bring ruin ("sinistrum et preiudicium . . . , periculum non modicum atque damnum in futurum") to the Grain Office in its role as a quasi-public bank; or perhaps more important in the minds of legislators was the desire to reserve the money deposited in the Grain Office by investors, local and foreign, for the needs of the state for quick credit.[205]

The last and very singular case is the loan of 30,000 ducats made by

---

indebtedness was surely greater, since the authorization of 1324 states that the salary advance was made because Gualtiero was "multis debitis aggravato et specialiter nostre camere frumenti et aliis" (doc. 165).

[202]ASV, Grazie, reg. 4, fol. 23 (14 April 1332).

[203]ASV, AC, reg. 21, fols. 57v (13 January 1319), 131v and 132v (8 and 10 March 1321), 142v, and Luzzatto in *PRV,* lxxvii–viii n. Count Doimo seems not to have been admitted to the Great Council during the process of its closing; see Rösch, *Der Venezianische Adel,* 182.

[204]ASV, AC, reg. 21, fol. 131 (21 February 1321), and reg. 22, fol. 64v (25 August 1327).

[205]*RES,* doc. 106 (1325) and p. lxvi; also ASV, MC, Spiritus, fol. 5 (29 May 1326).

Venice to the Empress Anna (of Savoy) and her minor son John V Pal-
aeologus at Constantinople in 1343, a loan taken over by the Grain Office
which in the end never was repaid. In the 1340s the office was in serious
economic straits, but the loan constituted an aspect of Venetian foreign
policy then and for many decades.[206]

In the spring of 1343 the rulers of Byzantium sought the loan to
strengthen their hand against the pretender John Catacuzeno and to prepare a fleet to face the Turks. By the early summer, seven Venetian nobles
present in Constantinople and two bankers who operated in Venetian Negroponte had made the loan in an unstated number of perperi (probably
52,500, at the rate of 1¾ perperi per ducat). The Signoria guaranteed
repayment in Venice of 30,000 ducats, with interest ("cum prode"), by 31
December. (The interest, which was not specified, may have been included
in the rate of exchange.) The crown jewels, carefully inventoried, certified,
turned over to the Venetian bailo, and transferred to Venice, constituted the
security on a promise to pay 10,000 ducats per year for three years (1343–
45), plus 5 percent interest.[207] In October the Senate ordered five "savi" to
find the money to repay the merchants, but on 1 December it admitted that
the Treasury did not have the necessary funds and so authorized the Grain
Office to contract loans with citizens or foreigners for 30,000 ducats, to
uphold the promise and thus the good name of the Commune. Optimistically, the Senate promised to turn over to the Grain Office the payments
received from Constantinople, but then it more realistically provided that if
creditors of the Grain Office desired repayment before installments were
received from the Palaeologi, the officials could contract further loans (that
is, accept further deposits) to meet demand for withdrawals; interest was to
be "secundum usum Camere."[208]

This loan aggravated problems. Almost immediately the sinking fund
for amortization of the consolidated debt had to be reduced in order to
channel money to the Grain Office. By May 1345 the loan was already
written off as a bad debt in the accounts of the office, as we have seen.[209]

[206]Unless otherwise indicated, the following account is based on the exemplary study, with
an extensive documentary appendix, by Tommaso Bertelé, "I gioielli della corona bizantina
dati in pegno alla repubblica veneta nel sec. XIV e Mastino II della Scala," in *Studi in onore di
Amintore Fanfani* (Milan, 1962), 2:89–177. An extensive summary with further bibliography
is in Setton, *Papacy and the Levant,* 1:317–20.

[207]The rate, taken for granted by the parties, is specified in extant documents only much
later. At simple interest, the value of the jewels, unstated, should have been 34,500 ducats;
Bertelé, "I gioielli," 96–101. The list of merchants is in his doc. 4; the bank of Negroponte is
that of Nicolò Gandolfo, who was also involved in the affair of Nicolò Zorzi, the feudatory of
Boudoniza (see above). Document 29, 1363, says that the loan had been made on 1 January
1343, twenty years previous. The role of the bailo is mentioned in Maltesou, *L'istituzione del
bailo di Venezia,* 229–31. See also Luzzatto in *PRV,* lxxxix.

[208]*RES,* docs. 168–69; Bertelé, "I gioielli," doc. 7; see also Thiriet, *Deliberations,* vol. 1, no.
506 and appendix, p. 310.

[209]*RES,* docs. 170, 178.

From that point on, the crown jewels became a pawn in the game of diplomacy: Venice insisted on repayment of the principal plus compound interest, threatened to sell the jewels (even at the peak of the Black Death!),[210] and offered to forgive the ever increasing debt, in toto or in part, principal or interest, in return for the destruction of the Genoese colony at Pera or for transfer of title to the much-sought-after island of Tenedos at the mouth of the Bosphorus.[211] Treaties between the two powers constantly repeated Venice's title to payment in full, while instructions given to the Venetian envoys aimed lower. At one point, Mastino II della Scala, whose son Cangrande II would deposit so much cash at the Grain Office, offered to repay the loan in order to appropriate the jewels, an offer not accepted.

The case sheds light on financial practices of the Grain Office. In 1350 the Senate ordered the envoy to insist on payment by the emperor, not of simple interest (1,500 ducats per year) but of compound interest, "prode prodis." Or, if payment could actually be had, he should be satisfied with simple interest, so long as he underscored Venice's right to compound interest, since that was what the office had to pay to its creditors.[212] Here the Senate referred to the practice of permitting depositors periodically (but not automatically) to add part or all of the interest due them to principal. (As was shown above, such permits sometimes constitute the only evidence we have that a given person was a depositor at the Grain Office.) In 1355 interest compounded annually for twelve years was stated as "circa 25,000 ducats" (the exact figure would be 23,877 ducats).[213] On the twentieth anniversary of the loan, the amount due was expressed as follows:

principal ("cavedal")	30,000
simple interest ("pro," at 5% for 20 yrs)	30,000
interest on interest ("pro' de pro'")	19,599
total	79,599 ducats

In 1370 Venice tried again to get John V, then a visitor in Venice, to cede Tenedos. Venice offered an additional sum of 25,000 ducats (which the Grain Office was ordered to come up with) plus remission of the earlier debt. An advance of 4,000 ducats was actually made. Rather unexpectedly, the emperor's economic position improved, and he was able to sail from Venice without ceding the island. The Senate, reconciled to the fact that the advance could not be recuperated, decided to write it off as a gift.[214]

[210]With a four-month ultimatum; ibid., doc. 195.

[211]Besides Bertelé, for the role of Marino Falier in negotiations in 1352, see Lazzarini, *Marino Faliero*, 114.

[212]Bertelé, "I gioielli," 110–11 and doc. 19: "instet suo posse ad habendum tam capitale quam prode, quam etiam prode prodis, sicut iustum est et sicut nos solvimus de hinc illis quibus mutuo fuit accepta pecunia."

[213]Ibid., 114 and doc. 21.

[214]Setton, *Papacy and the Levant*, 1:319–20.

Three times the jewels made their way back to Constantinople, on the assumption that either the repayment or the cession of Tenedos was imminent. They were never sold, despite the threats to do so. When Constantinople fell in 1453, the jewels were still on deposit in care of the Procurators of San Marco, so that after 110 years Venice had in hand only pawns worth at best the value of the principal. Thus the Grain Office was not able to recover either the principal or the interest it had repaid to the original lenders, and its balance sheet was destined to remain in the red.

These examples are sufficient to show how this institution, nearly a state bank and clearly administrator of the floating debt, was at the whim of government policy, foreign and local. If it had not been bailed out continually by the state, it would have failed, as did so many private banks. Perhaps the pressure of a run by depositors did not exist, given the six-month notice required and the rank of the depositors. Their very rank, however, placed a very particular kind of pressure on the Commune, once they began clamoring for withdrawal of their funds. In the period following the War of Chioggia the Grain Office outlived its usefulness in the eyes of the government. Thereafter, quick credit would be made available by private banks.

vii. RATES OF INTEREST AND CASES OF CONSCIENCE

Rates of interest paid and received and expressions of qualms of conscience by some persons who had accepted interest on their deposits have thus far been treated case by case, in the context of authorizations, petitions, and related sources. At this point, it may be useful to lift from their individual context some of the elements that have emerged and discuss them together.

Rates of Interest

First of all, the terminology: the authorities and clients referred to interest with the terms *presa, proficuum, prode, lucrum, utilitas,* that is, the same terms used generally in Venice in this period, without any intent of making distinctions. The terms are perhaps better rendered in English as "return" or "profit," but since what was practically involved was interest, that is the term used here.

The rates of interest paid by the Grain Office on loans and deposits during its history as a quasi-state bank can be seen at a glance in table 9.2. In general, the rates were at or very close to market rates from 1285 to 1310, when they moved between 8 and 12 percent;[215] thereafter, they seem to be 1

---

[215]Some of these rates, along with a brief sketch of the Grain Office, were included by Sidney Homer in his *History of Interest Rates* (New Brunswick, N.J., 1968), 97; Italian translation of the third revised edition, *Storia dei tassi di interese* (Milan, 1995), 135–37. Twelve percent was

TABLE 9.2

Rates of Interest Applied at the Grain Office, 1288–1426

Year	On Money Borrowed	Year	On Money Lent
1288	10%, 12%		
1289	10%		
1291	8%		
		1315	7%
		1316–18	6%
		1320	5.5%
		1327	6%
1329	5% on dowries		
1335	5%		
1343	5%	1343	5%
1345	3%		
1349	3% to foreigners		
1349	3% to foreigners (occasionally 4%, by "gratia") 4% to Venetian citizens (who had refused to lend at 3%) 5% on dowries		
1374	3–4–5% confirmed, with 6 months' notice to withdraw		
1426	4–5%		

to 3 points lower than the maximum rates that an investor could make on local colleganze, albeit with somewhat greater risk. Liquid dowry funds, which by a law of 1329 (later added to the statutes) had to be deposited in the Grain Office, earned a fixed 5 percent. Interest offered by the Grain Office to foreign depositors declined in 1345 to 3 percent, on account of the heavy demand to invest money in that way. Venetians refused to make deposits at that low rate and were offered 4 percent in 1349. In that year, then, the rates that would hold as long as the Grain Office depository functioned were fixed at 3 percent for foreigners, 4 percent for Venetians, 5 percent on dowries. Exceptions were occasionally made so that a foreigner could receive 4 percent or, on two occasions, even 5 percent: by granting him or her either Venetian citizenship or simply a special privilege. In 1374 these rates and the obligation of the depositor to give six months' notice of his or her desire to withdraw money were reconfirmed.[216] Interest rates could be kept low at the Grain Office because savings were more secure and demand was high — the same rationales that serve Swiss banks today. They can be compared to the fixed 5 percent applied by the Procurators on the

---

a legitimate return (called "interesse" or "beneficio") in 1304 also in Lucca; see Thomas Blomquist, "The Dawn of Banking in an Italian Commune: Thirteenth Century Lucca," *Dawn of Modern Banking*, 66.

[216]ASV, SM, reg. 34, fol. 73 (3 January 1374), and Cessi, in *RES*, cclix and n. 1.

investment of trust funds in local colleganze, beginning in 1347, and to government obligations, which earned a nominal 5 percent and yields of 5–8 percent at the time.

The rates of interest which the Grain Office charged for loans it extended are often expressly stated to be those that the magistracy itself paid on deposits. In other words, those industrial improvement loans were not meant to be a source of profit but a way of sustaining a certain kind of enterprise. The few quoted rates we have, for loans made in 1315–18 and 1327, were 7 and 6 percent, but generally the rate was simply the "usual" one "that the Grain Office itself" paid.

Simple interest was generally implied, whether owed to or by the Grain Office. In the case of the loan of 30,000 ducats made to the Byzantine emperor in 1343, however, compound interest comes into play. The government, while having in practice written off the loan as a bad debt, used it as a political lever for decades. In 1350 Venice already began asking for "interest on interest" [prode prodis] whenever it pressed the emperor for repayment, on the argument that the Grain Office itself was paying compound interest. This affirmation was never explicated in other contexts, but the procedure is reflected in some actual cases. The Grain Office normally paid out interest on deposits annually or semiannually, if a depositor or his representative came to collect. Oftentimes no one came but an explicit request was made that interest be added to principal; that way, of course, the Grain Office ended up in many cases paying "interest on interest."[217] Only a single case — to be discussed shortly, because it became a matter of conscience — has been found in which the depositor was informed that a given principal would earn a given return, which, by calculation, turns out to be compound interest.

Usury or Cases of Conscience

One gets the distinct impression reading the documents that Venetians were more practical and businesslike and on the whole rather less assailed by moral scruples about receiving interest from the state than citizens of some other cities, especially Florence.[218] On the other hand, only certain kinds of documentation have survived, and one ought not to be categorical when arguing from silence. While Venetians seem not to have been involved in the heated debates in Florence in the 1350s and 1360s about the admissibility of interest on forced loans, one participant in the debates, the Franciscan Guglielmo Centueri, cited a Venetian, the prestigious nobleman Zaccaria Contarini, as being contrary to receiving interest on forced

---

[217]Instructions on how to calculate compound interest are contained in a Venetian commercial arithmetic of about 1400: BMV, It. cl. IV, cod. 497 (5163), fol. 43; mentioned by Lane, "Investment and Usury," 66.

[218]Cf. Lane, "Investment and Usury," 56–68.

loans and yield on government obligations purchased on the open market. In the years 1355–61, it is true, Venetian authorities did debate the legality of the local colleganza contract, but the alternative — legalization of pawnbroking — was not accepted, and the popular form of loan was again declared legitimate (see above, Chap. 4, sec. iii, and below, Chap. 11, sec. v). In order to garner funds, the state was forced to offer a moderate interest schedule, both for the floating debt and for the funded debt.

As regards deposits at the Grain Office, extremes of concern and lack thereof are represented mostly by non-Venetians, the principal protagonists of what can be known about this institution. Guglielmo Castelbarco, for example, well known for usurious activity of his own, wanted no interest on his deposit of 20,000 florins made in 1319 and refused even the alternative of a gift of precious cloths. Most of his estate was earmarked for reparation of ill-gotten gain, and here, late in life, he obviously did not wish to add further to his guilt. On the other hand, another feudatory and money-lender, Pietro Nan da Marano of Vicenza, who deposited 10,000 ducats around 1336, did not shy away from an annual interest of about 4 percent — although he called it a discretionary gift ("aliquo dono"). The principal plus 2,153 ducats earned as interest were dispensed as conscience money by the executors, the Procurators of San Marco and two Franciscans (one of whom was inquisitor for the Veneto); some money went to pious causes, but most was destined for restitution to persons who could prove they had been victims of Pietro's usury and extortion. This is significant, for the inquisitor had jurisdiction over usury as well as heresy, and here interest, a moderate return on capital, was used for restitution of usury.[219]

It is worth recalling that the jurist Baldus remarked that his famous teacher, Riccardo Malombra, had been assailed by qualms of conscience for having accepted "usury" on loans. It could have been simply a snide remark on the part of a student, and the master's deposit at the Grain Office was not specifically mentioned, but Malombra had indeed received interest on his deposit.

On the Venetian side, an interesting case has come to light involving the widow of a man she considered possibly guilty of having accepted usury. Caterina, a noblewoman and widow of Marco di Gilberto Dandolo, was concerned about the interest her deceased husband had received from the Grain Office. In her testament of 1304, Caterina stated that her husband had lent (literally "given") an unspecified sum of money to the office and had received a return on it, an "utilitas," of 350 lire. Anxious about the legitimacy

---

[219]ASV, PSM, Misti, b. 4, reg. 1. Only shortly after Pietro's death the papacy in Avignon heard that there were several people in Venice ("nonnulle persone apud Venetias") who had earmarked funds for restitution of "male ablata" but that the precise victims of the extortion could not be identified; those funds were ordered collected, against a duplicate receipt valid as restitution, for use in the planned crusade against the Turks. Archivio Segreto Vaticano, Registri vaticani, 62, fol. 58v (8 August 1344).

of the return, she ordered that the sum be restored to the Commune. When she died, Marco's heirs seem to have petitioned for a derogation from the obligation to pay. The Forty and the Great Council granted the petition through the "grazia" procedure and were probably relieved to do so. For the Commune to have accepted the money would have been an admission that it was paying usury, and it had to keep its credit options open.[220]

Whereas this woman had been concerned for the soul of her husband, another woman, a non-noble, was concerned about her own soul. On 14 March 1347, on the eve of the Black Death from which she seems to have died, Cecilia, widow of Marco della Frescada of S. Stae, made a testament in which she referred to a deposit she was about to make at the Grain Office. The amount of the deposit was 1,200 lire di piccoli, and she states that in five years' time she would earn 10 lire di grossi on that amount. The sum, probably her dowry, earned 5 percent, so that the interest due, probably compounded annually, in fact comes very close to 10 lire or 100 ducats.[221] In her testament, Cecilia inserted a clause that she ordered her executors, the Procurators of San Marco, to read aloud before the Ducal Council, where she described the deposit and the promised interest, stated that she was anxious about it ("de hoc facto sit michi conscientia"), and ordered the interest to be turned over to the Signoria, to be used at its discretion. In addition, she left 10 ducats as reparation of uncertain usury ("pro male ablatis incertis"). The estate papers are extant, as are the minutes of the Ducal Council, when the clause was read, so that the matter can be followed further. In 1349, about six months after Cecilia's death, the Procurators withdrew more than 1,000 ducats from her deposit at the Grain Office, for principal and interest ("tam pro capitali quam pro prode"), which means she also had other assets in the office besides her dowry. The Ducal Councillors agreed in 1355 (with one negative vote) to accept the restitution of interest on the dowry and ordered the Procurators to turn it over to the Treasury. The Procurators then recorded the fact that they had paid with an offset against money the Camerlenghi owed them. Of the reparations bequest for uncertain usury, the Procurators paid 8 ducats "in auxilio" to the church of S. Angelo "de Zanparego." This woman knew what to expect in economic terms from her investments but did not wish it to compromise her status in the afterlife; her intervention with God and the civil authorities was very precise and self-conscious, and this time in a moment of particular concern in the city regarding the question of usury, the Signoria acceded to her wishes.[222]

Only somewhat more trusting is Bartolomeo Centrago of Chioggia,

---

[220]Favaro, *Grazie — novus liber,* doc. 494 (28 August 1304).

[221]The principal, 1,200 lire di piccoli, corresponds to 375 ducats; at 5 percent simple interest she would have earned 93.75 ducats, at compound interest, 103.61 ducats.

[222]ASV, PSM, Ultra, b. 135, commis. Cecilia qd. Marco della Frescada. The testament is also in NT, b. 1154, notaio de Brutis. For the Collegio, see CN, reg. 1, fol. 23 (19 October 1355).

who in his testament of 1342 ordered that all his liquid capital be deposited in the Grain Office and remain there as long as his executors saw fit — "as long as that deposit not be to the detriment of my soul."[223]

A similar concern was expressed in 1404 by Venice's newly named captain general, Malatesta di Pandolfo Malatesta of Pesaro, as we have seen above. Malatesta had for some time been benefiting from interest on 10,000 ducats deposited in the Grain Office by his father in 1372, some of which interest had been added to the principal, so that he occasionally received something approaching compound interest. In 1404 Malatesta wished to avoid the danger of having received interest ("prode") but did not mean for a moment to part with his income. A formal solution was found "in order to salve his conscience": the Senate issued a statement that restitution of the money had been received from Malatesta and simultaneously ordered the Signoria to "bestow" it upon the mercenary captain as a "gift." The deliberation is straightforward, but behind it must have been more than a few smirks of Venice's merchant-Senators at this foreigner's qualms and the solution that quieted them. Probably not a penny actually changed hands.[224]

Venetian males with similar preoccupations regarding deposits at the Grain Office have not turned up, and they are the ones who often benefited from the interest on dowries deposited there, even if they had made no deposits themselves. That persons concerned were foreigners and two Venetian women tends to reinforce the impression that, by and large, Venetians involved daily in manipulating money in some fashion did not consider their souls endangered by the moderate interest paid on deposits by the Grain Office.

---

[223]ASV, PSM, Misti, testamenti, b. ex-280. The passage reads: "Omnes mei denarii deponantur apud dominos officiales a frumento comunis Veneciarum qui remanere debeant apud ipsos dominos officiales usque dum appariuntur suprascriptis meis comissariis, tali condicione quod ipsa reposicio dictorum denariorum non fiat nec fieri possit in detrimento anime mee."

[224]ASV, SSec, reg. 2, fol. 22v. The rubric (SSec, Rubrica, reg. 1) is very concise: "Illi denarii quos habuit magnificus Dominus Malatesta capitaneus noster a Camera frumenti pro prode, de quibus habeat conscientiam, habeantur pro receptis et donentur sibi." The actual deliberation is quoted above (see p. 387, n. 100).

10

BANK LOANS TO THE STATE
IN THE FIFTEENTH CENTURY

i. INTRODUCTION

IN THE SPRING OF 1499 Venice was on the verge of another war against the Turks; in May the Lippomano bank followed the path taken by the Garzoni bank only three months earlier and declared bankruptcy; the third bank, that of the Pisani, was hard pressed by its depositors; the smallest of the four Rialto banks, that of the Agostini, resisted. Alvise Pisani, nearly a victim of the rush of depositors, called the Lippomano thieves, criticized the system of bank surety, and then, as the diarist Domenico Malipiero recounts, made a direct connection between the sad condition of the banks and the creditworthiness of the state: "When the banks are not trusted, the state has no credit" [quando i banchi no ha' fede, la Terra no ha credito].[1]

In order to drive home the idea of the essential symbiosis between the state and the Rialto banks, Malipiero made two points. First, he reported a debate that supposedly took place in the consistory, as we have seen above (Chap. 6). Having noted the clamorous bank failures, the pope drew the conclusion that Venice, having lost its lines of credit, was forced to withdraw from its treaty obligations and was finished as a major military power. True or spurious, the account indicates that Venice's capacity to carry on as a world power when its banking system lay in a shambles was being questioned. Second, he himself depicts the government at the time of the first failure as mobilizing to intervene in defense of the banks only when it saw its traditional opportunities to borrow from them volatilize. These four

---

[1]*Annali*, 716.

banks, he writes, used to be called the four pillars of the state: "se soleva chiamar . . . le quattro colone del tempio."[2]

In 1499 two "pillars" collapsed, and the other two were in danger of crumbling; was the state itself actually in danger of losing its trustworthiness as a result? Or could it be, as some suspected, that the government's failure to repay loans promptly had forced the banks to declare their insolvency? And again, just how important were the lines of credit offered by Rialto banks to the state? "Pecunia nervus belli" is a truism and holds for all times and all places. In the case of Venice, the readiness of Rialto banks to lend money in times of war was a crucial factor in maintaining its military strength.[3] But loans by private banks to the state became regular and almost daily operations in the fifteenth century, even in peacetime and for expenditures that can hardly be called extraordinary. In short, the banks took over from the Grain Office the management of Venice's floating debt and expanded it into an essential part of the banking system.

This topic is by no means new to Venetian historiography. In the nineteenth century, Francesco Ferrara, a leading political economist, dealt at length with the question, polemicizing with Elia Lattes in the debate over the "freedom" — or lack thereof — of the Italian banking sector.[4] On the basis of senatorial deliberations showing the banks constantly lending to the state, Ferrara argued that Venice's banks, besides being regulated according to a "monastic discipline," were enchained by their very role as cashier ("cassa comune"), that is, as administrators of the state's floating debt. For Ferrara, furthermore, the Venetian state itself was humiliated by its having to resort to bank loans to pay even petty expenses. The second half of the fifteenth century, the period of heaviest lending by the banks,

---

[2]"Vedando la Signoria che addesso la no ha da poderse valer del danaro dei Banchi ad imprestido, come l'ha fatto altre volte (che se soleva chiamar i quattro Banchi, le quattro colone del tempio), subito l'ha mandà chiamar i officiali." Ibid., 531–32. The phrase recalls Giovanni Villani's dictum according to which the largest merchant-banking firms of early-fourteenth-century Florence were "le colonne della cristianità." Giovanni Villani, *Cronica*, ed. F. G. Dragomanni, 4 vols. (Florence, 1844–45), bk. 11, lxxxviii, and de Roover, *Medici Bank*, 2.

[3]Particularly telling is this preamble to a senatorial deliberation, dating from the beginning of the Ferrara war: "Omnes intelligunt fundamentum omnium rerum nostrarum consistere precipue in habendis pecuniis necessariis pro possendo providere necessitatibus occurrentibus" — whereupon followed a request for a loan from the Soranzo bank for 10,000 ducats, guaranteed by revenues from two "decima" levies. Ferrara, "Documenti," doc. 88 (22 May 1482); also idem, "Antichi banchi," 210. It would, of course, be interesting to be able to compare the recourse to credit of both sides in a war. See, for example, Francesco Sforza's call for a loan of 60,000 ducats in 1454 in the war against Venice; two defeats were imputed to lack of money. See Francesca Levarotti, "Ricerche sulle origini dell'Ospedale Maggiore di Milano," *Archivio storico lombardo* 107 (1981): 80.

[4]Lattes held the view that private banks should be free to be banks of issue; to that extent, Venetian banks, relatively unregulated, could provide a model in the debate whether or not the state should be the only issuer of notes. *Libertà*, 24–25. The rebuttal is in Ferrara, "Antichi banchi," 458–66.

concluded Ferrara, corresponded with the period of Venice's unarrestable decline.[5]

This chapter reexamines the relationship between the banks of the Rialto and the Venetian state, dealing with such questions as the reasons for borrowing and how much was borrowed; which banks lent money and under what forms; what banks might have received in return for their loans. Before beginning, however, a word about the sources and the economic significance of this form of bank credit is in order.

The primary source consists of loan authorizations found among the deliberations of the Senate. Francesco Ferrara published 161 documents primarily of that kind. There are hundreds more among the very series exploited by Ferrara and in other legislative series of the Senate itself, in the Council of Ten, and in the Collegio alle Biave, which supervised the annona. At the same time, Ferrara's collection is sufficient for understanding the nature of the floating debt. Ferrara also took the trouble of adding up the loans, bank by bank, for which he had found authorizations. Such totals are meaningless, however, and misleading; what is significant is the volume of "float."[6]

In economic terms, therefore, it is important to stress the fact that the credit relationship between the state and the banks involved in practice the monetization of the floating debt. While many loans were made in cash, many others were made in bank money.[7] When what was lent was promises, a credit on the current account of a creditor of the state, then the banker was creating money. He was substituting his promise to pay for that of the state, on the basis of the state's promise to repay him. The supplier of goods and services to the state could then draw on the account to make his own payments by bank transfer. The same was true even without an authorized loan, when the banker discounted a private party's credit due from the state. The result was the creation and the potential multiple expansion of fiduciary money. Cash loans, on the other hand, to the extent that they reduced reserves, could cause a contraction — potentially multiple — of the money supply, particularly when the specie borrowed left the market, loaded onto ships headed, for example, for the Mediterranean's wheat-exporting regions.

In administrative terms, finally, the lines of credit which private banks made available to the state oiled the gears of government finance; they reduced red tape and delays, thus favoring private suppliers. Complication

---

[5]"Antichi banchi," 211–13; the author agreed with the pope's analysis and concluded, "Venezia è finita oramai."

[6]A spot check shows mentions of twenty-four loan authorizations in ASV, SMar, rubrica, reg. 2, fol. 44v, for regs. 11–12 (1478–84); a dozen more are in reg. 1, covering regs. 1–10 (1440–77).

[7]The verbs used in the deliberations do not distinguish between the two kinds of loan; most laws use *mutuare*, others *servire, accomodare, concedere, subvenire, promittere*.

and confusion, in any case, were postponed until it was the turn of the state to repay the banks. To what extent this kind of floating debt favored modernization and rationalization within the Venetian state machine remains an open question; a positive reply has been proposed for other areas.[8]

ii. SCOPE AND VOLUME OF LOANS

It is true, as Francesco Ferrara observed, that many senatorial requests for bank loans involved small sums, from as low as 25 ducats to a few hundred or a thousand ducats, to send off an ambassador or to receive a foreign dignitary or merely to send off a courier. These were expenditures, only superficially "extraordinary," which the central Treasury seems not to have been in a position to meet. The same, of course, had been true in the thirteenth and fourteenth centuries when especially ambassadorial expenses were often met with loans from the Grain Office when it functioned as a quasi-public bank. In the fifteenth century such relatively small loans often involved paying a draft or advancing the money needed for a remittance to facilitate the activity of diplomats abroad.[9] Or they might be needed for such unforeseen conspicuous expenditures as to wish a newly elected pope well or to welcome a visiting emperor,[10] or even for extraordinary charities.[11] Sizeable bank loans of 10,000–20,000 ducats are rather more under-

[8]Mario Del Treppo shows how the extension of credit by foreign, especially Florentine, merchant bankers in the kingdom of Naples in the fifteenth century, via a system of bank transfer (the "detta piana della Corte"), rationalized and modernized the finances of the realm; see his "I catalani a Napoli e le loro pratiche con la Corte," *Studi di storia meridionale in memoria di Pietro Laveglia* (Salerno, 1994), 71–97, and, more specifically on the role of the Strozzi bank, which did more than one-third of its business with the state, "Il re e il banchiere: Strumenti e processi di razionalizzazione dello stato aragonese di Napoli," in *Spazio, società, potere nell'Italia dei Comuni*, ed. Gabriella Rossetti (Naples, 1986), 229–304. Merchant bankers in Florence itself were also called upon to lend to the state, at least in the years of heavy military expenditures (1425–33); the bankers actually constituted an office of the floating debt, the Ufficiali del Banco, where they administered directly their own loans to the state, made via lucrative dry exchange contracts; see Molho, *Florentine Public Finances*, 166–82.

[9]For loans involving the use of bills of exchange, see, for example, Ferrara, "Documenti," docs. 13, 26, 29, 31–33, 131, 135, and numerous other such documents in ASV, SM and ST; for example, SM, reg. 60, fol. 162 (25 July 1439).

[10]Giovanni Soranzo lent 1,000 ducats "pro mantis sericeis seu veluteis decem oratorum designatorum ad summum pontificem" when the Venetian Pietro Barbo was elected Paul II. ASV, ST, reg. 5, fol. 94 (2 October 1464). Benedetto Soranzo, a clergyman in Rome, drew on his brothers in Venice so he could lend 1,500 ducats to the embassy to Pope Innocent VIII. Ibid., reg. 9, fol. 153 (23 July 1485). Banks in general were asked for 1,000 ducats in order to greet Emperor Frederick III "secundum dignitatem nostri dominii." Ibid., reg. 6, fol. 46v (10 January 1469).

[11]The state granted 1,000 ducats "amore Dei" to the Franciscans, who were holding their general chapter in Venice, but had to borrow the sum from the Garzoni. ASV, ST, reg. 6, fol. 43 (12 December 1468). When the salt pans were ruined in 1462, special loans were made to aid the "poor Chioggians." SMar, reg. 7, fols. 69v–70v.

standable, whether they were for arms suppliers, mercenaries, or seamen's salaries, prompt payment of which was critical for "national security" or for maintenance of social peace.[12] Loans that consolidated various government debts of these kinds could become quite large; in 1412, for example, the bank of Andrea Priuli offered to pay up to 60,000 ducats to suppliers of goods and services to the state.[13] Quite extraordinary was the request that the same bank advance the huge reward of 35,000 ducats offered for the assassination of Venice's mortal enemies, King Sigismund and Brunoro della Scala in 1415 (the banker was even commissioned by the Council of Ten to arrange the assassination).[14] Perhaps the largest single category of loans involved bank guarantees for wheat importers, as we shall see below in more detail.

Bank loans were meant to be mere advances of specific moneys that the state expected to receive from its revenue-collecting offices. Such specific future revenues were earmarked or "obligated" for repayment of the bank. Originally, the most commonly obligated funds came from forced loans, until around midcentury, when bank loans were often sought precisely in order to avoid having to impose forced loans on the taxpaying population. Then, when possible, repayment was more often than not promised from the Salt Office and the fiscal treasuries of the subject territories of the Terraferma.[15] Later in the century loans were often tied to specific numbered levies of the decima tax as a guarantee of their repayment.[16]

How much money might Venetian banks have made available to the state? To give an idea of the importance of bank credit in Venice, Francesco Ferrara compiled a table of loans, admittedly incomplete, for the half century 1457 to 1507. The total, a relatively meaningless figure, comes to nearly 770,000 ducats. The best observation that the list can support is a vague idea of the order in which lending banks appeared: preeminent was the Soranzo bank (40% of the total), second was the Bernardo-Garzoni bank (22%).

[12]Giovanni Soranzo came across with 680 ducats in order to pay the salaries of galeotti; these had "created a tumult" on the festive day of the "Sensa" around the doge and the Signoria, demonstrating to have their back pay. ASV, ST, reg. 4, fol. 73 (18 May 1458).

[13]See Mueller, "Role of Bank Money," 80.

[14]ASV, Consiglio dei Dieci, Miste, reg. 9, vol. 140 (3 July 1415); Sigismund is called "atrocissimus inimicus nostri dominii." The same banker, Andrea Priuli, in the role of inquisitor of the Council of Ten two years later, paid a reward of 2,000 ducats to those who had turned over Giorgio Bragadin, condemned traitor; he was then given a license to bear arms (ibid., fols. 160, 167). On the close rapport of Brunoro with Sigismund, see Wolf Weigand, "Gli Scaligeri dopo gli Scaligeri," in Varanini, *Gli Scaligeri,* 92. The charge given to Priuli is mentioned in the general context by Wolfgang von Stromer, "Landmacht gegen Seemacht: Kaiser Sigismunds Kontinentalsperre gegen Venedig, 1412–1433," *Zeitschrift für Historische Forschung* 22 (1995): 145–90.

[15]Bank loans were made in the mid-fifteenth century specifically "pro non faciendis impositionibus." See ASV, ST, reg. 2, fols. 133v, 141 (1450). For the whole gamut of repayment schemes, see Ferrara, "Documenti."

[16]See, for example, Ferrara, "Documenti," docs. 88–89 (1482).

Something like 40 and 20–25 percent respectively seems like a plausible proportion for these two banks, the most long-lived in Venetian banking history. At the time of the failure and rehabilitation of the Garzoni, however, that family of bankers asserted that they alone, between 1470 and 1499, had lent to the state "from time to time, at the request of the Signoria" a total of 1,200,000 ducats. That figure, best reformulated as a perfectly credible 40,000 ducats per year average, was presented as proof of the bank's merit and fidelity in support of an extraordinary petition; it was arrived at, they said, from ledgers that they brought to the Signoria as proof.[17] Should one wish to hazard deriving a hypothetical total for the whole banking system from this figure, as Ferrara let himself be tempted to do, a simple multiplication by four would give a total of about 5 million ducats in loans from all banks during the three decades considered.[18]

It is important to underscore immediately, however, that this or any long-term total is misleading and, in economic terms, meaningless. The sources on which a table like Ferrara's is based represent only one side of the balance sheet. Actually, the state was constantly, if irregularly, making payments on its obligations. True, hints of actual repayments are only rarely found in extant documents, but repayments on old loans were continual, and total outstanding obligations therefore were constantly changing; it was, after all, a floating debt, and in monetary terms it is the "float" that matters in any calculation of the level of the money supply.

Rather more useful, for forming an idea of the amounts of money involved in the banks' lines of credit, are totals of known loans for shorter periods. If we consider, for example, the activity of the bank of Giovanni Soranzo, cousin of Benetto, from June 1462 to October 1464, before and in the early stages of the war against the Turks (July 1463–79), we find that the bank was called upon at least thirty-two times, to lend a total of about 110,000 ducats, a low average of about 3,400 ducats per loan. To be sure, the amounts of single loans increased significantly once the war began, but low figures are still found.[19] If we look at a single year, 1465, on the other hand, we can see that Giovanni Soranzo was by no means alone. Piero Guerrucci, who had lent 15,200 ducats in March and 13,500 on 6 May, was recorded on

---

[17]Ibid., doc. 136, and "Antichi banchi," 208. The correct date is 30 January 1500 — the last day of their one-year moratorium and the day before they reopened. (The successful request was for a guarantee by the Signoria of 20,000 ducats, to add to the 50,000 ducats arranged with private guarantors.) Gerolamo Priuli reports that the petition was justified as follows: "cum sit che per il passato a li bisogni de la Signoria nostra questo bancho sempre sia stato cortese et voluntarosso a servirlla, dimostrando aver servito la Signoria veneta dal 1471 fino a questo giorno per li soi libri de bancho de duc. uno milion ed duc. 200 m. d'oro." Priuli, *Diarii,* 1:260.

[18]Assuming 1.2 million to be one-fourth of all loans; Ferrara toys, furthermore, with conversions into lire of the newly founded Italian state. "Antichi banchi," 208.

[19]Most of the data can be found in Ferrara, "Documenti," docs. 33–57. Twice the sum to be lent is unspecified. Of the ten unpublished documents, most come from the same sources cited by Ferrara, two from SMar.

8 May as being creditor for 17,700 when he offered to lend an additional 20,000, for a total debt of 37,700. On the same occasion the Garzoni extended 12,500 ducats of new loans. In mid-September the Soranzo bank was creditor for about 40,000 ducats. At the same date, Guerrucci lent another 10,000 ducats, and a few weeks later Agostino Ziera lent 9,000 ducats. In times of need, the whole Rialto was mobilized—the "pillars of the temple," indeed. Rival states, like Milan, were well aware, at this very time, of the reliance of Venice on its banks.[20]

A further sample period can be created with data of the mid-1470s, with Venice still at war against the Turks. In those years, four banks operated on the Rialto: Soranzo, Garzoni, Pisani, and Barbarigo. The latter is only rarely mentioned in senatorial authorizations for loans, but Malipiero says that it, too, lent money.[21] An incomplete list of sums lent, relatively evenly divided among the Soranzo, Garzoni, and Pisani banks (some deliberations read simply "all banks"), is given in table 10.1.

A minimum of some 300,000 ducats was lent in three years. Repayment of most of the loans was tied to the Salt Office, which usually paid in monthly installments—when it could.

A final example can be taken from information compiled by Sanudo in the first year of the Ferrara war. In six months, from 14 May to 29 November 1482, the Senate authorized loans totaling more than 115,000 ducats, from all four banks then operating.[22] In the second half of 1483, loans for at least 107,000 ducats are recorded[23]—and this at a time when the new forced loan fund, the Monte Nuovo, was functioning extremely well.

All these figures, undoubtedly high, are dwarfed, however, when they are compared, on the one hand, with gross annual receipts of more than 1 million ducats, in the second half of the fifteenth century, and, on the other hand, with the enormous costs of war. The latter were estimated by con-

---

[20]ASV, ST, reg. 5, fols. 113v (21 March) and 136 (16 September), 138 (23 September: 5,000 ducats "sibi restituendos cum nostra commoditate"!), 139 (1 October), 144 (7 December). See also Ferrara, "Documenti," docs. 62, 105, 157. Soranzo is indicated in July (doc. 59) as creditor for 19,000 ducats; on fol. 136, 16 September, as creditor for 41,310 ducats; a later document (doc. 62) says that on that same 16 September he had been creditor for 33,414 ducats. Galeazzo Sforza in 1466 said to the Venetian secretary Gonella, "We know you are in trouble; you cannot collect the decime and so you borrow from banks and private citizens." Romanin, *Storia documentata*, 4:329 (citing SSec, reg. 23, fol. 86).

[21]*Annali*, 69 (referring to 1471, when Guerrucci was still in business and before the Pisani had begun): "e cadaun d'essi i ha imprestà alla Signoria pur assai danari."

[22]*Vite*, 1:271–72, 281, 286, 300, 306, 311; for loans by private parties: 297–98. Sanudo's figures are almost exactly the same as those excerpted from Senate records and listed by Ferrara, "Antichi banchi," 206.

[23]Ferrara, "Antichi banchi," 206. A measure of the straits in which Venice found itself is this: the last loan of the year 1483, 6,500 ducats from the bank of Francesco Pisani, was to be repaid from coins struck from the necklaces and silverware that citizens were to bring to the mint. ASV, ST, reg. 9, fol. 48 (30 December).

TABLE 10.1

Bank Loans to the State, 1473–1475
(in ducats)

Date	Amount	Date	Amount
1473, 16.2	9,000	1475, 21.2	18,500
24.4	8,000	4.3	14,000
3.5	4,000	11.4–4.7	45,000
1.6	10,000	26.10	16,000
14.12	24,000	12.12	24,000
1474, 15.3	10,000	16.12	8,000
9.5	12,000		
17.6	10,000		Total: 297,500
26.10	23,000		
22.12	24,000		

Note: The years 1474–75 were not included in Ferrara's table. The data come only from senatorial deliberations, from ST (only the figure from 9 May 1474 was taken from SMar [reg. 10, fol. 7], which was not checked further); possible authorizations by the Council of Ten were not investigated here. ASV, ST, reg. 6, fol. 197v; reg. 7, fols. 5r–v, 8, 25, 31v, 42, 56v, 62v, 67, 68v, 72v, 78r–v, 93v–94, 99, 100v.

temporaries to be 700,000 (or even 1.2 million) ducats per year around 1470, during the naval war against the Turks, 2 million ducats total during the two-year Ferrara war.[24] Finally, if total obligations outstanding at any given moment to any single bank did not exceed about 40,000 ducats, which seems reasonable, that figure would have to be compared with total liabilities. At the end of the century, deposits in a large bank were probably about 300,000 ducats, perhaps 1 million ducats in the banking system as a whole.[25] The ability of the state to repay the banks on schedule, of course, was reduced during wartime; still, it seems true that borrowing by the government and eventual delays in repayments cannot be considered the cause of the financial difficulties or of the failures of Venetian banks. Only two instances point to a different conclusion. In 1473 the defaulting banker Piero Guerrucci, appearing before the Signoria to ask for a safe-conduct, blamed the state for his failure, or rather he blamed himself for having been too generous in lending to the state. When it came down to fixing what was owed, however, the banker turned out to be creditor of only 2,000 ducats outright, with another 8,000 ducats under lien, for a relatively small total (see above, Chap. 5, sec. v). When the Garzoni failed on 31 January 1499, it was rumored that the government was at fault for not having repaid loans. In fact, the state had repaid 30,000 ducats a few weeks earlier and was

[24]See Gaetano Cozzi and Michael Knapton, *Storia della Repubblica di Venezia: Dalla guerra di Chioggia alla riconquista della Terraferma* (Turin, 1986), 301–2.
[25]Lane, "Venetian Bankers," 72.

debtor for only 5,000 ducats at the time. Similarly, when Gerolamo Priuli failed in 1513, the state owed him only 6,000 ducats.[26] While only comparatively small sums were involved in these cases, however, the rumor that a bank was owed large sums by an impecunious government would certainly have contributed to the mania of a run (see above, Chap. 6, sec. ii).

As mentioned previously, a specific sector of the public economy in which bank credits became especially important was that of the annona. The claims of grain merchants had to be honored and on schedule, for the successful provisioning of the city and thus the very stability of the society was at stake. When the state demonstrated its incapacity to pay in cash according to the schedule agreed upon by contract, merchants began to insist on the inclusion, in the contract itself, of a "detta di banco," that is, of a guarantee that a named bank would step in to pay should the resources originally earmarked for payment be insufficient or even nonexistent. The guarantee might be requested by any creditor who doubted the solvency of the government: a hemp wholesaler, the seller of a palazzo intended as a gift for one of Venice's mercenary captains, or a seller of copper needed for casting bombards.[27] "Dette" were most commonly invoked, however, by importers of wheat for the annona. In practice, the guarantee meant that the bank would pay.

Take, for example, the case in 1468 when the annona was in arrears "for months and years" to importers who had been promised payment from the "tratta" or sale of the wheat they had delivered. Much of the wheat delivered had in fact not been sold but had been used to pay galeotti their back pay ("refusura") in kind and thus had not produced revenue. The Senate therefore ordered the grain officials to have Rialto banks pay sums totaling about 22,000 ducats "so that these merchants [would] continue to import wheat." Willing bankers were to be guaranteed repayment from the Camera Fiscale of Treviso — admittedly already burdened with similar obligations.[28] It was less complicated, however, to include the guarantee in the contract from the outset.

---

[26]Sanudo, *Diarii*, 17:354, 369.

[27]ASV, SM, reg. 59, fol. 20 (3 December 1433): all hemp merchants refused to sell "nisi sint caute et habeant aliquem banchum pro responsore solutionum suarum"; the Soranzo agreed to give their "promissio solutionis." Ferrara, "Documenti," doc. 130 (1484), where the Garzoni agree to pay the seller of a palazzo an unspecified sum of money in three annual installments; obligated to the Garzoni was the Salt Office, although it was already overburdened with similar debts. Sanudo says the palace ("casa . . . bellissima" on the Grand Canal at S. Giacomo), sold by the jeweler Domenico di Piero for 10,000 ducats, was paid for in two installments by the Pisani bank, in favor of Roberto Sanseverino. *Commentarii della guerra di Ferrara*, ed. Pietro Bettio (Venice, 1829), 108. In 1495 "German merchants," meaning in all probability the Fuggers, were ready to sell nearly 40 tons of copper to Venice as long as they had a "dicta banchi" to receive half on 1 August, half on 1 January 1496; again the Garzoni stepped in. Simonsfeld, *Der Fondaco*, 1:324–25, doc. 597.

[28]ASV, ST, reg. 6, fol. 19v (19 May 1468).

Scattered cases of bank guarantees are extant from the first half of the fifteenth century,[29] but they become very common in the second half of the century and are insisted upon by Venetians and foreigners alike. In 1472 Giovanni de Strigis, in the name of the marquis of Mantua, offered to sell wheat to Venice if he would receive "half in gold in advance and half in bank upon consignment."[30] A few years later Giovanni d'Orsino Lanfredini, manager of the Medici branch in Venice, contracted to deliver wheat on condition that a bank would promise to pay as each shipment arrived; the Garzoni guaranteed the needed 45,000 ducats.[31] In the 1480s many contracts were made with "detta di banco,"[32] backed generally with revenues from sales of the wheat itself and from the Camera of Treviso. The latter in 1486 was obligated to bankers and merchants for 30,000 ducats, while at the same time it was creditor for many "easily collectable dues." The Collegio delle Biave decided that the credits should be collected and the debts paid off so that the Camera's revenues could be used directly to guarantee contracts for wheat deliveries "so as to avoid the trouble of having to find banks that [would] agree to give their promise to pay."[33] But that was wishful thinking.

During the famine of 1496 and 1497, with wheat prices at record levels, Venetian firms like Andrea di Nicolò Loredan and Stefano and Teodosio Contarini, Spanish Jews like Alfonso and Giovanni Sanchez, and certain Marranos agreed to find and deliver wheat to Venice only if guaranteed with a "detta di banco" — and usually with a bonus. Sanudo praised the annona for its successful resolution of the crisis, despite the costs involved. Speculation in wheat placed the banks under pressure; risks were high as

[29]See, for example, ASV, SM, reg. 50, fol. 130 (19 July 1414); reg. 60, fol. 134 (28 March 1439); ST, reg. 2, fol. 27 (4 April 1447); CN, reg. 8, fol. 164 (13 July 1452): Marco Priuli and brothers had contracted to deliver wheat, "sed . . . volunt habere securitatem unius banchi sicut eis promissum est, ita quod ad terminum eis debite satisfiat"; the Ziera bank agreed.

[30]ASMN, Carteggio estero (da inviati a Venezia), b. 1431, under the date 31 May 1472, shortly after Venice had demonetized its silver.

[31]ASV, ST, reg. 7, fols. 72v, 73v, 78v (1475). Further imports, not guaranteed by a bank, were made in 1478 for which the state was indebted to the Medici for 12,000 ducats, to Angelo Baldesi for 6,000 ducats. Lanfredini is then called "socius Medicorum et Angeli Baldesi." Provveditori alle Biave, b. 2, libro 3, fol. 102r–v. In 1476 Angelo Baldese was in need of specie more quickly than the monthly installments of 1,000 ducats he had agreed upon with the grain officials, who agreed to help "in questo so bixogno" by having the Pisani bank advance the money; the bank was then to receive 2,000 ducats monthly from the Camera of Treviso and from the sale of wheat. Provveditori alle Biave, b. 2, libro 3, fol. 85v.

[32]ASV, Provveditori alle Biave, b. 2, libro 4, fols. 24v (12 February 1485, Council of Ten), 25v (7 May 1485, Collegio alle Biave), 28v (5 July 1486) — a sequel to Ferrara, "Documenti," doc. 134.

[33]ASV, Provveditori alle Biave, b. 2, libro 4, fol. 27 (18 May 1486): "Et volendo reintegrar el credito et la reputation a lo offitio de le biave, hora seria el tempo; . . . se troveria mercadanti che, vedendo la camera libera, venderiano a lo offitio senza detta de bancho, . . . senza haver più faticha de trovar banchi che facino la detta."

ships carrying specie to Sicily were threatened by pirates; finally, wheat had to be sold to the public below cost.[34] Between 1497 and 1499 prices declined, but the system remained the same: importers wanted bank guarantees that they would be paid in the cadenced form (now often twelve and eighteen months after delivery) stipulated in the contracts.[35] In 1499, contracts made before the failures of the Garzoni and Lippomano still called for payment via "dette di banco," but in February 1499, after the failure of the Garzoni, the remaining banks backed out of guarantees already provided, and other solutions had to be found quickly.[36]

iii. WHO LENT AND HOW?

One solution to financial problems which presented itself at various times during the century was that the state name a depositary to flank or even to substitute for the central Treasury. Had a Venetian bank or had the Rialto banks together been designated as the state's depositary, reliance on the banks even for petty credit would have been more efficient. But Venice refused to take the step that Francesco de' Medici, grand duke of Tuscany, would take in the second half of the sixteenth century, when he designated the de' Ricci bank of Florence to be official depositary. That privileged position as receiver and payer of the grand duchy's accounts greatly strengthened the bank's role in the local marketplace; in fact, the bank outdistanced all competitors.[37] In Venice, on the other hand, only rarely were state offices directed to deposit revenues in a bank independently of specific obligations they were to repay.

Proposals to inaugurate a service vaguely approximating that of a depositary were usually rejected outright or were restricted to simple, ad hoc operations, more like conditioned deposits.[38] A proposal made in 1388,

---

[34]On the famine and provisioning, see Sanudo, *Diarii*, 1:81, 261, 459, 507, 535, 554–55, 558, 605, 699, 709, 743 (mention of the corsairs), 751 (on the Marranos), 752, 755, 760, 771; on the deal with the Sanchez brothers, for a total of 60,000 ducats and 10,000 ducats "dono," see ibid., 535, and ASV, Provveditori alle Biave, b. 2, libro 4, fol. 59v (27 January 1497), when the Lippomano bank gave its "detta."

[35]Deliberations in the Council of Ten, agreements with the Lippomano bank, and the reckonning of deliveries can be found in ASV, Consiglio dei Dieci, Miste, filza 12, fol. 155 and allegati 1–4 (1497–98).

[36]Ibid., fol. 317, allegati 1–2; Andrea Loredan and the Contarini asked that "li sia dato una dicta de bancho, chè ai suo tempi i habia i suo danari senza niuna contradiction." Ibid., reg. 27, fol. 262r–v (20 February 1499): "et dapoi fatto cum essi banchi ogni debita experientia et non volendo essi banchi far le ditte promesse," the Council of Ten sought to resolve matters between its own treasury and the Camera of Treviso.

[37]See Carlo M. Cipolla, *La moneta a Firenze nel Cinquecento* (Bologna, 1987), chap. 6.

[38]The earliest case of a deposit for a specific reason dates from 1287 when the nobleman Pietro Sesendolo lent 2,000 lire for an embassy to Tunis, seemingly in Tunis itself. The Treasurers were ordered to deposit 200 lire per month in the shop (and bank) of the Bollani, who

for example, to deposit 6,000 ducats in two banks instead of in the Procuratia, clearly meant to favor them in return for their demonstrated readiness to lend to the state, was voted down.[39] Twice credits on bankers' books were withdrawn by the state "so that the money [would appear] on communal accounts."[40] An order to the Governatori delle Entrate in 1439 to pay 1,500 ducats per month into the Soranzo bank, which would in turn repay other creditors of the state, was rescinded after only six weeks.[41] A uniquely convoluted but isolated operation was a loan of 18,300 ducats from the Procurators de Citra—that is, from the estates they administered—to the state in 1427; the loan was made to pass through the Priuli bank.[42] In midcentury a proposal to deposit funds in the banks to facilitate their guaranteeing payment to wheat importers was passed almost unanimously, but there is no indication that the law was ever translated into practice.[43] At the end of the century relatively small sums were ordered deposited at Rialto banks in decisions that were seen as merited favors to the banks, favors that would make them more willing to lend further.[44] Such sums were too insignificant, however, to constitute more than a kind of moral support of

---

would repay the creditor at the end of a year, with interest at the rate they would normally pay depositors (to a maximum of 10 percent). *PRV,* doc. 47.

[39]ASV, SSec, reg. E, copia, fol. 99v (27 September 1388).

[40]ASV, SM, reg. 47, fol. 92 (19 February 1407); Ferrara, "Documenti," doc. 9 (1447). Both credits were on the Soranzo bank.

[41]ASV, SM, reg. 60, fols. 142, 152 (4 May, 16 June 1439); the Procuratori de Supra were then to collect the money and pay it out.

[42]Ibid., reg. 56, fols. 84v, 91v, 118v (6 March, 16 April, 17 August 1427). The bank was that of the Estate of Andrea Priuli and Bartolomeo Priuli. The loan was deposited in the bank; the Priuli were, in turn, to lend ("mutuare") the money to the state and to guarantee to the Procurators full restitution. The loan was originally declared "payable on demand," but when the Procurators pressed, the Senate told them not to "molestare vel astringere" the bank, for they did not have urgent need of the money.

[43]In 1451 a provision was passed—with only three abstentions—calling for the Provveditori alle Biave to deposit "in banchis Rivoalti" all the money received from sales of wheat flour, "tam pro plezaria sive securitate illorum qui dabunt de frumentis nostro communi, quam etiam pro solutione fienda de tempore in tempus de frumentis predictis sicut iuxta emptiones Venetias conducentur." ASV, ST, reg. 3, fol. 10 (27 November). More like a conditioned deposit is the order to the Patroni of the arsenal in 1449 to deposit 80 ducats per month in the Soranzo bank to pay for construction of a roof. CN, reg. 8, fol. 101.

[44]ASV, ST, reg. 11, fol. 105v (20 March 1492): 3,000 ducats were to be transferred from the Procurators' depository to the banks for the payment of importers of wine. "Et perchè si chome i banchi nostri hanno servito la Signoria nostra de bona summa de denari per el sfalchar del Monte nuovo, cossì etiam è conveniente accomodar quelli et maxime ne le cosse non sono detrimentose nè a la Signoria nostra, nè ad alcuno privato citadin nostro." In 1489 revenues from a tax on wheat imports, estimated at 200 ducats per month, were to be deposited in the banks. Provveditori alle Biave, b. 2, reg. 4, fols. 32v (12 August 1489, also in Banco giro, unnumbered volume entitled "Terminazioni e decreti, 1300–1738," fol. 3v) and 36v (25 February 1491). On the latter date, the Signoria called for cash from the deposit at Vettor Soranzo's bank and ordered those revenues to be deposited over the coming months at the Garzoni bank as repayment for bills of exchange the bank had honored.

the banks' liquidity. Finally, the Loan Office in 1488 was taken to task for the manner in which it handled the payment of interest, and officials were prohibited from borrowing money and from making deposits at banks; officials were threatened with heavy fines for contravening the order, making it probable that some kind of understanding had existed between this office and the banks.[45] But again, not enough was at stake that one could consider Rialto banks to have been depositaries for the state.

Even though Venetian banks did not become depositaries, they nonetheless played a role in state finance and had an influence on decision making which only rarely transpires from extant documentation but which must have been nearly quotidian. The occasions on which we get a glimpse inside the system all involve different generations of the Soranzo bank, which clearly held a position of preeminence during its long existence. It is worthwhile looking at the role of the Soranzo separately, therefore, even though it is important to remember that, despite its real preeminence, the Soranzo bank was never alone in oiling the wheels of government finance.

Gabriele Soranzo, along with his competitor on the Rialto Pietro Benedetto, probably inaugurated the practice of regular lending to the state in the years following the War of Chioggia.[46] When in the years 1387–90 the Senate granted special privileges to the two bankers, "considering their laudable comportment in favor of the state," the meaning is clear: they had been lending money to the Signoria.[47] Just how direct contacts between public and private financiers took place is not known, but one encounter is telling. In 1391 Gabriele Soranzo accompanied the ducal councillor Francesco Bragadin to the office of the Treasury (just a few steps away from the banks, at the Rialto) in order to check whether 500 ducats that he had offered to lend had been written to his credit. The treasurer Giacomo Tiepolo overheard Soranzo offer the councillor a further sum of money and felt bound to interject, "To borrow money from bankers in this manner is to act to the detriment of the Commune." An argument ensued, and Soranzo insulted the treasurer, for which he was fined. Very likely the treasurer was protesting against a relatively recent innovation in government finance, but evidence presented in court also shows that the banker moved — unofficially — in the highest circles of government and had no difficulty in gaining access to the books of the Treasury and in keeping track of his own interests.[48]

---

[45]ASV, ST, reg. 10, fols. 96–97 (17 May 1488).

[46]Evidence of bank loans to the state before the war is very rare. In 1358, when the Senate ordered repayment, inter alia, of remittances to Avignon, totaling 21,000 ducats, advanced by the banker Francesco Iuda, the deliberation asserted that he was always ready to lend: "Cum . . . semper fuerit et sit promptus ad complacendum nobis in subveniendo liberaliter de bancho suo in necessitatibus omnibus nostri comunis." ASV, SM, reg. 28, fol. 27v–28v (19, 22, 28 February). During the Chioggia war, Bartolomeo d'Acherisio, the banker who was later murdered, was said to have made many loans to the state from his bank.

[47]Lattes, *Libertà,* docs. 9–11 (1387–90).

[48]ASV, AC, reg. 3644, fol. 74v (12 July 1391).

Yet stronger ties are visible in the case of Benetto Soranzo, grandson of Gabriele, who was invited to sit in "at will" at meetings of the Signoria and of the Collegio, so as better to receive orders for payment to the state's creditors and at the same time to solicit the state for repayment. When that admission of the Signoria's dependency on the banks was made in 1440, Benetto was not yet the principal but acted in the name of the firm headed by his older brother, Luca Soranzo.[49] In that period the bank was in fact making many and large loans to the state. In one case, in the previous year, the state had put up, as security for a loan by the Soranzo bank, certain government obligations that had been sequestered from Mantuan citizens in reprisal for the marquis of Mantua's volte-face in the current war. On that occasion, the Soranzo were told they could dispose of the government credits as they saw fit, and the Senate ordered the officials of the Loan Office to follow any orders they might receive from the Soranzo bankers in that regard "as though they were orders made by the Signoria"![50] After Luca's death, Benetto continued the policy of lending in the role of principal of the bank. His recorded loans between 1448 and 1452 far outnumber those of other banks; at one point in 1449 his current credit was placed at 25,500 ducats.[51]

The next generation of the family bank appears to have been even more active in government finance. Official accounts of the Procurators and deliberations of the Collegio delle Biave mirror the continual presence in the corridors of government of Giovanni Soranzo, the cousin who upheld the family name by refounding the bank after Benetto had failed for the second time in 1455. Giovanni was always ready to lend to the state, begin-

[49] "Cum dominatio nostra habuerit multas pecunias mutuo a bancho de cha' Superantio, pro factis multum importantibus ad statum nostrum, et in futurum etiam opus erit habere de aliis pecuniis et serviciis ab ipso bancho secundum occurentia rerum et temporum, propter quas causas oportet quod unus ex dictis fratribus et presertim nobilis vir Benedictus Superantio, qui habuit et habet hanc practicam et sollecitudinem serviendi nostro dominio, nomine suo et fratrum, quotidie veniat et sit ad presentiam nostri dominii, ac in collegio, tam pro habendo ordinem a nostro dominio in dando ipsas pecunias, quam in sollicitando habere sollutiones suas de tempore in tempus, et pro diversis causis utilibus et necessariis ad facta nostra, infrascripti [sex] consiliarii terminarunt quod dictus ser Benedictus Superantio venire possit et stare ad benplacitum suum in collegio, non obstante quod non esset sapiens terre nove, sicut facere poterat et posset si esset in ipso officio." ASV, CN, reg. 7, fol. 23 (23 December 1440).

[50] "Et quod officiales nostri imprestitorum ad omnem voluntatem dictorum a bancho de cha' Superantio sine conditione et expensis, faciant sicut volent predicti a bancho, quemadmodum si fieret per nostrum dominium." The Soranzo had just lent 20,000 ducats; assigned were government credits worth 50,000 ducats at par or about 11,000 at the market price; the Signoria was obligated for the balance due. ASV, SM, reg. 60, fol. 134 (28 March 1439). For Soranzo loans made in 1440, see ibid., fol. 185 (2 January); CN, reg. 7, fols. 11 and 18v (29 April, 17 July, on rechange); SM, reg. 60, fols. 212v, 214 (both 11 May), 220r–v (3 and 10 June), 236 (28 July).

[51] ASV, ST, reg. 2, fols. 68, 71v, 75, 78, 98, 107, 124 (1 December 1449 — date of the trial balance), 133v, 164, 201; reg. 3, fols. 12r–v, 48v. Although no loan authorizations regarding the Ziera bank seem to be recorded in this register, that bank had outstanding credits of 19,000 ducats on 7 May 1450; reg. 2, fol. 141.

ning in 1456.[52] We have already seen above how often and for how much his bank could be a point reference for a credit-hungary state.

Whether Giovanni Soranzo continued to be an invited guest in decision-making bodies as Benetto had been earlier is not known, but a small official account book that has survived can help in defining his role. In early November 1461 a fund (called the "depositum inferius") maintained by the office of the Procurators of San Marco de Ultra was revived.[53] In administering this fund, the Procurators took in specie from the peripheral treasuries (Camere Fiscali) of Treviso, Brescia, and Crema, as well as from the Salt Office, and turned specific sums of money over to the state Treasurers (Camerlenghi di Comun); the latter, in turn, made the actual payment to creditors of the state or to specific projects. In the midst of several accounting entries we find Giovanni Soranzo "a bancho," not always with a clear reason for his being there. Under the revenues ("introitus") section of the Procurators' account book, in 1462, we find Giovanni paying money into the fund "in the name of the treasurer of the Salt Office."[54] Under the expenditures ("exitus") section at almost the same time we find a payment of 3,000 ducats by the Procurators to the Treasury, "which Giovanni Soranzo a banco carried and paid out to the Treasury."[55] Perhaps this involved a Soranzo loan to the Procurators, who might not have had enough in the till to pay as ordered. Such a loan is indeed meant in another entry in which Soranzo "carried" to the Treasury 450 ducats — entered as a payment by the Procurators to the Treasury — which he had long before promised to lend to the Signoria to cover the value of drafts sent from Rome.[56]

[52]When in 1457 he was sent for by the Collegio delle Biave and was asked to lend 1,720 ducats to the annona because a forced loan was not being paid in on time, Soranzo replied, "cum amplissimis et humanissimis verbis," that he was ready to lend 10,000 and more ducats, "libere et sine aliqua utilitate," as long as repayment was guaranteed; ibid., reg. 4, fol. 53 (3 October), and Provveditori delle Biave, b. 1, libro 2, fol. 113v. In the following year a repayment was ordered made promptly, "per render el dicto ser Zuane più prompto per l'avegnir a servir la Signoria ne li occorenti bisogni"; CN, reg. 9, fol. 126v (18 May 1458); see also fol. 74 and Ferrara, "Documenti," doc. 16.

[53]The deliberation, ordering the Salt Office to turn over to the Procurators 6,000 ducats per month "infallibiliter," was passed on 20 October; in ASV, SSec, reg. 21, fol. 62v; also mentioned in CN, reg. 10, fol. 40 (where Soranzo insisted on receiving his due from the Salt Office before that deposit was made). The account book, a small "quaderno," is in PSM, Ultra, b. 424, fasc. 2, and covers eighteen months, from November 1461 to July 1463); it is a chance survival. In the following notes it will be referred to simply as the PSM account book.

[54]PSM account book, fols. 5v–6 (23 July, 4 September). Earlier in July money owed to Soranzo was diverted to the support of Chioggians whose salt pans had been destroyed, and he made another loan, to be repaid from the PSM depository — which does not explain but only complicates understanding the entries. See ASV, SMar, reg. 7, fols. 69v, 70v.

[55]PSM account book, fol. 15v (28 June 1462); involved was part of a sum of 10,000 ducats which Venice had promised to Hungary as aid against the Turks, in ASV, SSec, reg. 21, fol. 88r–v (5 May 1462).

[56]Enabling legislation is in Ferrara, "Documenti," doc. 36 (26 October 1462); PSM account

Three further entries in the same account book are clearly repayments to Soranzo for specific loans, of seemingly short duration. In the first instance the Procurators recorded having paid 1,000 ducats to the acting treasurer as repayment for a loan made by the banker—in the name of Venice—to the (would-be) queen of Cyprus, Carlotta, daughter of John II; the one who according to the entry "carried" the money from the Procurators to the Treasury was Giovanni Soranzo, the beneficiary himself.[57] The second and third instances involve three loans registered in a similar manner; they were very small loans, respectively, of 60 ducats needed for a ship carrying troops to Nauplion, of 5 ducats needed to send a courier to Rome, and of 90 ducats for the purchase of ship biscuit.[58] It can legitimately be doubted that the actions of the persons concerned were quite as convoluted as the accounting entries indicate; probably Soranzo just took the money back to his bank while the Procurators simply informed the Treasury of the transaction, perhaps with a written memorandum. In any case, the prominent Rialto banker seems from these accounts often to have been present personally in important bureaus where he was needed for the smooth running of government finances, even though his bank was not a depositary.[59]

Among the operations facilitated by Giovanni Soranzo's lines of credit were purchases of wheat by the annona. The banker extended credit to importers of wheat or guaranteed payment for imports contracted by the state. Sometimes we find him (as we later find other bankers also) acting as an importer of wheat himself.[60] Other times he is actually authorized to deal with importers in the name of the powerful Collegio delle Biave itself and to promote the efficiency of the annona. In 1464 Soranzo was to make an agreement with the Venetian branch of the Florentine firm of Angelo Bal-

---

book, fol. 18 (15 March and 13 April 1463). The entry says that the money was paid to Andrea Boldù, chief Treasurer, on the basis of orders-to-pay ("cedule") sent by the Signoria.

[57]PSM account book, fol. 16 (4 September 1462). The order to make the loan, with money taken "ex omni loco," does not mention the banker; see SSec, reg. 21, fol. 107 (2 September). From the dates recorded, it would seem that this credit was only of one or two days' duration.

[58]PSM account book, fol. 18v (11 and 24 May 1463). For senatorial recognition that the loans had been made and for orders to repay from the Procurators' depository "subito . . . ut iustum est," see Ferrara, "Documenti," doc. 38 (7 May), and SMar, reg.7, fol. 116v (23 May).

[59]The Procurators' depository, during the twenty months for which the accounts are extant, took in about 230,000 ducats (in silver and in gold coins, carefully distinguished) and paid out about 225,000. For other references to loans made by Soranzo during the period covered by the accounts, see Ferrara, "Documenti," docs. 33–39, and ASV, Provveditori alle Biave, b. 2, libro 3, fol. 2v (9 July 1462). Several loans call for repayment from this "deposito inferiore"; see also ASV, ST, reg. 5, fols. 54, 55v. Ferrara's doc. 37 (1463) says that the Collegio had called for Soranzo: "collegium misit pro viro nobile Johanne Superantio a bancho et requisivit eum quod promittat solvere pecunias."

[60]ASV, Provveditori alle Biave, b. 2, libro 3, fols. 2v (July 1462), 31v (December 1465). Piero Guerrucci in 1470 (ibid., fol. 58) and Francesco Pisani in 1477 (ibid., fol. 94) also appear as wheat importers (as did Agostino Ziera, earlier).

dese for the importation of 20,000 staia of wheat, at the best price possible; then he lent 1,000 ducats to a member of the same Collegio who was to depart for the Marches of Ancona—under the cover of a pilgrimage to the Virgin of Loretto—in order to contract for an additional 10,000–20,000 staia.[61] Until his death, Soranzo continued to grant credits in the sector of provisioning, "according to his usual good custom," taking repayment from the sale of the wheat and from the Camera Fiscale of Treviso.[62]

When Giovanni Soranzo made his testament in 1468, he inserted the request that the doge, Cristoforo Moro, meet with his executors, including the Procurators of San Marco de Citra, to decide whether or not his sons should continue to operate the bank. The unusual request matches the unusual role that the Soranzo bank played in government finance; very likely the dying banker wanted to be sure that, if the bank was carried on, it would have the support of the highest authority of the land.[63] His sons indeed carried on and continued to extend lines of credit to the state.[64]

The only foreign bank that emerges as a lender to the Venetian state is the local branch of the Medici. To be sure, the relations between the Medici and Venice depended upon diplomatic and military relations between the two republics. In 1434 Cosimo, by way of thanking Venice for its hospitality during his exile, offered to lend Venice 30,000 ducats. As long as the alliance against Milan lasted, the Medici branch made some loans, presumably as representatives of Florentine policy. Thus in 1439 Venice asked Antonello Martelli, factor of the Medici branch, to pay 8,000 ducats to the mercenary captain Francesco Sforza; he replied that he could not do that unless Venice first paid him at least 3,000 ducats on the 10,000 ducats already outstanding.[65] Otherwise, the Medici branch lent smaller sums, acting in its capacity as international exchange bank, by accepting drafts sent by Venetian ambassadors and officials abroad. But smaller amounts could add up, and Venice in 1446 was concerned to repay "a good sum of money [as the deliberation reads] so that the Medici, who in the past have

---

[61]Ibid., fols. 13v, 16. In the same year the Baldesi firm supposedly declared insolvency during the financial crisis in Florence (de Roover, *Medici Bank,* 359), but in the following decades it continues to appear as an importer of wheat, in connection with the Venetian branch of the Medici.

[62]ASV, Provveditori alle Biave, b. 2, libro 3, fol. 27v: "segondo la solita suo bona costuma" (1465) and passim. Some marginal personal advantage is mirrored in the same record (fol. 27v) when the banker received a license to export grain from his estate in Castelfranco to Feltre and Belluno.

[63]ASV, NT, b. 1240, n. 203.

[64]In 1475 Pietro and Vettor Soranzo were said to have lent 6,000 ducats "cum exemplo parentis sui." ASV, ST, reg. 7, fol. 94 (26 October). Many loans they made to the state in the 1480s are mentioned in letters to their prelate brother; see dalla Santa, "Benedetto Soranzo patrizio veneziano," 310 n. 1, 317 n. 1.

[65]The Senate ordered payment of the 3,000 ducats. ASV, SM, reg. 60, fol. 157 (6 July 1439). On the current war against Milan, see Kretschmayr, *Geschichte,* 2:347–48.

so freely lent to our Signoria, will continue to do so."[66] In 1471 the branch lent 3,200 ducats by ordering the purchase of ship biscuit in Naples, and in 1478 it lent 3,200 ducats by ordering Florentine merchants in Constantinople to pay that much for the ransom of three Venetian mercenary captains captured by the Turks. In some cases — as in the last mentioned — Venetian banks were asked to advance sums necessary to repay the Medici.[67]

In the 1470s, when the branch was managed by Giovanni Lanfredini, most of Venice's debts with the Medici involved the importation of wheat by the annona. In fulfillment of one contract, the branch was paid 45,000 ducats (surely via a credit to their account) by the Garzoni bank.[68] Even though the branch defaulted and was forced into liquidation in 1477 (see above, Chap. 7, sec. iii), in the following year it was still completing deliveries of wheat presumably contracted earlier, alone and in partnership also with Angelo Baldesi, which placed Venice in its debt again.[69] Not long after, the Council of Ten arrested and expelled Lanfredini for revealing state secrets to Lorenzo the Magnificent, as we have seen above (Chap. 7), and the branch continued its process of liquidation under the direction of personnel of lesser rank.

iv. ACCOUNTING PROBLEMS

The constant, helter-skelter lending of large sums and small sums, of specie and of promises, for forecast expenditures and for debts already accrued or in arrears; authorizations of different organs, or of the same organ (the Senate) but registered in different series of deliberations; conflicting and parallel jurisdictions; the numerous sources of revenues and revenue-collecting offices that were juggled and "obligated" to the banks for repayment; the tendency of creditors to discount their credits with the government — all these aspects of bank lending often created confusion in the state's accounting, which sometimes occasioned the call for audits. The calls begin early but become particularly insistent toward the end of the Quattrocento.

---

[66]"Much money" was owed for drafts paid in 1435–36, and the Medici "insisted daily on repayment." ASV, SM, reg. 59, fols. 128r–v (10 September 1435), 147v (9 March 1436). Loans to ambassadors abroad, via drafts on Venice, were the part of Venice's debt in 1446 which the Senate ordered repaid promptly "ut dicta societas [Medicorum] que continue liberaliter servivit nostro dominio, sic in futurum facere continuet." ST, reg. 2, fol. 9 (22 November). The manager Alessandro Martelli was owed 350 ducats for a draft from the bailo of Constantinople in 1464. Ibid., reg. 5, fol. 79 (18 May).

[67]In 1471 the amount paid in Naples was 3,133 ducats, while Venice repaid 3,227 gold ducats, thus including 3 percent for exchange costs. ASV, ST, reg. 6, fol. 139 (19 August). For 1478, see ibid., reg. 8, fols. 31v (15 December) and 35 — where the Pisani are recorded as having lent the money required to repay the Medici loan.

[68]Ibid., reg. 7, fols. 72v, 78v, 80v, 93v–94, 106, 108v (1475–76), and Sanudo, *Vite,* 17.

[69]ASV, Provveditori alle Biave, b. 2, libro 3, fol. 102r–v; ST, reg. 8, fol. 21 (25 August).

In 1439 the Governatori delle Entrate were given a rather strange order: they were told to examine the books of the Soranzo bank in order to ascertain how much the bank was still owed by the state. That was a year of heavy borrowing; furthermore, it was June: the season of the termini was at hand, and the Senate recognized that the banks would be pressed for credit and specie and wanted to balance the accounts. One must recall that many loans were in the form of promises or current accounts opened to creditors of the state for indeterminate sums, for example, for imports of wheat, measurable only upon arrival, so it was reasonable that the state first determined the actual credit; it is strange, however, that the government had no independent system for keeping track of its debts.[70] In 1451, at the beginning of the war between Venice and Florence, the same Governatori were ordered to audit the books both of the banks and of Venice's mercenary captains, who had been ordered paid by banks. The state admitted it had no way of knowing whether the sums had actually been credited to the mercenaries by the bankers or how much was necessary from the state's coffers to liquidate the bank loans.[71]

Beginning in 1488 concern about confusion in the accounts increased. In that year one Savio del Collegio was ordered to direct the work of an accountant and a scribe to check all accounts, with the right to see the ledgers of both the Treasury and the banks.[72] That audit must have been only partially successful in registering sums already received by the banks but not so recorded at the Treasury if in 1494 two nobles (Benedetto Sanudo and Alvise Loredan) were elected to supervise the work of two accountants in auditing and balancing "all the accounts of the banks with the Signoria . . . from 1480 on, which were not debited to the banks on the books of the Treasury."[73] The group was at work for almost three years—not for the two months initially deemed necessary. In 1495 the nobles asked for the same wide authority to see the Treasury records as they had to see the

[70]ASV, SM, reg. 60, fol. 149 (5 June 1439). The need to repay was felt "maxime hoc tempore navium et galearum quod supervenit ipsis [Luca Soranzo and brothers]." One-third of interest due on the funded debt was withheld in order to repay the debt that the Governatori, within fifteen days, would ascertain.

[71]The deliberation begins: "Quia sicut notum esse potest, banchi nostri Rivoalti servierunt et dederunt de ordine nostro nonnullas pecuniarum summas in diversis temporibus et diebus plerisque conductoribus nostris, nec bene intelligitur si dicte pecunie sic date posite sunt ad computum ipsorum conductorum, nec etiam qualiter rationes illi procedunt." The Governatori were flanked by the auditors of Terraferma cameral accounts. ASV, ST, reg. 2, fol. 186 (15 May 1451).

[72]Ferrara, "Antichi banchi," 209–10; Malipiero, *Annali,* 684. Imagine the confusion that seven small loans totaling about 3,500 ducats must have caused: they were annotated in the margin of a deliberation of 8 December 1490, one in favor of the Pisani, the rest in favor of the Garzoni; *BG,* 1:162, doc. 128.

[73]Lattes, *Libertà,* doc. 29; original in ASV, ST, reg. 12, fol. 76v. After two months, all accounts not properly debited at the Treasury would be charged with a 10 percent fine.

bankers' books, and in 1496, with the task still incomplete, the accounts for the expansion of the Ducal Palace were added to their auditing duties.[74]

Clearly the bankers were better able to keep decent accounts of their loans to the state than was the Treasury. The latter seems to have had no way of overseeing its obligations, similar to that provided by the Garzoni ledgers, on the basis of which that bank could assert that it had lent, over a thirty-year period, 1.2 million ducats.

v. HOW WERE BANKS REIMBURSED?

As Ferrara noted correctly in the last century, there is not a hint of the state's paying any compensation or interest to the banks for their loans. On the contrary, the deliberations requesting or authorizing loans often assert that the banks offered to lend (the verb frequently used is "mutuare") without interest. Thus in 1396 the Commune agreed to back a guarantee it had requested from the bankers Pietro Benedetto and Gabriele Soranzo "so as not to occasion loss [it was stated] from something on which they do not profit."[75] During the mid-1450s, when bimetallic ratios vacillated, Giovanni Soranzo said he would lend "freely and without any profit," as long as he received repayment in gold if he lent gold, in silver if he lent silver; and the Signoria was again concerned to repay as agreed: "for it is not right that those who lend to the state suffer loss."[76] Interest-free loans were labeled "patriotic": bankers were "moved by love of fatherland" and lent "gratis and out of faith in — and love for — the fatherland."[77] Such statements force one to ask oneself, as did Francesco Ferrara, whether in fifteenth-century Venice there existed on the Rialto a peculiar brand of banker who, charitable and patriotic, had overcome greed and the desire for profit?[78]

Two loans for a total of 16,000 ducats made by the Soranzo bank in 1440 constitute an exception. Both loans, needed for paying mercenaries, were made "on exchange and rechange." The Governatori delle Entrate were to repay the company of Luca Soranzo and brothers the principal plus

[74]ASV, ST, reg. 12, fols. 88 (24 March 1495), 130 (22 March 1496), when it was said that the officials had done a good job but had not completed it. Francesco Foscari and Gerolamo Capello took the places of Loredan and Benetto Sanudo, as "revedadori di le raxon di la Signoria con li banchi." Ibid., reg. 13, fol. 30r–v, and Sanudo, *Diarii,* 1:850.

[75]ASV, SM, reg. 43, fol. 118 (1 March 1396): "Commune nostrum stet ipsis campsoribus complezium, ut non portarent damnum de re, de qua non lucrantur."

[76]ASV, CN, reg. 9, fol. 96 (30 January 1457); Ferrara, "Documenti," doc. 19; ST, reg. 4, fol. 53 (3 October 1457). See also CN, reg. 9, fol. 129 (2 June 1458): "ut serviendo nostro dominio non recipiat damnum."

[77]In 1475 the Soranzo lent 8,000 ducats "moti charitate patrie," and they and the Pisani lent 10,000 ducats each in order to meet the back pay of seamen, "sine ulla alicuius eorum utilitate sed ex precipua fide et caritate sua in patriam." ASV, ST, reg. 7, fols. 78 (20 April), 93v (26 October).

[78]"Antichi banchi," 208.

"'interesse' and expenses" as would be defined by the "returns" from London. Exactly how much the loans garnered after six months (twice the "usance" between Venice and London, "andata e ritorno") is not recorded, but about 15 percent annual interest was usual in that period.[79] Another exception involves a Jew lending in Mestre. Generally, in order to meet specific needs, extraordinary taxes were levied on the Jewish communities in areas under Venetian rule. In one case, however, not a tax but a forced loan was exacted from Moisè, a Jew operating in Mestre, in order to pay Gattamelata; the conditions were harsh (he had to come up with 4,000 ducats in only a few days, after which every delay of a day added 1,000 to the sum demanded), but Venice promised him repayment in four months at 12 percent annual interest, probably three points below the rate his condotta allowed him to charge to private borrowers.[80] How could the state agree to pay interest to a Jew while denying any profit to its Christian bankers — the "pillars of the state"?

Ferrara dismissed the possibility that the state passed on a profit to the bankers for their services through corruption or fraudulent accounting procedures. Similarly, we can reject the possibility that loans were regularly extended via dry exchange; the above-mentioned cases of 1440 seem to be exceptional. Also exceptional was the state's mediating free loans to the banks. One example of such a reversal of roles comes from the beginning of the Ferrara war, when the banks were pressed to make large and continual loans to the state. The Procurators of San Marco, executors of estates with cash assets on hand, made loans to the Pisani bank which the latter repaid only after six years, and without interest.[81] The sums of money thus made available, however, were only a small percentage of the loans made by the banks during the war. Another possibility for earning a profit presented itself when the banks lent specie in times of changing bimetallic ratios: they could lend in one metal and insist on repayment in the metal that was rising.

[79] "Item, quia necesse est etiam denarios accipere ad cambium . . . a viris nobilibus Luce Superantio et fratribus . . . ad denarios 48 de Londra pro ducato" for 10,000 ducats; to be repaid by the Governatori delle Entrate with "et interesse, et consto ad quod et quem redundaret cambium, tam eundo quam redeundo" when the returns from London fell due, that is, after six months. The second loan via rechange was at 47 sterling pennies per ducat; that is, the rate of the "andata" was given in the deliberation, and that of the "ritorno" was left to definition by market forces. ASV, CN, reg. 7, fols. 11, 18v; SM, reg. 60, fols. 203r–v, 236. For profits made on rechange operations between Venice and London in 1444–63, see above, graph 8.7. For recourse to borrowing via dry exchange by the Florentine republic in the years 1425–33, see Molho, *Florentine Public Finances*, 172–82.

[80] ASV, ST, reg. 60, fol. 156v (6 July 1439).

[81] A loan of 240 ducats by the Procurators on 13 May 1482 was registered on the account book of the estate of M. Morosini of S. Zulian in this manner: "Dedimus mutuo banco de Pixanis, quos portavit ser Franciscus Basadona, camerarius communis, de suo ordine." It was repaid on 9 February 1488. ASV, PSM, Citra, b. 179, fasc. 5, fols. 44v (dare) and 19 (recipere). Further examples could surely be found, but they would hardly change the picture.

This was the stipulation made by the banker Giacomo Corner in the 1450s; but in the same period, as we have just seen, Giovanni Soranzo polemically stated that for him it was enough to be repaid in the same metal that was lent, so as not to suffer loss.[82] That decade, however, was one of bullion famine, particularly of gold famine; betting on the future curve of bimetallic ratios cannot have been a means of earning a profit over the long term, when ratios were quite stable.

Favors were a typical way of repaying services rendered, and the state probably made favors in return for lines of credit. The biggest favor would have been that of making a bank depositary of the state; this would have greatly augmented its cash reserves and would have made possible a multiple increase in loans and investments; this was an option, however, which Venice chose not to try. But there were smaller favors. Families of bankers fined for late payment of taxes probably took for granted a certain degree of immunity.[83] Derogations from existing norms gave banks some freedom to invest as they desired. For example, bankers, forbidden to deal in silver in 1374, obtained exemptions in 1387 and 1390 which permitted them to export silver to the Levant.[84] A century later, beginning with the War of Ferrara, the Council of Ten adopted a different approach to the granting of favors: it permitted bankers to consign silver to the mint and have it struck into coin, an activity otherwise prohibited, as long as they would make large loans to the government—usually with the very coins struck. Each time a specific authorization was necessary, but there are dozens of such authorizations, from 1482 right up to the eve of the crash of 1499. The totals, expressed in marks of silver, went from a minimum of 15,000–20,000 ducats for the four banks then active to that same amount for each single bank. Such was the case in 1496, for example, when the mint was ordered to accept 12,000 marks from the four, for a value of some 72,000 ducats. In that case, the favor was expressed this way: the banks needed to increase their liquidity in order to meet demand for payments due both in the public and in the private spheres; since the right to consign 3,000 marks each depended on the readiness of the banks to lend to the state, one must assume that the authorities foresaw the relatively rapid restitution of the loans.[85]

[82]ASV, ST, reg. 3, fols. 85, 102, 152v–53.

[83]The families of Pietro Soranzo and Tommaso Lippomano were reported to the Governatori delle Entrate by the Dieci Savi alle Decime and fined for failure to pay on time; once they had paid the principal, they asked to be let off the fine, saying they had lent much more to the state during the Ferrara war than any debt that had accrued. ASV, CN, reg. 13, fol. 41v (19 December 1483).

[84]Lattes, *Libertà,* docs. 9–11.

[85]To what extent utility and profit were created by this system is not clear, although it promoted speculation. The law suspended was that of 14 March 1481; the system was in operation from 1482 until 1496. The loans, generally provided by all existing banks together, were on the order of 10,000–40,000 ducats each time. See *Cap. Broche,* 188–244, and ASV, Capi del Consiglio dei Dieci, Notatorio, reg. 2, fols. 45 (1492) and 88 (1495).

Another possible explanation of nominally free bank loans, mentioned by Ferrara, was more simple: as the state concluded business through the banks, it conferred on them added prestige in the eyes of their clients and, more important, it increased the mass of deposits on the bankers' books, which permitted bankers in good times to expand their "speculations," that is, their loans and investments.[86] It is difficult to imagine, however, that a banker would agree continually to make interest-free loans to the state for the mere prestige that might offer — and of course the prestige of one moment could easily turn into suspicion and a reduction of the "fiducia" of depositors, for the state could not at all times be equally creditworthy. A generic and unstable prestige, then, and the hope for an increase in the general level of business seem to be inadequate incentives for a banker.

More concrete were two kinds of agio, which constituted potential sources of profit. Bankers, as has been mentioned, made many loans in specie, to pay the salaries of soldiers and seamen, for example. One way a banker could earn on such loans was to lend underweight coins (mercenary captains sometimes complained of that) and to insist upon repayment in full-weight, mint coins. Even though the differential between current coins and mint coins might not have been large, even a small difference would constitute a desirable rate of return on a short-term loan.

The same is true of the other kind of agio, one that was surely exploited for a profit by bankers as often as possible, namely, that on good coin over bank money. When the banker lent promises, that is, opened an account to a supplier of goods and services to the state, and the creditor utilized it in making payments via bank transfers (today we would say by writing checks on it), the banker stood to gain if the state repaid the loan in coin, especially in mint coin; more than likely, that happened before the original creditor had used all the money available on his account.[87] This kind of differential did not exceed 1–2 percent, at least not before the early sixteenth century.[88] But, once again: a low rate of return on a short-term loan might have been sufficient to keep the bankers ready to lend.

A last possible explanation why a banker might agree to lend gratis to the state is discount, specifically the sale to a bank of an obligation the

---

[86]"Antichi banchi," 208–9.

[87]Delays in repaying could create problems. In one case a delay was agreed upon: in 1458 Giovanni Soranzo assented to the use of funds at the Salt Office, earmarked for him, for getting off the galleys as well as for paying the salaries of the chancery notaries; ASV, CN, reg. 9, fol. 131v (21 June 1458). On the other hand, the state recognized the importance of repaying in the season during which a bank's cash reserves were under particular pressure. Such an urgency was recognized in June 1439, "et maxime hoc tempore navium et galearum quod supervenit." ASV, SM, reg. 60, fol. 149. Loans of 8,000 mint ducats each were made by the Garzoni and by Piero Guerrucci in June 1468 on condition that they be repaid "ad tempus galearum," that is, in two to four weeks. ST, reg. 6, fols. 24, 25v (20 and 28 June).

[88]On this kind of agio, see Mueller, "Role of Bank Money," 84–94.

government had with a private party. That, of course, involves an agreement between the creditor and the banker, but it made the banker creditor to the state; the operation may have been sanctioned by the state as a way of assuring the banker a profit.

It has been seen that many government contracts, such as those for the delivery of wheat to the annona, involved deferred payment, up to twelve or eighteen months after delivery. To be assured of payment on schedule importers asked for bank "promises," which meant in practice that they were paid in bank. A merchant who wanted access to that money in advance of the schedule had only to ask a bank to discount the government's obligation. Or, if he did not have a bank guarantee in his contract, he could transfer his credit to a banker who would open an account in his name. Just how this form of discounting worked and what the "discount rate" was cannot be known, given the lack of suppliers' and bankers' account books. But it must be assumed that suppliers accepted a deposit credit of something less than their original credit with the state. That practice is mirrored in a law of 1485 which tried to regulate discounting while permitting it.

The law reads, in part:

> All our citizens, who happen to be our creditors for whatever reason, find ways of transferring their credits to banks; the banks, in turn, create demand deposits for them and adjust the accounts [at the Treasury] in such a way that the Signoria appears as the immediate debtor of the banks, for sums originally due only far in the future. That is, the banks thus appear as our creditors for loans and are repaid ahead of schedule.

The advantage to the banks of such a scheme is obvious. The Senate complained that the government was unable to free its revenue-collecting offices, such as the Salt Office, from obligations incurred during the war with Ferrara. The attempted remedy was this: creditors could indeed transfer their credits to banks or to anyone else, but the discounting banks were no longer to appear on the books of the Treasury as though they were original creditors for cash loans to the state but only as beneficiaries of transferred obligations on which the conditions originally negotiated remained in force. In short, banks would be repaid swiftly for loans actually made in cash ("in prompta pecunia") but would be repaid only according to the original schedule of deferred payments for credits transferred to them, even if — it must be assumed — the accounts opened in the name of the original creditor could have already been drawn upon directly.[89]

---

[89]ASV, ST, reg. 9, fols. 157v–58; also in Camerlenghi di Comun, reg. 2 (capitolare), fols. 3v–4. A corrupt text, derived from the capitolare of the Provveditori sopra Banchi, was provided by Lattes, *Libertà,* doc. xxviii. The lines translated in the text read: "nam omnes cives nostri, qui creditores reperiuntur Dominii nostri quacunque de causa hunc invenere modum quod

This solution, however, was insufficient to resolve the problems of liquidity faced by the government's financial administration. Only two years later the Senate suspended payments to banks for four months on all book loans; in the interim, only cash loans that fell due were honored.[90]

Unfortunately there is no way of watching how the system of discounting worked in practice. At the time of the failure of the banker and diarist Gerolamo Priuli in 1513, however, Sanudo reports how Priuli's credit with the state was subjected to particular scrutiny. The audit aimed at distinguishing, among the government obligations he held, between those that had fallen due, so that the creditor could draw on his account, and those that had not yet fallen due. For the former, the Council of Ten promised prompt payment to the bank; for the latter, it agreed to assume the obligations directly.[91]

Lines of credit made available by bankers to the state had taken the place, after the War of Chioggia, of that quasi-state bank of the Trecento, the Grain Office, in managing the floating debt. On the side of the private banking system, the monetization of government obligations meant the expansion of the money supply and an increase of business concluded at the banks. New business, enhanced reputation, and small agios were perhaps the only compensation banks realized for their loans. On the other side, the assurance of ready credit from the banks oiled the wheels of government; not only military expenditures but even quite simple expenses were met with loans. As regards the effect of the system on taxpayers, recourse to bank loans was an attempt to reduce the burden on that part of the citizenry

credita sua transferunt banchis per quos fiunt partite, et aptantur scripture per modum quod Dominatio nostra immediate constituitur debitrix ipsis banchis earum pecuniarum, que ad longa tempora sunt solvende, ed dicti banchi, qui vadunt cum nostro Dominio ad computum longum, apparent pro eisdem pecuniis creditores nostri de ratione impresti, et sic ante tempus solvuntur." The law concludes: "Remanere debeant ipsi bancherii in illamet conditione, et in illismet modis et obligationibus, in quibus reperiebantur illi primi veri creditores nostri Dominii, qui credita ipsa transtulerunt sive obligarunt et scripserunt banchis predictis, nec alio modo solvi possint ipsi bancherii, sub pena ducatorum mille contrafatientibus." Several years later a contract for saltpeter, which called for payment at the Pisani bank in installments of one and two years, specified that the bank would be repaid only according to that fixed schedule. ST, reg. 11, fol. 94v (25 January 1492).

[90]Venice, in the midst of the Rovereto war, was concerned "tam ad conservationem status et rerum nostrarum quam pro recuperatione honoris et extimationis nostre." ASV, ST, reg. 10, fol. 50r–v (1 June 1487).

[91]The state owed the bank 6,000–7,000 ducats for obligations "ch'è venuto il tempo di le promission fece"; "le ubligation avìa fato esso banchier per la signoria nostra a diverse persone, che non è venuto il tempo, i qual [the auditors] hanno contentà tuor quelle medeme ubligation a loro," for an amount left blank. The reason for Priuli's insolvency, says Sanudo, was that he "ha comprato crediti special e tolto in sì il credito de la signoria per vadagnar poi con pro' Monte nuovo." Hardly crystalline in its meaning, the phrase seems to refer to discounted obligations. Sanudo, *Diarii*, 17:354, 369.

subjected to forced loans and direct taxes; by contrast, indirect taxes and taxes on the subject territories were called upon, when possible, to repay the banks. All in all, privileged sectors of society in the capital city stood to gain from this form of floating debt.

The failures of 1499 and 1500, despite their drama, did not cause the loss of face of the Venetian state for long. The Rialto picked itself up and recovered from the shock only a bit more slowly than usual after recurrent bank failures. For the time being, however, the state had to resort to loans from Jews lending in the area of Padua; in May 1499, for example, Venice had to come up with security, as required by the great pawn bankers Anselmo (Asher Meshullam) and Salamoncin of Piove di Sacco, for a loan of 15,000 ducats.[92] Then ties between banking and politics became, if anything, even tighter, as exemplified by Alvise Pisani, a leading politician and leading banker who regularly extended credit to the government; in 1519 he alone held credits of 150,000 ducats.[93] The "temple," as Malipiero had referred to the state, could be sustained with both repaired and new "pillars." The banks regained fiducia; the state regained credit.

[92]Ibid., 2:742, 745.

[93]Lane, "Venetian Bankers," 82–86. The expanded role of bankers in the crisis of the War of the League of Cambrai is recounted by Gilbert, *The Pope, His Banker, and Venice,* 26, 34–35, 50, 60 (for the interest-free loan offered by Agostino Chigi, papal banker in Rome).

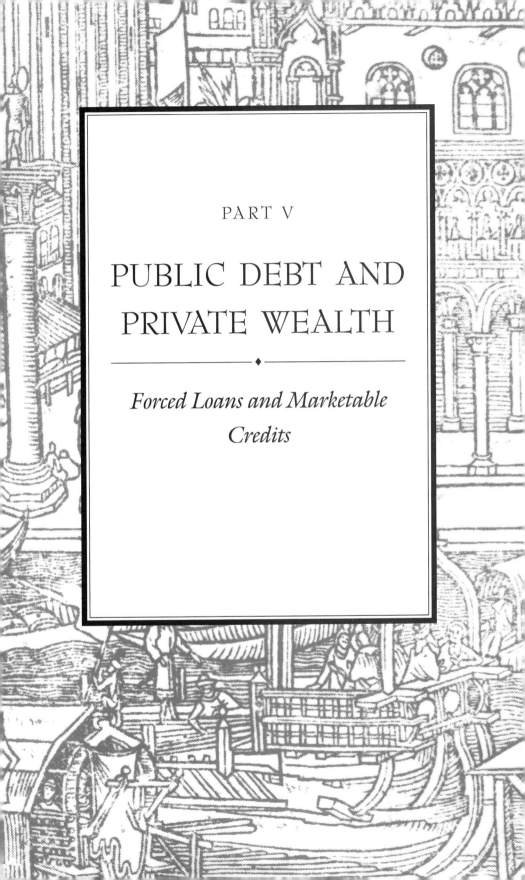

PART V

PUBLIC DEBT AND PRIVATE WEALTH

Forced Loans and Marketable Credits

11

VENICE'S MONTE VECCHIO
An Overview

HE PUBLIC DEBT AND private credit discussed in this part involves the funded debt, a practically perpetual deficit based on
forced loans, which gave the purchaser a marketable claim on the
state and a title to interest; today that claim would be called a government
bond (or share), except for the fact that it was not a certificate but a mere
entry in the ledgers of the state Loan Office. The history of Venice's first
funded debt was written, in exemplary fashion, by Gino Luzzatto. Faced
with the total loss of the archive of the Venetian monti, with the sole
exception of a few capitolari, Luzzatto was forced to reconstruct the story of
the Monte Vecchio (so called only when a new monte was inaugurated in
1482) completely on indirect evidence, namely, legislation regarding the
debt and accounts maintained by the Procurators of San Marco in their role
as executors of the estates of thousands of well-to-do Venetians. The author's study is especially valuable for its analysis of the relevant legislation
(much of it published in an appendix of nearly three hundred documents,
ranging from 1164 to 1483) and for the compilation of data regarding levies
of forced loans and market prices of state credits.[1] No other public debt, in

---

[1]*PRV,* introduction of 275 pages (Roman numerals) plus 289 documents (Arabic numbers
both for the pages and the documents), published in 1929. In the same year, Luzzatto published
an article on the public debt as a reply to a review by Corrado Barbagallo (expert in the early
history of Florentine public finance); it provides a still valuable overview: "Il debito pubblico
nel sistema finanziario veneziano dei secoli XIII–XV," reprinted in his *Studi.* The introduction
to the book was published separately, at the initiative of Armando Sapori, as *Il debito pubblico
della Repubblica di Venezia* (Milan, 1963), 272 pages (Arabic numbers). The pagination of the
latter is nearly but not exactly identical to the introduction to the large volume. In the separate
version only a few of the misprints were corrected, but the previously attempted correspondence of medieval monetary values to those of 1929 was dropped. Since in what follows I refer

Italy or in the rest of Europe, has been studied in such depth and breadth, despite the availability elsewhere of rich archives of the very institutions that administered the debts. As regards Venice, more recent studies, albeit not of the same monographic nature, have built on the foundation laid by Luzzatto by emphasizing the military demand for money in the Venetian system of deficit spending, the imposition of direct taxation ("dadie," "colte") in the subject territories on the Terraferma, the inauguration of direct taxation in Venice with the decima (1463), and the story of the Monte Nuovo (1482), the Monte Nuovissimo (1509), the Monte del Sussidio (1526), and later forms of public indebtedness.[2]

Some of the themes developed in what follows bring together material already dealt with by Luzzatto, in an attempt to aid the reader in understanding the history of the debt and its technical mechanisms. The major emphasis, however, is on themes not treated in depth by Luzzatto, in particular the impact of the system on persons and households actually involved, the functioning of the market in credits, and investment by foreigners. Exploitation of private account books, well known but never previously analyzed with the public debt in mind, as well as the use of grants of privilege (grazie) make possible the reconstruction of specific cases, both of payers of forced loans and of investors in the open market.

A rather fundamental error made by Luzzatto in his treatment of the moneys of account utilized in the administration of the debt has been rectified; the revision and a step-by-step justification of it can be found in Appendix D, sec. i.

i. EUROPE AND ITALY

In all of Europe during the Middle Ages and the Renaissance — and not only there and then — private patrimonies were considered somehow

---

to so many of the documents, I have used the first version of the introduction throughout, despite the unhandy Roman numbers; but readers who have only the 1963 version can readily trace any cited passage. The later edition concludes with an appendix by Frederic C. Lane: "Sull'ammontare del 'Monte Vecchio' di Venezia," in English as "The Funded Debt of the Venetian Republic, 1262–1482," in *Venice and History*. See also the summary treatment by periods in Luzzatto, *Storia,* 72–74, 111, 129–30, 141, 204–13. Terse summaries of Luzzatto's work, also by period, with the inclusion of useful tables, are in Homer and Sylla, *A History of Interest Rates*; Italian edition, *Storia dei tassi di interesse,* 134–36, 141–44,150–53.

[2] Besides Lane, "Funded Debt," see Michael Knapton, "Il fisco nello Stato veneziano di Terraferma tra il '300 e '500: La politica delle entrate," in *Il sistema fiscale veneto: Problemi e aspetti, XV–XVIII secolo,* ed. Giorgio Borelli et al. (Verona, 1982), with extensive bibliography; see also his contribution, entitled "Guerra e finanza (1381–1508)," to Cozzi and Knapton, *Storia*; Giuseppe Del Torre, *Il Trevigiano nei secoli XV e XVI: L'assetto amministrativo e il sistema fiscale* (Treviso, 1990); Luciano Pezzolo, "Dal prestito all'imposta: Verso lo Stato territoriale," forthcoming in *Storia di Venezia*. For surprisingly complete descriptions of the loan offices and their jurisdictions as well as the system of taxation around 1500, see *Traictie,* esp. chaps. 59, 61, 66.

sacred, and direct taxes were abhorred. Thus, rulers universally sought to meet regular expenditures with indirect taxes (such as those on salt, wholesale and retail wine, brokerage, customs duties, and the like). In lieu of direct taxes, loans were called for to meet extraordinary expenditures. Systems of public debt, where they were put into place, saved the well-to-do strata of the population from direct taxes and paid them interest on their economic support of initiatives of the state (primarily making war); indirect taxes, which notoriously weigh on the poor, were used to service the debt structure, that is, to pay interest and, occasionally, reimburse principal. This is what Karl Marx referred to as the "ancient thieving system" when he wrote of the public debts of medieval Genoa and Venice as levers of "primitive accumulation" of capital. The popular classes were well aware of the inequity of the system. In Genoa a popular revolt in 1339 burned the account books of the *compere,* the sole record of the state's obligations; in Florence, the revolutionary wool workers, the Ciompi, in 1378 demanded abolition of the funded debt and the reinstitution of direct taxes.[3]

In the cities of northern Europe in the Middle Ages, recourse by governments to extraordinary measures for meeting extraordinary expenditures, such as those for war and the annona, took the form almost universally of the open sale of annuities. Such sales, according to the Frydes, were issues more voluntarily subscribed to than purchased under duress. They were of two types, life annuities and perpetual annuities, the former largely unredeemable, the latter usually redeemable. In German cities life annuities generally bore 10 percent interest, perpetual annuities 5 percent. Annuities issued by the cities of the Low Countries and Burgundy were often purchased more by foreigners than by citizens (for example, annuities issued by Bruges or Ghent tended, in the late thirteenth century, to be purchased especially by financiers of Arras). Cities, of course, were more creditworthy than royal governments, for an urban patriciate guaranteed continuity, whereas a new king might well not honor the debts of his predecessor.[4]

On the Italian peninsula, cities requested more or less voluntary loans of leading wealthy citizens at various times, but a distinction quickly developed. Cities ruled by princes ("tyrants," according to republican humanist polemicists), such as the Milan of the Visconti and the Sforza or the Verona of the della Scala, seem to have continued to use an ad hoc system of

[3]Karl Marx, *Capital,* 3 vols. (Chicago, 1906–9), vol. 1, chap. 31. Day, *Medieval Money Market,* 157. Roberto Barducci, "Le riforme finanziarie nel tumulto dei Ciompi," in *Il tumulto dei Ciompi: Un momento di storia fiorentina ed europea,* acts of the congress of 1979 (Florence, 1981), 100–101.

[4]See Fryde and Fryde, "Public Credit," esp. pt. 8, "The Towns of Northern Europe," and Wim P. Blockmans, "Le crédit public dans les Pays-Bas méridionaux au bas moyen âge," in *Local and International Credit in the Middle Ages and the Sixteenth Century,* ed. Henri Dubois, acts of session B9 of the Ninth International Economic History Congress (Bern, 1986), 1–7. Universally overlooked on this theme but solid and still valuable is Usher, *Early History,* chap. 5, "Long Term Lending and Public Debts."

voluntary loans, organized into a floating debt, whereas city-republics, led by Venice, Genoa, and Florence, early changed to a system of forced loans, based on an assessment of ability to pay. In the case of Verona, for example, the citizens who lent some 27,000 ducats during the war against the coalition of Venice and Florence (1337–39) formed themselves into a consortium, the Universitas Civium, which established control over large parts of the public domain which had been pledged as surety; since the loans were not repaid, the consortium compensated itself from the rents it collected, at the time and for successive centuries.[5] Each of the three republics, by contrast, early consolidated their debts into a "monte," or fund of indebtedness, in which loans, imposed on the basis of assessed patrimony, lost their individuality and became claims, sometimes to repayment of principal but always to payment of interest. The claims were marketable, albeit just on the books of the loan administration; but in certain Lombard cities and in Vicenza in the thirteenth century small notarized declarations of urban debt, on parchment, constituted negotiable credit instruments.[6] The market for credits was often lively; sometimes the title to interest separated and became marketable on its own. Credits were an investment opportunity open to foreigners as well as to citizens, under certain conditions.

In the three Italian republics mentioned, the funded debt was of primary concern, not only to the governments, which became dependent on deficit financing, but to affluent citizens, both those forced to lend and those who invested in credits made available on the open market.[7] In Ven-

[5]The creditors were several hundred in number; Archivio di Stato, Verona, Università dei cittadini, reg. 6, described in Varanini, *Gli Scaligeri,* 386–87. For Milan, where some kind of estimo existed in the 1420s, of which, however, little trace remains, see Gigliola Soldi Rondinini, "Aspetti dell'amministrazione del ducato di Milano al tempo di Filippo Maria Visconti (Dal 'Liber Tabuli' di Vitaliano Borromeo, 1427)," in *Milano e Borgogna: Due stati principeschi tra Medioevo e Rinascimento,* ed. Jean-Marie Causchies and Giorgio Chittolini (Rome, 1990), 145–57.

[6]For Lombardy, see Jacob Wackernagel, *Städtische Schuldscheine als Zahlungsmittel im XIII. Jahrhundert,* Beiheft 2 to *Vierteljahresschrift für Sozial- und Wirtschaftsgeschichte* (Stuttgart, 1924), based on the statutes of Como, Milan, and Novara. For Vicenza, where more than five hundred actual obligations are extant, some of them negotiated, in a form of notarized ratification by the Commune, see Natascia Carlotto, *La città custodita: Politica e finanza a Vicenza dalla caduta di Ezzelino al vicariato imperiale (1259–1312)* (Milan, 1993), 200–214; the author has shown that the "obligationes nomine mutui" at the time were an instrument of ordinary, not extraordinary, financial administration.

[7]See the overviews by Day, *Medieval Money Market,* 154–59; Anthony Molho, "Tre città-stato e i loro debiti pubblici: Quesiti e ipotesi sulla storia di Firenze, Genova e Venezia," in *Italia, 1350–1450,* 185–215, and idem, "Lo Stato e la finanza pubblica: Un'ipotesi basata sulla storia tardomedioevale di Firenze," in *Origini della Stato: Processi di formazione statale in Italia fra medioevo ed età moderna,* ed. Giorgio Chittolini et al., Annali dell'Istituto storico italo-germanico, Quaderno 39 (Bologna, 1994), 225–80. See also Frederic C. Lane, "Public Debt and Private Wealth: Particularly in Sixteenth-Century Venice," reprinted in his *Profits from Power: Readings in Protection Rent and Violence-Controlling Enterprises* (Albany, N.Y., 1979), 72–81. For a bibliographical overview of Florentine finance, see Giovanni Ciappelli, "Il fisco

ice, which consolidated its debts in a single and lasting fund in 1262, the organs of the state proclaimed the Loan Office "the life and health of this blessed Signoria" in 1384; "the main foundation of our existence" in 1434; "the main foundation, the continual and everlasting equilibrium of our state, the glorious fame of our Signoria . . . , in which Office lie the trust of our Signoria and the everlasting preservation of our state" as late as 1458, when the system had already broken down under the heavy burden of continual forced loans for the exigencies of war.[8] In Genoa, where a first debt was funded in 1258 (it was consolidated with six further issues in 1340, and other issues were consolidated separately in later years), the debt was managed by the creditors themselves, organized in the famous Casa di S. Giorgio. S. Giorgio, Machiavelli remarked, was an autonomous construct more powerful, more respected, more durable than the state itself. "Should S. Giorgio take possession of the entire city," he wrote, "the result would be a republic more to be remembered than that of Venice."[9] In Florence, where the debt was consolidated only in 1343–45, it was the object of humanistic hyperbole; a law of 1470 used this metaphor: "The Monte is the heart of this body which we call city . . . ; every limb, large and small, must contribute to preserving this heart as the guardian fortress, immovable rock and enduring certainty of the salvation of the whole body and government of your state."[10] One could say, with Louis Marks, that the well-to-do citizen, in all three city-republics, was accustomed "to look on the state as a source of profit," understood as a modest return or income, which for forced lenders was interest on the nominal value of their credits, for investors a somewhat more substantial yield on credits purchased at lower market values. Citizens of Venice, Genoa, and Florence were happy to contribute to the functioning of the state as long as the support took the form of interest-bearing loans and as long as the pressure on liquid capital was relatively moderate. When the imposition of forced loans became heavy,

fiorentino nel '400: Note in margine al lavoro di Elio Conti sull'imposta diretta," in *La società fiorentina del basso Medioevo: Per Elio Conti,* Istituto storico italiano per il Medio Evo, Nuovi studi storici, 29 (Rome, 1995).

[8]"Camera nostra imprestitorum . . . semper fuit et est vita et salus istius benedicti dominii," *PRV,* doc. 196; "principale fundamentum status nostri," ibid., doc. 232; "Camera nostra imprestitorum . . . [est] principale fundamentum, continua et perpetua stabilitas nostri status, in qua consistit gloriosa fama nostri dominii . . . ; et . . . in ipsa Camera constitit fides nostri dominii et perpetua conservatio nostri status," ibid., doc. 276.

[9]Day, *Les douanes de Gênes,* xxxi–xxxiv; idem, *Medieval Market Economy,* 155–56.

[10]Quoted by Louis Marks, "The Financial Oligarchy in Florence under Lorenzo," *Italian Renaissance Studies,* ed. E. F. Jacob (London, 1960), 127. See also Becker, *Florence in Transition,* vol. 2, chap. 3, and Antonio Stella, "Fiscalità, topografia e società a Firenze nella seconda metà del Trecento," *ASI* 151 (1993): 797–862, who reveals a mechanism used in the fourteenth century by the wealthy for paying the forced loans of persons lacking ready cash, in order to earn the interest; the author does not explain, however, the rationale behind the choice of the wealthy for this mechanism rather than for simple purchases on the open market.

reaction to them was like the reaction against direct taxes — which they began to resemble, as soon as citizens, households, and institutions had to sell credits at a loss in order to have the liquidity necessary to meet successive levies; when the burden was judged insupportable, there could be active resistance to the fisc, similar to a tax strike, as occurred in Venice in 1442.[11] The diarist and banker Gerolamo Priuli spells it out clearly: taxpayers would take pains to come up with what was required, as long as they got something for their money, some annual return, "as had been observed of old in the republic of Venice."[12]

Under optimal circumstances, government credits constituted an investment for the forced lender, even though he could have earned considerably more in enterprise; they were nearly always attractive investments in the secondary market for speculators or for persons seeking a modest income. Government credits could be transferred by sale, by testamentary bequest, or by contract of gift or dowry; they could be lent, pledged as surety for nearly any kind of transaction, including bank loans, or used as money in payment of private obligations. Liens binding real estate could pass to public credits, once the owner received a special license to sell; credits thus encumbered were, of course, withdrawn from the open market as long as the conditions imposed remained in effect.[13]

In Venice in the first half of the sixteenth century, when the system of forced loans had outlived its usefulness, the authorities resorted to the system that had been widely used by the cities of northern Europe centuries earlier, namely, the issue of annuities open to voluntary purchase, the administration of which was handled by the Venetian mint.[14]

[11]*PRV,* ccli and doc. 253 (1442).

[12]He writes that people would have balked at paying a tax that was a dead loss: "volendo metere angarie . . . , bisognava trovare modo de dare qualche utillitade a quelli pageranno le angarie, come sempre hè stato observato *antiquitus* in la citade et Republica Veneta, . . . perchè la brigatta non vuol pagare di persso, ma, sperando avere qualche utillitade a l'anno, se sforzanno et astrengenno a pagar le loro angarie." *Diarii,* 332. For an earlier comment of the same tenor, see below, n. 19.

[13]For Florence, see Julius Kirshner, "Encumbering Private Claims to Public Debt in Renaissance Florence," in *The Growth of the Bank as Institution and the Development of Money-Business Law,* ed. Vito Piergiovanni (Berlin, 1993); the many possible uses of public credits as surety and as money in Florence outlined by the author are practically the same that one finds in Venetian practice. Loans of credits, or pegged to credits, or providing options on credits at maturity, were common in Venice in certain periods; they involved considerable risk. (See below, nn. 39–40.) A bank loan, later negotiated to a third party, which included an option on taking repayment in cash or in government credits at a given price led to a suit when the debtor judged the return to be exorbitant and earned "senza fadiga et senza perichlo"; the debtor lost on appeal. GP, Sg, reg. 55, fols. 18v–20v (22 March 1431). A dozen encumbrances of credits as security for bank loans, 1483–98, were registered in Camera degli Imprestiti, reg. 10, fols. 4v, 8v, 11v, 12v, 18, 32, 52, 73v, 85, 90; the banks were free to sell, if they wished.

[14]See Lane, "Public Debt and Private Wealth," and Luciano Pezzolo, *L'oro dello stato: Società, finanza e fisco nella Repubblica veneta del secondo '500* (Venice, 1990), index under "Debito pubblico."

ii. THE MONTE VECCHIO, FROM ITS ORIGINS TO 1482

In the period preceding consolidation, it was a practice to request more or less voluntary loans to meet extraordinary expenses. The first documented loan dates from 1164, when twelve men (in a list headed by the future doge Sebastiano Ziani) lent 1,150 marks of silver and received in return the revenues of the Rialto market (much of which had been part of the public domain since the end of the previous century). By 1207, however, the loans had already become forced, and they were levied on the basis of ability to pay; in other words, by that date an "estimo" already existed which listed the assessed patrimony of citizens according to their residence, by sestiere and parish. The loan of that year does not specifically mention interest, but all the other elements of the later system are already in place: the levy or imposition was a fixed percentage of the estimated patrimony; specific revenues were earmarked for repayment; amortization payments were to be made in March and September of each year; an account book of the loans was to be preserved at the office of the Procurators of San Marco. The Loan Office (Camera Imprestitorum) with specific jurisdiction over the public debt, namely, the collection of levies and payment of interest, was instituted sometime between 1224 and 1252. At the latest by 1262 the "monte" of debt earned 5 percent interest per year, paid semiannually in March and September; accounts were kept according to the sestiere of the fiscal residence of each forced contributor. A fund was set aside to service the debt. Technically, the system was not a perpetual debt from the outset, since amortization payments on principal continued to be made at par when possible; that procedure was suspended in 1363, and in 1375 amortization became occasional and much cheaper: when the state had available funds, it retired credits by buying them up at the market rate. In practice, however, the public debt can be considered perpetual as early as 1262, for repayments on principal never matched new levies — that is, the capital was continually added to and was not paid off for centuries; furthermore, amortization payments received by individuals and estates were readily reinvested in obligations available on the open market.[15]

Levies were imposed when needed by announcing to contributors the percentage (for example, ½ or 1 percent) of the assessment to be paid and the deadline for doing so. Each levy or issue was numbered, and, as we shall see, private contributors were careful to note the number when they registered payment in their account books; similarly, when an issue was amortized, its number was announced and noted. Over the history of the Monte Vecchio, numbered issues totaled 560, distributed as follows:

---

[15]Two attempts to establish perpetual incomes with government credits were made in 1319 and 1325; the solution was simply to have eventual payments received on the principal immediately reinvested on the open market. Luzzatto, *PRV,* lxi.

Fig. 17. Interior of the Venetian Loan Office, situated at the Rialto. Officials and staff are shown paying out interest on government obligations to a lay brother of the monastery of S. Maffeo di Murano. Detail of an illuminated manuscript of about 1390.

Catastico di S. Maffeo di Murano, Seminario Patriarcale, Venice. Photograph by Osvaldo Böhm.

from circa 1250 to February 1381	1–259
December 1381 to April 1432	1–132
May 1432 to August 1441	1–100
August 1441 to February 1454	1–69

When issues were purchased on the open market, their numbers were generally not recorded, at least not in extant documentation. Exceptional are the accounts prepared by the Loan Office for Ludovico Gonzaga (whose extensive purchases in the 1360s were numbered 200 to 208, issued in 1352–54, during the third war with Genoa). All issues were treated equally until the period following 1386, when distinctions were made between the "portfolios" of forced lenders and of those who were not.[16]

Venice paid interest regularly, twice per year, from 1262 to 1380, even during the severe financial crises caused by the War of Ferrara (1310–13) and the third naval war with Genoa (1350–54), as is clearly reflected in the accounts maintained by the Procurators of San Marco.[17] Claims to interest were called "paghe," as they were in Genoa and Florence; as with the credits themselves, paghe were mere registrations on the ledgers of the Loan Office. As long as interest was paid regularly and Venice maintained its promise to amortize occasionally some principal of the debt, government credits sold on the open market at relatively high prices, fluctuating between about 75 and par, with exceptional drops to 60–65 in years of war, including the two wars just mentioned (see graph 11.1). In 1344, when the spate of failures had shown Rialto banks to be untrustworthy depositories and after the state had been spending heavily to buy back forced loans, paying par value, credits reached a peak price of 102.[18]

The crisis of the War of Chioggia, however, inflicted a serious blow to the system. In less than four years between 1378–81, Venetians were forced to lend 41 percent (not 107 percent, as Luzzatto put it—on which see below, App. D, sec. i) of their assessed patrimony, equal perhaps to one-fourth or more of their real patrimony. Venetians had never had to pay so much; many forced lenders defaulted and saw their real estate sold at public auction by the Cazudi, the office with jurisdiction over tax delinquents.

---

[16]Since accountants at the Procurators of San Marco often did not note the numbers of issues, Luzzatto records only scattered numbers; private account books made possible the numbering of many more issues dated by Luzzatto in his tables, and it was a simple operation to fill in the gaps. The results show that only about thirty issues are missing in Luzzatto's tabulations, which cover more than two centuries (nineteen seem to be missing in the first period, eight in the second). Mentions of the numbering are in *PRV*, xcv, cxxxiv. Some issues received no number, but these were usually extraordinary forced loans made with the promise of restitution.

[17]See, for example, ASV, PSM, Citra, b. 260, commis. of Tommaso Querini.

[18]Luzzatto calculated that under Doge Bartolomeo Gradenigo (1339–42) the state used nearly half its revenues to amortize principal on the debt, thus reducing it by about 25 percent (*PRV*, lxxxvii); the contemporary *Venetiarum historia* (Cessi and Bennato, 224), however, sets the figure at 18 percent, still a large amount in a short time.

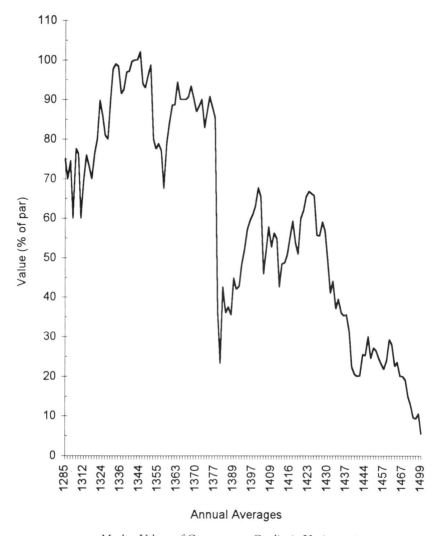

GRAPH 11.1. Market Values of Government Credits in Venice, 1285–1500

Bertolino de' Coldelupi, agent of Ludovico Gonzaga in Venice, reported this to his master, owner of perhaps the largest portfolio of credits in the Monte Vecchio. "Everyone complains of the heavy impositions," he wrote in 1381, in a very telling analysis, "but they are all the more oppressed because they were used to profiting from the funded debt rather than to being burdened by it."[19] This inflation of issues, the temporary suspension

---

[19]"Omnes conqueruntur de gravaminibus que nimia sunt; sed tamen plus gravantur, quia consueverant lucrari et non gravari." *PRV,* clxviii.

of interest payments and then the reduction of interest rates, the inauguration of a direct tax ("impositio") on holdings of government obligations — all these factors caused credits to fall to a low of 18 percent of par in 1381. The subsequent recovery was only partial; even after the resumption of interest payments, market values of credits fluctuated between 40 and 60 until 1429, after which the decline was inexorable; in the 1470s they were worth only from 15 to 8, and interest payments were already in arrears by nearly twenty years.

The seeming decline of the system after 1380, however, actually gave new life to open market operations, for even if interest paid to persons not inscribed in the estimo (especially foreigners) was reduced to 3 percent per year on par, when an individual bought credits at 50, his yield was 6 percent, as we shall see below in examining actual cases. Obviously, foreign investors quickly lost interest in depositing funds in the Grain Office at 3 percent when they could earn twice that by purchasing credits on the open market, albeit with the addition of considerable risk. That was an important factor in the decline of the Grain Office, which did not raise interest rates to meet the competition.

At the same time, many stolid Venetian families enrolled on the estimo must have begun to lose interest in the public debt as an investment opportunity that brought a modest but regular return. They were forced to purchase obligations at 100 which were subsequently worth only a fraction of that. Many were — or felt themselves to be — constrained to sell their holdings, either to be able to invest in more profitable commercial enterprises or simply to have the liquidity with which to meet future forced loans. If they sold at 30, for example, they absorbed a net loss of 70 percent, which could be considered a kind of direct tax. For such citizens, the system became a liability.

Households and institutions inscribed on the estimo which could afford to hold on to their "virginal" credits (the term *imprestiti vergini* was sometimes used in the fifteenth century) earned 4 percent on par for some decades. For them, as well as for purchasers on the open market, state credits were for quite some time, even after 1380, a source of respectable incomes, serving households, individuals (including orphans, minor children, widows), and charitable and religious foundations. Hospitals, confraternities, and religious houses often received credits as bequests left by dying benefactors or members or as dowries for nuns. Sometimes, when they had sufficient liquidity, they added to their portfolio by purchases on the open market. In his "poem" of 1442, Jacopo d'Albizzotto Guidi noted that many people lived off the interest income from government obligations and were quick to collect the "pro'".[20] Increasing arrears in the pay

---

[20]"A pigliar que' danari tutti son presti, / Che molti vivon di chotale entrata, / Sicch'a tor quelli ciaschedun si desti." Cessi and Alberti, *Rialto,* 443.

ment of interest claims, however, reduced incomes and potential yields about the time Guidi was writing.

The marketability of credits, guaranteed by the consolidation in 1262 but probably a reality earlier, created a flourishing and speculative financial market. Not that trust in the new type of asset was established immediately. Doge Raniero Zeno, for example, who died in 1268, leaving about 12 percent of his patrimony in the form of government credits (issued 1255–66), in his testament ordered the credits sold and the proceeds invested in real estate, so as to create a rent-producing endowment for his charitable bequests.[21] By the turn of the century, testators instead used their credits to fund endowments and tended to order the purchase of further credits on the open market from the proceeds of the sale of other assets. Between 1333 and 1407 laws were passed which eliminated altogether the possibility of funding perpetual pious endowments with real estate located in Venice and the Terraferma, in an effort to limit the passage of properties into the "dead hand" of religious and charitable institutions. The largest sale of real estate already so bequeathed and administered by the Procurators of San Marco was mandated by the Great Council and undertaken in 1353–54, during the third naval war with Genoa. Buyers could pay the purchase price in government credits at a favorable quotation, with the result that suddenly some 175,000 nominal ducats' worth of credits were encumbered for the specific endowments previously funded by real property and were thus withdrawn from the open market. Even though that capital alone brought nearly 9,000 ducats annual interest, at 5 percent, it was not large enough in itself to affect the nature of the public debt, but it reflects a strong and ever increasing tendency for credits to pass from potentially marketable assets into permanent trust funds, a tendency that would preoccupy Venetian officials later on, as we shall see.[22]

It is impossible to know the level of turnover on the market for government obligations at any given time, as a result of the loss of all the ledgers of the Loan Office. A single indication, for a single year, can be derived from a budgetary law of 1434 which placed a tax of 2 percent on transfers of ownership of obligations; the proponents estimated the take at 2,000 ducats over the year, which means they figured on a turnover of at least 100,000 ducats in market value or about 300,000 ducats in par value.[23] Although such totals are not small, in some years turnover was surely much higher, as examples of investments by foreigners analyzed below will make clear. The vivacious financial market gave work to numerous specialized

---

[21]Gino Luzzatto, "Il patrimonio privato di un Doge del secolo XIII," reprinted in his *Studi*, 85, and Lane, "Funded Debt," 97.

[22]For the laws, the sales, and specific exemplification, see Mueller, "Procurators of San Marco," 185–214.

[23]*PRV*, doc. 232; it is here presumed that the tax was on the market value transferred and not on nominal values.

brokers ("sensales imprestitorum") and even fostered their formation into companies, as is known from an example of 1408.[24]

Venice's wars against Milan in the first half of the Quattrocento created such a demand for credit that it became normal, in war years, to levy forced loans at an average rate of about 1 percent or more of assessed patrimony per month. The government realized that citizens and estates inscribed on the estimo could not support taxation at that pace for long. Whenever there was a peace, levies were quickly reduced to a minimum or stopped altogether. In the previous century the fiscal burden was also manipulated by rendering harsher or by relaxing the criteria on the basis of which patrimonies were periodically assessed. Only once was a certain portion of "impotentes," assessed households that were unable to meet their levies, permitted to pay a lower figure but as a direct tax, for which they received no interest-bearing asset. This solution, which was normal procedure in Florence (where the payment was called "ad perdendum," in contrast to payment "ad rehabendum"), was invoked only in 1380, during the War of Chioggia, when one-third of assessed households, judged to be in difficulty, paid only 40 percent of the levies, but *a fondo perduto*. The doge Andrea Contarini himself, assessed at the high figure of 14,000 lire d'estimo, had to apply for inclusion in the list, since he was seriously illiquid ("in maxima extremitate in facto denariorum"). A proposal of 1412 to have all households assessed at less than 500 lire pay 50 percent of each levy *a fondo perduto* was turned down by a majority of senators.[25] Individual heads of household who were unable to convince the Loan Office of their straits could petition for relief before the Forty and the Great Council, via the grazia procedure.[26]

The rhythm of annual impositions from 1406 to 1449, to limit our attention to the years of the wars in Lombardy, covered by two case studies analyzed below, can be read from column 4 of tables 13.1 and 13.2, below. The heaviest burdens were imposed in 1440 and 1448 (15 percent of assessed patrimony) and in 1412, 1426–27, 1438–39, and 1441 (12–14 percent). In twenty-eight years, 1425–54, the total imposed was 168 percent, or an average of 6 percent of assessed patrimony per year. The revenue from forced loans collected by the city as a whole is known only for the years 1425–27, when each levy of 1 percent produced about 40,000 ducats. That means annual totals of about 500,000 ducats in 1426, about 570,000 in 1427. Levies beginning in 1438 probably took in less, as the ability — and the

[24]The company was formed by two men, Marco Menegi, of Lucchese origin, and Giovanni Davanzo; ASV, CIN, b. 192, notary F. de Soris, imbreviatura, fol. 107v.

[25]*PRV*, clxiii–iv, ccxxiii, and doc. 220.

[26]See, for example, ASV, Grazie, reg. 16, fols. 20, 84v, 111v, cases of 1364–69, regarding, respectively, a commoner robbed by Catalan pirates, an eighty-year-old widow, and a commoner who had five children in seven years. Persons fined for late payment of levies could also appeal using the same procedure.

willingness — of households to liquidate assets in order to meet renewed impositions declined.[27]

The fiscal burden had been such during the wars in Lombardy and the tension in the Levant that shortly before the Peace of Lodi (signed on 9 April 1454) and the peace treaty with Mohammed II, conqueror of Constantinople (signed ten days later, on 19 April), the system of forced loans was suspended. The last levy on the Monte Vecchio was imposed in February 1454. Thereafter various expedients were used until 1463, when, under the pressure of a new war against the Turks which would last until 1479, Venice instituted a system of direct taxation, called the decima, based on a new and more precise assessment of patrimonies in the form of real estate; as we shall see in actual cases, the decima was also applied to government obligations and to certain kinds of merchandise. But in 1482, there was a partial return to the old system when Venice founded the Monte Nuovo, a new scheme — for garnering funds rapidly for the war against Ferrara — which met initially with great public enthusiasm: the old expedient, tantamount to promising to pay interest on taxes, was considered by the affluent preferable to paying direct taxes. In time, the first two impositions of the decima in a year were pure taxes: subsequent levies were credited to the Monte Nuovo and thus bore interest.[28] Issues of the old fund, now formally called the Monte Vecchio, continued to be traded on the open market, side by side with the new issues, each with its own market price.

iii. INTEREST, YIELD, AND DEBT SERVICE

Interest

In order to follow the payment of interest on the nominal value of credits over the long term, it is necessary to compare the laws that established the gross rates with accounts that registered the net rates of interest actually paid. The results constitute the premise for a discussion of yield on investments made on the discount market. The only surviving accounts that extend over centuries are those of perpetual foundations administered by the Procurators of San Marco, whose only income came from a portfolio of government credits; these, in turn, can be compared with incomes accounted for by families inscribed on the estimo.

As the basis for the tabulation of rates of interest summarized in table 11.1 I have chosen a small endowment, that of Jacopo Bertaldo. Venetian notary, legist, and, when he died in 1315, bishop of Veglia, Bertaldo left rents from his real property in Venice to support some ten different per-

---

[27]Although the annual levies derived from my sources differ slightly from those of Luzzatto, I have used his total for the whole period, 1425–54; see *PRV,* ccxxx–xxxiv, and *BG,* 1, doc. 86.

[28]*Traictie,* cap. 59.

petual bequests. In 1354 these properties were sold at public auction and paid for in credits at their nominal value; since their market price stood at about 80, the purchase of these houses was particularly advantageous. The Bertaldo properties were thus exchanged for some 790 ducats' worth of credits, bringing the principal of the estate's portfolio to 940 ducats. In the years following the War of Chioggia some unpaid interest was added to principal, and perhaps additional credits were purchased with interest income, so that the portfolio stood at 1,440 ducats in 1387, at 1,472.5 ducats beginning in 1421. In the table, the data have been broken up into uneven time spans defined by the homogeneity of actual annual returns. Data are available until 1576, when the interest for 1503 was paid; thereafter, interest payments on the Monte Vecchio were suspended and retirement of the capital begun. (It should be pointed out that no attempt has been made to account for inflation, given the absence for Venice of consistent wage and price series.)[29]

The process of paying interest to holders of government obligations took time. So as to avoid inequities, the order was decided by lot cast by the doge himself in the Great Council, solemnly, in the presence of one of the heads of the Ten. It was customary to establish the order of the six sestieri all at once; then, when the state went further into arrears, only one was chosen at a time, as recorded in the registers of the Great Council. Results of the drawing were news, anxiously awaited by citizens, trustees of endowments, and foreigners alike.[30]

Venetian financial authorities paid interest regularly, every March and September, from the funding of the debt in 1262 until 1380 at 5 percent per year, even during the financial crises caused first by the War of Ferrara (1308–11) and the resultant indemnity of 100,000 ducats owed to the papacy, then by the third naval war against Genoa (1350–54), when the Treasury was at most one or two months behind schedule. It was the fourth and decisive war against Genoa, known as the War of Chioggia (1379–81), which caused major changes in the Venetian public debt. On the eve of the war, in 1378 and 1379, the semestral interest payments of 2½ percent each were still made regularly every March and September. On the basis of a quickly revised estimo, with particularly burdensome criteria of assessment, assessed households were forced to turn over to the coffers of the state more than 40 percent of their assessed valuation over the duration of the war;

[29]On the sale of trust property in 1353–54 and the Bertaldo estate, see Mueller, "Procurators of San Marco," 196–200. The estate papers are now in ASV, PSM, Ultra, b. 45.

[30]Marin Sanudo (Le vite, 1:224) wrote under the date 30 October 1481, "Che li pro' di la Camera de Imprestidi si pagino li sestieri a l'anno, sicome sarano butadi a un a uno in Gran Conseio per il Serenissimo, presente uno Cao d'il Conseio d'i X . . . Prima si butavano tutti a un tratto." In his Diarii (6:267) in 1505 he wrote, "Fo gran consejo. Butà il pro' di setembrio 1474, vene Canarejo." For example, ASV, MC, Deda (reg. 25), fol. 43: "Proiectis texeris pro rendendo prode page martii 1475, venit pro secundo Dorsoduro."

TABLE 11.1

Interest and Rates of Interest Received by the Estate of Bishop Jacopo Bertaldo
(d. 1315), 1355–1576

Period	Gross Interest Rate p.a.	Claims Paid	Cash Paid (ave. p.a. in ducats)	Net Interest Rate p.a.	Comments
1355–79	5	1355–79	47	5	
1382–85	4	—	37.6	4	Arrears in the 1380s; some paghe consolidated
1386–1400	3	1386–1400	43.2	3	Reduction as tax, then confirmed
1401–20	3	1401–20	43.2	3	
1421–34	3	1421–33[a]	39.43	2.68	3 paghe in arrears, 6 paghe paid only half
1435–39	3	1433[b]–36[a]	26.4	1.8	No payment in 1439
1440–41	3	1436[b]–37[a]	14.75	1.0	No payment in 1441
1442–43	3	1438–39[a]	21.3	1.45	9 paghe in arrears; paga 1437[b] paid in 1445
1444–59	2	1439[b]–48[a]	17.16	1.17	Reduction plus 5% tax; 19 paghe in 31 semesters
1459–64	2	1448[b]–51	18.75	1.27	7 paghe in 11 semesters
1465–66	2	1452	13.25	0.9	14 years in arrears
1467–1534	2	1453–83	11.94	0.81	58 paghe in 68 years; none 1509–17
1535–48	2	1484–89[a]	9.05	0.61	Many paghe paid in installments
1549–76	2	1489[b]–1503	14.5	0.98	29 paghe; 73 years in arrears

Source: ASV, PSM, ultra, b. 45.
Note: Nominal value of portfolio: 940 du., 1355–79; 1,440 du., 1387–1420, 1,472.5 thereafter.
[a]March claim.
[b]September claim.

public and private indebtedness soared. After the September paga had been honored in 1379, interest payments were suspended; they were resumed only in February 1383, albeit at the reduced rate of 4 percent per year. In February 1386 the rate was further reduced to 3 percent for owners of government obligations and for estates — such as that of Jacopo Bertaldo — which were not inscribed on the estimo.[31] In the course of the 1380s, interest in arrears was either paid in cash or consolidated, at an arbitrary value of 60; claims due in 1380 were paid only in 1389, which was another way of attenuating potential profits of speculators who had bought obligations at low prices during the war. From 1390 to 1411 payments were

[31]Payments were obviously resumed at different dates in different cases, as the bureaucracy caught up with arrears; cf. *PRV,* cliii n. For the reductions in rates and for accounting fictions employed 1386–94, see ibid., clx, clxxxi–ii.

regular; interest, that is, was turned over in specie at most three to four months late. There were some exceptions owing to military exigencies: one-half the interest due on the September claims of 1405, 1409, and 1411 was not paid until 1413, 1414, and 1415 respectively. From 1415 to 1431 interest was paid in full at most six months late, with some exceptions: in certain semesters in the years 1412–15, 1426–27, and 1431–32, only one-half the interest was paid, the other half being withheld as a tax or credited to capital.[32]

Beginning in 1432, as a result of the wars in Lombardy, the state began falling behind in its interest payments; even the promised rates, eroded by deductions and taxes, came slowly to be halved on the average, until in practice only one semestral payment per year was made. Interest was in arrears by seven years in 1450, when the average annual rate paid on pious endowments was only slightly over 1 percent; in 1454, the year of the Peace of Lodi, which ended the war against Milan and Florence and which marks the last year in which a forced loan was levied, no interest was paid at all; in 1455 the claims of 1446 were paid, while those of 1455 were not paid until 1471, sixteen years late and at a rate of only 0.8 percent on the average. By the end of the long naval war against the Turks (1463–79), payments were twenty years behind; none were made in 1480. Soon thereafter began the war against Ferrara (1482–84), financed by the Monte Nuovo; the new series, which promised 5 percent on par, awakened considerable popular support and may have reduced concern for the paghe of what was now known as the Monte Vecchio. On that series in 1482 only one claim to interest was paid (that of 1461), in 1484 none at all. Beginning in 1487 the arrears lengthened: by 1500 the state was almost thirty years behind (the claim paid was that of March 1471). During the War of the League of Cambrai, between 1509 and 1517, no interest was paid to foundations (only one to households), so that interest was in arrears by fifty years in 1531, by sixty in 1550, when the average net rate rose once again to about 1 percent per annum; in 1576 the second claim of 1503 was paid. With that, interest payments on Monte Vecchio issues seem to have been suspended;[33] a short time later the state began liquidating that oldest of series, at the price of 2½ (the average market price since about 1520) for credits that had been ceded, of double that for "virginal" credits.[34]

[32]Bishop Miani of Vicenza complained in 1429 that in war years interest due was occasionally halved and sometimes added to principal; see Dieter Girgensohn, "Il testamento di Pietro Miani ('Emilianus'), vescovo di Vicenza († 1433)." *AV,* ser. 5, 132 (1989): 49–50, 55.

[33]Accounting in separate "quaderni" for each single estate administered by the Procurators of San Marco ended in that year, probably concomitant with the suspension of interest on the old debt, which had financed most of the old trusts.

[34]On repayment of the whole public debt in the course of the sixteenth century, see Lane, "Public Debt and Private Wealth," 80 and n. 11; idem, *Venice,* 324–27, and Pezzolo, *L'oro dello stato,* 200–7.

What happened to the incomes of foundations whose resources were limited to government credits can be read from table 11.1: revenues funding Bertaldo's bequests declined from 47 ducats per year in the mid-Trecento to about 18 ducats in the mid-Quattrocento, to 12–14 ducats in the mid-Cinquecento — the century of considerable inflation. The Great Council itself admitted openly in 1452 that the policy of reducing the rate of interest from 3 to 2 percent via a withholding tax, and from a promised 2 percent to an actual 1 percent, by paying an average of only one semestral claim per year put charitable and religious foundations in serious financial straits. It provided, however, for a single exception: the portfolio held by the "most excellent temple" of San Marco was to receive the full interest of 3 percent (1½% per paga) on the nominal value of its portfolio, in order to avoid its going to ruin.[35]

The continual reduction of gross rates of interest on portfolios held by persons and foundations not inscribed on the estimo, beginning in 1382 (as summarized in table 11.2), was motivated by an attempt to reduce the inequity between interest returns paid to forced lenders and the yields earned by persons, often speculators and foreigners, who escaped assessment and benefited from buying below par the credits that forced lenders were constrained to sell at a loss. The only efficient way of taxing such portfolios was by withholding part of the interest due; in fact, all reductions in interest rates originated as temporary taxation measures, via withholding, which became definitive in the course of time.

The same motivation was behind the reduction of interest rates on large portfolios, acquired in part on the open market by heads of households inscribed on the estimo. Table 11.2 delineates the ceilings established by the Senate, in the difficult years 1412–40, for holdings eligible for the full (gross) rate of 4 percent; the balance was payable at 3 percent. The practical result was that persons with low estimo figures and large portfolios earned 4 percent only on a given figure per 1,000 lire d'estimo; vice versa, persons with high estimo assessments and large holdings could earn 4 percent on much of them. To take Luzzatto's example for 1412: a person inscribed on the estimo for 5,000 lire and who owned 30,000 nominal ducats' worth of credits received 4 percent interest on 12,500 ducats' worth (five times the ceiling of 2,500) and 3 percent on the balance (17,500 ducats).[36] Obviously, holders of obligations would try to maintain their portfolios within the figures eligible for the higher rate.

In 1444 the nominal rate of interest on the holdings of persons and

[35]*PRV*, docs. 269 (1452) and 279 (1466). In 1452 it was stated that "page que fieri solebant de sex in sex menses fiunt in uno anno, ita quod dici potest quod ipsa ecclesia de tribus pro centenario habeat solam unam pro centenario, unde nisi provideatur ipsa ecclesia . . . ibit in desolationem."

[36]Ibid., ccxxii; see also the reference to this policy, under the year 1413, by Antonio Morosini, Cronaca, 1:780–84.

TABLE 11.2

Gross Rates of Interest on the Nominal Value Government Credits, 1262–1444

| Year | Owners of Record Inscribed on the Estimo | | Persons and Foundations Not Inscribed on the Estimo |
	ceilings per £1,000 of Estimo	rate	rate
1262–1381	Unlimited	5	5
1382	Unlimited	4	4
1386	Unlimited	4	3
1412	Up to 2,500 du.	4	
	Above	3	
1419	Up to 2,000 du.	4	
	Above	3	
1434	Up to 3,000 du.	4	
	Above	3	
1439	Up to 4,000 du.	4	
	Above	3	
1444			2

Source: PRV, ccxxii, doc. 225; ccxxxiv–v (n. 1); ccxxxvii–xli; ccxlix–l, doc. 260.

estates not inscribed on the estimo was definitively reduced to 2 percent. As is revealed by the Bertaldo accounts (see table 11.1), that meant a net rate of about 1 percent or, more precisely, slightly above that for the first twenty years, then, beginning in the 1460s, at 0.81 percent. This was just about half (0.46) the rate paid — all on paghe in arrears — to households, whose gross rate remained 4 percent; this is best revealed by comparison of the Bertaldo estate with the accounts kept by Nicolò d'Andrea Barbarigo for the years 1463 to 1482. In that period, Nicolò, who carefully recorded the nominal capital on which each paga was due, received an average annual return, at par, of 1.77 percent (see below, table 13.4).

After the last forced loan was levied in February 1454, obviously no "virginal" credits were available, nor was the estimo updated; any acquisitions had to be made on the open market. Prior to that date, the buyer on the open market was eligible for collecting the interest on his credits as soon as he became owner of record; that was the reason there was so much jockeying for position as 1 March and 1 September neared and an individual desired to be — or not to be, according his exigencies — owner of record when a given paga came due. After 1454, Venetians who purchased credits did not collect interest when the paghe for those credits fell due, but only when the date of purchase fell due, as though the credits had been acquired, not from previous owners, but directly from the state as forced loans. This, in any case, is what transpires from accounts of Nicolò Barbarigo, who received a yield on three packets of monte credits purchased, from private parties between 1457 and 1461, only between 1476 and 1482. No legislation has been found to explain the anomaly. Possibly Venetians were simply constrained to accept this imposition as part of the state's policy of reducing debt service, or conceivably they were given the option to receive 2 percent on par for two paghe immediately, as one must assume foreign buyers could, or await a rate of 4 percent for two paghe at some unpredictable future date, thus creating a fiction that the credits were "virginal." A third possibility exists, although it seems not to have been the case in the Barbarigo example, namely, that the paghe on particular issues had been sold separately to a third party. Be that as it may, Barbarigo only began realizing a yield on his purchases after almost twenty years (see table 13.4).

Yield

The reduction of nominal rates of interest after the War of Chioggia and the application of withholding taxes and surcharges reduced the cost of servicing the debt and moderated the disproportion between yields to capital invested in government obligations on the open market and the nominal interest owed to forced lenders. From 1262 through 1379, the full rate of 5 percent on par values was paid regularly; thus yields, calculated by dividing the net rate of interest by the market price of credits, fluctuated between a low of 4.90 percent (when government obligations exceptionally soared above par in 1344) and a high of 8.3 percent. (Again, no provision can be made here for the inflation that presumably followed the Black Death.)

When credits fell to 18 during the War of Chioggia, potential yields reached nearly 28 percent, an unacceptable rate that would have been owed largely to speculators not inscribed on the estimo. This would have mortified forced contributors, who, if they kept their credits, would earn only 5 percent, and if they had been constrained to sell, would have suffered a loss of some 80 percent. The reduction of interest on par to 4 percent in 1382, before payments were resumed, meant, for those who had bought at 18, a yield of 22 percent — still an unconscionable rate. Net returns were therefore further reduced by the irregular withholding of *impositiones*. These were legislated as reimbursable loans, but they were actually consolidated at 60 percent, again irregularly and in blocks, rather than repaid, which renders practically impossible the calculation of actual returns.[37] The rate at par for these portfolios was then further reduced to 3 percent in 1386, formally differentiating between the treatment accorded forced lenders and those not assessed. By that time, the strong demand provoked by hopes for high yields had already brought market prices back to about 40, thus reducing yield to 10 percent for investors who were also forced lenders, to 7.5 percent

---

[37]*PRV,* cxcviii n. 1. For the policy of *impositiones* in general, see Cessi, "La finanza veneziana," an important contribution, based almost exclusively on legislation, even though it lacks footnotes and provides no quantifiable data.

for those who were not. Given the arrears, consolidations, taxes, and reductions of interest, the yield rates for the 1380s shown in table 11.3 are more theoretical than real.[38]

By the end of the century, when the financial difficulties caused by the War of Chioggia had been overcome, yields, on the average, were in fact quite moderate. This result may reflect a policy of calibrating net rates of interest—to the extent possible—to market prices of credits. Of course, daily variations of prices, which are flattened by using averages, created speculative occasions for higher yields (for an actual case, see below, graph 14.1). As can be seen in table 11.3, yields to assessed households were one-third higher than yields to estates, as long as gross rates at par remained 4 and 3 percent, but double beginning in 1444, when the differential between portfolios of forced lenders and those not assessed was increased by setting theoretical rates at 4 and 2 percent respectively. Delays in paying interest began in 1432; payments were nine paghe (four and one-half years) in arrears in the mid-1440s. Thereafter, the delay increased progressively, and calculation of yield becomes problematic. It becomes quite impossible after the last forced loan was levied in 1454, when credits purchased on the open market were liable to be treated as "virginal" forced loans, whose claims to interest were eligible for the theoretical rate of 4 percent but which actually matured only after many years. Credits purchased in this manner were more similar to pension funds or trust funds, to be enjoyed in old age or by one's heirs. The only practical example found comes from the accounts of Nicolò Barbarigo, discussed in detail below (see Chap. 13, sec. iii). Claims to interest on his first purchase in 1457, at a price of 22, matured in 1476 and, over the next half century, earned an average yield of about 7 percent. Two subsequent purchases, at higher prices, yielded about 5.5 percent—again, beginning only twenty years after purchase. No wonder Nicolò, in his testament, insisted that his heirs hold on to that portfolio!

It is interesting to note that the rate of yield on government obligations at times was taken to define the current rate of interest on a loan. The rationale must have been as follows: the lender could have invested legitimately in such credits and could rightfully have profited from the yield on his investment; since he had to forgo that opportunity in order to make a private loan, the borrower could be asked to provide a comparable rate of return. Here are two examples, one a small private loan, the other a very large public loan, both from the 1390s. In 1391, Tommaso Talenti, whom we have encountered before, lent 200 ducats to two immigrants from Rimini; the notary gave the loan the form of a local colleganza, but it was in fact

---

[38] A useful table of market prices of Venetian government obligations and the respective rates of yield can be found in Homer and Sylla, *A History of Interest Rates*; Italian edition, *Storia dei tassi di interessi,* 142; since the authors had no accurate data for net rates of interest paid after 1379, they suspended their calculation of yields at that point.

TABLE 11.3

Rates of Interest and Yield on Monte Vecchio Credits, 1262–1576

Period	Gross Interest Rate p.a. contrib.	noncontrib.	Claims Paid	Net Interest Rate p.a. contrib.	noncontrib.	Yield at Given Market Prices of Credits (boldface) (yield rates in italics)				
1262–1379	5	5	1262–1379	5	5	**75** *6.67*	**80** *6.25*	**85** *5.9*	**90** *5.5*	**95** *5.3*
1382–85	4	4	—	4	4	**18** *22*	**25** *16*	**35** *11.4*	**40** *10*	**45** *8.9*
1386–1420	4	3	1380–1420	4		**40** *10*	**45** *8.9*	**50** *8.0*	**55** *7.3*	**60** *6.7*
					3	**45** *7.5*	**50** *6.7*	**55** *6.0*	**60** *5.45*	**65** *5.0*
1421–34	4	3	1421–33[a]	(3.7)		**45** *8.2*	**50** *7.4*	**55** *6.7*	**60** *6.2*	**65** *5.6*
					2.68	**45** *6.0*	**50** *5.4*	**55** *4.9*	**60** *4.5*	**65** *4.15*
1435–39	4	3	1433[b]–36[a]	(2.8)		**20** *14*	**25** *11.2*	**30** *9.3*	**35** *8.0*	
					1.8	**20** *9.0*	**25** *7.2*	**30** *6.0*	**35** *5.1*	
1440–41	4	3	1436[b]–37[a]	(2.0)		**20** *10.0*				
					1.0	**20** *5.0*				

						20	23	28	30
1442–43	4	3				12.3	10.7	8.75	8.2
			1438–39[a]	(2.45)	(1.45)	7.25	6.3	5.2	4.8
1444–59	4	2				10.0	8.7	7.1	6.7
			1439[b]–48[a]	2.0	1.17	5.85	5.1	4.2	3.9
1459–64	4	2				10.0	8.7	7.1	6.7
			1448[b]–51	2.0	1.27	6.35	5.5	4.5	4.2
1465–66	4	2				10.0	8.7	7.1	6.7
			1452	2.0	0.9	4.5	3.9	3.2	3.0
1467–1534	4	2				8.85	7.7	6.3	5.9
			1453–83	1.77	0.81	4.1	3.5	2.9	2.7
1535–48	4	2				3.1	2.7	2.2	2.0
			1484–89[a]		0.61				
1549–76	4	2				4.9	4.3	3.5	3.3
			1489[b]–1503		0.98				

Source: Tables 11.1, 13.3, and 13.4.

Note: Figures in parentheses were derived from the interest data. After ca. 1456 interest claims on new acquisitions on the open market began maturing only 20 years later, making it impossible to calculate yield; the figures from 1459 on show how yield oscillated over time on purchases made at the last-indicated market prices.

[a] March claim.

[b] September claim.

a mortgage, with interest tied to the yield on government obligations, "as though they had been bought at 40, their actual price yesterday." The resulting rate of interest was 7.5 percent. The interest was due in March and September, when the Loan Office paid interest to holders of government credits.[39] The approach taken was very similar when, in 1395, the Venetian state lent 50,000 ducats to Marquis Nicolò III d'Este of Ferrara. It was to be considered a free loan for five years; if he did not repay it at maturity, however, he owed Venice a return "at an annual rate equal to what he would have earned had he now invested that money in government credits, at the yield [the document continues] that his subjects in fact earn on the credits they purchase in Venice." After the necessary calculations, the rate was expressed as 7⅓ percent.[40]

Marketability of Paghe

Beginning with the mid-Quattrocento, there are clear indications that paghe had become marketable separately from the credits to which they had been attached. This fact is reflected especially in civil suits; I have not uncovered accounting records of actual purchases. Market prices of paghe were far different from prices of bonds and depended on the nearness or not of the maturity of a given paga. A lawsuit of 1455, when credits were valued at about 24, concerned interest claims bought at 50, 60, and 63, at unspecified earlier dates; a lawsuit of 1450 dealt with a sale of pro' at 72.[41] In 1465

[39]ASV, PSM, Citra, b. 141, commis. Tommaso Talenti, parchment of 1 March 1391; the borrowers were Fosco di Giovanni Santi and his son Giacomo of Rimini; the loan, made in the bank of Pietro Benedetto, used the phrase "ad negotiandum hic in Rivoalto," typical for local colleganze, but it was secured on two pieces of real estate; the borrowers promised "illud prode quod ex eis reciperetis a Camera imprestitorum" had you bought credits at 40, "sicut valebant heri." There are two ways of calculating the rate: 3 percent interest on par / 40 = 7.5 percent; 200 ducats would have purchased 500 ducats nominal credits, which, at 3 percent, gives 15 ducats, and 15/200 = 7.5. The notary was Marco Rafanelli, Talenti's principal notary, who was located "sub Camera imprestitorum"; his acts are in CIN, b. 168–70. The legality of such an approach was propounded in commercial court by a borrower, who affirmed that although interest on a cash loan, especially at fixed interest, was illegal, to set interest at the yield on government credits was permitted: "di denari non hè licito rende pro' et maxime a far patto, ma pur a raxon di imprestedi el se conziedi apresso i homeni, perchè nui rendemo raxon che queli se reze segondo el chorso di la Camera." The original lender was the banker Giovanni Orsini; with the failure of that bank, the credit was negotiated to a third party. The problem lay with the option to ask repayment in obligations or in cash. GP, Sg, reg. 55, fols. 18v–20v (22 March 1431).

[40]ASV, Commemoriali, reg. 9, fols. 1r–2v (3 April 1395): "quod, facto calcolo de precio quod nunc valent imprestita supradicta, sapit summam ducatorum 7 pro centenario." Since the interest on par for foreigners was 3 percent, the rate means government obligations were selling for 41 on that day (3/41 = 7.3 percent).

[41]The "pro'" was to have been collected by the Garzoni bank and turned over to the daughter of the plaintiff, while in fact it had been collected by a testamentary executor, here object of the suit. The former reported that, upon his return to Venice after an absence, he had

the Senate prohibited the auditing offices (the Raxon Vecchia and Raxon Nova) from accepting payment of fines in offsets of interest that would mature only after many years; the offices were to insist on payment in cash "or in paghe whose payment had already been designated by lot," that is, that would mature directly.[42] A final lawsuit that discusses at length the marketability of claims to interest dates from 1473, when the parties presented and debated extracts from the books of the Loan Office, prepared by the scribe of the office, Alvise Amadi, and copied into the court record. The extracts regarded the paga of March 1456, which, in fact, had been paid the previous year. They show, argued the defendant, that the accounting practice of the Loan Office was to use the verb *dire* when the pro' had simply been ordered payable to an agent, the verb *volere* (or *de volontà*) when the claim to interest had actually been sold and the seller had given orders for its "translation" or alienation to the purchaser. The defendant lost the case, but his explanation of the formulas used by the Loan Office was not contested.[43] It seems, in short, albeit on the basis of limited documentation, that the marketability of paghe in Venice was completely accepted and quotidian in the mid-fifteenth century, with discounts deriving from the ever increasing arrears in payments by the state. But there is no evidence that it ever reached anything like the popularity that it knew in Genoa, where interest (paghe) and credits (luoghi) were regularly negotiated separately and used for offsetting debits and credits with the state.[44]

Debt Service

No consistent data are available on the question of carrying charges, that is, the payment of interest on the funded debt. Early on a sinking fund

---

found "esser stadi compradi zerti pro' de imprestedi." ASV, GP, Sg, reg. 121, fols. 7–12v. An earlier though less explicit indication of marketability is in ibid., reg. 100, fol. 131v (31 May 1445). Finally, see AC, reg. 3650, fol. 19v (16 September 1450).

[42]ASV, ST, reg. 5, fol. 123v (17 June 1465). A case of just such a payment is recorded in the following year. One noble asked another to buy 100 ducats' worth of interest so that he could use it to pay a customs duty: "perché el comprasse di questi pro' di inprestedi del 1456, per satisfare e pagar a le Raxon Nove quelo che del dazio de l'oio condutto." GP, Sg, reg. 148, fols. 27v–30v (8 July 1467). Such a manner of paying a tax served as an immediate alieviation of carrying charges. Other instances of purchases of pro' are in ibid., reg. 149, fols. 97–100 (24 October 1467), and reg. 150, fols. 192–96v (16 September 1468).

[43]The defendant said he had transferred interest in the manner followed for sales: "i qual pro' io li fizi traslatar . . . a quel medemo modo se translata tuti i pro' che se vende, che dixeno 'de volontà' del vendedor. . . . Cussì fono notati nel scuoder contadi a mi de sua volontà, per quella rima, denotandovi, Signori, che la Camera de Imprestedi, ch'è uno offitio real, in su li pro' non uxita dir questa parolla de volontà, non, ma in caxo de alienacion, perchè coloro che schuodono i pro' per chomision se dixeno 'contadi al tal' et non se dixe 'de volontà' de colui del pro.'" The polize or extracts from the books of Dorsoduro and Castello provide, under the relevant paga, the instructions given on 2 May 1468 for disposition of the interest, when it should fall due, using just such formulas. ASV, GP, Sg, reg. 158, fols. 81–83.

[44]Day, *Medieval Market Economy,* 158–59.

was established to service the debt, the amount of which was changed at various times. As we have seen above, in the years around 1340 debt service (amortization plus carrying charges) probably absorbed half of total revenues.[45] For later years, we have chosen to narrow the discussion to data regarding carrying charges alone.

Totals paid as interest on obligations for thirteen years, 1386–98, have been preserved in a late chronicle. The figures go from peaks of 246,690 ducats in 1386 and 241,190 in 1393 to a minimum of 188,950 ducats in 1397. The high sums paid in the 1380s, of course, reflect the heavy burden of forced loans contracted during the War of Chioggia and the effort made to pay interest in arrears as well as current interest; in 1391–93 Venice was paying interest on theoretically reimbursable loans or *impositiones* levied on portfolios of noncontributors which were in fact consolidated, that is, added to the principal of those portfolios. The easing of the burden later in the century was the result of both reductions in interest rates and the insistent policy of retiring credits through purchases on the open market.[46]

Expansion on the Terraferma and the wars in Lombardy brought heavy impositions of forced loans, and carrying charges rose again as a result. Antonio Morosini records the figure of 224,000 ducats per year in 1413; an anonymous chronicle of about 1432–34 set the cost of interest at 320,000 ducats as a result of the wars and wrote that the Loan Office was finding it difficult to pay one paga every nine months rather than every six and thus was beginning to go into arrears on its obligations.[47]

---

[45]Luzzatto in *PRV,* lxxxvi–vii, and in "Il debito pubblico," 220–21. For the whole topic of the level of the funded debt, amortization, and carrying charges, see Lane, "Funded Debt."

[46]*BG,* 1, doc. 74, p. 85. Luzzatto writes that "certamente" the figures refer to the full legal interest of 5 percent, since the reductions in interest were considered taxes and recorded as revenues until 1394. There is no indication, however, that the figures were derived from account books of the type Luzzatto assumes, and one wonders whether the decline in debt service would have been as sharp simply as a result of amortization. *PRV,* clxxxix n. 1, cxcvii–cc. Even the effect of amortization on the level of debt service is open to question. The office charged with retiring credits through purchases on the open market was that of the Provveditori di Comun. Retirement and amortization are misnomers, however, for those credits were not really extinguished at all but kept active—for how long is not known; now it was the Provveditori as new owners of record who, in a strange game of Peter paying Paul, received the interest, possibly as a way of increasing the sinking fund. But the office was found to be defrauding the fisc by collecting a yield based on the full 4 percent of par even on credits that had been due only 3 percent; since they bought the credits at prices ranging from 40 to 60, they profited, like private speculators, from yields of 6.67 to 10 percent. The Signoria ordered an audit of the accounts in order to reduce to the legal rate of 3 percent the interest claims on that type of obligation and required restitution of the difference illegally collected. See ASV, CN, reg. 5, fol. 57v (5 September 1416). By contrast, a law of 1386 regarding amortization speaks of canceling such credits ("faciendo cancellari illa talia imprestita accepta nomine nostro Comunis"); *PRV,* clxxxix n. 3. The policy of not actually extinguishing obligations is reflected also in cases of sequester, as will be seen below; behind it is some combination of legal and accounting fictions and mentality.

[47]*Cronaca,* 1:780, and Biblioteca Civica, Padua, PD, C.M. 279, fol. 222r–v. The latter, a well-

Half a century passes before other figures become available. In 1488 the state paid 112,920 ducats for the September claim of 1464, according to a senatorial deliberation of that year. Sanudo in 1493 reported the exact same figure, with the same breakdown by sestiere, clearly from the same source. It is tantamount to an annual expenditure, since on the average only one claim in arrears of Monte Vecchio credits was paid in a year.[48] Considerably higher estimates are recorded for the period around 1500 in sundry balance sheets (one of them copied by Sanudo himself) and in the treatise by the anonymous French observer, namely, 150,000 ducats "more or less" per year for the Monte Vecchio for a single coupon and "nearly the same" for the Monte Nuovo, which, of course, paid two claims per year. Gerolamo Priuli, banker and diarist, records exactly the same figure for the Monte Nuovo in September 1509; he gives the capital as about 3 million ducats and the interest as 75,000 ducats per semester. On gross annual revenues of 1,150,000 ducats, those figures represent more than 25 percent. In the mid-sixteenth century, when the state paid the same amount, about 300,000 ducats, per year in interest and amortization, about double what Venetians were paying in direct taxes, that meant about 15 percent of total revenues.[49]

Terms of comparison for the relative costs of deficit finance are similarly scanty and scattered. In 1380 Florence earmarked 50,000 florins to payment of interest, while in 1415 the Arno city, then with less than half Venice's population, paid 185,000 florins in interest on prestanze and prestanzoni — equal to revenues from the four major gabelles. If the figure of about 400,000 florins for total revenues in peacetime, with reference to the year 1423, is credible, the Arno city consumed nearly half of its revenues in carrying charges alone.[50] Genoa, also about half the size of Venice, in the wake of the War of Chioggia paid the same amount as Venice, about 200,000 florins in carrying charges annually, which was about half of the city's total revenues.[51] In the early 1990s, the cost of interest on the public debt in the United States stood at 16–18 percent of gross revenues, while

---

informed and little used chronicle, states, "Camera degli imprestidi vuol de pro' ogni anno ducati 320.000, che si pagano in doi ratte ogni sei mesi ducati 160.000." Because of the wars, however, "l'è cresciuto tanto il debito della detta camera ch'el se paga con fatica una paga in mesi nove, la qual camera è debita' a 4 per cento — millioni de ducati et a 3 per cento — milliona." It would not be unreasonable to fill in the blank spaces thus: a total debt of 9.3 million ducats, of which 4 million at 4 percent and 5.3 million at 3 percent.

[48]*BG,* 1, doc. 127; Sanudo, *De origine,* 190–91.

[49]*BG,* 1, docs. 122 (dated 1464, which probably refers, however, to the interest claim due in 1488), 134 (dated 1500); *Traictie,* chap. 66, from which the quoted phrases are taken; only this text and Priuli mention the interest on the Monte Nuovo. Priuli, *Diarii,* 332–33. Cf. also Lane, *Venice,* 137, and idem, "Public Debt and Private Wealth"; also Cozzi and Knapton, *Storia,* 303.

[50]Molho, *Florentine Public Finances,* 54, 66 n, and 72 n; *BG,* 1, doc. 83, "Intrade di alcuni Principi Cristiani ne l'ano 1423," taken from Sanudo's *Vite dei dogi.*

[51]Day, *Les douanes de Gênes,* vol. 1, xxxi, xxxiv.

that in the Republic of Italy fluctuated around 27–30 percent and that in the Federal Republic of Germany stood at 9–10 percent.[52]

iv. FRAUDS AND PUBLIC OUTCRIES

Frauds involving the Loan Office were swindles by private operators and the usual embezzlements by officials and staff members. One case concerned a profit-making scheme for defending citizens from the increasing arrears in interest payments; it involved so many owners of government obligations as to constitute a threat to public order.

In 1359 the Senate dealt with the problem of false claimants to interest who presented themselves at the Loan Office before the arrival of the genuine owners of record. But instead of ordering the staff to pay out interest only to those third parties who presented a notarized power of attorney, it simply authorized the officials to proceed against offenders.[53] Two nobles were identified and condemned for swindling women who held government obligations. In 1370 Giovanni Venier was condemned *in absentia* to banishment from Venice and its territories for suborning a witness to make possible a theft. He sent the noblewoman Beriola Baffo to the Loan Office to attest that another noblewoman, Fiordalisa Moro, had agreed that he sell her portfolio, for the considerable amount of 5,400 nominal ducats in obligations, a fraud that he proceeded to perpetuate. Venier was to be hanged if he broke the ban, and Beriola Baffo was sentenced for false testimony. Just after the War of Chioggia a somewhat similar swindle was perpetrated by Filippo di Marco Bellegno to the detriment of Donna Elena Bon. Bellegno had once been authorized by Elena Bon, in the presence of two witnesses, to sell and transfer a certain number of her credits, which he did, probably as a professional dealer. When Elena was away in Padua, he pretended still to be her authorized dealer and fraudulently ("fraudolenter et dolose") sold her whole portfolio. He was sentenced to one year in prison, counting from the time that he had repaid the victim her capital and interest plus the 80 ducats he had earned on the operation. He applied for and received a grazia two years later and fulfilled the conditions in April 1385, when Elena Bon declared that she was satisfied and he paid the 40 ducat fine he owed to the state.[54] In a civil lawsuit of 1468 Isabetta, widow of Gerolamo da Viviano, sued Francesco Sagredo, to whom she had entrusted 300 ducats with which to purchase interest claims of 1454 for her. When the paga fell due and she went to the Loan Office to collect, she discovered that there was nothing in her name. The defendant was sen-

---

[52]These figures, extracted from national statistical abstracts, were kindly provided by my colleague Giuseppe Tattara.

[53]ASV, SM, reg. 29, fol. 24v.

[54]ASV, AC, regs. 3643, fol. 141 (31 October 1370), and 3644, fol. 50v (6 February 1383 and 22 January 1385).

tenced to restitution of the 300 ducats.[55] It is not hard to imagine how single women, especially widows who had just gotten back their dowries, could be victimized by swindlers and unprincipled sellers of investment schemes.

Selling pure air was another way of making money; it defrauded the state rather than individual holders of credits. In 1393 Leonardo Venier, son of the late Giovanni, that is, very likely the son of the above-named swindler, is identified as a habitual dealer or speculator in credits ("mercator imprestitorum"). He was discovered to have had himself accredited with government obligations and to have sold credits that were not his at all, for a total par value of more than 6,000 ducats. That took the connivance of a scribe at the Loan Office. For this fraud against the Commune, which consisted of inflating the debt with otherwise nonexistent credits, Venier was ordered held in prison until he repaid what he had taken. There is no indication that he paid.[56] A similar scheme was developed inside the office, by a scribe. In 1457 Simone Fioravanti was tried *in absentia* on two counts of fraud. First, he falsified the ledgers by adding zeros (actually a "C" for "centenario") to some accounts, thus inflating them for a total of 10,000 ducats. These nonexistent credits he then sold to connivers, who paid him the interest, as his cut. Second, he made out false orders-to-pay ("bolletini") to the Governatori delle Entrate, who were charged with retiring credits, in the name of bearers of the chits who actually owned no loan assets at all; he shared the take with these accomplices. One of the latter was identified and sentenced for complicity to a short prison term and a fine. But Fioravanti was banished *in perpetuo* and threatened with hanging should he be captured. Two years later a bill broker was similarly banished for making out two false orders-to-pay to the Governatori.[57]

Embezzlement was a more common form of fraud, for which officials were often tried and sentenced. In 1390 a noble official of the Loan Office, Giacomo Trevisan, was discovered to have stolen nearly 1,000 ducats from the brokerage tax due to the Commune and consigned to him by the brokers. He was condemned to restitute the money embezzled, fined for a sum equal to half the total, and banned from holding office for four years. A special commission charged with his "avaritia" prepared a list of all his landholdings in the Terraferma and authorized their sequester and sale. A marginal note testifies to the fact that the sum was paid in full.[58]

A final scheme, on the limits of legality but never clearly described in the pages and pages of text regarding the matter produced by the Council of Ten, was devised in 1456 by the nobleman Francesco dalle Boccole. What

[55]ASV, GP, Sg, reg. 150, fols. 192–96v (16 October 1468).
[56]ASV, AC, reg. 3645, fol. 4 (29 April 1393).
[57]Ibid., reg. 3651/I, fols. 4r–v, 68v.
[58]Ibid., reg. 3644, fols. 63, 76v–78.

seems to have happened is this. Dalle Boccole had been named to study the matter of balances due ("residua") to creditors of the Loan Office, meaning, or at least including, interest in arrears. Having finished the audit on the books of the Loan Office and of the auditors (Officium Rationum Veterum), instead of desisting, he decided to inform Venetians and foreigners alike of their balances, for a commission or fee to be paid in advance into his account at the bank of the de Colti brothers on the Rialto. On Saturday, 7 February, he and his cohorts ("attinentes") called a general meeting at the Rialto, where it seems he began providing the desired information, using the ledgers provided for him by obliging staff members of the Loan Office and the auditors. Easily hundreds, maybe thousands of persons crowded together (it was described as an "adunantia multarum personarum cum magno tumultu"), and he had already planned an adjournment to his own house the next day, to arrive at some decision on how to recoup the credits. The heads of the Council of Ten halted the proceedings, however, and arrested dalle Boccole on two counts, breaking a law of the Ten against illegal assembly and another of the Senate against holding a kind of private referendum ("ponere partitum") — laws that were not further specified, however. His system of seeking out and advising creditors of their dues had profited him much money, stated the Ten, to the detriment of the Signoria. The scribe of the Loan Office and the "famulus," or staff member, of the auditors were also arrested, and the three were subjected to torture more than once, to determine what was behind their scheme. Dalle Boccole confessed to having organized the large public assembly and to having invited it, including women ("in maximo numero, . . . cum dominabus"), to his house on Sunday, as well as to having "extorted" a large sum of money from foreign creditors of the state and suborning the scribe and the assistant ("famulus"). The nobleman was banished to Zara and the scribe to Sibenico, both for three years, and the "famulus" was deprived forever of his position with the auditors. Three further general provisions were made; first, the individuals connected with the case, as well as their relatives, were not permitted to talk about it; second, harsh punishment was threatened against anyone who would go to the Loan Office and claim a balance due which was not his (for money had been extorted, said the Ten, even from persons who actually had no claims); third, money deposited in the de Colti bank for the scheme was to be restored to its rightful owners. But only two days after the prohibition against talking about the case was passed, it had to be revoked, in order to allow members of the Ten to justify their case against dalle Boccole, in the face of much talk by his supporters in the city's squares ("super plateis") in favor of the man and his plan.[59] Even though he

[59]ASV, Consiglio dei Dieci, Miste, reg. 15, fols. 82v — 86v (9 February to 3 March 1456). The order to return the fees already paid reads: "Quod denarii depositati in manibus illorum de Coltis bancheriorum pro partito posito per ser Franciscum a Bocolis auctoritate istius

may have enriched himself, there was broad-based support among creditors of the state for dalle Boccole's scheme, which in itself seems not to have been illegal at all; clearly, to them he was not a swindler but one who agreed to advise them of their rights.

Records of the uproar cover a single month, after which silence falls on the matter; perhaps it was but a straw fire. Only one "victim" is mentioned, the agent of the Poor Clares of Pavia, who was collecting the interest due on the portfolio donated by Bianca di Savoia two generations earlier, when dalle Boccole's agents got hold of him and made him come up with the fee. The Loan Office did not subsequently accelerate the payment of interest. One possible echo of the matter, however, comes from the Council of Ten itself two and one-half years later, when, in an extraordinarily strongly worded statement, it reminded the ruling nobility, in all its organs, including the Ten itself, of the standing prohibition to divert, or merely propose to divert, funds earmarked for the payment of interest and for the amortization of principal of the funded debt. The preamble, which opens with a characterization of the Loan Office as the very foundation of the state and the glory of the Signoria (see sec. i of this chapter), closes with the recognition that any such discussion of a diversion of funds would surely have serious consequences for the public order: "certissimum est quod in statu nostro sequi possent inconvenientia maxima et periculosa."[60] If memory of the recent "tumultum" was alive in the Council of Ten, concern among owners of government obligations for the increasingly serious delays of the Loan Office in paying interest was similarly alive. Such stentorian proclamations, however, did not restrain the continuing tendency to reduce the net rate of payments via further delays and surtaxes. One wonders what discussions took place in the Barbarigo palace at S. Barnaba, where the young sons of Andrea and their tutors, at the very time of the "tumultum," were planning (as we shall see below) to invest in government credits, whose interest claims would mature only twenty years later.

v. USURY AND THE MORAL QUESTION

The theological and juridical problem of usury in regard to the public debts of medieval and Renaissance Italy has been studied in depth by Julius

---

consilii restituantur illis quorum sunt" (fol. 85, 26 February). For the meaning of "ponere partitum" as presenting a proposal to be voted on, see Charles Du Resne Du Cange, *Glossarium mediae et infinae latinitatis,* 10 vols., rev. ed. (Niort, France, 1883–87), s.v. "Partitum." The law against illegal assembly (promoted by "aliquis homo de Veneciis . . . ad domum suam nec alibi") applied in this case was passed by the Quarantia in 1289 and registered by the Council of Ten in 1329, in the wake of the Barozzi-Querini conspiracy. See Zago, *Consiglio dei Dieci,* 3:150, doc. 443.

[60]*PRV,* doc. 276.

Kirshner. Since I have uncovered no new material on this theme,[61] I can merely underscore here some of the major points developed in Kirshner's publications and occasionally relate them more closely to the history of the Venetian debt.[62]

Perhaps the earliest *quaestio* that uses the Venetian debt as the central example is one by the Dominican Nicholas de Anglia. On the basis of internal evidence, it seems to date from some time between 1359 and 1363 or, at the latest, 1375. First, the author uses in his Venetian example a market price of 80, which repeatedly turns up in those years; second and more important, he recounts that Venice still amortized principal at 100 percent ("restituit integrum capitale"), a practice that was suspended beginning in 1363 and was ended definitively in 1375, when government obligations began simply to be retired through purchase at the current market price.

Like almost all the moralists who concerned themselves with the public debt, this author defended the legitimacy of forced loans on the basis of the citizens' obligation to sustain the operation of the state ("necessitas" and "publica utilitas") and held that forced contributors could accept — and even hope for — a profit, as long as it was freely given as a gift or indemnification. The open market for credits, on the other hand, constituted a more difficult problem for the moralists. Some saw market purchases, below par, as voluntary loans to the state and thus as usurious, a misrepresentation of the facts to the extent that the buyer on the free market merely substituted himself for the original forced contributor as creditor of the state, without himself having lent the money. Nicholas, on the other hand, was much more concrete and upheld the legitimacy of the sale ("emptio-venditio") of a loan already legitimate in origin. He even considered the possibility that the sale at a discount involved an act of charity, on the part of the seller for making a gift of the discount, on the part of the buyer for helping someone in need of liquidity.

Pietro d'Ancarano (d. 1415), a jurist who was occasionally asked to

---

[61]There is the hint of an ongoing discussion on the matter in a letter of Mariano da Volterra, vicar of the Certosa of S. Andrea del Lido, to Agnolo di Zanobi Gaddi in Florence of 1 September 1442, in which the writer says he had prepared some "verses" "de monte Florentino et imprestitis Venetorum" for Gaddi, who probably owned credits in both cities. See de Marinis and Perosa, *Nuovi documenti*, letter 3.

[62]The present discussion is based primarily on the following two articles and the edited texts appended to each: "The Moral Theology of Public Finance: A Study and Edition of Nicholas de Anglia's *Quaestio disputata* on the Public Debt of Venice," *Archivium Fratrum Praedicatorum* 40 (1970): 47–72, and "Reading Bernardino's Sermon on the Public Debt," in *Atti del simposio internazionale cateriniano-bernardiniano, Siena, 1980*, ed. Domenico Maffei and Paolo Nardi (Siena, 1982), 547–622. See also "A *Quaestio de usuris* Falsely Attributed to Bartolus of Sassoferrato," *Renaissance Quarterly* 22 (1969): 256–61. I have not consulted Kirshner's Ph.D. thesis, "From Usury to Public Finance: The Ecclesiastical Controversy over the Public Debts of Florence, Genoa, and Venice" (Columbia University, 1970).

provide legal opinions in Venice, where he was granted citizenship, wrote a tract in 1398 (dated and analyzed by Kirshner) which used Nicholas's *Quaestio* but is dedicated more specifically to the Venetian debt.[63] The jurist supports completely the legitimacy of the debt, both the original forced loans and the market in obligations. The discount market in Venice existed "from time immemorial"[64] and was created, he says, "by just and devout Catholic men, who detest the vices more than [men] of any other city in which I have spent time." Furthermore, he says, Venetian obligations have been purchased by Christian princes and members of the Curia, whose investments are tolerated both by bishops of Venice and by popes. How can such holders of portfolios be guilty of usury? he asks. Government obligations are not loans at all, he affirms, since the state is obliged only to pay a return, not the principal. Finally, he poses the question whether investment in the public debt is to be condemned because it causes the flight of capital from agriculture; no, he replies, Venetians are not inclined toward agriculture, and the sea is the territory through which they provision themselves.[65]

D'Ancarano, Kirshner suggests, was probably writing in response to a recent and very negative tract by Guglielmo Centueri, a Franciscan of Cremona, which was taken up almost verbatim in Bernardino of Siena's *Sermo* XLI. Centueri denied the legitimacy of both forced loans and transactions in government obligations, or rather of earning a return (interest and yield) on them. In general terms, he stated that forced loans were not necessary instruments of public finance, for many (named) cities inside and outside Italy functioned without them — forgetting that the very same cities often had recourse to voluntary loans, much more heinously usurious. His references to Venice are specific. He relates the problem of conscience of the Venetian nobleman Zaccaria Contarini, reportedly contrary to receiving interest on forced loans, and assumes that many other Venetians, less illustrious, were similarly contrary to the public debt.[66] Contarini was indeed

[63]In "Reading Bernardino's Sermon," 565–72 and app. 3.

[64]In fact, the earliest capitolare, dating from the very funding of the debt, contains this paragraph: "De modo illorum qui aliorum imprestita emerant. De illis vero qui aliorum imprestita emerant iste modus debet observari, videlicet, quod ipsa habeant et habere possint cum honore quod habebant illi quorum fuerunt nec aliter habeant ea." *PRV*, doc. 20, p. 42.

[65]"Nec per dicta inprestita agricultura non deseritur, cum ibidem non tendant homines ad agriculturam, nam mare est territorium per quod navigantes frumentum, vinum et divicias sibi parant." "Reading Bernardino's Sermon," 571.

[66]The passage, not particularly limpid, reads: "Secundo, dico quod non de civitatibus illis consentiunt omnes, sicut in Venetiis habui [notitiam] a quodam spectabili et virtuoso et famoso viro domino Zacharia Contareno quod ex conscientia numquam aliquid habere voluerat ad mutua illa; et puto multi, non ita spectabiles, ex conscientia ibi nolunt habere, et multos per Domin[i]um coguntur ponere ibi pecunias, sicut factum est." The editor paraphrases the passage as saying that Contarini "did not at any time wish to make loans to his city," whereas the sense is "he never wanted to receive anything on such loans," for a citizen could always make a free loan to the state, while the crux of the matter is whether he might accept a return on that loan or not. Ibid., 574 and 601.

a prominent nobleman and diplomat. He was one of the four Venetian "Aristotelians" who discussed and debated with Petrarch during the latter's sojourn in Venice in the 1360s. In 1374, as one of the savi elected in the Senate to study the current banking crisis, he formulated a long, articulated proposal for the solution of the crisis; the proposal, which garnered only two favorable votes, meant to control and limit Rialto banks so as to avoid their becoming as powerful as those that were then in trouble by limiting but not prohibiting bank loans (see above, Chap. 3, sec. vi, and Chap. 4, sec. iv). He made no reference to usury on that occasion, and we know of no position taken by him on the matter, aside from the mention by Centueri, which may be pure hearsay. He paid forced loans on the basis of a high assessment of 10,000 lire d'estimo.[67] To be sure, Venetians were concerned about forms of usury, particularly in times of economic crisis, as in 1340, 1356–57, and 1366, but the system that formed the basis of deficit financing of the state was—understandably—never publicly called into question in Venice, as it was in Florence, similarly in the 1350s and 1360s.[68]

Centueri went so far as to condemn as "manifest usurers" those foreigners, "magni principes . . . de Ytalia," who invested in Venetian credits. He does not indicate anyone by name but obviously meant Ludovico Gonzaga and other tyrants of Burckhardtian memory, interim victors in plots and counterplots, who are discussed below. Two points are worth making in the present context, however. First, the precise rationale for such open market purchases by many princes is formulated by Centueri in terms we will see used almost verbatim, namely, the instability of their regimes and the desire to secure the future of their heirs.[69] Second, the Franciscan names a precise counterexample. Giangaleazzo Visconti, he reports, promoted a theological debate on his proposal to purchase Venetian government obligations in order to create a pious endowment. Some opinions were favorable, some contrary. Then the prince consulted Centueri in 1385, when the latter was bishop of Piacenza. Centueri, at his request, in turn consulted Urban VI, then in Genoa, and both were decidedly negative: such a purchase would be illicit, and the Conte di Virtù would do best to turn his

[67]*PRV*, 186; actually, there are two men of that name, one without patronymic, the other Zaccaria qd. Cristoforo, both assessed in the parish of S. Silvestro, for 10,000 and 1,000 lire respectively. It can be assumed that the "spectabilis et virtuosus et famosus vir" to whom Centueri referred was the former, but the problem of homynyms, especially among the Contarini, the most common noble surname in Venice, is often unresolvable.

[68]Centueri himself was present at the chapter general of the Franciscans in Florence in 1365 at which Florentine funded and floating debts were debated. Kirshner, "Reading Bernardino's Sermon," 576. For the legislation regarding usurious contracts in Venice, see Mueller, *Procuratori di San Marco*, pt. 3, chap. 2.

[69]"Aliqui etiam domini, dubitantes de instabilitate status sui, ponunt ad illa mutua magnas pecunias, credentes ex hoc suis filiis de periculo providere in casu in quo statum perderent vel similia adversa contingerent." Kirshner, "Reading Bernardino's Sermon," 601. Compare the formulation of the petition of Paolo Guinigi, discussed below, Chap. 14.

attention to other forms of pious giving. Giangaleazzo desisted, only to foster the exact same kind of investment by his own wife and by his courtiers (Kirshner speaks of a veritable "flight of Visconti capital into Venice," corroborated below). On these points, Centueri is silent, as he is silent about the investment in Venetian obligations in the 1370s by the bishop of his home city of Cremona, about which he similarly must have known (see below, Chap. 14).[70] At the same time, writes the moralist—creating a serious loophole in his line of argumentation—pious and religious institutions that receive such portfolios, or, rather, the returns on them, as alms from the parties that had purchased them may legitimately collect interest and have interest collected for them; only they, as ecclesiastical institutions, could legitimately transfer to others their claims on the funded debt. It is in this context that both Centueri and San Bernardino praise the Venetian system of pious trusts, administered by the Procurators of San Marco and largely endowed with government obligations.[71]

Outside of Centueri's reference to Zaccaria Contarini, there is no way of knowing what impact such learned theological treatises and sermons made on Venetian forced lenders to the funded debt and on purchasers of credits on the open market. It may be that interest in the matter declined as interest on credits declined. In other words, it is possible that at the time Centueri was writing, Venetian government obligations were an issue because, as market prices of bonds declined, yields rose. It would be logical, then, that they be less an issue in the mid-Quattrocento when interest was in arrears and yields were falling. In any case, the daily operations in Venice of creditors of the state, on the one hand, and those of the debtor state, on the other, knew no hiatus over the centuries as a result of such discussions.

[70]Kirshner, "Reading Bernardino's Sermon," 581–84, 596.

[71]Finally, Centueri held that government credits and interest claims could legitimately be used as money. Ibid., 585–87, 602, 606.

12

CRITERIA EMPLOYED IN ASSESSING PATRIMONIES

i. PRELIMINARY CONSIDERATIONS

IN ORDER TO UNDERSTAND just who had to contribute forced loans and the impact of forced loans on citizens and estates, it is necessary above all to know how the state estimated the value of a patrimony, that is, how it arrived at the assessment for which it inscribed a household on the estimo, for it was the assessment that constituted the basis for levies of forced loans. The terminology itself sometimes creates problems of comprehension in this area of public finance. The Latin terms *facere de imprestitis, facere de factionibus,* and *facere de impositionibus* all meant to pay forced loans. When a taxpayer wrote in Venetian "fo de fazion per £3,400," he meant that he contributed forced loans on the basis of an assessment of 3,400 lire d'estimo; he was *not* quoting a figure that he ever paid out as a loan. What he was required to contribute, in cash and within a given date, was a percentage of that sum — often ½ or 1 percent at a time, or whatever rate was decided upon by the Senate each time it legislated a forced levy. That is how the estimo of 1379, the only document of its kind extant in Venice, and the scattered estimo figures often declared by persons petitioning for a "grazia" are to be understood — not as loans but as assessed patrimony.

The Estimo of 1379

The list of names and figures known as the estimo of 1379 is one of the most consulted sources relating to the Venetian fourteenth century.[1] The

---

[1] It was published by Luzzatto in *PRV,* doc. 165, and before him by Gallicciolli, *Delle memorie*

document we have is not an original, alas, but a corrupt copy; or, better, we have two corrupt copies, with minor variants, one of the mid-sixteenth century, one of the early seventeenth century, neither of which indicates the nature of the source from which it was copied. It is an important record but not completely trustworthy. Most significant for social history are the document's characterizations of social rank. The copyists highlighted the names of heads of households they thought to be noble with the title "ser," in order to distinguish them from commoners. Thus most — but not all — of the thirty patriotic commoners coopted on 1 September 1381 into the Great Council, and thus ennobled, are indicated with the title "ser," even though the revision of the estimo, undertaken because of and during the War of Chioggia, had been completed earlier, when they were not nobles at all.[2] For the same reason, they labeled "ser" the three members of the Battaia (or Battaglia) family on the list, a family of new citizens, recent immigrants, not nobles then or later. This error is attributable to the fact that a man of the same family name, Piero Antonio Battagia (or Battaglia), was made a member of the Great Council in the year 1500 in recognition of his having turned over to Venice — instead of to Louis XII of France — the fortress of Cremona; the copyists simply applied to the Trecento family the noble title carried by their own contemporary and his heirs. In more than one case, furthermore, the same name is repeated, sometimes in different parishes, but here there is no way of knowing whether these are cases of homonyms or copyists' errors. There are probably also some errors or anomalies in the figures. For instance, two households are inscribed for 250 lire d'estimo, while the legal minimum was 300; these could be errors or simply exceptions. Again, Luzzatto wrote that estates ("commissarie") administered by the Procurators of San Marco were not included; while this seems largely to be the case, it is not always so. For example, a certain Nanticler Cristian is registered for 300 lire under the "contrada" of S. Marco as a living person; actually, this man had died without heirs in 1312, leaving his money and a small piece of property as an endowment for the hospital he had founded in the parish of S. Ternita. Records of that hospital, administered by the Procurators of San Marco, are extant for the years around the War of Chioggia; they show that it paid forced loans on an assessment of precisely 300 lire. Or again, the entry for "the heirs of Ser Renier Zen," assessed in the parish of S. Giovanni Crisostomo for 2,000 lire, seems to refer to the estate of the doge of that name (d. 1268), administered by the Procurators, which benefited

---

venete, 2:99–185, both from a miscellany now in the BMV, It. cl. VII, 90 (8029), a copy in the hand of Pietro Foscarini of the early seventeenth century. Luzzatto considered this the earlier of the two and noted the variations from the Cronaca Albergna of the BMCV, which is actually of the mid-sixteenth century. The variations he noted are in some names, not in figures.

[2] Todesco, "Aggregati ed esclusi."

the hospital of the Crociferi. The document, in short, needs to be used with caution.[3]

As we shall see shortly, a revision of the estimo could take a year or more. When there was great urgency to collect levies on the basis of new, generally raised assessments, the revised figures were passed along to the Loan Office as soon as they were defined between the assessors and the head of household, instead of waiting until the whole task was completed. That might have been the case also in 1379. Be that as it may, it is clear that a part, if not all, of the revision was completed by early spring of that year.[4]

Luzzatto's well-known breakdown of the list by social rank and tax bracket, despite the errors, is *grosso modo* valid, if one rounds off his tallies. Subtracting the 42 assessments of parishes, hospitals, and monasteries, included for their real estate holdings alone, leaves 2,141 households, including the estates. Rounded off, we have about 2,100 households, of which somewhat more than 1,100 were nobles, about 1,000 commoners. Despite the near parity in numbers, nobles held some two-thirds of taxable wealth, commoners one-third.[5] Estates administered by the Procurators of San Marco, of which there were perhaps hundreds that contributed forced loans, are generally not included — as we have just seen; the Procurators had longstanding and wide-ranging autonomy in determining the level of assessment of those estates; perhaps they had not concluded their internal census at the time the extant list was redacted.[6]

---

[3]Crossing two databases, CIVES (for citizenship privileges, 1300–1500) and ESTIMO (for the estimo of 1379), uncovered some of the anomalies. Donald Queller recently studied the estimo, but without providing any critique of the text or of the information it contains. See "The Venetian Family and the *Estimo* of 1379," in *Law, Custom, and the Social Fabric in Medieval Europe: Essays in Honor of Bryce Lyon*, ed. Bernard S. Bachrach and David Nicholas, Studies in Medieval Culture, 28 (Kalamazoo, Michigan, 1990), 185–210. Derogations from the legal minimum of 300 lire are not unheard of; an immigrant from Vienna, for example, was granted naturalization on the condition that he pay forced loans on an assessment of 200 lire, 100 below the minimum that still applied at that date; see ASV, Grazie, reg. 23, fol. 34 (31 August 1432). The accounts of the hospitals of Nanticler Cristian and Renier Zen have been studied by Pierpaolo Miniutti, "Povertà ed assistenza a Venezia dal Medio Evo all'Età Moderna: L'amministrazione di tre ospedali" (laurea thesis, University of Venice, 1993–94); for the entries in the estimo, see *PRV,* 149, 170.

[4]Molà, *La comunità dei lucchesi a Venezia,* 280–81, where the author, besides underscoring further anomalies in this estimo, pointed out that Tano Ridolfi, inscribed for 500 lire, died on 16 April 1379 and was buried two days later.

[5]Kedar, *Merchants in Crisis,* 53.

[6]*PRV,* clxiv; Luzzatto, *Storia,* 129–30. Donald Queller, *The Venetian Patriciate: Reality versus Myth* (Urbana, Ill., 1986), reproduced Luzzatto's breakdown, whereas he provided a new breakdown, into nine instead of seven categories, for the Italian version: *Il patriziato veneziano: La realtà contro il mito* (Rome, 1987), 64. He explains in "Venetian Family," 206 n. 8, that one of the errors corrected was Luzzatto's use of the same assessment figure "as the bottom of one category and the top of the succeeding one." The two versions are alas not comparable. Many more anomalies remain to be corrected before a more authoritative breakdown can be attempted.

It is apparent from a glance at the assessments listed in the estimo, furthermore, that the assessors were not required to identify every minute element of patrimony, down to the last lira or soldo. They rounded off assessments in the lower brackets to the nearest 50 or 100 lire d'estimo, in the higher brackets to the nearest 500 or 1,000 lire. The rare occasions on which one finds figures carried out to the tens and units are very often the result of a simple division of a previous assessment of a deceased father among his surviving sons.[7] The policy of rounding off assessment figures, confirmed in the scattered data remaining for other years in accounts and petitions, of course facilitated enormously the calculations of sums due on the basis of levies formulated in percentages and thus the keeping of accounts, public and private.

The estimo of 1379, finally, is almost the only remaining trace of a revision of assessments which was both heavy handed and hasty. The revision applied particularly onerous coefficients on house rents, thus adversely affecting owners of real estate, the component of patrimony most readily identified and taxed in that moment of life-or-death struggle of the republic. Although the final redaction is no more than a skeletal summary, a particularly unsatisfactory document when contrasted with the Florentine catasto of 1427, nevertheless it contains all the information the Loan Office needed to know for collecting each levy as it was imposed. Moreover, the data it provides make possible an interesting comparison between the two documents which is significant for the history of these city-republics: only about 12 percent of Venetian households and 14 percent of Florentine households had a net taxable patrimony (that is, after subtracting deductions and exemptions). A small part of the total population, in short, bore the burden of these two systems of forced loans. The picture looks like this:[8]

	Venetian estimo of 1379	Florentine catasto of 1427
households with net taxable wealth	2,100	1,400
percentage of total households	ca. 12%	14%
total net estimated patrimony	6,294,040 du. (d'oro)	7,613,274 fl. (di suggello)
average net patrimony per paying household	ca. 3,000 du.	5,400 fl.

[7]See, for example, the case of the three sons of Zuane Marcello of S. Vidal, each assessed for 1,133 lire (*PRV,* doc. 165, pp. 155–56).

[8]Florence, at the time of the catasto, had a population of 37,000, with an average of 3.7 persons per household. Venice's population can be guessed to have been about 70,000 in 1379 (see Kedar, *Merchants in Crisis,* app. 7); assuming about 4 persons per household, one arrives at about 17,500 households and 12 percent of this hypothetical total. For paying Florentine households, see David Herlihy and Christiane Klapisch-Zuber, *Tuscans and Their Families: A*

The rest of this chapter emphasizes the criteria employed in revisions of the estimo legislated after the turn of the century, the first for which surviving documentation is sufficiently clear, in order to compare the manner of arriving at assessments with two specific cases, one of them already studied by Luzzatto. In this way, we can get some idea of accuracy and evasion, or, perhaps, the variations between carefulness and laxity imposed by different financial and military conjunctures. We will see, in fact, that the burden of contributing forced loans derived not only from the percentage of levies imposed in a given period but from the criteria of assessment employed in a given revision and from the strict or loose definition of the criteria that the Senate thought acceptable at a given time.

I have underscored the criteria of assessment, finally, as a basis for comparison with the much better known Florentine catasto of 1427. This theme had to be confronted because the discussions leading to the institution of the catasto often cited the Venetian system of assessment as a precedent, sometimes as a model to be followed, first and foremost because of its statist philosophy.

ii. THE LEGISLATION

The first clearly expressed criteria for preparing a tax return or "condizione" are found in the reform of 1403 and successive revisions. That each head of household was to provide an accounting of his income and patrimony to the board of assessors in writing ("dare suas conditiones in scriptis") is specified only in 1419; since the assessors were authorized to demand an oath from each head of household beginning in the late thirteenth century, however, Luzzatto took it for granted that some kind of sworn written statement traditionally had been required much earlier. The earliest condizioni uncovered so far date from 1412 (for a religious house) and from 1439 and 1447–48 (for a household), as we shall see below.

In 1403 the Senate, concerned about the marauding of Admiral Boucicault and the Genoese fleets rather than about the imminent war that would make Venice a territorial state on the Italian mainland, elected a board of assessors to update the estimo. The board was made up of one representative per sestiere plus two officials elected at large; the number was

---

Study of the Florentine Catasto of 1427 (New Haven, 1985), 19. From this vantage point, it comes as much less of a surprise to learn from Herlihy and Klapisch that the upper 2 percent of Florentine households owned 60 percent of Monte credits. Of course, most of the 8,600 households whose net assessments lay below the minimum were recuperated in part via a head tax. The figure for total net patrimony was kindly provided by Judith Brown from the computer tape. Since the agio on the fiorino di suggello in 1427 stood at about 7 percent (see above, table 7.3, and Goldthwaite and Mandich, *Studi*, 93), the total for Florence was the equivalent of somewhat more than 7 million gold florins.

later raised to twelve, in order to constitute two subcommittees.[9] Members were to present their own "conditiones" before assuming office. They were given full authority to investigate the books of government offices (especially customs offices) and magistracies to check the veracity of particular condizioni. The books of customs and brokerage offices were especially useful for evaluating merchandise. There were two hurdles. The first, insuperable in 1403, was bank secrecy: they were not allowed to interrogate bankers concerning the accounts they held for third parties and could not place them under oath.[10] The second hurdle was one with a long tradition: the assessors were not to investigate the estates and tutorships administered by the Procurators of San Marco and could merely accept as veracious the condizioni presented by that office.

Families or households of citizens, including naturalized citizens, had to present their condizioni. The household was the typical Venetian "fraterna": fathers, sons, uncles, brothers, grandsons, and certain relatives ("attinentes"), as specified, for example, in the law of 1403. Each male who was formally emancipated from his father or "divided" from the fraterna had to present his condizione separately, and every family member was to be placed under oath individually, in order to prevent fraud in this regard. Persons who had no assessable patrimony other than government obligations were not to be inscribed on the estimo (they were usually taxed separately, as we have seen). No one who had not presented his condizione was to leave Venice without designating a procurator to act in his name.[11] Medical doctors and surgeons were traditionally exempt, as were probably also jurists; at the same time, if they wished to invest in the Levant trade, they had to be assessed and inscribed on the rolls.[12]

Clergy were not exempt from paying forced loans. The question of their benefices became acute after Venetian expansion on the Terraferma; in 1419, in response to their remonstrations against double taxation on the

[9]ASV, SM, reg. 46, fols. 112v–13v. The proponent of the bill voted into law on 2 November was Ramberto Querini; the officials elected on 13 November were Benedetto Capello (S. Croce), Paolo Nani "maior" (Castello), Alvise Morosini (S. Polo), Leonardo Mocenigo (S. Marco), Paolo Zulian (Cannaregio), Alvise Giustinian (Dorsoduro), and Luca Bragadin "maior" and Antonio da Mula, at large. The number was raised in June 1404 in the attempt to expedite matters (*PRV,* ccxx n. 4). Luzzatto paid more attention to the criteria deliberated in 1412, which he published (ibid., doc. 214), while those of 1403, unpublished, are more innovative and are thus emphasized here.

[10]ASV, SM, reg. 46, fols. 112v–13: "Verum bancherii non possint poni ad sacramentum nec peti de quantitate pecunie quam habent de aliqua alia persona in eorum banchis."

[11]Ibid., fol. 133v (27 April 1404); the provision was to be announced publicly at the Rialto, and severe penalties were applied.

[12]*BG,* 1:clxxxvii; *PRV,* doc. 128 (1328). See also *Traictie,* cap. 79. The college of medical doctors was required, however, to provide and fund one doctor for the captain general of the Adriatic patrol fleet and another for the Provveditori of the army.

same benefice, Venetian holders of benefices were exempted from paying local taxes, but serious consequences were threatened for those who evaded the obligation to declare their incomes to the assessors in Venice. Religious institutions, parish churches, and hospitals — like trusts — were inscribed on the estimo only for their revenues from real estate. That had been the case ever since 1258, and we find their house rents duly inscribed, for example, on the estimo of 1379. Beginning in 1403, religious houses were also assessed for their incomes from government obligations.[13]

Personal Property and Real Estate

Personal property (movables) and real estate (immovables) were assessed as patrimony, at least beginning about 1280, in the following manner.

Personal property was evaluated one to one, that is, 1,000 ducats of real value corresponded to 1,000 lire d'estimo. Expressly mentioned were cash, gems, silver, and silverware, which were considered "boni denari"; household furnishings that were not gold or silver were exempted.[14] The value of bad debts ("non . . . boni denari") was to be estimated and prorated. The net value of merchandise as estimated by brokers was to be considered as cash, with the exception of salt, which was to be appraised at the time the condizione was presented. Holdings in government obligations and interest income on them had traditionally been exempt; portfolios held by households and institutions inscribed on the estimo were assessed for the first time in 1403, and that at 50 percent (2,000 ducats

---

[13]The law of 1403 makes no express mention of clergy and trusts in this regard; their treatment was probably a matter of tradition. On the whole question, see *PRV*, xxi, ccxviii–xxv, and doc. 223. Bishop Miani of Vicenza complained about double jeopardy as late as 1429, ten years after the matter had supposedly been resolved; see Girgensohn, "Il testamento di Pietro Miani," 49, and, for the threats against evaders, 33 n. 147. An exemption of benefices held by cardinals, passed on 11 May 1413, is cited in ASV, CN, reg. 8, fol. 129 (30 December 1450). The authorities had to insist that the monasteries of S. Giorgio Maggiore and Pomposa pay their forced loans; see Grazie, reg. 16, fols. 11v, 26v (1364–65). The condizione prepared for the assessors in 1412 by the procurator of the convent of S. Lorenzo in Venice includes, after the listing of rents on real property, an entry for the capital held in government obligations and the respective interest income; see S. Lorenzo, b. 9, fasc. "Per graveze, 3," loose sheet entitled "Condiciom de le done munege del Monastero de San Lorenço," kindly brought to my attention by Federica Masè. See also Giuseppe Del Torre, "Stato regionale e benefici ecclesiastici: Vescovadi e canonicati nella terraferma veneziana all'inizio dell'età moderna," *Atti dell'Istituto veneto di scienze, lettere ed arti* 151 (1992–93): 1193–94.

[14]It should be noted that the figure of "100" ducats in specie and gems for 1,000 lire d'estimo in *PRV*, cxlvii, is a misprint, duely corrected to 1,000 ducats in *Debito pubblico*, 148; the law is discussed more thoroughly at ccxv–xviii. For the exemption of household furnishings that were not gold or silver, see *PRV*, xxv. Sumptuary laws were tied to assessments in the 1440s. In 1442 a proposal that tied varying values of female garb to increases in assessments was turned down, but a simpler proposal, which added 1,000 lire to the assessment of any head of household whose wife or daughters wore clothing of outlawed values, was passed. See Newett, "The Sumptuary Laws of Venice," 257–58.

nominal corresponded to 1,000 lire d'estimo); market values, which four months earlier had been closer to 65, since then had probably declined considerably. Unpaid interest claims had to be declared and included as credits beginning in 1438; by that date, the delay in making interest payments, which had begun in 1432, was obviously judged to be irreversible.

Real estate, both in Venice and elsewhere, was assessed by capitalizing the rents it produced. From at least 1280 and presumably as late as the onset of the War of Chioggia, the rate was 10 percent. During the revision of 1379, however, real estate was capitalized at the onerous rate of 4 percent (4 lire di grossi or 40 ducats in rents were to be registered as 1,000 lire d'estimo). In 1383, that burden was considered "gravissimum," and the rate was raised to 6 percent (that is, 6 lire di grossi or 60 ducats were to be registered as 1,000 lire d'estimo). In 1403 the rate was at first set at 10 percent, amended quickly to 11.1 percent: 100 ducats in rents were to be registered initially as 1,000 lire, reduced then to 900 lire d'estimo, in recognition of expenses for upkeep of rental property.[15] Real estate owned by Venetian citizens outside Venice and the dogado was treated in the same fashion; a list of fixed values of agricultural produce was prepared in early 1404 to aid the assessors in evaluating revenues in kind.[16]

[15]For reasons explained in detail in App. D, sec. i, Luzzatto's analysis in *PRV,* cxlvi and ccxvi, namely that 4 lire meant 10 lire a grossi (4 x 2.6 = 10.4) so that the rate was 10 percent, is completely incorrect. Briefly, the lira d'estimo was equal to 1 ducat; thus 4 lire di grossi, or 40 ducats, is *not* to be converted into lire a grossi.

[16]*PRV,* ccxvii n. 1, is a haphazard and untrustworthy transcription of part of the deliberation in ASV, SM, reg. 46, fol. 119v — not "11v" — (16 February 1404); it was not corrected in *Debito pubblico,* 216–17. It might be noted here that separate evaluations of house property, on the basis of unknown and probably changing criteria, were undertaken for the imposition of a very extraordinary tax on rents (a tax of one-third, for example, was imposed in 1453); Besta in *BG,* cxlvi–viii. Known total estimates (in ducats) are the following:

Year	Value	Source
1367	2,882,818	Romanin, *Storia documentata,* 3:384–85, by parish; cf. *PRV,* cxlv.
1423	7,050,000	Doge Mocenigo's "address," in *BG,* 1:95.
pre-1425	2,896,170	Morosini, Cronaca, 2:588–94, by parish.
1425	4,636,030	Ibid., "stima nova."
1455	3,588,950	Sanudo, *De origine,* 190–91.
1469 (?)	4,548,490	*BG,* 1:150, and Romanin, *Storia documentata,* 4:551 (both from the Cronaca Alberegna, mid-sixteenth century, by sestiere).

A fragment for two sestieri of what seems to be such an estimate, dateable in the 1360s, although the totals diverge from those of the "stima" of 1367, is extant in British Library, London, Ms. Egerton, 611. Cf. Kedar, *Merchants in Crisis,* 162. A copy of the summary by parish of the "stima nova" of 1425 indicates the exemptions: "non metando a conto le giese, nè hospedali, nè case de comun"; BMV, It. cl. VII, 48 (7143), fol. 160. A commission of noble "savi" and non-noble "magistri" was formed in 1460 to undertake a general evaluation of house property; see ASV, ST, reg. 4, fol. 151v. Cf. Cecchetti, *La vita dei veneziani nel 1300,* 34–35, 156–58.

Exemptions and Deductions

Citizens with an assessed patrimony of less than the following values, periodically revised, were exempt from paying forced loans: 50 lire d'estimo in personal property from at least 1280 until 1325, 100 lire from 1325 to 1339, 300 lire as an overall assessment from 1339 to 1446, and 200 lire thereafter.[17] Bank deposits, officially protected by bank secrecy in 1403, were de facto exempt; bankers could be called upon to give evidence only in 1427, and only in 1446 could they be interrogated (see above, Chap. 2, sec. v). Most important, the house that the declarant owned and in which he lived was exempt.

It was debated in 1403 whether to allow a deduction of 100 lire for each member of a household ("pro qualibet bucha quam haberent in domo"), but a proposal to that effect was defeated. Some kind of personal allowance was made, but it was at the discretion of the assessors.[18] A deduction was allowed, after some debate, for dowries, trousseaux, and marriage gifts, but contemporaneously one-half the value was to be added to the condizione of the receiver; only much later were widows permitted to declare two-thirds of the value of the dowry restored to them.[19] For the sake of equity, finally, house rents were deductible for the declarant who lived in a rented house, whether or not he owned revenue-producing property; again, only much later did houses rented to the "miserable poor" obtain a one-third reduction in assessment.[20]

The revision of the rolls according to the criteria explicated in 1403 took one and one-half years, by which time Venice was deeply involved in war against Padua, the beginning of expansion on the Terraferma. It was reported that a great many Venetians had become richer since the previous reform of 1383, and many new households had to be assessed. Initially the revised estimo was to be presented all at once, with back taxes and refunds owed from the date of the law (3 November 1403), but the pressure of military expenditures called for sending off individual results to the Loan Office as soon as they were ready, so that more revenue could be brought in immediately. To be sure, some contributors had lower assessments, and others had dropped below the minimum; they were protected when the

---

[17]*PRV,* docs. 120, 132. For certain kinds of estates, the minimum was set at 200 lire in 1412; ibid., doc. 219. See also Lattes, *Libertà,* 64. The oath of about 1280–1325 (*PRV,* xxi, xxiv) clearly defines the minimum as consisting of "personal property" below 50 lire; the laws mandating the increases of the minimum do not specify the type of patrimony, but it can be assumed that by 1339 it was to be calculated on both personal property and real estate. Actually, the minimum may have been changed at other times or in special cases (see above, n. 3).

[18]ASV, SM, reg. 46, fol. 117v (24 November 1403); it was stated that the assessors "debeant habere respectum ad familias."

[19]Ibid., fol. 117r–v.

[20]Ibid.

assessors quickly informed the Loan Office of that fact, and they were promised refunds if they had overpaid. Once the assessors had completed their task, two ad hoc committees were formed to deal with the fiscal effects in cases of enrichment, impoverishment, and transfers of wealth before the next general revision of the rolls. The first was made up of seven officials from three different offices; most of the Signoria itself was called upon to form the second.[21]

Successive revisions of the estimo consolidated the innovations of 1403 as well as the old but poorly documented traditions. In 1412 an exemption was added for silverware and jewelry, declared under oath as for personal use ("pro usu domus sue"), up to a maximum value of 200 ducats.[22]

Deductions were also increased and clarified. In 1412 the deduction for dependent children and grandchildren was fixed at 200 lire d'estimo, that is, at 200 ducats; it was set at 150 lire for each monk, friar, or nun in religious institutions in 1427. At the latter date, the deduction for dependent grandchildren, reduced to 100 lire, could be claimed only as long as they were legitimate, in the male line, and below age twenty.[23] No deduction is mentioned for the head of household or his wife. Freights and customs duties paid on merchandise were declared deductible in 1412, as were house rents, but only those paid by declarants who did not own a house. In 1439 the assessors found, in the course of inspecting rental properties, that many were declared to be almshouses ("quod dicuntur dari per elimosinam . . . miserabilibus personis"); they were ordered to investigate the veracity of the claim, and, if made available to the poor over the previous five years or bequeathed as almshouses, their assessed value was to be reduced by one-third, "ob reverentia Dei." As in the amendments passed in 1403, dowries, trousseaux, and gifts made "inter vivos" to the children of the declarant were deductible in full but had to be added at 50 percent of their value to the estimo of the beneficiary. The deduction for dowries of daughters, sisters, and granddaughters ("fie, sorelle, neze"), as long as they were "done verzene," and their inclusion in the assessment of the husband were confirmed in 1412, 1428, and 1433. Only in 1439 were widows, previously assessed for the full value of the dowry restored to them, assessed at two-thirds of that value, "per paura de l'ira de Dio," since forced loans consumed their patrimony before they received any interest on their credits and hunger could force them to prostitute themselves ("serano constrete per necessitade de fame a prender forsi mala via").[24] Since jewelry trans-

[21]Ibid., fols. 117r–v, 133v–34, 138v–39; reg. 47, fol. 5.

[22]*PRV*, ccxxvii and doc. 218.

[23]For 1412, ibid., ccxxii and doc. 214, p. 256: "pro quolibet filio et filia legitimis, nepotibus et neptibus qui starent in domibus suis et ad suas expensas." For 1427, ASV, SM, reg. 56, fol. 90r–v; children could be claimed as deductions only by their fathers or grandfathers.

[24]*PRV*, ccxxi and doc. 214 (1412), and ASV, SM, reg. 58, fol. 185v (19 March 1433). The legislator in 1439 recognized the flagrant injustice of counting only half for the husband and

ferred as surety for loans was being deducted as though it was for personal use by both the borrower and the lender, it was decided in 1427 that it could be deducted only by the lender; for the borrower, the secured loan would be treated in fiscal terms like a sale, until the piece was redeemed. Finally, debts were unequivocally declared deductible only in 1427, but at the same time the creditor could be interrogated under oath as to the veracity of the debtor's claim. This was a logical aspect of cross-checking between what one person had to declare and another could deduct.

Clarification concerning the treatment of landed estates came only in 1419, as a result of complaints lodged by Venetian landowners that they were subject to double jeopardy, that is, they were being taxed for the same property both locally (especially for the military tax, the "dadie delle lanze") and in Venice. The solution was formulated as a basic principle: Venetian landowners in the Terraferma were to pay only in Venice for the whole of their patrimony. The same held for ecclesiastical benefices, as we have seen. In order to aid the assessors in their task, adjunct assessors with particular expertise in the Terraferma were named. The result of the decision, of course, was to increase the fiscal burden of inhabitants of the subject territories by reducing the tax base on which to meet the impositions levied by the capital city.[25]

The latitude permitted by bank secrecy, carefully protected in 1403, was successively reduced and finally eliminated. At first, bankers could not be placed under oath nor their ledgers checked.[26] When in 1427 debts became officially deductible, it was logical that the veracity of bank loans claimed as debts would have to be checked. In fact, it was ruled that bankers could now be interrogated and placed under oath to verify such claims.[27] By midcentury, bankers were being accused of aiding and abetting tax evasion, by concealing taxable wealth of their clients. In 1446 the assessors were given full authority to interrogate any banker under oath in order to deter-

---

two-thirds for the widow but thought that the reduction allowed the widow would be sufficient "azochè le possano pagar i fitti de chaxa e fornirse de arnixe e sciave necessarie al so viver." Ibid., reg. 60, fol. 162v (27 July 1439).

[25]Venetian landowners complained "quod coguntur ad faciendum impositiones in duobus locis pro unamet re." They were thus ordered to "dare in scriptis Sapientibus nostris deputatis ad aptandum terram [that is, the assessors] omnes redditus quos habent singulo anno de possessionibus, decimis, feudis in territoriis, etc." *PRV,* ccxxiv–xxv and doc. 223. See also Michael Knapton, "I rapporti fiscali tra Venezia e la terraferma: Il caso padovano nel secondo '400," *AV,* ser. 5, 117 (1981): 5–65.

[26]"Verum, bancherii qui sunt ad presens et erunt infra hoc tempus non possint poni ad sacramentum nec peti de quantitate pecunie quam haberent de aliqua alia persona in eorum banchis." *PRV,* ccxv.

[27]"Se alguno nostro çitadin se darà per debitor a algun dei nostri banchi de scrita, sia tegnudi i diti banchieri la veritade dir ai nostri Savi da chi i serano rechiesti e con sacramento afermar quelo che serà la veritade del dito debito. E se i darà altri suo crededori, sia tegnudi i diti far clari i diti nostri Savii dei diti tal debiti." ASV, SM, reg. 56, fol. 90r–v.

mine the veracity of any condizione that they were investigating; further-more, they could examine the banker's account books regarding the specific matters under investigation. The assessors could even investigate bankers in general, if they suspected concealment of taxable wealth. It was specified, finally, that bankers themselves and all partners in banking companies had to present separately their own condizioni, so that they would not benefit from preferential treatment. Such treatment was probably normal, for in a lawsuit against two Garzoni brothers, partners in the Garzoni bank, an angry taxpayer said that bankers paid taxes at rates that suited them, and proceeded to advise the court of their very low estimo assessments.[28]

After the revision of 1426–27, others were undertaken on the basis of laws passed in 1431, 1434, 1438, and 1446. It had been decided that the estimo was to be renewed every five years; in 1444, following closely upon the tax strike of 1442 (see below), the system of the public debt was so hated and so contested that it took two years of heated debate to formulate the criteria of the survey. In 1446 the account books of brokers were subject to audit in order to ferret out merchants who were hiding their merchan-dise from the fisc, and a tariff was established for estimating the fiscal value of such crucial goods as pepper and wheat in the city itself — a procedure borrowed from the tariff used for evaluating rents in kind from landed estates. A distinction was made, furthermore, between rents in Venice and the dogado on the one hand and rents earned by Venetians from properties on the Terraferma on the other. The deliberation that passed states that the capitalization rate of 10 for Terraferma rents was the customary one ("prout poni consuetum fuit"). Finally, in order to include as many taxpayers as possible, exemption from payment of forced loans was set at patrimonies of 200 lire and below (it had been 300); a proposal to reduce the floor to 100 lire was voted down.[29] By that time, fiscal pressure had become unbearable; the system of deficit spending through exaction of forced loans was in decline; and the *boccatico*, literally a head tax but actually a hearth or house-hold tax, was well in place. Its imposition, begun in 1439, brought pitiful results when it was applied only to those who were not inscribed on the estimo, less the "impotenti."[30]

Two summary tables (tables 12.1 and 12.2) can facilitate an under-standing of some of the more repeated criteria employed by the fisc.

[28]Lattes, *Libertà*, docs. 19 (ASV, ST, reg. 1, fol. 187v) and 20 (ST, reg. 2, fol. 3v). The claimant in the suit said, "Questi da cha' di Garzoni non habuto angaria de tal raxione, perchè sono banchi de scripta e fano le angarie per quelo che i piaxe, avixando le reverentie vostre che uno di loro fratelli fano di £2000, l'altro di 2400, che dixe chotanto àno." GP, Sg, reg. 123, fols. 65–69v (24 May 1456). See also above, Chap. 2, sec. v.

[29]*PRV,* ccxxxv nn. Nearly the whole debate of 1444–46 was printed by Lattes, *Libertà*, 60–69; it was missed by Luzzatto. In the case of 1446, rates of capitalization were given as such, for the first time; previously, the rate was stated as a proportion between rents and assessments. Cf. table 12.1, columns 2–3.

[30]*PRV,* ccxxxii–xxxiii, and *BG,* 1:clvi–clvii and docs. 92, 94.

It is worth repeating that the estimo did not involve a tax on income but an imposition on patrimony, that is, on what the contributor of forced loans was worth or owned at the time of the general assessment, rather than on what he earned. Table 12.1 shows that the rate of capitalization at the time of the estimo of 1379 did indeed hit landowners very hard. To say that rent income on a house was worth only 4 percent of its taxable value as patrimony meant that a rent of 10 ducats was calculated as 250 lire d'estimo (equal to 250 ducats), a factor of 25; in other words, to rental property was applied a value corresponding to 25 years' rent. It is easy to see from the table just how arbitrary the criterion of capitalization was: it was manipulated so as to benefit or burden landowners, to facilitate the collection of revenues by the state or to make it more difficult, according to some feeling of the conjuncture and of the readiness of assessed households to contribute forced loans. Actually, the rate was pushed up, with a single exception (1412), in an attempt progressively to reduce the burden. A rate of 10 meant that 10 ducats in rent represented a house assessed at 100 lire d'estimo or 10 years' rent. Only in 1403 with the amendment raising the rate (thus lowering the burden) was any consideration of costs of upkeep expressed by the Senate; no statement about net returns to the landowner is possible. The much better known rate of capitalization, set by the Florentine catasto of 1427, has been added in brackets for the sake of comparison.

Table 12.2 shows how holdings in government obligations of persons inscribed on the estimo were assessed as part of patrimony, beginning in 1403–4. Comparison of the value applied to government credits for assessment purposes (col. 2) with market prices shows that the former were set at the lower end of a price range that was more or less foreseeable for the period during which the rolls would be revised. At the same time that assessment criteria were legislated, it was also decided to set a ceiling on the portfolios — of persons inscribed on the estimo — which were eligible for interest at the gross rate of 4 percent. That figure (col. 4) was set at between 2,000 and 3,000 lire in nominal value for every 1,000 lire d'estimo of assessed valuation; any amount above that ceiling would earn only 3 percent gross interest. Finally, as interest claims began to be paid with ever increasing delays and about the time that they became marketable separately from credits, they came also to be taxed separately. In 1438 interest claims in arrears beginning from September 1436 were to be assessed at 50 percent of their nominal value; in 1446, those beginning from September 1441 were to be assessed at 40 percent.[31]

---

[31]*PRV,* ccxxii, ccxxix, ccxxxv; for 1438, see table 12.3; for 1446, Lattes, *Libertà,* 65. Interest credits in arrears had to be declared and taxed also under the decima; see, for example, the accounts prepared by the Scuola Grande di S. Marco, for the estates it administered and of which it was beneficiary, in ASV, currently filed under Scuola di S. Maria del Rosario, b. 5 (it is destined to be reinventoried under the Scuola Grande di S. Marco). In 1474 the Scuola listed holdings exceeding 45,000 nominal ducats; among the estates, that of Nicolò d'Antonio Al-

TABLE 12.1

Estimating Real Estate Values: Rates of Capitalization, 1280–1446

Year	Rents	Assessment	Rate (%)	Factor
ca. 1280–1325	100	1,000	10	10
1379	40	1,000	4	25
1383	60	1,000	6	16.67
1403	100	1,000	10	10
	100	900	11.1	9
1412	110	1,000	11	9.9
[1427	70	1,000 Florence	7	14.3]
1446	120	1,000 Venice	12	8.3
	100	1,000 Terraferma	10	10

Note: For the sake of comparison, the well-known capitalization rate set by the Florentine catasto of 1427 was entered in brackets.

TABLE 12.2

Government Obligations and the Fisc, 1403–1446:
Assessments, Prices, and Portfolio Ceilings

Year Estimo Revised	Assessed Value of Obligations (in %)	Market Price (range)	Maximum Earning 4% (per £1,000)	Assessed Value of Interest Claims (in %)
1403–4	50	65–50		
1412	40	42–44	£2,500	
1419	50	56–60	£2,000	
1434	33⅓	40	£3,000	
1438	25	34–24		50
1446	25	25		40

iii. EVASION AND ASSESSMENT

Did Venetians declare their true worth to the fisc?[32] To what extent were declarations examined for correctness? The general wisdom is that no one pays taxes willingly; if it is possible to avoid telling the truth, one does, even under oath. But there are many ifs and buts. First of all, a system of

---

dioni alone had a portfolio of 29,900 ducats (fols. 60, 92, and passim). Some of the interest was encumbered ("fo obliga'") to banks, such as the Garzoni, Lippomano, and Pisani (see fol. 137, for example).

[32]For the sake of comparison, Conti (*L'imposta diretta,* 148–49) found some frauds but mostly trustworthy returns, in comparing the condizioni of Florentines in 1427 with account books of the firms involved. Real tax evasion in Florence, says the author, began with the successive catasti.

forced loans was not, in origin or in philosophy, a direct tax but rather a forced interest-bearing investment. In times when war was not overly costly, forced loans presented an acceptable way of investing some liquid funds at 5 percent annual interest. True enough, one could generally earn more than that in commerce, but a diversified portfolio of investments was as advisable then as now. The forced "investment" became a tax when it was levied so often and at such high percentages of assessed patrimony as to limit one's freedom of action by absorbing liquidity and forcing divestment in order to meet levies; when the state reduced net rates of interest from 5 to 4 to 3 and eventually to 1 percent; when the contributor had to, or decided he should, divest himself of his government obligations and he had to sell them, no longer between 80 and 100 as they were for a century before the War of Chioggia but at 60, 50, 30, or 20 percent of their nominal value, that is, of what he had paid—clearly, then, the balance or the loss was very similar to a direct tax. In that case, he would be ever less willing to allow his real worth to be known. Obviously, when it was possible to contribute at a lower rate but *à fonds perdu* ("ad perdendum," as it was put in Florence), that is, without having title to an income, then what was involved was a direct tax; but that option seems to have been created only as a temporary measure during the War of Chioggia.

Formulated differently, the question could be stated: How close did the state come to assessing the wealth of its citizens? It must be remembered, first of all, that cities were relatively small. Venice, one of the largest cities of Europe, had well below 100,000 inhabitants after the Black Death. Furthermore, only about 2,100, or 12 percent, of the city's households were inscribed on the estimo in 1379; the number was higher in 1403, but probably not relative to population. In short, it was not difficult to collect information and to check the veracity of the condizioni of such a small elite of citizens; it was more difficult to investigate properties on the Terraferma, but a specialized staff existed to handle eventual audits there. Second, there were large patrimonies that escaped paying forced loans, as the rulers of Venice often complained, not only at the time of revisions of the estimo. Those patrimonies were particularly liquid, containing little or no real estate and large portfolios of government credits acquired on the open market. They could be taxed only by lowering the nominal rate of interest due at least one point below that paid to forced lenders.

To be sure, real estate was hard to hide, whereas merchandise and liquid wealth could be more easily kept from the eyes of the fisc. Cash was a problem, but Venetians normally did not keep hoards of specie out of circulation. Banks could hide deposits, first by bank secrecy, then by holding accounts not registered in the official ledgers. Merchandise that was imported, however, could be tracked down at the customs offices; that which changed hands could be tracked down in the books of brokers and in those of the Messetteria, the brokerage tax office—and to all these the assessors had access. So straw men could be used. In 1398, for example, Zanobi Gaddi sent orders to the Datini branches in Majorca and Barcelona that agents not send wool in the names of Federico Corner and Antonio Contarini. These two noblemen were probably the biggest wool importers in Venice, and the latter owned a very large wool shop. The reason given is this: customs controls were being reinforced, and there was supposed to be a revision of the estimo, and the two did "not wish to be reputed wealthy" ("E' qui uno stento per dazi; poi si raconciono le prestanze e non vogliono esere tenuti richi").[33] The straw men had to be either foreigners or persons not on the rolls — persons perhaps ready to return a favor to Venetians who might have acted as stand-ins for foreigners illegally involved in the Levant trade. The government knew full well and legislated — literally for centuries — heavy penalties against stand-ins which were probably difficult to collect.

The problem of straw men was particularly pressing when limitations on free trade and on the use of commercial credit were applied by the Officium de Navigantibus in 1324, 1331–38, and 1361–63 and by legislation passed in 1404. The restriction stated that Venetians and residents could not invest in the Levant trade sums exceeding their assessed patrimony ("non navigetur ultra quam faciant de imprestitis"). With the demise of the Officium in 1363 and the lifting of the restriction for Venetians in general, the limitation to investment remained applied to naturalized citizens ("forenses facti cives"). In 1404, during a banking crisis, a ceiling of one and one-half times the estimo assessment was applied to bankers, thus drastically curtailing their ability to invest depositors' funds. The result of such restrictions, beyond the search for straw men, was that contributors interested in investing in the Levant trade or persons discovered to have invested more than their estimo figure were permitted to present themselves before the authorities (the Officium de Navigantibus or the Loan Office) asking to increase their assessment; they had to demonstrate their ability to pay forced loans at the higher rate and to condition real estate or government credits worth one-tenth the amount for which they requested the increase. If they were found to have a patrimony inferior to that claimed, their assessed valuation had to be reduced. In short, the assessment was manipulatable, and we are confronted with the anomaly of persons asking to pay a greater portion of forced loans — for the right to invest more in the Levant trade.[34] That this provision was enforced against naturalized citizens is reflected in the grazie requested by persons found to have dealt in merchandise of greater value, who sought relief from the fines that had been levied on them.[35]

---

[33]ADP, 712, Gaddi to Florence, 12 July 1398.

[34]Cessi, "L'ufficium de Navigantibus," in his *Politica ed economia*, 23–61, especially the documents on 50–51; for the bankers, see Lattes, *Libertà*, doc. 12 (original in ASV, SM, reg. 46, fol. 162v, the correct date of which is 28 November 1404).

[35]For example, ASV, Grazie, reg. 16, fols. 4v, 14 (1364).

During the Chioggia war the Rialto banker Bartolomeo d'Acarisio, an immigrant from Ferrara and naturalized citizen (he was made citizen de intus in 1375, de extra in 1378, originarius in 1382) moved by a spirit of patriotism for his new fatherland and perhaps by the desire to invest in the Levant trade after the Chioggia war, went on his own initiative ("sponte") to the Loan Office and offered to raise his estimo to 4,500 lire — the figure for which he is inscribed on the estimo of 1379 and on the basis of which he paid forced loans during the war.[36]

Luzzatto, convinced that Venetians in the three years of the War of Chioggia were forced to contribute 107 percent of their assessed patrimony, solved the apparent illogicality of the proposition by affirming that the estimo assessed only "about one-fourth of a household's real wealth." But first of all, as we have shown (see below, App. D, sec. i), the total figure for war loans in the years 1379–81 was actually 41 percent of assessed valuation, not 107 percent, still an extremely heavy burden but credible. Second, estimates of the possible relationship of the assessed patrimony of a forced lender to his real patrimony were based on pure guesses — Luzzatto's 25 percent, or Lane's 40 percent — guesses that were close to or far from the mark, according to different cases and contexts, as we shall see below.[37]

As an example of proven cheating on tax statements, Luzzatto used the situation surrounding the failure of the Orsini bank in September 1429. During the revision of 1426–27 it had been decided that bankers could be interrogated regarding condizioni that claimed deductions for bank debts; at the same time, it was discovered that audits were necessary, since debts claimed by one party had to appear as credits on the condizione of the other party. That kind of cross-checking was feasible and clearly was undertaken. In 1431 the authorities discovered that many people were exploiting the failure of the Orsini bank to claim large deductions for losses suffered in the failure — but falsely ("ficticie, dolose et fraudolenter"). The Senate authorized the board of assessors then at work to audit the books of the failed bank to find out who was evading taxes in this manner. While they worked, they discovered the other half of evasion: creditors of the bank were not declaring their credits, or, when they did so, they declared them for much smaller sums than were being uncovered during the audits. Similarly, they discovered that creditors were withdrawing cash by installments from the bank's liquidators without declaring those sums as cash in their condizioni. The assessors were told to proceed against evaders of both kinds — underreporting creditors and overreporting debtors of that failed bank and of others.[38]

---

[36]See ibid., reg. 17, fol. 127v, in his petition for the privilege of originarius.

[37]Lane, *Venice*, 151, where he suggests that the highest figure for 1379, namely the 60,000 lire at which Federico Corner of S. Luca was assessed, represented about 150,000 ducats in real patrimony. (Without warning the reader, Lane here assumed — correctly! — that 1 lira d'estimo was the equivalent of 1 ducat; the same is true of Queller — see App. D, sec. i, below.)

[38]*PRV*, ccxxxiv n. 1, citing ASV, SM, reg. 58, fol. 36v (9 March 1431). But see also ibid., fol.

On the side of the state, in sum, controls could be effective. That the periodically installed boards of assessors, elected by the Senate, evaluated constantly changing patrimonial situations and drew the logical consequences can be seen in their continual revision of the assessments of the Soranzo fraterna and of Andrea Barbarigo, discussed below. Between one general revision of the rolls and another, furthermore, there were standing committees that could be called into session to evaluate significant changes in individual patrimonies, on the basis of such events as marriages, inheritances, or shipwrecks.

Investigations on the part of the assessors of the veracity of citizens' *condizioni* could be quite thorough. A general inquiry regarding rental property declared to be almshouses was mentioned above, but there is also a rare lawsuit regarding an individual case in which proof of expenditures had to be provided to the assessors' office. When the executors of an estate petitioned for reduction of its assessment because some 1,600 ducats had been distributed as alms, as requested by the testator, the assessors asked for proof. The principal executor related that of 250 beneficiaries, from the years 1426–29, he was able to track down 100, while the rest, he claimed, had died of plague, especially in 1427. It took him fifteen days, by boat and on foot, to get the statements of those 100, for a total of 880 ducats. Upon receipt of the proof ("le confession de que[l]ori che avè le elemosine"), the assessors provided him with a written declaration of exemption for that amount and correspondingly reduced the assessment by 1,000 lire. Exemplary or not, the case provides a small insight into the investigative criteria actually employed.[39]

On the side of the contributor, the reaction against particularly heavy impositions could take the form not only of evasion but of more or less organized revolt against the fisc. One such very diffused revolt was serious enough that the Senate decided to intervene. The preamble to a law of 1442 — after eleven years of extremely onerous forced loans in Venice and of gabelles and direct taxes in the subject territories — states that recently there had been "insolent, bold and presumptuous" persons who not only refused

---

73: "Cum concessum fuerit Sapientibus nostris ad aptandum terram, quod deberent inquirere et procedere contra illos qui dolose et fraudolenter dedissent se pro debitoribus banchi de Ursinis"; they should proceed similarly "contra illos qui fuissent creditores dicti banchi et non dedissent se in condicionibus suis preteritis pro creditoribus ipsius banchi, aut dedissent se pro creditoribus in minori quantitate quam esse reperientur." The same jurisdiction was granted against those who, three to four days before turning in their "conditiones," received cash from the bank and did not declare it. Both orders were then extended, presumably to other banks that had failed in the recent past: "etiam intelligantur pro aliis banchis a scripta qui erant tempore sapientum predictorum" (9 August 1431).

[39]The lawsuit pitted executors of the estate of the papermaker Alvise di Nicolò Santo against each other and records some ten years of their contacts with the assessors ("i signori a conzar la terra"). ASV, GP, Sg, reg. 116, fols. 50–60 (17 March 1452).

to pay their own forced loans or gabelles but incited others to similar disobedience. Taking it as given that any open and organized opposition to the "long customary" impositions and taxes was illegal, the Senate declared that "no one, in private, dare condemn, contest or contradict any levy or gabelle, using such words as 'Don't pay!' 'Don't buy pawns!'" [utendo talibus verbis, "non pagè," "non comprè pegni"] and the like." An explosive situation had clearly developed not only in the city itself but also in the dominions of Terraferma and Mar—thus the reference to gabelles and pawns, as well as to levies of forced loans, calibrated according to wealth. Since a widely diffused tax revolt threatened Venetian interests and brought ignominy to the Signoria, the Senate ordered incarceration for one year or banishment for two years from the place where incitement to civil disobedience had been expressed, plus a fine of 300 ducats, of which one-third was offered to the informer. A hiatus in the wars in Lombardy at that very time made it possible over the next three years to extract forced loans at very low rates of levy, which certainly contributed more than a repressive law to defusing the immediate situation.[40]

iv. TWO CASES OF ASSESSMENT IN THE QUATTROCENTO

For Venice, only two condizioni for a single household have been uncovered, an incomplete one (for 1439) and a declaration of reduced patrimony (for 1448), preserved among the estate papers of Guglielmo Querini. Furthermore, only in the case of Andrea Barbarigo can we match levels of assessment with estimates of actual patrimony. The need here to exploit such limited and incomplete documentation merely underscores the poverty of extant fiscal sources in Venice, in comparison with the wealth of such documentation in the Florentine archives. It may be that written declarations prepared by each household and religious institution were consciously destroyed at the time of the subsequent revision.

The Condizioni of Guglielmo Querini

Guglielmo (Vielmo) Querini was a bachelor merchant who was born about 1400 and died in 1468. His interest in commercial investment, even as a younger man, was inconstant. Although his account books are not extant, various loose notes and a small notebook or ricordanza have survived among the papers of his estate, which was administered by the Pro-

---

[40]The importance of this law was underscored by Luzzatto, *PRV,* ccli, who published it as doc. 253. The reference to pawns seems to have to do with the Camere dei Pegni used in the Terraferma, where those who lacked the liquidity with which to pay a given tax could leave a pawn, which, of course, had to be either redeemed or sold. For the change in levels of imposition of forced loans (the last was of September 1442, the next would be only in August 1443), see Luzzatto's appendix, p. cclxxii, and table 13.2, below.

curators of San Marco. There Luzzatto found the documents, or copies thereof, which Querini took with him when he had to present himself before the board of assessors at the time of two revisions of the estimo.[41]

The statement for 1439 leaves blank several items that I have sought to complete; it is summarized in table 12.3. Most important, the merchandise and capital account (which includes a single bill of exchange for 160 ducats) totals 3,850 ducats but leaves blank the calculations for two kinds of raw silk and for pepper; the weight in pounds is entered, but the evaluation in money of account awaited his meeting with the assessors; I have entered a total of 4,000 ducats. As regards deductions, Querini noted that he would claim the maximum permitted of 200 ducats for jewels and silver ("chome conziede la tera"); being unmarried, he claimed no dependent children. He claimed ten years' rent (50 ducats × 10) on the house in which he lived (owner: Nicolò Sturion), while he declared income from rents of 21⅓ ducats (one-fourth of a palace at S. Zulian brought him nothing); he left a blank space, where I have entered the capitalization at 11 percent. Similarly left blank in the right-hand column were credits declared uncollectible ("per debitori dai qual non spiero mai aver niente"); I have entered the figure Querini reported in 1448, assuming it referred to the same situation. Finally, Querini alerted the assessors to the death of his two brothers since the last revision of the rolls and affirmed that their patrimony, which had passed to him, was included in his declaration. Although the declarant left this copy incomplete, the credit balance calculated here on the basis of various interpolations is close to the figure of 4,900 lire for which he was actually inscribed on the estimo by the assessors; the increase with respect to his previous assessment meant that he owed 106 ducats in back taxes.[42]

When Querini presented himself before the board of assessors on 28 February 1448, he brought two documents, a largely uncompleted "Chondizion" and a declaration of variations in patrimony in the seven years intervening between the previous revision of the estimo in 1439 and 9 July 1446, the date of the law that called for updating the estimo. In the condizione (summarized in table 12.4), he leaves the capitalization of rents received to the assessors and says he will explain orally ("a bocha") his business losses (registered as credits in the condizione, as debits on the balance sheet). In the latter (see table 12.5), he simply totals income and expenditures; he does not capitalize rents, but he adds a deduction of 200

---

[41]For his story, see Luzzatto, "L'attività commerciale di un patrizio."

[42]ASV, PSM, Citra, b. 271, loose sheet in dare-avere dated 16 February 1439, analyzed (somewhat differently) by Luzzatto in *PRV,* ccxxvi–xxvii, and in "L'attività commerciale di un patrizio," 170–71. Note that back taxes, or more precisely both over- and underpayments, are called "refusure," just like the back pay owed to sailers upon their return to the home port. Repayments were owed by the taxpayer or by the state for levies paid at a previous assessment during the time intervening between the date of the law mandating revision and the actual revision, if the assessment was changed.

TABLE 12.3

Summary of the Condizione of Guglielmo Querini, 1439 (in ducats)

Debits		Credits	
Four debts		Gov't credits: 5,796 du. at 25%	1,448
(creditors named)	1,140	Interest in arrears,	
Annual rent × 10	500	at 50%	199
	———	Merchandise and	
	1,640	capital investments	4,000
		Rents of 48 du. p.a.	
Exemption		from the Ferrarese	
Jewels and silverware	200	[capitalized at 10%]	480
		Rents from houses at	
		S. Zulian and S. Salvador	
		[capitalized at 11%]	211
		Business credits	
		"uncollectable"	479
	———		———
Total:	1,840		6,817
Balance:	4,977		
Estimo figure: £4,900			

Source: PSM, Citra, b. 271, fasc. 3, fol. 195.

ducats for each of six dependents ("boche") that he must have taken over from his brothers; this should more logically have gone into the "Chondizion." In declaring what he paid for house rents, he records that his former house was owned first by Nicolò Sturion, then by Alvise Diedo, while the house to which he had moved was owned by the estate of Giacomo Badoer. The liabilities were greater than the assets, and the assessors agreed to a reduction of his estimo from 4,900 lire to 2,800 lire.[43]

On both sheets Querini noted on 28 February 1448 that his assessment had been dropped to 2,800 lire and that he was owed a refund for levies totaling 18 percent, paid since 9 July 1446, on the figure of 2,100 lire for which his estimo figure had been reduced. On the first sheet he added that the order to make the refund, of 378 ducats, had been sent to the appropriate office on 2 March and stated that this meant his portfolio would be reduced by the amount of the cash refund.[44] The payment is not mentioned in Querini's miscellaneous papers, but we know from the con-

[43]ASV, PSM, Citra, b. 271, fasc. 3, fol. 192; haphazard versions by Luzzatto (transcription errors especially in the credit column) in *PRV,* ccxxvii–xxviii, and in his *Studi,* 171. Luzzatto did not discuss the incomplete condizione presented in 1448.

[44]He also mentioned the assessors before whom he discussed his condizione: Cristoforo Donà, Zorzi Zorzi, Vettor Barbaro, Marco Longo, Bernardo Balbi; of these the most important was surely the last named, brother and partner of Francesco Balbi, who had operated a bank on the Rialto until 1445.

TABLE 12.4

Summary of the Condizione of Guglielmo Querini, 1448 (until 9 July 1446)
(in ducats)

Debits		Credits	
Annual rent × 10	400	Gov't credits: 5,620 du. at 25%	1,405
		Interest in arrears,	
		at 40%	420
		Merchandise (woad)	100
		Rents of 48 du. p.a.	
Exemption		from the Ferrarese	480
Jewels and silverware	200	Rents from houses at	
		S. Zulian and S. Salvador,	
		21⅓ du. p.a.	211
		¼ palace at S. Zulian	
		with no rent income	—
		A credit at the Office	
		of the Estraordinari	16
		Two business credits,	
		"uncollectable"	479
Total:	600		3,111
Balance:	2,511		
Estimo figure: £2,800			

Source: PSM, Citra, b. 271, fasc. 3, fol. 191.

TABLE 12.5

The Revision of Guglielmo Querini's Condizione, 1447–1448 (in ducats)

Debits		Credits	
Forced loans paid, nos.		£2,900 in gov't credits sold	
27 (1435) to 75 (1439)	2,558	[ave. price: 21.67]	629
Direct taxes (boccatico,		Interest received on gov't credits	801
house rents)	126	Rents from Ferrarese	
Back taxes (refusure)		estate, for 5 years	240
on forced loans (1439)	106	House rents received	150
House rents paid	362	Salary, office of	
Living expenses for		Auditori vecchi, minus	
6 dependents (× 200)	1,200	a tax of ⅓	135
Purchase of a male slave	48	Commercial profits	
Two business losses	479	(under 8 headings)	110
Upkeep of rental houses,			
dredging canals	20		
Total:	4,899		2,065
		Negative balance:	2,834

temporary account books of Andrea Barbarigo that the fisc lived up to its obligations in this regard (see below, table 13.2).

It is doubtful that the condizioni normally consigned to the assessors in Venice were that incomplete. Querini's copies may have been just rough drafts. He does not even give the names and ages of the dependents he seems to have "inherited" at the death of his brothers, and he accounts for them only on the informal balance sheet, not on the condizione, where he might have claimed the deductions. Nor is it clear how the assessors evaluated these two documents in order to arrive at the reduction.

By contrast, condizioni prepared in Treviso and the Trevigiano in the same years show that in this area, close to Venice and subject to it since 1339, tax declarations were as complete as those of the Florentine catasto of 1427: they contain descriptions of each piece of real estate with its revenue, the number and ages of members of the household, the kind and number of livestock owned, debts and credits. Thousands have survived, including some from the city of Treviso based on the general estimo of 1434, despite the order — given to the local assessors in 1486 but probably long a tradition, conceivably also in Venice — that they be burned at the termination of the fiscal census.[45] Could authorities in the capital city have been satisfied with less precision?

Andrea Barbarigo's Patrimony and Assessments

There is only one case known to date in which we can match a man's patrimony as estimated from his own accounts with his estimo figure, that of Andrea Barbarigo. Lane calculated Barbarigo's net worth at three dates; he was unsure of how to evaluate the dowry that Cristina Capello brought to Andrea in 1439–40, of which only 1,000 (of 4,000) ducats seem clearly to have been in Andrea's name. The fisc, beginning in 1403, counted dowries at 50 percent of their value.[46] From the last column of table 12.6, we can see at a glance that the fisc assessed Andrea at between one-fourth and two-thirds of his actual net worth. Perhaps the assessment was low at first, to favor a young man just starting out. It went quickly to two-thirds, in the period of Venice's heavy military involvement in Lombardy, when the fisc had to be stricter. Mitigating factors in the seemingly low fiscal evaluation of Andrea's patrimony were the fact that he did not own a house and could claim a deduction for the rent he paid; the addition to the household of his wife, dependent but not deductible, in 1439; and the addition of two sons,

---

[45]The estimi concerned the subdivision of lump sums in direct taxes, the dadie delle lanze or colte ducali, allotted by Venice to each subject province. Del Torre, *Il Trevigiano,* esp. 64–96 and appendix, docs. 3 and 4. The condizioni or polizze were described and nearly six hundred of them exploited by Giuliano Galletti, *Bocche e biade: Popolazione e famiglie nelle campagne trevigiane dei secoli XV e XVI* (Treviso, 1994), pt. 2.

[46]*Andrea Barbarigo,* 28–29 and n. 66; also 184–85. On dowries and the fisc, see just above.

TABLE 12.6

Andrea Barbarigo's Estimo Figure and Net Worth in Given Years, 1431–1449
(in ducats)

Year	Estimo Figure	Rate of Levy (%)	Amount Paid	Net Worth	Tax as % of Net Worth	Relation: Estimo/ Net Worth
1431	500	12.25	61.25	1,537–1,673	4–3.6	⅓
1435	1,000	6.75	67.50	—	(4.4–4)	(⅔)
1440	4,500	15.50	697.50	6,866–7,532	10–9	⅔
1447	3,000	7.50	225.00	—	(3)	(⅖)
1449	3,000	6.75	202.50	12,000	2	¼

Sources: For the first four columns, see table 13.2. The figures for 1431 here include the 9 interest claims owed in back taxes, thus completing the year. Those for 1449 are for the last 12 months of levies (July 1448–July 1449) preceding Andrea's death. The net worth is drawn from Lane, *Andrea Barbarigo*, 182–86. Figures in parentheses were derived from the earlier calculation of net worth, in the absence of updated estimates.

born in 1440 (Nicolò) and 1443 (Alvise), for each of whom 200 ducats were deductible. The growth of the household, as well as the general recognition that fiscal pressure had reached the limits of supportability, probably contributed to the reduction granted in 1447.

Table 12.6 can also be analyzed from another vantage point, that of the actual burden of taxes levied and paid on Andrea's net worth. In four of the five years examined, taxes burdened the household for only 2–4 percent of net worth; in 1440, the peak year in which 15.5 percent was levied on the estimo and Andrea paid nearly 700 ducats, forced loans represented 9–10 percent of his net worth. In short, in the case of Andrea Barbarigo, a middling merchant with a very liquid patrimony, the fiscal burden cannot be judged unbearable in the years for which the data are sufficiently precise. Persons with a more illiquid patrimony, consisting of rent-producing real estate that was more easily assessed, were probably hit harder by the fisc.

v. THE "VENETIAN MODEL" FOR THE FLORENTINE CATASTO

Some of these criteria for the formation of the Venetian estimo were taken as a model for the Florentine catasto of 1427 — whose very name came from Venice.[47] This emerges from the debates in Florence regarding a re-

[47]The estimo or list of contributors was recorded in large books called "catastici," a word imported early from Byzantium (καταστιχον). They were so called in 1207 in an important law regarding the public debt (*PRV*, doc. 7); again, an accounting reform called for the compilation of a "catasticho" of all encumbered government credits, with the conditions (*PRV*, doc. 176). The term was also used closer to the time of the Florentine catasto in two rare tax lists for Venetian subject territories. The first was made for Scutari in 1416 under the count

form of the manner of levying forced loans and from the new law itself. The system previously used in Florence for levying "prestanze" had been based upon a rather vague presumption of resources and was manipulated — according to the government's need for credit on the one hand and according to the reputation of the wealth of a household on the other — by neighborhood committees charged with raising the amount of money which the government had imposed. It was judged inequitable and arbitrary by proponents of reform, who, by contrast, praised the efficiency of the Venetian fiscal administration, judged "the best governed of all." The point most underscored was the assessment of all forms of wealth in a catasto, "as is done in Venice," but it was also considered important that the assessors be elected officials of the city government, that is, responsible politically; only that way, the proponents stated, could a reform bring with it peace and concord among the citizenry.[48]

The debates began in Florence in August 1422 and were taken up periodically until the law was finally approved in 1427. References to Venice are terse and generic, with few exceptions. In 1422 the silk merchant Bartolomeo Corbinelli asserted that in Venice the house in which one lived and the foodstuffs consumed by the household were exempt and that persons and expenses were deductible; the assessment was made on the balance.[49]

---

and captain Albano Contarini by a notary of the Avogaria di Comun. Their mandate was to register, village by village, "in presenti cathastico, . . . nomina habitantium . . . et quantum teneatur solvere unusquisque eorum." ASV, Secreta, Materie miste notabili, reg. 108, fol. 1; edited by Fulvio Cordignano, S.J., *Catasto veneto di Scutari e Registrum Concessionum, 1416–1417* (2 vols., Scutari, Albania, and Rome, 1940–42); in vol. 2, which seems the only one to have survived (the author disavowed the first, which appeared full of errors), Cordignano writes (4–5) that the tradition of such registers came from the very exact Byzantine tax roll or "praktikon." The second extant register was drawn up when the Venetian conte or rector of Cattaro, Giovanni Balbi (in office 1427–29), had a "catasticus" made of all taxpayers, nobles and commoners, recorded according to a system of carats, for the town of Zupa Gerbili, in the county of Cattaro. See Bibliotéque Municipale de Roanne, France, Fonds Boullier, ms. no. 5, a large document of 130 fols., which gives only the names and the number of carats of assessment for each specific subdivision. In later centuries, the term *catasticus* was used in Venice for any list of properties.

[48]David Herlihy and Christiane Klapisch-Zuber, *Les Toscans et leurs familles: Une étude du Catasto florentine* (Paris, 1978), 56–58 (or 9–10 of the English edition, *Tuscans and Their Families: A Study of the Florentine Catasto of 1427* [New Haven, 1985]), and Conti, *L'imposta diretta*, 119–37. Herlihy and Klapisch were more convinced there was a Venetian model, whereas Conti, who studied the Florentine debates (not the Venetian system) more closely, held, "In realtà, malgrado diversi punti di contatto, i 'catasti' fiorentini furono molto diversi dagli 'estimi' veneziani" (119 n. 1). Cf. Molho, *Florentine Public Finances*, 79–80. Giuseppe Petralia makes the case that a more direct antecedent for the catasto reform was Florence's own imposition of a direct tax on Pisa and its contado in 1416; see "Imposizione diretta e dominio territoriale nella Repubblica fiorentina del Quattrocento," *Società, istituzioni, spiritualità: Studi in onore di Cinzio Violante* (Spoleto, 1994), 639–52. For the responsibility granted to the officials of the Venetian Loan Office, see the capitolare of 1262–78 in *PRV*, doc. 20.

[49]"Veneti onus non ponunt super domum habitationis et super victualia, et qualitatem personarum et expensas considerant. Et super eo quod superatur ponitur." Conti, *L'imposta*

The banker Averardo di Francesco de' Medici propounded the inclusion of all forms of wealth, including real estate, government obligations, and cash, saying that the Venetians, who had governed themselves independently for nine hundred years, observed that system and that it would be no dishonor to procure information from them.[50] The proposal to tax cash holdings disturbed opponents of the bill. In that context, the banker Nicolò Barbadori went so far as to state, "Venetians do not do business with borrowed money," by which he presumably meant cash loans.[51] That was hardly true, but perhaps in 1422 Venice had not yet inserted a deduction for debts. In 1425, by which time Barbadori had been converted to support for the catasto, terse mentions of Venice, by Barbadori and by Rinaldo degli Albizzi, who said he had heard the "Venetian catasto" discussed, concerned generically the justice of that model. For the latter, ambassador to Venice on various occasions, the success of the Venetian fiscal system was fundamental to the city's reputation as being the best governed and administered. The model, finally, was overextended in the intervention of Giovanni Minerbetti, who implied, erroneously, that Venice taxed directly the citizens of its subject territories.[52] Here, in fact, lies the most macroscopic difference between the Venetian estimo and the Florentine catasto: the former included, beginning in 1403, the landed estates of Venetian citizens, while leaving the assessment of non-Venetian subjects to local tradition and local responsibility; the catasto officials, on the other hand, undertook directly the assessment of the households of all subject territories.

The points of similarity are striking enough as to suggest conscious imitation of certain Venetian criteria. The assessment was to include all forms of wealth: not only real estate but also cash, merchandise, gold, silver and gems, and government obligations. The dwelling and its furnishings, considered non-revenue-producing, were exempt. A deduction of 200 florins was allowed for each member of the household (not counting servants, apprentices, or salaried labor), as in Venice, where the allowance for dependents was 200 lire d'estimo, that is, 200 ducats. Similarly, while credits had to be declared, debts could be deducted. Capitalization of house rents, how-

---

diretta, 121. The exemption for the house was certainly correct; foodstuffs for direct consumption are not mentioned in the laws.

[50]"Veneti sic agunt et per annos DCCCC regerunt. Et ut ipsi agunt et nos facere debemus. Nec debemus ad dedecus reputare ab ipsis notitiam habere." Ibid.

[51]"Veneti non cum credito mercantur." Ibid., 122.

[52]Ibid., 126–27. Rinaldo degli Albizzi declared, after outlining reforms, "Et Venetiis forma hec servatur et dicitur civitatem illam pro ceteris melius regi et gubernari." Giovanni Minerbetti said, after asking for the assessment of citizens and inhabitants of the subject territories alike, "Et Veneti sic agunt et subditi omnes eorum solvunt." Pietro Berti, "Nuovi documenti intorno al catasto fiorentino," *Giornale storico degli archivi toscani* 4 (1860): 38, 43–44, 46–47. Niccolò Barbadori insisted on the assessment of all forms of wealth and added, "Veneti sic faciunt: et Catastum habent,"—at which point Rinaldo degli Albizzi interpolated, "Et Veneti id observant." Guasti, *Le commissioni*, 2:323.

ever, was a factor that had already been applied in Florence under the pre-stanza system. Herlihy and Klapisch-Zuber concluded that even the under-lying fiscal philosophy was borrowed, namely, to include all forms of wealth, income-producing real estate, and commercial capital, without burdening productive activity. To this one should add the inclusion of real property owned in the subject territories in the declaration of the owner in the city, and the importance of instituting a centralized bureaucracy, with elected officials, substituting for the manipulatable neighborhood committees.

It is not surprising that Florentines should have been acquainted with the ins and outs of the Venetian system of forced loans well enough to cite it as an example, although it may well be doubted that official inquiries, suggested by Averardo de' Medici, were ever made. The highest echelons of government knew Venice through diplomatic experience, merchants and artisans resident in Venice through firsthand experience. Rinaldo degli Albizzi, for example, who propounded the Venetian model in debates, was ambassador to Venice in 1412, 1422, and 1423. It was he who reported, correctly, that each levy of 1 percent of assessed valuation as recorded on the estimo brought about 40,000 ducats to the coffers of Venice.[53] More intimate acquaintance with the Venetian fisc could be found within the large Florentine community in Venice. Dual citizenship in fact meant taxation in both cities.

Some kinds of war taxes, levied when the two republics were allied in the same war effort, caused enough persons to complain that the question of double jeopardy was taken up at the diplomatic level. In 1412 Rinaldo degli Albizzi himself was sent to Venice to negotiate an exemption for Florentines resident in Venice from a special head tax for the war against King Ladislaus of Hungary; in exchange, he promised that Florence would make a loan of any amount as long as the war continued. The Senate responded that the tax would remain applied to foreign brokers and shop-keepers living in Venice, but it exempted nonresident exchange dealers — that is, the big Florentine merchant bankers and their factors.[54]

More significant for the planning stages of the reform in Florence is the situation in which Florentines with dual citizenship found themselves: they had to contribute forced loans, on the basis of assessed valuations of

[53]"Et Veneciis exigitur summa florenorum XL millium; et hic exigitur 80 millium et ultra." In Berti, "Nuovi documenti," 44. The 1 percent levy of 11 December 1425 in Venice brought in 43,642 ducats; *BG,* 1, doc. 86, and *PRV,* cclxx. Prestanze in Florence at the same date were meant to bring in 20,000 florins; Molho, *Florentine Public Finances,* 90. One catasto in 1430 brought in 25,000 florins; Herlihy and Klapisch, *Les Toscans,* 28–29, 43.

[54]He complained against "la inposta posta sovra Fiorentini abitanti in Veniexia e simel tuti altri forestieri, con ziò sia che pur queli non voiando eser mesi ad alguna faciom per questa presente vera del re d'Ongaria." The Senate ruled "che i sanseri e botegieri over stazoneri abitase in Veniexia devese dar le suo faxion, e altri mestieri de chanbii viandanti no' s'entendese a la dita chondiciom per fin a la prexente vera." Morosini, Cronaca, 1:697–99. The tax involved would only later be called a "boccatico," or head tax, on those not inscribed in the estimo.

their property, in both cities. Two examples will suffice. The first concerns Taddeo di Zanobi Gaddi, born in Venice, son of a naturalized Venetian citizen, with a branch office of his business located in Venice. He declared to the catasto office in Florence that he was being taxed at 1½ percent per month on an assessed valuation of 3,000 lire; he hoped that the officials would consider that as a result he was already paying 45 ducats per month for the same war effort and grant him relief from "two torments." Francesco di Jacopo Arnoldi, who ran silk shops in both cities, had the same status as Taddeo Gaddi. He reported being inscribed on the Venetian estimo for 2,100 lire and showed that he had contracted debts on the exchange in order to pay his forced loans.[55] Gaddi, Arnoldi, and persons like them were not in the ruling group in Florence and did not participate in the debates, but they clearly were in a position to advise those who were most involved in preparing the reform concerning the nature of the Venetian fiscal system.

After the law of the catasto had already been rescinded, upon the return of the Medici from exile in Venice, further exemptions of Florentines from the Venetian boccatico were negotiated. In 1439, again only merchant bankers, the most capable of paying, succeeded in gaining exempt status: the Medici, Panciatichi, and Gaddi.[56] Others were surely still obliged to contribute to the forced loan administrations of both city-republics.

An examination of the criteria employed in assessing patrimony in Venice makes it clearer now that on many levels, surely not on all, Florentine lawmakers looked to Venetian experience and adopted and adapted assessment procedures. There was much more than mere "points of contact" between the two systems; behind the comments of the Florentines was a genuine interest in the "Venetian model." With the criteria in place, one can now turn to the impact of forced loans on specific households and on the workings of the free market in government credits.

[55]For a complete transcription of both passages, see p. 612, n. 4.
[56]Conti, *L'imposta diretta,* 46 n. 36.

13

FAMILY AND FINANCE
Forced Loans and the Open Market at Work

i. SPECULATION AND PRICES

I N VENICE AS ANYWHERE there was continual speculation on the open market in government obligations, ever since the debt was consolidated and marketability was guaranteed in 1262. Account books that would provide direct evidence of hard-nosed speculators in action, persons who bought low to sell high, however, are lacking. Gerolamo Priuli in the early years of the Cinquecento wrote — with disapproval — that there were many speculators who grew wealthy by buying and selling government credits "as though they were commodities." Many others, he continues, were forced to sell at the best price they could get in order to be able to pay the next impositions.[1] As will be seen below, however, on the basis of the limited documentation that survives, it seems that active merchants inscribed on the estimo tended to sell the issues they had been forced to buy, in order to increase their liquidity, rather than to pay new forced issues. On the other hand, some investors — estates, probably widows, certainly foreigners, sometimes institutions — bought with the aim of keeping the portfolio as a guaranteed source of a moderate income. Market prices of government credits fluctuated constantly, albeit less radically than those of foreign exchange, reflecting changing pressures of supply and demand. The

---

[1] It must be remembered that Priuli had just lost 10,000 ducats by buying Monte Nuovo credits at over par which then dropped to 60, which is why he says they were not worth the paper they were written on: "sonno carte dipincte et carta et ingiostro, senza fondamento alchuno." Priuli, *Diarii*, 332–33 (September 1509).

quotations on the "big board" at the Rialto were influenced, as anywhere, by news — and made news.

In their correspondence during the years 1392–1408, Ruggiero and Andrea Contarini often provide for their brother Giovanni in Oxford and Paris the current quotations of Venetian government credits. The letters show market prices to have moved about rapidly, between a low of 43 and a high of 58½. The rationales occasionally provided by Ruggiero for the variations have to do with peace and war, as when he awaited news from Bologna in 1392, or with economic crises, like the bankruptcy in 1393 of a Giovanni Morosini, which caused a decline in prices from 55 to 53. The interest shown by the Contarini brothers reflects the acumen of speculators but not actual speculation, for they had orders from their brother abroad to purchase government credits in his name, thus to reinvest the money they were to receive from selling off the spices he had left behind. They dallied for years with the spices, however, while Giovanni, who had departed in 1392 when government obligations were at 43–44 and had given orders to buy at those prices, failed to accept the advantageous offer they made him of their own holdings, as prices went above 55. The university student and future patriarch of Constantinople had enough business acumen to have his brothers sell high if they bought low, but he seems to have been more concerned with securing an income to support his studies.[2] By contrast, the correspondence of contemporary Florentines operating in Venice reflects no interest in Venetian government credits as an investment opportunity. In a rare mention, an agent of Francesco Datini reported from Venice in 1402 that a breakdown in peace negotiations had caused market prices to drop from 61 to 55 but that a resumption had brought them back to 60, "which [he wrote] is a good signal for peace." In short, he reported prices merely as a sign of the mood of the market in general.[3] Similarly, commercial letters of the Bembo family from the summer of 1418, during Venice's trade war with King Sigismund, describe the oscillations of the market: hopes for peace in late July had caused prices to rise to 58–59 until a

---

[2]Some of the letters, in ASV, San Giorgio Maggiore, b. 174, but not the dozen that discuss the market in government obligations, were published by Giuseppe Dalla Santa, "Uomini e fatti dell'ultimo Trecento e del primo Quattrocento: Da lettere a Giovanni Contarini, patrizio veneziano, studente a Oxford e Parigi, poi patriarca di Costantinopoli," *NAV,* ser. 2, 32 (1916): 5–105; see 20 n. 1 for a list of most of the letters containing such information. Luzzatto mentioned the correspondence in *PRV,* cciii–iv, as reflecting true speculation.

[3]ADP, 714, Bindo Piaciti to Florence and to Francesco (15 July 1402): "Per le novità di Bolongnia i danari del monte di chostoro che valevano 60 in 61 tornorono a 55; ora da parecchi dì in qua sono tornati a 60, ch'è buon sengnio di pacie." Again on 31 December 1403 he wrote, "Sono milgliorati i danari del monte 4 in 5 per cento, e il pevere basato; sichè ambedue sono buon sengni di pace." In general, however, the Datini correspondents in Venice, who reported rates of foreign exchange weekly, did not concern themselves with the local market in government obligations.

negative report, sent ahead by the Venetian ambassador, caused them to drop to 52; a few days later the price was reported as 50; in early August a letter from the pope brought renewed hope that caused a jump from 52 to 56; then when news reached Venice of Pandolfo Malatesta's alliance with Milan, already in Sigismund's camp, there was another drop to 53. There is nothing in the letters, however, to indicate that the writer was about to exploit variations in the price of government credits for his own investments.[4] A man who, in need of liquidity in May 1425, went to the Rialto with a mind to sell recounted that when he got there rumors of an alliance between Florence and Venice were beginning to spread and government obligations had dropped from 67 to 64½, causing him to decide otherwise.[5]

The case of foreign lords was rather different. Serious investors such as the Gonzaga of Mantua, beginning in the 1360s, and Paolo Guinigi of Lucca, beginning in 1411, had their agents keep them constantly apprised of conditions that could affect their portfolios, as we shall see in the following chapter. To mention a single example in the present context, in 1438 the ambassador to Venice of the marquis of Mantua reported that the price had fallen to 31 as a result of war with Ravenna—"which is a bad sign and everyone is dismayed," he wrote. Here the correspondent relayed information of direct concern to the marquis, regarding not only his financial investments but also diplomacy and military policy, which affected prices of government obligations. In fact, only a short time later, the marquis joined an alliance against Venice and saw his portfolio sequestered, along with that of many of his subjects.[6]

The influence of news of war and peace on prices of government credits was sometimes recorded by chroniclers as well. Antonio Morosini, for example, expressed dismay in late August 1430 at Florence's opening hostilities against Milan, since that inevitably involved Venice, and reported that government credits had dropped to 49 at the news. In June 1433 he wrote that the arrival in Venice of a Milanese peace delegation had been greeted with celebrations and caused the price to rise from 32¼ to 36, "which was great news," he wrote [che fo bonisima novela]. When a peace treaty was actually signed a month later, Morosini drew a nearly audible sigh of relief: it had been a long war, during which Venetians had had to contribute forced loans totaling 67 percent of their assessments; now credits stood at 43–44, and the ducat was stable at 108 soldi — "che Cristo ne sia senpre regraciado, Amen."[7]

---

[4]ASV, Miscellanea Gregolin, b. 13, copialettere Bembo, fols. 2v–4 (July–August 1418).

[5]ASV, GP, Sg, reg. 96, fols. 87v–96v (27 April 1444): "ma vignando a Rialto el commenzava a spanderse la voxe de la liga [fra nui e Fiorentini] e imprestedi chomenzava a chalar; dove i valeva £67 vene in 64½."

[6]ASMN, Archivio Gonzaga, b. 1431, letter of 21 April 1438.

[7]Cronaca, 2:1116: "e avemo inprestedi è già caladi in livre 49 lo cento, che Dio perdona a questi Fiorentini aver demeso e fato intraiade in vera per la liga avem con loro" (1430); with

The list of market prices published by Luzzatto, with the addition of many further prices culled from other sources, has been rendered in graphic form as annual averages (see above, graph 11.1). Averages, of course, cannot reflect the actual pulse of the market—not the prices reported by the Contarini and Bembo families or by the agents of Paolo Guinigi; they merely provide a summary image of trends and tendencies of the market.[8] As always, fluctuations created profits for some, losses for others.

Although we have not found a specific case of speculation on the market, there are some legislative provisions that reflect speculation to the extent that they tried to control it. Rumors were circulated in 1351, during Venice's naval war with Genoa, that there would be a diversion of money from the sinking fund and that interest payments were to be suspended— rumors designed to cause a fall in prices. That led to a provision that threatened heavy fines for anyone who would actually propose such legislation.[9] The military conflict and heavy forced levies exacerbated a financial crisis anyway, and although interest payments remained regular, the price of government credits plummeted from 98½ in 1350 to 76 in late 1355. Much later, in 1422, specialized brokers were called to order and required to register each transaction so that the brokerage tax (messetteria) could be correctly applied; as matters stood, it was said, credits sometimes changed hands as many as four times before the first—and only—transaction was actually registered, as a result of which the Treasury received only a single tax payment.[10] Speculative sales of government obligations on deferred payment were permitted, but repeated attempts were made—in 1390, 1404, and 1410—to control them, which is proof that such operations were quite normal. In 1404, during Venice's war with Carrara Padua, a head of the Forty accused investors on the open market of speculating on Venice's fate in a time of serious crisis ("et el no' sia ben ch'el se faza merchandantia del stado de Veniexia"); instead of calling for prohibiting such contracts, however, he merely proposed they be taxed. Fictitious contracts, such as loans of government credits, made to cover speculation, were banned in 1443. Finally, some attempt was made to control a practice akin to insider trading, when the doge and members of the Ducal Council were prohibited from buying or selling government credits except upon authorization—by the Senate for the doge, by the Ducal Council itself for council members.[11]

---

peace in sight, he speaks of a temporary increase of faith in government credits: "montando la creta d'inprestedi de livre 32¼ in livre 36 per cento, che fo bonisima novela, ma per avanti la saveremo meio" (2:1528); and 2:1542 for the market indicators at the signing of the peace.

[8]Prices could change quickly and considerably; credits purchased by the Procurators of San Marco for the estate of Tommaso Talenti in 1409, for example, went from 52½ on 31 August to 49¾ on 5 September to 44 on 19 October; ASV, PSM, Citra, b. 141, fasc. 4.

[9]*PRV*, xcviii–ix and doc. 138.

[10]Ibid., doc. 228.

[11]Ibid., ccii–iii and docs. 200, 207, 254; also ASV, CN, reg. 3, fol. 117r–v (February 1404), and ASV, SM, reg. 47, copia, fol. 24 (31 May 1405). A strongly worded prohibition was passed

Although we lack account books of speculators, we can study the daily activity of merchants who recorded their estimo rating, their forced purchases, their interest income, and how they subsequently divested and invested. Few private account books are extant in Venice, in contrast to the situation in Florence, but those available make possible the concatenation of individual "financial histories" to cover actual practice throughout most of the fifteenth century and beyond.[12]

ii. THE SORANZO FRATERNA

The earliest large ledger extant is the much studied "libro real novo" of the Soranzo fraterna, a family of four brothers (Donato, Jacopo, Pietro, and Lorenzo), sons of Vettor who died in the early years of the century. The brothers were principally involved in the importation of cotton from Syria; many, if not most, of their clients were German merchants. It is a strange ledger, compiled sometime between 1434 and 1445 at the order of the Giudici di Petizion, who were hearing a lawsuit; the accountant followed orders given by two arbiters on the basis of several particular account books and of loose sheets of paper prepared by the arbiters, to which the accountant often refers ("chome i zudixi albitri à notado su alguni foi"). Thus it is an anomalous source.[13] Just the same, the information regarding the relationship of the fraterna to the fisc is surprisingly complete from 1406 to the first months of 1430, despite the confusion resulting from the backdating of numerous entries.

As can be seen at a glance from table 13.1, the estimo figure of the fraterna was changed at each of the six revisions, generally but not always upward, from 4,600 lire d'estimo to 13,000 lire, reflecting both growing commercial success and increased fiscal pressure. The two reductions (1415 and 1426) follow periods during which no levies were imposed, and the state, as a result, owed no reimbursements; they may reflect a loosening of criteria for redacting a tax declaration. The increases, on the other hand, coincide with periods of costly warfare; they were made retroactive to the date of the deliberation to revise the rolls. Since a revision took longer than one year, on three occasions the fraterna had to pay back taxes ("refusure"),

---

again in 1410 to "vendere aliqua imprestita ad salvandum nec dare ad aliquem terminum vel repentagium, publice vel occulte"—practices the meaning of which is unclear, except for the reiterated ban on credit sales; ASV, SM, reg. 48, fol. 128v (3 March).

[12]The question of the tax burden in Florence, in individual cases (especially that of Datini), was addressed by Molho, *Florentine Public Finances*, 87–112, and Giovanni Ciappelli, "Il cittadino fiorentino e il fisco alla fine del trecento e nel corso del quattrocento: Uno studio di due casi," *Società e storia* 46 (1989): 823–72.

[13]Lane (*Andrea Barbarigo*, Critical Notes, 145–46, 155–58) overlooked the reason for the anomalous nature of the ledger; on that score see Tommaso Zerbi, *Le origini della partita doppia: Gestioni aziendali e situazioni di mercato nei secoli XIV e XV* (Milan, 1952), 372–77.

which, of course, were written to its credit in the Loan Office as part of the forced loans. The entry for each payment made at that office names the ranking official in charge and present at the time.[14]

The Soranzo ledger registers a total of 81 levies over the years 1406–30, for an average of 3.4 per year. The issues bear the numbers 31 to 108 (3 levies were unnumbered). Of course, the average indicates little: wars with Milan forced Venice to impose about 1 levy per month in 1412 and 1426–27, at slightly over 1 percent of estimated patrimony due in cash for each levy. The next heaviest years are 1413, 1418–19, and 1428, which register 4 to 9 levies each but at lower rates of about ½ percent per levy. The total imposition over the whole period was 63.25 percent of the various estimo figures; that is, the state asked an average of 0.78 percent of estimated patrimony for each regular levy, or about 2.6 percent per year over twenty-four years.

Included in the column "cash paid" are sums (indicated by the letter[d]) which, although based on the estimo like any forced loan, were exacted from the forced lender as reimbursable loans. They were made directly to a designated office then particularly in need: especially the grain administration (the Provveditori alle Biave), but also the Provveditori di Comun and the Estraordinari. The Provveditori alle Biave often repaid its loans in wheat, although that is not the case here.[15] Only one imposition, the first on the list (23 ducats), is recorded as having been repaid in cash; all the rest (for a total of 247 ducats) were consolidated, that is, added to capital (each time the accountant duly noted: "fo messo in chavedal") and are thus here included in the total, together with back taxes, as effectively normal forced loans.

Clearly the forced lender could bear the burden of large cash payments to the state only if limited in time. In fact, periods of heavy imposition of forced loans were followed by periods of few or no impositions, in order to give the citizens respite. The Soranzo ledger reflects this fact. After the very costly wars during which Venice began its conquest of the Terraferma in 1404–5, Venice allowed six years to go by without collecting a forced loan; again in 1414, after another war against the Visconti, no levy was imposed at all and only very few over the successive three years; another long respite, including three years with no imposition, followed the war that led to the inclusion of Friuli in the Terraferma state in 1420; finally,

---

[14]Luca Pacioli advised a more careful registration, in one's inventory, of activity at Venice's Loan Office: the person in whose name the obligations were registered, in what ledger, page, and entry, the name of the scribe, the date, and rate of interest due. *Trattato di partita doppia*, 61.

[15]One example will suffice, from the many that could be adduced from accounts kept by the Procurators of San Marco throughout the fourteenth and fifteenth centuries. After a levy paid in November 1450, we find the registration: "Notamus quod de restitutione suprascripti tertii de mensis novembris recepimus . . . staria 6½ et 1 quartarolum frumenti," at 5½ lire di piccoli per staio, which they passed on to the heirs of the estate of Filippo Marcello (d. 1448); PSM, Misti, b. 63, reg. 1.

TABLE 13.1

The Soranzo Fraterna and the Public Debt: Forced Loans and Activity on the Market in Government Credits, 1406–1430
(in ducats)

Year	Estimo	No. of Levies (issue nos.)	% of Estimo	Cash Paid	Back Taxes	Pro' Rec'd	Sales	Acqu.	Price	Proceeds	Cost
1406				504[a]							
1407							1,600		51.25	820	
1407–11[b]											
1412	4,600	12 (31–42)[c]	13	626		69					
				23[d]		5					
1413	7,400	8 (43–50)	5	370	336	30		1,500	50		
1414	5,400					20[e]	500		46.75	234	
1415		1 (51)	0.5	27		6	1,080		49.625	536	
1416		2 (52–53)	0.75	40.5		13	200		51.5	103	
1417		1 (54)	0.5	27		15	400		54.5	218	
				84[d]							
1418		6 (55–60)	2.75	148.5		16					
1419		9 (61–69)	4.75	256.5		9					
				54[d]							
1420	9,900	3 (70–72)	1.5	126	236[f]	70[g]	270		59.875	162	
				46[d]							
1421		1 (73)	0.5	49.5		36	600		60.25	362	
1422		3 (74–76)	1	99		55[h]					
				25[d]							
1425[i]											
1426	6,800	13 (77–89)	12.5	850							
	800[j]			100							

522

1427		12(90–101)	14.25	969		40				
				114						
				34^d						
				4^d						
1428^k	13,000	4(102–105)	5	340	715	90	925	60		554
1429		4(106–107)^l	0.917	40		192	1,000	56.8		568
1430		2(108)^m	0.33	119		210				
				43						
24 yrs.		81(31–108)	63.247	5,119 +	1,287	876	4,650	3,425	54.055	2,435	1,112
				= 6,406					(ave.)		

Source: Soranzo ledger, fols. 2, 5, 10, 42, 56, 90, 125–26, 135–36, 139, 146.

Note: acqu. = acquisition, present in only three years (the first by bequest, the remaining two by purchase).

^{a} Paid for the "commissaria" of Vettor Soranzo.

^{b} That there were no levies 1406 through 1411 is essentially corroborated by Luzzatto (who lists only one, April 1407, unnumbered).

^{c} First levy on new estimo: December 1412.

^{d} Formally reimbursable levies to the Provveditori alle Biave (a few went also to the Provveditori di Comun and the Estraordinari); a single cash refund (of 23 ducats, in 1409) from the Provveditori alle Biave is recorded; all other such levies were added to capital at the Loan Office, with the notation "fo messo in chavedal."

^{e} Figure includes 10 ducats interest on a loan of 500 ducats in government credits made to Benedetto Soranzo.

^{f} "Per refuxura de duc. 4500 fo achresudi a 5¼ pro C. se trovan esser sta' fato da marzo 1419 fino a questo di."

^{g} In 13 cash receipts from 4 different account sources.

^{h} Of which 13.5 ducats were offset on a later levy ("scontado in una fazion").

^{i} No levies recorded 1423–25 (Luzzatto records only one, in December 1425, *PRV*, cclxx), but also no interest recorded, although interest was paid regularly. The late Amadi record gives levies for 8½ percent in 1424 (BMCV, Cod. Gradenigo, 56).

^{j} "Heirs" registered at 6,800 lire, Lorenzo di Vettor separately at 800 lire.

^{k} 14 August: estimo "cresudo di £5,400" (6,800 + 800 + 5,400 = 13,000).

^{l} Two levies unnumbered.

^{m} One levy unnumbered; the second, no. 108, dated 20 February.

some relief came again after the war with the Visconti in 1426–28 which brought Bergamo and Brescia into the Venetian state.[16]

The effects of the state's domestic and foreign policy on the Soranzo fraterna as a forced lender are easily seen. The state exacted a total of 6,406 ducats in cash, or 267 ducats per year (22 ducats per month) on the average. But the sums due during war years were three and four times the average, probably requiring the Soranzo brothers — along with many of their compatriots — to liquidate other assets in order to meet the forced levies.

The accounts, despite their anomalous nature, are quite precise regarding the collection of interest and the management of the portfolio. The interest ("pro'") received by the fraterna from 1407 to July 1430 totaled 876 ducats. All was received in cash with a single exception: the amount due on 12 May 1422, namely 13.5 ducats, was offset against a forced levy of ¼ percent (the accountant noted: "pro' fo scontado in una fazion"). The actual figure was surely higher, since three years, 1423–26, were skipped by the accountant, years in which we know from other sources that interest was paid regularly. Despite the partial nature of the data, interest income amounted to nearly 14 percent of the total in cash that the fraterna turned over to the Loan Office. Since credits held by persons inscribed on the estimo were earning 4 and 3 percent on par, according to the ceilings indicated in table 12.2, the high percentage figure earned means that the fraterna's portfolio was considerably larger than that reflected merely by the amounts that the brothers were forced to contribute. In fact, they continued throughout the period to receive income from a portfolio inherited from their deceased father, Vettor.

The management of the portfolio was probably rather typical for noble families, for their negotiating on the open market does not reflect a speculative bent. The brothers sold some issues on seven occasions but bought on the open market only twice — and then in order to meet obligations that, despite the high price, they chose not to meet with their existing portfolio; a third lot was inherited, for a nominal total of 3,425 ducats. Sales, for a nominal value of 4,650 ducats, brought 2,435 gold ducats to the family's cash account, for an average price of 52. The decisions to sell seem rational. In 1413 the fraterna received 1,500 ducats par value (recorded as worth 50 percent) as a bequest from Agnesina Venier. Probably so as not to let their portfolio grow too large in the category that earned only 3 percent interest on par, the brothers sold credits for a comparable value within a year and lent a further sum of 500 ducats in government obligations. In 1420–21 they sold 870 ducats' worth at considerably higher market prices, as table 13.1 shows. Most of what they purchased in 1428–29 was almost immediately redistri-

---

[16]These data largely corroborate those collected by Luzzatto for the same period; they integrate his data for the years 1417–18, issues numbered 54–60, left out probably because of an error in printing the table. He records a single levy of 1 percent for 1407, which bears no number. *PRV,* cclxx.

buted to third parties. Only rarely is the reason for an alienation indicated: in 1414, 100 ducats in credits were sold to Leonardo Giustinian to pay part of their sister Marcolina's dowry (it was Marcolina who was later to sue her brothers); in 1425, 100 ducats' worth were transferred to Marina, Donato Soranzo's widow, for part of her dowry; in 1429, of the government obligations just purchased, 280 ducats' worth were transferred to the religious order of the Cruciferi (probably to honor a bequest made by Donato), and 800 ducats' worth were simply distributed among three different accounts registered in the names of the brothers. A summary of the fraterna's transactions, in nominal values, would look like this:

bought at par (forced loans)	6,406	transferred	
acquired (3 lots, nominal)	3,425	in the family	800
total	9,831	to a widow	100
		to the Cruciferi	280
		sold	4,650
		total	5,830

Of the total transferred on the books of the Loan Office, 5,030 ducats were alienated outright, while 800 were kept in family.

Some idea of the net fiscal burden sustained by the fraterna can be had by subtracting interest received and proceeds from sales from the total turned over in forced loans. The result is a loss of something more than 2,000 ducats in twenty-four years. In short, the brothers had to write off as a dead loss an average of under 90 ducats per year, which can hardly be judged oppressive.[17]

Interest payments made to the fraterna by the Loan Office reflect considerable confusion. Instead of consolidating accounts payable to the fraterna, we find in 1420, for example, interest being collected from five accounts registered under four different names, in the ledgers of three different sestieri! In fact, thirteen different cash receipts are recorded in that year, collected on four different dates, relative to three different paghe (March/September 1419, March 1420); the first was a year late, the others one-half year late.[18] In short, paying out—and thus collecting—interest, generally in both gold and silver coin at rates of exchange fixed by the Senate, was a lengthy process; the time lapse between the first sestiere to collect and the last, as decided by lot, could be considerable. It hardly comes as a surprise, then, to learn that the office was pleased when it could consolidate the lots purchased by foreign buyers; similarly understandable is Luca

---

[17]Interest (876) plus proceeds (2,435) = 3,311 gold ducats; subtracted from 6,406 ducats in forced loans gives a loss of 2,095 ducats over twenty-four years, an average of 87 ducats per year.

[18]The accounts in S. Marco are entitled: the male heirs of Vettor Soranzo, Donato and Jacopo Soranzo; in Dorsoduro: Donato Soranzo, Agnesina Venier; in S. Croce: Donato and Jacopo. See Soranzo ledger, fol. 10.

Pacioli's caution always to go to the Venetian Loan Office with careful documentation in hand and to note the name of the scribe with whom one contracted business!

iii. ANDREA BARBARIGO AND HIS HEIRS

The fine set of account books kept by Andrea di Nicolò Barbarigo begin in 1431, only months after those of the Soranzo end. They carry the story of Andrea's administration of his portfolio — paralleled for a few years by that of Jacomo Badoer — until his death in 1449. The extant ledger maintained by his son Nicolò reflects affairs on the market in government obligations from 1456 to 1482. The hiatus between Andrea's death and the coming-of-age of Nicolò is short but important, since it includes the last forced loan imposed on the Monte Vecchio (February 1454); it will be filled in from another source. Accounts of grandsons and great-grandsons bring the story up to the time of the redemption of the Monte Vecchio.

That Andrea began his career as merchant without the backing of a fraterna and quite impecunious was underscored by Frederic Lane in his biography. In fact, Andrea was first inscribed on the estimo in July 1431 at only 500 lire, barely above the minimum. Over nearly twenty years, as table 13.2 reveals, his assessment rose sharply to 4,500 lire in 1440 before being reduced to 3,000 in 1447 — a reduction, as we have already seen (above, Chap. 12, sec. iv), attributable rather to a policy of fiscal leniency following costly wars in Lombardy than to sudden impoverishment, for Andrea's actual patrimony grew steadily. For the sake of comparison, Andrea's highest figure did not match the lowest figure at which the Soranzo fraterna was assessed. In customary fashion, Andrea paid back taxes when his assessment was raised, and he received refunds when it was reduced, the date of reference being always that of the deliberation calling for reform of the rolls.

As the same table shows, over nineteen years Andrea paid 3,648 gold ducats in forced loans in 162 levies (numbered 124–130, 1–100, 1–55), plus four small, technically reimbursable levies to the Provveditori alle Biave and the Estraordinari (indicated by the letter [b]) for an additional 16.75 ducats. The tax burden of 147 percent of his various fiscal ratings comes in cash terms to an average of 23 ducats per forced loan or nearly 200 ducats per year. As in the case of the Soranzo fraterna, here again one can read off times of peace and war: the minimum paid (25 ducats) was in 1433, the maximum (619 ducats) in 1441. Once again, wars in Lombardy (1438–41, 1446–48) signal the heaviest periods of impositions. The level of impositions was so much higher here than in the period covered by the Soranzo ledger that Barbarigo's average annual cash payments were not far behind those of the Soranzo brothers, despite his much lower assessment figure.

Andrea's administration of his portfolio shows that he was little interested in holding on to government credits. His intent was to keep his assets as liquid as possible and available for a good investment opportunity. Even before his first ledger opens, he borrowed his mother's credits, worth 1,300 nominal ducats, and sold them for 714 ducats (at a price of 55). Then, between 1432 and 1442 he sold issues worth about one-third more than those he had been forced to purchase in the same period. In 1432 he sold 533.3 ducats par value as soon as he was released from the encumbrance that had conditioned them.[19] Among the further lots sold were 1,000 ducats retired by the Governatori delle Entrate. Total sales added almost 800 gold ducats to his working capital. But buying, forcedly, at 100 and selling, optionally, at an average price of 25 meant a loss of 75 percent. On two occasions, moreover, Andrea lent packets of government credits. The advantage was that he could insist on prompt payment of officially promised interest semiannually, at a time when the state was getting behind in payments, and then collect again, this time from the state, when he again was the owner of record. One of the borrowers was his banker Francesco Balbi, who was probably fronting for another client; Balbi credited the 4 percent annual interest to Barbarigo's account with great regularity.

Interest income due Andrea was very low at first. He delayed collecting the first 9 ducats, which were already in arrears. In contrast to the records kept by the Soranzo fraterna, Barbarigo did not keep a separate running account of interest income.[20] All told, he received 246 ducats, which corresponds to 6.7 percent of the forced loans made; this means he owned other credits (he never mentions his nominal capital at any given date), but it also reflects double receipts on his loan of credits, as mentioned above. The last interest claim accounted for, that of 1442, was collected in 1448, six years in arrears.

Actual payment of levies was handled in a wide variety of interventions and mediations, often involving Rialto banks. Andrea made most payments himself and in cash in the early years. Then, beginning in 1434, he gave orders to the Balbi bank to pay the levies for him; it was very often Lorenzo Loredan, a manager or cashier of the bank, who withdrew cash from Barbarigo's current account and made payments at the Loan Office when they fell due—that until the bank failed in 1445. Thereafter it was often Andrea's brother Giovanni who made the cash payment, until, in 1447, the Rialto banks of Bernardo Ziera and Company and Luca Soranzo and Brothers provided cash from Andrea's accounts and often made the payment directly in his name. This seemingly disinterested manner of handling his accounts with the fisc reflects this sedentary merchant's determina-

---

[19]The story is told in Barbarigo, ledger A, fol. 45, in a kind of ricordanza; summarized by Lane, *Andrea Barbarigo,* 23 n. 30.

[20]He began a proper account, entitled "Camera d'imprestedi, per conto del pro' d'imprestedi" on fol. 46 but closed it out soon to profit and loss; thereafter it is necessary to recuperate the figures from the profit and loss accounts.

TABLE 13.2

Andrea Barbarigo and the Public Debt: Forced Loans and Activity on the Market in Government Credits, 1431–1449 (in ducats)

Year	Estimo	No. of Levies (issue nos.)	% of Estimo	Cash Paid	Back Taxes	Refunds	Pro' Rec'd (Claim)	Dir. Tax (no.)	Sales	Loans	Price	Proceeds
1431	500	9(115–23)	9.00		45[a]							
		4(124–27)	3.25	16.25								
1432		12(128–30, 1–9)	12.50	62.50					533		44.5	237
				2.50[b]								
1433		7(10–16)	4.91	24.55			9(1431[c]–1432[d])[c]					
				2.50[b]								
1434		11(17–27)	7.25	36.25					200		39.5	79
1435	1,000	11(28–38)	6.75	63.75	58			2.5(1)		100[f]		
1436		12(39–50)	6.20	62.00				5.0(2–3)				
1437		10(51–60)	8.50	85.00				5.0(4–5)				
1438		12(61–72)	14.00	140.00			10.4 (1433[d]–1436[d])	2.5(6)				
1439		11(73–83)	12.58	125.8		3[g]	1	10.0(7–10) 10 Balbi		500[h]		
1440	4,500	11(84–94)	15.50	505.00	294		20 Balbi					
1441		11(95–105)	13.75	618.75			20 Balbi					
							10.75 (1437–38[d])					

Year						20 Balbi					
1442	7(6–12)		5.00	225.00				1,000	20.25	201
1443[i]	5(13–17)		3.25	146.25		8(1438[c])		1,400	20.00	280
1444	2(18–19)		1.50	67.50		15(11)				
1445	2(20–21)		1.25	56.25 / 11.25[b]		3(1440[d]) / 15(1440[c])				
1446	11(22–32)		7.16	322.50		47(1441)				
1447	7(33–39)	3,000	7.50	300.00						
1448	13(40–52)		14.80	444.00	85	73(1442)				
1449	3(53–55)		1.75	52.50	15					
19 yrs.	162		147.4	3,354 + 294	397 − 103	247	40	3,133	600	797
				= 3,648	= 294					

Source: Barbarigo ledgers A–B (for the fols., see rubrics, under the relevant key words).

aTaxes due beginning January 1431: "messo a fare d'imprestedi per £500 nel sestier d'Osoduro in S. Barnaba" (fol. 38).

bFormally reimbursable levies, the first two to the Provveditori alle Biave, the third to the Estraordinari; generally added instead to capital.

cMarch claim.

dSeptember claim.

eOne-half of the interest due on both claims was withheld as a tax.

fLoan to Bartolomeo da Mosto on demand, at 4 percent: "el me de'render a mio piaxer, el pro' come fa la Camera") (fol. 168). Lent on 13 August 1435, returned on 7 August 1438.

gRefund of 3.3 ducats credited to capital as 15.14 ducats in bonds at 22, the current price.

hLoan to or through the mediation of Balbi, who paid the interest promptly on the current claim even though the state was in arrears; in fact, Andrea earned 4 percent twice, once from Balbi and then, 4–5 years late, from the state. Bonds lent 12 May 1439, returned 31 August 1442.

iAndrea's brother Giovanni has an estimo of 400 lire, completely separate from that of Andrea (fol. 71).

tion to devote his time to the counting house, making his investable capital turn over as rapidly as possible; he was happy to have others handle his debits and credits with the state. No commission charge is registered for this service rendered by the transfer banks of the Rialto.

Two final points regarding table 13.2 are worth making. First is a hitherto unnoticed direct tax, lifted in eleven numbered exactions on the basis of the estimo, for a total of 40 ducats. Each payment was made directly to the Treasury, *à fonds perdu* ("che perdo," "se dona ai Texaurieri," records Andrea); usually the Balbi bank and Lorenzo Loredan were involved in making the actual payment. The second is the total absence of any purchases whatsoever on the open market. Andrea was not interested in keeping capital inactive at low rates of return.

As we have already seen (Chap. 12, sec. iii), these records offer a unique opportunity to ask how close the estimo came to assessing real wealth. Comparing Lane's calculations of Barbarigo's wealth at three different dates with the estimo figures shows that the assessment varied from a low of one-fourth to a high of two-thirds of Andrea's net worth. In other words, Barbarigo's actual tax burden ranged from about 4 to about 10 percent of his patrimony. These estimates can probably not be generalized for the class of forced lenders as a whole, however, since Barbarigo had a peculiar indisposition toward investing either in real estate or in government credits, the income on both of which was more readily assessable than commercial investments. Furthermore, he went into debt often in order to keep his capital turning over — and debts were deductible on the condizione. He was, therefore, probably more successful than many other noble and non-noble merchants in keeping his assessed patrimony low.

Interest income and proceeds from sales of government credits recouped less than one-third of what Andrea paid in forced loans. The loss he sustained totaled about 2,600 ducats, an average of some 140 ducats per year.

Corroboration of Andrea Barbarigo's choices in the fiscal sector comes from another well-known account book, that of Giacomo Badoer, kept in Constantinople from 1436 to 1439. It falls in the middle of the period covered by the Barbarigo ledgers and prompts a brief excursus. The picture, seen below in table 13.6, is very similar. Giacomo sold off his government credits as quickly as he could, at about one-third their nominal value, and a large number of older issues as well; in all, he sustained a loss of nearly 1,000 ducats. His brother Gerolamo, who handled his affairs in Venice, reported no interest over those years, for he had already sold off the issues whose interest would have matured in the years covered by the ledger. Giacomo's only receipt from the state was a 20 ducat refund, owing to a reduction of his assessment ("che fazo de fation") in 1435 to 2,800 lire.

The period between the death of Andrea Barbarigo, who paid his last levy (no. 55) in July 1449, and the death of his brother Giovanni in 1456, when Andrea's first son came of age, is easily covered by accounts kept by the Procurators of San Marco. The issues of 1449–54 (numbered 56 to 69) were for a combined 12.67 percent of the estimo. The largest were those levied upon arrival of news of the fall of Constantinople, collected between August and October 1453.[21] In 1452 and 1453 the coalitions of Venice and Naples on the one hand and Florence and Milan on the other were at war; when levies were not paid in full, other impositions were revived, such as the special tax on real estate rents. No interest was paid out to holders of portfolios between November 1451 (when the claim of September 1444 was paid) and May 1453 (claim of March 1445). The concrete possibility for peace in early 1454 convinced authorities finally to suspend the system of forced loans, but interest payments stuck to a rhythm of about one paga out of two per year, so that in 1456 and in 1458 the paghe for 1447 and 1448 were paid, ten years late.[22]

Despite this bad performance by the state, despite the demonstrated fact that even in peacetime there was no will to bring interest payments up to date — understandably, because of the wide differential between interest paid on par to forced lenders and yield to capital invested on the open market, despite Andrea's aversion to holding government credits and real estate, in 1457 someone who had the ear of Andrea's sons Nicolò and Alvise, aged seventeen and fourteen respectively, thought it best to invest funds from the estate in government obligations. Perhaps their uncle Giovanni had paved the way to this decision when, before his death in 1456, he arranged the purchase of a landed estate in Carpi Veronese, or perhaps Andrea da Mosto, the other tutor, also opted for a conservative solution. In any case, between 1457 and 1461 the boys purchased more than 1,000 gold ducats' worth of credits in thirteen lots on three different dates. According to Nicolò's accounts, the state treated that portfolio as though it bore the dates of his purchases, rather than those of the original issue (the last of which, as we have seen, had been levied in 1454). I have not found legislation that instituted such a procedure, but the accounts are unequivocal, and surely the buyer knew what he was getting into. Table 13.3, which summarizes the development of the portfolio, and table 13.4, which records in-

---

[21]*PRV,* cclxxiii.

[22]A useful observatory is the account book of the estate of Tommaso Talenti, which earned about 330 ducats interest per paga. ASV, PSM, Citra, b. 141, fasc. 4, fol. 5 ("Danari scossi di pro'"). The portfolio of this rich estate stands in sharp contrast to those of the merchants studied here; between 1425 and 1454, the estate paid 6,680 ducats in levies, while it received 23,200 ducats in interest, meaning net receipts of more than 16,500 ducats. See also the ledgers of Francesco Contarini, who succeeded in freeing a portfolio of some 4,000 nominal ducats from a lien in 1449–50 and sold it in 1450–52. BMCV, PD.C.912, ledger 1, fol. 18. In the later 1450s he turned around and bought 1,000 nominal ducats in government credits from Maestro Tommaso Lily of Cyprus, at practically the same price at which he had previously sold. BMCV, PD.C.911, ledger 2, fol. 33. Nowhere does he seem to keep an account of interest received.

come from interest, show how the interest claims matured only when the claim of the year of purchase first matured; in other words, paghe on purchases made in 1457 matured in 1476, while paghe of 1460–61 matured in 1481–82, already twenty years overdue. Had a speculative bent been behind the initiative, then, when the market price reached 29 in March 1460, the first lot, purchased at 22, should have been sold in order to realize the difference; instead, further lots were bought at 29 and 28.[23]

The last purchases, made in 1461, brought the nominal capital to 5,011 ducats; that figure would remain unchanged for more than a century, until the Monte Vecchio was paid off. What earnings accrued to Andrea's sons on this portfolio, and, at the same time, what were their taxes? In 1461, Nicolò and Alvise were earning interest of about 20 ducats per year on old inherited issues (table 13.3), and, of course, they did not have to contribute to the public debt, as had their father. In 1463 the old system of forced loans was replaced by the decima, a direct tax of 10 percent, based on a new and more careful evaluation of taxable patrimony. As table 13.4 shows, while the fraterna was earning about 2 percent per year on the nominal value of inherited credits, it was paying progressively increasing amounts in direct taxes, on continually increasing figures of estimated patrimony — for an annual average of 112.5 ducats over the period of twenty-one years. These decima exactions were made largely to finance Venice's costly naval war with the Turks (1463–79). Only in 1482, at the beginning of the War of Ferrara, did the last packet of government credits purchased when Nicolò was young begin to mature, bringing a net return of 60–70 ducats per year. In other words, the purchases of 1457–61 finally began producing a respectable yield, for even at a net annual interest rate of only 1.6 percent on par, the yields were about 7 percent of the price paid for the first packet, about 5.5 percent for the other two, over the next half century.[24] (On yields, see also above, Chap. 11, sec. iii.) Those would have been welcome yields, had the obligations produced immediately instead of only after twenty years. From 1482 on, the Barbarigo portfolio of Monte Vecchio credits, with its full nominal capital finally matured, would earn — gross — 100 ducats for each semester's paga; but only 22 of 40 paghe had been paid during the

[23]One might hypothesize that the two brothers had purchased only the bare capital of the obligations and that the usufruct was paid in the interim to the sellers or to third parties. No corroboration has been found, however, for differential market prices of government credits (a credit without a claim to interest should have cost less than one with such a claim), and there is no reference to deferred title to usufruct in the purchase or interest accounts.

[24]Between 1476, when the first packet matured, and 1482, when the last matured, Nicolò's portfolio earned an average of 1.5 percent net interest on par, which translates into an average yield on the first packet (purchased at 22) of 6.9 percent (0.0151 / 22 = 6.86). If we apply a slightly higher average (1.6, double the rate paid to the Bertaldo estate, which received half the rate due on "virginal" credits) to the half century after 1482, the year Nicolò's accounts end, the yield on the second and third packets (bought in 1460 and 1461 at 29 and 28 respectively) was 5.5 and 5.7 percent.

TABLE 13.3

Creating a Portfolio in Government Credits: Nicolò and Alvise d'Andrea Barbarigo, 1456–1462 (in ducats)

Year	Capital (nominal)	Interest Due[a]	Claim	Capital on Which Interest Was Paid	Interest Received	Rate of Interest on Claim (%)	Acquired (nominal)	Market Price	Cost
1456[b]	936	19	1447[c]	613	12	1.96			
1457[c]	851	17						22	
1457[b]	1,853	37	1447[b]	780	16	2.05	1,000	21.5–22	217.5
1458	1,853	74	1448[c]	910	18	1.98			
1459	1,853	74	1448[b]	1,055	20.5	1.94			
1460[c]	1,853	37	1449[c]	1,244	25	2.00	1,013	29	293.5
1460[b]	2,871	57							
1461[c]	2,871	57	1449[b]	1,213	24	1.98			
1461[b]	5,011	100	1450[c]	501	11.5	2.29	2,140	28	599
1462[c]	5,011	100	1450[b]	?	14	?			
1462[b]	5,011	100							
6 years					117		4,153		1,110
Average p.a.					19.5	2.03		26.7	

Source: ASV, Archivio Grimani-Barbarigo, b. 43, reg. 6.

Note: New acquisitions matured only between 1476 and 1482 (see table 13.7). For the 13 lots acquired, see table 13.4.

[a]At 2 percent per semester (4 percent p.a.).

[b]September claim.

[c]March claim.

533

TABLE 13.4

Interest Income and Direct Taxation: Nicolò Barbarigo's Portfolio of
Monte Vecchio and His Decima Exactions, 1463–1482 (in ducats)

Year	Claim	Capital (nominal)	Decima on Bonds	Interest Received	Net Interest (% per claim)	Decima Patrimoniale no.	amount
1463	1451[a]	619		12.4	2.00	1	30
1464	1451[b]	619	2.5	10.5	1.69	2	34
1465	1452[a]	590		11.5	1.95	3–4	64
1466	1452[b]	664		14	2.11	5–6	74
1467	1453[a]	749		15	2.00	7–9	249
1468	1453[b]	828		16.5	1.99	10	50
1469	1454[a]	904		18	1.99	11–12	99
1470	1454[b]	904	3.4	15	1.66	13–15	198
1470	1455[a]	904		18	1.99		
1471					0	16–18	153
1472	1455[b]	914	3.5	14.5	1.59	19–21	157
1472	1456[a]	936		18.6	1.99		
1473					0	22–23	104
1474	1456[b]	936	1.8	16.8	1.79	24–27	207
1475	1457[a]	851		17	2.00	28–29	102
1476	1457[b]	1,851	11	26	1.40	30	63
1476	1458[a]	1,851		37	2.00		
1477	1458[b]	1,851	14	22	1.19	31–33	112
1478					0	34–35	44
1479	1459[a]	1,851	37		0	36–37	153
1479	1459[b]	1,851	7.5	29	1.57		
1480	1460[a]	1,851	37		0	38–40	260
1481	1460[b]	2,871	27.5	30	1.04	41	77
1482	1461[a]	2,871		57.5	2.00	42–45	133
1482	1461[b]	5,011	30	70	1.40		
20 yrs.	1451–61		175.2	469.3		1–45	2,363
Average p.a.			8.8	23.5	1.77		118

Source: ASV, Archivio Grimani-Barbarigo, b. 43, reg. 6.
Note: When the nominal capital owned reached 5,011 ducats, interest was theoretically due at 200 ducats p.a. The Decima was imposed on real estate and government obligations ("case, possesion, imprestiti," as the account reads). A discount ("don") of 2% was applied on Decime nos. 8, 12–14, and 19; of 3% on nos. 17–18; no. 18 was refundable.
[a]March claim.
[b]September claim.

previous twenty years, and during the subsequent half century the average would be considerably less than one interest claim per year (compare table 11.1). With that ends the nearly continuous series of surviving Barbarigo account books; Nicolò's first ledger ends precisely when the war against Ferrara showed the decima to be an insufficient fiscal instrument and forced the state to inaugurate the Monte Nuovo. Nicolò's investment in obligations was tantamount to a purchase of pension or trust funds, the yield on which would be enjoyed later in life or by one's heirs. Thus it is hardly surprising, as was suggested above, that in his testament of 1496 Nicolò urged his sons to hold on to the portfolio of credits on the Monte Vecchio; his heirs — and their heirs — complied.[25]

When the accounts pick up once again with Giovanni Alvise Barbarigo, Nicolò's son, in 1506, the state was paying him 100 ducats on the interest claim of 1474. In twenty-three years, from 1506 to 1528, only 14 paghe (dated 1474–81), practically untaxed, were paid. No interest was paid during the War of the League of Cambrai (1508–17) except for a valiant attempt, in 1511–14, to pay two meager paghe — in seven installments. When that ledger was closed in 1528, the state was paying the claim of 1481, forty-seven years late. Looking at the whole period of twenty-three years, the fraterna received a total of 1,400 ducats in interest, an average of only 61 ducats per year — compared to the 200 ducats theoretically due. Just the same, the sum of 1,400 ducats was considerably more than the capital invested in 1457–61, and the low yearly average still meant a yield of 5.46 percent, hardly an unwelcome rent.[26]

Between 1542 and 1576, in a period of sustained inflation, Antonio Barbarigo, Giovanni Alvise's son, collected interest on claims of 1487–1503 which had been due in the lifetime of his grandfather. When the Monte Vecchio was paid off beginning in 1576, Antonio received a balance due of 777 ducats in the form of a deposit on the Salt Office.[27]

Despite the arrears and despite the policy of paying interest on obligations newly acquired on the open market only when the claim of the date of acquisition fell due, as though they were tied to new issues, the open market continued to attract buyers. Very likely, the government obligation itself, even though only potentially interest producing, maintained some attraction as an asset in itself. The latest purchases I have come across are those by Nicolò Donà dalle Rose. Between 1472 and 1476 he bought a nominal value of 3,258 ducats at six different dates, at prices ranging from 15 to

[25]Lane, *Andrea Barbarigo,* 32, 38, 40–42 (here Lane attributes to Giovanni Barbarigo purchases actually made after his death). See also Piergiovanni Mometto, *L'azienda agricola Barbarigo a Carpi: Gestione economica ed evoluzione sociale sulle terre di un villaggio della bassa pianura veronese (1443–1539)* (Venice, 1992), chaps. 1, 5.

[26]ASV, Archivio Grimani Barbarigo, b. 44, reg. 9, fols. 30, 81, 110.

[27]Lane, *Andrea Barbarigo,* 42. That means that only five years, or ten paghe (1482–86), were paid between 1528 and 1542. See also Pezzolo, *L'oro dello Stato,* 190–91.

8¾.[28] Since at the time of purchase the state was already twenty-five years in arrears in paying interest, the buyer could not have been surprised had his broker predicted that his purchases would begin yielding a return in the 1520s, fifty years hence, as must have been the case (see table 11.1). The yields then — but only then — ranged from 13.3 to 22.9 percent on the capital investment; another generation would profit from it.

iv. DEMAND AND SUPPLY

It is easy to justify the choices made by the Soranzo fraterna and by Andrea Barbarigo in administering their portfolios: they preferred to keep their money liquid and moving in commerce, so they did not hesitate to sell, even at considerable loss, the issues they had been forced to buy at par; generally, they seem to have had the liquidity necessary to meet new impositions as they came. By contrast, institutions, such as religious houses, which took in only rents and interest, had no choice but to sell obligations in order to have the necessary liquidity; the procurator of the convent of S. Lorenzo made this very clear to the assessors in 1412: at current levels of imposition, he wrote, with an assessment of 12,500 lire d'estimo, the nuns will have to sell all their government credits and then their house property; as it is, he continued, they once had a portfolio of 25,000 ducats, which was already down to 4,500 ducats.[29] It is more difficult to understand the motivations of Nicolò Barbarigo and successive generations, or of Nicolò Donà, in buying on the open market and in holding on to their portfolios. To be sure, credits fetched ever lower prices, which promised ever higher yields, albeit in a distant and nebulous future. At the same time, the trouble of keeping account of assets in Monte Vecchio credits, of interest claims on which the decima was exacted, and of seeing to the disposition of the assets via inheritance was considerable. The decision to hold on probably involved such intangibles as faith in the solvency of the state and concern both for future generations and for the payment of pious and charitable bequests — elements of a mentality to which expression was rarely given, if not in lire, soldi, and denari. In his testament of 1429, Pietro Miani, bishop of Vicenza, who reports that he had contributed more than 15,000 ducats (or 730 ducats per year) in forced loans over the previous two decades, complained that in wartime the Loan Office sometimes paid only half the interest due; this factor complicated the definition of his pious bequests and forced him

---

[28]ASV, Archivio Marcello, Grimani, Giustinian (Archivio Donà), b. 167, small ledger dated 1488–91, fol. 3.

[29]"Per vostra information, Signor, siè' zertissimi, durando la guera et façando il monastero de £12,500 como el fa, tuti l'enprestedi che ha el monastero se convegnirà vender per far le façion de la guera . . . ; soleva aver ducati 25,000 de inprestedi — le guerre li ha fato tuti perder." ASV, S. Lorenzo, b. 9, loose sheet in fasc. "Per gravezze, 3." S. Lorenzo had been inscribed for 25,000 lire d'estimo in 1379; *PRV,* 143.

to propose alternative solutions, should that eventuality repeat itself, as indeed it would; but recognition of the problem did not stop him from ordering his executors to make further purchases of government obligations to complete his endowments.[30]

Clearly, if some bought, others sold, largely for opposite reasons; let us now turn briefly to their side of the workings of the open market.

There are no extant archival series that could give us an idea of the normal, daily operations on the open market of owners of government credits. There are some insights, however, into the interplay of supply and demand. A lawsuit filed in 1463 relates the story of a widow, Isabetta Pessato, who let herself be convinced that she could earn a better return on her money by investing in business than by holding on to her portfolio. In 1420 Isabetta supported her family on the interest income she received from funds ("zerti dinari") she held as government credits at the Loan Office. Convinced by two non-noble drapers, Marco da Porto and Stefano Marioni, Isabetta sold credits worth 280 gold ducats, which she proceeded to invest in the drapers' shop, "placing hope in their convincing words to earn much more than what she would have earned at the Loan Office." During six years of operation (1420–26), the profits of the shop came to 1,251 ducats, of which the share due to the widow was 306 ducats, a welcome return of 18 percent per year — theoretically. In fact, for a longer but unspecified period, an accountant of the court discovered that the drapers owed the widow 586 ducats on her investment, while they had actually paid her only 212½ ducats. In short, they had swindled her, probably keeping her satisfied with something better than her previous income but not what was owed her. Isabetta's son and heir filed suit and won a settlement for the balance due — more than forty years after the government obligations had been sold.[31]

Such stories, probably commonplace, do not find their way into account books, which, however, provide lists of names of buyers, some of whom might well have been in Isabetta's position. Above we have seen two commercial companies, those of the Soranzo and of Andrea Barbarigo, which were much more apt to sell than to buy. If we examine, instead, the cases of some buyers, we can better see the nature of the supply side: whose portfolios did buyers find available on the open market? We can look at three cases, chronologically: that of Paolo Guinigi, lord of Lucca (whose purchases are dealt with more closely in the following chapter), the estate of the

[30]Girgensohn, "Il testamento di Pietro Miani," appendix. The bishop's father, Zuane, was inscribed in the estimo of 1379 for the considerable sum of 18,000 lire (*PRV*, p. 194). Miani also accounted for the fact that, while he was currently earning 4 percent on par as a forced lender, at least on a sizeable portion of his portfolio, his estate would earn only 3 percent.

[31]She invested "a utile e danno, sperando per le bone parolle i diti dixea conseguir asai mior utilità de quelo la dita feria a la dita Camera de Imprestedi." ASV, GP, Sg, regs. 134, fol. 10–12 (5 February 1462), and 140, fols. 48v–52 (17 June 1463).

bishop Giacomo Ziera, and the purchases of Nicolò Barbarigo, already mentioned above. In each case we get no more than a glimpse of who was selling on a given day; we cannot know what moved the person to sell, or whether he or she did not buy again at a lower rate later, in a speculative manner.

Paolo Guinigi, lord of Lucca from 1400 to 1430, made a large investment in Venetian credits in 1412–14 as a way of securing a liquid portion of his patrimony, far from the vagaries of local politics. His agent in Venice was the firm of the Guidiccioni brothers, immigrants from Lucca and naturalized citizens of Venice.

The Guidiccioni purchased a total of eighty-two lots on fifty-four different dates over those two years. For 40,551 ducats in cash, they bought a total nominal value of 89,528 ducats in credits, at an average price of 45. The agents' lists of the names of all sellers, the date and price of the lot, and the total paid are fortunately extant. Of the eighty different sellers named, sixty-eight were nobles and only twelve were non-nobles. Only six women are mentioned, five of them noble, of whom one sold the smallest lot (100 ducats nominal for 41 ducats cash); for three it is explicitly stated that males were acting in their name. The first and third highest lots (2,000 and 1,086 ducats cash) were sold by non-nobles, the latter a "lowly" master tailor. Two sellers were Rialto bankers, both non-noble (Guglielmo Condulmer and Antonio Miorati). One was "masser" or treasurer of the office of the Consoli dei Mercanti. Four were Lucchese, including Nicolò Guidiccioni, director of the same firm that was representing the lord of Lucca. One was a high-ranking ecclesiastic, the "primicerio" or head of the chapter of San Marco. Three sellers were estates of deceased nobles. Another was the humanist Zaccaria Barbaro.[32]

The lots were generally large — mostly of at least 1,000 ducats nominal value, which means the sellers were not necessarily those normally found on the Rialto. In fact, the Guidiccioni reported to Lucca that they purposely would avoid buying small lots, in order not to drive up the market price by continual interventions. Some seasonal variation is observable which would identify many sellers as long-distance merchants: a large number of sales take place in August, meaning that persons were trying to increase their liquidity in concomitance with the "termini" of the departure of the Beirut galleys, both for paying debts then falling due and for loading goods onto the departing galleys. The presence on the list of many noble merchants, contemporaries of the Soranzo brothers and of Andrea Barbarigo's father, men of the same impulse to sell their credits and invest in commodities,

---

[32]The tally of the sellers and the lots acquired, as reported by Nicolò Guidiccioni in 1414, is found in table 3 of Reinhold C. Mueller, "Foreign Investment in Venetian Government Bonds and the Case of Paolo Guinigi, Lord of Lucca (Early Fifteenth Century)," in acts of the symposium *Cities of Finance,* ed. David Reeder and Herman Diederiks, Konigliche Academie der Wettenschoopen (Amsterdam, 1996).

would help explain the concern of the government to stimulate the market by increasing demand on the part of foreigners, for higher prices meant a lower margin of loss for forced contributors to the public debt who preferred, or were obliged, to sell the issues they had been forced to buy at par.

A second case concerns the purchases made by an estate, in an accounting that survived by reason of its having been copied into the record of a civil suit.[33] Giacomo Ziera, member of an illustrious non-noble family, was bishop of the Venetian fortress colony at Coron in the Peloponnesus. When he made his testament in 1426, he ordered his executors to purchase government credits with which to endow several pious and charitable bequests (among them paying the salary of a schoolteacher in Coron). The suit was brought by his heirs and concerned the handling of the estate. The executor, Bernardo Ziera, who would later establish himself and his son Agostino as bankers on the Rialto (see above, Chap. 5, sec. v), proceeded in 1437 to purchase government credits, as ordered by his cousin; from 22 May to 27 August he intervened seventeen times on the open market to buy 14,670.5 nominal ducats' worth of credits for 5,256.5 gold ducats; market prices rose by small fractions throughout the summer from a minimum of 35 to a maximum of 36¾, pushed upward slightly by demand from buyers like the Ziera estate itself (see table 13.5).

Who were the sellers? The best known was, of course, Giacomo Badoer, the contemporary of Andrea Barbarigo, whose accounts, although kept in Constantinople, provide another view of the supply side. Most of the others are mere names, but a rapid overview reveals the following: of seventeen sellers, eleven were nobles, five were non-nobles, one was a government office; there is only one woman. Among the nobles are eight different families. Both the highest and the lowest lots were sold by nonnobles. On the bottom end is a carpenter (for 100 ducats par), a non-noble estate, and two noblemen (200 ducats par each for the first two, 350 for the third), and a noble widow (for 500 ducats par); there is no way of knowing whether the carpenter, Lorenzo di Lorenzo, was an artisan-investor or a forced lender inscribed in the estimo. At the top, at 2,000 ducats par each, we find the non-noble Giacomo Tataro and the nobleman Lorenzo Loredan, associate at the Rialto bank of Francesco Balbi and in that role administrator of the portfolio of Andrea Barbarigo, as we have seen above; the other sizeable lots were sold largely by nobles. On 28 June Bernardo Ziera was able to purchase three lots held by three brothers, sons of the deceased Nicolò Pisani. Two sellers were estates, both of non-nobles.

The rule of thumb indicated by the administrators of the Guinigi portfolio, namely, that holders of government obligations who were active merchants tended to sell in the summer in order to meet debts maturing at the departure of the galleys for the Levant, does not apply here, for the

---

[33]ASV, GP, Sg, reg. 158, fol. 20v.

TABLE 13.5

Sellers of Government Credits to the Estate of Bishop Giacomo Ziera, 1437

Date	Name	Amount Sold	Price	Cash Value
22.05	Lorenzo di Lorenzo, marangon	100	35.00	35
22.05	Provveditori di Comun	1,020	35.50	362.10
23.05	Estate of Venturin di Arzelini	200	35.50	71
24.05	Pantalon Davegia	1,000	36.00	360.00
30.05	Piero qd. Luca Contarini	800	35.75	286.00
28.06	Zuan qd. Nicolò Pisani	1,000	35.50	355.00
28.06	Carlo qd. Nicolò Pisani	200	35.50	71.00
28.06	Marino qd. Nicolò Pisani	350	35.50	124.25
03.07	Jacomo Badoer (2 *poste*)	1,000.5	35.50	355.18
08.07	Lorenzo Loredan	2,000	35.50	710.00
13.07	Antonio qd. Domenico Zane	1,000	35.50	355.00
15.07	Jacopo Tataro	2,000	35.50	710.00
31.07	Estate of Zuan Montana	1,000	36.00	360.00
07.08	Maria Nani, widow of ser Zorzi	500	36.75	183.75
19.08	Antonio Molin de la Madalena	1,500	36.75	551.25
27.08	Nicolò qd. Alvise Bragadin "a l'ixola"	1,000	36.75	367.50
	Total	14,670.50		5,257.03
	Average	916.91	35.83	328.56

Source: ASV, GP, Sg, reg. 158, fol. 20v.

market price actually rose, albeit only slightly, meaning that demand was stronger than supply.

The investment by the estate for the bishop's pious legacies promised 3 percent interest on par, or 8.3 percent yield on the investment; but in fact, the net rate actually paid in 1437 was only 1.8 percent on par, which made for a yield of 5 percent — still an acceptable return on capital. The testator's desires reflected considerable faith in the system, but by the time his will was executed, the state had already begun delaying payments of interest, and the yield was destined to decline.

As mentioned above, the man who sold two lots to Bernardo Ziera on 3 July was the well-known merchant Giacomo Badoer, a nobleman of relatively modest means whose activity in the Venetian colony at Constantinople in 1436–40 is covered by a published ledger. Giacomo's brother Gerolamo handled his affairs in Venice, paid his forced loans, and rendered accounts by letter, accounts that Giacomo promptly copied into his ledger (and converted into perperi of account). Table 13.6 shows that Giacomo was much like the other active merchants we investigated above: he was little interested in holding on to government credits; he sold to the Ziera

TABLE 13.6

Giacomo Badoer's Forced Loans, 1436–1439 (in ducats)

a. Payment of Forced Loans

Date	Total Levies ("fation") Paid	No. of Issue	Percentage	Total Paid
0.7–4.12.1436	4	47–50	2.50	70
18.1–28.6.1447	6	51–56	5.25	147
Before 5.12.1437	1	57	0.75	21
Until 31.8.1438	12	58–69	12.50	350
1.10.1438–31.8.1439	9	70–78	11.00	308
Total 1436–39	32	47–78	32.00	896

Average for 37 months: 1 percent or 28 ducats per levy, that is, 24.2 ducats per month or 290.4 ducats per year.

Assessment ("che faxo de fation"): 2,800 lire d'estimo
Receipts: interest — none; refunds ("refoxura") — 20 ducats.

b. Government Credits Sold by Gerolamo in Venice

Date	Buyer	Amount		Market Value
		par	cash	
27.8.1436	Polo Tron	200	75	37.5
3.7.1437	Giacomo Ziera estate	1,000.5	355.2	35.5
16.10.1438	Governatori delle Entrate	300	87	29.0
Total		1,500.5	517.2	
Average				34.5

Source: Dorini and Bertelè, *Il libro dei conti di Giacomo Badoer*, 316–17, 762–63.

estate alone a portfolio larger than that created by the forced loans he had to pay during the years covered by the ledger.

Whereas the Soranzo fraterna and Andrea Barbarigo sold 80–85 percent of the issues they had been forced to buy, Badoer sold nearly twice as many credits as he was forced to purchase in the three years covered by his accounts, in that he liquidated most of his previously existing portfolio at the same time; in fact, in three years, he seems to have received no interest whatsoever. Like other active merchants, he preferred to keep his assets moving. Gerolamo sold credits nominally worth 1,500 ducats in two lots, at 35.5 in 1437 and at 29 in the following year, for a total of 517 gold ducats, that is, at about one-third their par value. On the assumption that his portfolio was made up solely of obligations purchased at par, by selling, he sustained a loss of two-thirds. At the same time, proceeds from the sales of current and past issues, plus the small refund, recouped more than two-thirds of the cash he paid out in forced loans during the documented period.

The third case, which we have also looked at from the other side, is that of Nicolò Barbarigo — or of his tutors, assuming it was they who made the purchases. Here the situation is quite different. We are in the years after 1454, when there were no more forced issues to have to purchase; thus if one desired a portfolio, it had to be sought on the open market. The lots purchased by Nicolò are all rather small — an average of only 300 ducats nominal value. The thirteen lots were purchased from thirteen different sellers whose credits were registered on the ledgers of four sestieri; all were then transferred to Dorsoduro, the sestiere of Nicolò's residence at S. Barnaba. The sellers were of a completely different social makeup, compared with the cases discussed above. Of the thirteen sellers, nine were women, of whom six bore names of noble families; one was the daughter of a humble mason; three were widows. Only one was a nobleman, Castellan Minotto, who sold the largest lot; one was an estate. Only one name is familiar, that of Pantalon Davegia, very likely the same person who had sold credits to the Ziera estate twenty years earlier (see table 13.7).

These rare lists of sellers do not permit much generalization, but some observations might be hazarded. If in the first half of the Quattrocento active merchants tended to sell, and certain noble merchants, inscribed on the estimo, in fact sold, in the period after 1454, when forced levies ended, anyone who wanted a portfolio had to buy on the open market. Perhaps then noblemen became more apt to buy than sell; perhaps Nicolò d'Andrea Barbarigo was not unique, not only in buying but in holding on to his government obligations and counseling his heirs to do the same, despite the fact that a yield would materialize only in the distant future. Perhaps more women, many of them widows, who had their savings — often their dowries — tied up at the Loan Office and who supported their families on the income allowed themselves to be convinced, like Isabetta Pessato, to sell in the hope of getting a better return by investing in commerce or industry, especially as interest declined and payments were ever more in arrears. It is not surprising that the institution of the Monte Nuovo in 1482, despite the military crisis that occasioned it, was greeted with such widespread enthusiasm when it set a ceiling on indebtedness and guaranteed a return of 5 percent on par. Credits on the Monte Vecchio, by that time, could interest only far-sighted — or somewhat odd — investors, willing to buy at low prices and bet on good yields in the distant future, as with a modern pension fund or insurance policy.

The open market for government obligations on the Monte Vecchio in the century and a half before 1482, however, was constantly stimulated by demand from foreign lords and feudatories, from estates, and from pious and charitable endowments. While endowments were usually also passive

TABLE 13.7

Sellers of the Government Credits Purchased by Nicolò Barbarigo, 1457–1461
(in ducats)

Date	Seller	Amount Sold	Price	Cash Value
1457				
22.03	Lucia, daughter of Zuan Stecco, murer	100	21.75	21.75
24.03	Pantalon Davegia	500	22.00	110
04.04	Ixabetta Dolfin	400	21.50	86
1460				
11.03	Marietta Trevisan	100	29	29
11.03	Mattia and Battista Bolan, qd. Zuane	300	29	87
12.03	Commis. Marco Vizier	400	29	116
12.03	Lucia Zane, widow of Polo	113	29	32.8
14.03	Cecilia, wife of Jacomo Marin	100	29	29
1461				
29.07	Castellan Minotto	1,000	28	280
29.07	Jacomella, widow of Jacomello Longo	300	28	84
29.07	Maria Spandinoxe	240	28	67
29.07	Zuan Mosolin	500	28	140
30.07	Suordamor Dolfin, widow of Zuane	100	28	28
	Total	4,153		1,110.55
	Average	318	26.7	

Source: ASV, Archivio Grimani Barbarigo, b. 43, reg. 6.

beneficiaries of legacies, foreigners, of the same stamp as those we have already seen making deposits in the Grain Office, were active investors in the open market. We can trace the demand they created through the "grazie" or special licenses needed before they could acquire Venetian government credits.

14

INVESTMENT BY FOREIGNERS IN THE MONTE VECCHIO

i. ADVANTAGES AND DISADVANTAGES OF FOREIGN INVESTMENT

THE THEME OF INVESTMENT by foreigners in a city's funded debt is not a new one. Better known than the Venetian situation is that coming to light in the ongoing research on the Florentine Monte Comune. At present, we have few points of comparison, since the open market in Florentine Monte credits, which seem to have paid better and more regularly in the mid-Quattrocento than Venetian government obligations, has hardly been studied as regards foreign capital. What has been called "deposits in the Florentine Monte" were not purchases of Monte credits on the open market; often they were simple deposits in a floating debt, not dissimilar to the Venetian Grain Office, where cash received was used to amortize the funded debt, thereby reducing debt service. Florentine legislative provisions were not unequivocally favorable to the entry of foreign capital; in 1415 a tax of 10 percent was applied to the nominal value of credits purchased by foreigners.[1]

It comes as no surprise that the foreign investors in credits of the Monte Vecchio recall the depositors in the Grain Office — in fact, some are

---

[1] Julius Kirshner, "Papa Eugenio IV e il Monte Comune: Documenti su investimento e speculazione nel debito pubblico di Firenze," *ASI* 127 (1969): 340–82. The option open to licensed foreigners was to deposit money at 5 percent in the Ufficium Diminutionis Montium, a fund used for amortizing the Monte Comune through purchases at market prices. See also Molho, *Florentine Public Finances*, 141–50, and, for the Monte delle Doti, idem, *Marriage Alliance in Late Medieval Florence* (Cambridge, Mass., 1994), 80–81, 122–27.

the same people. As was the case in the Grain Office, persons turned to the Venetian funded debt both because they had no similar investment opportunity in their own capital cities and because they sought to put a safe distance between internecine struggles in their own courts and the hoards that could guarantee survival to themselves or their heirs in case of a change of political fortune. The major difference was that government obligations were discountable and thus available for purchase on the open market, and they had a fluctuating market price and thus varied returns to capital, whereas the deposits at the Grain Office were at fixed interest — generally lower than yields on government credits — and their cash value was always equal to their nominal value. On the open market, speculation in government credits was involved only to the extent that one tried to buy at low prices; buying low in order to resell at a higher price and earn from the difference seems not to have interested foreign purchasers. They were concerned about the security of their capital and about returns to capital; they sought an income while living, a safe patrimony to pass on to their heirs, and, in many cases, the opportunity to constitute a perpetual endowment for pious or charitable causes, whether religious or laic: a convent, a program of almsgiving, a college, or scholarships for university students. A funded debt that gave proof of credibility and security — as long as it did — provided the individual a rare opportunity for terminal and perpetual legacies alike. Institutions, especially religious institutions, also discovered the advantages of investing in government obligations. Their information about investment opportunities in Venice probably came both from local lords and from their confreres in Venice itself, for Venetian religious houses had to pay forced loans and received interest on further credits received from pious testators; but they also developed portfolios themselves, when they sold off rental properties that were unprofitable or falling into ruin and, with the license of the state, converted the sale price into conditioned government credits through the offices of the Provveditori di Comun.[2]

[2]For permissions granted by the Senate to sell properties that were in awkward locations or otherwise unprofitable and to invest the proceeds in government obligations, see, for example, ASV, SM, reg. 59, fols. 178v–79 (orphanage of the Pietà, bishop of Torcello, 1436); fol. 191 (S. Martino di Oderzo, 1437); reg. 60, fols. 47v and 55 (S. Michele di Murano, for properties in Capodistria and Tana, 1437); fol. 57 (Cruciferi); fol. 59v (S. Maria di Mazzorbo, S. Chiara di Conegliano, 1438). For a comparable grant by the Great Council, for dilapidated houses at S. Marcuola in Venice owned by the abbess and nuns of S. Chiara, the friars of S. Maria dei Frari, and the priest and chapter of S. Marcuola — Franciscans the first two, it is worth noting, and secular the third — in 1441, see Grazie, reg. 25, fol. 40. Of course, the massive sale of such properties administered by the Procurators of San Marco in 1353–54, using government credits as money, constituted an important precedent. Individual licenses were granted also to laymen to sell properties under lien or entail, with the obligation to buy credits with the proceeds and apply to them the same condition that had bound the properties, under a law that later was made a statute; see MC, Leona, fol. 62v (1392). Such oft repeated procedures increased demand for credits but then withdrew them from circulation, since they were no longer marketable.

The advantages of investment by foreigners were considerable. New money flowed into the urban economy and into the pockets of forced lenders, for the increased demand boosted market prices, thereby reducing the loss to individuals who had been required to buy at par and had to sell at a loss.[3] In fact, whereas purchase and sale agreements among Venetians could be paid for in bank (as in the case of the Barbarigo family), foreigners had to pay in cash. The agio on specie probably offset brokerage and scribal fees, so that transactions costs were in effect carried by the foreign party. Even a simplification of accounting procedures resulted: the innumerable lots acquired could be consolidated into a single, unified portfolio, which facilitated the work of the Loan Office. In the case of the bequest made by bishop of Cremona, discussed below, the officials asked specifically to intervene themselves in the open market with cash from the legacy, with the intent of buying up small lots that cluttered their ledgers.[4] On the diplomatic front, it is obvious that licenses granted to foreign princes, their courtiers, and leading citizens to invest in government credits could be a diplomatic tool in making or maintaining alliances. At the same time, when a ruler was bent on crossing over to the side of Venice's enemies, the risk that his portfolio would be sequestered, assurances to the contrary notwithstanding, did not detain him, as we shall see.

There were, of course, also negative aspects. First, while an increase in circulating media brought an immediate advantage to the economy, the state assumed the obligation of paying interest to foreigners, which would lead to an export of specie, unless the interest was used for purchases in Venice, which was sometimes the case. Second, the acquisition by foreigners and the conditioning of portfolios for perpetual endowments in effect reduced supply in the open market. Furthermore, credits acquired in the open market had a yield to capital superior to the nominal interest received by Venetians who were forced to contribute to the public debt. This was the objection made by an official of the Loan Office in 1375 when he voted against the granting of a grazia to the estate of a Dalmatian nobleman, whose executors wanted to invest money *ad pias causas*: "A very large portion of government credits is passing into the hands of foreigners," he

---

[3]This fact was expressed in the officials' support of the request of a widow to invest 1,000 ducats in government credits: "quod dicta gratia est facienda quia non est in damnum comunis set utile specialium personarum, quia quanto sunt plures emptores imprestitorum, tanto imprestita plus valent." ASV, Grazie, reg. 17, fol. 91v (1377). Similar rationales were used by Palla di Nofri Strozzi during the Florentine crisis of the 1430s, when, in serious straits for lack of cash, he asked permission to sell a large portion of his portfolio to foreigners; Molho, *Florentine Public Finances*, 157–60.

[4]The officials asked that the ducats "ponantur in manibus ipsorum . . . , de quibus possint emere imprestita in postis parvis, et eas de quaternis Camere Imprestitorum cancellare, et ipsas reducere in unam postam ad novissimum numerum, videlicet 228, et dicta imprestita per eos sic empta scribi facere cum conditione in peticione contenta." ASV, Grazie, reg. 17, fol. 41 (1375).

stated, "and granting the petition would only stimulate new requests, for these people can make a 6 percent yield on credits when once they were satisfied with the 3 or 4 percent interest offered by the Grain Office. To grant the request," he continued, "would be detrimental, since foreigners, the Procurators, religious houses, scuole and estates hold about two-thirds of all credits, which can never be further marketed." He suggested, as an alternative, that the Commune accept the money as a voluntary loan, issue government obligations at par, with the usual 5 percent interest, and use the money for amortizing the debt, at market rates.[5] The suggestion, which would have involved a considerable revision of the system and the creation of a fund somewhat resembling the Florentine Offitium Diminutionis Montium, was ignored, and the grazia was granted despite his objections. Acceding to such requests became common practice, whatever the opinion of officials of the Loan Office or the Provveditori di Comun, who were called upon to evaluate each request.[6]

There was a way of avoiding an unenthusiastic response to a petition to invest in Venetian government obligations: ask to be naturalized. Foreigners who applied for citizenship in the 1380s as a way of getting around the need for a license and of getting a freer hand in operating on the open market, however, were sometimes unmasked by investigating officials. With prospective yields particularly high in 1381, for example, a citizenship privilege was granted to a Veronese on condition that he not be allowed to buy government credits for four years. In two cases in 1385 certain Provveditori judged the acquisition of credits by recently naturalized citizens as detrimental to Venice, but the applicants received citizenship just the same. In a final case, citizenship was granted with a clause completely prohibiting the purchase of government credits. By and large, however, whether the

---

[5]"[Marinus Bono] dicit quod ista gratia nec consimilis amplius est fienda, quia reperitur hodie maxima quantitas imprestitorum in manibus forensium, et attendendo huiusmodi petitionibus multiplicabunt vehementer, quia petentes tales gracias continget habere annuatim de prode sex pro centenario, ubi solebant contentari ponere at Cameram Frumenti ad III vel IIII pro centenario, ed at presens sic ponerent nisi esset avantagium ponendi ad imprestita, ita quod multis respectibus tales gracie sunt dannose et nocive, nam forenses, Procuratores, monasteria, scole et commissarie habent circa duas partes imprestitorum que numquam venduntur; sed si tamen gracia deberet fieri istis commissariis non esset parva accipere denarios in comune et dare eis tot imprestita scripta ad Cameram Imprestitorum quot libre ad grossos capient denarii quos ipsi dabunt, ita quod continget eos habere V pro centenario annuatim; et de illis denariis posset fieri illud quod fit de ducatis 3000 in mense" [a reference to the sinking fund]. ASV, Grazie, reg. 17, fol. 47v (1375). Luzzatto calculated for 1386 that more than half of a total debt of 5 million ducats was conditioned; *PRV,* clxxxviii–ix.

[6]Twice previously two Provveditori di Comun, who supported requests of foreigners to buy real estate (on which they would then pay taxes [onera]), expressed opposition to granting licenses to buy obligations, but their reasons were not registered. One said, "Non videtur ei bonum nec racionabilem quod eidem aut alicui forensi fiat gratia emendi imprestita, propter malam consequenciam que perveniret." The other said simply it would be "valde periculosum statui nostro." ASV, Grazie, reg. 16, fols. 113, 116 (1370).

petition was to invest in the open market or to become a Venetian citizen — with that same goal in mind — the authorities tended to accede.[7]

ii. FOREIGN LORDS AND COURTIERS

That foreign rulers — "principes et dominorum mundi" — were the principal non-Venetian investors on the open market was expressed in 1442, when the requirement that foreigners apply for a license in order to invest was rescinded.[8] The presence of their agents on the market began at least a century earlier, however, and was a notorious fact. When Philippe de Mézières wrote in 1384 that there was hardly an Italian signore who did not leave a hoard in Venice ("il est pou de seigneurs et tyrans en Italie qui n'y tienne aucun tresor"), he must have had in mind especially their investments in government credits.[9]

The earliest mention is almost contemporaneous to the first deposits by foreigners in the Grain Office. Count Doimo Frangipani, deceased by 1318, had received permission from the Great Council to invest money in government obligations in order to create a perpetual income with which to guarantee the annual payment of a feudal tribute that the counts, as vassals of the doge, owed to Venice. Doimo's son Federico sent a procurator to Venice to make sure that the portfolio was properly conditioned and protected against sequester; he received the assurance of the Great Council in a long deliberation.[10]

Sometime before 1340 begins a most interesting rapport between Venice and the ruling houses of Milan and Savoy which would last more than a century and a half, as succeeding generations of both families continued to invest. A chronicler relates that Manfredo IV of Saluzzo in Piedmont, before his death in 1340, sold off plots of land in order to invest the enormous sum of 115,000 florins in Venetian government credits, in that period worth very close to par on the open market. The investment was made in favor of his sons.[11] One of these, Manfredo V, counsellor first of

---

[7]Ibid., reg. 17, fol. 112 (Nicolò de' Stancari from Verona, promoted by Giacomo Cavalli, 1381); fol. 176 (the Mantuan captain Giovanni de' Bazzi, 1384); fol. 176, 178 (Bonifacio Serego of Verona, 1385); fol. 196 (Aldobrandino de' Avosti of Bologna, 1385); fol. 224 (Vallus Johannes of Dulcigno, 1387). For grants of Florentine citizenship for similar reasons, see Kirshner, "Papa Eugenio IV," 345 n. 17.

[8]*PRV,* doc. 250.

[9]*Le songe de vieil pelerin,* 1:254.

[10]*PRV,* lxi and doc. 95 (1319). The tribute was still owed in 1493, after Veglia had been absorbed by Venice; see Sanudo, *De origine,* 233–34. The sources for the discussion of individual cases in this section and the next, unless otherwise indicated, are to be found in table E.2, below.

[11]Alessandra Sisto, *Banchieri-Feudatari subalpini nei sec. XII–XIV* (Turin, 1963), 27 n. 4. G. della Chiesa, *Cronaca di Saluzzo,* Historiae Patriae Monumenta, Scriptores (Turin, 1836), Tome 3, cols. 964 and 968, n. 2, relates that Manfredo sold land and "li dinary misse in logi a

Galeazzo II and then of Giangaleazzo Visconti of Milan, continually petitioned—in his own name and that of his wife, Eleanor of Savoy—for permission to acquire further credits, both for hereditary and for pious ends. Between 1373 and his death in 1389, he asked for permission to purchase at least 32,000 ducats' worth of government credits—over a period, that is, which witnessed a complete revolution in market values and in returns to capital.[12] Of this sum, 4,000 ducats (nominal value) were conditioned *in perpetuo* to fund charitable bequests of which the poor of Venice were the beneficiaries; accounts for the annual distribution of coarse woolen tunics and of bread by the executors (the Procurators of San Marco de supra) are extant for the years 1385–1425.[13] Such bequests *ad pias causas,* through which a certain portion of interest funds stayed in Venice, probably helped to keep Venetian authorities amenable to foreign investments.

Manfredo V's heirs, in their turn, continued the tradition: in 1392 his sons and grandsons purchased an additional 10,000 ducats' worth, the interest on which was devolved to another son, Antonio, archbishop of Milan (1376–1401) in his lifetime, in fulfillment of a clause in Manfredo's will. Permission was granted to the same heirs once again in 1403 to purchase 20,000 ducats' worth of credits. In 1426 Manfredo VI asked for a license to purchase further packets of credits for his portfolio, for the same value.[14] Some unspecified friction intervened in 1441, for the Signoria sequestered the interest on the holdings of three Saluzzo heirs, but five months later the decision was overturned by the Avogadori di Comun. Then in 1444 certain representatives of the house of Saluzzo ("de domo Salucii") came to Venice to stake a claim to interest on conditioned credits held by the estate, on the

---

Venecia per legarly a questi figloly e cossì fece cum effetto." A marginal note states that the portfolio passed at an unspecified later date into other hands: "Nota come sono venuti li luoghi di Venetia alli signori di Cardeto." The use of the Genoese term *luoghi* for shares in the public debt will derive from the nearness of Genoa and conceivably also from the fact that Manfredo IV married a Genoese, Isabella, daughter of Bernabò Doria.

[12]ASV, Grazie, reg. 17, fols. 8v, 11r, 15r, 163v, 201r, 225r, 234r. Very likely the petitions were more than those recorded. In 1380, during the Chioggia war, Pietro Corner, Venetian ambassador to Milan, was asked insistently that he intervene in support of Manfredo's requests to purchase Venetian credits: "he keeps plying me," wrote Corner, "and you do not reply." He is "bene dispositus . . . et est magnus homo," Corner reported. Lazzarini, *Dispacci di Pietro Cornaro,* docs. 81, 96, 113. Clearly the courtier was eager to buy while market prices were as low as 30, the figure reached in October at the date of Corner's last recommendation. No replies are extant; most documents concerning the war years were consciously destroyed after the war. A few particulars on Manfredo are in *Storia di Milano,* 6:69, 9:513.

[13]ASV, PSM, Supra, commissarie, b. 35, fasc. 5, which contains, besides the original account book, late copies of the acts of institution, dated 1385 and 1388, which are then simply confirmed in the testament made in Milan on 5 August 1389. Other accounts indicate that the capital was 4,090 ducats beginning 1420, that in 1609 the interest claim for 1520 was paid, and that in 1628, when the Monte Vecchio was paid off at 2.5 percent, the capital was reduced to 102¼ ducats.

[14]ASV, Grazie, reg. 18, fol. 27; reg. 19, fol. 39v; reg. 22, fol. 70.

basis of a testament that had been drawn up in Savoy. The Senate advised they return home and resolve the pending inheritance question according to the laws in force in Savoy; it promised that to the winner of the lawsuit Venice would pay the interest due on his holdings ("proficua imprestitorum suorum").[15] How that matter was resolved is not known, but the Saluzzo house continued to hold on to its investment; the portfolio, or part of it, was in the hands of Armand, viscount of Polignac, first son of Medea da Saluzzo, as late as 1499.[16]

The ties between Savoy, Milan, and the Venetian public debt become even tighter. About the same time that Manfredo IV was buying government credits on the open market, Azzo Visconti, lord of Milan (1329–39), who had married Caterina of Savoy in 1330 and was made an honorary citizen of Venice in 1332, had himself inscribed voluntarily on the Venetian estimo and paid a number of forced loans as a way of contributing to Venice's war effort against the Scaligeri of Verona (1337–39). Once on the estimo, he technically should have paid all the successive levies; since he did not do so, the officials of the Loan Office were opposed to recognizing the credits as appertaining to his heir, Luchino, but in 1342 they were ordered to do so and to cancel any fines imposed in the case.[17] Whether Luchino Visconti kept the portfolio — and if so, for how long — is not known, but it may be recalled that in the following year he established a deposit at the Grain Office, on the basis of silver coins imported to Venice, and that the deposit, however small, was sought after by claimants to the inheritance (see above, Chap. 9, sec. iv).

The person who had formally supported the petitions of Manfredo V of Saluzzo was Bianca of Savoy, sister of Amedeo VI, the Green Count, wife of Galeazzo II Visconti and mother of Giangaleazzo, in short, for decades an important member of the Milanese court. About one week before Manfredo V's petition of 1373, Bianca herself presented her first petition to purchase the par value of 30,000 ducats in Venetian government obligations — a petition granted "notwithstanding the fact [as it read] that she is not a citizen of Venice" and "on account of the unique friendship existing between Venice and the houses of Visconti and Savoy." At an unknown later date she was permitted to raise the nominal value to 40,000 ducats with further purchases — clearly with the intention of bringing the income back to a desired level after the reduction in interest rates decreed in 1382; in 1383 she reached her goal with the purchase of a final packet of 800 nominal

---

[15]ASV, AC, 3648, fol. 91v (the decision by the Signoria is not preserved in CN, reg. 7, where, at that date, some pages are missing. ST, reg. 1, fol. 138v (1444).

[16]ASV, CN, reg. 15, fol. 13v (6 November 1499); the matter involved the illegal appropriation of interest by two members of the Bembo family.

[17]These loans to Venice, effected in an unusual manner, were said to have been made by Azzo "ob reverenciam et amorem huius dominii tempore guerre" and simply "de sua curialitate"; ASV, Grazie, reg. 9, fol. 33.

ducats. That total corresponded—nominally and perhaps not accidentally—to the 40,000 gold florins that Bianca had brought as a dowry to her marriage in 1350.[18]

The petitions do not mention a rationale behind the creation of the noblewoman's portfolio, but we know she used it to endow the convent of S. Chiara la Reale of the order of Poor Clares in Pavia, which she founded in 1380. The endowment is mentioned in her testament of 1387 (principal executor was Manfredo di Saluzzo), in which she bequeathed the income ("redditus, prode et proventus") of the portfolio to the convent. The 3 percent that government credits earned for foreigners at that time (a further reduction, from 4 to 3 percent, had been decreed in 1386) meant an annual income of 1,200 ducats for the Franciscan convent. Agents were sent from Pavia to collect the money, which was probably frozen during the periods of war against Milan; we had a glimpse of one of these agents, when he was a victim of the schemer Francesco dalle Boccole in 1456 (see above, Chap. 11, sec. iv). The economic well-being of the foundation largely paralleled that of the Venetian public debt (not to speak of Venetian-Milanese diplomatic relations), and in fact the convent, seriously hurt by the gradual reduction in interest payments, collapsed definitively in the early seventeenth century when the Monte Vecchio was paid off at 2.5 percent of its nominal value.[19]

There are two further cases of investment in Venice by members of the Visconti family. In 1386 Giangaleazzo, son of Bianca of Savoy and Galeazzo II, the Conte di Virtù who, as we have seen, was praised by the Franciscan moralist Centueri for having decided not to purchase government obligations himself, petitioned the Venetian Signoria, through the Milanese ambassador and in the name of his second wife, Caterina (daughter of Bernabò Visconti), for the right to purchase the par value of 100,000 ducats (for a cost of some 35,000 gold ducats).[20] At least 70,000 nominal ducats'

---

[18]Ibid., reg. 17, fols. 7v (12 March 1373), 224 (17 March 1383); this last lot was "for about 300 ducats cash"— credits in fact were then worth about 40.

[19]For the testament, see Luigi Osio, ed., *Documenti diplomatici tratti dagli archivi milanesi,* 3 vols. (Milan, 1864–72), 1:260–66 (at 262). Carlo dell'Acqua, *Bianca Visconti di Savoia in Pavia e l'insigne monastero di S. Chiara la Reale* (Pavia, 1893), 21–22, 49, 56, 59; the appendix contains several documents, including the "fundatio" of the convent in 1380 and the testament. Dell'Acqua writes—erroneously—of the "Banco di S. Marco di Venezia" and the "Banco di Monte Vecchio"; probably the portfolio was inscribed in the ledger of the sestiere of S. Marco. See also ASMI, Fondo di religione, parte antica, 5959, for litigation regarding the endowment in the early fifteenth century (kindly passed on by Antonia Borlandi).

[20]ASV, Grazie, reg. 17, fol. 212 (16 January 1386). As was seen above, Kirshner has suggested that the praise bestowed by Guglielmo Centueri, bishop first of Piacenza and then of Pavia, on Giangaleazzo for having decided against purchasing Venetian obligations after provoking a debate on the matter in 1385 was spurious; here in fact we see him intervening personally in favor of the investments of his wife; "Reading Bernardino's Sermon," 582–84. Cessi writes, without citing a source, that Bernabò Visconti accepted payment of assets of

worth were purchased, as we learn from lawsuits pleaded by Caterina's sons after she died intestate in 1409. Actually, the portfolio had already been raided many times before Caterina's death, on the basis of decisions of both Milanese and Venetian courts (one ruling involved the transfer of a large sum to the Salt Office in payment for salt that Venice had delivered to Milan). In 1410 the transfers, made previous to the division of the inheritance, were ruled illegal by the Council of Forty, at the request of Filippo Maria Visconti, then count of Pavia. Later Caterina's debts were recognized as legitimate, however, and credits from her portfolio were sold to meet them. Again, the sequel is not known.[21]

Purchases made by Luchino Novello Visconti, in addition to the portfolio he may have inherited from his above-mentioned father and grandfather, gave him a total portfolio in Venetian government obligations of some 20,000 ducats par value. That is the amount (equal to the amount he held in shares of the Florentine Monte Comune) which he disposed of in his testament of 1399, made in Venice. The income on half was to go to his widow, the Florentine Maddalena Strozzi, and that on the remaining half was to be used for pious bequests in Venice. Since, like his forebears, he was an honorary citizen of Venice, he did not require a special license to intervene on the open market, in contrast to his relatives, who had exiled him from Milan when he was a boy.[22]

Another Milanese nobleman, Count Pietro Capello, bishop of Cremona, petitioned in 1374 and 1375 to purchase government credits for 4,000 ducats cash and condition them *in perpetuo* for charity. He ordered that the revenues be distributed as contributions to dowries for poor girls, half to inhabitants of Cremona, half to inhabitants of Venice. The rationales of the petition and the recommendation that it be accepted are interesting. Capello wrote that he wished to provide for the salvation of his soul, but since there were no opportunities in Lombardy for creating an endowment, he turned to this holy city, famous for liberty and justice. The officials of the Loan Office, granting the benign disposition of the supplicant, saw the chance to do some cleaning up in their account books: they recommended acceptance of the petition but asked that the money be given to them to invest, so that they could buy up small lots and consolidate them under a single new entry. The petitions were granted in 1375 and 1376. The Procurators of San Marco handled the almsgiving in Venice, specific confraternities the almsgiving in Cremona. In 1377 the bishop applied for—and

---

20,000 ducats held in the Grain Office in the form of government credits, at the market price; "La finanza veneziana," 214.

[21]ASV, AC, reg. 3646, fols. 85–86, 91 (16 July and 17 November 1410), and pt. 2, fols. 3v–4 (16 May 1412).

[22]See Osio, *Documenti diplomatici,* 1:348–56, and Mueller, "Espressioni di *status* sociale," 60–61.

received — Venetian citizenship; it is not known whether under that guise he made additional purchases.[23]

Farther south on the peninsula other lords invested in the Loan Office. The Este family of Modena and Ferrara were interested, beginning at least in 1364. In that year Azzone di Rinaldo d'Este and his wife, Tomasina, who had been granted citizenship shortly before, asked to purchase an unspecified amount in government credits notwithstanding the fact, as their petition stated, that they were not domiciled in Venice.[24] In 1407 Azzone di Francesco, of a collateral branch, took loans from the Venetian nobleman Vettor Marcello and, as surety, posted 3,200 nominal ducats' worth of government credits, on which he also owed the interest. Ten years later his sons Taddeo — by then a mercenary captain for Venice — and Francesco promised Marcello to continue paying interest on the credits as well as installments on the loan.[25] As regards the ruling branch of the family, Nicolò II d'Este (1361–88) exported wheat to Venice, and some of the proceeds may have been invested in credits. Sometime later Nicolò's widow, Verde della Scala, herself both a citizen and resident of Venice, acquired a large portfolio, of which she disposed in her testament of 1393.[26]

Mutual advantage constituted a close bond between the Gonzaga lords of Mantua, owners of some 8,000 hectares of prime wheat-producing land, and Venice, financial center and consumer of imported foodstuffs. Ludovico Gonzaga exported large amounts of wheat to Venice, for some of which he was credited with interest-bearing deposits at the Grain Office, where he also made further deposits in cash. At the very same time, begin-

---

[23]Copies of the bishop's letters to the doge are preserved in Cremona; see Giorgio Politi, *Antichi luoghi pii di Cremona,* 2 vols. (Cremona, 1979–85), 1:143; see also ibid., 77, for a request of 1592 that the Loan Office pay its due. The accepted petitions are in ASV, Grazie, reg. 17, fols. 41, 73, 82. The preamble, loosely paraphrased in the text, reads, "volens providere anime sue et considerans conditiones Lombardie, ac libertatem et iustitiam huius sancte civitatis." Citizenship de intus et extra was granted to Capello — who chose "this city above all others in the world" [ipsam civitatem preelegit ultra omnia loca mundi] — because the supplicant was "not a merchant" (fol. 82). The bishop's brother and administrator applied for citizenship in 1383 but seems not to have been successful (fol. 170). The accounts (in PSM, Ultra, b. 79) have the names of all beneficiaries from 1398 to 1460, after which there is merely a generic entry.

[24]ASV, Grazie, reg. 16, fol. 7 (30 July 1364); Azzone was made a citizen in 1359, his wife in May 1364. See also Trevor Dean, "Venetian Economic Hegemony: The Case of Ferrara, 1220–1500," *SV,* n.s., 12 (1986): 82 (where records in Modena are cited, without dates). The author relates that in the 1340s two members of the Este family had deposited some 5,000 ducats in the Procuratia de Supra. See also BMCV, cod. Cicogna, 2944, fasc. 1.

[25]ASV, CIN, b. 241, notaio Pietro Zane, fasc. 2, fol. 75r–v, an admission of debt by Taddeo d'Este in Venice, 6 April 1417. For the identification of these lines, see Trevor Dean, *Land and Power in Late Medieval Ferrara: The Rule of the Este, 1350–1450* (Cambridge, England, 1988), 52–55, and Mallett in Mallett and Hale, *Military Organization,* 30–31, 58.

[26]For wheat imported from Ferrara, see *PRV,* doc. 188; for Verde's estate, see ASV, PSM, Misti, b. 98A.

ning in 1367, he started buying Venetian government obligations. The figures for both investments make members of the Gonzaga family far and away the biggest foreign investors in Venice's financial market. An account prepared for Ludovico Gonzaga by a scribe of the Loan Office details his investments: in the years 1367–70 and 1373 he bought a nominal amount of more than 150,000 ducats' worth of credits, in 374 lots, or "poste," at prices ranging from 86 to 96 percent of par in the first years, then between 78 and 90. Of those purchases, 1,000 gold ducats' worth were signed over to the Franciscan convent of Mantua, in part to cover a legacy, in part for prayers for the souls of deceased and living members of the family.[27] The portfolio in government credits alone, then paying 5 percent on par, gave Ludovico an annual income of a startling 7,450 ducats per year, a return on capital, assuming an average price of 90, of 5.5 percent.[28] In early 1382, just after the War of Chioggia, the portfolio seems to have stood at about 90,000 ducats, which would have provided an annual income of 4,500 ducats had Venice been able to pay the 5 percent interest it had paid before the war began. After Francesco (who had married a daughter of Bernabò Visconti of Milan) inherited the marquisate from his father, he had an audit made in Venice in 1385 which showed him to be the owner of a portfolio worth 105,543 nominal ducats, for a revenue, at 3 percent, of 3,166 ducats; besides this, he had, as we saw above (Chap. 9), 86,667 ducats at the Grain Office, so that his total income from these two Venetian sources was 5,756 ducats per year, the fourth highest figure among the sources of revenue of the whole state of Mantua.[29] Of his capital at the Grain Office, Francesco Gonzaga transferred 20,000 ducats to Carlo di Galeotto Malatesta in 1387 as part of the dowry of his daughter Isabetta. Malatesta, in turn, had to condition a portfolio of 20,000 ducats in government credits at the Loan Office as surety for the dowry. When he became heavily indebted to the Signoria and

---

[27]Cenci, "I Gonzaga e i Frati minori," 26–29, and Kirshner, "Reading Bernardino's Sermon," 585.

[28]Romani, "Il credito," 191–99. The figures given in his table 1, p. 192, are in lire a grossi; I totaled the figures and converted the sum to ducats. The account book, in ASMN, Archivo Gonzaga, b. 409, does not give the running market price, but the scribe's subtotals include the total purchase price; for example, the cash value of purchases made in 1369 (Romani, "Il credito," 192 n. 4) shows that the average purchase price during that year was 90. The number of lots was reported by the Gonzaga agent in Venice, Bertolino de'Codelupi, as 370 in 1376, when the scribe was preparing the account book (*PRV*, clvii); the total nominal amount reported by Luzzatto (*PRV*, cliv and clv n. 1) as 19,240 ducats is a misinterpretation or refers only to a single year's purchases.

[29]Luzzatto in *PRV*, clv n. 1. The *translatio* of Venetian credits from father to son took place on 25 February 1383, shortly after Francesco succeeded his father. For the audit of 1385, from which the interest was calculated, and for the revenues of the Gonzaga, see Romani, "Il credito," 196–99. The author confused the nominal value of the portfolio with its market value (p. 197), which in 1385 stood at about 35 percent of par.

to individual Venetians in 1419, that sum in credits was ordered sequestered by the Senate.[30]

Investments by the Gonzaga lords were imitated by other members of the family and by other Mantuans, including Goncelario and Antonio, grandsons of Giacomo "a Toaleis," in a petition supported by Ludovico Gonzaga himself: Margarita di Guido Gonzaga (about 1381); Pietrobono Pomponazzi in 1432; and the convent of S. Chiara (upon petition by the marquis Gianfrancesco Gonzaga) in 1435. There were many others, for the sequester of the portfolios of all Mantuans in 1439 created general havoc, as will be seen below.

Relations between the Casali family, lords of Cortona, and the neighboring states of Siena and Florence were politically and militarily more important, but it is to Venice that the family turned for investments. Francesco di Bartolomeo was made a Venetian citizen in 1371. Probably in concomitance with his patent of citizenship, Francesco began investing in the Venetian public debt — perhaps for a value of 20,000 gold florins. At his death in 1375, the usufruct of all his goods, therefore including the income on the Venetian government credits, went by testament to his widow, while the signory passed to his first son, under guardianship. Later his brother Uguccio succeeded as lord of Cortona; he also held a portfolio, of unspecified value, as indicated by his testament of 1400, in which a bequest to his wife of 10,000 gold florins was secured on his holdings in Venetian government obligations.[31]

The last important investor in the class of the signori was Paolo Guinigi, lord of Lucca from 1400 to 1430. He was made an honorary noble citizen in 1408, and in 1411 he petitioned for the privilege of investing from 25,000 to 50,000 florins "in Venetian government credits or in the Grain Office." The request, made in his name in a harangue before the Great Council by his friend the powerful Procurator of San Marco Marino Caravello, was to constitute a very secure capital ("unum capitale firmissimum") in Venice for himself and his heirs, "given the precariousness and mutability of things in this world . . . and the fact that rulers are often constrained to undertake actions that one day are considered just, the next are considered unjust." A series of legal conditions was appended to make the portfolio safe from sequester and from claims lodged by persons or entities; only Guinigi or his immediate heirs were to be able to collect

---

[30]*PRV,* doc. 226.

[31]Franco Cardini, "Casali, Francesco," in *DBI,* 21 (1978), 78–80, reports the stated value of purchases but says the lord drew an annual income of 2,600 florins, which would have meant, in 1375, a nominal capital of 52,000 ducats; it is not clear what his source was for these figures or for the presumed rate of interest of 13 percent, which is not possible at that date, even as returns to capital. See also Vittorio Lazzarini, "Il testamento di Uguccio Casali, Signore di Cortona (16 Ottobre 1400)," *Polimnia* (Cortona), 3 (July–September 1932), offprint.

interest or to get their hands on the cash value of the nest egg; the only claims that could possibly be heard against these conditions were those of Venetian citizens, brought before Venetian courts with due process. Clearly, the lord of Lucca did not feel secure upon his throne and was hedging his bets on his future and that of his sons.[32]

Beginning the following year Guinigi transferred to Venice nearly 40,000 florins, almost all of which arrived by bill of exchange. The value of the bills was credited to current accounts on Rialto banks and later converted, with an agio, into specie, for foreign investments in government obligations were to be paid in cash. His agents on the Rialto were the three Guidiccioni brothers, immigrants from Lucca and naturalized citizens of Venice. These men carefully analyzed the conditions of the market and, over the next two years, timed their purchases as best they could to buy low. Their reports back to Lucca constitute a source comparable only to the letters of the Gonzaga agent in Venice, Bertolino de' Codelupi. Thus we know the names of the sellers of the eighty-two lots purchased, the market price, and all the transactions costs involved. In 1414 Guinigi held a portfolio of almost 90,000 nominal ducats in government credits, purchased at an average price of 45, on which he earned the very respectable income of 2,700 ducats, an average yield of 6.67 percent (see graph 14.1). A careful final accounting by Nicolò Guidiccioni shows that transactions costs, of which the heaviest was the agio for buying specie, came to 1.5 percent of the total invested. In 1425, at the time of a new audit, Guinigi's nominal capital stood at about 112,000 ducats, probably as a result of the capitalization of some interest or some undocumented further investments; his returns then were more than 3,000 ducats. But only two years later he took a dangerous step and crossed to the side of the Visconti, in their war against Florence and Venice. His support of the enemy was direct, for one of his sons led mercenary forces in attacks against Venetian territories. Venice immediately sequestered the portfolio, as we shall see.

The only non-Italian ruler, besides the neighboring count of Veglia, uncovered so far who petitioned to invest was John I of Portugal, whose request was granted in 1410, for an unspecified sum of money. The same John I held a portfolio of nearly 35,000 florins in the Florentine Monte Comune in 1415.[33]

[32]The Franciscan Guglielmo Centueri's phrase about foreign princes investing in Venetian government obligations in order to provide for their families is very close to the substance and the form of Guinigi's petition; Kirshner, "Reading Bernardino's Sermon," 580. The account that follows summarizes my paper "Foreign Investment in Venetian Government Bonds and the Case of Paolo Guinigi," in which the text of the petition is published and all references to the archives of Venice and Lucca can be found.

[33]Conti, *L'imposta diretta*, 31 n. 4; the crown still owned nearly 30,000 florins' worth of Monte Comune in 1470, on which it earned the privileged rate of 4.5 percent (ibid., 58). Cf. Kirshner, "Papa Eugenio IV," 342.

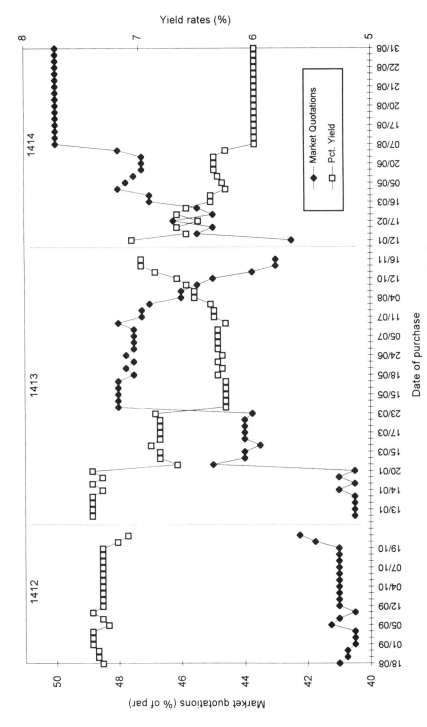

GRAPH 14.1. The Venetian Market in Government Credits, 1412–1414

An idea of the rapport there must have been, at least occasionally, among these foreign signori as holders of Venetian government obligations comes from February 1382, when the Signoria decided to reduce interest rates on par from 5 to 4 percent and to consolidate interest from the period of the War of Chioggia to capital at 60 percent. The consolidation was first made as an offer and then transmuted into a simple alternative: either accept the offer or lose interest in arrears. The Gonzaga agent, Bertolino de' Codelupi, opposed the move with all the force he could muster. Then he consulted the agents of the other big foreign holders of Venetian credits, only to discover that they had just agreed to the consolidation, and he names Bianca of Savoy, mother of Giangaleazzo Visconti; Manfredino di Saluzzo and his wife; and Verde della Scala. Finally he, too, had to concede, in the name of Ludovico Gonzaga. In that moment of crisis, they were all in the same boat.[34]

iii. OTHER CATEGORIES OF INVESTORS

Having introduced the theme of foreign investments in the Venetian funded debt by considering foreign lords, who seem in fact to have inaugurated the practice, I shall now touch upon other investors, by broad categories, with reference to table E.2, in Appendix E. The fact is, however, that the number of persons who petitioned for a license, or whose petition is extant, is inferior by far to the number of foreigners who actually invested in government obligations or who inherited a portfolio. A reflection of this reality is found in those cases in which Venice threatened some kind of reprisal against a foreign lord; not only his portfolio could be sequestered but also that of other citizens — generally unnamed — of his domains. Examples mentioned below regard subjects resident in Padua, Mantua, and Urbino.

A first category of owners of government obligations which stands out is that of mercenary captains. It is a group one would expect to find, since Florence, in times of crisis, is known to have paid salaries to mercenaries "in monte credits," usually deposits in the office of the floating debt (called the Ufficium Diminutionis Montium, whose liabilities were to be used to amortize the funded debt) but sometimes also in credits.[35] Of course, some of the signori discussed above — such as Taddeo d'Este or Gianfrancesco Gonzaga — were at times also in the pay of Venice qua captains. It does not seem that Venice paid its captains in government obligations, especially since they usually needed specie with which to pay their troops. Although there are no explicit examples, the possibility that such an option was occasionally exercised cannot be excluded.

Cases of mercenaries known to have held portfolios of government

---

[34]*PRV,* clii–vi and notes; Cessi, "La finanza veneziana," 214, 234.
[35]Molho, *Florentine Public Finances,* 143–44.

credits cover a period of some seventy years. Giacomo Cavalli, Venice's captain general of ground forces in the 1370s and during the War of Chioggia, had been made a citizen of Venice in 1367 along with his two brothers, soldiers of fortune themselves. Giacomo was coopted into the Great Council after the war for his services. He did not need to petition, therefore, for the right to purchase government obligations, but we know of his portfolio because in his testament of 1383 he disposes of an income of 600 ducats from such credits, which means he owned a par value of 15,000 ducats. It is not impossible that he received some of that amount as pay, during the tight-money situation that existed during the war.[36] Giacomo was well acquainted with open market operations in Venice, however, since in 1376 he mediated the petition of Anna, wife of his "nepos" Franceschino Cavalli, to invest 4,000 ducats. Luchino Novello Visconti, already mentioned above, was a soldier of fortune. Just how Guid'Antonio da Montefeltro, count of Urbino, formed a portfolio is not clear; we know that he held one because, about the time when Venice offered him a "condotta in aspetto" as captain general in 1424, he had a debt with Venice which the authorities threatened to make good "by withholding the interest he and other citizens of Urbino were due on government obligations."[37] The latest recorded cases were Lorenzo Attendoli, whose petition to invest 6,000 gold ducats in the open market was granted in 1436, after he had been released from Venetian service,[38] and Nicola da Todi and his brothers, who petitioned while they were stationed in Padua in 1440.

The case of the notorious mercenary captain Francesco Bussone, count of Carmagnola, can be singled out for special attention. In late 1420, while he was in the pay of Filippo Maria Visconti and so much part of the entourage of the duke of Milan after having married a Visconti that he himself was referred to as "de Vicecomitibus," Carmagnola applied for a license to invest in Venetian government obligations. Six months later, he sent letters via the Milanese ambassador petitioning that his portfolio be ruled immune from sequester, for his own assurance and that of his sons and heirs. Although the Great Council had agreed to the initial request with an overwhelming majority, many members had second thoughts when it was proposed to permit him to invest up to 30,000 gold ducats in government obligations, with the very same conditions and reservations applied earlier, in 1411, in the case of Paolo Guinigi, which was specifically invoked as a precedent. In fact, the proposal only barely passed, and only on the second ballot. Needless to say, after the famous trial and execution of Carmagnola for treason in 1432, the credits were indeed sequestered. The nominal value of 40,000 ducats was divided among the count's survivors.

---

[36]Mueller, "Veronesi e capitali veronesi," 371.
[37]Mallett and Hale, *Military Organization,* 32; ASV, SM, reg. 55, fol. 136.
[38]Mallett and Hale, *Military Organization,* 38.

His widow, Antonia, was credited with 10,000 ducats, to provide her with an income of 300 ducats, while each of their three daughters received a similar amount, as dowries then claimed to be worth 5,000 gold ducats each; until their marriage, the interest would serve for their support. The tradition of numerous members of the Visconti court in investing in Venetian government credits and the similar interests of mercenaries, regardless of their being in Venetian service or not, are combined in this important figure of Venetian historiography.[39]

Chivalric orders were also attracted by such investments. The Knights Hospitalers of St. John of Jerusalem, based on the island of Rhodes, asked in 1435 to purchase the nominal value of 200,000 ducats in government credits; with the market at about 36, that meant the considerable sum of 72,000 ducats in cash. The interest — 6,000 ducats at 3 percent on par, an 8.3 percent yield to capital — was to go to Rhodes to support the brothers there. The petition, made by the grand master Antonio Fluviano, left formulation of conditions to Venice; the Senate agreed that the credits purchased would be safe from sequester "except in extreme circumstances." That was to mean, replied the Senate to the grand master's request for clarification, the waging of open warfare against Venice.[40] Shortly thereafter the grand master of the Castilian Order of Calatrava, Ludovico de Gusman, and his son Numo asked for a license to purchase 100,000 and 25,000 ducats' worth of credits respectively. It is not clear whether the grand master was acting in his own name or in that of the order; in any case, he was to be free to dispose of the portfolio as he wished.

Citizens and institutions of certain cities and certain areas emerge as particularly interested in investing in the funded debt. Members of the Milanese court, as was seen above, were keen on investing both in government obligations and in the Grain Office. The same was true for citizens of Mantua under the Gonzaga and of Rimini under the Malatesta. Nine laymen and churchmen more or less directly connected with the royal court of Cyprus are also present on the list.

Merchants are not many, especially not persons labeled as such; merchants in full activity would have preferred to keep their money as liquid as possible or invested in operations that offered higher profits. The best known and most important was Alessandro Borromei, founder and direc-

---

[39]ASV, MC, Ursa, fols. 41, 44r–v (27 December 1420, 29 May 1421). See also Mallett and Hale, *Military Organization,* 32–37. For the decisions regarding his widow and daughters, see Consiglio dei Dieci, Miste, reg. 11, fols. 45v (23 July 1432), 70v (27 August 1433), and 87 (25 February 1433). Almost contemporaneously, in June 1421, Carmagnola petitioned for permission to make a five-year deposit of 30,000 florins in the Florentine floating debt; he actually deposited 15,000. See Molho, *Florentine Public Finances,* 145.

[40]ASV, Grazie, reg. 23, fol. 116v (31 December 1435); SM, reg. 59, fol. 138v (4 January 1436); *PRV,* doc. 236 (8 May). Very likely the funds seeking investment were already in the hands of the Venetian priory of the order.

tor of the important merchant-banking company headquartered in Venice; in 1430, a year before his death, he asked to invest 8,000 ducats in government obligations, to be rendered inalienable; the interest was earmarked for the Olivitani order at S. Elena, where, in the chapel of S. Elena, of which he was patron, he and several other members of the family are buried.[41] Nearly in the same class as the Borromei were the Gozzadini of Bologna, a firm represented in Venice around 1400 by Bonifazio Gozzadini; this family was interested in Venice's open market in government credits, but just how it intervened is not yet clear.[42]

Besides these exceptional cases of merchant bankers, several smaller merchants, from Germany, Italy, and Dalmatia, can also be identified among the prospective investors. Four German purchasers were clearly merchants familiar with the Venetian marketplace. Ulrich Samer of Salzburg in 1409 bought the portfolio of 12,000 ducats held until then by the burgomaster and the governors of the city hospital of Salzburg; the usufruct or "pro'" remained with the previous owners. The only condition connected with the licenses granted to Johannes Daga of Nuremberg, Johannes Maurino of Augsburg, and Peter Silber ("Argentus") of Freiburg was the customary one: they had to intervene in the market within four to six months.[43]

The Milanese Antonio da Galerate, who in his testament left 50 ducats to be invested "in lucrum sine peccato" for the altar of S. Orsola at SS. Giovanni e Paolo, was surely a merchant deceased in Venice; his executors asked in 1387 that the sum, the smallest for which a grazia was granted, be invested in government credits. Giacomo di Francesco Giuberti of Bologna, described as a merchant conversant with Venice for twenty-five years when he applied to invest 4,000 or 5,000 ducats in credits in 1402, declared that he was ready to come with his family to live permanently in Venice; he was given a full year to invest. The merchant Zupano de Bona of Ragusa and his compatriots Stefano da Ragusa and two brothers received permission to acquire credits in 1438. In the same year, Lisiolo Capoana, Venetian vice-consul in Manfredonia, in Apulia, was given a license to invest 2,000 ducats. Very likely Enrico Bunci, a citizen of Asti, was a merchant familiar with Venice when he applied in 1440. None of these active merchants declared that they were interested in establishing an endowment; they seem to have purchased government credits as a safe investment.

More interesting are two final categories. Thirteen women are listed as buyers. Those connected with the Visconti court have already been dis-

---

[41]ASV, Grazie, reg. 22, fol. 133v; Edler de Roover, "Borromeo, Galeazzo," 48–49.

[42]Biblioteca dell Arciginnasio, Bologna, Archivio Gozzadini, b. 58, fascicle of letters to Bonifacio Gozzadini in Venice; on 16 October 1398 Bonifacio's sister Filippa wrote him concerning a purchase of Venetian imprestiti.

[43]The four grazie were published by Simonsfeld, *Der Fondaco,* vol. 1, docs. 297, 329, 414, 424.

cussed. Of the thirteen, eight were widows who applied precisely for the opportunity to invest cash safely, perhaps the cash value of their dowries, and earn an income — a kind of pension — for their support. Two, who applied in 1377, were sisters-in-law: widows of Lorenzo and Antonio Maffei, Veronese but naturalized citizens of Venice and brothers of Filippo; Antonio and Filippo had been bankers on the Rialto, about 1349–59, when they represented the interests of Cangrande della Scala; Sofia declared specifically that she wished to continue residing in Venice.[44] Margherita of Arbe had requested the investment in her testament in order to endow works of charity.

About ten ecclesiastics are involved. Three were prelates. The Milanese bishop of Cremona was discussed above. Two cardinals, Pileo da Prata of Ravenna and Hugo de Lusignan of Nicosia, Cyprus, were concerned for university students. The cardinal of Ravenna founded a college, meant initially to be at the university of Bologna but which actually was instituted as the Collegio Pratense at the University of Padua, with an endowment of 12,000 ducats invested in Venetian government credits; the income was to permit the twenty-some students of the college to "vivere et perseverare in studio, pro acquirendo scientiam." With the price of credits at about 40, his investment could have acquired 30,000 ducats par value, for an income, at the time at 4 percent, of 1,200 ducats, a yield of 10 percent on capital. The cardinal of Cyprus established a scholarship fund with 2,000 ducats in 1431; in so doing, he followed the example of his compatriot Pietro di Cafrano, admiral of the kingdom, who in his testament, drawn up in Cyprus in 1393, had established a fund with his portfolio of 5,000 ducats in Venetian government obligations to support four Cypriot students (one in canon law, one in civil law, two in arts and medicine).[45]

There were three Franciscan institutions — two friaries and a con-

---

[44]For the Maffei, see Mueller, "Veronesi e capitali veronesi," 373.

[45]After permission had been granted in 1383 to Cardinal Pileo for the purchase of the credits for a project destined for Bologna, the patron changed his mind. In his testament of 1399, the college is identified as that of SS. Gerolamo e Prosdocimo, founded by him personally at Padua. See the documents of 1384, 1399, and 1407 collected in 1540 in *LCR*, 6, lib. 19, nos. 1–3, 48. Cafrano, who seems not to have petitioned for a license, refers to his Venetian government obligations with Genoese terminology, whereby the public debt is "columna mutuorum" or "conpra," obligations are "loca," and interest is "proventus" (Famagosta at the time was, in fact, under Genoese rule). Remaining documentation regards the selection of scholars a half century later and cites the relevant clause of the testament. See ASV, CIN, b. 123, no. 11, atti P. dalle Mole (1446) and Miscellanea atti notai diversi, b. 119 (1465). The cardinal of Cyprus also promoted the bid of Alvise da Tana in 1436 to purchase credits. A Venetian prelate at the same time also established a scholarship fund, but with the credits he already possessed. In his testament of 1426 Francesco Lando set up a much more lavish fund offering 120 ducats per annum (80 in living expenses, 40 for books) for students without any physical handicaps, for thirteen years if in both laws, seven years if only canon law; precedence was secured for members of his own family. See ASV, CIN, Miscellanea testamenti notai diversi, b. 19, no. 19bis, and PSM, Citra, b. 132, for the commissaria.

vent — in Forlì, Rimini, and Mantua, which invested in government obligations. The Franciscans of Forlì in 1433 merely increased the size of a portfolio already in existence. Those of Rimini invested money left them by a local merchant. The case of the Poor Clares of S. Chiara in Mantua was pleaded by the marquis Gianfrancesco Gonzaga, then mercenary captain in the pay of Venice. While the flexibility of many Franciscans in matters of moderate rates of interest is well known, in the context of their support of the Monti di Pietà a generation later, slightly more surprising is the investment of an unspecified amount by the Dominicans of Rimini, who in this case clearly followed the example of their local Franciscan confreres. In 1440 the prior of a Benedictine monastery in the Trevigiano received the right to purchase the nominal value of 1,500 ducats in government credits. In the following year the inhabitants of the town of Castel S. Lorenzo in Campo near Ancona, with the mediation of Sigismondo di Pandolfo Malatesta, sought to regularize their rent dues of 50 ducats by buying a portfolio that would produce that much annually for the monastery *in perpetuo*; at the time, that meant about 1,700 ducats par value. Finally, two Venetian priests received licenses: Guidone, canon of San Marco, in 1377, and the chaplain of the nuns of S. Secondo, who, in 1431, bought the small sum of 400 ducats nominal value.

The overwhelming majority of the foreigners who asked for and received the privilege of buying government obligations on the open market had the principal aim of keeping a liquid patrimony safe and earning a modest income; a minority endowed, with their portfolios, pious institutions and works of charity. Some, perhaps, foresaw the use of their credits as an eventual means of payment. There is not a single case of speculation among them. The market remained lively until about 1440, according to extant documentation. Thereafter, low market prices probably did not constitute a sufficient incentive to foreigners to purchase Monte Vecchio credits, for the arrears and irregularity of interest payments reduced their attractiveness for the ends, familial or pious, which earlier purchasers had expressed.[46]

iv. PORTFOLIOS AND REPRISALS

Despite clauses granting the portfolios of foreign princes exemption from sequester, there were situations in which Venice did not hesitate to freeze or sequester them outright. First of all, the sequester of credits or the interest due on them (or both) was a way of getting even with holders of credits who owed money to Venetian citizens or to the Venetian state; use

---

[46]Luzzatto (*PRV*, ccxlv–vi n. 1) refers to petitions — supposedly collected by Simonsfeld — made by German merchants as late as 1460, "when no one could have imagined to secure for himself a modest but safe income by buying Venetian government credits." The last of four petitions by Germans, however, is dated 1441. At the same time, the market, as we have also seen, was still considered viable in 1457–61 by Nicolò d'Andrea Barbarigo and his advisors.

of this lever, as a last resort, was mentioned above in the cases involving the mercenaries Carlo di Galeotto Malatesta and Guid'Antonio da Montefeltro. Much more serious was the situation in which an owner of government obligations waged war on Venice. It is obvious that no government could countenance paying interest to a foreign lord who had become its enemy. Credits might be frozen and then used as a lever in peace negotiations, or they might be confiscated and either maintained as gifts to be distributed or canceled definitively.

During the War of Chioggia, when the Carrara of Padua sided with Genoa, Venice froze the assets of Paduans. During the peace negotiations Francesco il Vecchio demanded that all be restored, especially a portfolio of about 20,000 ducats in the name of his deceased wife, Fina Buzacarini, of which he claimed to be heir. In the treaty itself, Venice promised to investigate what had happened to the assets and to determine the rights of Francesco.[47] Paduan assets were frozen once again during the war that ended in 1405 with the subjugation of Padua. Nicolò III d'Este supported the cause of his son-in-law, and, until the separate peace, his assets were similarly frozen. While any Carrara holdings remaining in Venice were surely sequestered definitively when Francesco Novello and his sons were executed, assets of other Paduans, having become Venetian subjects, were probably restored in time.[48]

Paolo Guinigi, lord of Lucca, had been careful to insist upon strict conditions in the pact he made with Venice: only Venetian debtors supported by Venetian courts could touch his portfolio. He probably believed that the pact would still hold when he decided to support the Visconti cause in 1427. When his son Ladislaus appeared as a mercenary captain in the pay of the enemy, Guinigi was formally reminded of his oath as a Venetian citizen and warned that if his son took the field, Lucca and its lord would be considered at war with Venice and Venice would react accordingly. There was no reply. When the son was involved in attacks on Venetian castles and territories, Venice did not hesitate to sequester the assets he was to have inherited. The portfolio, then worth some 112,000 ducats at par, was simply ordered canceled. All attempts made by Guinigi's son Agostino (who tried in 1445 to get approval of his membership in the Great Council, which he claimed he had inherited) and by the Commune of Lucca (Guinigi, overthrown in 1430, died in 1432) to have the nest egg restored were to no avail. The step was considered unique and of potentially serious consequences for the trust of foreigners in the funded debt should news leak out, so the

---

[47]The sixth demand made by the lord of Padua was "che i danari, che avea madona Fina Buziacarina sua mogliere in Venezia agl'inprestii, gli sia dadi e restituidi per tuto uno mexe, e così per simille ogn'altro dinaro dela ditta donna che fesse il signor fede che fusse in Venexia." Gatari, *Cronaca Carrarese*, 201–2, and above, Chap. 9, sec. iv.

[48]Vittorio Lazzarini, "Beni carraresi e proprietari veneziani," in *Studi in onore di Gino Luzzatto*, 1:274–88, mentions the sequester only of landed possessions in the "fattoria carrarese."

Senate's decision, approved by anything but a large majority, was ordered kept "secretissima."[49] Over the next century and a half, further attempts at recovering the investment were made, but all in vain.

In the same year as Guinigi's death, Carmagnola was tried by the Council of Ten and executed for treason. The case of the former had been considered a precedent at the time of the petition of the latter; both, that is, had been given the most solemn assurances that their portfolios would be safe from sequester and available, at their death, to their sons and heirs. Venice accorded the heirs of Carmagnola slightly better treatment than it accorded those of Guinigi, since the widow and daughters of the former resided initially in Venice, before the widow was interned in Treviso. Their inheritance of the portfolio was denied, but they were credited with enough of it to lead a respectable existence.

The successive Visconti war, during which Verona withdrew for a short time from the Venetian Terraferma state, brought two further confiscations from military leaders who, having passed to the enemy, were declared rebels. The Veronese captain Alvise Dal Verme deserted the Venetian ranks in 1436. In March 1437 the Senate ordered an inventory of all his possessions, real and personal, in Venice and on the Terraferma, and declared them sequestered. Specifically mentioned were his "imprestita," acquired under his inherited status as Venetian citizen. All income from his assets, including interest on government obligations, was to be used by the Governatori delle Entrate to purchase credits on the open market, that is, to amortize the funded debt. This time the credits themselves were not canceled from the books.[50] The same was true in the following year when Gianfrancesco Gonzaga, marquis of Mantua and longtime captain of Venetian forces, accepted a "condotta" from the enemy after retiring from Venetian service. In this case the portfolios of all Mantuan citizens, not only those of the Gonzaga, were sequestered, as were the "persons and goods" of all Mantuan merchants, in Venice and en route to and from Mantua.[51] The credits belonging to Mantuans, along with those of Alvise Dal Verme, were maintained and continued to earn interest; they were used for various purposes: as surety for bank loans (see above, Chap. 10), for loans from the Salt Office, and for those from the Procurators of San Marco; to provide an income for the children of a nobleman who had died in the service of Venice; to repay reimbursable forced loans. In the latter case, 50,000 ducats par value in obligations formerly owned by Mantuans were distributed in repayment of a forced loan that had brought in 11,000 ducats.[52] The sequester was suc-

---

[49]PRV, doc. 230, and ASV, AC, reg. 3649, fols. 76v–77.

[50]ASV, SSec, reg. 14, fol. 26v (23 March 1437); Mallett and Hale, *Military Organization*, 191.

[51]ASV, SSec, reg. 14, fol. 129 (9 July 1438); see also fol. 127v with a marginal note that Gonzaga had rendered himself a rebel on 7 July.

[52]PRV, ccxlvii.

cessfully appealed by individuals who, though of Mantuan origin, could prove that they were Venetian citizens or subjects. One such was Bartolomeo de Torchis, physician of Padua; another was Bonadomana della Volta, a citizen able to prove that her portfolio had been purchased eighty years earlier by Omnebono of Mantua, who in fact had become a naturalized Venetian citizen in 1358. Since the Mantuan holdings had all been transferred or sold by 1441, these claims had to be honored by purchases on the open market. Obligations held by religious houses and hospitals of Mantua were exempted.[53] There is nothing to indicate that, when the marquis later became reconciled to Venice, any offer was made to restore his portfolio.

From Licensed to Free Investments

On 22 February 1442 the Senate eliminated the need for foreigners to ask for a license in order to buy Venetian government credits and decreed a new anticonfiscation pact for foreign buyers. "Many concessions have been granted to princes and lords throughout the world," reads the preamble, "but without any profit to Venice, which is not the case in any other city." Now, instead of applying for a license, albeit gratis, and then intervening on the open market, foreigners would buy directly from the Governatori delle Entrate and pay a tax of 4 percentage points above the market price; in other words, the Governatori would buy, for example, at 20 and resell to a foreigner at 24. The rate of interest was, as before, the 3 percent gross rate still promised to holders of credits who were not inscribed on the estimo; while that rate was already wishful thinking, however, the net rate of nearly 2 percent actually paid at the time still meant, on government credits purchased at 20, a yield of 10 percent. In order that foreigners would opt more freely ("liberiori animo") to buy such credits, all purchasers were guaranteed against confiscation, even in case of open war or reprisals. Furthermore, foreigners currently holding portfolios could acquire the same guarantee by paying the 4 percent tax on their holdings. To convince would-be buyers of their sincerity, the senators threatened anyone who would propose revocation of the new law with heavy fines.[54]

It is impossible to know what effect this law had on demand in the market. It is a fact that the prices recovered, bouncing from 20 to 28 in 1443. But the law eliminated the need for a license, which was in many cases

[53]ASV, SM, reg. 60, fols. 133 (16 March 1439), 134 (28 March, the decree that told the Governatori to accept orders from the Soranzo bank as to the disposition of 50,000 ducats' worth of obligations), 134v (31 March, for the orphans of Marino q. Alessandro Contarini), 136 (15 April), 138 (23 April), 143 (9 May, exemption of religious houses and hospitals), 249 (6 September 1440). For the claims, see CN, reg. 7, fols. 21 (22 November 1440), 37v (3 December). Among the grazie to religious houses discussed above, for Mantua only the convent of S. Chiara was mentioned; others obviously received portfolios from benefactors, with or without special license.

[54]PRV, doc. 250.

the only documentation we had. Hints exist that there was demand. In 1444, for example, Bishop Giovanni de Dominis of Arbe in Dalmatia, desirous to buy "a certain quantity" of Venetian obligations, inquired whether he fell under the provisions of the law regarding foreigners; the Collegio responded that no, as a citizen of Arbe he was to be treated as a Dalmatian and thus with the rights of a Venetian citizen de intus.[55] And in 1451 exemption from the tax was accorded to Messer Pietro da Nosceto, who wished to purchase such obligations.[56] Obviously, yields were still sufficiently attractive, even though interest payments were in arrears.

[55]ASV, CN, reg. 8, fol. 11v; the privilege accorded to all citizens of Zara was to apply to all Venice's Dalmatian subjects. See also Cozzi and Knapton, *Storia*, 137.

[56]*PRV,* doc. 268.

CONCLUSION

THE FERVENT ACTIVITY in all the financial sectors discussed in this book is practical evidence that citizens and foreigners, women included, knew that in Venice they could make money with money ("pecuniam ad multiplicandum seminare"), as Matthew Paris put it when he commented on the collaboration between magnates and "Lombards" in England in the early thirteenth century; and Venice did not need the "exemplum Romanae curiae" sarcastically invoked by Matthew.[1]

Venetians and foreigners active in Venice had three major preoccupations regarding the marketplace. First, they needed institutions suitable for bringing together persons with excess, lendable capital and those looking for credit. That was essential not only for trade and manufacture but also for persons who were not active in these areas, such as widows and orphans and also princes and feudal lords, who sought opportunities for keeping their money safe and making it work for them at the same time. A prime customer for credit was the state, which did not trade but which produced protection for those who did. Second, both Venetians and foreigners were concerned lest success in affairs of this world, especially in the money market, preclude their attaining salvation in the next. This was an area of constant confrontation between theory and practice, as full of risk as the credit market itself. Third, active and passive investors alike looked to the state, perhaps more in Venice than elsewhere, for judicial and regulatory institutions and for a philosophy that would promote a proper balance between regulation and freedom, so as to maintain an environment conducive to investment and making profits.

Local deposit and transfer banks, international merchant banks, float-

---

[1]Quoted in Postan, "Credit in Medieval Trade," 85–86 n. 75.

ing debts, public deposit banks, and the funded debt were the principal structures that sustained the money market in medieval and Renaissance Venice. Some of them were relatively unique, others less so, but even those found in other major urban commercial centers attained in Venice a particular renown.

Local transfer banks active on the Rialto became famous across Europe, as "banchi di scritta" or giro banks, for their central position in the whole payments system in the year-round fair that was the Venetian marketplace. Even though they operated on a strictly local basis, their service of transferring assets from one account to another cleared international debits and credits and, in the process, created fiduciary money.

The international merchant banks, which organized the foreign exchange market in Venice as elsewhere, were in the hands of Florentines. These experts in lending money to long-distance merchants and in facilitating the circulation of assets throughout Europe, however, made Venice, for a century and a half, one of the most important exchange markets of the West. Florentine preeminence in this sector was not called into question; Venetians concerned themselves only with safeguarding their traditional monopoly of trade — and exchange — with the Levant.

The approach taken by Venice — as always, by experimentation over time rather than by decree — to guarantee to the state apparatus a functional floating debt was original. Initially, the decision makers of the city raised a traditional annonary administration, the Grain Office, to the level almost of a state bank, which attracted investors from north-central Italy and beyond, rather like a Swiss bank today; then, when it had outlived its usefulness after a century and more, they simply coopted the existing system of local private banks, which proceeded to monetize much of the state's short- and medium-term obligations. It was logical, therefore, that the strength or weakness of the Rialto banks in the marketplace and in their role as "pillars of the state" would be carefully observed by foreign powers, preoccupied with the question whether to form military alliances with Venice or to wage war against it.

A full-fledged public deposit and transfer bank was instituted only in the late sixteenth century, when it, too, gained renown and became a model. But the feasibility or advisability of such an institution was discussed several times centuries earlier, given the perennial weakness of deposit banks in the face of eventual runs by depositors. Venetian lawmakers seem never to have entertained the possibility of having the Grain Office open current accounts, which would have been a logical development, and those debates always ended with acceptance of the status quo, leaving the marketplace in the hands of private entrepreneurs in the banking sector.

Finally, the funded debt, based on forced loans paid by the wealthiest portion of the population on the basis of an assessment of ability to pay, was similar to that of other major Italian city-republics. While the first known recourse to deficit financing (a loan of 1164, underwritten by 12 wealthy citizens and validated by the signatures of 112 leading nobles and citizens) and the first forced loan (1177) place Venice in the forefront of this development, the formal act of funding the debt, and making it for all practical purposes a perpetual debt (in 1262), vied with the funding of the first Genoese issue of government obligations for chronological primacy and antedated that of Florence by nearly a century. When Florence, moreover, set about to reform its system of assessment in the 1420s, its decision makers looked to Venice for ideas, some even for a model. The important point for the Venetian economy and society, as for those of other Italian communes, as Luzzatto insisted, was the substitution of direct taxation with a forced investment of capital at a moderate rate of interest, a return made possible by indirect taxation. When a large portion of marketable government obligations passed into the hands of institutions and persons who were not subject to making forced loans, and heavy impositions constrained lenders to sell at a loss, then lawmakers became less preoccupied with supporting the system in its pristine state. It may well be that Venice in the mid-Quattrocento was less faithful in paying interest and more burdensome on forced lenders than Genoa or Florence. At the same time, the yields to capital offered by the open market in Venetian government obligations were considered attractive by foreign as well as local investors for a long time after nominal interest rates declined and interest claims were increasingly paid in arrears.

Distinctions among the major types of credit institutions that sustained the Venetian money market and made it, in organization and sheer volume, one of the foremost of Europe have been utilized here in order to organize the material and clarify legal and institutional aspects. The distinctions were real enough. We have seen, for example, that merchant bankers and pawnbrokers needed the services of the Rialto banks in transferring assets from one account to another. The fact that Florentine companies, expert lenders in the exchange market, often lost heavily when Rialto banks failed (as in 1400 and 1405) means that they had left assets with those banks, counting on the services of "giro" which the latter provided and which the Florentine companies in Venice did not provide; similarly, the Florentines explained to their correspondents that when the local banks were closed, because of snow or a local feast day, they could not conclude foreign exchange operations. Jewish pawnbrokers, albeit resident in the city only for a short time during the period here considered, also had recourse to the Rialto banks when they lent money, assigned by transfer, on personal surety rather than on collateral. Most independent and distinct was the administration of the public debt, even though government obligations could be used as money and portfolios might be administered by deposit banks. It should be recalled, however, that the public debt did not constitute a bank, despite the penchant of historians of the nineteenth century to call it the Bank of Venice.

These distinctions, at the same time, should not be exaggerated, for competencies of each type of figure or institution were entangled with those of another. Strict specialization did not and could not exist; the medieval urban *homo oeconomicus* was first and foremost a merchant, and that was the case with most of the operators we have encountered in the money market. A certain overlapping of roles, therefore, was normal. Deposit bankers on the Rialto, while they were not habitual or "manifest" lenders on collateral, might insist on having concrete security for their loans; for example, the banker Francesco Balbi readily granted overdrafts to Andrea Barbarigo, but the latter then often shipped wares in Balbi's name, as Frederic Lane observed. One could find objects of worked silver, especially belt buckles, and gems on the counters of moneychangers, who thus functioned also as retailers and—more often than was discovered by the police—as fences for stolen valuables. The inventories of transfer bankers, when they failed, always listed gems and jewelry, accumulated as unredeemed collateral taken for occasional loans to important, usually foreign, borrowers.[2] Merchant bankers and other lenders who extended credit on rechange contracts sometimes hedged their risks by asking the borrower to provide collateral or personal guarantees. The state itself insisted on collateral for the extraordinary loans it made, as an instrument of diplomacy—such as that to the rulers of Byzantium in 1343, in the midst of a general banking crisis. According to the anonymous French tract of around 1500, the Treasury guarded by the Procurators of San Marco contained unredeemed rings worth half a million ducats, taken in the past as collateral by the Signoria for just such loans made to foreign lords.[3]

These are instances of a confusion, or fusion, of roles and functions that were quotidian. I have reserved for these concluding remarks a more exceptional case that eludes categorical distinctions, as it eluded more traditional sources for the study of credit; it is suggestive because many kinds of operators in the money market and several Venetian public institutions became involved. During the first barons' conspiracy in southern Italy, in the years 1459–61, both sides sought financial aid from the government of Venice;[4] when their entreaties proved vain, belligerents were forced to seek credit on the marketplace. Soon after he had become king of Naples and Sicily in 1458, Ferdinando I (or Ferrante "il bastardo") sent an envoy with a valuable jeweled collar to Venice to deal with certain Jews, headquartered in Mestre, for a loan of 30,000 ducats. Piero Guidiccioni, wealthy merchant and silk entrepreneur, got wind of the mission and saw a chance to make

[2]"News on the Rialto," 8, and "Venetian Bankers," 73–75.

[3]*Traictie,* cap. 18.

[4]For requests by Ferrante and the prince of Taranto, see ASV, SSec, reg. 21, fols. 3r–v, 7r–v, 8v, 17, 37r–v; the last indicated, of 10 March 1461, is a request by the prince of Taranto for a loan of 30,000 ducats, turned down with the excuse of the impending Turkish threat.

money. He formed a "societas" with a member of another family of Lucchese origin, Francesco Pardini, and with the eminent Rialto banker Giovanni di Vettor Soranzo, in which the former two would supply one-quarter each of the value of the loan, the latter one-half. It was the banker who presented himself to the ambassador, acting as though he were a mere intermediary, and concluded a patently illicit contract: Pardini would buy the collar, with a repurchase option, and pay 5,000 ducats in Venice, 5,000 in Florence, 10,000 in Naples, and he would supply 10,000 ducats' worth of silks and woolens in Siena. After sixteen months, the king could repurchase the collar, for 35,000 ducats, or 12.8 percent annual interest on the face of it. The option of eventual extensions prior to repurchase of the collateral was foreseen, on the basis of rechange operations ("stando super cambiis et interesse"). A fictitious contract was drawn up by the notary of the Sicilian ambassador. Probably the king or his envoy reacted when the goods delivered in Siena were actually sold and discovered to be worth only half the promised sum of 10,000 ducats, a fraud that greatly increased the cost of the loan. In any case, the operation came to the attention of the authorities. The Avogadori, the state's attorneys, arrogated the case to themselves, judged the contract illicit and usurious, and brought the matter before the Senate itself, saying that "the Venetian republic had always abhorred such usurious contracts" and that the partners had acted "in disregard of God, the Signoria and charity in making the illicit and usurious contract with the envoy of the king." The three were sentenced to heavy fines: Giovanni Soranzo "a banco" 800 ducats, Piero Guidiccioni 500, Francesco Pardini 300. The collar was deposited in the Procuratia di San Marco for six months, where it could be redeemed for such a figure as would be set by the Avogadori.[5]

Here we have nearly all the elements of the Venetian credit market, from a point of view that generally remained hidden: two important non-noble merchants of immigrant stock and a nobleman who was the leading deposit banker on the Rialto — Christians secretly in competition with the licensed Jewish lenders headquartered in Mestre; remittances by bill of exchange and the prospect of defining interest by rechange; partial payment in textiles in Siena, distant from both parties; a valuable pawn and, upon discovery of the illicit contract, its precautionary deposit in the hands of the Procurators of San Marco; finally, the intervention of the state's attorneys to preserve its honor and the "officium caritatis" in what had probably become some kind of diplomatic incident, otherwise information about the loan, made via a fictitious purchase-and-resale contract, might not have surfaced at all.

No party to the affair seems to have suffered any further conse-

---

[5]ASV, AC, reg. 3651, fol. 87v (23 June 1460). The vote showed many senators to be unconvinced: the sentence passed 94 to 16, with 60 absentions.

quences. Guidiccioni was a financial wheeler-dealer before, and he would continue to be one. Giovanni Soranzo, the Rialto banker, continued to operate as though nothing had happened. Only Pardini, the second silk merchant, seems later to have encountered economic difficulties, but they were probably extraneous to the affair.[6] And King Ferrante, in dire need of credit, instructed his envoy to return to Venice in the following year with even more jewels (including a thousand pearls and a jeweled cross) in search of even more credit, this time directly with Christian lenders, including three members of the Loredan family and one of the Garzoni, partner in the Bernardo-Garzoni bank. This was the same bank chosen by the Signoria in 1461 as depositary for all the king's jewels for a period of two months, during which time Ferrante had the option of redeeming them; thereafter, they could be freely sold by the owner of record. Despite having been defrauded earlier on the Rialto, the king was back for more, and this time the state intervened as mediator from the start.[7]

The practice of usury, as this case shows, was a matter of intense interest in certain conjunctures; concern about it in Venice would merit further study. Manifest usury, the public extension of consumption credit on collateral, was the financial sector most controllable by the state. Venetian authorities handled the problem very simply, by banning manifest usury from the city during most of the period covered by this study. Between 1254 and 1508, pawnbanks were permitted in the city only for fifteen years, 1382–97, when they were run by Jews. Otherwise, they were kept at bay, in Mestre and other nearby mainland cities, where they were run first by Christians labeled "Tuscans," often but not always Florentines, and then, from the mid-fourteenth century on, by Jews. Venetians boasted from an early date that Venice and Venetians were more free of the taint of usury than other peoples. In the late fifteenth century, Marin Sanudo noted with undisguised satisfaction that Jews were banned from lending in Venice and were relegated to Mestre: "Et nota una eccellente cosa di Venetia che niun Zudìo, sotto grandissime pene, puol tegnir banco d'imprestar qui a Venetia danari, ma ben a Mestre." By that time, charitable pawnbanks, the Monti di Pietà, were already springing up in cities of the Venetian Terraferma, with the blessing of the Venetian Senate. But the same authorities outlawed the Christian institution in Venice itself and, as Brian Pullan has shown, preferred licensing Jewish pawnbroking in the city, after Jewish lenders had taken refuge there in 1508, at the outset of the War of the League of Cam-

---

[6]ASV, CN, reg. 10, fols. 125v, 136v (1465), regarding the failure of Antonio Pardini, which involved "alii de Pardinis."

[7]Ibid., fol. 46 (16 November 1461). Involved were, besides the bank, Fantino, Giovanni, and Matteo di Giovanni Loredan and a certain Ludovico di Giovanni, probably a Florentine.

brai. It was judged easier to control foreign infidels, lacking rights of citizenship, than a large local entity established under private initiative, however pious.[8]

The state could obviously not control hidden usury, although it had a lay court, the Piovego, which, alongside its jurisdiction over encroachments in the public domain, heard accusations of usury and investigated suspicious contracts, at the Rialto, three afternoons per week, as needed. Its archive has not survived, but its sentences and fines were often commuted on appeal, or, when the judges were working on an important case, jurisdiction was arrogated by the Avogadori. Such was the case, discussed above (Chap. 7), of the extensive lending operation of the Frescobaldi, the Florentine merchant bankers who used the cover of Jews in Mestre in the late 1490s — another situation in which institutional distinctions were very blurred.[9] Gouging usury and extortion generally escaped the control of magistrates and thus remain hidden, along with their social consequences.

It is difficult to assess the mentality of the men who operated in the money and financial markets of Venice or that of their clients — male and female; concerns that might readily be expressed in the private forum, confession, were only rarely aired publicly before a notary or magistrate. The pricked consciences of a few foreigners and two Venetian women regarding interest received from the Commune for deposits made in Grain Office, however, found written expression and could therefore be treated above in the context of that institution. In a contrasting case, two Franciscan confessors — one of them an inquisitor — and civil trustees were perfectly content to use interest, received from a similar deposit, to save the depositor's soul by making restitution of those ill-gotten gains that his victims could prove. The exchange of coins by campsores was universally accepted as a legitimate and fundamental service in the marketplace, but moneychanger-bankers also lent money. The legality of bank loans and

---

[8]"Terra nostra et cives nostri sunt inter omnes alios huius mundi ab usurae maculis mondiores." A. S. Minotto, *Documenta ad Bellunum, Cenetam, Feltria, Tarvisium spectantia* (Venice, 1871), sec. 1, p. 84 (the context was a suit heard about 1301, concerning a penalty formula then commonly used in notarial loan contracts). Also about 1301 a memorandum on usury applied practical standards to the analysis of commercial loans; see Mueller, *Procuratori di San Marco,* app. 1. See also Sanudo, *De origine,* 136; *Traictie,* cap. 34; Pullan, *Rich and Poor,* pt. 3; and Mueller, "Jewish Moneylenders of Late Trecento Venice."

[9]Sanudo wrote in 1515 that the court of the Piovego was located in the ducal palace but that the judges held court in a shop ("volta") at the Rialto on the three afternoons "dove aldeno le querele presentatoli contra li merchati usurarij et feneraticij, sopra le qual examinano testemonij, et *formato processu,* fa citar il reo ala difesa, e tuor' le sue justification, poi sententiano come li par, taiando li merchadi et condanando l'usuraro *juxta* la forma dile leze." *De origine,* 258. Jurisdiction over loans by Jews was in the hands of the Sopraconsoli, "zudexi di deferentie si ha con li Hebrei banchieri sopra li pegni." Ibid., 266. The *Traictie,* which dates from before 1508, locates the Jews in Mestre (cap. 34); as regards usurious contracts, it states (cap. 35) that serious cases were heard by the Avogadori rather than by the Piovego — very likely a direct reference to what happened in the Frescobaldi case.

overdrafts seems not to have been debated by jurists and theologians. I have found only one Rialto banker, of secondary importance, who in the mid-Trecento left money for reparation of ill-gotten gain ("pro male ablatis"); but his brother, active at the same bank, expressed no similar preoccupation when he made his testament.[10]

The acceptability — or not — of receiving interest on loans via re-change and on government credits was treated above on the basis only of theoretical works by jurists and theologians. The Trevisan jurist who de-cided for the legitimacy of such investments said that his investigation of the matter had been stimulated by Venetian "friends," without offering any indication that might lead to their identification. One could imagine that Guglielmo Querini, whom we have encountered, not only when he paid forced loans but also when he guaranteed lenders on rechange operations, was one of them. In his testament of 1457, shortly after both tracts had been terminated, he left 25 ducats, 14 grossi a oro to Giovanni Panciatichi, a Florentine merchant banker who operated in Venice, in the name of his — long since — deceased brother Bartolomeo Querini and "for [the latter's] conscience." The deal ("merchado") very likely involved a loan on rechange on which Bartolomeo had earned a comparable, very specific sum. Gugli-elmo himself left open the possibility that someone might make a claim on his estate for similar earnings; sums needed for eventual restitution (the term was deliberately avoided) were to be deducted from other legacies.[11] Venetian courts were probably anxious to evade the issue, which was liable to unsettle the money market. The Avogadori, for example, overturned on appeal a condemnation for usury passed down by the Piovego court con-cerning a draft on Bruges from the year 1395; a witness had testified that the bill had been partially secured — by a deposit in the Grain Office — a practice that would be branded as illegal by the law of 1411. All the parties, accuser, accused, and witnesses, were foreigners from Lombardy.[12]

Again, only a foreigner, Giangaleazzo Visconti, seems to have been much concerned about the legality of buying Venetian government obliga-tions on the open market, even for a charitable cause. The Franciscan moral-ist Centueri, as we have seen, lauded the decision of the Conte di Virtù not to invest but ignored altogether the investments made by the count's own wife and courtiers in Venetian government credits, about which he surely was well informed. In support of his condemnation of purchases on the open market and of receiving interest on government obligations, he men-

---

[10]Mueller, "Sull'establishment bancario veneziano," 54 (for the banker Adoldo) and passim for bankers' concern for their security in the afterlife.

[11]"Item lasso a Zuan Panzatichi da Fiorenza per uno merchado el dito mio fradelo feze con lui per so consienzia ducati 25, denari 14 di grossi. Ma se io havesse fato queste chosse hover parte in mia vita, sia desfalchado dei diti legati." ASV, PSM, Citra, b. 271.

[12]ASV, AC, reg. 3645, fol. 24 (1 August 1401). The draft had been paid at the bank of Gabriele Soranzo.

tioned the concern supposedly expressed by a prominent Venetian noble-man, Zaccaria Contarini, who had been one of Petrarch's erstwhile Vene-tian "friends." Contarini's testament has not turned up, and it is doubtful that corroboration on this score will be forthcoming. Another member of the same group of Aristotelian intellectuals condemned by Petrarch, how-ever, admitted having pangs of conscience. Tommaso Talenti, an immigrant from Florence, wealthy merchant and entrepreneur, and founder of the school of logic and philosophy situated at the Rialto, had often lent money, sometimes on the basis of contracts that pegged earnings to the market in government obligations. In his testament of 1397, he ordered the restitu-tion of all certain claims of extortion, "de iure vel de bona conscientia," and left a total of 620 ducats to be distributed to charities in Venice, Bologna, and Ferrara for uncertain ill-gotten gain ("pro male ablatis incertis"). That is a large sum of money, especially when compared with the bequest of his immigrant father, Giovanni di Filippo Talenti, who had left a mere 20 ducats, similarly "pro male ablatis incertis."[13] But once again, it was for-eigners and immigrants, more than native Venetians, who tended to give similar expression to their qualms of conscience.

The single aspect that most characterizes Venetian history and histo-riography is the dominant role of the state in the life of the city and the symbiosis between public and private sectors of the economy, between public and private interests. Frederic Lane underscored the use made by the ruling class of the state and its organs for increasing their own profits. To that end, a primary concern of civil authorities was to create an atmosphere of competitive opportunity on the Rialto conducive to investment, that is, to the influx of money and goods, their turnover in Venice, and their eventual outflow. The exportation of coin and bullion to the Levant was helped rather than hindered. If there was protectionism, it lay in defending the monopoly of Venetian citizens in the Levant trade; trade to the West was nearly unrestricted. In this book, we have often seen how the state intervened in financial institutions and practices in order to increase their security and thus the trust of citizens and foreigners alike, potential inves-tors in one form or another. This might be considered a preoccupation of any civil government; perhaps Venice was merely more insistent in apply-ing controls and regulations.

The deposit and transfer banks of the Rialto — similar to institutions that existed in Genoa, Barcelona, Bruges, and elsewhere — quickly became famous across Europe for the centrality of their position in the whole sys-tem of payments. The creation and maintenance of trust in this financial

---

[13]ASV, PSM, Citra, b. 141, commis. Tommaso Talenti; the testament of his father is in CIN, b. 144, fasc. 5, no. 11 (13 March 1362). Tommaso's testament was published, with some errors, by Nardi, "Letteratura e cultura," 130–35.

institution involved, first of all, public licensing and insistence on sureties, a kind of insurance for depositors ("pro maiore cautione omnium"). These were normal steps taken by local authorities anywhere. While the law passed in 1318 requiring bankers to provide sureties was of limited efficacy for a century or more, the Senate stepped in forcefully beginning in 1455, by insisting on regular, triennial investigation of the trustworthiness, first of the guarantors, later of the aspirant bankers themselves. The new law may indeed have contributed to increasing trust, for between 1455 and 1499 there was only one failure, without serious repercussions; thereafter, however, the rhythm of bankruptcies increased sharply. The Signoria itself occasionally stepped in as co-guarantor for a bank pressed by its depositors. Or, if it was already too late to save the bank, the state often named two Procurators of San Marco, persons of the very highest prestige in the structure of government, to be official receivers of the bankrupt institution. In the end, no system of bank surety could protect depositors from a banker's tendency to overextend himself or, for that matter, protect a banker from the nervousness of depositors, always ready to participate in a run. Other attempts to regulate banking, by placing limits on the level of bank investments or on the kinds of commodities in which banks could invest, must have proved difficult, if not impossible, to police.

Investments by foreigners, usually screened and voted upon, were facilitated and attracted both in the Grain Office and in the secondary market in government credits. Foreign demand sustained market prices of those credits, thus containing losses incurred by Venetian forced lenders who had to buy at par and were constrained to sell at market prices. In both structures, the authorities guaranteed the integrity of these portfolios — as long as their holders did not go over to the enemy. They did not hesitate to pay in cash the interest earned on obligations purchased in the secondary market simply because specie might leave Venice, adding to the revenues of foreign lords; at the same time, the availability of interest-bearing assets in Venice served as an incentive to investors to spend at least part of their earnings on the Rialto.

The capital necessary for trade, manufacture, and making war in a metropolis like Venice came largely from the local credit markets. On the degree of success of the markets and their organization in making capital available at the right time to the right people and institutions depended the well-being of the city and its economic life in general. The reputation of trustworthiness which the financial system developed, at home and abroad, was made possible by that constant collaboration of public and private, of regulation and economic freedom, which characterized Venetian institutions.

APPENDIX A

LOCAL DEPOSIT BANKERS AND PARTNERSHIPS

ABLE A.1 IS MADE UP of all persons identified in any kind of document as a campsor or bancherius or is called "dal banco" or "de la tola," as long as the document reflects an economic activity; in other words, if a campsor was sentenced for violent crime and no other documentation was found which could better define his activity, his name was not entered. There are 146 names of individuals, partnerships, and dynasties of bankers.

It is often not clear if the person so identified rented a bank from the Commune himself, or whether he was a subletter, partner, managing factor, or cashier. Some men might have been partners of — or worked for — others, although this does not emerge from the documents found. For the small operators, only one or two documents were found; that can be seen from the single year or restricted period indicated in column one. For others, a more accurate description was possible.

I have not investigated the social rank of each entry. When in doubt, I entered a question mark in the last column. The matter is of interest, since quite a few moneychangers, especially but not only at San Marco, were not noble even though they bore noble surnames. This is the case of the Zancani bank of the 1370s and of Marino Dandolo in 1415.

The sources from which this information was collected are so varied that it made no sense to try to mention them all for each entry. Especially rich in information were private account books, estate accounts maintained by the Procurators of San Marco, grazie, raspe (criminal sentences), and the deliberations of various legislative organs.

TABLE A.1

Chronological Listing of Moneychangers, Bankers, and
Bank Partnerships, 1225 to about 1550

Dates	Name or Style	Loc.	Cat.	Rank
1225	Marino Decazatus	R	M	C
1225	Zordanus	R	M	C
1225	Vidoto Sinolo	R	M	C
1285–1319?	Ca' Bollani (Andrea, Bartolomeo, Domenico, Tommaso, brothers)	R	B	N
1294	Bernardo (de) Bernardo	R	B	N
1300	Marco Trevisan	SM	B	C
1300	Nicolò Pizzamano	R	B	N?
1301	Bertuccio Diedo	R	B	?
1311	Giovanni Bondumiero	R	B	N
1319–38	Pantaleone, Bertucci, Bianco Capello	R	B	?
1324	Francesco Baffo	R	M	?
1324–39	Nicolò Lanzolo	R	B	C
1324–36	Andrea e Francesco Corner	R	B	N
1324	Bonaventura Rizzo	R	M	C
1325–30s?	Nicoletto Zuccuol	R	B	C
1325–29	Donato Bobizo "Galina"	R	B	C
1325–48	Caterino Ghezo	R	B	C
1326–31?	Nicoletto Sanino	R	M	C
1326–27	Nicolò Michiel (renter of tabula: Nicolò Diedo)	R	M	??
1326	Francesco "Rizzo" Contarini	R?	M	N
1329?–42	Marco Bobizo "Galina," grandson of Donato; revived 1357–66	R	B	C
1329–42	Giovanni qd. Marco Stornado	R	B	C
1330–31	Zonino Alberegno	R	B	N
1331–32, 1369	Zanino, Andrea Acotanto	SM	M	N
1331–47	Pietro Alberegno	R	B	N
1333–38	Marco (d'Antonio) Arian	R	B	C
1333–38	Mafeo e Giannino Gritti; a Marco Gritti, campsor, mentioned 1358	R	B	?
1334–36	Nicoletto De Lorenzo	SM	M	C
1335–41	Piero Serafini	R	B	C
1336–42	Marino Vendelino	R	B	N?
1337–60	Mafeo, Jacomello, Andriolo Gabriel, brothers (Jacomello banned from banking 1355, Andriolo in 1360)	R	B	N
1337–58	Nicoletto, Marco ("Bianco"), Guido, Pietro Michiel	R	B	N
1338–41	Marco Storlado	SM	M	?
1338?–1345	Ca' De Buora (six brothers)	SM	M	C
1339–55	Giacomo e Armellino Da Mosto	R	B	C
1340	Nicoletto Onorato	R	B	N?
1340	Marco Rosso	SM	M	C
1340–42	Filippo Marmora	R	B	N
1340	Donato Quintavalle	R	B	N
1340–48	Giovanni e Marino Baffo	R	B	?

TABLE A.I   (*Continued*)

Dates	Name or Style	Loc.	Cat.	Rank
1341–48–54	Stefano e Marco Trevisan (partner of Marino Baffo in 1354)	R	B	?
1343–63	Pietro De Mortisio	SM R	M	C
1344	Guernerio Volpe	R	M?	N?
1345–59	Andreolo e Alvise Sanador	R	B	C
1346–59	Francesco Spirito	SM	M	C
1348–56	Alessandro Agolanti e Donato Alemanni	R	B	C
1348	Giovanni Papaziza	SM?	M	N
1348?–55	Marino Baffo e Marco Trevisan	R	B	?
1349–59	Antonio e Filippo Maffei, bros.	R	B	C
1350–52	Pietro Pazo	R	M	C
1350–52	Donato Alemanni (then partner of Agolanti)	R	B	C
1350?–53?	Vettor Stornado	R?	M	?
1351–56	Matteo Spiati	SM	M	C
1351	Ughetto De Cavariis	R	M	C
1352–69	Giovanni Rizzo	R	M	C
1352–61	Alvise Viaro e Co.	R	B	N
1352	Francesco Teldi	R	M	C
1353	Marco Corner	R	B	N?
1354–76	Pietro qd. Marco Zancani (d. 1364) (partners: Donato dell'Agnella, Francesco de' Buoni) Jacomello Zancani and Brothers (Andriolo, Alvise "el Negro," Simone, "nevodi" of Pietro)	R	B	C
1354–63	Francesco "Rizzo" Contarini	SM	M	N
1355–56	Zanino, Marino Soranzo	R	B	C
1355–60	Francesco Iuda e Pietro Da Mosto	R	B	CN
1355–57	Jacopo Da Lisca	R	B	C
1356?–84	Marco qd. Andrea Stornado (sometimes also Storlado) (ennobled in 1381)	R	M	CN
1356–74	Gasparino Soranzo	R	B	N
1357–64	Jacomello and Pietro Zeno	SM	M	N
1358?–82	Zanino Amizo	R	M	N
1359	Andreolo Sainben	R	R	C
1359? –69	Franceschino Spirito	R?	M	C
1361	Bernardo d'Arsengo	R	B	C
1361	Bertolino Da Molin	R	M	N
1363–75 '82	Pietro, Bernardo, Alvise Emo	R	B	N
1364	Jacobello Falcone	R?	M	C
1367–1400	Pietro Benedetto	R	B	N
1368–71	Bartolomeo Micheli e Giovanni Bugni	R	B	CC
1369	Nicolò Zini	R	M	C
1371	Giovanni De Buora	R	M	C
1374–1455	Gabriele qd. Giovanni Soranzo, 1374–1410 Estate of Gabriele Soranzo, 1410–29 Cristoforo (di Gabriele) Soranzo e fratelli, 1429–1432 Banco da ca' Soranzo, 1432–38 Luca (di Cristoforo) Soranzo e fratelli, 1438–49	R	B	N

TABLE A.I   (*Continued*)

Dates	Name or Style	Loc.	Cat.	Rank
	Benetto (di Cristoforo) Soranzo e fratello, 1449–55			
	Continued by cousins: see 1455			
1374	Franceschino Signolo	R	M	N?
1377	Zanino Morosini	SM	M	?
1378–83	Bartolomeo Da Carixe (d'Acarisio)	R	B	C
1380–83	Pietro Barbafella	R	B	C
1386–90	Antonio qd. Francesco Contarini	R	B	N?
1389–1413	Guglielmo qd. Nicolò Condulmer	R	B	C
1390	Agostino Micaletto	R	M	C
1390–91	Cristoforo Zancani	SM	M	N
1390	Silvestro di Dante da Firenze	R	M	C
1391–97	Andriolo, Donato Grioni	SM	M	?
1391	Tomasino Zancaruolo	SM	M	N?
1391	Cristoforo Minio	SM	M	N?
1391	Pietro Contarini	SM	M	?
1392	Bernardo Foscari	SM	M	?
1393–1406	Bartolomeo Darmano	R	B	C
1394	Gerolamo Gaffaro	R	M	C
1397	Francesco Da Mosto	SM	M	?
1397–1424?	Gerolamo qd. Nicolò Morosini	R	M	N
1399–1410	Zan Corner e Antonio Miorati. Partner: Donato di Filippo Nati	R	B	NC
1399–1429	ser Roberto Priuli e fratelli, 1399–1402	R	B	N
	Commissaria di ser Roberto Priuli e fratelli, 1402–5			
	ser Andrea Priuli e fratelli, 1405–24			
	Commissaria di ser Andrea Priuli e fratelli, 1424–25			
	Commissaria di ser Andrea Priuli e ser Bartolomeo [Priuli], 1425–29			
	ser Leonardo e ser Jacomo Priuli, 1425–28			
	Commissaria di ser Leonardo Priuli e ser Jacomo Priuli, 1428			
	ser Jacomo Priuli e ser Zan Orsini e compagni, 1428–29.			NC
1400	Marco Signolo	R	M	N?
1400–1405	Estate of Pietro Benedetto e Marco Condolmer e compagni	R	B	NC
1403	Marco (d'Antonio di Nicolò) Arian	R	M	C
1409–24	Bernardo qd. Pietro Giustinian	R	B	N
1410–24	Nicolò Cocco e Antonio Miorati	R	B	NC
1412–16	Giovanni qd. Filippo Della Torre	R	M	C
1415	Marino Dandolo	SM	M	C
1415–19	Pietro qd. Andrea Venier	R	B	N?
1417–20	Pietro qd. Bernardo d'Arsengo	R	M	C
1420	Francesco di Bonaventura	SM	M	C
1421	Antonio di Paolo Salvazzo (?)	SM	M	C
1425–28	Zan Orsini e fradelli, banchieri (Giovanni, Francesco, Bernardo, Agostino)	R	B	C

TABLE A.1   (*Continued*)

Dates	Name or Style	Loc.	Cat.	Rank
1430–45	Francesco Balbi e fratelli	R	B	N
1430–68	Nicolò (Di) Bernardo e fratelli e ser Matio e ser Zan Garzoni e Co.	R	B	NC
	Nicolò Di Bernardo el Procurator e compagni (the Garzoni), 1465–68.			
	Continues under the style Garzoni; see 1468.			
1441–55–76?	Melchiore De Colti e nipoti	R	B	C
1442–68	Bernardo Ziera and Partners (until 1454)	R	B	C
	Agostino qd. Bernardo e Giacomo Corner (d. by 1464)			N
1448	Jacopo e Marco Maraschino, brothers	SM?	M	C
1450	Antonio Zane	R	M	C
1450?–54	Nicolò Orsini e compagni. Partners Antonio e Cosmo de Tomasi	R	M	C
1452–60	Stefano Marino	R	M	C
1453–54	Giacomo qd. Donato Corner	R	B	N
1455	Piero Dalle Pole	SM	M	C
1455–91	Giovanni di Vettor Soranzo, 1455–68	R	B	N
	Pietro qd. Giovanni Soranzo e fratelli (Francesco, Vettor), 1468–91			
1460–61	Alvise Venier "a banco"	R	B	?
1460–73	Piero Guerrucci (Veruzzi)	R	B	C
1460–66	Melchiore "claudus" qd. Nascimbene	R?	M	C
1467–81	Andrea Barbarigo "Brocca," with Vettor and Giovanbattista Contarini	R	B	N
1468	Nicolò Alemanni	R	M	C
1468–99	Garzoni (extended family); Bernardo family seems to be silent partner.	R	B	CN
1471	Nicolò Rainaldi di Treviso	SM	M	C
1475–1500	Francesco e Giovanni qd. Almorò Pisani	R	B	N
1476–84	Francesco Fedele	R	B	C
1478	Antonio Fantino	R	M	C
1480–85 ca.	Tomà Lippomani e Andrea Capello e fratelli (qd. Vettor)	R	B	NN
1485 ca. –99	Tomà Lippomani e fioli	R	B	N
1490?–1508	Matteo Agostini	R	B	C
1491	Giovanni Trevisan	B	M	?
1494–97–99	Alvise Nichetta	R	M	C
1499	Andrea e Gerolamo Rizzo	R	M	C
1504–28	Alvise qd. Giovanni Pisani	R	B	N
1507–30?	Antonio e Silvan Capello (qd. Leonardo) e Luca Vendramin	R	B	NN
1508–13	Gerolamo di Lorenzo qd. Piero Priuli	R	B	N
1521–24, 1529–46?	Mafeo and Benetto Di Bernardo	R	B	N
1522–51	Antonio Priuli el Procurator	R	B	N
1523–26	Andrea e Piero Da Molin	R	B	N
1523–26	Andrea Arimondo	R	B	N

Note: Abbreviations used in this table: Loc. = Location: R = Rialto, SM = San Marco; Cat. = Category: B = banker, M = moneychanger; Rank: C = commoner, N = nobleman.

APPENDIX B

FAILURES OF LOCAL DEPOSIT BANKS

ABLE B.1 SPECIFIES NAMES, dates, and known causal factors of the bank failures discussed above, in Chapters 4–6.

TABLE B.1

Failures of Deposit Banks in Venice, 1327–1500

Date	Name	Causal and Related Factors
1327, ca. Feb.	Lorenzo di Nicolò Diedo; cashier: Nicolò Michiel	Diedo sublet bank to Michiel, campsor, who failed within 4 months
1331	Zonino Alberegno	
1340 (before July)	Donato Quintavalle	Scaliger war; expulsion of Florentine merchant bankers, 1340
1341 (before Nov.)	Piero Serafini	Beginning of failures in Florence; famine; speculation in silver
1342	Marco Bobizo Marco and Guido Michiel Filippo Marmora e frat. Marino Vendelino Giovanni Stornado	Same as 1341, and instability of bimetallic ratios; divergence between official and market rates of ducat
1355, Oct.	Marino Baffo e Marco Trevisan	Third maritime war against Genoa; debates on usury and pawnbroking
1359, July?	Francesco Spirito Andreolo Sanador Andreolo Sainben	Famine followed by glut of wheat; speculation in silver; law against fraudulent bankruptcy in general
Nov.–Dec.	Francesco Iuda	
1361, Aug.	Alvise Viaro	Public bank proposed; coin clippers sentenced
1363 (Jan.?)	Marco Gritti	Speculation in silver?
1364	Pietro Mortisse	Death and liquidation of bank
1369	Franceschino Spirito	
1375, 21 Apr., June	Jacomello Zancani e frat. Pietro e Bernardo Emo	In payments difficulties already previous August; generalized famine; war with Austria; public bank debated; speculation in silver. Failures also in Florence.
1390, Jan.	Antonio Contarini	Little turnover on the Rialto the whole year. Speculation in "Viennese" pennies.
Dec.–Jan. 1391	Cristoforo Zancani (S. Marco)	
1400, 30 Oct.	Piero Benedetto	Death from plague. 1399 failure of Soldani bank in Barcelona
1405, 12 Jan.	Benedetto Estate Bank	Had guaranteed bills of Foscherari bank, which failed in Bologna and Venice
1415, Oct.	Marino Dandolo, campsor at S. Marco	(Non noble)
1424 (?)	Bernardo Giustinian	Voluntary liquidation
1424, 1 Sept.	Nicolò Cocco e Antonio Miorati	Miorati died of plague 31 Aug.; Cocco liquidates; Miorati estate declared bankruptcy on 12 March 1425

TABLE B.1 (*Continued*)

Date	Name	Causal and Related Factors
1424, late Aug.	Andrea Priuli e fratelli	Liquidated upon death of Andrea; successor bank founded
1425, 14 May	A. Priuli Estate Bank	Quarreling among brothers probably produced a run; forced liquidation
1429, 12 Oct.	Jacomo Priuli e Giovanni Orsini e Co.	Run; speculation in silver; pressure on Venetian currency leads to
26 Oct.	A. Priuli Estate e Bartolomeo Priuli	monetary reform
1445, Aug.	Francesco Balbi e frat.	Papal legate withdrew cash on remittances for crusade, forcing bank to close
1450	Antonio Zane	Accused of counterfeiting; forced to liquidate
1453, 10–11 Oct.	Benetto Soranzo e frat.	Swindle and flight of cashier; fall of Constantinople; rise of gold; general bullion famine; ducat to 120s
1455, 1 Oct.	Benetto Soranzo successor bank	Flight by banker and family; tight money; ducat to 124s
1468, Dec.	Agostino di Bernardo Ziera	Sentenced for accounting fraud; court-imposed liquidation
1473, 21 Oct.	Piero Guerrucci	Survived a run in May 1472 monetary crisis; cashier accused of clipping. Claimed loans to state forced him to liquidate.
1481–82?	Andrea Barbarigo "Brocca"	Voluntary liquidation
1491, 21 Apr.	Piero e Vettor Soranzo	Voluntary liquidation; division of the fraterna
1497, 2 Aug.	Alvise Nichetta, moneychanger	
1499, 1 Feb.	(Bernardo) e Garzoni	Last run began Monday 28 January;
2 Feb.?	Andrea Rizzo e fratello	tight money, speculation in silver;
15 May	Gerolamo Lippomano	chains of indebtedness
17 May	Alvise Nichetta (no. 2)	
1500, 16 Mar.	Andrea Garzoni (no. 2)	Six weeks after the reopening.
23 Mar.	Alvise Pisani	Announces voluntary liquidation (reopens in 1504).

FOREIGN EXCHANGE IN VENICE DURING THE DATINI YEARS, 1383–1410

i. INTRODUCTION

AS HAS BEEN SEEN ABOVE, exchange rates reacted to demand for specie as well as to demand for credit; and demand was largely foreseeable, according to the rhythm of the activity of the port, as the authors of merchant manuals noted and as is reflected in the commercial correspondence. A detailed year-by-year chronicle of the money market, based on the practically weekly observations of the cambisti operating in Venice, would be useful to underscore those aspects that deviated from the usual seasonal fluctuations (for examples, see above, Chap. 8). At the same time, such a chronicle would be repetitive and tedious. Deviations from the norm, that is, unusual peaks and troughs, can be identified on the graphs in this appendix as well as those in Chapter 8. This appendix is dedicated, therefore, simply to the presentation of the sources of the data and of graphs that register the pulse of the market.

The source of the data is the correspondence preserved in the archive of Francesco di Marco Datini. Out of a total of about 150,000 letters extant, some 7,000 were written in Venice by various agents and addressed to branches and agencies in the whole Datini network. The earliest series is that directed to Pisa: some 900 letters, 1383–1402 (buste 548–550); the most important series consists of letters directed to Florence (some 2,100), which begin in 1386, become rare in 1405, and stop altogether in 1407 (buste 709–

715); the correspondence with Barcelona (some 1,400 letters) begins in 1395 and continues until February 1411, that is, even after Francesco di Marco Datini's death in 1410 (buste 926–929). In gathering data, I perused the first two series completely and the third, which provides particularly complete listings of exchange rates in Venice, only beginning in July 1405. About 400 letters written by Venetians are extant, most of them to Majorca, Barcelona, and Valencia; especially concerned with purchases of raw wool (any study of the wool industry in Venice might well begin here, in identifying interested parties), these letters are surprisingly uninformative on matters of foreign exchange and even of commodity prices. In fact, Venetians preferred working through Florentine commission agents represented in Venice rather than having to deal directly with agents abroad.[1]

I culled quotations or exchanges for 1,229 observation dates, 1383–1411. The rates for Florence are continuous, those of ten other major European banking places much less so. The observations total 7,326 for the twenty-seven-year period. For the frequencies, see below, tables C.2 and C.3.

In order not to burden the apparatus further, the rates themselves will not be printed here. They will be on deposit at the Rutgers Medieval and Early Modern Data Bank, Department of History and the University Library, Rutgers University, New Brunswick, New Jersey 08903), where they will be available on diskette. Here they are presented solely in graphic form. Actual rates quoting Florence are published in Spufford, *Handbook,* 89–91, from my data base but with his criterion of selection (namely, the first business day of each month); those quoting Pisa are mentioned by the same author (xlviii). The rates have been reduced to graphs (see below, graphs C.4–C.8) depicting monthly averages; plots of raw data were too unwieldy for publication. While transactions were not made on average prices, neither should "market rates" quoted in commercial letters be fetishized: "contractual leverage" was sometimes a factor, so that in practice a client with a better credit rating than his competitor might receive a slightly more advantageous rate on a given day or time of day, for opening, midday, and closing quotations often differed in active markets like Venice.

Paired Cities

The relationship between the fluctuation of exchange rates and the availability of specie is particularly clear when one examines the banking places that were situated in geographic proximity. These paired cities, no more than one or two days' postal time apart, are identified in the merchant manual of Giovanni da Uzzano (ca. 1420): Venice-Bologna, Florence-Pisa, Avignon-Montpellier, Barcelona-Valencia, Bruges-Paris.[2] News of a sharp

---

[1]Exact figures will be available at the conclusion of the inventory by Bruno Dini and Elena Cecchi (see above, Chap. 7, n. 32).

[2]*Pratica della mercatura,* 154.

rise in foreign exchange rates in one city arrived quickly in the other, where the operators immediately responded by sending off specie in order to profit from the rise. Arrival of the specie had the effect of lowering rates, so that in normal equilibrium the rates of the two cities were very close and moved in parallel fashion. This situation is corroborated by the market reports and the rates actually quoted.

ii. THE MANNER IN WHICH EXCHANGE RATES WERE RECORDED

By Percentage, Above, At, or Below Par

PISA, LUCCA, BOLOGNA, ROME

The simplest fashion was the relationship of gold coin to gold coin, on the contemporary assumption that one gold ducat (of Venice, of Rome) equaled in value one gold florin (of Florence, of Pisa) wherever it circulated; thus, par was one to one; when ducats were rated above par, the quotation in Venice was given as a percentage "meglio questi"; when they were below par, they were quoted as a percentage "peggio questi." This manner of quoting rates in Venice was used for the markets of Pisa, Lucca, Bologna, and Rome.[3]

Actual bills are extant both to and from Pisa, which can serve as examples. On 1 October 1393 Zanobi Gaddi in Venice drew a bill for 20 lire di grossi, payable to Lapo di Messer Lapo in Pisa as 205 gold florins, plus 6s 8d a oro, "at the rate of 2⅔ percent, ducats higher (meglio questi)." An extant Pisan draft on Venice dated 20 March 1396 confirms that the exchange was between gold florins and gold ducats but shows that in this case ducats were lower: the Pisan branch ordered Gaddi to pay Guaspar della Vaiana e Co. in Venice 414 ducats "for 400 gold florins received here from Giovanni Canpolini e Co."; the Pisan florin, that is, was rated 3.5 percent higher than the ducat (at the same time, in Venice, the Pisan florin was rated at ⅔ of 1 percent).[4]

For Pisa, Lucca, and Bologna, all of whose gold currency was largely Florentine, the rates in Venice were generally "meglio questi"; an increase meant an increase in exchange and in interest. As regards Bologna, "paired" with Venice, the rates remained low and ranged generally between 1 and at most 4 percent above par. For Rome, the rates were generally quoted "peggio questi"; thus a rate of 2 percent would mean that for 100 ducats paid out

---

[3]It should be noted that Raymond de Roover discovered the manner of quoting rates by percentage of par only very late; see his "Renseignements complémentaires sur le marché monétaire à Bruges au XIVᵉ et au XVᵉ siècle," *Handelingen van het Genootschap "Société d'Emulation" te Brugge* 109 (1972): 55.

[4]ADP, 1143, two drafts on Pisa; 1142 for the draft on Venice; for the corresponding letters to Pisa, see 549; for those to Florence, see 710–11.

in Venice the remitter had 98 ducats "da camera" in Rome. In the Datini circuit, direct exchange dealings with Rome from Venice were rare; such business was probably handled by the various Alberti and Medici branches.

Pisa's role as a banking place or exchange market, an important role, as seen from the Venice correspondence, was ended when Pisa was subjugated by Florence in October 1406. It was quoted from Venice regularly until August 1405, when it was placed under siege. The last time it was quoted (at 4 percent) was 12 August; on the 22d and then on 7 December 1406, as a tacit comment on the conquest, Pisa was recorded as "H," meaning no business, or no business possible. Pisa seems, however, to return to the status of a banking place of some kind when its rates are again quoted in Venice beginning in August 1409.[5] And one or more of the remittances sent by the agents of Paolo Guinigi of Lucca for the purchase of Venetian government credits between 1412 and 1414 were sent from Pisa (see above, Chap. 14).

Lucca was quoted quite regularly, from 1399 until 1410. Its actual role as a banking place remains questionable, however, if one considers that Paolo Guinigi's agents, in the case just mentioned, never chose to remit directly from Lucca; instead, they shipped gold florins from Lucca to Florence, and sometimes from there to Pisa, from where the assets were then remitted by bill of exchange to Venice.[6]

The exchange rates in Venice on Pisa, Bologna, and Lucca are depicted in graph C.4.

MILAN AND GENOA

Much more complex were the rates quoted by percentage but between a gold-based money of account (Venice) and a silver-based one (Milan and Genoa). As long as a fixed monetary standard or a nearly stable bimetallic system was in place, the rates quoted varied *grosso modo* from 1 to 3 percent "Venice higher" [meglio questi], just like the other cities that used percentages expressing a gold-to-gold parity. When extensive debasement of silver ended the stability of the domestic exchange rate in Milan, the foreign exchange rates began to soar in somewhat parallel fashion, thus clearly showing that they were not based on a gold parity at all (see graph C.5).

Here the discussion of specific data is limited to Milan, where the major debasement and then a "monetary earthquake" took place, under the reign of Giangaleazzo Visconti. For Milan, furthermore, we can present the quotations in that market on Venice for the crucial years (1394–1402); those

---

[5]Ibid., 929, Paoluccio to Barcelona (12 August); 715, Paoluccio to Florence (22 August); 929, Commissaria Gaddi to Barcelona (7 December 1406). For the period 1409–10, see 930, letters from Venice to Barcelona.

[6]De Roover, *Medici Bank,* 237, makes the same point without indicating a date, although the passage seems to be in the context of 1460.

rates, as is clear from graph C.5, were generally some two points below rates in Venice. High rates denote low demand, low rates high demand.[7]

To buy a bill in Venice on Milan meant paying a ducat in Venice in order to receive a Milanese ducat at usance (about fifteen days). Although the rate was quoted as a simple percentage over par, the ducat in Venice was paid in lire di grossi a oro and generally in bank money, whereas the ducat in Milan was paid according to its quotation in silver-based lire imperiali. When the money-of-account system in Milan was still stable at 1 ducat = 32 soldi imperiali, parity with Venice in money of account was 2 soldi di grossi a oro = 32 soldi imperiali. While Milan was not quoted often in the years 1384–94, the rates moved between 1 and 3 percent. A progressive debasement was undertaken as part of war finance by Giangaleazzo beginning in 1395. Domestic exchange rates began to rise, pushing up foreign exchange rates, until the decree of 21 February 1400, as in table C.1.[8]

While it is not meaningful to index fluctuating exchange rates in Venice, the relative parallelism of the two exchanges is evident. That both series were interconnected is particularly clear from the effects of the decree of 21 February 1400, the thrust of which — the crying down of silver currency by one-third — was known and reported to Venice immediately, although it went into effect on 1 March. The peak of 52 percent in Venice (50 percent in Milan) was reached during an extremely easy market ("larghezza grande" was reported at the time); the comment "bocie" after the rate meant that there was no demand whatsoever on Milan, presumably as a result of the monetary uncertainty reflected in the high rate. The ducal decree aimed at reinstating the value — artificial as it had often been — of 32 soldi imperiali per ducat. The effect in Milan was to lower the value of silver coin and thus also the value in silver-based lire imperiali of gold coin; the immediate effect on the exchange markets of both Milan and Venice was to compensate — or overcompensate — with a sharp drop in rates expressed in percentages. That is clear proof that the exchange rate expressed formally the relationship between two comparable gold coins, of which one, however, was paid in gold-based money of account (the Venetian ducat), the other (the Milanese florin or ducat) in silver-based money of account.[9]

---

[7]Luciana Frangioni, *Il carteggio milanese dell'Archivio Datini di Prato*, 2 vols. (Florence, 1994). The letter of 11 October 1396, which quotes Venice at a very low 1¼ percent, notes high demand: "c'è al presente fame di danari, come pe' canbi vedete."

[8]Tommaso Zerbi, *Moneta effettiva e moneta di conto nelle fonti contabili di storia economica* (Milan, 1955), 77–84; Gigliola Soldi Rondinini, "Politica e teoria monetarie dell'età viscontea," *Nuova rivista storica* 59 (1975): 298–302; Franca Levarotti, "Scritture finanziarie dell'età sforzesca," in *Squarci d'archivio sforzesco: Mostra storica documentaria* (Como, 1981), 134, table 2. For 28 March 1400: Melis, *Documenti*, doc. 21, where the author was confused between the foreign rate (10 percent) and the domestic rate (35 soldi imperiali per ducat). For April–May 1407: ADP, b. 807. These rates supplement Spufford, *Handbook*, 99.

[9]It is thus clear why the anonymous writer of a merchant manual, when he explained the parameters of exchange in Venice, reported that Milan was quoted at 7–8 percent, when the

TABLE C.1

Domestic and Foreign Exchange in Milan Compared, 1395–1410

Date	The Milanese Ducat (in soldi imperiali)		Venice Quoting Milan (in %)
	Soldi	Index	
Before 1395	32	100	min. 2–4, max. 5–6
1395 24 Aug.	33.2	103.75	same
1396 —	33	103	4–5
1397 —	34	106	rise 5 to 10
1398 mid-Feb.	35	109	10.5
Mar.	36	112.5	11–12
Apr.–Dec.	—	—	13–17
1399 Feb.	—	—	18–21
Apr.	—	—	25.5–28.5
Oct.–Dec.	rise	—	29–40
1400 Jan.	44	137.5	—
mid-Jan.	47	147	47
Feb.	48–49	151.6	—
14 Feb.	—	—	52 "bocie"
19 Feb.	—	—	9
21 Feb.–1 Mar.	36	112.5	—
28 Mar.	35	109	10
late July	35–34	108	12
1405 —	41	128	12.5 (1 rate only)
1406 —	42	131	(no further rates)
1407 21 Apr.	48.5	151.6	Milan quoting Venice: 25–26
4–10 May	49	153	26–26.5
1410 —	48	150	—

Graph C.5 shows the curves of rates in Milan and Venice often super-imposed or with only a slight lag.

Milan is no longer quoted in the Datini correspondence after 1404 in Venice, nor was Venice quoted after 1402 in Milan, for reasons that are not clear. Continued monetary instability in Milan probably hurt that market as a banking place, but Milanese merchants earlier had preferred to deal through the Venetian exchange market and would do so again later.[10]

Milanese florin had a value of 60 soldi imperiali (a level reached about 1430). BNF, cod. Palatino 601, fol. 66.

[10]See Tommaso Zerbi, *Il mastro a partita doppia di un'azienda mercantile del '300* (Como, 1936), 74–75, with eight bills on Venice, 1395–98, including an example of rechange; also the studies of Patrizia Mainoni, "Un mercante milanese" (the author mistakenly thought the exchange in Milan to be anchored to gold coin [364]), and *Mercanti lombardi tra Barcellona e Valenza nel basso medioevo* (Bologna, 1982). For scattered exchange dealings with Milan by Andrea Barbarigo, see ledger B, fols. 133 (1444) and 179 (1446).

The situation in Genoa was quite similar to that in Milan. A stable rate of exchange was maintained for much of the fourteenth century between the gold genovino and silver-based soldi di genovini piccoli, at 1 to 25. The domestic rates became unglued about 1397, judging from the foreign rates (see graph C.5), but too few domestic rates have been collected to be able to know just when and how the rise above 25 soldi developed and for what reasons, whether from depreciations or decrees.[11] From 1400 to 1404, in particular, foreign exchange rates for Genoa parallel almost perfectly the rates for Milan, which is sufficient proof that, also in this case, the rate between Venice and Genoa, quoted in percentage above par, was between a gold ducat expressed in gold-based money of account and a gold genovino expressed in silver-based money of account.

Florence

Venice usually quoted Florence certain for uncertain: one ducat, expressed in lire di grossi a oro (1 lira = 10 ducats), was worth a variable number of lire affiorino (1 florin = 1.45 lire affiorino, 10 florins = £14 10s affiorino). Parity of 10 gold ducats to 10 gold florins, therefore, was 1 lira di grossi a oro = £14 10s affiorino.

As long as the lira manca, also called lira di grossi manchi (1 lira = 239 grossi) was still in use in Venice, until about the middle of the fourteenth century, however, parity of the ducat to the florin was slightly different: 1 lira manca, worth $9^{23}/_{24}$ ducats, = £14 8s $9^{1}/_{2}$d affiorino.[12] After midcentury the lira manca disappeared, and the monetary basis for foreign exchange from then on was the lira di grossi complida, of 240 grossi.

There were also complications on the other end. Florentines used as the basis of their lira affiorino, not the full-weight gold florin, but the fiorino di suggello, of slightly less and then of ever diminishing value; the differential between it and full-weight gold florins was called an agio. In the years 1336–40, studied by Giulio Mandich, the agio was about 2 percent, which would have shifted further "par value."[13] In practice, rates of exchange made up for the difference by rising with the agio. This explains the rising trend in rates in the years covered by the Datini correspondence, 1383–1411 (when rates ranged between about 15 lire [3,600 denari] and £15 15s [3,780 denari]; see graph C.6); in the years 1415–17, covered in de Roover's study of cambium ad Venetias (range: between £15 12s, and 16

[11]Spufford, *Handbook,* 112, and de Roover, *Bruges Money Market,* 75. For extant drafts on Genoa by Zanobi Gaddi in 1385–86 (at rates of 1¼ and ⅞ percent respectively), see ADP, b. 1144; the correspondence with Genoa is not extant, so that it cannot be known just how common it was to find a direct relationship between Florentine cambisti resident in the two maritime and rival cities.

[12]Mandich, "Per una ricostruzione," clii.

[13]See "La prassi delle assegnazioni," 43.

lire); and about 1443, when an anonymous merchant manual gives the range in Venice as £15 12s to £16 10s affiorino for 1 lira di grossi.[14] In 1455–56, rates were given in percentages and ranged 19–21 percent in Florence, 23–23½ percent in Venice.[15]

That was the system — certain for uncertain — which Datini's agents in Venice used in reporting to the head office in Florence the rates current on the Rialto. When they wrote to branches and agents in cities whose exchanges were quoted as percentages over par, however, they quoted also Florence in percentage over par. The conversion between the two systems is not difficult. Since par was considered to be 1 lira di grossi = £14 10s affiorino, or 3,480 denari affiorino, the equation is the following:

$$(3,480 \times \%) + 3,480/240 = N \text{ lire aff.}$$

For example, on 10 December 1394 Gaddi wrote contemporaneously to Pisa that Florence was quoted 6 percent, and to Florence that the rate was £15 7s 6d affiorino, which jibes $[(3,480 \times .06) + 3,480/240 = 15.37$ lire, or £15 7s 3d].[16]

Bruges and Paris

The exchange relationship between Venice and Bruges involved three different ways of quoting rates, each way specific to a chronological stage of development.

The two bills of 1360, of which a transcription can be found in Appendix G, documents 1–2, themselves involved two approaches: Venice gave Bruges certain, in that a variable number of Venetian denari grossi a oro (of 24 to the ducat) corresponded to one Flemish gold réal, probably already a money of account, similarly subdivided into 24 groats Flemish. In fact, Pegolotti speaks of par as being "a denaro per denaro."[17] In the other direction, Bruges quoted the Venetian ducat in deniers tournois, but as a percentage over par (on 13 October 1360 the rate was 28¼ percent). Mandich (as cited in App. G, below) calculated that par in that case was 16.5 gros tournois per ducat.

The second manner was that employed at the time of the Datini firm's operation, about 1380–1410: each city gave the other certain! Bruges quoted Venice in groats Flemish per ducat, while Venice quoted Bruges in

---

[14]On the fiorino di suggello and the agio between it and the gold florin, see Goldthwaite and Mandich, *Studi,* 52–54 and table 2. See also de Roover, "Cambium ad Venetias," and BNF, cod. Palatino, 601, fol. 66. It will be recalled that the partnership capital of the Medici branch in Venice, expressed in fiorini affiorino di suggello, also reflected the rising agio (see above, table 7.3).

[15]ASF, MAP, 134/3, Quaderno dei cambi, tavola di Firenze.

[16]ADP, 550, Gaddi to Pisa, and 710, Gaddi to Florence, at the stated date.

[17]*Pratica,* 248; Spufford, *Handbook,* 213.

grossi a oro per Flemish gold franc (of 33 groats).[18] If we base ourselves on grossi as fractions of the ducat and on groats as fractions of the gold franc (a money of account), the calculations become simpler. A rate of 22 grossi per franc in Venice means $^{22}/_{24}$ ducat (or 0.916 ducat) = 33 groats flemish; or, turning it into certain, 1 ducat = 0.916 × 33, that is, 30.228 groats. That figure then becomes perfectly comparable to the return rate Bruges-Venice of, say, 35 groats Flemish per Venetian ducat. And rates in Bruges were regularly higher than those in Venice. A *de*crease in the number of Venetian grossi per franc meant an *in*crease in exchange rate and thus in the interest rate, which is how the mirror-image oscillations in graph C.7 are to be interpreted. In this graph de Roover's rates for Bruges quoting Venice have been added to the Venetian series quoting Bruges.

The third manner, which must have been introduced around 1420 and which lasted as long as Bruges remained a banking place, has Bruges giving certain to Venice, so that in both markets rates were quoted as a variable number of Flemish groats per Venetian ducat. From this point on, rates in Venice were almost invariably higher than those in Bruges (see above, Chap. 8, sec. vi, and graph 8.6).[19]

Here again we have a gold-based money of account over against a silver-based one, as is clear from the rise in the rate of the ducat in Venice for exchange on Bruges, from 35 groats in 1400 to 50 in 1451 to 60 in 1474.

The system of registering exchange rates in the first two periods was sufficiently complicated as to discourage any extensive operations of rechange or dry exchange between the two cities; the third system, on the other hand, seems to have been made to order so that the Venice-Bruges axis could take over for the traditional Venice-Florence axis, where the one-month "cambium ad Venetias" had reigned supreme for nearly a century. The substitution of a four-month rechange (two months' usance in each direction) for the traditional one-month rechange clearly required streamlining and fixing anew the rules of the game; the manner of quoting rates was changed in order to facilitate making the now more popular longer-term loans—and making a profit on them.

Paris was "paired" with Bruges, that is, their rates were close together, although Paris was clearly second in importance as a banking place; they quoted each other in percentage of par. During the years of operation of the Datini firm, Venice gave Paris certain: a French gold franc was quoted as a

---

[18]R. de Roover recognized this anomaly in "Renseignements," 57. Of course, his *Bruges Money Market* is the standard work for the Bruges side. Two bills for 1,000 ducats each were drawn by the Hansa merchant Hildebrand Veckinchusen in Bruges on his agent Peter Karbow in October–November 1410, at 40 groats Flemish per ducat. Michail P. Lesnikov, ed., *Die Handelsbücher des Hansischen Kaufmannes Veckinchusen*, Forschungen zur Mittelalterlichen Geschichte, vol. 19 (Berlin, 1973), 352–53.

[19]De Roover, *Medici Bank,* 116–22, and above, Chap. 8, sec. vi.

variable number of Venetian grossi a oro of account. This means that rates on Paris behaved like those on Bruges in the second stage: a *de*crease in the number of Venetian grossi per franc meant an *in*crease in exchange rate and thus in the rate of interest. As is obvious from graphs C.2 and C.7, the curves for both cities move in parallel fashion; any rise in one market or the other was quickly reequilibrated by the movement of specie. In the years 1393–98 the two curves are practically superimposed.

Paris was quoted regularly in the Datini letters from 1392 to 1410. Zanobi Gaddi wrote to Pisa in 1399, "Per Parigi si canbia spesso, e sì per Bruggia."[20] After the English victory at the battle of Agincourt (1415), Paris ceased to be a banking place.[21]

Barcelona

Barcelona also "gave certain" to Venice: a variable number of soldi and denari of the lira of Barcelona for one Venetian gold ducat. The range around 1400 was between 15 soldi and 16s 8d per ducat. An example of an actual bill: on 14 June 1398 Bernardo Alberti and Company drew 100 lire di grossi (1,000 ducats) on Barcelona, at 16s 2d per ducat. After two months' usance, the beneficiary was to receive in Barcelona £808 6s 8d Barcelona currency.[22]

Graph C.8 provides two curves, one for Venice quoting Barcelona, the other, using data that de Roover published, for Barcelona quoting Venice. It should be noted that the Venice-Barcelona axis was not normally utilized for rechange operations. On the contrary, Venice remitted to Barcelona primarily to pay for raw wool, and the biggest remitters during the Datini years were the wool importers Antonio Contarini, lanaiuolo in his own right, and the partnership of Giorgio Corner and Gabriele Soranzo (the banker), who remitted funds when they gave orders for purchases at each new shearing.[23] The Medici continued over the following decades to sell drafts in Venice to importers of wool and saffron from Spain.[24] Barcelona as an exchange market, on the other hand, dealt with the West: with Montpellier, with

[20]ADP, 550, 11 October 1399.

[21]See the overview in Raymond de Roover, "Le marché monétaire a Paris du régne de Philippe le Bel au début du XVe siècle," in *Académie des inscriptions et belles-lettres: Comptes rendus* (séances of November–December 1968, published 1969, Paris), 548–58.

[22]ADP, 1145bis; in decimals: 16.167 × 1,000/20 = 808.3.

[23]Zanobi Gaddi wrote to Pisa on 11 October 1399, "Di qui a Barzalona si canbia rade volte ora, ma qua al Natale questi Viniziani vi voranno rimetere, sichè alora potrete dare le comesioni; ora non c'è se non canbiatori, siatene avisati." As regards usance, he continued: "Fàsi di qui dal dì a 2 mesi, o dì 30 vista, m'al più vogliono 2 mesi a la fata." On the 25th there were already takers. ADP, 550. That Barcelona rarely drew on or remitted to Venice can be seen from the fact that Venice is not mentioned once among the thirty-eight bills contracted by the Datini branch in Barcelona in the first four months of 1396; see the table in Enrico Bensa, *Francesco di Marco da Prato: Notizie e documenti sulla mercatura italiana del sec. XIV* (Milan, 1928), 466.

[24]De Roover, *Medici Bank*, 245.

Genoa, but especially with Bruges.[25] And there was clearly a triangular relationship, Barcelona-Bruges-Venice, which de Roover always maintained was a commonly used route for settling international balances.[26] Finally, the Venice-Barcelona axis interested cambisti involved in arbitrage and triangular relationships with Valencia, as we saw above (Chap. 8) in the example provided by Benedetto Cotrugli.

London

Venice quoted London certain for uncertain: a variable number of sterling pence per gold ducat. The range in this period was about 38 to 42 pence per ducat; around 1450 the range was 45 to 47 pence (see above, graph 8.7). Rates were almost invariably higher in Venice than in London, which made possible the longest loan on a single rechange, one of six months' duration (three months' usance in each direction). See graph C.9.

Other Cities Mentioned

Besides the eleven major cities discussed above, very occasionally rates for other cites, such as Verona, Perugia, and Viterbo, were mentioned in the Datini correspondence. These were not "banking places," and they were quoted only in extraordinary circumstances, such as when troops had to be paid in Verona in January 1389. Similarly exceptional were remittances to Ferrara (during the Chioggia war for the purchase of wheat), Palermo, and Avignon.[27]

iii. APPARATUS: TABLES AND GRAPHS

Tables

FREQUENCY TABLE: OBSERVATION DATES

As can be readily seen in table C.2, in twenty-eight years one or more rates were extracted from letters at 1,229 different dates. During Datini's

---

[25]ADP, 823 (1395–96) and 841 (1398–99), account books devoted exclusively to the bill trade in Barcelona.

[26]He always held that "northwest Europe" had an unfavorable balance of trade in relation to Italy; see "La balance commerciale entre les Pays-Bas e l'Italie au quinzième siècle," *Revue belge* 37 (1959): 374–86, and *Bruges Money Market*, 43–46. The thesis was criticized by W. B. Watson, "The Structure of the Florentine Galley Trade with Flanders and England in the Fifteenth Century: Some Evidence about Profits and the Balance of Trade," *Revue belge* 39 (1961) and 40 (1962), and Edmund B. Fryde, "Anglo-Italian Commerce in the Fifteenth Century: Some Evidence about Profits and the Balance of Trade," *Revue belge* 50 (1972): 345–55.

[27]ASV, PSM, Citra, b. 141, account book of Tommaso Talenti, fol. 19r: cash was paid to Giovanni Portinari in Venice, "per scrittura di Bartolomeo da Carixe" (an immigrant from Ferrara, recently established as a banker on the Rialto), to remit 600 ducats to Ludovico Avvenati in Ferrara (6 June 1380). Regarding Palermo and Avignon, see the information sent to Florence by Gaddi on 21 July and 25 October 1386 (ADP, 709); for Perugia, see Piaciti's letter of 29 April 1402 (ADP, 714).

lifetime, the low came in 1390, a bad year for business, the high in 1399, when his international banking operation was in high gear. The distribution over the months is relatively uniform, although the months of greater and lesser activity are clearly reflected. September was the month following the departure of the last galleys for the Levant, and business was slow.

Given the importance of the rhythm of supply and demand, graphs were prepared which reflect seasonal patterns. Graphs C.1, C.2, and C.3 continue the series begun with graphs 8.1 and 8.2 above. The curve that most clearly registers the pulse of the money market is, of course, that for Florence (see graph 8.1). The peak months are July and August, because of the departure of the galleys for the Levant, and December, for the Christmas fair that often coincided with the return of the galleys from the East. The low month is September, when all cambisti took time to get their accounts in order. The departure of the Flanders galleys, which was hardly foreseeable but sometime in early spring, did not affect the rates of exchange. Graphs C.1 and C.2 portray the seasonal patterns, respectively, for Genoa and Milan and for London, Paris, and Bruges.

In graph C.3, where there are two parallel curves for rates in Barcelona (from de Roover) and in Venice, the seasonal pattern highlights the peaks and troughs: the tendency is for rates to move in opposite directions, meaning that exchange was economical in early spring, dear for the rest of the year. To understand the causal factors of this phenomenon, one would have to study the rhythm of wool production and trade between the two cities. In any case, the pattern does not have anything to do with the money market in Venice, for lenders and borrowers did not use the Barcelona axis for rechange arrangements.

Graphs C.4–C.9 give the fluctuations of exchange on the basis of monthly averages of the data. In graph C.6, concerning Florence, one can clearly note a rising trend, the result largely of the increasing agio of the fiorino di suggello against the fiorino d'oro.

TABLE C.2

Frequency of Observation Dates between Venice and Eleven Cities, by Year and Month, 1383–1411

Year	Jan.	Feb.	Mar.	Apr.	May	June	July	Aug.	Sept.	Oct.	Nov.	Dec.	Year Total
1383	0	0	0	0	0	0	0	0	0	0	2	0	2
1384	1	1	2	3	5	4	5	4	2	5	6	5	43
1385	5	3	3	2	4	6	5	6	2	4	5	5	50
1386	4	3	3	2	3	3	4	4	3	4	2	3	38
1387	4	3	4	4	6	6	5	6	3	7	3	6	57
1388	5	3	4	4	5	6	2	5	4	5	4	7	54
1389	6	5	5	2	3	3	4	0	2	1	1	3	35
1390	2	0	2	0	1	1	0	2	0	0	0	1	9
1391	5	5	6	3	3	3	4	3	2	2	4	5	45
1392	1	2	5	0	0	4	5	6	4	2	3	3	35
1393	2	2	5	3	3	1	6	3	1	6	6	6	42
1394	4	3	4	3	4	5	6	6	7	8	6	7	63
1395	4	4	5	5	5	5	5	6	5	5	5	6	60
1396	5	6	5	6	7	7	5	6	8	7	4	7	73
1397	5	5	4	4	5	6	4	4	5	3	4	5	54
1398	7	6	7	4	4	5	5	5	1	5	3	4	56
1399	5	6	6	7	6	3	12	7	6	7	7	6	78
1400	6	6	6	3	5	5	5	2	4	3	3	4	52
1401	7	5	3	5	4	3	5	4	5	6	4	5	56
1402	4	4	4	5	4	5	4	4	5	3	3	5	50
1403	4	3	5	3	4	5	4	4	5	4	3	5	49
1404	4	4	5	4	5	5	4	5	5	5	3	2	46
1405	3	3	2	3	3	4	5	4	2	2	2	3	36
1406	4	2	3	4	3	1	2	4	2	4	2	2	33
1407	3	3	3	4	3	3	2	3	3	3	3	3	36
1408	2	2	4	0	2	4	3	1	2	4	2	1	27
1409	2	2	3	3	3	3	3	2	3	1	2	1	26
1410	1	3	4	3	3	2	1	2	0	1	0	0	20
1411	2	2	0	0	0	0	0	0	0	0	0	0	4
Grand Total	107	96	112	89	103	107	111	108	88	107	91	110	1,229

TABLE C.3

Exchange in Venice, 1383–1411: Frequency of Observations, by City

Year	Florence	Pisa	Bologna	Genoa	Bruges	Paris	Milan	Rome	Lucca	Barcelona	London	Year Total
1383	2	1	1	1								5
1384	43	42	4	37	29							162
1385	50	49	10	44	9							164
1386	38	37	12	36	35		6					164
1387	57	55	14	55	35		5					221
1388	54	52	44	52	31	4	22					259
1389	35	28	26	27	25	19	26					186
1390	9	9	6	9	4							37
1391	45	41	33	41	24							184
1392	35	25	21	28	9							118
1393	42	40	39	37	13	2	1					174
1394	63	62	60	60	45	40	40	24				394
1395	60	49	44	45	38	37	41	9				323
1396	73	57	39	50	17	17	32	5				290
1397	54	23	15	26	3	2	16	6				145
1398	56	33	29	32	8	8	28	4				198
1399	78	66	67	67	61	61	66	57	52	59		636
1400	52	47	45	46	40	40	41	38	18	41	2	408
1401	56	54	51	55	54	54	50	51	42	55		522
1402	50	49	47	48	49	48	48	47	47	48		481
1403	49	47	46	46	47	47	47	45	46	48	16	484
1404	46	35	44	44	44	44	13	43	44	43	25	425
1405	36	23	33	29	32	30	3	20	32	35	2	275
1406	33	1	33	32	33	33		19	30	33	13	260
1407	36		33	35	31	36		18	27	36	13	265
1408	27		23	26	25	24			21	27	14	187
1409	26	6	22	24	24	24			18	25	19	188
1410	20	13	14	20	19	18			12	20	18	154
1411	4		1		3	4				4	1	17
City Total	1,229	944	856	1,052	787	592	494	386	389	474	123	7,326

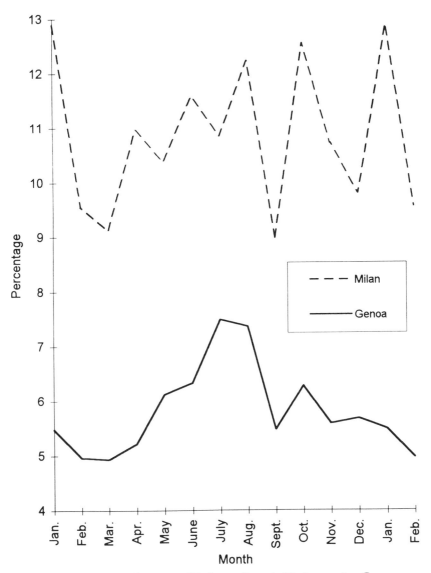

GRAPH C.1. Seasonal Pattern of Exchange Rates in Venice quoting Genoa
and Milan, 1384–1410

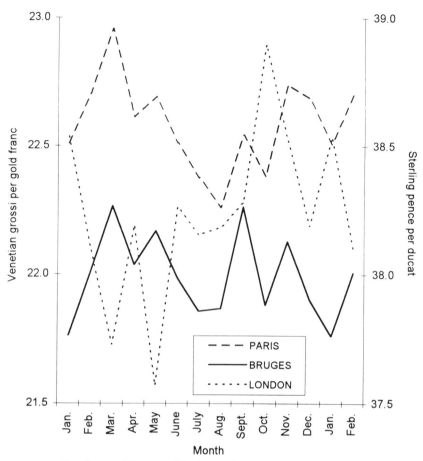

GRAPH C.2. Seasonal Pattern of Exchange Rates in Venice quoting London,
Paris, and Bruges, 1399–1410

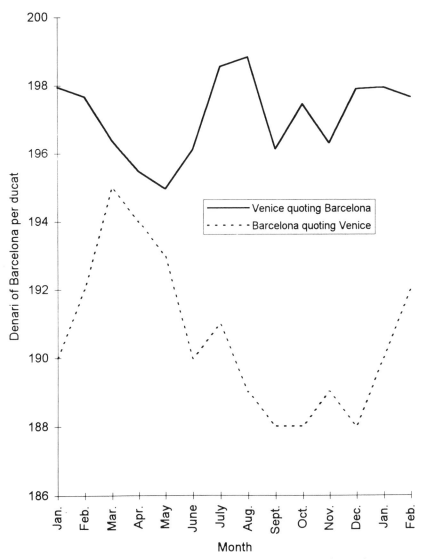

GRAPH C.3. Seasonal Pattern of Exchange Rates in Venice and Barcelona, 1399–1410

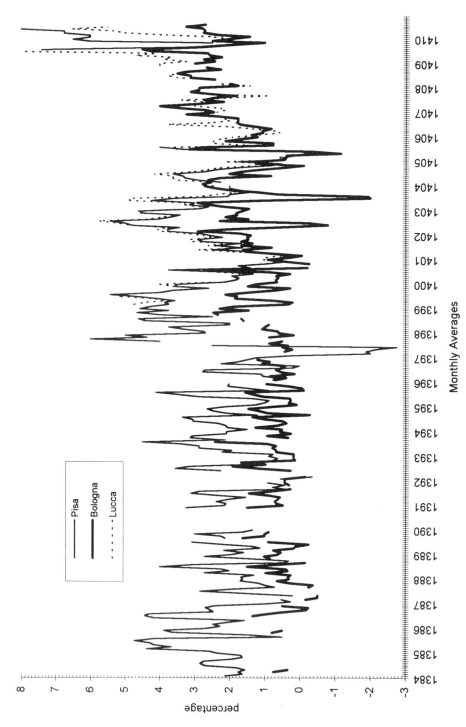

GRAPH C.4. Exchange Rates in Venice quoting Pisa, Bologna, and Lucca, 1384–1410

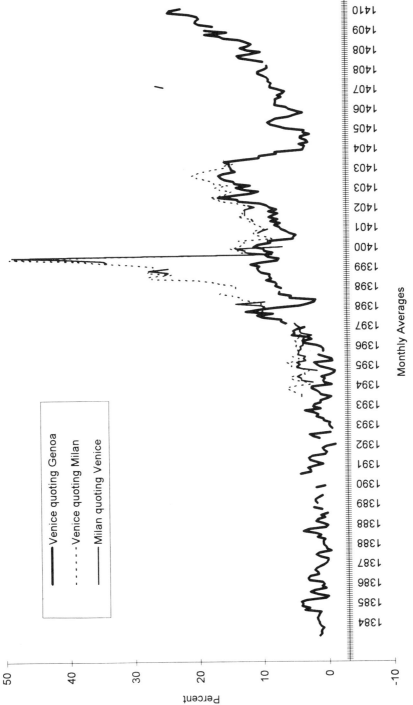

GRAPH C.5. Exchange Rates in Venice quoting Genoa and Milan, and in Milan quoting Venice, 1384–1410

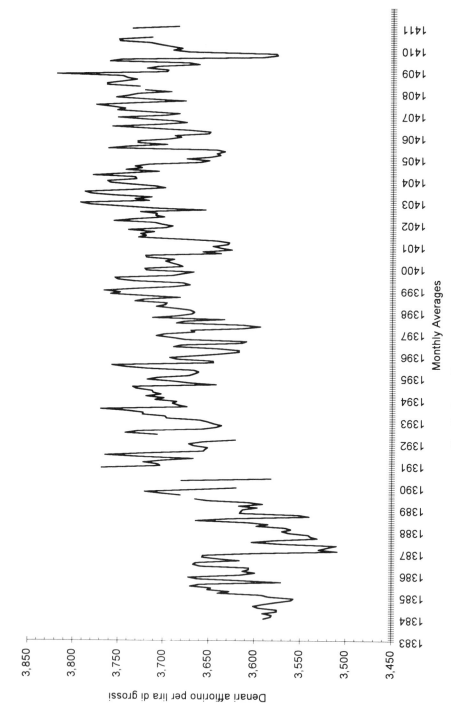

GRAPH C.6. Exchange Rates in Venice quoting Florence, 1383–1411

Monthly Averages

Denari affiorino per lira di grossi

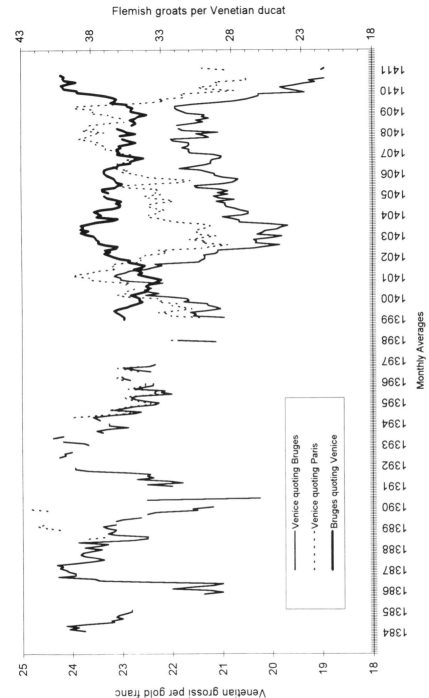

Flemish groats per Venetian ducat

Venetian grossi per gold franc

Venice quoting Bruges
Venice quoting Paris
Bruges quoting Venice

Monthly Averages

GRAPH C.7. Exchange Rates in Venice quoting Bruges and Paris, and in Bruges quoting Venice, 1384–1411

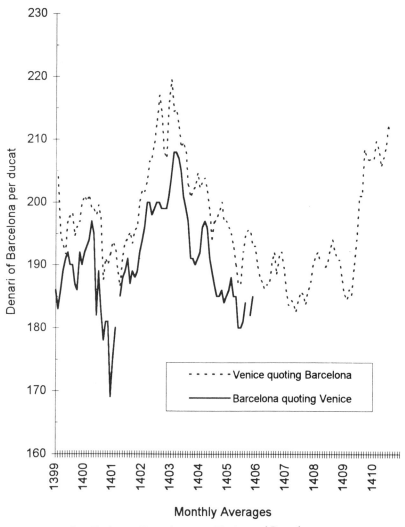

GRAPH C.8. Exchange Rates between Venice and Barcelona, 1399–1410

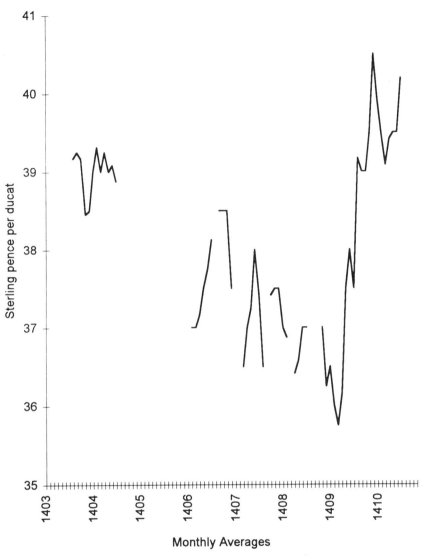

GRAPH C.9. Exchange Rates in Venice quoting London, 1403–1410

APPENDIX D

MONEYS OF ACCOUNT REVISITED

i. THE MONEY OF ACCOUNT USED BY THE LOAN OFFICE

GINO LUZZATTO'S TREATMENT OF THE lira used by the Senate in levying forced loans, by the Loan Office (Camera degli Imprestiti) in collecting them, and by the ad hoc boards of assessors (Sapientes ad Aptandum Terram or ad Augendum et Diminuendum de Imprestitis) in evaluating patrimonies is at best ambiguous and often simply erroneous. His doubts and hesitations have led historians, myself included, into numerous misunderstandings and errors of fact.[1] It is the aim of this appendix to rectify and clarify the matter once and for all.

For the sake of simplicity, let me begin with the conclusion and then proceed with the proof. The Senate and the Loan Office used the lira a grossi when imposing forced loans, in percentages, as N lire a grossi (of 2.611 lire a grossi per ducat) per 100 lire d'estimo, until July 1404; after that

---

[1] The short statement in Vol. 1, pp. 358–59, derived from Luzzatto, is itself at best ambiguous. Similarly, Lane's appendix to Luzzatto's *Debito pubblico* (in English as "The Funded Debt of the Venetian Republic, 1262–1482," in *Venice and History,* 87–98), based as it is on Luzzatto, reproduced his errors and ambiguities. My "Effetti della guerra di Chioggia," 29, reproduced Luzzatto's erroneous total of "107 percent" for levies made during the War of Chioggia. See also Cozzi and Knapton, *Storia,* 324. Queller ("The Venetian Family," 185–86) and Lane (*Venice,* 151), whom the former interprets, actually came close to the proper solution, on a hunch and in passing. At the basis of the problem was the failure to understand that a completely separate money of account had been employed in this sector, namely the "lira d'estimo," equivalent, as we shall now see, to 1 ducat. Luciano Pezzolo was able to rectify in time the data he had derived from Luzzatto for his contribution to the *Storia di Venezia* ("Dal prestito all'imposta").

date, levies were formulated as N ducats per 100 lire d'estimo. Both before this accounting reform and after, the undefined lira used by the boards of assessors was the equivalent of 1 ducat; in other words, beginning in July 1404 impositions were finally stated in true percentages, that is, practically speaking, in the same money: N ducats per 100 ducats. This means that both before and after the reform an assessed valuation, for example, of 1,000 "lire," so recorded in the estimo, was the equivalent of 1,000 ducats. I call this otherwise undefined lira, the equivalent of 1 ducat, the lira d'estimo, in order to distinguish it from other, very different lire and reduce the risk of confusion. To continue the list begun in Volume 1 (pp. 488–89), this would be money of account number 12.

Luzzatto, to the contrary, reasoned on the basis of logic: the lira used in levying individual forced loans (before July 1404), namely, the lira a grossi, must be the same lira as that in which assessments were expressed. Alas, that line of reasoning was wrong. The anomaly of the system in force before the reform, which can be understood only from accounting practice and not from the state's terse deliberations for levying forced loans in "percentages" of undefined and unequal units (lire a grossi per 100 lire d'estimo), led him astray. The deliberations regarding assessments and revisions of the estimo, in fact, speak simply of "lira" without ever undertaking to define the type.[2] On the other hand, the Loan Office itself seems to have used the lira a grossi in its own accounting, of which no fragment has yet been uncovered; all we know of that is the directive imparted to the Loan Office during the Chioggia war to switch to lire di grossi: "so that each person may better understand his situation"[3] — an order that probably was implemented only after the military crisis, but how long after is unclear. To be sure, the complete substitution of the lira a grossi in the sector of forced loans came only with the reform of July 1404, which itself was merely the last act of the general accounting reform aimed at eliminating the use of the lira a grossi from the marketplace, implemented in the spring of the same year (see Vol. 1, pp. 357–58).

The parts of Luzzatto's monograph most often consulted are his tables, in which the ambiguities are immediately reflected. To begin with, while he entitled the rate column in his first table properly (*PRV*, app. 1, p. cxvii) as "misura del prestito ([£-s-d] per 100 lire d'estimo)," the title of the same column in the table that continues the analysis (app. 1, p. cclxix) reads simply "per cento," giving the impression that the figures following thereupon are to be read as normal percentages. This is incorrect and misleading, for that column should read "lire a grossi per 100 lire d'estimo." In order to

---

[2]*PRV*, docs. 79 (1311), 120 (1325), 125 (1326), 132 (1339), 154 (1361), 160 (1374), 214 (1412), and so forth.

[3]"Item che le raxon che se livre a grossi se reduga a libre de grossi, azò che chadaun meio se possa entender." Ibid., doc. 176.

understand better the impositions made before July 1404, one need merely divide by 2.611 (that is, 2.611 lire a grossi per ducat, since 1 lira di grossi = 10 ducats = 26⅑ lire a grossi) to arrive at the actual percentage. The impositions made beginning in July 1404 are already given as true percentages in the very documents exploited by Luzzatto; but instead of leaving them in percent (N ducats per 100 lire d'estimo, that is, per 100 ducats), he proceeded to convert the percentages into lire a grossi by multiplying them by 2.6 (he simplified the operation by dropping the ⅑—see sec. ii, below). Thus he recorded 1 percent as 2.6; 2 percent as 5.2; ½ percent as 1.3; ⅓ percent or 8 grossi as 0.87 percent, and so forth. The author's aim was to make the table homogeneous, but he failed to advise his reader that the original form of the data had changed and that he had undertaken to manipulate it.

It was the comparison of data for forced loans recorded in private account books with the data provided by Luzzatto which made clarification impelling. Information culled from the accounts of the Soranzo, Badoer, and Barbarigo books, presented in tabular form above (see above, tables 13.1, 13.2, and 13.6), shows that the assessed valuation for which the family was inscribed in the estimo, although given in "lire," meant "ducats." The individual levies, then, are given in straight percentages. For example, Giacomo Badoer records that he was inscribed for 2,800 lire; a 1 percent levy, not surprisingly, is registered as 28 ducats, but the same levy is entered on Luzzatto's table as "2.6 percent." The same situation can be seen in Taddeo di Zanobi Gaddi's catasto return in Florence in 1427, in which he says he is inscribed for 3,000 "lire" in Venice and that he pays an average of 1.5 percent per month, that is, 45 ducats; or, again, in the return of Francesco d'Andrea Arnoldi, who says he is inscribed in Venice for 2,100 "ducati"— clearly different ways of expressing the same money of account, namely, the lira d'estimo.[4] Finally, the very estate accounts of the Procurators which

---

[4]Gaddi addressed the catasto officials thus: "Ma notate honorevoli cittadini che, in su e sopradetti danari contanti tutti che io mi truovo perchè io sono cittadino viniziano, per chagione che llà naqui, e questo non si può in nessun modo richusare; mi truovo eziandio avere le gravezze e fare le fazioni, perchè sapete che llà lungamente abiano auto trafiho, e fo al presente di £3000, sichè a uno per C. pagho ducati trenta; benchè io cercho ora con quelli che llà raconc[i]ano di ritornare a meno, ma lloro pure stanno duri. Apare la mia posta là nel sestiere di Santa Croce e nella contrada di Santo Chasciano, sotto nome di Taddeo di Zanobi Ghadi e fassi ogni mese al presente 1½ per cento, che sono ducati 45 il mese in fino a ora. S'è fatto ora nella present ghuera 22 per cento, sicchè per Dio fatemi di ciò lo sbattito ragionevele, perchè a due tormenti in questo modo in veruna maniere potrei [?] sofrire; preghando l'altissimo Dio e in questo et in ogni altra cosa vi do ben a fare." ASF, Catasto, 55 (portata), fol. 883r–v, and 79 (campione), fols. 616–17. For the Arnoldi silk firm, with shops in Florence and Venice, see ibid., 29 (portata), fols. 178–80; concerning Venice, Francesco wrote: "Alla sopradetta sustanza paghiamo di graveza per la valuta di ducati 2100, che ogni mese paghiamo una per cento e al presente s'è comminciato a paghare uno e meza per cento, che tutti danari paghiamo cie gli conviene torre a chambio per el sinestro si troviamo." For the same firm, see also Conti, *L'imposta diretta,* 119 n. 1, for the catasto of 1433 and the "census" of 1447.

provided the statistical basis for Luzzatto's study show how, beginning in July 1404, the system passed from quoting levies as "lire a grossi per 100 lire d'estimo" to "ducats per 100 lire d'estimo." In short, after the reform they used simple percentages, the same usage one finds in private accounts (the earliest of which, however, begins only in 1406).[5] Estate accounts show that a similar change had already been introduced at least one year earlier in registering special taxes or "impositiones" payable on assessed patrimony to other offices, such as the Provveditori alle Biave or the Provveditori di Comun (levies that were sometimes stated in mills ["ducati pro miliario"] rather than in percent ["pro centenario"]).

In order to exemplify the nature of the accounting reform, let us take the estate accounts of Marino di Nicolò Zen (ASV, PSM, Misti, b. 80A), under the heading "Facere imprestita," where we learn that the estate was inscribed for an assessment of 900 lire d'estimo. Before July 1404, the accountants entered what they owed for the estate in the following manner — using here the last entry thus made:

> 1404, 13 iunii, dedimus dominis imprestitorum pro faciendo imprestita ad 5 pro centenario de £900, £45 ad grossos, n. 14, val. £1 14s 5d 23p

It involved not a little arithmetic to transform 45 lire a grossi (that is, 5 lire a grossi for each 100 lire d'estimo), the money of account of the Loan Office, into lire di grossi a oro, the money used by the accountants of the Procurators, owing to the odd fraction of ⅑. Stated in terms of ducats, in order to facilitate comparison with the next levy, the result was about 17.2 ducats.[6]

Beginning in July, the accountants registered the assessment on the same estate as follows — using the first entry made after the reform:

---

[5]In fact, Luzzatto himself sometimes speaks of "percentages per year" in his text. He probably used two sets of notes, or, more likely, he completed his tables only after having written his text; he did not always check that the data jibed. For example, in his text (*PRV,* ccxxxiii, or *Debito pubblico,* 232), for the years 1439–54 he gives the annual imposition in percentage. For 1439, he gives a total of "9 percent"; in his table for the same year his figures total 25.57 "percent" — which, divided by 2.6, comes to 9.83. For 1440 in the text (same page) he gives 14½, while the figures in the table tally 40.95 "percent" or, divided by 2.6, 15.75. Comparison of Luzzatto's figures on the table with data from private account books, however, shows that the table is, with the exception of some few years, quite nearly complete. For example, see table 13.6, above, for the years 1436–39; there, where Badoer records levies totaling 32 percent, Luzzatto's total is 83.6, which, divided by 2.6, = 32.1 percent.

[6]Using decimals and a hand-held calculator, we can easily make the conversion as follows: 45/26.11 = 1.7234775; the integer is 1 lira di gr. — subtract it; multiply the balance by 20 (20 soldi di gr. make 1 lira), result: 14 soldi; subtract the integer, multiply the balance by 12 (12 denari per soldo), result: 5 denari; subtract the integer, multiply the balance by 32 (32 piccoli in 1 denaro grosso), result: 20.3 piccoli. Altogether: £1 14s 5d 20p — very close indeed to the accountant's £1 14s 5d 23p. Using 2.6 as the divisor brings a different result, namely £1 14s 7d 12p, sufficiently different to show that the relationship used was 1 to 26⅑, not 1 to 26.

1404, 15 iulii, dedimus dominis imprestitorum pro faciendo
imprestita ad ducatos 2 pro centenario de £900, n. 15, val.

£1 16s 0d 0p

In other words, 2 ducats per 100 ducats on 900 lire d'estimo meant in fact 2 percent on 900 ducats, that is, 18 ducats, registered as £1 16s di grossi a oro without the need of any arithmetic.

The result of the two methods of assessment was very similar: 17.2 ducats before the reform (levy no. 14, at 5 lire a grossi per 100 ducats, or 1.9 percent), 18 ducats after the reform (levy no. 15, at 2 percent). The intent was to maintain basically the same result (in that year of heavy military expenditures) while simplifying procedures and benefiting from a small (less than 4 percent) increase in revenue.

The comparison of the two accounting procedures constitutes incontrovertible proof that, both before and after the reform, 1 lira d'estimo stood for 1 ducat. In other words, assessed valuations registered in the estimo, the figures on the basis of which taxes were levied, were expressed in lire or lire d'estimo, actually the equivalent of ducats. The figure for which a contributor was inscribed on the estimo, therefore, is *not* to be divided by 2.6 (or 2.611) in order to reduce it to ducats: it is already the equivalent of ducats. On the other hand, individual levies upon that assessed patrimony were in lire a grossi per lira d'estimo, that is, per ducat, before the reform. To understand the data from before July 1404 in the documents, then, the levy must be divided by 2.611. To understand Luzzatto's table beginning in July 1404, it is necessary to divide by 2.6 (the multiplier he used in transforming percentages).

Just how (just why? remains a mystery) Luzzatto fell into this trap emerges from his own reasoning about accounting entries in the estate books of the Procurators in 1419–21. His errors are macroscopic. He states (p. ccxi and n. 3) that the laws imposing levies and the registration of the levies coincide when they speak of ½ or ¼ "percent"; this means, he continues — correctly for the moment — "effectively ½ or ¼ ducat per 100 lire d'estimo." He then proceeds, however, to insist that to arrive at a real percentage it is necessary to multiply by 2.6, since he continued to insist that the lira d'estimo was a traditional lira a grossi. Thus he shows that the levies in two years, 1419–21, totaled 6⅓ ducats per 100 lire, "equivalent, that is, to 17½ percent"! His note to the text represents the ultimate contortion. For proof, he quotes from the accounts of an estate that was liable for "impositiones" on 2,500 lire.[7] The estate, in paying ½ "percent," had to turn over 12½ ducats (or £1 5s di grossi a oro). That is perfectly correct, so that Luzzatto's note is actually unequivocal proof that the lira d'estimo means

---

[7] ASV, PSM, Ultra, b. 104, commis. Pietro di Nicolò Contarini, whose accounts begin in 1413.

one ducat, since both the authorities and the accountants dealt with real percentages ($0.5\% \times 2,500 = 12.5$). In short, the author himself provided the reader with the very proof why he should *not* have tampered with levies imposed after July 1404, multiplying them by 2.6; a new table, or at least a new column in the same table, should have been added beginning with the accounting reform. Or again (p. ccxxxiv), when summarizing the levies of the last twenty-eight years of the system of forced loans, that is, up to 1454, he states that the total was about 168 ducats per lira d'estimo and then adds: "Since the estimo continues to be expressed in lire a grossi, and the ducat corresponds to £2 12s a grossi, the total levy was actually 434 percent of the estimo." Since such a burden — "434 percent" — is unthinkable, the only solution, he concludes, was that taxpayers never declared anything approaching their actual wealth, especially in personal property and commercial profits. To be sure, 168 percent, the correct figure, in twenty-eight years still represents a heavy fiscal burden, but it is more significant to see it as an annual average of 6 percent. The author's attempt to maintain consistency in his reasoning, as one can see, merely vitiates his further considerations.

Luzzatto encounters the same problem with regard to the capitalization of rents in establishing assessed patrimony. Since he reads the lira d'estimo as a traditional lira a grossi, he states (in *PRV*, cxlvi and ccxvi) that a capitalization rate prior to 1383 of "4 lire di grossi assessed as 1,000 lire d'estimo," as the law read, was actually a rate of 10 percent ($4 \times 2.6 = 10.4$), which is blatantly incorrect. It is similarly incorrect to say that the reform of 1403, which stated that 100 ducats in rents were to be calculated as 900 lire d'estimo, set the rate as "poco più del triplo (260/900)." On the contrary, the rate of capitalization was not "about one-third" but 11.1 percent. To repeat once again, the lira d'estimo was equal to 1 ducat; thus neither the 4 lire di grossi or 40 ducats of 1383 nor the 10 lire di grossi or 100 ducats of 1403 should have been converted into lire a grossi.[8]

Moving backward for a moment, the question as to when the lira d'estimo as worth 1 ducat was introduced arises from a consideration of the fact that the ducat was first coined only well after the rules for assessing property had been formulated and after the consolidation of the public debt. Here a reply can only be hazarded. Luzzatto's table for the earlier period (app. 1, chap. 2) reveals that up to the year 1325 fractions of lire ($\frac{1}{2}$, $\frac{1}{4}$, $\frac{1}{10}$) were used in expressing levies, while, when levies pick up again beginning in 1335, they are always expressed as integers. Although this is only a guess, that decade of void includes the year 1328, when the ducat was made legal tender for 24 grossi, a possible occasion for introducing an

---

[8]It is worth pointing out that Luzzatto made these ill-considered conversions, as we have seen, using the relationship 1 lira di grossi = 26 lire a grossi, in order to simplify his calculations, while the accountants of the Procurators of San Marco, prior to July 1404, used the relationship 1 to 26⅑ (see above, n. 6).

accounting reform. Before that time, according to the oath required of merchants between about 1280 and 1325, the example of a levy is stated as a simple percentage: "If my assessment is 1,000 lire and the levy is 1 percent, then I will pay 10 lire" (in *PRV*, xxiv).

The line of reasoning pursued so far makes it possible to affirm, now without ambiguity or hesitation, that the equivalence of the lira d'estimo with 1 ducat was already in place by the mid-fourteenth century. Given that fact, some reconsiderations are in order. First, the burden of taxation during the third Genoese war (1350–54), for a total of 40 lire a grossi per lira d'estimo, was in fact a burden of 15.3 percent of the estimo — as Luzzatto himself wrote (*PRV*, p. c). Second, the impositions of the War of Chioggia (1379–81), for a total of 107 lire a grossi per lira d'estimo, meant a burden of 41 percent — as Luzzatto conceded (*PRV*, cxlix), but only after trying to convince the reader that the figure was indeed 107 "percent" (*PRV*, cxxxiii–xxxiv). Third, individual assessed patrimonies registered on the estimo in lire (that is, in lire d'estimo) are to be read as ducats; and, logically, the total for the only estimo that has survived, that of 1379, namely 6,290,000 lire, means 6,290,000 ducats — as Luzzatto himself conceded (*PRV*, cxli–xlix), but only after much hesitation and after trying to convince the reader, just the same, that it was "beyond all doubt" that the lira used in public records, and thus also in the case of the public debt, was the lira a grossi, worth $10/26$ of a ducat (*PRV*, cxliv–v).

The ambiguities that remained in Luzzatto's mind were so strong as to block out his own often correct deductions. Thus, in his *Storia* he returns to state categorically that the impositions during the War of Chioggia totaled "44 percent in the year 1381, for a sum total, 1377–81, of 107 percent of assessed patrimony" (p. 141). To explain the anomaly of having to contribute more than one owned, Luzzatto estimated that "real" patrimonies were "on the average about four times assessed patrimonies" (*Storia*, 132, 141). That hypothesis, namely, that the estimo assessed only about 25 percent of real patrimony, seems to derive in part from his reasoning about the lira a grossi; but the capacity — or the desire — of the system of assessments to identify real patrimony can be tested only on the basis of actual cases, such as that of Andrea Barbarigo, presented above (see table 12.6).[9]

The correct understanding of the lira d'estimo as equivalent to the ducat is, finally, the only possible way for making sense of the limitations on free trade applied first in 1318 on naturalized citizens and then by the Officium de Navigantibus in 1324, 1331–38, and 1361–63 on all Venetians and residents, after 1363 on naturalized citizens alone, and in 1404 on Rialto bankers. The restriction stated that the above-mentioned categories of Venetians could not invest in the Levant trade sums exceeding the

---

[9]See also his *Studi*, 183, where he states that the seventeen levies from December 1439 to March 1441 totaled "59½ percent of the estimo."

amount "on the basis of which they contributed forced loans" [non navigetur ultra quam faciant de imprestitis], that is, their assessed patrimony. That ceiling would have been impossibly low had it actually been expressed in lire a grossi.[10]

ii. LIRE MANCHE, LIRE A GROSSI, AND THEIR SUBDIVISIONS

Giulio Mandich published an article on Venetian moneys of account on the basis of an analysis of the "libro nero" of Duccio di Banchello and Company, 1336–39 (discussed above, Chap. 7 and 8), which appeared nearly contemporaneously with Volume 1.[11] That article discusses, among other things, a subdivision of the lira manca which Frederic Lane and I did not bring to light. This note presents a brief summary of the author's argument as presented in the article and in subsequent correspondence.[12]

Around 1250, the lira di grossi complida (240 denari grossi) had risen to 26⅑ (or 26.11) lire a grossi. The lira di grossi manca (239 denari grossi "compiuti" or 240 "grossi manchi," both moneys of account), on the other hand, continued to be worth 26 lire a grossi. This fact, which ought to have been entered in table 5 of Volume 1 (p. 131), requires (Mandich argued) a consideration of the ducat of account as a subdivision of both of these lire and a reconsideration of the manner of quoting certain commodity prices which I had left unresolved.

Some time after the coining of the ducat (1284–85), the lira di grossi manca (239/240 of a lira di grossi complida) was worth 10 ducats of account, each worth an uneven 23.9 grossi compiuti, or an even 24 grossi manchi, or an even 2.6 lire a grossi (or 52 soldi a grossi), or 10 gold ducats less 1 grosso. The lira di grossi complida was also worth 10 ducats of account, but each of them was worth an even 24 grossi "compiuti" (later "a oro") of account or an uneven 2.611 lire a grossi (or 52⅖ soldi a grossi); this ducat is recorded as number 10 on the list of moneys of account begun in Volume 1 (pp. 488–89).[13] The missing money of account, then, is the ducat of the lira di grossi manca, worth ⅒ of that lira or 24 grossi manchi; in specie, it was worth 23.9/24 of a gold ducat or 23.9 silver grossi (as long

[10]Cessi, "L'ufficium de Navigantibus"; Lattes, *Libertà,* doc. 12 (original in ASV, SM, reg. 46, fol. 162v; the correct date is 28 November 1404).

[11]"Monete di conto veneziane in un libro di commercio del 1336–39," *SV,* n.s., 8 (1984): 15–36. The matter was picked up again in his "Delle prime valutazioni del ducato d'oro veneziano (1285–1346)," *SV,* n.s., 16 (1988): 15–31.

[12]On 5 August 1994, just ten days before his stroke, Mandich kindly wrote me a position paper of two pages on the relationship between the lira manca, its "ducat," and the lira a grossi, as well as a covering letter with further explanations, in response to my draft of this section and a discussion held in his home one month earlier.

[13]In his unpublished note, Mandich exemplifies these relationships on the basis of an entry in the libro nero of Duccio di Banchello (ASF, Del Bene, 64, fol. 22v, 6 March 1338).

as they circulated, that is, until about 1320); it could be added (as number 14) to the above-mentioned list. The lira di grossi manca was the lira used in the 1330s to state the value of exchange operations with Florence, the price of which (or rate of exchange of which) was formulated in a varying number of Florentine lire a fiorini (see, besides Mandich's article, Vol. 1, pp. 308–9). In exchange operations, the sums owed and paid in lire manche were generally credited to accounts maintained with Rialto bankers; an agio was charged for the difference between bank money and specie.

The accounts that Mandich transcribed from the Florentine "libro nero," however, never mention expressly the ducat of the lira manca (or the "ducato di grossi manchi," as the author calls it on p. 27), but only lire manche. The lira manca, however, the author argues, is a multiple of the "ducato di grossi manchi"; he so argues on the basis of logic, (a) because of the parallelism with the lira di grossi complida (made legal tender for 10 gold ducats in 1328) and (b) because of the even equivalence of the lira manca as 2.6 lire (52 soldi) a grossi, as well as on the basis of texts. The agio quotations for the ducat which Mandich provides are derived by calculation from figures given in lire, in grossi, in piccoli — not from direct quotations of the "ducat of the lira manca."

Mandich adduced two texts to support his argument. The first is a conversion found in the libro nero between lire di grossi compiuti and lire di grossi manchi; again, this involves two kinds of lire, however, not their eventual subdivision into ducats.[14] The second is a passage from Pegolotti which described, around 1328, how exchange was quoted between Venice and Constantinople and how the price of pepper was quoted in Venice; although the text seems to refer to actual coin, Mandich shows that actually money of account was meant. The text referred to by Mandich reads: "varrebbe il pipero . . . tanti soldi a grossi di Vinegia, di soldi 52 a grossi di Vinegia uno fiorino d'oro o vero ducato, di denari 26 a grossi il grosso di Vinegia." A very similar text can also be adduced from Pegolotti's discussion of Famagosta: "E vagliendo in Vinegia il fiorino d'oro o vero ducato d'oro soldi 52 a grossi, di denari 26 a grossi il grosso d'argento di Vinegia."[15] These conversions, Mandich showed, would have been erroneous had they actually referred to ducat and grossi coins; they are correct and understandable only if referred to accounting subdivisions of the lira manca.

---

[14]ASF, Del Bene, 64, fol. 89 (30 December 1337).

[15]*La pratica della mercatura*, 50, 97. In his article ("Monete di conto veneziane," 20 n. 9) Mandich dismissed one of these passages as "un testo forse scorretto" when it was cited from an early and admittedly uncritical edition of Pegolotti's *Pratica*; later, on the basis of Evans' text, he admitted that the cause of confusion was not a corrupt text but the mistaking (by Pegolotti perhaps, by Evans for sure) of a money of account for a coin. Finally, the list of five moneys of account used in Venice provided by Saminiato de' Ricci around 1380 (Borlandi, *Il manuale*, 99–100) includes a "libra di grossi [which should read "a grossi"] di s. 52 il fiorino."

Giulio Mandich, in correspondence and conversation, held further-more that the equivalence 1 ducat = 2.6 lire a grossi or 52 soldi a grossi used by Florentine operators in the conversion to ducats of certain commodity prices quoted in Venice before 1404 means they were calculating in ducats of the lira manca — this in reference to table 11 in Volume 1 (p. 357) and its note. In fact, I had found only one instance in which a calculation was made which tried to account for the odd fraction of ⅑; otherwise, both in price lists and in letters, particular prices were quoted in lire and soldi specified as "a grossi, of 52 soldi to the ducat,"[16] the very same equivalence we have seen reported both by Pegolotti, who wrote prior to about 1340, when the lira di grossi manca was still used in Venice in the foreign exchange market, and by Saminiato de' Ricci, who wrote about the time that Francesco di Marco Datini began to deal with agents in Venice, when the lira manca had long since been replaced in the foreign exchange market with the lira di grossi complida, that is, a oro.

If we accept Mandich's reasoning, which is extremely rigorous, the lira manca continued to exist after midcentury in its subdivision, the ducat of the lira di grossi manca, for those three commodities (pepper, silver, silk) quoted on the Rialto, until the spring of 1404, in lire a grossi. My assumptions, (a) that the lira manca did not survive the middle of the fourteenth century in any form and (b) that Florentine merchants tended to drop the odd fraction as a savings in transactions costs for these commodities, were probably wrong. Had Florentines, out of frustration with the complexity of Venetian accounting conventions, figured the ducato d'oro (¹⁄₁₀ of the lira di grossi a oro) as 52 soldi a grossi rather than as 52⅖ soldi, the difference would have amounted to 0.42 percent. Even though the bookkeepers of the Procurators of San Marco were perfectly capable of dealing with the fraction (see sec. i of this appendix), Venetian authorities admitted that use of the lira a grossi "induced confusion and fraud" in government offices and promised that its elimination would save the state money by permitting the dismissal of accountants and scribes. And Florentines expressed their satisfaction with the accounting reform of 1404 which substituted the gold ducat for the lira a grossi in quoting commodity prices, which was "better and more expedi-tious" (see Vol. 1, pp. 356, 358). The frustration of merchants, accountants, and historians is understandable under the circumstances.[17]

[16]Besides the lists in ADP, 1171, cited in Vol. 1, 357, table 11, see also ADP, 709, letter of Zanobi Gaddi to Florence, of 15 January 1387, which states that cordovan hides were sold in Venice at N soldi per centinaio di libbre grosse, "di s. 52 [al] ducato"; and letter of Antonio di Benincasa and Jacopo di Tedaldo to Florence, 14 November 1387, which states that pepper was sold in "lire a grossi di soldi 52 il fiorino."

[17]It might be recalled that even Gino Luzzatto, whether consciously or not, dropped the fraction when he converted ducats into lire a grossi in recording the levies of forced loans "more expeditiously."

iii. QUOTATIONS OF THE DUCAT IN LIRE AND SOLDI DI PICCOLI IN VENICE AND MESTRE

Not surprisingly, new quotations of the ducat in lire and soldi di piccoli have been brought to light since the publication of Appendix D in Volume 1. I shall merely refer the interested reader to the compilations, without reproducing them.

First, Giulio Mandich culled more than one hundred "values" of the ducat, 1337–39, from the "libro nero" of Duccio di Banchello and Company. These are important years, for which I had only a few figures (actually from the same source). The quotations range between 65 and 68 soldi di piccoli, still quite close to the par rate of 64 soldi.[18]

Second, Alessandra Checchin culled several hundred quotations of the ducat from account books of the scuola and hospital of S. Maria dei Battuti of Mestre, 1382–1455. Those quotations for the marketplace of Mestre overlap almost completely with those published in Appendix D of Volume 1. It was necessary to collect them, however, in order to verify their relationship to quotations on the Rialto market. The overlapping values of the ducat on the two very close marketplaces, it might be added, are not matched by wheat prices, which were higher in Mestre than in Venice, in periods in which comparisons are possible.[19]

Other values have been collected for Venice and for other cities on the Terraferma and Lombardy, moving well into the sixteenth century. Those for Venice again merely confirm the rates previously published in Appendix D of Volume 1.

iv. THE LIRA DI PICCOLI OF VENICE AND THE SUBJECT TERRITORIES

Venice permitted the subject territories to maintain their respective traditional moneys of account. On the Terraferma, the cities closest to Venice, Treviso (taken in 1338, lost in 1381, and retaken in 1388) and Padua (taken in 1405), used the same lira di piccoli as Venice. Verona and Vicenza (subjected in 1405) used a lira that was one-third larger than that of Venice. Brescia and Bergamo (conquered in 1426–28) used the lira imperiale, later called the lira di planeti, which had a value of exactly twice the Venetian lira. Venice minted the coins for all the subject territories, precisely to fit each of these moneys of account.[20] The relationships between these moneys can be summarized as follows:

[18]"Delle prime valutazioni del ducato d'oro," 29–30, appendix.

[19]*La scuola e l'ospedale di S. Maria dei Battuti di Mestre,* table 17 (to be read horizontally rather than vertically).

[20]See my "L'imperialismo monetario," 277–97. It is interesting to note that the first known crack in the Carolingian lira system, in 972, set an equivalence between the Milanese lira and that of Venice — just devalued — of precisely one to two; see Gherardo Ortalli, "Il mercante e lo

1 lira di piccoli of Venice = 1 lira di piccoli of Treviso
= 1 lira di piccoli of Padua
= 0.75 lire di piccoli of Verona and Vicenza
= 0.50 lire di piccoli of Brescia and Bergamo
4 lire veneziane = 3 lire veronesi = 2 lire bresciane
1 lira veronese = 1.33 lire veneziane
1 lira bresciana = 2 lire veneziane

The "lira dalmata" used in Zara (Zadar) and the other cities of Dalmatia, purchased or reconquered between 1409 and 1420, was supposedly worth two-thirds the Venetian lira di piccoli. Not surprisingly, the Venetian soldini sent there in the role of the soldo of the Dalmatian lira were immediately taken out of circulation and hoarded. A special soldo, devised in 1410 but perhaps actually produced in Venice for Zara only beginning in 1414, was worth slightly less than two-thirds of the Venetian soldino. Beginning in 1486, the Venetian mint also struck special denari piccoli or bagattini, one for each of the five major centers, which were slightly heavier than Venetian denari piccoli. But the identification of actual equivalences in money of account will have to await the corroboration of documentary sources.[21]

Cattaro (Kotor) was also permitted to keep its money of account, the Dalmatian perpero. But its circulating coins were produced in the local mint, under Venetian supervision and with the symbols of Venetian sovereignty and with the initials of the Venetian governors. That mint privilege of 1423 for Cattaro ("quod in Catharo cudatur moneta iuxta suas consuetudines") was unique for the whole Venetian empire. Its grosso or grossetto was supposedly worth two-thirds of that of Venice. Just how the coins struck there fit into the local perpero system and what the equivalences were between that system and Venice's await, once again, documentary corroboration.[22]

v. THE LIRA DI PICCOLI, THE DUCATO D'ORO, AND THE DUCATO CORRENTE, 1331–1797

Tables D.1 and D.2 show the devaluation of the lira di piccoli, first by giving the decreasing silver content, then the increasing value of the ducat

---

stato: Strutture della Venezia altomedievale," *Mercati e mercanti nell'alto Medioevo: L'area euroasiatica e l'area mediterranea,* Settimane di Studio (Spoleto, 1993), 129–30, citing the work of Andrea Saccocci.

[21]For this paragraph and the next, see my "Aspects of Venetian Sovereignty in Medieval and Renaissance Dalmatia," in *Quattrocento Adriatico: Fifteenth Century Art of the Adriatic Rim,* ed. Charles Dempsey, Villa Spelman Colloquia, 5 (Bologna, 1996), 41–44.

[22]Vincenzo Lazari, *Le monete dei possedimenti Veneziani di oltremare e di terraferma, descritte ed illustrate* (Venice, 1851), 43–51, provides equivalences but gives no hint of how they were derived or by whom.

in lire di piccoli, and finally the mirror image, the decreasing gold value of the lira di piccoli. After 1517, the same information is continued, but, with the birth of the money of account known as the ducato corrente, worth a fixed 124 soldi di piccoli of Venice (or £6 4s, or 6.2 lire), the same calculations are provided for it: its fine silver content, the value of the zecchino or "ducato d'oro in oro" in ducati correnti, and the declining value in zecchini of 100 ducati correnti. These values held for Venice, the Trevigiano, and the Padovano.[23]

From 1517 to the fall of the republic, 1 ducato corrente was the equivalent of 93 soldi veronesi. The Brescian lira, which came to be called the lira di planeti, was worth (as noted above) twice the Venetian lira, which means that 1 ducato corrente was the equivalent of 62 soldi of Brescia.

The data elaborated in tables D.1 and D.2 were derived from Volume 1, Appendix A (through 1407) and from Papadopoli, *Le monete di Venezia,* tables in appendices to vols. 1, 2, and 3. Following Papadopoli, the gold ducat, or, after 1517, the zecchino, was rated as 3.556 grams until 1517 and thereafter 3.49 grams, even if the variations were three, for a drop of 1.74 percent in gold content between 1491 and 1526 (ibid., 2:62, 100, 145). The years selected here in column 1 in both tables are those during which there was a change in mint standards or in the value of the ducat/zecchino (or both) which caused a change in other parameters. Values of the ducat/zecchino in lire and soldi di piccoli are provided in Volume 1, Appendix D, until 1517; for the following period, rates of domestic exchange — for more years than those here selected — can be found in eighteenth-century printed sources cited in the same place and by Pezzolo, *L'oro dello stato,* 323, who provides from the same sources rates covering the years 1548 to 1607.

vi. UNSPECIFIED VENETIAN LIRE AND THEIR VALUATION

A sentence of the Curia di Petizion in 1396, regarding the manner in which a bequest ordered in a testament of 1338 was to be paid, stated that it was "usually" the practice to consider a sum stated in lire but with no further specification to be lire a grossi (see Vol. 1, p. 355, and its app. G, doc. 7). I have since found an earlier document, of 1304, which states that it was normal practice in Venice to consider a sum given simply in "lire" to be the smallest lira of account used, namely, the lira di piccoli; similarly, it states, if simply "lire di grossi" were indicated, the sum was to be judged the smaller of the two then in use, namely, the lira di grossi manca, not the lira di grossi complida. (If this second affirmation actually held true in 1304, it was certainly no longer true by 1350, when the lira di grossi complida was

---

[23]These tables were originally published, with explanations, in Reinhold C. Mueller, "Monete coniate e monete di conto nel Trevigiano: Medioevo e epoca moderna," in *Due villaggi della collina trevigiana: Vidor e Colbertaldo,* ed. Danilo Gasparini, 4 vols. (Vidor, 1989), 2:323–35.

TABLE D.I

Devaluation of the Lira di Piccoli and Its Relation to the Gold Ducat, 1331–1517

(1)	(2)	(3) Value of the Gold Ducat in Lire di Piccoli		(4)	(5)
Year	Grams Fine Silver in £1 di Piccoli	£/s	decim.	Gold Value of £1 di Piccoli (grams)[a]	Bimetallic Ratio[b]
1331	12.820	3/10	3.5	1.016	12.6
1333	12.820	3/4	3.2	1.111	11.5
1349	11.610	3/4	3.2	1.111	10.5
1353	10.660	3/4½	3.225	1.103	9.7
1369	9.760	3/14	3.7	0.961	10.2
1379	9.440	3/16	3.8	0.936	10.1
1382	9.440	4/	4.0	0.889	10.6
1391	8.920	4/4	4.2	0.847	10.5
1399	8.640	4/13	4.65	0.765	11.3
1407	8.340	4/16	4.8	0.741	11.3
1417	7.706	5/	5.0	0.711	10.8
1421	7.583	5/3	5.15	0.690	11.0
1429	7.290	5/4	5.2	0.684	10.7
1443	6.646	5/14	5.7	0.624	10.7
1456	6.646	6/4	6.2	0.574	11.6
1472-1517	6.180	6/4	6.2	0.574	10.8

[a]3.556 grams pure gold per ducat, divided by column 3.
[b]Column 2 divided by column 4.

understood when a sum was stated simply in lire di grossi.) The document of 1304 is not Venetian but Sicilian in origin; it was registered in the Venetian chancery without comment, and no continuation of the case (which concerned reparations payments) has been found that states Venice's eventual reply to the affirmation. The solution proposed in 1304 seems the more logical of the two; and the statement of 1396 was not relevant to the case at hand (in fact, lire di piccoli had been specified in the testament, and the litigation involved deciding the rate of exchange in ducats which was to be applied to that lira). I have found no document, however, which would resolve the doubt raised by the contradiction between the two statements regarding lire *tout court,* formulated a century apart. The difference between the lira di piccoli and the lira a grossi was 18.4 percent, for 1 lira di grossi was worth 26⅑ lire a grossi or 32 lire di piccoli. The difference between lire di grossi manca and complida was only 0.42 percent (1/240).

For the sake of completeness, I am providing a transcription of the first paragraph of the document of 1304, a "responsio" of King Frederick II of Sicily to Filippo Belegno, ambassador of Venice, concerning reparations for the sacking of a Venetian galley by subjects of the Sicilian crown. The

TABLE D.2

Devaluation of the Lira di Piccoli and the Ducato Corrente and Their Relation to the Gold Zecchino, 1517–1797

(1) Year	(2) Grams Fine Silver in £1 di Piccoli	(3) Value of Zecchino in Lire di Piccoli £/s	(3) decim.	(4) Gold Value of £1 di Piccoli (grams)	(5) Bimetallic Ratio	(6) Grams Fine Silver in 1 Du. Cor.	(7) Value of Zecchino in Duc. Correnti	(8) Value of 100 Duc. Correnti in Zecchini
1517	5.781	6/10	6.5	0.537	10.8	35.842	1.048	95.42
1519	5.781	6/14	6.7	0.521	11.1	35.842	1.081	92.51
1519	5.781	6/16	6.8	0.513	11.3	35.842	1.097	91.16
1525	5.151	7/6	7.3	0.478	10.8	31.936	1.177	84.96
1544	5.151	7/12	7.6	0.459	11.2	31.936	1.226	81.57
1562	5.030	8/	8.0	0.436	11.5	31.185	1.290	77.52
1570	5.030	8/12	8.6	0.406	12.4	31.185	1.387	72.10
1572	4.292	8/12	8.6	0.406	10.6	26.610	1.387	72.10
1584	4.292	9/12	9.6	0.364	11.8	26.610	1.548	64.60
1593	4.292	10/	10.0	0.349	12.3	26.610	1.613	62.00
1608	4.591	10/	10.0	0.349	10.3	26.264	1.613	62.00
1621	3.591	12/10	12.5	0.279	10.3	26.264	2.016	49.60
1635	3.242	15/	15.0	0.233	13.9	20.100	2.419	41.34
1635	3.242	16/	16.0	0.218	14.9	20.100	2.581	38.74
1643	3.242	17/10	17.5	0.199	16.3	20.100	2.823	35.42
1643 Nov.	3.242	16/	16.0	0.218	14.9	20.100	2.581	38.74
1665	3.142[a]	17/	17.0	0.205	15.3	19.480	2.742	36.47
1665	3.117[b]	17/	17.0	0.205	15.2	19.325	2.742	36.47
1704	2.723	20/5	20.25	0.172	15.8	16.883	3.266	30.62
1717	2.723	22/	22.0	0.159	17.1	16.883	3.548	28.18
1733-97	2.416	22/	22.0	0.159	15.2	14.979	3.548	28.18

Note: Calculations were made as follows: column 4 = 3.49 grams pure gold per zecchino divided by column 3; column 5 = column 2 divided by column 4; column 6 = column 2 multiplied by 6.2 lire di piccoli per ducato corrente; column 7 = column 3 divided by 6.2; column 8 = 100 divided by column 7.

[a]Scudo d'argento.

[b]Ducatello.

legal rule of thumb formulated by the Sicilians for the bilateral negotiations had supposedly been confirmed by "persons knowledgeable about Venetian customs," who had been "questioned under oath" on the matter.

ASV, Commemoriali, reg. 1, c. 74v
s.d. [1304]

Primo est ad capitulum de errore commisso in calculo, qui error est *a grossos, ad parvos,* etc., non obstantibus[24] rationibus responsionis domini ducis nuper adductis per dictum dominum Phylipum, et etiam non obstantibus allegationibus dicti domini Phylipi, dicunt quod responsio domini regis primiter facta esse bona et iusta nam asserunt se habuisse per homines fidedignos, sacramento astrictos et conscios de consuetudinibus veneciarum, quod quotienscumque in aliquibus scripturis de calculo exprimuntur libre ad grossos alique rationes, alie libre scripte sic simpliciter nichil addendo intelliguntur libre ad parvos; et hoc idem dicunt de libris grossorum completis et non completis et dicunt quod hec etiam sunt secundum iura, quod semper quando alique monete specificantur, ille qui non exprimuntur nec specificantur debent glosari ad minorem monetam.

[24]The phrase "dicti domini Phylipi allegationibus," which follows, was crossed out.

APPENDIX E

FOREIGN INVESTORS IN VENETIAN CREDIT INSTITUTIONS

i. THE GRAIN OFFICE

TABLE E.1

Authorizations for Borrowings and Deposits in the Grain Office, 1283–1411

Date		Amount	Interest (%)	Source
1283,	2/4	?	?	*DMC*, 3:24 (for 50,000 staia of wheat)
1288,	8/4	£20,000	10	*DMC*, 3:201, and *PRV*, doc. 49
	22/5	£20,000	10–12	*DMC*, 3:204, 207
1289,	19/7	?	10	*DMC*, 3:238, and *PRV*, doc. 52
1293,	3/3	?	?	*DMC*, 3:334
1315,	13/2	£10,300 a gr.	?	*RES*, doc. 71; loan by ser Fabius de Florentia for Zara action; Grain Office not mentioned, but likely agency
1316,	20/9	?	?	*RES*, doc. 78
1317		20,000 fl.	0	See text re. Castelbarco
1320,	5/6	£300 di gr.	?	*PRV*, doc. 102 (see text re. Rizzardo Malombra)
1323,	11/9	£12,800 di p.	?	*PRV*, doc. 112 (re. Marsilio da Carrara); cf. *RES*, doc. 97
1323,	20/12	£20,000	?	*RES*, doc. 99
1345,	18/7	12,000 du.	?	*RES*, doc. 179: if the office is unable to lend the sum from funds on hand, it is to borrow
1346?		1,233 du.	?	SM, rub. I, f. 187v
1347,	4/9	5,000 du.	u	SM, 24, f. 33v: from dowries held by the Procurators.
1349,	15/2	10,000 du.	3 or 4	SM, 24, f. 119v
	20/3	10,000 du.	3 or 4	*RES*, doc. 200
	6/6	12,000 du.	3 or 4	*RES*. docs. 203, 204
1351,	5/2	20,000 du.	u	SM, 26, f. 50
1355,	5–12	90,000 du.	u	SM, 27, fols. 10, 51 (clearly re. Cangrande II della Scala)
1363,	15/11	10,000 du.	u	SM, 31, f. 46
1364,	10/3	1,800 du.	3	SM, 31, f. 53v (O. Forzetta)
1365,	7/1	10,000 du.	u	SM, 31, f. 87v
	2/3	10,000 du.	u	SM, 31, f. 91 (for grain)
1366,	9/3	3–5000 du.	u	SM, 31, f. 132v
1367,	11/5	6–10,000 du.	u	SM, 32, f. 48 (re. estate of L. Soranzo)
1368,	2/7	600 du.	3	SM, 32, f. 129 (re. Pietro da Parma)
	21/11	3,000 du.	3	SM, 32, f. 155v
1370,	21/7	25,000 du.	u	SM 33, f. 66v (conditional to an agreement with Byzantine Emp.)
1371,	25/7	20,000 du.	3	SM, 33, f. 124 ("pro factis bladi")
1374		33,334 du.	3	Re. Ludovico Gonzaga

TABLE E.1 *(Continued)*

Date		Amount	Interest (%)	Source
1375,	13/1	5,000 du.	u	SM, 34, f. 153 (Stefanino Ponzoni)
	6/11	10,000 du.	3	SM, 35, f. 55v
1376,	20/5	3,000	u	SM, 35, f. 100v
1377,	10/1	11,000 du.	?	SM, 35, f. 136v
	23/3	700 du.	?	SM, 35, f. 151v
	16/7	3,000 du.	u	SM, 36, f. 22v
	19/11	5,000 du.	u	SM, 36, f. 45
1378,	13/4	3,000 du.	?	SM, 36, f. 56
1379,	13/1	1,000 du.	?	SM, 36, f. 70v (Roger de Anglia)
1380,	28/9	21,000 du.	4	SM, 36, f. 100 (Donnina de Porris, for grain imports)
1381,	29/11	12,000 du.	4	SM, 37, f. 36
1382,	15/2	12,000 du.	4	SM, 37, f. 52 (Pietro Stampa)
	7/3	20,000 du.	3	SM, 37, f. 56 (credit for grain imports of Ludovico Gonzaga)
1411,	10/5	12,000 du.	4	SM, 49, f. 20 (Sandalo of Zara; 4% is "per privilegium")
	8/11	25–50,000 du.	?	MC, Leona, f. 210v (re. Paolo Guinigi's investment, in Grain Office or in bonds)

Note: u = at usual rate (ad prode solitum).

TABLE E.2

Some Known Depositors in the Grain Office, 1317–1411

Name	Area	Year	Amount	Interest %	Source
Guglielmo (qd. Azzone) da Castelbarco	Trent	1317	20,000 fl.	0	See text
Rizzardo Malombra da Cremona	Padua/Ve	pre 1320	£300 gr.	?	*PRV*, doc. 102
Marsillo da Carrara	Padua	1323	£12,800 p.	?	*PRV*, doc. 112
Barnaba de la Paga	Mantua	1327	?	?	AC 3641, f. 45
Nona Nani (S. Polo)	Venice	1328	£1,000	?	PSM, U, Test.b. 3
Avensore de' Fanti	Cervia	1331	?	0	*Sen.Misti,* 1:460
Enrico Scrovegni	Padua/Ve	pre 1336	£1,000 p.	4	PSM, M75
Gregorio di Curiaco, count of Corbavia[a]	Dalmatia	1335	10,000 du.	5	SM, 40, f. 15; 59, f. 168v
Pietro Nan da Marano[a]	Vicenza	1330s	10,000 du	4?	PSM, M4 (left for male ablata)
Luchino Visconti[b]	Milan	1343	?	?	SM, 21, f. 13; cf. vol. 1:194, 372
Nelipcio, count of Knin[a]	Dalmatia	1343	£20,000	5	SM, 43, f. 27

TABLE E.2 (*Continued*)

Name	Area	Year	Amount	Interest %	Source
Pietro and Sachetto Campagnola	Padova	1344	3,185 fl. + 3,000 du.	?	Commem., 7, f. 80
Oliviero Forzetta	Treviso	1345–74	37,150 du.	3	See text (left for hospital)
Nicolò Giorgio, Marquis of Bodonitsa	Greece	1346	1,233 du.	?	SM, 23, f. 26, 30
Cangrande II della Scala	Verona	1355–59	80,000 du.	?	See text
Jacobina d'Este (widow of Enrico Scrovegni)	Venice	pre 1365	1,150 du.	?	PSM M88; heir: Ugolino. For Caterina, cf. SM, 37, f. 53v (1382)
Estate of Lorenzo Soranzo	Venice	1367	6–10,000 du.	u	SM, 32, f. 48
Estate of Tomà Lippomani	Venice	1367	1,500 du.	?	SM, Rub. 1, f. 216bv
Magister Petrus de Parma	Parma	1368	600 du.	3	SM, 32, f. 129
Pandolfo II Malatesta	Pesaro	pre 1372	10,000 du.	3	SM, 36, f. 18v
Ludovico Gonzaga	Mantua	1374	33,334 du.	3	SM, 34, f. 73r–v, plus credit for grain imported and other money: f. 146v
Stefanino di Giovanni Ponzoni	Cremona	1375	5,000 du.	u	SM, 34, f. 153
Roger Buchiberch, filius Johannis de Anglia	England	1379	1,000 du.	?	SM, 36, f. 70v
Donnina de Porris (mistress of Bernabò Visconti)[b]	Milan	1380	20,000 du.	4	SM, 36, f. 100 and Com., 8, f. 37v (for grain?)
Pietro Stampa	Milan	1382	12,000 du.	4	SM, 37, f. 52
Ludovico Gonzaga [b]	Mantua	1382	20,000 du.	3	SM, 37, f. 56 (for grain)
Antonio della Scala	Verona	pre 1388	3,000 du.	?	SSec, E, f. 18
Giovanni della Torre	Verona	pre 1389	?	u	SM, 41, f. 18; for balance due heir Domenico: SM, 47, f. 105v
?Crown of Hungary?	Hungary	1394	110,000 du.	3	BMV, Cr. Morosini, 8332, f. 483–84
Sandalo, voivoda of Bosnia	Bosnia	1411	12,000 du.	4	SM, 49, f. 20
Paolo Guinigi[a]	Lucca	1411	25,000– 50,000 du.	?	Here or in bonds: MC, Leona, f. 210v

[a]Citizen.
[b]Citizen with privileges of a noble.

ii. THE MARKET IN GOVERNMENT OBLIGATIONS

TABLE E.3

Foreigners Licensed to Invest in Venetian Government Obligations, 1318–1451
(in ducats)

| Year | Name | Provenance or Residence | Amount | | Source |
			Nominal	Market	
pre 1318	Doimo Frangipane, count of	Veglia	?	?	*PRV,* doc. 95
pre 1339	Azzone Visconti	Milan	?	?	G9:33
pre 1340	Manfredo IV	Saluzzo		115,000	chap. 14
1364	Azzone d'Este	Ferrara	?	?	G16:7
1365	Caterina, wife of Giovanni of	Val Venosta		2,000	G16:36
1365–73	Ludovico Gonzaga	Mantua	151,000		chap. 14
1370	Nicolò qd. Simone Bonasi	Pola	?	?	G16:113
1370	Goncelario and Antonio qd. Giacomo a Toaleis	Mantua	?	?	G16:116
ca. 1371	Francesco Casali	Cortona		20,000	chap. 14
1373–83	Bianca di Savoia	Milan	40,000		G17:7, 151v
1373–87	Manfredo V di Saluzzo	Milan		32,000	chap. 14
1374	Bonaventura di Rustighello, physicus	Pola		1,000	G17:37
1374–76	Pietro Capello, bishop of Cremona	Milan		4,000	G17:41
1375	Traversina, widow of Nicolò de Cortelariis	Padua		385	G17:43
1375	Pietro Siroba (citizen of Venice)	Famagosta		1,000	G17:44v
1375	qd. Dragogna qd. Pietro de Balbas	Cherso		1,500	G17:47v
1375	Felixina de Trivisana	Venice		150	G17:56v
1375	Caterina, widow of Marcolo de Testa	?		500	G17:57
1376	Francesco de Torenzo	Rimini		1,000	G17:69
1376	Anna, wife of Franceschino Cavalli	Verona		4,000	G17:76v
1377	Sofia, widow of Lorenzo Mafei (citizen of Venice)	Verona/Venice		800	G17:80v
1377	Zaccaria, widow of Antonio Mafei (citizen of Venice)	Verona/Venice		1,000	G17:82v
1377	Guidone, canon of S. Marco	Venice		600	G17:82v
1377	Teodoro Durachin and wife Giovanna Moro	Arcadia		5,000	G17:89
1378	Nicoletta, widow of Aristotile, scriptor	Venice		1,000	G17:91v
1382	Lanzarotto	Treviso		3,000	G17:143
1383	Pileo da Prata, cardinal of	Ravenna		12,000	G17:164v
1385	Lucia qd. Andrea d'Anzolo	Trieste/Venice		300	G17:193

TABLE E.3 *(Continued)*

Year	Name	Provenance or Residence	Nominal	Market	Source
			Amount		
1385	Caterina, widow of Antonio Bevilacqua, citizen of Venice	Verona/Venice		1,000	G17:196v
1385	Rambaldo di Collalto, count	Treviso		1,000	G17:201v
1386	Caterina Visconti, wife of Giangaleazzo	Milan	100,000		G17:202
1387	Carlo Malatesta (dowry from Francesco Gonzaga)	Rimini		20,000	G17:224
1387	qd. Antonio da Galerate	Milan/Venice		50	G17:227
1391–92	Pietro de Cassiano, admiratus regni Cipri	Cyprus		10,000	G18:10v, 14
1392	Raniero de Scolaribus, bailus regni Cipri	Cyprus		5,000	G18:25v
1392	Tommaso, Giovanni, Galeaz-zo, heirs of Manfredo V	Saluzzo		10,000	G18:27
1394	Nicolò di Filippo	Fano		2,000	G18:100
pre 1399	Luchino Novello Visconti	Florence	20,000		PSM, Ultra, b. 305
1402	Giacomo Giuberti, merchant	Bologna		4–5,000	G19:31
1403	Tommaso and other heirs of Manfredo V	Saluzzo		20,000	G19:39v
1403	Cristoforo, schoolmaster in	Muggia	2,000		G19:41v
1404	Bonamente Aliprandi	Mantua	2,000		G19:45v
1404	Nascimbene qd. Zambono	Padua	10,000		G19:45v
1409	Ulrich Samer	Salzburg	12,000		G20:37
1410	Giovanni da Francia	Capodistria		2,000	G20:41v
1410	John I, King of	Portugal	?	?	PRV, doc. 211
1411	Paolo Guinigi, lord of	Lucca		40,000	chap. 14
1412	Agostino Fornari	Vicenza		4,000	G20:58
1420	Francesco Bussone, Count of Carmagnola	[Milan]		30,000	chap. 14
1423	Abbondio di Leonardo de Cograriis	Como		2,000	PRV, doc. 229
ca. 1424	Guid'Antonio da Montefeltro	Urbino	?	?	SM, reg. 55:136
1423	Johannes Daga	Nuremberg	10,000		G21:68v
1423	Giacomo Aguto (?)	Mantua		8,000	G22:2
1426	Manfredo di Manfedo	Saluzzo	20,000		G22:70
1428	Bianca, widow of Raffaele Raimondi, doctor utriusque	[Padua?]		2,000	G22:96v
1429	Giovanna de Caria, qd. Antonio, widow of Raffaele Fulgosi, doctor utriusque	Padua		3,000	G22:119
1429	Giovanni Secretico, magister fisicus	Cyprus		2,000	G22:126v
1430	Alessandro Borromei (for the church of Sant'Elena)	Milan/Venice		8,000	G22:133v
1431	qd. Margherita qd. Francesco	Arbe		1,200	G23:9

TABLE E.3   (*Continued*)

Year	Name	Provenance or Residence	Amount Nominal	Amount Market	Source
1431	Stefano da Francia, chaplain of S. Secondo	Venice	400		G23:10v
1431	Hugo de Lusignan, Cardinal	Cyprus	2,000		G23:12v
1432	Pietrobono Pomponazzi	Mantua	10,000		G23:29
1432	estate of qd. Domenico di Tommaso	Florence / Venice	2,000		G23:29
1432	Friary of S. Francesco	Forli	2,000		G23:56v
1435	Knights Hospitallers of St. John of Jerusalem	Rhodes	200,000		G23:116v
1436	Convent of S. Chiara	Mantua		600	G23:120
1436	Lorenzo Attendoli, captain	Codignola		6,000	G23:130v
1436	Stefano Pignolo, miles	Cyprus		6–8,000	G23:131
1436	Tommaso Bibi, M.D., advisor of the King of	Cyprus		6,000	G23:132v
1436	Alvise da Tana "de partibus pedemontium"	Cyprus?		6,000	G23:139
1437	Franciscan friary	Rimini		900	G23:150
1437	Johannes Maurino (?)	Augsburg	10,000		G24:13
1437	Stefano Pignolo, advisor of the King of	Cyprus		6–8,000	G24:18
1438	Lisiolo Capoana, Venetian viceconsul in	Manfredonia	2,000		G24:36
1438	Numo de Gusman, son of the Grand Master	Castile	25,000		G24:36
1438	Ludovico de Gusman, Grand Master, Order of Calatrava	Castile	100,000		G24:44v
1438	Zupano de Bona, merchant	Ragusa		2,000	G24:44v
1438	Stefano Magno and brothers	Ragusa		1,000	G24:46v
1439	Giovanni de Mileto Soldani, majordomo of Eugenius IV	Florence	10,000		G24:48v
1439	Wenceslaus, son of count Zachan	Corbavia	10,000		G24:51
1439	inhabitants of Castel S. Lorenzo in Campo	Marches of Ancona	1,700		G24:60
1439	Dominican friary	Rimini	?	?	G24:63
1440	Dom Nicola Manenti, prior of S. Maria del Pero	Monastier (Treviso)	1,500		G25:8v
1440	Giacomo de Petrocco	Montesanto		1,000	G25:9v
1440	Bartolomeo Brancacci	[Florence]		10,000	G25:10
1440	Enrico qd. Gabriele Bunci	Asti		4,000	G25:16
1440	Nicola da Todi and brothers	Todi / Padua		1,000	G25:18
1441	Petrus Silber	Freiburg	8,000		G25:30v
1441	Magister Pietro Magnano	Codignola	1,000		G25:30v
1451	Pietro da Nosceto	?		*ad libitum*	PRV, doc. 268

Note: G = ASV, Grazie, followed by register number and folio number.

APPENDIX F

RATES OF INTEREST ON CREDIT SALES, 1383–1405

T IS OBVIOUS FROM THE discussion above of the various credit institutions and the investors who exploited the opportunities offered that Venetians of middling status, not only merchants and not only males, were conversant with interest and its calculation. Manuals of commercial arithmetic posed problems on interest and taught students how to make the necessary calculations, for both simple and compound interest. One could also consult a handy table of interest rates, such as one that has survived from the first half of the Trecento.[1] Less obvious and rarely discussed is the interest included in sales on credit.

The Venetian series of Datini letters provides thousands of prices of commodities in the wholesale market; prices for certain commodities have been culled and elaborated for use in a future study. The prices of some commodities were occasionally quoted in the letters in a differential fashion: one price for payment in cash on delivery or only shortly thereafter, another for payment on credit, that is, on deferred payment. Pepper, a highly speculative commodity with volatile prices, was by law to be sold only for cash.

Cases in which both the credit terms and the cash prices are sufficiently clearly stated in the correspondence as to permit calculation of the rate (or approximate rate) of interest are listed in table F.1. Some of the quotations give the period in months, others simply "until the galleys," that is, until the legal termini for loading and departure of the Beirut galleys, namely, 4–15 July; some set the due date at the Christmas fair.

---

[1] It provides a table of rates, from 1 to 20 percent, from one to twenty years, and explains how long it takes to double one's money. BMV, It. cl. XI, 18 (7438). In general, see Postan, "Credit in Medieval Trade."

633

Levantine products predominate. The ginger is of the "michino" variety. The cotton is Sarmin ("asciamo") cotton, with a single exception when, in May 1399, interest on the Hamath ("amano") variety was quoted on the same day at nearly two points lower. The wool is Spanish, in all but one case of San Matteo; the exception concerned Minorcan wool, quoted in April 1402 at a low rate of interest.

In economic terms, little can be said about the level of these rates. They do not form a series; they do not reveal trends; they represent an indistinguishable mix of supply and demand both for commodities and for credit in different moments. The compilation is presented here simply to indicate just one other very common form of credit, credit sales, about which too little, in concrete terms, is known. It is worth pointing out, at the same time, that the widely varying rates range, more than half of the time, between about 10 and 14 percent; this dominant middle range, as well as the rates scattered above and below it, is perfectly comparable to the middle range of interest rates which can be found in any series derived from the medieval exchange market (see the discussion, above, in Chap. 8, and the relevant tables).

TABLE F.I

Rates of Interest on the Sale of Commodities at Deferred Payment, 1383–1405

Date of Letter	Commodity	Term	Interest (% p.a.)
26.11.1383	Sugar	3 months	10.5
01.12.1383	Sugar	3 months	10.5
31.03.1384	Sugar	4 months	12.9
05.08.1384	Cloves	3 months	10.8
06.02.1386	Cloves	Until galleys (5 months)	8.3
05.04.1386	Cloves	3 months	20.3
06.10.1386	Cloves	3 months	13.8
18.12.1387	Cloves	4 months	5.1
27.02.1388	Cloves	4 months	4.5
22.10.1388	Cloves	3 months	13.8
23.12.1388	Cloves	4 months	10.7
27.02.1389	Cloves	4 months	10.3
10.09.1389	Cotton	4 months	18.8
11.03.1394	Cloves	4 months	8.8
07.01.1396	Cloves	4 months	14.6
19.02.1396	Wool	8 months	11.6
08.02.1398	Ginger	Until galleys (5 months)	14.7
13.02.1398	Cloves	Until galleys (5 months)	10.7
21.02.1398	Ginger	Until galleys (5 months)	10.9
22.10.1398	Wool	16 months	9.7
16.01.1399	Wool	Until galleys (6 months)	19.6
16.01.1399	Wool	Until Christmas (11.5 mo.)	14.3
22.03.1399	Wool	16 months	17.9
15.04.1399	Wool	12 months	29.4
13.05.1399	Cotton	Until Christmas (7 mo.)	13.3
13.05.1399	Cotton	Until Christmas (7 mo.)	11.5
05.07.1399	Cotton	6 months	10.9
26.07.1399	Sugar	4 months	13.0
16.01.1400	Cloves	Until galleys (6 months)	12.5
16.01.1400	Ginger	Until galleys (6 months)	13.5
10.02.1400	Cloves	Until galleys (5 months)	9.5
23.07.1401	Cloves	4 months	23.1
23.07.1401	Cloves	5 months	23.0
25.02.1402	Cloves	4 months	18.4
08.04.1402	Wool	12 months	5.5
22.04.1403	Wool	Until Christmas (8 mo.)	12.5
22.03.1404	Wool	4 months	37.5
22.03.1404	Wool	8 months	25.0
23.02.1405	Wool	6 months	8.0
23.02.1405	Wool	8 months	18.0

Source: ADP, letters sent from Venice, at the dates.

APPENDIX G

DOCUMENTS

i. EARLY BILLS OF EXCHANGE

WO EARLY BILLS OF EXCHANGE, one drawn in Bruges on Venice, the other in Venice on Bruges, survive in the original as part of the estate papers of one of the parties, Giacomello Gabriel, who died in Bruges when the bills were under way. Both were published by Giulio Mandich in "Mercanti veneziani in Bolzano secondo una cambiale del 1360 (ma trattasi di un errore di lettura)," *Cultura atesina* 2 (1948): 13–23, and the second of them is also included in his *Le pacte de "ricorsa,"* 118–19. See above, figure 12a–b and Chapter 8, section ii.

1. Bill of Exchange on Venice: Bruges, 13 October 1360.
ASV, PSM, Misti, b. 67, commis. of Giacomello Gabriel.

address side:
Çacharia Chabriel in Veniesia, prima.
De duc. 200 d'oro, per dì 13 dic. 1360
[*the Gabriel merchant seal*]
[*annotation by the executors:*] 1360, mensis decembris, die 13 intrante, presenta fuit presens littera cambii per manum Bartholomei Micheli.

text side:
In nome de Dio, Amen. 1360, die 13 otubrio in Broça. Chacharia Chabriel Jacomo Chabriel saludo. Darà e pagerà in Veniesia a ser Bo[r]tolamio Michele e compangni a dì tredese decebrio prossimo duchatti dusento

d'oro de çusto peso, per questa prima letera, e son per la vaiuda de libre disesete e soldi 12, denari grossi 8¼ to[r]nesi, a raxo[n] de 28¼ per 100, a nue ava[n]taço, che i'òe reçevudo in B[r]oça da ser Piero de Bon da Luccha e de ço li desa bon pagamento. Dio t'alengra, amen.

[*in another hand:*] Salutum fuit die 13 Januarii de hoc millesimo.

2. Bill of Exchange on Bruges: Venice, 18 November 1360.
ASV, ibid.

address side:
A lo nobele e savio misser Jacomo Gabriel ha Bruzes
de reali 300
[*the Gabriel merchant seal*]

text side:
In nome de Dio, amen. 1360, dì 18 novembre in Veniexia. Misser Jacomo Gabriel, pagere' per questa prima leterea in Bruzea a mezo luio prosimo a ser Bortolamio de Goldio riali trisento, a florini do per rial, scontando scudi tre per florini quatro, segondo usanza de canbio, de li qual io son ben pagado de qua da ser Piero Morexini de santo Antolin, libre XLIII, soldi XV, denari — de grossi, a raxon de denari XXXV lo rial. Priegove che li fe bon pagamento al dito termene. Dio v'aliegra senpre.

Zacharia Gabriel fio vostro se recomanda a vuii.

ii. WRITTEN ORDERS-TO-PAY

Nothing like a bank check has survived in Venice, nor has any accounting entry made any reference to such an order. Deposit banks operated on the basis of oral orders; clients periodically compared their accounts with those of their bankers. At the same time, there are references to deposit receipts, although nothing that is unequivocally such has been uncovered. It might be that Venetians had an aversion to written orders, whereas Florentines were attracted by the use of written "polize."

Survival may be a factor, however. In 1390, there was a criminal case against the servant (Polo di Belluno) of a lumber merchant (Rizzardo) for having falsified two orders-to-pay in his master's name, one of them made out to a Rialto banker. The first "cedula" was for 3 ducats; the servant brought it to the house of Franceschino Pisani, who paid it on the spot, as though he was used to honoring similar orders; Pisani then went to the Rialto to recoup the sum, and the forgery was discovered. The second, a "scripta" for 10 ducats, he made out in the name of Andreolo "a telis," a draper with a shop at the Rialto, and he presented it to Silvestro di Dante, the Florentine deposit banker situated near the shops of the furriers ("qui tenet banchum in Rivoalto penes varotariam"); Silvestro, "credens hoc," also promptly honored the order-to-pay, which was later discovered to be false. The same servant hoodwinked shopowners in a similar manner, convincing them to turn over goods, such as meat and shoes. He would not have gotten as far as he did had there not been a certain familiarity with written orders that the signer "sent for collection" [mittebat ad petendum], as is recorded in the record of the trial.[1] Such orders-to-pay would be called "mandati all'incasso" in modern Italian accounting terminology. There are some examples.[2]

3. Order-to-pay of 1430. A tiny slip of paper.
ASV, PSM, Citra, b. 282, commis. Lorenzo Dolfin, tomo III.

[*recto:*]
Carissimo fratello Lorenzo Dolfin. Per questo messo, à nome Tomaxo, fameio di Zan Moressini, condam misser Zillio, vui pode' dar el ducato ve domandai ieri sera imprestedi. Et chussì ve priego.

Benedetto di ser Andrea da Pozo *subscripsi*

[*verso:*]
1430, 15 novembre
Ser Lorenzo Dolfin
[*in another hand:*] Ser Benedetto da Pozo

4. An IOU with a bearer clause.
ASV, GP, Sg, reg. 163, fol. 102v (case of 1 June 1476)
Date of the IOU: 5 August 1469

1469, a dì 5 avosto in Veniexia
Nota faxo mi Antonio Nadal qd. misser Zacharia a chadauna persona che vederà el prexente scrito, chome mi Antonio sorascritto prometo de dar e pagar a chi me aprexenterà el presente scrito ducati 100, zoè ducati zento,

---

[1]ASV, Signori di Notte al Criminal, reg. 12, fol. 6v (25 February 1390).
[2]Besides the Dolfin commissaria, cited for doc. 1, see also ASV, PSM, Ultra, b. 95, commis. Alberto Colletto; here there is a small envelope, marked "Bolletini dei Governadori," 1519–20.

da mo' per fina anni 3 prosimi, zoè ani tre, i qual sono per altratanti me scrisse ser Piero Corner qd. miser Jacomo a l'Ofizio di Straordenarii a le 3 per zento, chomo apar nel dito libro. E mi Antonio Nadal sorascrito ò scrito el prexente scrito a dì e mileximo sorascrito de mia man propria.

The claimant in the lawsuit is Melchiore de Coltis e nevodi, a fraterna that had been active as banker-moneychanger on the Rialto, at least in 1441–55 and conceivably thereafter; later it seems to have been more of a speculator in bills of exchange.[3] The IOU was initially given to Piero Corner, qd. Giacomo (probably the Rialto banker who had been partner of Agostino Ziera), in return for a credit of 100 ducats transferred on the books of the office of the Estraordinari, for the customs duty of 3 percent;[4] since it was a bearer note, Corner passed it on to the de Coltis fraterna, as Melchiore stated: "el qual scritto per le chosse havemo a far con misser Piero Chorner n'è sta' datto dal ditto misser Piero, e però dimandemo el ditto misser Antonio sia per le Vostre Magnificenzie sentenziato per vertude del ditto scritto in ditta summa de ducati cento et in expensis cause." The note had a limitation of three years, but the date was not considered by the judges. The defendant did not respond to the suit, and the judges ordered Nadal to pay as originally promised.

5. IOU with bearer clause, of 1480.
ASV, GP, Sg, reg. 173, fol. 2.
Date of the IOU entered in the court record: 20 October 1480.

Sia manifesto a chi vederà questo scritto chome mi Panthalon Zorzi, fo de misser Domenico, ho recevudo per imprestedo da ser Ieronimo Amai ducati 80, zoè ducati octanta, i qual prometto darli e pagarli ad ogni suo bon piazer, sì a lui *etiam* a colui me presenterà ditto scritto; et per suo chiareza, io ho fatto questo scritto de mia man propria.

io Panthaleon Zorzi, fo de
misser Domenico *subscripsi*

[3]The family were immigrants from Pisa. See Giuseppe Petralia, *Banchieri e famiglie mercantili nel Mediterraneo aragonese: L'emigrazione dei Pisani in Sicilia nel Quattrocento* (Pisa, 1989), 171–74. Melchiore and his brothers Gasparre and Baldassare received the de intus privilege in 1422.

[4]On this customs house and the practice of transferring credits on its books, see Mueller, *Procuratori di San Marco*, 215–19.

APPENDIX H

GENEALOGIES OF THE GADDI, SORANZO, AND PRIULI FAMILIES

ABLE H.1 SHOWS AT A glance how the important merchant banking family of the Gaddi originated from a family of artists and how its rise to economic and political power began in Venice and developed there, as well as in Florence, before the focal point of family interests shifted to Rome. It is also clear how Vasari confused the two Agnolos—the painter, brother of Zanobi, and the merchant, son of Zanobi—eliding them into the same sketch in his *Lives*. Names of family members known to have been in Venice or to have had business enterprises there (or both) are indicated in boldface. For the sources of this genealogy, see above, Chapter 7, section ii, and Mueller, "Mercanti e imprenditori fiorentini," 44–47 and the notes. Birth dates were derived from ASF, Tratte, 39 and 443bis, with the kind help of Sig. Merendoni and his personal files. See also Pompeo Litta, *Famiglie celebri d'Italia* (15 vols., Milan, 1819–1902), vol. 3. Lodovico, most likely Zanobi di Taddeo's first son, conceivably born in Venice, was called "nobilis vir" when his business partner in Venice, Lorenzo di Francesco di Vanni, named him testamentary executor (ASV, NT, b. 1233, no. 388; 10 September 1423); similarly, Maddalena—or her notary—calls her husband Agnolo "dominus" in her testament of 1450 (NT, Miscellanea testamenti notai diversi, b. 25, no. 1994); there is no hint in the humble testament that she was a Ridolfi. Two sons, Luigi I and Gerolamo I, obviously died young and have been omitted from the table. In the catasto of 1427, Agnolo listed his wife Maddalena as age twenty-one and three children (Caterina, three and a half years; Niccolò, two years; Giovanni nine months). Gerolamo II was probably born of a third wife, assuming the correctness of the birth date.

Table H.2 records the remarkably short life span of the bank founded in 1399 by Roberto di Lorenzo Priuli. (Missing from the table are two other brothers of Roberto, Costantin and Alessandro, mentioned in Marco Barbaro's genealogy [ASV, "Priuli, branch 'O' "], left out here for lack of space but also because they were never recalled in the documents concerning the banks and had probably died young.) After only three years, the management passed to Andrea, who held it until his death in 1424. The estate bank, managed by Bartolomeo, lasted only one year, when it failed and the estate was divided: Leonardo and Giacomo split off on their own, while Bartolomeo continued with Andrea's sons Alvise and Alessandro. According to the Avogaria's marriage records, in 1409 Piero married Cateruza, daughter of Pietro d'Almorò Venier, who seems, therefore, to have nothing to do with Pietro di Maffeo Venier, partner of Andrea, whose heirs continued as late as 1481 to sue the heirs of Andrea for the failed bank's liabilities. In 1428 Giacomo merged with Zan Orsini and brothers. Both this bank and that managed by Bartolomeo failed in September 1429. Despite the demographic strength of this family, its several banks did not survive a generation. Names in boldface are mentioned in the documents as having been active in banking or formed part of the styles of the bank. For the sources, see above, Chapter 5, section ii. For the company styles, see table A.1, under 1399. Many testaments of the family were found in ASV, in CIN and NT.

The marriages were found in AC, regs. 106–7 (the dates are given in parentheses); wives of unknown first name are indicated as "f." for "figlia di" (daughter of) (as in table H.3). Maria, an elder daughter of Andrea Priuli, married the twenty-two-year-old Francesco Foscari, future Procurator of San Marco and doge, in 1395, before the bank was founded; she died sometime before 1411, when Foscari married a second time.

Table H.3 is divided into two parts, the first for the bank founded by Gabriele and brought to ruin by his grandson Benetto in two insolvencies (1453, 1455), the second for the branch of the family which refounded and continued the bank, until liquidating it in 1491. It is clear in this manner that the Giovanni Soranzo dal banco who appears in the documents after 1456 is not the son of Cristoforo, who in fact was in voluntary exile at the time, having fled from justice along with his brother Benetto and the latter's family, but the son of Vettor, brother of the founder, Gabriele. (The homonyms had created confusion for Francesco Ferrara, "Antichi banchi," 191.)

Again, names that appear in the documents as part of the styles of the bank are in boldface.

The information on marriages was culled from ASV, AC, regs. 106–7. Some marriages stand out as examples of alliances with potent or wealthy families. Vettor di Zuane married the granddaughter of a Rialto banker, Giovanni de' Bugni, the wealthy immigrant from Cremona. Cristoforo di Gabriele, who ran the bank from 1410 until his death in 1432, married the daughter of a Procurator of San Marco, of another branch of the large Soranzo clan. Benetto di Cristoforo married the granddaughter of Francesco di Marco Corner, Gabriele's major business partner around 1400, himself son of a doge. Nicolò di Mafio di Gabriele married the niece of the wealthy future doge Andrea Vendramin. For the second marriage of Pietro di Giovanni di Vettor to Clara, daughter of the "magnifica domina" Paula Dal Verme of Verona, who brought in dowry extensive possessions in the Veronese, see PSM, Ultra, b. 79, commis. Capello, bound parchment book, fol. 27v, act of 22 February 1467. Finally, a son of Vettor di Zuane di Vettor (whose marriages were indicated differently in AC 106 and 107 — I have entered both, with a question mark) married the niece and namesake of Caterina Corner, queen of Cyprus, albeit after the successful liquidation of the bank.

Several of the Soranzo testaments are discussed in Mueller, "Sull'establishment bancario veneziano," where they are also cited.

The Gaddi Family between Florence and Venice, Fourteenth to Sixteenth Century

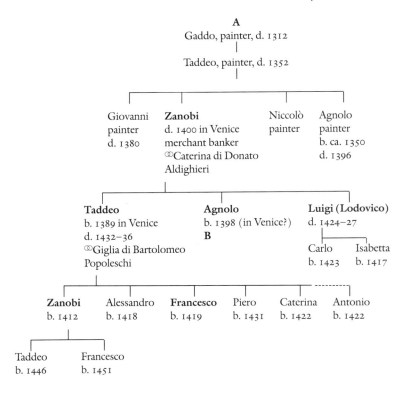

A

Gaddo, painter, d. 1312

|

Taddeo, painter, d. 1352

|

Giovanni painter d. 1380 — **Zanobi** d. 1400 in Venice merchant banker ∞Caterina di Donato Aldighieri — Niccolò painter — Agnolo painter b. ca. 1350 d. 1396

Taddeo b. 1389 in Venice d. 1432–36 ∞Giglia di Bartolomeo Popoleschi — **Agnolo** b. 1398 (in Venice?) **B** — **Luigi (Lodovico)** d. 1424–27

Carlo b. 1423 — Isabetta b. 1417

Zanobi b. 1412 — Alessandro b. 1418 — **Francesco** b. 1419 — Piero b. 1431 — Caterina b. 1422 — Antonio b. 1422

Taddeo b. 1446 — Francesco b. 1451

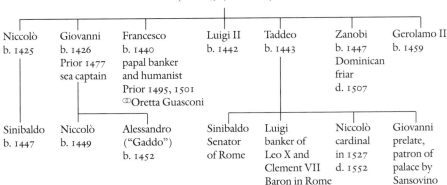

B

Agnolo di Zanobi
b. 1398 (in Venice?)
merchant banker and humanist
Prior 1437, 1442, 1451
∞1Isabella Adimari
∞2**Maddalena Ridolfi**
(test. 1450, in Venice)

| Niccolò b. 1425 | Giovanni b. 1426 Prior 1477 sea captain | Francesco b. 1440 papal banker and humanist Prior 1495, 1501 ∞Oretta Guasconi | Luigi II b. 1442 | Taddeo b. 1443 | Zanobi b. 1447 Dominican friar d. 1507 | Gerolamo II b. 1459 |

| Sinibaldo b. 1447 | Niccolò b. 1449 | Alessandro ("Gaddo") b. 1452 | Sinibaldo Senator of Rome | Luigi banker of Leo X and Clement VII Baron in Rome | Niccolò cardinal in 1527 d. 1552 | Giovanni prelate, patron of palace by Sansovino |

TABLE H.2

The Priuli Family, Bankers on the Rialto, 1399–1429

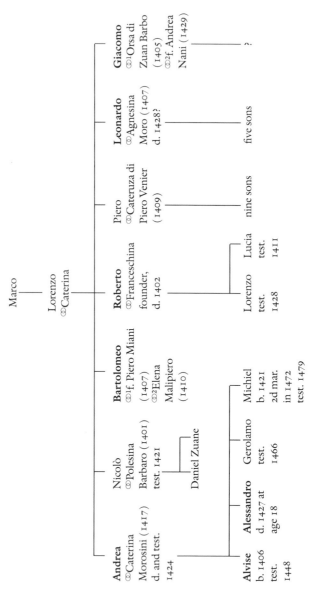

Marco

Lorenzo
⚭Caterina

Andrea
⚭Caterina
Morosini (1417)
d. and test.
1424

Nicolò
⚭Polesina
Barbaro (1401)
test. 1421

Daniel Zuane

Bartolomeo
⚭1f. Piero Miani
(1407)
⚭2Elena
Malipiero
(1410)

Roberto
⚭Franceschina
founder,
d. 1402

Lorenzo
test.
1428

Lucia
test.
1411

Piero
⚭Cateruza di
Piero Venier
(1409)

nine sons

Leonardo
⚭Agnesina
Moro (1407)
d. 1428?

five sons

Giacomo
⚭1Orsa di
Zuan Barbo
(1405)
⚭2f. Andrea
Nani (1429)

?

Alvise
b. 1406
test.
1448

Alessandro
d. 1427 at
age 18

Gerolamo
test.
1466

Michiel
b. 1421
2d mar.
in 1472
test. 1479

TABLE H.3

The Soranzo Family, Bankers on the Rialto, 1374–1491

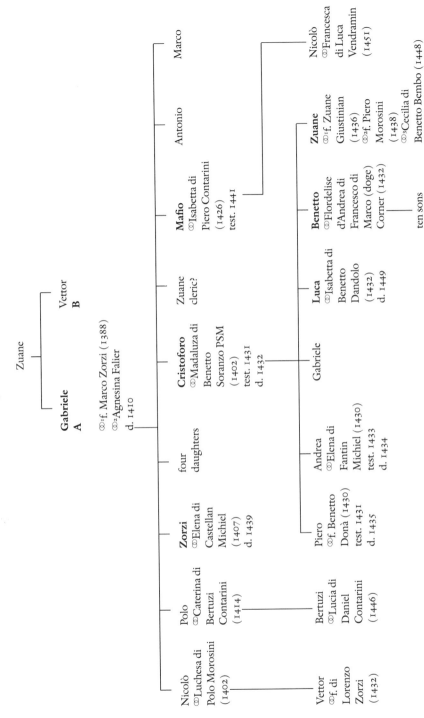

(continued)

645

B

Vettor di Zuane
∞Bianca di Pino
de' Bugni (1401)
test. 1419

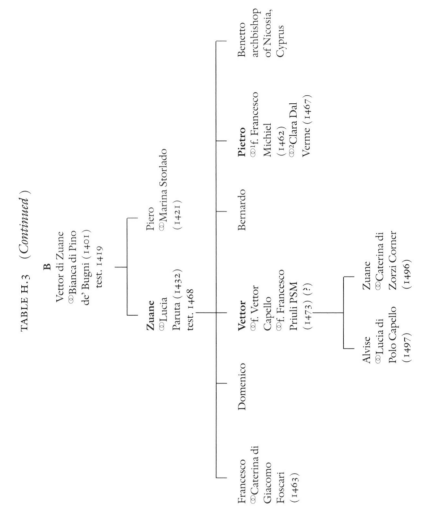

Piero
∞Marina Storlado
(1421)

Zuane
∞Lucia
Paruta (1432)
test. 1468

Domenico

Francesco
∞Caterina di
Giacomo
Foscari
(1463)

Vettor
∞f. Vettor
Capello
∞f. Francesco
Priuli PSM
(1473) (?)

Alvise
∞Lucia di
Polo Capello
(1497)

Zuane
∞Caterina di
Zorzi Corner
(1496)

Bernardo

Pietro
∞1f. Francesco
Michiel
(1462)
∞2Clara Dal
Verme (1467)

Benetto
archbishop
of Nicosia,
Cyprus

APPENDIX I

THE VALUE OF MONEY AND THE COST OF LIVING

INCE SUMS OF MONEY, large and small, have been mentioned in numerous and diverse contexts during the nearly three centuries covered by this book, it may be useful to provide some idea of the value of money, that is, its purchasing power, at scattered dates. The data provided and manipulated in this appendix are largely unscientific; the basic research necessary for a clarification of this theme remains to be done before anything comparable to Giuliano Pinto's exemplary study for Florence can be undertaken.[1]

It was reported earlier (Vol. 1, pp. 32–33) that Venice lacked long-term, homogeneous wage and price series and that studies of the cost of living were few and far between. The intervening decade has produced some five relevant contributions. The one covering the earliest period, by Louise Buenger Robbert, provides tables of official commodity prices and salaries of government officials and employees which supply "overwhelming evidence" of inflation over the century 1172–1282, conceivably stimulated by an increase in the quantity of money in circulation. The second, by Susan Connell, lists quite a number of wages of masters and workers in the building trades between 1392 and 1505, derived from actual building accounts; nominal wages, the author shows, remained at the same level for almost a century from 1390 to the 1470s. The third study, chapter 17 in Goy's *House of Gold* (entitled "The Building Industry: Money, Wages, and

---

[1]"I livelli di vita dei salariati fiorentini (1380–1430)," reprinted in his *Toscana medievale: Paesaggi e realtà sociali* (Florence, 1993), 113–49.

Standards of Living"), is the first to discuss real wages, for the period about 1425–32, but the author does so using Venetian wages and Florentine prices; that mistaken procedure merely underscores the poverty of Venetian price data currently available. In her contribution, Ester Zille draws some wages but especially salaries paid by the government in the late fifteenth and early sixteenth centuries almost exclusively from official deliberations. Finally, a study by Donald Queller, covering a brief but important period in the late Trecento, has been announced but has not yet appeared.[2]

More essential for this appendix, however, and for any future study of the cost of living in Venice is the important series of day wages of building workers, 1377–1540, collected by Susan Connell and presented in Appendix J, below.

Two obvious factors influencing the cost of living which must be kept in mind are inflation and the rise in the value of the gold ducat in silver-based soldi di piccoli. The latter was studied in Volume 1, Appendix D, and has been taken up again briefly above, in Appendix D of the present volume. Both salaries and wheat prices are generally given in lire di piccoli, beginning in the mid-Trecento, which simplifies calculations. As regards periods of inflation prior to the sixteenth century, on the other hand, the data so far collected are at best indicative of trends.

The half century after 1348 was characterized by a fairly consistent price inflation; in fact, wine prices in 1382–93 (when the alimentary crisis of the War of Chioggia had already been overcome) are double and triple those of 1341–48, and the same is true of fava beans; wheat prices between 1382 and 1395 hold and even exceed the price level reached during the serious famine of 1346–48, during which prices had already doubled the preceding level. But there are as yet no Venetian wage data for artisan labor in the period before the Black Death. Some idea can be had from the wages of two service personnel who worked in a small hospice for twenty widows. Before the plague, they earned the equivalent, in silver coins, of 2½ ducats per year, whereas between 1378 and 1395 they earned the equivalent of 4½ to almost 5 ducats.[3]

Household accounts are not abundant, but not even these have yet been studied systematically in order to cull the prices of consumables which

[2]Louise Buenger Robbert, "Money and Prices in Thirteenth-Century Venice," *Journal of Medieval History* 20 (1994): 373–90. Susan Connell, *The Employment of Sculptors and Stonemasons in Venice in the Fifteenth Century* (Ph.D. diss., 1976; New York, 1988), 162–84. Ester Zille, "Salari e stipendi a Venezia tra Quattro e Cinquecento," *AV,* ser. 5, 138 (1992): 5–29. Donald E. Queller, "A New Approach to the Pre-modern Cost of Living: Venice, 1372–89," forthcoming in the *JEEcH.* Still useful is the collection of prices by Cecchetti, *La vita dei veneziani,* pt. 2: Il vitto.

[3]These data were collected and elaborated by Pierpaolo Miniutti, "Povertà ed assistenza a Venezia dal Medio Evo all'Età Moderna: L'amministrazione di tre ospedali" (laurea thesis, University of Venice, 1993–94), esp. tables 3.15, A.3.1, A.3.5, A.3.8.

can be matched with wage rates; for the time being, the following indications may be useful.

From an early and very rare record of living expenses for a modest noble family in 1343, Gino Luzzatto evinces that a household of nine persons (a widow, five sons, and three daughters, mostly minors, plus a maid-servant) spent 103 ducats for food alone in six months; with the addition of clothing, medicine, a tutor, and service, the total rises to 137 ducats.

> An isolated purchase of wheat by the family cost 60 soldi or 3 lire per staio in 1343, shortly before the onset of the famine.
>
> A maidservant earned 3 ducats per year, besides board and lodging.
>
> A tutor for three children earned 3 denari piccoli per lesson — enough to purchase two eggs — or 3 ducats per year.
>
> A doctor, called in to assist a sick person around the clock for extended periods (ten to thirty days at a time), earned 0.8 ducats per day in 1343, 1 ducat per day in 1367. Medical visits in 1343 were paid about ½ ducat each.[4]

For the period embracing the lifetime of Andrea Barbarigo and his son Nicolò, nearly a century later, Frederic Lane (*Andrea Barbarigo,* 32–33) provided a list that is still useful:

Oarsman's wage, if he served a full year on a war galley in peacetime:	ca. 1420	28 du.
Ordinary master shipwright (highly skilled labor), whole year:	1407–47	48 du.
Salary of a top marine architect:	1424	100 du.
Cash salary, besides perquisites, of expert galley builder from Crete:	1424	200 du.
Estimated net worth of Andrea Barbarigo, at his death:	1449	15,000 du.
Dowries for daughters of Doge Andrea Vendramin:	ca. 1476	6,000–7,000 du.
Estimated patrimony of Doge Andrea Vendramin:	1476	160,000 du.

To this list, one might add:

> A head of the caulkers (proto dei calafati) earned 100 ducats in 1392 (ASV, Grazie, reg. 18, fol. 35) and exactly the same in 1519 (Zille, "Salari"); this is a reminder that wages in the arsenal are often somewhat out of the ordinary.
>
> The salaried factor of the Corner-Miorati transfer bank on the

---

[4]"Il costo della vita a Venezia nel Trecento" reprinted in his *Studi*.

Rialto (the Florentine Domenico di Masino di Manetto) about 1405 earned 100 ducats per year.

The salaried manager of the Medici branch in Venice in 1417 (Giovanni d'Adoardo Portinari) earned 150 florins (di suggello). In the same position, Francesco Davizi in 1440 earned 60 ducats per year (de Roover, *Medici Bank,* 242, 248).

The salary of a proto or protomaistro in the building trades ranged from 50 to 150 ducats between 1450 and 1550; the sculptor Antonio Rizzo received 200 ducats per year as architect (soprastante) of the doge's palace, 1491–95 (Connell, *Employment,* 163).

Master craftsmen and laborers in the building trades earned nominal wages that were quite stable from about 1370 to 1470; projected to a 200-day year (out of 270 working days), a master earned about 320 lire di piccoli, a laborer about half that. The value in gold of the master's wage was 80 ducats in 1388, 60 ducats in 1430, 52 ducats in 1468, that of the laborer, again, just half that (see below, App. J).

Dalmatian valets hired by Guglielmo Querini in the 1460s earned 3 to 4½ lire di piccoli per month, or 5.8 to 8.7 ducats per year (Mueller, "Aspects," 55).

The valet (Bartolomeo da Trento) of Marino Contarini, builder of the Ca' d'Oro, earned 100 lire di piccoli, or 19 ducats per year, in the 1420s (Goy, *House of Gold,* 93).

The cost of building the Ca' d'Oro (1425–32) has been estimated at about 7,000 ducats (ibid., 245), not much higher than the 6,000 florins that Francesco Datini calculated in 1399 as the cost of his palace in Prato. The Ca' d'Oro was valued at 12,000 ducats in 1479.

The church of S. Maria della Carità, built around the middle of the fifteenth century, cost 7,433 ducats (Connell, *Employment,* 171).

A woman's silk dress, especially if cloth-of-gold, could cost as much as 300–500 ducats about the mid-fifteenth century.

About 1460, a pair of chickens cost 9 soldi, a fat goose 12 soldi; a "pound" of cherries 1 soldo, of dried figs 2 soldi, of raisins 2–4 soldi; an "excellent" eel 3 soldi, "eleven pairs" salted eels £1 4s, 100 squid 5–6 soldi (Cecchetti, *Vita dei veneziani,* 102–3, 115, 189).

Marin Sanudo's family earned the fabulous sum of 800 ducats per year in rent from a small hostel (l'hostaria "Della Campana") at the Rialto in the late fifteenth century; any other well-situated hostel, Sanudo reported, would have been let for about 250 ducats—more than the rent any patrician palace could have gotten at the time (*De origine*, 29).

The price ceiling on beef was 2 soldi the pound (477 grams), on oil 4 soldi for the same kind of pound, on firewood 28 soldi per "carro," all around the year 1493 (ibid., 30).

A haircut by a barber at the same time was normally 4 soldi (ibid.).

Monthly wage rates of galley rowers depended on whether they could trade goods or hope for booty.[5] But basically, in the Quattrocento, the direction was downward:

Year	Type of Galley Duty		
	war	*patrol*	*merchant*
1400		£13	
1402		£14–18	
1427		£13	
1482–83	£12		£7–9
1499	£8		
1500	£12		
1519		£6–8	

The wages of 1499–1500 were for merchant galleys pressed into service in the naval war against the Turks. If the oarsmen worked a full year, at current exchanges they would have earned, in gold ducats, in 1400, 36 ducats; in 1427, 30 ducats; in 1482, 15.5 ducats; in 1500, 23 ducats; in 1519, 14 ducats.

Hans Keller, factor of the Fugger company, on a business trip to Venice in 1489, spent 1 ducat, £5 16s di piccoli (or 1.935 ducats) in seventeen days for food alone; projected to a full year, in the unlikely case of a businessman living "out" the whole time, this comes to 42 ducats.[6]

The costs of tutoring children, at home and at school, were as follows:

Tutors, schoolmasters, and schools (per year, in ducats):[7]

1343	tutor of 3 children (nonresident)	3
1364	tuition in a school, for one child	1
1381–85	resident tutor of one child (salary: 21.5 du., living costs: 25 du.)	46.5
1385–88	tuition in school, one child	12

---

[5]The first two rates were kindly provided by S. Piasentini; the others are from Frederic C. Lane, "Wages and Recruitment of Venetian Galeotti, 1470–1580," reprinted in his *Studies*, art. X.

[6]Bruder, "Reiserechenbuch des Hans Keller," 837.

[7]Gherardo Ortalli, *Scuole, maestri e istruzione di base tra Medioevo e Rinascimento: Il caso veneziano* (Vicenza, 1993), see index, under "salari."

| 1400–17 | communal schoolmaster in Chioggia according to the exigencies of the Venetian war budget: | 80-40-60 |
| 1427 | salary of tutor, plus living costs: | 40 |

Wheat prices do not abound for Venice; prices current in Mestre, for which a relatively good series has been collected for many of the years between 1384 and 1519, cannot be considered characteristic of the Venetian marketplace until more is known about price ceilings in Venice and the nature of its market or markets. Whereas Mestre was provisioned from the surrounding countryside, Venice was provisioned by sea, and price controls were a part of government policy.[8] L. Buenger Robbert lists prices offered by the Commune to importers (in soldi of the libra denariorum venetialium) which rise from about 18 soldi in the 1220s to about 40 soldi in 1282. Thereafter, wheat, like other bread grains and dried beans, is quoted in lire di piccoli. The prices provided below were derived from only isolated purchases (in the first case) or sales (in the second case); although they do not form a series, they are not completely without value, to the extent that someone actually paid or received or registered that price at some point in a given year. (The data are so scarce that where there is more than one datum, the average was calculated per calendar year beginning 1 January. In fact, the agricultural year — beginning 1 July — is of less importance in a city like Venice, which, before the sixteenth century, imported wheat primarily by sea from as far away as Apulia, Sicily, and the Black Sea.)

The Saluzzo charitable endowment for the distribution of bread provides, besides wheat prices, the costs per unit of bread produced, including the pay due the baker for having the wheat ground and for making bread of it, which passed from 14 soldi per staio in 1389 to 20 soldi in 1405. The baker baked 350 small loaves or "panini" (each made of 0.24 liters of wheat and weighing about 180 grams) from one staio throughout the period. The cost per loaf changed with the price of wheat, in these contracts by the job, from a minimum of 0.19 soldi (2.28 denari) to a maximum of 0.40 soldi (4.8 denari). To give an example, in 1413 the contract was for baking 70,000 loaves, at 6 "light ounces" (ca. 180 grams) each, from 200 staia of wheat that cost 105 soldi per staio; the total cost of that year's charitable dole, with the ducat at 100 soldi, was 210 ducats.[9]

---

[8]Checchin, *La scuola e l'ospedale di S. Maria dei Battuti di Mestre*; the appendix contains prices, not only of wheat, but also of flour, wine, oil, and wax. On only one occasion do the months of price quotations on the two markets overlap, and on that occasion even the date coincides: on 24 December 1472 wheat in Mestre sold for 90s (Checchin), in Venice for 68s (Mometto). The wide differential, not accounted for at all by the difference of only 4 percent in the larger staio used in Mestre, does not seem to be unusual. During the famine years of the 1490s, prices in Venice were again considerably lower on close dates, but more solid data are needed before a true comparison can be made.

[9]I have the basic data from an unpublished study of the Saluzzo endowment by Edoardo

Even though these were, for all practical purposes, wholesale prices, we can compare them with builders' wages. In 1389 the builder (muraro) Zane earned 32 soldi per day, the carpenter Jacomo 40 soldi (but he surely had to pay his own helper from that). That is, with wheat at 82 soldi, Zane could buy 0.4 staia (33.3 liters), Jacomo 0.5 staia (41.7 liters), or 119 and 148 wholesale "panini" respectively, with a day's wage and at that year's unit costs. The very next year, with wheat at an average of 112 soldi (it was 125 soldi in March, 100 soldi in September), Zane could have bought only 0.28 staia (23.3 liters) or 82 panini, Jacomo 0.36 staia (30 liters) or 103 panini.

A century later, in 1473, with wheat at 94 soldi, a master builder, earning from 18 soldi to 24 soldi could buy from 0.19 to 0.26 staia (15.8–21.7 liters) of wheat.

The decline in nominal wages becomes much more serious if a wage is transformed into its gold value. In 1389, with the ducat at 82 soldi, our master builder could earn a ducat in 2.6 days' work, while in 1474, with the ducat at 124 soldi, it took him 5.2 to 6.9 days to earn a ducat—that is, double to triple the time. Even if the artisan and the laborer earned in a silver-based money of account and took home silver coin as pay, the gold value is significant, for it is the measure of what Carlo Cipolla long ago pointed to as profit inflation; relative to gold, men and women who did manual work lost 200–300 percent in a century.

The cost of living needs to be placed in a wider setting, and I experimented here with comparing nominal and real wages in Venice and Florence, in scattered and rather randomly chosen years, of high, low, and average prices in each city. The procedure is not quite as simple as was thought by Richard Goy (*House of Gold,* 97–98), who based his optimistic comments regarding Venetian wages and the cost of living on Goldthwaite's data for Florence, on the assumption that the Venetian soldo was the equivalent of the Florentine soldo (which, of course, it was not). The author concluded that a Venetian artisan in the building trades spent only a quarter of his wage on essentials and may well have been able to save money for a rainy day. These calculations will have to be redone with Venetian prices of consumables — not only wheat — and housing rents, which, taken together, may well have been relatively higher in Venice than in Florence. Still, wages in Venice were high in this sector, and Goy's optimism may well be confirmed even by the use of proper data.

If one looks at the last column of table I.3, one sees that in two of the six years analyzed (1421 and 1462) unskilled laborers in Florence and Venice were able to purchase exactly the same amount of wheat—in liters— with their respective wages. In the other four years considered, Venetian

Demo, provisionally entitled "Lana e pane a Venezia tra il 1387 e il 1425," presented at a seminar at San Miniato. At the bakery, it is worth recalling, the price of retailed bread remained stable, while the weight of a loaf varied according to the price of wheat.

TABLE I.1

Price of Wheat Purchased by the Saluzzo Endowment, 1389–1425
(in scattered months)

Year	Price (decimalized)		Year	Price (decimalized)	
	soldi	lire		soldi	lire
1389	82	4.1	1401	88	4.4
1390	112.5	5.6	1402	80	4
1391	90	4.5	1403	88	4.6
1392	80	4	1404	80	4
1393	77	3.9	1405	80	4
1394	67	3.4	1407	98	4.9
1395	59	3	1408	100	5
1396	52	2.6	1413	105	5.3
1397	94	4.7	1417	128	6.4
1399	91	4.6	1419	125	6.3
			1421	143	7.2
			1425	83	4.2

Source: ASV, PSM, Supra, Commissarie, b. 35, commis. Manfredo di Saluzzo.
Note: A total of 35 purchases in 22 years, 40–250 staia at a time for a charitable bread dole. Annual averages where more than one quotation per year. (Culled and elaborated by E. Demo.) One Venetian staio = 83.3 liters = 2.36 bushels.

laborers could purchase between about 150 and 250 percent the amount of wheat which their Florentine counterparts could afford. Of course, wheat prices were volatile, and the situation in either city at any given observation date could have been considerably different.

Another approach is to translate wages into grams of fine silver, as in the third to last column in the table. These calculations moderate the Venetian workers' advantage, which now ranges from a minimum of 122 percent to a maximum of 167 percent; on the other hand, the Venetians' advantage in fine silver of 135 and 156 percent in 1421 and 1462, respectively, was neutralized by particularly high prices for wheat, with the result that in those years workers in both cities earned the same real wages. That seems to be rather an exception, however; the rule seems to be that Venetian workers earned relatively more in real terms, a tendency that was sometimes aided by their being able to buy wheat at relatively lower prices than was the case in Florence. As will be seen below in Appendix J, contemporaries were very aware that wages were relatively higher in Venice than elsewhere.

The comparisons made here are mere approximations of reality, it must be remembered. In order to begin refining the data and making them effectively comparable, more solid and especially homogeneous series of wheat prices will be needed for Venice. More will have to be known of the extent to which the government of Venice, perhaps to a greater extent than elsewhere, controlled wheat prices as a social policy by absorbing eventual

TABLE I.2

Price of Wheat sold in Venice by the Barbarigo Family, 1462–1479
(in scattered months)

Year	Price (decimalized)		Year	Price (decimalized)	
	soldi	lire		soldi	lire
1462	65.3	3.3	1470	57	2.8
1463	66.5	3.3	1471	43.2	2.2
1464	112.4	5.6	1472	55	2.75
1465	106	5.3	1473	95	4.7
1466	72.5	3.6	1474	94.4	4.7
1468	71	3.6	1475	87	4.4
1469	56	2.6	1476	58.5	2.9
			1477	84.2	4.2
			1478	112	5.6
			1479	46	2.3

Source: Mometto, *L'azienda agricola Barbarigo*, 200–201.
Note: 52 sales in 17 years, in amounts of 1 to 137 staia, but generally about 20–25 staia per sale.
Annual averages.

losses between retail prices and the wholesale prices on imports which it guaranteed and on which it offered bonuses. Finally, given the difficulty of policing prohibitions against the export of wheat to the mainland, first of all to nearby Mestre, where prices seem regularly to have been higher, it will be necessary to investigate in depth the nature of contiguous markets and the possible price differentials within circuits (merchants, millers, bakers, and the like) in one and the same market.

At the same time, other data for the capital cities of the northern Italian "quadrilateral" also show Venetian builders' wages to be very high. Scattered data on master builders' day wages collected by Carlo Cipolla for the late Quattrocento, when reduced to grams of fine silver, reveal the following:

City	Wage and Currency (Master Builders)	Grams Fine Silver
Milan	10–12 soldi imperiali	4.3–5.2
Florence	16–18 soldi di piccioli	4.6–5.1
	13–15 soldi di piccioli	4.3–4.9*
Genoa	8–10 soldi Genoese	5.2–6.5
Venice	22–26 soldi di piccoli	6.8–8.1

(*The second set of figures for Florence, derived from Goldthwaite's data on wages and the Florentine soldo ca. 1494, would drop Florence to the lowest position, below Milan.)[10]

[10]Carlo M. Cipolla, *Le avventure della lira* (Bologna, 1975), 58 and n. 29 (the grams of fine silver, reported above, were calculated on the basis of data provided by Cipolla himself).

TABLE I.3

Nominal and Real Wages in Venice and Florence Compared, 1389–1499
(in scattered years)

Year	City	Ducat/ Florin in S. Pic.	1 s. in Grams Fine Silver	Wheat Prices		Wages of Unskilled Workers		Wages in Wheat	
				Soldi per Staio	Grams Fine Silver	Soldi per Day	Grams Fine Silver	Staia	Liters
1389	VE	82	0.472	82	38.7	14	6.6	0.17	14.2
	FI	74	0.542	43	23.3	9.9	5.4	0.23	5.7
1390	VE	84	0.472	112	52.9	14	6.1	0.13	10.4
	FI	75	0.480	33	15.8	8.5	4.1	0.26	6.4
1421	VE	103	0.380	143	54.3	16	6.1	0.11	9.3
	FI	81	0.450	26	11.7	10	4.5	0.38	9.4
1462	VE	124	0.332	65	21.6	16	5.3	0.25	20.5
	FI	108	0.382	11	4.2	9	3.4	0.82	20.2
1464	VE	124	0.332	112	37.2	18	6.0	0.16	13.4
	FI	106	0.382	25	9.6	9.3	3.6	0.37	9.2
1499	VE	124	0.309	65	20.1	12	3.7	0.18	15.4
	FI	137	0.328	26	8.5	8.8	2.9	0.34	8.4

Sources: For Venice (VE): Volume 1, p. 527, table A.2 and App. D; Papadopoli, *Le monete di Venezia,* 2:2–5, 12, 20, 25, 51–52, 77–78; below, table J.1. For Florence (FI): Goldthwaite, "I prezzi del grano a Firenze," 33–34; idem, *The Building of Renaissance Florence*, apps. 1, 3; Goldthwaite-Mandich, *Studi,* 86, table 2.

Note: Dry measures: after the formation of the Italian state, the staio of Venice was calculated as 83.3 liters, the staio of Florence as 24.7 liters; no more credible figures for making conversions are available. In comparative terms, 1 staio Venetian = 3.37 staia Florentine. Discrepancies in the decimal places are due to rounding off.

These figures confirm the conclusions derived above from table I.3, and they are themselves corroborated, in turn, by the advice given to Duke Francesco Sforza in the 1460s, namely, that to complete the palace he had purchased on Venice's Grand Canal he could save 30–50 percent on labor costs if he hired artisans in Milan and sent them to Venice. His ambassador in Venice wrote: "serà mandare de là et maistri de muro et marangoni et lavoratori anchora, perchè forsi se avantagiarà el terzo de manifactura, perchè qua guadagnano molto ingrosso, forsi el dopio, o al mancho el terzo più che non hano de là." And his architect confirmed the judgment even as regards house carpenters: "Avisandovi che in questa terra se paghino molto bene li magistri — se paghe el dopio più de quello se pagarìa a Milano." Lombard building workers in fact immigrated to Venice in large numbers, leading in the second half of the Quattrocento to loud complaints by local artisans about the competition. Just how they made ends meet is difficult to say, but many — as the Venetian artisans complained — came to Venice without their families and did not settle down for good. Despite the high general cost of living in Venice, experienced by travelers then as today, they were still able to earn a living and presumably earned more in Venice than they could have earned at home. The arrival of the immigrants, combined with the general increase in demographic growth experienced throughout Europe, began in the 1460s and 1470s to depress nominal salaries in the building trades, as is revealed in table J.1, below.[11]

[11]Anne M. Schulz, *Niccolò di Giovanni Fiorentino and Venetian Sculpture of the Early Renaissance* (New York, 1978), 3 and nn. 3–6. See also Connell, *Employment of Sculptors*, 72–79.

APPENDIX J

BUILDERS' WAGES FROM THE LATE TRECENTO TO THE EARLY CINQUECENTO

HIS APPENDIX IS DUE solely to the research and generosity of Susan Connell. My reduction of the large sheets she provided to the scant table J.1 meant reducing also the wealth of detail provided in the notes for the type of work being done in each case, not to speak of the names of the artisans themselves and the sources. Some of the detail can be found in the author's *Employment,* 162–84. There one will also find a large number of the sources from which the rates presented here were derived; the general trend of the rates was already indicated by the author's short table of wages (pp. 183–84). I have exploited here not only her figures but her incisive critique of a first draft of this appendix and her suggestions.

Master stonemasons (tagliapietra), builders (mureri), and carpenters (marangoni) were paid at day rates that could vary considerably according to their skill and fame, the type and quality of work to be done, the time of year, that is, according to the length of the working day, and, at times, whether or not the employer would provide a ration of wine. Just the same, there often seems to be no rhyme or reason for the differences in wages accorded, even to the same person, but contractual leverage was obviously important. A stonemason generally graduated from a day wage to a piece rate or contract; he had a shop, if he could afford one, and supplied his own stone, which distinguishes him from the builder or carpenter. The range in wages contracted and paid is often so considerable that calculating averages, weighted or otherwise, for masters was impracticable.

The situation was somewhat different for assistants, an umbrella term used here to cover unskilled and semiskilled workers who were often called "lavoranti" or, for stonemasons, also "fregadori" or "manoali," for builders and carpenters also "manoali," "fachini," "fanti," and "schiavoni." "Garzone" and "fante" were terms used also for apprentices. The wages of such laborers varied only within a much smaller range, so that averaging them — as did Goldthwaite for Florence — is more justifiable. The very lowest wages were reserved for apprentices and children and were sometimes indicated separately, rather than included in the master's wage; these low figures, of 10 soldi per day or less, have been omitted from table J.1 for the century preceding 1470, when rates began to fall.

Despite the relative scantiness — in statistical terms — of the data, they are sufficient to warrant some generalizations. First, nominal wages were "sticky" once they rose after the Black Death, as was everywhere the case. A typically good master builder or carpenter earned a stable wage of 32 soldi per day in 1388, 1428–29, 1438, 1468; in the same years, a good laborer earned 16 soldi, even though his wages were more variable from about 1390 to 1420, then more stable from about 1420 to 1470. Thereafter, nominal wages of both masters and laborers declined, as was mentioned in the previous appendix, to 20–24 soldi for masters, to 12–14 soldi for laborers. An increase begins in the 1520s and becomes somewhat more marked in the 1530s, probably as wages tried to keep pace with inflation. A rather similar pattern emerges from the Florentine data gathered by Goldthwaite: the decline in nominal wages begins in the 1470s for skilled artisans, in the 1490s for unskilled laborers; the marked increase for both begins in the 1530s (*Building of Renaissance Florence,* app. 3).[1]

Projection of the day wage of an artisan in the building trades to a year is somewhat arbitrary; inclement weather and irregular employment meant that no one in that sector, outside of stonemasons, who could often work in sheds or shops, was ever employed all the approximately 270 working days in a normal year, and a long-term average of about 200 days, as suggested by Domenico Sella, is much more reasonable.[2] In order to facilitate comparisons, we can say that a master's day wage of 32 soldi in Venice in the 1380s meant 320 lire di piccoli, or about 80 ducats, in a 200-day year. The same salary in 1430 was worth in gold only about 60 ducats, in 1468 about 52 ducats. A day wage of 26 soldi in 1470 meant 260 lire di piccoli, or only 42 gold ducats in a year. The projections for laborers are just about half

---

[1]For Venice in the following period, outside our present scope, see Brian Pullan, "Wage-Earners and the Venetian Economy, 1550–1630," reprinted in idem, ed., *Crisis and Change in the Venetian Economy in the Sixteenth and Seventeenth Centuries* (London, 1968), 146–74.

[2]*Salari e lavoro nell'edilizia lombarda durante il secolo XVII* (Pavia, 1968), 19–20; the author cites this explanation for the short year written in 1594: "de questi [270 giorni] ne va persa buona parte, massime nell'invernata et anco in altri tempi per piogge et nevi. Un'altra ne va persa a molti, puoichè tutti non trovano senpre da lavorare." Sella constructed an index of real wages for his period by dividing a wage index by a cost-of-living index calculated on the prices of bread, wine, and wool cloth (table 11, pp. 149 ff.).

these figures for masters. It goes without saying that the paymaster calculated salaries in silver-based money of account; if a worker desired payment in ducats (or florins), he did not avoid the declining gold value of his pay, for he was charged the inexorably rising rate of exchange current on the local marketplace.

In the summer months of longer days, wages ought to have been higher; this is by no means always the case. In the detailed table J.1, where the months were summer months (practically from March through October), the wage is followed by an "S." If the wage clearly included an assistant, it is followed by a superscript a; if two assistants, a superscript b. Probably many of the high wage rates included a helper, even when this was not stated in the accounts and contracts.

Table J.2, which concludes the appendix, provides the promised simplification, namely, the average day wages of undifferentiated semiskilled and unskilled workers in all three sectors of the building trades.

TABLE J.1

Day Wages of Stonemasons, Builders, and Carpenters, 1377–1540
(in soldi di piccoli)

Year	Stonemasons		Builders		Carpenters	
	Master	Assistant	Master	Assistant	Master	Assistant
1377			48,[a] 26–30			
1382			56[a], 40, 28	14		
1384			32			
1388					32S	16S, 12S
1389			32		26	
1392					32S	18S
1393			32S, 40S	18	32	18m
1394			35, 41	18	38	12
1395			20, 44S		40S	
1398			24, 34S		29S	
1399			24–25, 32S, 35S	12, 13, 14S		
1400			24, 26	14		
1401			24	11	44, 48	16
1402			32S	16S, 18S		
1404			25, 28	14, 16, 20	35[a]	14
1408					52S, 16	
1412			36	14		
1417			36S[a]			
1418			29, 60[b]	16S	27S, 40[a]S	
1421			40			
1422			16, 24, 26, 28	16		
1423			37[a], 32S, 34S	14S	33S, 34S	
1424			27S, 36S	15S	24, 32S, 36S, 64[b]	16,20
1425	five at 20S–36S	18S	28S, 32S, 40[a]S	14S	28S, 33S, 36S	14S
1426	16, 18, 20, 24	17	20, 36	13	four 16–32	
1427	six at 13S–28S	5, 8			26S, 32S, 36S	
1428	15–20		32, 32[a]	16	27, 40[a]	
1429	five 20–31	12, 15S	32–48	14–18	thirteen at 20–32	15, 20
1430	20–26		36–48S			
1431	22		14–18, 32, 44[a] 52–54, 62[a]	12, 15–16		
1432					20	14
1436	26		32		32, 40[a]	
1437			32–36		36	
1438			32	16		
1439			32	16		

TABLE J.1 *(Continued)*

Year	Stonemasons		Builders		Carpenters	
	Master	Assistant	Master	Assistant	Master	Assistant
1443	48S		24–32, 44S	16	27S–32S, 33.3ªS, 56ᵇS	
1447			40			
1451			40ª			
1453			36ª	12		
1458	26	18	20–28		26S, 28S, 30ªS, 40ªS	
1459	23S–30S	18S				
1460	24		32	14	34ª	
1462	26S, 28, 28S, 36	16S	25S–28S	14S	28S	20S
1463	26S					
1464			32Sª			
1465	24		28	18		
1467			24	16		
1468			34	14, 18	32	
1470	five at 26	14–16				
1471			40ª		20, 36	12
1472			18–24, 40ª	10–12	20, 36	
1473	20, 24		18–24	10–12	20	
1474	22S–25S					
1477	22S–24S		five at 17–30	13, 20S		
1478		16S	24S	12S		
1480	20, 24					
1483	20, seven at 24S, 26S				34ªS	
1484	20	15S				
1485	25S					
1486	20, 25, 26ªS	12S	28S			
1490	28, 31					
1492	25					
1493		20				
1499	22	12–13	28	13		
1500	20, 26	five at 12–13	20, 26			
1505			three at 20; 24, 32ª	three at 12, three at 15	14, 25	
1506			36ªS	10S, 12S	24S	
1508			21S–22S, 24S–25S	12S–14S, 17S, 21S–22S	20S, 24–25S; 32ªS	
1509	24S			13S	20S, 24S	
1515			24	14		
1516	20				24	

TABLE J.I   (*Continued*)

Year	Stonemasons		Builders		Carpenters	
	Master	Assistant	Master	Assistant	Master	Assistant
1517	18S					
1518			19–20S, 23S			
1520	30					
1521	two at 30S		30S, 34[a]–36[a]S	15S		
1524		ten at 10S–12 and 15–16S	24, 26S, 28S	13, 15–16S	26	12
1525	22	14	20, 24		20, 24	
1526	20; five at 24–30S					
1528			20–23S, 24, 28	15, 17S		
1529	24		24	18–19		
1530		four at 16–18S				
1532	24S		35S	22S	30S	
1533			30S	16; four at 21S		
1535	27½		30, 32, 36	16; six at 20	24	12, 16, 20
1536	31½					
1537	44S					
1540	24S		30S	16S	28S, 36[a]S	20S

[a]Wage includes one assistant.
[b]Wage includes two assistants.
m = manovale (manual laborer).
S = summer wage.

TABLE J.2

Average Wage Rates of Unskilled and Semiskilled Workmen, 1388–1540
(in soldi di piccoli)

Year	Rate	Year	Rate	Year	Rate
1388	14 (2)	1438	16	1500	12.5 (2)
1393	18 (2)	1439	16	1505	13.5 (6)
1399	13.25 (4)	1443	16 (6)	1506	11 (2)
1400	14	1453	12	1508	16.5 (7)
1401	13.5 (2)	1458	10	1509	13
1402	17 (2)	1460	14	1515	14
1404	14.67 (3)	1462	16.3 (6)	1521	15
1412	14	1465	18	1524	13.9 (15)
1418	16	1467	16 (2)	1525	14
1422	16 (2)	1468	15.3 (3)	1526	16.5 (2)
1423	14	1470	15 (2)	1528	16 (2)
1424	15.5 (2)	1472	12	1529	18.5 (2)
1425	15.3 (3)	1477	16.5 (2)	1530	16.75 (4)
1426	13	1478	14 (2)	1532	22
1428	16	1484	15	1533	20 (5)
1429	15.75 (8)	1493	20	1535	18.2 (11)
1431	15.75 (4)	1499	12 (2)	1540	18.67 (3)
1432	14				

Note: The number of quotations, when more than one, is entered in parentheses.

BIBLIOGRAPHY

PRIMARY SOURCES

Manuscript Sources

The reader is referred to the notes for complete references to documents culled from numerous series, public and private, in the Archivio di Stato, Venice (ASV), the Archivio Datini, Prato (ADP), and many other archives and collections.

The unfinished manuscript history entitled "I banchi privati" by Mario Brunetti and Giovanni Orlandini, mentioned in the Preface, can be found in BMCV, P.D. C. 2368/8.

Conspicuous by its absence from the notes is ASV, Capitular dell'Offitio di Sopra Banchi. This register, last cited by Roberto Cessi (*PMV*) in 1937, has been lost. Begun in 1553 and containing documents from 1318 to 1799, this capitulary, consisting of 206 folios, contained almost exclusively copies of Senate deliberations. Nearly all the entries up to 1530 were published by Lattes (*Libertà*), who described it in detail. It was microfilmed by Florence Edler and Raymond de Roover for Abbott P. Usher in the 1930s. The microfilm collection was discovered by Alexander Gershenkron in the office in Harvard's Widner Library which he had inherited from Usher, and he passed it on to Frederic C. Lane. The films of this capitulary, numbered 37–41 (no. 37 has unfortunately been lost), today form part of the Lane Collection in the Archive of the Johns Hopkins University Library. A rudimentary transcription of the unpublished deliberations contained in the capitulary, originally made for Usher and passed on to me by Lane when I was a graduate student, is currently in my possession.

Published Sources

Alberti, Leon Battista. *I libri della famiglia*. Edited by Ruggiero Romano and Alberto Tenenti. Turin, 1980.

Baroni, Manuela, ed. *Notaio di Venezia del sec. XIII (1290–1292)*. FSV. Venice, 1977.

Berti, Pietro, ed. "Nuovi documenti intorno al catasto fiorentino." *Giornale storico degli archivi toscani* 4 (1860): 32–62.

Besta, Fabio, ed. *Bilanci generali della Repubblica di Venezia*. Vol. 1. Venice, 1912. Abbr.: *BG*.

Biancolini, G. *Serie cronologica dei vescovi e governatori di Verona*. Verona, 1760.

Bonfiglio Dosio, Giorgetta, ed. *Il "Capitolar dalle broche" della zecca di Venezia (1358–1556)*. Padua, 1984. Abbr.: *Cap. Broche*.

Borlandi, Antonia, ed. *Il manuale di mercatura di Saminiato de' Ricci*. Genoa, 1963.

Braunstein, Philippe, and Reinhold C. Mueller, eds. *Description ou traictie du gouvernement de la cité et seigneurie de Venise*. Forthcoming. Abbr.: *Traictie*.

Brown, Rawdon, ed. *Calendar of State Papers — Venetian*. Vol. 1. London, 1864.

Bruder, Adolf, ed. "Reiserechenbuch des Hans Keller aus den Jahren 1489–90." *Zeitschrift für die gesammte Staatswissenschaft* 37 (1881): 831–51.

Cassandro, Michele, ed. *Il libro giallo di Ginevra della compagnia fiorentina di Antonio Della Casa*. Florence, 1976.

Cessi, Roberto, ed. *Deliberazioni del Maggior Consiglio di Venezia*. 3 vols. Bologna, 1931–50. Abbr.: *DMC*.

———, ed. *Problemi monetari veneziani fino a tutto il secolo XIV*. Padua, 1937. Abbr.: *PMV*.

———, ed. *La regolazione delle entrate e delle spese (sec. XIII–XIV)*. Padua, 1925. Abbr.: *RES*.

———, ed. *Gli statuti veneziani di Jacopo Tiepolo del 1242 e le loro glosse*. Istituto veneto di scienze, lettere ed arti, *Memorie*, 30. Venice, 1938.

Cessi, Roberto, and Fanny Bennato, eds. *Venetiarum historia vulgo Petro Iustiniano Iustiniani filio adiudicata*. Venice, 1964.

Cessi, Roberto, et al., eds. *Le deliberazioni del Consiglio dei Rogati (Senato), serie "mixtorum."* 2 vols. Venice, 1960–62.

Cordignano, Fulvio, S.J., ed. *Catasto veneto di Scutari e Registrum Concessionum, 1416–1417*. 2 vols. Scutari, Albania, and Rome, 1940–42.

Cornet, E., ed. *Giornale dell'assedio di Constantinopoli, 1453*. Vienna, 1856.

Cotrugli, Benedetto. *Il libro dell'arte di mercatura*. Edited by Ugo Tucci. Venice, 1992.

da Cerea, Parisio. *Chronacon veronense.* Rerum Italicarum Scriptores, 8. Milan, 1728.

Dandolo, Andrea. *Andree Dandoli Chronica per extensum descripta.* Edited by E. Pastorello. Rerum Italicarum Scriptores, 12, pt. 1. Bologna, 1941.

da Uzzano, Giovanni. *Pratica della mercatura.* In *Della decima,* edited by G. F. Pagnini. Vol. 4. Lucca, 1766.

Davanzati, Bernardo. *Notizia de' cambi.* Florence, 1581. Reprinted in *Scisma d'Inghilterra, con altre operette del signor B. Davanzati.* Padua, 1729.

de Caresinis, Raffaino. *Chronica.* Edited by E. Pastorello. Rerum Italicarum Scriptores, 12, pt. 2. Bologna, 1923.

de Franceschi, Camillo, ed. "Chartularium piranense — Raccolta dei documenti medievali di Pirano." *Atti e memorie della Società istriana di archeologia e storia patria* 44 (1932–33): 271–320.

della Chiesa, G. *Cronaca di Saluzzo.* Historiae Patriae Monumenta, Scriptores. Tome 3. Turin, 1836.

de Marinis, Tammaro, and Alessandro Perosa, eds. *Nuovi documenti per la storia del Rinascimento.* Florence, 1970.

de Mézières, Philippe. *Le songe du vieil pelerin.* Edited by G. W. Coopland. 2 vols. Cambridge, England, 1969.

Dorini, Umberto, and Tommaso Bertelè, eds. *Il libro dei conti di Giacomo Badoer.* Rome, 1956.

Faldon, Nilo, ed. *Gli antichi statuti e le provvisioni ducali della magnifica comunità di Conegliano (1488).* Conigliano, 1974.

Favaro, Elena, ed. *Cassiere della bolla ducale: Grazie-novus liber (1299–1305).* FSV. Venice, 1962.

Ferrara, Francesco. "Documenti per servire alla storia de' banchi veneziani." *AV* 1 (1871): 106–53, 332–63. Abbr.: Ferrara, "Documenti."

Frangioni, Luciana. *Il carteggio milanese dell'Archivio Datini di Prato.* 2 vols. Florence, 1994.

Gatari, Galeazzo, Bartolomeo Gatari, and Andrea Gatari. *Cronaca carrarese.* Rerum Italicarum Scriptores, ser. 2, vol. 17, pt. 1. Città di Castello, 1909–31.

Genuardi, Luigi, ed. "La 'Summula statuorum floridorum Veneciarum' di Andrea Dandolo." *NAV,* n.s., a. 11, 21 (1911): 436–67.

Goldthwaite, Richard A., Enzo Settesoldi, and Marco Spallanzani, eds. *Due libri mastri degli Alberti: Una grande compagnia di Calimala, 1348–1358.* 2 vols. Florence, 1995.

Guasti, Cesare, ed. *Le commissioni di Rinaldo degli Albizzi.* 3 vols. Florence, 1867–73.

Lanfranchi Strina, Bianca, ed. *Codex publicorum (Codice del Piovego).* FSV. Vol. 1. Venice, 1985.

Lattes, Elia. *La libertà delle banche a Venezia dal secolo XII al XVII.* Milan, 1869. Reprint, Milan, 1977. Abbr.: Lattes, *Libertà.*

Lazzarini, Vittorio, ed. *Dispacci di Pietro Cornaro, ambasciatore a Milano durante la guerra di Chioggia*. Venice, 1939.

Lesnikov, Michail P., ed. *Die Handelsbücher des Hansischen Kaufmannes Veckinchusen*. Forschungen zur Mittelalterlichen Geschichte, vol. 19. Berlin, 1973.

Ljubić, Šime, ed. *Listine o odnošajih izmedju Južnoga Slavenstva i Mletačke republike*. 10 vols. Monumenta spectantia historiam Slavorum meridionalium (vols. 1–5, 9, 12, 17, 21–22). Zagreb, 1868–91.

Lombardo, Antonino, ed. *Le deliberazioni del Consiglio dei Quaranta della Repubblica di Venezia*. 3 vols. Venice, 1957–68. Abbr.: *DQ*.

Lünig, I. C., ed. *Codex Italiae diplomaticus*. 4 vols. Frankfurt, 1725–35.

Luzzatto, Gino, ed. *I prestiti pubblici della Repubblica di Venezia (sec. XIII–XV)*. Padua, 1929. Abbr.: *PRV*.

Machiavelli, Nicolò. *Le opere*. Edited by Luigi Passerini et al. 5 vols. Rome and Florence, 1873–79.

Malipiero, Domenico. *Annali veneti dall'anno 1457 al 1500*. Edited by Agostino Sagredo. *ASI* 7 (1843–44). Abbr.: Malipiero, *Annali*.

Mazzei, Ser Lapo. *Lettere di un notaro a un mercante del secolo XIV*. Edited by Cesare Guasti. 2 vols. Florence, 1880. Reprint, Prato, 1979.

Melis, Federigo. *Documenti per la storia economica dei secoli XIII–XVI*. Florence, 1972.

Minotto, A. S. *Documenta ad Bellunum, Cenetam, Feltria, Tarvisium spectantia*. Venice, 1871.

Monticolo, Giovanni, ed. *I capitolari delle arti veneziane (dalle origini al 1330)*. 3 vols. Rome, 1896–1914.

Monumenta Hungariae Historica. Series IV/A, Acta extera andegavorum. 3 vols. Budapest, 1874–76.

Morozzo della Rocca, Raimondo, ed. *Lettere di mercanti a Pignol Zucchello (1336–1350)*. FSV. Venice, 1957.

Morozzo della Rocca, Raimondo, and Antonino Lombardo, eds. *Documenti del commercio veneziano nei secoli XI–XIII*. 2 vols. Turin, 1940. Reprint, Turin, 1971.

———, eds. *Nuovi documenti del commercio veneto dei sec. XI–XIII*. Venice, 1953.

Osio, Luigi, ed. *Documenti diplomatici tratti dagli archivi milanesi*. 3 vols. Milan, 1864–72.

Pacioli, Luca. *Trattato di partita doppia*. Edited by Annalisa Conterio. Venice, 1994.

Pegolotti, Francesco Balducci. *La pratica della mercatura*. Edited by Allan Evans. Cambridge, Mass., 1936.

Pertusi, Agostino, ed. *La caduta di Costantinopoli*. 2 vols. Milan, 1976.

———, ed. *Testi inediti e poco noti sulla caduta di Costantinopoli*. Edited posthumously by Antonio Carile. Bologna, 1983.

Piacentino, Jacopo. *Cronaca della guerra Veneto-Scaligera*. Edited by Luigi Simeoni. Venice, 1931.

Predelli, Riccardo, ed. *I libri commemoriali della Repubblica di Venezia — regesti*. 8 vols. Venice, 1876–1914. Abbr.: *LCR*.

Princivalli, Alessandra, ed. *Capitolare degli Ufficiali sopra Rialto: Nei luoghi al centro del sistema economico veneziano (secoli XIII–XIV)*. With an essay by Gherardo Ortalli. Milan, 1994.

Priuli, Gerolamo. *I diarii*. Edited by Arturo Segre et al. Rerum Italicarum Scriptores, 2d ser., 24, pt. 3. Città di Castello and Bologna, 1921–41.

Quartine in lode di Venezia tratta fidelmente da un'antica stampa di Treviso, 1473. Nozze Albrizzi-Galvagna. Venice, 1839.

Relazioni di Guglielmo da Castelbarco con Venezia (Documenti del R. Archivio di Stato in Venezia). Nozze Jacob-Schizzi. Trent, 1887.

Roberti, Melchiore, ed. *Le magistrature giudiziarie veneziane e i loro capitolari fino al 1300*. 3 vols. Padua and Venice, 1906–11.

Sacchetti, Franco. *Il trecentonovelle*. Edited by Antonio Lanza. Florence, 1984.

Santoro, Caterina, ed. *La politica finanziaria dei Visconti: Documenti*. Milan, 1976.

Sanudo, Marin. *Commentarii della guerra di Ferrara*. Edited by Pietro Bettio. Venice, 1829.

———. *De origine, situ et magistratibus urbis Venetae ovvero la città di Venetia (1493–1530)*. Edited by Angela Caracciolo Aricò. Milan, 1980. Abbr.: Sanudo, *De origini*.

———. *I diarii*. Edited by Rinaldo Fulin et al. 58 vols. Venice, 1879–1903. Abbr.: Sanudo, *Diarii*.

———. *Vite de' duchi di Venezia*. Rerum Italicarum Scriptores, vol. 22. Milan, 1733.

———. *Le vite dei dogi (1474–1494)*. Edited by Angela Caracciolo Aricò. Vol. 1. Padua, 1989.

Sapori, Armando, ed. *I libri di commercio dei Peruzzi*. Milan, 1934.

———, ed. *Libro giallo della compagnia dei Covoni*. Milan, 1970.

Sarayna, Torello. *Le historie e fatti de Veronesi nei tempi del popolo e signori scaligeri*. Verona, 1542.

Simonsfeld, Heinrich. *Der Fondaco dei Tedeschi in Venedig und die deutsch-venetianischen Handelsbeziehungen*. 2 vols. Stuttgart, 1887. Reprint, Aalen, 1968.

Stussi, Alfredo, ed. *Zibaldone da Canal: Manoscritto mercantile del sec. XIV*. FSV. Venice, 1967.

Tamba, Giorgio, ed. *Bernardo de Rodolfis, notaio di Venezia (1392–1399)*. FSV. Venice, 1974.

Thiriet, Freddy, ed. *Deliberations des assemblées vénitiennes concernant la Romanie*. 2 vols. Paris, 1966–71.

———, ed. *Regestes des délibérations du Sénat de Venise concernant la Romanie.* 3 vols. Paris, 1958–61.

Thomas, Georg M. "Belagerung und Eroberung von Constantinopel im Jahre 1453." *Sitzungsberichte der königlichen bayerischen Akademie der Wissenschaften* 2 (1868).

Verci, Gianbattista. *Storia della marca trevigiana e veronese.* 17 vols. Venice, 1786–90.

Villani, Giovanni. *Cronica.* Edited by F. G. Dragomanni. 4 vols. Florence, 1844–45.

von Harff, Arnold. *Die Pilgerfahrt des Ritters Arnold von Harff . . . in den Jahren 1496 bis 1499.* Edited by E. von Groote. Cologne, 1860.

Zago, Ferruccio, ed. *Consiglio dei Dieci, deliberazioni miste.* 3 vols. FSV. Venice, 1962–93.

SECONDARY WORKS

Ashtor, Eliahu. "Aspetti della espansione italiana nel Basso Medioevo." Reprinted in his *Technology, Industry, and Trade: The Levant versus Europe, 1250–1500.* London, 1992.

———. "Le taux d'intérét dans l'orient médiéval." Reprinted in his *The Medieval Near East: Social and Economic History.* London, 1978.

———. "The Volume of Levantine Trade in the Later Middle Ages (1370–1498)." Reprinted in his *Studies on the Levantine Trade in the Middle Ages.* London, 1978.

Avogadro, G. A. "La congiura Tiepolo-Querini." *AV* 2 (1871): 214–18.

Azzoni Avogaro, Rambaldo. "Delle monete di Trivigi." In Zanetti, *Nuova raccolta delle monete e delle zecche d'Italia,* vol. 4.

Ballardini, Gaetano. "L'insigne 'piatto Leverton' con un episodio della spedizione di Carlo VIII in Italia." *Faenza* 10 (1922): 132–43.

Banchi pubblici, banchi privati e monti di pietà nell'Europa preindustriale. Atti del Convegno, Genova 1990. 2 vols. Genoa, 1991.

Barbagli Bagnoli, Vera, ed. *La moneta nell'economia europea, secoli XIII–XVIII,* Acts of the Settimane di Studio, Istituto Datini, Prato, 7. Florence, 1981.

Barbieri, Gino. "Donne ed affari a sostegno della signoria viscontea." In *Scritti in onore di Catarina Vasalini.* Verona, 1974.

Barducci, Roberto. "Politica e speculazione finanziaria a Firenze dopo la crisi del primo Trecento (1343–58)." *ASI* 137 (1979).

———. "Le riforme finanziarie nel tumulto dei Ciompi." In *Il tumulto dei Ciompi: Un Momento di storia fiorentina ed europea,* acts of the congress of 1979. Florence, 1981.

Becker, Marvin. *Florence in Transition.* 2 vols. Baltimore, 1967–68.

Bensa, Enrico. *Francesco di Marco da Prato: Notizie e documenti sulla mercatura italiana del sec. XIV.* Milan, 1928.

Bergier, Jean-François. "From the Fifteenth Century in Italy to the Six-teenth Century in Germany: A New Banking Concept?" In *Dawn of Modern Banking*, 105–29.

Bernardi, Giulio. *Monetazione del Patriarcato di Aquileia*. Trieste, 1975.

Bertelé, Tommaso. "I gioielli della corona bizantina dati in pegno alla re-pubblica veneta nel sec. XIV e Mastino II della Scala." In *Studi in onore di Amintore Fanfani*. 6 vols. Milan, 1962. 2:89–177.

Besta, Enrico. *Riccardo Malombra, professore nello studio di Padova, consultore di stato in Venezia*. Venice, 1894.

Bevilacqua, Eugenia. "Un particolare aspetto del passato nella laguna di Venezia: I molini." *Memorie dell'Accademia patavina di scienze, lettere ed arti,* classe morale, 72 (1959–60): 155–60.

Billanovich, Maria Chiara. "Carrara, Marsilio da." In *DBI,* 20 (1977), 688–91.

Bini, Teleseforo. *I lucchesi a Venezia*. 2 vols. Lucca, 1853–56.

Biscaro, Gerolamo. "Il banco Filippo Borromei e compagni di Londra." *Archivio storico lombardo,* a. 40, fasc. 37 (1913): 37–126, 283–386.

———. *L'ospedale [di Treviso] ed i suoi benefattori*. Treviso, 1903.

Blockmans, Wim P. "Le crédit public dans les Pays-Bas méridionaux au bas moyen âge." In *Local and International Credit in the Middle Ages and the Sixteenth Century,* edited by Henri Dubois, 1–7. Acts of session B9 of the Ninth International Economic History Congress. Bern, 1986.

Blomquist, Thomas. "The Dawn of Banking in an Italian Commune: Thir-teenth Century Lucca." *Dawn of Modern Banking*.

Bratchel, M. E. *Lucca, 1430–1494: The Reconstruction of an Italian City-Republic*. Oxford, 1995.

Braudel, Fernand. *Civilization matérielle, économie et capitalisme*. 3 vols. Paris, 1979.

———. "L'Italia fuori d'Italia: Due secoli e tre Italie." In *Storia d'Italia,* 2:2092–2248. Turin, 1974.

Braudel, Fernand, and Alberto Tenenti. "Michiel da Lezze, Marchand Veni-tien (1497–1514)." *Wirtschaft, Geschichte und Wirtschaftsgeschichte: Festschrift zum 65. Geburtstag von Friedrich Lütge*. Stuttgart, 1966.

Braunstein, Philippe. "Les entreprises minières en Vénétie au XVᵉ siècle." *Mélanges d'archéologie et d'histoire,* Ecole Française de Rome, 77 (1965): 529–607.

———. "Le marché du cuivre à Venise à la fin du Moyen-Age." In Kellen-benz, *Schwerpunkte,* 78–94.

———. "Relations d'affaires entre Nurembergeois et Venitiens à la fin du XIVᵉ siècle." *Mélanges d'archéologie e d'histoire,* Ecole Française de Rome, 76 (1964): 227–69.

Brucker, Gene. *The Civic World of Early Renaissance Florence*. Princeton, 1977.

———. *Florentine Politics and Society, 1343–1378*. Princeton, 1962.

Brunetti, Mario. "Banche e Banchieri veneziani nei 'Diari' di Marin Sanudo (Garzoni e Lippomano)." In *Studi in onore di Gino Luzzatto*, 2:26–47.

———. "Nuovi documenti viscontei tratti dall'Archivio di Stato di Venezia: figli e nipoti di Bernabò Visconti." *Archivio storico lombardo*, s. 4, 12 (1909): 5–90.

Buenger Robbert, Louise. See Robbert, Louise Buenger.

Calabi, Donatella, and Paolo Morachiello. *Rialto: Le fabbriche e il Ponte*. Turin, 1987.

Candotto Mis, Maria Grazia. "Leonardo da Udine, un domenicano del Quattrocento." Laurea thesis, University of Padua, 1983–84.

Cardini, Franco. "Casali, Francesco." In *DBI*, 21 (1978), 78–80.

Carlotto, Natascia. *La città custodita: Politica e finanza a Vicenza dalla caduta di Ezzelino al vicariato imperiale (1259–1312)*. Milan, 1993.

———. "I da Marano: Una famiglia vicentina dall'età ezzeliniana al dominio veneto." In Ortalli and Knapton, *Istituzioni, società e potere*.

———. "Pietro Nan da Marano, miles e civis veneto: Accumulazione e restituzione di un patrimonio nel primo Trecento." Laurea thesis, University of Venice, 1983.

Carpentier, Elizabeth. "Autour de la Peste Noire: Famine et épidémies dans l'histoire du XIV^c siècle." *Annales, économies, sociétés, civilisations* 17 (1962): 1062–92.

Cassandro, Giovanni. "Breve storia della cambiale." Reprinted in his *Saggi*.

———. "Note minime per la storia del 'cambio.'" Reprinted in his *Saggi*.

———. *Le rappresaglie e il fallimento a Venezia nei secoli XIII–XVI*. Turin, 1938.

———. *Saggi di storia del diritto commerciale*. Naples, 1976.

———. "Vicende storiche della lettera di cambio." Reprinted in his *Saggi*.

Cecchetti, Bartolomeo. "Appunti sulle finanze antiche della Repubblica Veneta." *AV* 35 (1888): 29–55, and 36 (1888): 71–98.

———. "La medicina in Venezia nel 1300." *AV* 26 (1883). Reprinted in his *La vita dei Veneziani*.

———. *La vita dei Veneziani nell 1300*. First published in *AV* and then separately, in fascicles, Venice, 1870–86. Reprint, Bologna, 1980.

Cenci, Cesare. "I Gonzaga e i Frati minori." *Archivium Franciscanum Historicum* 58 (1965).

———. "Senato veneto: 'Probae' ai benefizi ecclesiatici." In C. Piana and C. Cenci, *Promozioni agli ordini sacri a Bologna e alle dignità ecclesiastiche nel Veneto nei secoli XIV–XV*. Quaracchi, 1968.

Cessi, Roberto. "Alcuni aspetti della crisi economica veneziana al principio del secolo XV." *Economia: Rassegna mensile di politica economica* (Trieste), 1 (July 1923): 145–58.

———. "La finanza veneziana al tempo della guerra di Chioggia." In his *Politica ed economia*.

———. "Note per la storia delle società di commercio nel medioevo in

Italia." *Rivista italiana per le scienze giuridiche* 59 (1917). Also published separately as a book, Rome, 1917.

——. *Politica ed economia di Venezia nel Trecento.* Rome, 1952.

——. "Studi sulla moneta veneta: II. La coniazione del ducato aureo." *Economia: Rassegna mensile di politica economica* 2 (1924): 1–11.

——. "L'ufficium de Navigantibus e i sistemi della politica commerciale veneziana nel sec. XIV." Reprinted in his *Politica ed economia.*

Cessi, Roberto, and Annibale Alberti. *Rialto: L'isola, il ponte, il mercato.* Bologna, 1934.

Checchin, Alessandra. *La scuola e l'ospedale di S. Maria dei Battuti di Mestre, dalle origini al 1520.* Quaderno di studi e notizie, n.s., no. 6, of the Centro Studi Storici, Mestre. Venice, 1996.

Chojnacki, Stanley. "In Search of the Venetian Nobility." In Hale, *Renaissance Venice,* 47–90.

Ciappelli, Giovanni. "Il cittadino fiorentino e il fisco alla fine del trecento e nel corso del quattrocento: Uno studio di due casi." *Società e storia* 46 (1989): 823–72.

——. "Il fisco fiorentino nel '400: Note in margine al lavoro di Elio Conti sull'imposta diretta." *La società fiorentina del basso Medioevo: Per Elio Conti.* Istituto storico italiano per il Medio Evo, Nuovi studi storici, 29. Rome, 1995.

Cipolla, Carlo M. *Le avventure della lire.* Bologna, 1975.

——. *La moneta a Firenze nel Cinquecento.* Bologna, 1987. Reprinted in his *Il governo della moneta a Firenze e a Milano nei secoli XIV–XVI.* Bologna, 1990.

——. *Studi di storia della moneta.* Vol. 1, *I movimenti dei cambi in Italia dal secolo XIII al XV.* Pubblicazioni dell'Università di Pavia, Studi nelle scienze giuridiche e sociali, 101 (Pavia, 1948).

——. "Uomini duri." In his *Tre storie extra vaganti.* Bologna, 1994.

Ciscato, A. *Gli ebrei in Padova (1300–1800).* Padua, 1901.

Cognasso, Francesco. "L'unificazione della Lombardia sotto Milano." In *Storia di Milano,* vol. 5.

Cogo, Gaetano. "Fregnano della Scala bastardo di Cangrande II." *Atti dell'Accademia di Udine,* ser. 2, 3 (1896): 33–51.

Collodo, Silvana. "Credito, movimento della proprietà fondiaria e selezione sociale a Padova nel Trecento." Reprinted in her *Una società in trasformazione: Padova tra XI e XV secolo.* Padua, 1990.

Coniglio, Giuseppe. *I Gonzaga.* Milan, 1967.

Connell, Susan. *The Employment of Sculptors and Stonemasons in Venice in the Fifteenth Century.* Ph.D. diss., 1976; New York, 1988.

Conti, Elio. *L'imposta diretta a Firenze nel Quattrocento (1427–1494).* Istituto storico italiano per il Medio Evo, Studi storici, 136–39. Rome, 1984.

Corazzol, Gigi. "Varietà notarile: Scorci di vita economica e sociale." In *Storia di Venezia,* vol. 6.

Cozzi, Gaetano, and Michael Knapton. *Storia della Repubblica di Venezia: Dalla guerra di Chioggia alla riconquista della Terraferma*. Turin, 1986.

Cracco, Giorgio. *Società e stato nel medievo veneziano*. Florence, 1967.

dalla Santa, Giuseppe. "Benedetto Soranzo patrizio veneziano, arcivescovo di Cipro e Gerolamo Riario: Una pagina nuova della guerra di Ferrara degli anni 1482–1484." *NAV,* n.s., 28 (1914): 308–87.

——. "Uomini e fatti dell'ultimo Trecento e del primo Quattrocento: Da lettere a Giovanni Contarini, patrizio veneziano, studente a Oxford e Parigi, poi patriarca di Costantinopoli." *NAV,* ser. 2, 32 (1916): 5–105.

The *Dawn of Modern Banking* . Edited by Center for Medieval and Renaissance Studies, University of California, Los Angeles. New Haven, 1979.

Day, John. *Les douanes de Gênes, 1376–1377*. 2 vols. Paris, 1963.

——. "The Great Bullion Famine of the Fifteenth Century." Reprinted in his *Medieval Market Economy*.

——. "Late Medieval Price Movements." Reprinted in his *Medieval Market Economy*.

——. *The Medieval Market Economy*. Oxford, 1987.

——. "Monetary Contraction in Late Medieval Europe." Reprinted in his *Medieval Market Economy*.

——, ed. *Etudes d'histoire monétaire*. Lille, 1984.

Dean, Trevor. *Land and Power in Late Medieval Ferrara: The Rule of the Este, 1350–1450*. Cambridge, England, 1988.

——. "Venetian Economic Hegemony: The Case of Ferrara, 1220–1500." *SV,* n.s., 12 (1986): 45–98.

Degrassi, Donata. "I rapporti tra compagnie bancarie toscane e patriarchi d'Aquileia (metà XIII secolo–metà XIV secolo)." In *I toscani in Friuli,* edited by Alessandro Malcagni. Florence, 1992.

De Leonardis, G. "Tra depressione e sviluppo: Tendenze dell'economia fiorentina nel secolo XIV, attraverso la storiografia più recente." *Bollettino dell'Istituto storico italiano per il medioevo e Archivio muratoriano* 84 (1972–73): 275–311.

dell'Acqua, Carlo. *Bianca Visconti di Savoia in Pavia e l'insigne monastero di S. Chiara la Reale*. Pavia, 1893.

Del Torre, Giuseppe. "Stato regionale e benefici ecclesiastici: Vescovadi e canonicati nella terraferma veneziana all'inizio dell'età moderna." *Atti dell'Istituto veneto di scienze, lettere ed arti* 151 (1992–93): 1171–1236.

——. *Il Trevigiano nei secoli XV e XVI: L'assetto amministrativo e il sistema fiscale*. Venice, 1990.

Del Treppo, Mario. "I catalani a Napoli e le loro pratiche con la Corte." In *Studi di storia meridionale in memoria di Pietro Laveglia*. Salerno, 1994.

——. "Il re e il banchiere: Strumenti e processi di razionalizzazione dello stato aragonese di Napoli." In *Spazio, società, potere nell'Italia dei Comuni,* edited by Gabriella Rossetti, 229–304. Naples, 1986.

Dennis, George T. "Venezia e le signorie feudali nelle isole greche." In *Venezia e il Levante fino al secolo XV,* edited by Agostino Pertusi, 219–35. Florence, 1973.

Dentici Buccellato, Rosa M. "Forestieri e stranieri nelle città siciliane del basso Medioevo." In *Forestieri e stranieri nelle città basso-medievali.* Florence, 1988.

Denzel, Markus A. *"La pratica della cambiatura": Europäischer Zahlungsverkehr vom 14. bis zum 17. Jahrhundert.* Stuttgart, 1994.

de Roover, Raymond. "A Florence: Un projet de monetisation de la dette publique au XVe siècle." In *Histoire économique du monde mediterranéen, 1450–1650 (Mélanges Braudel),* 511–19. Toulouse, 1973.

——. "The Antecedents of the Medici Bank: The Banking House of Messer Vieri di Cambio de' Medici." Reprinted in his *Business, Banking, and Economic Thought.*

——. "La balance commerciale entre les Pays-Bas e l'Italie au quinzième siècle." *Revue belge* 37 (1959): 374–86.

——. *The Bruges Money Market around 1400.* Brussels, 1968.

——. "Bueri, Gherardo." In *DBI,* 14 (1972), 792–93.

——. *Business, Banking, and Economic Thought in Late Medieval and Early Modern Europe.* Edited by Julius Kirshner. Chicago, 1974.

——. "Cambium ad Venetias: Contribution to the History of Foreign Exchange." In his *Business, Banking, and Economic Thought.*

——. "Early Accounting Problems of Foreign Exchange." *Accounting Review* 19 (1944): 398–99.

——. "Le marché monétaire a Paris du régne de Philippe le Bel au début du XVe siècle." In *Académie des inscriptions et belles-lettres: Comptes rendus.* Séances of November–December 1968. Paris, 1969.

——. "Le marché monétaire au Moyen Age et au début des temps modernes." *Revue historique* 244 (1970): 5–40.

——. *Money, Banking, and Credit in Mediaeval Bruges: Italian Merchant-Bankers, Lombards, and Money-Changers: A Study in the Origins of Banking.* Cambridge, Mass., 1948.

——. "New Interpretations of the History of Banking." Reprinted in his *Business, Banking, and Economic Thought.*

——. *La pensée économique des scolastiques: Doctrines et méthodes.* Montreal, 1971.

——. "Renseignements complémentaires sur le marché monétaire à Bruges au XIVe et au XVe siècle." *Handelingen van het Genootschap "Société d'Emulation" te Brugge* 109 (1972): 51–91.

——. *The Rise and Decline of the Medici Bank, 1397–1494.* Cambridge, Mass., 1963. Abbr.: de Roover, *Medici Bank.*

——. "The Story of the Alberti Company of Florence." Reprinted in his *Business, Banking, and Economic Thought.*

——. "La structure des banques au Moyen Age." In *Third International Conference of Economic History, Munich 1965,* vol. 5. Paris, 1974.

Di Lernia, Nicola. "Il giornale di Lorenzo Priuli e figli (1505–1533): Aspetti economici e sociali di una fraterna veneziana." Laurea thesis, 2 vols, University of Venice, 1988–89.

Dizionario biografico degli italiani. Rome, 1960–. Abbr.: *DBI.*

Doumerc, Bernard. "La crise structurelle de la marine venitiénne au XVᵉ siècle: Le probleme du retard des 'mude.'" *Annales, économies, sociétés, civilisations* 40 (1985): 605–23.

Du Cange, Charles Du Resne. *Glossarium mediae et infinae latinitatis.* 10 vols. Revised ed. Niort, France, 1883–87.

Edler de Roover, Florence. "Borromeo, Galeazzo." In *DBI,* 13 (1971), 47–49.

English, Edward. *Enterprise and Liability in Sienese Banking, 1230–1350.* Toronto, 1988.

Fano, Nellie. "Ricerche sull'arte della lana a Venezia nel XIII e XIV secolo." *AV,* ser. 5, 18 (1936): 73–213.

Felloni, Giuseppe. "I primi banchi pubblici della Casa di San Giorgio (1408–1445)." In *Banchi pubblici, banchi privati,* 1:225–46.

Ferrara, Francesco. "Gli antichi banchi di Venezia." *Nuova antologia* 16 (1871): 177–213, 435–66. Reprint, Palermo, 1970.

Ferrari, Giorgio. "Agostini, Agostino" and "Agostini, Maffio." In *DBI,* 1 (1960), 459, 468–69.

Fortini Brown, Patricia. *Venetian Narrative Painting in the Age of Carpaccio.* New Haven, 1988.

Franceschini, Gino. *I Malatesta.* Milan, 1973.

Fryde, Edmund B. "Anglo-Italian Commerce in the Fifteenth Century: Some Evidence about Profits and the Balance of Trade." *Revue belge* 50 (1972): 345–55.

——. "Financial Resources of Edward III in the Netherlands, 1337–1340." Reprinted in his *Studies.*

——. *Studies in Medieval Trade and Finance.* London, 1983.

Fryde, Edmund B., and M. M. Fryde. "Public Credit, with Special Reference to North-Western Europe." In *The Cambridge Economic History of Europe,* vol. 3. Cambridge, England, 1963.

Galletti, Giuliano. *Bocche e biade: Popolazione e famiglie nelle campagne trevigiane dei secoli XV e XVI.* Treviso, 1994.

Gallicciolli, G. B. *Delle memorie venete antiche profane ed ecclesiastiche.* 8 vols. Venice, 1795.

Gallo, Rudolfo. "Marco Polo, la sua famiglia e il suo libro." In *Nel VII Centenario della nascita di Marco Polo.* Edited by the Istituto veneto di scienze, lettere ed arti. Venice, 1955.

Gargan, Luciano. *Cultura e arte nel Veneto al tempo del Petrarca*. Padua, 1978.

Geremek, Bronesław, ed. *Truands et misérables dans l'Europe moderne (1350–1600)*. Paris, 1980.

Gerola, Giuseppe. "Guglielmo Castelbarco." *Annuario degli studenti trentini* 7 (1901).

Giannasi, Laura. "Ciera, Bernardo" and "Ciera, Agostino." In *DBI*, 25 (1981), 443–47.

Gilbert, Felix. *The Pope, His Banker, and Venice*. Cambridge, Mass., 1980.

Girgensohn, Dieter. "Il testamento di Pietro Miani ('Emilianus'), vescovo di Vicenza (†1433)." *AV*, ser. 5, 132 (1989): 5–60.

Gloria, Andrea. *La pietra del vituperio nel salone di Padova: Lettera*. Padua, 1851.

Goldthwaite, Richard A. *Banks, Palaces, and Entrepreneurs in Renaissance Florence*. London, 1995.

——. *The Building of Renaissance Florence: An Economic and Social History*. Baltimore, 1981.

——. "Local Banking in Renaissance Florence." *JEEcH* 14 (1985): 5–55. Now also in his *Banks, Palaces, and Entrepreneurs*.

——. "The Medici Bank and the World of Florentine Capitalism." *Past and Present* 114 (1987). Now also in his *Banks, Palaces, and Entrepreneurs*.

——. "I prezzi del grano a Firenze nei secoli XIV–XVI." *Quaderni storici*, n. 28 (1975). Now also in his *Banks, Palaces, and Entrepreneurs*.

——. "Urban Values and the Entrepreneur." In *L'impresa: Industria commercio banca, secc. XIII–XVIII*. Acts of the Settimane di Studio, Istituto Datini, Prato, 22. Florence, 1991. Now also in his *Banks, Palaces, and Entrepreneurs*.

Goldthwaite, Richard A., and Giulio Mandich. *Studi sulla moneta fiorentina (secoli XIII–XVI)*. Florence, 1994.

Gonnelli, P. "Momenti e aspetti dell'economia veneziana, rivissuti attraverso la corrispondenza Venezia-Firenze dell'azienda fiorentina di Bindo Piaciti, 1394–1407 (con trascrizione di 445 lettere)." Laurea thesis, Istituto di Storia Economica, University of Florence, 1971.

Goy, Richard. *The House of Gold: The Contarini and the Ca' d'Oro: Building a Palace in Medieval Venice (1420–1440)*. Cambridge, England, 1993.

Gullino, Giuseppe. *I Pisani "dal banco" e "moretta": Storia di due famiglie veneziane in età moderna e delle loro vicende patrimoniali tra 1705 e 1836*. Rome, 1984.

Günther, Karl. *Die städtischen Wechselbanken Deutschlands im Mittelalter und im 16. Jahrhundert*. Munich, 1932.

Hale, John R., ed. *Renaissance Venice*. London, 1973.

Herlihy, David, and Christiane Klapisch-Zuber. *Les Toscans et leurs familles: Une étude du catasto florentin*. Paris, 1978. Abridged English edition: *Tuscans and Their Families: A Study of the Florentine Catasto of 1427*. New Haven, 1985.

Hernandez Esteve, Esteban. "Aspectos organizativos, operativos, administrativos y contables del proyecto de erarios publicos." In *Banchi pubblici, banchi privati,* 2:971–74.

Heyd, Wilhelm. *Histoire du commerce du Levant au Moyen-Age.* 2 vols. Leipzig, 1886. Reprint, Amsterdam, 1959.

Hocquet, Jean-Claude. "Guerre et finance dans l'etat de la Renaissance (la Chambre du Sel et la dette publique à Venise)." In *Actes du 102ᵉ Congrès National des Sociétés Savantes, Limoges 1977,* vol 1. Paris, 1979.

———. *Le sel et la fortune de Venise.* 2 vols. Lille, 1978–79. Vol. 2 is entitled *Voilliers et commerce en Méditerranée* and may be catalogued separately.

Holmes, George. "Anglo-Florentine Trade in 1451." *English Historical Review* 108 (1993): 371–86.

———. "How the Medici Became the Pope's Bankers." In *Florentine Studies,* edited by Nicolai Rubinstein. London, 1968.

Homer, Sidney. *A History of Interest Rates.* New Brunswick, N.J., 1968. Third revised and expanded edition: S. Homer and Richard Sylla, New Brunswick, 1991. Italian translation: *Storia dei tassi di interesse.* Milan, 1995.

Hoshino, Hidetoshi. *L'arte della lana in Firenze nel basso Medioevo: Il commercio della lana e il mercato dei panni fiorentini nei secoli XIII–XV.* Florence, 1980.

———. "Francesco di Iacopo Del Bene cittadino Fiorentino del Trecento." *Annuario* of the Istituto giapponese di cultura, 4 (1966–67).

Howard, Deborah. *Jacopo Sansovino: Architecture and Patronage in Renaissance Venice.* New Haven, 1975.

Hunt, Edwin S. *The Medieval Super-companies: A Study of the Peruzzi Company of Florence.* New York, 1994.

Italia, 1350–1450: Tra crisi, trasformazione, sviluppo. Tredicesimo convegno di studi, 1991, Centro italiano di studi di storia e d'arte. Pistoia, 1993.

Jacoby, David. "Les Juifs à Venise du XIVᵉ au Milieu du XVIᵉ Siècle." In *Venezia centro di mediazione tra oriente e occidente (secoli XV–XVI),* Acts of the congress of 1973, 1:163–216. Florence, 1977.

Jones, Philip J. *The Malatesta of Rimini and the Papal State: A Political History.* Cambridge, England, 1974.

Kedar, Benjamin. *Merchants in Crisis: Genoese and Venetian Men of Affairs and the Fourteenth-Century Depression.* New Haven, 1976.

Kellenbenz, Hermann. "Europäisches Kupfer, Ende 15. bis Mitte 17. Jahrhundert: Ergebnisse eines Kolloquiums." In idem, *Schwerpunkte,* 290–351.

———. "Le miniere di Primiero e le relazioni dei Fugger con Venezia nel Quattrocento." *Il Trentino in età veneziana,* in *Atti dell'Accademia roveretana degli agiati* 238 (1988). Rovereto, 1990.

———. "Die Münzen und die internationale Bank, Ende 15. bis Anfang 17

Jahrhundert (Das oberdeutsche Beispiel)." In Barbagli Bagnoli, *La moneta.*

——, ed. *Schwerpunkte der Kupferproduktion und des Kupferhandels in Europa 1500–1650.* Cologne, 1977.

Kindleberger, Charles. *Manias, Panics, and Crashes: A History of Financial Crises.* New York, 1978. Revised edition, New York, 1989.

Kirshner, Julius. "The Moral Theology of Public Finance: A Study and Edition of Nicholas de Anglia's *Quaestio disputata* on the Public Debt of Venice." *Archivium Fratrum Praedicatorum* 40 (1970): 47–72.

——. "Papa Eugenio IV e il Monte Comune: Documenti su investimento e speculazione nel debito pubblico di Firenze." *ASI* 127 (1969): 340–82.

——. "A *Quaestio de usuris* Falsely Attributed to Bartolus of Sassoferrato." *Renaissance Quarterly* 22 (1969): 256–61

——. "Raymond de Roover on Scholastic Economic Thought." In de Roover, *Business, Banking, and Economic Thought,* 15–36.

——. "Reading Bernardino's Sermon on the Public Debt." In *Atti del simposio internazionale cateriniano-bernardiniano, Siena, 1980,* edited by Domenico Maffei and Paolo Nardi, 547–622. Siena, 1982.

Klaić, V. *Geschichte Bosniens.* Translated from the Croat. Leipzig, 1885.

——. "Rodoslovje knezova Krbavskih od plemena Gusić." *Rad Jugoslavenske akademije znanosti i umjetnesti,* 134 (1898).

Knapton, Michael. "Il fisco nello Stato veneziano di Terraferma tra il '300 e '500: La politica delle entrate." In *Il sistema fiscale veneto: Problemi e aspetti, XV–XVIII secolo,* edited by Giorgio Borelli et al. Verona, 1982.

——. "I rapporti fiscali tra Venezia e la terraferma: Il caso padovano nel secondo '400." *AV,* ser. 5, 117 (1981): 5–65.

Kretschmayr, Heinrich. *Geschichte von Venedig.* 3 vols. Gotha, 1905–34.

Lane, Frederic C. *Andrea Barbarigo, Merchant of Venice, 1418–1449.* Baltimore, 1944.

——. "The Enlargement of the Great Council of Venice." Reprinted in his *Studies.*

——. "Exportations vénitiennes d'or et d'argent de 1200 à 1450." In Day, *Etudes.* Reprinted in Lane, *Studies.*

——. "Family Partnerships and Joint Ventures." Reprinted in his *Venice and History.*

——. "The Funded Debt of the Venetian Republic, 1262–1482." In English in his *Venice and History.* This is a slightly corrected version of "Sull'ammontare del 'Monte Vecchio' di Venezia," first published as an appendix to Luzzatto's *Il debito pubblico.*

——. "Investment and Usury." Reprinted in his *Venice and History.*

——. "Naval Actions and Fleet Organization, 1499–1502." Reprinted in his *Studies.*

——. "Pepper Prices before Da Gama." Reprinted in his *Studies.*

——. "Public Debt and Private Wealth: Particularly in Sixteenth-Century Venice." Reprinted in his *Profits from Power: Readings in Protection Rent and Violence-Controlling Enterprises.* Albany, N.Y., 1979.

——. "Rhythm and Rapidity of Turnover in Venetian Trade of the Fifteenth Century." In his *Venice and History.*

——. *Studies in Venetian Social and Economic History.* Edited by Benjamin G. Kohl and Reinhold C. Mueller. London, 1987.

——. "Venetian Bankers, 1496–1533." Reprinted in his *Venice and History.*

——. *Venice: A Maritime Republic.* Baltimore, 1972.

——. *Venice and History: The Collected Papers of Frederic C. Lane.* Baltimore, 1966.

——. "Wages and Recruitment of Venetian Galeotti, 1470–1580." Reprinted in his *Studies.*

Lane, Frederic C., and Reinhold C. Mueller. *Money and Banking in Medieval and Renaissance Venice.* Vol. 1, *Coins and Moneys of Account.* Baltimore, 1985. (Abbr.: Vol. 1.)

La Roncière, Charles-M. de. *Un changeur florentin du Trecento: Lippo di Fede del Sega (1285 env.–1363 env.).* Paris, 1973.

Lattes, Alessandro. *Il diritto commerciale nella legislazione statutaria delle città italiane.* Milan, 1884.

——. *Il fallimento nel diritto comune e nella legislazione bancaria della Repubblica di Venezia.* Venice, 1880.

Law, John. "La caduta degli Scaligeri." In Ortalli and Knapton, *Istituzioni, società e potere,* 83–98.

Lazari, Vincenzo. *Le monete dei possedimenti Veneziani di oltremare e di terraferma, descritte ed illustrate.* Venice, 1851.

Lazzarini, Vittorio. "Beni carraresi e proprietari veneziani." In *Studi in onore di Gino Luzzatto,* 1:274–88.

——. *Marino Faliero.* Florence, 1963.

——. "Il testamento di Uguccio Casali, Signore di Cortona (16 ottobre 1400)." *Polimnia* (Cortona), 3 (July–September 1932).

Levarotti, Franca. "Ricerche sulle origini dell'Ospedale Maggiore di Milano." *Archivio storico lombardo* 107 (1981): 77–113.

——. "Scritture finanziarie dell'età sforzesca." In *Squarci d'archivio sforzesco: Mostra storica documentaria.* Como, 1981.

Litta, Pompeo. *Famiglie celebri d'Italia.* 15 vols. Milan, 1819–1902.

Lopez, Roberto S. "Venezia e le grandi linee dell'espansione commerciale." In *La civiltà veneziana nel secolo di Marco Polo.* Florence, 1955.

Luzzati, Michele. *Una guerra di popolo: Lettere private del tempo dell'assedio di Pisa (1494–1509).* Pisa, 1973.

Luzzatto, Gino. "L'attività commerciale di un patrizio veneziano del Quattrocento." Reprinted in his *Studi.*

——. "Les banques publiques de Venise: Siècles XVIᶜ–XVIIIᶜ." Reprinted in his *Studi*.

——. "La commenda nella vita economica dei secoli XIII e XIV, con particolare riguardo a Venezia." Reprinted in his *Studi*.

——. "Il costo della vita a Venezia nel Trecento." Reprinted in his *Studi*.

——. *Il debito pubblico della Repubblica di Venezia*. Milan, 1963. This is a reprint of the introduction to *PRV*; the pagination, Arabic in the former, Roman in *PRV*, is nearly but not exactly identical.

——. "Il debito pubblico nel sistema finanziario veneziano dei secoli XIII–XV." Reprinted in his *Studi*.

——. "Il patrimonio privato di un Doge del secolo XIII." Reprinted in his *Studi*.

——. "Politica ed economia nella storia di Venezia." *Atti dell'Istituto veneto di scienze, lettere ed arti* 121 (1962–63): 495–511.

——. *Storia economica di Venezia dall'XI al XVI secolo*. Venice, 1961. Reprint, with a preface by Marino Berengo, Venice, 1995. (References here are to the 1961 edition.)

——. *Studi di storia economica veneziana*. Padua, 1954.

——. "Sull'attendibilità di alcune statistiche economiche medievali." Reprinted in his *Studi*.

——. "Tasso d'interesse e usura a Venezia nei sec. XIII–XV." *Miscellanea in onore di Roberto Cessi*. Rome, 1958.

——. "Vi furono fiere a Venezia?" Reprinted in his *Studi*.

Magalhaes Godinho, Vitorino. "Le repli vénitien et égyptien et la route du Cap, 1496–1533." *Eventail de l'histoire vivante: Hommage à Lucien Febvre*. 2 vols. Paris, 1953.

Magnocavallo, Arturo. "Proposta di riforma bancaria del banchiere veneziano Angelo Sanudo (secolo XVI)." In *Atti del Congresso internazionale di scienze storiche, Roma, 1–9 Aprile 1903*, vol. 9. Rome, 1904.

Mainoni, Patrizia. "Un mercante milanese del primo Quattrocento: Marco Serraineri." *Nuova rivista storica* 59 (1975): 331–77.

——. *Mercanti lombardi tra Barcellona e Valenza nel basso medioevo*. Bologna, 1982.

——. "Milano di fronte a Venezia, un'interpretazione in chiave economica di un rapporto difficile." *Venezia Milano*. Milan, 1984. Reprinted in her *Economia e politica nella Lombardia medievale: Da Bergamo a Milano fra XIII e XV secolo*. Cavallermaggiore, 1994.

Mallett, Michael, and John Hale. *The Military Organization of a Renaissance State: Venice c. 1400 to 1617*. Cambridge, England, 1984.

Maltesou, Chryssa A. *L'istituzione del bailo di Venezia a Costantinopoli, 1268–1453* [in Greek]. Athens, 1970.

Mandich, Guilio. "Delle prime valutazioni del ducato d'oro veneziano (1285–1346)." *SV*, n.s., 16 (1988): 15–31.

———. "Mercanti veneziani in Bolzano secondo una cambiale del 1360 (ma trattasi di un errore di lettura)." *Cultura atesina* 2 (1948): 13–23.

———. "Monete di conto veneziane in un libro di commercio del 1336–1339." *SV*, n.s., 8 (1984): 15–36.

———. *Le pacte de "ricorsa" et le marché italien des changes au XVIIIᵉ siécle.* Paris, 1953.

———. "Per una ricostruzione delle operazioni mercantili e bancarie della compagnia dei Covoni." In *Libro giallo della compagnia dei Covoni,* edited by Armando Sapori. Milan, 1970.

———. "La prassi delle assegnazioni e delle lettere di pagamento a Venezia nel 1336–1339 (da un libro di conti)." *SV*, n.s., 11 (1986): 15–46.

———. "Le privative industriali veneziane (1450–1550)." *Rivista del diritto commerciale*, a. 34 (1936): 509–47.

———. *Studi sulla moneta fiorentina.* See under Goldthwaite.

———. "Una compagnia fiorentina a Venezia nel quarto decennio del secolo quattordicesimo (un libro di conti)." *Rivista storica italiana* 96 (1984): 129–49.

Manfredi, Fulgentio. *Degnità procuratoria di San Marco di Venetia.* Venice, 1602.

Manzini, Vincenzo. "La bancarotta e la procedura fallimentare nel diritto veneziano, con cenni sui grandi fallimenti del secolo XV." *Atti dell'Istituto veneto di scienze, lettere ed arti* 85 (1925–26): 1091–1135.

Marchesan, Angelo. *Treviso medievale.* 2 vols. Treviso, 1923.

Marks, Louis. "The Financial Oligarchy in Florence under Lorenzo." In *Italian Renaissance Studies,* edited by E. F. Jacob. London, 1960.

Martines, Lauro. *The Social World of Florentine Humanists.* London, 1963.

Marx, Karl. *Capital.* 3 vols. Chicago, 1906–9.

Masè, Federica. "Patrimoines immobiliers ecclésiastiques dans la Venise médiévale: Une lecture de la ville." Doctoral thesis, Université de Paris-II, 1996.

Mayer, Theodor. *Der auswärtige Handel des Herzogtums Österreich im Mittelalter.* Innsbruck, 1909. Reprint, Aalen, 1973.

Melis, Federigo. *Aspetti della vita economica medievale: Studi nell'Archivio Datini di Prato.* Siena, 1962.

———. "Intensità e regolarità nella diffusione dell'informazione economica generale nel Mediterraneo e in Occidente alla fine del Medioevo." In *Mélanges en l'honneur de Fernand Braudel,* 2 vols., 1:389–424. Toulouse, 1973. Reprinted in *Quaderni di storia postale* 2 (1983), and in his *I trasporti e le comunicazioni nel Medioevo,* edited by Luciana Frangioni. Florence, 1984.

———. *Note di storia della banca pisana nel Trecento.* Pisa, 1955. Reprinted in Melis, *La banca pisana e le origini della banca moderna,* edited by Marco Spallanzani. Florence, 1987.

———. "Le società commerciali a Firenze dalla seconda metà del XIV al XVI secolo." Reprinted in Melis, *L'azienda nel Medioevo,* edited by Marco Spallanzani. Florence, 1991.

Merores, Marghereta. "Un codice veneziano del secolo XIV nell'Haus-Hof- und Staatsarchiv di Vienna." *NAV,* n.s., 29 (1915): 139–66.

Miglio, L. "Cavalli, Giacomo." In *DBI,* 22 (1979), 727–31.

Mihelić, Darja. *Neagrarno gospodarstvo Pirana od 1280 do 1320 [La produzione non rurale di Pirano dal 1280 al 1320].* Academia scientiarum et artium slovenca, cl. I, 27. Ljubljana, Slovenia, 1985.

Miller, William. "The Marquisate of Boudonitza (1204–1414)." In his *Essays in the Latin Orient.* Cambridge, England, 1921. Reprint, Amsterdam, 1964.

Minchinton, W. E. "Early Tide Mills: Some Problems." *Technology and Culture* 20 (1979): 777–86.

Miniutti, Pierpaolo. "Povertà ed assistenza a Venezia dal Medio Evo all'Età Moderna: L'amministrazione di tre ospedali." Laurea thesis, University of Venice, 1993–94.

Molà, Luca. *La comunità dei lucchesi a Venezia: Immigrazione e industria della seta nel tardo Medioevo.* Istituto veneto di scienze, lettere ed arti, *Memorie,* 53. Venice, 1994.

Molà, Luca, and Reinhold C. Mueller. "Essere straniero a Venezia nel tardo Medioevo: Accoglienza e rifiuto nei privilegi di cittadinanza e nelle sentenze criminali." In *Le migrazioni in Europa, secoli XIII–XVIII,* edited by Simonetta Cavaciocchi. Acts of the Settimane di Studio, Istituto Datini, Prato, 25. Florence, 1994.

Molho, Anthony. *Florentine Public Finances in the Early Renaissance.* Cambridge, Mass., 1971.

——. *Marriage Alliance in Late Medieval Florence.* Cambridge, Mass., 1994.

——. "Lo Stato e la finanza pubblica: Un'ipotesi basata sulla storia tardo-domedioevale di Firenze." In *Origini dello Stato: Processi di formazione statale in Italia fra medioevo ed età moderna,* edited by Giorgio Chittolini et al., 225–80. Annali dell'Istituto storico italo-germanico, Quaderno 39. Bologna, 1994.

——. "Tre città-stato e i loro debiti pubblici: Quesiti e ipotesi sulla storia di Firenze, Genova e Venezia." In *Italia, 1350–1450,* 185–215.

Mometto, Piergiovanni. *L'azienda agricola Barbarigo a Carpi: Gestione economica ed evoluzione sociale sulle terre di un villaggio della bassa pianura veronese (1443–1539).* Venice, 1992.

Mosher Stuard, Susan. "The Adriatic Trade in Silver, c. 1300." *SV* 17–18 (1975–76): 95–143.

Mueller, Reinhold C. "Aspects of Venetian Sovereignty in Medieval and Renaissance Dalmatia." In *Quattrocento Adriatico: Fifteenth Century Art of the Adriatic Rim,* edited by Charles Dempsey, 29–56. Villa Spelman Colloquia, 5. Bologna, 1996.

——. "I banchi locali a Venezia nel tardo Medioevo." *Studi storici* 28 (1987): 145–55.

——. "Bank," "Larghezza," "Ricorsa," "Strettezza," and "Trockenwechsel." In North, *Von Aktie bis Zoll.*

——. "La Camera del frumento: Un 'banco pubblico' veneziano e i gruzzoli dei signori di terraferma." In Ortalli and Knapton, *Istituzioni, società e potere,* 321–60.

——. " 'Chome l'ucciello di passaggio': La demande saisonnière des espèces et le marché des changes à Venise au Moyen Age." In Day, *Etudes,* 195–219.

——. "Il circolante manipolato: L'impatto di imitazione, contraffazione e tosatura di monete a Venezia nel tardo Medioevo." In *Italia, 1350–1450,* 217–32.

——. "La crisi economica-monetaria veneziana di metà Quattrocento nel contesto generale." In *Aspetti della vita economica medievale: Atti del convegno di studi nel X anniversario della morte di F. Melis,* 541–56. Florence, 1985.

——. "Domanda e offerta di moneta metallica nell'Italia settentrionale durante il Medioevo." *Rivista italiana di numismatica e scienze affini* 97 (1996): 149–66. Also published in *Die Friesacher Münze im Alpen-Adria-Raum/La moneta frisacense nell'Alpe Adria,* edited by Reinhard Härtel. Acts of the conference of Friesach, 1992. Graz, 1996.

——. "Effetti della guerra di Chioggia (1378–1381) sulla vita economica e sociale di Venezia." *Ateneo veneto* 19 (1981): 27–41.

——. "Espressioni di *status* sociale a Venezia dopo la 'Serrata' del Maggior Consiglio." In *Studi veneti offerti a Gaetano Cozzi.* Venice, 1992.

——. "Foreign Investment in Venetian Government Bonds and the Case of Paolo Guinigi, Lord of Lucca, Early Fifteenth Century." Acts of the symposium *Cities of Finance,* edited by Herman Diederiks and David Reeder, Koninklijke Nederlandse Akademie van Wetenschappen, Amsterdam, 1996.

——. "L'imperialismo monetario veneziano nel Quattrocento." *Società e storia* 8 (1980): 277–97.

——. "The Jewish Moneylenders of Late Trecento Venice: A Revisitation." In *Intercultural Contacts in the Medieval Mediterranean: In Honour of David Jacoby.* Edited by Benjamin Arbel. London, 1996. Also as a special number of the *Mediterranean Historical Review* 10 (1995): 202–17.

——. "Mercanti e imprenditori fiorentini a Venezia nel tardo Medioevo." *Societa e storia* 55 (1992): 29–60.

——. "Monete coniate e monete di conto nel Trevigiano: Medioevo e epoca moderna." In *Due villaggi della collina trevigiana: Vidor e Colbertaldo,* edited by Danilo Gasparini, 2:323–35. Vidor, 1989.

——. "Les prêteurs juifs de Venise au Moyen Age." *Annales, économies, sociétés, civilisations* 30 (1975): 1277–1302.

——. *The Procuratori di San Marco and the Venetian Credit Market: A Study of the Development of Credit and Banking in the Trecento.* Ph.D. diss., 1969; New York, 1977.

——. "The Procurators of San Marco in the Thirteenth and Fourteenth Centuries: A Study of the Office as a Financial and Trust Institution." *SV* 13 (1971): 105–220.

——. "The Role of Bank Money in Venice, 1300–1500." *SV,* n.s., 3 (1979): 47–96. Revised and expanded version of "Bank Money in Venice, to the Mid-fifteenth Century," in Barbagli Bagnoli, *La moneta.*

——. "The Spufford Thesis on Foreign Exchange: The Evidence of Exchange Rates." *JEEcH* 24 (1995): 121–29.

——. "Sull'establishment bancario veneziano: Il banchiere davanti a Dio (secoli XIV–XV)." In *Mercanti e vita economica nella Repubblica Veneta (Secoli XIII–XVIII),* edited by Giorgio Borelli, 2 vols., 1:45–103. Verona, 1985.

——. "Veronesi e capitali veronesi a Venezia in epoca scaligera." In Varanini, *Gli Scaligeri.*

Munro, John H. "Wechsel." In North, *Von Aktie bis Zoll,* 413–16.

Nardi, Bruno. "Letteratura e cultura veneziana del Quattrocento." In *La civiltà veneziana del Quattrocento.* Florence, 1957.

——. "La scuola di Rialto e l'umanesimo veneziano." In *Umanesimo europeo e umanesimo veneziano,* edited by Vittore Branca. Florence, 1963.

Netto, Giovanni. *Nel '300 a Treviso: Vita cittadina vista nell'attività della "Scuola" Santa Maria dei Battuti e del suo Ospedale.* Treviso, 1976.

Newett, Margaret M. "The Sumptuary Laws of Venice in the Fourteenth and Fifteenth Centuries." In *Historical Essays by Members of Owens College, Manchester,* edited by T. F. Tout and J. Tait, 245–78. London, 1902.

Nicol, David M. *Byzantium and Venice.* Cambridge, England, 1989.

Noonan, John T. *The Scholastic Analysis of Usury.* Cambridge, Mass., 1957.

North, Michael, ed. *Von Aktie bis Zoll: Ein historisches Lexikon des Geldes.* Munich, 1995.

Nystazopoulou Pélékidis, Marie. "Venise et la Mer Noire du XIe au XVe siècle." In *Venezia e il Levante fino al sec. XV,* edited by Agostino Pertusi, 541–82. Florence, 1973. Also in *Thesaurismata* (Venice), 7 (1970): 15–51.

Occhipinti, Elisa. "Castelbarco, Guglielmo." In *DBI,* 21 (1978), 570–74.

Olivieri, Achille. "Cavalli, Sigismondo." In *DBI,* 22 (1979), 758–60.

Origo, Iris. *The Merchant of Prato.* London, 1957.

Ortalli, Gherardo. "Il mercante e lo stato: Strutture della Venezia altomedievale." In *Mercati e mercanti nell'alto Medioevo: L'area euroasiatica e l'area mediterranea*. Settimane di Studio, 40. Spoleto, 1993.

———. *Scuole, maestri e istruzione di base tra Medioevo e Rinascimento: Il caso veneziano*. Vicenza, 1993.

Ortalli, Gherardo, and Michael Knapton, eds. *Istituzioni, società e potere nella marca trevigiana e veronese (secoli XIII–XIV): Sulle tracce di G. B. Verci*. Istituto storico italiano per il Medio Evo, Studi storici, 199–200. Rome, 1988.

Padovan, Vincenzo. *Le monete dei Veneziani: Sommario*. Venice, 1881.

Papadopoli-Aldobrandini, Nicolò. *Le monete di Venezia*. 4 vols. Venice, 1893–1919. Abbr.: Papadopoli.

Pecchioli, Renzo. "Uomini d'affari fiorentini a Venezia nella seconda metà del Cinquecento." In his *Dal "mito" di Venezia alla "ideologia" americana*. Venice, 1983.

Perret, Paul M., ed. *Histoire des relations de la France avec Venise du XIIIe siècle a l'avènment de Charles VIII*. 2 vols. Paris, 1896.

Pesce, Luigi. *La chiesa di Treviso nel primo Quattrocento*. 2 vols. Rome, 1987.

———. "Filippo de Mézières e la Certosa del Montello." *AV* 134 (1990): 5–44.

———. *Vita socio-culturale della diocesi di Treviso nel primo Quattrocento*. Venice, 1983.

Petralia, Giuseppe. *Banchieri e famiglie mercantili nel Mediterraneo aragonese: L'emigrazione dei Pisani in Sicilia nel Quattrocento*. Pisa, 1989.

———. "Imposizione diretta e dominio territoriale nella Repubblica fiorentina del Quattrocento." In *Società, istituzioni, spiritualità: Studi in onore di Cinzio Violante*, 639–52. Spoleto, 1994.

Peyer, Hans Conrad. *Zur Getreidepolitik oberitalienischer Städte im 13. Jahrhundert*. Vienna, 1950.

Pezzolo, Luciano. "Dal prestito all'imposta: Verso lo Stato territoriale." Forthcoming in *Storia di Venezia*.

———. *L'oro dello stato: Società, finanza e fisco nella Repubblica veneta del secondo '500*. Venice, 1990.

Piasentini, Stefano. *Alla luce della luna: Il furto a Venezia, 1275–1403*. Venice, 1992.

Piergiovanni, Vito. "Banchieri e falliti nelle 'Decisiones de mercatura' della Rota civile di Genova." In *Diritto comune, diritto commerciale, diritto veneziano*, edited by Karin Nehlsen-von Stryk and Dieter Nörr, 17–38. Centro tedesco di studi veneziani, Quaderni, 31. Venice, 1985.

———. "I banchieri nel diritto genovese e nella tecnica giuridica tra Medioevo e Età Moderna." In *Banchi pubblici, banchi privati*, 1:205–23.

Pinto, Giuliano. "I livelli di vita dei salariati fiorentini (1380–1430)." Reprinted in his *Toscana medievale: Paesaggi e realtà sociali*. Florence, 1993.

——. *La Toscana nel tardo Medio Evo: Ambiente, economia rurale, società*. Florence, 1982.

——, ed. *Il libro del Biadaiolo: Carestia e annona a Firenze dalla metà del '200 al 1348*. Florence, 1978.

Pistarino, Geo. "Banchi e banchieri del '300 nei centri genovesi del Mar Nero." *Cronache Finmare*, no. 5/6 (May–June 1974): 8–13.

Pitteri, Mauro. *Segar le acque: Quinto e Santa Cristina al Tiveron: Storia e cultura di due villaggi ai bordi del Sile*. Treviso, 1984.

Politi, Giorgio. *Antichi luoghi pii di Cremona*. 2 vols. Cremona, 1979–85.

Postan, M. M. "Credit in Medieval Trade." Reprinted in *Essays in Economic History*, edited by E. M. Carus-Wilson, 2 vols., 1:61–87. London, 1954–62.

Praga, Giuseppe. *Storia della Dalmazia*. Zara, 1941. New ed., Varese, 1981.

Pullan, Brian S. "The Occupations and Investments of the Venetian Nobility in the Middle and Late Sixteenth Century." In Hale, *Renaissance Venice*.

——. *Rich and Poor in Renaissance Venice: The Social Institutions of a Catholic State, to 1620*. Oxford, 1971.

——. "Wage-Earners and the Venetian Economy, 1550–1630." Reprinted in *Crisis and Change in the Venetian Economy in the Sixteenth and Seventeenth Centuries*, ed. B. S. Pullan, 146–74. London, 1968.

Queller, Donald. "A New Approach to the Pre-modern Cost of Living: Venice, 1372–1389." Forthcoming in the *JEEcH*.

——. "The Venetian Family and the *Estimo* of 1379." In *Law, Custom, and the Social Fabric in Medieval Europe: Essays in Honor of Bryce Lyon*, edited by Bernard S. Bachrach and David Nicholas, 185–210. Studies in Medieval Culture, 28. Kalamazoo, Michigan, 1990.

——. *The Venetian Patriciate: Reality versus Myth*. Urbana, Ill., 1986. Italian translation, somewhat revised: *Il patriziato veneziano: La realtà contro il mito*. Rome, 1987.

Ravid, Benjamin. "The Legal Status of the Jew In Venice to 1509." *Proceedings of the American Academy for Jewish Research* 54 (1987): 169–202.

Reichert, Winfried. "Mercanti e monetieri italiani nel regno di Boemia nella prima metà del XIV secolo." In *Sistema di rapporti ed élites economiche in Europa (secoli XII–XVII)*. Edited by Mario Del Treppo. Naples, 1994.

Riedmann, Josef. *Die Beziehungen der Grafen und Landesfürsten von Tirol zu Italien bis zum Jahre 1335*. Österreichische Akademie der Wissenschaften, Sitzungsberichte, 307. Vienna, 1977.

Riu, Manuel. "Banking and Society in Late Medieval and Early Modern Aragon." In *Dawn of Modern Banking*, 131–67. Expanded and updated as "La banca i la societat a la corona d'Aragó, a finals de l'edat mitjana i començaments de la moderna." *Acta mediaevalia* 11–12 (1990–91): 187–224.

Robbert, Louise Buenger. "Money and Prices in Thirteenth-Century Venice." *Journal of Medieval History* 20 (1994): 373–90.

Romanin, Samuele. *Storia documentata di Venezia*. 2d ed. 10 vols. Venice, 1925.

Romani, Marzio A. "Il credito nella formazione dello stato gonzaghesco (fine XIV sec.)." *Studi storici Luigi Simeoni* 33 (1983): 191–99.

Rösch, Gerhard. *Der Venezianische Adel dis zur Schließung des Großen Rats: Zur Genese einer Führungsschicht*. Sigmaringen, 1989.

Rossi, Vittorio. "Jacopo d'Albizzotto Guidi e il suo inedito poema su Venezia." *NAV* 5 (1893): 397–451.

Rossini, Egidio. "La signoria scaligera dopo Cangrande." In *Verona e il suo territorio,* vol. 3, pt. 1. Verona, 1975.

Ruggiero, Guido. *The Boundaries of Eros: Sex Crime and Sexuality in Renaissance Venice*. Oxford, 1985.

———. *Violence in Early Renaissance Venice*. New Brunswick, N.J., 1980.

Runciman, Steven. *The Fall of Constantinople, 1453*. Cambridge, England, 1965.

Ruskin, John. *Venezia*. Translation and notes by M. Pezzè Pascolato. Florence, 1901.

Sambin, Paolo. "La guerra del 1372–73 tra Venezia e Padova." *AV* ser. 5, 38–41 (1946–47): 1–76.

Santarelli, Umberto. *La categoria dei contratti irregolari: Lezioni di storia del diritto*. Turin, 1990.

Sapori, Armando. *La crisi delle compagnie mercantili dei Bardi e dei Peruzzi*. Florence, 1926.

———. "La famiglia e le compagnie degli Alberti del Giudice." Reprinted in his *Studi,* 2:975–1012.

———. "Il personale delle compagnie mercantili del Medioevo." In his *Studi,* 2:695–763.

———. *Studi di storia economica*. 3 vols. Florence, 1955–67. (Vols. 1 and 2 were reprinted, Florence, 1982)

Sardella, Pierre. *Nouvelles et spéculations a Venise au début du XVIe siècle*. Paris, 1948.

Savelli, Rodolfo. "Between Law and Morals: Interest in the Dispute on Exchanges during the Sixteenth Century." In *The Courts and the Development of Commercial Law,* edited by Vito Piergiovanni, 39–102. Berlin, 1987.

Schalk, Carl. "Rapporti commerciali fra Venezia e Vienna." *NAV,* n.s., 23 (1912): 52–95, 285–317.

Schulz, Anne M. *Niccolò di Giovanni Fiorentino and Venetian Sculpture of the Early Renaissance*. New York, 1978.

Scialoija, A. "Un precedente medioevale dei 'pools' marittimi." In *Studi in memoria di B. Scorza*. Rome, 1940.

Segre, Arturo. "Di alcune relazioni tra la Repubblica di Venezia e la S. Sede ai tempi di Urbano V e di Gregorio XI (1367–1378). *NAV* 9 (1905): 200–214.

Sella, Domenico. *Salari e lavoro nell'edilizia lombarda durante il secolo XVII,* Pavia, 1968.

Setton, Kenneth M. *The Papacy and the Levant (1204–1571).* 4 vols. Philadelphia, 1976–84.

Simeoni, Luigi. "La ribellione di Fregnano della Scala e la politica generale italiana." *Studi storici veronesi* 11 (1961): 5–62.

Sisto, Alessandra. *Banchieri-Feudatari subalpini nei sec. XII–XIV.* Turin, 1963.

Skrzinskaja, E. C. "Storia della Tana." *SV* 10 (1968): 3–45.

Smith, Adam. *Wealth of Nations.* New York, 1937.

Soldi Rondinini, Gigliola. "Aspetti dell'amministrazione del ducato di Milano al tempo di Filippo Maria Visconti (Dal 'Liber Tabuli' di Vitaliano Borromeo, 1427)." In *Milano e Borgogna: Due stati principeschi tra Medioevo e Rinascimento,* edited by Jean-Marie Causchies and Giorgio Chittolini, 145–57. Rome, 1990.

———. "Politica e teoria monetarie dell'età viscontea." *Nuova rivista storica* 59 (1975): 288–330.

Soranzo, Giovanni. *La guerra fra Venezia e la Santa Sede per il dominio di Ferrara (1308–1313).* Città di Castello, 1905.

Spallanzani, Marco. "L'apside dell'Alberti a San Martino a Gangalandi: Nota di storia economica." *Mitteilungen des kunsthistorischen Institutes in Florenz* 19 (1975): 241–50.

———. "A Note on Florentine Banking in the Renaissance: Orders of Payment and Cheques." *JEEcH* 7 (1978): 145–68.

Spufford, Peter. *Handbook of Medieval Exchange.* London, 1986.

———. *Money and Its Use in Medieval Europe.* Cambridge, England, 1988.

Stahl, Alan M. "Office-holding and the Mint in Early Renaissance Venice." *Renaissance Studies* 8 (1994): 404–15.

Stefanutti, Ugo. *Documentazioni cronologiche per la storia della medicina, chirurgia e farmacia in Venezia dal 1258 al 1332.* Venice, 1961.

Stella, Antonio. "Fiscalità, topografia e società a Firenze nella seconda metà del Trecento." *ASI* 151 (1993): 797–862.

Storia di Milano. 17 vols. Milan, 1953–66.

Storia di Venezia. Rome, 1992–.

Strnad, A. A. "Cavalli, Antonio di." In *DBI,* 22 (1979), 714–16.

Stuard: See Mosher Stuard.

Studi in onore di Gino Luzzatto. 4 vols. Milan, 1949.

Szekely, G. "Hongrie et Venise à l'epoque de Sigismond." In *Venezia e l'Ungheria nel Rinascimento,* edited by Vittore Branca. Florence, 1973.

Teja, Antonio. *Aspetti della vita economica di Zara dal 1289 al 1409.* 3 vols. Zara, 1936–42. Vol. 1, *La pratica bancaria* (1936).

Tentori, Cristoforo. *Saggio sulla storia civile, politica, ecclesiastica e sulla cor-*

ografia topografica degli stati della repubblica di Venezia. 12 vols. Venice, 1785–90.

Thiriet, Freddy. *La Romanie vénitienne au Moyen Age*. Paris, 1959.

Todesco, Maria Teresa. "Aggregati ed esclusi: Le cooptazioni al Maggior Consiglio al tempo della guerra di Chioggia." Laurea thesis, University of Venice, 1986–87.

Trivellato, Francesca. "La missione diplomatica a Venezia del fiorentino Gianozzo Manetti a metà Quattrocento." *SV,* n.s., 28 (1994): 203–35.

Tucci, Ugo. "Il Banco della Piazza di Rialto, prima banca pubblica veneziana." Reprinted in his *Mercanti, navi, monete nel Cinquecento veneziano,* 231–50. Bologna, 1981.

———. "Il banco pubblico a Venezia." In *Banchi pubblici, banchi privati,* 1:309–25.

———. "Cappello, Andrea" and "Cappello, Antonio," In *DBI,* 18 (1975), 738–40, 743–48.

———. "I primi viaggiatori e l'opera di Marco Polo." In *Storia della cultura veneta,* vol. 1. Vicenza, 1976.

Usher, Abbott P. "Deposit Banking in Barcelona, 1300–1700." *Journal of Economic and Business History* 4 (1931): 121–55.

———. *The Early History of Deposit Banking in Mediterranean Europe*. Cambridge, Mass., 1943. Reprint, New York, 1967.

———. "The Origins of Banking: The Primitive Bank of Deposit, 1200–1600." Reprinted in *Enterprise and Secular Change: Readings in Economic History,* edited by Frederic C. Lane and Jelle C. Riemiersma, 262–91. Homewood, Ill., 1953.

van der Wee, Herman, general editor. *La banque en occident*. Antwerp, 1991. In English: *A History of European Banking*. Antwerp, 1994.

Vannini Marx, Anna, ed. *Credito, banche e investimenti, secoli XIII–XX*. Acts of the Settimane di Studio, Istituto Datini, Prato, 4. Florence, 1985.

Varanini, Gian Maria. "Patrimonio e fattoria scaligera: Tra gestione patrimoniale e funzione pubblica." In his *Gli scaligeri,* 383–87.

———, ed. *Gli Scaligeri, 1277–1387*. Verona, 1988.

Verlinden, Charles. "La colonie vénetienne de Tana, centre de la traite des esclaves au XIVe et au debut du XVe s." In *Studi in onore di Gino Luzzatto,* 2:1–25.

Volpe, Gioachino. "L'Italia e Venezia." In *La civiltà veneziana del Trecento*. Florence, 1956.

von Stromer, Wolfgang. "Funktionen und Rechtsnatur der Wechselstuben als Banken im internationalen Vergleich." In Vannini Marx, *Credito, banche e investimenti.*

———. *Die Gründung der Baumwollindustrie in Mitteleuropa*. Stuttgart, 1978.

———. "Landmacht gegen Seemacht: Kaiser Sigismunds Kontinentalsperre gegen Venedig, 1412–1433." *Zeitschrift für Historische Forschung* 22 (1995): 145–90.

———. "Das Zusammenspiel Oberdeutscher und Florentiner Geldleute bei der Finanzierung von König Ruprechts Italienzug, 1401–02." In *Forschungen zur Sozial-und Wirtschaftsgeschichte,* edited by Hermann Kellenbenz, vol. 16. Stuttgart, 1971.

Wackernagel, Jacob. *Städtische Schuldscheine als Zahlungsmittel im XIII. Jahrhundert.* Beiheft 2 of *Vierteljahresschrift für Sozial-und Wirtschaftsgeschichte.* Stuttgart, 1924.

Watson, W. B. "The Structure of the Florentine Galley Trade with Flanders and England in the Fifteenth Century: Some Evidence about Profits and the Balance of Trade." *Revue belge* 39 (1961) and 40 (1962).

Weigand, Wolf. "Gli Scaligeri dopo gli Scaligeri." In Varanini, *Gli Scaligeri.*

Weitnauer, Alfred. *Venezianischer Handel der Fugger, nach der Musterbuchhaltung des Matthäus Schwarz.* Studien zur Fugger-Geschichte, 9. Munich, 1931.

Wurthmann, William B. "The Council of Ten and the Scuole Grandi in Early Renaissance Venice." *SV,* n.s., 18 (1989): 15–66.

Zanetti, Guid'Antonio, ed. *Nuova raccolta delle monete e delle zecche d'Italia.* 4 vols. Bologna, 1775–89.

Zen Benetti, Francesca. "Prestatori ebraici e cristiani nel Padovano fra Trecento e Quattrocento." *Gli Ebrei e Venezia, secoli XIV–XVIII.* Milan, 1987.

Zerbi, Tommaso. *Il mastro a partita doppia di un'azienda mercantile del '300.* Como, 1936.

———. *Moneta effettiva e moneta di conto nelle fonti contabili di storia economica.* Milan, 1955.

———. *Le origini della partita doppia: Gestioni aziendali e situazioni di mercato nei secoli XIV e XV.* Milan, 1952.

Zille, Ester. "Salari e stipendi a Venezia tra Quattro e Cinquecento." *AV,* ser. 5, 138 (1992): 5–29.

Zordan, Giorgio. *I visdomini di Venezia nel secolo XIII.* Padua, 1971.

INDEX

Market days: at S. Marco, 29, 77; at S. Polo, 29

Marks, L., 457

Marmora, Filippo, 11n. 28, 129, 132–33

Marranos, 237; expulsion of, 249–50; wheat imports by, 434

Martelli: Alessandro, 284; Antonio di Niccolò, 258, 279, 441

Martin V, 290

Martini, Martino, 164

Martini (di), Mons. Andrea, 348

Marx, K., 455

Mattei, Leonardo, 343–45, 349–50

Maurino, Johannes, 561

Maximilian (emperor), 251

Medici (de'): Averardo di Francesco, 272, 276, 279, 513–14; Francesco, 279; Francesco (grand duke), 435; Giovanni di Bicci, 272, 276, 290, 311; Giuliano, 284; Lorenzo di Giovanni, exile in Venice, 195, 258, 279–80; Lorenzo il Magnifico, 282–83; Piero di Lorenzo, 283–84; Vieri di Cambio, 276, 309–10

—bank: in Naples, 180, 354; in Rome, 354

—bank, Venice branch, 197–98, 227–28, 274–85, 296, 312–13, 335, 354–55, 515, 590, 650; bankruptcy and liquidation of, 281–83, 285; capital and profits of, 278; and loan to Venice, 280, 441; as patrons of S. Giorgio Maggiore, 280; and rechange, 333–36; staff of, 277; and wheat imports, 434

—Cosimo, 4n. 2, 258, 279, 290, 312, 441; alliance with F. Sforza, 274, 284; exile in Venice, 195, 258, 279; return from exile, 515

Menegi, Jacomello, 165

Mercenaries, payment of, 126, 218

Merchant bankers: Bolognese, 169–70, 186; Florentine, in Naples, 428n. 8; Milanese, 197, 242, 245, 275, 327

—Florentine, in Venice, 22–23, 57, 122, 129, 132–33, 159–60, 163–64, 166, 184, 255–87, 514, 517, 574–75; confraternity of, 257–58, 284–87; current accounts on Rialto banks, 22–23, 129–30, 155, 163–64; expelled in 1313, 259; expelled in 1340, 130, 133, 136, 260–61, 265; expelled in 1451, 214, 284; and failures of 1499, 240–41, 244; "nation" of, 257–58, 284–87; and ransoms in Constantinople, 442; and Venetian exchange market, 288–355. See also Exchange, foreign

Merchant manuals, 32, 288, 290, 296, 346, 355, 588, 594, 618–19

Mercury, 236

Meshullam, Asher, 233, 450

Messetteria, 502, 519

Mestre, 91, 259, 412; hospital of S. Maria dei Battuti of, 620; pawnbroking in, 142, 233, 240, 445, 571–74; prices of consumables in, 620, 652

Miani, Pietro, forced loans of, 536–37

Micheli, Bartolomeo, 91, 95, 159

Michiel: Federico, 167, 173; Gerolamo, 338; Giovanni, 412; Guido, 131; Marco, 131; Nicoletto

Milan: alliance with, 247; ambassador of, 241–47, 280; builders' wages in, 655–56; counterfeit coin of, 189; immigration from, 656; and public debt, 455–56; quoting exchange with, 590–93, 601, 605

—court of: and Grain Office deposits, 384–87; and portfolio, 548–52, 575

—wars with, 202, 211, 214, 258; and effect on obligations market, 518; and forced loans, 465–66, 521, 526. See also under Merchant bankers

Miliotto, Bartolomeo, 222

Mills, and milling, 406–12

Minerbetti, Giovanni, 513

Mining, of silver, in Vicentino, 193

Minotto: Castellan, 542–43; Giovanni, 416

Mint of Venice. See Zecca

Miorati: Antonio, 82, 91–92, 99–100, 102, 110, 126, 182, 538; Benedetto, 92; Ranieri di Antonio, 92, 176. See also Cocco-Miorati bank; Corner-Miorati bank

Mocenighi (1 lira coins), 234

Mocenigo: Leonardo, 104, 180; Tommaso (doge), 256

Modena, 206, 208

Mohammed II, 466

Moisè, Jew of Mestre, 445

Moneychangers, 574; list of, 580–83; public, 31; at Rialto, 3–9, 26–32, 61, 243

—at S. Marco, 3–9, 26–32; bankruptcies of, 65, 143, 157, 160; and bullion, 27–28; clientele of, 41, 51; guarantors of, 52–62; hours of, 51; and jewelry, 29; list of, 580–83; partnerships of, 83, 93, 97; quarters of, 70, 77–78; regulation of, 8–9; rentals, 41–42; robberies at, 70–80; staff of, 93, 97. See also under individual moneychangers

Moneys of account: at Loan Office, 610–17;

Library of Congress Cataloging-in-Publication Data
Mueller, Reinhold C.
The Venetian money market : banks, panics, and the public debt,
1200–1500 / Reinhold C. Mueller.
p.   cm.
Includes bibliographical references (p.   ) and index.
ISBN 0-8018-5437-7 (alk. paper)
1. Money — Italy — Venice — History.   2. Banks and banking — Italy —
Venice — History.   3. Money market — Italy — Venice — History.
4. Economic history — Medieval, 500–1500.   5. Economic history — 16th
century.   6. Renaissance — Italy — Venice.   I. Title.
HG1040.V46M84   1997
332.1'0945'31 — dc21
96-36921
CIP